DATE DUE

OC 28 '02			

DEMCO 38-296

THE WOMEN'S DESK REFERENCE

THE

WOMEN'S

DESK

REFERENCE

•

BY IRENE FRANCK &
DAVID BROWNSTONE

VIKING

VIKING
Published by the Penguin Group
Penguin Books USA Inc., 375 Hudson Street,
New York, New York 10014, U.S.A.
Penguin Books Ltd, 27 Wrights Lane,
London W8 5TZ, England
Penguin Books Australia Ltd, Ringwood,
Victoria, Australia
Penguin Books Canada Ltd, 10 Alcorn Avenue,
Toronto, Ontario, Canada M4V 3B2
Penguin Books (N.Z.) Ltd, 182–190 Wairau Road,
Auckland 10, New Zealand

Penguin Books Ltd, Registered Offices:
Harmondsworth, Middlesex, England

First published in 1993 by Viking Penguin,
a division of Penguin Books USA Inc.

1   3   5   7   9   10   8   6   4   2

LIBRARY OF CONGRESS CATALOGING IN PUBLICATION DATA
Franck, Irene M.
The women's desk reference / by Irene Franck and David Brownstone.
p.   cm.
ISBN 0-670-84513-2
1. Women's rights—United States—Handbooks, manual, etc.
2. Women—United States—History—Handbooks, manuals, etc.
3. Women—Services for—United States—Handbooks, manuals, etc.
4. Women—History—Handbooks, manuals, etc.   I. Brownstone. David M. II. Title
HQ1236.5.U6F73   1993
305.4′0973—dc20   93-17515

Printed in the United States of America
Set in Minion
Designed by Liney Li

PREFACE

From abortion to zygote, women have special interests and concerns on a host of issues, but over the years we had never found a single work that took up the whole range of social, legal, psychological, medical, and other issues relating to women and from a special women's perspective. Our aim in *The Women's Desk Reference* is to provide just such a basic reference and resource book on the key women's concerns, speaking to *all* women, whether they see themselves as "radical feminists" or "traditional women," or more commonly somewhere in between; and to women of any age, from those approaching adulthood all the way through those in mid-life—and these days often mid-career—on to those in their later years.

The Women's Desk Reference is an A-to-Z encyclopedia covering the whole spectrum of women's concerns, and the key people, organizations, works, and events associated with them. In each entry, we have aimed to provide a balanced overview of the topic, the controversies surrounding it, and its importance to women, emphasizing personal and practical relevance in women's own lives. Throughout the book, especially for major topics, such as *infertility, breast cancer, divorce, adoption,* and *displaced homemakers,* readers will be offered additional resources for help, information, and action; these include organizations (many themselves treated in separate entries, such as the *National Women's Health Network* and *National Organization for Women*), suggestions for further reading, and special tabular and other material in highlighted boxes, ranging from illustrated exercises for pregnant women to a list of warning signs for bulimia.

Following the article on *sexual harassment,* for example, readers will find organization and reading references in a special box called the "Sexual Discrimination and Sexual Harassment Help, Information, and Action Guide," offering women places to turn to for practical guidance and support when they or someone they know is facing such problems. In addition, they will find a box called "Sexual Harassment: What Every Working Woman Needs to Know," and will be referred to an article on the *Equal Employment Opportunity Commission* and its accompanying box, "How to File an EEOC Complaint."

To aid readers in finding entries directly on their concerns, we have throughout the book used small capital letters (such as EQUAL PAY FOR EQUAL WORK) as cross-references, to indicate where additional discussions of related topics can be found. In the article on sexual harassment, for example, readers will find small capital letters used for topics such as the TAILHOOK SCANDAL, Anita Faye HILL, POLITICAL PARTICIPATION, and TITLE VII OF THE 1964 CIVIL RIGHTS ACT. These cross-references (normally at the first mention in an article) indicate that fuller discussion will be found under that entry head. Throughout the book, we have also included brief entries as cross-references to major topics, so readers looking under *sexual abuse* will find a cross-reference entry directing them to major articles on RAPE, BATTERED WOMEN, SEXUAL HARASSMENT, and CHILD ABUSE AND NEGLECT.

The "Special Information Section" at the back of the book offers additional material of interest, including the text of some key documents on women's rights; a statistical "portrait" of American working women; a tabular overview of the main aspects of women's lives around the world, from child care and unpaid housework to quality of living conditions; an international overview of women's access to political life; and a timeline of *Highlights in the Fight for Women's Rights*.

Our thanks to our editors, Nan Graham and Courtney Hodell; to designer Liney Li; to cover designer Evan Gaffney; and to the whole production staff, who have so capably seen this book through the publishing process. We also thank the staff of the Chappaqua Library—Director Mark Hasskarl; the expert reference staff, including Martha Alcott, Teresa Cullen, Carolyn Jones, Paula Peyraud, Mary Platt, and Carolyn Reznick; and the circulation staff, including Marilyn Coleman, Lois Siwicki, and Jane McKean—and their colleagues throughout the northeastern library network, who are ever-helpful in fulfilling our research needs.

Irene Franck
David Brownstone
Chappaqua, New York

CONTENTS

abandonment, in general, the act of leaving behind something to which one has legal rights, or someone to whom one has legal ties, with no expressed intention of returning.

In relation to MARRIAGE, abandonment—often called *desertion*—is generally grounds for DIVORCE. In such cases the court generally requires proof:

- that abandonment has actually occurred. If one party moves out but the couple meet several times for SEXUAL INTERCOURSE, abandonment may not have occurred, depending on the laws in that jurisdiction.
- that the abandoned spouse had not agreed to a SEPARATION. If the two parties agreed to separate, it is not considered abandonment.
- that it was voluntary, rather than being provoked by the abandoned spouse. Such provocation cannot be trivial but generally refers to acts that would give grounds for divorce, if desired (see DIVORCE).
- that attempts at RECONCILIATION have failed. However, some states do not accept attempt at a reconciliation by the abandoning party when it is being presented only to prevent abandonment being used as a basis for divorce.

Abandonment can be a tricky question. Traditionally courts assumed that a wife must always follow her husband. As a result, a woman might be charged with abandonment if she failed to relocate to another state with her husband, even if she had sound reasons, as in one case being near the end of a nurse's training program. The man could not be unreasonable, however; for example, courts have variously ruled that he must give his wife preparation time, provide transportation for her and the household goods, and provide a home in the new location. In recent years rulings assuming that the wife should follow the husband have been challenged on the basis of SEXUAL DISCRIMINATION and constitutional protection to equal rights under the law.

Also grounds for divorce is *constructive abandonment,* in which one spouse denies the "comforts and benefits" of marriage to the other spouse, but without leaving the couple's home. This often means denial of sexual relations, though not where the accused has ill health or where the situation has gone on for years and so has been accepted, or *ratified,* by the complaining party. It may also be a pattern of behavior that evidences destruction of the relationship's marital character, as in cases where a wife's relatives spent every evening and weekend with the couple over the husband's objections; a husband had contracted severe

SEXUALLY TRANSMITTED DISEASES; or a woman changed the locks on the door one day after her husband left for work. In one case a woman was judged to be abandoned even though *she* was the one who left home, because her husband beat her and had a sexual relationship with a live-in servant.

Where divorce is based on guilt and blame, as was usual in the past, charges of abandonment are commonly brought before courts. Today many countries, such as the United States, have adopted liberalized "no fault" divorce laws, which do not require proof of abandonment. However, abandonment can still have significant legal implications for marital partners. A woman who is legally found to have abandoned her husband may, in some circumstances, lose her rights to his pension or insurance, for example, or the ability to act as administrator of or to contest his will. Women in such situations will want to seek advice from a professional specializing in marital and divorce questions (see DIVORCE AND SEPARATION HELP, INFORMATION, AND ACTION GUIDE on page 238, for referrals to women's groups or public interest law firms specializing in women's concerns) and especially arrange for a SEPARATION AGREEMENT covering all property and financial matters.

In family law, abandonment may also refer to deserting a child or to leaving the child without effective supervision and provision for basic needs for what the state judges to be too long a time. This judgment varies from state to state and depends partly on the child's age, the nature (or complete lack) of the supervision, and the length of time involved. If abandonment of the child is judged to have occurred, a suit may be brought to terminate PARENTS' RIGHTS. In the past some courts have followed the *flicker of interest rule,* indicating that a parent who shows even a flicker of interest in a child's welfare has not abandoned that child. Other courts judge that abandonment has occurred when the parent demonstrates a desire to be rid of all parental obligations. Stepparents or foster parents sometimes initiate abandonment proceedings when they wish to adopt a child in their care but cannot locate the child's biological parent or parents for permission to do so (see ADOPTION).

In cases of physical abandonment, as when the child is left on a doorstep or in a garbage can, the parent can be subject to criminal prosecution. Historically, abandonment in this manner was a common form of INFANTICIDE; in a practice called *exposure,* an unwanted or unaccepted child would be left out in the open to die or to survive only if someone else chose to care for it. In some parts of the world, children with disabilities or disputed parentage are still frequently abandoned in this way, if not killed outright. So are female children in those parts of the world where SON PREFERENCE is strong, especially where there is also pressure to have smaller families.

In some cases parents—generally mothers—are attempting not infanticide, but better provision for an infant than they themselves can give. They may leave a child, for example, at a hospital, church, or orphanage, once called foundling homes because they cared specifically for abandoned children. (See INFANTICIDE; PARENTS' RIGHTS.)

Abbott, Edith (1876–1957) and **Grace** (1878–1939), two sisters joined throughout their lives in a considerable range of social reform movements; both became feminists, leading social workers and social work educators, and writers.

Grace Abbott studied at the University of Chicago before beginning her career as a powerful advocate of social justice for women and children and especially for the millions of poor immigrant women and children during the floodtide period of American immigration. In 1908 she and her sister Edith joined Jane ADDAMS at Chicago's Hull House. In that same year Grace Abbott became director of the Chicago-based Immigrant's Protective League (1908–1917), also working with the U.S. Children's Bureau during and after World War I. Later she headed the Children's Bureau (1921–1934) and during the early years of the New Deal strongly influenced the development of PROTECTIVE LEGISLATION for women and children in the workplace.

Edith Abbott, a labor economist whose work included *Women in Industry* (1910) and *The Tenements of Chicago* (1936), studied at the University of Chicago and the London School of Economics before she and her sister moved to Hull House. In the same period she joined Sophonisba Breckenridge at the Chicago School of Civics and Philanthropy, beginning a long career as a pioneer in social work education, from 1924 to 1942 as dean of University of Chicago's School of Social Work Administration. From 1927 to 1953 she and Breckenridge edited the influential *Social Work Review*.

abdominal delivery, an alternative name for CESAREAN SECTION.

abdominoplasty, removal of excess skin and fatty tissue from the abdomen (see COSMETIC SURGERY).

abortion, the ending of a PREGNANCY, either spontaneously or deliberately. Abortions that occur naturally are called MISCARRIAGES or *spontaneous abortions,* happening most often because genetic defects in the EMBRYO are so severe as to be incompatible with life (see GENETIC DISORDERS). These occur at a surprisingly high rate, in at least 10 percent and perhaps as much as 30 percent of all pregnancies but often so early that the woman does not even realize she has been pregnant.

However, the main area of controversy is the deliberate termination of a pregnancy, medically called an *elective* or *induced abortion*—and by opponents termed *feticide* or INFANTICIDE. For much of history abortions have been illegal and are still so in many parts of the world, often with the highly restricted exception of a *therapeutic abortion,* when the mother's life or health is threatened—though in some countries not even then, as a 1992 vote in Ireland confirmed. Despite that, abortions have been performed for as long as any humans have known how to do so.

Abortions have always carried some risks for the woman, especially of life-threatening infections or hemorrhages; but where the operations were being performed illicitly, in back alleys and other nonsterile settings, the risks were magnified. In desperation some women tried to perform abortions on themselves or each other, using everything from coat hangers to chemically caustic douches. It has been images of women dead from illegal or self-induced abortions gone wrong that have caused many people to seek legalization of abortion. On the other hand, it has been images of death for tiny, though recognizably formed fetuses that have spurred many people opposed to abortion, quite apart from any specific religious prohibition.

Advocates of legalization of abortion are "pro-choice" rather than pro-abortion; that is, they endorse the woman's right to decide for herself whether or not to have an abortion. Many people believe that the abortion question does not stand in isolation. They note, in particular, that widespread provision of BIRTH CONTROL information and devices would eliminate many unwanted pregnancies, and that, if abortion and birth control are both restricted, society must accept a responsibility to help care for children brought into the world against their MOTHER's will. Indeed, many of those who choose abortions—teenagers, SINGLE WOMEN, and married women alike—do so because they feel unable to cope with the personal, family, social, and economic problems posed by the new life.

There are a number of key abortion-related questions that are exercising societies around the world in these decades:

- Under what circumstances shall an abortion be allowed, and how restricted?
- When during a pregnancy should an abortion be allowed and when restricted?
- Who should decide whether or not a woman has an abortion, and should notification or consent be required, as from a husband or (for a teenager) a parent?
- More generally, when does life begin, or to put it another way, at what point in a pregnancy does society have a right or duty to protect the new being?

People around the world are trying to answer these and other extraordinarily difficult questions, through legislation, public policy, protests, and moral persuasion. And the answers they are coming to change as society changes.

In the United States, the watershed year was 1973, when, in the *Roe* v. *Wade* decision, the U.S. Supreme Court for the first time legalized abortion. Based on the "right of privacy" between a woman and her doctor, the ruling provided for a woman's unrestricted right to an abortion during the first three months (trimester) of pregnancy; for state regulation of abortion in the second trimester; and for state regulation or prohibition of abortion in the third trimester, except for therapeutic abortions to protect the mother's life or health. The trimester system was set up on the premise that the state's interest in the fetus essentially begins at the point when the new being becomes *viable*—that is, able to exist outside the womb—a time taken to be approximately at the end of the second trimester, or six months into the pregnancy. In the wake of *Roe* v. *Wade,* thousands of clinics were established to offer both abortions and birth control information. For many women these became prime sources for reproductive services in general; in the early 1990s PLANNED PARENTHOOD alone had about nine hundred clinics around the United States.

However, a series of court decisions over the years—while continuing to reaffirm the constitutionality of the right to an abortion—have modified and restricted *Roe v. Wade*. In *Beal v. Doe* (1977), the Supreme Court ruled that states were not required to use public funds to pay for abortions (introducing different polices in different states), and in *Harris v. McRae* (1980), it upheld the Hyde Amendment, providing that Medicaid could not be used to pay for medically unnecessary abortions. Both of these rulings made abortions more difficult for poor women to obtain. In 1988 the Reagan administration issued regulations designed to bar federally funded clinics from providing pregnant women with information about abortion, including the fact that it was a legal option; this so-called gag rule was invalidated by the courts late in 1992 and later rescinded under the Clinton administration. In *Webster v. Reproductive Health Services* (1989), the Court upheld a Missouri law barring the use of public hospitals or clinics for abortions.

Some rulings have focused on consent or a waiting period. In *Planned Parenthood v. Danforth* (1976), the Court struck down a Missouri law that required a married women to obtain her husband's consent for abortion. In *Bellotti v. Baird* (1979), it ruled that the state could not require a teenager to get a parent's consent, unless an alternative was provided, such as getting consent from a judge. In *Ohio v. Akron Center for Reproductive Health* (1990), it upheld a state law requiring that a teenager notify one parent before obtaining an abortion. However, in *City of Akron v. Akron Center for Reproductive Health* (1983), it struck down a law requiring a twenty-four-hour wait before an abortion, because the statute asserted "the unborn child is a human life from the moment of conception."

In *Planned Parenthood v. Casey* (1992), the Court specifically reaffirmed *Roe v. Wade*, indicating that laws prohibiting all or most abortions would be considered unconstitutional; but it affirmed the states' rights to place restrictions on the provision of abortions, as long as they do not pose an "undue burden." Among the provisions approved in the Pennsylvania law involved in the case were a delay of twenty-four hours after a woman hears a presentation attempting to persuade her to change her mind about having an abortion (involving information about and pictures of fetal development and details about the procedure and its risks) and requirement that a teenager get the consent of one parent or a judge; it also described medical emergencies when other requirements would be waived and required the doctor or clinic to make statistical reports to the state. The Court struck down a fifth provision that would have required a married woman to tell her husband that she intended having an abortion. (The Court had struck down an earlier version of Pennsylvania's Abortion Control Act in *Thornburgh v. American College of Obstetricians and Gynecologists* [1986].) The ruling also rejected the "rigid trimester framework of *Roe v. Wade*," indicating that with modern medical advances the point of *viability* has been growing earlier and so therefore has the state's interest in the new life. (See U.S. SUPREME COURT ON ABORTION on page 9.)

Abortion rights activists at both poles were unhappy with the *Planned Parenthood v. Casey* ruling: anti-abortion, or pro-life, advocates because it upheld the right to abortion; pro-choice advocates because it allowed increasing restrictions, opening the door also for further court cases. Though they hoped to see on the Supreme Court more judges with their point of view to rule on future cases, both groups quickly turned toward legislation to press their viewpoints. Pro-life activists focused on passage of restrictive laws in the states, while pro-choice activists concentrated on the federal level, seeking a Freedom of Choice Act that would replace judicial rulings with a law encompassing the essentials of *Roe* v. *Wade.*

But legality is one thing, practical availability quite another. While the fight continues in legislatures, many individual women—especially the poor, the young, and the rural—have had increasing difficulty obtaining abortions in recent years. Seemingly minor restrictions, such as a one-day waiting period, can pose an almost insuperable obstacle for a poor teenage girl from a small town two hundred miles from the nearest abortion clinic, for whom the expense and travel time are already burdensome. Even though clinics are relatively low cost, for poor women it takes time to obtain sufficient money to obtain an abortion—sometimes so long that they are unable to have a relatively inexpensive first trimester abortion locally but must have a much more expensive later abortion in a hospital-like setting, if they have the funds to obtain one at all.

Parental consent is likewise a significant problem. In some states with parental consent laws, young women who wish to do so can obtain the consent of a judge relatively easily; in other states, while that is a legal option, it is virtually never granted. Unwilling to face their parents with an unwanted pregnancy, some young women have gone the old route of self-induced or back-alley abortions, and some have paid with their lives. One particularly poignant instance was that of a model young woman who did not want to "disappoint" her parents; after her death they went public to fight against parental consent laws, commenting, "She died because of a law we would have voted for."

As small, widely dispersed, isolated clinics increasingly took over not just abortion but also gynecological care once provided in doctor's offices or hospitals, they also became more vulnerable to pressure from anti-abortion activists. These are not just nationally known, highly organized groups but also local groups and individuals who put pressure on clinics, using everything from changing building codes and zoning laws to bombing and personal threats to force closure of such clinics. In the wake of the 1992 rulings, pro-life activists became increasingly involved in direct action, with escalating acts of violence, especially chemical damage, bombing, or arson of clinics or homes of providers, and harassment, threats, and attacks on providers and recipients, in at least one case involving murder, that of Florida doctor David Gunn. That caused something of a split in the anti-abortion movement, as such violence seems to many incompatible with a truly "pro-life" stance. Pro-choice activists, in response, turned to the courts and legislatures for protection from or at least limitation of such attacks, a knotty question involving balancing of the pro-life activists' right to free speech against the right to privacy (one of the bases for *Roe* v. *Wade*) of those seeking and providing abortions. Physical damage to persons or property is, of course, covered by existing laws, unrelated to the abortion question itself.

Complicating matters still further, some abortion opponents set up dummy clinics, ostensibly to offer abortions, but in actuality to pressure and persuade women to continue their pregnancies. Some pro-choice individuals and groups have actively taken on the job of protecting both providers and women seeking abortion, even to the point of establishing an "overground railway" to help women overcome physical, economic, and geographical barriers to exercising their right to an abortion.

Meanwhile, with most abortions being performed in such clinics and with increased controversy, many medical schools no longer routinely provided all new doctors with training in performing abortions, so the skills necessary are no longer so widely available. Some medical schools have reversed that trend, putting back into their curriculum courses on abortion skills; some have made special arrangements for medical students to train in clinics such as those of Planned Parenthood. One problem is that doctors who specialize in providing abortions, rather than performing them as part of a wider medical practice, make far less money and waste many of their skills on repetitions of relatively simple procedures. To meet the shortage of abortion providers, some areas, notably Vermont, have moved to allow specially trained physicians' assistants or nurses to perform abortions. The hazard is that women are vulnerable if an emergency occurs during an abortion, unless a doctor is immediately available on the premises. Because of obstacles to abortion, and in fear that *Roe* v. *Wade* might be overturned if the composition of the Supreme Court became more conservative, some women developed self-help techniques of abortion (see below).

The status of abortion around the world ranges from the two extremes. In some countries abortions are not available under any circumstances. One example is Ireland, where a 1992 cause célèbre involved a young woman who had been raped having to go to the High Court for permission to go to Britain for an abortion, after she had been barred from leaving the country on stating her intention. At the other extreme are countries where abortion is allowed at any time before birth for any reason. This was the case in the former Soviet Union, where contraceptive information and devices were in such short supply that abortion was the main form of birth control. West and East Germany were examples of the two extremes; when they reunited, it took many months before a compromise set of regulations was worked out.

One complicating factor is the widespread use of genetic screening tests, such as AMNIOCENTESIS, CHORIONIC VILLUS SAMPLING (CVS), ALPHA FETOPROTEIN (AFP), and ULTRASOUND, which can indicate the presence of BIRTH DEFECTS. If a child is expected to be badly deformed, many couples now choose to have an abortion and try again for a healthy baby—a difficult decision and one criticized by many, including people born with birth defects or GENETIC DISORDERS who might not be alive today if their parents had opted for abortion. Genetic screening tests also indicate the sex of a child, and parents can decide to abort a child based on gender alone. Sometimes male fetuses are aborted this way, especially where a couple already has a boy and want a girl, for example. But in many cases it is female fetuses that are aborted. The situation is extreme in some countries where SON PREFERENCE is especially pronounced; in India, for example, so many female fetuses are aborted by families wanting sons that there are estimated to be over 25 percent fewer women than men in the age brackets affected. There the choice to abort female fetuses, in a culture where women have extremely low status and where many do what their husbands command, is very far from the kind of "choice" abortion rights activists envision.

The abortion fight has had other social implications as well. Because most fetal tissue used in medical research comes from aborted fetuses, the U.S. government, under the Reagan and Bush administrations, barred such research, significantly slowing the rate of medical research on such disorders as Parkinson's disease and Alzheimer's disease. And because abortion is among the birth control alternatives presented and performed by many international health organizations, the U.S. government in that same period withheld support from international family planning efforts. Such restrictions were eased or removed under the Clinton administration.

By contrast with the moral, social, economic, and philosophical issues posed by abortion, the actual procedures involved are relatively simple. Basically most procedures aim to remove the fetus and its nourishing PLACENTA from the uterus; it is important to remove all such tissue, to avoid possibly life-threatening infection.

During the first trimester, many abortions are carried out by *vacuum extraction,* in which a machine called a *vacuum extractor* or *ventouse* is used to suck out the contents of the UTERUS. This is often combined with an operation called a D&C (dilatation and curettage), involving curettage or scraping of the uterine lining to see that no tissue remains; this is performed under general or regional ANESTHESIA.

Some women's self-help groups have developed a "homemade" version of vacuum extraction, using a thin tube *(cannula)* inserted through the CERVIX and a syringe to remove the contents. This procedure, called MENSTRUAL EXTRACTION, was developed in the early 1970s before *Roe* v. *Wade* and has been revived in recent years as abortion rights have been threatened; it is popular among some women who wish to lessen reliance on gynecologists. Critics, including some abortion rights proponents and providers, are concerned that no testing has been done to show the safety or efficacy of the technique, used through the eighth week of pregnancy. Some regard it as a return to the "bad old days," noting that nonprofessionals are unprepared to manage medical complications that can result from an abortion and expressing concern about possible infection and damage in the REPRODUCTIVE SYSTEM. In addition, some are concerned that women performing such a procedure could be prosecuted for practicing medicine without a license, while others speculate on the results of a possible successful lawsuit for damage or death during a menstrual extraction. Others, while noting that it involves relatively simple technical skills, stress the importance of adequate training and of a system of referral in case of medical complications.

During and after the second trimester, when abortions are more difficult and hazardous, vacuum extraction may be used in combination with a D&C, with the procedure then being called *dilatation and evacuation.* But often, especially after the fifteenth week, a saline solution or HORMONE is injected into the fluid contained in the AMNIOTIC SAC, to induce contractions in the uterus, which usually expels the fetus in about twelve hours. This type of procedure, called *amnioinfusion, amniocentesis abortion,* or *intra-amniotic infusion,* normally requires remaining in a hospital for one to two days afterward.

When performed under hospital or clinic conditions, the mortality rate for abortion is relatively low, during the first trimester, under 1 in 100,000 abortions, though rising later in pregnancy. Women who have an abortion, especially more than one, also have an increased risk of later miscarriage or INFERTILITY.

Many questions about abortion may become moot, if so-called abortion pills come widely into use (see RU486). (See ABORTION HELP, INFORMATION, AND ACTION GUIDE on page 10.)

THE U.S. SUPREME COURT ON ABORTION

It must be stated at the outset and with clarity that Roe's essential holding, the holding we reaffirm, has three parts. First is a recognition of the right of the woman to choose to have an abortion before viability and to obtain it without undue interference from the state. Before viability, the state's interests are not strong enough to support a prohibition of abortion or the imposition of a substantial obstacle to the woman's effective right to elect the procedure. Second is a confirmation of the state's power to restrict abortions after fetal viability, if the law contains exceptions for pregnancies that endanger a woman's life or health. And third is the principle that the state has legitimate interests from the outset of the pregnancy in protecting the health of the woman and the life of the fetus that may become a child. These principles do not contradict one another; and we adhere to each....

Men and women of good conscience can disagree, and we suppose some always shall disagree, about the profound moral and spiritual implications of terminating a pregnancy, even in its earliest stages. Some of us as individuals find abortion offensive to our most basic principles of morality, but that cannot control our decision. Our obligation is to define the liberty of all, not to mandate our own moral code....

Source: *Planned Parenthood* v. *Casey* (1992), decision jointly written by U.S. Supreme Court Justices Sandra Day O'Connor, Anthony M. Kennedy, and David H. Souter.

ABORTION

Help, Information, and Action Guide

Organizations

◨ **FOR PRACTICAL ADVICE, INFORMATION, AND REFERRALS**

▶ PLANNED PARENTHOOD® (800-829-7732; 212-541-7800). Operates over 900 clinics supplying information, counseling, and services, including abortions. Publishes *Abortion: Questions and Answers.*

▶ NATIONAL WOMEN'S HEALTH NETWORK (**NWHN**) (202-347-1140). Operates the **Women's Health Information Service.** Publishes *Abortion Then and Now: Creative Responses to Restricted Access, Childbearing Policies with a National Health Program: An Evolving Consensus for New Directions* and the information packets *Abortion* and *RU486.*

▶ INSTITUTE ON WOMEN AND TECHNOLOGY (413-367-9725). Publishes *RU486: Misconceptions, Myths, and Morals.*

▶ FEDERATION OF FEMINIST WOMEN'S HEALTH CENTERS (916-737-0260). Network of organizations that perform MENSTRUAL EXTRACTION abortions and other self-help procedures.

▶ NATIONAL BLACK WOMEN'S HEALTH PROJECT (**NBWHP**) (404-681-4554).

◨ **FOR LEGAL ADVICE AND REFERRALS**

▶ EQUAL RIGHTS ADVOCATES (**ERA**) (415-621-0672; advice and counseling lines, 415-621-0505). A national women's law center.

▶ NORTHWEST WOMEN'S LAW CENTER (206-682-9552; for information and referral, 206-621-7691). For the Washington State area.

▶ WOMEN'S JUSTICE CENTER (**WJC**) (313-961-5528). For the Detroit area.

◨ **PRO-CHOICE ORGANIZATIONS**

▶ **National Abortion Federation (NAF)** (1436 U Street, NW, Suite 103, Washington, DC 20009; 202-667-5881; toll-free hot line 800-772-9100; Barbara Radford, executive director), an organization of people and institutions providing abortion services, setting standards and guidelines in the field. It provides information and makes referrals and publishes various materials for professionals and the public, including *Consumer's Guide to Abortion Services* (in English and Spanish).

▶ **National Abortion Rights Action League (NARAL)** (1101 14th Street, NW, Washington, DC 20005; 202-408-4600; Kate Michelman, executive director), an organization founded in 1969 "to keep abortion safe, legal, and accessible for all women." The NARAL-PAC (Political Action Committee) directly supports pro-choice candidates at all levels of government, while the NARAL Foundation supports research, legal work, leadership training, and public education problems. NARAL publishes various materials, including the books *Who Decides? A Reproductive Rights Issues Manual, Who Decides? A State By State Review of Abortion,* and *The Voices of Women;* the brochures *Congressional Votes on Abortion* and *Choice—Legal Abortion: Arguments Pro & Con;* and the video *Voices.*

▶ NOW LEGAL DEFENSE AND EDUCATION FUND (NOW LDEF) (212-925-6635). Publishes the *State Index of Women's Legal Rights, Facts on Reproductive Rights: A Resource Manual, Protecting Young Women's Right to Abortion: A Guide to Parental Notification and Consent Laws, Attorney Referral Services List,* and the legal resource kit *Reproductive Rights.*

▶ Religious Coalition for Abortion Rights (RCAR) (100 Maryland Avenue, NE, Washington, DC 20002; 202-543-7032; Ann Thompson Cook, executive director), an organization of religious groups supporting a woman's legal right to abortion. It publishes various materials, including the quarterly newsletter *Options;* legislative alerts and fact sheets; manuals such as *Youth Talk About Sexuality and Abortion: Training Manual for Religious Educators;* booklets such as *Words of Choice;* and booklets such as *We Affirm* (statements from 32 national religious organizations on abortion rights).

▶ WOMEN'S ACTION COALITION (WAC) (WAC voice mail 212-967-7711, ext. WACM [9226]).

▶ FUND FOR THE FEMINIST MAJORITY (617-695-9688; or 703-522-2214; or 213-651-0495). Publishes the videos *Abortion: For Survival* and *Abortion Denied: Shattering Young Women's Lives.*

▶ NATIONAL ORGANIZATION FOR WOMEN (NOW) (202-331-0066).

▶ WOMEN'S MINISTRY UNIT (WMU) (502-569-5382). Publishes or distributes packets such as *What It Means to Be for Choice, Christian Reflection on the Issues of Abortion,* and the video *Whose Choice?*

▶ NATIONAL INSTITUTE OF CHILD HEALTH AND HUMAN DEVELOPMENT (NICHD) (301-496-5133).

▶ LEAGUE OF WOMEN VOTERS (202-429-1965). Publishes *Public Policy on Reproductive Choices* and *Coping with Conflict: Reproductive Choices and Community Controversy.*

▶ COMMISSION FOR WOMEN'S EQUALITY (CWE) (212-879-4500).

▶ INTERNATIONAL WOMEN'S HEALTH COALITION (IWHC) (212-979-8500). Publishes *Reproductive Choice in Jeopardy: International Policy Perspectives.*

▶ NATIONAL CENTER FOR POLICY ALTERNATIVES (202-387-6030). Publishes *Choice After* Webster: *An Overview of State Abortion Legislation, Comprehensive Reproductive Choice Legislation: Examples from the States, Eroding the Constitutional Right to Abortion: The* Webster *Decision of 1989*

and Minors' Access Decisions of 1990, Health Care Access for Low-Income Women, Minors' Access to Abortion: 1990 Supreme Court Decisions, The Politics of RU486: States Look for Ways to Counter Anti-Choice Opposition, and *The State Legislative Agenda of the National Anti-Choice Movement.*
▶ Ms. FOUNDATION FOR WOMEN (MFW) (212-353-8580).

◪ FOR SUPPORT OF PRO-CHOICE CANDIDATES

▶ NATIONAL WOMEN'S POLITICAL CAUCUS (NWPC) (202-898-1100). Bipartisan. Publishes *Mobilizing the Pro-Choice Vote: A Basic Phonebanking Guide* and *Your Campaign and Abortion Rights.*
▶ WOMEN'S CAMPAIGN FUND (WCF) (202-544-4484). Bipartisan.
▶ EMILY'S LIST (202-887-1957). Democrats.
▶ WISH LIST (WOMEN IN THE SENATE AND HOUSE) (908-747-4221). Republicans.

◪ FOR ALTERNATIVES TO ABORTION FOR CRISIS PREGNANCIES

▶ NURTURING NETWORK, THE (TNN) (208-344-7200 or 800-TNN-4MOM [866-4666]. Provides counseling and aid for those who decide *against* having an abortion.
▶ CHILD WELFARE LEAGUE OF AMERICA (CWLA) (202-639-2952). Its **Florence Crittenton Division** offers a national residential adolescent pregnancy service.
▶ BIRTHRIGHT, UNITED STATES OF AMERICA (609-848-1819; Birthright hot line 800-848-LOVE [5683]). Urging alternatives to abortion. Offers childbirth and parenting classes. Publishes the newsletter *Life-Guardian.*

◪ PRO-LIFE ORGANIZATIONS

▶ **National Right to Life Committee (NRLC)** (419 Seventh Street, NW, Suite 500, Washington, DC 20004; 202-626-8800; Dr. Wanda Franz, president), an organization opposing abortion and euthanasia and supporting alternatives to abortion, including counseling and adoption. It maintains a library and publishes the biweekly *National Right to Life News* and pamphlet *Challenge to Be Pro-Life.*
▶ **Americans United for Life (AUL)** (343 South Dearborn, Suite 1804, Chicago, IL 60604; 312-786-9494; Guy Condon, president), an organization that opposes abortion and euthanasia and maintains the AUL Legal Defense Fund. It maintains a library and publishes various materials, including the newsletters *AUL Forum* and *Lex Vitae.*
▶ HUMAN LIFE INTERNATIONAL (HLI) (301-670-7884).

Other resources

☑ **GENERAL WORKS**

A Woman's Book of Choices: Abortion, Menstrual Extraction, RU486. Rebecca Chalker and Carol Downer. Four Walls Eight Windows, 1992. Downer was executive director of the FEDERATION OF FEMINIST WOMEN'S HEALTH CENTERS.

Abortion: A Positive Decision. Patricia Lunneborg. Greenwood, 1992.

Abortion: Pro-Choice or Pro-Life?. Gary Crum and Thelma McCormack. American University Press, 1991.

Abortion: The Clash of Absolutes. Laurence H. Tribe. Norton, 1990.

The Abortion Question. Hyman Rodman and others. Columbia University Press, 1990.

Abortion and Woman's Choice: The State, Sexuality and Reproductive Freedom, rev. ed. Rosalind P. Petchesky. New England University Press, 1990.

Over Our Live Bodies: Preserving Choice in America. Shirley Radl, Steve Davis, 1989.

☑ **ACTION-ORIENTED WORKS**

The Pro-Choice Victory Handbook: How to Keep Your Abortion Rights. Craig Chilton. Boiled Owl, 1991.

Keep Abortion Safe and Legal: The Postcard Activist. PGW Staff. Postcard Activist, 1991.

☑ **PERSONAL EXPERIENCES**

Bitter Fruit: Women's Experiences of Unplanned Pregnancy, Abortion, and Adoption. Ann Perkins and Rira Townsend. Hunter House, 1992.

The Choices We Made: 25 Women and Men Speak Out About Abortion. Angela Bonavoglia, ed. Random House, 1991.

Post-Abortion Trauma. Jeanette Vought. Zondervan, 1991.

Crusaders: Voices from the Abortion Front. Marian Faux. Birch Lane, 1990.

Contested Lives: The Abortion Debate in an American Community. Faye D. Ginsburg. University of California Press, 1990.

☑ **ON LEGAL ISSUES**

Abortion, Medicine and the Law, 4th ed. J. Douglas Butler and David F. Walbert, eds. Facts on File, 1992.

Life Before Birth: The Moral and Legal Status of Embryos and Fetuses. Bonnie Steinbock. Oxford University Press, 1992.

The Law Governing Abortion, Contraception and Sterilization. Irving J. Sloan. Oceana, 1988.

Mother-Love and Abortion: A Legal Interpretation. Robert D. Goldstein. University of California Press, 1988.

◪ ON RELIGIOUS AND PHILOSOPHICAL ISSUES

Our Right to Choose: Toward a New Ethic of Abortion, rev. ed. Beverly W. Harrison. Beacon Press, 1991.
Abortion: The Crisis in Morals and Medicine. Nigel M. Cameron and Pamela F. Sims. InterVarsity, 1991.
A Time to Be Born and a Time to Die: The Ethics of Choice. Barry S. Kogan, ed. Aldine de Gruyter, 1991.
Matters of Life and Death: Calm Answers to Tough Questions About Abortion and Euthanasia. Frank Beckwith and Norman L. Geisler. Baker, 1991.
Confessing Conscience: Churched Women on Abortion. Phyllis Tickle, ed. Abingdon, 1990.
Abortion and Catholicism: The American Debate. Patricia Beattie Jung and Thomas H. Shannon, eds. Crossroad, 1990.

◪ REFERENCE WORKS

Contraception and Abortion from the Ancient World to the Renaissance. John M. Riddle. Harvard University Press, 1992.
Pro-Choice—Pro-Life: An Annotated, Selected Bibliography (1972–1989). Richard Fitzsimmons and Joan P. Diana, eds. Greenwood, 1991.
Abortion: A Reference Handbook. Maria Costa. ABC-CLIO, 1991.

abruptio placentae, premature separation of the PLACENTA from the wall of the UTERUS during a PREGNANCY.

acquired immunodeficiency syndrome, the full name of the disease better known as AIDS.

Action Plan for Women's Health: See PHS ACTION PLAN FOR WOMEN'S HEALTH.

Addams, Jane (1860–1935), for almost five decades one of the world's leading women, whose honors included a 1920s Daughters of the American Revolution denunciation as "the most dangerous woman in America today" and a Nobel Peace Prize (shared with Nicholas Murray Butler) in 1931.

In 1889 Addams and Ellen Gates Starr founded Chicago's Hull House, the pioneering settlement house that became central to the developing American social work movement, as testing place and training ground. There Addams wrote her seminal *Twenty Years at Hull House* (1910), as well as the earlier and scarcely less influential *Democracy and Social Ethics* (1902). She was founder and first president (1911–1935) of the National Federation of Settlements.

Addams was a leading WOMEN'S RIGHTS advocate, pacifist, and civil libertarian. She was a vice-president of the NATIONAL AMERICAN WOMAN SUFFRAGE ASSOCIATION from 1911 to 1914, turning her major attention to antiwar activities with the outbreak of World War I. During the war, she chaired the WOMEN'S PEACE PARTY and was president of the Women's Peace Congress at the Hague. In 1919 she chaired the second Women's Peace Congress and was in that year a founder and first president of the WOMEN'S INTERNATIONAL LEAGUE FOR PEACE AND FREEDOM. In 1920 she was a founder of the American Civil Liberties Union.

Old-fashioned ways which no longer apply to changed conditions are a snare in which the feet of women have always become readily entangled.

JANE ADDAMS, 1907
IN "UTILIZATION OF WOMEN IN CITY GOVERNMENT,"
IN NEWER IDEALS OF PEACE

•

adoption, raising as one's own a child born to someone else. The child's *biological parents*, also called *birth* or *natural parents*, would initially have PARENTS' RIGHTS and associated responsibilities, including CUSTODY. In most adoptions, the parents or (if unmarried) the single MOTHER gives up parental rights voluntarily, as in cases of unwanted PREGNANCY or SURROGATE PARENTING; sometimes the state may terminate the rights, as in cases of CHILD ABUSE AND NEGLECT, including ABANDONMENT; less commonly in these days, the biological parents may have died.

In formal adoption, the parents' rights are transferred legally to the *adoptive parents*, making the adopted child formally part of a new family. The child's legal rights, such as INHERITANCE RIGHTS, are also transferred, but these vary widely from one state to another, so adoptive parents must be sure that all legal documents relating to the family, such as insurance policies and wills, specifically include the adopted child; such references as *next of kin, descendants, heirs of the body, born to* or *issue*, need to be changed in many cases, since they refer to biological children, unless the particular state provides otherwise.

Adoption may be handled in a wide variety of ways, among them:

▶ *sealed adoption,* in which the adoptive parents and child are brought together by a neutral organization, generally a private or public adoption agency, and all records of the adoption are kept strictly confidential, generally being unavailable to biological or adoptive parents or adopted child, as well as the public, except by court order. Agencies generally conduct a long and intensive investigation of the prospective parents' suitability as adopters, aiming to screen out those who are unsuitable, as for financial or psychological reasons; their home-study report is then sent out to whatever other agencies are involved when a family applies for adoption. Agencies also frequently provide counseling to adoptive and birth parents, and parenting preparation courses for adopters.

Usually, adoptive parents—and later the adopted child—learn only general information about the birth parents, though this is becoming more precise as GENETIC COUNSELING has become more common and people seek more information about their family medical history. Among the kinds of information normally made available are age, race, ethnic background, religion, educational and occupational background, general medical and psychiatric history, information on intellect and personality, and some circumstances surrounding the birth and planned adoption, including whether the child was born outside marriage. Some also include information on any medical examinations the birth parents had within the year before the child was placed for adoption, the birth mother's PRENATAL CARE, and the child's medical condition at birth. However, some information may be withheld, such as whether one or both birth parents are imprisoned or INCEST or RAPE was involved.

Sealed adoption is a twentieth-century development, designed to ease the problems of older forms of adoption. Its main advantage is that it provides a clean break with the past for all parties involved in what is called the *adoption triangle:* adoptive parents, birth parents, and adopted child. The identity of the birth parents is protected, and the child has a single family, rather than a possibly confusing two.

In recent decades, however, many adoptees—as teens or adults—have sought access to information about their birth parents. Similarly, some birth parents have sought to find their biological children, in regret over having given them up. Also, some parents and siblings have sought information on relatives lost when the state terminated parents' rights and placed a child for adoption. Various organizations have been formed to help such people in their search for each other (see ADOPTION HELP, INFORMATION, AND ACTION GUIDE on page 19). In some states adopted children—on reaching adulthood—are able to obtain certain information. The question is not simple, however. Many birth parents do not *want* to be found, and some have complained bitterly that their privacy has been violated, as the legal understanding that applied at the time of the adoption has been broken. Some states that have liberalized information on adoption have made it conditional on the consent of the birth parents.

▶ *open adoption,* in which birth parents and adoptive parents often meet and get to know each other during PREGNANCY, sometimes also mediated by an agency. What happens after that varies widely. At its most open, the parents maintain full contact, including letters, photographs, and perhaps even meetings, as the child grows. Sometimes the initial contact is made without full names, addresses, and phone numbers, and contact ends after the adoption. In other cases letters and photographs are exchanged confidentially through the adoption agency. Open adoption is especially common with older children, as when they have living relatives, such as a sibling or grandparent (see GRANDPARENTS' RIGHTS).

The main problem with open adoption is that the relationships may be unstable. Birth parents can later have a change of heart and attempt to reverse the adoption, disrupting everyone involved, and (in the most open form) the child may be torn by two sets of parents.

▶ *private, independent,* or *direct adoption,* in which the connections between adoptive and birth parents are made outside the agency system, often through relatives, friends, or acquaintances and sometimes through doctors, lawyers, and even personal advertisements. The adoption must be registered with the court to be official. This is the older, traditional approach to adoption, which sealed adoption was designed to replace. Perfectly legal, it is today "nonstandard," so many call it *gray-market adoption.* The two sets of parents often deal through a lawyer, but in some states such intermediaries are forbidden.

For many people private adoption is very attractive because it avoids the intervention of agencies, with their home studies and evaluations. For people who would be unlikely to pass agency scrutiny—for example, single people (see SINGLE WOMAN), older people, poor people, LESBIANS, gay men, or people who already have large families—this may be the only route to adoption. In private adoption of newborns, the child often goes to the adoptive parents directly from the hospital. The hazard for adoptive parents is that the adoption does not become permanent for a period of time, specified by state law, and the birth parents may change their mind and take the baby back.

▶ *identified* or *designated adoption,* a form of private adoption in which the would-be adoptive parents engage an adoption agency to handle the adoption details for a child privately located. The agency then performs its normal services: home study, counseling the birth parents, obtaining adoption consent papers, and arranging for payment of the birth mother's expenses.

▶ *legal risk adoption* or *foster/adoption,* in which the child is placed in the home of the prospective adoptive parents, who act as *foster parents* until the adoption can be arranged. Used especially for older children, this approach allows child and adoptive parents to live together as soon as possible, rather than keep the child in limbo for the months or even years (in extreme cases) it can take to finalize adoption. But legal risk adoption can—as the name indicates—be very risky for both, because adoption may in the end fall through, if the birth mother or child's other relatives decide not to sign adoption consent papers.

▶ *subsidized adoption,* in which adoptive parents receive subsidies to adopt children who are otherwise not so easy to place, such as older children, siblings who wish to stay together, children of minority ancestry, or children with special health needs. Plans vary widely, but many include a monthly sum or coverage of specific medical, psychiatric, or other costs, and sometimes also Medicaid benefits. Moving from one state to another can be a problem, except where the states belong to the Interstate Compact on Adoption and Medical Assistance.

▶ *international adoption,* in which prospective adopters look abroad for children to adopt. This has been an increasingly common choice, but it involves long, tangled, frustrating dealings with two sets of international authorities and differing state laws as well (see below).

▶ *baby brokering,* adoptions in which often large amounts of money are paid to the birth parents or guardians and especially to the intermediaries, also called *black-market adoptions.* They have become more common in recent decades, where ABORTION has been legalized, because fewer infants are available for adoption. To the problems associated with traditional adoptions are added the fact that these often illegal adoptions do not have legal protections built in for both sets of parents and for the child.

Whatever form of adoption is involved, the sheer amount of paperwork can be daunting, both in connection with the initial home study (if there is one) and the later adoption application itself. Among the documents generally required for a home study are certified copies of birth certificates and, where applicable, marriage certificates, divorce records, death records of former spouse, and sometimes birth certificates of other children in the family; physicians' statements on the prospective parents' physical health and sometimes also their mental health and information on possible infertility; notarized financial statements, such as bank statements, accountants' reports, and federal income tax returns; employment statements indicating position, length of service, salary, and stability of job; personal autobiographies from the prospective parents; photographs of the parents, any other children, and their home; proof of naturalization, where appropriate; and a check of police files for a clear police record, especially regarding child abuse. Obtaining certified copies of birth, marriage, divorce, and death certificates is not always easy; the U.S. government publishes a pamphlet, *Where to Write for Vital Records: Births, Deaths, Marriages, and Divorces,* to help with the process. Many of the required documents can take weeks or months to obtain, and two or three are required of many, so parents are advised to get multiple copies to begin with. Where the child is being given up for adoption at birth, adoptive parents often arrange to pay the birth mother's living and medical expenses.

The adoption agency or birth parents will have to supply adoption consent forms from the birth parent (or other legal authority) and medical consent giving the new adoptive parents the rights to provide medical treatment for the child. A petition for adoption must be filed in state court, to be followed by a final order of adoption from the court (sometimes with a temporary, or *interlocutory* order first), after which the adopted child is given a new birth certificate, with new name and parents.

For international adoption many of those same forms are required, but they must be translated, notarized, verified, and authenticated at the consulate of the child's country of birth. In addition, parents must file numerous forms required by the U.S. Immigration and Naturalization Service (INS), including the I-600, "Petition to Classify Orphan as an Immediate Relative"; the I-600A, "Application for Advance Processing of Orphan Petition," filed even before parents have identified a specific child for adoption, to speed processing; Form N-402, "Application to File Petition for Naturalization in Behalf of Child," with a thirty-day-old photograph of the child; Form N-600, "Application for Certificate of Citizenship," where both adoptive parents are U.S. citizens; Form FD-258, showing the fingerprints of the adoptive parents; Form G-641, "Certification of Birth Data," to act as a birth certificate; certified copies, with certified translation, of the child's birth certificate or other proof of age, the death certificate of the child's birth parent(s), release of the child by the surviving parent, evidence of a surviving parent's inability to provide for the child, evidence of the child's abandonment, and/or the foreign adoption decree; evidence that the parents have met preadoption requirements of the proposed state of residence, as by posting a bond; a U.S. passport and alien registration for the child; and application for readoption of the child in the United States. In addition, parents must meet requirements set by the laws in the child's country of birth and the prospective parents' home state. The INS publishes a special booklet, *The Immigration of Adopted and Prospective Adoptive Children,* to help parents through the maze. In some cases of international adoptions, the child keeps in touch with family members in the home country.

Numerous organizations have been formed that will help prospective parents through the long, complicated adoption process; some of the main ones are listed in ADOPTION HELP, INFORMATION, AND ACTION GUIDE, below.

ADOPTION
Help, Information, and Action Guide

Organizations

▶ **National Council for Adoption (NCFA)** (1930 17th Street, NW, Washington, DC 20009; 202-328-1200; hot line 202-328-8072; William L. Pierce, executive director), an organization for adoptees, adoptive and birth parents, and professionals in the field; formerly the National Committee for Adoption. It supports confidentiality of adoption information and opposes nonstandard adoptions, seeking to influence legislation on these and other adoption concerns. The NCFA also gathers information, maintains a library, and publishes various materials for professionals and individuals, including *Adoption Factbook: United States Data, Issues, Regulations and Resources.*

▶ **American Adoption Congress (AAC)** (1000 Connecticut Avenue, NW, Suite 9, Washington, DC 20036; 800-274-OPEN [6736]; Kate Burke, president), an organization concerned with adoption, founded in 1978 for adopted people, adoptive parents, and biological parents. AAC sponsors research and educational conferences; gathers and disseminates information, acting as a national clearinghouse; and publishes various materials; including the quarterly *Decree,* an annual *Legislative Report,* and directories of search/support groups, special services, and regional directors.

▶ NATIONAL ADOPTION INFORMATION CLEARINGHOUSE (NAIC) (202-842-1919). Publishes *National Adoption Directory.*

▶ Families Adopting Children Everywhere (FACE) (P.O. Box 28058, Northwood Station, Baltimore, MD 21239; 410-488-2656; C. A. Tolley, president), an organization of people and agencies involved in adoption. It educates current or would-be adoptive families, as through the course "Family Building Through Adoption," and publishes a newsletter and other materials, such as *They Became Part of Us.*

▶ THE NURTURING NETWORK (TNN) (208-344-7200 or 800-TNN-4MOM [866-4666]). Offers an alternative to ABORTION for a crisis PREGNANCY.

☑ ON SPECIAL ADOPTION SITUATIONS

▶ Committee for Single Adoptive Parents (CSAP) (P.O. Box 15084, Chevy Chase, MD 20815; 202-966-6367; Hope Marindin, executive director), an organization for current or would-be single adoptive parents. It makes referrals; offers help in dealing with agencies; and publishes *Handbook for Single Adoptive Parents.*

▶ SINGLE MOTHERS BY CHOICE (SMC) (212-988-0993).

▶ RESOLVE, INC. (617-623-0744). Offers adoption services, in addition to infertility treatments.

▶ LESBIAN MOTHERS NATIONAL DEFENSE FUND (LMNDF) (206-325-2643). Provides information to lesbians who wish to adopt.

▶ LAMBDA LEGAL DEFENSE AND EDUCATION FUND (212-995-8585). Provides legal counsel for lesbians wishing to adopt.

▶ NATIONAL CENTER FOR YOUTH LAW (NCYL) (415-543-3307).

▶ NATIONAL CENTER FOR LESBIAN RIGHTS (NCLR) (415-621-0674).

☑ ON RELATIONSHIPS BETWEEN ADOPTEES AND BIRTH PARENTS

▶ Concerned United Birthparents (CUB) (2000 Walker Street, Des Moines, IA 50317; 515-263-9558; Janet Fenton, president), an organization for birth parents and others who support adoption reform. It seeks the opening of birth and adoption records for both adoptees and birth parents and publishes newsletters and other materials.

▶ Origins (P.O. Box 556, Whippany, NJ 07981; 201-428-9683; Mary Anne Cohen, co-founder), an organization for women whose children have been adopted, offering support and assistance to them and other relatives in searching for information about their children. It also publishes a newsletter.

Other resources

■ GENERAL WORKS

There Are Babies to Adopt. Christine A. Adamec. Windsor (NY), 1991.
Adopting a Child. Brown O'Neil. W. Gladden Foundation, 1991.
The Adoption Option: A Practical Handbook for Prospective Adoptive Parents. Kalynn George. C. C. Thomas, 1990.
Ideal Adoption: A Comprehensive Guide to Forming an Adoptive Family. S. C. Samuels. Plenum, 1990.
Adopt the Baby You Want. Susan Shultz. Simon & Schuster, 1990.
The Private Adoption Handbook. Stanley B. Michelman and Meg Schneider. Dell, 1990.
Adoption Resource Guide. Julia L. Posner. Child Welfare, 1990.
Making Sense of Adoption. Lois Ruskai Melina. Harper & Row, 1989.
Beating the Adoption Game, rev. ed. Cynthia D. Martin. Harcourt Brace Jovanovich, 1988.
The Adoption Resource Book, rev. ed. Lois Gilman. Harper & Row, 1987.
Successful Adoption: A Guide to Finding a Child and Raising a Family, rev. ed. Jacqueline Plumez. Harmony, 1987.
Adoption: Parenthood Without Pregnancy. Charlene Canape. Holt, 1986.

■ ON BIRTH MOTHERS AND LATER CONTACTS

Birth Mother Search: Some Day I'll Find Her. E. B. Schumacher and others. Larksdale, 1992.
The Other Mother: A Woman's Love for the Child She Gave Up for Adoption. Carol Schaefer. Soho Press, 1991.
Wanted: First Child: A Birth-Mother's Story. Rebecca Harsin. Fithian Press, 1991.
Pregnant by Mistake: The Stories of Seventeen Women, rev. ed. Katrina Maxtone-Graham. Remi Books, 1990.
I Wish You Didn't Know My Name: The Story of Michele Launders and Her Daughter Lisa. Michele Launders and Penina Spiegel. Warner, 1990.
Birthbond: Reunions Between Birthparents and Adoptees—What Happens After. . . . Judith S. Gediman and Linda P. Brown. New Horizon, 1989.
Lost and Found: The Adoption Experience, rev. ed. Betty Jean Lifton. Harper & Row, 1988.

■ ON OPEN ADOPTION

Unlocking the Adoption Files. Paul Sachdev. Free Press, 1990.
An Open Adoption. Lincoln Caplan. Farrar, Straus & Giroux, 1990.

Children of Open Adoption. Kathleen Silber and Patricia Martinez Dorner. Corona, 1990.

Open Adoption: A Caring Option. Jeanne Warren Lindsay. Morning Glory Press, 1987.

▨ **PERSONAL STORES**

Bitter Fruit: Women's Experiences of Unplanned Pregnancy, Abortion, and Adoption. Ann Perkins and Rira Townsend. Hunter House, 1992.

Open Adoption: My Story of Love and Laughter. Ann K. Anderson. Tyndale, 1990.

Adoption Story. Marguerite Ryan. Tudor (NY), 1990. Reprint of 1989 ed.

Waiting for Baby: One Couple's Journey Through Infertility to Adoption. Mary Earle Chase. McGraw-Hill, 1989.

Whose Child Am I? Adults' Recollections of Being Adopted. John Y. Powell. Tiresias Press, 1985.

▨ **BACKGROUND BOOKS**

Adoption Project. A. Brodzinsky. Doubleday, 1992.

Encyclopedia of Adoption. Christine A. Adamec and William Pierce. Facts on File, 1991. Pierce is president of the National Council for Adoption (see above).

Intercountry Adoption: A Multinational Perspective. Howard Altstein and Rita J. Simon, eds. Greenwood, 1990.

Adoption: The Facts, Feelings and Issues of a Double Heritage, rev. ed. Jeanne DuPrau. Simon & Schuster, 1990.

The Psychology of Adoption. David M. Brodzinsky and Marshall D. Schecter, eds. Oxford University Press, 1990.

The Adoption Triangle: Sealed or Open Records: How They Affect Adoptees, Birth Parents, and Adoptive Parents. Arthur D. Sorosky and others. Texas Monthly Press, 1989.

adultery, SEXUAL INTERCOURSE between a married person and someone other than his or her legal SPOUSE; legally sometimes called *criminal conversation.* For women, adultery refers only to voluntary sex and so does not apply to a woman who has been raped (see RAPE) but *does* apply to a man who rapes a woman other than his wife. If a spouse is living with someone other than a marital partner, it is called *adulterous* COHABITATION.

Adultery is the oldest of grounds for DIVORCE. In places where SEPARATION, DIVORCE, and related questions such as ALIMONY, CUSTODY, CHILD SUPPORT, and division of MARITAL PROPERTY are sharply contested in court, adultery may still be considered grounds for a divorce or may lead to loss of alimony or custody.

Though such rulings generally apply to HETEROSEXUAL intercourse, in some cases men have successfully used their wives' LESBIAN experiences as adultery (and vice versa). Because adultery is hard to prove, the court sometimes accepts a pattern of behavior that showed both the opportunity and the inclination to commit adultery. In the days before so-called no-fault divorces, where adultery was virtually the only grounds for divorce, courts routinely accepted "rigged" evidence of adultery, in which the husband and wife agreed that he should allow himself to be photographed with another woman, both in nightclothes, in a hotel, with the photograph then being used as presumptive evidence of adultery.

Traditionally, rulings regarding adultery much favored men over women. In some parts of the United States, for example, a husband was allowed to divorce his wife simply for "lewd and lascivious behavior," without proving adultery, though wives were unable to bring similar suits. Some states required more than a single instance of adulterous behavior, and in one case a woman was unable to divorce her husband on grounds of adultery, even though he had contracted a SEXUALLY TRANSMITTED DISEASE and passed it on to her, with the court ruling that she could have the divorce only if her husband's behavior brought her public scandal and disgrace. In most Westernized countries, courts have been doing away with such gender bias, if only because no-fault divorces largely circumvent such questions. However, in many other parts of the world, a woman may be cast aside in cases of proven or suspected adultery, though she often does not have a similar right to divorce her husband on the same grounds. (See also DIVORCE; also DIVORCE AND SEPARATION HELP, INFORMATION, AND ACTION GUIDE on page 238.)

affinity, a legal term for kin relations by MARRIAGE (see INCEST).

AFP, an abbreviation for ALPHA FETOPROTEIN.

African-American feminism: See FEMINISM.

afterbirth, the PLACENTA expelled from a woman's body after a baby has been born.

Against Our Will: Men, Women and Rape: See Susan BROWNMILLER.

age of consent, the age at which a woman (or man) can legally marry without obtaining consent from a parent or guardian; also the age at which a person can legally agree to have SEXUAL INTERCOURSE. The precise age depends on the laws in a particular state; in the United States it is usually sixteen or eighteen. Someone who has sexual relations with a girl under the specified age is liable to a charge of statutory RAPE, regardless of the girl's previous sexual experience and of her consent, which the law generally does not acknowledge as valid. In practice, with the change of sexual mores in Western countries over the last several decades, charges of statutory rape are seldom brought regarding sex between consenting adolescents. However, if an underage girl has sex with an older man, charges of statutory rape or child sexual abuse (see CHILD ABUSE AND NEGLECT) may be brought.

AIDS (acquired immunodeficiency syndrome), infection with a deadly virus that cripples defensive cells in the IMMUNE SYSTEM and leaves the body prey to abnormal cellular behavior, such as CANCER and opportunistic infections, so-called because they are present in the body normally and become dangerous only under special circumstances. The virus that causes AIDS is called *human immunodeficiency virus,* or HIV, sometimes *human T-cell lymphotropic virus III,* HTLV-III, or LAV. It works by attacking vital defensive cells called T cells, which produce disease-fighting antibodies (see IMMUNE SYSTEM).

AIDS is a new and devastating disease, and much about it is still unknown. There are at least two viruses known, HIV-1 and HIV-2. Also, different strains of HIV exist, some of which are readily transmitted while others are not. The virus exists in various body fluids, including BLOOD, SEMEN, saliva, tears, BREAST milk, secretions from female GENITALS, and tissue in the nervous system (see BRAIN AND NERVOUS SYSTEM). Intensive study of all known cases of AIDS indicates that HIV is not spread by casual contact, or in home, office, school, or other public places. It is *not,* for example, spread through the air, as a cold or flu might be, and AIDS experts regard touching, hugging, *closed-mouth* kissing, and *giving* blood as no-risk activities.

HIV *is* spread from one person to another through exchange of body fluids, most notably blood (including menstrual blood) and semen. The most common means of transmission are SEXUAL INTERCOURSE, especially rough or anal sex, making AIDS a kind of SEXUALLY TRANSMITTED DISEASE; by blood transfusions (see BLOOD); and by sharing needles, as among drug users or reuse of unsterilized needles (as has been common in Eastern Europe). However, HIV can be passed between any two people with open cuts or sores, including health care workers and patients. In addition, HIV can be transmitted to a woman through semen from a SPERM bank and from mother to FETUS by way of the PLACENTA.

Total abstinence from any of these activities or situations is the only sure way to avoid exposure to HIV (see TIPS FOR PREVENTING AIDS on page 31). However, the risk can be reduced in various ways: blood for transfusions can be tested for presence of antibodies to the virus; mothers can be tested before or during PREGNANCY; sexual partners can be tested; a CONDOM can be used during sex (see CONDOMS: WHAT WOMEN NEED TO KNOW on page 188); health care workers can use protective gear to avoiding giving or receiving the virus; and so on.

But like all medical tests, AIDS tests are fallible. They can give a false negative, indicating no sign of the virus when it actually is present, or a false positive, indicating signs of the virus when it is *not* present. Also, the tests may not pick up evidence of antibodies if infection has been very recent, but the disease may still be communicable. In addition, especially with such a serious disease, no one should ever rely on a single test. For all these reasons, a positive result is often double-checked with a second test; and a negative result is followed up by another test a few months later. Such double testing is also often done on blood and semen in sperm banks (see ARTIFICIAL INSEMINATION). Women trying to protect themselves from exposure, however, should never be dissuaded from using condoms by someone's claim to have been tested and found free of the virus. AIDS experts estimate that as many as 90 percent of heterosexuals infected with HIV do not know it, not getting tested because they do not consider themselves at risk. So they not only spread the disease, but may lose the chance to prolong their lives by starting medication early.

Exposure to HIV virus does not automatically and immediately bring on AIDS. For unknown reasons, some people appear to be more susceptible than others. Certainly having other sexually transmitted diseases, which often involve open sores, greatly increases the likelihood of HIV infection. It is not known, however, whether everyone exposed to the virus becomes infected; whether everyone who has signs of initial infection will ultimately develop AIDS; and whether everyone who develops AIDS will die from it.

Early signs of infection with HIV result from mild impairment of the immune system. These include swollen lymph nodes (see IMMUNE SYSTEM), SKIN disorders, weight loss, fever, diarrhea, opportunistic infections such as *candidiasis* (see YEAST INFECTION), and increased susceptibility to diseases such as HERPES or tuberculosis. This mild condition is called *AIDS-related complex,* or ARC. Full-blown AIDS involves progression to more serious problems, including rare CANCERS such as Kaposi's sarcoma and lymphoma of the brain and infections such as toxoplasmosis, CYTOMEGALOVIRUS (CMV), and pneumonia, especially the type caused by the usually innocuous *Pneumocystis carinii.*

What actually constitutes AIDS has, in fact, been a matter of some dispute. The early definition was based on male symptoms and so did not include many women who were clearly infected. In the United States the definition was expanded somewhat in late 1992 to include invasive cancer of the CERVIX (see UTERINE CANCER), pulmonary tuberculosis, and two or more episodes of bacterial pneumonia. Under this expanded definition, many more women and drug users would be considered to have AIDS, and inclusion of such groups in the AIDS population should lead to more equitable distribution of funding for care and prevention of AIDS. Many insurance companies and government agencies have been covering such people already, but the change should allow women with AIDS to more readily get disability benefits. Some women's groups want the definition widened even further, to include PELVIC INFLAMMATORY DISEASE and YEAST INFECTIONS, common in women, which can become lethal in women with AIDS.

When AIDS was first recognized, many people thought of it as associated primarily with gay men and drug users, because it was among those populations that the largest number of cases were first recognized in developed countries. But in fact AIDS has been and remains very much a heterosexual disease. AIDS experts estimate that of the ten million people infected with HIV in the world, about one in three is a woman. In the United States overall the ratio is one in eight, but in some eastern states it is also one in three. Why such regional differences exist is unclear but may have to do with NUTRITION and the increased presence of opportunistic diseases, among other factors. Though in the United States, only about 6 percent of all AIDS cases have resulted from heterosexual sex, this is the fastest-growing segment of the AIDS population, especially among women.

What has become very clear is that women are more likely to become infected by men than vice versa. One reason for this is that semen contains more of the virus than cervical fluid, and the semen remains in the woman's body for some days, while the man's PENIS is in contact with cervical fluid only during intercourse. Women also die from the disease twice as quickly as do men, again for unknown reasons but perhaps partly because many women AIDS victims are poor, SINGLE PARENTS, and lack ready access to health care. Women are also less able to participate in trials of experimental drugs, if they might become pregnant; many of them are against ABORTION, and in any case companies are concerned about liability for possible BIRTH DEFECTS.

The children of mothers with AIDS pose a special problem. Many were infected with AIDS at birth and themselves live only as long as medical care allows. Many others are orphaned when the mother—often the sole provider—dies of AIDS. In some parts of Africa AIDS has been called the "grandmother's disease," because it is that older generation of women that often assumes the responsibility for raising orphaned grandchildren. The same pattern may be found in the developed world.

Globally the areas of greatest AIDS concentration are in Africa, where the disease is believed to have originated; in the hardest-hit country, Uganda, an estimated 1.5 million people out of a total of 16 million are believed to be infected with HIV. In many parts of the world, notably Africa and Asia, social observers have seen a rise in child PROSTITUTION as adult males seek sexual contacts with females less likely to be infected with AIDS.

Much remains to be learned, however. In late 1992 health officials reported that they had found people with AIDS-like symptoms but no sign of the HIV. There was wide concern that a new, as yet unrecognized strain of virus was being spread, but early reports seemed to indicate that was not so. However, also in late 1992, other researchers reported that five people known to have been infected with AIDS-tainted blood had no symptoms seven to ten years later, suggesting that some strains may be nonvirulent or that HIV infection does not always lead to AIDS and is not always fatal. Also unexplained were why fewer than half of the babies born to mothers with AIDS are infected with HIV.

In any case, women seem to be increasingly conscious of the dangers and the need for care. Recent studies have shown that at least a third of unmarried women have changed their sexual behavior; many are having intercourse less often, only with men they already know, or just with a single partner. Above 5 percent have stopped having intercourse altogether. Black and Hispanic women are more likely to have changed their behavior than White women, who perhaps mistakenly believe they are not at risk.

Treatment with some antiviral drugs has shown some promise in prolonging life; other drugs and treatment are also being used and tested, but none so far offers a cure. Some studies have suggested that the sooner AIDS is recognized and treatment begun, the longer the survival and the better the quality of life; other studies have found no such benefit. Researchers are also developing possible vaccines, including one made from a harmless copy of the HIV, which has shown promise in experiments on monkeys. In 1991 an experimental human vaccine began testing in several countries where AIDS is prevalent, but a vaccine for general use is thought to be years away, and there are questions whether such a vaccine can be developed, since different strains exist. (See **AIDS HELP, INFORMATION, AND ACTION GUIDE,** below; also SEXUALLY TRANSMITTED DISEASES; CONDOM; also **WHAT YOU CAN DO TO AVOID STDS** on page 660; **CONDOMS: WHAT WOMEN NEED TO KNOW** on page 188; **SEXUALLY TRANSMITTED DISEASES HELP, INFORMATION, AND ACTION GUIDE** on page 658.)

AIDS

Help, Information, and Action Guide

Information lines

▶ **National AIDS Hotline** (24 hours, 800-342-AIDS [2437]; in Spanish, 8 A.M.–2 A.M., 800-344-7432; TTY/TDD for hearing impaired, 10 A.M.– 10 P.M., 800-243-7889), a service offering recorded information on the prevention and spread of AIDS.
▶ **CDC National AIDS Clearinghouse (CDC NAC)** (P.O. Box 6003, Rockville, MD 20850; 800-458-5231; TDD for hearing impaired, 800-243-7012; international calls, 301-217-0023), a service of the Public Health Service (PHS) and Centers for Disease Control (CDC), established to gather, classify, and disseminate information on AIDS. It distributes publications from various public and private organizations and makes referrals to local information numbers for specific information on AIDS and treatment service. Material can be accessed directly through the **CDC NAC Online,** using a computer and modem.
▶ **AIDS Clinical Trials Information Service** (800-TRIALS-A [874-2572]; TDD for hearing impaired, 800-243-7012; for international calls, 301-217-0023), a federally sponsored service providing current information on clinical trials for people with AIDS or those infected with HIV.
▶ **National Criminal Justice Reference Services** (800-851-3420 or 301-251-5500), a service that provides information about AIDS in a criminal justice setting.
▶ **National Indian AIDS Information Line** (800-283-AIDS [2437]), a service to provide printed material about AIDS and AIDS prevention in the Indian community.

Organizations

▶ NATIONAL WOMEN'S HEALTH NETWORK (NWHN) (202-347-1140). Operates the **Women's Health Information Service.** Publishes *AIDS: What Every Women Needs to Know, Women, AIDS, and Public Health Policies,* and various reprints.

▶ NATIONAL INSTITUTE OF ALLERGY AND INFECTIOUS DISEASES (NIAID) (301-496-5717).

▶ NATIONAL CLEARINGHOUSE FOR ALCOHOL AND DRUG ABUSE INFORMATION (NCADI) (301-468-2600 or 800-729-6686). Publishes *Acquired Immunodeficiency Syndrome and Chemical Dependency, AIDS and Drug Abuse,* and *Alcohol and AIDS: Update.*

▶ WOMEN'S MINISTRY UNIT (WMU) (502-569-5382). Publishes *Women and AIDS.*

▶ ACLU AIDS Project (American Civil Liberties Union, 132 West 43rd Street, New York, NY 10036; 212-944-9800, ext. 545; William B. Rubenstein, project director), an organization that "undertakes precedent-setting litigation, public policy advocacy, and public education on civil liberties issues raised by the AIDS crisis." It also acts as a backup to ACLU affiliates work on AIDS around the nation and functions as an AIDS policy center, as through its AIDS Policy Network, supplying legal and policy documents to advocates and policy makers.

▶ National Association of People with AIDS (NAPWA) (1413 K Street, NW, 10th Floor, Washington, DC 20006; 202-898-0414; William J. Freeman, executive director), an organization of people who have AIDS or AIDS-related conditions. It acts as advocate for people with AIDS and publishes materials, including a monthly newsletter.

▶ MS. FOUNDATION FOR WOMEN (MFW) (212-353-8580).

▶ CENTER FOR WOMEN POLICY STUDIES (CWPS) (202-872-1770). Has *National Resource Center on Women and AIDS.*

▶ NATIONAL BLACK WOMEN'S HEALTH PROJECT (NBWHP) (404-681-4554).

▶ ACT UP (AIDS COALITION TO UNLEASH POWER) (135 West 29th Street, New York, NY 10014; 212-564-2437), an organization concerned with people with AIDS or HIV infection. It acts as an advocate; carries out direct political action; and publishes various materials, including a newsletter, quarterly ACT UP Reports, *Women, AIDS and Activism,* and handbooks.

▶ PLANNED PARENTHOOD® (212-541-7800). Publishes *AIDS and HIV Questions and Answers; How to Talk with Your Child About AIDS; The Condom: What It Is, What It Is For, How It Works;* and *It Can't Happen to Me!: True Stories About AIDS,* a comic-book-style pamphlet for teenagers.

▨ ON MOTHERS, CHILDREN, AND AIDS

▶ NATIONAL CENTER FOR EDUCATION IN MATERNAL AND CHILD HEALTH (NCEMCH) (703-524-7802) and NATIONAL MATERNAL AND CHILD HEALTH CLEARINGHOUSE (NMCHC) (703-821-8955). Publish *Women and Infants at Risk for HIV Infection: Guidelines and Protocols for Prevention and Care.*

▶ MARCH OF DIMES BIRTH DEFECTS FOUNDATION (914-428-7100; local chapters in telephone directory white pages). Publishes *Congenital AIDS.*

▶ **Pediatric AIDS Foundation (PAF)** (2407 Wilshire Boulevard, Suite 613, Santa Monica, CA 90403; 213-395-9051; Elizabeth Glaser, chairperson), an organization concerned with AIDS in children. It encourages research in pediatric AIDS and seeks programs to meet the special needs of children with AIDS.

▶ **Mothers of AIDS Patients** (1811 Field Drive, NE, Albuquerque, NM 87112-2823; 619-544-0430; Barbara Peabody, executive officer), an organization for the families of people with AIDS, providing information and encouraging the formation of local mutual support groups.

▶ **Child Welfare League of America (CWLA)** (202-639-2952). Publishes *Courage to Care: Responding to the Crisis of Children with AIDS.*

▨ ON LESBIANS, GAYS, AND AIDS

▶ NATIONAL CENTER FOR LESBIAN RIGHTS (NCLR) (415-621-0674). Publishes *AIDS and Child Custody: A Guide to Advocacy.*

▶ DIGNITY/USA (202-861-0017 or 800-877-8797).

▶ HUMAN RIGHTS CAMPAIGN FUND (202-628-4160 or 800-777-HRCF [4723]).

▶ **LAMBDA** LEGAL DEFENSE AND EDUCATION FUND (**LLDEF**) (212-995-8585). Publishes *AIDS Update.*

Other resources

▨ GENERAL WORKS

What You Can Do to Avoid AIDS. Earvin "Magic" Johnson. Times Books, 1992.

AIDS-Proofing Your Kids: A Step-by-Step Guide. Loren E. Acker and others. Beyond Words, 1992.

How to Find Information About AIDS, 2nd ed. Jeffrey T. Huber, ed. Haworth, 1991.

The Essential AIDS Fact Book. Columbia University Health Service. Pocket Books, 1990.

Living with AIDS. Stephen R. Graubard, ed. MIT Press, 1990.

AIDS and Schoolchildren in America's Communities. David L. Kirp. Rutgers University Press, 1990.

In the Absence of Angels: A Hollywood Family's Courageous Story. Elizabeth Glaser and Laura Palmer. Putnam, 1990. By the founder of the Pediatric AIDS Foundation (see above).

◪ FOR OR BY ADOLESCENTS

Risky Times: How to Be AIDS-Smart and Stay Healthy. Jeanne Blake. Workman, 1990. For teenagers, with parents' guide.

The Impact of AIDS. Ewan Armstrong. Watts/Gloucester Press, 1990.

AIDS: What Does It Mean to You?, 3rd ed. Margaret Hyde and Elizabeth Forsyth, M.D. Walker, 1990.

Coping with Health Risks and Risky Behavior. Alan R. Bleich. Rosen, 1990.

Fighting Back: What Some People Are Doing About AIDS. Susan Kuklin. Putnam, 1988.

AIDS: Trading Fears for Facts: A Guide for Teens. Karen Hein and others. Consumer Reports, 1989.

Lynda Madaras Talks to Teens About AIDS: An Essential Guide for Parents, Teachers and Young People. Lynda Madaras. Newmarket Press, 1988.

◪ ON PROGRAMS AND SERVICES

AIDS and the Law: A Basic Guide for the Non-Lawyer. Allan H. Terl, 1992. (Address: Taylor & Francis Group, 1900 Frost Road, Suite 101, Bristol, PA 19007-1598; 800-821-8312.)

The AIDS Benefits Handbook: Everything You Need to Know to Get Social Security, Welfare, Medicaid, Medicare, Food Stamps, Housing, Drugs, and Other Benefits. Thomas P. McCormack. Yale University Press, 1990.

Take These Broken Wings and Learn to Fly: The AIDS Support Book for Patients, Family and Friends. Steven D. Dietz and M. Jane Parker Hicks, M.D. Harbinger House, 1989.

Local AIDS-Related Services National Directory. Available from The United States Conference of Mayors, 1620 Eye Street, NW, 4th floor, Washington, DC 20006; 202-293-7330.

◪ BACKGROUND WORKS

Acquired Immune Deficiency Syndrome: Biological, Medical, Social, and Legal Issues. Gerald J. Stine. Prentice-Hall, 1993.

AIDS: The Making of a Chronic Disease. Elizabeth Fee and Daniel M. Fox, eds. University of California Press, 1992.

Dictionary of AIDS-Related Terminology. Jeffrey T. Huber. Neal-Schuman, 1992.

AIDS, Sexual Behavior, and Intravenous Drug Use. National Academy Press, 1989.

The AIDS Epidemic: Private Rights and the Public Interest. Padraig O'Malley, ed. Beacon Press, 1989.

Report of the Presidential Commission on the Human Immunodeficiency Virus Epidemic. U.S. Government Printing Office, 1988.

(See also SEXUALLY TRANSMITTED DISEASES; also SEXUALLY TRANSMITTED DISEASES HELP, INFORMATION, AND ACTION GUIDE on page 658.)

TIPS FOR PREVENTING AIDS

The U.S. Public Health Service recommends that people take these precautions to reduce the risk of exposing themselves or others to the AIDS virus:

- The best protection against sexually transmitted infection by the virus is, of course, to abstain from sex or to have a mutually monogamous relationship with an uninfected person. Avoiding sex with people who have AIDS, people who have tested positive for the AIDS virus antibody, or people at risk of infection would also eliminate the risk of sexually transmitted infection.
- Unless you're absolutely sure that your sex partner is not infected, avoid contact with his or her blood, semen, urine, feces, saliva, and vaginal secretions:

Use condoms, which will reduce (but not eliminate) the possibility of transmitting the virus.

Avoid sexual practices that may cause tears in the vagina, rectum, or penis.

Avoid oral-genital contact without a condom.

Avoid openmouthed, intimate kissing.

- Do not have sex with multiple partners. The more partners you have, the greater the risk of infection.
- Do not use illegal intravenous drugs. If you do, never share needles or syringes.

If you think you may be infected, or you have engaged in risky sexual or drug-related behavior:

- Seek counseling and a medical evaluation. Consider taking the AIDS antibody test, which would enable you to know your status and protect yourself or—if you are infected—your sex partner.

- Do not use illegal intravenous drugs. If you do, never share needles or syringes.
- Do not donate blood, plasma, body organs, other body tissues, or sperm.
- If you are a woman at increased risk, seriously consider delaying plans for pregnancy until more is known about AIDS and transmission of the AIDS virus. A pregnant woman infected with the AIDS virus has a 30 percent to 50 percent chance of passing the virus on to her unborn child. Women at increased risk of AIDS should take the antibody test before deciding to become pregnant.

For people who have received a positive result on the AIDS antibody test:

- See a doctor. There are medical steps you can take to protect your health. Either avoid sex or tell your prospective sex partner your AIDS test result and take the precautions listed above to protect him or her from infection.
- Inform anyone whom you may have exposed to the AIDS virus— through sex or drug use—of their potential exposure, and encourage them to seek counseling and antibody testing.
- Do not share toothbrushes, razors, or other items that could become contaminated with blood.
- If you use drugs, enroll in a treatment program. Never share needles or other drug equipment.
- Do not donate blood, plasma, sperm, or other body tissues or organs.
- Tell your doctor, dentist, and eye doctor that you are infected with the AIDS virus so that proper precautions can be taken to protect you, them, and others.
- Women with a positive antibody test should avoid pregnancy.

Source: "Tips on Preventing AIDS," Public Health Service, 1988.

PRECAUTIONS FOR AIDS CAREGIVERS

AIDS is not easy to catch. It is *not* transmitted from person to person by shaking hands, hugging, preparing and serving food, or even coughing and sneezing. No cases have been found where the virus has been transmitted by casual household contact.

Even if you are infected, however, you should take steps to avoid reexposure to the AIDS virus. You can care for a person with AIDS at home and minimize or eliminate the chances of putting yourself or others at risk if you observe some simple precautions:

- Do not share toothbrushes, razors, tweezers, or other items that could have blood on them.
- Use freshly diluted household bleach (1 part bleach to 9 parts water) or other disinfectants (hospital strength) to clean surfaces soiled with blood or other body fluids. Bleach should not be used on upholstery or carpets, and it is corrosive to metal objects. For some spills, soap and water or a household detergent solution can be used.
- Wear rubber gloves and a coverall or smock when handling materials soiled with the patient's blood, semen, or vaginal secretions, or urine or feces in which blood is visible. Household rubber gloves can be decontaminated and reused, but disposable medical gloves cannot.
- Wash soiled clothes, sheets, and towels in soapy water until no visible soiling is present. This may require several wash cycles. Water should be at a minimum temperature of 160°F, and the wash duration should be at least 25 minutes.
- If the person with AIDS has been your sexual partner, the only *certain* way to avoid further risk of exposure to the virus is to have no more sexual contact with that person. The exchange of body fluids—especially semen, blood, or vaginal secretions—is particularly risky. If you find it impossible to abstain from sexual contact with a person who has AIDS, it is *extremely* important to use a condom and spermicidal gel from start to finish.
- Be careful to avoid exposure to the patient's blood by a cut, needle stick, or a splash in the eye or mouth. If you are so exposed, wash with plenty of soap and water, then call your personal physician.
- You also may wish to obtain AIDS virus testing and counseling for yourself.

Source: *When Someone Close Has AIDS*. National Institute of Mental Health, 1989.

Aid to Families with Dependent Children (AFDC), a U.S. welfare
program for families with needy children under eighteen, sometimes called *Aid to Dependent Children* (ADC). Established under SOCIAL SECURITY to aid children who have been deprived of support from a parent, as by death, disability, unemployment, ABANDONMENT, or nonpayment of CHILD SUPPORT, the AFDC program provides financial assistance to the custodial parent or to whoever has assumed CUSTODY, such as a grandparent, stepparent, or other relative. Though federally funded, the program is state-administered, so rules and requirements vary widely. In some states AFDC payments are made to any family living below the poverty level, even when both parents are employed; in other states payments are made only when neither parent at home is employed.

Most AFDC payments go to women who are SINGLE PARENTS. The law requires the state to try to find the child's legal FATHER and to get from him the child support that is his legal responsibility (see PARENTS' RIGHTS); specifically they will ask him to sign a *consent agreement*. If the children's parents are unmarried, and the father has not acknowledged the child, the law requires the woman to aid the state in its search, as a condition of receiving payments. If the father, once found, does not acknowledge the child as his and begin making support payments, the state may institute a *paternity suit* to establish if he is, in fact, the legal father. (See CHILD SUPPORT.)

"Ain't I a woman?," refrain from an 1851 speech by Sojourner TRUTH (for
full text, see page 723).

alcohol and drug abuse, physical and psychological dependence on alco-
holic drinks or on drugs, legal or illegal; more generally called *substance abuse*. Such abuse is characterized by long-term, excessive drinking or use of drugs; by the felt need to continue such use; and by withdrawal symptoms on discontinuing use. Increasingly people are addicted to more than one substance, a condition called *cross-addiction;* many people also smoke, adding yet another addiction (considered separately, under SMOKING).

Drug and alcohol abuse have long been common among women—as witness the many women who in the nineteenth century were dependent on doctor-supplied opiates—but often silently and out of sight. Only in recent decades—as substance abuse has been widely recognized as a major social problem, as such abuse has been reaching ever-younger populations, and as more is being learned about the effects of the abuse—has the nature and extent of abuse among women come fully to light.

In general, fewer women than men drink heavily; in the United States, women make up about one-third of people classed as alcohol-abusing or alcohol-dependent. Women also tend to consume less alcohol and experience fewer problems than men, though women who drink heavily tend to experience greater problems than men. The highest rates of alcohol dependence are found among middle-aged women (thirty-five to forty-nine), especially those who are not married; though genetic factors are increasingly understood to underlie substance abuse, the National Institute on Alcohol Abuse and Alcoholism notes that a "marriage or marriagelike relationship lessens the effect of an inherited liability for drinking."

Dependence on drug and alcohol are also linked with sexual abuse, especially RAPE and INCEST, reported by nearly three-quarters of substance-dependent women. Indeed, many women are drawn into alcohol or drug abuse by addicted partners, often after failing to change the partner's behavior, though the reverse is also true. Because substance abuse has both hereditary and learned components, addictive behavior is often seen in several generations within a family. Some older women have found themselves bearing special burdens when their children become drug addicts, leaving them to raise young grandchildren for the "lost generation."

Only recently, researchers have been recognizing that alcoholism is more widespread among the elderly—most of whom are women—than was previously thought, with symptoms often mistaken by senility or even Alzheimer's disease. Drug and alcohol dependence among the elderly is likely to receive increasing attention in the coming years, with the graying of the population.

Women are more likely than men to be cross-addicted with both alcohol and other drugs. Often such drugs were originally prescribed for therapeutic reasons or are available legally over-the-counter. The National Council on Alcoholism and Drug Dependence (NCADD) reports that two-thirds of all the psychoactive drugs—notably tranquilizers—legally prescribed by doctors are for women; in the United States alone, over one million women are dependent on them. Among teenagers, more girls than boys are known to have used illicit drugs, such as crack. Many women athletes have illicitly and dangerously abused STEROIDS in pursuit of body strength.

The dangers of alcohol and drug abuse among women are widespread. Women's bodies respond differently, often in stronger ways, from men's. For example, the NCADD notes that if a man and a woman of similar weight drink the same amount of alcohol, 30 percent more alcohol will actually enter the woman's bloodstream, because women have less of a stomach enzyme needed for alcohol digestion; some alcoholic women completely lack the enzyme. As a result, even drinking less, women are more likely to have health problems, especially liver disease, and have a greater risk of dying once liver disease has developed. NCADD notes that alcoholic women are more frequently disabled and for longer periods than alcoholic men, partly because their dependence is not normally recognized as quickly. Problems are more common among Black women who drink and much more common among Native American women.

The effects of drug use are far more various, since so many different kinds of drugs exist. But it has long been recognized that women's bodies respond more strongly to drugs in general; they are more likely to have drug reactions, and such reactions are more likely to be fatal (see ALLERGIES). That makes it all the more reprehensible that so much testing of legal drugs has been done primarily on men, including few or no women (see HEALTH EQUITY). Added to all this is the new and lethal danger of contracting AIDS directly from sharing needles in drug use or from a drug-using sex partner.

Serious as such problems are, alcohol and drug abuse affect not only women, but often the children they bear. Only in recent decades has it been understood that alcohol is a—perhaps *the*—leading cause of mental retardation in newborns. At least one to three of every one thousand babies born each year in the United States is affected with *fetal alcohol syndrome* (FAS), which involves central nervous system disorders, deficient growth before and after birth, and facial malformation; less serious effects, called *fetal alcohol effects* (FAE) affect at least three times as many babies.

Many women understand the need to avoid taking any drugs—licit or illicit—during pregnancy and carefully avoid taking any that have not been specifically cleared for safe use during pregnancy. But women addicts are not always able to control their needs; the NCADD notes that in one recent survey, 11 percent of pregnant women used drugs, including heroin, methadone, cocaine, amphetamines, PCP, and marijuana. Neonatal hospitals and intensive care units have been bulging with infants born addicted to the drugs their mothers took during the pregnancy and who have been damaged in many and various ways by the drugs' effects.

Unfortunately, women's addiction is often recognized later than men's, and women are less likely to receive treatment, partly because their addiction problems have traditionally been viewed as less serious. Less than a quarter of publicly funded alcohol treatment admissions and under a third of drug treatment admissions are women, though their proportion of the addicted population is much higher. One reason for this is that few treatment programs provide any assistance for women who are MOTHERS, such as CHILD CARE or flexible programs to meet their needs. Indeed, in one New York City survey, over half of the drug treatment programs denied treatment to addicted women who were pregnant; over two-thirds to such women on Medicaid; and 87 percent to pregnant women on Medicaid and addicted specifically to crack.

Much research in the area of chemical dependence continues to focus on the genetic differences that make some people especially susceptible to substance abuse. Meanwhile, social efforts in the community stress early diagnosis and intervention—always the best hope for treatment—and provision of wider services to those who need them, especially women with young children, and the elderly. Much attention has also been focused on helping people who are *co-dependents*—those who, by supporting and covering for the addict, actually and unwittingly encourage continuation of the addiction. In both earlier times and today, women have been leaders in the fight against addiction, as in the TEMPERANCE MOVEMENT that was so closely intertwined with the nineteenth-century WOMEN'S RIGHTS MOVEMENT. (See ALCOHOL AND DRUG ABUSE HELP, INFORMATION, AND ACTION GUIDE, page 37.)

ALCOHOL AND DRUG ABUSE

Help, Information, and Action Guide

▨ ON SUBSTANCE ABUSE IN GENERAL

▶ **National Institute on Drug Abuse (NIDA)** (5600 Fishers Lane, Rockville, MD 20857; 301-443-1124, Community and Professional Education Branch; Richard A. Millstein, acting director), one of the National Institutes of Health, focusing on substance abuse. Information and federal publications for the public and professionals are available from **National Clearinghouse for Alcohol and Drug Information (NCADI)** (P.O. Box 2345; Rockville, MD 20857-2345; 800-729-6686 or 301-468-2600).

▶ **Center for Substance Abuse Treatment (CSAT), Drug Information Treatment Referral Hotline** (800-662-HELP [4357]; in Spanish, 800-66A-YUDA; TDD [telecommunications devices for the deaf], 800-228-0427; all available 9 A.M.–3 A.M. Mon.–Fri.; noon–3 A.M. Sat.–Sun.), a federal service; formerly part of the National Institute on Drug Abuse (NIDA).

▶ **National Council on Alcoholism and Drug Dependence, Inc. (NCADD)** (12 West 21st Street, New York, NY 10010; 212-206-6770; or 1511 K Street NW, Washington, DC 20005; 202-737-8122; or 800-NCA-CALL [622-2255]; Paul Wood, president), an organization founded in 1944 that seeks to prevent alcoholism and other drug addictions, and to help addicted people. It provides information and publishes *The Alcoholism Report,* the *NCADD Medical/Scientific Quarterly,* and various materials on alcoholism and drug dependence. Its 800-NCA-CALL offers referrals to over 200 state and local affiliates that provide counseling.

▶ **800-COCAINE** [262-2463], a service offering treatment referrals to public and private programs nationwide; no counseling. It is operated by National Medical Enterprises, parent of Fair Oaks Hospital, Summit, New Jersey.

▶ WOMAN'S CHRISTIAN TEMPERANCE UNION **(WCTU)** (708-864-1396 or 800-755-1321).

▶ **National Association for Prenatal Addiction Research and Education (NAPARE)** (200 North Michigan Avenue, Suite 300, Chicago, IL 60601; 312-541-1272 or helpline 800-638-BABY [2229]; Ira Chasnoff, president), an organization that focuses on addiction during pregnancy. It gathers and disseminates information; sponsors research; operates a clinic; and publishes the monthly *NAPARE Update.*

☑ SPECIAL SUBSTANCE ABUSE PROGRAMS

▶ **Alcoholics Anonymous World Services (AA)** (P.O. Box 459, Grand Central Station, New York, NY 10163; 212-870-3400 [see White Pages for local number]; George Dorsey, Administrative General Manager), a key network of mutual-support groups for recovering alcoholics. It publishes numerous books and other materials, including *A Message for Teenagers,* book *Alcoholics Anonymous,* and monthly *AA Grapevine.* A related network of groups for families and friends is **Al-Anon Family Group Headquarters (AAFGH)** (1372 Broadway, New York, NY 10018; 212-302-7240 or 800-356-9996; Myrna Hammersley, director).

▶ **Drugs Anonymous (DA)** (P.O. Box 473, Ansonia Station, New York, NY 10023; 212-484-9095; Mary Lou Phippen, secretary), a network of mutual-support groups for recovering drug abusers, modeled on Alcoholics Anonymous (see above); formerly called Pills Anonymous. Related programs include **Pil-Anon Family Program** for families of drug abusers.

▶ **Narcotics Anonymous (NA)** (P.O. Box 9999, Van Nuys, CA 91409; 818-780-3951 [see telephone directory or information for local numbers, including hot lines in major cities]; Joe Gossett, director), a network of mutual-support groups for recovering narcotic addicts, modeled on Alcoholics Anonymous (see above). It operates hot lines and publishes various materials, including *NA Way Magazine* and book *Narcotics Anonymous.*

▶ **Hazelden Foundation (HF)** (Box 11, Center City, MN 55012; 612-257-4010; for treatment programs, 800-262-5010; for publications, U.S. except Minnesota, 800-328-9000; Minnesota, 800-257-0070), an organization offering treatment and rehabilitation for substance-dependent people of all ages, with special programs for groups with special needs. It also trains counselors; sponsors research; and publishes numerous materials.

☑ INFORMATION FROM OTHER ORGANIZATIONS

▶ FOOD AND DRUG ADMINISTRATION (301-295-8012).
▶ NATIONAL WOMEN'S HEALTH NETWORK **(NWHN)** (202-347-1140). Operates the **Women's Health Information Service.** Publishes the information packets *Women and Alcohol* and *Women and Smoking.*
▶ CHILD WELFARE LEAGUE OF AMERICA **(CWLA)** (202-639-2952). Its **Florence Crittenton Division** offers a national adolescent pregnancy service, including drug-related pregnancies.
▶ WOMEN'S SPORTS FOUNDATION **(WSF)** (212-972-9170; Women's Sports Infoline, 800-227-3988). Publishes the packet *Drug Use.*
▶ NATIONAL CENTER FOR POLICY ALTERNATIVES (202-387-6030). Publishes

Women, Babies and Drugs: Family-Centered Treatment Options and *Public Health Solutions to the Problem of Drug Use by Pregnant Women: A Review of the 1991 Legislative Sessions.*

Other resources

GENERAL WORKS

Straight Talk About Alcoholism: A Doctor Explains Its Causes, Its Effects, and What You Can Do About It. Robert A. Liebelt. Pharos Books (NY), 1992.
Beyond AA: Dealing Responsibly with Alcohol. Clarence Barrett. Positive Attitudes, 1991.
Good News About Drugs and Alcohol: Curing, Treating and Preventing. Mark S. Gold. Random, 1991.
Drugs and Pregnancy: It's Not Worth the Risk, rev. ed. Paddy Cook. American Council for Drug Education, 1991.
Surviving Addiction: A Guide for Alcoholics, Drug Addicts, and Their Families. Dennis Daley. Gardner Press, 1989.
Everything You Need to Know About Chemical Dependence: Vernon Johnson's Complete Guide for Families. Vernon Johnson. Johnson Institute, 1990.
Family Addictions: A Guide for Surviving Alcohol and Drug Abuse. Charles R. Norris, Jr. PIA Press, 1990.
Drug Dependence. Jason M. White. Prentice-Hall, 1990.
Addicted? A Guide to Understanding Addiction. Tom O'Connell. Sanctuary, 1990.
Pills, Potions, People: Understanding the Drug Problem. Liz Byrski. Meyer Stone Books, 1989.
Straight Talk About Drugs and Alcohol. Elizabeth A. Ryan. Facts on File, 1989.
Women and Drugs: Getting Hooked, Getting Clean. Emanuel Peluso and Lucy S. Peluso. CompCare, 1988.

ON RECOVERY

Recovery from Alcoholism: Beyond Your Wildest Dreams. Jerome D. Levin. Aronson, 1991.
Why Don't I Feel Better? Healing the Recovering Alcoholic. Joyce Bismack. Bear and Co., 1991.
Alcoholism: Time and Recovery. Donald L. Carriere and Muriel Doehr-Hadcock. Vantage, 1991.
The Recovery Resource Book: The Best Available Information on Addictions and Co-Dependence. Barbara Yoder. Simon & Schuster/Fireside, 1990.
The 800-COCAINE Book of Drug and Alcohol Recovery. James Cocores. Villard Books, 1990.

Recovery from Addiction. John Finnegan and Daphne Gray. Celestial Arts, 1990.

Overcoming Chemical Dependency. Robert S. McGee. Word Inc., 1990.

Rx for Recovery: The Medical and Health Guide for Alcoholics, Addicts, and Their Families. Jeffrey Weisberg and Gene Hawes. Watts, 1989; Ivy/Ballantine, 1990.

Jolted Sober: Getting to the Moment of Clarity in the Recovery from Addiction. Sylvia Cary. Lowell House, 1989.

Kicking the Drug Habit: A Comprehensive Self-Help Guide to Understanding the Drug Problem and Overcoming Addiction. Michael A. Corey. C. C. Thomas, 1989.

Kick the Drug Habit: The Basic Guide, 3rd ed. Clifton J. Alexander. Antler, 1989.

Unhooked: Staying Sober and Drug-Free. James Christopher. Prometheus, 1989.

◪ ON HEALTH EFFECTS OF ADDICTION

You Are What You Drink: The Authoritative Report on What Alcohol Does to Your Mind, Body and Longevity. Allan Luks and Joseph Barbato. Villard, 1989.

To Your Body: The Health Effects of Illicit Drugs and Alcohol. L. A. Chotkowsky. Learning Publications, 1989.

Mental Illness and Substance Abuse. Wrynn Smith. Facts on File, 1988.

◪ REFERENCE WORKS

A Handbook of Drug and Alcohol Abuse, 3rd ed. F. Hofman and others. Oxford University Press, 1992.

Encyclopedia of Alcoholism, 2nd ed. Glen Evans, Robert O'Brien, and Morris Chafetz. Facts on File, 1991.

Encyclopedia of Drug Abuse, 2nd ed. Glen Evans, Robert O'Brien, and Sidney Cohen. Facts on File, 1990.

Women's Recovery Programs: A Directory of Residential Treatment Centers. Oryx Press, 1990.

Drug, Alcohol and Other Addictions: A Directory of Treatment Centers and Prevention Programs Nationwide. Katherine Clay. Oryx Press, 1989.

◪ BACKGROUND WORKS

The Nature of Alcohol and Drug-Related Problems. Malcolm Lader and others, eds. Oxford University Press, 1992.

Alcohol in America: Drinking Practices and Problems. Walter B. Clark and Michael E. Hilton, eds. State University of New York Press, 1991.

America's Alcohol Dilemma. Phyllis A. Langton. Allyn, 1991.
Illegal Drugs and Alcohol—America's Anguish. Carol D. Foster and others,
eds. Information Plus (TX), 1991.

alimony, money paid by one SPOUSE to another after a SEPARATION or DIVORCE;
also called *maintenance* or sometimes SPOUSAL SUPPORT. It is intended to cover
household, personal, and recreational expenses as well as costs of training and
education. An allowance made while a divorce is pending is called *temporary alimony* and may include—if the woman has negotiated for it—money for preparing the divorce suit. Once the divorce is granted, the payments are called
permanent alimony. When negotiating for alimony, women should keep in mind
that alimony is taxable income to the person who receives it and a tax deduction
to the one who pays it. Alimony should be kept separate from child support,
which is not taxable to the receiver but is a tax deduction to the payer.

Traditionally alimony was virtually always paid by the husband to the wife,
in a practice dating from the time when women were usually unable to earn
money on their own and men were designated as their prime support not only
during MARRIAGE, but afterward (see SPOUSAL SUPPORT). Well into the mid–
twentieth century, alimony continued to be paid primarily from husband to wife,
regardless of the woman's ability to support herself, though occasionally it might
be paid to a husband by a high-earning or rich wife. Also traditionally, the granting of alimony was very much dependent on which partner was at fault in adversarial divorce proceedings. If a woman was at fault, she might receive little or
nothing, but if the man was judged the guilty party, she would receive a larger
amount.

But with the increasing number of two-career families, the liberalization of
divorce laws, and increasing sex equity in the law, alimony has become less common. In fact, contrary to popular opinion, in the United States alimony is today
granted to only about 15 percent of divorced women, according to the **NOW LE-
GAL DEFENSE AND EDUCATION FUND (NOW LDEF)**, and an estimated one-quarter
of those actually receive no payments. Alimony is most often awarded where the
family has been affluent or rich and where the wife has been primarily a HOME-
MAKER. But, **NOW LDEF** reports, the average annual payment is only $3,733, or
about $72 a week. Those most hurt by this change are older women who are nei-
ther trained nor geared for finding and holding any job, but especially one that
would allow them to maintain a style of living anywhere near what they previously had. These are a new underclass of the twentieth century: DISPLACED HOME-
MAKERS.

Not only that, but alimony now is generally granted only for a limited period of time. Previously alimony was paid to a woman for her lifetime or until
she remarried—or until she did something that allowed her husband to challenge
her right to alimony, such as having a sexual relationship with someone else (see

ADULTERY; COHABITATION; DIVORCE). Today, however, especially for marriages that have lasted under fifteen years, alimony is more often regarded as *rehabilitative*, intended to provide temporary support for a woman while she gets training or prepares herself in other ways to enter the workforce. After two to three years she is on her own.

In addition, in some states, an ex-spouse—usually a woman—who is living with someone else can have her alimony payments reduced or terminated. In some places this is a carryover from the old judgments of *fault;* but in other places courts have argued that the new partner provides support, eliminating or lessening the need for alimony. Notably, however, courts seldom recognize subsequent same-sex relationships for purposes of alimony reduction.

In the United States, under the model Uniform Marriage and Divorce Act, the court is advised to consider the following in assessing whether to award alimony and, if so, how much:

- the financial resources of the person asking for alimony, usually the woman.
- how long it would take to obtain the necessary education or training for appropriate employment.
- the couple's standard of living during the marriage.
- how long the couple had been married.
- the age and physical and emotional condition of the person seeking alimony.
- the ability of the other spouse, usually the man, to meet his own needs and still support his ex-spouse.

The model law recommends that alimony be awarded only when the person requesting it has insufficient property or earning ability to provide for personal needs or when that person has CUSTODY of a young child and so should not be forced to be work outside the home. This law has not been adopted by all states, but its approach is influential nevertheless.

Many women's rights organizations point out that such thinking fails to take into account the fact that a woman who has stayed at home full-time—or worked only part-time or at a job with modest demands—has given up her chance to develop or increase her own earning power, in order to care for the family home, raise the children, and aid her husband in increasing *his* earning power. They stress that alimony is not a *gift,* but an *entitlement,* a way of compensating the woman for that work and of equalizing the earning capacities of wife and husband after a divorce. They recommend that women going through a divorce thoroughly document their contributions to the marriage, their standard of living during the marriage, and the difficulty of earning enough to maintain anywhere near that standard after marriage. An experienced divorce lawyer can help a woman prepare such a case before a court. For starters, see PREPARING FOR DIVORCE: A WOMAN'S GUIDE on page 236. (See also DIVORCE; also DIVORCE AND SEPARATION HELP, INFORMATION, AND ACTION GUIDE on page 238.)

allergies, hypersensitivities to various substances. More precisely, allergies are an excessive response by the body's IMMUNE SYSTEM to a foreign substance, called an *allergen,* or more generally an *antigen.* The number of substances that can trigger an allergic reaction sometimes seems endless; it includes pollen, mold spores, insects, insect bites, animal dander, food additives, and various kinds of drugs. Some kinds of foods can also trigger bodywide responses that are still not fully understood, often involving severe headaches and other associated symptoms, such as nausea, vomiting, and vertigo. Among the common culprits are eggs, milk and cheese, nuts, wheat, fish, shellfish, corn, and peaches. Other kinds of reactions more loosely called "allergies" are actually food intolerances, in which the body lacks certain substances necessary to break down the particular food (see DIGESTIVE SYSTEM). Beyond that, our modern environment includes a wide range of chemicals that can trigger sensitivities.

A tendency to allergic reactions seems to be inherited, but the precise substances that trigger reactions can vary from one generation to the next. Both genetic predisposition and exposure seem to be involved. A person often develops an allergy in adulthood (though seldom after age forty) in response to a changing exposure pattern, such as a seafood allergy after emphasizing sushi in the diet, an allergy to cats several years after getting one as a pet, or a latex allergy several years after adopting CONDOMS as safety devices. Women are more susceptible to some kinds of allergic problems than others—they are more likely to have hay fever than asthma, for example—and in general have more and often more severe reactions to drugs and foods. Some women find that their reactions are somewhat cyclical, with sensitivity increasing and decreasing in response to the monthly hormonal changes (see MENSTRUATION) and may become less intense in later years, especially after MENOPAUSE.

Some reactions are barely noticeable or produce only mild symptoms (see SKIN), but some can be life-threatening. The basic mechanism is this: The presence of an offending substance triggers the body's immune system to manufacture defensive antibodies; it also releases chemicals called *histamines,* which cause BLOOD vessels to widen, tissues to fill with fluid, and muscles to go into spasm. These histamines are responsible for many allergic symptoms—including swelling and watering of EYES, nose, and skin, and breathing difficulties (see RESPIRATORY SYSTEM)—commonly counteracted with drugs called *antihistamines.* In some people the symptoms are centered on the respiratory system and especially involve constrictive spasms of the bronchial muscles and swelling of bronchial tissue, in a syndrome called *asthma.* When foods are involved, symptoms may also include vomiting, abdominal cramps, hives, and severe headaches.

But in some people reactions to certain substances can cause *anaphylactic shock,* a severe, life-threatening drop in blood pressure, which requires emergency treatment, notably by injection of a drug called *epinephrine,* to relax the bronchial muscles and "jump-start" the heart. People who have suffered such a severe reaction must be extremely careful to avoid the allergy triggers and must always carry a dose of the medication so it can be injected immediately if necessary; the medication must be kept *immediately at hand,* because the reaction may be so swift as to immobilize people before they can go even the short distance from backyard to house. Such people are advised to wear a medical identification bracelet such as Medic Alert and to carry a card to give out appropriately, as in restaurants. For example, one person carries a card that reads "I have an acute allergy to peanuts. Any contact with peanuts or peanut oil could kill me immediately. Please double-check your recipes." Among the substances that cause such potentially fatal allergies are penicillin; the sting of various insects, notably yellow jackets, hornets, honeybees, wasps, fire ants, and (in the U.S. Southwest) kissing bugs; and some foods, such as peanuts, the flavor enhancer monosodium glutamate (MSG), and food preservatives called sulfites. More recently, latex has been added to the list. This is a particular concern because almost all CONDOMS and DIAPHRAGMS are made of latex; people who have irritation in the GENITALS after using latex protective devices should turn to other protections immediately and arrange for prompt consultation with a doctor regarding a possible allergy.

One traditional test for allergic response to a substance is a *patch test,* in which a sample of the substance is taped to the skin and the area then checked for reactions such as redness or swelling. Blood tests can also sometimes be used to check for the level of antibodies to particular allergens. These help identify only a limited number of allergies, however.

The best defense is an offense: if you know or suspect that you are allergic to a substance, try as much as possible to eliminate it from your environment. That may be easier said than done, as by someone who has a reaction to eggs or wheat (in so many foods), nuts (including nut-derived oils used in cooking), or latex (used in many tools and devices). Many women have to be very careful about using COSMETICS (see **PREVENTING SKIN INFLAMMATION** on page 691).

Where avoidance is not possible, many people undergo desensitization treatment, called *immunotherapy* or *allergy shots,* which involves injecting small, diluted doses of the allergen periodically, gradually increasing the size of the dose over several years, to build up the body's tolerance to the allergen. This has proved effective in many people but is an expensive, delicate process, because the injections themselves can cause allergic reactions. Doctors also may prescribe antihistamines, other drugs that inhibit production of histamines, and STEROIDS used in topical sprays, though those can lose their effectiveness or cause side effects with long-term use.

For people who have more generalized reactions to foods, finding which food or foods are causing the problems takes some detective work. Many people keep a food diary, noting precisely what they have eaten so they can look for patterns when they have reactions. Some put themselves on an *elimination diet,* in which they limit themselves for a day or two only to foods they are *sure* cause them no problem, such as chicken or rice. Then they gradually add foods to their diet, one at a time, and observe their reactions. For infants this is also the recommended strategy when moving to solid food: add foods one at a time, and monitor the child for any adverse reactions. Infants who have early food sensitivities, if they are not severe, may outgrow them, as their immune system matures.

Much remains to be learned about allergies. As recently as 1988, the **NATIONAL INSTITUTE OF ALLERGY AND INFECTIOUS DISEASES** noted that some people can trigger allergic responses by EXERCISE. In addition, allergies and especially asthma can be triggered by other factors at various times in various people, including respiratory infections, stress, excitement, aspirin and other anti-inflammatory drugs, weather changes, temperature changes including sudden drafts, and a wide range of airborne substances, among them various kinds of outdoor and indoor pollutants, such as automobile exhaust, industrial pollution, and chemicals of all kinds. (See ALLERGIES HELP, INFORMATION, AND ACTION GUIDE, below.)

ALLERGIES

Help, Information, and Action Guide

Organizations

▶ NATIONAL INSTITUTE OF ALLERGY AND INFECTIOUS DISEASES (NIAID) (301-496-5717).

▶ **Asthma and Allergy Foundation of America (AAFA)** (1125 15th Street, NW, Suite 502, Washington, DC 20005; 202-466-7643; Mary Worstell, executive director), an organization concerned with allergies and asthma. It supports research and gathers and disseminates information, as through various materials, including a bimonthly newspaper.

▶ **American Academy of Allergy and Immunology** (611 East Wells Street, Milwaukee, WI 53202; 414-272-6071 or 800-822-2762 for information or referral; Donald MacNeil, executive director), a professional organization of physicians specializing in allergy, asthma, and immunology.

▶ **Human Ecology Action League (HEAL)** (P.O. Box 49126, Atlanta, GA 30359; 404-248-1898; Ken Dominy, president), an organization founded in 1977 by and for people who have been exposed to environmental chemicals, or who have strong chemical sensitivities. It publishes numerous resource materials, including the magazine *The Human Ecologist* and the brochure *Chemicals Can Affect Your Health*.

Other resources

◪ GENERAL WORKS ON ALLERGIES

Allergies: Complete Guide to Diagnosis, Treatment, and Daily Management. Consumer Reports Books, eds., Stuart Young and others. Consumer Reports, 1992.

Allergies. Gerald Newman and Eleanor Newman Layfield. Watts, 1992.

Random House Personal Medical Handbook: For People with Allergies. Paula Dranov. Random, 1991.

All About Asthma and Allergy. H. Morrow Brown. Trafalgar Square, 1991.

The Whole Way to Allergy Relief and Prevention: A Doctor's Complete Guide to Treatment and Self-Care. Jacqueline Krohn and others. Hartley & Marks, 1991. (Address: P.O. Box 147, Point Roberts, WA 98281.)

An Alternative Approach to Allergies: The New Field of Clinical Ecology Unravels the Environmental Causes of Mental and Physical Ills, rev. ed. Theron G. Randolph and Ralph W. Moss. HarperCollins, 1990.

Allergy Environment Guidebook: New Hope and Help for Living and Working Allergy-Free. Judy L. Bachman. Putnam, 1990.

A Doctor Discusses Allergy Fact and Fallacies. Lou Joseph and Alice S. Mills. Budlong, 1990.

Understanding Allergy, Sensitivity, and Immunity: A Comprehensive Guide. Janice Vickerstaff Joneja and Leonard Bielory. Rutgers University Press, 1990.

◪ ON FOOD ALLERGIES

The Complete Guide to Food Allergy and Intolerance. Jonathan Brostoff and Linda Gamlin. Crown, 1992.

The Allergy Discovery Diet: A Rotation Diet for Discovering Your Allergies to Food. John E. Postley and Janet M. Barton. Doubleday, 1990.

Food Allergies and Adverse Reactions. Judy E. Perkin. Aspen, 1990.

Overcoming Food Allergies. Gwynne H. Davies. Avery, 1990.

Hidden Food Allergies: How to Find and Overcome Them. Stephen Astor. Avery, 1988.

◪ ON ASTHMA

The Asthma Self-Help Book. Paul J. Hannaway. Prime, 1992.

The Asthma Self-Care Book: How to Take Control of Your Asthma. Geri Harrington. HarperCollins, 1991.

Asthmatic's Action Plan: Practical Advice for Gaining Relief from Distressing Symptoms. John Chapman. Thorsons, 1991.

What You Can Do About Asthma. Nathaniel Altman. Dell, 1991.

Asthma and Hay Fever: Proven Drug-Free Methods to Combat the Causes. Leon Chaitow. Thorsons, 1990.

Asthma Resources Directory. Carol Rudoff. Allergy Publications. 1990.

◪ BACKGROUND WORKS

Migraine and the Allergy Connection: A Drug-Free Solution. John Mansfield, M.D. Inner Traditions, 1990.

Allergy Products Directory, 2nd ed. American Allergy Association, 1987. (Address: Allergy Publications Group, P.O. Box 640, Menlo Park, CA 94026.)

Genetic and Environmental Factors in Clinical Allergy. David G. Marsh and Malcolm N. Blumenthal, eds. University of Minnesota Press, 1990. (See also IMMUNE SYSTEM.)

alpha fetoprotein (AFP), a type of PRENATAL TEST designed to screen for some kinds of GENETIC DISORDERS; more formally called the *maternal serum alpha-fetoprotein test* (MSAFP). The alpha fetoprotein (AFP) is a protein produced by the liver of the FETUS but passed into the mother's BLOOD, a sample of which can easily be taken and analyzed.

Abnormally high levels of AFP are associated with some types of fetal abnormalities, especially neural tube defects such as spina bifida (open SPINE) and anencephaly (see BRAIN AND NERVOUS SYSTEM); malformation of the esophagus (see DIGESTIVE SYSTEM); and some kidney abnormalities (see URINARY TRACT). High AFP levels are also found in multiple pregnancies or where MISCARRIAGE is imminent. Because AFP levels rise and fall, peaking between weeks fifteen and twenty, abnormally high AFP can also mean that the due date has been miscalculated (see PREGNANCY). Abnormally *low* levels of AFP are associated with DOWN'S SYNDROME.

Women should be aware that the AFP test is *not* a precise test, but only a general screen to indicate the presence of *possible* problems and the advisability of further testing, with more reliable procedures such as AMNIOCENTESIS. Indeed, the AFP test is notoriously unreliable, especially at low AFP levels. It often gives *false positives,* indicating that problems exist when they do not, and *false negatives,* failing to indicate that a problem does exist. The test continues to be widely used, however, because it is a simple, relatively noninvasive type of screening test. If abnormal levels are found, a second AFP test is often done before further tests are ordered. (See PRENATAL TEST; also GENETIC INHERITANCE AND BIRTH DEFECTS HELP, INFORMATION, AND ACTION GUIDE on page 314.)

alternative birthing centers, an alternative name for maternity centers (see CHILDBIRTH).

alternative fertilization, an alternative name for ARTIFICIAL INSEMINATION (AI).

Amazons, in Greek mythology, a nation of warrior women who were said to have fought the Greeks on several occasions. Speculation placed them to the east of Greece, in the lands surrounding the Black Sea. Later speculation focused on the possibility of there having been women soldiers among the Sarmatians, who occupied much of the area north of the Black Sea from approximately the fourth century B.C. to the fourth century A.D. As late as the sixteenth century, armed encounters with Amazons were reported in South America, near the mouth of what was to be called the Amazon River. No hard evidence supports the existence of the Amazons, although some twentieth-century feminist theorists feel otherwise, most notably Helen Diner in her *Mothers and Amazons* (1932).

ambiguous genitals, a condition in which a person's SEXUAL IDENTITY is not immediately apparent.

amenorrhea, lack or cessation of MENSTRUATION.

American Association of Retired Persons (AARP)(3200 East Carson Street, Lakewood, CA 90712; or 601 E Street, NW, Washington, DC 20049; 202-434-2277; Horace B. Deets, executive director), an organization founded in 1958 for people fifty or older, retired or (despite the title) working. Though it deals with every aspect of over-fifty life, its focuses include women's concerns, health care, worker equity, and minority concerns. It has numerous programs, including group health insurance offerings, auto rental and hotel discounts, and preretirement planning; many more are sold through advertising mailings to AARP lists. AARP publishes the newsletters *AARP Bulletin* and *Working Age,* the magazine *Modern Maturity,* and various books, on topics such as retirement and financial planning, EXERCISE, health, housing, and travel and recreation.

American Birth Control League: See Margaret SANGER.

American Booksellers Association v. Hudnut, a 1986 U.S. Supreme Court case striking down an Indianapolis antipornography ordinance as an unconstitutional violation of First Amendment free speech guarantees. (See PORNOGRAPHY.)

American College of Obstetricians and Gynecologists (ACOG) (409 12th Street, SW, Washington, DC 20024-2188; 202-638-5577; Ralph Hale, executive director), a professional organization of obstetricians, gynecologists, and subspecialists such as maternal-fetal specialists, reproductive endocrinology, and gynecology oncology. ACOG is allied with the **Organization for Obstetric, Gynecologic, and Neonatal Nurses (NAACOG)** and is also a member of the HEALTHY MOTHER, HEALTHY BABIES NATIONAL COALITION (HMHB). ACOG makes referrals; maintains a resource center for the general public, on obstetrical and gynecological questions; and publishes various materials, including ACOG Patient Education Pamphlets and a Healthy Mother's Food Wheel.

American Fertility Society (AFS) (2140 11th Avenue South, Suite 200, Birmingham, AL 35205; 205-933-8494; Nancy C. Hayley, administrative director), a professional organization acting as an information clearinghouse on fertility and INFERTILITY. It provide information and makes referrals to specialists in areas such as fertility workups, ARTIFICIAL INSEMINATION, reversing vasectomies (see STERILIZATION), and IN VITRO FERTILIZATION. AFS publishes various materials, including the monthly *Fertility and Sterility Journal, Vasectomy: Facts About Male Sterilization,* and professional materials such as *How to Organize a Basic Study of the Infertile Couple* and *Report of the Ad Hoc Committee on Artificial Insemination.*

American Medical Women's Association (AMWA) (801 North Fairfax Street, Suite 400, Alexandria, VA; 703-838-0500; Eileen McGrath, executive director), an organization of women physicians and medical students founded in 1915 and "dedicated to improving the personal and professional well-being of its members and increasing the influence of women in all aspects of the medical profession." AMWA also seeks to enhance women's health care in general, offering a Women's Health Curriculum program providing continuing education for physicians seeking to deepen or update their knowledge of women's health, in areas such as BREAST CANCER and treatment with ESTROGEN. It publishes the newsletter *What's Happening in AMWA* and the *Journal of the American Medical Women's Association (JAMWA).*

American Woman Suffrage Association (AWSA), an organization founded in November 1869 as an alternative to the newly formed NATIONAL WOMAN SUFFRAGE ASSOCIATION (NWSA). AWSA was organized by Lucy STONE, her husband, Henry Blackwell, and other members of the Equal Rights Society, many of them former abolitionists who had criticized the NWSA's Elizabeth Cady STANTON, Susan B. ANTHONY, and other radical feminists for putting women's rights ahead of African-American rights during the Reconstruction period. The AWSA confined its efforts to WOMAN SUFFRAGE rather than the wide range of WOMEN'S RIGHTS issues taken up by the for-women-only NWSA and relied largely on political action through the Republican party, rather than building a mass women's movement. AWSA's first president was Henry Ward Beecher; Julia Ward HOWE was a later president. In 1890 it merged with the much larger NWSA to form the NATIONAL AMERICAN WOMAN SUFFRAGE ASSOCIATION, as the two wings of the American women's suffrage movement reunited. (See also WOMAN SUFFRAGE; WOMEN'S RIGHTS MOVEMENT.)

amniocentesis, a type of PRENATAL TEST used to identify possible GENETIC DISORDERS or CHROMOSOMAL ABNORMALITIES. In the procedure a needle is inserted through the pregnant woman's abdomen (the physician is guided by ULTRASOUND images), and a sample of fluid is taken from the AMNIOTIC SAC surrounding the FETUS. The amniotic fluid contains cells "shed" from the fetus, which can be analyzed for as many as seventy-five possible disorders, such as DOWN'S SYNDROME or spina bifida (literally, "open SPINE"). The doctor must specify which types of disorders to test for, often guided by the results of previous GENETIC COUNSELING. Tests can also help genetic counselors assess the risk of sex-linked genetic disorders (see GENETIC DISORDERS), because the sex of the fetus is shown in the cells.

Amniocentesis is performed later than some other prenatal tests (such as CHORIONIC VILLUS SAMPLING), generally fourteen to sixteen weeks into the PREGNANCY, by which time sufficient amniotic fluid is available for testing. Laboratory analysis takes somewhat longer as well, often 10 days or more, since cells must be cultured. This means that if a woman chooses to terminate a pregnancy on the basis of test results, she faces a possibly difficult late ABORTION, in the second trimester. Unlike some other prenatal tests, amniocentesis is considered quite reliable.

Amniocentesis involves some discomfort or pain, including cramps afterward. There is a small risk of MISCARRIAGE, infection, maternal or fetal hemorrhage, and complications where mother and child have Rh incompatibility (see BLOOD). As a result, the procedure is recommended in specific situations, such as when
- the pregnant woman is over thirty-five, checking especially for Down's syndrome.
- either parent has a personal or family history of chromosomal abnormalities or genetic disorders, especially sex-linked diseases (see GENETIC INHERITANCE), such as hemophilia (see BLOOD), affecting primarily boys.
- the woman has previously had several miscarriages.
- the woman has abnormally high ALPHA FETOPROTEIN levels, which may indicate neural tube defects, such as spina bifida.
- mother and baby have Rh incompatibility.

The test is sometimes also done late in pregnancy, to check on the baby's lung development, when delivery is being induced prematurely (for other reasons, such as PREECLAMPSIA) or done by CESAREAN SECTION. (See PRENATAL TEST; also GENETIC INHERITANCE AND BIRTH DEFECTS HELP, INFORMATION, AND ACTION GUIDE on page 314.)

amnioinfusion, a type of procedure used in a late ABORTION.

amniotic sac, the fluid-filled membrane in which a FETUS grows in the UTERUS during PREGNANCY. Shortly after IMPLANTATION, when the EMBRYO attaches to the lining of the uterus, this saclike membrane begins to form and gradually fills with *amniotic fluid*. Floating in the fluid-filled sac, the fetus is cushioned from outside injury and pressure from the mother's internal organs. The fetus also swallows some of the fluid, absorbing fats and other substances from it, and excretes urine into it. The PRENATAL TEST called AMNIOCENTESIS involves taking a sample of the amniotic fluid and analyzing waste fetal cells from it for signs of some kinds of GENETIC DISORDERS or CHROMOSOMAL ABNORMALITIES. The amniotic sac was traditionally called the "bag of waters," which breaks before CHILDBIRTH. The fetus does not drown because the lungs are undeveloped and are not used for breathing until after CHILDBIRTH (see RESPIRATORY SYSTEM; HEART AND CIRCULATORY SYSTEM).

Both too little amniotic fluid *(oligohydramnios)* or too much *(hydramnios* or *polyhydramnios)* can cause problems during pregnancy. Too little fluid may result if the fetus has kidney or URINARY TRACT problems, if the PLACENTA is not providing proper nourishment, if the mother has PREECLAMPSIA or eclampsia, or if the fetus is postmature (beyond about forty-one weeks; see GESTATION). It brings an increased risk of MISCARRIAGE, especially early, and some physical deformities, such as clubfoot.

Excess fluid can accumulate when the fetus has a problem that prevents normal swallowing, if the MOTHER has DIABETES, and sometimes in cases of multiple births. Hydramnios brings an increased risk of premature DELIVERY and abnormal FETAL PRESENTATION. (See PREGNANCY.)

androcentric, an assumption or attitude that places the male at the center of things; in practice, a synonym for such terms as *male supremacist, male chauvinist,* and PHALLOCENTRIC. The early American feminist economist Charlotte Perkins GILMAN popularized the term in her book *The Man-Made World: Our Androcentric Culture* (1911). (See PATRIARCHY.)

androgens, a group of male sex HORMONES, most notably TESTOSTERONE.

androgyny, the combining of both feminine and masculine behaviors, actions, and perceptions in a single person. This is an ideal posed as an alternative to traditional SEX ROLES, proposing instead that females and males, while retaining their biologically derived SEXUAL IDENTITY, would be free to develop their own life roles individually. Women who prefer androgyny will have to carefully "deprogram" or "counterprogram" themselves and their children, since social "programming" of SEX ROLES is so powerful.

anesthesia, use of drugs to deaden sensation of pain and sometimes to induce unconsciousness during CHILDBIRTH or a medical procedure; literally, "without feeling." Anesthesia may be topical, local, regional, or general.
- ▶ *topical anesthesia* generally involves applying a sense-deadening substance to the surface of the skin, or perhaps part of the eye. It is the most minor type of anesthesia.
- ▶ *local anesthesia* generally involves injection of a substance to deaden sensation in just a small area of the body, as in dental surgery. Sometimes, as during some kinds of minor COSMETIC SURGERY, a patient may also be given a sedative.
- ▶ *regional anesthesia* affects a whole area of the body, generally involving an injection called a *nerve block,* given to deaden sensation in the main nerve serving that region of the body.

▶ *general anesthesia* affects the whole body, causing the patient to lose not only feeling, but consciousness as well.

General anesthesia is used in many surgical operations and was in decades past very widely used during CHILDBIRTH as well. However, general anesthesia has some risks. Some people have a rare, life-threatening reaction to anesthetics, a GENETIC DISORDER called *malignant hyperthermia.* Other complications, though rare, include potentially fatal heart irregularities; low BLOOD pressure; breathing problems, which during childbirth can affect both mother and baby; and, of course, possible error in administration. In addition, with general anesthesia mothers are asleep and so unable to experience the actual birth. Whether for childbirth or surgery, general anesthesia requires supervised time in a recovery area, although modern drugs have greatly reduced the nausea and vomiting that were once routine.

Regional anesthesia is becoming increasingly common. In place of local anesthesia, it is especially useful when the area involved is very large or hard to reach directly by injection. It also avoids some of the risks of general anesthesia. Many women in childbirth see it as a godsend, because it offers them relief from pain but leaves them conscious during the birth experience. Regional anesthesia does, however, involve at least one small but significant risk—nerves can be damaged by the injections.

There are several main types of nerve blocks, depending on the site of the injection and the area anesthetized:

▶ *epidural,* with injection into the SPINE's epidural space between the vertebrae and spinal cord, affecting the pelvic area, lower abdomen, and GENITALS. A thin, flexible tube called a *catheter* is sometimes left in place for giving more anesthetics or *analgesics* (pain-killing drugs) when desirable during childbirth or long surgical procedures.

▶ *pudendal,* with injection in the wall of the VAGINA to anesthetize the VULVA. This is often used during LABOR, to kill pain without adversely affecting the contractions of the UTERUS.

▶ *paracervical,* with injection into the CERVIX, also commonly used during childbirth, since it does not affect uterine contractions.

▶ *spinal,* with injection into the cerebrospinal fluid between the vertebrae of the spine, affecting the lower limbs and abdomen.

▶ *caudal,* with injection into the lower spinal cord through the sacrum (the part of the spine just above the "tailbone"), affecting the genital or rectal area. Often epidural block is used instead, since the caudal block is less reliable. During childbirth, a caudal block can adversely affect contractions; it also carries the risk of accidental and dangerous injection of the FETUS.

▶ *intercostal,* involving injection between two ribs, affecting the chest area.

▶ *brachial plexus,* involving injection into the nerve network serving an arm.

Before any operation, the person who will be administering the anesthesia should discuss with the patient the type of anesthesia to be used. The discussion should include the obsetrician's or surgeon's recommendation, the risks and possible side effects of the choices appropriate for that procedure, the patient's preferences, and any special medical history. Patients who have strong feelings for or against any particular kind of anesthesia—or use of anesthesia at all, as during childbirth—should be sure to make their views known well beforehand. And if the obstetrician, surgeon, or anesthesiologist does not initiate discussion of anesthesia choices, the patient should do so. Some surgeons prefer to use general or regional anesthesia, even where local anesthesia is an option, so they will have a specialist administering the anesthetic and monitoring the patient's vital signs, allowing the surgeon to concentrate totally on the procedure itself, whether surgery or childbirth. (See also CHILDBIRTH; PREGNANCY; also PREGNANCY AND CHILDBIRTH HELP, INFORMATION, AND ACTION GUIDE on page 580; WOMEN'S HEALTH HELP, INFORMATION, AND ACTION GUIDE on page 334.)

anovulatory periods, periodic vaginal bleeding, or MENSTRUATION, that occurs even when no egg (OVUM) has been ripened in the OVARIES or released for FERTILIZATION, in the process called OVULATION. Anovulatory periods are common in young girls, in the first few years after the onset of menstruation, called MENARCHE, and also in older women, in the last few years before MENOPAUSE, part of a longer-term set of changes called the CLIMACTERIC. Anovulatory periods also occur in women who are on BIRTH CONTROL PILLS or ESTROGEN REPLACEMENT THERAPY (ERT), in which ovulation is suppressed. Failure of ovulation is also a common cause of INFERTILITY and can occur from a variety of reasons, including OBESITY, stress, heavy physical EXERCISE, DIETING, thyroid gland problems, and excess production of some HORMONES, especially PROLACTIN and some male sex hormones (androgens). Anovulatory periods can also occur with overgrowth of the uterine lining, a condition called endometrial hyperplasia. (See MENSTRUATION; MENOPAUSE; UTERUS.)

annulment, a legal declaration that something is void; in relation to MARRIAGE, a judicial ruling that the marriage never existed (as opposed to a DIVORCE, which ends an existing marriage), and that a couple never were husband and wife. In the past, and still in those places with restrictive divorce laws, annulment cases were common, as they provided the main means of voiding a marriage and allowing the parties to marry again. Annulments are much less common today where divorce laws are liberal.

Annulments are most readily granted before COHABITATION, especially before the marriage is consummated—that is, before the couple have had SEXUAL INTERCOURSE—especially in cultures where VIRGINITY is regarded as important in a bride. Traditionally this approach has been to protect the woman, since (unlike divorce) an annulment—in many places—simply sweeps away the marriage, with no ALIMONY, no sharing of MARITAL PROPERTY, no right to share in the other person's estate, and no right to legitimacy for the couple's children, if any. Many states today have laws to provide for such property settlements and legitimacy of children. Where they do not, women may well be advised to seek a SEPARATION or divorce, rather than an annulment.

Some marriages are void from the start, as when they violate state laws. For example, if a man attempts to marry a woman while he is already married to someone else, the second marriage is void. The same is true if either the man or woman is under the AGE OF CONSENT, or if the man and woman are too closely related according to state INCEST laws, though special exceptions are sometimes made. In such cases anyone, including parents or neighbors, with knowledge of the defect in the marriage can bring that to the attention of the court.

Other marriages are described as *voidable,* meaning that the marriage exists as valid unless someone seeks an annulment. A suit seeking this kind of annulment can generally be brought only by the deceived or injured party, not by the other party. One exception is that adult children may seek an annulment on the ground that an elderly parent was mentally incompetent to marry, as where a substantial estate is involved. State laws vary widely on grounds for annulment, but often include

▶ *fraud,* in which one party lies or misleads the other on a question so central that the innocent party would not have proceeded with the marriage except for the deceit. Such grounds often involve religion, children, or sexual problems, such as falsely claiming to be Catholic or hiding a fixed intention not to have children or an inability to do so. By contrast, less essential frauds are generally rejected, such as learning that one's partner is not rich or is bald. If a woman is pregnant with another man's child, an annulment will generally be granted. However, if a man married a woman thinking she was pregnant with *his* child, and either she never was pregnant or she miscarried, the court may *not* grant annulment; the argument is that by marrying the woman, the man had reason to believe he was the father and so did not come before the court with "clean hands" in the matter. Exceptions to this have been made in some states where the couple has not lived together and neither wanted to stay married. Acknowledgment of homosexuality (see LESBIAN) is also often grounds for annulment.

▶ *physical and emotional conditions,* most often inability to have normal SEXUAL INTERCOURSE or to bear children, if such conditions are learned after (but not *before*) the marriage. In some states other conditions may be grounds for annulment, including serious SEXUALLY TRANSMITTED DISEASES, ALCOHOLISM, incurable insanity (see MENTAL DISORDERS), "feeblemindedness" (now more often called "mental retardation"), and epilepsy.

▶ *conditions appearing after marriage,* including incurable insanity for a certain number of years or unexplained absence (see ABANDONMENT) with indications of possible death, though in the latter case some states prefer *dissolution* of the marriage (see DIVORCE) to annulment.

▶ *lack of consent,* as when someone is forced into marriage by physical threats or is incompetent to give consent, because of mental illness or senility.

▶ *duress,* as when someone is forced into marriage at gunpoint.

▶ *mistake,* as when either party was so drunk or high on drugs as to be unable to make a rational decision or when a joke or dare was involved. Again, minor "mistakes" are generally not considered.

▶ *prohibition against remarriage,* as when a second marriage violated the terms of a court order in a previous divorce, though courts disagree sharply on their handling of such questions.

An annulment case must be brought within a certain time period set by law, called the *statute of limitations,* and will generally not succeed if the complaining party has accepted the marriage (and the situation being complained about) for a period of time, an acceptance called *ratification*. A case that has been brought and decided in another court will generally not be reheard in a different state, so if there is a choice about where to file a suit—as between the state of the original marriage or the present state of residence, for example—a woman will want to seek legal advice about which state's laws and precedents are more generally favorable to her situation.

In some special cases, Catholic couples who have received a legal divorce ask the Church to grant them an annulment. Though this annulment has no standing in the civil law, it circumvents the Church prohibition on divorce and leaves the parties free to marry again. (See DIVORCE AND SEPARATION HELP, INFORMATION, AND ACTION GUIDE on page 238.)

anorexia nervosa, a type of EATING DISORDER that involves self-starvation, through general avoidance of food and obsessive EXERCISE to burn up calories. In perhaps one out of two cases it is linked with induced vomiting and use of laxatives (as in the related eating disorder BULIMIA), in a condition called *bulimarexia* or *bulimic anorexia.*

The name *anorexia* literally means "without appetite" and is sometimes applied more generally to people who have lost a taste for food, such as a CANCER patient undergoing chemotherapy. But people with *anorexia nervosa* are actually obsessed with food, often hoarding it secretly. They cut their food intake drastically, not because food is unattractive, but because they have an intense fear of gaining weight and "being fat"—even though before anorexia developed, few would have been considered "fat" by common social standards and only about a third would have been considered even mildly overweight. However, they persist in seeing themselves as fat, even when they have reduced their body weight 15–25 percent or even more below the normal body weight for their age, becoming so emaciated that they look like inmates of a concentration camp.

It is this distorted body image that causes anorexia to be classed and treated as a MENTAL DISORDER. Some observers charge that anorexia is simply an extreme expression of Western society's widespread obsession with thinness, dieting, and generally unrealistic images of physical attractiveness for women. In the United States, for example, a recent study showed that approximately two-thirds of teenage girls were attempting to lose weight, though most of them were already of normal weight. Other studies suggest that girls with eating disorders are imitating their mother's pattern of eating and dieting and view of physical attractiveness.

Though anorexia can affect people of either sex or any age, only 5–10 percent of the cases are among males, and few are found before adolescence and above age thirty. The National Center for Health Statistics (NCHS) reported that in 1989 about 11,000 anorexia cases were diagnosed in the United States and that 67 people had died of anorexia in the previous year. However, some American researchers estimate that as many as 1 in 100 females may have anorexia, often undiagnosed. The disorder is by far most common among adolescent girls. Some psychologists suggest that anorexia results when such young women suppress their normal adolescent feelings of rebellion, in their striving for independence, control, and perfection. Some researchers report that anorexia is increasing among children eight to eleven years old. DEPRESSION and some other MENTAL DISORDERS, such as *bipolar disorders* (popularly called manic-depression), are more than usually common among the families of people with anorexia. Anorexia patients themselves also are more likely to be depressed or socially withdrawn and have an increased risk of suicide.

Meanwhile, some researchers are searching for possible physical causes for the disorder. One focus of their research is the *hypothalamus,* a gland that controls or affects many key functions in the body. Malfunctions in the hypothalamus are frequently associated with anorexia, and researchers are exploring the possibility that they precede and help trigger the disorder. At present, however, the causes of anorexia remain obscure. The NATIONAL INSTITUTE OF CHILD HEALTH AND HUMAN DEVELOPMENT (NICHD) concludes simply, "A combination of psychological, environmental, and physiological factors are associated with development of the disorder."

Among women, one of the first signs of anorexia—even before striking weight loss—is the cessation of MENSTRUATION; some even suggest that the disorder may result partly from a desire to forestall adulthood; the disorder also slows the long-term processes associated with sexual maturation, including growth and development of SECONDARY SEX CHARACTERISTICS, such as adult BREASTS. As weight drops drastically, other major body functions are also affected. Temperature and BLOOD pressure drop; heartbeat and circulation slow, leading to buildup of fluid, or *edema* (see HEART AND CIRCULATORY SYSTEM); HAIR is lost and replaced with fine, downy hair called *lanugo* (like that on a newborn child); digestive processes are disrupted, leading to severe malnutrition, as well as bloating and constipation (see DIGESTIVE SYSTEM); SKIN becomes dry and NAILS brittle; muscle and other body tissues waste away (see MUSCULAR SYSTEM); bone is lost, leading to increased risk of fractures and later OSTEOPOROSIS (see SKELETAL SYSTEM).

If unchecked, the self-starvation leads to failure of vital systems, such as the kidneys (see URINARY TRACT), and in extreme cases to death. The NICHD estimates that "about 10–15 percent of anorexia nervosa patients die, usually after losing at least half their normal body weight." Others give estimates ranging from 2 percent to over 20 percent; the figures are so uncertain because many deaths occur not immediately, but over the next few decades, from damage done to vital organs, such as the kidneys, during extreme anorexic episodes. Many cases of anorexia are believed to go undiagnosed. When the disorder first came to public attention, it was thought to be found primarily among previously "model" children from White middle- and upper-class families who emphasized achievement. But the disorder is now being found among all social classes and is strongly on the increase in Western societies, though it is rarely found in societies where there is an actual shortage of food. At particular risk are women such as dancers, athletes, models, and actresses, where thinness is regarded as desirable.

Since, almost by definition, people with anorexia are unable to see that they have a problem and do not seek medical help, recognition of the disorder often comes from family and friends (see ANOREXIA: DANGER SIGNS on page 57). Once anorexia is recognized, the first concern is to get the patient to eat and gain weight, to restore normal functioning of the body's systems and attempt to avert serious, sometimes fatal organ damage. That is easier said than done. In extreme cases the patient may need to be hospitalized and given controlled nutritional therapy, often using drugs and special diets to promote weight gain, with feeding done by tube or intravenously, if necessary. On occasion, parents have even gone to court to get their daughter declared mentally incompetent, to force medical treatment.

But for long-term recovery, individual psychotherapy and often also family counseling are vital—and often very difficult, because of the patient's resistance even to acknowledge a problem. Mutual-support groups have proved invaluable to anorexics—and to their families and friends—in the long and difficult process of recovery. Some of those who recover from anorexia go on to lead largely normal lives, but in others anorexia becomes a chronic illness, with recurrent episodes. Long-term studies indicate that up to half have continuing problems, with the prognosis for full recovery best for teenagers whose anorexia has been diagnosed early, before abnormal patterns have become fully established and the body has been damaged by emaciation. (See EATING DISORDERS HELP, INFORMATION, AND ACTION GUIDE on page 58.)

ANOREXIA: DANGER SIGNS

Eating disorders may be prevented or more readily treated if they are detected early. A person who has *several* of the following signs may be developing or has already developed an eating disorder.

The individual
- has lost a great deal of weight in a relatively short period.
- continues to diet, although bone thin.
- reaches diet goal and immediately sets another goal for further weight loss.
- remains dissatisfied with appearance, claiming to feel fat even after reaching weight-loss goal.
- prefers dieting in isolation to joining a diet group.
- loses monthly menstrual periods.
- develops unusual interest in food.
- develops strange eating rituals and eats small amounts of food (for example, cuts food into tiny pieces or measures everything before eating extremely small amounts).
- becomes a secret eater.
- becomes obsessive about exercising.
- appears depressed much of the time.
- begins to binge and purge.

Source: American Anorexia/Bulimia Association, Inc. 1989.

EATING DISORDERS

Help, Information, and Action Guide

Organizations

▶ **National Association of Anorexia Nervosa and Associated Disorders** (P.O. Box 7, Highland Park, IL 60035; hot line number 708-831-3438; Vivian Meehan, president), an organization focusing on anorexia and related disorders. It provides information and referrals, operating a hot line, generally staffed by recovered anorexics or their family members. It also publishes the newsletter *Working Together* and various fact sheets.

▶ **American Anorexia/Bulimia Association (AABA)** (418 East 76th Street, New York, NY 10021; 212-734-1114; Randi Wirth, executive director), a network of mutual-support, professionally led groups for people with eating disorders. The AABA provides counseling, referrals, links between new and recovered members, and information, as through its newsletter, fact sheets, and pamphlets.

▶ **National Anorexic Aid Society (NAAS)** (1925 East Dublin-Granville Road, Columbus, OH 43229; 614-436-1112; Laura Hill, director), an organization for anorexics and their families, linked with an outpatient organization, **the Center for the Treatment of Eating Disorders** (at same address and number). The NAAS provides information, makes referrals, and publishes various materials, including the quarterly *NAAS Newsletter*.

▶ NATIONAL INSTITUTE OF CHILD HEALTH AND HUMAN DEVELOPMENT **(NICHD)** (301-496-5133). Publishes *Facts About Anorexia Nervosa*.

▶ NATIONAL INSTITUTE OF DIABETES, DIGESTIVE AND KIDNEY DISEASES **(NIDDK)** (301-496-3583). Publishes *Obesity and Energy Metabolism*.

▶ WOMEN'S SPORTS FOUNDATION **(WSF)** (212-972-9170; Women's Sports Infoline, 800-227-3988). Publishes expert packets entitled *Eating Disorders* and *Nutrition/Weight Control*.

Other resources

◪ **GENERAL WORKS**

Eating Disorders: The Facts, 3rd ed. Suzanne Abraham and Derek Llewellyn-Jones. Oxford University Press, 1992.

Eating Disorders. Steven Spotts. Rapha, 1991.

Obesity and Anorexia Nervosa: A Question of Shape. Peter Dally and Joan Gomez. Faber and Faber, 1991.

The Beauty Myth. Naomi Wolf. Morrow, 1991. Suggests a "cult of the anorexic."

Freedom from Food: The Secret Lives of Dieters and Compulsive Eaters. Elizabeth Hampshire. Prentice-Hall, 1990.

Eating Disorders. L. George Hsu. Guilford Press, 1990.

Compulsive Eating. Donna LeBlanc. Health Communications, 1990.

Compulsive Eaters and Relationships. Aphrodite Matsakis. Hazelden, 1990.

Never Too Thin: Why Women Are at War with Their Bodies. Roberta Pollack Seid. Prentice-Hall, 1989.

Bulimia Nervosa. James Mitchell. University of Minnesota Press, 1989.

Fasting Girls: The Emergence of Anorexia Nervosa as a Modern Disease. Joan Jacobs Brumberg. Harvard University Press, 1988; NAL, 1989.

You Can't Have Your Cake and Eat It Too: A Program for Controlling Bulimia. Lillie Weiss and others. R & E Publishers, 1986.

Bulimia: A Guide to Recovery. Lindsey Hall and Leigh Cohn. Gurze Books, 1986.

Fat Is a Family Affair. Judi Hollis. Hazelden, 1985.

The Anorexia Nervosa Reference Book. Roger Slade. Harper & Row, 1984.

Starving to Death in a Sea of Objects: The Anorexia Nervosa Syndrome. John A. Sours. Jason Aronson, 1980.

The Best Little Girl in the World. Steven Levenkron. Contemporary Books, 1978.

◪ ON TREATMENT AND RECOVERY

Controlling Eating Disorders with Facts, Advice, and Resources. Raymond Lemberg, ed. Oryx Press, 1992.

No More Black Days: Complete Freedom from Depression, Eating Disorders and Compulsive Behaviors. Lauri A. Mallord. White Stone, 1992.

Bulimia: A Guide to Recovery, rev. ed. Lindsey Hall and Leigh Cohn. Gurze Books, 1992.

It's Not Your Fault: Overcoming Anorexia and Bulimia Through Biopsychiatry. Russell Marx. Random, 1991; NAL-Dutton, 1992.

Living with Anorexia and Bulimia. James Moorey. St. Martin's, 1991.

Eating Without Fear: A Guide to Understanding and Overcoming Bulimia. Lindsey Hall. Bantam, 1990.

Inner Harvest: Daily Meditations for Recovery from Eating Disorders. Elisabeth L. Harper & Row/Hazelden, 1990.

Food Trips and Traps: Coping with Eating Disorders. Jane Claypool and Cheryl D. Nelsen. CompCare, 1989.

When Will We Laugh Again? Living and Dealing with Anorexia Nervosa and Bulimia. Barbara P. Kinoy and others. Columbia University Press, 1989.

The Deadly Diet: Recovering from Anorexia and Bulimia. Terence Sandbek. New Harbinger, 1986.

Bulimia: A Guide to Recovery. Lindsey Hall and Leigh Cohn. Gurze Books, 1986.

Bulimia: A Systems Approach to Treatment. Maria Root, Patricia Fallon, and William Friedrich. Norton, 1986.

You Can't Have Your Cake and Eat It Too: A Program for Controlling Bulimia. Lillie Weiss and others. R & E Publishers, 1986.

Anorexia Nervosa: Finding the Life Line. Patricia Stein and Barbara Unell. CompCare, 1986.

Anorexia Nervosa: The Turning Point. Barbara Unell. CompCare, 1985.

The Fear of Being Fat: The Treatment of Anorexia and Bulimia. Charles Philip Wilson and others. Jason Aronson, 1983.

◪ BACKGROUND WORKS

Anorexia and Bulimia: Anatomy of a Social Epidemic. Richard A. Gordon. Basil Blackwell, 1990.

Compulsive Eaters and Relationships. Aphrodite Matsakis. Hazelden, 1990.

Obesity and the Family. David Kallen and Marvin Sussman. Haworth Press, 1984.

Feeding the Hungry Heart: The Experience of Compulsive Eating. Geneen Roth. Bobbs-Merrill, 1983.

The Golden Cage: The Enigma of Anorexia Nervosa. Hilde Bruch. Harvard University Press, 1977.

Eating Disorders, Obesity, Anorexia Nervosa and the Person Within. Hilde Bruch. Basic Books, 1973.

◪ PERSONAL EXPERIENCES

Hope and Recovery: A Mother-Daughter Story About Anorexia Nervosa, Bulimia, and Manic Depression. Becky Thayne Markosian and Emma Lou Thayne. Watts, 1992.

Conversations with Anorexics. Hilde Bruch, Danita Czyzewski, and Melanie A. Suhr, eds. Basic Books, 1989.

Starving for Attention. Cherry Boone O'Neill. Continuum, 1982.

◪ FOR PARENTS AND OTHER ADULTS

A Parent's Guide to Eating Disorders and Obesity. Martha Jablow. Delacorte, 1992.

Eating Disorders and Athletes: A Handbook for Coaches. AAHPERD Staff. Kendall-Hunt, 1991.

Overweight Children: Helping Your Child Achieve Lifetime Weight Control. Michael D. LeBow. Plenum, 1991.

A Parent's Guide to Eating Disorders: Prevention and Treatment of Anorexia Nervosa and Bulimia. Brett Valette. Avon, 1990.

Anorexia, Bulimia, and Compulsive Overeating: A Practical Guide for Counselors and Families. David Swift and Kathleen Zraly. Continuum, 1990.

Bulimia: A Guide for Family and Friends. Robert T. Shermand and Ron A. Thompson. Free Press, 1990.

Helping Obese Children: Weight Control Groups That Really Work. Roselyn Marin. Learning, 1990.

A Parent's Guide to Anorexia and Bulimia: Understanding and Helping Self-Starvers and Binge/Purgers. Katherine Byrne. Henry Holt, 1989.

Fat-Proofing Your Children . . . So That They Never Become Diet-Addicted Adults. Vicki Lansky. Bantam, 1988.

Surviving an Eating Disorder: New Perspectives and Strategies for Family and Friends. Michele Siegel, Judith Brisman, and Margot Weinshel. Harper & Row, 1988.

◪ FOR ADOLESCENTS

Straight Talk About Eating Disorders. Michael Maloney and Rachel Kranz. Facts on File, 1991.

Everything You Need to Know About Eating Disorders. Rachel Kubersky. Rosen, 1991.

Coping with Eating Disorders. Barbara Moe. Rosen Group, 1991.

Eating Disorders. Don Nardo. Lucent Books, 1991.

Weight: A Teenage Concern. Elaine Landau. Lodestar, 1991.

So You Think You're Fat. Alvin Silverstein and Sylvia Silverstein. HarperCollins, 1991.

Eating Disorders. John R. Mathews. Facts on File, 1990.

Eating Habits and Disorders. Rachel Epstein. Chelsea House, 1990.

(See also WOMEN'S HEALTH HELP, INFORMATION, AND ACTION GUIDE on page 334.)

antenuptial agreement, an alternative name for PRENUPTIAL AGREEMENT, commonly used in the law.

antepartal care, an alternative term for PRENATAL CARE.

Anthony, Susan B. (1820–1906), a social reformer who became an outstanding leader in the long, ultimately successful battle for American WOMAN SUFFRAGE. While teaching at a "female academy" in Canajoharie, New York (1846–1849), she became a WOMEN'S RIGHTS activist, attending the landmark first women's rights convention at Seneca Falls, New York, in 1848. With her lifelong associate Elizabeth Cady Stanton, she was a founder of the New York Women's

State Temperance Society in the early 1850s and an active abolitionist before and during the Civil War.

After the war she focused on woman suffrage and quickly emerged as the leading militant of the American WOMEN'S RIGHTS MOVEMENT. With Elizabeth Cady Stanton she founded the periodical *The Revolution* (1868–1870) and the NATIONAL WOMAN SUFFRAGE ASSOCIATION (NWSA) in 1869. From the late 1870s she led the fight for the Woman Suffrage Amendment to the Constitution, which became known as the Anthony Amendment. Formally introduced in 1878, and first voted on and defeated in 1886, it ultimately became the NINETEENTH AMENDMENT in 1920. Anthony, Stanton, and Matilda GAGE were authors of *THE HISTORY OF WOMAN SUFFRAGE* (1886).

The somewhat more conservative AMERICAN WOMAN SUFFRAGE ASSOCIATION had been organized as an alternative to the NWSA in 1869. The two wings of the movement rejoined in 1890, and from 1892 to 1900 Anthony was president of the unified NATIONAL AMERICAN WOMAN SUFFRAGE ASSOCIATION. Anthony was also a leader of the international women's movement, in 1888 founding the INTERNATIONAL COUNCIL OF WOMEN, and in 1904 joining Carrie Chapman CATT in founding the INTERNATIONAL WOMAN SUFFRAGE ALLIANCE. (See also WOMEN'S RIGHTS MOVEMENT.)

Of all the old prejudices that cling to the hem of the woman's garments and persistently impede her progress, none holds faster than this. The idea that she owes service to a man instead of to herself, and that it is her highest duty to aid his development rather than her own, will be the last to die.

SUSAN B. ANTHONY, 1897
IN "THE STATUS OF WOMEN, PAST, PRESENT,
AND FUTURE"

•

antifeminist, a very broad pejorative term used by some feminists and WOMEN'S RIGHTS advocates to characterize the beliefs of those who oppose them ideologically and practically. Among those so characterized have been a very wide range of thinkers, from Aristotle to Freud and his female and male disciples, as well as those who are simply woman haters or male-ascendant jungle-law proponents.

"Antifeminist" also characterizes some of those movements and organizations that have opposed WOMEN'S RIGHTS during the past two centuries, as the worldwide struggle for women's rights has developed. Most highly visible have been such largely female nineteenth- and early twentieth-century American movements as those opposing WOMAN SUFFRAGE, which (with many male and dual-sexual groups) tried unsuccessfully to defeat suffrage for women. Led by the National Association Opposed to Woman Suffrage, the antifeminist movement defeated woman suffrage in many states before it ultimately became law with ratification of the NINETEENTH AMENDMENT in 1920.

Half a century later, the mainly White fundamentalist Protestant, middle-aged, religious constituency of that earlier movement was joined by large numbers of Catholic, lower-middle-income, and working-class women, all together part of the New Right's "silent majority," which defeated the EQUAL RIGHTS AMENDMENT (ERA). They were led by such newly emergent women leaders as Phyllis SCHLAFLY, in such single-issue organizations as her Stop ERA, in alliance with the wide range of conservative religious and political organizations that provided the basis of Republican support during the Reagan and Bush administrations.

arbitration, a procedure in which two people in conflict present their dispute to a neutral third party for resolution. The arbitrator, often from the American Arbitration Association, may be selected by the parties themselves or appointed by the court. Unlike MEDIATION, arbitration results in a decision that is binding on both parties. The arbitration procedure is informal, but each side presents evidence and brings witnesses. The main advantages of arbitration are that it avoids the cost, delay, hard feelings, and even trauma involved in court cases. In some cases, *mediation,* in which the mediator attempts to help the disputants themselves solve their problem, may be preferable; many turn to arbitration only if mediation fails. Many SEPARATION AGREEMENTS and living-together agreements (see COHABITATION) include mediation and arbitration clauses. (See DIVORCE AND SEPARATION HELP, INFORMATION, AND ACTION GUIDE on page 238.)

areola, the circle of pigmented skin surrounding the nipple on a breast (see BREAST).

arthritis, inflammation of the joints—places where bones meet and often move—affecting one part of the body or many and typically causing pain, stiffness, and redness; actually a general name for over one hundred joint disorders with a wide variety of causes.

Some joints, such as those in the skull, are not meant to move, but others are movable—and therein, literally, lies the rub. These mobile joints contain a fibrous capsule lined with a special membrane called the *synovium,* which produces *synovial fluid* to fill the capsule, some of it being stored in packets called *bursae.* Normally these fluid-filled capsules act as cushions or shock absorbers between the bones; the ends of the bones themselves are covered with a slippery cartilage, so the combination allows for nearly friction-free movement. But if the joint tissues deteriorate in any way, inflammation results—in a word, arthritis, which literally means "joint inflammation."

The most common form is *osteoarthritis,* also called *degenerative joint disease,* which affects approximately sixteen million people in the United States alone. In those affected, the slippery cartilage at the bone ends wears away, so the dry bones grate and produce pain when they move. This is commonly a disease of old age—sometimes even called the wear-and-tear disease—affecting both men and women, but women disproportionately because they live longer. But it can also be brought on earlier, by injury or trauma; GENETIC DISORDERS, including metabolic disorders; and possibly by occupational or sports-related activities (see EXERCISE).

The second most common form, affecting about three million Americans, is *rheumatoid arthritis*, in which the body's own IMMUNE SYSTEM mistakenly attacks tissue in the joints, as if it were a foreign invader; as a result it is called an *autoimmune disorder*. The joints become inflamed and swollen, weakening the ligaments, causing fingers and thumbs to spread apart (and so making grasping difficult), and throwing muscles generally out of alignment. Rheumatoid arthritis is a progressive disease, though its rate of development varies. In the early stages various kinds of white blood cells are attracted to the synovial membrane, their numbers alone causing swelling and their activity also causing excessive growth in the synovial membrane and some of their products beginning to attack the joints. Symptoms include malaise, fatigue, and mild joint stiffness, along with swelling. Drugs to reduce inflammation and inhibit production of cells in the affected area can at this stage prevent cartilage loss and joint deformity. But if the disease is undiagnosed and untreated, the synovial membrane and cartilage become so grossly overgrown—sometimes the synovial membrane reaches one hundred times its normal weight—and bones become so damaged that the supporting ligaments are thrown out of position. Once this happens, at the present stage of medical knowledge, the effects are irreversible.

Some kinds of arthritis—sometimes only temporary, if treated—can also be caused by infections, such as the bacteria-caused Lyme disease; Kawasaki disease; and infection with strep A *(Streptococcus pyogenes)*. These are normally treated with antibiotics. Various disorders of the spine, collectively called *spondyloarthropathies*, are also today considered forms of arthritis, as is gout; these predominantly affect men. An autoimmune type of arthritis primarily affecting children, and focusing on knees, is *juvenile rheumatoic arthritis*, which sometimes passes by PUBERTY. An arthritic, autoimmune disorder affecting predominantly women is LUPUS (systemic lupus erthyematosus).

Therapy aims primarily to protect affected joints; strengthen adjacent muscles, especially through exercise (such as swimming) that does not place weight on affected joints; and in general maintain as much mobility as possible. Support devices such as canes or crutches can also ease weight-bearing pressure on affected joints, as will losing weight for those who are overweight (see OBESITY); numerous devices can help with everyday living. While corticosteroid drugs can reduce inflammation, they have various adverse side effects (see STEROIDS) and offer only temporary relief. Drug therapy tends to rely on *nonsteroidal anti-inflammatory drugs* (NSAIDs), including aspirin and ibuprofen. For some rheumatoid arthritis patients, for whom NSAIDs no longer serve, gold is injected into joints; this provides relief for about half of the patients, for unknown reasons, for a few years. Some other drugs attempt to halt excessive cell production in the synovial membrane or suppress the immune system response that is causing the attacks on the joint.

People with advanced cases of arthritis today can choose to have the joint replaced with an artificial implant. These are made of various materials and shaped according to the type of joint being replaced. (See SKELETAL SYSTEM for a description of the types of joints.) Small hinge-type implants used in fingers are often made of silicon, while larger ball-and-socket-type implants, as for a hip, are often made of metals or special ceramics. Implant surgery is not simple, and it is not a panacea. After healing, patients must exercise and take physical therapy for perhaps a year for maximum rehabilitation. And sometimes the implants themselves can cause problems, if the materials of which they are made trigger a further immune system reaction. Some of the problems related to silicon BREAST IMPLANTS have also been experienced by people with joint implants, though these are solid devices, as opposed to the gel-filled breast implants. But artificial implants can, for some people, be a godsend, restoring long-lost mobility.

Another common joint problem is *temporomandibular joint (TMJ) disorder* (see TEETH). (See ARTHRITIS HELP, INFORMATION, AND ACTION GUIDE, below; also SKELETAL SYSTEM; IMMUNE SYSTEM.)

ARTHRITIS

Help, Information, and Action Guide

Organizations

► **Arthritis Foundation** (1314 Spring Street, NW, Atlanta, GA 30309, 404-872-7100; Don Riggin, director and CEO), an organization focusing on arthritis and related diseases. It provides information and makes referrals; sponsors self-help programs through local chapters; and publishes many materials, including the quarterly newsletter *Arthritis Basic Facts* and *Arthritis: Diet and Nutrition.*

► NATIONAL INSTITUTE OF ARTHRITIS AND MUSCULOSKELETAL AND SKIN DISEASES **(NIAMS)** (301-496-8188); **AMS Clearinghouse** (301-495-4484); **Office of Research on Women's Health** (301-402-1770). Publishes *How to Cope with Arthritis, Arthritis: Medicine for the Layman,* and *Arthritis, Rheumatic Diseases and Related Disorders.*

► **Problem Reporting Program** (12601 Twinbrook Parkway, Rockville, MD 20852), an organization for receiving reports about implants. (See IF YOU HAVE IMPLANTS . . . on page 119.)

Other resources

■ **GENERAL WORKS**

If It Runs in Your Family, Arthritis: Reducing the Risk. Mary D. Eades. Bantam, 1992.

Fight Back Against Arthritis. Robert Bingham. Harbor House West, 1992.

Take Charge of Your Health: Arthritis. Mike Samuels and Nancy Samuels. Summit, 1991.

Arthritis: What Works. Dava Sobel and Arthur C. Klein. St. Martin's, 1991.

Winning with Arthritis. Harris McIlwain and others. Wiley. 1991.

Taking Control of Arthritis: A Noted Doctor Tells You Everything You Need to Know to Triumph . . . Fred G. Kantrowitz. Harper Collins, 1990.

Arthritis Helpbook, 3rd ed. Kate Lorig. Addison-Wesley, 1990.

■ **ON TREATMENT APPROACHES**

Freedom from Arthritis Through Nutrition: A Guide to Pain-Free Living, with Original Recipes, 6th ed. Philip J. Welsh and Bianca Leonardo. Tree Life Publications, 1992.

Oigong for Arthritis: A Chinese Way for Healing and Prevention. Jwing-Ming Yang and Alan Dougall. Yangs Martial Arts, 1991.

Arthritis Relief at Your Fingertips: Your Guide to Relieving Aches and Pains Without Drugs. Michael R. Gach. Warner, 1990.

The Arthritis Exercise Book: Gentle, Joint-by-Joint Exercises to Keep You Flexible and Independent. Gwen Ellert. Contemporary Books, 1990.

Doctor Discusses Learning to Cope with Arthritis Rheumatism and Gout. Robert E. Dunbar. Budlong, 1990.

Free Yourself from Chronic Arthritis. The Dell Medical Library Staff. Dell, 1990.

Arthritis: The Allergy Connection. John Mansfield. Thorsons SF, 1990; G. K. Hall, 1991.

Arthritis: A Practical Guide to Coping. Richard Price. Trafalgar Square, 1989.

Arthritis Relief. Jean Wallace. Rodale, 1989.

Arthritis Relief at Your Fingertips: The Complete Self-Care Guide to Easing Aches and Pains Without Drugs. Michael R. Gach. Warner, 1989.

Exercise Can Beat Your Arthritis: A Guide to Overcoming Arthritis Through Exercise. Valerie Sayce and Ian Fraser. Avery, 1989.

Coping with Osteoarthritis: A Guide to Living with Arthritis for You and Your Family. Robert H. Phillips. Avery, 1989.

Coping with Rheumatoid Arthritis: A Guide to Living with Arthritis for You and Your Family. Robert H. Phillips. Avery, 1988.

◪ **PERSONAL EXPERIENCES**

The Long Journey: Personal Stories of Living with Arthritis. William E. Byrd. Aegina Press, 1991.

Meeting the Challenge of Arthritis: A Motivational Program to Help You Live a Better Life. George Yates and Michael Shermer. Lowell House, 1990.

Arthritis Self-Preservation: Arthritis Can't Make Me Cry. Toni Spencer. Jigsaw, 1989.

Osteoarthritis: A Step-by-Step Success Story to Encourage Others to Help Themselves. Fred L. Savage. Gordon Soules Books, 1989.

(See also **WOMEN'S HEALTH HELP, INFORMATION, AND ACTION GUIDE** on page 334.)

---

artificial insemination (AI), the process of attempting FERTILIZATION not through SEXUAL INTERCOURSE, but by introducing SPERM-containing SEMEN into a woman's VAGINA through an instrument such as a tube or syringe. Some women prefer the term *alternative fertilization,* but the usage has not caught on. To maximize the chances of CONCEPTION, this procedure is undergone at the time of OVULATION, using methods such as those in NATURAL FAMILY PLANNING, and may be repeated over several days. Semen is sometimes held in place for a few hours by a small cup. The success rate is highest when the procedure is performed at a doctor's office or special clinic, but it can also be done at home. AI may be done with either fresh or frozen semen, using one of two main approaches.

Artificial insemination–husband (AIH) or *homologous insemination* involves using sperm from the woman's husband or sex partner. AIH is sometimes used by heterosexual couples when the man has a physical disability that prevents vaginal intercourse; when he will be undergoing medical treatment, such as radiation or chemotherapy (see CANCER), that can cause STERILITY, and in cases of INFERTILITY. Artificial insemination is especially useful where the sperm count is low, where the sperm needs special treatment before being introduced, or where the procedure is necessary to bypass some of the hostile fluids in the woman's vagina. Generally fresh semen is used for AIH, produced by the man through MASTURBATION in the doctor's office, temporarily placed in a sterile container, and then inserted near the woman's *cervix.* However, the man's semen may sometimes be frozen and stored for later use; in that case the procedure is much the same, but the timing of insemination at ovulation is even more crucial, since frozen sperm have a somewhat shorter life span.

The biological FATHER of a baby produced through AIH is also the legal father. Some legal disputes may occur, however, as over ownership of stored sperm when a couple has split but the woman still wants a child. In one example of the potential complexity of artificial insemination, a woman became inseminated with frozen semen that had supposedly been obtained from her husband (who had since died of cancer), but genetic analysis proved that the woman had actually been impregnated with someone else's semen. Some states have implicitly or explicitly limited artificial insemination to married women, though some unmarried women have successfully challenged such laws in some instances.

Legal and biological questions are both more complicated with *artificial insemination–donor (AID),* also called *donor insemination* or *heterologous insemination,* in which the semen used is from someone who is not the woman's husband or sex partner. This approach is often taken by heterosexual couples who have a medical history of GENETIC DISORDERS or Rh incompatibility (see BLOOD), or by a SINGLE WOMAN or a LESBIAN couple who wishes to have children.

Generally the sperm used comes from private organizations known as *sperm banks* or *cryobanks.* These collect sperm from donors, sometimes for a fee, freeze it in liquid nitrogen, and later sell it to women or doctors for use in artificial insemination. But sometimes the sperm comes from personally chosen donors, such as a friend or, in the case of a lesbian couple, perhaps a partner's brother or other male relative.

In this age of AIDS, one significant concern for women is that artificial insemination is as dangerous as having sex without a CONDOM; SEXUALLY TRANSMITTED DISEASES, including AIDS, and also the liver disease *hepatitis* can be transmitted to a woman during AI. The danger is less with AIH, if the woman's husband or sex partner has been tested for AIDS on two widely spaced occasions and does not have sexual relations with other people, men or women. But with donor insemination, a woman may have less ability to assure her safety. Because of past problems, many sperm banks use only sperm that have been stored frozen for a considerable period of time, from donors who have tested negative for at least AIDS and hepatitis on two tests spaced a considerable time apart. Women considering donor insemination should explore such protections very carefully with their doctor and arrange for similar tests if they are using a known donor, rather than an anonymous donor through the sperm bank. The identity of donors to sperm banks generally remains confidential, unless *both* the donor and the donee—the inseminated woman—agree to reveal it. However, sperm banks normally gather and keep on file full medical histories of the donors, for later reference by the woman or her child, as for information on GENETIC INHERITANCE.

Sperm banks generally attempt to see that donors are in good health and screen them for known physical and MENTAL DISORDERS. A woman or couple can sometimes select the donor, based on anonymous information about the person's health, intellect, background, and achievement, sometimes attempting to match her own characteristics and sometimes attempting to have a "superchild" with genes linked to high achievement (see EUGENICS). No one can guarantee, however, that the donor may not unknowingly be carrying a defective gene. For donor insemination, doctors generally obtain sperm from a bank elsewhere in the country, to lessen the possibility that two children in the same locality will have the same biological father, which could lead to serious genetic disorders in the next generation should they conceive a child. Women should get very specific information from their doctor on the source of the sperm. In one notorious case, a doctor who had performed artificial insemination on over 180 women had used his *own* sperm, rather than sperm from a bank, so that many children in one region had, genetically, been fathered by a single man.

With donor insemination of a married woman, the woman's husband is generally considered the child's legal father; the anonymous biological father does not have PARENTS' RIGHTS. Beyond that simple statement, confusion abounds. Where women use sperm donated by known male friends, various state laws may come to different conclusions as to the question of the child's legal father; similar questions are involved in SURROGATE PARENTING, which often uses artificial insemination.

Among lesbian couples, the partner who actually bears the child is the biological MOTHER; the other partner may have no legal parental rights and, if the couple splits, may have no basis for CUSTODY or VISITATION RIGHTS. Couples can attempt to cover such eventualities by making preinsemination agreements, but these may or may not stand up in court, depending on the law in the state where they are living at the time. They may well want to consult lesbian rights specialists before having a child on this basis. (See LESBIAN HELP, INFORMATION, AND ACTION GUIDE on page 397.)

One alternative approach to artificial insemination is *intrauterine insemination* (IUI), in which the sperm is deposited directly into the woman's UTERUS through the CERVIX. Before IUI, sperm must be "washed," however. This is because the seminal fluid, which usually remains in the vagina, contains a hormone called *prostaglandin,* which can cause strong contractions and cramping in the uterus. IUI is used primarily when some aspect of the cervix is the bar to conception.

A variation on donor insemination is EMBRYO TRANSFER, in which a woman agrees to donate an egg (OVUM) to another woman. First she is inseminated by sperm from the woman's husband or sex partner; then, if fertilization occurs, the embryo is transferred to the other woman. (See INFERTILITY AND REPRODUCTIVE TECHNOLOGY HELP, INFORMATION, AND ACTION GUIDE on page 368.)

Asian-American feminism: See FEMINISM.

Atkinson, Ti-Grace (1939–), a radical feminist and leading figure of the first wave of the modern American woman's movement. She was briefly president of the New York chapter of the NATIONAL ORGANIZATION FOR WOMEN (NOW), until her breakaway in 1968, when she co-founded The Feminists, a utopian radical feminist group without specified leaders, strongly committed to the elimination of the institutions of MARRIAGE and the FAMILY and to the development of a classless society without PATRIARCHY. The vehicle was to be a leaderless structured organization, resembling in theory and partly in practice some of the earlier anarchist models. Her affiliation with the group lasted only until 1970, though she continued to work with other radical feminists in the decades that followed. Atkinson published *Amazon Odyssey* (1974), a collection of her speeches and papers.

augmentation mammoplasty, breast enlargement (see COSMETIC SURGERY).

Augspurg, Anita (1857–1943), a German feminist, a campaigner against legalized PROSTITUTION, and a leader of the Federation of German Women's Associations in the mid-1890s, who then moved toward radical action. In 1902 she co-founded and became first president of the German Women's Suffrage Association, working with her companion Lida HEYMANN. Augspurg was a co-founder and vice-president of the INTERNATIONAL WOMAN SUFFRAGE ALLIANCE in 1904. In 1907 Heymann and Augspurg became active in the German Women's Suffrage League, organizing the kinds of mass demonstrations then being led in Britain by Emmeline PANKHURST and in the United States by Harriet Stanton Blatch (see Elizabeth Cady STANTON). Augspurg and Heymann were pacifists, whose opposition to World War I ultimately cost them much of their mass support (see PACIFISM AND NONVIOLENCE); ultimately they were silenced—their offices closed and their writings censored—though not imprisoned by the German government. Both resumed WOMEN'S RIGHTS activity during the Weimar period and fled to Switzerland after the Nazi takeover of their country.

autoimmune disorder: See IMMUNE SYSTEM.

azoospermia, a rare condition involving total lack of SPERM and resulting in STERILITY (see INFERTILITY).

Baby Doe law, a 1984 U.S. federal law mandating medical care for all infants, including those with severe disabilities, deformities, or disorders, many of whom would previously be allowed to die (see INFANTICIDE).

back problems: See SPINE; OSTEOPOROSIS; MUSCULAR SYSTEM.

bacterial vaginosis, a common bacterial infection of the VAGINA; also called *nonspecific vaginitis*. Symptoms commonly include a vaginal discharge with a somewhat fishy odor, especially after SEXUAL INTERCOURSE, and often vaginal irritation, burning, or itching. Bacterial vaginosis can be transmitted through sexual contact and so is often classed as one of the SEXUALLY TRANSMITTED DISEASES (STDs), but it can also result in women, including young girls, who are not sexually active. This occurs when the normal balance of bacteria in the vagina is disrupted for unknown reasons. Bacterial vaginosis can be a signal that other infections are present, including other STDs or YEAST INFECTION (candidiasis).

For diagnosis, a sample of vaginal fluid is examined under a microscope for presence of bacteria. Usually just the infected woman is treated; partners are not treated, unless the original infection does not respond to drug therapy. Although it is relatively benign, it should be treated promptly because of its possible links to PELVIC INFLAMMATORY DISEASE (PID), which can cause INFERTILITY and possibly life-threatening ECTOPIC PREGNANCY, and its adverse impact on PREGNANCY, where it can lead to premature or low-birth-weight babies. (See SEXUALLY TRANSMITTED DISEASES; also SEXUALLY TRANSMITTED DISEASES HELP, INFORMATION, AND ACTION GUIDE on page 658; WHAT YOU CAN DO TO AVOID STDs on page 660.)

bag of waters, a traditional name for the AMNIOTIC SAC.

Band-Aid surgery, a popular name for LAPAROSCOPY, especially a type of TUBAL LIGATION.

Bartholin's glands, a pair of glands on either side of the opening to the VAGINA, also called *vulvovaginal glands* or *vestibular glands*. When a woman is sexually aroused, these pea-size glands secrete a fluid that lubricates the region, easing SEXUAL INTERCOURSE. On occasion, one or both glands can become infected and are generally treated with antibiotics, warm baths, painkillers, sometimes drainage, and on rare occasions removal. (See VULVA.)

battered women, females who are routinely subjected to physical or psychological abuse from their husbands, partners, or ex-partners; also called *spouse abuse, wife abuse,* or (especially when it also includes CHILD ABUSE AND NEGLECT) *domestic violence* or *family violence.*

Despite the fact that much wife battering is still hidden, the experience of recent decades has made it clear that it cuts across all lines—racial, ethnic, age, regional, educational, and socioeconomic. No less a body than the American Medical Association said in 1992 that domestic violence was "a public health problem that has reached epidemic proportions," noting that in the United States nearly one out of four women will be abused by a current or former partner at some time during their lives, with about four million women assaulted each year. U.S. Surgeon General Dr. Antonia Novello said in 1991, "The home is actually a more dangerous place for American women than the city streets," noting that one-third of the women murdered each year are killed by their current or former husbands or partners. She noted that domestic violence causes more injuries to women than automobile accidents, muggings, and RAPE combined. Wife abuse is found the world over and is widely condoned in some places. In India it is sometimes a part of a tacitly accepted pattern of harassment and abuse from the husband's family designed to extort additional money from a woman's family and sometimes resulting in DOWRY murder.

Some sociologists and psychologists have identified several kinds of characteristics that are commonly found in abuser profiles, among them
- a family history of abuse, either child abuse or wife abuse, is the most important single characteristic, since this is often learned behavior.
- low self-esteem, which is assuaged by controlling their partners.
- use of threats, force, or violence to solve problems or control their partners.
- ALCOHOL AND DRUG ABUSE.
- jealousy of their partners' relationships with other people.
- blaming the abused partners for their violence.

The pattern of abuse is often cyclical, with building of tension, anger, blaming, arguing, then battering; this is often succeeded by a calm stage, with denial of the violence, promises that it will never happen again, excuses of drunkenness, and the like; then gradually the tension builds and the cycle starts again. The cycles shorten, and the battering tends to grow more violent over time.

Women are often drawn into abusive relationships unknowingly and may be deeply involved before they realize that they are in trouble. Often the woman herself suffers low self-esteem, made even lower by continual abuse, and typically fears planning and acting on her own, tendencies accentuated by the abusive partner, who often makes the abused woman totally dependent on him. Abuse

frequently starts or becomes worse during PREGNANCY and can lead to MISCAR-
RIAGE. The abusive man characteristically shows several types of physical or psychological violence toward the woman, including

- *controlling behavior*—trying to completely control what she does, where she
  goes, whom she sees, whom she talks to.
- *isolation*—attempting to cut her off from family and friends.
- *intimidation*—using threatening looks, actions, gestures, shouts, and smashing
  or destroying things, especially her property.
- *emotional abuse*—putting the woman down, calling her names, undermining
  her self-confidence, making her think she is crazy, playing "mind games."
- *economic abuse*—trying to keep her from getting or keeping a job, taking her
  money, giving her a strict allowance, making her ask or even beg for money.
- *sexual abuse*—making her do sexual acts against her will, attacking the sexual
  parts of her body, treating her like a SEX OBJECT.
- *using male privilege*—treating her like a servant, making all the major decisions.
- *threats*—making and sometimes carrying out threats to do things that will
  hurt her, threatening to take the children or report her to welfare, threatening
  to commit suicide.
- *using the children*—making her feel guilty about the children, using the children to pass messages, abusing (or threatening to abuse) the children, using
  VISITATION RIGHTS as a way to harass her (after a SEPARATION or DIVORCE).
- *blaming others for problems*—saying that she (or someone else) is always to
  blame, out to get him, keeping him from concentrating.

Often the relationship starts out as a whirlwind involvement, with the woman
"swept off her feet"; she often feels guilty if she wants to slow down or break off
the involvement. The abuser often explains his exaggerated behavior as stemming
from great love or concern, which can at first be very flattering, especially if she
has low self-esteem, and only later appears dominating or excessively controlling.

Once a situation turns abusive, many women are too demoralized, frightened, and resourceless to leave. Partly as a result of the abuse, many doubt their
own judgment and ability to make decisions. Often friends, family, and society—
not realizing the seriousness of the situation—urge that the woman try to keep
the family together. And, in fact, many women try to do just that; they see that
as their role and are encouraged by remembrances of previously loving relationships, periodic apologies, and promises to reform. Many women are ashamed of
what they see as their own failure and come to accept blame for causing the violence. Some psychologists have likened the abusive situation to a concentration
camp, where the prisoners try to behave and accommodate and placate their cap-
tors. Many, in fact, do not even recognize that they are in an abusive relationship
(see ARE YOU ABUSED? on page 76). Many withdraw into alcohol or drug abuse
and develop emotional problems, such as DEPRESSION.

More practically, many abused women have no financial resources, no marketable skills, no means to support themselves and their children, no money for
CHILD CARE if they were to work, and no place to go. Even if they go to a shelter,
they fear—and with good reason—losing the children in a CUSTODY battle, especially since they cannot match their partners in funds for prolonged legal battles.

Given the odds against them, it is not surprising that women often tend to stay in such relationships.

As society has come to understand the dimensions of the problem, however, and to supply resources to help them, many battered women are seeking new lives. At the heart of this support system is a network of battered women's shelters. Specific shelters vary, but generally they offer women and children basic shelter and food (though many do not take children); a safe, violence-free environment; twenty-four-hour crisis intervention and support; counseling services; child care; transportation assistance; legal assistance and referral; financial assistance; victim advocacy services; information; and medical assistance. For women still in the abusive home, many centers also offer individual counseling and nonresident mutual-support groups, so women can share experiences with and draw strength from other women who are or have been in similar circumstances. Some programs also offer sexual assault services and counseling for batterers. In some states social workers ask women a series of questions as part of a *danger assessment*, to evaluate the danger of homicide in a particular case.

Leaving is not easy, however. Nor does it end the violence. In fact, in many cases the danger escalates, and women who try to escape are increasingly likely to be seriously hurt or killed. Because of that, a woman should—where possible—plan her move carefully. Experts in spouse abuse recommend that women

- get expert advice about how to leave the home safely by consulting with a lobattered women's shelter or the NATIONAL COALITION AGAINST DOMESTIC VIOLENCE.
- engage legal support, getting referrals from the local shelter.
- prepare friends and family and seek their moral support for a smooth transition.

Abused women should, in any case, have an emergency plan—some extra money and copies of important documents hidden away, car keys, the police number, and a place to go, such as a shelter or trusted relative. They should also seek medical attention, since some internal injuries may be serious but not apparent. They should also take photographs of the injuries, should they wish to press legal charges at any time.

Women preparing for long-term SEPARATION or DIVORCE may also want to look at PREPARING FOR DIVORCE: A WOMAN'S GUIDE (page 236), which discusses what kinds of moves to make and information to gather before leaving home, if they may not be able to, or want to, return. Note that if they want to retain custody of any children, women should take the children when they go, since otherwise they may risk losing custody immediately. If they do get a separation, they should remember that visitation brings with it new occasions for possibly abusive contact (see TIPS FOR MAKING VISITATION WORK on page 744).

Some women may choose to stay in their homes with the children but seek a court order protecting them from the husband, in some cases barring the husband from the home. Enforcement of court orders is spotty, however. Though police departments are becoming more sensitive to domestic violence, and many have special officers to handle such cases, they cannot prevent violence from occurring. In at least fifteen states, in reaction to years of no action on domestic abuse cases, police are under orders to jail husbands in domestic abuse cases; however, at least one recent study shows this practice has limited usefulness. In 1,200 domestic violence cases in Milwaukee, repeat assaults occurred in almost 60 percent of the cases where the man was just warned, and where the man was arrested, the repeat rate was still over 50 percent. If the men were unemployed on release from jail, the rate for repeat assaults jumped to 75 percent. Some suggest that the police should have more latitude in arrests, including taking the victim to a safe place temporarily, having the man leave for several hours, or just giving a warning.

In many other states without such stringent rules, however, abusers are often either not arrested or released by disbelieving judges. Many pursue and hound their former partners, often even after the women have changed addresses and phone numbers and have sought protective court orders. In some places women have even hired professional bodyguards. In the end, many women lack the personal, financial, and social resources to remain on the run and about half return to the abusive relationship.

It is among those women who feel utterly trapped, who have failed to find a way out of the abusive situation, that we generally find the few who finally, in despair and desperation, may turn and grievously injure or kill the abuser. Some have attempted to use the psychological profile of a battered woman, called the *battered woman syndrome,* as a defense for such killings; acquittals so far are rare. In several states clemency drives by women's organizations and latterly government officials themselves have resulted in early release of battered women who killed their abusers. Some battered women turn their desperation inward; U.S. Surgeon General C. Everett Koop noted in 1989 that battered women are four to five times more likely to require psychiatric treatment and more likely to commit suicide than women who were not battered.

It is also true that men are not the only abusers. Women frequently use physical and emotional abuse toward their spouses; in one study of six thousand married and cohabiting couples, women were slightly more likely to have used some kinds of violence. One major difference is that the men, generally being bigger and stronger, are more likely to seriously injure women than vice versa; and when men leave the situation, the abusing woman does not generally continue to hound the man. Men in that situation have no comparable battered men's shelters and get even less support from the community at large, though some have formed a Domestic Rights Coalition to seek comparable treatment. Clearly any person who abuses adults of either sex, as well as children or the elderly, should seek counseling to learn nonviolent ways to resolve conflicts. (See VIOLENCE AGAINST WOMEN HELP, INFORMATION, AND ACTION GUIDE on page 612; women seeking help in controlling their own violent behavior should see also CHILD ABUSE AND NEGLECT HELP, INFORMATION, AND ACTION GUIDE on page 152.)

ARE YOU ABUSED?

Victim Services (see below) says that a woman who answers "yes" to any of these questions may be in an abusive relationship.

Does your partner

- constantly criticize you and your abilities?
- become overprotective or extremely jealous?
- threaten to hurt you, children, pets, family, or friends?
- prevent you from seeing family or friends?
- have sudden bursts of anger?
- destroy personal property?
- deny you access to family assets or control all finances and force you to account for what you spend?
- use intimidation or manipulation to control you or your children?
- hit, punch, slap, kick, or shove you?
- prevent you from going where you want when you want?
- force you to have sex when you don't want to?
- humiliate or embarrass you in front of others?

Source: Victim Services operates a 24-hour phone line for victims of domestic violence in New York State, at 212-577-7777. (See also VIOLENCE AGAINST WOMEN HELP, INFORMATION, AND ACTION GUIDE on page 612.)

Beal v. Doe, the 1977 U.S. Supreme Court decision, ruling that states were not required to use public funds to pay for ABORTIONS.

Beard, Mary Ritter (1876–1958), an American historian, co-author (with Charles Beard) of the magisterial *The Rise of American Civilization* (1927), and also a leading writer on women in history, whose work in that area includes *On Understanding Women* (1931) and *Women as a Force in History* (1946). Her latter book focused largely on the question of COVERTURE, which she saw as essentially the husband's common-law ownership of all of his wife's assets and rights in law, giving little weight to what others have seen as a considerable body of equity and statutes, particularly relating to the law of wills and trusts (see IN-HERITANCE RIGHTS), that some people felt checked and qualified that ownership. Beard accepted the probable existence of earlier matriarchal societies, though she did not accept the theory put forward by many feminists regarding replacement of such societies by entirely patriarchal, wholly inimical societies, feeling that

some women in later societies continued to exercise great power. (See also WOM-
EN'S STUDIES.)

---

*... the personalities, interests, ideas and activities of women must receive an atten-
tion commensurate with their energy in history. Women have done far more than exist and bear and rear children. They have played a great role in directing human
events as thought and action. Women have been a force in making
all the history that has been made.*

MARY BEARD, 1946
IN WOMEN AS A FORCE IN HISTORY

•

Beauvoir, Simone de (1908–1986), a French philosopher, writer, and
leading twentieth-century feminist theoretician, whose *The Second Sex* (1949) became a worldwide centerpiece of feminist thinking as the new women's movement began to unfold in the 1960s. Her study of the roots of women's oppression
and the possibility of rising to personal independence continues to attract new
generations of feminists, who also reach for her four-volume autobiography:
Memoirs of a Dutiful Daughter (1958), *The Prime of Life* (1960), *Force of Circumstance* (1963), and *All Said and Done* (1972). In short, de Beauvoir posits the centrality of men and the marginality or "otherness" of women in modern societies,
the victimization of women as being intrinsic to those societies, and women's
need (and ability) to find and choose independent, fulfilling roles.

With Jean-Paul Sartre (her lifetime companion) and Albert Camus, de
Beauvoir was at the heart of the existential movement in the years following
World War II; her novel *The Mandarins* (1954) is about the leaders of that move-
ment. Other novels are *She Came to Stay* (1943) and *The Blood of Others* (1945).
Later she wrote about the treatment of the aged in modern society in *The Com-
ing of Age* (1970). (See also WOMEN'S RIGHTS MOVEMENT.)

---

*Society, being codified by man, decrees that woman is inferior; she can do away with
this inferiority only by destroying the male's superiority.*

SIMONE DE BEAUVOIR, 1949
IN THE SECOND SEX

•

Bellotti v. Baird, the 1979 U.S. Supreme Court ruling that a state could not
require a teenager to get her parent's consent for an ABORTION, unless an alternative was provided, such as getting consent from a judge.

belly-button surgery, a popular name for LAPAROSCOPY, a type of TUBAL LIGATION.

benign breast disease, various kinds of noncancerous lumps in the BREASTS.

bigamy, the condition of a woman having two husbands at the same time, or a man two wives, in places where that is a crime. Having two or more SPOUSES is called POLYGAMY, and that term is most often used to refer to those cultures where having multiple spouses simultaneously is legal and socially accepted. In popular usage, bigamy generally refers to illegal multiple marriages. By contrast, having a single husband or wife at one time is called MONOGAMY.

In the simplest terms, if a MARRIAGE exists and one of the parties then marries someone else, bigamy has occurred. Sometimes a person will intentionally and knowingly commit bigamy, including men or women out to bilk innocent victims of their resources, before moving on. But bigamy can also result by mistake. One or both parties to the original marriage may not believe that the first marriage exists. They may, for example, have been under legal age when married; but unless an ANNULMENT has taken place, the marriage exists. They may believe that because no WEDDING ceremony took place, no marriage exists; but in some places bigamy can also apply if the first union was a COMMON-LAW MARRIAGE. They may believe that an annulment or DIVORCE has been obtained in the first marriage; but if the divorce is not legal in that state or was obtained fraudulently, the second marriage is bigamous. In a few places, honest and reasonable belief that a divorce was legal is a defense against bigamy. But in most places, as in many other situations, ignorance of or a mistaken understanding of the law is no defense.

In many jurisdictions, if a spouse disappears, is absent without explanation or contact for a certain period of time (such as seven years), and is believed to be dead, he or she may be presumed dead, and the other spouse may legally remarry after that time period; however, in other jurisdictions, this might be considered bigamy. Sometimes, instead, a divorce is granted, ending the first marriage and leaving the deserted spouse free to remarry. (See MARRIAGE; also COUPLES AND FAMILIES HELP, INFORMATION, AND ACTION GUIDE on page 418.)

binge eating disorder, a pattern of compulsive eating characterized by recurrent episodes of excessive, out-of-control eating, with associated feelings of distress, disgust, guilt, or DEPRESSION. Quite different from an occasional "splurge," such binges may involve huge amounts of food—sometimes as much as 20,000 calories, far more than an adult should need for a whole day—in a single sitting or day-long orgy of food, consumed even when not physically hungry. The person may feel unable to stop eating or control consumption, once into a binge, except in embarrassment when "discovered" by others in midorgy. In its binge aspects this disorder is similar to BULIMIA but without the associated "purge" response, in which binge eaters attempt to rid their bodies of excess calories, as by vomiting. As a result, the large number of calories build up excess weight in the body; in this respect, it overlaps with OBESITY, though it seems to involve some different behavior mechanisms. Some eating disorders specialists have suggested that binge eating should be recognized as a distinct disorder, so that therapies might be developed to treat it. (See EATING DISORDERS HELP, INFORMATION, AND ACTION GUIDE on page 58.)

birth control, the making of deliberate choices about when, and when not, to have a child; also called *family planning*. Actually several choices may be involved: first, whether or not to allow possible CONCEPTION to take place unimpeded; second, if conception occurs, whether to continue the PREGNANCY or to have an ABORTION; and possibly also whether or not to take various PRENATAL TESTS, which can also influence the second decision. Birth control is also an umbrella term for the approaches or devices that allow a person to make those choices. In a wider sense, it also refers to the social goal of limiting population growth.

Among the many forms and approaches to birth control are

▶ NATURAL FAMILY PLANNING, several approaches that are alike in avoiding the use of any artificial or mechanical means to block conception.

▶ CONTRACEPTION, several methods that focus on preventing conception from taking place, including BIRTH CONTROL PILLS (oral contraceptives), CONDOMS, DEPO-PROVERA, DIAPHRAGM, DOUCHING, CERVICAL CAP, INTRAUTERINE DEVICE (IUD), NORPLANT, SPERMICIDE, SPONGE, and VAGINAL POUCH (female condom).

▶ STERILIZATION, which involves surgical intervention to prevent egg (OVUM) and SPERM from meeting, as in vasectomy or TUBAL LIGATION.

▶ ABORTION, the termination of a pregnancy, once begun, which also may be achieved by several different methods, including RU486.

▶ MORNING AFTER PILL, a drug given after SEXUAL INTERCOURSE that is designed to block a PREGNANCY by preventing a fertilized egg (OVUM) from implanting in the UTERUS.

The various currently used methods of birth control have different degrees of effectiveness; some depend more than others on consistency and care in use; and some have other health implications, positive or negative. BIRTH CONTROL: A GUIDE TO THE PROS AND CONS on page 87 gives an overview of the estimated effectiveness, risks, subsidiary benefits, convenience, and availability for a number of traditional methods. New approaches and new variations are being developed, however, so any woman wishing to exercise birth control should consult her doctor on what is best for her specific situation.

Information on and access to birth control has been hard won by women. Distribution of birth control information has often been barred by law. In the United States, for example, the nineteenth-century Comstock Laws classed contraceptive literature as obscene and therefore unlawful to send through the mails; not until 1917 were U.S. physicians legally able to give their patients birth control information, and not until 1936 could they prescribe contraceptive devices. The key figure in the court cases that brought these freedoms was Margaret SANGER, who in 1914 coined the phrase *birth control*. She opened her first birth control clinic in 1916 (it was quickly closed and Sanger arrested) and her first permanent clinic in 1923; the **PLANNED PARENTHOOD** movement sprang largely from her work. In Britain, the comparable figure was Marie **STOPES,** who founded the first birth control clinic there in 1921. As late as 1965, in *Griswold* v. *Connecticut,* the U.S. Supreme Court struck down a law that would have banned use of contraceptives by married couples; it established the "right of privacy" between the married couple and their doctor. The **REPRODUCTIVE RIGHTS** confirmed were then extended to unmarried people in 1972 with *Eisenstadt* v. *Baird* and to minors in 1977 with *Carey* v. *Population Services International.* By the late twentieth century, birth control was generally available to women in most affluent countries. Indeed, innovations such as birth control pills, introduced in 1955, brought substantial changes in sexual mores. Where birth control has been readily available, it has significantly increased the **LIFE EXPECTANCY** of women, already generally higher than that for men.

The fight over birth control still rages, however. In many countries, both rich and poor, some groups of people—often with strong religious and even governmental support—still seek to restrict the availability of birth control information and devices, except for natural family approaches. Opposition has been softening somewhat as it becomes clear that some kinds of birth control approaches, such as **CONDOMS,** offer some protection from **SEXUALLY TRANSMITTED DISEASES,** especially the lethal **AIDS.** Indeed, for maximum protection, many health experts now recommend use of a condom during **SEXUAL INTERCOURSE,** even if a woman is using some other form of birth control, such as "the pill."

In some countries, such as Ireland, contraceptive information and devices have been barred or discouraged for religious or cultural reasons. In others, contraceptive information has been withheld for political reasons, as in Romania before the fall of the Ceausescu regime, where the government sought larger families. In many developing countries, quite apart from cultural resistance to birth control, contraceptive information and devices are unavailable because of sheer poverty, though that is the focus of considerable international attention, since population is becoming an increasingly urgent worldwide problem.

On the other hand, some forms of contraception, such as Norplant or Depo-Provera, can be misused by governments for social control—as in the earlier twentieth century, notably in Germany, the Scandinavian countries, and the United States, where sterilization was used legally to prevent reproduction among certain groups of people, often for racist or otherwise biased ends (see **EUGENICS**). Where population control is a major concern, as in India and China, the government sometimes exerts strong pressure for the use of contraception to keep family size down. So it is that, in an ironic twist, some feminists in such areas have found themselves *resisting* birth control, so women can retain their reproductive rights, the key issue being that the woman—not the government or anyone else—should be the one to decide if and when to have a child.

As long as reproductive rights are preserved, however, women who are concerned about worsening of living conditions and further damage to a fragile environment by rapidly rising world populations continue to urge the spread of access to and information about birth control in all countries. It is a crucial need: the **INTERNATIONAL WOMEN'S HEALTH COALITION (IWHC)** estimates that of eight hundred million couples of reproductive age in the world, most of whom live in the Third World, only 40 percent use modern contraception, though 2–5 percent use abstinence, withdrawal, or other traditional methods (see NATURAL FAMILY PLANNING). By region, IWHC estimates the rate of contraceptive use among reproductive-age couples to be 10 percent in sub-Saharan Africa; 20–40 percent in developing Asian countries (except China); 25 percent in North Africa and the Middle East; 40–50 percent in Latin America and the Caribbean; and above 70 percent in China and most developed countries. (See BIRTH CONTROL AND FAMILY PLANNING HELP, INFORMATION, AND ACTION GUIDE, below; see also specific entries on types of birth control mentioned above.)

No woman can call herself free who does not own and control her body. No woman can call herself free until she can choose consciously whether she will or will not be a mother.

———————————— MARGARET SANGER, 1913 ————————————

●

BIRTH CONTROL AND FAMILY PLANNING
Help, Information, and Action Guide

Organizations

☑ **FOR PRACTICAL ADVICE, INFORMATION, AND REFERRALS**

► PLANNED PARENTHOOD® (212-541-7800). Publishes *Facts About Birth Control* and *Teensex: It's OK to Say No Way.*
► FOOD AND DRUG ADMINISTRATION (**FDA**) (301-472-4750). Publishes *Comparing Contraceptives,* including natural family planning.
► NATIONAL INSTITUTE OF CHILD HEALTH AND HUMAN DEVELOPMENT (**NICHD**) (301-496-5133). Publishes series of "Facts About" booklets on topics such as *Oral Contraceptives* and *Vasectomy Safety.*
► NATIONAL WOMEN'S HEALTH NETWORK (**NWHN**) (202-347-1140). Operates the **Women's Health Information Service.** Publishes or distributes *Childbearing Policies within a National Health Program: An Evolving Consensus for New Directions, Women and the Crisis in Sex Hormones,* and the information packets on new reproductive technology and on contraceptives, including *Cervical Cap, Depo-Provera, Diaphragm, Intrauterine Device (IUD), New Methods, Norplant, Pill, Spermicide,* and *Sponge.*
► INSTITUTE ON WOMEN AND TECHNOLOGY (413-367-9725).

► NOW Legal Defense and Education Fund (**NOW LDEF**) (212-925-6635). Publishes *Facts on Reproductive Rights: A Resource Manual* and the Legal Resource Kit *Reproductive Rights*.

► **Choice** (1233 Locust Street, 3rd Floor, Philadelphia, PA 19107; 215-985-3355; hot line for health information 215-985-3300; hot line for day care information 215-985-3302; Lisa Shulock, executive director), an organization to educate the public on reproductive health care. It offers seminars and workshops; maintains a resource information center; provides telephone counseling and referrals; publishes various materials for adolescents and for parents as sex educators.

► National Black Women's Health Project (**NBWHP**) (404-681-4554). Produced the documentary film, *On Becoming a Woman: Mothers and Daughters Talking Together*.

► Federation of Feminist Women's Health Centers (916-737-0260).

► Ms. Foundation for Women (**MFW**) (212-353-8580).

◪ ON SPECIFIC TECHNIQUES

► **Association for Voluntary Surgical Contraception (AVSC)** (79 Madison Avenue, New York, NY 10016; 212-561-8000; Hugo Hoogenboom, president), an organization that encourages voluntary sterilization internationally. It gathers and disseminates information and publishes various materials, including fact sheets on both male and female sterilization.

► **Family of the Americas Foundation (FAF)** (P.O. Box 1170, Dunkirk, MD 20754; 301-627-3346 or 800-443-3395; Mercedes Wilson, executive director), an organization encouraging use of the Billings ovulation method (see NATURAL FAMILY PLANNING). It trains teachers to instruct others in the method and offers sex education to teenagers and help to parents as sex educators. It maintains a library; provides referral services; and publishes various print and audiovisual materials, in English, Spanish, French, Portuguese, Chinese, and Arabic.

► **Couple to Couple League (CCL)** (P.O. Box 111184; Cincinnati, OH 45211; 513-661-7612; John F. Kippley, executive director), an organization for couples interested in using natural birth control. It trains teaching couples, who instruct others in local groups. In addition to a newsletter, it publishes *The Art of Natural Family Planning* and *Sex and the Marriage Covenant: A Basis for Morality*.

► Human Life International (**HLI**) (301-670-7884). Publishes *The Best of Natural Family Planning, Deceiving Birth Controllers, Birth Control: Why Are They Lying to Women?, A Cooperative Method of Birth Control, The Art of Natural Family Planning, Family Planning the Natural Way: Complete Guide to Sympto-Thermal Method, Natural Family Planning: Nature's Way, God's Way,* and *The New No-Pill Birth Control*.

◪ POLITICAL AND SOCIAL ORGANIZATIONS

▶ **National Family Planning and Reproductive Health Association (NFPRHA)** (122 C Street, NW, Suite 380, Washington, DC 20001; 202-628-3535; Judith M. DeSarno, executive director), an organization concerned with family planning and reproductive health. It acts as an advocate, seeking to influence public policy, and publishes various materials.

▶ **Center for Population Options (CPO)** (1025 Vermont Avenue, NW, Suite 210, Washington, DC 20005; 202-347-5700; Margaret Pruitt Clark, executive director), an organization seeking to reduce adolescent pregnancies, through education about birth control and parenting. It attempts to influence legislation and public policy, and publishes various materials, including fact sheets in English, Spanish, and French.

▶ NATIONAL CENTER FOR POLICY ALTERNATIVES (202-387-6030).

▶ FUND FOR THE FEMINIST MAJORITY (617-695-9688; or 703-522-2214; or 213-651-0495).

▶ WOMEN'S ACTION COALITION (WAC) (WAC voice mail 212-967-7711, ext. WACM [9226]).

▶ LEAGUE OF WOMEN VOTERS (202-429-1965). Publishes *Public Policy on Reproductive Choices* and *Coping with Conflict: Reproductive Choices and Community Controversy.*

▶ COMMISSION FOR WOMEN'S EQUALITY (CWE) (212-879-4500).

▶ INTERNATIONAL WOMEN'S HEALTH COALITION (IWHC) (212-979-8500). Publishes *Women's Health in the Third World: The Impact of Unwanted Pregnancy, Population Control and Women's Health: Balancing the Scales, Reproductive Health and Dignity: Choices by Third World Women, Reproductive Choice in Jeopardy: International Policy Perspectives, The Contraceptive Development Process and Quality in Reproductive Health Services, Creating Common Ground: Report of a Meeting Between Women's Health Advocates and Scientists on Women's Perspectives on the Introduction of Fertility Regulation Technologies,* and *Cervical Cancer and Contraceptive Safety.*

▶ WOMEN'S INTERNATIONAL NETWORK (WIN) (617-862-9431). Publishes *A Picture Story of Reproduction from a Woman's View.*

Other resources

◪ PERSONAL AND PRACTICAL GUIDES

The Fertility and Contraception Book. Julia Mosse and Josephine Heation. Faber and Faber, 1991.

Preg-Not: A Guide for Modern Women, rev. ed. Do it Now, 1990.

Birth Control and You. Elizabeth K. White. Budlong, 1990.
Contraception: A Guide to Birth Control Methods. Vern L. Bullough and Bonnie Bullough. Prometheus, 1990.
How Not to Get Pregnant. Sherman J. Silber. Warner, 1990.
Your Fertility Signals: Using Them to Achieve or Avoid Pregnancy, Naturally. Merryl Winstein. Smooth Stone Press, 1990.
The Billings Method. Evelyn Billings and Ann Westmore. Ballantine, 1989.
Natural Birth Control. Frank Richards. Meyer Stone Books, 1989.
The New Birth Control Book. Howard Shapiro. Prentice-Hall, 1988.
Fertility: A Comprehensive Guide to Natural Family Planning. Elizabeth Clubb and Jane Knight. Sterling, 1988.

◢ GUIDES FOR TEENS

T.A.P.P. Sources: A National Directory of Teenage Pregnancy Prevention Programs. Dominique Treboux. Scarecrow, 1989.
Coping with Birth Control. Michael D. Benson. Rosen Group, 1988.
Birth Control. Alan E. Nourse. Watts, 1988.

◢ ON ORAL CONTRACEPTIVES (BIRTH CONTROL PILLS)

Oral Contraceptives and Breast Cancer. Institute of Medicine, Committee on the Relationship Between Oral Contraceptives and Breast Cancer Staff. National Academic Press, 1991.
The Pill: The Most Misunderstood Drug in the World. G. Samisoe, ed. Parthenon (NJ), 1990.

◢ ON STERILIZATION AND EUGENICS

The Surgical Solution: A History of Involuntary Sterilization in the United States. Philip R. Reilly. Johns Hopkins, 1991.
Guaranteeing the Good Life: Medicine and the Return of Eugenics. Richard J. Neuhaus, ed. Eerdmans, 1990.

◢ BACKGROUND BOOKS

Predicaments of Love. Miriam Benn. Paul and Co., 1992.
Family Planning. Tim Parks. Grove Weidenfeld, 1991.
Fertility Control: New Techniques, New Policy Issues. Robert H. Blank. Greenwood, 1991.
Handbook of Family Planning, 2nd ed. Nancy B. Loudon, ed. Churchill, 1991.
Family Planning and the Law. Kenneth M. Norrie. Ashgate, 1991.
Woman's Body, Woman's Right: Birth Control in America, rev. ed. Linda Gordon. Penguin Books, 1990.

Preventing Birth: Contemporary Methods and Related Moral Controversies. James W. Knight and Joan C. Callahan. University of Utah Press, 1989.

What You Need to Know About Planned Parenthood: What Is It? How Does It Affect You and Your Children? What Can You Do About It? JoAnn Gasper. Servant, 1989.

The Law Governing Abortion, Contraception and Sterilization. Irving J. Sloan. Oceana, 1988.

Birth Control Choices, rev. ed. Gloria M. Bertacchi. National Medical Seminars, 1988.

◪ REGIONAL STUDIES

Population and Development Planning in China. Wang Jiye and Terence H. Hull, eds. Paul and Co., 1991.

Population Planning in India: Policy Issues and Research Priorities. Ashish Bose and P. B. Desai, eds. South Asia Books, 1990.

Slaughter of the Innocents: Coercive Birth Control in China. John Aird. American Enterprise, 1990.

Pregnancy, Contraception, and Family Planning Services in Industrialized Countries. Elsie Jones. Yale University Press, 1989.

Improving Family Planning, Health, and Nutrition in India: Experience from Some World Bank Assisted Programs. Richard Heaver. World Bank, 1989.

Family Planning and Population Problems in India. S. K. Srivastava. South Asia Books, 1989.

Choosing a Contraceptive: Method Choice in Asia and the United States. Rodolpho Bulatao. Westview, 1989.

Regional Development and Family Planning. S. Siva Raju. Apt Books, 1988.

Family Planning and Child Survival Programs: 100 Developing Countries. John A. Ross and others. CUCFP and FH, 1988.

Population Control and Family Planning in India. Mamta Lakshmana. South Asia Books, 1988.

◪ RELIGIOUS VIEWS

Six Billion and More: Human Population Regulation and Christian Ethics. Susan P. Bratton. Westminster John Knox, 1992.

Powerful Conceptions: A Series on Bishops and Birth Control. Denise Shannon and Maggie Hume. Catholics for Free Choice, 1991.

A Full Quiver: Family Planning and the Lordship of Christ. Rick Hess and Jan Hess. Wolgemuth and Hyatt, 1990.

Abortion, Birth Control, and Surrogate Parenting: An Islamic Perspective. Abul F. Ebrahim. Am Trust Publications, 1989.

Is There a Solution to the Catholic Debate on Contraception? James Arraj. Inner Growth Books, 1989.

◪ HISTORICAL WORKS

Contraception and Abortion from the Ancient World to the Renaissance. John M. Riddle. Harvard University Press, 1992.

A Fertility Awareness and Natural Family Planning Resource Directory, 2nd ed. Suzannah C. Doyle, ed. FA Services, 1991.

A History of Contraception: From Antiquity to the Present. Angus McLaren. Blackwell, 1991.

An Illustrated History of Contraception. W.H. Robertson, ed. Parthenon (NJ), 1989.

The Legacy of Planned Parenthood: Excerpted from Grand Illusions. George Grant. Wolgemuth and Hyatt, 1990.

(See also ABORTION HELP, INFORMATION, AND ACTION GUIDE on page 10.)

Birth Control: A Guide to the Pros and Cons

Efficacy rates given in this chart are estimates based on a number of different studies. Methods that are more dependent on conscientious use and therefore are more subject to human error have wider ranges of efficacy than the others. For comparison, 60 to 80 percent of sexual active women using no contraception would be expected to become pregnant in a year.

Type	Estimated Effectiveness	Risks	Noncontra-ceptive Benefits	Convenience	Availability
Condom	64–97%	Rarely, irritation and allergic reactions	Some protection against sexually transmitted diseases, including herpes and AIDS	Applied immediately before intercourse	Nonprescription
Vaginal spermicides	70–80%	Rarely, irritation and allergic reactions	May give some protection against some sexually transmitted diseases	Applied no more than one hour before intercourse; can be "messy"	Nonprescription
Sponge	80–87%	Rarely, irritation and allergic reactions; difficulty in removal; very rarely, toxic shock syndrome	Spermicides may give some protection against some sexually transmitted diseases	Can be inserted hours before intercourse, let in place up to 24 hours; disposable	Nonprescription
Diaphragm with spermicide	80–98%	Rarely, irritation and allergic reactions; bladder infections; constipation; very rarely, toxic shock syndrome	Spermicides may give some protection against some sexually transmitted diseases	Inserted before intercourse; can be left in place 24 hours but additional spermicide must be inserted if intercourse is repeated	Rx
Cervical cap with spermicide	80–98%	Abnormal Pap test; vaginal or cervical infections; very rarely, toxic shock syndrome	Spermicides may give some protection against some sexually transmitted diseases	Can remain in place for 48 hours, not necessary to reapply spermicide upon repeated intercourse; may be difficult to insert	Rx

Type	Estimated Effectiveness	Risks	Noncontra- ceptive Bene- fits	Convenience	Availability
IUD	95–96%	Cramps, bleeding, PID (pelvic in- flammatory disease), in- fertility; rarely, perfo- ration of the uterus	None	After inser- tion, stays in place until physician re- moves it	Rx
Birth-control pills	97% (mini) 99% (comb.)	Blood clots, heart attacks and strokes, gallbladder disease, liver tumors, water retention, hy- pertension, mood changes, diz- ziness and nausea; not for smokers	Less men- strual bleed- ing and cramping; lower risk of fibrocystic breast dis- ease, ovarian cysts, and pelvic inflam- matory dis- ease; protects against can- cer of the ovaries and lining of the uterus	Pill must be taken on daily sched- ule, regard- less of the infrequency of inter- course	Rx
Periodic absti- nence (NFP)	Very variable, per- haps 53–98%	None	None	Requires fre- quent moni- toring of body func- tions and pe- riods of abstinence	Instructions from physi- cian or clinic
Vasectomy (male sterilization)	Over 99%	Pain, infec- tion; rarely, possible psy- chological problems	None	One-time procedure	Minor sur- gery
Tubal ligation (fe- male sterilization)	Over 99%	Surgical complications; some pain or discomfort; possibly higher risk of hysterectomy later in life	None	One-time procedure	Surgery

Source: *Comparing Contraceptives*, by Judith Levine Willis (1989). Prepared by the Food and Drug Administra- tion for the Public Health Service. **Note:** The author of this chart meant it to be used in conjunction with discus- sions of each method, not alone.

birth control pills (oral contraceptives), pills containing HORMONES that act on the body in various ways to block CONCEPTION. Primarily they block release of an egg (OVUM) from a woman's OVARIES, by steadying the levels of key female sex hormones, since it is the rising and falling levels of these hormones that normally trigger OVULATION during the reproductive cycle (see MENSTRUATION).

Birth control pills come in different forms, the two main kinds being

▸ *combination pills,* which block the release of an egg. The earliest oral contraceptives were made primarily of ESTROGEN, but these were found to cause various adverse side effects, so today's combination pills also include *progestin,* a synthetic form of PROGESTERONE. Even so, some women still experience side effects, including nausea, high BLOOD pressure, and blood clots, which in some cases can cause severe problems, including blindness and death. Newer *biphasic* and *triphasic* forms, designed to follow a woman's normal hormonal variations, may lessen such side effects.

▸ *minipills,* which also suppress release of an egg, though not as effectively as the combination pill, and in addition act to make the CERVIX and UTERUS more hostile to SPERM. These are made only from progestin. Side effects include spotting and bleeding between periods.

Oral contraceptives must be taken every day for twenty-one days, regardless of how often a woman has SEXUAL INTERCOURSE, and then discontinued for seven days, allowing normal MENSTRUATION to occur. Taken regularly, they are regarded as among the most effective forms of *temporary* BIRTH CONTROL methods; the FOOD AND DRUG ADMINISTRATION (FDA) estimates that combination pills have a 99 percent effectiveness rate, while minipills are 97 percent effective. By comparison, STERILIZATION, which is intended to be permanent, had over 99 percent effectiveness. Some kinds of birth control pills are also given as MORNING AFTER PILLS on an emergency basis, following sexual intercourse.

From their introduction in the 1960s, "the pill" has been the contraceptive of choice for many sexually active young women and has had a great deal to do with the revolution in sexual mores since that era. It is not for everyone, however, and the decision to go on the pill should not be taken lightly. Individual women considering birth control pills should review the question carefully with their doctor, weighing their personal and family medical history against the potential adverse and beneficial effects of the pill.

Because they face increase risk of heart attack and stroke, and of some kinds of cancers, the FDA recommends *against* oral contraceptives for women who smoke (see SMOKING); are over thirty-five; have high blood pressure, heart problems, or blood clots (see HEART AND CIRCULATORY SYSTEM); have unexplained vaginal bleeding; or have BREAST CANCER or CANCER of the uterus (see UTERINE CANCER). Women who take combination pills also have increased risk of GALLBLADDER problems, liver problems, DEPRESSION, dizziness, vomiting, severe headaches, water buildup (*edema*), missed menstrual periods, and adverse reactions to some medications (such as some barbiturates and antibiotics). A woman who is or may be pregnant should not take oral contraceptives, since they may cause BIRTH DEFECTS. If a woman misses a period while on the pill, a pregnancy test may be advised; if she is not pregnant and periods continue to be skipped, she may need a pill with a different balance of hormones. Similarly, some women experience side effects such as growth of facial HAIR, acne, and oily SKIN; they, too, may be switched to a different kind of pill.

On the other hand, many people experience no such problems with birth control pills, and some reap substantial health benefits. Women on the pill have menstrual periods that are lighter, less painful, and also more predictable, since they are triggered when women stop taking the pills. Women on the pill are also less likely to have fibrocystic breast disease (see BREASTS), ovarian cysts (see OVARIES), PELVIC INFLAMMATORY DISEASE, ECTOPIC PREGNANCY, and possibly cancer of the ovaries or endometrium (the lining of the uterus). One 1991 study from the Alan Guttmacher Institute, balancing the general risk of death against the likelihood of death being prevented by use of the pill, actually concluded: "The average woman who has ever used the pill is less likely to get cancer and die as a result before age fifty-five than a woman who has never used the pill."

Birth control pills do not protect against cervical cancer and SEXUALLY TRANSMITTED DISEASES (STDs), including AIDS, unlike barrier forms of birth control, such as the CONDOM, DIAPHRAGM, and VAGINAL POUCH, used with SPERMICIDES. In fact, some countries, notably Japan, ban the use of birth control pills, fearing that condom use would decline and AIDS would increase. In many other countries, some women on the pill are being advised to also use one of the barrier methods, to reduce exposure to AIDS and other STDs.

Because of the numerous and potentially serious side effects, the FDA urges: "Women prescribed birth control pills should acquaint themselves with the information in the patient package insert accompanying the prescription [good advice, in general]. They should also have their blood pressure checked and should have physical examinations and a PAP SMEAR at least yearly. Because the risk of serious side effects in many cases decreases with a reduced hormone dose, patients should discuss with their physicians using the lowest effective dose." (See BIRTH CONTROL AND FAMILY PLANNING HELP, INFORMATION, AND ACTION GUIDE on page 81.)

birth defects, malformations, malfunctions, or disorders of any kind that are *congenital,* or present in newborns. This includes GENETIC DISORDERS, stemming from defective genes from one or both parents; CHROMOSOMAL ABNORMALITIES, resulting from problems in the separation, combination, and duplication of genetic material; and the many even more complicated and subtle problems that result from the impact on the child's genetic material of outside influences, such as radiation, drugs, disease, or injury during PREGNANCY or during CHILDBIRTH itself.

Well over three thousand distinct kinds of birth defects have been identified, but many others are suspected. Some are obvious at birth; some become apparent only months or even decades later. Some are lethal—so lethal that the FETUS is aborted spontaneously, so early in the pregnancy that the woman does not yet even know she is pregnant (see MISCARRIAGE). Others lead to death shortly before birth, resulting in STILLBIRTH, or shortly after, as with babies born with anencephaly, or absence of a brain. Of the surviving babies, an estimated 5–9 percent have some sort of birth defect. Though many types of defects are known or suspected, no one type is regarded as common. (For a full discussion of many specific types of birth defects, as well as organizations and references for help and information, see our *Parent's Desk Reference,* Simon & Schuster, 1990; see also GENETIC INHERITANCE AND BIRTH DEFECTS HELP, INFORMATION, AND ACTION GUIDE on page 314.)

The causes of most defects are still unknown, though most seem to result from a combination of GENETIC INHERITANCE and environmental influences. No absolute predictions can be made. Two women with otherwise similar life-styles and home settings may drink while pregnant, and one may have a child with fetal alcohol syndrome (see ALCOHOL AND DRUG ABUSE) and the other will not, the difference presumably being the way their individual metabolisms handled the alcohol.

Much of the information we have about birth defects is statistical—and it shows surprising variations. For example, spina bifida (a disorder in which the SPINE is not completely enclosed) occurs in approximately 1 out of every 575 births in northern Ireland, every 3,333 births in the United States, and every 20,000 births in Japan. The reasons for these variations are unknown but serve as clues for researchers, who try to make connections between environmental conditions and other factors, to act as guides to behavior. It is study of such statistical associations that lies behind many of the general guidelines for women during pregnancy. It has been shown, for example, that large doses of vitamin A during pregnancy, especially the first trimester, are linked to birth defects (see KEY VITAMINS AND MINERALS on page 502).

Though much remains unknown, increasing amounts of information is now available about the causes of birth defects, the transmission of genetic disorders, and the likelihood of chromosomal abnormalities. In PRENATAL CARE, this accumulated medical knowledge is used in setting guidelines and cautions for women who are or intend to become pregnant, such as having a properly balanced diet and avoiding exposure to environmental hazards that have direct effects on the developing fetus—all classed as *reproductive hazards.* These include virtually all drugs. In general, a woman who is pregnant or is even considering pregnancy should take *no* medications—prescription or over-the-counter—without first consulting her gynecologist or obstetrician about the possible side effects on a developing fetus. Some drugs can cause birth defects at any stage in a pregnancy, but often the most vulnerable period is the first few weeks, before a woman even realizes she is pregnant. Other known or suspected reproductive hazards include toxic chemicals, SMOKING, alcohol, SPERMICIDES used around the time of CONCEPTION, rubella (German measles), toxoplasmosis, viral diseases such as hepatitis, radiation (not only from X-rays or industrial use, but also from high-altitude flying), ANESTHESIA, and stress.

In GENETIC COUNSELING, new and growing knowledge about birth defects helps counselors give practical guidance to prospective parents and others concerned about birth defects. Genetic counseling is most helpful *before* CONCEPTION, so a couple can make appropriate life-style changes ahead of time, to reduce their risk of having a child with birth defects. Some men and women may even decide to make at least a temporary change of work, to shield the fetus during the most vulnerable first three months (*trimester*); a flight attendant—male or female—may arrange a ground transfer to avoid high-altitude radiation, for example.

Increasing medical knowledge has resulted in a series of PRENATAL TESTS, such as AMNIOCENTESIS, ALPHA FETOPROTEIN (AFP), CHORIONIC VILLUS SAMPLING (CVS), and ULTRASOUND, which can give parents advance warning of possible birth defects. Such genetic screening tests are often given early in pregnancy, so ABORTION is an option, if desired. Some people have ethical concerns about the use of reproductive technology (see EUGENICS). Some kinds of birth defects can actually be repaired during the pregnancy, with relatively new and still-developing techniques of FETAL SURGERY. (See GENETIC INHERITANCE AND BIRTH DEFECTS HELP, INFORMATION, AND ACTION GUIDE on page 314.)

birthing center, an alternative name for maternity centers (see CHILDBIRTH).

birth rate: See FERTILITY.

Birthright, United States of America (686 North Broad Street, Woodbury, NJ 08096; 609-848-1819; Birthright Hotline 800-848-LOVE [5683]; Denise Cocciolone, executive director), a network of volunteer groups urging alternatives to abortion. It offers pregnant women classes in childbirth and parenting and publishes various printed materials, including the newsletter *Life-Guardian.*

birth without violence, an alternative name for the LeBoyer method (see CHILDBIRTH).

bisexual, someone who is sexually attracted to persons of both sexes; also a synonym for HERMAPHRODITE, a person who has both male and female genitals. Bisexuals may experience sexual and emotional fulfillment from both HETEROSEXUAL and HOMOSEXUAL relationships, though they are often more active with one sex than the other. An unknown but apparently substantial portion of people do have both types of relationships at various times during their lives, often because they are attracted by individuals of both sexes, but sometimes because they have responded to social pressure. In particular, many women and men who have felt themselves to be primarily homosexual have been pressured into heterosexual relationships by social expectation and often by fear of openly expressing a homosexual preference (see LESBIAN).

Blackwell, Elizabeth (1821–1910), the first woman to gain a degree from an American medical college (Geneva College), in 1849. She did her residency in Paris and London, began her New York practice with great difficulty in

1851, and in 1857 opened the New York Infirmary for Indigent Women and Children, with her sister, Dr. Emily Blackwell. In 1868, the sisters opened an attached women's medical college. She moved to London in 1869, there becoming a founder of the London School of Medicine for Women.

bladder control: See URINARY TRACT.

Blatch, Harriet Stanton: See Elizabeth Cady STANTON.

blepharoplasty, eyelid surgery (see COSMETIC SURGERY).

blood, the fluid that circulates in the HEART AND CIRCULATORY SYSTEM, supplying oxygen and other vital elements throughout the body, removing carbon dioxide and other waste products, helping to keep the body's chemistry in balance, and ferrying other vital substances from site to site.

Blood cells originate in the BONE marrow (see SKELETAL SYSTEM). It is red blood cells (RBCs), called *erythrocytes*, that give blood its characteristic color; these cells carry a special protein called *hemoglobin*, which attracts and carries oxygen and also contains iron vital for health. Less numerous but larger are white blood cells (WBCs), or *leukocytes*, which fight infection in the body; of special importance are *lymphocytes*, which play an important role in the body's IMMUNE SYSTEM. Some other white cells, called *phagocytes*, are charged with ingesting and destroying bacteria and cell fragments. The smallest blood cells are *platelets* or *thrombocytes*, which control bleeding through blood clotting and speed repairs of damaged blood vessels.

Blood comes in different types, which are distinguished by protein markers called *antigens*. The immune system uses these markers to identify what substances belong in the body and which are foreign and should be attacked. The two main kinds of markers are A and B, and the four main kinds of blood are
- Type A, with A markers only.
- Type B, with B markers only.
- Type AB, with both A and B markers.
- Type O, with neither A nor B markers.

Blood can also be distinguished by the presence or absence of a marker called the *Rh factor*. About 85 percent of the population has blood with the marker, called *Rh positive*, but the rest of the population does not, called *Rh negative*. When blood is taken for blood transfusions, it is identified by ABO type and Rh factor; people with blood type O and Rh negative are called *universal donors*, because— since their blood lacks special markers—it can be used for transfusions on virtually anyone. If people get blood that does not match their type, the donor cells can self-destruct by bursting (*hemolysis*), resulting in shock, a possibly life-threatening drop in blood pressure, or kidney failure. The blood of a pregnant women and her developing fetus are routinely tested as part of PRENATAL CARE, to see if they are incompatible for the Rh factor. In cases of Rh incompatibility, hemolysis may result in the child at birth; in that case, an *exchange transfusion* may be performed, to replace virtually all of the infant's blood to prevent permanent damage.

Because blood is in touch with every organ and tissue in the body, it can easily spread infectious organisms that enter the body, as through an injury. When bacteria enter and multiply in the blood, the result is a potentially life-threatening *septicemia,* or more generally *blood poisoning.* In some types the bacteria produce toxins, substances that act as poisons in the body, producing an infection called *toxemia.* Examples are TOXIC SHOCK SYNDROME and PREECLAMPSIA, also called *toxemia of pregnancy.*

Blood also carries other kinds of infections. Probably of greatest public concern today is HIV, the virus that causes AIDS; for prevention, the primary aim is to prevent blood or other fluids of an infected person from mixing with someone else's blood or body fluids. Before the disease was recognized and the danger widely known, many people contracted AIDS from transfusions received for hemophilia (see below), during CHILDBIRTH, or during an operation.

Blood is routinely tested for infections—for HIV, hepatitis B, and SYPHILIS, among other diseases—to keep the blood supply as safe as possible. No test is absolutely foolproof, however, and some risk exists from receiving transfusions. As a result, many hospitals allow people to donate some of their own blood over several weeks before an elective operation, to allow for what is called an *autologous blood transfusion.* Others allow family and friends to donate blood specifically designated for use by a particular patient, though at least one recent study has shown that this approach is no safer than screened blood from a bank.

Some disorders affect the blood itself, among them
- ▶ *anemia,* too few red blood cells.
- ▶ *polycythemia,* too many red blood cells.
- ▶ *leukemia,* too many white blood cells, a form of CANCER.
- ▶ *hemophilia,* a group of bleeding disorders that result from defective platelets and ineffective clotting.
- ▶ *thrombosis,* excess clotting, which can cause circulatory problems (see HEART AND CIRCULATORY SYSTEM).

Though any of these disorders may affect women, anemia is the most common. Blood cells have a limited life; as red blood cells grow old they are gradually filtered out of the blood and destroyed by the lymphatic system (see IMMUNE SYSTEM), while new ones are formed in the bone marrow. The process can go awry, however, and lead to anemia when more old RBCs are destroyed than are formed; when some RBCs self-destruct in the bloodstream; when large amounts of blood have been lost, as from hemorrhage or during surgery; or when the blood cells themselves are defective and incapable of carrying oxygen efficiently.

Symptoms of anemia include headaches, fatigue, difficult breathing during EXERCISE, paleness, and in more serious cases pain from too little oxygen to the heart, dizziness from too little oxygen to the brain, heart palpitations, and sometimes *jaundice,* in which the body has excess amounts of the yellow pigment *bilirubin,* formed when RBCs are destroyed. In extreme cases, anemia can be life-threatening. Treatment focuses on restoring the proper balance and efficiency of the person's RBCs by giving blood transfusions, but also, where possible, identifying and treating the underlying cause of the problem.

The most common type of anemia results from insufficient iron in the diet (see KEY VITAMINS AND MINERALS on page 502), needed in the manufacture of hemoglobin. This is especially a problem among women, who lose extra blood each month during their reproductive years (see MENSTRUATION). Women are often advised to take iron supplements to avoid iron-deficiency anemia. During PREGNANCY a woman may also become anemic but should then not take any supplements before specific discussion with the doctor. Testing for iron-deficiency anemia is a routine part of PRENATAL CARE.

Megaloblastic anemia can result from deficiency of certain key vitamins, especially vitamin B_{12} and folic acid, which causes production of deformed, abnormally large RBCs (*macrocytes*). This sometimes results from poor NUTRITION; as a side effect of other disorders such as DIABETES, Crohn's disease, or celiac sprue (see DIGESTIVE SYSTEM); or from the body's inability to absorb vitamin B_{12}, a condition called *pernicious anemia.*

In *aplastic anemia,* the body has too few of all types of blood cells, because the production sites—the bone marrow—have been damaged. This can occur with some kinds of viral infections, but also with some anticancer therapies, such as radiation and chemotherapy, or exposure to some kinds of chemicals. If severe and irreversible, aplastic anemia can be fatal; in some cases, however, it may be treated by bone marrow transplant (see CANCER).

Some kinds of anemia are GENETIC DISORDERS. In *sickle-cell anemia,* the hemoglobin is abnormal and distorts the red blood cells into a distinctive crescent or sickle shape, making them not only less efficient at carrying oxygen, but also more likely to clog small blood vessels. The result can severely damage vital organs and even be life-threatening; it is often treated with blood transfusions. Sickle-cell anemia is most often found among those of Black African or Mediterranean descent and generally must be passed by both parents. In *thalassemia,* the RBCs are fragile and smaller than usual and self-destruct prematurely. Sometimes called *Mediterranean anemia,* it is most often found among people of Mediterranean descent but is also found in those from Southeast Asia. Various forms exist, some mild, some life-threatening. Blood transfusions are sometimes given but can cause damaging excess iron to be stored in body organs. Both kinds of anemia can be identified by genetic screening tests (see GENETIC COUNSELING; GENETIC INHERITANCE).

Many forms of hemophilia are also GENETIC DISORDERS. They result from a deficiency or total lack of one or more enzymes, called *coagulation factors.* Normally, blood heals any breach in its defenses by forming a clot, but in hemophiliacs the blood keeps on flowing. This means an external cut, even a minor one, can lead to dangerous loss of blood, but bleeding also proceeds internally as well, with blood causing painful swelling as it gathers in areas such as the knees and elbows. Some forms of these bleeding disorders affect both men and women, but some of the most common are carried by women but affect only their male children. Hemophilia can also be a secondary effect of other disorders, including leukemia. The main treatment is to provide blood transfusions to supply the missing factors, though this carries the risk of infection from blood transfusions (see above).

Leukemia is a form of CANCER that involves uncontrolled production of white blood cells in the bone marrow. Because it gradually crowds out both RBCs and platelets, it leads to severe anemia and hemorrhages. It strikes both men and women, and (contrary to popular expectation) more adults than children. Among women, leukemia is the tenth most common and eighth most lethal form of cancer. The five-year survival rate is only 35 percent; however, in one type of leukemia, dramatic improvements have been made, bringing the survival rate up from about 4 percent to 50 percent in twenty years. Common early symptoms are fatigue, paleness, weight loss, repeated infections, nosebleeds and other hemorrhages, and easy bruising. However, the disease can progress slowly and show few symptoms and so may be missed or misdiagnosed. Treatment generally includes chemotherapy, transfusions, and antibiotics and sometimes bone marrow transplants. The causes of leukemia are not known, but some forms are apparently triggered by a virus or by exposure to environmental hazards such as certain cancer-causing chemicals (*carcinogens*) or radiation. People with some genetic disorders or CHROMOSOMAL ABNORMALITIES, such as DOWN'S SYNDROME, have an increased risk of leukemia. (See BLOOD AND BLOOD DISORDERS HELP, INFORMATION, AND ACTION GUIDE below.)

BLOOD AND BLOOD DISORDERS
Help, Information, and Action Guide

Organizations

▶ NATIONAL HEART, LUNG, AND BLOOD INSTITUTE (NHLBI) (301-496-4236). **Sickle Cell Disease Branch** (301-496-6931). Publishes *Adolescents with Sickle-Cell Anemia and Sickle-Cell Trait, The Family Connection,* and *Sickle Cell Fundamentals.*

▶ **National Hemophilia Foundation** (NHF) (Soho Building, 110 Greene Street, Suite 406, New York, NY 10012; 212-219-8180 or the HANDI hot line 800-424-2634; Alan P. Brownstein, executive director), an organization concerned with hemophilia and related bleeding disorders. It acts as an information clearinghouse and advocate; operates the HANDI hot line (Hemophilia and AIDS-HIV Network for the Dissemination of Information); provides support for patient and families; supports research; and publishes various materials, including the quarterly *Hemophilia Newsnotes,* directories of treatment centers, and pamphlets such as *What*

You Should Know about Hemophilia, Comprehensive Care for the Person with Hemophilia, and *Control of Pain in Hemophilia.*

▶ **National Association for Sickle Cell Diseases (NASCD)** (3345 Wilshire Boulevard, Suite 1106, Los Angeles, CA 90010-1880; 213-736-5455 or 800-421-8453; Lynda Anderson, executive director), an organization focusing on sickle cell diseases. It acts as an information clearinghouse and advocate and publishes various materials, including quarterly *Sickle Cell News.*

▶ **March of Dimes Birth Defects Foundation** (914-428-7100; local chapters in telephone directory White Pages). Publishes fact sheets *Sickle-Cell Anemia* and *Thalassemia.*

▶ **Leukemia Society of America** (600 Third Avenue, New York, NY 10017; 212-573-8484 or 800-955-4572; Dwayne Howell, president), an organization focusing on leukemia, lymphomas, and multiple myelomas. It provides direct financial aid, transportation, and other services to patients; supplies information; and publishes various materials, including the bimonthly *Society News.*

▶ **National Leukemia Association** (585 Stewart Avenue, Suite 536, Garden City, NY 11530; 516-222-1944, Gilbert Schwab, president), an organization concerned with leukemia. It funds research and provides financial aid.

(See also CANCER.)

Other resources

Diet, Demography, and Disease: Changing Perspectives of Anemia. Patricia Stuart-Macadam and Susan Kent, eds. Aldine de Gruyter, 1992.

Safe Blood: Purifying the Nation's Blood Supply in the Age of AIDS. Joseph Feldschuh with Doron Weber. Free Press, 1989.

Health Care U.S.A. Jean Carper. Prentice-Hall, 1987. Lists major hemophilia treatment and research centers.

◪ ON LEUKEMIA

Looking Down from the Mountain Top: The Story of One Woman's Fight Against All Odds. Christine Michael. Spirit of Success, 1992. On fighting leukemia.

Fight the Good Fight. Philip Bedsworth and Joyce Bedsworth. Herald Press, 1991.

Borrowed Blood: Victory over Leukemia. Shawn S. Riley. Lion Press (NY), 1991.

(See also **WOMEN'S HEALTH HELP, INFORMATION, AND ACTION GUIDE** on page 334.)

Bodichon, Barbara Leigh-Smith (1827–1891), a British feminist, artist, writer, teacher, and WOMAN SUFFRAGE activist. In 1852 she opened Portland Hall, her experimental coeducational school. Two years later, in 1854, she emerged as a major feminist in the fight for women's property rights, publishing *A Brief Summary in Plain Language of the Most Important Laws Concerning Women*, which led to the successful fight for the Married Women's Property Bill (1857) (see COVERTURE; MARITAL PROPERTY). A year later, in 1858, she helped found the *English Woman's Journal*. She was one of the organizers of the first petition for woman suffrage, presented to Parliament by John Stuart MILL in 1866. During the late 1860s, she worked with Emily Davies to found the English woman's college that in 1874 became Girton College and continued to help develop the college in the years that followed, at the same time continuing to work for woman suffrage. (See also WOMEN'S RIGHTS MOVEMENT.)

body lift, a type of COSMETIC SURGERY.

bonding, the formation of special emotional ties between two people, especially between a MOTHER and her baby, called *maternal-infant attachment* (see MOTHER).

bone marrow transplant (BMT), a technique for treating patients with leukemia or some other types of CANCER.

bourgeois feminism, a pejorative term used by Marxists and some other revolutionaries, some of them feminists, to attack liberals in the feminist movement for being middle-class (*bourgeois,* in French) reformers instead of revolutionaries. As a pejorative term, it is a straightforward carryover from earlier political uses, though heard much less often since the end of Soviet communism. (See also FEMINISM.)

brachioplasty, removal of excess skin and fatty tissue from the arms (see COSMETIC SURGERY).

Bradley method, a popular natural childbirth approach (see CHILDBIRTH).

brain and nervous system, the body's intelligence and communications network; the brain is the command center of the network of nerves feeding information back and forth to part of the body.

The main line of communication runs through what is called the *spinal cord,* a column of nerve tissue that runs up the back of the body, housed in a column of small, cylindrical bones called the SPINE. The brain itself is made up of three main parts:

▶ the ***brain stem***, in the back of the head, which connects the spinal cord and the rest of the brain. The important cranial nerves, serving the EYES, EARS, mouth, and other areas of the face and throat, are connected directly to the brain stem, which also controls heartbeat and breathing (see HEART AND CIRCULATORY SYSTEM; RESPIRATORY SYSTEM).

▶ the ***cerebrum***, the largest part of the brain, where most conscious thoughts occur and deliberate actions are generated. Some functions, such as seeing, hearing, or smelling, seem to be centered in specific areas; other activities seem to be carried on in many parts, and both halves, of the brain, including memory. In relation to motor activities and sense impressions, the left half of the brain primarily controls the right side of the body, and vice versa. In general, the "left brain"—dominant in right-handers and many left-handers as well—seems to focus on word comprehension, language, speech, and numbers, while the "right brain" focuses on spatial relationships and feelings. Much of what is known about the cerebrum's functioning, however, is still quite rudimentary and conjectural. Longtime conjectures posing as fact, about brains of women and men being significantly different in size or function, have been disproved or called deeply into question but have not yet been replaced by firm new information.

▶ the ***cerebellum***, the second largest portion of the brain, lying below the cerebrum. Here many subconscious activities are centered, including those involving balance and coordination of movement.

The brain and spinal cord, which together make up the *central nervous system,* are both covered by protective membranes called the *meninges.* As the spinal cord is protected by the spine, the brain is protected by a rigid bony housing called the *cranium* or *skull,* which forms fully only after birth (see SKELETAL SYSTEM).

Significant damage or danger can result if injury or disease causes inflammation and swelling of the brain or spinal cord, including inflammation of the meninges (*meningitis*) and the brain itself (*encephalitis*), since the rigid skeletal housing offers little room for expansion. Direct damage to the spinal cord, or pressure from BLOOD clots and accumulated fluid after an injury, can lead to partial or complete paralysis of parts of the body. People with a possible spinal cord injury should not be moved unless absolutely necessary until a trained medical professional has had a chance to assess the severity of the injury and the probable danger of further damage. It is most important to stabilize the bones and take action to minimize swelling; actions taken—or not taken—here can affect a lifetime.

The functioning of the brain itself may be affected in many ways. GENETIC DISORDERS, including CHROMOSOMAL ABNORMALITIES, may damage or interfere with the brain's operation, resulting in mental retardation; cause structural defects; or lead to degeneration of brain tissue, as in Huntington's chorea. Brain cells may also be damaged by lack of oxygen, as during CHILDBIRTH. Tumors may also grow in and around the brain; even when they would normally be classified as benign, not malignant, they can have severe effects and can be life-threatening (see CANCER).

In some diseases, nerve or brain tissue degenerates, often for unknown causes, as in MULTIPLE SCLEROSIS and Alzheimer's disease. In addition, many kinds of MENTAL DISORDERS, sleep problems, and EATING DISORDERS such as ANOREXIA NERVOSA and BULIMIA, are also linked with brain functioning, but how and why they develop is so far mostly unclear. Some researchers believe that DEPRESSION and schizophrenia stem from underlying disorders in the chemistry of the brain; such disorders are sometimes called *organic brain syndromes.*

For more help, information, and action

▶ NATIONAL INSTITUTE OF NEUROLOGICAL DISORDERS AND STROKE (NINDS) (301-496-5751).

Other resources

The Brain Has a Mind of Its Own: Insights from a Practicing Neurologist. Richard Restak. Harmony/Crown, 1991.
The Brain and Nervous System. Charles B. Clayman, ed. RD Association, 1991.
The Three-Pound Universe: Revolutionary Discoveries About the Brain—From the Chemistry of the Mind to the New Frontiers of the Soul. Judith Hooper and Dick Teresi. Tarcher, 1991.
The Amazing Brain. Robert Ornstein and Richard F. Thompson. Houghton Mifflin, 1991.

breast (mammary gland), one of a pair of rounded structures protruding from the chests of mature females. They are composed largely of fatty tissue cushioning fifteen to twenty milk-producing glands called *lobes,* arranged somewhat like spokes around a wheel. This tissue is surrounded by a layer of SKIN, which includes a nipple through which milk is funneled. The nipple is set in a circle of pigmented skin called the *areola;* this contains smooth muscle that causes the nipple to become erect when it is stimulated. Apart from that, the breasts contain no muscle but are supported by ligaments attached to the chest wall; these overlie the *pectoral muscles* that cross the chest, with the breasts generally positioned above the second to sixth ribs. (See THE FEMALE BREAST on page 101.)

THE FEMALE BREAST

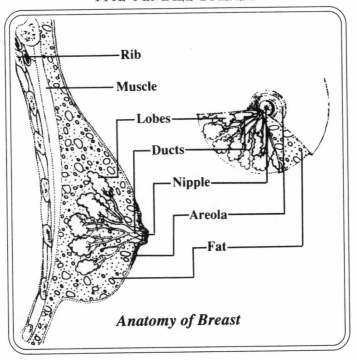

Rib

Muscle

Lobes

Ducts

Nipple

Areola

Fat

Anatomy of Breast

Source: *FDA Consumer*, July–August 1991.

Breasts are one of the most obvious symbols of the mature female. Actually modified sweat glands, they are undeveloped in children (and men), only developing during PUBERTY, as the breasts' fat cells enlarge in response to the ESTROGEN that the OVARIES then begin to pump into the body. The growth of these key SECONDARY SEX CHARACTERISTICS are clear markers of sexual maturity. The breasts, and especially the nipples and areola, are EROGENOUS ZONES, closely associated with sexual pleasure.

Breasts vary widely in size, shape, and position from person to person, depending on the individual's genetically patterned response to the female HORMONES, as well as her age and percentage of body fat. All women generally have approximately the same amount of glandular tissue in their breasts; what varies is the amount of fatty tissue that develops during puberty. Breast size and shape are unrelated to a woman's sexual sensitivity or the amount of milk produced after a birth. A woman's breasts are seldom identical; often one, commonly the left, is slightly larger than the other, sometimes markedly so.

A woman's breasts also change over time. They change in size, feel, and sensitivity with the monthly hormonal changes that are part of the cycle of MENSTRUATION; in particular, they often feel heavier, more tender, and even lumpy before the period starts (see PREMENSTRUAL SYNDROME). That is why breast self-examination (BSE) should be done at the same time each month (see page 104), preferably a few days after menstruation ends. During PREGNANCY, the breasts, including the nipples, grow noticeably larger, responding to new floods of estrogen and PROGESTERONE, and the hormone PROLACTIN, which activate the milk-producing glands to prepare for their main physiological function, BREAST-FEEDING. With the swelling, the breasts sag and often continue to do so afterward, though they may shrink. In any case, responding to the force of gravity, breasts gradually sag with age. After MENOPAUSE, with less female hormones and resulting loss of fat, the breasts shrink and sag further; skin and breast tissue also thins and loses elasticity.

Though breasts cannot be enlarged or their shape changed by EXERCISE, the sag that comes over time can be lessened by the wearing of a bra during maturity and especially pregnancy, to ease the strain on the supporting ligaments. Bras have been the subject of considerable controversy within the modern women's movement. Some women feel that bras are—with high heels, girdles, curlers, and the like—symbols of female enslavement to society's repressive notions of physical attractiveness. Others feel that bras are a symbol of modern freedom, allowing women to lead active lives without the discomfort of bobbing breasts. In personal terms, some women feel more comfortable, as well as more attractive, wearing a bra; others feel hamstrung and unnatural. As with so much else relating to women's lives, the choice of whether to wear a bra is a very individual one, made for a variety of reasons.

Many women are dissatisfied with the shape, size, or orientation of their breasts. Some use bras to orient their breasts into what they feel is a more attractive position; some also use padding to increase the size or change the shape of their breasts. Some go further, using surgery to change their breasts (see COSMETIC SURGERY; BREAST IMPLANTS).

The breasts are subject to a variety of disorders, mostly found in adult women. Many of these are quite common and cause no severely adverse effects, though some may be uncomfortable and require treatment. They are often grouped under the general heading *benign breast disease,* or the development of noncancerous lumps in the breasts, including

▶ *cysts,* fluid-filled pockets around the areola, often resulting from the blockage of one of the ducts from the breast's milk-producing glands. These may collapse when pierced with a needle; otherwise they may be removed surgically, in a *cystectomy*. These are most common in women thirty-five to fifty years old. If a cyst becomes infected, the result is a *breast abscess,* which is generally treated with antibiotics, hot and cold compresses, and if necessary surgical drainage.

▶ *fibroadenoma,* thickening of milk-producing glands, causing painless, apparently movable lumps within the breast.

▶ *lipomas,* single, soft, painless, movable, slow-growing lumps of fatty tissue sometimes found in older women.

▶ *intraductal papillomas,* small, wartlike growths in the lining of ducts near the nipple, sometimes causing bleeding from the nipple, usually found in women forty-five to fifty years old.

▶ *mammary duct ectasia,* an inflammation of the ducts, involving a thick, sticky, grayish-green discharge from the nipple, a condition that can become painful unless treated.

► *fibrocystic disease,* also called *cystic mastitis, chronic cystic mastitis,* or *cystic disease,* development of nodular lumps, ranging in size from that of orange pips to about an inch. Most women have some fibrocystic development just before menstruation (see above), but in some it becomes chronic. Though benign, the condition calls for careful monitoring, including periodic mammograms, since large, solid fibrocystic masses are associated with increased risk of malignancy.

► *traumatic fat necrosis,* painless, round, firm lumps, often under red or bruised skin, that results from a bruise or blow to the breast, even if the woman does not remember a specific injury; generally found in older women or those with very large breasts.

► *galactorrhea,* production of milk from the breasts of a woman who has *not* just given birth, often due to a hormonal imbalance, which should be investigated promptly (see PROLACTIN).

► *mastitis,* or *postpartum mastitis,* inflammation of the breast common among nursing mothers (see BREASTFEEDING).

The National Cancer Institute cautions women who find a change in their breasts not to use such descriptions to try to diagnose it themselves. There is no substitute for a doctor's evaluation.

Of major concern, of course, is BREAST CANCER (see separate entry). From puberty, women should for their own self-protection become very familiar with the look and feel of their own breasts and check them routinely for any changes, seeking medical advice immediately if any changes take place (see BREAST SELF-EXAMINATION on page 104). Many women are confused about self-examination, because their breasts normally feel "lumpy." But that is precisely why regular self-exams are important—so you will recognize any change, especially a new, persistent lump.

Periodic mammograms are also recommended for adult women (see MAMMOGRAMS). Several other screening methods are sometimes used, including ULTRASOUND, using high-frequency sound; *diaphanography,* or *transillumination,* shining a light through the breast; and *thermography,* using heat patterns to produce an image of the breasts' internal tissues. But at present none of these has the accuracy of mammography. In addition, the American Cancer Society advises women to have a doctor physically examine their breasts at least every three years for women twenty to forty and every year for those over forty.

In the end, there is only one sure way to learn whether a breast lump or suspicious area is cancerous: have a doctor take a biopsy, or sample of tissue, and analyze it (see BREAST CANCER). Women should take heart from the fact that 80 percent of all breast lumps are *not* cancerous; but they should be sure to take recommended precautions to identify and deal with those that are. Also, about 70 percent of women with benign breast conditions are *not* at any increased risk of cancer. Often benign lumps are surgically removed for safety, however, so they do not obscure possible cancerous lumps in future mammograms. (See BREAST AND BREAST IMPLANTS HELP, INFORMATION, AND ACTION GUIDE on page 122; also BREAST CANCER; BREAST IMPLANTS; MAMMOGRAM.)

BREAST SELF-EXAMINATION

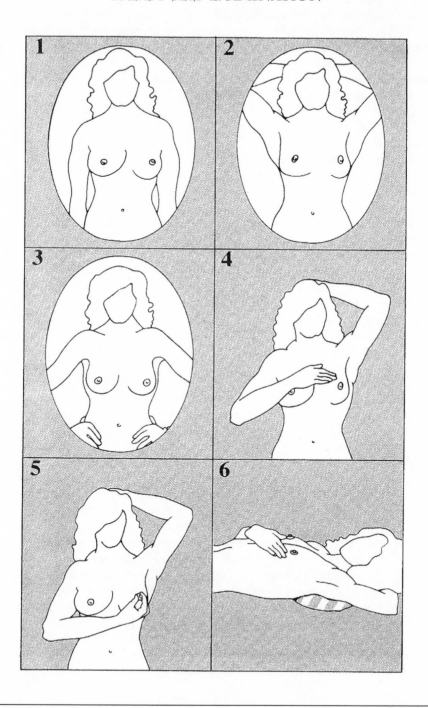

Breast self-examination should be done once a month so you become familiar with the usual appearance and feel of your breasts. Familiarity makes it easier to notice any changes in the breast from one month to another. Early discovery of a change from what is "normal" is the main idea behind BSE. If you menstruate, the best time to do BSE is two or three days after your period ends, when your breasts are least likely to be tender or swollen. If you no longer menstruate, pick a day, such as the first day of the month, to remind yourself it is time to do BSE.

1. Stand before a mirror. Inspect both breasts for anything unusual, such as any discharge from the nipples, puckering, dimpling, or scaling of the skin.

The next two steps are designed to emphasize any change in the shape or contour of your breast. As you do them you should be able to feel your chest muscles tighten.

2. Watching closely in the mirror, clasp hands behind your head and press hands forward.

3. Next, press hands firmly on hips and bow slightly toward your mirror as you pull your shoulders and elbows forward.

Some women do the next part of the exam in the shower. Fingers glide over soapy skin, making it easy to concentrate on the texture underneath.

4. Raise your left arm. Use three or four fingers of your right hand to explore your left breast firmly, carefully, and thoroughly. Beginning at the outer edge, press the flat part of your fingers in small circles, moving the circles slowly around the breast. Gradually work toward the nipple. Be sure to cover the entire breast. Pay special attention to the area between the breast and the armpit, including the armpit itself. Feel for any unusual lump or mass under the skin.

5. Gently squeeze the nipple and look for a discharge. Repeat the exam on your right breast.

6. Steps 4 and 5 should be repeated lying down. Lie flat on your back, left arm over your head and a pillow or folded towel under your left shoulder. This position flattens the breast and makes it easier to examine. Use the same circular motion described earlier. Repeat on your right breast.

Source: *Why Women Don't Get Mammograms (And Why They Should)*, by Judith Willis. *FDA Consumer*, May 1987, revised October 1988.

breast cancer, malignant tumors in the BREASTS. Among women, this is the most common kind of CANCER and in the United States the main cause of death among women between the ages of thirty and fifty, killing over 44,000 in 1991. At least one in every nine American women develops breast cancer; that is, of every one hundred women alive today at least eleven will have breast cancer somewhere between birth and age eighty-five. According to the National Cancer Institute, the incidence of breast cancer has been increasing at about 1 percent a year since the early 1970s, for reasons that are unclear, though perhaps partly because increased screening programs have detected more tumors at previously undetectable early stages. Putting it another way, the American Cancer Society (ACS) notes that the incidence of breast cancer rose from 84.8 per 1,000 in 1980 to 109.5 in 1988. At the same time, however, the ACS points out that death rate from breast cancer has held rather steady over the past fifty years, presumably because of early detection and improved treatment.

Breast cancer can strike *any* woman at any time, regardless of age or background. An early 1980s study by the American Cancer Society found that *three-quarters of all breast cancers cannot yet be attributed to any known specific cause.* However, women who are statistically at increased risk are those who have early onset of MENSTRUATION (before age twelve); go into MENOPAUSE after age fifty; have their first child after age thirty or never bear a child; are tall and heavy, rather than short and thin; have a history of benign tumors; have experienced high radiation exposure to the breasts, especially when young, as from multiple X-rays for tuberculosis or SCOLIOSIS (curved SPINE); or have a family history of breast cancer, especially if relatives developed cancer before menopause or the cancer affected both breasts. Women who bottlefeed (rather than breastfeed) their children or are over forty have increased risk, as do women of Caucasian and European Jewish ancestry and women of high socioeconomic status in North America and northern Europe. There are indications that a diet heavy in fats is also linked to increased risk of cancer; in general, breast cancer risk is higher for women in countries and socioeconomic classes that have diets rich in fat and animal protein. Overall, the risk of breast cancer increases with a woman's age.

Scientists are still researching whether or not other factors increase the risk of breast cancer, including BIRTH CONTROL PILLS, ESTROGEN REPLACEMENT THERAPY, Reserpine (a drug for high blood pressure), chemicals in HAIR dyes, and alcohol consumption (see ALCOHOL AND DRUG ABUSE). Genetic factors clearly play some role in the development of breast cancer, though it is still unclear how much and in what ways.

Women with lower risk of breast cancer are those who bear their first child before age eighteen; have their OVARIES removed before age thirty-five and so become menopausal early; or are of Asian descent, though Western-style high-fat diets sharply increase their risk. There are strong suggestions that a diet high in cruciferous vegetables, such as broccoli, cabbage, and bok choy, have a lower risk of estrogen-fueled breast cancers.

Cancers may occur anywhere in the breast but for unknown reasons occur about half of the time in the upper outer quadrant of the breast. (See SITE OF BREAST CANCERS on page 107.) Approximately 90 percent of breast cancers arise from the milk ducts, the tubes that carry milk from the glands to the nipple.

When the cancer is confined to the duct, it is called *in situ* or *intraductal* cancer; when it spreads to surrounding tissue, it is called *invasive ductal cancer.* Approximately 5 percent of breast cancers arise from lobules in the milk-producing glands; these are *lobular carcinomas.* Most ductal or lobular cancers are painless and grow slowly.

Two other types of breast cancer are less common. *Inflammatory breast carcinoma* is painful and progresses rapidly; the breast is warm and red, as with an infection, and the skin may appear pitted, like orange peel. *Paget's disease* involves a malignancy deep in the breast, with cancer cells growing along the milk ducts; a common symptom is a crusted nipple.

SITE OF BREAST CANCERS

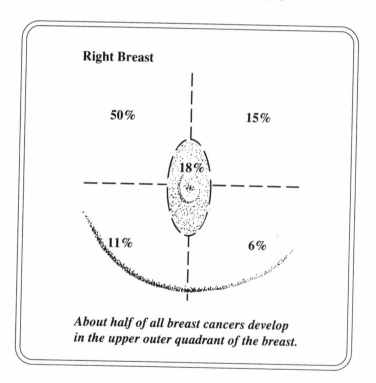

Right Breast

50%   15%

18%

11%   6%

About half of all breast cancers develop in the upper outer quadrant of the breast.

Source: *FDA Consumer,* July–August 1991.

Whether an abnormality is detected by manual examination or MAMMOGRAM, a common first step is to take a biopsy, a tissue sample sent for laboratory analysis. In the past, the biopsy was performed as a surgical procedure, in which part or all of the lump or suspicious area was removed; a woman was asked to sign a consent form that authorized the doctor to remove the breast if, during the taking of the biopsy, the growth was found to be cancerous. Since at least the late 1970s, however—in large part due to agitation by women themselves—a two-step procedure has become more common: a biopsy is taken and analyzed; if the tumor is found to be cancerous, the woman has time to explore her treatment options, get a second opinion, and generally prepare herself for substantial surgery. In some areas this two-step approach is even required by law. And, increasingly, the initial biopsy is being done not with surgery, but by *fine needle aspiration,* using a special hollow needle to withdraw sample cells, a procedure that can be done on an outpatient basis under local ANESTHESIA. Approximately 80 percent of breast lumps biopsied are benign, not cancerous.

Treatment depends on the size, spread (*metastasis*), and nature of the cancer, so any malignancies found are classified as a guide to treatment. The classifications as to size and spread are

▶ *carcinoma in situ:* very early cancer that has not invaded nearby tissues
▶ *Stage I:* a localized tumor no larger than 2 centimeters (cm), or about 1 inch.
▶ *Stage II:*
  • a tumor under 2 cm, but where cancer has spread to the underarm lymph nodes, *or*
  • a tumor 2–5 cm (about 2 in.), which may or may not have spread to the lymph nodes, *or*
  • a tumor larger than 5 cm, but where cancer has not spread to the lymph nodes.
▶ *Stage III:*
  • a tumor larger than 5 cm, which has spread to underarm lymph nodes, *or*
  • a tumor smaller than 5 cm, where underarm lymph nodes have grown into each other or into other tissues, *or*
  • a tumor that has spread to tissues near the breast (such as the chest muscles and ribs) or to lymph nodes near the collarbone, *or*
  • inflammatory breast carcinoma (see above).
▶ *Stage IV:* cancer that has spread to other organs of the body, usually the lungs, liver, bone, or brain.

Carcinoma *in situ* has a cure rate approaching 100 percent with surgery alone. The prognosis is also good with tumors of 1 cm or less; these have less than 10 percent recurrence in ten years. In its *Cancer Facts and Figures 1992,* the American Cancer Society (ACS) reports that the five-year survival rate for people with localized breast cancer "has risen from 78 percent in the 1940s to 92 percent today." Beyond that, the ACS notes that with regional spread the survival rate is 71 percent, but for people "with distant metastases, the survival rate is 18 percent." The risk of recurrence rises with the size and lymph node spread, which is why early detection is so important.

Breast tumors have other characteristics, or "markers," that help doctors assess the aggressiveness of the cancer, as a guide to determining therapy. Among these markers are

▶ *estrogen and progesterone receptors,* indicating that the cancer growth is "fueled" by these hormones and therefore may be receptive to hormone therapy (see below).
▶ *histologic type,* cell types characteristic of different rates of growth and patterns of spread.
▶ *DNA disruption,* the amount of DNA disarray in the cell, with the greater

disarray and rate of cell division indicating more aggressiveness and poorer prognosis for cancer recurrence.

▶ **HER-2 oncogene,** a gene present in some patients, indicating greater likelihood of spread and therefore the importance of aggressive treatment.

▶ **Cathepsin D,** a substance secreted by cancer cells that may aid spread within the body and so indicates a poorer prognosis.

In decades past, any breast cancer meant an immediate *Halsted radical mastectomy,* meaning removal of not only the entire breast, but also the underlying chest muscles, the underarm (*axillary*) lymph nodes, and other fat and muscle, the aim being to remove all possible avenues by which cancer might spread. But with better understanding of how breast cancer develops, by the 1970s—earlier in Europe than in the United States—surgeons began to use a wider variety of alternatives, designed to preserve the breast as much as possible.

The most limited breast cancer surgery is the *lumpectomy,* also called a *segmental mastectomy* or *tylectomy,* in which only the tumor and its closely surrounding tissue is removed. In a *partial* or *segmental mastectomy,* also called a *segmentectomy,* the tumor is removed with a wedge of surrounding tissue, including some skin and the lining of the chest muscle underlying the tumor. In a *total mastectomy,* or *modified radical mastectomy,* the breast and possibly the lining over the chest muscles are removed.

In all of these procedures, some or all of the underarm lymph nodes are often removed for examination, to check for possible spread of cancer. In a 1990 review, the National Institutes of Health (NIH) found that for women with early-stage breast cancer, lumpectomy is preferable because it provides "survival equivalent to total mastectomy and also preserves the breast." However, the panel also found that only one out of every five women eligible for the procedure chose a lumpectomy; some suggest that surgeons have been slow to accept or offer the newer procedures, though for many women it is simply that the fear of recurrence is greater than the cosmetic benefits of retaining the breast.

Women facing breast cancer surgery will want to weigh the alternatives carefully, in consultation with their doctors, friends, and family, to reach the decision that is best for them. For women with cancers in several locations within the breast, or a large tumor relative to breast size, lumpectomy and partial mastectomy are not realistic alternatives. Some women who are at extremely high risk of breast cancer, especially those with a family history of breast cancer, have chosen to have their breasts removed as a preventive, in what is called *prophylactic mastectomy.* This is, however, a controversial approach, to be considered very carefully; many doctors will instead recommend frequent examinations to monitor for any breast changes.

Lumpectomy or mastectomy are often supplemented by *adjuvant* (additional) *therapy*—radiation treatments, chemotherapy, and/or hormone therapy to kill any remaining cancer cells. Controversy exists as to whether such therapy should be given to women who are *node-negative*—that is, who have no sign of cancer in their lymph nodes. Approximately seven out of ten such women will have no recurrence; current studies indicate that adjuvant therapy will prevent recurrence in one of the remaining three. Unfortunately, doctors are so far unable to tell which women will fit in which category, so therapy has often been given to all, though the side effects can be substantial, especially of radiation and chemotherapy, and studies of long-term effects are still to be conducted.

In addition to various drugs used in chemotherapy, doctors may also use hormone therapy, such as *tamoxifen* (*Nolvadex*), which blocks estrogen-fueled cancer cells in the breasts from getting the estrogen they need to grow. In some cases a woman's OVARIES may be removed or deactivated for the same purpose, in a procedure called *ovarian ablation* (see MYOMECTOMY). Tamoxifen is also being studied as a possible preventive for at least some types of breast cancer. Some small early studies suggest that it may also have other beneficial effects on the body, such as lowering cholesterol level and lessening risk of heart disease (see HEART AND CIRCULATORY SYSTEM and OSTEOPOROSIS); however, adverse effects such as DEPRESSION, BLOOD clots, potentially blinding EYE disorders, and increased risk of cancer of the UTERUS (see UTERINE CANCER) or liver have also been suggested by tamoxifen use. A major study of Tamoxifen, involving 16,000 women, was announced in 1993. Some organizations hail the study as a breakthrough in women's health; others, such as the NATIONAL WOMEN'S HEALTH NETWORK, have protested the study and tamoxifen use in general, as "trading one kind of cancer for another." Another drug, the yew-derived taxol, has shown some early promise in halting tumor growth, or even causing regression. Advanced cancers may also be treated with other approaches, such as *bone marrow transplant* (see CANCER).

After major breast cancer surgery, many women have difficulty adjusting to the loss of one or both breasts, given the central role they play in women's appearance and sexuality. Some women choose to live openly with the loss, rejecting any "camouflage" on principle. Others choose to wear breast forms (*prostheses*) under their clothes, for cosmetic reasons. Still other women choose to have some form of breast reconstruction. Sometimes this is done at the same time as the mastectomy, with the cancer surgeon and plastic surgeon working together. But many surgeons recommend waiting for three to six months, to give the incision time to heal and to allow time for adjuvant therapy.

Traditionally, breast reconstruction has involved implants. In the simplest and most traditional form of reconstruction, a gel- or liquid-filled sac is sewn into the chest of patients who have enough remaining chest muscle and skin in the area to cover the implant. For women who have had more radical surgery, and therefore lack chest muscle and skin, some new alternatives have been developed. In *latissimus dorsi* reconstruction, surgeons move muscles of that name from the back to the chest, along with skin and other tissue, to form an "envelope" for the implant. This, of course, leaves scars on the back as well as the chest. In *rectus abdominus* reconstruction, a similar approach uses muscle, skin, and tissue from the abdomen, which are used to shape a breast. If sufficient abdominal tissue is available, no implant is needed. In the process, the woman gets an *abdominoplasty,* popularly called a *tummy tuck* (see COSMETIC SURGERY), with abdominal as well as chest scars. Skin and tissue may also be taken from elsewhere in the body, in what is generally termed *flap surgery.* These operations generally rebuild the shape of the breast but do not always include a nipple and its encircling areola. Plastic surgeons have developed techniques that allow them to reconstruct these structures as well; however, sensation is not restored, and it requires an additional or extended operation. Though breast reconstruction is still widely performed on women who have mastectomies, in recent years major controversy has erupted about the safety of implants used in breast reconstruction (see BREAST IMPLANTS), leaving open the question of future approaches.

Some studies suggest that the long-term prognosis for breast cancer surgery varies according to when during the woman's menstrual cycle the surgery is performed, though research data are so far conflicting. As a result, some people suggest that women have breast cancer surgery during the OVULATION portion of the menstrual cycle (days 7–20), rather than the portion closer to actual MENSTRUA-TION (days 0–6 and 21–36), counting from the first day of the previous period. Women will want to discuss this with their doctors.

Some people have suggested that women who had silicone-gel breast implants have an increased risk of breast cancer, but at least one major Canadian study released in 1992 indicated no such finding, though the study did not explore prognosis for other types of cancer or long-term survival of women who had breast cancer after receiving implants.

BREAST CANCER

Help, Information, and Action Guide

Organizations

▶ **National Cancer Institute (NCI)** (Cancer Information Service 800-4-CANCER [422-6237]). Publishes *Breast Exams: What You Should Know* and *Questions and Answers About Breast Lumps, Questions and Answers About Choosing a Mammography Facility, Breast Biopsy, What You Should Know About Breast Cancer: Understanding Treatment Options, Mastectomy: A Treatment for Breast Cancer, Radiation Therapy: A Treatment for Early Stage Breast Cancer, After Breast Cancer: A Guide to Follow-up Care,* and *Breast Reconstruction: A Matter of Choice.* (See CANCER.)

▶ NATIONAL WOMEN'S HEALTH NETWORK **(NWHN)** (202-347-1140). Operates the **Women's Health Information Service.** Publishes the information packets *Breast Cancer* and *Mammography.*

▶ **National Alliance of Breast Cancer Organizations (NABCO)** (1180 Avenue of the Americas, 2nd Floor, New York, NY 10036; 212-719-0154; Amy Schiffman Langer, executive director), a central resource on all aspects of breast cancer, including detection, treatment, and resources, through its **Breast Cancer Information Network**. NABCO seeks to influence public and private policies relating to breast cancer, including

---

health insurance, discrimination, and informed consent. It publishes the quarterly *NABCO News* and a *Resource List.*

▶ **Y-Me** (18220 Harwood Avenue, Homewood, IL 60430; 800-221-2141, 9–5 Central Time weekdays; 708-799-8228, 24 hours; Sharon Green, executive director), a breast cancer support organization founded in 1978. It provides information, hot-line counseling (see numbers above or other regional hot lines) with callers matched to counselors with similar experiences where desired, presurgical counseling and referral services, educational programs, and self-help group meetings for breast cancer patients, their families, and friends. Y-Me also maintains a speakers bureau; gives workshops; offers in-service programs for health professionals on the psychosocial needs of breast cancer patients; and has a selection of donated prostheses and wigs for women with limited financial resources. Y-Me publishes the newsletter *Y-Me Hotline,* as well as *Guidelines for Breast Cancer Support Programs* and a video, to aid development of new groups.

▶ **ENCORE** (ENCORE Supervisor, National Board, YWCA, 726 Broadway, New York, NY 10003; 212-614-2827; see telephone directory White Pages for local programs), a program for women who have had breast cancer surgery, including exercise to music, water exercise, and group discussions, sponsored by the YWCA.

▶ COMMISSION FOR WOMEN'S EQUALITY (**CWE**) (212-879-4500).

Other resources

◪ FOR WOMEN AT RISK

Beating the Odds Against Breast and Ovarian Cancer: Reducing Your Hereditary Risk. Mary M. Kemeny and Paula Dranov. Addison-Wesley, 1992.
Challenging the Breast Cancer Legacy: A Program of Emotional Support and Medical Care for Women at Risk. Renee Royak-Schaler and Beryl L. Benderly. HaperCollins, 1992.
Make Sure You Do Not Have Breast Cancer. Philip Strax. St. Martin's, 1991.
Relative Risk: Living with a Family History of Breast Cancer. Nancy C. Baker. Viking Penguin, 1991.

◪ FOR WOMEN WHO HAVE OR HAVE HAD BREAST CANCER

The Race Is Run One Step at a Time: Every Woman's Guide to Taking Charge of Breast Cancer. Nancy Brinker and Catherine M. Harris. Simon & Schuster, 1991.
Affirmations, Meditations, and Encouragements for Women Living with Breast Cancer. Linda Dackman. Lowell House, 1991.

Up Front: Sex and the Post-Mastectomy Woman. Linda Dackman. Viking, 1990.

Chemo and Lunch. Susan Winn. Fithian Press, 1990.

◪ FOR FRIENDS AND FAMILY

Helping the Woman You Love Recover from Breast Cancer. Andy Murcia. St. Martin's, 1991.

Man to Man: When the Woman You Love Has Breast Cancer. Andy Murcia. St. Martin's, 1990.

◪ PERSONAL EXPERIENCES

My Breast. Joyce Wadler. Addison-Wesley, 1992.

Breast Cancer in the Life Course: Women's Experiences. Julianne Oktay and Carolyn Walter, eds. Springer, 1991.

A Slice of Life: A Personal Story of Healing Through Cancer. Lee Sturgeon-Day. Lifeways, 1991.

Cancer in Two Voices. Sandra Butler and Barbara Rosenblum. Spinsters Books, 1991.

Spinning Straw into Gold: Your Emotional Recovery from Breast Cancer. Ronnie Kaye. Simon & Schuster, 1991.

Moms Don't Get Sick. Pat Brack. Melius, 1990. A mother and ten-year-old son alternate views of her fight against breast cancer.

No Less a Woman: Ten Women Shatter the Myths About Breast Cancer. Deborah H. Kahane. Prentice-Hall, 1990.

Women Talk About Breast Surgery: From Diagnosis to Recovery. Amy Gross, Amy and Dee Ito. HarperCollins, 1990.

◪ BACKGROUND WORKS

Breast Cancer—Literature for Nonmedical People: A Bibliography. Rama K. Rao. Ramdil, 1992.

Understanding Breast Cancer Risk. Patricia T. Kelly. Temple University Press, 1991.

(See also CANCER; CANCER HELP, INFORMATION, AND ACTION GUIDE on page 133.)

breast enlargement, augmentation mammoplasty (see COSMETIC SURGERY).

breastfeeding, giving a baby milk from the mother's BREASTS as the main source of NUTRITION.

During PREGNANCY, the mammary glands in a woman's breasts develop, in response to various HORMONES, especially ESTROGEN and PROGESTERONE; this is responsible for the enlargement of the breasts. By late in the pregnancy, the breasts begin to produce *colostrum,* a yellowish fluid that contains white BLOOD cells, protein, minerals, fats, sugars, and antibodies. To absorb this fluid (and later milk) and prevent staining of clothes, some women place a small, clean pad in their bras. The breasts should be kept washed and clean, to avoid infection. Colostrum continues to be produced until a few days after CHILDBIRTH.

At that point, production of actual milk begins, in a process known as *lactation.* Two key hormones are involved in lactation: PROLACTIN, which signals the mammary glands to produce milk, and OXYTOCIN, which causes milk to be pushed through the breast glands to be available for the nursing infant, in what is called the *let-down reflex.* Production of both hormones is stimulated by the infant's sucking on the breast, so the breasts will continue to produce milk as long as breastfeeding continues. If a woman decides not to breastfeed her child, lactation will stop; she may experience some discomfort from the fullness of the breasts, normally treated with ice bags and painkillers for a few days, until the *engorgement* subsides. On rare occasions, lactation can be reestablished after it has stopped, as when the mother was ill or had a breast infection (*mastitis*); it has even sometimes been induced in a woman who has not given birth, recently or ever, as when a woman wishes to nurse an adopted infant.

Breastfeeding has many advantages, as the Public Health Service outlined in its booklet *Infant Care:*

- Mother's milk normally has just the right amount of the right nutrients to help the baby grow, with no worry about whether it is "too rich" or "too thin."
- It is easy for the baby's immature system to digest.
- Mother's milk contains antibodies that give the baby a temporary immunization protecting against viruses and bacteria. [See IMMUNE SYSTEM.]
- Breastfeeding lessens the likelihood that a child will later develop ALLERGIES.
- Mother's milk is clean, uncontaminated, and served at the right temperature.
- Mother's milk is ready when the baby is hungry, needing no equipment, preparation, or cleanup.
- Breastfeeding is inexpensive and costs less than bottlefeeding with formula.
- Mother's milk is the only food a baby needs for the first four to six months.
- Breastfeeding uses some of the extra fat stored for this purpose in the body during PREGNANCY and so helps mothers to lose weight.
- Breastfeeding also helps the UTERUS resume its normal size more quickly.
- Nursing provides a natural form of BIRTH CONTROL, since the reproductive cycle [see MENSTRUATION] does not normally begin again until after she ceases to breast-feed.
- Breastfeeding helps with BONDING, the building of the special emotional and physical relationship between mother and child.

Breastfeeding is the natural and traditional form of feeding and continues to be so around the world.

In developed countries, many infants are fed with modified cow's milk (whole milk is too rich for a baby to digest) or on a milklike fluid called *formula*. For some decades in midcentury, bottlefeeding was even recommended as superior to breastfeeding, before scientists understood that mother's milk provides temporary immunity to disease. Today, many public health experts recommend breastfeeding, where possible. However, many women—especially working women—find breastfeeding too inconvenient, unattractive, or difficult to arrange and so choose bottlefeeding. Where properly prepared, formula offers all the necessary nutrition, though not the temporary immunity to disease. Proper sterilization of containers and storage of the formula are vital, however, to avoid contamination, which can pass digestive diseases—sometimes very serious—on to the infant. One advantage of bottlefeeding is that MOTHER and FATHER can both share the feeding and may establish equally close bonding with the baby.

Working women, who spend large portions of the day apart from their baby, can still breastfeed, if they wish, by *expressing* (squeezing) milk from the breast by hand or using a breast pump, so the baby can be given the milk in a bottle while they are away. The Public Health Service notes:

> [Milk] can safely be left at room temperature for forty minutes, in the refrigerator for forty-eight hours, or in your freezer for up to three months. Store it in a sterile glass or a hard plastic container (such as a bottle) or a disposable bottle. If the milk is cooled or frozen, bring it to room temperature by placing it in warm water. Don't heat breast milk in a microwave or over boiling water.

Such a choice often takes considerable planning and determination, however. Where they are lucky, working women have special CHILD CARE arrangements at or near their employment, allowing them to breastfeed the baby periodically through the workday.

Not all women who wish to breastfeed are able to do so; it is a shared learning process between mother and baby and does not always work. Sometimes the milk supply is inadequate, or the infant has a physical problem that prevents nursing. If a mother develops mastitis, she will need to bottlefeed her baby temporarily; if she wishes to resume breastfeeding after the infection is treated, she needs to continue to express milk (to be discarded) during this period. Some women seek advice from friends and family, from *lactation specialists*, or from organizations such as La Leche League (see below). Breastfeeding is normally supplemented by solid foods by about age six months, but some mothers continue breastfeeding for a year or longer.

For more help, information, and action

▶ **La Leche League International (LLLI)** (9616 Minneapolis, P.O. Box 1209, Franklin Park, IL 60131; 708-455-7730 or 800-525-3243; Mary Lawrence, executive director), an organization dedicated to breastfeeding babies, founded in 1956. Actually an international network of women's groups, it trains group leaders; maintains libraries and resource centers; provides information and referrals; and publishes many materials, including general brochures such as

When You Breastfeed Your Baby, Does Breastfeeding Take Too Much Time?, The Breastfeeding Father, Breastfeeding after a Cesarean Birth, Nutrition and Breastfeeding, Positioning Your Baby at the Breast, Increasing Your Milk, Preparing Your Nipples, Establishing Your Milk Supply, Manual Expression of Breast-Milk—Marmet Technique, Medications for the Nursing Mother, and *Legal Rights of Breastfeeding Mothers, USA Scene;* materials for families in special situations, such as a *Breastfeeding Rights Packet* for mothers whose continued breastfeeding is threatened by legal situations, such as DIVORCE or a CUSTODY dispute; and numerous books such as *A Practical Guide to Breastfeeding, The Womanly Art of Breastfeeding, Nighttime Parenting, Of Cradles and Careers: A Guide to Reshaping Your Job to Include a Baby in Your Life, Drugs in Pregnancy and Lactation, Breastfeeding and Drugs in Human Milk, Mothering Your Nursing Toddler, Mothering Multiples: Breastfeeding and Caring for Twins,* and *A Special Find of Parenting: Meeting the Needs of Handicapped Children;* and various products to aid breastfeeding, such as breast pumps and breast shields.

▶ NATIONAL CENTER FOR EDUCATION IN MATERNAL AND CHILD HEALTH (NCEMCH)(703-524-7802), and NATIONAL MATERNAL AND CHILD HEALTH CLEARINGHOUSE (NMCHC) (703-821-8955). Publish *Art and Science of Breastfeeding* (Manual and Slide Set) and *Breastfeeding Catalog of Products.*

▶ NATIONAL WOMEN'S HEALTH NETWORK (NWHN) (202-347-1140). Operates the **Women's Health Information Service**. Publishes the information packet *Breastfeeding.*

▶ **Human Lactation Center (HLC)** (666 Sturges Highway, Westport, CT 06880; 203-259-5995; Dana Raphael, director), an organization encouraging breastfeeding of babies. It conducts research on lactation and maternal and infant NUTRITION; maintains a library; and publishes various materials.

Other resources

Doctor Discusses Breast Feeding. Marie P. Warner and Miriam Gilbert. Budlong, 1992.
Keys to Breast Feeding. William Sears. Barron's, 1991.
A Practical Guide to Breastfeeding. Janie Riordan. Jones & Bartlett, 1991.
Breastfeeding Today: A Mother's Companion, 2nd ed. Candace Woessner and others. Avery, 1991.
The Nursing Mother's Companion, rev. ed. Kathleen Huggins. Harvard Common Press, 1991.
Nursing Your Baby, rev. ed. Karen Pryor; Jane Chelius, ed. Harper & Row, 1990.
Breastfeeding Your Baby. Sheila Kitzinger. Knopf, 1989.
Babies, Breastfeeding and Bonding, rev. ed. Ina May Gaskin. Bergin & Garvey, 1989.
Successful Breastfeeding, rev. ed. Nancy Dana and Anne Price. Meadowbrook Press, 1989.

▨ BACKGROUND WORKS

The Nature of Birth and Breastfeeding. Michel Odent. Bergin & Garvey/Greenwood, 1992.

Nutrition During Lactation. Institute of Medicine, Committee on Nutritional Status During Pregnancy and Lactation Staff. National Academy Press, 1991.

The Impact of Diet and Physical Activity on Pregnancy and Lactation: Women's Work in the Developing World. Institute of Medicine Staff. National Academy Press, 1991.

Women's Experience of Breast Feeding. Heather Maclean. University of Toronto Press, 1990.

Will It Hurt the Baby? The Safe Use of Medications During Pregnancy and Breast-feeding. Richard S. Abrams. Addison-Wesley, 1990.

(See also PREGNANCY AND CHILDBIRTH HELP, INFORMATION, AND ACTION GUIDE on page 580; WOMEN'S HEALTH HELP, INFORMATION, AND ACTION GUIDE on page 334.)

breast implants, liquid- or gel-filled sacs inserted into a woman's natural BREASTS for enlargement (see COSMETIC SURGERY) or into the reconstructed breasts of women who have had a partial or total mastectomy (see BREAST CANCER). Breast implants have been performed since approximately 1962, most for enlargement, the rest usually for reconstruction after cancer surgery. In the United States alone, somewhere between one and two million women have had breast implants, some 80 percent for enlargement. Figures are so imprecise because, astonishingly, no one—not government, medicine, manufacturing, or consumer groups—had systematically registered who was having implants or monitored their experiences with them.

Early breast implants were made of rubbery silicone, but by 1972 implants containing silicone in a fluid-gel form were developed. These became the most widely used type of breast implants—and the most controversial. Though many women had silicone gel-filled implants without apparent problems, and expressed satisfaction with the results, some implant recipients and some researchers began reporting problems shortly after the silicone-gel implants were introduced. Among the types of problems or adverse effects reported are

- *capsular contracture,* or the development and then shrinking of scar tissue around the implant, causing painful hardening of the breasts.
- leaks and ruptures in the implants, releasing the gel into the body, with possibly harmful consequences, such as disruption of the IMMUNE SYSTEM, leading to *autoimmune disorders,* in which the body mistakenly attacks its own tissue; among these are connective-tissue disorders such as scleroderma.
- concerns that implants might obscure some parts of the breast, making MAMMOGRAMS ineffective in showing possible cancerous tissue.
- concerns about CANCER risk, especially from implants that were coated with polyurethane foam. (These were taken off the market in April 1991; see IF YOU HAVE IMPLANTS ... on page 119.)

These questions and concerns were largely ignored by implant manufacturers and by most plastic surgeons specializing in implants, as was later revealed to the general public. Controversy grew as to whether or not silicone gel-filled breast implants should remain on the market, a question fueled by U.S. court cases in which some women won judgments against implant manufacturers. What was manifestly clear was the absence of and vital need for solid research data regarding the safety and long-term effects of such implants.

In the United States, the FOOD AND DRUG ADMINISTRATION (FDA)—which established jurisdiction over the implants as "medical devices" only in 1988—called for a review of safety data and eventually for a moratorium on use of the silicone gel implants until properly constructed safety studies were carried out. Then, after a preliminary review of current data, the FDA allowed use of silicone-gel implants to proceed, but only under heavy restrictions. Except for women who were in "urgent need," such as those who were in the midst of a breast reconstruction process or needed an implant replacement for medical reasons, the FDA ruled that silicone-gel implants would only be available to women enrolled in one of the safety studies, with informed consent and enrollment in a patient registry. Some other countries followed suit, halting or heavily restricting use of gel-filled breast implants. Some manufacturers also announced that they were ceasing production of the implants. Women who have had implants will want to read carefully the FDA's advice in IF YOU HAVE IMPLANTS . . . , page 119.

In previous decades, starting in the 1950s in Japan, liquid silicone had been directly injected into the body, notably into breasts for enlargement. This practice was later stopped as women experienced a wide variety of problems from bits of silicone drifting around their bodies, including reports of cases of silicone-inflamed lung tissue causing suffocation and death (see RESPIRATORY SYSTEM). Even after silicone breast injections were largely abandoned, some doctors continued to inject silicone directly into facial and neck SKIN as a wrinkle remover; in the United States, this was finally halted by the FDA in the wake of the breast implant controversy, though such injections are still given illegally by some doctors.

Still available to women who want them are implants filled with saline solution (salt water); less attractive cosmetically than the silicone-gel type, these have accounted for only 10 percent of the market. Leak or rupture of a saline implant releases only harmless salt water into the tissues, though if the deflation is rapid, additional surgery may be required (as is also true with the silicone-gel implants). Also, the saline implants use a silicone rubber envelope, with unknown effects in the body. In 1991 federal officials seized a new kind of inflatable implant, brand name Misti Gold, because it failed to get FDA approval to market the device and made false and misleading claims for the product. (See BREAST AND BREAST IMPLANTS HELP, INFORMATION, AND ACTION GUIDE on page 122; also COSMETIC SURGERY; BREAST; BREAST CANCER.)

IF YOU HAVE IMPLANTS . . .

Most women with silicone gel-filled breast implants do not experience serious problems. *If you are not having problems, there is no need to have your implants removed.* But you should have regular checkups by a physician or plastic surgeon. If you have any breast discomfort, changes in size or shape of your breast, or any symptoms you think may be related to your implants, see your doctor.

Regarding specific concerns, the agency [FOOD AND DRUG ADMINISTRATION] advises the following:

- **You should be checked periodically by your physician for as long as you have implants.**

  Implants can last from a very short time to many years, depending on the patient and the implant. In any case, they should not be expected to last a lifetime.

- **A ruptured implant should be removed.**

  The percentage of implants that rupture is not certain. An FDA advisory panel concluded that the rupture rate may be higher than previously thought. Manufacturers' reports suggest a range between 0.2 and 1.1 percent; the medical literature contains figures ranging between 0 and 25 percent; and individual doctors have said the implants fail in as many as 32 percent of their patients.

  The panel also noted that rupture may go undetected in some patients. In some undetected ruptures the gel may be contained within the fibrous tissue that forms around the implant. Also, the implants "bleed," or leak, silicone, but the significance of the leakage is uncertain.

  Routine mammograms are not recommended to detect such "silent" ruptures. Other methods of detection, such as ultrasound, computerized axial tomography (CAT) scans, and magnetic resonance imaging (MRI), are being studied but are not now recommended on a routine basis.

  The chance for rupture may increase the longer the implant is in the body. Injury to the breast may also increase the chance of rupture, as may capsular contracture (shrinking of scar tissue around the implant that makes the breast feel hard). Closed capsulotomy—a nonsurgical technique sometimes used to reduce the contracture—may also increase the likelihood of rupture.

- **The value of tests to detect silicone in blood and urine is uncertain.**

  Since small amounts of silicone "bleed" even from intact implants, these tests cannot tell whether your implant has ruptured. Also, silicone is found in many products, including commonly used medicines and cosmetics, so the source of silicone detected may not be clear.

- **If you have symptoms of connective tissue or immune-related disorders, see your doctor.**
  It is not known whether implants can cause or contribute to the development of connective tissue and immune-related disorders. But you should be aware of symptoms that can occur with these disorders. They include
  - joint pain and swelling
  - skin tightness, redness, or swelling
  - swollen glands or lymph nodes
  - unusual and unexplained fatigue
  - swollen hands and feet
  - unusual hair loss

  People who have immune-related disorders generally have a combination of these and other symptoms. These symptoms can also occur with a variety of other health problems, however, and a doctor's evaluation can rule out other possible causes.

- **Although the possibility cannot be ruled out, there is currently no evidence that silicone gel-filled implants increase the risk of cancer in humans.**
  Studies now under way should shed more light on this matter in the next few years.

  About 10 percent of women have silicone gel-filled implants coated with polyurethane foam, intended to reduce the risk of capsular contracture. These implants have not been used since April 1991, because studies showed the polyurethane coating could break down to release very small amounts of TDA [2,4-toluenediamine], a substance that can cause cancer in animals. It is not known whether women with this type of implant have an increased risk of cancer. However, based on current evidence, FDA does not recommend removing polyurethane-coated implants because of cancer concerns. The agency is requiring the manufacturer of these implants to conduct studies analyzing blood, urine, and breast milk for TDA.

- **It is not known whether the silicone that "bleeds" from an implant gets into breast milk and, if so, whether it could affect a nursing child.**
  Research is being planned to resolve these concerns.

- **As is recommended for all women, you should have regular breast examinations by a trained health professional, and you should do monthly self-exams.... [See BREAST SELF-EXAMINATION on page 104.]**
  Pay particular attention to changes in the firmness, size, or shape of the breasts. Also, note pain, tenderness, or color changes in the breast area, or any discharge or unusual sensation around the nipple. Report them, or any other concerns about your breasts, to your doctor.

- **You should have screening mammography at the same intervals recommended for all women in your age group.** [See MAMMOGRAMS.] Good-quality mammograms are essential to detect cancer in any women—with or without breast implants. (If you have had breast cancer surgery, ask your doctor whether mammograms are still necessary.) Mammography is *not* recommended to detect implant rupture. The radiation exposure to younger women is not justified for this purpose.

Mammographic examination of women with breast implants requires special expertise, however, because implants can often obscure breast tissue, impairing the ability to detect cancer. By taking extra views of the breast and pushing the implant backward and breast tissue forward, visibility is improved. Be sure the mammography facility you go to has personnel trained and experienced in the special techniques needed for women with implants.

Tell the radiologist and the technician that you have implants before they take the mammograms so they know to use the special techniques and can take extra care when compressing the breasts to avoid rupturing the implant.

Facilities accredited by the American College of Radiology (ACR) are likely to have appropriately trained staff. For names and locations of ACR-accredited facilities, call the Cancer Information Service (toll-free 1-800-4-CANCER) or your local American Cancer Society chapter. Then doublecheck with the facility to make sure it can perform the needed techniques.

Reporting Implant Problems

To report a problem with an implant, write to the Problem Reporting Program, 12601 Twinbrook Parkway, Rockville, MD 20852. A copy of your report will be forwarded to the manufacturer and to FDA [the Food and Drug Administration]. If you have documentation you feel would be helpful, please enclose it with your report. Include the following information, if known:

- manufacturer's name
- product brand name
- style, size, and lot number
- dates of all implant surgeries
- patient's age at time of first implant
- whether the procedure was done for augmentation [enlargement] or reconstruction
- date of problem
- nature of problem

- time between implant and onset of symptoms
- name and address of surgeon and facility where surgery was performed
- your name, address, and telephone numbers (optional)

For information about what kind of implant you have, ask your surgeon or contact the facility where you had the surgery.

Source: *FDA Consumer,* June 1992

BREAST AND BREAST IMPLANTS

Help, Information, and Action Guide

Organizations

▶ NATIONAL WOMEN'S HEALTH NETWORK (**NWHN**) (202-347-1140). Operates the **Women's Health Information Service.** Publishes the information packets *Fibrocystic Breast Conditions* and *Breast Implants,* with separate packets for reconstruction or augmentation.

▶ NATIONAL INSTITUTE OF CHILD HEALTH AND HUMAN DEVELOPMENT (**NICHD**) (301-496-5133).

◪ ON BREAST IMPLANTS

▶ FOOD AND DRUG ADMINISTRATION (**FDA**) (301-472-4750). Operates **Breast Implant Information** (Office of Consumer Affairs, HFE-88, 5600 Fishers Lane, Rockville, MD 20857; 301-443-3170), a key federal source of information about breast implants.

▶ **Problem Reporting Program** (12601 Twinbrook Parkway, Rockville, MD 20852), an organization for receiving reports with implants. (See IF YOU HAVE IMPLANTS . . . on page 119.)

▶ **Breast Implant Registry, Medic Alert Foundation International** (2323 Colorado Avenue, Turlock, CA 95381–9986; 800-892-9211; Mon.–Fri. 6:30 A.M.–4:30 P.M., Pacific Time), a nonprofit confidential registry for women with breast implants, independent of manufacturers and funded by registration fees. It provides women with information about implants as it becomes available (though not medical advice). Registrants have the option of participating in future medical research studies.

▶ **Command Trust Network, Inc.** (P.O. Box 17082, Covington, KY 41017), an advocacy organization offering support and information about breast implants and breast implant surgery. (Send self-addressed, stamped envelope and $1 to above address.)

Other resources

Healthy Breasts: Every Woman's Birthright! Iris A. Michael. Clarke, 1991.

Breast Care Options for the 1990s, rev. ed. Paul Kuehn. Newmark, 1991.

Breast Self-Examination and You. P. G. Nama. Budlong, 1991.

How to Examine Your Breasts: A Guide to Breast Health Care. Judith Tetzleff and Prabharathie G. Nama. Budlong, 1991.

Your Breasts: A Complete Guide. Jerome Levy with Diana Odell Potter. Noonday Press/Farrar, Straus & Giroux, 1990.

Dr. Susan Love's Breast Book. Susan M. Love with Karen Lindsey. Addison-Wesley, 1990.

bridegift, in some traditional societies, payment made by a groom or his family or kinship group to the bride or her family or kinship group, including property, goods, services or money. The term is sometimes used just for gifts to the bride herself, while those to the family or kinship group are called *bridewealth*. The previously common term, *brideprice*, is rarely used today because it suggests the buying of a wife; some feminists feel that is precisely what it *is*, regarding this as evidence for the notion of MARRIAGE as legalized PROSTITUTION. By contrast, in *brideservice*, the groom provides his in-laws with services and gifts from his own labor. (See MARRIAGE.)

Briffault, Robert: See *THE MOTHERS*.

browlift: See COSMETIC SURGERY.

Brown, Rita Mae (1944–), a novelist and essayist, a radical LESBIAN feminist of the late 1960s who emerged as a popular lesbian novelist with her largely autobiographical novel *Rubyfruit Jungle* (1973), which expressed the view that a strong, successful feminist movement can be developed only by radical lesbians. She has also published several other novels, all on radical lesbian themes, including *Six of One* (1978), *Southern Discomfort* (1982), *Sudden Death* (1983), *High Hearts* (1986), and *Bingo* (1988). Her essays are collected in *A Plain Brown Wrapper* (1976).

Brownmiller, Susan (1935–), an American feminist, best known for her widely read study *Against Our Will: Men, Women and Rape* (1975). The book takes the position that all men use RAPE, the threat of rape, and other aspects of sexual force and violence as a means of subjugating all women. Brownmiller rejects passive acceptance of rape, counseling active resistance; regards rape as so widespread as to be considered "normal" male behavior; and is against PROSTITUTION and PORNOGRAPHY. Her position on outlawing pornography has taken her into sharp conflict with many women's movement leaders and other civil libertarians.

bulimia, a type of EATING DISORDER that involves binge eating and then expulsion of food, in a *binge-purge cycle;* sometimes called *bulimia nervosa.* A person with bulimia commonly eats very large amounts of food in a short time—not the usual sort of "splurge," such as gobbling a pint of ice cream in one sitting, but more food than an adult would eat in an entire day—and then expels the food from the body through vomiting, induced by hand or by using ipecac, or through use of laxatives or diuretics. Binges involve rapid, out-of-control eating, often in secret and over several hours, sometimes halted only by vomiting, abdominal pain, sleepiness, or discovery. Instead of the normal 2,000–3,000 calories in a day, someone with bulimia might eat as much as 20,000 calories in an eight-hour binge. In between binges, the person often diets strenuously (see DIETING), fasts, and EXERCISES obsessively in attempts to burn away fat. In fact, bulimia is sometimes linked with ANOREXIA NERVOSA, in a condition called *bulimarexia* or *bulimic anorexia.*

Unlike the self-starvation of anorexia, bulimia is not so likely to be immediately life-threatening, but it can damage the body severely, leading to long-term health problems and shortened LIFE EXPECTANCY. Persistent vomiting can cause irritation, overstretching, and possible rupture of the stomach and esophagus (see DIGESTIVE SYSTEM); dental decay from stomach acid (see TEETH); and pneumonia from vomited material being breathed into the lungs (see RESPIRATORY SYSTEM). Perhaps the most serious danger, both immediate and long term, is the generalized disturbance of the body's chemical balance, which can trigger severe health problems; in particular, overuse of ipecac to induce vomiting can cause such severe loss of potassium that it can trigger heart irregularities, which can cause death.

Like anorexia, bulimia is more common among women than among men, occurring generally in adolescence or early adulthood; it often starts in the late teens (generally somewhat later than anorexia) and persists for years. The National Center for Health Statistics (NCHS) estimates that in 1989 ten thousand bulimia cases were diagnosed in the United States. Other American studies indicate that by their first year of college, 4.5–18 percent of women and 0.4 percent of men have a history of bulimia. Unlike people with anorexia, many with bulimia were overweight by normal standards before onset of the disorder. During the disorder, their weight is often above normal or in the normal range, even though they have starved their bodies of vital nutrients. Their weight tends to fluctuate widely above and below the normal body weight for their age and height. Common signs of bulimia include calluses on the upper surfaces of the hand, especially the knuckles, from inducing vomiting; puffy face and bloating and tenderness elsewhere, especially in the feet and abdomen; dental cavities and erosion and discoloration of enamel; and general weakness and muscle aches (see MUSCULAR SYSTEM).

The causes of bulimia are unknown, and its occurrence is not apparently linked with either socioeconomic status or race. People with bulimia (and their relatives) are more than usually likely to have a history of *affective disorders* such as DEPRESSION; ALCOHOL AND DRUG ABUSE; OBESITY; shoplifting; and attempted suicide. While bulimia is generally treated as a MENTAL DISORDER, often through individual or group therapy and antidepressants, researchers are exploring genetic, physiological, and environmental factors that may be involved in triggering the disorder. One focus of research is levels of the HORMONE *serotonin;* the somewhat lower levels among people with bulimia may be linked with binging. Long-term studies suggest that half or more bulimics may continue to have chronic problems; the prognosis is best for people diagnosed in an early stage of the disorder. (See BULIMIA: DANGER SIGNS, below; EATING DISORDERS HELP, INFORMATION, AND ACTION GUIDE on page 58.)

BULIMIA: DANGER SIGNS

Eating disorders may be prevented or more readily treated if they are detected early. A person who has *several* of the following signs may be developing or has already developed an eating disorder.

The individual

- binges regularly (eats large amounts of food over a short period of time), and
- purges regularly (forces vomiting and/or uses drugs to stimulate vomiting, bowel movements, and urination).
- diets and exercises often, but maintains or regains weight.
- becomes a secret eater.
- eats enormous amounts of food at one sitting, but does not gain weight.
- disappears into the bathroom for long periods of time to induce vomiting.
- abuses drugs or alcohol, or steals regularly.
- appears depressed much of the time.
- has swollen neck glands.
- has scars on the back of hands from forced vomiting.

Source: American Anorexia/Bulimia Association, Inc., 1989.

Business and Professional Women/USA (BPW/USA) (2012 Massachusetts Avenue, NW, Washington, DC 20036; 202-293-1100; Legislative Hotline, 202-833-5524; Barbara Sido, deputy executive director), a national organization founded in 1919, more formally called the **National Federation of Business and Professional Women's Clubs, Inc.** With over three thousand local groups, the BPW describes itself as the "voice of America's working women," promoting "full participation, equity and economic self-sufficiency through legislative advocacy, member training, dissemination of information, and member support programs." It aids member organizations in developing advocacy programs and building local coalitions; offers personal and professional skill building workshops; and operates a Legislative Hotline for members. Members also have "access to business and personal loans, group medical, disability, and life insurance options, discounts on office products, publications, travel, and eyewear." The BPW Political Action Committee (BPW/PAC) "provides contributions and endorsements to women and pro-women national candidates who support BPW's legislative priorities," among them passage of the EQUAL RIGHTS AMENDMENT, PAY EQUITY, equal treatment and economic equality in employment, equal educational opportunity, access to BIRTH CONTROL, maintenance of REPRODUCTIVE RIGHTS, and available, affordable health care and dependent care. The **BPW Foundation** (202-293-1200), founded in 1956, is an education and research organization that offers scholarships, loans, fellowships, and research grants, also assisting women entering nontraditional career fields and offering education and training for members "on such topics as starting a business, leadership development, career strategies, work and family issues, and work force 2000." It maintains the **Marguerite Rewalt Resource Center,** a key library on working women's issues. BPW/USA publishes the quarterly magazine *National Business Woman.*

Caesarean section, an alternative spelling for CESAREAN SECTION.

cancer, a group of diseases that have in common uncontrolled growth of cells. Precisely why and how abnormal cell growth starts is unclear. Within cells are special genes called *oncogenes*, which turn on and off to control normal growth; sometimes, when they or their regulators are damaged, these oncogenes fail to turn off, so cells keep multiplying unchecked. At least some of the time, the malfunctioning is triggered by cancer-inducing substances called *carcinogens*. If not removed or checked, the masses of abnormally growing cells, called *tumors* or *neoplasms*, crowd out normal cells, in the process killing the tissues or organs involved.

If the cancer is detected early, is localized in a single site, has not invaded nearby tissues, and is removed quickly, the prognosis is generally good. Cancerous growths "shed" abnormal cells, however; these can travel elsewhere in the body, notably in BLOOD or lymph fluid (see IMMUNE SYSTEM), and can start other *secondary cancers*, a process called *metastasis*. If the cancer has, indeed, spread to other parts of the body, the long-term prognosis varies widely depending very much on the site or sites of the cancer, the type of treatment given, and the response of the individual body to that treatment.

Cells are found everywhere in the body, so cancer can occur anywhere. But the patterns of cancer incidence vary widely around the earth, by sex, age, race, diet, geographical location, exposure to known or suspected carcinogens, genetic susceptibility (see GENETIC INHERITANCE), and many other factors, often for reasons that are unknown. In the period 1986–1988, for example, the death rate from BREAST CANCER per 100,000 women ranged from a high of 29.3 in England and Wales, to a low of 1.0 in Thailand.

Not all tumors are cancerous. Some grow so slowly and are so confined that they are not considered life-threatening and are labeled *benign*—though even they can be lethal if they affect a vital structure, such as the brain. However, *malignant* tumors, or cancers, are expected to grow, spread, and, if untreated or unresponsive to treatment, cause death. Some cancers are more dangerous than others because they are in less easily treatable locations, in hard-to-detect sites, or of less easily treatable types. Those most treatable are small; are limited to the original, or *primary,* site; and are *encapsulated,* meaning distinct from the surrounding tissue. The danger increases as the growth moves beyond the capsulelike confines, because abnormal cells are "shed" into the BLOOD stream and lymphatic system (see IMMUNE SYSTEM). Though many of these will be killed by the body's immune system, some can trigger *secondary tumors* or *metastases* elsewhere in the body. That is why early detection is so vital.

For an overview of the most common and the most deadly cancers in males and females in the United States, see CANCER INCIDENCE AND DEATHS BY SITE AND SEX—1992 ESTIMATES on page 129. As that table indicates, the most common types of cancers among American women today are

▶ *breast cancer,* for over forty years, until 1987, the major cause of cancer death among American women (see BREAST CANCER).

▶ *colon and rectum cancer,* still the second most frequent type of cancer found in women, but in the last thirty years at a declining rate, for unknown reasons, possibly partly because of improved screening (see DIGESTIVE SYSTEM).

▶ *lung cancer,* since 1987 the most deadly cancer among American women, and the third most common, largely because of increased SMOKING (see LUNG CANCER). The American Cancer Society (ACS) reports that the death rate from lung cancer among women increased 425 percent (from 5.4 to 28.2 deaths per 100,000 annually) from the late 1950s to the late 1980s.

▶ *uterine and cervical cancer,* the fourth most common type of cancer in women, affecting the UTERUS and its neck, the CERVIX; however, death rates have "decreased more than 70 percent over the past forty years, due mainly to the Pap test for early detection of cervical cancer and regular checkups," the ACS reports (see UTERINE CANCER).

▶ *lymphoma,* affecting the lymphatic system, including Hodgkin's disease, which has a sharply declining death rate among women, and non-Hodgkin's lymphoma and multiple myeloma, which have a sharply increasing death rate (see IMMUNE SYSTEM).

▶ *ovarian cancer,* the fifth most common type of cancer overall among women and the second among gynecological cancers, but the deadliest, largely because symptoms do not appear until late in development (see OVARIES).

▶ *melanoma,* a highly dangerous type of skin cancer, sharply on the increase, with early detection vital (see SKIN).

▶ *pancreatic cancer,* a "silent" form of cancer, with symptoms not appearing until late in development; incidence and death rates have been relatively steady since the early 1970s, the ACS reports, though they have increased slightly among Black women (see DIGESTIVE SYSTEM).

▶ *bladder cancer,* more common among men than women, and among Whites than Blacks, and among smokers, people living in urban areas, and workers exposed to dyes, rubber, or leather (see URINARY TRACT).

▶ *leukemia,* affecting the blood-forming bone marrow, which strikes not just children but people of all ages and both sexes, often difficult to diagnose because its symptoms initially seem to be those of less serious conditions (see BLOOD).

▶ *kidney cancer* (see URINARY TRACT).

▶ *oral cancer* (see SMOKING).

C

CANCER INCIDENCE AND DEATHS
BY SITE AND SEX—1992 ESTIMATES

CANCER INCIDENCE BY SITE AND SEX*	
PROSTATE 132,000	BREAST 180,000
LUNG 102,000	COLON & RECTUM 77,000
COLON & RECTUM 79,000	LUNG 66,000
BLADDER 38,500	UTERUS 45,500
LYMPHOMA 27,200	LYMPHOMA 21,200
ORAL 20,600	OVARY 21,000
MELANOMA OF THE SKIN 17,000	MELANOMA OF THE SKIN 15,000
KIDNEY 16,200	PANCREAS 14,400
LEUKEMIA 16,000	BLADDER 13,100
STOMACH 15,000	LEUKEMIA 12,200
PANCREAS 13,900	KIDNEY 10,300
LARYNX 10,000	ORAL 9,700
ALL SITES 565,000	ALL SITES 565,000

*Excluding nonmelanoma skin cancer and carcinoma in situ.

CANCER DEATHS BY SITE AND SEX	
LUNG 93,000	LUNG 53,000
PROSTATE 34,000	BREAST 46,000
COLON & RECTUM 28,900	COLON & RECTUM 29,400
PANCREAS 12,000	PANCREAS 13,000
LYMPHOMA 10,900	OVARY 13,000
LEUKEMIA 9,900	UTERUS 10,000
STOMACH 8,000	LYMPHOMA 10,000
ESOPHAGUS 7,500	LEUKEMIA 8,300
LIVER 6,600	LIVER 5,700
BRAIN 6,500	BRAIN 5,300
KIDNEY 6,400	STOMACH 5,300
BLADDER 6,300	MULTIPLE MYELOMA 4,500
ALL SITES 275,000	ALL SITES 245,000

Source: *Cancer Facts & Figures 1992*, American Cancer Society, 1992.

In cancer, early detection and treatment are keys to survival. For women, the American Cancer Society recommends a checkup with a physician at least every three years from age twenty to thirty-nine and annually over age forty, including examinations of the BREASTS, uterus, CERVIX, colon and rectum, mouth, skin, thyroid, and lymph nodes. However, people at particular risk for cancerous conditions may be advised to have screening tests more often.

Such early detection and treatment are medically termed *secondary prevention*. But for *primary prevention* people must take steps to avoid exposures that have the potential to initiate or promote cancers. No one yet knows how to actually prevent cancer, but among the general guidelines to reduce your risk of getting cancer are

▶ *avoid smoking*, which is considered responsible for nearly 80 percent of all lung cancer cases in women, according to the American Cancer Society. Overall, the ACS notes, people who smoke two or more packs of cigarettes a day have cancer mortality rates fifteen to twenty-five times that of nonsmokers. Nonsmoking forms of tobacco, such as snuff and chewing tobacco, are also dangerous, being linked to cancers of the mouth, larynx, throat, and esophagus. All such risks are much further magnified by heavy consumption of alcoholic beverages.

▶ *avoid unprotected exposure to sunlight,* which is believed to be implicated in almost all cases of skin cancer.

▶ *avoid radiation exposure,* which can cause cell damage and increase cancer risk. One major area of concern that has come to light only in recent years is the effect of the radioactive gas *radon,* which is present in many houses, being released from rocks in the ground. People who live in private dwellings, or on the lower floors of apartment buildings, may well want to have their air tested to determine if they have unacceptable radon levels and, if so, to take appropriate action. Radiation from nuclear activities is also a substantial concern, especially since information about dangerous emissions has often been kept from people in nearby communities, so they were unable to leave the area for safety or to press for safer operations. Medical and dental X-rays are designed to give minimal exposure to radiation, which in any case is far outweighed by the health benefits.

▶ *eat a low-fat, high-fiber diet,* which is believed to lower the risk for breast and colon cancer (as well as prostate cancer in men). High-fiber diets are especially helpful in reducing colon cancer risk, but a varied diet eaten in moderate amounts is now believed to reduce the risk of many types of cancer (see NU-TRITION). Some people estimate that 35 percent of all cancer deaths are related to diet.

▶ *eat plenty of fruits and vegetables,* which are associated with lessened risk of lung, bladder, esophagus, stomach, and some other cancers.

▶ *avoid smoked, nitrite-cured, or salt-cured foods,* which have been linked to cancers of the esophagus and stomach.

▶ *maintain a weight in the proper range of your age and height* (see page 516), since OBESITY is linked with increased risk of many cancers, including colon, breast, GALLBLADDER, ovary, and uterus cancer.

▶ *consult carefully with your doctor about any medications that may be linked with cancer risk.* An example is ESTROGEN, often used to treat symptoms of MENOPAUSE, though the risk of cancer can be lessened by including progesterone in hormone replacement therapy. Each woman will have to balance her own possible need or desire for such treatment against the risk of cancer, given her personal and family history. Medications such as the AIDS drug zidovudine (AZT) have been linked with cancer risk but are used anyway because the disease they fight is immediately life-threatening.

▶ *avoid exposure to carcinogenic chemicals,* the problem being that it is not always known which chemicals do or do not increase cancer risk—and which new, unintended, and unknown chemicals are formed in the "chemical stews" that have been created in polluted areas around the world. Certainly most at risk are people working with dangerous chemicals, but people living near plants and dumps are also in danger, such as those living in "cancer alley," a stretch of Louisiana full of chemical plants. Some food additives have also been found to raise the risk of cancer. While some government agencies attempt to identify carcinogenic chemicals and remove them from the market, individuals must act defensively to protect themselves. Numerous works are available to assist people in identifying and removing or avoiding environmental dangers (among them our own *The Green Encyclopedia,* Prentice-Hall,

1992). The cancer risk of chemical exposure can be sharply increased by cigarette smoking.

Suspected cancers are often detected visually, as in a medical examination of the skin or cervix; manually, as by a breast self-examination (see page 104); or through a screening or scanning process, such as an X-ray, ULTRASOUND, NMR imaging, or CAT (CT) scan. To confirm the existence of cancer, a *biopsy* or sample of tissue is generally taken for analysis; for internal growths, this traditionally meant an operation, but often now some cells can be removed using a long, hollow *aspiration needle*. Laboratory tests then confirm whether the growth is benign—as it is in the majority of the cases—or malignant.

If cancer is diagnosed, a medical team develops a treatment plan called a *protocol,* which takes into account the type of cancer, how early or advanced it is, the part of the body involved, and the patient's general medical condition. A variety of therapies are used, including

▶ *surgery,* cutting out the tumor completely, if its size and location make that possible, or partially, to reduce the number of malignant cells remaining to be treated. Traditionally surgery generally meant complete removal of a whole body part, as of a breast or uterus, or an arm or leg, and sometimes creating a new body opening, called an *ostomy,* as for colon or rectal cancer. But increasingly surgeons have been developing more limited surgical techniques, to remove the cancer while leaving more of the body intact (see BREAST CANCER; HYSTERECTOMY). This has become possible partly because of advances in other therapies used after surgery; these additional therapies are called *adjuvant therapies.*

▶ *chemotherapy,* the use of poisonous chemicals to kill cancer cells, which are more vulnerable to the chemicals than normal cells are. The problem is that the poisons affect the rest of the body as well, though not so much, and their side effects cause difficulties, including loss of appetite, loss or distortion of taste and smell (called *mouth blindness* or *anosmia*), nausea and vomiting, severe weight loss and wasting of body tissues, loss of hair, water retention (*edema*), diarrhea, constipation, dehydration, dry mouth (*xerostomia*), and tooth decay. Often chemotherapy is given as adjuvant treatment, after surgery, but sometimes it is offered before surgery, to shrink the tumor so it is easier to excise surgically.

▶ *radiation therapy,* using radiation to destroy cancer cells. Like chemotherapy, in doses concentrated enough to do the job, radiation poses significant health hazards and difficulties for patients. Modern computer imaging techniques, however, have allowed more pinpoint radiation, sparing more of the normal tissue. Other new approaches include *interstitial radiation* or *bracytherapy,* in which radioactive materials are implanted directly into the tumor.

▶ *immunotherapy,* a treatment using substances from the body's own disease-fighting system, the immune system, to fight the cancer cells; this is a new treatment, so far applied only to a few types of cancers and in a limited way.

▶ *bone marrow transplantation (BMT),* long a technique used for leukemia patients who are able to find donors with bone marrow similar enough to their own for it to be used in a transplant. A newer, promising, but very risky twist on this approach takes advantage of the devastating effects of some treatments, such as chemotherapy or radiation therapy, with the patient as her own donor, in what is medically called an *autologous bone marrow transplant.* A portion of the patient's blood-making *bone marrow* (see SKELETAL SYSTEM) is removed and stored; the patient is then treated with therapies intended to be strong enough to destroy the cancer cells and remaining bone marrow. Later the bone marrow previously "harvested" is restored to the patient. The whole process is extremely delicate, and during it the patient is at considerable risk of infection, but for increasing numbers of cancer patients, the procedure has indeed been a lifesaver. Researchers are also experimenting with giving patients *growth factors* to help the bone marrow cells survive concentrated chemotherapy.

▶ **steroid therapy,** use of various kind of STEROIDS to ease swelling of sensitive tissues, as in the case of brain tumors.

▶ **hyperthermia,** use of heat to kill cancer cells or to make them more susceptible to radiation therapy; still an experimental approach.

▶ **photoradiation,** in which a patient is given a light-sensitive drug and placed under a special light; also still an experimental technique.

Among other approaches being explored are the use of genetically engineered cells to produce substances called *monoclonal antibodies,* which will specifically target and kill cancer cells; use of *retinoids,* vitamin A derivatives, for possible cancer prevention; and use of medicines specifically designed to fight or prevent specific types of cancers. The drug *taxol* has shown early promise against ovarian and breast cancer, slowing tumor growth and sometimes even causing regression, though it seems to have little effect on some other cancers. Originally derived from yew bark, newer forms come from yew needles, which do not require killing the tree, and some forms may be synthesized. The main side effects of taxol are neurological, especially numbness and tingling of fingers and hands, and loss of fine muscle coordination.

In addition, much progress has been made in meeting the psychological and social needs of patients and their families during and after treatment. Much remains to be done, however. Even after cancer patients are pronounced "cured"—meaning their bodies have shown no sign of cancer for a specific time, often five years, and their life expectancy is once again roughly that of someone who has never had cancer—they still face problems, in returning to employment, advancing normally in their careers, maintaining relationships with friends and family, getting medical and life insurance, and a host of similar questions. Because the problems are substantial and similar, many cancer patients—present and former—have joined groups to gain not only mutual support, but also a voice in changing public perceptions and policies (see CANCER HELP, INFORMATION, AND ACTION GUIDE on page 133; WOMEN'S HEALTH HELP, INFORMATION, AND ACTION GUIDE on page 334).

CANCER

Help, Information, and Action Guide

Organizations

▶ **National Cancer Institute (NCI)** (9000 Rockville Pike, Building 31, Room 10A18, Bethesda, MD 20892; Cancer Communications Office 301-496-5583; Cancer Information Service 800-4-CANCER [422-6237], Samuel Broker, director), a key U.S. center for research and public policy regarding cancer. It provides information to the public and professionals through its **Cancer Information Service (CIS),** including up-to-date information, prevention guidelines, referrals, emotional support; its computerized data base (Physician Data Query, or PDQ) of current experimental treatments; and its many free publications, many in Spanish as well as English. Among these are general materials such as *What You Need To Know About Cancer;* pamphlets and fact sheets on specific types of cancers; cancer prevention and detection materials such as *A Time of Change* (directed at young women); *Diet, Nutrition and Cancer Prevention: The Good News; Good News, Better News, Best News . . . Cancer Prevention; The Pap Test: It Can Save Your Life!;* patient materials such as *Advanced Cancer: Living Each Day, Cancer Treatments: Consider the Possibilities, Chemotherapy and You—A Guide to Self-Help During Treatment, Radiation Therapy and You—A Guide to Self-Help During Treatment, Eating Hints: Tips and Recipes for Better Nutrition During Cancer Treatment, Facing Forward: A Guide for Cancer Survivors, Help Yourself: Tips for Teenagers with Cancer, Patient to Patient: Cancer Clinical Trials and You* (videocassette), *What Are Clinical Trials All About?, Taking Time: Support for People with Cancer and the People Who Care About Them, When Cancer Recurs: Meeting the Challenge Again,* and *When Someone in Your Family Has Cancer;* special materials for children with cancer; and a series of information sheets of anticancer drugs. (See also BREAST CANCER; SMOKING.)

▶ **American Cancer Society (ACS)** (1599 Clifton Road, NE, Atlanta, GA 30329; 404-320-3333 or 800-227-2345; John R. Seffrin, executive vice-president), a key organization of people concerned with cancer. It provides support services to cancer patients and their families, such as programs for people with specific types of cancers, as well as **Cansermount,** which matches current cancer patients with cancer survivors, and **I Can Cope,** which educates people about living with cancer. It sponsors research and provides information to public and professionals, as through numerous print and audiovisual materials, including newsletter *Cancer News, When Your Brother or Sister Has Cancer* (for ages 7 through early teens), *Pain Control,* and booklets *Helping Children Understand: A Guide for a Parent with Cancer, What Happened to You Happened to Me* (for cancer patients aged 7 through early teens), and on specific types of cancer, such as *Facts on Bone Cancer* and *Facts on Leukemia.*

▶ **Cancervive, Inc.** (6500 Wilshire Boulevard, Suite 500, Los Angeles, CA 90048; 213-203-9232; Susan Nessim, president and executive director), a network of support groups of cancer survivors.

▶ **National Cancer Care Foundation** (NCCF) (1180 Avenue of the Americas, New York, NY 10036; 212-221-3300; Diane Blum, executive director), an organization that offers "professional social work counseling and guidance to help patients and families cope with the emotional and psychological consequences of cancer," also providing eligible families with financial assistance in some home care, child care, transportation and medical treatment expenses, as well as assistance in pain management. It offers various special programs, as for children or teens from families facing cancer, and for cancer patients with AIDS. Primarily serving the tristate area of New York, New Jersey, and Connecticut, NCCF also offers consultation and education programs for professionals and the wider community and is a key member of the **National Alliance of Breast Cancer Organizations** (NABCO) (see BREAST CANCER HELP, INFORMATION, AND ACTION GUIDE on page 111).

▶ **American Institute for Cancer Research** (AICR) (1759 R Street, NW, Washington, DC 20009; 202-328-7744; Marilyn Gentry, president), an organization for cancer research. It publishes the AICR Information Series of booklets and pamphlets, including *All About Fat and Cancer Risk, Dietary Fiber to Lower Cancer Risk,* and *Dietary Guidelines to Lower Cancer Risk.*

▶ **DES Action** (415-826-5060). Sponsors the **DES Cancer Network.** (See DES.)

▶ **Skin Cancer Foundation** (245 Fifth Avenue, Suite 2402, New York, NY 10016; 212-725-5176; Mitzi Moulds, executive director), an organization concerned with skin cancer; it publishes *Sun Sense: A Complete Guide to the Prevention, Early Detection, and Treatment of Skin Cancer.*

▶ **National Marrow Donor Program** (100 South Robert Street, St. Paul, MN 55107; 800-654-1247; David Stroncek, president), a registry of donors for people in need of bone marrow transplants from unrelated people. The program is sponsored jointly by the American Association of Blood Banks, American Red Cross, Council of Community Blood Centers, and the National Heart, Lung, and Blood Institute. It publishes *The Chance of a Lifetime: Questions and Answers about Marrow Transplants.*

▶ **American Brain Tumor Association** (ABTA) (3725 North Tallman Avenue, Chicago, IL 60618; 312-286-5571, or for patients 800-886-5571; Gail

Segal, president), an organization concerned about brain tumors. It sponsors mutual-support groups; supports research; provides information and referrals; and publishes various materials, including the bibliography *Living with a Brain Tumor,* and booklets such as *A Primer of Brain Tumors* and *Coping with a Brain Tumor.*

▶ **Corporate Angel Network** (Westchester County Airport, Building 1, White Plains, NY 10604; 914-328-1313; Priscilla Blum, president), an organization that arranges for cancer patients (and one family member or attendant) to fly free on corporate airplanes to NCI-approved treatment centers, when seats are available.

▶ INSTITUTE ON WOMEN AND TECHNOLOGY (413-367-9725).

Other resources

▨ **GENERAL WORKS**

Cancer A to Z. Roberta Altman and Michael J. Sarg. Facts on File, 1992.
Challenging Cancer: From Chaos to Control. Nira Kfir and Maurice Slevin. Routledge, 1991.
Cancervive: The Challenge of Life after Cancer. Susan Nessim and Judith Ellis. Houghton Mifflin, 1991. Nessim founded Cancervive (see above).
Understanding Cancer. Jay S. Roth. Academic Press, 1991.
A Family Doctor's Guide to Understanding and Preventing Cancer. S. R. Kaura. Health Press, 1990.
Cancer: Your Questions Answered. Charles Dobree. Trafalgar Square, 1990.
Cancer. Joann Rodgers. Chelsea House, 1990.
Understanding Cancer, 3rd ed. Mark Renneker. Bull Publishing, 1988.
The Cancer Reference Book, rev. ed. Paul M. Levitt and others. Facts on File, 1983.

▨ **PRACTICAL GUIDES**

Coping with Cancer: Twelve Creative Choices. John E. Packo. Christian Publications, 1991.
When Someone You Love Has Cancer. Dana R. Pomeroy. IBS Press, 1991.
The Road Back to Health: Coping with the Emotional Aspects of Cancer, rev. ed. Neil A. Fiore. Celestial Arts, 1991.
Charting the Journey: An Almanac of Practical Resources for the Cancer Survivor. Fitzhugh Mullan. Consumer Reports, 1990.
The Complete Book of Cancer Prevention: Foods, Lifestyles and Medical Care to Keep You Healthy. Prevention Magazine Health Books eds. Rodale Press, 1990.

Cancer as a Turning Point: A Handbook for People with Cancer, Their Families, and Health Professionals. Lawrence LeShan. Dutton, 1989.

Your Defense Against Cancer: The Complete Guide to Cancer Prevention. Henry Dreher. HarperCollins, 1989.

Protect Yourself from Cancer: A Physician's Comprehensive Plan for Cancer Prevention. Howard R. Bierman. Dodd, Mead, 1988.

How to Improve Your Odds Against Cancer. John F. Potter. Frederick Fell, 1988.

Health Care U.S.A. Jean Carper. Prentice-Hall, 1987. Provides general and specific health care information for different types of cancers, cancer treatments, and major centers for treatment or research.

Coping Magazine, for cancer patients and families, on cancer research, services, and personal experiences. Available from 2019 North Carothers, Franklin, TN 37064; 615-790-2400.

◪ BACKGROUND WORKS

Let's Get the Fear Out of Cancer: A Holistic Approach to Illness and to Life. Vernon Templemore. Atrium, 1991.

Cancer and Its Psychological Influences: Index of Modern Authors and Subjects with Guide for Rapid Research. John C. Bartone. ABBE Publications Association, 1991.

In Search of Safety: Chemicals and Cancer Risk. John D. Graham and others. Harvard University Press, 1991.

Cancer and Consciousness. Barry Bryant. Sigo Press, 1990.

Cancer Sourcebook: Basic Information on Cancer Types, Symptoms, Diagnostic Methods, and Treatments, Including Statistics on Cancer Occurrences Worldwide and the Risks Associated with Known Carcinogens and Activities. Frank E. Bair, ed. Omnigraphics, 1990.

The Cancer Industry: Unraveling the Politics. Ralph W. Moss. Paragon House, 1989.

◪ PERSONAL EXPERIENCES

Healing Journey. O. Carl Simon. Bantam, 1992.

Rainbow Man, rev. ed. Richard G. Rockman, Jr., and R. G. Rockman, 1992.

Life in the Shadow. Bill Soiffer. Chronicle Books, 1991.

The Power Within: True Stories of Exceptional Patients Who Fought Back with Hope. Wendy Williams. HarperCollins, 1990; Simon & Schuster, 1991.

The Jason Winters Story: Killing Cancer, In Search of the Perfect Cleanse, Breakthrough, The Ultimate Combination, 2nd ed. Jason Winters. Vinton, 1991.

Making Miracles: Finding Meaning in Life's Chaos. Paul Pearsall. Prentice-Hall, 1991.

Courage: The Testimony of a Cancer Patient. Barbara Creaturo. Pantheon, 1991.

First Cancer, then Lupus: The Courageous Story of One Woman's Journey Through Illness, Chemotherapy, Steroids, and Pain Control. Anne O'Connell. A. O'Connell, 1991.

Between Hello and Goodbye: A Life-Affirming Story of Courage in the Face of Tragedy. Jean Craig. Tarcher, 1990.

Loving Medicine: Patients' Experiences of the Holistic Treatment of Cancer. Rosy Thomson. Atrium, 1990.

Cancer Stories: Creativity and Self-Repair. Esther Dreifuss-Kattan. Analytic Press, 1990.

One Dark Mile: A Widower's Story. Eric Robinson. University of Massachusetts Press, 1990.

The Cancer Conqueror: An Incredible Journey to Wellness. Greg Anderson. Andrews and McMeel, 1990.

In the Face of Death. Peter Noll. Viking Penguin, 1990.

Dr. Anne's Journal. Robert Lloyd. Davar, 1990.

Remember, I Love You: Martha's Story. Charlie W. Shedd. Harper SF, 1990.

candidiasis, a main type of YEAST INFECTION.

cap, a type of BIRTH CONTROL device (see CERVICAL CAP).

capsular contracture, development and shrinking of scar tissue around an implant (see BREAST IMPLANT; COSMETIC SURGERY).

carcinogens, substances that trigger CANCER.

Carey* v. *Population Services International, a 1977 U.S. Supreme Court ruling extending to minors the right to contraceptives and the right to privacy with their doctor (see BIRTH CONTROL).

Catalyst (250 Park Avenue South, New York, NY 10003; 212-777-8900; Felice Schwartz, president), an organization that consults with organizations on issues related to women employees. It sponsors research; operates an information center; and publishes various materials, including the monthly *Perspective on Current Corporate Issues* and reports such as *The Corporate Guide to Parental Leaves.*

Catt, Carrie Chapman (1859–1947), a major figure in the successful fight for WOMAN SUFFRAGE, who emerged as a leading political action organizer with the NATIONAL AMERICAN WOMAN SUFFRAGE ASSOCIATION (**NAWSA**) in 1895, and succeeded Susan B. ANTHONY as its president (1900–1903), then becoming president of the International Woman's Suffrage Alliance (1904–1923). In 1916, with the NAWSA and the American fight for woman suffrage in great difficulty, she returned to the NAWSA presidency, during the next three years leading a growing movement that in 1919 resulted in the winning of woman suffrage, with passage of the NINETEENTH AMENDMENT. In 1919, its single-issue work done, the NAWSA dissolved. Catt then led in the formation of the LEAGUE OF WOMEN VOT-ERS, a successor organization.

Although a pacifist, Catt supported American entry into World War I and the American war effort, returning to her pacifism in the 1920s and 1930s, in 1925 founding the National Committee on the Cause and Cure of War and in 1935 publishing *Why Wars Must Cease.*

There are two kinds of restrictions upon human liberty—the restraint of law and that of custom. No written law has ever been more binding than unwritten custom supported by popular opinion.

CARRIE CHAPMAN CATT, 1902
—————————— IN THE SPEECH "FOR THE SAKE OF LIBERTY" ——————————

•

celiac sprue, a type of digestive disorder involving intolerance to wheat and other grains (see DIGESTIVE SYSTEM).

Center for the American Woman and Politics (CAWP)
(Eagleton Institute of Politics, Rutgers, State University of New Jersey, New Brunswick, NJ 08901; 908-828-2210; Ruth B. Mandel, director), an organization founded in 1971 as a unit of the Eagleton Institute of Politics, to compile information about women in government and politics and to study and monitor the status and prospects of those women. It acts as an information clearinghouse, responding to both calls and letters; conducts research and surveys; maintains a data bank on women in public office and the Women in American Politics library, open to the public; provides consulting services; and holds conferences, seminars, and special programs for women lawmakers and for college and high school students. Through its Subscriber Information Service (SIS), subscribers receive three packets a year, each including the newsletter *CAWP News & Notes,* as well as fact sheets on women in elective and appointive office at levels from municipal to federal, including special topics such as the gender gap, sex differences in voter turnout, and women of color in elective office, reports such as *Gender and Policymaking: Studies of Women in Office, The Impact of Women in*

Public Office, and *Reshaping the Agenda: Women in State Legislatures;* reprints of articles, and other timely information. Many of these materials are also available directly from CAWP, as are audiotapes of various programs.

Center for Women Policy Studies (CWPS) (2000 P Street, NW, Suite 508, Washington, DC 20036; 202-872-1770; Leslie R. Wolfe, executive director), an organization founded in 1972 as "an independent policy research and advocacy institution" for "women's equality and empowerment." It holds the general premises that all issues affecting women are interrelated, that sex and race bias must be addressed simultaneously, and that analyses of women's status and needs must "recognize their diversity—by race and ethnicity, by economic status, by disability, by sexual identity, and by age." Among its various advocacy, research, policy development, and public education programs are

▶ *Educational Equity Policy Studies (EEPS),* seeking to identify and remove barriers to equal education and work preparation for women and girls;

▶ *National Brain Trust on Economic Opportunity for Low Income Women,* stressing higher education and entrepreneurship;

▶ *Work and Family Policy Program,* researching "how women of color define and experience work and family issues," to guide future policies;

▶ *National Resource Center on Women and AIDS,* acting as a centralized information resource on policies and strategies, working with other coalitions, and producing policy papers;

▶ *The Law and Pregnancy—Implementing Policies for Women's Reproductive Rights and Health,* seeking to convey policy recommendations to legislators, judges, and advocates on issues such as the legal status of a FETUS, coerced medical treatment of pregnant women, living wills, and substance abuse, with special focus on women of color and low income, again working with other coalitions;

▶ *Violence Against Women as Gender Bias Motivated Hate Crime,* conducting research, analyzing legislation, and shaping civil rights remedies;

▶ *Girls and Violence,* exploring causes of girls' violent actions and recommending programs and strategies; and

▶ various *leadership development programs.*

CWPS publishes various materials, including

• on education, economic opportunity, and family policy: *Women of Color in Mathematics, Science, and Engineering: A Review of the Literature, The SAT Gender Gap: Identifying the Causes, How Does the SAT Score for Women?, More Than Survival: Higher Education for Low Income Women, Earnings Sharing in Social Security: A Model for Reform, Federal Laws and Regulations Prohibiting Sex Discrimination in Educational Institutions* (a wallchart), *The Restoration of Title IX: Implications for Higher Education, It's All in What You Ask: Questions for Search Committees to Use, Looking for More Than a Few Good Women in Traditionally Male Fields;*

• on women's health policy: *The Guide to Resources on Women and AIDS* (published annually), *Fighting for Our Lives: Women Confronting AIDS* (a video, with an accompanying *Action Kit*), *More Harm Than Help: The Ramifications*

for Rape Survivors of Mandatory HIV Testing of Rapists, *The Law and Pregnancy: Protection or Punishment? A Resource Collection, The Politics of Reproduction in 1992: Contraceptive and Reproductive Technologies, A Resource Collection, Women, Pregnancy and Substance Abuse;*
- on violence against women: *Violence Against Women as Bias Motivated Hate Crime: Defining the Issues, Legal Help for Battered Women, The Letter and the Spirit: Federal and State Legal and Policy Issues—Violence Against Women, A Resource Collection, Court-Mandated Counseling for Men Who Batter, Sexual Assault Reform Legislation: An Assessment From the Field, "Friends" Raping Friends: Could It Happen to You?, Campus Gang Rape: Party Games?, In Case of Sexual Harassment . . . A Guide for Women Students, Sexual Harassment Action Packet,* and *Peer Harassment: Hassles for Women on Campus.*

certified nurse–midwife, a specially trained registered nurse who acts as a birth attendant and also often gives PRENATAL CARE and education. (See CHILDBIRTH.)

cervical cancer, CANCER of the CERVIX, the neck of the UTERUS (see UTERINE CANCER).

cervical cap, a small rubber cup that fits tightly over the CERVIX, generally used with SPERMICIDE as a form of BIRTH CONTROL. The FOOD AND DRUG ADMINISTRATION (FDA) estimates that the cervical cap-spermicide combination is approximately 80–98 percent effective in preventing PREGNANCY. The cervical cap has been widely used for some years in Europe, though it was not approved for use in the United States until 1988.

Like the diaphragm, the cervical cap must be fitted by a doctor and is available only by prescription. The cap is harder to insert and remove than a diaphragm, though it can remain in place for forty-eight hours and (unlike the diaphragm) does not require additional spermicide to be added if intercourse is repeated. Also unlike the diaphragm, the cervical cap should not be inserted or used during MENSTRUATION or just after CHILDBIRTH or an ABORTION. Either the woman or her partner can have irritation or allergic reaction to either the rubber (latex) or the spermicide and should discontinue use in case of any genital burning or irritation (see ALLERGIES). The cervical cap with spermicide gives some protection against SEXUALLY TRANSMITTED DISEASES, though they should not be regarded as any protection against AIDS; also, spermicide has been linked with BIRTH DEFECTS (see SPERMICIDE). The cervical cap carries some increased risk of vaginal or cervical infections (see VAGINA) and TOXIC SHOCK SYNDROME and can cause the PAP SMEAR to give less reliable results.

Several other forms of cervical cap are also in development, including the *Fem cap,* also of silicone rubber, with a "brim" that helps create an airtight seal with the vaginal walls, which would require fitting by a doctor; and two over-the-counter products: the *Oves cervical cap,* made of clear, flexible silicone rubber and disposable; and *Lea's Shield,* a silicone-rubber cap that is reusable more than twenty times, with a special loop to allow for easy insertion and removal. (See BIRTH CONTROL AND FAMILY PLANNING HELP, INFORMATION, AND ACTION GUIDE on page 81.)

cervical smear, an alternative name for the PAP SMEAR.

cervical sponge, a type of BIRTH CONTROL device (see SPONGE).

cervix, a cylinder of fibrous tissue, actually the neck and bottom of the UTERUS, which protrudes into the VAGINA. Though only an inch or so long and normally less than that in diameter, the cervix is the all-important passageway between the inner body and the vagina, which connects to the outside. Through the cervix regularly flow the unused contents of the uterus, as MENSTRUATION. After vaginal SEXUAL INTERCOURSE, SPERM pass this way from the vagina to the uterus and FALLOPIAN TUBES, to where an egg (OVUM) may be available for FERTILIZATION. The cervix, with the vagina, also form the *birth canal* by which a baby emerges to independent life during CHILDBIRTH.

The cervix changes in various ways to perform these functions. Glands lining the inside of the cervix produce secretions that change during the reproductive cycle (see MENSTRUATION). Often thick, opaque, and sticky and distinctly hostile to sperm, it changes to clear and slippery—like raw egg white—around the time of OVULATION, then easing passage of sperm. In the *cervical (vaginal) mucus method* or *Billings method* of NATURAL FAMILY PLANNING, couples chart these changes to target the time of ovulation, whether their aim is BIRTH CONTROL or CONCEPTION.

The most dramatic changes come during PREGNANCY. At first the cervix becomes longer and more muscular, to support and hold the developing FETUS in the uterus. Its blood supply increases, changing the end of the cervix from its normal pink to bluish, a common quick sign of pregnancy. Then, just before LABOR and DELIVERY, the cervix becomes very short and widens to allow passage of the baby, afterward never quite resuming its original shape.

Because of its key role as guardian of a woman's inner reproductive organs, the cervix is subject to a variety of disorders, among them

▶ *cervicitis,* inflammation of the cervix. This can result from many infections, including SEXUALLY TRANSMITTED DISEASES, such as CHLAMYDIA, GONORRHEA, HERPES, and the *human papillomaviruses* (HPVs) that cause GENITAL WARTS. Some of these may spread to interior organs to become PELVIC INFLAMMATORY DISEASES, affecting the uterus and fallopian tubes and causing possible INFERTILITY; some also increase the risk of CANCER. Some infections can be passed on to the baby at birth, with disastrous consequences, including pneumonia and blindness. Women are normally tested for such conditions during routine PRENATAL CARE but should alert their doctor if they have any unusual symptoms, such as lower abdominal pain, vaginal discharge, or fever, which might indicate active infection. To prevent damage to the baby, a CESAREAN SECTION may be recommended.

▶ *injury,* tears or strains in the cervix, as may occur during childbirth or a badly performed ABORTION. If the injuries are severe enough, they can cause hemorrhaging, at times life-threatening, and may require surgery to repair.

▶ *incompetent cervix,* a cervix that cannot hold a fetus properly in place, which can lead to MISCARRIAGE. Sometimes this is because muscles have been weakened by earlier injuries, but in some women the cervix widens prematurely, months before delivery; this can be detected on ULTRASOUND. A woman who has an incompetent cervix, or who has had previous miscarriages, may have the end of the cervix stitched in a minor surgical procedure, normally done in a hospital under epidural ANESTHESIA at around the fourteenth week of pregnancy; she will also be advised to limit activity during the pregnancy. Later the suture will be removed, so she can deliver normally.

▶ *polyps,* small benign growths in the interior passageway of the cervix, called the *cervical canal.* These can be symptomless, but some women experience bleeding or spotting between periods or after MENOPAUSE. Large polyps can cause cramps during and sometimes between menstrual periods and sometimes bleed after vaginal SEXUAL INTERCOURSE. Single polyps that protrude into the vagina can readily be removed in a doctor's office or clinic. Numerous or persistent polyps are sometimes removed during a procedure called a D&C (*dilatation and curettage*).

▶ *cancer,* malignant growths in and around the cervix (see UTERINE CANCER; CANCER).

▶ *cervical eversion,* the replacement of tissue on the cervix's surface with tissue that normally grows in the cervical canal. Because the internal tissue contains more glands, heavier mucous secretions result, especially when the woman has high levels of ESTROGEN, as during PUBERTY or PREGNANCY, or when taking BIRTH CONTROL PILLS. Some feel this increases the risk of infection; others feel the minor risk is less than that posed by the destruction of such abnormal tissue.

(See WOMEN'S HEALTH HELP, INFORMATION, AND ACTION GUIDE on page 334; BIRTH CONTROL AND FAMILY PLANNING HELP, INFORMATION, AND ACTION GUIDE on page 81.)

cesarean section, a surgical procedure to deliver a baby through an incision in the mother's abdomen; also called *Caesarean section, C-section, abdominal delivery,* or *surgical delivery.* C-sections are most commonly performed when DELIVERY through the VAGINA is impossible or so difficult as to pose a danger for mother, child, or both.

Before modern times, cesarean sections were used only in extremis, usually if the mother was already dead, since before the development of abdominal surgery, blood transfusions, and antibiotics, the operation almost always resulted in the mother's death. Today, however, it is widely performed, and often for reasons of its safety, in comparison with a difficult CHILDBIRTH that could injure the mother and damage the child, as in the case of abnormal FETAL PRESENTATION.

Traditionally a C-section was done using a vertical cut high on the abdomen, called the *classical uterine incision*. For some situations, some doctors used a *low vertical incision*, low on the abdomen, or an *inverted-T incision*, with two cuts, one vertical, one horizontal. All of these types can lead to rupture of the UTERUS in future pregnancies and laid the basis for the traditional medical maxim "Once a cesarean, always a cesarean."

However, in recent decades, physicians have increasingly been using less damaging alternatives, most commonly the *low transverse uterine incision*, a horizontal cut low on the abdomen, also called the *bikini cut*. One enormous advantage of this approach is that women who have previously delivered by cesarean are often able to deliver later children normally through the vagina. Such an approach, called *vaginal birth after cesarean section* (VBAC), is possible because the conditions that made a C-section right for one birth are often not present in a later one. (Groups like those below can provide information and referrals to doctors who support VBAC.) The classical incision is quicker and allows more maneuvering room, however, so it is still used in special cases, especially in emergency situations where time is critical, where placenta problems affect the lower uterus, where the baby is large or in an awkward position, or in multiple births.

Among the conditions when a C-section might be indicated are

▶ *fetal distress,* in which the baby has insufficient oxygen during a difficult LABOR, often indicated by electronic devices called *fetal monitors.*

▶ *problems with the* PLACENTA, the organ that nourishes the fetus, including *placenta previa* or *abruptio placenta.*

▶ *infection in the mother,* which might be passed to the child, such as active HERPES infection.

▶ *abnormal fetal presentation,* potentially anything other than the ideal vertical, head-down presentation, but especially *breech presentation,* with feet or buttocks down, or *transverse lie,* a horizontal position (see FETAL PRESENTATION).

▶ *cephalopelvic disproportion,* in which the baby is too large to emerge normally from the mother's pelvis, as may become clear late during LABOR.

▶ *multiple births,* which may involve various difficulties, especially fetal distress and abnormal presentation.

▶ *prolapse of the* UMBILICAL CORD, in which the cord drops down into the VAGINA, potentially endangering the baby's oxygen supply.

▶ *dystocia,* LABOR so difficult it ceases to progress, as when the mother is too weak or her reproductive organs are abnormally shaped.

▶ *previous cesarean section,* with an incision of a type that could cause problems during a possible vaginal delivery.

▶ *Rh incompatibility,* or a mismatch in BLOOD factors between mother and child, which can lead to self-destruction of the child's red blood cells and consequent organ damage (see BLOOD).

▶ *maternal distress,* serious conditions affecting the mother, including PREECLAMPSIA or eclampsia, DIABETES, or heart disease (see HEART AND CIRCULATORY SYSTEM).

A C-section is still major surgery, but it is far safer and requires far less recovery time than in the past, not only because of improved surgical techniques,

but also because it is often performed under regional (epidural) ANESTHESIA.
Partly because it is safer, and because obstetricians are concerned about possible
malpractice charges resulting from difficult labor, the number of cesareans has
risen dramatically in the past two decades. This is especially so in the United
States, where most obstetricians are trained as surgeons, where some doctors
(and even some mothers) have chosen C-section for their convenience, and—
certainly a factor in at least some cases—where health insurance pays more for
a surgical delivery than a vaginal one. The rate of cesareans varies widely among
areas, doctors, and socioeconomic levels, with the highest rate being found in affluent areas.

A woman should discuss the question of C-sections—when they should
and should not be used—with her obstetrician. If she is not comfortable with the
doctor's approach, she should switch to another doctor—but sooner rather than
later. In addition, she may want to discuss the rate of cesareans in that obstetrician's practice and consider another doctor if the rate is above 15 percent. A
woman and her partner will also want to explore a hospital's policy on having
partners attend C-sections. Some do not allow it—and for good reasons, including increased risk of infection, crowded operating-room space, and the possibility
of the partner fainting. On the other hand, since the mother is often under only
a regional anesthetic, the partner can give useful emotional support. Because cesarean can be a shock for a woman who has prepared for vaginal delivery, some
hospitals and some prepared childbirth classes (see DELIVERY) educate and counsel women about the possibility beforehand.

Also important to explore is the doctor's and hospital's policy on vaginal
birth after cesarean, for later children. Some automatically assume that any subsequent child will be by cesarean as well. However, some hospitals will allow a
trial of labor, on the understanding that if difficulties occur, a cesarean may be
necessary. Trial of labor has the advantage that it will occur when the baby is actually ready to be born. Otherwise, when the due date is uncertain or miscalculated, a doctor may perform a cesarean section when the baby is premature and
so cause needless medical problems.

For more help, information, and action

▶ **C/SEC (Cesareans/Support, Education, and Concern)** (22 Forest Road,
Framingham, MA 01701; 508-877-8266), an organization focusing on cesarean
deliveries. It seeks to prevent unnecessary cesareans and stresses vaginal birth
as a later alternative. It provides information; makes referrals; encourages mu-
tual support; and publishes various materials, including a newsletter; pam-
phlets such as *Education for Vaginal Birth After Cesarean* and *Planning for
Birth*; and books such as *Frankly Speaking, The Cesarean Myth, The Vaginal
Birth After Cesarean (VBAC) Experience, Essential Exercises for the Childbearing
Year, Having Twins,* and *Special Delivery: A Book for Kids About Cesarean and
Vaginal Birth.*

▶ **International Cesarean Awareness Network (ICAN)** (P.O. Box 152, University
Station, Syracuse, NY 13210; 315-424-1942; Esther Zorn, director), an organi-

zation concerned with the increased rate of cesareans; formerly Cesarean Prevention Movement. It makes referrals; stresses mutual support; and publishes various materials, including a quarterly newspaper and *Cesarean Facts.*

Other resources

Recovering from a "C" Section. Margaret Blackstone and Tahira Humayun. Longmeadow Press, 1991.
The Expectant Parent's Guide to Preventing a Cesarean Section. Carl Jones. Bergin & Garvey/Greenwood, 1991.
Birth After Cesarean: The Medical Facts. Bruce L. Flamm. Prentice-Hall, 1990.
The Cesarean Myth: Choosing the Best Way to Have Your Baby. Mortimer Rosen, M.D., and Lillian Thomas. Penguin, 1989.
Silent Knife: Cesarean Prevention & Vaginal Birth After Cesarean. Nancy Wainer Cohen and Lois J. Estner. Greenwood, 1983; C/SEC, 1983.
(See also CHILDBIRTH; DELIVERY; also PREGNANCY AND CHILDBIRTH HELP, INFORMATION, AND ACTION GUIDE on page 580.)

chancroid, a bacterial infection of the GENITALS; one of the SEXUALLY TRANSMITTED DISEASES. Painful open sores appear on the genitals, often with swollen and tender lymph nodes in the groin. The open sores are called *soft chancres,* to distinguish them from the *hard chancres* of SYPHILIS, though it is often hard to distinguish chancroid from syphilis or genital HERPES sores. Diagnosis must be made by analyzing a sample of the infectious microorganism. It responds to any of several antibiotics. (See SEXUALLY TRANSMITTED DISEASES; also WHAT YOU CAN DO TO AVOID STDs on page 660; SEXUALLY TRANSMITTED DISEASES HELP, INFORMATION, AND ACTION GUIDE on page 658.)

chastity, virtue in relation to sexual matters. If a woman is unmarried, the term *chastity* is used virtually synonymously with VIRGINITY. But chastity can also apply to a sexually active woman, if she is married, or to a woman who has previously been married, if widowed or divorced, the essential point being that the sexual activity is confined to legally recognized unions (see MARRIAGE).

chemical peel (chemosurgery), a SKIN procedure (see COSMETIC SURGERY).

Chesler, Phyllis: See *Women and Madness.*

Chicago, Judy (Judy Cohen, 1939–), an American feminist artist, best known for her production of the massive women's historical ceramics, embroidery, and photography project *The Dinner Party* (1978), created by a large number of people, most of them women, under her direction. The work honors 999 women, some of them mythical figures, and singles out 39 for special honor. Another well-known work is *The Birth Project* honoring the process of CHILD-BIRTH and associated mythologies.

Chicana feminism: See FEMINISM.

child abuse and neglect (CAN), "the physical or mental injury, sexual abuse, negligent treatment, or maltreatment of a child under eighteen by a person who is responsible for the child's welfare," as defined in the U.S. federal Child Abuse Prevention and Treatment Act of 1974. Women may be concerned with child abuse and neglect in several ways. Many women were abused as children themselves. Many are mothers who are concerned that their children not be abused, as by CHILD CARE workers or others in a position of trust supervising their children. They may have to confront the fact that some members of their own families are child abusers. Some women are themselves abusers—often having been abused in their own youth and repeating a cycle of mistreatment. Some may be falsely accused of child abuse, as by a malicious ex-spouse in a CUSTODY fight. And all are friends, neighbors, and citizens, who wish to be alert for signs of abuse in their communities.

In general, child abuse refers to acts of *commission,* while child neglect refers to acts of *omission.* More precisely, child abuse encompasses deliberate acts that harm—or threaten to harm—a child's health and welfare, while neglect includes failure to protect a child and especially to provide for the child's basic needs.

Among the acts that constitute child abuse and neglect are

▶ *physical abuse,* the most obvious kind of abuse, involving acts that produce internal or external physical injuries, such as bruises, welts, cuts, fractures, and burns. Often intended as discipline or punishment, these may be inflicted by hand, fist, foot, or some object such as a strap, switch, or pipe. Internal and external injuries tend to form recognizable patterns, such as the *battered child syndrome.* Society's view of corporal punishment is changing, and some actions long accepted as harmless or useful are being sharply questioned as their full effects have come to be known. For example, violent shaking of a child was not previously thought to be dangerous but is now understood to produce a group of brain and neck injuries known as *whiplash-shaken child syndrome,* which can even be fatal in some infants. Sociopsychological effects include suppressed anger, DEPRESSION, apathy, lack of compassion, and low self-esteem, even self-hatred.

▶ *sexual abuse,* a more silent, hidden type of abuse, often unrecognized within families. The National Center on Child Abuse and Neglect (established by the 1974 act) defines these acts of a sexual nature as "contacts or interactions between a child and an adult when the child is being used for the sexual stimulation of the perpetrator or another person. Sexual abuse may also be committed by a person under the age of eighteen when that person is either significantly older than the victim or when the perpetrator is in a position of power or control over another child." The age of the child and the context are important here. Sex between consenting adolescents, even though under eighteen, may legally be considered statutory RAPE but in practice is today not viewed very seriously in legal or social terms. At the other extreme, the most reprehensible type of sexual abuse is adults sexually abusing young children, sometimes young boys but much more often young girls. Estimates of how many American women were sexually abused as children run as high as 20, or even 50, percent, half of them under age eleven.

Great fears have been raised about sexual abuse in CHILD CARE settings, given some highly publicized cases in recent years. Certainly child abuse does exist in many types of settings where young people are in the care of adults or older children, and parents will wish to be aware of the possible signs of abuse (see below). But the numbers involved are relatively small and can serve to direct attention away from the main area of concern. The overwhelming number of child sexual abuse cases takes place within the family and is labeled INCEST. Incest laws are more restrictive and generally apply only where SEXUAL INTERCOURSE (or MARRIAGE) has taken place, so familial sexual abuse is generally prosecuted under the broader child sexual abuse laws, which include genital touching, or is treated as statutory RAPE.

▶ *psychological and emotional abuse,* perhaps the most insidious and among the most deeply damaging kinds of abuse. This includes rejection, isolation, long-term verbal harassment, denigration, making unrealistic demands, and encouraging self-destructive behavior. Children subjected to such abuse generally have a negative self-image, a variety of behavioral problems, and often MENTAL DISORDERS.

▶ *physical neglect,* failure to provide food, clothing, shelter, hygiene, supervision, and other such necessities of life. Physical neglect, especially failure to provide enough food, is especially obvious in infants or small children, who often show a pattern of characteristics known as *failure to thrive.* But what constitutes physical neglect varies greatly from one locality to another and also depends on the age of the child, the nature of the arrangements made (if any) for emergencies, the length of time, and the time of day. A mother who leaves her infant with no food or supervision may be charged with neglect and in some cases with ABANDONMENT, which can lead to loss of PARENTS' RIGHTS. But the mother of a twelve-year-old latchkey child, who has established backup plans in case emergencies arise during the time between the end of school and the time she returns from work, is unlikely to be charged with physical neglect.

▶ *medical neglect,* failure to get a child medical or dental care for a condition that, if untreated, could cause death or serious damage. Generally this is intertwined with physical neglect. Charges of medical neglect alone are most often directed at parents whose religion, such as Christian Science, leads them to disavow treatment for themselves and their children, in cases of severe or life-threatening situations, where courts and social agencies believe that the parental responsibilities to provide essential medical care outweighs parents' rights to make decisions about medical care for their children, in general.

▶ *educational neglect,* failure to provide for a child's intellectual development, including regular school attendance or state-approved home schooling. Parents are legally responsible for seeing that their children attend school or for providing for their education in some other state-approved way. In some areas government agencies are experimenting with reduction or elimination of welfare payments for families of children who are regularly absent from school without a valid excuse.

▶ *moral neglect,* failure to teach basic social values, especially the principles of right and wrong. In practice this applies primarily to parents who encourage or knowingly allow their children to commit crimes, such as stealing, drug dealing, or PROSTITUTION.

▶ *psychological or emotional neglect,* failure to support a child's psychological and emotional growth and development. This is sometimes called failure of *nurturance,* or responsiveness to the child's needs, hopes, fears, and aspirations, and is the hardest of all to define or prove.

Overall, in the United States alone, in 1991, the National Committee for the Prevention of Child Abuse estimated that nearly 2.7 million children were reported for abuse or neglect, and that nearly 1,400 of them died; how many cases were unrecognized or unreported is unknown. According to data collected during the 1980s by the Children's Division of the American Humane Association (CD/AHA), about 40 percent of reports are generally found to be substantiated after investigation; though some of the others may have been false allegations or reports, most simply could not be substantiated—for example, because the family could not be located or inadequate information was available. Even in many unsubstantiated cases, the family receives some sort of services.

The CD/AHA figures for 1986 indicate that of substantiated cases, almost 55 percent involve neglect, over 16 percent sexual abuse, under 3 percent major physical injury, 25 percent minor or other physical injury, and 16 percent emotional or other maltreatment. (Figures total more than 100 percent, since more than one type of maltreatment could be found in a single case.) The average age of an abused or neglected child was seven years old, and over 53 percent were girls; the abuser's average age was thirty-one and in four out of five cases was a parent. Overall, the abuser was a woman in nearly 54 percent of the substantiated cases.

For many adult women, child abuse is a directly personal question. Millions of grown women alive today were abused as children. Their numbers are unknown because most such cases were unreported. This is especially true of sexual abuse. Many silently carried into adulthood the pain, unhappiness, and obscure feelings of their *own* guilt—the common childhood idea that they had somehow been responsible for their own sexual abuse. Many completely blocked out the experience. As has only recently been widely understood, many young girls repress the memory of incest as a coping mechanism, which allows them to survive the trauma; some recall it only years later, perhaps during therapy or when the memory is triggered by other events. As the question of child abuse has been brought out into the open, many more young girls may feel free to seek and get help—and often to bring their abusers to justice.

In the past, even when such cases have been reported, few were prosecuted successfully. Most states have a statute of limitations, whereby a woman can bring a civil suit only if she files suit within a few years after the end of the abuse or after she reaches the age of majority (usually eighteen), whichever comes later. Some groups, such as the **NOW LEGAL DEFENSE AND EDUCATION FUND,** are working in the courts and legislatures, seeking a change in that approach, to allow the statue of limitations to begin to run only when the victim *discovers* the abuse, in what is called a *delayed discovery* approach. Some states have already adopted such laws, so an adult woman should not automatically assume it is too late to bring a suit. And because state laws differ, she should consider in which state to bring a suit—for example, the state of current residence, the state of residence at the time of abuse, or other states in which abuse occurred, as during vacations. Child sexual abuse is also a criminal offense, but is rarely reported while it is occurring, also has a statute of limitations, and is difficult to prove in court, though court cases have had some notable successes against continuing abuse by people in institutions, such as churches or schools. Though at present many women abused as children have little or no legal redress, increasing numbers of them are now bringing their experiences into the open and receiving support from other victims, through mutual-support groups to help each other deal with childhood traumas (see CHILD ABUSE AND NEGLECT HELP, INFORMATION, AND ACTION GUIDE on page 152).

As mothers, many women are also concerned to protect their own young children from abuse, especially sexual abuse. Many of the same organizations also work to help parents and community workers be alert to signs of possible child abuse and to take steps to protect their children through education. They should be familiar with the kinds of injuries and warning signs that could alert them to possible abuse (see INDICATORS OF CHILD ABUSE AND NEGLECT on page 160). Children often do not report abuse because they have been frightened into silence, by threats to themselves or others dear to them, so adults should be watchful of any symptoms or changes in behavior that might be warning signs. One of the problems in cases regarding abuse of young children is the difficulty of obtaining evidence that is reliable enough to stand up in court; many young children are susceptible to suggestion, so jurors are unsure how much credence to give a young child's testimony.

Adult women and men who were abused as children are at risk for becoming abusers themselves. Health and social work professionals increasingly are trying to act preventively, intervening with help or counseling to relieve stress before a family's problems become too severe. Child abuse occurs in all kinds of families, of every racial, ethnic, and socioeconomic background. However, sociological research has shown that various kinds of *risk factors* increase the likelihood of child abuse within a family. In addition to previously abused parents, these factors include ALCOHOL AND DRUG ABUSE; MENTAL DISORDERS, mental retardation, or anomie (essentially, social disconnection) in a parent; failure of BONDING between mother and infant; the family's social isolation; unemployment or extreme stress and dissatisfaction in work; lack of child care; immature parents; parental ignorance of infant care and child development; a child who was unwanted or has physical or emotional disorders or health problems such as colic; strife and discord between the parents; and family disruptions, such as death, illness, or separation. If a child's health or welfare is threatened by the immediate situation, social workers may make crisis intervention. Women who have abused their children, or fear they may do so, should seek help from local community services or from the various child abuse organizations and mutual-support groups. These can help families try to break the cycle of child abuse and neglect by easing current stress and problems, by linking them with other families facing similar problems, and by teaching new methods of family interaction, including nonviolent ways of training and disciplining children.

Most countries today have laws against child abuse and neglect, but they differ widely in coverage and enforcement. In the United States, all states have laws requiring that child abuse and at least some forms of neglect be reported and filed in a *central register,* but they have different definitions of what is considered abuse, who should report it and when and how; and what actions should then be taken. There is the most agreement on physical abuse, sexual abuse, physical neglect, and educational neglect; there is much less uniformity on psychological and emotional abuse, medical neglect, moral neglect, and psychological or emotional neglect, all of which are harder to define and prove.

In most parts of the United States, reports of abuse—such as a neighbor's concerned call or a suspect hospital admission of a child—are turned over for investigation to a Suspected Child Abuse or Neglect (SCAN) team, often including at least a pediatrician, a social worker, and a psychiatrist or psychologist. If a report is not verified or confirmed, it is termed *unfounded* and is supposed to be cleared from the central registers, though in practice that is not always done. If reports are confirmed or verified, they are called *founded.* Procedures for handling a founded report vary widely, and the description below outlines an *ideal* situation, which assumes availability of social services and timely judicial and administrative decision making, both of which are often lacking in hard-pressed communities.

In general, the child is taken out of the situation; where the allegation of abuse or neglect is against a family member or guardian, this means out of the home and into protective or emergency CUSTODY, also called *detention.* Where crisis intervention services exist, the whole family may be taken to a twenty-four-hour residential family shelter, for short-term diagnosis and treatment. Within a day or two—again *ideally*—a government official, such as a social worker or probation officer, files a detention request, calling for a *detention hearing* in the next day or two, to decide whether the child should be kept away from the family until a full court has a chance to consider the case.

In the same few days, various government officials evaluate the situation and hold a *dispositional conference* to recommend what longer-term actions should be taken to protect the child and to provide treatment for the family, and to assess whether or not the court needs to be involved. If so, a juvenile or family law court will hold a *dispositional hearing* to decide whether the child should be returned to the home and, if so, under what conditions, or instead sent elsewhere, as to another relative's home, a foster family, or a group home. Where the situation is regarded as sufficiently dangerous or destructive, the dispositional conference may recommend that the state take temporary custody of the child, while both child and family receive counseling and therapy, the aim being ultimately to reunite the family.

The court considers such a recommendation during what is called a *dependency hearing*. Courts have long tended to keep the child in the home, regarding that as providing the most emotional stability and being overall in the best interests of the child. That court predilection continues, though social anger and concern about cases of death and severe injury of children returned to an abusive home have caused some courts to reconsider what *is*, in fact, in the child's best interests. Where such services are available, the court may order that the child and some or all family members be given day treatment services including psychological and social counseling, structured supervision, and specially designed activities. The aim is to break the cycle of abuse and begin to repair the damage, not only in the child but also in other family members; this is based on the understanding that many abusive parents were themselves once abused and need to learn new ways of carrying out their rights and responsibilities as parents. If such attempts ultimately fail, however, the state may seek termination of PARENTS' RIGHTS. In some cases, foster families may initiate such proceedings, where they wish to adopt a child in their care; in one notable 1992 Florida case, twelve-year-old Gregory Kingsley sued his mother for termination of parental rights, the first child to do so in his own name.

Child abuse and neglect seems like a virtual epidemic, at least since it is now much more widely reported. But it is also a very sensitive, subjective, and complicated area and unfortunately itself subject to abuse. Some parents have found themselves wrongly charged with child abuse and neglect, sometimes with malice, as by ex-spouses, but often by overzealous neighbors, health professionals, or social workers, some of whom may be well-meaning but confused or mistaken. Caregivers, teachers, and others in positions of responsibility with children may also be mistakenly charged with child abuse and neglect. Women who care for children or share CUSTODY of children with a vindictive ex-spouse should be careful to protect themselves against possible charges of child abuse and neglect (see VISITATION RIGHTS). Conversely, if a woman feels that someone has abused her child, she should be very sure of her facts, and seek counsel over how to proceed, before making any such allegations.

The National Center on Child Abuse and Neglect has recommended that people accused of such child abuse or neglect should have their legal rights protected, including the right to

- be informed of their legal rights.
- receive written notice and information on legal rights regarding protective custody.
- have counsel from an attorney during any court trial or administrative hearing.
- appeal a decision.
- have material in a child abuse and neglect report kept confidential.

In essence, the center is encouraging that the rights to *due process* provided in the Constitution be applied to such family law situations, including administrative hearings where they have seldom applied in the past. Women who have been charged with child abuse or neglect should be sure to seek legal counsel at all phases of the proceedings, to protect their rights as strongly as possible. At the center's recommendation, the child's interests are often represented separately at court by a court-appointed legal adviser, called a *guardian ad litem* (at law); the government's child protective services also generally have legal counsel. (See CHILD ABUSE AND NEGLECT HELP, INFORMATION, AND ACTION GUIDE below.)

CHILD ABUSE AND NEGLECT
Help, Information, and Action Guide

Organizations

🗹 GENERAL ORGANIZATIONS

▶ **National Center on Child Abuse and Neglect** (Children's Bureau/ Administration for Children, Youth and Families, U.S. Department of Health and Human Services, 330 C Street, SW, Washington, DC 20201; Mailing address: P.O. Box 1182, Washington, DC 20013; 202-205-8586; David Lloyd, director), an agency established under the federal 1974 Child Abuse Prevention and Treatment Act. It conducts research; gathers and disseminates national statistics, as through its National Child Abuse and Neglect Data System (NCANDS); provides technical assistance; funds pilot prevention, identification, and treatment projects, including parent self-help projects. Affiliated with it is the **Clearinghouse on Child Abuse and Neglect Information** (703-385-7565 or 800-394-3366), which provides information and publishes various materials.

▶ **Children's Division of the American Humane Association (CDAHA)** (63 Inverness Drive East, Englewood, CO 80112-5117; 303-792-9900 or 800-227-4645; Patricia Schene, director), an organization that seeks to prevent child abuse and neglect; formerly known as the **American Association for Protecting Children (AAPC)** of the AHA. It promotes stronger child protection services; offers training to community professionals; seeks to change public policy; and publishes various materials, including the quarterly *Protecting Children,* and books and pamphlets, for professionals and for the public, including the leaflet *Guidelines to Help Protect Abused and Neglected Children* and the booklet *Responding to Child Neglect and Abuse.* It operates the **National Resource Center on Child Abuse and Neglect (NRCCAN)** (800-227-5242), responding to requests from the public and the social welfare system for information on child abuse and neglect, distributing various fact sheets, and making referrals.

▶ **National Committee for Prevention of Child Abuse (NCPCA)**

(332 South Michigan Avenue, Suite 1600, Chicago, IL 60604; 312-663-3520; Anne Cohn Donnelly, executive director), an organization to educate the public and shape public policy regarding child abuse, sexual, physical, or emotional. It provides information and referrals; conducts child abuse prevention programs and media campaigns; and publishes various materials, including *A Future Filled with Healthy Minds and Bodies: A Call to Abolish Corporate Punishment in Schools.*

▶ **International Society for Prevention of Child Abuse and Neglect (ISPCAN)** (332 South Michigan Avenue, Suite 1600, Chicago, IL 60604; 312-663-3520; Richard Krugman, president), an organization concerned with preventing child neglect and abuse, especially sexual abuse. It holds international congresses and publishes the quarterly *International Journal: Child Abuse and Neglect.*

▶ CENTER FOR WOMEN POLICY STUDIES (**CWPS**) (202-872-1770). Has *Child Abuse Resource Collection.*

▶ NATIONAL CENTER FOR EDUCATION IN MATERNAL AND CHILD HEALTH (**NCEMCH**) (703-524-7802), and NATIONAL MATERNAL AND CHILD HEALTH CLEARINGHOUSE (**NMCHC**) (703-821-8955). Publishes *Child Sexual Abuse: Implications for Public Health Practice, Childhood Injury: State-by-State Mortality Facts, Data Book of Child and Adolescent Injury,* and *Surgeon General's Letter on Child Sexual Abuse.*

▶ NATIONAL COUNCIL ON CHILD ABUSE AND FAMILY VIOLENCE (**NCCAFV**) (202-429-6995 or Helpline 800-222-2000).

▶ NATIONAL COALITION AGAINST DOMESTIC VIOLENCE (**NCADV**) (303-839-1852).

▶ NATIONAL LEGAL RESOURCE CENTER FOR CHILD ADVOCACY AND PROTECTION (202-331-2200). Publishes *Sexual Abuse Allegations in Custody and Visitation Cases.*

▶ CHILD WELFARE LEAGUE OF AMERICA (**CWLA**) (202-639-2952).

▶ MS. FOUNDATION FOR WOMEN (**MFW**) (212-353-8580).

◪ **ON PREVENTION AND TREATMENT PROGRAMS**

▶ **Childhelp U.S.A., Inc. (CUI)** (6463 Independence Avenue, Woodland Hills, California 91370; 818-347-7280 or National Child Abuse Hotline 800-4-A-CHILD [422-4453]; Sue A. Meier), an organization founded in 1959 that focuses on prevention and treatment of child abuse. It operates two Village of Childhelp residential treatment centers; provides family services; sponsors research; and publishes various materials, including recommended reading lists and national statistics and a brochure on the CHILDHELP/IOF Foresters National Child Abuse Hotline.

▶ **Committee for Children (CFC)** (172 20th Avenue, Seattle, WA 98122; 206-322-5050; Karen Bachelader, executive director), an organization that seeks to educate the public about sexual abuse. It develops a curriculum for children K–12, seeking to prevent child abuse, and publishes various print and video materials, including *Prevention Notes, Talking About Touching, A Personal Safety Curriculum, Talking About Touching with Preschoolers,* and *Yes, You Can Say No.*

☑ ON PROGRAMS FOR ABUSE VICTIMS

▶ **Parents United** (c/o Institute for Community as Extended Family, 232 East Gish Road, 1st floor, San Jose, CA 95112; 408-453-7616; Henry Giaretto, executive director), a network of professionally guided mutual-support groups of people with experience of child molestation, including incest. It provides therapy for individuals or a whole family, as well as medical, legal, and vocational counseling. Affiliates include **Daughters and Sons United,** for sexually abused children (5–18) and their families, and **Adults Molested as Children United (AMACU),** for people over 18 who were abused as children.

▶ NATIONAL ORGANIZATION FOR VICTIM ASSISTANCE **(NOVA)** (202-232-6682). Publishes the *NOVA Newsletter* and the *Victim Service Program Directory.*

☑ FOR CHILD-ABUSING PARENTS

▶ **Parents Anonymous (PA)** (520 South LaFayette Park Place, Suite 316, Los Angeles, CA 90057; 213-410-9732 or 800-421-0353 or 800-775-1134 or call 800-555-1212 for the nearest group; Lisa Pion-Berlin, executive director), an organization started in 1970 for child-abusing adults, modeled on Alcoholics Anonymous, encouraging formation of "parent-led, professionally facilitated" free and confidential mutual-support groups for rehabilitation of parents, with groups also for children and other special groups, such as teen parents, minority parents, grandparents, and parents themselves sexually abused as children. It publishes a newsletter and other materials.

▶ **Sexaholics Anonymous** (P.O. Box 300, Simi Valley, CA 93062; 805-581-3343), a network of mutual-support groups, modeled on Alcoholics Anonymous, for people addicted to destructive or self-destructive sexual behavior, including incest. It publishes various materials, including a newsletter.

☑ FOR LEGAL ADVICE AND REFERRALS

▶ NOW LEGAL DEFENSE AND EDUCATION FUND **(NOW LDEF)** (212-925-6635). Publishes a statistical fact sheet on child sexual abuse and *Incest and Child Sexual Abuse Legal Resource Kit,* including a state-by-state list of helping organizations, case references, and legislative review, and a directory of attorneys for civil suits on incest and sexual abuse.

C

▶ NATIONAL CENTER ON WOMEN AND FAMILY LAW (**NCOWFL**) (212-674-8200). Publishes *Guide to Interstate Custody Disputes for Domestic Violence Advocates, Effects of Battery of the Mother on Children: Psychological and Legal Authority, Child Sexual Abuse,* and *Legal Issues and Legal Options in Civil Child Sexual Abuse Cases: Representing the Protective Parent.*
▶ NATIONAL LEGAL RESOURCE CENTER FOR CHILD ADVOCACY AND PROTECTION (202-331-2200).
▶ NATIONAL CENTER FOR YOUTH LAW (**NCYL**) (415-543-3307).

Other resources

▢ GENERAL WORKS ON CHILD ABUSE AND NEGLECT

Understanding Child Abuse and Neglect. 2nd ed. Cynthia C. Tower. Allyn, 1993.
Too Scared to Cry: Psychic Trauma in Childhood. Lenore Terr. Basic Books, 1992.
For Their Sake: Recognizing, Responding to and Reporting Child Abuse. For Kids Sake, Inc. Staff and Rebecca Cowan Johnson. American Camping Association, 1992. (Address: 5000 State Road, 647 North, Martinsville, IN 46151; 317-342-8456.)
Save the Family, Save the Child: What We Can Do to Help Children at Risk. Vincent J. Fontana and Valerie Moolman. NAL-Dutton, 1991.
Straight Talk About Child Abuse. Susan Mufson and Rachel Kranz. Facts on File, 1991. For teens.
Fine Line: When Discipline Becomes Child Abuse. David A. Sabatino. TAB/Human Services Institute, 1991.
Recognizing Child Abuse: A Guide for the Concerned. Douglas J. Besharov. Free Press/Macmillan, 1990.
The Abusing Family, rev. ed. Blair Justice and Rita Justice. Plenum, 1990.
Too Old to Cry: Abused Teens in Today's America. Robert J. Ackerman and Lee Marvin Joiner. TAB, 1990.
Violence and the Family. Gilda Berger. Watts, 1990. For teens.
Child Abuse. William A. Check. Chelsea House, 1989. For teens.
Spare the Rod: Breaking the Cycle of Child Abuse. Phil E. Quinn. Abingdon, 1988.

▢ GENERAL WORKS ON CHILD SEXUAL ABUSE

Helping Your Child Recover from Sexual Abuse. Caren Adams and Jennifer Fay. University of Washington Press, 1992.
Everything You Need to Know About Incest. Karen Spies. Rosen, 1992.
Stranger Danger. Priscilla Larson. Tyndale, 1991.

The Best-Kept Secret: Sexual Abuse of Children. Florence Rush. TAB, 1991.

Coping with Sexual Abuse, rev. ed. Judith Cooney. Rosen, 1991. For teens.

Sexual Assault and Child Sexual Abuse: A National Directory of Victim/ Survivor Services and Prevention Programs. Linda Webster, ed. Oryx, 1989.

When Your Child Has Been Molested: A Parents' Guide to Healing and Recovery. Kathryn Hagans and Joyce Case. Lexington, 1988.

The Mother's Book: How to Survive the Incest of Your Child. Carolyn Byerly. Kendall/Hunt, 1987.

Incest and Sexuality: A Guide to Understanding and Healing. W. Maltz and B. Holman. Lexington, 1987.

The Secret Trauma: Incest in the Lives of Girls and Women. Diana E. H. Russell. Basic Books, 1985.

Protect Your Child from Sexual Abuse. Janie Hart Rossi. Parenting Press, 1984.

◪ ON BREAKING THE ABUSE CYCLE

I'll Never Do to My Kids What My Parents Did to Me: A Guide to Conscious Parenting. Thomas Paris and Eileen Paris. Lowell House, 1992.

How to Avoid Your Parents' Mistakes When You Raise Your Children. Claudette Wassil-Grimm. Pocket, 1992.

Forgiving Our Parents, Forgiving Ourselves. David Stoop and James Masteller. Servant Publications, 1991.

◪ ON ADULTS ABUSED AS CHILDREN

Transcending Turmoil: Survivors of Dysfunctional Families. Donna F. La Mar. Plenum/Insight, 1992.

Reach for the Rainbow: Advanced Healing for Survivors of Sexual Abuse, rev. ed. Lynne D. Finney. Perigee, 1992.

Beyond the Darkness: Healing for Victims of Sexual Abuse. Cindy Kubetin and James Mallory, Jr. Word, 1992.

The Sexual Healing Journey: A Guide for Survivors of Sexual Abuse. Wendy Maltz. HarperCollins, 1991.

Breaking Down the Wall of Silence: The Liberating Experience of Facing the Painful Truth. Alice Miller. NAL-Dutton, 1991.

Breaking the Cycle: Survivors of Child Abuse and Neglect. Pamela Fong. Norton, 1991.

Allies in Healing: When the Person You Love Was Sexually Abused as a Child. Laura Davis. Harper, 1991.

Growing Through the Pain: The Incest Survivor's Companion. Anonymous. Prentice-Hall, 1990.

Soul Survivors: A New Beginning for Adults Abused as Children. J. Patrick Gannon. Prentice-Hall, 1990.

The Courage to Heal Workbook: For Women and Men Survivors of Child Sexual Abuse. Laura Davis. Perennial Library, 1990.

Adult Children of Abusive Parents: A Healing Program for Those Who Have Been Physically, Sexually, or Emotionally Abused. Steven Farmer. Ballantine, 1990.

Reclaiming the Heart: A Handbook of Help and Hope for Survivors of Incest. Mary Beth McLure. Warner, 1990.

Abused! A Guide to Recovery for Adult Survivors of Emotional/Physical Abuse. Dee Anna Parrish. Station Hill Press, 1990.

The Healing Way: Adult Recovery from Childhood Sexual Abuse. Kristin A. Kunzman. Hazelden, 1990.

Forgiveness: How to Make Peace with Your Past and Get On with Your Life. Sidney B. Simon and Suzanne Simon. Warner, 1990.

Strong at the Broken Places: Overcoming the Trauma of Childhood Abuse. Linda T. Sanford. Random House, 1990; Avon, 1992.

Reclaiming Our Lives: Adult Survivors of Incest. Carol Poston and Karen Lison. Little, Brown, 1989.

Secret Scars: A Guide for Survivors of Child Sexual Abuse. Cynthia Crosson Tower. Viking, 1988.

The Courage to Heal: A Guide for Women Survivors of Child Sexual Abuse. Ellen Bass and Laura Davis. Harper & Row/Perennial, 1987.

◪ PERSONAL STORIES

Daddy, Please Say You're Sorry. Amber. CompCare, 1992. A handwritten, self-illustrated book by a woman survivor of incest.

Dancing with Daddy: A Childhood Lost and a Life Regained. Betsey Petersen. Bantam, 1991.

Please, Somebody Love Me! Surviving Abuse and Becoming Whole. Jillian Ryan. Baker Book House, 1991.

Cry Hard and Swim: The Story of an Incest Survivor. Jacqueline Spring. Trafalgar Square, 1991.

Not My Child: A Mother Confronts Her Child's Sexual Abuse. Patricia Crowley. Doubleday, 1990; Avon, 1991.

Love Letters: Responding to Children in Pain. Doris Sanford and Graci Evans. Multnomah, 1991.

What Lisa Knew: The Truths and Lies of the Steinberg Case. Joyce Johnson. Putnam, 1990.

Nap Time: The True Story of Sexual Abuse at a Suburban Day Care Center. Lisa Manshel. Morrow, 1990.

Understanding Survivors of Abuse: Stories of Homeless and Runaway Adolescents. Jane Levine Powers and Barbara Weiss Jaklitsch. Lexington, 1989.

Kiss Daddy Goodnight: Ten Years Later. Louise Armstrong. Pocket Books, 1987. A follow-up to *Kiss Daddy Goodnight: A Speak-Out Book on Incest.* (1979).

I Never Told Anyone: A Collection of Writings by Survivors of Child Sexual Abuse. Ellen Bass and Louise Thornton, eds. Harper & Row, 1982.

◪ ON LEGAL QUESTIONS

Shifting the Burden of Truth: Suing Child Sexual Abusers—A Legal Guide for Survivors and Their Supporters. Joseph Crnich and Kimberly Crnich. Recollex Publishing, 1992.

On Trial: America's Courts and their Treatment of Sexually Abused Children. Billie Wright Dziech and Charles B. Schudson. Beacon, 1991.

Legal Aspects of Child Abuse. Elizabeth Butler-Sloss and A. E. Levy. Waterlow/Macmillan, 1991.

The Child Sexual Abuse Case in the Courtroom, 2nd ed. James Selkin. J. Selkin, 1991.

◪ BACKGROUND BOOKS

Interdisciplinary Perspectives in Child Abuse and Neglect. Faye F. Untalan and Crystal S. Mills, eds. Praeger/Greenwood, 1992.

The Kasper Hauser Syndrome of "Psychosocial Dwarfism": Deficient Statural, Intellectual, and Social Growth Induced by Child Abuse. John Money. Prometheus, 1992.

Spare the Child: The Religious Roots of Punishment and the Psychological Impact of Physical Abuse. Philip Greven. Random House, 1992.

The Assault on Truth: Freud's Suppression of the Seduction Theory. Jeffrey M. Masson. HarperCollins, 1992. Reprint of 1984 ed.

When a Child Kills: Abused Children Who Kill Their Parents. Paul A. Mones. Pocket, 1991.

With the Best of Intentions: The Child Sexual Abuse Prevention Movement. Jill D. Berrick and Neil Gilbert. Guilford, 1991.

The Effects of Child Abuse and Neglect: Issues and Research. Raymond H. Starr and David A. Wolfe, eds. Guilford, 1991.

Ritual Child Abuse: Discovery, Diagnosis, and Treatment. Pamela S. Hudson. R and E Publishers, 1991.

Man-Child: An Insight into Child Sexual Abuse by a Convicted Molester, with a Comprehensive Resource Guide. Howard Hunter. McFarland, 1991.

Slaughter of the Innocents: Child Abuse Through the Ages and Today. Sander J. Breiner. Plenum, 1990.

Soul Murder: The Effects of Childhood Abuse and Deprivation. Leonard Shengold. Yale University Press, 1989.

The Encyclopedia of Child Abuse. Robin E. Clark and Judith Freeman. Facts On File, 1989.

Triumph Over Darkness: Understanding and Healing the Trauma of Childhood Sexual Abuse. Leslie Hatton and Wendy Wood. Beyond Words, 1988.

The Battle of the Backlash: The Child Sexual Abuse War. David Hechler. Lexington, 1988.

Incest and Sexuality: A Guide to Understanding Healing. Wendy Maltz and Beverly Holman. Lexington, 1988.

Intimate Violence: The Definitive Study of the Causes and Consequences of Abuse in the American Family. Richard J. Gelles and Murray A. Straus. Simon & Schuster, 1988.

The Politics of Child Abuse. Paul Eberle and Shirley Eberle. Lyle Stuart, 1986.

The Kids Next Door: Sons and Daughters Who Kill Their Parents. Gregory Morris. Morrow, 1985.

(See also INCEST; RAPE; BATTERED WOMEN; CHILDREN'S RIGHTS; also VIOLENCE AGAINST WOMEN HELP, INFORMATION, AND ACTION GUIDE on page 612; COUPLES AND FAMILIES HELP, INFORMATION, AND ACTION GUIDE, page 418, under "On Problem Families," page 420.)

Indicators of Child Abuse and Neglect

Category	Child's appearance	Child's behavior	Caretakers's behavior
Physical abuse	Bruises and welts (on the face, lips, or mouth; in various stages of healing; on large areas of the torso, back, buttocks, or thighs; in unusual patterns, clustered, or reflective of the instrument used to inflict them; on several different surface areas) Burns (cigar or cigarette burns; glove- or socklike burns or doughnut-shaped burns on the buttocks or genitalia indicative of immersion in hot liquid; rope burns on the arms, legs, neck, or torso; patterned burns that show the shape of the item [iron, grill, etc.] used to inflict them) Fractures (skull, jaw, or nasal fractures; spiral fractures of the long [arm and leg] bones; fractures in various states of healing; multiple fractures; any fracture in a child under the age of two) Lacerations and abrasions (to the mouth, lips, gums, or eye; to the external genitalia) Human bite marks	Wary of physical contact with adults Apprehensive when other children cry Demonstrates extremes in behavior (e.g., extreme aggressiveness or withdrawal) Seems frightened of parents Reports injury by parents	Has history of abuse as a child Uses harsh discipline inappropriate to child's age, transgression, and condition Offers illogical, unconvincing, contradictory, or no explanations of child's injury Seems unconcerned about child Significantly misperceives child (e.g., sees him as bad, evil, a monster, etc.) Psychotic or psychopathic Misuses alcohol or other drugs Attempts to conceal child's injury or to protect identity of person responsible
Neglect	Consistently dirty, unwashed, hungry, or inappropriately dressed Without supervision for extended periods of time or when engaged in dangerous activities Constantly tired or listless Has unattended physical problems or lacks routine medical care Is exploited, overworked, or kept from attending school Has been abandoned	Is engaging in delinquent acts (e.g., vandalism, drinking, prostitution, drug use, etc.) Is begging or stealing food Rarely attends school	Misuses alcohol or other drugs Maintains chaotic home life Shows evidence of apathy or futility Is mentally ill or of diminished intelligence Has long-term chronic illnesses Has history of neglect as a child

Category	Child's appearance	Child's behavior	Caretakers's behavior
Sexual abuse	Has torn, stained, or bloody underclothing Experiences pain or itching in the genital area Has bruises or bleeding in external genitalia, vagina, or anal regions Has veneral disease Has swollen or red cervix, vulva, or perineum Has semen around mouth or genitalia or on clothing Is pregnant	Appears withdrawn or engages in fantasy or infantile behavior Has poor peer relationships Is unwilling to participate in physical activities In engaging in delinquent acts or runs away States he/she has been sexually assaulted by parent/caretaker	Extremely protective or jealous of child Encourages child to engage in prostitution or sexual acts in the presence of caretakers Has been sexually abused as a child Is experiencing marital difficulties Misuses alcohol or other drugs Is frequently absent from the home
Emotional maltreatment	Emotional maltreatment, often less tangible than other forms of child abuse and neglect, can be indicated by behaviors of the child and the caretaker.	Appears overly compliant, passive, undemanding Is extremely aggressive, demanding, or rageful Shows overly adoptive behaviors, either inappropriately adult (e.g., parents other children) or inappropriately infantile (e.g., rocks constantly, sucks thumb, is enuretic) Lags in physical, emotional, and intellectual development Attempts suicide	Blames or belittles child Is cold and rejecting Withholds love Treats siblings unequally Seems unconcerned about child's problems

Source: *Interdisciplinary Glossary on Child Abuse and Neglect: Legal, Medical, Social Work Terms* (1980). Prepared for the National Center on Child Abuse and Neglect, Childrens' Bureau, Administration of Children, Youth and Families, Department of Health and Human Services, by the Midwest Parent-Child Welfare Resource Center (now Region V Child Abuse and Neglect Resource Center).

C

childbirth, the birth of a baby, including not only the physical stages of LABOR and DELIVERY, but also the wider questions of the MOTHER's role, the FATHER's role, the setting, and the nature and function of the birth attendants.

For most of history, women had few choices in childbirth but simply followed the pattern in their society and culture. In most periods they were attended by women called *midwives,* who were generally experienced, having given birth themselves and attended at the births of others, but were not formally trained. In early centuries men (except for astrologers) were generally barred from labor and delivery rooms, and sometimes their presence was even a capital crime. But with the rise of modern science and technology in the seventeenth century—when university education was almost universally restricted to men— male doctors took over much of the obstetrical and gynecological care of women among affluent, well-educated populations. Better anatomical and physiological understanding, the development of tools such as forceps (see LABOR), and scientifically based training in delivery techniques helped save the lives of many women and babies. Poorer women the world over continued—indeed, still continue—to rely on midwives, who generally were denied access to training in newer techniques. But in the twentieth century, at least in developed countries, medical care came to be concentrated in hospitals. Use of ANESTHESIA, painkillers (*analgesics*), and forceps delivery had been widespread by the nineteenth century, and the twentieth century added newer techniques, such as fetal monitoring and vacuum extraction (see LABOR), and wider use of older techniques, including EPISIOTOMY and CESAREAN SECTION (in earlier centuries used primarily to save the child, when the mother seemed beyond hope, since such surgery then was almost always fatal). By the late twentieth century many women—and some men as well—had come to feel that childbirth had become too "medicalized"; that medical technology was being overused and invasive; that the hospital was too cold and impersonal; and that obstetricians (mostly male) had taken control of the birth process away from the woman herself. The result was the development of a whole range of alternatives for women giving birth.

Many of these alternatives form what is called the *natural childbirth* or *prepared childbirth* movement. In general, these approaches stress avoiding medical intervention in the birth process whenever possible and emphasize education for pregnant women and their birth partners—generally their husbands or sex partners, but sometimes a relative or friend. Childbirth classes focus especially on relaxation techniques for dealing with labor pains, through breathing EXERCISES that lessen tension in the body and other exercises to improve muscle tone and stamina in preparation for childbirth. These help women lessen or deal more rapidly with pain and lessen the need for anesthesia or analgesics. But more widely, the classes diminish tension, fear, and anxiety by teaching women and their partners about the anatomy and physiology of PREGNANCY and delivery; about PRENATAL CARE; about parenting skills; and about early choices that must be made, such as BREASTFEEDING vs. bottlefeeding, or circumcision (see PENIS).

Among the main natural childbirth approaches are

▶ *Lamaze method* or *Lamaze-Pavlov method,* which spurred the natural childbirth movement in the 1960s in the United States and today is the most widespread such approach. To ease consciousness of pain and keep oxygen flowing smoothly to the baby and the muscles of the UTERUS, pregnant women are trained to concentrate on a focal point so as to block out pain during labor. The birth partner acts as a coach, supporter, and occasional masseur. This approach, also called *psychoprophylaxis* or *psychophysical preparation for childbirth,* was developed by French physician Fernand Lemaze, based partly on Ivan Pavlov's work on conditioned reflexes. Several variations on this approach are taught, often in a series of weekly classes relatively late in pregnancy, attended by the pregnant woman and, if possible, her birth partner.

▶ **Read (Dick-Read) method,** developed in the 1930s by English obstetrician Grantly Dick-Read, who believed that what he called the *fear tension pain syndrome* was responsible for much of the pain of labor and delivery. To counter this, he established classes teaching special breathing patterns for different stages of labor as well as physical exercises and general education, stressing visualization of the internal stages of birth. It was Dick-Read who first brought men into the delivery room as birth partners and who coined the phrase *natural childbirth.* His was the first natural childbirth method popular in the United States, from the 1950s.

▶ **Bradley method,** also called **husband-coached childbirth,** which relies most heavily on the woman's husband or sex partner (or other birth partner) as coach, stressing the training of both partners, and encouraging deep abdominal breathing and relaxation techniques to use during labor. Developed in the 1940s by American obstetrician Robert Bradley, this method normally involves one class in the third or fourth month of pregnancy and the rest in the last trimester (three months).

▶ **LeBoyer method,** also called **birth without violence** or **gentle birth,** which seeks to minimize the trauma of birth for the baby, with delivery in a darkened, quiet room and with a minimum of interference, such as pulling on the baby's head. French obstetrician Frederick LeBoyer, who developed the approach around 1970, recommended that the newborn be placed on the mother's abdomen and massaged immediately after birth, to facilitate maternal-infant BONDING, and then gently washed by the father in warm water, resembling its previous environment of amniotic fluid; only then is the infant dried and wrapped.

As prepared childbirth approaches have become more popular, many of their principles have been adopted by hospitals, where most births still take place. But a related main set of choices for pregnant women and their partners concerns the choice of health care providers and birth sites.

In recent decades, the midwife movement has been revived in many affluent countries. Midwives today are generally specially trained and often state-certified registered nurses, in the United States called *certified nurse–midwives* (CNMs). Working originally in maternity centers (see below) or attending at home births, these modern midwives are now often found in clinics, health maintenance organizations (HMOs), public health departments, and hospitals as well. From inner cities to rural areas—especially where money and medical practitioners are scarce, but also where women are turning away from "high-tech" pregnancy and childbirth—they bear increasing responsibility for educating women about pregnancy and childbirth; providing basic prenatal care; counseling on such related matters as NUTRITION and EXERCISE; and giving afterbirth instruction on self-care and infant care, including breastfeeding and bottlefeeding. CNMs deal only with normal pregnancies, however; high-risk pregnancies (see below) are referred to a physician early in the pregnancy, often an obstetrician, but in special cases a *fetal and maternal specialist.* If unanticipated problems or complications develop during childbirth, either a doctor is brought in or the woman is transported to a hospital for emergency care.

In the United States, some nurse-midwives practice independently, but their ability to do so depends very much on state regulations and the attitude of the community, including the physicians. Many states require that CNMs make provisions for backup medical care in case of problems, but when physicians and hospitals refuse to serve as backups, they may be unable to practice—or their backup hospitals may be so far away as to jeopardize the health of mother and baby in case of an emergency during delivery. Mothers who wish to have a CNM attend their delivery should carefully inquire into backup arrangements; sometimes mothers must arrange for their own transport to the hospital in emergencies. Certified nurse–midwife services are covered by most public and private insurance plans. However, fees of traditional uncertified *lay midwives*—who still work in many parts of the world—generally are not.

Maternity centers, sometimes called *alternative birthing centers* or just *birthing centers,* developed in recent decades as alternatives to hospitals. Often staffed by certified nurse–midwives, these are free-standing institutions where a woman gives birth. In general, maternity centers have a more relaxed, personal atmosphere, with birth taking place in a relatively homelike environment. Not only are birth partners welcome to attend the birth (which they are not in all hospitals), but sometimes other family members are as well. Again this alternative is for low-risk, normal pregnancies, and the main hazards are the loss of time getting to a hospital for emergency care, if complications arise, and the possibility of infection, since the setting cannot (of necessity) be as germ-free as a hospital's delivery room.

Responding to popular demand, many hospitals are meeting these concerns by establishing birthing centers with a homelike atmosphere but attached to the hospital. Others have done away with the traditional separation between the labor room and delivery room, offering a single *labor/delivery room* or even a combined *labor/delivery/recovery room,* so the mother is not disturbed by being shunted from one room to another during labor. Some maternity centers and hospitals offer homelike *birthing rooms,* with amenities such as stereos and rocking chairs. Pregnant women and their birth partners should carefully examine the possible options available to them and what restrictions, if any, the hospital places on birth partners' activities.

Even more traditional is *home birth,* in which the baby is delivered at home, generally under the care of a midwife. The twin hazards—risk of infection and loss of time in emergency—are even greater here. Women and their partners considering home birth should be especially careful about prenatal care and checkups, to spot any complications early and make certain of backup emergency care.

The above alternatives are for women with normal pregnancies, with no indications of any complications and no particular risk factors in their life situation that would make complications likely. Most women between the ages of twenty and thirty-five will have normal pregnancies. And, in fact, with proper prenatal care, most women who have so-called *high-risk pregnancies* also bear healthy, full-term babies without damage or hazard to their own health or their babies'. But various risk factors indicate that they are somewhat more likely than normal to have difficulty during pregnancy or childbirth, including an increased risk of BIRTH DEFECTS, and that prenatal care should be especially alert to possible complications. Among the most common risk factors are adolescent pregnancy; the mother being over thirty-five years old; a pregnancy before a woman's body has fully recovered from the previous one; the use of BIRTH CONTROL PILLS or devices, including INTRAUTERINE DEVICES (IUDs) and SPERMICIDES, at the time of CONCEPTION; multiple births; incompatibility of BLOOD type between mother and child (*Rh incompatibility*); DES daughters (whose mothers took the medication *diethylstilbestrol*); a previous premature baby (see GESTATION); or various diseases or disorders that can affect development of the FETUS or leave the mother herself in poorer medical condition, including DIABETES, HERPES, and other SEXUALLY TRANSMITTED DISEASES (STDs), hypertension or heart problems (see HEART AND CIRCULATORY SYSTEM), LUPUS, MULTIPLE SCLEROSIS, epilepsy, hepatitis, asthma (see ALLERGIES; RESPIRATORY SYSTEM), and thrombocytopenia (see BLOOD).

For women with such risk factors, or with known complications, such as abnormal FETAL PRESENTATION or diagnosed birth defects or other health problems in the baby, a different set of choices exists. They must decide, with the help of their obstetrician or fetal and maternal specialist which level of hospital care is wisest for them. Normal, low-risk pregnancies are generally handled by Level I hospitals, also called *primary-care facilities,* including many community hospitals, which are oriented toward basic care and handling of routine medical emergencies. Most appropriate for pregnant women with risk factors are Level II and III hospitals.

Level II hospitals, called *secondary-care facilities,* serve larger areas and populations, have more sophisticated medical equipment and laboratory facilities, and sometimes include a *neonatal intensive care unit* (NICU) for newborns with health problems. Level II hospitals serve normal or moderate-risk pregnancies, but women with known complications or high risk are referred to a Level III hospital, or *tertiary-care facility.* These have the most sophisticated facilities for diagnosis and treatment, the most extensive support systems, and the most highly specialized staff, often associated with university research and training facilities, called *university-affiliated facilities* (UAFs). These are best equipped to handle any pregnancy and childbirth complications.

For normal or high-risk pregnancies alike, women who choose to give birth in a hospital will want to explore the institution's policies on such matters as administration of enemas, fetal monitoring, episiotomies, intravenous supplements, and birth partners—especially who will be allowed to attend the birth and who will not and what training, if any, is required of birth partners.

Pregnant women have yet one more set of options: childbirth position. Whether in a home or hospital, giving birth in bed, with the woman lying on her back, has been the standard mode only for the last few centuries. In hospital births the woman is often in the *dorsal lithotomy* position used in a pelvic examination (see GYNECOLOGICAL EXAMINATION), with the legs spread wide apart and the feet in stirrups. This allows for easiest visibility and examination. However, some critics are concerned that the position places the baby's weight over the key vein, the *vena cava* (see HEART AND CIRCULATORY SYSTEM), and so may allow less oxygen through to the baby between contractions; there is also a concern that the position may strain the perineum and make EPISIOTOMY more necessary. Some recommend what is known as the *Sims position* or *left lateral position,* in which the woman lies on her left side during labor, especially when labor pains are strong in the lower back.

Going back at least to biblical times, before the bed came in fashion, a *birthing chair* was used; this was a high-backed chair with a hole or semicircular cut in the seat, which allowed gravity to aid in the delivery. The birthing chair has been revived by some people in recent years and has inspired a newer approach, a reclining bed with a bottom that drops down for the actual delivery. Some people have also experimented with having a woman give birth in a tub of warm water, an environment that will approximate that of the amniotic fluid the baby has been swimming in.

Pregnant women and their birth partners will want to learn more about these various choices so they can decide which best suits their needs, desires, and inclinations, understanding that any risk factors will limit the choices. (See also LABOR; PREGNANCY; CESAREAN SECTION; also PREGNANCY AND CHILDBIRTH HELP, INFORMATION, AND ACTION GUIDE on page 580.)

child care, supervision and nurturing of infants and young children by people other than their parents. Because MOTHERS are traditionally and still in most families the prime caregiver, the provision of child care is a major concern for women who wish to be free for other activities, such as to pursue a career for its professional rewards, or increasingly to provide all or part of a FAMILY's basic financial support. In decades past, when most married women were HOMEMAKERS, staying home to care for their young children, child care concerns were primarily questions of finding a baby-sitter, neighbor, or relative to come in for a few hours. But for today's working mothers and especially SINGLE PARENTS, child care is a much different concern and normally mounts up to more than forty hours a week. Even where the caregiver is not working full-time, child care is necessary to enable the mother to take advantage of various kinds of programs that are not now usually geared to the needs of women with young children, such as ALCOHOL AND DRUG ABUSE programs or training programs designed to upgrade job skills. Many working single mothers have, in fact, been obliged to go on welfare because they have no available, affordable, reliable child care. As a result, child care has become a major social concern.

In some European countries, notably France and Scandinavian countries, the government has recognized and tried to meet the need for child care by providing a nationwide network of child care centers. In most other countries, certainly the United States, child care is a haphazard, patchwork affair. Some employers offer on-site child care, either full-time and permanent, or emergency and temporary, designed only to fill in when a parent's usual arrangements have fallen through; those who provide such services find them a significant asset to attracting and retaining skilled employees. In addition, some communities have local provisions for child care, sometimes privately run and for-profit but often run in and by churches, community centers, and schools. Indeed, when comparing prospective employers or selecting areas in which to live, many couples include in their assessment the availability of child care.

Where it is possible and affordable, many parents prefer to have children cared for in their own home. A highly paid, professional parent often hires a woman as a *nanny* to care for the child full-time, sometimes coming in by the day, sometimes living with the family; many of these are young women from abroad, called *au pairs*. The difficulty of finding in-home caregivers was highlighted in early 1993, when President Bill Clinton's original nominee for U.S. attorney general, Zoë Baird, was forced to withdraw after acknowledging that she had used an undocumented Peruvian woman to care for her child. In some cases women who would not be able to afford a full-time nanny may have a relative, such as a grandmother, come into the home to care for the child.

One major alternative is child care is someone else's home, with five or six children, in what is called *family day care*. The main advantages of this are that children receive individual attention in a homelike setting, that hours can be more flexible (though sometimes less so), and that it is generally less expensive than either a nanny or a more formal child care center. The main disadvantage is that emergency alternatives will be necessary if the main caregiver or someone in her family is ill. Such family day care centers are sometimes run by experienced older women in their own homes but are also attractive to many young mothers, allowing them to be with their own young children and still have an income and occupation.

The other common alternative is to place the child in a separate child care center, which provides care for larger groups of young children. One advantage is that such centers have backup staff, so if one person is sick, others will still be there to provide care. Traditionally centers have been open for more limited hours, but some are providing longer, more flexible hours for working parents who need child care nights and evenings. Another main concern is with personnel, since parents cannot know and personally evaluate the reliability of the people who will provide the primary care. Though no one can guarantee safety, parents are advised to seek licensed child care centers, where possible, since that indicates that the center at least meets basic minimum standards.

In the United States, about half of all preschool-age children are cared for in their own homes, by family members or hired caregivers, a figure down from over three-quarters in the 1960s. About one-quarter are in family day care settings as described and one-quarter in child care centers. Whatever the options, parents will generally have to plan months ahead for child care arrangements, since waiting lists are common in many areas. Local friends and relatives, and community agencies, can be good sources of information about individual child care providers, family day care, or child care centers. Many centers charge a sliding fee, depending on the family income. Parents can sometimes get income tax credits—federal or state—for child care expenses; they should check with their accountant or the taxing agencies for current information.

In evaluating child care, inside or outside the home, parents will want to be sure that the caregiver has compatible views in such matters as providing stimulation, helping develop skills, providing discipline, maintaining discipline, toilet training, and the like. In addition, they will want to be sure that the caregiver is healthy and able to care for children, that he or she has taken first-aid and cardiopulmonary resuscitation (CPR) courses (advised today for parents themselves, as well) and has first-aid supplies available, and that telephone and emergency procedures are in place. Parents will want to feel comfortable with the caregiver and be sure that the child will be treated with loving care.

A major concern, whatever the type of child care, is CHILD ABUSE AND NE-GLECT. Parents should be alert to any unusual accidents or injuries, or changes in the child's behavior, especially a child's unusual discomfort, fear, or upset in the caregiver's presence, apart from any normal anxiety a child feels on separation from a parent or in the presence of a stranger (see INDICATORS OF CHILD ABUSE AND NEGLECT on page 160.) Parents should learn how long a facility has been in operation and how long specific caregivers have been on the staff. They will want to choose a place where they are welcome to visit at any time, even unexpectedly, and where caregivers and children alike seem to be happy and alert.

Parents should be sure that the home or center to which they bring a child is safe, clear, well aired, and sufficiently roomy for the number of children; that the center has a sufficient number of people to care for the children—at least one person for every four to five babies, though fewer for older children—at all times of the day; that the children have age-appropriate toys to play with; that regular snacks and meals will be provided; that the center provides regular reports on the children; and that the center reports any accidents involving the child or diseases in the child's group.

Most important of all, parents should check the references of any child care workers, in or out of the home, by actually talking with parents whose children have been cared for by the individual or center being considered. Once they have made a child care decision, they should not change lightly, since each such disruption can be major in a young child's life. But they should be alert to signs of problems between child and caregiver, understanding that infants and young children are often unable to communicate that a problem exists, and make a change where that is appropriate. (See CAREGIVER'S HELP, INFORMATION, AND ACTION GUIDE on page 454.)

children's rights, a developing area of the law. In general, the law labels a minor child an *infant* with little or no independent legal status, apart from receiving basic INHERITANCE RIGHTS at birth; a child traditionally has had no ability to make a contract, consent to medical treatment, or make a will, for example. But as family law matters increasingly come before courts, with concerns that involve children, the courts have gradually been recognizing certain rights. In the United States, since 1967 children have been entitled to *due process of the law* guaranteed by the Constitution, which includes the rights to hear charges against them, to not incriminate themselves (including the right to remain silent), to have an attorney (court-appointed, if necessary), and to confront and cross-examine witnesses.

Though traditionally barred as witnesses at court, children today be called in cases involving them, such as CUSTODY, VISITATION RIGHTS, CHILD ABUSE AND NEGLECT, and possible termination of PARENTS' RIGHTS. Generally a judge will evaluate the child's maturity, ability to recall and communicate, and understanding of principles such as right and wrong, truth or falsity. Increasingly courts are appointing an attorney or a specially trained volunteer called a *court-appointed special advocate* (CASA) or a *guardian ad litem* (at law), to represent the interests of the child, which may differ from those of the parents, especially in an acrimonious dispute or where the court is taking into account the child's views on questions such as custody or child abuse and neglect.

Though traditionally barred from suing or being sued, except where an adult acted as a guardian or "next friend," children today can sometimes act in their own names. In a landmark 1992 Florida case, twelve-year-old Gregory Kingsley was the first child to sue in his own name (successfully) for termination of parents' rights, so he could be adopted by his foster parents.

In addition, with the much increased sexual activity of adolescents, many teenage girls have been faced with an unplanned, generally unwanted PREGNANCY and the possibility of having an ABORTION. In these cases the traditional parents' rights to make medical decisions regarding their children (see PARENTS' RIGHTS) come into conflict with the girl's REPRODUCTIVE RIGHTS. Some abortion laws require a girl to obtain a parent's consent, or a judge's, before having an abortion. With the increasing rate of adolescent pregnancy, many young women who choose to bear a child rather than have an abortion may become MOTHERS while they are still legally children themselves.

More generally, children have a widely accepted right—though not a legally guaranteed one—to a relatively stable home and adequate care (see PARENTS' RIGHTS) and are expected to accept reasonable supervision by their parents. They have a right to expect to be supported by their parents until they reach the *age of maturity,* usually eighteen, or unless they become *emancipated,* as by supporting themselves and supervising their own conduct, or as by marrying.

Young women seeking the aid of the court system should contact some of the women's organizations listed in this book under the particular topics that concern them, such as ABORTION or CHILD ABUSE AND NEGLECT.

For more help, information, and action

▶ **National Court Appointed Special Advocates Association (National CASA Association, or NCASAA)** (2722 Eastlake Avenue, East, Suite 220, Seattle, WA 98102; 206-328-8588; Beth Waid, executive director), an organization for specially trained court appointed special advocates (CASAs). It provides training seminars and other assistance to local groups and publishes various materials, including the quarterlies *CASA Connection* and *Feedback,* the semiannual directory, and *NCASAA Communications Manual.*

▶ NATIONAL LEGAL RESOURCE CENTER FOR CHILD ADVOCACY AND PROTECTION
(202-331-2200).

Other resources

Children, Rights, and the Law. Philip Alston and others, eds. Oxford University
Press, 1992.
As a Child: Safeguarding Children's Rights. Elizabeth D. Shetina. Rourke, 1992.
In Their Best Interest? The Case Against Equal Rights for Children. Laura M. Purdy.
Cornell University Press, 1992.
*Who Speaks for the Children? The Handbook of Individual and Class Child Advo-
cacy.* Jack C. Westman, ed. Pro Resource, 1991.
Rights of Children. D. D. Rawstron, ed. State Mutual Books, 1989.

▨ BACKGROUND WORKS

Human Rights for Children. Amnesty International, Human Rights for Children
Committee Staff. Hunger House, 1992.
*Children's Rights: Crisis and Challenge: A Global Report on the Situation of Chil-
dren in View of the U.N. Convention on the Rights of the Child.* Dennis Nurkse
and Kay Castelle, eds. DCI USA, 1990.
In the Spirit of Peace: A Global Introduction to Children's Rights. Dennis Nurkse
and Kay Castelle. DCI USA, 1990.
Advocating for the Child in Protection Proceedings: A Guide for Child Advocates.
Donald N. Duquette. Free Press, 1990.
(See also CHILD ABUSE AND NEGLECT HELP, INFORMATION, AND ACTION GUIDE on
page 152; ABORTION HELP, INFORMATION, AND ACTION GUIDE on page 10.)

Children's Rights Council (CRC) (220 I Street, NE, Suite 230, Washington, DC 20002; 202-223-6227 or 800-787-KIDS [5437]; David L. Levy, president), an organization seeking more equitable DIVORCE, CUSTODY, and CHILD
SUPPORT arrangements, especially joint custody, enforcement of VISITATION RIGHTS,
and MEDIATION; formerly **National Council for Children's Rights (NCCR)**. It
gathers and disseminates information, as through various publications, including
the newsletter *Speak Out for Children.*

child support, money that parents must pay for the care of their child, to
cover expenses for such things as food, clothing, shelter, medicine, education,
and insurance; part of the responsibilities associated with PARENTS' RIGHTS.
Whether the child's parents are married or unmarried (see COHABITATION), the legal MOTHER and FATHER both have support obligations. The support obligation
extends at least until the child reaches legal adulthood, often age eighteen, or becomes formally emancipated (see CHILDREN'S RIGHTS), though in practice most
parents continue to support their children through college and sometimes beyond, especially if the child is disabled or incapacitated. Before then, child sup-

port obligations end only if parental rights are terminated, as they would be if the child is given up for ADOPTION and might be in cases of ABANDONMENT.

Most parents take child support for granted, as part of family support. It generally becomes an issue only in cases of SEPARATION or DIVORCE—but there it has become a major thorn in the side of broken families and society as a whole. There are two main aspects to the problem: the amount of child support awarded and the amount actually paid.

Where separating or divorcing parents can agree between themselves (usually with advice from lawyers) how much child support is reasonable, the court will generally accept their decision as part of their SEPARATION AGREEMENT. To some extent, child support hinges on who has CUSTODY of the child. In most cases—90 percent in the United States—the mother gets custody and the father is asked to pay child support; the reverse is rarer. Joint custody is becoming increasingly common, but one substantial problem for women is that child support payments are often much lower in joint custody, on the assumption that the child will spend much time with the father. However, that fails to take into account the cost to the woman of maintaining full-time quarters for the child. And, in practice, the woman often ends up with full-time custody anyway—and less money to cover expenses. Sometimes fathers use joint custody only as a ploy to lower support payments.

Women must be very aware of such potential pitfalls during separation negotiations, to try to ensure that they will have sufficient child support payments. In this, strong legal advice is vital. They should also get advice as to the best proportions of ALIMONY (if any) and child support payments. They must pay taxes on alimony they receive, but not on child support payments; on the other hand, fathers can deduct alimony from their income tax, but not child support. (The same applies in those cases where the woman is the partner making alimony or child support payments.) Women should also remember that alimony is often, these days, relatively short-term, lasting perhaps only two to three years, where it is awarded at all; child support lasts until the child is eighteen, but then also stops.

Where parents cannot agree on what is proper child support, the court will decide. The parent who is ordered to pay child support, generally the father, is called the *obligated* or *responsible parent*. Court child support orders have traditionally varied widely, based on vague notions of each spouse's ability to earn and ability to pay. The 1984 Child Support Enforcement Act encouraged the formation of state guidelines on what is a fair amount of child support. But, in fact, the guidelines have been ill defined and open to quite different ideas about what is fair and feasible. The court ruling on child support is crucial because, once made, it is rarely changed, except in special circumstances, such as a sharp decrease in a parent's income or when a child's health problems require expensive medical care. It is extremely important for women to have advice from an attorney experienced in representing women in such situations.

One peculiar recent twist has been that low child support payments can later lead to loss of custody. As courts have come to view custody as "sex neutral," they have given more weight to other issues, especially to a parent's financial ability. So, later on, perhaps when a father remarries and sues to gain custody of the child, some courts have been awarding it, since the mother has less income and so is a poorer "provider"—ignoring the fact that the two would be more equal if the child support payments were increased. And, in a classic Catch-22, when the woman works outside the home to provide for herself and her family, the court often regards her as a "less fit" parent, when the father has remarried; in such cases the court's assumption (correctly or incorrectly) is often that the new stepmother will be available as HOMEMAKER.

Sometimes reopening of custody suits is, in fact, triggered by women's attempts to get promised child support payments. And that is the other major problem relating to child support: much of it never gets paid. In the United States, over 41 percent of all mothers with custody receive *no* support from the children's father; and of those who do receive support, only about half receive the full amount. Some fathers, even when they are able to pay, also end support when the child is eighteen, leaving children feeling—not surprisingly—abandoned, though most fathers continue to provide support for a child's further education. Nonpayment stretches across all education and socioeconomic brackets and is not linked to either the amount of child support granted or to the father's ability to pay. Well over a third of these families therefore exist below the poverty level, and many depend on government assistance.

Various federal and state programs have been put into place to try to ease the strain on custodial mothers and to get noncustodial fathers to pay their proper share of child support. In 1975, under Title IV-D of the SOCIAL SECURITY Act, the federal government established the Office of Child Support Enforcement (OCSE), which works through regional and state OCSE agencies to find the delinquent parent, often using its PARENT LOCATOR SERVICE (PLS). The 1984 Child Support Enforcement Amendments to this act went beyond this first step to give women—through the OCSE—ways of collecting support, once the delinquent parent was found. These include

- withholding child support payments automatically from paychecks.
- withholding tax refunds to pay overdue child support, called *arrears.*
- requiring that the delinquent parent post bonds or securities to guarantee payment.
- government seizure of property, or *sequestration,* for sale to cover arrears.
- reporting delinquent parents to credit agencies, when amounts are over $1,000.

Like the comparable act regarding custody, the Uniform Reciprocal Enforcement of Support Act (URESA) and its revised form (RURESA) provide for enforcement of child support payments when the obligated parent lives in a different state from that of the custodial parent and children. If the father ignores court orders to pay, he is held in contempt of court and can be sent to jail, though that is, in fact, rarely done.

Where custodial women and their children are receiving government assistance under the AID TO FAMILIES WITH DEPENDENT CHILDREN program, the state will institute a search for the delinquent parent, to obtain reimbursement for that aid. The law requires women receiving aid to cooperate in the state's search. If the delinquent parent is located, the custodial parent will be asked to sign an *assignment of support rights,* so that support payments and arrears are paid to the state, in exchange for AFDC grants and other benefits. If the absent parent is an unwed father, the state will ask the father to sign a *consent agreement* acknowledging the child and his support responsibilities. If he refuses, the state may institute a paternity suit to establish his support obligations (see FATHER). (See DIVORCE AND SEPARATION HELP, INFORMATION, AND ACTION GUIDE on page 238.)

Child Welfare League of America (CWLA) (440 First Street, NW, Washington, DC 20001; 202-639-2952; David S. Liederman, executive director), an organization established in 1920 that seeks to raise the level of care for dependent children, especially those deprived, abused, or neglected; provides information and referrals, as to adoption agencies. CWLA is actually a "federation of over 650 public and voluntary child welfare agencies, community-based and regionally organized, who work with children and their families on critical issues such as child abuse, adolescent pregnancy, adoption, out-of-home care, child day care, and homelessness." Among its current special initiatives are child protection, family foster and kinship care, group care for children, multicultural sensitivity, and HIV infection and AIDS. CWLA's **Center for Program Excellence** offers a training institute and a wide range of program services.

CWLA's **Institute for the Advancement of Child Welfare Practice** does research; sets child welfare standards; acts as accrediting body for child welfare services; maintains a library and information service; facilitates exchange of innovative program ideas; provides peer and field consultation; and seeks to shape public policy. Its **Florence Crittenton Division** (Jean Tucker Mann, program director; same phone and address) was formed after CWLA's 1976 merger with the Florence Crittenton Association (founded in 1883) and is a national adolescent pregnancy service, which also focuses more widely on adolescent sexuality and self-esteem, youth EMPOWERMENT, substance abuse, and male adolescent parents. CWLA also publishes newsletters, a scholarly professional journal, and numerous books and reports, as well as training videos, workbooks, and curricula.

chin augmentation, a type of COSMETIC SURGERY.

chlamydia, infection with the bacteria *Chlamydia trachomatis;* a type of SEXUALLY TRANSMITTED DISEASE (**STD**). Chlamydial infection is probably the most common STD, with three to four million new cases annually in the United States alone. It is spread by vaginal or anal sexual contact between adults (see SEXUAL INTERCOURSE) or by a mother to her baby during CHILDBIRTH. Like many other STDs, early symptoms are nonexistent or mild and often mistaken for other illnesses, so chlamydia is sometimes called the "silent STD." Symptoms affect only one of every two infected women and one of every four men. Women may have pain during urination, vaginal discharge, or abdominal pain; men commonly have a discharge of mucus or pus from the PENIS, pain during urination, and pain and swelling around the scrotum, reflecting *epididymitis,* inflammation of the epididymis, part of the male REPRODUCTIVE SYSTEM. Both sexes may also have inflammation of the rectum (*proctitis*) or the lining of the EYE (*conjunctivitis*). The bacteria may also affect the throat, and some strains cause *lymphogranuloma venerium (LGV)*, involving swelling and inflammation of the lymph nodes of the groin (see IMMUNE SYSTEM).

Though often silent, chlamydia can cause serious complications. Among them is PELVIC INFLAMMATORY DISEASE (**PID**), which is a major cause of INFERTILITY and potentially life-threatening ECTOPIC PREGNANCY. A baby infected with chlamydia during delivery may develop health problems such as conjunctivitis or pneumonia; because of that, testing for chlamydia is routinely recommended as part of PRENATAL CARE for pregnant women.

Chlamydia is often confused with GONORRHEA, and the two infections frequently occur together. It can be diagnosed through various laboratory tests and treated with various antibiotics, though penicillin is not effective against it. Both partners need to be treated, to prevent reinfection and spread of the disease. Patients generally return to the doctor or clinic one to two weeks after finishing a course of medication to be sure the infection has been cleared up. Use of CONDOMS and DIAPHRAGMS can help prevent the disease from spreading. (See SEXUALLY TRANSMITTED DISEASES; also WHAT YOU CAN DO TO AVOID STDs on page 660; SEXUALLY TRANSMITTED DISEASES HELP, INFORMATION, AND ACTION GUIDE on page 658.)

CHOICES: Clearinghouse on Implementation of Child Care and Eldercare Services, an arm of the WOMEN'S BUREAU.

chorionic villus sampling (CVS or chorion biopsy), a relatively

new type of PRENATAL TEST used to identify GENETIC DISORDERS, CHROMOSOMAL ABNORMALITIES, and some other types of BIRTH DEFECTS. As with AMNIOCENTESIS, a needle is inserted into the pregnant women's abdomen, the physician being guided by ULTRASOUND; but here what is withdrawn is not amniotic fluid but a sample of tissue from the *chorion*, the outer membrane of the PLACENTA; alternatively, a flexible tube, also guided by ultrasound, may be inserted through the women's VAGINA for the tissue sample. More specifically, the procedure seeks cells from fingerlike projections called *villi* on the chorion; since these cells are identical with those of the FETUS, they can be examined for the presence of various genetic disorders.

Chorionic villus sampling can be done earlier than amniocentesis, at ten to twelve weeks instead of fourteen to sixteen weeks, and results can be derived more quickly—normally in just a few days, rather than ten or more. That is a distinct advantage, when a woman is contemplating a possible ABORTION if birth defects are found. However, fewer genetic disorders can be identified through CVS. Also, because the procedure is relatively new, its long-term effects on the fetus are not fully known, though it seems to carry a somewhat higher risk of MISCARRIAGE and other complications. Research suggests that CVS may be linked with increased risk of limb or facial abnormalities in the fetus. As a result, the

FOOD AND DRUG ADMINISTRATION recommended in late 1992 that the test be done only after ten weeks, not as early as eight weeks, and required that women be given warning of the risks.

Side effects include abdominal aches and cramps. CVS, like amniocentesis, is used primarily for women who are over thirty-five or have a personal or family medical history suggesting risk of abnormalities. (See PRENATAL TEST; also GENETIC INHERITANCE AND BIRTH DEFECTS HELP, INFORMATION, AND ACTION GUIDE on page 314.)

chromosomal abnormalities, any type of GENETIC DISORDER that results from errors in the duplication of the chromosomes that carry an individual's GENETIC INHERITANCE. Humans normally have twenty-three pairs of chromosomes: one pair of sex chromosomes (with two X chromosomes for a female and an X and a Y chromosome for a male) and twenty-two pairs of other chromosomes, called *autosomes.* In the sperm and egg (OVUM) that form a new individual, chromosomes divide, join together, and duplicate themselves (see GENETIC INHERITANCE). Sometimes this complicated process goes awry, and pieces get detached or attached in the wrong places (*translocation*), or there will be too many chromosomes or too few. The result is that vital genetic information is not available to the new being or is somehow scrambled.

Many chromosomal abnormalities are so serious that the FETUS is unable to develop, and the pregnancy is aborted spontaneously, in what is called a MISCARRIAGE, though it sometimes occurs so early that a woman is not even aware that she is pregnant. Other chromosomal abnormalities may cause the death of a child just before or shortly after birth (see STILLBIRTH), while others allow the child to survive but have serious effects on health and development.

A normally lethal condition called *polyploidy* results when a child possesses one or more extra full sets of chromosomes. However, some children with three chromosomes instead of two, a condition called *trisomy,* are able to survive, sometimes depending on precisely which chromosome is a triplet. The most common trisomy involves a triplet for chromosome 21, or *trisomy 21;* this condition is better known as **DOWN'S SYNDROME.** Other trisomies are rarer, including Patau's syndrome (trisomy 13), and Edwards' syndrome (trisomy 18). Some rare syndromes result when all or part of a chromosome is deleted; one example is the *cri du chat* syndrome, so-called because the baby's cry is like the "cry of a cat." Some special syndromes result when the abnormalities occur in the sex chromosomes, including TURNER'S SYNDROME, in which a girl has only one X chromosome, and Klinefelter's syndrome, in which a boy has one or more extra X chromosomes.

Some other chromosomal abnormalities have only slight effects on health and development and may even go undetected, though they will be passed on to the next generation. Chromosomal abnormalities are increasingly common as prospective parents get older, especially when the woman is over thirty. Because of that, many people without a personal or family history of GENETIC DISORDERS may have GENETIC COUNSELING and various PRENATAL TESTS to alert them to any potential chromosomal abnormalities that might affect the health and develop-

ment of a child. (See GENETIC INHERITANCE AND BIRTH DEFECTS HELP, INFORMA-
TION, AND ACTION GUIDE on page 314.)

chronic fatigue immune dysfunction syndrome (CFIDS), a
newly discovered debilitating, but not life-threatening, disease of still-unknown
origin. CFIDS—pronounced *"SEE-fids"*—is so recently recognized and so hard to
diagnose that it goes by several other names, including *chronic fatigue syndrome*
(*CFS*, the name still used by government agencies), *chronic mononucleosis, myalic
encephalomyelitis* (in Britain and Canada), *low natural killer cell syndrome* (in Japan), and *chronic Epstein-Barr virus* (*CEBV*), though many researchers now believe that Epstein-Barr infection *follows,* rather than triggers, onset of the disease.
Though newly recognized as a disease, CFIDS may have been around for over
one hundred years, under different names such as *neurasthenia* and *Iceland disease.*
    Symptoms include severe fatigue and persistent flulike symptoms—most
commonly low-grade fever, sore throat, swollen and painful lymph glands, weak
and painful muscles, joint pain, headaches of a previously unknown type or severity, abdominal cramps, and a variety of neurological symptoms, such as
numbness and tingling in various parts of the body, dizziness, disorientation, seizures, memory loss, DEPRESSION, sleep disturbance, vision problems, and inability
to concentrate. A person is considered to have CFIDS if such symptoms last for
over six months and reduce a person's ability to function by 50 percent or more.
In the United States alone, estimates of the number of people affected range from
two to five million. CFIDS affects more women than men, by an estimated ratio
of three to two, and more adults than children, and is believed to leave perhaps
one-third totally bedridden, one-third disabled but able partly to care for themselves at home, and one-third functional but with major adjustments in activity
level and life-style. Symptoms often come on quite suddenly, though they can appear gradually and sometimes go into remission for a time, but whether the disease is progressive or degenerative in the long term is as yet unknown. Some
researchers suggest that people with CFIDS may be at greater risk of developing
disorders such as CANCER and MULTIPLE SCLEROSIS, and for committing suicide,
with depression also regarded as an effect, not a cause.
    The pattern of transmission—with clusters of cases in families and
communities—suggests that the cause is viral; however, the fact that many people
in close contact with CFIDS patients do *not* develop the illness suggests that an
individual's susceptibility depends on genetic predisposition (especially immune
system disorders, such as ALLERGIES), environmental poisons, level of exposure,
and perhaps other as-yet-unknown factors. (Though it also affects the immune
system, early research indicates that CFIDS is *not* spread the way AIDS is, nor is
it life-threatening.) Medical research suggests that it somehow causes the IMMUNE
SYSTEM to overreact to some bodily threats, remaining in a permanently activated
state, and producing the adverse symptoms experienced; another theory is that
the triggering virus hides in the brain and so resists detection. Other research indicates that people with CFIDS have deficiencies in HORMONES in the endocrine
system.

The disorder is hard to diagnose and is often mistaken for other disorders, such as AIDS, multiple sclerosis, LUPUS, Lyme disease, fibromyalgia, various MENTAL DISORDERS, or the effects of MENOPAUSE. Indeed, many patients have been told the problem was all "in their head." The disorder was, early on, trivialized with the name "yuppie disease," perhaps partly because young professionals were best able to pay for the enormous medical costs of seeing doctor after doctor in search of a diagnosis. In fact, the disease cuts across all races, ethnic backgrounds, and income groups. No test exists, nor is there as yet any cure, though CFIDS responds to some extent to antiviral drugs. (See CHRONIC FATIGUE IMMUNE DYSFUNCTION SYNDROME HELP, INFORMATION, AND ACTION GUIDE, below.)

CHRONIC FATIGUE IMMUNE DYSFUNCTION SYNDROME
Help, Information, and Action Guide

Organizations

▸ **Chronic Fatigue Syndrome Line** (404-332-4555), a service offering taped messages, from the Centers for Disease Control.
▸ **CFIDS Association** (P.O. Box 220398, Charlotte, NC 28222; 704-362-CFID [2343] or CFIDS 800-44-CFIDS [442-3437]; Marc Iverson, president), an organization concerned with CFIDS. It funds research; gathers and disseminates information; makes referrals; and publishes *The CFIDS Chronicle* and video- and audiocassette tapes. It also operates the **CFIDS Information Line,** 900-988-2343 (charges $2 for the first minute, $1 for each additional minute).
▸ NATIONAL INSTITUTE OF ALLERGY AND INFECTIOUS DISEASES (**NIAID**) 301-496-5717.

Other references

Chronic Fatigue Syndrome. David M. Dawson and Thomas D. Sabin, eds. Little, Brown, 1993.
Chronic Fatigue Syndrome: How and Where to Find Facts and Get Help. Pamela Jacobs. R & E Pubishers, 1992.
Fifty Things You Should Know About Chronic Fatigue Syndrome. Neenyah Ostrom. That New Mag, 1992.
Chronic Fatigue Syndrome and the Yeast Connection: A Get-Well Guide for People with this Often Misunderstood Illness and Those Who Care for Them. William C. Crook. Professional Books Future Health, 1992.

Running on Empty: Chronic Fatigue Immune Dysfunction Syndrome. Katrina Berne. Hunter House, 1992.

Solving the Puzzle of Chronic Fatigue Syndrome. Murray Susser and Michael Rosenbaum. Life Sciences Press, 1992.

Living with Chronic Fatigue: New Strategies for Coping with and Conquering CFS. Susan Conant. Taylor, 1990.

Hope and Help for Chronic Fatigue Syndrome: The Official Book of the CPS-CFIDS Network. Karyn Feiden. Prentice-Hall, 1990.

Chronic Fatigue Syndrome: A Natural Healing Guide. Steve Wilkinson. Sterling, 1990.

Chronic Fatigue Syndrome: A Victim's Guide to Understanding, Treating and Coping with This Debilitating Disease. Gregg Fisher and others. Warner, 1989.

The Chronic Fatigue Story: Medical Cover-Up of the Century. Neenyah Ostrom. That New Mag, 1989.

Chronic Fatigue Syndrome: The Hidden Epidemic. Jesse Stoff. Random House, 1988.

CFIDS: The Disease of a Thousand Names. David Bell. Available from: Pollard Publications, P.O. Box 180, Lyndonville, NY 14098; 716-765-2060. Dr. Bell is one of the doctors who recognized an initial outbreak of CFIDS in Incline Village, Nevada, near Lake Tahoe, in 1984.

(See also IMMUNE SYSTEM.)

Church and the Second Sex, The: See Mary DALY.

Church Women United (CWU) (Ecumenical Development Office, 475 Riverside Drive, New York, NY 10115; 212-870-2347; Pat Rumer, general director), a "national, ecumenical movement that brings Protestant, Roman Catholic, Orthodox, and other Christian women into one community of prayer, advocacy, and service," working for "global justice and peace" and "committed to the empowerment of women," with special focus on alleviating poverty. CWU publishes the magazine *Churchwoman*, the quarterly newsletter *UN Update*, action alerts on national legislation affecting women and children, and various study materials and audiovisual resources.

circumcision, removal of the FORESKIN, the partly retractable hood of SKIN covering a sexual organ, in a man the PENIS, in a woman the CLITORIS. The term is also used to refer to genital mutilation of girls (see FEMALE CIRCUMCISION).

City of Akron v. *Akron Center for Reproductive Health*, a 1983 U.S. Supreme Court decision that struck down a law requiring a twenty-four-hour wait before an ABORTION, because the statue asserted "the unborn child is a human life from the moment of conception."

Civil Rights Act of 1964, Title VII: See TITLE VII OF THE CIVIL RIGHTS ACT OF 1964.

Clearinghouse on Women's Issues (CWI) (P.O. Box 70603, Friendship Heights, MD 20813; 301-871-6016 or 202-363-9795; Elaine L. Newman, president), an organization established in the early 1970s "by a diverse group of women's organizations to provide a channel for dissemination of information on a variety of issues of mutual concern to all women." These include equality in the workplace, equal legal rights, advancement of educational opportunities for women, status of the HOMEMAKER, problems of older women, elimination of prejudice and discrimination in all areas of society, women and health, protection of human and civil rights, special concern with problems of low-income women, and a national and world plan of action. CWI takes no action or position but only gathers and provides information, through educational materials, public discussion forums, and its nine-times-a-year newsletter, and makes referrals.

climacteric, the period of years preceding MENOPAUSE, when a woman's body begins to undergo various changes that will result in the end of her reproductive capability. The climacteric generally begins in a woman's early forties but can start as early as her mid-thirties, and usually lasts ten to fifteen years. During these years, HORMONE levels decline gradually and then sharply; the OVARIES gradually stop producing, maturing, and releasing eggs (see OVUM; ANOVULATORY PERIODS); and menstrual periods become more irregular and lighter, with periods sometimes being skipped and finally ceasing altogether (see MENSTRUATION).

clitoridectomy, surgical removal of the CLITORIS, sometimes in cases of CANCER (see VULVA); also a form of FEMALE CIRCUMCISION.

clitoris, a small organ in a woman's external GENITALS, lying in the upper part of the VULVA; the main organ of sexual pleasure in women. The clitoris is a button of tissue—the same sort of tissue as forms a man's PENIS—richly supplied with blood vessels and nerve endings and thus extremely sensitive to the touch, especially at the tip. When stimulated, it fills with blood and become erect, though still being less than an inch long. The SKIN covering the clitoris is a moist mucous membrane, and the structure itself is protected by a partly retractable hood, called a *foreskin* or *prepuce*, formed by the meeting of the small inner "lips" of the vulva, the LABIA *minora*. The clitoris is also somewhat protected by the pubic bone and its associated fatty tissue, called the MONS VENERIS, or mound of Venus, which lies above it.

Direct stimulation of the clitoris, as by hand or tongue, brings sexual pleasure, sometimes leading to the climactic sensations known as an ORGASM; so can indirect stimulation, as during vaginal SEXUAL INTERCOURSE. Over the centuries, people in some cultures have disliked or feared the idea of a "good" woman having an orgasm or, indeed, any sexual pleasure; thus the clitoris has been the subject of some particular attacks.

Most seriously, some cultures adopted the practice of surgically removing part or all of the clitoris in an operation called a *clitoridectomy;* some have gone further to remove associated parts of the VULVA and seal up the LABIA. These practices, which go under the general name of FEMALE CIRCUMCISION, stretch back at least to the time of the pharaohs in Egypt and continue today in parts of Africa and western Asia, primarily in Arab-Muslim and Black countries, affecting an estimated 85 million women even as recently as the mid-1980s, despite years of international protests over the barbarity and health dangers of the practice.

Clitoridectomies were also performed in Western countries in the nineteenth century and at least into the 1930s, as a treatment for MASTURBATION and "nymphomania" in women. Even after such operations generally ceased to be performed, except in cases of CANCER of the VULVA, many physicians and sex experts made much of the supposed differences between a clitoral orgasm—that is, one involving direct stimulation of the clitoris—and a vaginal orgasm, involving indirect stimulation. The clitoral orgasm was widely dubbed "immature" and the vaginal orgasm the "proper" kind for adult women, an argument that caused many women considerable anguish but has somewhat died away in more recent decades as men and women have become more comfortable with and open to a multiplicity of sexual activities and responses. (See ORGASM; VULVA.)

cohabitation, living together in the same home. In general usage this usually means a couple sharing living quarters without being married—a woman and a man or a couple of the same sex. Legally known as *cohabitants,* the partners may be never married, separated, divorced, widowed, or even married to other people, in which case their situation is legally termed *adulterous cohabitation.*

In the law, cohabitation does not *necessarily* mean that a cohabiting couple has a sexual relationship. However, in some cases the court will often presume a sexual relationship, whether or not one exists. If a woman is seeking a DIVORCE on the grounds of ABANDONMENT, she may have to testify that she and her husband have not cohabited for a specified period of time. A woman who is living unmarried with a man may be at a disadvantage in a case involving CUSTODY or ALIMONY and in some cases can lose either or both.

Unmarried partners also face legal difficulties. As late as 1977, in a classic case that went before the Supreme Court, a couple were fired from their library jobs for living together. In later cases several state courts have upheld the rights of people to live together, though as late as 1979 a woman living unmarried with a man had to go all the way to the Virginia Supreme Court to get the right to become an attorney. Unmarried partners may also have trouble getting credit, even though court rulings have said that discrimination on the basis of marital status, including unmarried status, is illegal.

Unlike common-law marriage, where a couple live together as wife and husband even without a formal WEDDING ceremony, in cohabitation the partners do not intend to be married—more precisely, they intend to be *not* married. Many states no longer recognize common-law marriage, but some do (see COMMON-LAW MARRIAGE). Couples who are cohabiting in a state that *does* and who do not wish to be recognized as married should sign an agreement to that effect and should also be careful to retain their separate last names and keep their property separate, including credit, bank accounts, car ownership, and the like (see *The Living Together Kit* on page 420).

Historically society has frowned on cohabitation as being outside the established social and legal structures and not providing for legitimacy of children. That view still holds in many traditional societies, especially those that retain a cult of VIRGINITY. Even in many Western countries, cohabitation is illegal in many places, including (as late as 1990) Arizona, Florida, Michigan, New Mexico, North Carolina, and Virginia, and an extremely negative view of it is written into many laws still on the books. Some laws in this area have been voided in recent years on the basis of the right to privacy, but others still stand.

But in Western societies, since the revolution of sexual mores that started in the 1960s, large numbers of heterosexual couples have chosen to live together "without benefit of clergy." The arrangement became so widespread that the U.S. Census Bureau developed a new category to count it, called Persons of Opposite Sex Sharing Living Quarters (POSSLQ). The 1960 census count found 439,000 unwed couples living together, and that figure jumped to 2,856,000 in 1990 (even this figure was felt to be far too low, since it did not include the many couples where one partner had an "official" residence elsewhere, as in a dormitory or separate apartment). In 1990 over half of these cohabiting couples were under thirty-five years old; also, over half—56 percent—had never been married, while 34 percent had been divorced. (See ADULTS IN UNMARRIED-COUPLE HOUSEHOLDS, BY AGE, SEX, AND MARITAL STATUS: 1990 on page 184.) In 1960 approximately 30 percent of all cohabiting couples had homes that included children, a proportion that declined over the next three decades. (See UNMARRIED-COUPLE HOUSEHOLDS, BY PRESENCE OF CHILDREN: 1960–1990 on page 185.)

Many couples live together on a trial basis, in relationships that may last several years, often because one or both are not ready to make the more serious, longer-term commitment to MARRIAGE. Indeed, these days many couples live together for several years and marry only later, often when they decide they want to have children. In Sweden an estimated 99 percent of all married couples lived together for a time before marriage. Whether couples who live together before marriage have a higher or lower divorce rate in the long run than other couples is a matter of some dispute among researchers.

Some couples live together unmarried for financial reasons. Under United States tax codes, where both partners are working, their taxes will be lower than what they would pay if they were married; the difference is sometimes called the *marriage tax* or *marriage penalty*. In some cases one or both partners might lose benefits of various kinds if they were married, including ALIMONY, welfare benefits, food stamps, Medicare, and the like. Another financial consideration, especially where one or both of the partners is elderly or disabled, is that neither will become legally liable for the other's health and nursing home care if both remain unmarried.

Some couples—especially partners without children—choose to remain unmarried to be free of legal entanglements and state involvement in their private lives. However, that freedom can often be an illusion—or can at least cost far more than anyone anticipated—because it means that the partners individually and together lack *protection* from the law. If one partner becomes so ill as to be unable to make medical and other basic care decisions, the other will have no legal right to do so; under law, those decisions would have to be made by the nearest legally recognized relative (see CUSTODY) or someone appointed by a court. Similarly, if the couple should split up, or if one of them should die, the standard rules applied by law to cases of SEPARATION, DIVORCE, and inheritance (see INHERITANCE RIGHTS) would not be applied; so the partners have no legal assurance of equitable division of MARITAL PROPERTY and no recourse in court if one partner—or a late partner's surviving relatives—take more than their share. The couple may not (depending on the state and the court) be able successfully to sue for loss of *consortium*—loss of company, cooperation, affection, and sexual companionship—if one partner is injured in an accident, as a married couple could (see MARRIAGE). Also a major concern is that Social Security, health insurance, pensions, and other benefits generally do not cover partners except in legally recognized marriage. These are all concerns not just of heterosexual couples, but of same-sex couples, LESBIANS or gay men, for in the same decades many homosexuals began to cohabitate openly.

To provide for some such eventualities, but on their own terms, many unmarried couples—heterosexual or homosexual—draw up legal documents of their own, laying out their wishes in regard to key concerns such as handling of income and expenses, property ownership, insurance, CHILD CARE, custody, inheritance, and HOUSEWORK and more generally the role of each partner in the management of daily life. These documents are often called *living together agreements* or *relationship contracts*. (If the couple later decides to marry, most states will disregard this agreement and simply apply the state's marriage and divorce laws, as appropriate; however, some states allow partners to convert a living together agreement into a PRENUPTIAL AGREEMENT, if they wish.) Many couples include a *conflict resolution clause* or *mediation and arbitration clause*, outlining how they will attempt to solve disputes, if they occur, without going to court (see MEDIATION; ARBITRATION). In many cases each partner will give the other a *durable power of attorney* or similar document that will allow them to make decisions in specified situations, such as when one is injured and in a coma, but within specified limitations. The partners should also draw up and maintain separate property lists, not only to avoid disputes in case of a split, but also to avoid being caught up in the other's financial concerns, including bankruptcy. The agreement might also cover whether the partners will make loans to each other and how these would be handled. Note that if either partner has children from a prior marriage, and would like to ensure that in case of death the other partner will be able to raise the children, this must be put in the form of a will, since custody provisions of living together contracts are traditionally not legally enforceable. All such agreements should be drawn up only after consultation with a lawyer, to be sure they meet the legal situation in the couple's state of residence.

Failure to draw up living together arrangements has led to some lengthy, often very nasty court cases, especially when a couple has cohabited for a number of years and a substantial amount of money is involved.

One landmark 1973 California case involved a couple who, though not formally married, had lived together as husband and wife for eight years, with him supporting the family and her bearing four children; all records showed the wife and children with the husband's last name, including deed to the house, mortgage, and joint tax returns all showing them as man and wife. When the couple split, the man claimed all the property for himself because California does not recognize common-law marriages; if the couple had been legally married, the wife would have been entitled to half the property, under California's community-property laws. The court eventually ruled that the husband could not take everything, because the man had accepted the woman's unpaid efforts for the family.

In another California case, actor Lee Marvin and singer Michelle Triola had lived together for six years. Triola claimed that the two had agreed to combine and share equally their efforts and earnings, but that she had given up her career as singer, working as his companion, housekeeper, and cook, while Marvin had agreed to support her financially. When he left her she sued for half of his earnings during that period. The courts had historically ruled that payment in such situations would amount to PROSTITUTION. In this case, however, the court awarded Triola $104,000 for her "rehabilitation" and transition to a separate, independent life. It was this case that gave rise to the popular term *palimony* for payments to a former cohabitation partner, establishing that contracts between people living together unmarried were no longer illegal, except where the contract is explicitly based on sexual services by one partner. Many states now follow this approach, though some still regard contracts between cohabiting partners as "immoral," and some require proof of an oral contract, which is difficult to provide. The Marvin case also involved the principle of *unjust enrichment,* in which he benefited from Triola's labor and efforts in the relationship and so should compensate her. Some other states, though not as many, have also adopted this principle in compensating partners in unmarried relationships.

In some states, a person who has been deceived into thinking that a legal marriage exists when in fact it does not—as in a case of BIGAMY—may also receive some protection under the law, under the *putative spouse doctrine.*

A few places, mostly metropolitan cities, allow unmarried couples to register as *domestic partners.* This allows them to share various benefits, such as health insurance coverage for city employees, the right to visit each other in public hospitals, and bereavement leave for city employees. Some states regard such registration as an implied contract to share property; if that is not what the partners wish, except for day-to-day expenses, they will need to specify that in a separate agreement. (See also COUPLES AND FAMILIES HELP, INFORMATION, AND ACTION GUIDE on page 418; also DIVORCE AND SEPARATION HELP, INFORMATION, AND ACTION GUIDE on page 238.)

ADULTS IN UNMARRIED-COUPLE HOUSEHOLDS, BY AGE, SEX, AND MARITAL STATUS: 1990

(Numbers in thousands)

Male partner	Total	Female partner				
		Under 25 years	25-34 years	35-44 years	45-64 years	65 years and over
Total..............	2,856	788	1,170	494	320	83
Under 25 years	530	381	141	8	3	-
25 to 34 years	1,189	333	726	113	15	3
35 to 44 years	618	55	236	270	55	2
45 to 64 years	390	19	54	100	195	24
65 years and over.....	129	4	13	4	55	54
Percent	100.0	27.6	41.0	17.3	11.2	2.9
Under 25 years	18.6	13.3	4.9	0.3	0.1	-
25 to 34 years	41.6	11.7	25.4	4.0	0.5	0.1
35 to 44 years	21.6	1.9	8.3	9.5	1.9	0.1
45 to 64 years	13.7	0.7	1.9	3.5	6.8	0.8
65 years and over.....	4.5	0.1	0.5	0.1	1.9	1.9

Male partner	Total	Never married	Married		Widowed	Divorced
			Separated	Other		
Total..............	2,856	1,595	149	8	142	963
Never married	1,584	1,178	62	3	30	311
Married: Separated.....	184	70	43	-	18	55
Other	20	7	-	3	1	8
Widowed	95	27	1	2	34	32
Divorced	973	285	44	-	60	555
Percent	100.0	55.8	5.2	0.3	5.0	33.7
Never married	55.5	41.2	2.2	0.1	1.1	10.9
Married: Separated.....	6.4	2.5	1.5	-	0.6	1.9
Other	0.7	0.2	-	0.1	-	0.3
Widowed	3.3	0.9	-	0.1	1.2	1.1
Divorced	34.1	10.0	1.5	-	2.1	19.4

Represents zero.

Source: U.S. Bureau of the Census, Current Population Reports, Series P-20, No. 450. *Marital Status and Living Arrangements: March 1990.* U.S. Government Printing Office, 1991.

UNMARRIED-COUPLE HOUSEHOLDS, BY PRESENCE OF CHILDREN: 1960-1990

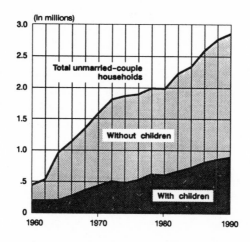

Source: U.S. Bureau of the Census, Current Population Reports, Series P-20, No. 450. *Marital Status and Living Arrangements: March 1990.* U.S. Government Printing Office, 1991.

collusion, agreement to deceive, as when a married couple "rigs" evidence to obtain a DIVORCE.

Commission for Women (CW), Evangelical Lutheran Church in America (ELCA) (8765 West Higgins Road, Chicago, IL 60631-4191; 312-380-2860; Joanne Chadwick, executive director), an organization to help the Evangelical Lutheran "church to realize the full participation of women, to address sexism, and to advocate justice for women in this church and in society." Among its other activities are to "identify and build community among women of all cultures and to encourage the full acceptance of the gifts of African American, Asian, Hispanic, and Native American women;" to advocate legislative reforms affecting women; to make the church a "safe place" for all who are vulnerable to harassment, abuse, or violence; and to identify women and skills and experience to act as resources, in addition to ELCA clergywomen. CO/ELCA publishes various materials, including *Call the Laborers: A Congregational Resource on Women and Ordained Ministry, If You Have Been Sexually Abused or Harassed . . . A Guide to Getting Effective Help in the ECLA, Twenty Years After the Ordination of Women: Reports on the Participation of Ordained Women, A Cloud of Witnesses* (on Lutheran women's history), and bibliographies on the ordination of women, inclusive language, and sexual abuse and sexual harassment.

Commission for Women's Equality (CWE) (c/o American Jewish Congress, Stephen Wise Congress House, 15 East 84th Street, New York, NY 10028; 212-879-4500; Hanita Blumfield, director), an organization that seeks to "end sex-biased discrimination and address the feminist issues of the 1990s in a Jewish context." Areas of special concern include political empowerment, women's health issues, especially REPRODUCTIVE RIGHTS, BREAST CANCER, and fetal tissue research; women and the media, women and work, domestic violence, and religious-feminist issues. Working through task forces, discussions, direct actions, and coalitions, the commission seeks to "ensure that women are present and their perspectives and experiences are heard and considered in all areas of secular and Jewish life." CWE publishes the *International Directory of Jewish Feminists.*

common-law marriage, a form of MARRIAGE in which a woman and a man live together as wife and husband for a period of time (such as seven or ten years) specified by law, without going through a formal WEDDING ceremony or exchange of vows. It is not enough for a couple to live together, they must also put themselves forward to the world as married—for example, by calling themselves "Mr. and Mrs." Historically, common-law marriages were widespread, but they are found far less often today, even though the number of unmarried couples living together has grown enormously (see COHABITATION). This is because many countries no longer recognize common-law marriages, though in the United States some states still do. In general, if a marriage is recognized as valid by the couple's state of residence, it is recognized in other states; for example, if a couple has a legally recognized common-law marriage in Ohio, the marriage would be recognized in California, even though the common-law marriage could not be established in California. (See MARRIAGE; COHABITATION; also COUPLES AND FAMILIES HELP, INFORMATION, AND ACTION GUIDE on page 418.)

Compassionate Friends, The (TCF) (P.O. Box 3696, Oak Brook, IL 60522; 708-990-0010; Susan Salisbury-Richards, executive director), a network of nondenominational mutual-support groups for parents who have lost a child, of whatever age or cause of death. It offers counsel and support for survivors, including siblings, often through "telephone friends"; and publishes a newsletter and other materials.

conception, an alternative term for FERTILIZATION, the union between a SPERM and an egg (OVUM) to form a new individual. Conception is a broader term, in this context often referring to the man and woman's efforts to conceive, rather than simply the biological sperm-egg union. In cases of INFERTILITY, various kinds of techniques can be used to help a couple conceive, such as ARTIFICIAL INSEMINATION or IN VITRO FERTILIZATION. Conversely, a wide variety of methods are used to avoid conception; these go under the general name of BIRTH CONTROL, *contraception*, or *family planning*. (See FERTILIZATION; INFERTILITY; BIRTH CONTROL.)

concubine, a woman who is legally recognized as living with a man but whose rights are inferior to those of a wife; a status encountered historically and in some modern cultures, often as part of a system of POLYGAMY. The concubine is, in fact, a greatly disadvantaged wife, easily cast aside. (See MARRIAGE.)

condom, a thin, stretchable sheath that acts a physical barrier; a form of BIRTH CONTROL with many other names, including *prophylactic, rubber,* and *safe.* The term generally refers to a condom worn by males; the so-called *female condom* is more precisely called a VAGINAL POUCH.

In the traditional form of condom, the sheath is placed over the man's PE-NIS as soon as it is erect—for full protection, before it touches any part of his partner's body. During SEXUAL INTERCOURSE, the condom prevents the penis and the SPERM released during EJACULATION from making direct contact with the woman's VAGINA and any egg (OVUM) that might be available for FERTILIZATION. Condoms are made of various materials, generally either rubber or natural material, such as lamb intestines; some have SPERMICIDE added to them. As a contraceptive, the condom has an effectiveness that varies from 64 to 97 percent, according to the FOOD AND DRUG ADMINISTRATION. Various studies have shown that condoms fail, through tearing or slippage, 1–12 percent of the time.

The condom also offers some protection against SEXUALLY TRANSMITTED DIS-EASES (STDs), including AIDS and HERPES, since it largely prevents either partner from coming into direct contact with blood or fluids from the other. The protection is not 100 percent—the only truly safe sex is *no* sex—but condoms offer *safer* sex. For that purpose, latex rubber condoms are far more effective, since natural materials have pores large enough for viruses to pass through. Some men have an allergic reaction to rubber condoms, however, and are unable to use them; women may also have latex sensitivities (see ALLERGIES). These reactions can become serious, in rare cases even life-threatening, so anyone who experiences a reaction should switch to another type of birth control and consult a doctor—understanding that they will not be protected against AIDS and other STDs.

Except for oral sex (see SEXUAL INTERCOURSE), condoms generally need lubrication, if only to help prevent breakage; only *water-based* lubricants should be used; check the package or ask your doctor or pharmacist for recommendations. Oil-based lubricants—including petroleum jelly, vegetable oil, baby oil, hand lotion, massage oils, dairy oils, and the like—should not be used, because they can damage the condom, making it vulnerable to tears and so ineffective as any kind of protection. For maximum effectiveness, condoms should be kept cool, dark, and dry in unopened packages, opened only when about to be used, and certainly never re-used. Condoms may sometimes slip during or after sex; if so, they should be held in place at the rim until withdrawal. If the condom breaks during sex, the penis should be withdrawn immediately and the condom removed; the penis and surrounding area should be washed and a new condom put on before continuing intercourse. (See CONDOMS: WHAT WOMEN NEED TO KNOW on page 188.)

Before the age of AIDS, condoms were seldom discussed. Even today—even as AIDS rages and adolescent pregnancy is a major social problem—some people still resist spreading information about condoms. But most people now realize that condoms can be lifesavers, and public and private organizations in many countries are attempting to educate the public about the importance of using them. Even when a woman uses some other form of CONTRACEPTION, she is urged to have her male partner use a condom for disease protection, and many women—enough to account for at least 25 percent of condom sales in the United States alone—have begun to carry condoms for that purpose. This is easier said than done, since some men still resist using a condom. Much recent anti-AIDS education has, indeed, been focused on how to convince a male partner to use a condom for mutual protection. For women, that has always been the main drawback of the condom as a birth control device—it is literally out of their hands. That was one of the spurs to development of the vaginal pouch for women. The main advantages of the condom are that it is easily accessible over-the-counter, relatively easy to use, inexpensive, and disposable. Under development is a kind of *Unisex Condom Garment* (see VAGINAL POUCH). (See BIRTH CONTROL AND FAMILY PLANNING HELP, INFORMATION, AND ACTION GUIDE on page 81.)

CONDOMS: WHAT WOMEN NEED TO KNOW

Though condoms are meant to be used by men, women should know how to select and use them, for their own self-protection.

Condom Shopping Guide

Use this handy shopping guide as a reminder of what to look for when buying condoms, lubricant, and spermicides:

Be sure to choose
- ☑ **Latex**
- ☑ **Disease prevention claim on package label**

Also consider
- ☐ With spermicide
- ☐ Separate spermicide
  - ☐ Gel
  - ☐ Cream
  - ☐ Foam
- ☐ With lubricant
- ☐ Separate lubricant (Select only **water-based** lubricants made for this purpose.)

Guidelines for Using a Condom

For maximum safety, both for disease prevention and birth control, the U.S. Public Health Service has developed these guidelines for men using condoms:

- Use a new condom for every act of intercourse.
- If the penis is uncircumcised, pull back the foreskin before putting on the condom.
- Put on the condom after the penis is erect (hard) and before *any* contact is made between the penis and any part of the partner's body.
- If using a spermicide, put some inside the condom tip.
- If the condom does not have a reservoir tip, pinch the tip enough to leave a half-inch space for semen to collect.
- While pinching the half-inch tip, place the condom against the penis and unroll it all the way to the base. Put more spermicide or lubricant on the outside.
- If you feel a condom break while you are having sex, stop immediately and pull out. Do not continue until you have put on a new condom and used more spermicide.
- After ejaculation and before the penis gets soft, grip the rim of the condom and carefully withdraw from your partner.
- To remove the condom from the penis, pull it off gently, being careful semen doesn't spill out.
- Wrap the used condom in a tissue and throw it in the trash where others won't handle it. Because condoms may cause problems in sewers, don't flush down the toilet. Afterward, wash your hands with soap and water.
- Finally, beware of drugs and alcohol! They can affect your judgment, so you may forget to use a condom. They may even affect your ability to use a condom properly.

Source: Adapted from *Condoms and Sexually Transmitted Diseases . . . Especially AIDS*, Department of Health and Human Services, Public Health Service, Food and Drug Administration, Center for Devices and Radiological Health, 1990.

condonation, forgiveness of an offense; a traditional defense in an adversarial DIVORCE.

condylomata acuminata, an alternative name for GENITAL WARTS.

congestive dysmenorrhea, an alternative term for *premenstrual syndrome* (see MENSTRUATION).

Congressional Caucus for Women's Issues (Congress of the United States, 2471 Rayburn Building, House of Representatives, Washington, DC 20515; 202-225-6740), a "bipartisan legislative service organization" founded by the women members of Congress in 1977 to promote women's economic and legal rights, primarily by promoting "legislation to improve the status of women and eliminate discrimination from federal programs and policies." It focuses especially on economic issues such as PAY EQUITY, FAMILY AND MEDICAL LEAVE, dependent care, pension reform (see INSURANCE AND PENSION EQUITY), CHILD SUPPORT enforcement, and, more recently, health issues, including BREAST CANCER, OSTEOPOROSIS, and adolescent PREGNANCY. The caucus also serves as an information clearinghouse on such issues through its weekly congressional activity report and monthly newsletter *UPDATE* (both for caucus members only, though some may make copies available to their constituents), as well as background papers and briefings.

conjugal rights, the rights of a wife and a husband to have from each other mutual love, affection, comfort, companionship, and sexual relations in a MARRIAGE.

consciousness-raising (c-r), a WOMEN'S LIBERATION MOVEMENT adaptation of a widely used development or manipulative technique, most notably used in politics, self-help organizations, and group therapy. For whatever purposes the technique is used, the common thread is the development of the small group as an entity, with its own dynamics of motion and conviction, and a group and individual commitment to complete and often brutal honesty in the group situation, so that all participants can bare and understand their true motives and the roots of those motives and so be able to change.

As used in political organizations, the direction of change is a given; in women's liberation groups, for example, the direction of change was always toward greater—that is, raised—consciousness of multiple male oppressions and a shared desire to take action for the current goals of the women's liberation movement. In the late 1960s and early 1970s, the radically oriented women who had worked in the NEW LEFT organizations of the period took with them the New Left consciousness-raising technique, sometimes called "criticism and self-criticism," used by such organizations as the Students for a Democratic Society and its Maoist Progressive Labor party component, which adapted the technique from its long use in the world communist movement. The technique had been used perhaps most effectively during the latter development of the Chinese Communist party, and throughout China after the communist victory in 1949. In the women's liberation movement, use of the technique was generally more open-ended than it had been in the rigidly led communist movement and somewhat more open-ended than in the more anarchist-oriented New Left.

Consciousness-raising was very popular in the women's movement of the late 1960s and early 1970s, far beyond the small women's liberation movement organizations from which it came, and continued to be popular in the 1990s, though by then often shading over into a call for fruitful dialogue in working party and study group situations. (See also WOMEN'S LIBERATION MOVEMENT.)

consent, age of: See AGE OF CONSENT.

constructive abandonment: See ABANDONMENT.

contraception, an approach to BIRTH CONTROL that focuses on blocking CONCEPTION from taking place. It includes BIRTH CONTROL PILLS (oral contraceptives), CONDOM, DIAPHRAGM, CERVICAL CAP, INTRAUTERINE DEVICE (IUD), NORPLANT, SPERMICIDES, SPONGE, DOUCHING, DEPO-PROVERA, and VAGINAL POUCH (female condom). (See BIRTH CONTROL; also BIRTH CONTROL AND FAMILY PLANNING HELP, INFORMATION, AND ACTION GUIDE on page 81.)

Convention for the Suppression of the Traffic in Persons and of the Exploitation of the Prostitution of Others, a 1949 United Nations–sponsored international agreement relating to PROSTITUTION and sexual slavery.

Convention on the Elimination of All Forms of Discrimination Against Women, a 1979 United Nations–sponsored agreement outlining the types of SEXUAL DISCRIMINATION ideally to be ended. (For the text of the convention, see page 796.)

Copenhagen World Conference for Women (1980), the interim conference generated by the United Nations Decade for Women, to report on progress to that point. Like the 1975 Mexico City Conference (see INTERNATIONAL WOMEN'S YEAR), it was effectively destroyed by the great attention paid to Cold War, Middle East, and North-South political and economic issues. Again, little eventuated; the United States even refused to sign the Conference's World Plan of Action, which included Middle East issues among the women's resolutions, calling Zionism racism, as per the Cold War and Arab nations' political stance of the time.

cordocentesus (percutaneous umbilical cord sampling), a relatively new type of PRENATAL TEST used to identify some kinds of GENETIC DISORDERS. A needle is inserted through the pregnant woman's abdomen, with the physician guided by ULTRASOUND, and a sample of blood is withdrawn from the UMBILICAL CORD. Because the BLOOD cells are virtually identical with those of the FETUS, they can be analyzed quickly for the presence of serious BLOOD disorders, such as hemophilia, thalassemia, or sickle-cell anemia. (See PRENATAL TEST; also GENETIC INHERITANCE AND BIRTH DEFECTS HELP, INFORMATION, AND ACTION GUIDE on page 314.)

corpus luteum, the two outer protective layers shed by an egg (OVUM) when it leaves one of the OVARIES during OVULATION; the name is Latin for "yellow body." The corpus luteum triggers release of the female sex hormone PROGESTERONE, which increases the thickening of the *endometrium,* the lining of the UTERUS, to prepare for a possible fertilized egg. During a normal reproductive cycle, the corpus luteum will continue to produce progesterone for about two weeks; then it will wither away, and the resulting drop in progesterone levels will help trigger MENSTRUATION and the start of a new cycle. However, if FERTILIZATION does occur, the corpus luteum will continue to pump out progesterone for several weeks, until the PLACENTA that nourishes the new FETUS takes over that job.

corticosteroids, a type of HORMONE produced by the adrenal gland (see STEROIDS; HORMONES).

cosmetics, substances that may be "rubbed, poured, sprinkled, or sprayed on, introduced into, or otherwise applied to the human body for cleansing, beautifying, promoting attractiveness, or altering the appearance without affecting the body's structures or functions," as defined by the 1938 U.S. Federal Food and Drug and Cosmetics Act. This wide category excepts soaps but includes a very broad range of products, among them skin-care preparations, such as creams, lotions, powders, and sprays; fragrances; manicure products; HAIR products, including coloring preparations, shampoos, permanent wave products, conditioners, and hairstyling preparations; deodorants; shaving products; baby products; bath oils and bubble baths; mouthwashes; sunscreens; and all the items classified as "makeup"—foundation, blusher, face powder, EYE shadow, eyeliner, mascara, lipstick, and the rest. However, substances designed to change "the body's structure or function," such as a cream sold as a liver-spot remover, would be classed as a drug, not a cosmetic.

Whether cosmetics or drugs, such items have long been regulated by governments for the safety of consumers; in the United States that job falls to the FOOD AND DRUG ADMINISTRATION (FDA). Under FDA regulations, labels on cosmetic products must include a list of the ingredients, so people can avoid substances to which they may have ALLERGIES. However, some kinds of flavorings and fragrances may be listed unnamed, if they constitute a trade secret. As a result, women with sensitivities must use a trial-and-error method of checking out cosmetics. They may want to look for *hypoallergenic,* which may be less likely to cause reactions, or *fragrance-free* products, though these may still contain small amounts of fragrances to mask unattractive odors. "Natural" products sound attractive, if they are indeed made from plant or animal products rather than synthetics; however, many people can also be allergic to natural substances. Consumers should also understand that such terms, and such other label claims as "dermatologist-tested," "sensitivity-tested," "allergy-tested" or "nonirritating," are not government-regulated and so can be used freely by marketers. In general, the best approach is to test a cosmetic on a small part of the body, to see if any reaction results, before using it widely. (For more suggestions, see PREVENTING SKIN INFLAMMATION on page 691.)

The FDA does mandate safety testing of some kinds of substances in cosmetics. One of the main tests used is the Draize test, in which the substance is placed directly into the eyes of animals, usually rabbits, to identify the severity of allergic reactions, if any. Among environmentalists and animal rights advocates, such animal testing has become a major issue; many companies have been swayed by protests to make products using only substances that have been shown safe on the basis of previous testing and history of use, allowing them to advertise their products as "cruelty-free." Numerous researchers are also attempting to develop alternatives to animal testing of cosmetics. Certain types of ingredients are absolutely prohibited, such as mercury compounds (except as preservatives in eye cosmetics), hexachlorophene, vinyl chloride and zirconium salts in aerosol products, biothionol, and chloroform. Color additives must be tested. Beyond that, the *FDA Consumer* reports, "a cosmetic manufacturer may use any ingredient or raw material and market the final product without government approval."

Women who use makeup can follow some basic safety rules to protect themselves:

- Keep makeup containers tightly closed.
- Keep makeup out of sunlight; light can degrade preservatives.
- Don't use eye cosmetics if you have an eye infection, such as conjunctivitis, and throw away all products you were using when you first discovered the infection.
- Never add any liquid to bring the product back to its original consistency. Adding water or, even worse, saliva could introduce bacteria that could easily grow out of control.
- Never share [that includes at shared-use makeup-testing counters].
- Throw away makeup if the color changes or an odor develops. Preservatives can degrade over time and may no longer be able to fight bacteria.

(Source: "Cosmetic Safety: More Complex Than at First Blush," by Dori Stehlin, *FDA Consumer,* November 1991.)

Contamination of makeup, either because products are misused or have inadequate preservatives, is a substantial problem. Perhaps the most vulnerable to both contamination and injury are the eyes. The FDA stresses the importance of exercising care in applying eye makeup. In particular they urge women not to apply makeup while driving, the cause of numerous eye injuries. (See SKIN, HAIR, NAILS, AND COSMETICS HELP, INFORMATION, AND ACTION GUIDE on page 689.)

cosmetic surgery, surgical procedures performed on SKIN and underlying tissue and bone to change the look and shape of the body, performed primarily for reasons of appearance, as opposed to *reconstructive surgery* performed for medical reasons (see PLASTIC SURGERY). In general, excess skin, tissue, cartilage, or bone are removed or reshaped, or implants are inserted, and the cuts are then stitched together to form new contours. The actual incisions are usually made with scalpels, though high-intensity light beams called *lasers* are sometimes used.

The main reasons for performing cosmetic surgery are to alter genetically inherited traits, often the nose, EARS, and facial structure; to blunt the effects of aging, again focusing on the face, as well as HAIR; and to change the shape of the body, especially the BREASTS and the abdomen but also other areas where fat is deposited. Among the most common cosmetic procedures are

▶ *nose surgery (rhinoplasty),* in which the nasal cartilage, bone, and skin are reshaped to new contours, such as a smaller, straighter nose or a differently shaped tip. This operation involves few scars, since most work is done from inside the nose.

▶ *ear surgery (otoplasty),* to reshape the ear; most commonly to make large ears lie closer to the head, by cutting segments of skin and sometimes cartilage from the back of the ear and then stitching together the two sides, generally leaving an insignificant scar.

▶ *reshaping of the facial skeleton,* modifying the chin, jaw, eyebrows, and cheekbones to change the balance between various parts of the face, often using implants to augment chin and cheekbones. Implants may be shaped from the patient's own cartilage or bone, but for various reasons nonhuman materials, including silicones, coral, and plastics, are more often used. Some scarring results, though surgery on the cheek may be done through incisions inside the mouth.

▶ *eyelid surgery (blepharoplasty),* the removal of fat and sometimes excess skin and muscle, from the upper and lower eyelids, the aim often being a younger, more alert appearance. One adverse result may be difficulty in closing eyes during sleep, in some cases a long-term and occasionally even permanent condition.

▶ *browlift,* making an incision above the hairline, removing excess tissue, and stitching together the remaining skin in such a way as to reduce sagging eyebrows and forehead creases.

▶ *facelift (rhytidectomy),* taking "tucks" in the skin around the face, jaws, and neck to reduce the sagging that comes with age, focusing especially on the crease between the nose and mouth (the *nasolabial fold),* slack skin around the jawline, and folds and fatty deposits around the neck. Where possible, incisions and therefore scars are made above the hairline or behind the ears and so kept out of sight.

▶ *hair-replacement surgery,* the transplantation of hair to bald spots from elsewhere on the scalp, a procedure used far more by men than women (see HAIR).

▶ **breast surgery (mammoplasty),** various types of changes or reconstruction of one or both breasts, all leaving some kinds of scars. The main types of breast surgery are

• **breast lift (mastopexy),** cutting excess skin to tighten the "envelope" enclosing the breast and thus reduce sagging, in the process moving the nipple and areola higher on the breast. This operation is often performed on women after PREGNANCY, when breast tissue shrinks inside stretched skin. The operation is not generally recommended if the woman is planning another pregnancy. Effects of the operation are also temporary, since gravity and bodily changes will inevitably lead to more sagging, especially if the breasts are relatively large.

• **breast enlargement (augmentation mammoplasty),** insertion of gel- or liquid-filled sacs into the breast. This has long been considered the simplest and most common type of breast surgery, and for women the most popular type of cosmetic surgery, after liposuction (see below). However, recent concern about implant problems has changed that picture dramatically (see BREAST IMPLANTS).

• **breast reconstruction,** the rebuilding of a breast, often involving breast implants, generally performed after a mastectomy (see BREAST CANCER).

• **breast reduction (reduction mammoplasty),** removal of fat and glandular tissue to reduce uncomfortably oversized breasts, with the nipple and areola being moved higher. This is a long, complicated procedure, which leaves scars; may also cause loss of sensation in nipples and breast skin; and will bar the possibility of BREASTFEEDING. However, it is attractive to some women whose breasts are so large as to cause psychological or medical problems, including back pain, breathing difficulties, or deformation of the skeleton.

▶ **suction-assisted lipectomy (liposuction),** using suction devices to remove localized accumulations of fat through tubes called *cannulas,* as from double chins, hips, thighs, abdomens, buttocks, and legs; now the most commonly performed cosmetic surgery procedure in the United States. Because the procedure is imprecise, some asymmetry may result; also, the skin above the suctioned areas may become rippled, baggy, or discolored. Scars are generally small and placed out of sight, in the navel, groin, or bottom of the buttocks.

▶ **body lifts,** involving removal of baggy excess skin and fatty tissue from the arms *(brachioplasty),* thighs, buttocks, and abdomen *(abdominoplasty).* Because these procedures leave long, permanent scars, many people have turned to liposuction, though body lifts may be used to deal with baggy skin remaining *after* liposuction. Abdominoplasty is a substantial operation, involving tightening of the abdominal muscles and requiring a long convalescence, a situation belied by the light nickname "tummy tuck." A "minituck" is a partial abdominoplasty involving only the lower abdomen.

More than one type of procedure may be done as part of the same reshaping process—for example, chin augmentation and rhinoplasty often go together—but sometimes several separate operations will be involved.

Cosmetic surgeons also perform various other procedures to smooth skin and blunt the effects of aging or scars, as from injuries or acne. Two procedures—*chemical peel* and *dermabrasion*—do this by removing the damaged surface skin, to allow creation of a smoother surface as the skin heals and regenerates. In a chemical peel, also called *chemosurgery*, a caustic solution is applied to the face; new skin then regenerates under the deliberately damaged skin. In dermabrasion, the surface skin is actually scraped or "sanded" away with a hand-held machine, with new skin then forming gradually. Both procedures involve considerable discomfort during the healing process, often for two to three weeks afterward, though milder peels have a shorter recovery time, as would more localized treatment. Because of the great potential for infection and damage, chemical peel and dermabrasion should not be done lightly, and only by trained surgeons. Such procedures affect only the skin's surface and do nothing for sagging skin, but they are done often along with other kinds of facelifts. People with sensitive skin or skin-related conditions that may flare up should avoid such procedures, as should anyone with dark or sallow complexions, since even among fair-skinned women the new skin will be lighter, and the line between treated and untreated areas will need to be covered by makeup.

In an attempt to smooth away wrinkles, some cosmetic surgeons also use injections of various substances, even though this often has not been sanctioned by governmental oversight authorities. One popular substance, silicone (see BREAST IMPLANTS), is now specifically barred for such use. The vitamin A derivative Retin-A *(tretinoin* or *retinoic acid)* is a newer popular choice but (as of this writing) has not been approved by the Food and Drug Administration. The natural protein *collagen,* derived from cowhides, is sometimes injected to supply support to skin sagging from breakdown of its own collagen. One of the great hazards with all of these substances is the possibility of allergic reaction by the body, which can last for months and is suspected of triggering long-term connective-tissue disorders, such as LUPUS or rheumatoid ARTHRITIS. The "plumping" effects of these injections are also quite temporary, often disappearing in a year or less. Even more temporary, though unlikely to trigger allergic reactions, are injections of fat taken from elsewhere in a woman's body.

Another ancient type of cosmetic surgery is *tattooing,* in which a special needle is used to inject an indelible dye into the skin, a technique medically termed *surgical skin pigmentation.* Cosmetic surgeons have begun performing some special tattoos, giving women permanent eyelid lining and eyebrows. Some have also developed techniques of *reverse tattooing,* using surgical removal, dermabrasion, chemical peel, bleaching, or even special lasers to get rid of unwanted tattoos.

Though the approaches vary for different ends, all cosmetic surgery will involve pain and some disfigurement (such as swelling or bruises) during the healing process and also some permanent scarring, even when performed by the most skilled of surgeons. In addition to the hazards associated with the necessary use of ANESTHESIA, not all operations are successful; further surgery is sometimes required, as when an implant shifts out of place, though not all failures can be repaired. Medical problems may also result, such as infection, BLOOD clots, bleeding, accumulation of fluids, damage to internal organs, or nerve damage causing temporary and in rare instances permanent loss of feeling in the affected area. In some cases patients develop abnormally heavy scarring called *keloids* or capsules of scar tissue form around implants, a condition called *capsular contracture*. Laser surgery carries special dangers, since a misdirected beam can cause deep and heavy damage, including possible blindness during eyelid surgery. Women considering cosmetic surgery should determine whether their desire for cosmetic change is strong enough to outweigh the risks involved—including the risks associated with anesthesia.

Critics of cosmetic surgery point out that surgery is surgery—that *any* surgical operation entails some risk, if only from the use of ANESTHESIA—and lament that people's self-esteem and body image are so poor or distorted that they need to change their outward appearance to look and feel "attractive." Proponents counter that since the techniques have been developed and refined, why shouldn't people take advantage of them?

For women considering cosmetic surgery, the first step is to locate a doctor who specializes in the type of operation they seek and "vet" the surgeon carefully. They should be sure that their doctor has been specially trained to perform the specific procedures being considered and is affiliated with a local hospital, even if the procedure may be performed at a free-standing surgical facility. (Note that any licensed doctor can legally do plastic surgery, but some have little or no special training in doing so.) In particular, beware of inflated claims of success, especially about being the first or only doctor to perform a particular procedure. Another "red flag" is any attempt to rush into surgery, as by discovering a "cancellation" the next day.

The consultation with a cosmetic surgeon should involve a full discussion of the procedure being considered; a description of the risks involved, including scars, pain, and potential complications; and an estimate of the probability that the operation will achieve what the patient desires. Women should be wary of any doctor who does not fully discuss the potential risks of the operation. Not all of the changes a patient might seek are technically feasible. If the doctor and patient agree that the operation has a good chance of success and decide to proceed, the woman will be asked to sign an *informed consent* form; in the case of a minor, a parent may also need to sign the form.

Women considering cosmetic surgery should also be realistic and not expect their whole lives to be transformed by the procedure. It is important for patients to define what they hope to achieve. Surgeons can sometimes use photographs or computer-imaging machines to suggest the results that might appear, but patients should take such tools with a grain of salt. Patients can maximize their chances of success by assuring that they are in generally good health at the time of the operation and leaving adequate time for healing. They should also exercise care for some months after surgery, avoiding exposure to direct sunlight and SMOKING, for example. Where surgery has been successful, women may also need to guard against becoming what some have called "scalpel slaves," who are almost addicted to surgery and go back again and again for more operations.

For more help, information, and action

▶ **American Society of Plastic and Reconstructive Surgeons (ASPRS)** (444 East Algonquin Road, Arlington Heights, IL 60005; 708-228-9900; for referrals, 800-635-0635; Thomas R. Schedler, executive director), a professional society for plastic surgeons, affiliated with the Plastic Surgery Educational Foundation, gathering and disseminating information on techniques and procedures for professionals and their patients. It operates a toll-free hot line providing information brochures on various procedures and referrals to plastic surgeons performing specific procedures in the caller's region.
▶ Food and Drug Administration **(FDA)** (301-443-3170).

Other resources

The American Society of Plastic and Reconstructive Surgeons' Guide to Cosmetic Surgery. Josleen Wilson. Simon & Schuster, 1992.
The Teen Face Book: A Question and Answer Guide to Skin Care, Cosmetics, and Facial Plastic Surgery. American Academy of Facial Plastic and Reconstructive Surgery. Acropolis, 1989.
Plastic Surgery: The Kindest Cut. John Camp. Holt, 1989.
The Complete Book of Cosmetic Surgery: A Candid Guide for Men, Women and Teens. Elizabeth Morgan. Warner, 1988.

coverture, in the English and American common law, the status of a married woman, who in most significant respects lost her property rights on MARRIAGE, as well as most other rights independent of her husband. In the law she became a *feme covert*—a woman covered or protected by her husband. That made her in the law quite literally a nonentity, something other than a chattel that could be bought and sold but with little more than a chattel's status. As a practical matter, that status was somewhat modified by courts operating under the concept of equity—that is, fairness—and married women therefore had some inheritance law protections (see DOWER; INHERITANCE RIGHTS); but these only slightly affected their basic status. On occasion, where the husband was away for a long time, as at sea or war, or where he approved, the court might grant a married woman the status of a SINGLE WOMAN *(feme sol)*, but that was rare.

In the first half of the nineteenth century, as WOMEN'S RIGHTS MOVEMENTS began in the newly independent United States, the long campaign for married women's property legislation began. In Mississippi in 1839, women first won the right to hold property in their own name, with their husband's permission; then in several other states before the Civil War, Married Women's Property Acts were passed. In England the first Married Women's Property Bill was enacted in 1857. These and other bills gradually extended married women's property rights, until—in these countries, at least—they could not only own property freely and without interference from their husbands, but could also enter into contracts, sell

C

land, sue and be sued, and write wills. As the law continues to change, so do married women's rights (see MARRIAGE).

crab lice, an alternative name for PUBIC LICE.

credit equity: See EQUAL CREDIT OPPORTUNITY ACT.

Crohn's disease, a type of digestive disorder (see DIGESTIVE SYSTEM).

cross-dressing, the wearing of clothes that, in a particular culture, are normally associated with the other sex, for a variety of reasons; sometimes called *transvestitism*. For some HETEROSEXUALS or HOMOSEXUALS, cross-dressing can bring sexual excitement; where the dressing becomes a compulsion, it is sometimes called *fetishistic transvestism* or *transvestic fetishism*. For some people who resist their socially assigned GENDER IDENTITY, cross-dressing may be part of living as the sex they feel themselves truly to be. For some feminists, cross-dressing may be a blow for freedom and liberation from the constraints of SEX ROLES. For many others, the clothes of the opposite sex may simply be more functional, convenient, or enjoyable for various living and working purposes.

C-section, an abbreviation for CESAREAN SECTION.

cultural feminism, a nonpolitical, separatist, female-supremacist body of theory, which declares the supremacy of women over men by virtue of women's shared cultural inheritance, rather than by biological inheritance, though just as inflexibly (see FEMALE SUPREMACY), and seeks to build a separate women's society reflecting that superiority, calling it "womanculture." Charlotte Perkins GILMAN described that kind of utopian matriarchal society in her novel *Herland* (1915). In the early 1970s some of the women in the radical feminist movement turned the theory into a movement, with women-only businesses and organizations, and many also with the separate religion of SPIRITUAL FEMINISM, as developed by Mary DALY and others. (See also ESSENTIALISM; FEMINISM; RADICAL FEMINISM.)

curtesy, under common law, a husband's continuing lifetime interest in his wife's property after her death, if they had surviving children who could inherit it. The husband could occupy the land and benefit from it, as from using it or renting it out, but could not sell it or will it away from the natural heirs. The comparable provision for a wife is called a DOWER.

In many places this common-law approach has been replaced by laws that provide for a husband to receive a certain share (usually one-third to one-half) of his wife's estate outright, if the wife dies without a will. In some states the law applies only in the absence of a will, so a wife could leave her husband a much smaller amount, called a *distributive share.* In some states, however, the curtesy applies *in addition* to any provisions in the will. Many states, however, include a RIGHT OF ELECTION, allowing the surviving SPOUSE a choice among the possibilities. Personal property as well as real estate may be included in these laws.

custody, the legal right and responsibility to care for and make basic decisions about children or disabled adults. Custody is usually thought of in connection to children, and that certainly is where enormous contention exists in modern DIVORCE courts; but custody may also apply to adults who are so disabled as to be unable to discharge those tasks themselves, such as a mentally retarded grown child, an elderly mother no longer competent to make daily decisions, or a brain-damaged partner, HETEROSEXUAL or same-sex. Custody may also apply to other living things that require care, such as a pet.

Custody is a two-sided coin, with both rights and responsibilities. These include provision of food, clothing, shelter, basic medical care, education, and control or discipline. *Legal custody* is the right and responsibility to make basic decisions, as about medical care or education, and may be exercised by one person alone or held jointly. By contrast, the person who provides day-to-day care and control, and who actually shares the child's living quarters, is said to have *physical custody.* Where a SINGLE PARENT raises a child alone from the time of birth or ADOPTION, that parent has *sole custody,* which includes both legal and physical custody. Parents in a stable marriage share *joint custody* of their children; this, too, includes both legal and physical custody.

Problems come, however, when a couple with children separates or divorces. At that point they must agree between themselves—or the court must decide for them—who will have custody and with what limitations. In general, the *custodial parent* is the parent the child lives with. The other—the *noncustodial parent*—still has CHILD SUPPORT obligations but may or may not have the legal right to participate in major decisions regarding the child, depending on the agreement reached. Among the main types of arrangements between parents are

▶ *sole custody,* in which one parent has both physical and legal custody of the child. The other parent has VISITATION RIGHTS but generally no legal right to participate in major decisions, though that parent will often do so informally.

▶ *shared or joint custody,* in which the parents generally share custody and the child spends a substantial amount of time with each parent. Actual arrangements vary, but may include spending the school year with one parent and most of the holidays with the other; or spending alternate weeks, months, or years with each parent. Many courts—and many parents—favor joint custody because a child has continuing contact with and support from both parents during the crucial childhood years. Some states routinely award joint legal custody, while giving one parent physical custody. One disadvantage is that children's lives, and their network of friends and contacts, are so frequently disrupted.

Ideally, joint custody can ease the parental burdens of the custodial parent by shared responsibility, but any form of joint custody requires substantial co-operation between parents and so has little chance of working well in an extremely acrimonious relationship. In practice, joint custody can work out very badly for the woman. Some men seek joint custody for the purpose of lowering child support payments, arguing before the court that lower amounts are justified because the children will spend much of their time with him. Later, in fact, the woman often ends up with de facto sole custody but with less money for support. Also, with joint custody the woman does not have the sole authority to make key decisions in a timely way, especially if the couple are unable to agree on questions affecting the children.

▶ *bird's nest custody* or *nesting,* a less common form of joint custody designed to ease disruption of children's lives. Here children stay in their home, and the parents shuttle in and out at agreed-upon intervals, such as one during the week and the other on weekends. This provides a more stable base for the children but disrupts the parents' lives. It is also expensive and complicated, since each parent must maintain separate living quarters or have temporary living arrangements outside the family home.

▶ *splitting,* also a less common option, for families with several children, in which some children live with the MOTHER full-time and the others with the FATHER, with each parent exercising sole custody of the children they live with. This avoids some of the abrasions of joint custody and eliminates shuttling back and forth by all. But the absolute breaking up of the family is disruptive to the children, and often *all* children feel short-changed by having contact with only one parent. The two sets of siblings can also develop strong resentment and rivalries, as over the perceived advantages and disadvantages of each home.

Often arguments over custody are continuations of the battles that caused the split in the first place and are further complicated when—as is common today—one or both parents have new partners and often new children or stepchildren as well.

Where parents are unable to work out custody arrangements on their own, a court will make the decision for them, generally a *family court* or *domestic relations court.* In the nineteenth century courts generally awarded custody of the children to the father. Later, as the law came to recognize the marriage partners as more equal, custody was awarded to the "most fit" parent; that was interpreted as the one who could best provide for the child, materially and emotionally. Gradually the courts developed the general presumption that the interests of the child were best served if the mother was awarded custody. That presumption, sometimes called the *tender-years doctrine,* was followed for much of the twentieth century. When it held sway, fathers in a contested custody suit generally had to prove the mother "unfit" in order to win their case.

Only since the 1960s have the courts, in the United States, at least, taken a more evenly balanced approach to awarding custody. Some states have gone so far as to forbid courts to take a parent's sex into account when awarding custody. Mothers are still commonly granted custody—in the United States, approximately 90 percent of the time—but this is often because fathers do not object. However, when fathers *do* choose to contest custody, they are today often favored, some estimate by two to one. In fact, some women's groups argue that the current court approach takes insufficient account of the special relationship that normally exists between mother and child (see MOTHER).

The courts have considerable latitude in deciding custody questions regarding a child. A court may award sole custody to one parent and visitation rights to the other, may decide on a form of joint custody, or may award custody to a third party as *guardian,* such as a grandmother or stepfather who has cared for the child. Where dispute is especially acrimonious, the court may appoint a *guardian ad litem* (at law) or some other representative to act on the child's behalf during the custody suit (see CHILDREN'S RIGHTS). The court's overriding concern is the emotional and financial stability of the child; this is called the doctrine of the *best interests of the child,* or sometimes more realistically the *least detrimental alternative.* In line with these principles, courts have developed a wide variety of considerations to take into account when awarding custody, among them

▶ *established living pattern.* The court tends to favor whichever custody arrangement will provide the most continuity and stability, especially the same family home and school, community, and religious ties. For similar reasons, the court tends to keep siblings together.

▶ *emotional ties.* The court tends to favor the person with whom the child appears to have the strongest emotional ties, the one who has been closest to the child's day-to-day hopes and fears; this person—parent or guardian—is sometimes called the *psychological parent.*

▶ *child's age, sex, health, and physical condition.* The court tends to favor the person who seems best able to deal with the particular needs of the child, including any special health needs.

▶ *parent's health and physical condition.* The court tends to favor the parent who is physically best equipped to care for the child. This works against a parent with weakness, handicap, or ill health, although theoretically disability is not supposed to be a bar to custody.

▶ *parent's ability to supply basic necessities.* The court does not necessarily choose the more wealthy contestant, since child support is arranged separately, but wishes to assure that the child's basic needs for food, clothing, shelter, and medical care are met. If such needs are not met, a parent could later lose custody.

▶ *parent's plan for education.* The court tends to favor the parent who makes plans for the child's education, especially college, generally regardless of that parent's own level of education or skills.

▶ *parent's behavior.* The court tends to favor the parent whose behavior has been most in keeping with traditional standards and who has regular religious involvement. Such considerations have changed somewhat, with the post-1960s revolution in social and sexual mores, but many courts still give great weight to a circumspect and unobtrusive life-style. Courts still tend to look with disfavor on ADULTERY during MARRIAGE, especially by the mother, and in some places either parent could lose custody for living unmarried with another sex partner. LESBIANS and gays who, after marriage, openly acknowledge their homosexuality have had particular difficulty in custody fights, though in recent years they have also had occasional successes. In addition, parents who have had problems with drugs, alcohol, money handling, and so on have also been at a disadvantage in custody fights. Several groups (see CUSTODY HELP, INFORMATION, AND ACTION GUIDE on page 205) have formed to help parents fight for custody against such disadvantages.

▶ *parent's acrimony.* The court favors continuing contact between the child and both parents and so looks with disfavor on a parent who wishes to sever such contacts, as by making bitter personal attacks on the other parent, denying visitation rights, or engaging in parental kidnapping, temporary or long-term. Such actions can lead to reconsideration by the court and loss of custody.

▶ *blood ties.* The court tends to favor the person with the strongest blood ties to the child—a mother over a grandmother, for example, or a father over a stepfather—where other considerations do not tip the balance. Among unmarried couples, with no legally recognized relationship, the mother tends to be favored in custody disputes. With lesbian couples, where one woman actually bore the child, she tends to be favored in a custody dispute.

▶ *citizenship.* The court tends to favor the parent who intends to remain in the country. In the United States, this is especially true for children born outside of the United States and with only one parent a U.S. citizen, who risk loss of U.S. citizenship if they do not live in the United States for a specified period of time.

▶ *child's preference.* The court tends to give less weight to a younger child's preferences of parent or guardian and more to an older child's. The judge may, however, interview the child *in camera* (in chambers), for information not only on preferences, but also on other aspects of the relationship. The records of such conversations are normally sealed.

Based on an overview of the child's situation, including these considerations, the judge makes a custody decision. In rare instances the judge may even override a parents' prior agreement and order different custody arrangements.

Once the court has given a custody decision, it is not lightly modified. Changed circumstances, such as the temporary hospitalization of a parent, may cause a temporary modification. But permanent modifications are seldom ordered, except where the changed circumstances directly and adversely affect the child. If the custodial parent loses a job because of alcoholism (see ALCOHOL AND DRUG ABUSE) or is convicted of a crime, the court may make a permanent change. But the reverse is not true. Individuals who have lost custody for such reasons should not assume that because they "reform" they will be able to reverse a custody decision, since the questions of stability and continuity for the child continue as major principles.

One of the major custody problems of recent decades has been parental kidnapping of children by a parent who feels unjustly deprived of custody or visitation rights. Hundreds of thousands of American children have been abducted by parents or other family members in recent years, causing a great deal of personal anguish and public furor. Often the children are returned within a week, but sometimes the parent and child go underground, breaking all communication with the other parent or the court system for long periods, or disappearing permanently. Many parents have resorted to kidnapping in the hope that a court in a different jurisdiction would award them custody.

In the United States, two key laws were passed to undercut this practice. These are the Parental Kidnapping Prevention Act (PKPA) and the Uniform Child Custody Jurisdiction Act (UCCJA), adopted by all fifty states (except Massachusetts, which has a similar law). The UCCJA provides rules for deciding which court has jurisdiction; if a custody decision has already been made, it stresses enforcement of the original order, under the principle of *continuing jurisdiction*, or modifies it in special circumstances, rather than making a new and perhaps different decision. Perhaps most important, the UCCJA specifies that the parent who kidnaps a child, except in very special circumstances, will be denied custody. The parent will not be charged with kidnapping, however; a federal law labeled Title 18, Section 1201A, exempts them from such charges—though many custodial parents who have lost their children to kidnapping are attempting to change the law. Some states also have laws against parental kidnapping.

Another serious problem is that in no-holds-barred custody fights, some parents have taken to making allegations of child abuse, especially sexual abuse (see CHILD ABUSE AND NEGLECT).

In some cases of possible child abuse and neglect, the state itself may temporarily take *emergency* or *protective custody* of children. If the situation remains destructive and dangerous to the children, the parents may lose custody permanently (see PARENTS' RIGHTS).

Adults can also be the focus of custody fights, when an adult is judged incompetent to handle everyday self-care. Where such adults are in legally recognized relationships—husband and wife or mother and daughter—they are legally able to assume care for each other, making necessary medical decisions, for example, and the court rarely needs to be involved. But where adults are living together unmarried (see COHABITATION), in heterosexual or homosexual relationships, they do not automatically have the legally recognized right to care for each other—even if they have been living together for years—depending on the laws in the state where they live. If one partner becomes so seriously ill as to be unconscious or unable to communicate desires, the other partner often has no legal standing to make the necessary medical and other decisions; these can be made only by the nearest legally recognized relative—no matter how estranged. Some of the most bitter and poignant cases of recent years have involved fights over custody of a severely disabled person between parents and unmarried partner. Where an unmarried woman wants her partner—heterosexual or homosexual—to be able to assume her care in case of incapacity, she should make legal arrangements for that.

Various organizations can advise women on custody questions, in whatever kind of situation. (See CUSTODY HELP, INFORMATION, AND ACTION GUIDE on page 205; DIVORCE AND SEPARATION HELP, INFORMATION, AND ACTION GUIDE on page 238; also VISITATION RIGHTS; SURROGATE PARENTING; COHABITATION.)

CUSTODY

Help, Information, and Action Guide

Organizations

▶ **Joint Custody Association (JCA)** (10606 Wilkins Avenue, Los Angeles, CA 90024; 213-475-5352; James A. Cook, president), an organization concerned with child custody and related issues. It gathers and disseminates information and offers support to those seeking to establish joint custody.

▶ **Parents Sharing Custody (PSC)** (420 S. Beverly Drive, Beverly Hills, CA 90212-4410, 310-286-9171; Linda Blakeley, president), an organization for divorced parents who have joint custody of children and others interested in such arrangements; aims to educate others about shared custody, through seminars and other programs.

▶ **Mothers Without Custody (MWOC)** (P.O. Box 27418, Houston, TX 77227-7418; 713-840-1622; Angie Mease, executive director), a network of mutual-support, self-help groups for mothers who do not live with their children for whatever reason, as by choice, by judicial or social agency intervention, by loss of custody, or by abduction of the child by an ex-husband; provides information, referrals, and legal help; publishes newsletter *Mother-to-Mother*.

▶ **Committee for Mother and Child Rights (CMCR)** (210 Old Orchard Drive, Clear Brook, VA 22624; 703-722-3652; Elizabeth Owen, national coordinating director), an organization offering "emotional support and guidance for mothers with child custody problems." It seeks to educate the public and influence public policy on custody concerns, especially on recognition of the primary caregiver—usually the mother—and on "mental, physical, and sexual abuses often associated with contested custody."

▶ National Center on Women and Family Law (**NCOWFL**) (212-674-8200). Publishes *Representation in Interstate Child Custody Disputes and Parental Kidnapping: Policy, Practice and Law, Guide to Interstate Custody Disputes for Domestic Violence Advocates,* and *Custody Litigation on Behalf of Battered Women.*

▶ Parents Without Partners (**PWP**) (301-588-9354 or 800-637-7974). Publishes information kits on family law for noncustodial fathers and noncustodial mothers.

▶ National Legal Resource Center For Child Advocacy and Protection (202-331-2200). Publishes *Sexual Abuse Allegations in Custody and Visitation Cases.*

▶ WOMEN'S LEGAL DEFENSE FUND (WLDF) (202-887-0364). Publishes *Custody Handbook.*

▶ NATIONAL COUNCIL FOR CHILDREN'S RIGHTS (NCCR) (202-547-NCCR [6227]).

☑ ON PARENTAL KIDNAPPING

▶ **Citizen's Committee to Amend Title 18** (P.O. Box 936, Newhall, CA 91321; 805-259-4435; Beth Kurrus, coordinator), an organization of parents granted custody, whose children were kidnapped by the other parent. It aims to change the law (Title 18, Section 1201A of the U.S. Code) that exempts parents from kidnapping charges regarding their children under 18.

▶ **National Center for Missing and Exploited Children (NCMEC)** (2101 Wilson Boulevard, Suite 550; Arlington, VA 22201; 703-235-3900; [voice; U.S. and Canada] 800-843-5678 or [for hearing-impaired; U.S. and Canada] 800-826-7653; Ernest Allen, president), an organization that acts as clearinghouse for parents and agencies searching for missing children and helps individuals arrange for return of the children, once found. It seeks to influence public policy and publishes various materials, including a handbook on parental kidnapping and material on searching techniques.

▶ **Missing Children . . . Help Center (MCHC)** (410 Ware Boulevard, Suite 400, Tampa, Florida 33619; 813-623-5437 or 800-USA-KIDS [872-5437]; Ivana DiNova, executive director), an organization that serves as contact point for missing children, parents, and private and public agencies, gathering data on missing children and on child search agencies nationwide. It seeks to influence government policy.

▶ **Missing Children of America (MCA)** (P.O. Box 10-193B, Anchorage, AK 99510; 907-248-7300; Dolly Whaley, executive director), an organization to help find missing children. It maintains computer files and advises parents on preparing identification packages and getting media coverage. It publishes various materials.

▶ **Child Find of America (CFA)** (P.O. Box 277, New Paltz, NY 12561; 914-255-1848 or 800-I-AM-LOST [426-5678]; Carolyn Zogg, executive director), a network of individuals and groups that provides a contact point for separated children and parents. It pools information from other organizations around the country in a registry of missing children and publishes a newsletter and annual directory with physical descriptions and photographs.

☑ ON CUSTODY PROBLEMS OF LESBIANS

▶ NATIONAL CENTER FOR LESBIAN RIGHTS (NCLR) (415-621-0674). Publishes *A Lesbian and Gay Parents' Legal Guide to Child Custody, Lesbian Moth-*

er Litigation Manual, and *AIDS and Child Custody: A Guide to Advocacy.*

▶ **Lambda Legal Defense and Education Fund (LLDEF)** (212-995-8585).

Other resources

◢ **ON CUSTODY**

Understanding Child Custody. Susan N. Terkel. Watts, 1991.

The Joint Custody Handbook, rev. ed. Miriam G. Cohen. Running Press, 1991.

Humanizing Child Custody Disputes: The Family's Team. Gordon B. Plumb and Mary E. Lindley. C. C. Thomas, 1990.

Parent vs. Parent: How You and Your Child Can Survive the Custody Battle. Stephen P. Herman. Pantheon, 1990.

How to Handle Your Child Custody Case: A Guide for Parents, Psychologists, and Attorneys. Leonard Diamond. Prometheus, 1989.

Child Custody. James C. Black and Donald Cantor. Columbia University Press, 1989.

How Could You? Mothers Without Custody of Their Children. Harriet Edwards. Crossing Press, 1989.

My Kids Don't Live with Me Anymore: Coping with the Custody Crisis. Doreen Virtue. CompCare, 1988.

Sharing the Children: How to Resolve Custody Problems and Get On with Your Life. Robert E. Adler. Farrar, Straus & Giroux, 1988.

Mothers Without Custody. Geoffrey L. Greif and Mary S. Pabst. Lexington Books, 1988.

Child Custody: A Complete Guide for Concerned Mothers. M. Takas. Harper & Row, 1987.

◢ **ON PARENTAL KIDNAPPING**

Hilary's Trial: The Morgan Case and the Betrayal of Our Children by America's Legal System. American Lawyer Staff and Jonathan Groner. Simon & Schuster, 1991.

Missing Children: Rhetoric and Reality. Martin L. Frost and Martha-Elin Blomquist. Free Press, 1991.

A Cry of Absence: The True Story of a Father's Search for His Kidnapped Children. Andrew Ward. Viking, 1988.

◢ **BACKGROUND BOOKS**

Uniform Child Custody Jurisdiction Act: A State-by-State Guide. Roger A. Kessinger. Kessinger Publishers, 1990.

Child Custody Disputes: Searching for Solomon. American Bar Association, 1989.
Child Custody and the Politics of Gender. Carol Smart and Selma Sevenhuijsen. Routledge, 1989.
Custody and the Courts: Mental Health and the Law. William Wittlin and Robert T. Hinds, eds. Irvington, 1989.
(See also DIVORCE AND SEPARATION HELP, INFORMATION, AND ACTION GUIDE on page 238; LESBIAN HELP, INFORMATION, AND ACTION GUIDE on page 397.)

CVS, an abbreviation for CHORIONIC VILLUS SAMPLING.

cyst, a sac filled with fluid or gelatinous material, as in the OVARIES, SKIN, BREASTS, or URINARY TRACT; if surgically removed, the operation is called a *cystectomy*. Cyst is also a general name for the bladder.

cytomegalovirus infection (CMV), infection with the *cytomegalovirus*
(CMV), related to that causing HERPES. CMV can be spread in many ways, including by kissing, but because it is found in both SEMEN and cervical secretions (see CERVIX), it is often spread by sexual contact and so is considered one of the SEXUALLY TRANSMITTED DISEASES. Almost everyone has been exposed to CMV by late adulthood; most people have no symptoms of infections or perhaps only swollen lymph glands, fever, or fatigue, which might be easily mistaken for many other mild viral infections. But for people whose IMMUNE SYSTEMS are impaired— including people who receive chemotherapy for CANCER, take immunosuppressant drugs for organ transplants, or have AIDS—the disease can have severe effects, including blindness (see EYES), and can even be life-threatening.

Also very much at risk is a FETUS or newborn baby, since they have immature immune systems. Like some other viruses, CMV remains in the body and reactivates occasionally. If that happens during PREGNANCY, or if the first infection occurs during pregnancy, the fetus may become infected. Though some infected babies will have no symptoms, severe BIRTH DEFECTS can result, including mental retardation, blindness, deafness (see EARS), and epilepsy; the baby may even die. This is one of the leading causes of congenital infections, so doctors recommend that pregnant women limit sexual contact with multiple partners during pregnancy. An infected baby can also easily spread the virus to others, through saliva or urine, for example.

CMV infection is normally detected by the presence of antibodies in the BLOOD. Researchers are seeking drugs that might be effective against CMV. (See SEXUALLY TRANSMITTED DISEASES; also WHAT YOU CAN DO TO AVOID STDs on page 660.)

Daly, Mary (1928–), an American radical feminist theologian, who began her career as a Catholic philosopher and theologian but moved from Catholicism to SPIRITUAL FEMINISM in the late 1960s and the 1970s. She published her first book, *The Church and the Second Sex* (1968), while teaching at Boston College; it was so highly critical of perceived Catholic practice that only a strong mass protest saved her job. Her second book, *Beyond God the Father* (1974), was even more critical and signaled her move away from Catholicism, a move completed in her next book, *Gyn/Ecology: The Metaethics of Radical Feminism* (1978), in which she declared her spiritual feminism and outlined her radical feminist theology. During the late 1980s she became a major figure in the religious movement that developed out of spiritual feminism in the 1970s and 1980s (see RELIGION AND WOMEN'S RIGHTS).

D&C (dilatation and curettage), a surgical procedure that involves mechanically widening *(dilating)* the CERVIX (the neck of the UTERUS) enough to admit insertion of a small, spoon-shaped scraper *(curet* or *curette)*, which is used to scrape away part or all of the uterine lining *(endometrium)*. In the United States this is the single most common surgical operation performed; an estimated nineteen out of twenty women will have a D&C at some time during their lives.

The D&C is so common because it is used for a wide variety of diagnostic and preventative reasons, among them to
- check for possible UTERINE CANCER.
- check for possible FIBROIDS.
- more generally, to check for causes of abnormal bleeding or staining.
- remove small growths called *polyps.*
- stop heavy bleeding, as from overgrowth of the endometrium, called *endometrial hyperplasia* (see UTERUS).
- see if OVULATION has occurred, in cases of INFERTILITY.
- remove any remaining tissue, as from the PLACENTA or AMNIOTIC SAC, after CHILDBIRTH, MISCARRIAGE, STILLBIRTH, or ABORTION.
- perform an early abortion, though that is now generally done using a procedure called *vacuum extraction* (see ABORTION); for a later abortion, generally thirteen to eighteen weeks, a D&C may be combined with vacuum extraction, the procedure then being called a *dilatation and evacuation* (D&E).

Though relatively safe, a D&C is still surgery and involves some risk, notably from infection, damage to nearby organs, or problems with ANESTHESIA, and so should not be done lightly and without medical cause. A D&C is generally performed only when the woman has no apparent infection or inflammation, and of course when she is not pregnant, unless she does not wish to continue a PREGNANCY. It is done under general, regional, and sometimes local anesthesia, while the woman is in the same *dorsal lithotomy* position used in a GYNECOLOG- ICAL EXAMINATION, with the VAGINA held open by a device called a *speculum*. The cervix is steadied with a special clamp called a *tenaculum* and then gradually widened, often by insertion and withdrawal of a graduated series of rods. Then the curette is inserted through the cervical passage, to remove the tissue. The procedure takes only fifteen to twenty minutes and requires no stitches.

After a D&C, a woman will generally have mild cramps or a backache for a couple of days and bleeding or staining for perhaps two weeks. During that pe- riod, until the cervix returns to its normal position protecting the internal or- gans, she is often advised to avoid vaginal SEXUAL INTERCOURSE, DOUCHING, and use of tampons (see MENSTRUATION). Any sign of a fever, heavy bleeding, smelly discharge, or severe cramps can signal a serious problem, especially an infection, and should trigger immediate consultation with the doctor, who should in any case give a postoperative checkup after two weeks. (See WOMEN'S HEALTH HELP, INFORMATION, AND ACTION GUIDE on page 334.)

D&E, the abbreviation for the surgical procedure called *dilatation and evacuation* (see D&C; ABORTION).

dating: See MATE SELECTION.

Davison, Emily Wilding (1872–1913), a British militant feminist known for her hunger-striking tactics. An activist in the WOMEN'S SOCIAL AND PO- LITICAL UNION, Davison was arrested frequently from 1906 on; she moved to ar- son and violence somewhat earlier than the organization itself, which did not fully go over to guerrilla tactics until 1913. She tried to commit suicide at Holloway prison in 1911 to dramatically protest against force-feeding and in 1913 succeeded in martyring herself by jumping before the horse of King George V at the Epsom horse races and being trampled to death. Her burial was the occasion of a large WOMAN SUFFRAGE march.

Decade for Women: See INTERNATIONAL WOMEN'S YEAR.

Declaration of Sentiments and Resolutions, a centrally important document in the history of women and the worldwide fight for women's rights, introduced and signed at the SENECA FALLS WOMEN'S RIGHTS CONVENTION in 1848. (For the full text, see page 793; see also WOMEN'S RIGHTS MOVEMENT.)

Declaration of the Rights of Women, a document written by Elizabeth Cady STANTON and Matilda GAGE, for presentation at the 1876 Philadelphia Centennial celebration of the Declaration of Independence; the new declaration ended, "We ask justice, we ask equality, we ask that all the civil and political rights that belong to citizens of the United States, be guaranteed to us and our daughters forever." Although officials denied them permission to read their statement from the platform, they printed and distributed it widely. Their declaration had a considerable impact on the WOMEN'S RIGHTS MOVEMENT of the day.

Declaration of the Rights of Women and Citizens: See Olympe de GOUGES.

delivery, in PREGNANCY, the actual bringing forth of a baby from a mother's body and the expulsion of the PLACENTA (afterbirth). These actions correspond with the second and third stages of LABOR. Most children are delivered by vaginal birth, sometimes with assistance, but sometimes CESAREAN SECTION is required. (For a discussion of the stages, see LABOR; for a discussion of a woman's main birthing choices, see CHILDBIRTH.)

Depo-Provera, an injectable form of BIRTH CONTROL, consisting of a STEROID—*depo-medroxy progesterone acetate*—which mimics the effects of PROGESTIN, the synthetic form of PROGESTERONE used in BIRTH CONTROL PILLS and NORPLANT. Depo-Provera's main effect is to suppress OVULATION, or release of a woman's egg (OVUM), and so prevent PREGNANCY. The drug is contained in tiny crystals that, after injection in a water-based solution, dissolve in the woman's body.

A woman should receive an injection of Depo-Provera within five days of the beginning of her menstrual period. If she has just had a baby, she should get the injection five days after the birth if she is not BREASTFEEDING, but should wait for six weeks if she is, as a precaution, although World Health Organization studies so far have indicated no adverse effects on breast milk or on a nursing infant's health.

The most common side effect is a change in the menstrual cycle, which declines to irregular bleeding or spotting, and often disappears after several injections, which many women regard as a major plus; where MENSTRUATION continues, adverse symptoms, such as cramps and pain, including ovulatory pain, are often lessened. Many women taking Depo-Provera also have some weight gain, for unknown reasons, and may experience headache, dizziness, weakness, fatigue, nervousness, or abdominal pain. Women are advised *not* to take Depo-Provera if they have BREAST CANCER, BLOOD clots, unexplained vaginal bleeding, or liver disease. Women at risk for OSTEOPOROSIS should also discuss their options carefully with their doctor, since at least one study has indicated possible loss of bone density with long-term use of Depo-Provera.

If a woman decides she wants to get pregnant, she stops getting injections.

Normal menstrual periods will usually return within a few months. The length of time before CONCEPTION varies from four to thirty-one months, with the median time being ten months.

As of mid-1992 Depo-Provera was approved for use and available in approximately ninety countries. In the United States, the Food and Drug Administration did not approve it for use until 1992, although panels of experts had recommended approval twice in the 1970s. Approval was delayed because some international studies have indicated that women using Depo-Provera have a somewhat increased risk of breast cancer; that is the main basis for opposition to Depo-Provera by organizations such as the NATIONAL WOMEN'S HEALTH NETWORK. However, Dr. David Thomas, the leader of a World Health Organization (WHO) international study, reported that among *all* women, no additional breast cancer risk was found; and that although risk of breast cancer in women under thirty-five was slightly increased, it was no greater than that associated with BIRTH CONTROL PILLS, and that risk of cancer of the endometrium (the lining of the UTERUS; see UTERINE CANCER) was lessened, enough to lead overall to a decreased risk of CANCER.

Many family-planning organizations support use of Depo-Provera because of its convenience as a contraceptive. The main advantages of Depo-Provera are that it is injected only four times a year, eliminating birth control concerns for the rest of the year; it is as reliable as birth control pills in pregnancy prevention, with nearly 99 percent effectiveness; and it can be used privately, without a sexual partner's knowledge. The injections cost about $30 each, or $120 a year. One problem with Depo-Provera is that it has the potential to be misused as a form of social control (see EUGENICS). (See BIRTH CONTROL; also BIRTH CONTROL AND FAMILY PLANNING HELP, INFORMATION, AND ACTION GUIDE on page 81.)

depression, a condition characterized by feelings of hopelessness, worthlessness, dejection, apathy, pessimism, fatigue, and general lack of well-being. Many people, women and men alike, can experience minor and temporary depression in particular circumstances, often stressful events and situations such as bereavement, SEPARATION and DIVORCE, chronic medical illnesses, and changes in role, as with retired people or DISPLACED HOMEMAKERS. In most such cases, the depression is temporary and not deep, and people are able to recover on their own, often with the support of friends and family.

But sometimes the depression is so deep or long-lasting as to qualify as a MENTAL DISORDER. In general, the National Institute of Mental Health (NIMH) indicates that a clinical case of depression may exist if at least four of the symptoms below are apparent nearly every day for at least two weeks:
- change in appetite or weight.
- change in sleeping patterns, such as inability to sleep through the night or unusually long sleep.
- speech or movement with unusual speed or slowness (motor agitation or retardation).
- loss of interest or pleasure in usual activities.
- decrease in sexual drive.

- fatigue and loss of energy.
- depressed or irritable mood.
- feelings of worthlessness, self-reproach, or guilt.
- diminished ability to think or concentrate, slowed thinking, or indecisiveness.
- thoughts of death, suicide, wishing to be dead, or suicide attempt.

The NIMH notes that most people who attempt suicide are depressed, though many people who are depressed never attempt or even consider suicide. In some people, depression alternates with a hyperactive, manic state, the resulting condition being called *manic-depression,* or, medically, a *bipolar disorder;* research suggests that this condition is linked to a genetic defect (see GENETIC DISORDER).

The causes of depression are still obscure, but recent studies do make some things clear—most importantly, that depression is not an inevitable part of the aging process, nor is it triggered solely by emotional or social factors in the person's life. Indeed, researchers are finding more and more evidence that major depression is associated with changes leading to abnormal functioning in the brain, which can actually be seen on certain kinds of brain scans. These changes can be caused by genetic or environmental factors, illnesses such as stroke, side effects of medications (such as those used to control high BLOOD pressure), or genetic, environmental, or other as-yet-unknown factors. Often if a person experiences one episode of depression, more will follow; indeed, some doctors think of clinical depression as a chronic disease, with periodic episodes of acute symptoms.

Among adult women, one major trigger for depression is CHILDBIRTH, with many new MOTHERS experiencing a post-delivery condition called *postpartum depression,* or the *baby blues.* This usually short-lived condition is believed to be triggered by the massive hormonal changes that follow a pregnancy, as well as life-style changes from the new child. In some cases, the condition is so serious that the woman may harm herself or her baby, the disorder then being termed *puerperal psychosis.*

Other kinds of depression may appear at any time. Though long thought a condition primarily affecting adults, depression has now been shown to be common among young people as well, especially among adolescent girls, and often linked with other disorders. Older women, especially those living alone, are also often subject to depression, which may be associated with ALCOHOL AND DRUG ABUSE.

Fortunately, various medications have been developed that can help ease the symptoms of depression for many sufferers by altering brain chemistry, though it is not clear just how they work. Several major kinds of antidepressants exist, including tricyclics, tetracyclics, MAO inhibitors, and other drugs; the FOOD AND DRUG ADMINISTRATION (FDA) notes that no one type of drug has yet been shown to be significantly more effective than the others. In deciding which to prescribe, doctors must analyze the particular patient's medical condition, including other medications and the likelihood of side effects in the individual.

The drugs do not work immediately, and can take weeks to built up sufficiently to reduce symptoms—perhaps three to six weeks among younger adults, but six to twelve weeks in older people, who require smaller doses, since they may have more drug reactions and also respond more slowly. A problem is that many people fail to take the full prescribed dose of their medications needed to be effective. After symptoms have subsided, many doctors slowly reduce the levels of medication. However, at least one recent study has shown that patients kept on the steady level of medication had significantly fewer recurrent episodes of depression.

One controversial approach to people for whom antidepressant medications are for some reason not appropriate is electroconvulsive therapy (ECT), in which electrical currents are sent through the brain while the patient is anesthetized, the aim being to produce a brain seizure, to "shock" the brain back into proper functioning. Once widely used and abused, ECT fell into disfavor in the mid-twentieth century, though it is still sometimes employed. The FDA has expressed concern about side effects such as confusion, memory lapses, headaches, muscle soreness, nausea, and, more seriously, heart disturbances and possible loss of memory, short- or long-term. Another concern is that psychiatrists need no special license or certification to use ECT.

Beyond that, depression is treated with therapy, counseling, and sometimes temporary hospitalization. Whether they are recovering from major or minor depression, many people are substantially aided by mutual-support groups (see MENTAL HEALTH HELP, INFORMATION, AND ACTION GUIDE on page 442). (See also MENTAL DISORDERS.)

dermabrasion, a procedure done to remove outer layers of SKIN (see COSMETIC SURGERY).

Deroin, Jeanne (1810–1894), a trailblazing French feminist and socialist who participated in the 1848 revolution and became the first woman candidate for the National Assembly in 1849. Deroin was a pioneer on social and political issues, keeping her own name after MARRIAGE (see NAMES IN MARRIAGE) and speaking sharply on many aspects of women's condition in France, both as editor of the women's newspaper *L'Opinion des Femmes* and in such essays as *Cours de droit social pour les femmes* (1848). Self-exiled in 1852, she continued to speak from Britain, in works such as *Almanach des femmes* (1854) and *Lettre aux travailleurs* (1856). (See also WOMEN'S RIGHTS MOVEMENT.)

... the revolutionary tempest, in overturning at the same time the throne and the scaffold, in breaking the chain of the black slave, forgot to break the chain of the most oppressed of all—of Woman, the pariah of humanity....

JEANNE DEROIN, 1851
IN A LETTER FROM A PARIS PRISON

•

DES (diethylstilbestrol),

a synthetic form of the female hormone ESTRO-GEN, which was prescribed as a medication to many women between 1941 and 1971, especially women with a previous history of MISCARRIAGE, premature DE-LIVERY, bleeding during PREGNANCY, or DIABETES. However, DES was later found to have strongly adverse health effects on the women taking it and on their children.

In particular, DES mothers have an increased risk of having BREAST CANCER. DES daughters are more likely to have miscarriages, premature delivery, or EC-TOPIC PREGNANCY; they may have malformations in the CERVIX or VAGINA that make CONCEPTION more difficult (see INFERTILITY); and they have an increased risk of a rare CANCER of the vagina or cervix, called *clear-cell adenocarcinoma* (see UTERINE CANCER). DES sons are also likely to have problems or malformations of the GENITALS, including underdeveloped or undescended TESTES, and low SPERM counts. Some recent research also suggests a higher rate of IMMUNE SYSTEM disorders among DES children.

Unfortunately, the problems surfaced many years after the drug was widely prescribed, and many women no longer remembered being given DES during pregnancy. Young women who are considering pregnancy may want to check with their mother about medications and problems experienced during pregnancy; they may want also to check the mother's medical records at the doctor, pharmacy, or hospital, if those are still accessible. Many DES sons and daughters have had not problems with conception and pregnancy and have borne normal, healthy children. However, they are advised to have regular medical checkups to screen for possible changes in the body. In particular, many doctors advise DES daughters to avoid estrogen-containing BIRTH CONTROL PILLS or ESTROGEN REPLACE-MENT THERAPY, since the estrogen can increase their risk of cancer.

In some places, despite knowledge of the long-term adverse effects, DES was prescribed as late as 1980 as a MORNING AFTER PILL, especially on some college campuses. Women in their thirties who remember being given such medications should check their medical records and consult their doctors for advice.

For more help, information, and action

▶ **DES Action** (1615 Broadway, Oakland, CA 94612; 510-465-4011; Nora Cody, executive director), an organization for DES mothers and their children. It gathers and disseminates information about effects of DES; provides for mutual support through DES Cancer Network for DES daughters; and publishes various materials, including *DES Exposure: Questions and Answers for Mothers, Daughters and Sons, Fertility and Pregnancy Guide for DES Daughters and Sons, Preventing Preterm Birth: A Parent's Guide, Every Woman's Guide to Tests During Pregnancy,* and *Natural Remedies for Pregnancy Discomforts.*

▶ NATIONAL WOMEN'S HEALTH NETWORK (NWHN) (202-347-1140). Operates the **Women's Health Information Service,** which publishes the information packet *Diethylstilbestrol (DES).*

▶ **National Cancer Institute** (800-4-CANCER [422-6237]). Publishes *Questions and Answers About DES Exposure During Pregnancy and Before Birth* and *Were*

You or Your Daughter or Son Born After 1940? (See CANCER HELP, INFORMATION, AND ACTION GUIDE on page 133.)

Other resources

To Do No Harm: DES and the Dilemmas of Modern Medicine. Roberta J. Apfel and Susan M. Fisher. Yale University Press, 1984.
Daughters at Risk: A Personal DES History. Stephen Fenichell and Lawrence S. Charfoos. Doubleday, 1981.
(See also CANCER; BIRTH DEFECTS; GENETIC COUNSELING; INFERTILITY; also WOMEN'S HEALTH HELP, INFORMATION, AND ACTION GUIDE on page 334.)

desertion, an alternative term for ABANDONMENT.

development and women's rights, concerns about inequities in the distribution of natural and human resources intended to improve the quality of life. Though in this environmentally conscious world "development" has become a tarnished word, in fact, the concept includes many of the basic improvements in life that all people seek, including better provision of food, fuel, shelter, and other necessities. In recent decades, richer countries have been providing assistance to poorer or "developing" countries around the world. However, much of those funds has gone to massive projects, such as dams, and high-technology approaches, such as pesticide-dependent grains, rather than to the kinds of small-scale, locally oriented projects that directly affect the lives of the community and that are less disruptive of the environment as a whole, such as projects for sustainable farming—where the land is not used up or destroyed, but renewed—and health care projects. Many people, including those in WOMEN'S RIGHTS organizations, have pointed out that the smaller projects are often under the control of women, and suggest that some SEXUAL DISCRIMINATION may be involved in the traditional funneling of money into male-controlled massive projects. Whether or not women are uniquely suited to preserve the environment, as some believe (see ECOFEMINISM), pressure has been building around the world for reevaluation of how development priorities are to be decided, how funds are to be allocated, who is to allocate them, and (when originating elsewhere) what conditions, if any, should accompany them. Such matters as the scale of projects, sustainability, environmental implications, enormous population pressures, huge international debts, agricultural methods, and in some nations current and impending famines and pandemics loom large and are very real—indeed, so large that, in many countries, concerns about women's status and rights can often be overwhelmed by questions of sheer survival.

But improving the political, social, and economic status of the world's women is not simply social justice; it can also lead to massive benefits for all. For example, the funding of programs providing information about and access to BIRTH CONTROL and ABORTION can alone improve the lives of millions of women and men, with women having increased LIFE EXPECTANCY from controlling their reproduction, and with whole families not strained by new mouths to feed. More widely, such programs can help bring under control the population explosion that has been causing the growth of enormous, utterly unmanageable slums, havens for disease, around every major city in the developing world. Similarly, the development of sustainable farming practices, which recognize the vital role of women as farmers in most developing countries, can begin to transform the severely damaged ecologies and economies of such countries, improving the lot of all, not only women.

Some women's rights advocates and feminists also demand that the concept of development itself be reexamined from several different revolutionary feminist points of view, many of which assert that the earth and humanity cannot be saved without radical political solutions. Others, more reformist than revolutionary, seek women's participation in positions of power and decision making and pursue practical gains in such areas as family planning, PROTECTIVE LEGISLATION for women and children workers in industry and agriculture, and real equality before the law and in every aspect of life. Both the revolutionary and the reformist approach tend to be leanings, rather than hard positions. There are very few strongly separatist women's theorists and organizations to be found in the world's poorer countries and very few committed reformers who do not advocate what are in their countries radical new departures. (See POVERTY AND WOMEN HELP, INFORMATION, AND ACTION GUIDE on page 287; WORKING WOMEN'S HELP, INFORMATION, AND ACTION GUIDE on page 779.)

diabetes (diabetes mellitus), a disorder that results when the body is unable to use sugar available in the BLOOD to meet energy needs. This happens when the body has too little or no *insulin,* a HORMONE produced by the pancreas (see DIGESTIVE SYSTEM) that breaks down *glucose,* the sugar that is the body's main form of energy. While sugar builds up in the blood, energy-starved cells begin to burn the body's store of fat and protein, in the process producing toxic waste products called *ketones,* which also build up in the blood. If untreated, the person will become dehydrated, drowsy, and disoriented and in severe cases may lapse into a coma and die. In general, treatment involves maintaining a proper level of glucose in the blood, sometimes through injections of insulin.

Two main forms of diabetes mellitus exist. In *noninsulin-dependent diabetes,* the pancreas does make some insulin. The most common type of diabetes, it may appear at any age but usually emerges after age forty. It is also called *type II, adult-onset, maturity-onset, ketosis-resistant,* or *noninsulin-dependent diabetes mellitus (NIDDM).* Less common but more severe is *insulin-dependent diabetes,* in which the pancreas makes little or no insulin. This form may also appear at any age but generally appears suddenly and often before the age of thirty, so it is called *juvenile-onset, type I, ketosis-prone,* or *insulin-dependent diabetes mellitus (IDDM).*

Both forms of diabetes run in families, but not everyone who has a hereditary disposition toward diabetes actually gets the disorder. Type II seems to be triggered primarily by OBESITY. Type I is thought to result from an autoimmune reaction (see

D

IMMUNE SYSTEM) that destroys insulin-producing cells in the pancreas; the causes of the reaction are unclear, but suspects include a viral infection and, a recent study suggests, possibly even an allergic reaction to milk (see ALLERGIES).

In any form, diabetes is controllable. For many people with type II diabetes, careful diet and plenty of regular exercise may be sufficient. For others with type II, a daily injection of insulin may be required; people with type I diabetes will generally need one or more injections a day. For all diabetics, monitoring of the blood sugar level is critical, and most use do-it-yourself home testing kits. The emphasis, of course, is to see that the body has enough insulin to use blood glucose for its main energy needs. But people with diabetes must also be careful not to let their glucose levels fall too low, a condition called *hypoglycemia* or *insulin shock*. Symptoms include weakness, dizziness, confusion, and, in severe cases, unconsciousness and seizures.

Women with diabetes can have relatively normal pregnancies but must be especially careful in monitoring and managing glucose levels as the growing baby also draws on the body's blood glucose. Diabetes can also appear for the first time during pregnancy, sometimes previously undetected but sometimes triggered specifically by the pregnancy, a condition called *gestational diabetes*. It generally disappears after birth, though it signals a likelihood that type II diabetes may develop later in life. If any form of diabetes is present, the pregnancy will be treated as a high-risk one (see CHILDBIRTH), requiring special care.

If diabetes is not recognized or well controlled during pregnancy, the baby may grow faster and larger than normal, possibly causing difficulty during DELIVERY. Babies of diabetic mothers are somewhat more likely to be premature and to have higher risk of dying shortly after birth, especially from respiratory distress syndrome. Mothers are also at higher risk of maternal complications, but these risks have been much reduced with skilled PRENATAL CARE, as well as postnatal care.

Typical symptoms of diabetes include excessive thirst and hunger, frequent urination, fatigue, weight loss (as fat is burned up for energy), blurred vision, dehydration, and tingling or numbness in hands and feet. Women may also have inflammation, irritation, or itchiness in the GENITAL area and recurrent vaginal or URINARY TRACT infections. A woman who suspects she may have diabetes should see her doctor immediately; it is quickly diagnosed through a urine test. Many medical experts recommend that an oral glucose tolerance test be given to all women between the twenty-fourth and twenty-eighth weeks of pregnancy, or earlier for women at special risk because of family history or other predispositions.

If diabetes is not diagnosed and carefully controlled, it can lead to other serious health problems. Vision may be lost from damage to the retina, a condition called *retinopathy* (see EYES); sensation can be lost from damage to nerve fibers, in *neuropathy*; periodontal problems can develop (see TEETH); the kidneys can be affected (see URINARY TRACT); feet can can develop raw sores (*ulcers*) that can turn gangrenous and in severe cases may require amputation. High BLOOD pressure, cataracts (see EYES), and HEART AND CIRCULATORY SYSTEM problems are somewhat more common among people with diabetes, who have a slightly lower-than-normal life expectancy. (See DIABETES HELP, INFORMATION, AND ACTION GUIDE on page 219.)

DIABETES

Help, Information, and Action Guide

▶ NATIONAL INSTITUTE OF DIABETES, DIGESTIVE AND KIDNEY DISEASES
(NIDDK) (301-496-3583). Publishes the newsletter *Diabetes Dateline*;
operates the **National Diabetes Information Clearinghouse**
(301-468-2162); and distributes materials such as *Facts About Insulin-
Dependent Diabetes, Sports and Exercise for People with Diabetes,
Noninsulin-Dependent Diabetes, Periodontal Disease and Diabetes, A
Guide for Patients, Dental Tips for Diabetics, The Diabetes Dictionary*, and
Diabetic Retinopathy.

▶ **American Diabetes Association (ADA)** (National Service Center, P.O.
Box 25757, 1660 Duke Street, Alexandria, VA 22314; 703-549-1500 or
800-232-3472; John Graham, executive vice-president), an organization
concerned with diabetes. It provides information and services and publishes numerous materials, including the magazines *Diabetes Forecast* and
Kid's Corner, a series of *Diabetes and You* booklets, and books such as *Diabetes in the Family, Diabetes and Pregnancy: What to Expect, Gestational
Diabetes: What to Expect, Diabetic Foot Care, Caring for Children with Diabetes, The Journey and the Dream: A History of the American Diabetes
Association*, and diet guidelines and cookbooks.

▶ **Juvenile Diabetes Foundation International (JDFI)** (432 Park Avenue
South, 16th Floor, New York, NY 10010; 212-889-7575 or 800-223-1138;
Ken Farber, executive director), an organization for people concerned
with insulin-dependent diabetes. It funds research; provides information
and services; and publishes many materials, including the quarterly
newsletter *Tie Lines*, the magazine *Countdown*, and booklets such as
*Pregnancy and Diabetes, What You Should Know About Diabetes, Informa-
tion About Insulin*, and *Self Blood Glucose Monitoring.*

▶ **Joslin Diabetes Center (JDC)** (1 Joslin Place, Boston, MA 02215;
617-732-2400; Kenneth Quickel, president), a private center specializing
in the research and treatment of diabetes. It provides information and
publishes various materials, including *Joslin Magazine* and books such as
*A Guide for Women with Diabetes Who are Pregnant . . . Or Plan to Be,
Know Your Diabetes, Know Yourself*, and *Joslin Diabetes Manual.*

▶ **La Leche League International (LLLI)** (312-455-7730). Publishes *The Diabetic Mother and Breastfeeding*. (See BREASTFEEDING.)

Other resources

Diabetes from the Inside Out: A Resource Manual. Char Gast. Diabetes Education, 1992.

What You Can Do About Diabetes. Norra Tannenhaus. Dell, 1991.
Learning to Live Well with Diabetes. Donnell D. Etzwiler. Chronimed, 1991.
It's Time to Learn About Diabetes. Jean Betschart. Chronimed, 1991.
A Doctor Discusses Diabetes. Lou Joseph and John J. Lynch. Budlong, 1991.
Diabetes Mellitus: A Practical Handbook. Suellyn K. Milchovich and Barbara D. Long. Bull, 1990.
The Diabetic's Book: All Your Questions Answered, rev. ed. June Biermann and Barbara Toohey. Tarcher, 1990.
Diabetes Type Two: Living a Long, Healthy Life Through Blood-Sugar Normalization. Richard K. Bernstein. Prentice-Hall, 1990.
Reversing Diabetes. Julian M. Whitaker. Warner Books, 1990.
The Diabetes Sourcebook: Today's Methods and Ways to Give Yourself the Best Care. Diana W. Guthrie and Richard A. Guthrie. Lowell House, 1990.
The Diabetes Self-Care Method: The Breakthrough Program of Self-Management That Will Help You Lead a Better, Freer, More Normal Life. rev. ed. Charles M. Peterson and Lois Jovanovic-Peterson. Lowell House, 1990.
Diabetes: Actively Staying Healthy: Your Game Plan for Diabetes and Exercise. Marian Franz. Chronimed, 1990.

Dialectic of Sex: The Case for Feminist Revolution, The: See Shulamith FIRESTONE.

diaphragm, a special muscle that divides the chest from the abdomen and helps move air in and out of the lungs (see RESPIRATORY SYSTEM); more generally, any membrane that divides or separates two areas. As a form of BIRTH CONTROL, a diaphragm is a disk of soft rubber, shaped like a shallow cup with a flexible rim, that fits over the CERVIX, forming a physical barrier between a man's SPERM and a woman's egg (OVUM); it is relatively loose-fitting, compared to the CERVICAL CAP. The diaphragm is generally filled with a SPERMICIDE jelly or cream, which acts as a chemical barrier. According to the FOOD AND DRUG ADMINISTRATION, the diaphragm and spermicide together are 80–98 percent effective at preventing PREGNANCY. Spermicides may also give some protection against SEXUALLY TRANSMITTED DISEASES, though they may be associated with some BIRTH DEFECTS if pregnancy occurs (see SPERMICIDE). Some women also wear diaphragms if they wish to have sex during MENSTRUATION, to hold back the BLOOD flow.

Diaphragms must be specially fitted by a doctor and are sold only by prescription, but they can be used and reused for some months. They must be kept cool, clean, and dry for maximum effectiveness and to prevent damage to the rubber. Women should be careful of sharp nails and rings during handling or insertion, so the rubber is not damaged. The diaphragm should be inserted before intercourse and left in place for at least six hours afterward; it can be left in place for up to twenty-four hours, but if intercourse is repeated, additional spermicide should be added to the VAGINA (without removing the diaphragm). If lubricants are desired, only *water-based* kinds should be used, since other kinds can damage the rubber.

The main inconvenience of the diaphragm-and-spermicide combination is that the "run-up" to SEXUAL INTERCOURSE must be interrupted for insertion of the diaphragm; many women put in the diaphragm "on spec" to avoid that distraction, if sex is a possibility. Either way, some women feel use of a diaphragm detracts from sexual spontaneity. Some people have irritation or allergic reactions (see ALLERGIES) to rubber or spermicide; use should be discontinued in case of any genital burning or irritation, and a doctor should be consulted. Diaphragms may also be associated with bladder infections (see URINARY TRACT), constipation (see DIGESTIVE SYSTEM), and, very rarely, TOXIC SHOCK SYNDROME. Some women, especially those with ARTHRITIS in their hands or problems such as carpal tunnel syndrome (see MUSCULAR SYSTEM), find diaphragms messy and difficult to insert and remove. But the diaphragm-spermicide combination is generally considered safe and effective and is widely used. A new product, the VAGINAL POUCH, combines some features of the diaphragm and the CONDOM. (See BIRTH CONTROL AND FAMILY PLANNING HELP, INFORMATION, AND ACTION GUIDE on page 81.)

diethylstilbestrol, the full chemical name of the drug DES.

dieting, the effort to lose weight, specifically by diminishing the amount of fat carried on the body. This process is complicated by the fact that the body gains weight easily but fights weight loss (see OBESITY for a discussion of how). The problem faced by any diet is overcoming that resistance.

Hundreds of diet approaches and programs exist. Unfortunately, though they may offer a quick initial loss, many popular diets do little for long-term weight loss; and, if too much weight is lost too fast, this can be truly hazardous to health and even life. No one should undertake any type of diet without consulting their doctor, to be sure that they are in good health and that the diet approach will not do them harm. This is especially important for those starting a new diet and a strenuous EXERCISE program at the same time. Either one, and certainly both, should be gone into only gradually and with medical advice. One of the main hazards is that the body's rather delicate chemical balance will be thrown off by too little potassium, magnesium, or selenium (see KEY VITAMINS AND MINERALS on page 502); this can cause possibly fatal irregular heart rhythm (arrhythmia), which can occur in people with otherwise healthy hearts (see HEART AND CIRCULATORY SYSTEM).

Basically, diets fall into several main types:
▶ **high-protein, low-carbohydrate diets:** These promote a quick initial drop in weight, as water is excreted with excess protein. However, they do not provide balanced NUTRITION, leading to vitamin and mineral deficiencies; they may cause constipation from lack of roughage (see DIGESTIVE SYSTEM); are generally high in fat and cholesterol; stress the kidneys with excess protein; and may

lead to loss of bone mass, a special problem among women at risk for OSTEO-
POROSIS. Also, as fats are burned, toxic *ketones* are released into the blood,
causing nausea, dizziness, low BLOOD pressure, fatigue, and apathy.

▶ *low-protein, high-carbohydrate diets:* These also promote a quick initial
weight loss. However, they are nutritionally unbalanced, leading to vitamin
and mineral deficiencies while robbing the body of needed protein.

▶ *liquid or powdered protein diets:* These also promote rapid initial weight loss.
Many people are attracted by the total substitution for "real food," avoiding
the need to make food choices. These are, however, very unbalanced nutritionally and also promote excess ketones (see above). They can cause symptoms
such as sluggishness, headaches, and bad breath but also serious problems
such as heart arrhythmia, which has caused some deaths. Close supervision by
a doctor is vital if these are to be used at all.

▶ *fasting:* This is starvation, plain and simple. Some people are attracted by the
avoidance of all eating decisions and by the rapid weight loss. But this has the
substantial dangers noted with the liquid protein diets (above), as well as lack
of protein. Dieters also risk gout and DEPRESSION and sudden death from loss
of vital nutrients, dangers also faced by people with ANOREXIA NERVOSA and
BULIMIA.

▶ *reduced calorie diets:* These promote gradual weight loss with nutritional balance and can be continued indefinitely, as long as the basic minimum nutritional needs are met (see RECOMMENDED DAILY DIET on page 498). The
problem is that "calorie counting" can become tedious, and it assumes that all
calories are created equal, which is now understood to be false (see below).

▶ *reduced-fat diets:* These also promote gradual weight loss with nutritional balance and can be continued indefinitely. They are based on the relatively new
understanding that different types of calories are treated differently in the
body; in particular, that carbohydrates and proteins are converted into glucose
for energy and only the excess stored, while almost all fats are stored immediately in fat cells. (See FIGURE OUT YOUR FAT on page 496.)

Many researchers have found that the quick-loss diets are both dangerous
and generally doomed to failure in the long run, as are the drastically low-calorie
diets. A large proportion of those who have "success" with such diets do so only
in the short term, regaining all the weight and more in the long term. Unfortunately, the body's metabolism is such that the resulting weight gain is even easier
and later weight loss even harder.

In fact, so-called yo-yo dieting—cycles of weight losses and gains from successive diets—have proved to be a major health hazard in themselves. A 1991
study showed that repeated changes in weight—whether dieters were slim or
obese to start with—were linked to an increased death rate and double the risk
of death from heart disease. Another study indicated that people experiencing
weight cycling of more than twenty-five pounds had a higher risk of premature
death than smokers (see SMOKING).

Some turn to pills for weight loss. Most over-the-counter diet pills contain
a drug called *phenylpropanolamine* (PPA). Though this was found safe in at least
one 1991 study, some doctors are concerned that PPA can worsen hidden health
problems, such as DIABETES and hypertension (high BLOOD pressure). The FOOD

AND DRUG ADMINISTRATION has since 1990 been reviewing the safety of PPA and meanwhile cautioned dieters to follow label directions carefully, observing warnings about PPA use and not exceeding recommended dosages.

One type of diet pill was made from a vegetable-based commercial thickener, called *guar gum,* which swells when it absorbs moisture. It was designed to swell in the stomach, making a dieter feel full. Unfortunately, if taken with too little water, the substance could and did swell and obstruct the throat; some people had to have surgery to remove the resulting mass, and at least one died from complications of the operation. The product was taken off the United States market by the Food and Drug Administration.

Some people choose to have weight removed surgically. One approach is to have the fat literally sucked out of incisions in the body, a process called *liposuction* (see COSMETIC SURGERY). From the mid-1950s on, an operation called *jejunoileal bypass* was performed, involving disconnection of much of the small intestine, where nutrients are absorbed into the bloodstream. But by the late 1970s, long-term follow-up studies showed that the operation was associated with significant and sometimes fatal health problems, so the operation is now rarely performed.

Two other surgical approaches are *gastroplasty,* in which staples are inserted to narrow the size of the opening into the stomach, so reducing the amount of food entering, and *gastric bypass,* where staples divide the stomach into pouches, lessening the amount of food it can hold, and moving the intestinal connection from the lower pouch to the upper one. Both of these procedures, popularly called *stomach stapling,* are extreme measures and certainly should not be tried until other weight-loss programs have been tried without success and probably only in cases where the obesity is so extreme as to be potentially life-threatening. Long-term safety and effectiveness remain to be seen, in the absence of a behavior change.

The safest and ultimately most successful approach to lifelong weight loss is the reduced fat/reduced calorie approach, with balanced nutrition accompanied by a modest exercise program and sometimes behavior modification programs, resulting in slow but steady weight loss—ideally one-half to one pound a week—and long-term maintenance. In general, dieters should be wary and skeptical of fad diets and "miracle" weight-loss approaches, and of the doctors, firms, and writers who make their living from them and who may pay more attention to a dieter's money than to her well-being. As in most other areas of life, anything that seems too good to be true probably is. Some women (and men) take a different approach, rejecting dieting and the negative feelings that come from failure, and propose instead that people accept themselves (and others) as they are. (See EATING DISORDERS HELP, INFORMATION, AND ACTION GUIDE on page 58; see also NUTRITION; OBESITY; DIGESTIVE SYSTEM.)

digestive system, the system that processes food in the body, extracting vital nutrients and eliminating the remainder. This is a complex process, vulnerable to disorders at many stages.

The basic process is this: Food is taken in at the mouth, where it is chewed and softened with saliva, which begins the process of breaking down the food with chemicals called *enzymes*. As each mouthful is swallowed, it passes through the throat and a long tube called the *esophagus*. Here and all along the system, the food is propelled along by muscle contractions (*peristalsis*) and, when appropriate, held in place for "processing" by ringlike muscles called *sphincters*. All the organs through which the food passes have a mucous lining. In the stomach and small intestines, the mucous membranes produce and release HORMONES, which trigger the production of digestive enzymes by various organs and orchestrate the system's muscular movements.

In the stomach the food encounters acids and other digestive enzymes; the stomach's muscle action mixes them together for two to four hours. The resulting semiliquid mass gradually moves on into the *duodenum* and then the rest of the small intestine. There more digestive enzymes are added, some from the pancreas and liver, including bile stored in the GALLBLADDER. These continue to break down the food into small enough molecules to be used by the body; the lining of the small intestine absorbs these resulting nutrients.

The remaining material is moved on from the last part of the small intestine, the *ileum*, into the large intestine, the *colon*. There the lining absorbs most of the remaining fluid and some other vital chemicals, while the balance—now mostly waste—moves into the final part of the large intestine, the *rectum*, and is held there until excretion through the outer opening, the *anus*, as *feces* or *stool*.

THE HUMAN DIGESTIVE SYSTEM

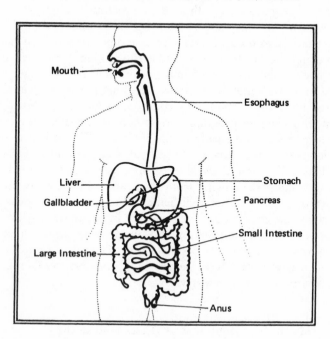

Source: *Facts and Fallacies About Digestive Diseases*,
National Digestive Diseases Information Clearinghouse,
1986.

Such a complicated process can go awry in many ways. If food is moved too quickly through the system, for whatever reason, the body fails to get proper nutrients from it and also has insufficient time to absorb water and reabsorb chemicals; the resulting *diarrhea* can, if unchecked, become dangerous because it dehydrates the body and robs it of vital chemicals. On the other hand, if food moves too slowly, the result will be stool so dry that it is hard to pass, known as *constipation.* The lining of the intestinal tract can become inflamed, keeping sufficient nutrients from being absorbed, or excess acid may "burn" *ulcers*—small cavities surrounded by an inflamed area—into the lining. Sometimes the inflammation and ulceration occur together, as in the chronic disorders generally called *inflammatory bowel disease* (IBD), including *ulcerative disease* and *Crohn's disease.*

Complicated, often subtle, sometimes extremely serious problems can also result from disruption of the chemical and physical processes by which food is broken down to extract nutrients. Dozens of *metabolic disorders* are known to be genetically inherited (see GENETIC INHERITANCE), often involving a defect in the production of just one enzyme or protein. *Storage disorders* result in the damaging and sometimes deadly accumulation of certain compounds in the body. Some such conditions are treatable, once diagnosed, simply by avoiding particular types of foods or other substances that strain the digestive system; enzymes taken orally or by injection can also sometimes overcome the deficiency. People with *celiac sprue,* an inherited intolerance for *gluten,* a substance in wheat, rye, barley, and probably oats, avoid products made from those grains, for example. People with *lactose intolerance,* an inability to digest a sugar found in milk, choose to avoid milk and milk products, while others take pills to help them digest the lactose. Researchers are also experimenting with *gene therapy,* which would involve insertion of genetically engineered cells to replace the defective ones.

Digestive disorders can also result from problems with major related organs, notably the liver, gallbladder, and pancreas. The inability of the pancreas to produce *insulin,* the substance needed to break down sugar in the body, leads to the disorder called DIABETES, sometimes triggered during PREGNANCY. Sometimes, for a variety of reasons, the liver becomes damaged or scarred, in what is called *cirrhosis of the liver.* Then it becomes inefficient or ineffective in carrying out its hundreds of functions, including production of key chemicals and proteins; regulation of the chemistry of the BLOOD; storing the sugar *glucose* (as *glycogen*) until needed; and clearing unwanted substances, including poisons and drugs, from the blood (a function it shares with the kidneys). When the liver is operating normally, these waste substances are excreted in a fluid called *bile,* some of which passes into and is temporarily stored in a small organ called the *gallbladder,* which frequently causes problems for women (see GALLBLADDER). During digestion, bile is released into the small intestine to help in the breakdown and absorption of fats.

Although digestive disorders are found among people of any age or sex— and in the United States send more people to the hospital than any other group of disorders—some are especially common among women, especially during PREGNANCY. Among them are

▶ **heartburn,** production of excess acid in the stomach, causing discomfort as some acid is released backward, or *refluxed,* into the esophagus. Changes during pregnancy, including slowing of the digestive system and relaxation of the connection between the stomach and the esophagus, make this more common, as does the pressure of the enlarged UTERUS late in pregnancy. In general, antacids can help; those containing calcium may also help prevent OSTEOPOROSIS. However, no pregnant woman should take any antacids without consulting her doctor. In general, women are advised to have light meals rather than large, heavy, rich, spicy ones; small, nonfatty snacks and occasional sips of milk may help to neutralize excess acid.

▶ **hiatal hernia,** where the opening (*hiatus*) between the stomach and esophagus relaxes, allowing part of the stomach and sometimes its contents to push back through it. As in heartburn, this irritates the esophagus, which lacks natural protection against the stomach's acid. Hiatal hernia is a common condition, caused by coughing, vomiting, straining at bowel movements, or sudden physical exertion. Often linked with OBESITY, pregnancy, or age, it occurs in most people over age fifty. Sleeping with the upper body raised will help prevent reflux during sleeping. Suggestions for heartburn (above) should also help.

▶ **vomiting,** expulsion of the stomach's contents through the esophagus and the mouth. Often preceded by the uneasy feeling called *nausea,* vomiting is generally involuntary, produced by contractions of the DIAPHRAGM, the sheet of muscle through which the esophagus passes. It is frequently triggered by irritation of the stomach, as from excess amounts of food or alcohol, overly rich or spicy food, or allergic reactions to food (see ALLERGIES), though it may result from many other disorders or imbalances in the body. During the early months of pregnancy, with the body's massive hormonal changes, many women experience nausea and vomiting popularly called *morning sickness,* though it may occur at any time of the day. TIPS FOR FIGHTING MORNING SICKNESS on page 229 has some helpful suggestions, but any woman who has severe vomiting and inability to keep fluids down should contact her doctor. Vomiting also often occurs along with other menstrual problems; these same tips can help during MENSTRUATION. Vomiting can sometimes be induced voluntarily to relieve nausea or as part of the binge-purge cycle of BULIMIA. If done persistently, vomiting can damage and even rupture the esophagus, robbing the body of vital nutrients, and degrade the teeth.

▶ **flatulence,** expulsion of intestinal gases through the intestines. Air swallowed during eating or intestinal gases formed during digestion may be released through the esophagus as a burp or hiccough; otherwise it must pass through the system, sometimes causing temporary abdominal discomfort. It tends to build up during pregnancy as the intestinal action slows somewhat. Avoiding gas-producing foods such as beans, onions, and fried foods should help.

▶ **hemorrhoids,** swelling of veins in the rectum, which sometimes protrude, or *prolapse,* outside the anus, and often bleed. Hemorrhoids generally occur when people strain to clear their bowels; in women they also often occur during PREGNANCY, when the enlarged UTERUS restricts flow of blood in the rectal area, or during the straining of CHILDBIRTH, generally easing after DELIVERY. Symptoms include soreness, irritation, or itching around the rectum, sometimes a clear mucus, and small amounts of red blood. Any woman with bleeding from the rectum should check with her doctor to be sure it is not a sign of something more serious, such as colon CANCER. If that is ruled out, the hemorrhoids can be treated with soothing substances and a diet designed to produce soft stool. In severe cases, especially where the swollen vein becomes twisted and painful, a *hemorrhoidectomy* might be performed to remove the hemorrhoids.

▶ *constipation,* difficulty or infrequency in passing dry stool. This is a common problem, which may result from a wide variety of causes, including improper diet, lack of EXERCISE, too little fluid intake, or pain from hemorrhoids or anal fissure (an ulcer in the anus). It is common in pregnancy when hormones relax the muscles needed to move the bowels normally. Poor bowel action is also common in older people and is a side effect of some medicines. Gradually increasing the amount of water and high-fiber foods in the diet, especially fruits such as figs and prunes, will generally help. So may stool-softening laxatives. Use of laxatives and purgatives should be limited, however, as too frequent use can actually lead to constipation as the bowel muscles lose their natural reflexes. Constipation can also be a sign of serious disorders, so any change in bowel action should be checked out with a doctor.

Another problem, twice as common among women as men, is *irritable bowel syndrome* (IBS), also called *spastic colon* or *nervous bowel,* in which malfunctioning of the muscles that move matter along through the intestines causes spasms and pain. This sometimes involves both diarrhea and constipation, generally decreasing the amount of nutrients absorbed. Many cases of IBS are now suspected of stemming from an allergic reaction to certain foods (see ALLERGIES).

In general, no woman who experiences gastric distress should lightly accept the "diagnosis" that her psychological behavior is the cause, but she should pursue physical causes with her doctors. Interestingly, many digestive disorders long thought to result from "emotional problems" or "stress" are now believed to stem from physical causes; for example, at least some types of stomach ulcers are now thought to be triggered by bacteria.

Like the rest of the body, the digestive system is also subject to malignant growths called *cancers*. Among women, colon and rectal cancer is the second most common kind of cancer, and the third most deadly, though the death rate has been declining in recent decades. Those with a personal or family history of cancer, or of polyps of the colon or rectum, are at increased risk, as are people with inflammatory bowel disease and those with high-fat, low-fiber diets. Warning signals include bleeding from the rectum, blood in stool, or a change in bowel habits. The American Cancer Society (ACS) recommends an annual physical examination by a doctor for people over forty; an annual stool slide test for hidden fecal blood for people over fifty, and a *proctosigmoidoscopy,* a procedure using a flexible, hollow, lighted tube to inspect the colon and rectum every three to five years for people over fifty or when advised by their doctor. Questionable results might lead to further tests, including a *colonoscopy,* or inspection of the entire colon; or a *barium enema,* a procedure allowing an X-ray view of the complete intestinal tract. (See also CANCER.)

Other types of tests used on the digestive system include an *upper GI series* or *small bowel studies,* using ingested barium to X-ray the esophagus and stomach or small intestines, respectively; *arteriograms,* to examine the solid organs, including the liver and pancreas, and their connecting blood vessels; *CT scan* or *CAT scan* for examining the solid organs and abdominal lymph nodes; and *ultrasound*, using sound waves to depict digestive organs. (See **Digestive Disorders Help, Information, and Action Guide,** below.)

DIGESTIVE DISORDERS
Help, Information, and Action Guide

Organizations

▶ **National Institute of Diabetes, Digestive and Kidney Diseases (NIDDK)** (301-496-3583). Operates the **National Digestive Disease Information Clearinghouse** (301-468-6344), and distributes materials such as *Your Digestive System and How It Works, Facts and Fallacies About Digestive Diseases, Digestive Health and Disease: A Glossary, Irritable Bowel Syndrome, About Stomach Ulcers, Inflammatory Bowel Disease, IBD and IBS: Two Very Different Problems, Diarrhea: Infectious and Other Causes, What Is Constipation?, What Is Hiatal Hernia?, Lactose Intolerance, Resources on Dietary Fiber, Digestive Health and Disease: A Glossary, Smoking and Your Digestive System,* and *Diagnostic Tests for Digestive Diseases: X-Rays and Ultrasound.*

▶ **Digestive Disease National Coalition (DDNC)** (711 Second Street, NE, Suite 200, Washington, DC 20002; 202-544-7497; Dale P. Dirks, Washington representative), a coalition of digestive disease organizations, founded in 1979, seeking to educate the public and the health care community, and secure funding for additional research, treatment, and education.

▶ **American Liver Foundation (ALF)** (1425 Pompton Avenue, Cedar Grove, NJ 07009; 201-256-2550 or 800-223-0179; Thelma King Thiel, president), an organization of people concerned with liver diseases. It provides information and referrals; encourages formation of local mutual-support groups; operates the Gift of Life Organ Donor Program; sponsors network for parents of children with liver diseases; and publishes many materials on liver diseases.

Other resources

A Healthy Digestion. Charles B. Clayman, ed. RD Association, 1992.
Gastrointestinal Health: A Self-Help Nutritional Program to Prevent, Alleviate, or Cure the Symptoms of Irritable Bowel Syndrome, Ulcers, Heartburn,

Gas, Constipation, and Many Other Digestive Disorders. Steve R. Peikin. HarperCollins, 1991.

Understanding Your Digestive System. Michael F. Elmore. Creative Ideas, 1991.

Complete Guide to Digestive Disorders: End Poor Digestion with This Self-Help Plan. Kathleen Mayes. Thorsons SF, 1990.

The Complete Book of Better Digestion: A Gut-Level Guide to Gastric Relief. Michael Oppenheim. Rodale, 1990.

Eating Right for a Bad Gut: The Complete Nutritional Guide to Ileitis, Crohn's Disease and Inflammatory Bowel Syndrome. James Scala. NAL, 1990.

Gut Reactions: Understanding Symptoms of the Digestive Tract. Plenum, 1989.

The Wellness Book of I.B.S.: A Guide to Lifelong Relief from Symptoms of One of America's Most Common and Least-Talked-About Ailments: Irritable Bowel Syndrome. Deralee Scanlon and Barbara Cottman Becnel. St. Martin's, 1990.

Irritable Bowel Syndrome: One Disease, Several, or None? Porro G. Bianchi and N. W. Read. Raven, 1990.

The Hemorrhoid Book. Consumer Reports Books eds. and others. Consumer Reports, 1991.

Hemorrhoids: A Book for Silent Sufferers. Jager Rama. Colon and Rectal Care, 1990.

TIPS FOR FIGHTING MORNING SICKNESS

- Eat some dry cereal, a piece of toast, or a cracker about a half hour before getting out of bed in the morning.
- Move slowly when you first get out of bed.
- Divide your food into five small meals a day rather than three large ones, since keeping food in your stomach seems to control nausea.
- Avoid greasy and highly spiced foods, or any food that disagrees with you.
- Drink liquids between meals instead of with your food.
- Let plenty of fresh air into the house, to get rid of cooking and other household odors.

Source: Adapted from *Prenatal Care,* Bureau of Health Care Delivery and Assistance. Division of Maternal and Child Health, for the Public Health Service, 1989.

D

Dignity/USA (1500 Massachusetts Avenue, NW, Suite 11, Washington, DC 20005; 202-861-0017 or 800-877-8797; Kevin Calegari, president), an organization founded in 1969 by gay, lesbian, and bisexual Catholics and their families and friends. Dignity works nationally and through local chapters to "overcome fear and prejudice," seeks to create "liturgical expressions of lesbian and gay spirituality, and explores linkages with other justice movements through attention to women's concerns, inclusive language, and multiculturalism." It provides educational materials; offers programs "to help heal those who have been alienated by ministers of the church;" and makes referrals to local chapters for support and counseling, including one-on-one HIV/AIDS crisis support. It also publishes the *Dignity/USA Journal.*

dilatation and curettage, the full medical name for the surgical procedure called a D&C.

dilatation and evacuation (D&E), a surgical procedure combining a D&C with vacuum extraction, as during an ABORTION.

Dinner Party, The: See Judy CHICAGO.

discrimination against women: See SEXUAL DISCRIMINATION; for sexual orientation discrimination, see LESBIAN.

displaced homemakers, people who have spent years caring for home and family, performing unpaid labor at home (see HOUSEWORK), and suddenly lose the financial support that has been coming from other family members. Most are women, though a very small number are men. They may be married or single; they may have young children or grown children or be childless. They may have lost their partners through DIVORCE, SEPARATION, or death (see WIDOW); experienced long-term unemployment, disability, or financially crippling illnesses; or lost vital public assistance. They may have been rich or poor, lived in mansions or been homeless, and may be from any kind of ethnic or socioeconomic background. But what they have in common is this: They are obliged to make their living with little or no skills that are valued in the world of employment, despite the fact that they have, in fact, been *working* all their lives (see WORK AND WOMEN; HOUSEWORK). In recent decades, as DIVORCE rates have climbed and women have more and more outlived their husbands (see LIFE EXPECTANCY), the number of such displaced homemakers has grown sharply.

Displaced homemakers have often been out of the labor market for many years, or have never been in the labor market, and have few or no marketable skills. What such women need—and too few have had—is support, counseling, training, and placement in jobs that pay sufficiently well to make them self-supporting. As the need has become clear, programs have been established on many levels—local, region, and national, both public and private—in many countries. In the United States, a major resource is the Displaced Homemaker Network, which provides information on many helping organizations that provide assistance, aided by the 1973 federal Employment and Training Act. In addition, many states have passed laws designed to help displaced homemakers. Congress passed the Displaced Homemakers Self-Sufficiency Assistance Act (DHSSA) in 1990, establishing the first federal training program designed specifically for displaced homemakers and SINGLE PARENTS, though it was not immediately funded. The 1990 Perkins Act (Carl D. Perkins Vocational and Applied Technology Education Act) aims to provide equitable vocational education opportunities for women and girls (see EDUCATION EQUITY). The NON-TRADITIONAL EMPLOYMENT FOR WOMEN ACT (NEW) may also benefit displaced homemakers, along with other women. Even so, such programs have so far only scratched the surface. In many parts of the world it is precisely fear of losing vital support, of becoming homeless, that keeps many BATTERED WOMEN in abusive, unequal family relationships. (See CAREGIVER'S HELP, INFORMATION, AND ACTION GUIDE on page 454; DIVORCE AND SEPARATION HELP, INFORMATION, AND ACTION GUIDE on page 238; OLDER WOMEN'S HELP, INFORMATION, AND ACTION GUIDE on page 374; WORKING WOMEN'S HELP, INFORMATION, AND ACTION GUIDE on page 779; SEXUAL DISCRIMINATION AND SEXUAL HARASSMENT HELP, INFORMATION AND ACTION GUIDE on page 642.)

divorce, the legal termination of a MARRIAGE, resulting from a formal court judgment sought by a couple unable to continue as wife and husband. Unlike ANNULMENT, divorce ends a legally existing marriage and the rights and responsibilities associated with it. The former husband and wife must decide between themselves—or ask the court to do so—as to their new relationships on continuing matters, such as CUSTODY of any children, CHILD SUPPORT, ALIMONY, division of MARITAL PROPERTY, and possible share in each other's estate at death (see INHERITANCE RIGHTS). Such matters are best laid out formally in a legal document called a SEPARATION AGREEMENT.

The full and final termination of a marriage, which allows both partners to remarry, is legally called a *divorce a vinculo* or *a vinculo matrimonii*, meaning "divorce from the bonds of matrimony." Sometimes the wife and husband no longer wish to live together but do not want to legally end the marriage, as when they have religious prohibitions against divorce. In that case they may arrange a formal SEPARATION, or *limited divorce*, legally called *divorce a mensa et thoro*, or "divorce from bed and board." Divorces are granted under the laws of the state or nation where the couple lives. If the parties wish to get a *foreign* or *migratory divorce*, from another state or country, they should get legal advice to be sure that their home state accepts such a divorce; if the foreign divorce is regarded as invalid and either party marries someone else, the resulting marriage may be illegal (see BIGAMY). Church divorces, such as a *get* in the Jewish religion or an annulment from the Catholic church, also have no legal validity.

Traditionally, society has had strong pressures to maintain marriage and family units, and divorces were frowned on. Where divorces were allowed, they often favored and were easier for the husband than for the wife. In pre-Christian Rome and Greece, a wife or husband could end a marriage by a public act called *repudiation,* and in early Jewish law a man could cast out his wife at will (a practice that still exists in some Islamic societies). In early Christian societies, divorce came to be more strictly controlled, though men were still favored. For example, a man could repudiate his wife if she had committed ADULTERY, tried to murder her husband, or had committed a serious crime; a wife had the same rights—but if she exercised them, she had to wait for five years before remarrying.

During medieval times, as the Christian church developed the view of marriage as a sacrament, divorces came to be judged on a case-by-case basis by Church courts and were very rare, partly because remarriage and extramarital sexual relations alike were forbidden. In some areas, notably Spain and parts of South America, divorce is still handled largely by Church courts, though governments provide divorces for civil marriages. In other countries divorce proceedings were gradually taken over by civil courts, which acknowledged only limited legal bases, or *grounds,* for divorce, such as adultery or ABANDONMENT. Whatever the misery of the marriage, or the real reasons for wishing a divorce, the parties could not get a divorce without proving to the court that such *grounds* existed. A woman whose husband beat her could not sue for divorce unless she could prove *other* grounds, such as adultery. And a couple could not mutually agree between themselves that their marriage was beyond repair and seek a divorce. To get a divorce, the "innocent" party had to prove fault on the part of the "guilty" party. Over time, more grounds were added, making divorce somewhat more common, and sometimes couples would collude to "rig" evidence of divorce grounds. But the adversarial nature of divorce proceedings continued to dominate into the twentieth century. In fact, some states would not grant divorce if both parties were guilty, under what was called the *clean-hands doctrine,* which obliged the complaining party to be innocent of like offenses.

Today, many states have instituted nonadversarial—so-called *no-fault*—divorces (see below), in which the parties can mutually agree to dissolve the marriage. But many states still have guilt-based divorce; guilt-based proceedings are also common where related questions are being contested. In such adversarial proceedings, the so-called guilty party often fares less well in court decisions on contested issues, including custody, child support, alimony, and property division (see CUSTODY for a fuller discussion).

The precise grounds for divorce vary state by state, nation by nation, but often include the following:

▶ *adultery,* having voluntary sex with someone other than a legal SPOUSE. Living with someone else is called *adulterous* COHABITATION. (See ADULTERY.)

▶ *bigamy,* being still legally married to another person. In some states an annulment is provided for the illegal marriage; other states grant a divorce. (See BIGAMY.)

▶ *abandonment,* intentional desertion of a spouse without a valid legal reason, not always a straightforward question. (See ABANDONMENT.)

▶ *imprisonment,* where a convicted spouse has been sentenced to prison for a specified time, such as one to three years.

▶ *unintentional desertion,* as when a soldier or sailor goes missing and fails to return, though abandonment was not intended. Traditionally, under *Enoch Arden laws,* so-named after Alfred Lord Tennyson's poem "Enoch Arden" about such a situation, the missing partner was presumed dead after seven years, and the surviving partner could remarry, though if the wanderer returned, the original marriage would still exist. Modern laws tend to grant divorce on proof of disappearance, generally after a specified time, which can be shortened if there is circumstantial evidence of death, though no body.

▶ *constructive abandonment,* where one partner denies the other the "comforts and benefits" of marriage, sometimes sexual relations alone but often stretching to wider disaffection. (See ABANDONMENT.)

▶ *gross neglect of duty,* where one of the partners fails to perform the duties involved in a marriage relationship (see MARRIAGE). Where husband and wife have a traditional sexual division of labor within a marriage, a wife might be sued for refusing to keep house and prepare meals, for example. Such matters are quite subjective and variously interpreted by the courts, however, which often seek a pattern of actions, not a single type of neglect, such as refusal of sexual relations. One common type of neglect is *nonsupport,* usually charged by a wife against her husband (see SPOUSAL SUPPORT).

▶ *mental and physical cruelty,* including a pattern of physical violence or threats to safety, or patterns of ridicule, contempt, or maltreatment, all variously defined in particular states (see BATTERED WOMEN). Some states recognize as grounds an overlapping category of acts called *personal indignities,* involving patterns of ridicule, contempt, rudeness, disdain, and vulgarity.

▶ *alcoholism and drug addiction,* usually where the addiction has continued for some time, such as over a year, but sometimes not where the complaining partner knew about the condition before the marriage and so had accepted it. (See ALCOHOL AND DRUG ABUSE.)

▶ *insanity,* where the condition makes normal marital relations impossible, in some states where the condition has continued for a specified number of years (not necessarily uninterrupted), often where the person is hospitalized; in others only where it has been diagnosed as incurable. In some states the person who obtains the divorce remains responsible for supporting the insane person. (See MENTAL DISORDERS.)

Divorce may also be granted in a variety of situations where a person was deceived about a matter so important that it would have affected the marriage decision, such as inability to have children, being pregnant with another man's child at the time of the wedding, or being underage at the time of the marriage. In many such situations a state may grant an annulment instead of a divorce (see ANNULMENT for a discussion of other grounds for dissolving a marriage).

In an adversarial divorce, the accused could traditionally mount a defense against the charges, to defeat the action for divorce. Over time, various categories of defenses developed that were accepted in divorce courts, all largely based on attacking the other partner. Some of these defenses are still allowed in some places, but in many states much of the liberalization of divorce has included elimination of such pass-the-blame defenses. These defenses included

▶ *recrimination,* in which the partner charged as guilty proved that the other partner was guilty as well. Traditionally, if both partners were judged "guilty," divorce was not granted. When grounds for divorce were increased, this sometimes had the intended effect of making divorce *harder* to obtain, since recrimination was easier to prove.

▶ *provocation,* if the action being complained of was in fact provoked by the complainant.

▶ *condonation,* earlier forgiveness of an offense, as when one partner has an affair and the other partner accepts the situation and maintains or resumes marital relations. In such a case divorce would usually not be granted, though some courts would add the proviso that the offense not be repeated.

▶ *connivance,* where the partner seeking the divorce shared in, promoted, or condoned the event being complained of, as when one partner "sets up" a grounds-giving situation, such as adultery, and encourages the other to fall into it.

▶ *lack of intent,* showing the defending party's inability to comprehend the offense or control its occurrence. A woman might defend herself against a charge of adultery by proving she was raped, for example, or a man might claim insanity as a defense against charges of beating his wife.

▶ *invalid marriage,* where a partner seeks to halt a divorce action, and possible economic loss, by claiming that the original marriage was invalid (see ANNULMENT for a discussion of applicable situations).

▶ *collusion,* where the parties secretly agreed to deceive the court. Before divorce liberalization, such collusion was common and largely winked at by the courts, though technically the parties could be subject to perjury charges. Sometimes one of the parties had a change of heart and used evidence of collusion against a suit for divorce.

A divorce action could also be halted if legal action was not started within a certain period of time after the offense complained of, under rules called *statutes of limitations* or more loosely *laches.*

During the twentieth century, as society has groped toward divorce liberalization, various states and nations have developed approaches that allow couples to get divorced without playing pass-the-guilt. These have in common the notion of incompatibility, irreconcilable differences, or irretrievable breakdown of the marital relationship. They vary markedly, however, both in law and interpretation, since some courts will not apply this approach if one of the parties is strongly at fault in the failure of the marriage. Some states allow virtual *divorce on demand,* where both parties or sometimes just one party says that the marriage is unsalvageable, and often when the parties have lived apart voluntarily for a period of time. In some states divorce is allowed if the parties have lived apart for a specified time, such as a year, as long as they have a mutual separation agreement or a court-ordered separation decree, covering such matters as child support, custody, alimony, and property division. This kind of divorce is called a *conversion divorce,* designed to recognize the fact that the marriage is dead. In some places, the parties need not even live in separate residences but must affirm that they "pursue separate lives and share neither bed nor board." The separation agreement or decree is also vital to protect the interests of a party who does not wish to be divorced.

In the past, many people chose to get a divorce in a foreign country; this so-called *migratory divorce* was easier, cheaper, and quicker, sometimes involving brief residence. It was not, however, always accepted in the state where the divorced parties lived. With liberalization of divorce laws, many more couples choose to get a divorce in the state where they live, if the state laws allow the type of divorce they are seeking. Most divorces today are uncontested; the parties reach a settlement on the key issues between them, generally with advice from separate attorneys; the evidence for the divorce and the settlement are presented to a judge at a hearing, and unless the judge finds reason to question their truth or equity, a divorce judgment will be granted. Some states recommend or mandate marriage counseling or attempts at RECONCILIATION before granting a divorce.

The main problems come in contested divorces, where the parties disagree over whether or not to get a divorce, or about the terms of the separation, especially custody, child support, property division, and alimony. In such cases, a civil trial—with witnesses, evidence, and attorneys for both sides—may take place before a judge and in some cases a jury.

One result of divorce liberalization has been a massive change in family structure. Where once divorce was exceedingly rare, and carried a social stigma, in many Western countries today at least one out of three marriages ends in divorce—in the United States, it is nearer one out of two. Women initiate separation and divorce more often than men do, even though they generally have greater economic hardship afterward. Men are also likely to remarry faster.

In the United States, the divorce *rate*—the number of divorces granted in a given year per one thousand people—rose with liberalization, but then declined somewhat after the early 1980s, partly because young people were marrying later. More useful is the divorce *ratio*, or the number of people who have divorced (at any time in the past) but were not remarried at the time of the survey; that figure took an enormous jump from 35 per 1000 in 1960 to a whopping 142 in 1990. The divorce ratio is higher for women than for men, because women are less likely to remarry, a differential that increases with age, and the divorce rates for Black women are twice that of White women. In actual numbers, that translated to 15,128,000 currently divorced people in 1990, with 8,845,000 of them women. Put still another way, of all the people who had ever been married, as of 1985, 23 percent had experienced a divorce. Divorce is most common among younger and middle-aged adults, but especially in teenage marriages. More than half of all divorces involve one or more children. (See DIVORCE AND SEPARATION HELP, INFORMATION, AND ACTION GUIDE on page 238; also PREPARING FOR DIVORCE: A WOMAN'S GUIDE on page 236.)

PREPARING FOR DIVORCE:
A WOMAN'S GUIDE

Divorce is a messy, unpleasant business, and nothing can change that. But it is also a process that can change a woman's life drastically, so it is worth preparing for as much as for any of the other major life decisions, such as college, career, and marriage.

Before formally beginning the process of getting a divorce—before seeing an attorney and often before opening discussions with her husband—a woman who has decided to get a divorce should, where possible, do a number of basic things to prepare herself for this major undertaking. Many of these relate to finances, both for general support and child rearing expenses.

Dos and Don'ts

- **Do** read and make copies of any statements relating to the family's finances, such as bank statements, brokerage account statements, loan documents and statements, wills, trust documents, mortgage applications, insurance policies (including health and life), your husband's pension plan, property appraisals, medical and dental plans, and financial statements relating to your husband's business.
- **Do** carefully read any income tax return and copy all of it—including schedules and attached forms—before signing it.
- **Do** review all mail and copy down return addresses of those related to finances, including insurance companies, credit card companies, brokerage houses, and banks.
- **Do** keep copies of statements and receipts for payment of household and family expenses involving you, your home, or your children, such as mortgage or rent payments, insurance premiums, utilities, repairs, medical and dental care, food and clothing, transportation, education, and child care.
- **Don't** sign anything without reading it and without making a copy of it.
- **Don't** sign any blank forms (good advice in any case).
- **Do** keep your assets liquid, so you have funds available for legal costs and divorce-related expenses.
- **Do** open your own bank account and put into it as much money as you can.
- **Do** arrange for a credit card or charge account solely in your own name, if you do not already have one.
- **Do** review your financial position and make plans to meet your living

expenses and legal fees; consider who might provide loans if needed, such as family, friends, or a bank.

- **Do** make an inventory of the contents of the family safe-deposit box, if any.
- **Do** keep all your personal papers, and all the financial documentation noted above, in a safe place, preferably outside the home.
- **Do** open a private safe-deposit box for your personal valuables and papers, if it seems necessary or advisable.
- **Do** open a private mail box, at the post office or a mail drop, for personal mail, including materials from your attorney.
- **Do** have a complete medical examination, to be sure you are in good physical health before you start what may be a grueling process.
- **Do** give your car a tuneup and checkup, to be sure you will be mobile.
- **Do** research the separation and divorce laws in your state; your local library and women's organizations can help. (See **DIVORCE AND SEPARATION HELP, INFORMATION, AND ACTION GUIDE** on page 238.)
- **Do** stay in the family home, if possible. But if you and your children are being subjected to abuse by your husband, go to a women's shelter (contact local women's organizations or your attorney for referrals; see also **BATTERED WOMEN**).
- **Do** take the children with you, if at all possible, should you have to move out of the house, if you want custody.
- **Do** maintain close contact with your children, providing continuing care and support, especially if you plan to seek custody.
- **Do** keep your job, if you have one, for the continuity as well as the paychecks.
- **Do** maintain close relationships with your friends and family, for support and companionship.
- **Do** take good care of your health. Stay in control, calm, and alert—it's good for you, and you'll be less subject to possible intimidation.
- **Do** use time to your advantage. Don't rush the divorce process, especially if your husband seems to be in a rush. If you respond to pressure, you may be stuck with an unfair settlement early in the negotiation.
- **Do** reach out for support if you have trouble coping. Friends, family, support groups, therapists, and many other kinds of resources (again, see local women's organizations) can offer understanding and experience, since many have gone through similar experiences.
- **Do** find an attorney to represent *your* interests. Get referrals from friends and local women's groups.
- **Don't** let the divorce run your life.

Source: Adapted from *Divorce and Separation Legal Resource Kit,* NOW Legal Defense and Education Fund (1992) and other materials.

DIVORCE AND SEPARATION

Help, Information, and Action Guide

Organizations

▨ ON LEGAL AND FINANCIAL QUESTIONS

▶ NOW LEGAL DEFENSE AND EDUCATION FUND (NOW LDEF)
(212-925-6635). Co-sponsors the National Judicial Education Program to Promote Equality for Women and Men in the Courts (NJEP). Publishes the *State Index of Women's Legal Rights, Attorney Referral Services List, Divorce Mediation: A Guide for Women, Divorce Planning: A Guide for Women,* and *Child Support Guidelines: How You Can Make a Difference*; a statistical fact sheet on separate and divorce; and the Legal Resource Kits *Child Custody, Child Support, Separation and Divorce—General,* and *Separation and Divorce—Pensions.*

▶ NATIONAL CENTER ON WOMEN AND FAMILY LAW (NCOWFL)
(212-674-8200). Publishes the newsletter *The Women's Advocate, Representation in Interstate Child Custody Disputes and Parental Kidnapping: Policy, Practice and Law, Guide to Interstate Custody Disputes for Domestic Violence Advocates, Custody Litigation on Behalf of Battered Women, Child Support: A Manual for Attorneys, Child Support and You, Mediation and You,* and resource packets on family law issues.

▶ PENSION RIGHTS CENTER (202-296-3776). Operates the Clearinghouse on Pensions and Divorce; publishes *Your Pension Rights at Divorce: What Women Need to Know;* maintains a computerized index of state court cases dealing with pensions and divorce.

▶ NATIONAL LEGAL RESOURCE CENTER FOR CHILD ADVOCACY AND PROTECTION
(202-331-2200).

▶ Help Abolish Legal Tyranny (HALT) (1319 F Street, NW, Suite 300, Washington, DC 20004; 202-347-9600; Bill Fry, executive director), an organization of people interested in citizens acting as their own lawyers (termed *pro se*) in areas such as divorce. It publishes various citizen's legal manuals.

▨ ON LIFE AFTER DIVORCE

▶ PARENTS WITHOUT PARTNERS (PWP) (301-588-9354 or 800-637-7974). Publishes the magazine *The Single Parent*; the book *My Mom and Dad Are Getting a Divorce*; bibliographies on divorce and single parenthood; information kits on family law for noncustodial fathers, noncustodial mothers, and parents raising children alone; and information sheets on topics such as child support and visitation.

▶ OLDER WOMEN'S LEAGUE (OWL) (202-783-6686; OWL POWERLINE, 202-783-6689, a weekly update on congressional activities). Publishes *Divorce and Older Women.*

▶ CHILDREN'S RIGHTS COUNCIL (CRC) 202-547-6227 or 800-787-KIDS [5437].

▶ NATIONAL ORGANIZATION FOR WOMEN (NOW) (202-331-0066). Publishes a Lesbian Rights Resource Kit and Lesbian Rights Lobby Kit.

▶ NATIONAL ORGANIZATION FOR WOMEN'S LEGAL DEFENSE AND EDUCATION FUND (212-925-6635). Publishes the Legal Resource Kit *Lesbian Rights.*

◪ ON CHILD SUPPORT

▶ **National Child Support Enforcement Association (NCSEA)** (Hall of State, 400 North Capitol, NW, Suite 372, Washington, DC 20002; 202-624-8180; Kathy Duggan, executive director), an organization of people and agencies involved in enforcing child support laws. It publishes a newsletter, biennial referral guide, and administrative procedures handbook.

▶ CONGRESSIONAL CAUCUS FOR WOMEN'S ISSUES (202-225-6740).

▶ NATIONAL CENTER FOR YOUTH LAW (NCYL) (415-543-3307).

◪ ABOUT MEDIATION OR ARBITRATION OF FAMILY DISPUTES

▶ **Academy of Family Mediators (AFM)** (P.O. Box 10501, Eugene, OR 97440; 503-345-1205; Nancy Thode, executive director), an organization of legal and mental health professionals promoting mediation of family disputes, including divorce. It provides information, makes referrals, and publishes a newsletter and quarterly.

▶ **Association of Family and Conciliation Courts (AFCC)** (c/o Ann Milne, 329 West Wilson, Madison, WI 53703; 608-251-4001), an organization of professionals concerned with constructive resolution of family disputes involving children, in law, social work, education, and related areas. It supports research and aids professionals and publishes various materials, including a quarterly newsletter, a semiannual journal, and an annual directory, as well as special studies on child support, custody, and visitation, such as *Joint Custody: A Handbook for Judges, Lawyers and Counselors.*

▶ **American Arbitration Association (AAA)** (140 West 51st Street, New York, NY 10020; 212-484-4100; Robert Coulson, president), an organization that focuses on resolving disputes by voluntary methods, as by arbitration or mediation. It makes referrals; conducts workshops and seminars; maintains a library; and publishes various newsletters, manuals, pamphlets, books, and audiovisual materials.

Other resources

■ ON TRYING TO AVOID DIVORCE

Reconcilable Differences: Mending Broken Relationships, rev. ed. Jim Talley. Nelson, 1991.
Divorce Won't Help, rev. ed. Edmund Berlger. International Universities Press, 1991.
Alternative to Divorce, 4th ed. James R. Hine. Interstate, 1990.
The Case Against Divorce. Diane Medved. Fine, 1989.
How to ... Salvage Your Marriage or Survive Your Divorce. Tanist Newton. New Vistas, 1988.

■ PRACTICAL GUIDES

How to Get Your Uncontested Divorce: On Your Own and Without an Attorney. Sherry Wells. Venture Press (NC), 1992.
Divorce Yourself: The National No-Fault Divorce Kit, rev. ed. Daniel Sitarz. Nova Pub (IL), 1991. Original Title: *Divorce Yourself: The National No-Fault No-Lawyer Divorce Handbook.*
Practical Divorce Solutions: A Guidebook, 2nd ed. Charles E. Sherman. Nolo Occidental, 1990.
A Woman's Guide to Divorce and Decision Making: A Supportive Workbook for Women Facing the Process of Divorce. Christina Robertson. Simon & Schuster, 1989.
The Complete Legal Guide to Marriage, Divorce, Custody, and Living Together. Steven M. Sack. Fisher Books, 1988.

■ FINANCIAL QUESTIONS—CHILD SUPPORT, ALIMONY, MARITAL PROPERTY

The Dollars and Sense Guide to Divorce: The Financial Guide for Women. Judith Briles. Ballantine, 1991.
How to Do Better at Collecting Child Support and Alimony. Robert S. Sigman. Legovac, 1991.
Getting Your Share: A Woman's Guide to Successful Divorce Strategies. Lois Brenner. NAL-Dutton, 1991.
How to Modify and Collect Child Support, 3rd ed. Joseph Matthews and others. Nolo Press, 1990.
The Economics of Divorce: A Financial Survival Kit for Women. Libbie Agran. Trilogy Books, 1990.
A Marital Property Handbook, 2nd ed. June Weisberger and Teresa Meuer. Center for Public Representation, 1989.
Divorce: Play the Game to Win. Jan E. Ross and Dianna J. Kremis. Freedom Enterprises, 1988.

Child Support: A Complete, Up-to-Date Authoritative Guide to Collecting Child Support. Marianne Takas. Harper & Row, 1985.

◪ GENERAL WORKS ON DIVORCE

Between Love and Hate: A Guide to Civilized Divorce. L. Gold. Plenum, 1992.

Vicki Lansky's Divorce Book. Vicki Lansky. NAL-Dutton, 1991.

Answers: A Divorce–Separation Survival Handbook. Divorce Support Services, Inc. Staff. Divorce Support, 1991.

Divorce Without Guilt. Robert Preston and Cheryl Preston. Center for Dynamic Living, 1991.

On Divorce. Louis De Bonald. Transaction Publishers, 1991.

When a Friend Gets a Divorce: What Can You Do? Sharon G. Marshall. Baker Books, 1990.

The Parent-Child Manual on Divorce. Maria Sullivan. St. Martin's, 1988; Tor Books, 1988.

No-Fault Divorce, An Exposé. Isabelle Andrews. Carlton, 1988.

Divorce. Sharon J. Price and Patrick C. Mckenry. Sage, 1988.

The Divorce Revolution: The Unexpected Social and Economic Consequences for Women and Children in America. Lenore J. Weitzman. Free Press, 1985.

◪ ON LIFE AFTER DIVORCE

Divorce and New Beginnings: An Authoritative Guide to Recovery and Growth, Solo Parenting, and Stepfamilies. Genevieve Clapp. Wiley, 1992.

The Complete Divorce Recovery Handbook: Grief, Stress, Guilt, Children, Co-dependence, Self-Esteem, Dating, Remarriage. John P. Splinter. Zondervan, 1992.

Divorce Hangover: A Step-by-Step Prescription for Creating a Bright Future After Your Marriage Ends. Anne Walther. Pocket Books, 1991.

Ms. Conceptions: The Trials and Travails of the Divorcée. Marylynn G. Williamson. Williamson (IN), 1991.

The Ex-Wife Syndrome: Cutting the Cord and Breaking Free after the Marriage Is Over. Sandra S. Kahn. Random, 1990.

Divorced Women, New Lives. Ellie Wymard. Ballantine, 1990.

Divorced Families: Meeting the Challenge of Divorce and Remarriage. Constance R. Ahrons and Roy H. Rodgers. Norton, 1989.

Parents Divided, Parents Multiplied. Margaret O. Hyde and Elizabeth H. Forsyth. Westminster John Knox, 1989.

Growing Up with Divorce: Helping Your Child Avoid Immediate and Later Emotional Problems. Neil Kalter. Free Press, 1989.

Helping Your Child Through Separation and Divorce. Glenda Banks. Meyer Stone Books, 1989.

Divorce: How You Can Survive and Thrive in Spite of It. G. D. Lundahl and Ruth C. Lundahl. How Publishers (CA), 1989.

Ex Familia: Grandparents, Parents and Children Adjust to Divorce. Colleen L. Johnson. Rutgers University Press, 1988.

Learning to Leave: A Woman's Guide. Lynette Triere and Richard Peacock. Warner, 1988.

Journey Through Divorce: Five Stages Toward Recovery. Harvey A. Rosenstock and others. Human Sciences Press, 1988.

▨ RELIGIOUS VIEWS

Children, Divorce, and the Church. Doug Adams. Abingdon, 1992.

Beyond Divorce: Hope and Healing in a World of Despair. Don Baker. Harvest House, 1992.

Marriage and Divorce: God's Call, God's Compassion. M. G. McLuman. Tyndale, 1991.

Beyond the Crocodiles: Reflections on Being Divorced and Being Christian. Patricia Wilson. Abingdon, 1990; Upper Room, 1990.

Divorce and Remarriage: Four Christian Views. H. Wayne House, ed. Inter-Varsity, 1990.

Divorce and Remarriage: Religious and Psychological Perspectives. William P. Roberts. Sheed and Ward (MO), 1990.

When Divorce Happens: A Guide for Family and Friends. James Greteman and Joseph Dunne. Ave Maria, 1990.

Tough Talk to a Stubborn Spouse. Stephen Schwambach. Harvest House, 1990.

Through the Whirlwind: A Proven Path to Recovery from the Devastation of Divorce. Bob Burns. Oliver-Nelson, 1989.

Divorce and Remarriage in the Catholic Church. Gerald D. Coleman. Paulist Press, 1988.

Divorce Recovery. Anita Brock. Word Inc., 1988.

Life After Divorce. Gayle C. Foster. Pacific Press, 1988.

Beyond a Broken Promise. Gregg Lewis. Tyndale, 1988.

Surviving Separation and Divorce. Sharon Marshall. Baker Books, 1988.

▨ LEGAL ASPECTS

Handbook of Divorce Mediation. L. Marlow and S. R. Sauber. Plenum, 1990.

Family Law: The Ground for Divorce. HMSO Staff. Unipub, 1990.

You're Entitled: A Divorce Lawyer Talks to Women. Sidney M. DeAngelis. Contemporary, 1989.

Divorcing. Melvin Belli and Mel Krantzler. St. Martin's, 1988.

◪ BACKGROUND BOOKS ON DIVORCE

Growing Up with Divorce. Neil Kalter. Free Press, 1989; Fawcett, 1991.

The Consequences of Divorce: Economic and Custodial Impact on Children and Adults. Craig A. Everett. Haworth Press, 1991.

After Marriage Ends: Economic Consequences for Midlife Women. Leslie A. Morgan. Sage, 1991.

Women and Divorce—Men and Divorce: Gender Differences in Separation, Divorce, and Remarriage. Sandra S. Volgy. Haworth Press, 1991.

Divorce: An American Tradition. Glenda Riley. Oxford University Press, 1991.

The Encyclopedia of Marriage, Divorce, and Family. Margaret DiCanio. Facts on File, 1989.

Second Chances: Men, Women, and Children a Decade after Divorce. Judith S. Wallerstein and Sandra Blakeslee. Ticknor and Fields, 1989; Houghton Mifflin, 1990.

Women, Work, and Divorce. Richard R. Peterson. State University of New York Press, 1989.

Divorce and Divorce Therapy Handbook. Martin R. Textor, ed. Aronson, 1989.

Marriage, Divorce, and Children's Adjustment. Robert E. Emery. Sage, 1988.

Putting Asunder: A History of Divorce in Western Society. Roderick Phillips. Cambridge University Press, 1988.

Impact of Divorce, Single Parenting and Stepparenting on Children. Mavis Hetherington and Josephine Arasteh, eds. L. Erlbaum Associates, 1988.

Impasses of Divorce: The Dynamics and Resolution of Family Conflict. Janet R. Johnston and Linda E. Campbell. Free Press, 1988.

(See also CUSTODY; DISPLACED HOMEMAKERS; also CUSTODY HELP, INFORMATION, AND ACTION GUIDE on page 205; CAREGIVER'S HELP, INFORMATION, AND ACTION GUIDE on page 454.)

domestic feminism, a nineteenth-century approach to some WOMEN'S RIGHTS matters, by way of redefining "women's work" as including admission to previously male-only occupations, especially in white-collar work. Domestic feminists were early organizers of women's vocational educational programs, although they generally disavowed the equal rights advocacy of the women's movement. (See also FEMINISM.)

domestic violence: See BATTERED WOMEN; CHILD ABUSE AND NEGLECT.

Donovanosis, an alternate name for GRANULOMA INGUINALE.

dorsal lithotomy, a position where the woman lies on her back, with legs spread wide apart and feet in stirrups, as during the pelvic portion of a GYNECOLOGICAL EXAMINATION or CHILDBIRTH.

douching, use of a fluid to rinse out a woman's VAGINA, often using a tube placed in the vagina through which the rinse runs under pressure, such as the force of gravity from a bag held above waist height. Douching is done for a variety of reasons, among them

▶ *hygiene,* the idea being that bathing the vagina is comparable to washing the rest of the body; however, the vagina is self-cleansing, and douching is not necessary nor medically recommended, so many women do not douche. Those who do frequently do so after MENSTRUATION or use of a SPERMICIDE. Many health professionals note, however, that douching reduces the natural acidity of the vaginal fluids and so may allow readier growth of infectious organisms. The pressure of the fluid used may also push disease-causing organisms farther into the UTERUS and FALLOPIAN TUBES, making PELVIC INFLAMMATORY DISEASE more likely.

▶ *fighting disease,* as a home remedy for vaginal infections. But the above concerns apply here as well. In addition, except where a sterile disposable device is used, the douche tube can *introduce* infection into the vagina.

▶ BIRTH CONTROL, though it is quite unreliable for these purposes, with estimates of the success rate ranging from 60 percent down to near zero. This is because SPERM can travel very quickly, often passing beyond the vagina and into the CERVIX in only a minute or two. In addition, the pressure of the douching fluid can even speed the sperm on their route. Women attempting to become pregnant should also realize that douching *before* SEXUAL INTERCOURSE or ARTIFICIAL INSEMINATION can decrease the chances of conception by washing away cervical mucus that helps draw sperm into and through the cervix.

▶ SEX SELECTION, attempting to alter the acidity-alkalinity balance of the vaginal fluids to favor sperm carrying chromosomes for the desired sex, a technique of doubtful value, at least so far.

Women who wish to douche for personal cleanliness should discuss with their doctor when, how often, with what fluids, and with what procedures. This is important because some over-the-counter sprays and douches can cause irritation or ALLERGIES and can mask symptoms of infection, allowing it to spread internally unnoticed. If standard nondisposable douche bags are used, they should be washed carefully and stored clean and dry so as not to provide a growing place for bacteria or other disease-causing organisms. Certainly women should not douche if they suspect they may be pregnant; after any gynecological procedure, such as a D&C or ABORTION; after CHILDBIRTH, until the doctor approves; and before a GYNECOLOGICAL EXAMINATION, since it may flush away signs of infection before they can be recognized and analyzed. (See VAGINA; also BIRTH CONTROL and Family Planning Help, Information, and Action Guide on page 81; Women's Health Help, Information, and Action Guide on page 334.)

dower, under common law, a wife's continuing lifetime interest in her husband's property after his death (see INHERITANCE RIGHTS); by contrast, a DOWRY is a payment by the bride's family to the husband. In medieval Europe the dower was originally a BRIDEGIFT, which became transformed into promises of the use of and profits from a portion (often one-third) of her husband's property. The comparable provision for a husband is called CURTESY. The main consideration has traditionally been to provide for a wife who survives her husband, a continuing concern given the difference in LIFE EXPECTANCY and the usual gap of years between a husband's and wife's age.

In many places the common-law approach has been replaced by laws that specify the wife's minimum share in her husband's estate. Under such laws, if a man dies without a will (*intestate*), his wife generally inherits one-third, sometimes one-half, of her husband's property at his death. In some states, if the provisions of a will granted her much less than that, in what is called a *distributive share,* the law would not take effect. However, in many places she would be able to choose the dower portion, under the RIGHT OF ELECTION. Some women's groups are seeking to replace the dower laws with fully equitable MARITAL PROPERTY laws. (See WIDOW; also OLDER WOMEN'S HELP, INFORMATION, AND ACTION GUIDE on page 374.)

Down's syndrome, a type of GENETIC DISORDER that results from a CHROMOSOMAL ABNORMALITY: the possession of three copies (*trisomy*) of the twenty-first chromosome, instead of the normal two. It is also called *trisomy 21, Down syndrome, congenital acromicria,* or (formerly) *mongolism.* Down's syndrome occurs in approximately 1 of every 600–650 births and is the most common cause of mental retardation; it is also associated with a wide variety of other physical problems serious enough that few with Down's syndrome lived to become fully mature adults before modern medical advances.

Women who are over thirty-five or who have a personal or family history of Down's syndrome are at special risk of having a child with the disorder. According to the March of Dimes, the odds of a woman having a child with Down's syndrome rise from 1 in 1,250 in her twenties, to 1 in 365 at age thirty-five, to 1 in 110 at age forty, and 1 in 30 at age forty-five, regardless of whether the pregnancy is her first or tenth. Because of that, many seek GENETIC COUNSELING before PREGNANCY and later take various PRENATAL TESTS that will indicate whether a child has Down's syndrome. (See GENETIC INHERITANCE AND BIRTH DEFECTS HELP, INFORMATION, AND ACTION GUIDE on page 314.)

dowry, in traditional societies, payment made by the bride's family at her MARRIAGE, which some consider a form of *premarital inheritance.* Although administered by the husband, the principal was generally supposed to be kept intact and at the woman's death to be passed on to her children or otherwise revert to her family. In case of DIVORCE, a dowry might be returned to the wife or her family, though part might be reserved for her children, if any; but in some cases a woman might lose all or part of the dowry on divorce, if, for example, she was found guilty of ADULTERY. Some girls never married because their parents could not afford to give them proper dowries. Dowries as such are not given in most modern societies; rather, both parents tend to give substantial gifts to the bride and groom, sometimes including a *settlement* of a certain amount of money in affluent families. In some instances the money that might have been paid as a dowry now goes toward a woman's education or to pay for a large WEDDING.

However, the practice of giving dowries is still prevalent in India and several other Asian and African countries and creates a bitter and despicable social situation called *dowry murder*. When a husband and his family have not—or claim they have not—received all of a promised dowry, the husband rains attacks on his wife, ranging from verbal abuse all the way to officially prohibited but socially sanctioned murder as a means of pressuring the wife's family for additional payments. Statistics on the incidence of dowry murder are impossible to verify, but there is widespread agreement that at least one thousand women a year die this way in India alone. (See MARRIAGE; WEDDING; also COUPLES AND FAMILIES HELP, INFORMATION, AND ACTION GUIDE on page 418.)

Duke's test, one of a battery of tests in a *fertility workup*, performed to discover the causes of INFERTILITY.

Dworkin, Andrea (1946–), a radical feminist writer whose work perceives most of human history as stemming from a false definition of male-female roles where males are defined as superior and enforce that definition by violent means, including the mass murders of women. She calls for a revolution that will destroy the concepts of male and female, replacing them with what she defines as a multisexual continuum. In practice her major focus has been on sexual violence directed against women (see RAPE; BATTERED WOMEN; CHILD ABUSE AND NEGLECT; SEXUAL HARASSMENT) and the outlawing of what she considers to be violence-inducing PORNOGRAPHY. Her best-known work includes *Our Blood: Prophecies and Discourses on Sexual Politics* (1970), *Woman Hating* (1974), and *Pornography: Men Possessing Women* (1981). (See also WOMEN'S LIBERATION MOVEMENT.)

dysmenorrhea, painful or difficult MENSTRUATION.

ears, the pair of structures on either side of the head that receive sounds, translate them into signals, and transmit them to the brain, in the process we call hearing.

The *outer ear,* the part visible on the outside, funnels sound waves into the ear, where they strike the *eardrum,* so-called because it vibrates when struck by sound. The vibrations are passed on to the *middle ear,* where the sound is amplified by a set of tiny bones called the *ossicles,* specifically the *malleus,* the *incus,* and the *stapes.* The amplified sound then passes into the *inner ear,* to a fluid-filled, bony structure called the *cochlea,* shaped somewhat like a snail's shell. This houses the *organ of Corti,* the actual organ of hearing, which is a minute passageway filled with microscopic hair cells. These register the sound vibrations and transform them into electrical signals, which are picked up by nearby nerve cells and transmitted along the *auditory nerve (eighth nerve)* to the brain, where they are "decoded." A narrow canal connecting the middle ear with the throat, the *Eustachian tube,* works to protect the eardrum and ossicles from potentially damaging loud noises or dramatic changes in pressure, as in an airplane descent.

There are two types of hearing loss: *conductive loss,* resulting from problems with the gathering and passing on of sound vibrations by the outer and middle ear, and *sensori-neural losses,* which stem from problems in the inner ear, especially with the sound-receiving hair cells or with the transmitting nerves.

One of the most common types of conductive loss is *otosclerosis,* in which excess bone forms in the middle ear, making the stapes immobile and therefore incapable of transmitting sound waves. This progressive hearing loss often runs in families and affects more women than men; it often starts in early adulthood, in women sometimes during PREGNANCY, and increases with age, producing muffled sounds. It may be associated with ringing in the ears (*tinnitus*) or dizziness (*vertigo*) and can sometimes lead to sensorineural deafness. The condition can often be aided by a hearing aid. Ear specialists (*otologists* or *otolaryngologists*) can sometimes remove the excess bone and replace the stapes with an artificial part, a procedure called a *stapedectomy,* though there is a risk of total deafness in the operated ear.

Conductive loss may also result from a variety of other causes:

▶ **infection,** most common in children, and generally treatable with antibiotics, though surgery is sometimes necessary for drainage. Chronic or severe infections can cause hearing loss.

▶ a **ruptured eardrum,** as from an injury or drastic drop in pressure. Using modern surgical techniques, ear specialists can often repair or rebuild the eardrum in many such cases.

▶ *external blockage,* as with a buildup of wax or an object in the ear. These should be removed only by a medical specialist, since the eardrum may be damaged.

More serious, and generally permanent, are *sensori-neural losses.* These can be present at birth, caused by disease during pregnancy. To protect her future children against hearing loss, a woman who has not had measles *(rubeola)* and German measles *(rubella)* should be sure that she has been vaccinated against both well before becoming pregnant. Unfortunately, no vaccinations exist against some other diseases, so a woman will need to exercise care in avoiding those associated with hearing loss in babies, such as CYTOMEGALOVIRUS and genital HERPES, both SEXUALLY TRANSMITTED DISEASES.

Hearing damage can also result at any time during life from diseases such as mumps, measles, chicken pox, meningitis, encephalitis, and any prolonged high fever, and from some kinds of medications. Tumors called *acoustic neuromas* or *eighth nerve tumors* can cause sensori-neural loss; some can be removed without hearing damage if caught early enough. Physical injury to the head or directly to the ear, as well as excessive or intense noise, can result in hearing loss, sometimes temporary and reversible, but sometimes permanent, especially if the assault is prolonged. A person who experiences any change in hearing, including dizziness, balance problems, or ringing in the ears should check immediately with a doctor.

Hearing loss is also associated with various GENETIC DISORDERS, appearing sometimes at birth, sometimes later. If either partner has hereditary deafness in their personal or family history, prospective parents may want to seek GENETIC COUNSELING to assess the risk of having a child with impaired hearing. Sensori-neural loss can also result from difficult CHILDBIRTH, especially with temporary lack of oxygen to the baby.

Because sensori-neural loss can affect some frequencies more than others, hearing aids can help some people. So can the newer *cochlear implant,* which uses a computerized microprocessor to simulate the cochlea's operations.

In truth, few people have total loss of hearing. Most people with hearing problems are classed not as *deaf,* but as *hard of hearing* or *hearing-impaired.* In ideal situations—facing one other person in an otherwise quiet room, for example—they may be able to understand speech through hearing alone or hearing combined with lip reading. Beyond lip reading and sign language, those with severe hearing loss can now benefit from a whole range of new aids, including telecommunication devices for the deaf (TDDs), alerting systems, electronic mail operating over telephone lines from computer to computer, computers that translate spoken words into words in screen and vice versa, systems that funnel sound directly into a hearing aid, closed captions for visual materials, and even "hearing dogs" that act as alerting systems, all designed to help people with hearing impairment lead independent lives.

For people who suffer gradual hearing loss with age, the most important advice is not to let the impairment isolate you. Consult your doctor, your friends, and groups like those listed below, to get whatever aid or training you need to remain fully active and in control of in your own life. (See EARS AND HEARING HELP, INFORMATION, AND ACTION GUIDE 249.)

EARS AND HEARING

Help, Information, and Action Guide

Organizations

▶ **American Speech-Language-Hearing Association (ASHA)** (10801 Rockville Pike, Rockville, MD 20852; 301-897-5700, voice and TDD [telecommunication devices for the deaf]; or Hearing and Speech Helpline, 800-638-TALK [8255]; Thomas O'Toole, president), an organization concerned with hearing and speech problems; **National Association for Hearing and Speech Action (NAHSA)**. It provides information, makes referrals, and publishes materials such as *Noise and Hearing Loss* and *About Tinnitus.*

▶ **National Institute of Deafness and Other Communication Disorders (NIDCD)** (9000 Rockville Pike, Building 31, Room 3C35, Bethesda, MD 20892; 301-496-7243; James B. Snow, Jr., director), one of the U.S. National Institutes of Health. It provides information and publishes materials such as *Hearing Loss: Hope Through Research.*

▶ **Better Hearing Institute (BHI)** (Box 1840, Washington, DC 20013; 703-642-0580; Hearing Helpline, 800-EAR-WELL [327-9355]), an organization concerned with hearing impairments. It provides information and publishes materials such as *Sounds or Silence?, Tinnitus or Head Noises,* and *Nerve Deafness and You.*

▶ **International Hearing Society (IHS)** (20361 Middlebelt, Livonia, MI 48152; 313-478-2610; Hearing Aid Helpline, 800-521-5247; Robin Holm, executive director), a professional association of hearing instrument specialists. It provides information on hearing aids and possible sources of financial aid; makes referrals to local hearing-aid specialists; and distributes the pamphlet *Facts About Hearing Aids.*

Other resources

Now Hear This: A Consumer's Guide to Testing for Hearing Loss, and the Selection and Purchase of a Suitable Hearing Aid. Lindsay L. Pratt and Dominic Quinn. Forum, 1991.

Hearing Aids—Who Needs Them? What They Can Do For You, Where to Buy Them, How to Use Them. David P. Pascoe. Big Bend Books, 1991.

Living with a Hearing Problem: Coping Strategies and Devices for the Hearing-Impaired. Fred M. Roberts. F. M. Roberts, 1990.

The Hearing-Aid Handbook. Donna S. Wayner. Gallaudet University Press, 1990.

How to Survive Hearing Loss. Charlotte Himber. Gallaudet University Press, 1989.
Health Care U.S.A. Jean Carper. Prentice-Hall, 1987. Includes general and specific health care information on hearing loss and related disorders.
Legal Rights of Hearing-Impaired People. National Center for Law and the Deaf. Gallaudet University Press, 1982.

☒ BACKGROUND WORKS

Dancing Without Music: Deafness in America. Beryl Lieff Benderly. Gallaudet University Press, 1990.
Living with Deafness. Barbara Taylor. Watts, 1989.
Seeing Voices: A Journey into the World of the Deaf. Oliver Sacks. University of California, 1989.

eating disorders, a group of disorders involving abnormal behavior regarding food. The causes of and relationships among these disorders are obscure, despite intensive study in recent decades. Traditionally, most eating disorders have been regarded and treated primarily as MENTAL DISORDERS, but several or all may have as-yet-unidentified physiological triggers, which suggest hope for more effective medical treatments in the future. Because eating disorders are major concerns for women, we have covered the individual types of eating disorders extensively in separate articles; see ANOREXIA NERVOSA; BULIMIA; OBESITY; PICA; BINGE EATING DISORDER.

eclampsia, a rare, life-threatening form of the condition PREECLAMPSIA.

ecofeminism, in general, the idea that women are better than men at being able to recognize and solve Earth's ecological problems. Ecofeminists believe that PATRIARCHY and masculine consciousness have been primarily responsible for devaluing the natural world; that the dominance of culture and technology over nature and life in the man-centered world is linked to the dominance of men over women; and that women are nature-oriented, life-affirming—especially spiritual feminists, who worship the goddess as the deity of earlier matriarchal culture—and so are uniquely suited to save the Earth (see GODDESS WORSHIP; MATRIARCHY; SPIRITUAL FEMINISM). Many go further, to posit that a world run by women—or at least one in which women have full equality—is necessary if the Earth is to be saved. The term *ecofeminism* is also sometimes used to describe any and all environmentalist actions taken by women.

For further information

Reweaving the World: The Emergence of Ecofeminism. Irene Diamond and Gloria Feman Orenstein, eds. Sierra Club Books, 1990.
Healing the Wounds: The Promise of Ecofeminism. Judith Plant, ed. New Society, 1989.

ectopic pregnancy, the abnormal IMPLANTATION and growth of a fertilized egg outside the UTERUS, usually in the FALLOPIAN TUBES (a *tubal pregnancy*), but sometimes in an OVARY, in the CERVIX, or elsewhere in the abdominal cavity.

Ectopic pregnancy normally occurs when the fallopian tubes have been damaged, misshapen, or blocked with scar tissue, which prevents the egg (OVUM) from moving normally from the ovaries to the uterus via the tubes. If the tubes are completely blocked, of course, the SPERM cannot reach the egg, and INFERTILITY results, though a surgical operation called TUBOPLASTY may clear the passageway. However, if SPERM do get through and the egg is fertilized, the EMBRYO may be unable to pass on through to the uterus and begins to develop in the fallopian tubes or migrates elsewhere, propelled by the tubes' muscular movements. As in other pregnancies, sometimes the fertilized egg has such serious defects that its growth ends quickly at a very early stage and the tissue is reabsorbed into the body. But if the pregnancy progresses in an abnormal place, especially in the fallopian tubes, it may grow for two or three months undetected. The tube may rupture when it can no longer expand to hold the growing embryo, possibly resulting in a life-threatening hemorrhage.

Ectopic pregnancies occur in as many as one to two out of every one hundred pregnancies. Any woman might be affected, but women face increased risk of an ectopic pregnancy if they have had severe infections and inflammations, such as PELVIC INFLAMMATORY DISEASE or SEXUALLY TRANSMITTED DISEASES, such as GONORRHEA; any gynecological surgery, including a CESAREAN SECTION; or related disorders, such as a ruptured appendix or ENDOMETRIOSIS. Any of these might lead to scar tissue or adhesions, where skin heals together abnormally, which could block the tubes. Use of an INTRAUTERINE DEVICE (IUD) or BIRTH CONTROL PILLS at the time of CONCEPTION is also associated with a higher-than-normal risk of ectopic pregnancy.

Diagnosis of ectopic pregnancy is not always easy. In some cases a woman will have abdominal pain and a positive pregnancy test—but sometimes she will not. Some have the traditional symptoms of pregnancy, while others may miss one or two periods before resuming MENSTRUATION, with no other symptoms before the tube ruptures. Women who have missed menstrual periods and have irregular light bleeding or spotting and especially sharp or persistent pain in the lower abdomen, especially on one side, should check with their doctor immediately.

An ectopic pregnancy is often confirmed by ULTRASOUND or LAPAROSCOPY and treated on an emergency basis. *How* it is treated depends on the woman's age, her future childbearing desires (if any), and whether she has an active abdominal infection. In an operation called a *laparotomy* (see LAPAROSCOPY), the embryo and any associated tissues are removed; the tube is repaired, where possible, but more often the affected fallopian tube must be removed. If a woman still hopes to bear children, however, the surgeon will try to save the ovaries, the uterus, and the other fallopian tube. In case of rupture and hemorrhage, blood transfusions may be needed to prevent shock and death. If fallopian tubes are partly blocked, or if a woman has lost both fallopian tubes to ectopic pregnancies, she may still become pregnant through use of modern reproductive technology, such as IN VITRO FERTILIZATION, which involves fertilization of an egg outside the body, which is then implanted directly into the uterus, bypassing the need for the tubes. (See INFERTILITY AND REPRODUCTIVE TECHNOLOGY HELP, INFORMATION, AND ACTION GUIDE on page 368.)

education equity, equal access to and opportunity to benefit from learning in any form; until the nineteenth century this was only very rarely available to women, and in the past two centuries education equality has been one of the great goals of the emerging WOMEN'S RIGHTS MOVEMENT. In her SERIOUS PROPOSAL TO THE LADIES (1701), Mary Astell called for the establishment of educational institutions for women. In A Vindication of the Rights of Woman (1792), Mary WOLLSTONECRAFT strongly linked the development of full equality to the opening up of the professions and the whole wide world to women, which in turn depended greatly on developing a system of women's education that went far beyond the kind of "charm school" education then available, and even then only to a few elite women. Key figures in the fight for women's access to learning were such pioneering women educators as Emma Willard, who introduced a then-revolutionary curriculum that included mathematics, the sciences, history, and literature at her Troy (New York) Female Seminary in 1821; Catharine Beecher, who founded the Hartford Academy in 1823; Mary Lyon, who founded Mt. Holyoke Seminary (later College) in 1837; and in Britain, Barbara BODICHON, who founded Portland Hall in 1852; and Emily Davies, who in 1869 founded the college that in 1874 ultimately became Girton College. Their work, in the twentieth century, led to widespread higher education for women. A major event in the history of women's education was the 1865 opening of Vassar College, the first of the top-ranked American women's colleges and the full academic equal of any other American college.

By the middle of the nineteenth century there were more girls than boys in American high schools, and the female lead continued to grow in the twentieth century. African-American women gained the right to education with emancipation; by 1900 more than twice as many were graduating from high school than African-American men.

Although great numbers of American women graduated from high school, and considerable numbers were college graduates by the mid–twentieth century, most found themselves on career tracks that led via courses in home economics and clerical skills to unpaid household labor (see HOUSEWORK), motherhood (see HOMEMAKER), and low-paid labor in such sex-segregated occupations as teaching and the several varieties of administrative support (see WORK AND WOMEN). The rampant SEXUAL DISCRIMINATION of the post–World War II period finally began to give way to the new WOMEN'S RIGHTS MOVEMENTS of the late 1960s, buttressed by such new antidiscrimination laws as TITLE VII OF THE CIVIL RIGHTS ACT OF 1964

WOMEN'S LITERACY IN THE DEVELOPING WORLD

Three-quarters of women aged 25 and over in much of Africa and Asia are still illiterate.

Illiterate women 25 and over, 1990 (%)

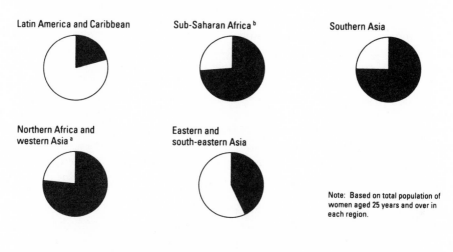

Latin America and Caribbean

Sub-Saharan Africa [b]

Southern Asia

Northern Africa and western Asia [a]

Eastern and south-eastern Asia

Note: Based on total population of women aged 25 years and over in each region.

Illiteracy rates are falling for young women but are still much higher for young women than men.

Over 40 per cent of young women are still illiterate in Africa and southern and western Asia.

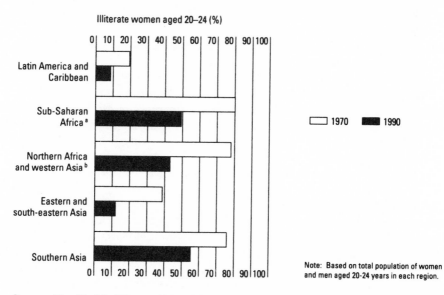

Illiterate women aged 20–24 (%)

☐ 1970   ■ 1990

Latin America and Caribbean

Sub-Saharan Africa [a]

Northern Africa and western Asia [b]

Eastern and south-eastern Asia

Southern Asia

Note: Based on total population of women and men aged 20-24 years in each region.

Source: *The World's Women 1970–1990: Trends and Statistics,* United Nations, 1991.

and TITLE IX OF THE 1972 EDUCATION ACT AMENDMENTS, and women were at last able to move in far larger numbers into more attractive and higher-paying jobs and young women to function in a less inimical educational system and work-place. The Perkins Act (Carl D. Perkins Vocational and Applied Technology Education Act of 1990) aims to provide equitable vocational education opportunities, not only for girls in school, but for older SINGLE PARENTS, including DISPLACED HOMEMAKERS.

In the world's developed countries, existing patterns of education parallel those of the United States with a few variations. In many Asian, Latin American, and Caribbean countries, universal primary schooling is close to being achieved, and secondary schooling advances are being made. In many developed and developing countries, women considerably outnumber men in higher education enrollment.

On the other hand, progress in even basic literacy has been very slow throughout sub-Sahara Africa and south Asia, especially for women. Throughout the poorer countries of the world, exploding populations have created severe social crises, in some countries making it difficult to keep pace in education and literacy. United Nations estimates in 1990 indicate that approximately 75 percent of all women aged twenty-five and over in Africa and Asia are still illiterate, and that more than 40 percent of young women are still illiterate in Africa and southern and western Asia, although some progress is being made. For example, the most recent reports available for 1990 indicate that for women over twenty-five, illiteracy rates are at 84.7 percent in Egypt, 85.7 percent in Algeria, 97.9 percent in Mali, 60.6 percent in Bolivia, 76.4 percent in Haiti, 97.6 percent in Afghanistan, 86.7 percent in Bangladesh, 85.4 percent in Iran, and 80.6 percent in enormous India. The illiteracy rates for younger women (fifteen to twenty-four) are scarcely more encouraging—for example, 72.8 percent in Bangladesh and 59.7 percent in India. There are considerably more illiterate women than men, generally by factors of 15–30 percent. (See WOMEN'S LITERACY IN THE DEVELOPING WORLD on page 253.)

In practical terms the figures are quite understated, for the definition of literacy used is very basic, and many of those described as literate by their countries are, in fact, functionally illiterate. As long as great masses of the world's women are illiterate or barely literate, and are buffeted by growing poverty, a runaway population explosion, and the ever-growing threat of pandemics, the promise of liberation through universal education and equality will be little more than an empty dream.

For more help, information, and action

► PROJECT ON EQUAL EDUCATION RIGHTS (PEER) (212-925-6635). Publishes the *Equal Education Alert, Cracking the Glass Slipper: PEER's Guide to Ending Sex Bias in Your Schools, Beyond Title IX: PEER's State-by-State Guide to Women's Educational Equity Laws,* and *Title IX Packet,* including *Anyone's Guide to Filing a Title IX Complaint.*

► NOW LEGAL DEFENSE AND EDUCATION FUND (NOW LDEF) (212-925-6635). Sponsors the PROJECT ON EQUAL EDUCATION RIGHTS (PEER), (202-332-7337), and publishes a statistical fact sheet on women in education and the Legal Resource Kit *Education.*

▶ NATIONAL COUNCIL FOR RESEARCH ON WOMEN (NCRW) (212-570-5001). Publishes *Opportunities for Research and Study, International Centers for Research on Women, Risk, Resiliency, and Resistance: Current Research on Adolescent Girls, Women in Academe: Progress and Prospects, A Task Force Report.*

▶ WOMEN'S INTERNATIONAL RESOURCE EXCHANGE (WIRE) (212-741-2955). Publishes *The Literacy Issue: Feminine Perspectives on Reading and Writing.*

▶ WOMEN'S SPORTS FOUNDATION (WSF) (212-972-9170; Women's Sports Infoline, 800-227-3988). Publishes *Playing Fair: A Guide to Title IX in College and High School Sports.*

Other resources

Perspectives on Minority Women in Higher Education. Lynne B. Welch. Praeger/ Greenwood, 1992.

Women in Academe: Progress and Prospects. Mariam K. Chamberlain. Russell Sage, 1991.

Smart Choices: A Woman's Guide to Returning to School. Anne Bianchi. Petersons Guides, 1990.

Changing Education: Women As Radicals and Conservators. Joyce Antler and Sara K. Biklen, eds. State University of New York Press, 1990.

Educating the Majority: Women Challenge Tradition in Higher Education. Carol S. Pearson and others, eds. ACE-Macmillan, 1989.

Women of Academe: Outsiders in the Sacred Grove. Nadya Aisenberg and Mona Harrington. University of Massachusetts Press, 1988.

Reconstructing the Academy: Women's Education and Women's Studies. Elizabeth Minnich and others. University of Chicago Press, 1988.

The Higher Education of Women. Emily Davies. Hambledon Press, 1988.

(See also TITLE IX OF THE 1972 EDUCATION ACT AMENDMENTS; SEXUAL DISCRIMINATION; SEXUAL HARASSMENT [for cases in educational settings]; also SEXUAL DISCRIMINATION AND SEXUAL HARASSMENT HELP, INFORMATION, AND ACTION GUIDE on page 642.)

egg donor, a woman who gives an egg (see OVUM) for use by another woman, who is unable to produce eggs of her own but can carry a PREGNANCY to term. (See IN VITRO FERTILIZATION.)

Eisenstadt* v. *Baird, a 1972 U.S. Supreme Court ruling extending to unmarried people the right to contraceptives and the right to privacy with their doctor (see BIRTH CONTROL).

ejaculation, the forceful release of SEMEN from a man's PENIS at ORGASM; during SEXUAL INTERCOURSE it deposits the fluid into a woman's VAGINA; if it contains active

SPERM and the woman has an egg (OVUM) available for FERTILIZATION, CONCEPTION may take place. At least some women seem to experience a form of ejaculation, in which the urethra forcibly expels a fluid (see SEXUAL RESPONSE; ORGASM).

Electra complex, the supposed sexual feelings of a daughter for her FATHER, a stage that, in Freudian psychology, is resolved by the daughter identifying with the MOTHER and adopting her appropriate SEX ROLE. In boys, the analogous theoretical relationship with the mother is called an *Oedipus complex*. Both names are taken from characters in Greek tragedies.

El Saadawi, Nawal (1930–), an Egyptian doctor and writer who emerged in the 1970s as a rare major feminist figure in the Arab world, with the publication of her powerful *Women and Sex* (1972), which resulted in the loss of her job at the Egyptian Health Ministry but found her a worldwide audience. Another major work was her trailblazing *The Hidden Face of Eve: Women in the Arab World* (1979). Her fiction on feminist themes also shocked many in the Arab world, most notably the novel *Woman at Point Zero* (1978), a sympathetic view of a woman imprisoned for killing a pimp. A founder of the feminist magazine *Confrontation*, she was jailed in 1981 and in 1982 founded a Pan-Arab women's group.

embryo, the scientific name for a new being in the early stages of growth in the UTERUS, during a PREGNANCY. Some people use the term from the time the ZYGOTE (fertilized egg) begins to subdivide, in a matter of hours after conception; most begin to use the name *embryo* after the new being implants itself in the uterus, in about a week; still others wait to use the term *embryo* until another four weeks into development, when organs begin to develop. The term *embryo* continues to be used through the first six to eight weeks of GESTATION, after which the new being is called a FETUS. One relatively new treatment for infertility is EMBRYO TRANSFER. (For a stage-by-stage description of growth, see **WHAT HAPPENS DURING PREGNANCY** on page 557.)

embryo implant, a type of reproductive technology that is used with IN VITRO FERTILIZATION.

embryo transfer, an approach to INFERTILITY in which a woman agrees to donate an egg (OVUM) to another woman, volunteering to be inseminated with a man's SPERM (see ARTIFICIAL INSEMINATION). The PREGNANCY is allowed to proceed until the fertilized egg has been implanted in the donor's UTERUS for a few days. At that point the developing EMBRYO is flushed out and implanted into the uterus of the other woman, usually the man's wife or sex partner.

This is a complicated and delicate procedure taking exquisite timing. Both women must have their reproductive cycles precisely in unison (see MENSTRUA-

TION). The procedure requires no surgery, but presents several potential dangers for the donor:

- The embryo may resist flushing, leaving the woman with an undesired pregnancy, the possibility of a SURROGATE PARENTING arrangement, or an ABORTION.
- The embryo may be flushed up into the donor's FALLOPIAN TUBES, which may result in a potentially life-threatening ECTOPIC PREGNANCY, necessitating emergency surgery.
- The woman may be exposed to SEXUALLY TRANSMITTED DISEASES, including AIDS as well as the liver disease *hepatitis*, from the sperm (see ARTIFICIAL INSEMINATION).

Also unresolved is the question of which woman is the legal mother and which the biological mother (see MOTHER). Despite long use with animals, the procedure is still so new that its success rate in humans is unclear and the related legal questions still unresolved. Embryo transfer has been used by some relatives— mother and daughter, or sisters, for example—in cases where a woman had nonfunctioning OVARIES or carried genetic defects (see GENETIC DISORDERS). (See INFERTILITY; also INFERTILITY AND REPRODUCTIVE TECHNOLOGY HELP, INFORMATION, AND ACTION GUIDE on page 368.)

Emily's List (1112 16th Street, NW, Suite 750, Washington, DC 20036; 202-887-1957; Ellen Malcolm, president), a "donor network and political resource for pro-choice Democratic women," founded in 1985. The acronym EMILY stands for "Early Money Is Like Yeast"—it makes the dough rise. Emily's List identifies viable candidates for key federal and statewide offices and provides them with direct contributions from members and also "strategic campaign support, as in conducting surveys and political research, developing resource materials, and providing technical assistance to support planning, fund-raising, media and message development." Members make a $100 contribution at membership and agree to make gifts of $100 or more to two or more candidates per election cycle. Emily's List researches candidates and provides members with issue analyses and campaign assessments as guide to deciding which candidates to support. It also publishes a quarterly newsletter and *Thinking of Running for Congress? A Guide for Democratic Women.*

empowerment, for modern women, a word with a wide range of meanings, including the ability to control one's own life and body; the individual's ability to hold positions of power and to exercise power; and the emergence of women as a group to positions of equal power with men throughout the world and in every aspect of life.

Individual women have held political, social, and economic power before the modern period, especially as rulers in hierarchical lines; Elizabeth I of England, Irene of Byzantium, and Catherine of Russia are three prime examples. But they have held power over male-dominated elites and societies, ultimately because the problem of legitimizing the family succession is so difficult to solve consistently in any other way. The establishment of a legitimate succession, whether democratic or autocratic, avoids what can amount to a constant state of civil war and in autocracies has mandated the reign of queens as well as kings.

Only in the modern period, and in the democracies, have large numbers of women gained political, social, and economic power—and that is still very recent, very limited, and very much in the process of becoming established. The number of women who lead nations is increasing but leaders such as Benazir Bhutto, Margaret Thatcher, and Corazon Aquino are still very much exceptions to the worldwide rule of men. The number of businesswomen leading large organizations is increasing—but is still only a small fraction of those led by men. Yet those women who have achieved significant power are scarcely tokens, but rather trailblazers. Large numbers of voting, independent women have emerged in many countries during the twentieth century and have entered the world of work—in fact and in law—increasingly as equals, with social and political status following the facts of the matter. But power in any of these senses has not yet come to the overwhelming majority of the world's women, and especially to the poorest and most disadvantaged in the developing countries of Asia, Africa, and South America, and throughout the Muslim world, though women's movements of some kind have begun in most countries. (See also POLITICAL PARTICIPATION; also POLITICAL PARTICIPATION HELP, INFORMATION, AND ACTION GUIDE on page 547; SEXUAL DISCRIMINATION AND SEXUAL HARASSMENT HELP, INFORMATION, AND ACTION GUIDE on page 642.)

endocrine glands, organs that produce and secrete HORMONES directly into the body's bloodstream (see HORMONES).

endogamy, an anthropological term for a culture's set of rules indicating those people a woman or man is allowed to marry. Closely related is the idea of EXOGAMY, rules describing people one is forbidden to marry. (See MATE SELECTION.)

endometriosis, the growth elsewhere in the body of tissue (*endometrium*) that normally lines the UTERUS. Areas commonly affected are the OVARIES, the surface of the FALLOPIAN TUBES, the external wall of the uterus, and the pelvic area between the uterus and rectum (see DIGESTIVE SYSTEM). This tissue breaks down and bleeds just as the endometrium does during the menstrual cycle (see MENSTRUATION); but because the blood has no outlet, blood-filled CYSTS often form; these are not only painful, but are also a leading cause of INFERTILITY.

What causes the abnormal growth is unknown, though some suggest it may be triggered by a malfunction in the IMMUNE SYSTEM. It commonly appears between ages twenty-five and forty-five and often involves painful or abnormal menstrual periods and sometimes painful vaginal SEXUAL INTERCOURSE and persistent pain. The amount of pain varies with the menstrual cycle but is not necessarily correlated with the amount of abnormal growth. Where it is widespread, scar tissue can virtually bind reproductive organs in place, sometimes trapping eggs (see OVUM) within the ovaries.

Because symptoms are general, endometriosis is generally confirmed by LAPAROSCOPY, visual examination of the abdominal area through a small incision, or during exploratory surgery. If the pain is not too great, the condition does not require treatment, unless the woman wishes to become pregnant. The main treatment is by a variety of HORMONES, which cannot cure the disease but can bring it under control. Pregnancy can also cause the symptoms of endometriosis to decline sharply.

Unfortunately, only about half the women with the condition are able to conceive normally, and those who do suffer three times the normal rate of MISCARRIAGE and sixteen times the normal rate of ECTOPIC PREGNANCY. Laparoscopic surgery can be used to burn, scrape, or otherwise remove abnormal endometrial tissue and restore fertility to up to one of every two to three women. At the same time the doctor may use other techniques to limit adhesions and pain. Sometimes laser surgery is used in an attempt to free ovaries to perform normally. Women who wish to have children are advised to do so as quickly as possible, because endometriosis is a progressive condition, worsening until MENOPAUSE, when symptoms generally subside. If, before then, the symptoms are too difficult to bear, HYSTERECTOMY—removal of the whole uterus—is an option.

For more help, information, and action

▶ **Endometriosis Association (EA)** (8585 North 76th Place, Milwaukee, WI 53223; 414-355-2200 or 800-992-ENDO [3636]; Mary Lou Ballweg, executive director), an organization focusing on endometriosis and infertility. It provides information; makes referrals; and publishes a newsletter, pamphlets, and information sheets.
▶ NATIONAL WOMEN'S HEALTH NETWORK **(NWHN)** (202-347-1140). Operates the **Women's Health Information Service.** Publishes the information packet *Endometriosis.*
▶ **RESOLVE, INC.** (617-643-2424). Publishes the fact sheet *Endometriosis.*

Other resources

Coping with Endometriosis. Lyle J. Breitkopf and Marion G. Bakoulis. Prentice-Hall, 1988; Borgo Press, 1989.
The Endometriosis Answer Book: New Hope, New Help. Neils H. Lauersen and Constance DeSwaan. Rawson, 1988; Ballantine, 1989.
Endometriosis and Infertility and Traditional Chinese Medicine: A Laywoman's Guide. Bob Flaws. Blue Poppy, 1989.
(See also UTERUS; INFERTILITY; also INFERTILITY AND REPRODUCTIVE TECHNOLOGY HELP, INFORMATION AND ACTION GUIDE on page 368; WOMEN'S HEALTH HELP, INFORMATION, AND ACTION GUIDE on page 334.)

endometrium, the lining of the UTERUS. (See UTERUS; ENDOMETRIOSIS; MENSTRUATION.)

engagement, a promise to marry, generally a publicly stated intention, solemnized by the man giving the woman a gift, such as a ring. In CHILDBIRTH engagement is the "dropping" or "falling" of a baby into position for DELIVERY (see FETAL PRESENTATION).

In modern societies engagement is a personal affair between the two partners, coming at the end of a process of MATE SELECTION. MARRIAGE is the clear intent, and the engagement may be marked by celebratory gatherings of family and friends, but society has no particular role to play in the progress of the engagement, or in how long or short it is. If, in the end, the WEDDING does not take place, one or both parties may experience considerable anguish, but the social impact will be small. Until recent decades, if one party ended the engagement, the other could sue for money damages in a *breach of promise to marry* suit. Such suits are no longer allowed in many places, though some allow suit for return of an engagement ring or other gift, given with the understanding that it was a precursor to marriage.

In some traditional cultures, however, engagement is a highly regulated process, often occurring in several stages, including elaborate exchanges of gifts and ceremonial feasts and involving whole families, clans, and sometimes villages. Among the Tharu people of India, for example, a girl and boy are engaged during childhood, at a betrothal ceremony; later, as the couple near or reach PUBERTY, there is a confirmation ceremony, to fix the date of the wedding, held some days later. In a culture such as this, ending an engagement can be a serious business, tantamount to DIVORCE. In traditional cultures betrothal is often marked by a gift from the man and his family to the woman or her family; among anthropologists this is called the BRIDEGIFT. Sometimes the gifts are services the man renders to his in-laws after the wedding, called *brideservice*.

In the past, engagements were sometimes quite long, allowing time for a woman to build up the collection of clothing and linens, called a *trousseau*, which she would bring with her from her parents' home to the marriage. The man, meanwhile, was supposed to be saving money to provide a proper home for the couple to occupy. Today many Western men and women are working and living on their own at the time of the engagement and often move into rented quarters together before or during their engagement (see COHABITATION). Buying a home and furnishing it is frequently put off until some time into the marriage, often in preparation for having children.

For people who have been previously married, and especially those with children, the engagement period is a time for readjustment. Certainly if young children are involved, they should be among the first, if not *the* first, to be told, since they are most intimately affected. They will often initially resist the idea of a remarriage, but especially so if they learn of it from someone else. (See COUPLES AND FAMILIES HELP, INFORMATION, AND ACTION GUIDE on page 418.)

Enoch Arden laws, laws covering a situation in which a spouse has gone missing unintentionally, as in the case of a shipwrecked sailor (see DIVORCE).

epididymis, a long, coiled tube behind a man's TESTES, where SPERM mature (see REPRODUCTIVE SYSTEM).

episiotomy, a surgical incision made in the *perineum,* the tissue between a woman's VAGINA and anus (see DIGESTIVE SYSTEM) during CHILDBIRTH; a subject of considerable controversy and debate. Proponents of the practice note that the delicate perineal tissues often tear during birth, and repair may be difficult and lead to complications. They say that making a neat incision enlarges the vaginal opening to ease pressure on the baby's head and is easier to repair afterward. Episiotomies are especially common to ease and speed the birth when the perineal tissue is under pressure and seems likely to tear, as in cases of abnormal FETAL PRESENTATION or forceps delivery, where a larger opening is needed, or when the fetus is showing signs of distress, especially lack of oxygen. Critics, however, say that episiotomies have been overused, and that they "medicalize" natural birthing processes, with some obstetricians performing them on virtually every birth. A pregnant woman will want to discuss with her doctor and hospital their policies on using episiotomies. (See CHILDBIRTH; DELIVERY; also PREGNANCY AND CHILDBIRTH HELP, INFORMATION, AND ACTION GUIDE on page 580.)

Equal Credit Opportunity Act, a U.S. federal law, passed in 1975 and in effect since 1977, prohibiting creditor discrimination on the basis of race, ethnic origin, religion, age, sex, marital status, or welfare status. For women, it became a powerful barrier against what had been pervasive personal and business credit discrimination. Under the law, it is illegal for creditors to discount a woman's income from such sources as employment, DIVORCE and SEPARATION AGREEMENTS, retirement, and public assistance; to ask demeaning personal questions about BIRTH CONTROL and family plans; to tie credit to her husband unless it was jointly granted; to tie credit to MARITAL STATUS or change of status; and to deny a woman a separate credit history and the right to examine that history.

In practical terms, the law did not succeed in barring all credit discrimination against women, for at least part of every credit-granting decision has to do with a lender's estimate of "character," leaving considerable scope for bias in the lending process. That is especially true for women of color, older women, women living on fixed sources of income, women in unmarried relationships (see COHABITATION), and women receiving public assistance, all of whom might be the objects of discrimination for more than one reason. (See also SEXUAL DISCRIMINATION AND SEXUAL HARASSMENT HELP, INFORMATION, AND ACTION GUIDE on page 642; OLDER WOMEN'S HELP, INFORMATION, AND ACTION GUIDE on page 374.)

equal employment opportunity: See TITLE VII OF THE CIVIL RIGHTS ACT OF 1964.

Equal Employment Opportunity Commission (EEOC) (1801 L Street, NW, Washington, DC 20507; 202-663-4900 or 800-669-EEOC [3362]; TDD [telecommunications for the deaf], 202-663-4494 or 800-800-3302), a federal agency created by the U.S. Congress to enforce TITLE VII OF THE CIVIL RIGHTS ACT OF 1964, prohibiting employment discrimination based on race, color, religion, sex, or national origin, and the PREGNANCY DISCRIMINATION ACT, an amendment to Title VII. Since 1979 it has also been charged with enforcing the Age Discrimination in Employment Act of 1967, protecting employees age forty or older; the Equal Pay Act of 1963 (see EQUAL PAY FOR EQUAL WORK); and Section 501 of the Rehabilitation Act of 1973, prohibiting federal sector discrimination against people with disabilities; and as of 1992 also the Americans with Disabilities Act, prohibiting discrimination in the private sector or state and local governments. In all these areas, the EEOC "provides oversight and coordination of all federal regulations, practices and policies," receiving and investigating employment discrimination charges, attempting conciliation where appropriate, and, where it finds it warranted, filing a suit. The EEOC's policy is "to seek full and effective relief for each and every victim of employment discrimination, whether sought in court or in conciliation agreements before litigation, and to provide remedies designed to correct the discrimination and prevent its recurrence." In fact, the EEOC's effectiveness depends very much on the commitment of the administration under which it serves, and it has often been criticized for finding cause for action in only a very small proportion of the charges filed. The EEOC publishes various brochures designed to help people considering the filing of a complaint. For an overview, see HOW TO FILE AN EEOC COMPLAINT, below.

HOW TO FILE AN EEOC COMPLAINT

If you think you have been treated unfairly in an employment situation and the reason for the action was your sex, race, color, religion, or national origin, you may file a complaint or charge with the Equal Employment Opportunity Commission. The complaint form asks for your name and address; the name and address and other information about the employer, union, or employment agency; and a brief description of the discriminatory practice or action. You must file the complaint within 180 days of the action you are complaining about. If there is a State or city fair employment practices (FEP) law offering comparable protection (most States have such FEP laws), the EEOC will send a copy of the complaint to the agency that enforces the State or local law. If the State agency does not complete action on the complaint within 60 days, EEOC may proceed to process the charge. If you send the complaint to the State agency first, the deadline for filing with EEOC is 300 days from the date of the unlawful act, or within 30 days of a notice that the State agency has finished its proceedings, whichever happens first. Some actions may be continuing violations of Title VII, and are not then subject to the usual time limits.

EEOC's enforcement process begins with an interview with an equal opportunity specialist who talks with you about what happened. The EEO specialist then fills out the charge form, provides counseling on legal rights, and explains the EEOC enforcement procedures. After the charge is filed, EEOC notifies the employer, who is often asked to come to the Commission office to discuss the charge with you and EEOC staff. If a satisfactory settlement cannot be reached, EEOC will investigate the charge further and make a decision on whether there is reasonable cause to believe the discrimination occurred. If the Commission finds no reasonable cause, it will give you a "right-to-sue" letter, which permits you to initiate a private suit, if you want to do so. If reasonable cause is found, and EEOC is not able to reach settlement through conciliation efforts, Commission attorneys review the case again and decide whether the Commission should sue the employer. If they decide against going to court, they issue a right-to-sue letter so you can sue privately. You do not have to wait for this entire process to be completed before you begin a private suit. You may begin your own suit any time after EEOC has had jurisdiction to act on the case for 180 days. However, you must have a right-to-sue letter before any action may be started in court. After getting the right-to-sue letter, you have 90 days to file in court. You should try to secure an attorney before requesting a letter. EEOC will try to help you find a lawyer if you are unable to find one on your own. If a court finds that discrimination occurred, it can order reinstatement or hiring, with or without back pay or anything else it feels is appropriate.

Because time is crucial in the Title VII cases, if you think you have been discriminated against, it is important to contact the EEOC soon after the discriminatory action occurs, to find out if there may be grounds for filing a complaint. You can reach the EEOC at 800-669-EEOC (669-3362) for the local number in your state or region.

It is also against the law to discriminate against anyone for starting proceedings under Title VII, opposing an illegal practice, or participating in an investigation. A person who is discriminated against in this way may file a complaint or charge.

Source: *A Working Woman's Guide to Her Job Rights*, U.S. Department of Labor, Women's Bureau, 1988.

Equal Pay Act: See EQUAL PAY FOR EQUAL WORK.

equal pay for equal work, the payment of equal amounts to women and men doing jobs calling for substantially equal skill, effort, and responsibility. In the United States, this principle was made into law by the Equal Pay Act of 1963, the first federal law against SEXUAL DISCRIMINATION. The law prohibited lowering wages to end differentials and defined wages widely enough to include such factors as fringe benefits, overtime, and equipment, though it did not prohibit setting wage differentials for other reasons, such as seniority and piecework.

Although a major advance, the Equal Pay Act left untouched the massive wage discrimination created by the sex-segregated jobs held by more than two-thirds of American working women (see WORK AND WOMEN). From the late 1970s, the related question of PAY EQUITY—equal pay for work of comparable value—therefore became hotly contested. The Equal Pay Act is enforced by the EQUAL EMPLOYMENT OPPORTUNITY COMMISSION. (See WORKING WOMEN'S HELP, INFORMATION, AND ACTION GUIDE on page 779; SEXUAL DISCRIMINATION AND SEXUAL HARASSMENT HELP, INFORMATION, AND ACTION GUIDE on page 642.)

Equal Rights Advocates (ERA) (1663 Mission Street, San Francisco, CA 94103; 415-621-0672; advice and counseling line, 415-621-0505; Nancy Davis, executive director), a national women's law center founded in 1974 by women lawyers "committed to working for social justice by providing high quality legal services free of charge to the people who need them most: women, minorities and especially women of color." ERA fights sex and race discrimination in various ways, including legal representation, technical assistance, advice and counseling, student internships in public interest law, public education and public policy, and active involvement in community-based coalitions. In addition to its broad range of equal rights work, ERA has recent focused especially on obtaining adequate pay (including equal pay, PAY EQUITY, and minimum wage); SEXUAL HARASSMENT; discrimination against parents in the workplace; affirmative action/access to nontraditional jobs; and immigrant women's rights in the workplace, with Spanish/English bilingual services on economic justice issues as well as special programs for equal economic opportunity for women of color. It publishes *The Equal Rights Advocate* providing up-to-date news on legal and other social developments affecting the status of women; *The Affirmative Action Handbook: How to Start and Defend Affirmative Action Programs* (co-published with the San Francisco lawyers' Committee for Urban Affairs); and "Know Your Rights" brochures, such as *Pregnancy Discrimination* and *Sex Discrimination* (both in English and Spanish).

Equal Rights Amendment (ERA), a proposed amendment to the U.S. Constitution. It was first proposed in 1923 by Alice PAUL, head of the NATIONAL WOMAN'S PARTY, and was debated for almost half a century before its 1972 passage through Congress. In its final form it read: "Equality of rights under the law shall not be denied or abridged by the United States or by any State on account of sex."

Initially, the proposed amendment was opposed by many women's groups, including the LEAGUE OF WOMEN VOTERS and the National Women's Trade Union

League, and by organized labor, who feared it would destroy hard-won women workers' PROTECTIVE LEGISLATION. The women's organizations also were concerned that it would legalize the drafting of women into the armed forces and for combat. But with the dawning of the quite different social and political context of the 1960s, and after invalidation of much protective legislation by laws that made employment and workplace discrimination illegal, the main women's organizations dropped their opposition to the ERA.

In 1967, the then-new NATIONAL ORGANIZATION FOR WOMEN (NOW) declared its support for the ERA and began a campaign that at first met with great success. The amendment was passed by the House of Representatives in 1971 and by the Senate in 1972, both by huge majorities. Then the ERA was ratified in thirty states within a year, before coming to what was very nearly a dead stop, as conservatives mounted a very effective counterattack, primarily in the South and West. Conservative leaders such as Phyllis SCHLAFLY successfully attacked the ERA as a "step down," arguing that if it became law, women would be forced to serve in the armed forces and would lose the protection of hard-won financial support laws. Portraying the ERA as "antifamily" and using or adapting some of the same concerns earlier voiced by women's organizations, the conservatives stopped the ERA, in spite of a massive campaign for its passage led by NOW, which in the late 1970s became very nearly a single-issue organization. By 1982, even after a three-year extension beyond the seven years normally allowed to secure state ratification, the ERA had been ratified by only five more states—three short of the thirty-eight needed—and several states were seeking to nullify their previous ratifications.

The ERA was wounded, but by no means entirely dead, as many states had passed equal rights amendments during the course of the long fight, including Alaska, Colorado, Connecticut, Hawaii, Illinois, Maryland, Massachusetts, Montana, New Hampshire, New Mexico, Pennsylvania, Texas, Utah, Virginia, Washington, and Wyoming. Meanwhile, the ERA continues to be placed before the Congress annually, and an informal coalition of women's organizations—among them the National Woman's Party, National Organization for Women, the League of Women Voters, BUSINESS AND PROFESSIONAL WOMEN/USA, FEDERALLY EMPLOYED WOMEN, and NATIONAL ASSOCIATION OF COMMISSIONS FOR WOMEN—hold regular ERA Summits to plan strategy for passage.

erogenous zones, those parts of the body that are especially sensitive to caresses and help to create sexual arousal and begin the cycle of SEXUAL RESPONSE. The primary erogenous zones, where many nerve endings make the area extremely responsive to touch, include the GENITALS, BREASTS, lips, and buttocks. But any area of the body may be a source of sexual arousal, and an individual woman will discover her own most sensitive areas, such as the inner thighs, palms of the hand, or the area known as the G SPOT. (See SEXUAL RESPONSE.)

escutcheon, the triangle of HAIR that grows after PUBERTY on the MONS VENERIS, the fatty mound of tissue over the pubic bone.

essentialism, for feminists, a form of FEMALE SUPREMACY theory, holding that women are innately superior to men because of their biological inheritance; it is a kind of biological determinism. Those who believe in women's innate superiority because of their cultural rather than biological inheritance are CULTURAL FEMINISTS. (See CULTURAL FEMINISM; FEMALE SUPREMACY.)

estrogen, the main female sex hormone—actually a group of HORMONES—that regulate normal female sexual development and the health of the REPRODUCTIVE SYSTEM. Estrogen is produced primarily in the female and male sex glands (GONADS), in women by the OVARIES and in men by the TESTES. In young girls and in men it is produced only in small amounts, but around the time of PUBERTY that changes in women. Triggered by increased production of FOLLICLE-STIMULATING HORMONE (**FSH**), the ovaries begin to develop eggs (see OVUM) in ovarian follicles, which then begin to produce estrogen. This stimulates the development of distinctive female SECONDARY SEX CHARACTERISTICS, such as larger BREASTS, growth of the UTERUS and FALLOPIAN TUBES, the laying down of fat to produce in the typical adult female distribution, the growth of pubic and underarm air, and the eventual ending of growth in the long bones, notably the arms and legs.

Estrogen levels are not steady, however. From the time of a girl's first MENSTRUATION through MENOPAUSE, except during PREGNANCY or severe illness or stress, estrogen levels will rise and fall in a monthly cycle. After the beginning of the menstrual period, as new eggs ripen, the ovaries produce estrogen, which triggers thickening of the *endometrium,* the lining of the uterus, to prepare for a possible fertilized egg. Later in the cycle, if fertilization does not take place, estrogen production will decline until the cycle comes around again.

During pregnancy, estrogen is also produced and maintained at high levels by the PLACENTA, the tissue that nourishes the developing FETUS. Some estrogen is also produced by the adrenal glands and by fatty (*adipose*) tissue; such production continues after menopause and may be the reason why larger, heavier women have fewer problems during menopause.

Both naturally derived and synthetic estrogen are used in treating women for a variety of symptoms and disorders, including menstrual irregularities, suppression of lactation after CHILDBIRTH, some forms of CANCER (though it fuels others), and menopausal problems (see ESTROGEN REPLACEMENT THERAPY). They also form the basis for various types of contraceptive medications, including BIRTH CONTROL PILLS, NORPLANT, and DEPO-PROVERA. Estrogen can cause significant side effects, however, and should be used only after careful consideration of a woman's total medical situation (see BIRTH CONTROL PILLS for more on the pros and cons). (See also MENSTRUATION and MENOPAUSE HELP, INFORMATION, AND ACTION GUIDES on pages 439 and 432; WOMEN'S HEALTH HELP, INFORMATION, AND ACTION GUIDE on page 334.)

estrogen replacement therapy (ERT), use of the female hormone ESTROGEN as a medication to counteract the effects of MENOPAUSE, especially hot flashes, vaginal dryness (see VAGINA), risk of OSTEOPOROSIS, and hormone-related atherosclerosis (see HEART AND CIRCULATORY SYSTEM). Estrogen medications, often pills or creams, have been used since the late 1940s, and many women feel they have benefited greatly from its use. Supporters note that historically, when LIFE EXPECTANCY was much shorter, women did not generally live into menopause and so did not routinely have the range of effects experienced by women of today, who live decades past their last menstrual periods.

Critics worry that doctors prescribe ERT as if menopause were a disease, not a natural process; they are also concerned about the side effects of estrogen treatment, which have become evident with decades of use. In particular, ERT is contraindicated if a woman has any personal or family history of estrogen-fueled CANCER (see BREAST CANCER; UTERINE CANCER); blood-clotting disorders (*thromboembolic disease*); side effects from estrogen, such as severe headaches; acute or chronic kidney or liver disease (see URINARY TRACT; DIGESTIVE SYSTEM); or unexplained vaginal bleeding. Many doctors also feel that ERT should not be used where a woman has benign estrogen-fueled growths (see FIBROIDS); a history of ENDOMETRIOSIS; or benign breast disease (see BREASTS), as their risk of cancer may be increased.

In each individual case, a woman and her doctor must carefully weigh the pros and cons to see what is best for her—and review their decision periodically as new medical information on the long-term risks and benefits of ERT becomes available. (See MENOPAUSE; also WOMEN'S HEALTH HELP, INFORMATION, AND ACTION GUIDE on page 334.)

eugenics, deliberate plans to alter the human genetic makeup, with the intention of improvement, as by preventing or hindering some people from having children while encouraging others to do so. *Positive eugenics* refers to the fostering of desirable genes; *negative eugenics,* to the suppression of undesirable ones. The ideas of eugenics are based on experience in animal breeding and plant propagation programs, which are designed to produce desired changes. Considering such ideas in relation to humans is not new, going back at least to Plato, but became widespread in the twentieth century, where it became intertwined with racist beliefs, especially belief in the superiority of Whites over other races, and in a person's GENETIC INHERITANCE being dominant over environmental influences. As a result, many countries passed laws calling for the STERILIZATION of whole groups of people, notably those labeled as "feeble-minded," insane, criminal, or epileptic, especially if they belonged to a group regarded as "inferior," such as Jews in Germany or Blacks in the United States. In the United States, sterilizations were widely performed on both women and men in the South and in California, which alone had performed 10,000 sterilizations by 1935. Many thinkers sharply attacked the movement's basic assumptions, but it was the actions of the German Nazis during World War II—not only sterilization but mass extermination—that caused general revulsion against eugenics.

But in fact, the ideas have not died. In recent decades, some judges and politicians have suggested that long-term forms of BIRTH CONTROL, such as NORPLANT or DEPO-PROVERA, be pressed on or even made mandatory for certain people, such as drug abusers or welfare MOTHERS. So far those proposals have been rejected, but they keep returning in new guises.

Ironically, in the post–World War II decades, new techniques in biology and medicine have given individuals the ability to be selective with their own reproduction. With AMNIOCENTESIS and other kinds of PRENATAL TESTS, parents can get information about possible birth defects and decide either to continue the PREGNANCY or to have an ABORTION—a kind of negative eugenics. With ARTIFICIAL INSEMINATION and IN VITRO FERTILIZATION, some women choose to use SPERM from sperm banks, which collect semen from supposedly "superior" men—in a sense, positive eugenics. The techniques of GENETIC ENGINEERING open the possibility of making alterations in the genes themselves before IMPLANTATION. A crucial difference here is that the individual, not the state, is making the choice; and that the decision is voluntary, not compulsory, the upshot being that the woman keeps control of her own REPRODUCTIVE RIGHTS. Even so, many people have been concerned about the ethics of becoming involved with reproductive technology. (See also STERILIZATION; ARTIFICIAL INSEMINATION; also BIRTH CONTROL AND FAMILY PLANNING HELP, INFORMATION, AND ACTION GUIDE on page 81.)

Eve, the archetype of the doomed or fallen woman, whose curse by the God of the Old Testament was explicit and extended to all the generations of women to come. In the story told by the Bible, Eve is seduced by the serpent, eats of the forbidden fruit, and convinces Adam to do the same, for which they are both cast out of Eden by their male God. Both, and by extension their entire race of beings, are cursed by all the afflictions known as the human condition; women are additionally cursed, with motherhood, love of men, and submission to men. The first woman, Eve, is placed second to Adam in the story, which holds that she was created from material taken from his side.

Taken literally, the tale of Eve creates in modern parlance a "no win" situation for all women who are believers in the religions involved or who are in any significant way attached to those religions. Far more seriously, the story and curse of Eve have been the ideological underpinning of the thinking and institutions of massive male supremacist systems (see PATRIARCHY) for some thousands of years. Although attitudes and interpretations have been softened by later generations of less-than-literal Christians and Jews, the story and the system it helps support remain operative at the ideological base of these groups of religions. Recognizing the centrality of this, many women have still elected to work within and build equality within their religious institutions; others have departed, some to alternative religions, many to agnostic or nontheistic views. (See also SPIRITUAL FEMINISM; RELIGION AND WOMEN'S RIGHTS.)

exercise, performance of physical activities designed to improve the body's general health and efficiency.

For most of history, women did not have to worry about getting enough exercise. Cleaning house; washing, hanging, and ironing clothes; carrying and preparing food; often planting, weeding, growing, and picking food as well; carrying and running after young children; and other such activities kept women active all day, at "work that was never done." That remains the pattern in many parts of the world (see HOUSEWORK; HOMEMAKER), but in many affluent countries women now have numerous labor-saving devices, and even when they work outside the home, their jobs are more likely to be sedentary (see WORK AND WOMEN). The result is that many women have felt the need for exercise to improve their health and fitness.

Done primarily to improve the strength and endurance of the MUSCULAR SYSTEM and the HEART AND CIRCULATORY SYSTEM, exercise aids the body in many other ways. Weight-bearing exercise helps prevent bone loss (see OSTEOPOROSIS); helps to control some mild disorders, including DIABETES and (in pregnant women) PREECLAMPSIA; keeps weight under control (see OBESITY); often eases discomforts associated with MENSTRUATION; helps prevent or ease VARICOSE VEINS; helps maintain or regain mobility during ARTHRITIS; helps avoid or correct incontinence (see URINARY TRACT); and has many other benefits.

That is not to say that exercise has no adverse effects. Exercise that is too strenuous and stressful can damage the SKELETAL SYSTEM and can sometimes even produce allergic reactions (see ALLERGIES). People who exercise excessively or even obsessively, often combined with DIETING and poor NUTRITION, can damage their bodies; in extreme cases, as with ANOREXIA NERVOSA or BULIMIA, menstrual periods may stop (see ANOVULATORY PERIODS), bone loss may occur (see OSTEOPOROSIS), and vital organs can be damaged. Such effects are a special risk among dancers and athletes concerned with thinness. On the other hand, some athletes concerned with bodybuilding harm their health through use of STEROIDS.

Exercise can be especially helpful to women during PREGNANCY, in preparation for and recovery from CHILDBIRTH. (See EXERCISES DURING AND AFTER PREGNANCY on page 561.) Some of these exercises, especially the Kegel (or pelvic floor) exercise, can also help strengthen the muscles that control urination, so helping to prevent incontinence, a common problem, especially among older women. Some pregnant women use those exercises as a warm-up for more strenuous exercises. Ideally, women will have been in an exercise program before becoming pregnant. They should not start a new exercise program at any time, and especially during pregnancy, before having a medical examination. Doctors may recommend exercise restrictions for some, such as those with heart problems, multiple births, or at risk for MISCARRIAGE or premature DELIVERY.

In general, the AMERICAN COLLEGE OF OBSTETRICS AND GYNECOLOGY (ACOG) recommends that pregnant women should exercise no more than three times a week, for no more than fifteen minutes (not including warm-up and cool-down), and only up to 140 heartbeats a minute, and that they should stop if they feel any adverse symptoms, including dizziness, faintness, bleeding, contractions or cramps, nausea, chest pain, or strain in general. More specifically, pregnant women are advised to avoid strenuous activities involving twisting, turning, bouncing, jerky motion, and deep flexion or extension; high-risk activities such as diving or skiing; competitive sports requiring stamina and endurance; and activities requiring balance, because of the danger attending a fall. Pregnant women should also beware of activities that could raise their body temperature too high (including not just exercise, but also the use of a sauna, steam room, or heated whirlpool) or of lying flat on the back, since that could hamper the flow of blood to the FETUS (see HEART AND CIRCULATORY SYSTEM).

Though the benefits of exercise are widely accepted and seem obvious, some recent studies have produced some illuminating findings. One major study of a large group of healthy people—both women and men—divided into five categories by fitness, found that the "least fit" group had overall death rates three times that of the "most fit" group, such as people who run thirty to forty miles a week. This study found that the greatest health gains were found among people who went from the least fit category, being largely sedentary, to modest activity, such as walking thirty to sixty minutes a day. In terms of LIFE EXPECTANCY, the benefits were greater for men than for women, who tend to live longer. However, exercise can be extremely important to women's quality of life, especially since many older women have physical problems that hinder their mobility and physical freedom. Nor is exercise only for the young. Studies indicate that even women in their nineties can gain increased mobility and independence from a modest exercise program. In fact, studies have shown that—at whatever age—simply moving from a sedentary life to one a bit more active can have substantial health gains, lessening the risk of dying from heart disease, CANCER, and some other causes. (See EXERCISE AND FITNESS HELP, INFORMATION, AND ACTION GUIDE, below.)

EXERCISE AND FITNESS

Help, Information, and Action Guide

Organizations

▶ WOMEN'S SPORTS FOUNDATION (WSF) (212-972-9170; Women's Sports Infoline, 800-227-3988). Publishes expert packets on *General Fitness, Pregnancy and Exercise,* and *Kid's Packet.*
▶ AMERICAN COLLEGE OF OBSTETRICIANS AND GYNECOLOGISTS (ACOG) (202-638-5577). Publishes Patient Education Pamphlets, for example on exercise during pregnancy.
▶ NATIONAL COUNCIL ON THE AGING (NCOA) (202-479-1200 or 800-424-9046). Publishes *A Resource Guide for Fitness Control Programs for Older Persons.*
▶ NATIONAL WOMEN'S HEALTH NETWORK (NWHN) (202-347-1140). Operates the **Women's Health Information Service.**
▶ PROJECT ON EQUAL EDUCATION RIGHTS (PEER) (212-925-6635). Publishes *"Like She Owns the Earth"—Women and Sports.*

Other resources

◪ **GENERAL WORKS**

The Safe Exercise Handbook. Toni T. Branner. Kendall-Hunt, 1991.

Better Bodies After Thirty-Five: A Common Sense Approach to Healthful Living. Irving A. Beychok. Mills Sanderson, 1991.

Living with Exercise. Steven N. Blair. American Health, 1991.

The Bodywise Woman: Reliable Information About Physical Activity and Health. Melpomene Institute for Women's Health Research Staff. Prentice-Hall, 1990.

✒ ON STRETCHING, STRENGTHENING, TONING, AND RANGE OF MOTION

Stretch and Strengthen: A Safe, Comprehensive Exercise Program to Balance Your Muscle Strength. Judy Alter. Houghton Mifflin, 1992.

Self-Help for Stress and Pain: Simple Energy Balancing Exercises for Home, School, Office, and Athletics, Repetitive Stress Injury, Learning Disability, Environmental Sensitivity, 3rd ed. Elizabeth Barhydt and Hamilton Barhydt. Loving Life, 1990.

✒ FOR OLDER OR PHYSICALLY LIMITED PEOPLE

Angela Lansbury's Positive Moves. Angela Lansbury. Thorndike Press, 1991.

Reach for It . . . A Handbook of Health, Exercise and Dance Activities for Older Adults, 2nd ed. David E. Corbin and Josie Metal-Corbin. E. Bowers, 1990.

Walking Medicine: The Lifetime Guide to Preventive Therapeutic Exercise-walking Programs. Gary Yanker and Kathy Burton. McGraw-Hill, 1990.

✒ ON EXERCISE DURING PREGNANCY

Elisabeth Bing's Guide to Moving Through Pregnancy: Advice from America's Foremost Childbirth Educator on Making Pregnancy as Physically Comfortable as Possible, at Home and at Work. Elisabeth Bing. Farrar, Straus & Giroux, 1991.

Fitness for Two: Guidelines for Exercise During Pregnancy. Gayle Brannon. R & M Press (WA), 1990.

✒ ON DEVELOPING MUSCLE POWER

Recovery Power: Advanced Nutrition and Training Methods for Competitive Athletes. Rick Brunner and others. Sports Focus, 1989.

Practical Approach to Strength Training. Matt Brzycki. Masters Press (MI), 1989.

How to Develop Muscular Power. Cedric X. Bryant. Masters Press (MI), 1988.

✒ BACKGROUND BOOKS

Exercise: For the Health of It, 5th ed. F. Compton Jenkins. Kendall-Hunt, 1991.

The Exercise Habit. James Gavin. Leisure Press, 1991.
Exercise, Fitness, and Health. Charles B. Clayman, ed. RD Association, 1991.
(See also WOMEN'S HEALTH HELP, INFORMATION, AND ACTION GUIDE on page 334.)

exogamy, an anthropological term for a culture's set of rules indicating those people a woman or man are forbidden to marry. Almost all societies have prohibitions against INCEST, which is SEXUAL INTERCOURSE or MARRIAGE between near blood relations, and sometimes also near relations by marriage (called *affinity* relations). But the rules for both incest and the wider exogamy vary tremendously. Closely related is the idea of ENDOGAMY, rules describing people one is allowed to marry. (See MATE SELECTION.)

eyes, the organs of sight, a pair of mechanisms protected by heavy bony sockets and eyelids, which provide further protection with eyelashes and thin, flexible membranes called *conjunctiva.* Glands from the eyelid and conjunctiva coat the eyes, lubricating and cleansing them, a process furthered by blinking.

The whitish *sclera,* which makes up most of the eyeball, serves primarily to hold and cushion the working parts. The transparent *cornea,* in the center of the sclera, controls the focusing of images; behind it is a depression filled with fluid (*aqueous humor*). Set into this is the *iris,* the colored part of the eye, with a central opening (*pupil*); this controls reception of light, contracting in the light and widening (*dilating*) in the dark. Behind the iris is the *lens,* surrounded by a ring of tiny muscles (the *ciliary body*) that help the eyes focus by changing the shape of the lens, and behind that a jellylike substance called the *vitreous humor.* Finally there is the *retina,* nourished by a network of blood vessels called the *choroid plexus,* which receives the image that was originally received and focused by the cornea and lens. Using light-sensing structures called *rods* and *cones,* the retina converts light impulses into electrical impulses, which are then transmitted along the *optic nerve* to the brain, where they become the images we call sight. Other sets of muscles help coordinate the messages from the two eyes, to form a single image and allow judgment of distances, in what is called *stereoscopic* or *binocular vision.*

Both delicate and intricate, the eyes are subject to many disorders. The most common are problems with focusing of the eye: with *nearsightedness* (*myopia*) a person has clear vision of objects up close but blurry far vision, while with *farsightedness* (*hyperopia*) the reverse is true. Both problems are corrected easily with specially ground lenses, either in eyeglasses or contact lenses, artificial plastic lenses that are placed over the cornea. Often the cornea's shape is distorted slightly, resulting in distortion and blurring of vision, called *astigmatism;* this, too, is correctable by glasses, though for strong distortion sometimes hard contact lenses or special soft lenses are more effective. If both near and far vision need correction, the solution is some form of *bifocals*. Accentuation of such problems is normal with age, as the eyes lose their elasticity, often producing a kind of nearsightedness called *presbyopia;* changes may sometimes temporarily be toward more normal vision, as when a previously farsighted person comes to need less strong correction for near vision, as in reading.

As they age, women are likely to have other eye problems as well. Most common are *cataracts,* clouded, opaque areas that develop in the lens, gradually blocking light from reaching the retina and lessening vision. Fortunately, most cases can now readily be corrected surgically, involving removal of the degenerated lens and replacing it with an artificial lens, sometimes correcting for other vision problems as well. Long-term exposure to sun is linked with formation of cataracts later in life; use of wraparound or closely fitting sunglasses specially formulated to screen out ultraviolet rays is strongly recommended. If cataracts develop in one eye, they are likely to develop in the other as well.

With *glaucoma*, abnormally high pressure builds up in the aqueous fluid, damaging the optic nerve and leading to loss of sight if not detected and treated early. It is one of the strongest reasons for having regular annual eye examinations, certainly after age forty and especially if glaucoma or diabetes are in the family medical history.

At some time during their lives, most people have some kind of infection or inflammation in the eye. These commonly involve inflammation of the eyelid membrane (*conjunctivitis*) or infection in an eyelash follicle, called a *sty*. These may heal themselves or require medical treatment; but nothing in or around the eyes should be self-treated with over-the-counter medications; the potential hazards are too great. More than one person has caused blindness by putting into their eyes substances they thought were medications. In addition, eye inflammation, pain, or other problems can be signals of even more serious problems. Some SEXUALLY TRANSMITTED DISEASES, for example, can cause blindness if undetected and untreated. Eye inflammation may occur with other disorders, such as ALLERGIES.

Particularly sensitive is the retina, which can become damaged or detached from the layer behind it, allowing leakage of vitreous humor. Women with long history of high BLOOD pressure or DIABETES are at substantial risk of *retinopathy,* a generalized disorder of the retina that can cause blindness. The retina is also affected in some types of GENETIC DISORDERS, such as *retinitis pigmentosa,* in which the retina's rods and cones degenerate and become pigmented, progressively reducing vision; and *color blindness,* a sex-linked disorder (see GENETIC IN-HERITANCE) involving reduced ability to perceive colors, especially to distinguish colors in the red and green ranges. Excessive exposure to direct sunlight can also damage the retina, causing blindness.

Women who choose contact lenses over glasses to correct vision should exercise great care. Some people are allergic to the materials used in them; have eyes too dry to wear them for long; or work around materials that may damage the lenses, such as in pharmaceuticals or chemicals. Women taking BIRTH CON-TROL PILLS may also have problems with contact lenses. Hard lenses are the most durable kind of contacts; softer lenses are more expensive, mold to the shape of the cornea, and can be worn longer. But therein lies a trap: if lenses are worn longer without proper cleansing, they may promote infection in the eyes, sometimes causing very serious damage.

Women who wear eye makeup should also exercise great care in applying it and should never borrow brushes, pencils, or other items, since they may spread infection (see COSMETICS). Some women choose to have COSMETIC SURGERY to adjust or lift eyelids or even to have permanent lines drawn on their eyelids for emphasis; such operations are very much a personal question, and each individual woman will have to weigh the possible benefits against the risks of surgery.

For more help, information, and action

► **National Society to Prevent Blindness (NSPB)** (500 East Remington Road, Schaumburg, IL 60173; 312-843-2020 or 800-221-3004; Robert Bolan, executive director), an organization of people concerned about blindness and preserving sight. It offers information about proper eye care, eye diseases, and treatments; supports research and operates screening programs; publishes various materials such as *Home Eye Injuries, Hereditary/Congenital Conditions, Diabetic Retinopathy, Cataract,* and *Glaucoma: Sneak Thief of Sight.*
► **National Eye Institute (NEI)** (Building 31, Room 6A32, Bethesda, MD 20892; 301-496-5248), one of the U.S. National Institutes of Health. It sponsors research; provides information; and publishes various materials on eyes and vision disorders.

Other resources

The Complete Guide to Eye Care, Eyeglasses, and Contact Lenses. Walter J. Zinn and Herbert Solomon. Lifetime, 1992.
Your Eyes! A Comprehensive Look at the Understanding and Treatment of Vision Problems. Thomas L. D'Alonzo. Avanti, 1991.
20/20 Is Not Enough: The New World of Vision. Arthur S. Seiderman and others. Knopf, 1990.
Encyclopedia of Blindness and Sight Impairments. Jill Sardegna. Facts on File, 1990.
The Eyes Have It: A Self-Help Manual for Better Vision. Earlyne Chaney. Instant Improve, 1991. Reprint of 1987 ed.

facelift, a type of COSMETIC SURGERY.

fallopian tubes, a pair of narrow tubes, each about four inches long, that curve outward from either side of the UTERUS, in the lower abdomen. Stopping just short of the ovaries, the tubes flare at the end, like upside-down lilies; and like lilies, the ends have petal-like projections called *fimbriae*. (For an illustration, see page 621.) When an egg (OVUM) is released from one of the OVARIES, these fimbriae draw it inside the nearest fallopian tube, helped by the wavelike movements of millions of hairlike cells (*cilia*) that line their inner surface. The egg then begins its slow movement through the tubes to the uterus, propelled by muscular contractions, a journey that takes approximately four to five days. If sperm enter the fallopian tube during the journey in the twenty-four hours when the egg is viable, or receptive, fertilization may take place. The fallopian tubes function mainly to provide a protected place for fertilization and to move the egg—fertilized or not—into the uterus.

The main problems associated with the fallopian tubes hamper those functions. These include

▶ *salpingitis,* inflammation of the fallopian tubes, often from infection with one of the SEXUALLY TRANSMITTED DISEASES or with PELVIC INFLAMMATORY DISEASE (PID), or from infection caused by an INTRAUTERINE DEVICE (IUD), ABORTION, or CHILDBIRTH, which can result in the blockage described below.

▶ *blockage of the fallopian tubes,* a common result from infections and inflammations such as those noted above, where scar tissue or adhesions (where skin heals together abnormally after surgery) bar the passageway. It can also result from a ruptured appendix, ENDOMETRIOSIS (growth of uterine tissue in the tubes), or various types of gynecological surgery, including a previous CESAREAN SECTION. Sometimes the tubes are completely blocked, so fertilization cannot take place; however, sometimes the sperm can get through, but not the fertilized egg. Then an ECTOPIC PREGNANCY results, also called a *tubal pregnancy,* when the growth takes place in one of the tubes; this is a potentially life-threatening situation and must be treated urgently as soon as it is recognized (see ECTOPIC PREGNANCY). In cases where tubal blockage causes INFERTILITY, the passageway can sometimes be cleared or rebuilt (see TUBOPLASTY).

▶ *cancer of the fallopian tubes,* a rare disorder, except when it has spread from the uterus or ovaries. In that case the tubes are generally removed surgically in a *salpingectomy;* if the uterus and ovaries are also removed, the combined operation is called a *hystero-salpingo-oophorectomy* (see HYSTERECTOMY; OOPHO-RECTOMY).

Because the fallopian tubes are so vital to fertilization, women who wish to have a permanent form of BIRTH CONTROL sometimes have an operation to have their "tubes tied," called a TUBAL LIGATION. One alternative is a *fimbriectomy,* in which the petal-like fimbriae are removed. (See REPRODUCTIVE SYSTEM; also WOMEN'S HEALTH HELP, INFORMATION, AND ACTION GUIDE on page 334.)

family, two or more people living together, related to each other by blood, ADOP-TION, MARRIAGE, or mutual agreement (see COHABITATION) and with shared re-sponsibilities and obligations regarding each other's physical, emotional, social, and economic care. Families come in many shapes and forms. Indeed, sociolo-gists and anthropologists—and, as was seen in the 1992 U.S. presidential cam-paign, politicians as well—disagree on precisely what a family *is.* Some people restrict the term to people related by blood or marriage who live together. Some seek to expand the term to include, formally, those who have agreed, in the ab-sence of blood or legal ties, to live together and care for each other. In a wider sense, a family may refer to all one's relatives, however far-flung geographically, or to all the descendants of a common ancestor.

Because family is defined so differently, laws relating to the family often spec-ify what does, and does not, constitute a family for purposes of the law. Such legal definitions are being challenged by people in nontraditional relationships who re-gard themselves as a family, such as a LESBIAN couple or an unmarried heterosexual couple living together (see COHABITATION). At stake is more than acceptance by so-ciety but often very practical benefits, such as being able to share in insurance and pension benefits or being able to rent a house in a single-family zone.

To sociologists, the most basic type is the *nuclear family,* centering around a wife and a husband and any children they might have. A single parent and child also form a nuclear family, as may a lesbian couple, even if their relation-ship is not recognized legally.

A *polygamous* family (see POLYGAMY) is one centered on a husband with several wives *(polygyny)* or a wife with several husbands *(polyandry).* Some kinds of collective families, such as communes or kibbutzes, have all adults share the rearing of all the children; these are sometimes called *multiparent families.* Less formally, *surrogate families,* familylike networks of friends, can provide mutual support, often based on shared work, culture, interests, or communities.

An *extended* family is one that includes three or more generations in the same household, as where a family includes a grandparent, grandchild, aunt, or cousin. Sometimes "extended family" refers more generally to the whole network of relatives with whom the family is in regular contact and whom the family can call on for help and support, whether or not they live in the same house. This was the traditional family form and remains so in much of the world. In the United States, nuclear families have predominated in much of the twentieth century, but three-generation households are becoming more common with the complex patterns of DIVORCE and remarriage, with many adolescent pregnancies, and with the need in many families to care for an elderly parent.

Families exist in most societies, though their forms and functions may vary widely. In some, men traditionally dominate women (see PATRIARCHY), though an individual couple may have an equal or role-reversed relationship; a society where women generally dominate men, in families and otherwise, is labeled a MATRIARCHY. Similarly, if the succession of power or inheritance in a family runs through the male side, it is termed *patriliny*; through the female, *matriliny*. If, on MARRIAGE, a newly formed family lives with or near the husband's family, that is termed *patrilocality*, in socioanthropological terms; if near the wife's, *matrilocality*. In modern mobile societies, of course, such terms have little relevance, and a family may establish residence thousands of miles away from either set of parents, or *in-laws*. In those places where parents do not live with the children, or where the husband and wife do not constitute a separate economic unit, as on a kibbutz or commune, sociologists differ as to whether a family does or does not exist.

The *head of the household* is the person who primarily supports one or more other members of the family—for income-tax purposes, contributing over half of the necessary support of a family member—and has significant authority within the family. Traditionally, the head of the household has been a male; indeed, until the nineteenth century women and children were "covered" by the man legally (see COVERTURE) and had virtually no separate legal status. With many modern two-career families, the head of household description is not only less useful, but also runs counter to any egalitarian feelings of the couple.

One enormously significant change in the family in recent decades has been the number of women who act as heads of households in the absence of males. Many are divorced women raising their children with little or no CHILD SUPPORT; many are SINGLE PARENTS raising children on their own; and increasing numbers are SINGLE WOMEN—many of them elderly—living alone. This phenomenon is seen all around the world. In *The World's Women: Trends and Statistics 1970–1990*, the United Nations estimates that over 20 percent of all households in developed countries, Africa, Latin America, and the Caribbean are headed by women. The actual percentage is probably higher, since in many countries, if any male is living in the household, he is considered its head, regardless of his contribution to or authority in the family. The living patterns differ, however: in developed countries, a majority of woman-headed households consist of single women living alone; in developing countries, woman-headed households are likely to include children.

Woman-headed households around the world have this in common: They are generally poorer than those headed by men. In multiperson households, the woman is often the sole working-age provider and often has the responsibility to support not only children, but also other ill or aging relatives, a responsibility that continues through life. Among the poorest are elderly women living alone, who have little or no pension or other income, few marketable skills, and meager job prospects.

A family unit that has not experienced a DIVORCE or SEPARATION is sometimes called an *intact family*, while one that has been split is called a *broken family*. Many people, especially single parents and their children, object to the term *broken* because it implies that the family needs to be "fixed." Many broken families regroup themselves into new family units when a parent remarries; in addition to the wife and husband, either or both previously married, the resulting *stepfamily* may include children from previous relationships and children from the new one. With various kinds of CUSTODY and VISITATION RIGHTS, the living arrangements of reconstituted families can sometimes be rather complicated, as can the legal relationships (see MOTHER; FATHER).

Intact or broken, most families function reasonably well on their own, without intervention from the government's social support system. Those that do not are termed *dysfunctional*. Health and social work professionals draw on knowledge of family dynamics to help identify problem areas where crisis intervention and counseling might be needed, as in cases of possible CHILD ABUSE AND NEGLECT or INCEST. (See MOTHER; FATHER; MARRIAGE; SINGLE PARENT; SINGLE WOMAN; also CAREGIVER'S HELP, INFORMATION, AND ACTION GUIDE on page 454; COUPLES AND FAMILIES HELP, INFORMATION, AND ACTION GUIDE on page 418; SINGLE PARENT'S HELP, INFORMATION, AND ACTION GUIDE on page 676; OLDER WOMEN'S HELP, INFORMATION, AND ACTION GUIDE on page 374.)

family and medical leave, unpaid time off from a job to care for a sick FAMILY member or for a medical condition, including PREGNANCY. Generally, health insurance and sometimes other benefits continue. A MOTHER would traditionally be granted *maternity leave* before and after CHILDBIRTH.

The last several decades have brought significant changes in family patterns, including higher rates of DIVORCE and SEPARATION, leading to more SINGLE PARENT families; a larger proportion of women working outside the home; and also much longer life spans, meaning more elderly relatives that need care. As these changes have been felt around the world, various countries have established family and medical leave programs. The specifics differ widely. Some places still offer only maternity leave. In others, a plan might also cover time off in case of serious illness of a family member, such as a child, spouse, or elderly parent. Still others, as in parts of Scandinavia, give time off to *both* parents around the time of a child's birth, ADOPTION, or serious illness.

As of 1992 the United States has no national family and medical leave policy. Some states and some individual firms have leave policies, but many do not. More often mothers who wish to be with family members at crucial times must make patchwork arrangements of vacation time, sick days, and personal days; the same is true of fathers, though men are less often caregivers. Both may be formally or informally penalized in the workplace for carrying out caregiving duties.

Many other firms, especially smaller ones, do not guarantee even basic maternity leave. Indeed, many a pregnant woman has been fired summarily on announcing her pregnancy. The PREGNANCY DISCRIMINATION ACT was designed to prevent this but is hard to enforce and does not cover the smallest firms. Even where maternity leave is granted, many women who return to work after giving birth find that they have been moved out of line, often onto a slower promotion line, called the MOMMY TRACK.

A family and medical leave bill twice passed by the U.S. Congress only to be vetoed by President Bush was quickly passed and signed under the Clinton administration in 1993. Its importance is highlighted by the statistics that, in the 1990 census, women made up over 45 percent of the workforce; and nearly 60 percent of women with children under six, and 75 percent of those with children six to seventeen, were working mothers. (See CAREGIVER'S HELP, INFORMATION, AND ACTION GUIDE on page 454; also CHILD CARE.)

family violence: See BATTERED WOMEN; CHILD ABUSE AND NEGLECT.

Families and Work Institute (330 Seventh Avenue, New York, NY 10001; 212-465-2044; Dana Friedman and Ellen Galinsky, founders), a research and planning organization founded in 1989 to "develop new approaches for balancing the changing needs of America's families with the continuing need for workplace productivity." It conducts policy research; provides management training; and acts as a national clearinghouse on work and family life, including "the entire life-cycle of the family, from prenatal care through child care and elder care." Among its publications are books and reports such as *The Corporate Reference Guide to Work-Family Programs, The State Reference Guide to Work-Family Programs for State Employees, Beyond the Parental Leave Debate: The Impact of Laws in Four States, Parental Leave and Productivity: Current Research, Public-Private Partnerships for Child Care: A Feasibility Study for New York State, The Six Stages of Parenthood,* and *The Preschool Years;* international-oriented works such as *The Family-Friendly Employer: Examples from Europe, Families at Work: Practical Examples from 140 Businesses, The Implementation of Flexible Time and Leave Policies: Observations from European Employers, The Relevance of British Career Break Schemes for American Companies,* and *The Family in Transition: An International Symposium;* and numerous articles and papers.

father, the male who legally exercises PARENTS' RIGHTS regarding a child. In the narrowest sense, the father is the man who contributed half of the child's genes (see GENETIC INHERITANCE); he is known as the child's *biological father, natural father,* or *birth father.* If he and the child's mother are married at the time of the birth, he is also the *legal father.* If the mother is married to someone other than the biological father, her husband is the child's *stepfather;* though he may have informal authority in the home, he does not become the child's legal father unless he adopts the child (see ADOPTION).

If the child's mother is unmarried, and the father recognizes the child as his, he is called the *acknowledged father.* But if the child has not been acknowledged, the state legally calls the man presumed to be the father the *putative father* or, more generally, the *unwed father.* If the biological father gives up his parents' rights and allows the child to be adopted, the male who adopts the child is called the *adoptive father;* if the placement is temporary or pending final adoption, the male may be called the *foster father.*

Complications can occur with some kinds of modern reproductive technology, such as ARTIFICIAL INSEMINATION or *IN VITRO* FERTILIZATION. If a woman is inseminated with SPERM from her husband, then the biological father of the baby is also the legal father. If a married woman is inseminated with sperm from a donor—someone other than her husband—the woman's husband is generally considered the legal father, and the biological father has no legal rights. That poses no problem when the sperm comes from an anonymous donor but can produce complications if sperm was donated by a male known to the woman; in that case, laws may vary as to whether the known donor is the legal father or if the child has *no* legal father.

The biological father, whether the legal father or an unwed father, has no legal rights—in the United States, at least—regarding the mother's decision as to whether to continue the PREGNANCY or have an ABORTION. That is for the woman to decide, as part of her REPRODUCTIVE RIGHTS, though governments have attempted to restrict such decisions in a variety of ways. After the birth, the legal father assumes parents' rights, including the responsibility to care for and support the child; and the child has the right to inherit from the father (see INHERITANCE RIGHTS). If the father dies before the birth, the child inherits from the father at birth and is called a *posthumous child.*

An unwed father has VISITATION RIGHTS and CHILD SUPPORT obligations, but the unwed mother can—without his consent—place the child for ADOPTION, which terminates parents' rights. At that point, if he wishes, the unwed father can ask the court for CUSTODY; his chances of success are uncertain and depend on state laws that differ markedly on such questions. Most will allow the adoption to proceed, especially if the child is a newborn.

In the United States, the question of paternity has become entwined with public support. If an unwed mother is receiving benefits under some government programs, such as AID TO FAMILIES WITH DEPENDENT CHILDREN (AFDC), the government will try to locate the putative father, for reimbursement of money paid by the state for child support. If the putative father is located, the government will ask him to sign a *consent agreement,* acknowledging the child and his own child support responsibilities. If he refuses, the government may institute a *paternity suit* to establish that he is, in fact, the *legal father* or *acknowledged father.*

Because the questions of parentage are complicated, many states have adopted the Uniform Parentage Act, which puts forward common court procedures, definitions, and standards on parentage issues, as in a paternity suit. Under this act, a man is presumed to be a child's father if

- he has acknowledged the child as his own, as by raising the child in his own home as his child.
- he and the mother were married at the time of the child's birth, or the child was born within three hundred days of the end of the MARRIAGE.
- he and the mother married, or tried to do so, after the child's birth, and he either acknowledged in writing that the child was his; allowed his name to appear on the birth certificate; or had court-ordered or voluntarily assumed child support obligations.

Traditionally, the man married to a child's mother at the time of the birth was automatically considered the child's legal father, whatever evidence might have existed to the contrary. However, since modern blood tests are accurate enough to indicate when a man could *not* have been a child's biological father (even if they cannot say precisely who *was*), the courts have allowed some challenges to that assumption in suits involving such paternity questions.

Many men have become far more active as fathers in the past few decades. Once generally barred from DELIVERY rooms (as they still are in some hospitals), many men have become active coaches, supporters, masseurs, and general aides in their role as *birth partners* with the rise of natural CHILDBIRTH. Many among the new generation of fathers also tend to be more closely involved with their children from birth, building a close relationship from the start and trying to know their children intimately as they grow—an experience earlier generations of fathers often missed.

When both parents work, fathers these days are more likely to be actively engaged in their children's day-to-day care, from feeding and dressing to playing and putting to bed.

Some have actively sought *paternity leave* (see FAMILY AND MEDICAL LEAVE) and more flexible work schedules so they can spend more time with the new baby, though such alternatives are rarely available for fathers. Society gives little support for male parents; employers rarely approve of fathers taking time off from work to care for a sick child or visit a child's school, for example, and few programs exist that help fathers learn how to care for their new children and share experiences with others. Despite the many changes that have taken place, the primary responsibility for child rearing still tends to fall on the MOTHER.

This is especially true if the parents DIVORCE. Most fathers do not request CUSTODY, though courts will often grant it when they do. When the mother has custody, as nine out of ten do in the United States, many fathers fail to keep up a fatherly attachment with their children and do not even regularly exercise VISITATION RIGHTS. In a 1991 study of 1,400 children from divorced families in the United States, an astounding 23 percent of fathers had *no* contact at all with their children in the previous five years, and another 20 percent had not seen their children at all during the previous year. Many also fail to meet their CHILD SUPPORT obligations. (See COUPLES AND FAMILIES HELP, INFORMATION, AND ACTION GUIDE on page 418; DIVORCE AND SEPARATION HELP, INFORMATION, AND ACTION GUIDE on page 238; see also CHILD SUPPORT.)

father right, another name for the whole body of rights stemming from a patrilineal line of succession (see PATRIARCHY).

fecundity, the biological capacity to bear children (see FERTILITY).

Federally Employed Women (FEW) (1400 Eye [I] Street, NW, Suite 425, Washington, DC 20005-2252; 202-898-0994; Carolyn M. Kroon, president), an organization founded originally in 1968 to represent female federal employees, though its members now include both men and women, civilian and military personnel of all grades and from all government agencies. FEW's primary goal is to end sexual discrimination and promote equal employment opportunities for women in the federal workforce and to influence legislation and public policy at the chapter, regional, and national levels. Other issues of special concern include pay equity; dependent care; retirement, pension, and other employee benefits; economic empowerment; education; health care; violence against women; and repeal of combat exclusion laws and inclusion of gynecological care as part of veteran's benefits for women in the military. FEW strongly supports passage of the EQUAL RIGHTS AMENDMENT. It also continues its original focus on career advancement by offering leadership training and career development programs. The FEW Legal and Education Fund (FEW LEF), founded in 1977, undertakes test proceedings or provides legal assistance to individuals in cases affecting opportunity or advancement in government employment; it also undertakes research on government employment and discrimination.

FEW publishes various materials, including the bimonthly national newsletter *News & Views;* the *FEW Policy and Procedures Manual, Report of a Survey on Women and the Federal Women's Program in the Federal Government, FEW Legislative Agenda,* and videotape *Balancing the Scales of Equality,* and various brochures.

Federation of Feminist Women Health Centers (FFWHC)

(3401 Folsom Boulevard, Suite A, Sacramento, CA 95816; 916-737-0260; Beverly Whipple, president of executive board), a network of women's health clinics and individuals seeking to improve women's health care, founded in 1975, especially concerned about ensuring REPRODUCTIVE RIGHTS and with educating women about their own bodies, and stressing self-help procedures, such as menstrual extraction (see MENSTRUATION). Its publications include *A New View of a Woman's Body, Woman-Centered Pregnancy and Birth,* and *How to Stay Out of the Gynecologist's Office.*

female circumcision

, the traditional mutilation of a woman's external GENITALS, the aim being to destroy a woman's capacity for sexual pleasure and so attempt to ensure CHASTITY and fidelity; an extreme form of SEXUAL DISCRIMINATION indeed. The practice is today mostly associated with Arab-Muslim cultures in Africa and western Asia, but in fact it is not mentioned in the Quran (Koran), the holy book of Islam, and predates Mohammed. Its roots stretch back at least to the time of the pharaohs in early Egypt and is also found among some non-Muslim peoples of the region. Female circumcision was even used in Western countries in the nineteenth century and into the 1930s as a "treatment" for MASTURBATION and "nymphomania." Today the practice is widely condemned internationally but continues to be tolerated and even encouraged at the national and local level, where many men believe that it is necessary to a "pure" marriage. In the mid-1980s an estimated 84 million women in thirty countries had been circumcised, perhaps 74 million of them in Africa, with the highest percentage of female circumcision in Somalia. Some areas have had some success in eradicating the practice through education and modern health care, notably in urban areas of Egypt. Some Western countries, notably France, have been attacking the problem among immigrants by bringing criminal charges against the mothers and midwives who carry out operations on their children.

The three main kinds of female genital mutilation are

▶ *Sunna circumcision,* which involves removing the tip of the CLITORIS, the main organ of sexual pleasure in a woman, similar in sensitivity to a man's PE-NIS. The term "circumcision" is something of a misnomer, since that term more properly refers to removal of the FORESKIN, the partly retractable hood of skin over the clitoris, analogous to male CIRCUMCISION.

▶ *clitoridectomy,* which involves removal of the entire clitoris and parts of the *labia minora,* the "small lips" that partly enclose it (see LABIA). Sometimes the *labia minora* are removed completely, and so are parts of the *labia majora,* the larger, outer lips; then the remaining tissue is stitched together, with an opening left for SEXUAL INTERCOURSE and urination. In Western societies, clitoridectomy is rarely performed today, except in cases of CANCER of the VULVA.

▶ *infibulation,* also called *Pharaonic* or *Sudanese circumcision,* which involves complete removal of the clitoris and also removal of the labia minora and majora, or their mutilation so that they adhere together in a lengthwise strip of scar tissue. In rural Sudan, for example, a local midwife removes a girl's clitoris with a knife, razor blade, or other sharp (though generally rough and nonsurgical) instrument, then scrapes the skin off the labia majora and stitches them together with string using acacia thorns. She leaves a small opening at the base, through which a small stick or twig is inserted, to allow for passage of urine (see URINARY TRACT) and blood from MENSTRUATION. The girl's legs are then tied together down to her ankles and remain so until the labia have healed so as to completely close over the genital area. At marriage this scar will be cut open, generally with no ANESTHESIA, to allow for sexual intercourse and possible CHILDBIRTH. Sometimes the labia will be resutured after birth and cut open again later.

The most common of these operations is the *clitoridectomy;* the most dangerous, *infibulation.* Such operations are performed at different times in different societies, as early as infancy and as late as shortly before marriage, but commonly between ages seven and thirteen, often as a rite of PUBERTY.

The health problems resulting from genital mutilation are extensive. The initial operation can cause life-threatening problems such as infections, hemorrhaging, or tetanus, apart from the pain itself, which also can cause severe psychological trauma. Longer-term health effects include anemia (see BLOOD), retention of menstrual blood and urine (which can lead to kidney or cardiovascular problems), and painful MENSTRUATION. In MARRIAGE, many circumcised women have difficult or painful intercourse, or *dyspareunia,* with scar tissue sometimes forming a virtually impenetrable barrier to vaginal intercourse. Infections can result in PELVIC INFLAMMATORY DISEASE (PID), which can lead to INFERTILITY and potentially life-threatening ECTOPIC PREGNANCY. Women who do become pregnant often have difficulty in CHILDBIRTH, with increased risk of STILLBIRTH, and sometimes are unable to give birth normally. With the repeated infibulation operations, some women become unable to have normal vaginal intercourse and are sometimes then cast aside by their husbands.

For further help, information, and action

Psychological Effects of the Female Circumcision. Ahmed I. Ballal. Vantage, 1992. (See WOMEN'S HEALTH HELP, INFORMATION, AND ACTION GUIDE on page 334; SEXUAL DISCRIMINATION AND SEXUAL HARASSMENT HELP, INFORMATION, AND ACTION GUIDE on page 642; see also Alice WALKER.)

female condom, popular name for the VAGINAL POUCH.

Female Eunuch, The: See Germaine GREER.

female supremacy, the theory that women are innately superior to men, whether through biological or cultural inheritance. It is a mirror image of the theory of male supremacy (see PATRIARCHY), although scarcely the ideological basis of a worldwide and historic pattern of SEXUAL DISCRIMINATION, as male supremacy has been. The idea of female supremacy does serve as the basis of CULTURAL FEMINISM and ESSENTIALISM, as well as of some earlier utopian feminist theories, hopes, and plans, and is part of the underpinning of several separatist theories and groups. (See also FEMINISM; ESSENTIALISM; CULTURAL FEMINISM.)

feme covert, formerly in common law, the legal status of a married woman (see COVERTURE).

Feminine Mystique, The: See Betty FRIEDAN.

feminism, a movement likened to a tree with many branches; also a group of often ill-defined, overlapping self-descriptions. In the most general sense, feminism is a worldwide movement for the right of women to enjoy complete equality in every economic, legal, social, and institutional way—in short, in every aspect of life in every society. Anyone who believes in those principles, man or woman, is a *feminist.* The term has been most used in the twentieth century; earlier, a more common term describing the struggle for WOMEN'S RIGHTS was "woman movement."

Largely because feminism is a very political term, it has also become a very spongy one. For the overwhelming majority of those who believe in women's rights, feminism is simply the accepted way of describing that belief as it has developed during more than two centuries of struggle for social reform. For them, feminism is a worldwide reform movement, and they are equality seekers who see no need to prescribe revolutionary solutions. Such reformers are sometimes called *liberal feminists.* In the United States, from the early 1970s, some of these reformers sought to distinguish themselves from the several radical feminist groups, describing themselves as part of *mainstream feminism.*

Some of those who are uneasy about being thought "radical," especially in periods of backlash against WOMEN'S RIGHTS MOVEMENTS, find it politic to go farther, avoiding the term *feminist* and instead calling themselves "believers in women's rights," as did women's rights advocates in the nineteenth century. This is not always entirely a matter of backlash, for the worldwide feminist movement embraces a very wide range of views and groups, and people at both ends of the spectrum are often quite uneasy allies, however strong their basic commitment to equality.

Feminism is also a very indistinct term for the other end of the range of feminist beliefs and actions, for here, as in so many other political and social movements, the revolutionary feminists tend to regard mainstream feminists as "mere" reformers who inadequately understand the need for radical change. Some revolutionary feminists work with reformers on common issues but also attempt to "radicalize" the much larger body of reformers. Others work with reformers only as very uneasy allies, being essentially separatist in their outlook. The several nineteenth- and twentieth-century socialist and communist movements provide illuminating parallels, with their beliefs and organizations ranging widely from different kinds of utopian separatists to a variety of activist reformers and direct revolutionaries.

So it is possible to find groups calling themselves "feminists" whose interests are concentrated on other issues as well as women's rights; the Marxist-oriented feminists of the early twentieth century, for example, strongly believed that socialism had to come first, before women could possibly gain their legitimate rights; they attempted to bend women's rights movements to socialist or communist organizational ends, with some success in many countries, though (where they won power) with at best very mixed results. Where women won political and employment rights, they still generally were left their traditional responsibilities as well (see HOUSEWORK). Modern Marxist feminist groups, advocating what seems essentially the same position, have in recent years often acted differently in practice, after the full impact of the Soviet, Eastern European, and Chinese experience on women has become apparent. There are also a few sectarian radical feminists who deny the validity of the whole range of feminist belief and action, describing their feminism as the only "true" feminism.

In addition, a considerable range of ethnic-oriented feminist groups exists; the African-American, Asian-American, Chicana, and Native American feminists of the United States have on their agenda several kinds of problems at once, including ethnic and racial discrimination and poverty, as well as pervasive SEXUAL DISCRIMINATION. Many ethnic women's rights advocates, in America and worldwide, continue to sharply criticize American feminist movements as being far too oriented to American White middle-class problems and issues and too little concerned with such worldwide questions as poverty (see FEMINIZATION OF POVERTY), sustainable economic development (see DEVELOPMENT AND WOMEN'S RIGHTS), recurrent famines, the terrible public health conditions that spur the growth of pandemics, and the enormous environmental damage and unchecked population explosion that underlie all other dilemmas. Feminism being a central concern, various types of feminism are discussed fully in separate articles throughout this book. (See BOURGEOIS FEMINISM; CULTURAL FEMINISM; DOMESTIC FEMINISM; ECOFEMINISM; ESSENTIALISM; LESBIAN FEMINISM; MARXIST FEMINISM; METAPHYSICAL FEMINISM; RADICAL FEMINISM; SOCIALIST FEMINISM; SPIRITUAL FEMINISM; MALE FEMINIST; POSTFEMINIST; WOMANISM; WOMEN'S RIGHTS MOVEMENT; WOMEN'S LIBERATION MOVEMENT.) (See also WOMEN'S RIGHTS HELP, INFORMATION, AND ACTION GUIDE on page 767.)

People call me a feminist
whenever I express sentiments that differentiate me
from a doormat or a prostitute.

REBECCA WEST, 1913
———— IN THE CLARION ————

•

feminist health center: See HEALTH EQUITY.

Feminists Concerned for Better Feminist Leadership

(FCBFL) (P.O. Box 1348, Madison Square Station, New York, NY 10159; 212-796-1467; Mia Albright, director), an organization that represents nationalist feminism, which is described as going "beyond traditional feminism and a remedy for pseudofeminism," in a rapidly deteriorating worldwide "malist society" and "wifist population." It rests on the premises that "the malist society is finished and is taking us and the environment down with him"; that "wifism destroys our lives, relations, and organizations"; and that "wifist leadership cannot understand that malist society is dangerous." FCBFL sponsors meetings, forms networks with individuals and organizations, and distributes nationalist feminist literature, including the FCBFL quarterly *The Gold Flag Bulletin* and the book *Feminism: Freedom From Wifism*, published by the Nationalist Feminist Studies Institute.

feminization of poverty, a phrase in common use in the United States from the late 1980s, recognizing the explosion of absolute and relative numbers of women living below the poverty level. Many are SINGLE PARENTS, some also welfare-dependent, reflecting the more than doubling of births to unmarried mothers in the United States in the 1970s and 1980s. Others are divorced working women, many of them with minimal skills, unable to make enough to support their families above the poverty level when they can get jobs (see DISPLACED HOMEMAKERS). Many of these suffer from the outcome of "equalizing" DIVORCE settlement laws, which effectively destabilize their family situations and rob them of support (see CHILD SUPPORT; ALIMONY); others do not receive legally due support. Many older women, with or without living husbands, find SOCIAL SECURITY payments insufficient to keep them above the poverty level (see WIDOW; SINGLE

WOMAN). Plunging far below the poverty level are some narcotics addicts (see AL-COHOL AND DRUG ABUSE) and AIDS victims. Former mental patients, essentially on their own on the street, swell the increasing numbers of homeless women, many of whom have children, (see MENTAL DISORDERS); others edge toward becoming homeless. All continue to suffer from the massive 1980s federal cutbacks and cut-offs of social service funds and vitally needed programs, which occurred as the United States sailed through the false prosperity of the 1980s and then slid into a long, deep recession, which, for many poor people, resembled the Great Depression of the 1930s.

The United States by 1992 has become one of the worst social service network providers in the industrialized world, with conditions that in some stricken urban and rural areas echo those found in some of the world's poorest countries. But the United States is one of the wealthiest countries on earth, and it is in these poorer countries that the great masses of poor women, children, and men can be found, huddled in shantytowns and worse around scores of the world's major cities. Inadequate food, water, shelter, or clothing, and plague-producing sanitation conditions count among their woes. They have little or no hope of making a living in these countries that continue to experience runaway population growth. United Nations–developed housing, human settlements, and environment indicators (see page 824) show the magnitude of the problem. Even though these figures are understated and unavailable from some countries, it is clear that the worldwide situation of poor people, among them many of the world's women, continues to worsen. (See also SINGLE PARENTS; DISPLACED HOMEMAKERS; DEVELOPMENT AND WOMEN'S RIGHTS; also POVERTY AND WOMEN HELP, INFORMATION, AND ACTION GUIDE, below).

POVERTY AND WOMEN

Help, Information, and Action Guide

Organizations

► NATIONAL HOOK-UP OF BLACK WOMEN (NHBW) (312-643-5866).
► NATIONAL DISPLACED HOMEMAKERS NETWORK (NDHN) (202-467-6346).
► CLEARINGHOUSE ON WOMEN'S ISSUES (CWI) (301-871-6016 or 202-363-9795).
► CENTER FOR WOMEN POLICY STUDIES (CWPS) (202-872-1770). Has *National Brain Trust on Economic Opportunity for Low Income Women*.
► NATIONAL CENTER FOR YOUTH LAW (NCYL) (415-543-3307).
► WOMEN AND FOUNDATIONS/CORPORATE PHILANTHROPY (WAF/CP)

(212-463-9934). Publishes *Statements From the Grass Roots: Women Breaking the Continuum of Poverty.*

▶ LEAGUE OF WOMEN'S VOTERS (202-429-1965). Publishes *Meeting the Employment Needs of Women: A Path Out of Poverty?.*

▶ CHURCH WOMEN UNITED (CWU) (212-870-2347). Publishes the quarterly newsletter *UN Update* and action alerts on national legislation affecting women and children.

◤ FOR LEGAL ADVICE AND REFERRALS

▶ EQUAL RIGHTS ADVOCATES (ERA) (415-621-0672; advice and counseling line, 415-621-0505). A national women's law center.

▶ LAWYERS' COMMITTEE FOR CIVIL RIGHTS UNDER LAW (202-371-1212).

◤ WOMEN AND DEVELOPMENT

▶ UNITED NATIONS DEVELOPMENT FUND FOR WOMEN (UNIFEM) (212-906-6400). Publishes *The World's Women: Trends and Statistics 1970-1990, Women, Law and Development: Action for Change, Tools for Community Participation, Women Working Together for Personal, Economic, and Community Development, Navamaga: Training Activities for Group Building, Health, and Income Generation, Learning to Teach, Women and World Development: An Education and Action Handbook,* and handbooks on business skills for "microenterprises."

▶ INTERNATIONAL CENTER FOR RESEARCH ON WOMEN (ICRW) (202-797-0007). Publishes *Women, Poverty and Environment in Latin America, Mothers on Their Own: Policy Issues for Developing Countries,* and *Low-Income Housing: A Woman's Perspective.*

▶ INTERNATIONAL WOMEN'S TRIBUNE CENTRE (IWTC) (212-687-8633).

▶ WOMEN'S INTERNATIONAL NETWORK (WIN) (617-862-9431).

▶ WOMEN'S ENVIRONMENT AND DEVELOPMENT ORGANIZATION (WEDO), (212-759-7982).

▶ INTERNATIONAL CENTER FOR RESEARCH ON WOMEN (ICRW) (202-797-0007). Publishes *Women, Work, and Child Welfare in the Third World.*

▶ NATIONAL CONFERENCE OF PUERTO RICAN WOMEN (NACOPRW) (CONFERENCIA NACIONAL DE MUJERES PUERTORRIQUENAS, INC.) (202-387-4716).

Other resources

Women, the State, and Welfare. Linda Gordon, ed. University of Wisconsin Press, 1991.

Short-Changed. Rhonda Sharp and Ray Broomhill. Paul and Co., 1991.

Poor Women, Poor Families: The Economic Plight of America's Female-Headed Households, rev. ed. Harrell R. Rodgers, Jr. M. E. Sharpe, 1990.

Women's Life Cycle and Economic Insecurity: Problems and Proposals. Martha N. Ozawa, ed. Praeger/Greenwood, 1989.

American Women in Poverty. Paul R. Zopf, Jr. Greenwood, 1989.

Women, Housing and Community. Willem Van Vliet. Ashgate, 1989.

Welfare Is Not for Women: Toward a Model of Advocacy to Meet the Needs of Women in Poverty. Diana M. Pearce, Institute for Women's Policy Research, 1989.

Biting the Hand That Feeds Them: Organizing Women on Welfare at the Grass Roots Level. Jacqueline Pope. Praeger/Greenwood, 1989.

☑ **WOMEN AND DEVELOPMENT**

Gender Analysis in Development Planning: A Case Book. Aruna Rao and others, eds. Kumarian Press, 1991.

Women and Development in the Third World. Janet Momsen. Routledge, 1991.

Women, Development and Survival in the Third World. Haleh Afshar, ed. Longman, 1991.

Women in the Developing World: Thoughts and Ideas. Hasna Begum. Apt, 1990.

Women in Rural Development: Critical Issues, 4th ed. International Labour Office, 1990.

Persistent Inequalities: Women and World Development. Irene Tinker, ed. Oxford University Press, 1990.

Women, Poverty and Progress in the Third World. Mayra Buvinic and Sally W. Yudelman. Foreign Policy, 1989.

Women and Economic Development: Local, Regional and National Planning Strategies. Kate Young, ed. Berg, 1989.

Women in the Third World: Gender Issues in Rural and Urban Areas. Lynne Brydon and Sylvia Chant. Rutgers University Press, 1989.

Seeds: Supporting Women's Work in the Third World. Ann Leonard, ed. Feminist Press, 1989.

(See also OLDER WOMEN'S HELP, INFORMATION, AND ACTION GUIDE on page 374; WORKING WOMEN'S HELP, INFORMATION, AND ACTION GUIDE on page 779.)

Femmes Chefs D'Entreprises Mondiales, Les (FCEM), the

World Association of Women Entrepreneurs, of which NATIONAL ASSOCIATION OF WOMEN BUSINESS OWNERS (NAWBO) is the official U.S. member.

fertility, for a woman, the ability to conceive and bear a child; for a man, the ability to impregnate a woman. Like INFERTILITY, fertility is a relative matter. Normally, a woman is most fertile—that is, most readily able to conceive and least likely to have problems carrying a child to term—in her mid-twenties, with her fertility declining slowly through her thirties and more rapidly after that, ending with MENOPAUSE, generally in her early fifties. For men the pattern is quite different; though they peak in their early twenties, their decline in fertility is slower and more gradual, with some fertility remaining into the old age. Many people have trouble conceiving, however, for a variety of reasons (see INFERTILITY).

In terms of wider population questions, the *fertility rate* or *childbearing rate* is an estimate of the number of children a woman would have on the average, given current patterns. This reflects not simply biological capacity for pregnancy, sometimes called *fecundity* in population circles, but also the many choices that women make regarding childbearing, especially in relation to BIRTH CONTROL and ABORTION. The fertility rate among women declined worldwide between 1970 and 1990, and bids fair to continue doing so. In developed countries, the rate in 1990 is about 1.8, or a little under the rate at which the population stabilizes. In undeveloped countries, the rate has remained considerably higher, falling from a range of five to seven births per woman in 1970 to three to six in 1990, with the smallest drop and the highest rates occurring in sub-Saharan Africa, and the largest decline in eastern Asia, especially China, which has had strong population control policies. (See PREGNANCY AND CHILDBIRTH, HELP, INFORMATION, AND AC-TION GUIDE on page 580.)

fertility specialists, physicians who specialize in treating INFERTILITY; also called *sterologists.*

fertility workup, a battery of tests performed to discover the causes of INFER-TILITY.

fertilization, the union of a woman's egg (OVUM) and a man's SPERM, which normally takes place in a woman's FALLOPIAN TUBES; also called *conception.* With this joining, a unique being is created with genetic material from each parent (see GE-NETIC INHERITANCE). The sex of the new being is determined at this stage; it will receive an X sex chromosome from the mother's egg. If the sperm from the father carries an X chromosome also, the being will be a girl; if a Y chromosome, a boy.

Fertilization is the beginning of a PREGNANCY but also the end of a long process. Both egg and sperm have been formed by special subdivisions so that each has only half of the genetic material needed for a new individual (see GE-NETIC INHERITANCE) and is incomplete without the other. The egg is the single survivor of a group of eggs—perhaps twenty or so—that begin ripening each month during a woman's fertile years (see OVULATION), from the many hundreds of thousands of eggs existing in potential form at a woman's birth. The sperm is one of millions released in an EJACULATION at a man's ORGASM.

During the woman's monthly cycle (see MENSTRUATION), various HORMONES trigger the ripe egg to burst out of the woman's OVARIES and move into the fallopian tubes, and cause the mucus in her VAGINA and CERVIX to change consistency and texture to allow for passage of sperm. The sperm cross the relatively vast expanse of the VAGINA, the usually hostile passageway of the CERVIX, the also vast UTERUS, and on into the fallopian tubes. Once there, a single sperm uses special chemicals in its head to penetrate the two outer protective layers of the egg; then the egg's membrane changes chemically in unknown ways to immediately bar other sperm from entering. The result is called a ZYGOTE or *fertilized egg*. This quickly begins to subdivide, and the resulting ball of cells (sometimes called a *blastocyte*) travels slowly down the fallopian tubes. In about seven to ten days it reaches the uterus, and there the egg implants itself in the uterine wall and begins to develop as an EMBRYO.

On occasion, two or more eggs will be present and fertilized by different sperm. The result is twins or multiple births, called *dizygotic, nonidentical,* or *fraternal*. On rarer occasions a single zygote will separate into two separate embryos; the result is *monozygotic* or *identical* twins or multiple births. However, if by some chance two sperm enter a single egg, the zygote will contain too much genetic material and will be incapable of normal development. Then a spontaneous ABORTION occurs, and the tissue is either reabsorbed into the body or flushed out in menstruation.

The same will happen if the fertilized egg has BIRTH DEFECTS or GENETIC DISORDERS that are at an early stage obviously incompatible with life. Some of these disorders are built into the genetic material from one or both parents; but some CHROMOSOMAL ABNORMALITIES occur during the various cell division processes, in which bits of genetic material may be lost, reattached improperly to the wrong place, or otherwise duplicated incorrectly.

Although fertilization normally takes place in the fallopian tubes, sometimes it takes place in the ovaries or elsewhere in the body, or the developing embryo fails to move into the uterus. The result is a potentially life-threatening ECTOPIC PREGNANCY, which requires emergency surgery. In cases of INFERTILITY, especially affecting the fallopian tubes, fertilization may take place outside the body, in a laboratory dish, a process called *IN VITRO* FERTILIZATION (meaning "in glass"); the resulting fertilized egg is implanted into the uterus by the doctor. Sometimes ARTIFICIAL INSEMINATION may be used to help a couple achieve conception.

When a woman is unable to produce eggs, or when she carries severe genetic disorders, but her REPRODUCTIVE SYSTEM is otherwise healthy, another woman may donate an egg. In a process known as EMBRYO TRANSFER, the donor is inseminated artifically with sperm from the infertile woman's husband or sex partner, and the resulting embryo is transferred to the infertile woman's uterus for implantation and—it is hoped—normal development. (See PREGNANCY AND CHILDBIRTH HELP, INFORMATION, AND ACTION GUIDE on page 580; INFERTILITY AND REPRODUCTIVE TECHNOLOGY HELP, INFORMATION, AND ACTION GUIDE on page 368.)

fetal and maternal specialist, a physician who specializes in complications of high-risk pregnancy (see CHILDBIRTH).

fetal presentation, the position a FETUS takes in the UTERUS at the time of CHILDBIRTH. Normally a fetus is oriented with the head upward during most of the pregnancy. But late in the term, perhaps two to three weeks before DELIVERY but possibly not until the beginning of LABOR, the fetus moves into a new position in preparation for delivery. This is called *engagement,* or the baby *falling* or *dropping.*

Ideally, and most often, the fetus settles head downward in the pelvis, so that during delivery the top of the head emerges first through the *birth canal* formed by the much widened CERVIX and VAGINA. This *vertex presentation* is by far the easiest and safest for delivery. Any other kind of presentation increases the difficulty and risk of delivery and is called *abnormal.*

Among these are forms of *cephalic presentation* in which a different part of the head appears first. In *face presentation* or *chin presentation,* the baby's head is bent toward the back. If the angle of extension is not too great and the woman's pelvis is normal in size and shape, vaginal delivery is often possible, perhaps with use of forceps (see DELIVERY). Otherwise passage may be blocked as the chin catches on the woman's pubic bone *(symphysis pubis),* and CESAREAN SECTION may be necessary. *Brow presentation,* with the forehead first, is a rare type of cephalic presentation. Often during delivery, the baby moves into either a vertex or face presentation. If not, vaginal delivery is generally possible only if the baby is relatively small. Otherwise cesarean section is commonly required.

In about 3 percent of all births, and especially common with twins or other multiple births, a baby's buttocks, feet, or knees appear first in the birth canal. This is called *breech presentation* (breech meaning "buttocks"), which may occur in several forms.

▶ *complete breech,* with the legs crossed over the thighs and tucked up toward the abdomen.

▶ *frank breech,* with the legs straight and the body bent at the hips, so the feet are near the shoulder.

▶ *footling breech,* with feet tucked backward under the buttocks; if one foot, called *single footling;* if both, *double footling.*

Whatever the form, breech presentation is considerably riskier for the baby, with particular danger to the baby's head and of blocking oxygen flow through the UMBILICAL CORD. Breech births are more common in premature babies, who are at increased risk for health problems already, because of their incomplete development. Sometimes the doctor may use pressure on the outside of the woman's abdomen to try to maneuver the fetus into a vertex position (*external cephalic version.*) Often, however, the baby returns to a breech position (sometimes because the pelvis is too small or the uterus abnormally shaped), and the risk is that the PLACENTA will be separated prematurely. Breech births often require some assistance, such as use of forceps or vacuum extraction (see DELIVERY) or EPISIOTOMY, and FETAL MONITORING is often used to ensure that the baby's oxygen supply is undiminished. A cesarean section may be needed in the end, especially if this is a woman's first birth; such operations are increasingly performed to avoid damaging the baby's brain and other organs.

Both cephalic and breech presentations are known as *longitudinal lies,* since the baby's body lies vertically in the uterus. But on rare occasions—less than one in two hundred births—the baby lies horizontally or crosswise in the uterus. This is called a *transverse lie* or a *shoulder presentation.* If the doctor cannot turn the baby, cesarean section is generally required to prevent damage or death to the infant or mother. Sometimes, also, a baby will present more than one part first, such as a hand with the head, in what is called a *compound presentation.* (See LABOR; DELIVERY.)

fetal surgery, an operation performed by a physician on a FETUS still in the womb (UTERUS) and so also called *in utero surgery.* This astonishing kind of surgery, developed from LAPAROSCOPY and more specifically FETOSCOPY, involves cutting small incisions in a pregnant women's abdominal wall and uterine wall. Through one incision a thin, rigid, lighted, periscopelike device called a *laparoscope* is inserted, guided by ULTRASOUND; normally surgical instruments are inserted through another incision.

Though *in utero* surgery is still relatively new and a limited number of operations have been performed, it has saved the lives of many babies. One of the most common *in utero* procedures performed is insertion of a thin tube called a *catheter* to bypass a fetus's blocked URINARY TRACT, which would otherwise cause kidney damage. In cases where mother and fetus have an Rh incompatibility in their BLOOD types, the baby's blood may be replaced in what is called an *exchange transfusion,* to prevent long-term damage. One recently developed operation corrects a usually fatal birth defect called *hernia of the diaphragm,* which affects 1 out of every 2,500 fetuses. A hernia, or hole, in the diaphragm allows abdominal organs to push into the chest cavity, preventing lung growth, so without surgery most babies with the defect die shortly after birth.

Astonishingly, for unknown reasons, fetal surgery leaves no scars. The techniques of fetal surgery are still very new, however, and entail some risks to the health of both mother and fetus and possibly to the mother's future childbearing possibilities, from the general ANESTHESIA and from the incision in the uterus. As a result, *in utero* surgery is (at least so far) normally limited to correction of very serious or life-threatening conditions. (See PREGNANCY AND CHILDBIRTH HELP, INFORMATION, AND ACTION GUIDE on page 580.)

feticide, the killing of a FETUS; an inflammatory term for ABORTION used by pro-life activists.

fetoscopy, a type of PRENATAL TEST, allowing the physician to visually examine a FETUS; a special type of LAPAROSCOPY. Requiring only local ANESTHESIA, the procedure involves making a small incision in a pregnant woman's abdomen and the wall of the UTERUS, generally just above the pubic bone or below the navel; into this is inserted a thin, rigid, periscopelike lighted device called a *laparoscope,* guided by ULTRASOUND. This allows the doctor to examine the fetus for visible signs of abnormal development and in some cases to repair BIRTH DEFECTS (see FETAL SURGERY). Samples of BLOOD, fluid, and fetal cells are also removed; this is incidental, however, since they would normally be obtained more easily and with less risk through other prenatal tests. Because fetoscopy carries a relatively high risk of MISCARRIAGE, it is not generally undertaken without good reason to suspect physical abnormalities. (See PRENATAL TEST; FETAL SURGERY; also GENETIC INHERITANCE AND BIRTH DEFECTS HELP, INFORMATION, AND ACTION GUIDE on page 314.)

fetus, the developing being in a woman's UTERUS during PREGNANCY after the embryonic stage; literally "little one" or "offspring." The new individual formed by FERTILIZATION—the union of a woman's egg (OVUM) and a man's SPERM—is first known as a ZYGOTE, or fertilized egg, and then an EMBRYO. The term FETUS is used from about six to eight weeks into the pregnancy until birth. The development of the fetus during those seven months or so is called GESTATION. (For a stage-by-stage description of fetal growth, see WHAT HAPPENS DURING PREGNANCY on page 557.)

fibroadenoma, a disorder that involves thickening of milk-producing glands, causing benign lumps in the BREAST.

fibrocystic disease, development of benign nodular lumps in the BREASTS.

fibroids, benign growths in a woman's UTERUS; one of the most common reproductive disorders, affecting perhaps two to three out of every ten women over age thirty-five.

The names *fibroids* or *fibroid tumors* are something of a misnomer, since they actually grow not from fibrous tissue, but from the muscle wall of the uterus. As a result, fibroids are known medically by a number of different names, including *myomas* (*myo-* means "muscle"), *leiomyomas, fibromyomas,* or *meiomyofibromas.* More precisely, fibroids are classified by their location. Fibroids may occur singly or in multiple growths. Most remain within the uterine muscle wall and are called *intramural* or *interstitial.* Less common are *subserous* or *subperitoneal* fibroids, which grow out from the outside wall. Rarest are *submucous* fibroids that grow into the uterus's interior, while those near the CERVIX, or neck of the uterus, are called *cervical* fibroids.

Some fibroids grow on a stalk or stem, called a *pedicle;* these can move around within the pelvis. If the stem becomes twisted, the BLOOD supply to the fibroid may be cut off, resulting in swelling, pressure, extremely heavy bleeding, the death of all or part of the tissue, and often acute pain and a thin, brownish, bad-smelling discharge.

Fibroids are often found during a GYNECOLOGICAL EXAMINATION by the doctor *palpating*—that is, feeling—the abdominal area from inside and outside. Sometimes an ULTRASOUND test will be needed to distinguish between fibroids and a tumor (see CANCER) or CYST in the OVARIES. A large, soft fibroid, especially one that has partly degenerated, may readily be mistaken for a PREGNANCY, and a pregnancy test may be needed to properly diagnose the condition. Fibroids have long been thought to grow more rapidly during PREGNANCY, raising concerns about the difficulty of carrying a pregnancy to term and of CHILDBIRTH, but some more recent studies showed such a result in only a small number of women.

Any woman, of any size, shape, age, personal history, or ancestry, can develop fibroids. But in general, women who weigh less than 120 pounds are less likely to have fibroids, and the risk rises sharply as weight increases. In fact, one of the few preventive actions a woman can take against fibroids is to keep her weight down, especially through a low-fat, low-sugar, high-fiber, largely vegetarian diet (see DIETING). The more pregnancies a woman has had, the less likely she is to have fibroids. Fibroids are found most often in women over forty, and women of African ancestry are estimated to be three to nine times more likely to have fibroids than those of Caucasian ancestry. Fibroids are less common among women who smoke, since SMOKING reduces ESTROGEN levels.

The relationship between fibroids and BIRTH CONTROL PILLS is not entirely clear. Many people believe that birth control pills cause fibroid growth, though that has not been clearly demonstrated in controlled studies. Others believe that birth control pills lessen fibroid risk. The confusion may stem from the fact that birth control pills vary in hormonal composition: some contain only estrogen as an active ingredient, but some have PROGESTERONE as well. In general, birth control pills are not recommended for older women with fibroids, nor is ESTROGEN REPLACEMENT THERAPY after MENOPAUSE.

Once, a diagnosis of fibroids meant a routine removal of the whole uterus in a surgical operation called a HYSTERECTOMY. But a much wider variety of options is now available, depending on the woman's age and the nature of the fibroids, particularly their size and speed of growth. One of the main alternatives is a MYOMECTOMY, which involves removal of fibroids only, not the uterus. A single fibroid on a stalk may be easy to remove, but multiple fibroids are much more difficult, sometimes impossible. Women considering a myomectomy should understand that it is a riskier operation than a hysterectomy, with a special risk of hemorrhaging, and that fibroids may well recur, especially in younger women; indeed, some women have had two or more myomectomies. A myomectomy requires special skills and is often performed by an INFERTILITY specialist, using techniques to minimize scar tissue that may cause *adhesions* (the abnormal binding together of internal organs), which can lessen fertility and cause chronic pain. Drugs are sometimes used to shrink fibroids before a myomectomy.

In emergency situations, where a woman's health precludes surgery, radiation has sometimes been used to destroy the OVARIES, and so produce artifical MENOPAUSE, to shrink the fibroids. This can fail, however, causing tissue death and infections, sometimes damaging the rectum (see DIGESTIVE SYSTEM), and possibly increasing the risk of pelvic CANCER.

Many fibroids are small and cause no medically worrisome symptoms.

Their causes are unknown, though they do tend to run in families (see GENETIC INHERITANCE), are apparently fueled by estrogen, and tend to grow in spurts, stabilizing in between. Fibroids in themselves are not harmful, and they generally cease to be a concern after MENOPAUSE, when—with falling estrogen levels—they shrink and often dwindle away. Fibroids should, however, be monitored carefully, often with checkups every six months, to see that no potentially serious changes have taken place. Among the potential problems are

▶ INFERTILITY *or difficult childbirth.* Fibroids on the inner wall of the uterus may hinder implantation of an EMBRYO; the thinly stretched endometrium (uterine lining) may provide insufficient blood supply for a growing FETUS; large fibroids may crowd the area and possibly lead to MISCARRIAGE; premature contractions may jeopardize the pregnancy; breakdown of the tumor (common during pregnancy) can cause pain; large fibroids, especially near the CERVIX, can make DELIVERY difficult, often necessitating a CESAREAN SECTION; and fibroids increase the risk of bleeding after delivery. A hysterectomy, and total loss of the uterus, would mean an end to childbearing, so women who may wish to have a child often choose some form of myomectomy.

▶ *abnormally long, heavy, often painful menstrual periods.* This is one of the most common complaints from fibroids. It results partly because the fibroids create more surface tissue, therefore more lining is formed and expelled each month (see MENSTRUATION), and the flow often contains heavy clots, resulting in iron-deficiency anemia (see BLOOD). Other sources of bleeding can be the distortion of blood flow, especially in areas of lining overgrowth (*endometrial hyperplasia*). Pain results from contractions as the uterus tries to expel the fibroids the same way it does the endometrial lining.

Women late in their menstruating years can often bear the inconvenience of this until menopause. But for many active women, and especially where the flow becomes an unmanageable flood, such excessively heavy menstruation is a major problem. Though sometimes treated with progesterone-related drugs or an operation called a D&C (*dilatation and curettage*), excessively heavy menstrual flow is a major reason for many women to have a hysterectomy.

▶ *abdominal discomfort.* Fibroid size alone is not necessarily a problem, though gynecological textbooks show occasional massive fibroids weighing dozens of pounds. But these are rare. For many doctors, the general rule of thumb is that when fibroid mass exceeds the size of a twelve-week FETUS, a hysterectomy is recommended; myomectomy is no longer an option at that size, since the fibroids cannot be removed with a single incision and damage is greater when the uterus has been much enlarged. Even at lower levels, fibroids produce discomfort equivalent to that of pregnancy, including heaviness in the pelvis, abdominal swelling, pressure on the bladder, frequency of need to urinate and sometimes incontinence (inability to control urine flow; see urinary tract), occasionally varicose veins (see HEART AND CIRCULATORY SYSTEM), gastrointestinal disturbances, hemorrhoids (see DIGESTIVE SYSTEM), and general aches in abdomen, lower back, and upper legs. Large fibroids can distort or damage other organs and on rare occasions may actually cause blockage of the urinary tract or bowels. ULTRASOUND tests can reveal some of these problems.

▶ CANCER. Malignancies, called *leiomyosarcomas,* are not common in fibroids, occurring in about one case in two hundred. They are more likely if the fibroids are growing rapidly, a prime reason for carefully monitoring size and growth rate through regular checkups. Where no urgent problems are present, many doctors today, rather than operate, prefer to closely monitor fibroids through periodic examinations, especially when the woman is at or near MENOPAUSE. And many women today strongly desire to avoid any unnecessary surgery involving their reproductive organs. The main hazard of waiting is that the fibroids will grow so large that myomectomy is no longer an option and a hysterectomy is necessary. An associated hazard is that with enlarged fibroids, cancer of the OVARIES could go undetected, since the doctor can no longer feel them during a GYNECOLOGICAL EXAMINATION; these areas can be checked by scanning, if ultrasounds are part of the periodic checkup.

For more help, information, and action

▶ NATIONAL WOMEN'S HEALTH NETWORK (NWHN) (202-347-1140). Operates the **Women's Health Information Service** and publishes the information packet *Fibroids.*

(See also HYSTERECTOMY; MYOMECTOMY; HYSTEROSCOPY; also HYSTERECTOMY HELP, INFORMATION, AND ACTION GUIDE on page 358; WOMEN'S HEALTH HELP, INFORMATION, AND ACTION GUIDE on page 334).

fimbriectomy, a surgical operation in which the petallike ends of the FALLOPIAN TUBES are removed so they cannot draw an egg (OVUM) into the tubes; a type of STERILIZATION.

Firestone, Shulamith (1945–), a leading radical feminist, whose *The Dialectic of Sex: The Case for Feminist Revolution* (1970) became a central theoretical work for the heterosexual portion of the radical feminist movement of the late 1960s and early 1970s. Canadian-born Firestone was active in civil rights and antiwar groups before co-founding RADICAL WOMEN (1967–1968), REDSTOCKINGS (1969–1970), and New York Radical Feminists (1969–1971).

In *The Dialectic of Sex,* Firestone stated that her application of the Marx-Engels principles of dialectical and historical materialism to the development of all human societies led her to this conclusion: Sexual oppression resulting from the existence of the biological FAMILY was at the root of all women's and children's subservience to male dominance, and the only solution was a feminist revolution that left women in full control of REPRODUCTION, shunning PREGNANCY and using other means than biological ones to reproduce. (See also WOMEN'S LIBERATION MOVEMENT.)

First Sex, The (1971), Elizabeth Gould Davis's highly speculative book on MATRIARCHY theory, in which she described early societies as matriarchies and posited the development of a single great matriarchy in the Mediterranean that was destroyed by a natural disaster, in the Atlantis-Lemuria "lost civilizations" vein. She further stated that although some survivals of matriarchy continued into historic times, women were ultimately enslaved in PATRIARCHY and predicted a return of matriarchy soon.

flicker of interest rule: See ABANDONMENT.

follicles, egg-producing structures in a woman's OVARIES; if a ripened egg (OVUM) fails to be released, a follicular cyst may form (see OVARIES). Follicle is also a term for the site from which HAIR grows.

follicle-stimulating hormone (FSH), a hormone produced by the pituitary gland. Production of FSH signals a woman's OVARIES to ripen eggs (see OVUM) as part of the reproductive cycle (see MENSTRUATION) and to produce the female sex hormone ESTROGEN. Later in the cycle, a fall in the levels of estrogen and PROGESTERONE at the onset of the menstrual period signals production of more FSH to begin the next cycle. In men, FSH is involved in the maturation of SPERM. (See HORMONES.)

follicular phase, an alternative name for PROLIFERATIVE PHASE (see MENSTRUATION).

Food and Drug Administration (FDA) (5600 Fishers Lane, Rockville, MD 20857; 301-472-4750; Office of Consumer and Professional Affairs, 301-295-8012), an arm of the U.S. Department of Health and Human Services with responsibility for regulating:
- foods, including labeling and safety.
- drugs, including approval, packaging, and prescription drug advertising.
- COSMETICS, including safety.
- biological products, such as vaccine and BLOOD.
- medical devices, approval and registration.
- radiological devices, providing safety standards and practices for such things as X-ray equipment, microwave ovens, television receivers, and lasers.
- veterinary products, including foods, drugs, and devices.

In addition to specific concerns, it has general responsibility in all these areas for maintenance of good manufacturing practices.

The FDA also has offices on topics of special concern. Two of particular interest to women are:
- **Breast Implant Information Office** (Office of Consumer Affairs, HFE-88, 5600 Fishers Lane, Rockville, MD 20857; 301-443-3170), a key federal source of information about breast implants.

- **Center for Food Safety and Applied Nutrition, Division of Colors and Cosmetics** (200 C Street, SW, Washington, DC 20204), for reporting adverse reactions to cosmetics.

The FDA also publishes various materials, including the consumer-oriented magazine *FDA Consumer*, with informative articles and also alerts on recalls and product safety, and professionally oriented reports such as the *FDA Drug Bulletin*, the *FDA Federal Register*, and the *FDA Enforcement Report*. Printed materials are often available free, with a modest sum charged for periodicals. People with computers and modems may also access such periodicals free on the FDA's Bulletin Board Service (BBS); for more information, contact the FDA Press Office, HFI-20, Rockville, MD 20857; 301-443-3285. To hook up, contact BT Tymnet, 6120 Executive Boulevard, Rockville, MD 20852; 800-872-7654. By making certain requests, people can also access most unpublished FDA documents under the Freedom of Information Act, including summaries of safety and effectiveness data, regulatory letters regarding violations, and enforcement records; the address is: Freedom of Information Staff, HFI-35, FDA, Room 12A-16, 5600 Fishers Lane, Rockville, MD 20857.

foreskin (prepuce), a partly retractable hood of skin covering or partially covering a sexual organ, in men the PENIS and in women the CLITORIS. In females, this hood is formed by the meeting of the upper ends of the *labia minora* (see LABIA). In males, the foreskin is sometimes removed for hygienic or religious reasons, in an operation called CIRCUMCISION. An analogous operation, called FEMALE CIRCUMCISION, is performed in some parts of the world, but in fact not just the foreskin is removed, but often much more.

fornication, a legal term referring to voluntary SEXUAL INTERCOURSE between two people of the opposite sex who are are unmarried; the term is sometimes applied, in law, to COHABITATION.

French, Marilyn (1929–), an American feminist writer who emerged as a popular figure with her largely autobiographical novel *The Women's Room* (1977), in which she described the journey of a middle-class woman out of MARRIAGE and a housewife's role into life as a mature student, wage earner, and single mother, who ultimately chooses not to pursue what she feels will be a stifling new relationship in favor of her new independence. The underlying thesis was similar to that expressed by Simone de BEAUVOIR nearly two decades earlier in *The Second Sex*, though French went in a somewhat different direction, stating essentially that men destroy women when they can, a theme that would dominate her later work. Among her other works are *The Bleeding Heart* (1980), the essays in *Beyond Power: On Women, Men and Morals* (1985), and *The War Against Women* (1992), in which she charged that the overwhelming majority of men in all countries are quite literally engaged in a systemic, institutional, cultural, and personal war against all of the world's women and have been doing so since approximately the fourth millennium B.C., when, she charged, PATRIARCHY succeeded the MATRIARCHY that she believes had earlier ruled human societies.

Friedan, Betty Goldstein (1921–), a central figure in the modern American women's movement. Friedan is the author of *The Feminine Mystique* (1963), in which she called upon women to solve what she called the "problem that had no name," by rejecting their stereotypical roles as wives and mothers to move out beyond home and FAMILY and achieve independent status as fully equal professionals and wage earners. Her focus was on those women, like herself, who had attended college, moved into family roles, and had not seriously used their educations; but her call for equality in all aspects of life struck a chord in women of many backgrounds and helped spark a new American women's movement, ready to be born in the socially turbulent 1960s. Her book became a best-seller, and she was soon hailed as a founder of that new movement.

In 1966 Friedan helped found and became first president of the NATIONAL ORGANIZATION FOR WOMEN (**NOW**) and during the four years that followed led a powerful and growing movement as its chief spokesperson. But as a reformer who sought to build the widest-possible popular base, she soon found herself at odds with many in NOW who felt themselves to be more revolutionary and with those who wanted the organization to fully support radical LESBIAN causes. In 1970 she resigned her presidency of NOW, while continuing to be active on such issues as the EQUAL RIGHTS AMENDMENT (**ERA**) and in the development of such organizations as the First Women's Bank and the National's Women's Political Caucus (see POLITICAL PARTICIPATION).

In *The Second Stage* (1981), Friedan continued to favor reform and to oppose what she saw as negative tendencies in the modern women's movement, calling for rejection of the "feminist mystique," which she felt had been wrongly interpreted to mean rejecting family relationships and values. Instead Friedan called for homes and relationships in which equality could be practiced by women and men. In 1993 she turned to the question of aging in a new book, *The Fountain of Age.* (See also WOMEN'S RIGHTS MOVEMENT; WOMEN'S LIBERATION MOVEMENT.)

The problem that has no name—which is simply the fact that American women are kept from growing to their full human capacities—is taking a far greater toll on the physical and mental health of our country than any known disease.

BETTY FRIEDAN, 1963
———————————— *IN* THE FEMININE MYSTIQUE ————————————

•

FSH, an abbreviation for FOLLICLE-STIMULATING HORMONE.

Fuller, Margaret (1810–1850), an American writer, editor, and early feminist who was editor of the major New England transcendentalist publication, *The Dial* (1840–1842). Her Boston "conversations" with a group of women subscribers (1839–1844) on a wide range of subjects were much admired and brought her considerable attention. She was a literary critic with Horace Greeley's *New York Herald Tribune* (1845–1846), then became a foreign correspondent for the newspaper—a first for a woman. Active in the Italian democratic revolutionary movement (1847–1849), she met and married revolutionary aristocrat Giovanni d'Ossoli and bore a child. All three died in 1850 when the ship bringing them to America sank off Fire Island.

Fuller's major lasting work was the book *Woman in the Nineteenth Century* (1845), which was an expansion of "The Great Lawsuit: Man versus Men, Woman versus Women," an essay published in *The Dial* in 1843. Its then-revolutionary call for equality became a centerpiece of the first American women's movement, born at the SENECA FALLS WOMEN'S RIGHTS CONVENTION only three years later, in 1848. (See also WOMEN'S RIGHTS MOVEMENT.)

Fund for the Feminist Majority (186 South Street, Boston, MA 02111; 617-695-9688; or 1600 Wilson Boulevard, Arlington, VA 22209; 703-522-2214; or 8105 West Third Street, Suite 1, Los Angeles, CA 90048, 213-651-0495; Eleanor Smeal, president; Peg Yorkin, chair), an organization founded in 1987 to "devise long-term strategies and permanent solutions for the pervasive social, political, and economic obstacles women face." It conducts research and disseminates information to "explode myths and expose sources of opposition to women's equality" and to "transform the public debate on issues of importance to women's lives and to empower women" in all sectors, including government and law, business, medicine, and the media, as through its Feminization of Power Campaign. It works to defend women's health clinics, women's reproductive choices, and WOMEN'S RIGHTS in general and also promotes WOMEN'S STUDIES programs through its Feminism and Public Policy internships. It sponsors the Memorial Bracelet Project, in remembrance of women worldwide who have died because of U.S. restrictions on ABORTION and withdrawal of funding for international agencies supporting abortions. The Foundation's Feminist Media Center monitors media coverage of feminist issues, maintaining a library of information, and publishes various materials, such as the quarterly newsletter *Feminist Majority Report, Empowering Women, The Feminization of Power: 50/50 By the Year 2000, The Feminization of Power: An International Comparison, Empowering Women in Business, Empowering Women in Medicine, Empowering Women in Philanthropy,* and the videos *Abortion: For Survival* and *Abortion Denied: Shattering Young Women's Lives.*

Gage, Matilda Joslyn (1826–1898), a leading U.S. WOMEN'S RIGHTS organizer and writer, a contemporary and collaborator of Elizabeth Cady STANTON and Susan B. ANTHONY. With them, she was an early leader of the NATIONAL WOMAN SUFFRAGE ASSOCIATION (**NWSA**) and contributed to Stanton's 1876 DECLARATION OF THE RIGHTS OF WOMEN. Gage, Stanton, and Anthony coauthored THE HISTORY OF WOMAN SUFFRAGE (1886). Gage did not, however, fully join her colleagues in their merger with the more conservative NATIONAL AMERICAN WOMAN SUFFRAGE ASSOCIATION in 1890. She turned her focus instead toward religious matters, organizing the feminist National Woman's Liberal Union in 1890 and in 1893 publishing *Woman, Church, and State,* a full-scale attack on patriarchal church attitudes and institutions. (See RELIGION AND WOMEN'S RIGHTS.)

galactorrhea, secretion of milk from the BREASTS of a woman who has *not* just given birth, often accompanied by lack of MENSTRUATION *(amenorrhea).* This can indicate an underlying hormonal problem, and a woman who experiences galactorrhea should see a doctor promptly (see PROLACTIN).

gallbladder, a pear-shaped organ that lies underneath the liver, in the upper right side of the abdomen; part of the DIGESTIVE SYSTEM (see page 224 for illustration), it is the source of many health problems, especially for women. The gallbladder is actually a sac that stores and concentrates *bile,* a liquid that digests fats. The liver produces bile, which passes into the gallbladder through a small tube called the *cystic duct.* When fat-containing foods appear in the stomach, bile is pumped back through the cystic duct and into the *common bile duct,* which it shares with the liver, and then into the *duodenum,* the first part of the small intestine. Chemically, bile is alkaline and is vital for neutralizing acids produced by the stomach.

 The most common gallbladder problem is *gallstones,* lumps of solid matter formed largely of cholesterol, but sometimes of other substances. Gallstones result when bile's chemical composition is disrupted, though the precise triggers are unknown. They are two and a half times more likely in women; appear more frequently with age; and are strongly linked with OBESITY. But the risk of getting gallstones is also increased with prolonged fasting (see DIETING) and use of BIRTH CONTROL PILLS.

 With gallstones present, the gallbladder may become inflamed by the presence and movement of the stones, a condition called *cholecystitis*. Often a chronic condition, it can become acute and serious if the gallbladder becomes infected and extremely painful if a large stone moves through the bile duct. If a stone becomes stuck and blocks the duct, especially the common bile duct, emergency surgery may be required to remove the gallbladder to prevent it from rupturing. Symptoms of acute cholecystitis include nausea, vomiting, sweating, and pain, especially intense in the upper right-hand side of the abdomen and up toward the shoulder blades.

Less severe gallbladder disease can often be treated without surgery. A low-fat, high-fiber diet is recommended. Medications are also available to dissolve some types of small gallstones, with progress monitored on periodic ULTRASOUND scans.

Luckily, not all gallstones cause problems. Many are "silent" and cause no problems, appearing only when the body is examined for other reasons, as during an abdominal ultrasound scan. Autopsies have shown that gallstones are generally present in 20 percent of women (as opposed to 8 percent of men), but only one in five women with gallstones actually experiences symptoms or complications during their lifetimes. Medical opinion has been somewhat divided for years about whether gallstones should be treated in the absence of symptoms. Some have argued that treatment, including surgery, should be undertaken when the patient is otherwise in good health, since emergency surgery later in life is more risky. Others argue that treatment may never become necessary, a view that seems to be predominating. (See DIGESTIVE DISORDERS HELP, INFORMATION, AND ACTION GUIDE on page 228.)

THE GALLBLADDER

Source: *Facts and Fallacies About Digestive Diseases,* National Digestive Diseases Information Clearinghouse, 1986.

gamete intrafallopian tube transfer (GIFT), a medical procedure to circumvent INFERTILITY. As in *IN VITRO* FERTILIZATION (IVF), a woman's OVARIES are stimulated to ripen many eggs (see OVUM), some of which are then removed, either by LAPAROSCOPY or *aspiration* through a hollow needle. However, instead of FERTILIZATION taking place in a laboratory dish, as in IVF, the eggs and SPERM (from the woman's husband or sex partner, or a donor) are mixed together while the woman is still on the operating table and injected into her FALLOPIAN TUBES, the normal site for fertilization, in hopes that PREGNANCY will then proceed as usual. It is important to monitor the developing EMBRYO to be sure that implantation takes place in the UTERUS and not elsewhere, which would cause a potentially life-threatening ECTOPIC PREGNANCY, requiring emergency surgery.

GIFT is appropriate only for women with at least one functional fallopian tube and is most appropriate when infertility is caused by the woman's cervical mucus being hostile to the man's sperm, by the woman having antibodies to the man's sperm (see IMMUNE SYSTEM), and in some types of male infertility or otherwise unexplained infertility. GIFT is somewhat less expensive than IVF; it is also still fairly new, so its long-term success rate is not yet known but is still very low, approximately 20 percent. (See *IN VITRO* FERTILIZATION; also INFERTILITY AND REPRODUCTIVE TECHNOLOGY HELP, INFORMATION, AND ACTION GUIDE on page 368.)

gastric bypass, an operation to promote weight loss, whereby a surgeon uses staples to divide the stomach in two and reduce its size (see DIETING).

gastroplasty, an operation to promote weight loss where the surgeon inserts staples that narrow the stomach's opening (see DIETING).

gender bias, discrimination on the basis of sex (see SEXISM; SEXUAL DISCRIMINATION; SEX ROLES; HEALTH EQUITY; INSURANCE AND PENSION EQUITY; EDUCATION EQUITY; WORK AND WOMEN; RELIGION AND WOMEN'S RIGHTS; DEVELOPMENT AND WOMEN'S RIGHTS).

gender identity, a person's inner sense of being male or female, a feeling some psychologists think is established by the time a child reaches two to three years old and generally irreversible by two and a half years of age. By contrast, SEXUAL IDENTITY is determined by one's biological attributes. Not everyone has a strong sense of gender identity; some are ambivalent or even neutral regarding their gender (see HERMAPHRODITE). Whereas gender identity is an internal feeling, *gender role* is the role established for the person by society, in sex assignment, training, and expectation (see SEX ROLE).

Although individuals may stretch, bend, or even rebel against their assigned gender roles, for most people gender identity and gender role are identical. For some people, however, they are totally contradictory. A young person may have the external GENITALS of a girl and be dressed, trained, and reared as a girl but maintain the inner conviction of being a boy; and vice versa. Such a feeling has been variously called *transsexualism, eonism, psychic hermaphroditism, metatropism,* and *severe intersexuality;* to some psychiatrists, it is a *gender identity disorder.* That characterization of gender identity questions, however, is disputed by many, including most of those in the gay and lesbian communities, who deny that any "disorder" is present. Such feelings are quite different from nonconformity with gender roles (such as acting like a tomboy), feeling inadequate to meet the social expectations, or wishing to have the other sex's real or presumed social advantages. People with such self-identifications feel that in their innermost beings they *are* a sex other than that perceived by the world around them and are intensely distressed about their gender "assignment." Such feelings and attitudes often appear in childhood and generally involve repudiation of clothing and activities thought proper for their sex, as well as an insistence that they will grow up to be the sex they feel themselves to be. Many routinely wear the clothes society normally associates with the "other" sex (see CROSS-DRESSING), and in adulthood, many become HOMOSEXUAL (see LESBIAN). For some, the feeling is so strong that they undergo a SEX CHANGE operation, also called *sex reassignment surgery.* (See SEX AND SEXUALITY HELP, INFORMATION, AND ACTION GUIDE on page 665; LESBIAN HELP, INFORMATION, AND ACTION GUIDE on page 397.)

gender role: See SEX ROLE.

General Commission on the Status and Role of Women in the United Methodist Church (GCSRW-UMC) (1200 Davis Street, Evanston, IL 60201; 708-869-7330; Kiyoko Kasai Fujui, general secretariat), a commission established in 1972 "to address the discrimination against, and underutilization of, women at all levels of" the United Methodist church. The members "wrestle, on behalf of the whole church, with issues of sexism, the linkages of racism-sexism, male-female dynamics, and inclusive language; and seek to "foster an awareness of issues, problems and concerns of women throughout the church; redress inequities in personnel, programs, policies, and publications; ensure inclusiveness of women in the total life and mission of the church in power and policy-making at all levels; and empower women to claim responsibility for and to take leadership in the mission and ministry of the church." GCSRW-UMC publishes a quarterly newsletter, *The Flyer.*

genetic counseling, a service providing practical information on genetic risks for individuals and families. Such counseling is often sought by prospective parents who want to assess their risks of having a child with a GENETIC DISORDER or a BIRTH DEFECT, but many individuals also want to know about their own lives and health—specifically the likelihood that they will be affected by a disorder or the risk of certain kinds of habits or exposures, as to toxic chemicals or radiation.

People who seek counseling are most often those from high-risk groups. These include prospective parents who
• have a FAMILY or ethnic history of genetic disorders, such as sickle-cell anemia

(see BLOOD) or cystic fibrosis, and wish to assess their own risks of developing the disorder or passing it on to their children;

- already have a child with a genetic disorder or other birth defect, including mental retardation, and want to know the likelihood that it might also appear in another child;
- are near blood relations, with greater likelihood of passing on identical defective genes;
- are somewhat older, generally over thirty or thirty-five, since they are more likely to have genetic problems, especially CHROMOSOMAL ABNORMALITIES;
- have experienced a previous MISCARRIAGE, STILLBIRTH, or infant death, which might have resulted from an unrecognized genetic disorder;
- work in occupations that expose them to environmental hazards possibly damaging to genetic material, including exposure to radiation, medications, chemicals, infection, drugs, or known carcinogens (see CANCER);
- have had an elevated ALPHA FETOPROTEIN test, indicating the possibility of complications or birth defects.
- have—or are concerned that they themselves may have—inherited a disorder or birth defect.

Counselors are often physicians trained in medical genetics but may also be nurses or other health professionals with special training. Basically, they explain how GENETIC INHERITANCE works (see PATTERNS OF GENETIC INHERITANCE on page 311), explore the likelihood of various kinds of BIRTH DEFECTS (if PREGNANCY is being contemplated), and—after eliciting and organizing specific medical information—explain how all this applies to the person's particular situation. The overall aim is to give people the information they need to make vital personal decisions. In the case of prospective parents, this may involve the decision of whether or not to try to have a child, and possibly to change life-style or work setting before attempting a pregnancy. It may also mean taking preventive action; in some cases, early diagnosis and treatment of a genetic disorder can prevent serious, irreversible damage.

Generally counselors start by gathering information on the families of the prospective parents. Of particular interest, of course, is any personal family history of *known* genetic disorders. But very often genetic disorders go unrecognized, or undiscussed within the family, so genetic counselors generally gather extensive information on the physical traits, characteristics, and medical problems on all close blood relatives, including

- ▶ *eyes*—blindness, farsightedness or nearsightedness, cataracts, glaucoma, retinal detachment or other retinal problems, thick glasses, eye surgery, eye patches, color blindness, night blindness, and unmatching eyes (for example, one blue and one brown).
- ▶ EARS—unusual shape, hearing loss, hearing aids.
- ▶ *absent sense of smell.*
- ▶ *general numbness.*
- ▶ HAIR, SKIN, and TEETH—psoriasis, eczema, birthmarks (pink, brown, white), moles, skin tags, premature balding or graying, white patch of hair, extra or missing teeth, misshapen teeth.
- ▶ *nerve, muscles, and bone*—"slow learners," learning disabilities, mental retar-

dation, seizures, convulsions, fits, epilepsy, MENTAL DISORDERS (especially DE-PRESSION or schizophrenia), speech difficulties, migraine headaches, shaking or twitching, weakness, dystrophy, back problems, brittle bones, club feet, dislocated hips at birth, tall or short stature, pilonidal cysts, loose joints, double joints, ARTHRITIS. (See MUSCULAR SYSTEM; SKELETAL SYSTEM; BRAIN AND NERVOUS SYSTEM; SPINE.)

▶ *respiration*—ALLERGIES, asthma, sinus problems, emphysema, cystic fibrosis. (See RESPIRATORY SYSTEM.)

▶ *digestion and metabolism*—ulcers, colitis, high cholesterol count, GALLBLAD-DER problems, restricted diet, goiter or other thyroid problems, DIABETES. (See DIGESTIVE SYSTEM.)

▶ REPRODUCTION AND EXCRETION—bladder or kidney infections, variation in size or number of kidneys, prostate problems, undescended TESTES, INFERTILITY, unusual reproductive organs (internal or external), hemorrhoids. (See URINARY TRACT; REPRODUCTIVE SYSTEM; DIGESTIVE SYSTEM.)

▶ *circulation*—heart murmurs, varicose veins, clotting, hemophilia or other bleeding disorders, anemias, high blood pressure (hypertension). (See BLOOD; HEART AND CIRCULATORY SYSTEM.)

▶ *other*—cysts, lumps, growths, tumors, extra fingers or toes *(polydactyly),* webbing of fingers or toes, hole in the heart or other congenital heart defects, spina bifida (open spine), hydrocephalus ("water on the head"), hernia.

▶ *surgeries and serious illnesses,* including leukemia (see BLOOD) and other types of CANCER, AND ALCOHOL AND DRUG ABUSE.

▶ *exposure to known or suspected reproductive hazards* (see BIRTH DEFECTS), including toxic chemicals, SMOKING, alcohol, drugs, SPERMICIDES used around the time of CONCEPTION, rubella (German measles), toxoplasmosis, viral diseases such as hepatitis, radiation (not only from X-rays or industrial use but also from high-altitude flying), ANESTHESIA.

▶ *pregnancies*—successful pregnancies, stillbirths, miscarriages (spontaneous ABORTIONS), infant deaths.

▶ *deaths*—age and cause of death, with particular attention to siblings and close blood relatives.

In addition, counselors often conduct laboratory tests to gain direct genetic information on the individual.

All this information is used in the construction of a specialized kind of family tree, called a *pedigree* or *genealogy,* for each of the prospective parents. This is designed to show up patterns of genetic inheritance of known disorders and of various traits that may be clues to unrecognized disorders. Though not completely standardized, pedigrees use some common symbols and arrangements. Males are shown as squares and females by circles, with a solid-line diamond used for sex unknown and a broken-line diamond for a pregnancy in progress. Those affected by a specific defect are shaded in, while a female carrier of the defect is indicated by a center dot within her circle. Members of each generation appear on the same line; siblings are attached by "branch bars," in order of birth, if known. (See COMMON PEDIGREE SYMBOLS and SAMPLE OF A PEDIGREE on page 308.)

People often have to search family records for medical clues. The MARCH OF

COMMON PEDIGREE SYMBOLS AND SAMPLE OF A PEDIGREE

COMMON PEDIGREE SYMBOLS AND SAMPLE OF A PEDIGREE

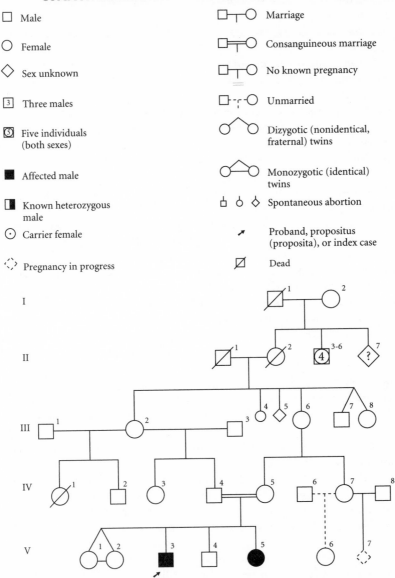

Siblings are indicated by arabic numerals from left to right in order of birth. Generations are represented by roman numerals, the earliest at the top.

Source: *Genetic Family History: An Aid to Better Health in Adoptive Children* (1984). Published by the National Center for Education in Maternal and Child Health (NCEMCH), for the Public Health Service's Genetic Diseases Service Branch, Division of Maternal and Child Health, from materials from a conference sponsored by Wisconsin Clinical Genetics Center and Waisman Center on Mental Retardation and Human Development, University of Wisconsin-Madison.

DIMES has free *Family Medical Record* forms covering three generations, which can help organize appropriate information ahead of time. But information necessary for pedigrees is not always readily available, given today's mobile and fractured society. In many countries, various government agencies help in gathering genealogical data; in the United States, the Public Health Service's National Center for Health Statistics has published *Where to Write for Vital Records: Births, Deaths, Marriages, and Divorces,* which can help in locating and obtaining copies of key records relating to family ancestry. Lack of genealogical information has traditionally been a problem for people who were adopted. However, many ADOPTION agencies now recognize the importance of family medical histories and provide such medical information (though without names attached, except in open adoptions) for use in future genetic counseling for the adopted person. (See GENETIC INHERITANCE AND BIRTH DEFECTS HELP, INFORMATION, AND ACTION GUIDE on page 314; PRENATAL TESTS.)

genetic disorder, a disease or abnormality that results from defects in a person's GENETIC INHERITANCE. The disorder often results from a defective gene that is passed to the child from one or both parents, though sometimes it results from a defect, or *mutation,* that appears spontaneously. Disorders that result from mistakes in the duplication of genetic material are called CHROMOSOMAL ABNORMALITIES.

Defects that are triggered by a single gene are called *unifactorial.* If the defect appears on a sex chromosome, generally the X chromosome (see GENETIC INHERITANCE), it is called *X-linked, sex-linked,* or *sex-limited,* because it is passed on by unaffected mothers, who are *carriers,* but usually affects only male children. Single genes on any other chromosomes, or *autosomes,* are called *autosomal disorders.*

If the defect need only be passed on to the child by one parent, it is called *dominant.* But if the defect must be passed on by both parents, it is termed *recessive.* (See PATTERNS OF GENETIC INHERITANCE on page 311.) Many genetic disorders, however, are caused by not a single gene, but by several genes, perhaps also affected by environmental influences. Information on patterns of inheritance is used in GENETIC COUNSELING, to help parents assess the risk of their having a child with a particular disorder. Once a child is conceived, various PRENATAL TESTS can be used to assess the health of the FETUS, in particular looking for information on genetic or other disorders.

genetic inheritance, the set of information that determines a person's physical characteristics, passed from parents to child. In each child's individual blueprint, this information is carried in "units of inheritance" called *genes,* themselves formed of molecules of DNA *(deoxyribonucleic acid)* and RNA *(ribonucleic acid),* which actually embody the information in chemical codes. Genes are arranged in pairs—with one of each pair from the mother and one from the father—in a regular linear sequence on twenty-three threadlike pairs of structures called *chromosomes.*

Most of the individual's genetic inheritance is carried on twenty-two chromosome pairs, called *autosomes*. The twenty-third pair is called the *sex chromosome,* because it determines the individual's sex; a normal female carries two X chromosomes, while a normal male carries an X and a Y chromosome.

The individual's genetic blueprint is written at CONCEPTION and includes equal genetic contributions from each parent. In preparation for reproduction, the father forms SPERM and the mother an egg (OVUM); in a cell-dividing process called *meiosis,* the chromosomes in the nucleus of the "mother cell" are first duplicated, then divided, creating four "daughter cells." The result is that each of these daughter cells (in both father and mother) has half of the chromosomes that will be needed to form a new being. Each cell also has a different selection of genetic material, which is incorporated into various sperm and eggs. Later, at the end of the long obstacle run known as FERTILIZATION, the "winning" or at least surviving sperm and egg join together. The resulting fertilized egg has received 50 percent of its genes from its mother and 50 percent from its father. Because the mother's and father's genetic inheritance resulted from the same process, 25 percent of the new being's genes were contributed by each of its four grandparents. The genetic pattern of the new individual will be duplicated over and over and will be present in the nucleus of the new being's every cell.

The actual characteristics of the new being depend on the nature of each gene and its relation to its pair and to other genes. If both of a pair of genes (called *alleles)* are identical—if both code for blue eyes, for example—the being is called a *homozygote* for that gene. If paired genes differ—if one codes for blue eyes, the other for brown—the person is a *heterozygote* for that gene.

Genes have different abilities to affect the future of an individual. Some genes are *dominant,* meaning that its characteristics will appear in an individual no matter what the other gene is. The gene for brown eyes is dominant, for example, so a baby will have brown eyes if *either* of the relevant genes is coded for brown eyes. Other genes are *recessive,* meaning that its characteristics will appear in the individual only if it is paired with an identical gene. Since blue eye color is a recessive trait, a baby with blue eyes has received a gene for blue eyes from both of her parents (whatever their own eye color). (See PATTERNS OF GENETIC INHERITANCE on page 311.)

The sex chromosomes in males are a special case. The X chromosome carries a full range of genetic information. But the Y chromosome carries little more than genetic information relating to male sexual development. That means that if a recessive gene appears on an X chromosome in a male, the coded characteristics will appear in the male, because no dominant gene is paired with it. The dominant-recessive rule operates normally in women. For example, the gene relating to baldness is recessive and is found on the X chromosome. If a male's mother passes on the baldness gene, he will become bald; but for a woman to be affected by the baldness, she would have to receive the recessive gene from both of her parents, which rarely happens.

Some traits, such as eye color or baldness, are controlled by a single gene; these are called *unifactorial.* But many characteristics and processes are far more complicated and are affected by many genes and also by the individual's environment; these are called *multifactorial.*

Errors sometimes occur in the complicated transmission of genetic information from parents to child. If errors occur in cell division *(meiosis)*, the result is CHROMOSOMAL ABNORMALITIES. Defects in the genetically coded information passed on from parent to child lead to GENETIC DISORDERS. If such defects are carried on the X chromosome, affecting primarily males, they are called *X-linked, sex-limited,* or *sex-linked disorders.*

Sometimes a spontaneous change, called a *mutation,* occurs in the genes of sperm or egg. Some of these can have positive benefits—that is, after all, how human variability and natural selection are believed to occur—but many have adverse, and sometimes lethal, effects. One of the main concerns with the level of environmental pollution in today's world, especially with radiation and toxic chemicals, is that it tends to increase the risk of genetic mutations.

In the human species' complete set of genes, called the *genome,* each gene occupies a specific site on a specific chromosome. The precise location of some has been identified, and researchers are actively seeking to map the position of others. Gene position has a very practical value: Scientists can use these sites, or *genetic markers,* to help healthy parents identify if they carry defective genes, which they could pass on to their children. Genetic markers are already used in various PRENATAL TESTS, to see if a FETUS has, in fact, inherited a defective gene. And the information in general is extremely valuable in GENETIC COUNSELING of prospective parents who are concerned about genetic risks. In addition, researchers are exploring the use of genetic engineering—inserting "corrected" genes to replace defective ones—to correct genetic disorders. (See GENETIC INHERITANCE AND BIRTH DEFECTS HELP, INFORMATION, AND ACTION GUIDE on page 314.)

PATTERNS OF GENETIC INHERITANCE

Genes are carried in the body on twenty-three pairs of chromosomes: one pair of *sex chromosomes,* an X chromosome and a Y chromosome; and twenty-two pairs of *autosomes.* If the trait coded for in a single gene will appear no matter what the paired gene, it is called *dominant.* If a trait will appear only if both of the paired genes are identical, it is called *recessive.* If the defect appears on the sex chromosomes, generally the X chromosome, it is called *X-linked, sex-linked,* or *sex-limited,* because they are passed on by unaffected mothers, who are *carriers,* but usually affect only male children. (For more, see GENETIC INHERITANCE.) Many traits are not coded for by a single gene, but rather by a combination of genes, perhaps also with environmental influences.

But those traits that are controlled by a single gene, called *unifactorial,* show up in regular patterns. It is these patterns that are studied as part of GENETIC COUNSELING, since some key genetic disorders are unifactorial. Note that the percentages given for each pattern are *for each child;* the fact that an older child has a genetic disorder *has no effect on the risks for a later child.* For example, if a child is born with a disorder that involves a 25 percent (one-in-four) risk, that does *not* mean that the next three children will be free from the disorder; rather the one-in-four risk applies to each new child. Note also that disorders sometimes appear unexpectedly, through a spontaneous change, or *mutation,* in a gene.

The main genetic inheritance patterns are

Autosomal Dominant (AD)

Only one gene of a gene pair is required for the trait or disorder to appear. Each child has a 50 percent likelihood of inheriting the AD gene from a parent. That means that if a parent has Huntington's disease, each child has a one-in-two chance of inheriting the disorder. Typically, an AD gene will show up in every generation, affecting males and females equally. However, the AD gene—a trait or disorder—will be expressed differently in various affected members of the same family, depending on the rest of their genetic inheritance. Also, if the child receives *two copies* of the gene, expression is stronger, so any genetic disorder may be more serious. Examples of autosomal dominant disorders are achondroplasia, a growth disorder; Huntington's disease, progressive degeneration of the nervous system; hypercholesterolemia, high cholesterol levels and heart disease risk; polydactyly, extra fingers or toes; osteogenesis imperfecta, brittle bone disease; and neurofibromatosis (Elephant Man disease), numerous benign tumors. The probability that a child will inherit an AD genetic disorder from an affected parent can be expressed schematically this way:

D = *dominant gene*
n = *normal gene*

AFFECTED FATHER		NORMAL MOTHER	
Dn		**nn**	
Dn	**nn**	**Dn**	**nn**
AFFECTED CHILD	NORMAL CHILD	AFFECTED CHILD	NORMAL CHILD

Autosomal Recessive (AR)

The trait or defect must be carried on both paired genes for it to appear in a child. If parents are carriers of the AR trait, any child of theirs has a 25 percent chance of having the trait or disorder; a 25 percent of having a "double dose" of the gene and so possibly a more serious form of the disorder; and a 50 percent chance of being an unaffected carrier of the gene. An AR trait or disorder does not appear in every generation, and males and females are affected equally often. The likelihood of having the trait or disorder increases if the parents are closely related; some kinds of AR disorders also appear more frequently among certain groups. Examples are Tay-Sachs disease (a fatal disorder affecting the brain) and Gaucher disease (a chronic disorder affecting various organs), found most often among people of East European Jewish background; thalassemia, a blood disorder affecting primarily people of Mediterranean ancestry; cystic fibrosis, a disorder affecting the mucus and sweat glands, more common among people of Caucasian background; and sickle-cell anemia, a blood disorder affecting primarily people of Black African ancestry. Other common AR disorders include galactosemia, problems in metabolizing milk sugar; phenylketonuria (PKU), malfunctioning of a liver enzyme; and albinism, lack of skin pigmentation. The probability that a child will inherit an AR genetic disorder from two unaffected carrier parents can be expressed schematically this way:

r = *recessive gene*
N = *normal gene* (takes precedence)

CARRIER FATHER		CARRIER MOTHER	
Nr		**Nr**	
NN	**Nr**	**Nr**	**rr**
NORMAL CHILD	CARRIER CHILD	CARRIER CHILD	AFFECTED CHILD

X-Linked Inheritance

X-linked disorders, also called *sex-linked* or *sex-limited inheritance,* are recessive, so the trait will be masked in the presence of a dominant gene. Such traits rarely affect women, because they must receive the recessive trait on both of their X chromosomes. Males have one X chromosome and one Y chromosome, which carries little genetic information beyond that relating to male sexual development. Any trait on a male's X chromosome, then, will be expressed; if the gene is defective, he will have the disorder. A sex-linked trait or disorder does not necessarily appear in every generation; males cannot pass it on: it is passed only through females. Each male child of a carrier mother has a 50 percent chance of having the trait or disorder. Each female child of a carrier mother has a 50 percent chance of becoming a carrier. Examples of X-linked disorders are color blindness, inability to distinguish certain colors; agammaglobulinemia, lack of immunity to infection; fragile X syndrome, involving mental retardation; hemophilia, a blood disorder; some forms of muscular dystrophy, progressive muscle wasting;

and spinal ataxia, spinal cord degeneration. The probability that a child will inherit an X-linked defect from a carrier mother can be expressed schematically this way:

X = faulty gene on X chromosome (from carrier mother)
x = normal gene on X chromosome
y = Y chromosome (lacks genes to counteract most genes on X chromosomes)

NORMAL FATHER   CARRIER MOTHER
xy   Xx

Xy   Xx   xy   XX
AFFECTED BOY   CARRIER GIRL   NORMAL BOY   NORMAL GIRL

Multifactorial Inheritance

These involve traits or disorders that depend not on a single gene, but on a number of factors—including several genes and some environmental influences—in order to appear in the offspring. Unlike unifactorial patterns shown above, these traits and disorders appear with no discernible pattern in families. The frequency varies with sex and race, the conditions vary in severity, and the risks that a particular person will have a disorder depends on complex statistical data, rather than on one-in-two or one-in-four predictions. Examples of multifactorial disorders include cleft lip or palate; clubfoot; congenital dislocation of the hip; congenital heart defects; asthma; DIABETES; spina bifida, incomplete spinal cord; hydrocephalus, water on the brain; pyloric stenosis, narrowed opening between the stomach and small intestine; some forms of CANCER, ARTHRITIS, and epilepsy; and some heart problems.

GENETIC INHERITANCE AND BIRTH DEFECTS

Help, Information, and Action Guide

Organizations

▶ NATIONAL CENTER FOR EDUCATION IN CHILD AND MATERNAL HEALTH (NCEMCH) (202-625-8400) and NATIONAL MATERNAL AND CHILD HEALTH

CLEARINGHOUSE (202-625-8410). Provides information about genetic diseases and referrals to specific support groups, and publishes various materials, including *Genetic Screening for Inborn Errors of Metabolism, a Guide to Selected National Genetic Voluntary Organizations, Genetic Family History: An Aid to Better Health in Adoptive Children,* and *Learning Together: A Guide for Families with Genetic Disorders.*

▶ **National Genetics Federation** (180 West 58th Street, New York, NY 10019; 212-245-7443; Ruth Y. Berini, executive director), an organization to foster medical genetics. It acts as a clearinghouse for information, computerized analyses, and referrals to a genetic counseling network and publishes various materials, including the brochures *How Genetic Disease Can Affect You and Your Family* and *Can Genetic Counseling Help You?*

▶ MARCH OF DIMES BIRTH DEFECTS FOUNDATION (**MDBDF**) (914-428-7100; local chapters in telephone directory White Pages). Provides information and referrals for genetic counseling. Publish materials such as *International Directory of Genetic Services, Genetic Counseling, Birth Defects: Tragedy and Hope, Your Special Child, Drugs, Alcohol and Tobacco Abuse During Pregnancy, Will My Drinking Hurt My Baby?, Babies Don't Thrive in Smoke-Filled Wombs, Family Medical Record, Family Health Tree, Fetal Alcohol Syndrome, Pregnancy Over 35, Rh Disease, Fitness for Two, Newborn Screening Tests, Infections During Pregnancy: Toxoplasmosis and Chlamydia, Stress and Pregnancy, Teen-Age Pregnancy,* and flyers on many specific problems or disorders.

▶ **National Organization for Rare Disorders (NORD)** (P.O. Box 8923, New Fairfield, CT 06812; 203-746-6518 or 800-999-6673; Abbey S. Meyers, executive director), an organization concerned with rare disorders. It provides information; makes referrals to organizations on specific disorders; and monitors availability of medicines for rare disorders. It publishes the quarterly *Orphan Disease Update* and the occasional legislative newsletter *NORD On-Line.*

Other resources

▰ ON GENETIC INHERITANCE

Nature's Thumbprint: The New Genetics of Personality. Peter B. Neubauer and Alexander Neubauer. Addison-Wesley, 1990.
Genome. Jerry E. Bishiop and Michael Waldholz. Simon & Schuster, 1990.

▰ ON GENETIC COUNSELING AND PRENATAL TESTING

Backdoor to Eugenics. Troy Duster. Routledge, 1990.
Before Birth: Prenatal Testing for Genetic Disease. Elena O. Nightingale and Melissa Goodman. Harvard University Press, 1990.

The Ethics of Genetic Control: Ending Reproductive Roulette. Joseph Fletcher.
  Prometheus, 1988.
The Tentative Pregnancy: Prenatal Diagnosis and the Future of Motherhood.
  Barbara Katz Rothman. Viking, 1986.

◪ ON GENETIC DISORDERS AND BIRTH DEFECTS

The Encyclopedia of Genetic Disorders and Birth Defects. Mark D. Ludman
  and James Wyndbrandt. Facts on File, 1990.
The Parent's Desk Reference. Irene Franck and David Brownstone. Prentice-
  Hall, 1990. Discusses many specific genetic disorders, with organizations
  and references for help and information.
The Family Genetic Sourcebook. Benjamin A. Pierce. Wiley, 1990.
Family Diseases: Are You At Risk. Myra Vanderpool Gormley. Genealogical
  Publishing, 1989.
*Peace of Mind During Pregnancy: An A-to-Z Guide to the Substances That
  Could Affect Your Unborn Baby.* Christine Kelley-Buchanan. Facts on File,
  1988.

◪ BACKGROUND BOOKS

Genetic Engineering: Opposing Viewpoints. William Dudley, ed. Greenhaven,
  1990.
Genethics: The Clash Between the New Genetics and Human Values. David
  Suzuki and Peter Knudtson. Harvard University Press, 1989.

genetic screening, the process of giving a pregnant woman PRENATAL TESTS
aimed at ruling out or identifying possible GENETIC DISORDERS or other BIRTH DE-
FECTS.

genital mutilation, an alternative term for FEMALE CIRCUMCISION.

genitals, a general name for all the organs of the REPRODUCTIVE SYSTEM but most
commonly referring to the external reproductive organs; also called *genitalia*. In
women, the external genitals are called the VULVA; they include the LABIA, the CLI-
TORIS, the opening to the VAGINA, and BARTHOLIN'S GLANDS. A woman's internal
reproductive organs include the OVARIES (female sex glands, or GONADS), FALLO-
PIAN TUBES, UTERUS, and VAGINA (for an illustration, see page 621). The condition
of having undeveloped or underdeveloped genitals, as appears in some kinds of
GENETIC DISORDERS or disorders of the sex glands (GONADS), is called *hypogenital-
ism*.

In men, the genitals include the TESTES, the male sex glands (gonads) that manufacture SPERM; the *scrotum*, the loose sac surrounding the testes; the *epididymis*, a "holding area" where the sperm mature; the *prostate gland*, which produces secretions that help make up seminal fluid; the *vas deferens*, a long tube through which sperm move into the seminal fluid; and the *penis*, through which the sperm-containing seminal fluid is ejaculated at the male's ORGASM and which is also the passageway for urine. (See REPRODUCTIVE SYSTEM; SPERM; also specific female organs mentioned.)

genital warts, an infection caused by *human papillomaviruses* (HPVs), one of the SEXUALLY TRANSMITTED DISEASES; also called *condylomata acuminata* or *venereal warts*. Symptoms are small, hard spots, which develop within three weeks to three months after exposure, on the lips of the VAGINA, around the anus (see DIGESTIVE SYSTEM), inside the VAGINA, and on the CERVIX, where they appear at first as invisible flat lesions. Warts can also appear on the mouth, if a person has had oral sex (see SEXUAL INTERCOURSE). On men the warts generally appear on the tip of the PENIS, though the shaft, the scrotum, and the anus may also be affected. Warts often occur in groups and can form large masses on genital tissues. However, like many other STDs, genital warts often produce no symptoms; in one study almost half the women infected were symptomless. Unfortunately that means they can be spread to others and, while undetected, can cause various health problems, especially for women.

During PREGNANCY genital warts can enlarge, making urination difficult (see URINARY TRACT) and causing problems during CHILDBIRTH because they make the vaginal wall less elastic and can even obstruct the birth canal. Infants born to mothers with genital warts can develop warts in the throat *(laryngeal papillomatosis)*, a rare but potentially life-threatening condition that sometimes requires surgical correction. In addition, genital warts are associated with increased risk of CANCER of the CERVIX and VULVA, as well as the penis. Indeed, cervical warts are a common trigger of an abnormal PAP SMEAR, which involves examining cells microscopically for signs of possible cancerous or precancerous tissue.

Warts are often treated with a chemical solution, though not during pregnancy since this can cause BIRTH DEFECTS. Small warts may be treated with freezing or burning; larger ones may be treated with surgery, including laser surgery. However, warts often return after treatment. (See SEXUALLY TRANSMITTED DISEASES; also WHAT YOU CAN DO TO AVOID STDs on page 660.)

gentle birth, an alternative name for the LeBoyer method (see CHILDBIRTH).

gestation, the full period of development in a PREGNANCY, from FERTILIZATION to CHILDBIRTH; also called the *term*. The average gestation is approximately 266 days from the date of fertilization. But because the precise date of fertilization is often unknown or uncertain, the *due date* or *delivery date* has traditionally been calculated from the *last menstrual period* (LMP), even though that is often two weeks *before* fertilization. As a result the due date is calculated as if the full term were 9⅓ months, 40 weeks, or 280 days.

The development of a fetus—called *gestational age*—is indicated by the number of weeks of development from that LMP. A baby born with a gestation age of thirty-six weeks is called *premature* or *preterm* and is subject to a variety of health problems because development is not complete. Birth at forty-two weeks or more is considered *postmature* and also carries hazards for both mother and child. (For a fuller discussion, see PREGNANCY; also WHAT HAPPENS DURING PREGNANCY on page 557.)

gestational diabetes, a form of DIABETES that occurs during PREGNANCY.

Gilman, Charlotte Perkins (1860–1935), an American feminist writer whose thinking embraced both practical social reform and utopian socialism. The first of her highly regarded series of practical works was *Women and Economics* (1898), in which she advocated such revolutionary reforms as ending women's work at home (see HOUSEWORK; HOMEMAKER) in favor of a shared, communal set of housekeeping and child-raising tasks, with men's and women's work treated equally, so women would be able to develop their lives as independent, fully respected economic members of society. She published several other works along similar lines, including *Concerning Children* (1900) and *The Home: Its Work and Influence* (1903).

Gilman founded the magazine *The Forerunner* in 1909 and edited it until 1916, in 1915 publishing her utopian novel *Herland,* in which she described a beneficent MATRIARCHY as a model society. Earlier she had written the famous short story "The Yellow Wallpaper," (1899), in which a woman trapped by her marriage goes slowly mad. Her work also included such books as *The Man-Made World, or Our Androcentric Culture* (1911) and *His Religion and Hers: A Study of the Faith of our Fathers and the Work of Our Mothers* (1923).

The labor of women in the house, certainly, enables men to produce more wealth than they otherwise could: and in this way women are economic factors in society. But so are horses.

CHARLOTTE PERKINS GILMAN, 1898
———————————— IN WOMEN AND ECONOMICS ————————————

•

glass ceiling, widespread continuing discrimination against the promotion of women to higher jobs traditionally held by men, as when a high-achieving woman executive finds that she is informally but very firmly barred from the board of directors of her large company; or a standout woman lawyer finds that she cannot become a partner in her law firm; or a very successful regional sales manager finds that those running her company will not appoint her to the national sales manager's job, no matter how well qualified she may be. The glass ceiling—so-named because it is invisible—can still prove an absolute bar to all women who rise to a certain level, though many who discriminate in this covert way try to appear nondiscriminatory by opening jobs to a few token women in order to deflect legal attack and criticism (see TOKENISM). Although such practices are illegal, and are being attacked on many fronts, proving that they exist can be a very difficult task. (See also SEXUAL DISCRIMINATION; WORK AND WOMEN; also WORKING WOMEN'S HELP, INFORMATION, AND ACTION GUIDE on page 779; SEXUAL DISCRIMINATION AND SEXUAL HARASSMENT HELP, INFORMATION, AND ACTION GUIDE on page 642.)

goddess worship, a formal construct developed by some feminist historians; also a modern alternative religion or set of religions attractive to people, especially feminists, who want to believe in deity but reject the major modern religions as essentially instruments of patriarchal repression (see PATRIARCHY). Such nineteenth-century system builders as historian Johann Bachofen and anthropologist Lewis Henry Morgan, and such twentieth-century feminists as Robert BRIFFAULT, Elizabeth Gould Davis, Evelyn Reed, and Merlin Stone, developed theories of early matriarchies (see MATRIARCHY), basing them largely on the "Venus" figurines found at many Neolithic archaeological excavation sites, on interpretations of cave paintings, and on inferences drawn from scattered and fragmentary allusions in the classical literature and religious writings of several Near Eastern and Mediterranean cultures. Several writers, perhaps most notably Briffault in *The Mothers* (1927) and Merlin Stone in *When God Was a Woman* (1976), have linked matriarchy with goddess worship theory; the goddess is also called the "mother goddess." Stone and several others have written of a monotheistic religion accompanying matriarchy, based on worship of a great goddess. Some called it the "old religion," and some have stated or inferred that goddess worship as the main form of worship was worldwide and stretched back from as recently as the middle of the first millennium B.C. to as far as 25,000 years ago. Others called it a religion set in the Mediterranean and Near East.

On the other hand, the overwhelming majority of historians and anthropologists, including many feminists, have called the evidence for goddess worship cultures—like the evidence for the existence of matriarchy—far too scanty to be taken very seriously and have at best reserved judgment until more persuasive evidence is developed.

For the great goddess theory there is an additional problem, in that the construct is a kind of back formation, placing monotheism where it is unlikely to belong, into a body of early pantheistic cultures, worshiping many female and male gods, as did all the major cultures before the coming of the idea of the single male God.

But flawed or not, the idea of "the Goddess" has struck a responsive chord in some modern feminists, who share the worldwide, fully demonstrated will to believe in some kind of deity, preferably one with ancient roots. Not for them the single male God; instead a powerful female Goddess, reviving what are perceived as ancient beliefs. For spiritual feminists like Mary **DALY** and others, the new spirituality is life-affirming and liberates the "Goddess within." (See SPIRITUAL FEMINISM; RELIGION AND WOMEN'S RIGHTS.)

Goldman, Emma (1869–1940), one of the leading anarchist women of her time, also a leading early-twentieth-century radical WOMEN'S RIGHTS crusader who advocated sexual freedom for women equal to that granted men, a very radical departure that in her time was almost universally castigated as "free love." She also advocated BIRTH CONTROL and the dissemination of information on birth control techniques, an equally radical idea, and spoke against the institution of MARRIAGE as a device used to enslave women. Her thinking on birth control, in particular, powerfully influenced that of Margaret SANGER and other American public health women's rights advocates.

Goldman, known in her time as "Red Emma," was one of the best-known anarchists in the world. Her companion from 1889 was anarchist Alexander Berkman, imprisoned from 1892 to 1906 for his attempt to assassinate industrialist Henry Clay Frick after the Homestead Steel strike. She and Berkman worked together in New York (1906–1919), a period in which she founded and edited the magazine *Mother Earth* (1906–1917) and published *Anarchism and Other Essays* (1910). During the 1919 Red scare, the U.S. government deported both of them to the Soviet Union. Goldman soon left the Soviet Union, greatly disillusioned; unable to reenter the United States, she died in Canada.

> *Merely external emancipation has made of the modern woman an artificial being. . . . Now, woman is confronted with the necessity of emancipating herself from emancipation, if she really desires to be free.*
>
> EMMA GOLDMAN, 1911
> "THE TRAGEDY OF WOMEN'S EMANCIPATION," IN
> ANARCHISM AND OTHER ESSAYS

●

gonadotropins, HORMONES that stimulate the action of sex glands, or GONADS—in women, OVARIES; in men, TESTES. One example is HUMAN CHORIONIC GONADOTROPIN (hCG).

gonads, the SEX GLANDS, vital parts of the human REPRODUCTIVE SYSTEM, which actually produce the cells that join together at CONCEPTION. The female gonads are the OVARIES, which produce eggs (see OVUM); the male gonads are the TESTES, which produce SPERM.

gonorrhea, a bacterial infection in moist, warm areas of the body, including the CERVIX, mouth, throat, URINARY TRACT, and rectum (see DIGESTIVE SYSTEM); one of the SEXUALLY TRANSMITTED DISEASES (STDs). The infection can be spread by various kinds of SEXUAL INTERCOURSE, including vaginal, oral, and anal sex; by the fingers from the GENITALS or mouth; and by a mother to her baby during CHILD-BIRTH. When found in young children, it can be a warning of possible sexual abuse (see CHILD ABUSE AND NEGLECT; INCEST). In the United States alone, over one million cases of gonorrhea are reported each year, and at least as many are believed to go unreported, many among teenagers and young adults.

As in many STDs, early symptoms are mild or even nonexistent, so an infected person can unknowingly infect others. Where symptoms appear, generally within two to ten days of contact with an infected partner, they include pain or a burning sensation when urinating and a yellowish vaginal discharge; later symptoms include abdominal pain, vaginal bleeding between periods (see MEN-STRUATION), vomiting, and fever; rectal infection may involve itching, discharge, and painful bowel movements.

Gonorrhea is diagnosed by examination or culture of samples from the infected area to detect presence of the *gonococcus* bacteria; tests are about 90 percent accurate, though that means one in ten cases is not detected. The disease is treated with penicillin or other antibiotics. The full course of medication must be taken, with a retest a week later to ensure that the infection has been eliminated. Doctors advise that all of an infected person's sex partners should also be tested and treated, even if they have no symptoms of infection.

Undetected and untreated, the infection can spread to the OVARIES and FAL-LOPIAN TUBES, causing PELVIC INFLAMMATORY DISEASE, which can lead to INFERTILITY or set the scene for a potentially life-threatening ECTOPIC PREGNANCY. If the bacteria spread into the bloodstream, they can infect the joints (see ARTHRITIS), heart valves (see HEART AND CIRCULATORY SYSTEM), and brain (see BRAIN AND NERVOUS SYSTEM). A baby infected during CHILDBIRTH faces possible blindness. To prevent this, many states require that the eyes of newborns be treated with silver nitrate or other medications immediately after birth. Most doctors recommend that a woman have at least one test for gonorrhea during a pregnancy (see PRENATAL CARE). Previous infection provides no immunity; a person can get gonorrhea many times and so must continue to exercise care in all sexual contact. Limiting the number of sex partners and using CONDOMS, DIAPHRAGMS, and SPERMICIDES containing nonoxynol-9 can reduce the risk somewhat. (See SEXUALLY TRANSMIT-TED DISEASES; also WHAT YOU CAN DO TO AVOID STDs on page 660; SEXUALLY TRANSMITTED DISEASES HELP, INFORMATION, AND ACTION GUIDE on page 658.)

"Goodbye to All That" (1970), an essay by Robin MORGAN. (*Good-bye to All That* was also a 1929 Robert Graves autobiography.)

Gouges, Olympe de (Marie-Olympe Gouze, 1748–1793), a
French writer who in 1789 became one of the leading women of the French Revolution and in 1790 the author of a pioneering call for WOMEN'S RIGHTS, the *Dec-*

laration of the Rights of Women and Citizens. She was soon devoured by her own Revolution, becoming in 1793 one of Robespierre's many victims guillotined during France's Reign of Terror. (See also WOMEN'S RIGHTS MOVEMENT.)

Graafian follicle, the site in a woman's OVARY where a dominant egg (OVUM) grows, as part of the reproductive cycle.

Grafenberg spot, the full name for the G SPOT.

grandparents' rights, the right of a grandmother or grandfather to visit a grandchild, even if the parents are separated or divorced or if grandparents and parents are estranged. Traditionally, when several generations of a family lived in close proximity, grandparents' rights were so widely accepted that they needed little legal support. Even today most parents wish to foster continuing relationships between children and their grandparents. However, the increasingly complicated pattern of DIVORCE and remarriage have led to increasingly bitter fights for child CUSTODY, with hard feelings often reaching out to affect grandparents as well.

As a result, grandparents have been lobbying widely for legal protection of their VISITATION RIGHTS, which most states have now provided in one form or other. Most of these apply to cases of SEPARATION or divorce, but the state of Illinois was the first to go beyond this to guarantee grandparents' visitation rights while the parents remain married, even if the parents would wish it otherwise, as when parents and grandparents are estranged. As in many other conflict areas, family members sometimes seek MEDIATION or ARBITRATION to resolve their disputes.

However, if PARENTS' RIGHTS are terminated, as in cases where a child is placed for ADOPTION, grandparents' rights also generally end as well. Some states continue to protect grandparents' visitation rights when the child is adopted by another relative or in some cases of open adoption. In practice, many grandparents become—formally or informally—the guardians or adoptive parents of their grandchildren, when the natural MOTHER and FATHER are having difficulty coping with their lives.

For more help, information, and action

▶ Grandparents'/Children's Rights (GCR) (5728 Bayonne Avenue, Haslett, MI 48840; 517-339-8663; Lee and Lucille Sumpter, study directors), an organization to protect the rights of children and grandparents to have access to each other. It works to protect grandparents' visitation rights and other rights affecting children's emotional, mental, and physical health, especially regarding child abuse; and serves as information clearinghouse.

Other resources

The Grandparent Book: A Guide to Changes in Birth and Child Rearing. Linda B. White. Gateway Books, 1990.

Congratulations! You're Going to Be a Grandmother. Lanie Carter. Pocket Books, 1990.

Grandparent Visitation Disputes: A Legal Resource Manual. American Bar Association, 1989.

Grandparenting: Understanding Today's Children. David Elkind. Scott, Foresman, 1989.

Grandparenting for the Nineties: Parenting Is Forever. Robert Aldrich and Glenn Austin. Robert Erdman, 1989.

A Survival Manual for New Grandparents. Linda B. White. Gateway Books, 1989.

The New American Grandparent: A Place in the Family, A Life Apart. Andrew J. Cherlin. Basic Books, 1988.

(See also OLDER WOMEN'S HELP, INFORMATION, AND ACTION GUIDE on page 374.)

granuloma inguinale, a chronic, progressive bacterial infection of the GEN-ITALS; one of the SEXUALLY TRANSMITTED DISEASES, also called *Donovanosis* or *granuloma venerium*. It occurs most often in tropical areas and is rare in the United States. The main symptom is one or more beefy-red sores in the genital area; these are generally painless and enlarge slowly. Like most STDs, granuloma inguinale can be spread in its early stages, even before symptoms are obvious. Serious complications can be avoided with antibiotic treatment. (See SEXUALLY TRANSMITTED DISEASES; also WHAT YOU CAN DO TO AVOID STDS on page 660; SEXUALLY TRANSMITTED DISEASES HELP, INFORMATION, AND ACTION GUIDE on page 658.)

Greer, Germaine (1939–), an Australian writer and critic who emerged as a leading feminist with the publication of her book *The Female Eunuch* (1970), in which she strongly urged women to take full control of their own lives by rejecting MARRIAGE and MONOGAMY, consumerism, and their accompanying sexual and economic self-definitions. She also rejected such larger social solutions as socialism and the development of new forms of religious belief, relying instead on individual thought and action. Her ensuing argument with many other feminists took up some of the same issues that had involved anarchist Emma GOLDMAN and many reform and social revolutionary feminists of the early twentieth century. Greer's feminist-related work also includes *The Obstacle Race: the Fortunes of Women Painters and their Work* (1979), *Sex and Destiny: the Politics of Human Fertility* (1984), and *The Change: Women, Aging, and the Menopause* (1992).

Grimké, Angelina (1805–1879) and **Sarah** (1792–1873), sisters born of a slave-holding family in Charleston, South Carolina, whose hatred of slavery brought them north and made them two of the leading abolitionists of their time. During the course of their shared antislavery careers, they became the first women lecturers of the American Anti-Slavery Society. But their political activity and especially their lectures to mixed male-female audiences brought powerful criticism, including that of the Massachusetts Congregational clergy. They responded in their classic *Letters on the Equality of the Sexes and the Condition of Women* (1838), a very early landmark feminist work that defended the right of women to engage in political action, refuted the scriptural grounds on which the clergy had based their criticism, and strongly advocated the full equality of women. (See POLITICAL PARTICIPATION.)

I ask no favors for my sex.... All I ask of our brethren is that they will take their feet from off our necks.

——————————— *SARAH GRIMKÉ, 1838* ———————————

•

Griswold v. Connecticut, a 1965 U.S. Supreme Court ruling that struck down a law that would have banned use of CONTRACEPTIVES by married couples and that established the "right of privacy" between the married couple and their doctor.

group B streptococcal infections (GBS), a bacterial infection of the GENITALS; one of the SEXUALLY TRANSMITTED DISEASES. GBS infections are widely found, most often among those with high levels of sexual activity; in the United States, the NATIONAL INSTITUTE OF ALLERGY AND INFECTIOUS DISEASES (NIAID) estimates that 20 to 35 percent of all otherwise healthy young women have GBS infection. Most adults have no symptoms. The greatest concern is with infants born to infected women; approximately one to two percent of them become seriously ill; about one-third of these babies die, and many of the others have mental retardation or other serious problems. Babies with early-onset GBS (symptoms occurring within five days of birth, often after premature or otherwise complicated DELIVERY) often suffer respiratory distress, shock, and coma. Those with late-onset GBS (occurring generally about twenty-four days after birth) often have fever and meningitis, or infection of the membranes covering the brain and spinal cord. Researchers seek a preventive vaccine and are exploring the treatment of pregnant women with antibiotics before delivery and at-risk infants soon after birth. (See SEXUALLY TRANSMITTED DISEASES; also WHAT YOU CAN DO TO AVOID STDs on page 660; SEXUALLY TRANSMITTED DISEASES HELP, INFORMATION, AND ACTION GUIDE on page 658.)

G spot (Grafenberg spot), a small area of very sensitive tissue just inside the VAGINA, on the upper front wall, alongside the urethra. Little is known about it because it has not been widely recognized and studied; Masters and Johnson, among others, did not mention the G spot in their *Human Sexual Response.* It is not even known, for example, if it occurs in all women. Where it does, it responds to manual stimulation and swells to several times its normal size. Some believe it is analogous to the male prostate gland (see REPRODUCTIVE SYSTEM; SEXUAL RESPONSE).

gynarchy, a woman-dominated or woman-centered government. The term is often expanded in use to mean a woman-dominated whole social system, including its government (see MATRIARCHY).

gynecological examination, a medical examination of a woman, focusing on the REPRODUCTIVE SYSTEM and special female structures, such as the BREASTS. It is often done by a gynecologist but may also be done by the family doctor— internist, general practitioner, or family practice physician—as part of a more general physical checkup.

The first gynecological examination should be performed when a girl becomes sexually active or by about age sixteen, especially if she has not begun MENSTRUATION by then. Checkups should then be done on a regular schedule. The frequency will depend on the woman's age; her personal and family medical history, especially her risk of CANCER; and the current medical recommendations, all of which change over time. At least some tests, however, should be done annually throughout life, notably the PAP SMEAR.

Like any general medical checkup, a gynecological examination begins with the taking of a *medical history,* or a review of the woman's health and that of her immediate family. Often a woman will be asked to fill out a form beforehand and then discuss it with the doctor. Among the topics covered by the medical history are age; personal medical history, including specific illnesses, hospitalizations, and surgery; menstrual history; previous gynecological problems, if any; type of BIRTH CONTROL used, if any, both past and present; number of pregnancies, if any, and their outcomes; medications being taken; any adverse reactions to medications; any past use of DES (diethylstilbestrol) by the woman or her mother; use of alcohol, drugs, or cigarettes (see ALCOHOL AND DRUG ABUSE; SMOKING); incidence of certain key illnesses in near blood relations (see GENETIC COUNSELING); and current complaints or illnesses, if any. This history will be taken in full at the first visit and will be reviewed and changes noted in subsequent visits.

After the history comes a general *physical examination,* where information such as height, weight, temperature, pulse, and BLOOD pressure is taken. If the woman has received a recent checkup from a general doctor, a gynecologist will do only an abbreviated version, focusing on women's concerns. The breasts will be examined for signs of any disorder; this is a professional's version of the examination a woman should be performing herself monthly (see BREAST SELF-EXAMINATION on page 104). Especially if a woman is or will be taking BIRTH CONTROL PILLS, the examination should include listening to heart and lungs with a stethoscope (see HEART AND CIRCULATORY SYSTEM; RESPIRATORY SYSTEM); many doctors will also check the inside of the mouth and throat and will feel the neck for any problems with the thyroid glands or lymph nodes (see IMMUNE SYSTEM).

Then follows the *pelvic examination.* Before this the woman normally should empty her bladder and bowels, to make her more comfortable and to allow the doctor to feel her internal organs more precisely. She then lies down on the examining table in the *dorsal lithotomy* position, with legs spread wide apart and feet in stirrups, to allow the doctor best access and visibility. For some women, such as those with scoliosis (see SPINE) or ARTHRITIS in the hip, the dorsal lithotomy position is difficult or impossible. One alternative is *Sims position,* in which the woman lies on her side, with her upper leg held or propped up in the air.

During the pelvic, the doctor visually examines and feels (*palpates*) the external GENITALS, looking for anything abnormal, including lumps, sores, growths, discoloration, discharges, infection, or infestation. Then the doctor inserts a two-armed metal or plastic device called a *speculum* into the VAGINA; once inside, the speculum is widened to hold the vaginal walls apart and allow the doctor to examine the vagina and CERVIX for abnormalities, such as redness, irritation, swelling, or discharge. The insertion of the speculum may be somewhat uncomfortable but for almost all women is not painful, even if the woman has not had vaginal SEXUAL INTERCOURSE and has never used tampons (see MENSTRUATION). But if it *is* painful, a woman should say so and ask the doctor to adjust it or use a smaller speculum. At this time, the doctor may use a swab or small spatula to remove tissue, especially from the cervix, for testing, as for a Pap smear. Before an examination, the woman should not douche for at least twenty-four hours, since DOUCHING could wash away evidence of infection.

Before or after the speculum examination, the doctor will perform several other examinations:

▶ **bimanual examination,** inserting two fingers of one hand into the vagina and feeling the abdomen with the other. Here the doctor is checking for the position, size, firmness, and mobility of internal reproductive organs—the UTERUS, FALLOPIAN TUBES, and OVARIES—and any possible tenderness or lumps in the abdominal area.

▶ **rectovaginal examination,** inserting one finger into the vagina and another into the rectum. Here the doctor is checking the wall between the vagina and the rectum (see DIGESTIVE SYSTEM) and feeling the internal organs from a different angle.

▶ **rectal examination,** inserting one finger into the rectum alone. This is to check for any abnormalities, such as growths.

During a pelvic examination, women can help ease discomfort by relaxing their abdominal muscles as much as possible, as through open-mouth deep breathing. If the gynecologist is male, as more than 85 percent still are in the United States, a female nurse is often present during the pelvic examination. A woman who is embarrassed or uneasy with a particular doctor should "shop around" to find another doctor—male or female—with whom she will feel more comfortable or who she feels will be more responsive to her needs and concerns. She may also, if she desires, have a relative, friend, or patient's advocate present during the examination.

The doctor may order various laboratory tests to be performed. This will often include a Pap smear annually, and a MAMMOGRAM regularly, and may include a wide variety of other tests, depending on the woman's particular condition and history, such as urine tests, BLOOD tests, and laboratory cultures when infections are suspected.

Either in the examining room or, more likely, back in the consulting office, the doctor will generally discuss the findings of the physical examination; explain the tests ordered and what is expected to be learned from them; prescribe medications or contraceptives, as needed; answer the woman's questions, if any; discuss any necessary follow-up to the treatment; and schedule any further visits. If the woman is pregnant, this examination will be the beginning of her PRENATAL CARE. In some clinics, a specially trained nurse practitioner, often a CERTIFIED NURSE-MIDWIFE, may conduct gynecological examinations.

Though gynecologists are trained in general medicine, their main specialty is in problems with a woman's reproductive system. For general medical care, women should see a general physician. If they rely on their gynecologist for their general medical care, they should make it clear that they are doing so, so appropriate measurements and tests can be taken.

Conversely, general physicians are trained to handle routine gynecological care, though they they have less experience and training in it. If a woman is not routinely seeing a gynecologist, she should alert her regular doctor, so the standard breast and pelvic examinations are included in a regular checkup.

Sometimes the two doctors work together as part of a medical group, with other specialists available as well, providing a full range of care. But in other cases, the two doctors are quite separate. Many people have criticized this split in medical care for women, and some are recommending the establishment of a new medical specialty in women's health, so a woman will be able to get all her medical care from a single doctor without loss of special skills and training (see HEALTH EQUITY). (See WOMEN'S HEALTH HELP, INFORMATION, AND ACTION GUIDE on page 334; SEX AND SEXUALITY HELP, INFORMATION, AND ACTION GUIDE on page 665.)

Gyn/Ecology: The Metaethics of Radical Feminism: See Mary DALY.

Hainisch, Marianne (1839–1936), an Austrian educator and a leader of the WOMEN'S RIGHTS MOVEMENT in Austro-Hungary, later in Austria. Hainisch was a founder and president of the General Austrian Women's Association and from that position led campaigns on a wide range of issues, including WOMAN SUFFRAGE and MARRIAGE law reform. She was also a pacifist who opposed the onset of World War I.

hair, strands of material that grow out of the SKIN, actually formed from dead specialized skin cells, made up largely of the protein *keratin*. Each strand grows from a separate site, called a *follicle;* oil (sebaceous) and sweat glands release their secretions at the same sites, lubricating hair.

Though we are not generally aware of it, hair of various types actually covers our whole bodies, apart from the palms of the hand and the soles of the feet. *Lanugo* is the silky, downlike hair found on an EMBRYO or FETUS before birth and sometimes on newborns; it also may appear in women with severe ANOREXIA NERVOSA. The body and scalp hair of children is generally fine and silky, then, in response to the hormonal changes of PUBERTY, hair on arms and legs darkens and becomes coarser. At the same time, hair begins to grow in under the arms and in the pubic area and among men also on the face (see SECONDARY SEX CHARACTERISTICS).

Scalp hair is the fastest-growing type of hair, with the growth coming in cycles. The average person has approximately one hundred thousand strands of hair; at any one time, an estimated 80–90 percent of these hairs are in a two- to seven-year growing phase, while the rest are in a two- to four-month "resting" phase. At the beginning of a growth phase, the old hair is pushed out and replaced by a new hair, at the rate of perhaps twenty to one hundred hairs each day.

Hair color, determined by GENETIC INHERITANCE, depends on the amount, type, and concentration of pigment in the hair. Production of pigment in the hairs tends to slow with age, the result being gray hair. About one person in four has some gray hair by age twenty-five, and about one in four (not necessarily the same people) will eventually turn totally gray. Various substances can be used to change the color of hair. Some can simply be sprayed on and brushed out; some coat the hair strand, lasting through several shampoos; some dye the hair strands themselves, lasting until the hair grows out. Women should be cautious and careful about using chemical dyes at home or in beauty shops; some have been found to cause CANCER, and many others are possible carcinogens.

Various substances can be used to straighten, relax, wave, or curl the hair. Shampoos can change hair's appearance by removing excess dirt and oil and so allowing hairs to fluff away from the scalp and from each other, appearing fuller. Conditioners and cream rinses coat hair to make it seem thicker, often camouflaging frayed or split ends. Substances used for styling also coat the hair and help it hold the shape it has been given by combing or curling; some also contain a sunblock to protect hair from ultraviolet rays (see SKIN).

Age and inheritance affect questions of thinning or loss of hair. This is most common among men, since *male pattern baldness* is a *sex-linked trait* carried by women and passed on to men (see GENETIC INHERITANCE). But women, too, experience some receding hairlines, often as early as in their twenties or thirties, and gradual thinning; this is accentuated after MENOPAUSE with cessation of the production of HORMONES.

If the hair is deprived of necessary nutrients, many hairs at once may stop growing and then fall out two to four months later. This can result from major surgery or severe illness; traumatic experiences such as an accident or the death of a loved one; thyroid disorders; iron-deficiency ANEMIA (see BLOOD); and extreme vitamin and mineral deficiencies (see NUTRITION), as may result from anorexia nervosa or BULIMIA. Some medical treatments can also have the same effect, most noticeably the chemotherapy medications used to treat many types of CANCER. In sufficient doses, ionizing radiation can produce permanent baldness, as can some skin-related disorders, such as shingles or ringworm, and some chemicals, if they destroy the hair follicles. Conversely, the HORMONES produced during PREGNANCY or found in BIRTH CONTROL PILLS can extend the growing phase for many of a woman's hairs; afterward, more than the usual number of hairs may go into the resting phase at once, leading to thinning over two to four months before the hair returns to its previous fullness.

Women can cause hair thinning by mistreatment as well. Constant use of braids, cornrows, tight ponytails, hot combs, curling irons, tight barrettes, and the like can pull or strain the strands enough to cause hair loss. Hair thinning and damage can also result from too frequent or improper use of chemicals to straighten, curl, or color hair. Using a peroxide bleach and then a permanent dye is more damaging to the hair than using a mild color rinse. Excess sun can also make hair dry and brittle.

Hair loss can also result from other types of disorders. Some people, especially preteen girls, have a nervous habit of yanking hairs from part of their scalp, a disorder called *trichotillomania*. In *alopecia areata,* the body's IMMUNE SYSTEM apparently attacks hair follicles, mistaking them for foreign matter; hair is temporarily lost in patches, though with recurring episodes loss may become permanent. The cause of the disorder is unknown, though a family history of the problem is common.

Until recent years, treatments for baldness were largely quackery. However, since the late 1980s, a drug called *minoxidil* has been used to treat hair loss, with at least some success among some users, though it is still too early to gauge the extent or permanence of the hair regrowth. Others use *hair-replacement surgery,* in which still-active hair follicles from the back of the head are transplanted to the balding areas, especially in the top front of the head. Another approach has been to swing "flaps" of hair from the back to the top front of the head. Though used most often by men, these procedures are also sometimes used by women. For people who have hair loss or thinning—or some who simply want a different look—a wig is often the answer.

More often, women have excess unwanted hair, not on their heads, but elsewhere on their bodies, such as legs, forearms, chest, and face. Where it grows rapidly or appears in a new area suddenly, excess hair growth may signal a medical problem, such as a tumor of the adrenal glands or OVARIES, both of which produce male hormones, or occur among athletes who take drugs such as anabolic STEROIDS. Beyond such causes, hair growth is determined largely by genetics, and women who grow more hair than is expected for their sex, age, and ancestry often wish to remove some of it. Traditionally this has meant periodically shaving legs and underarm areas, for temporary removal of hair; contrary to popular opinion, this does not increase either the growth or the coarseness of the hairs, though as hairs grow back they will initially be short and stand up, seeming bristly.

Another means of temporary removal includes use of a *depilatory*, a chemical mixture to dissolve hairs above the skin. These should be used cautiously, on a patch of skin first to test for sensitivity (see ALLERGIES); they should never be used immediately after a bath or shower, while the skin's pores are open, and should be removed with cool water only, not warm or hot. A longer-lasting, though still temporary, approach is the use of wax or tape applied to the skin; hairs stick to the substance and are then removed with the wax or tape as it is stripped off. This is a painful approach, and again the skin should be tested for sensitivity. Other scattered hairs, as in eyebrows or on the face, may be removed by selected plucking or tweezing.

The only permanent method of hair removal is *electrolysis*, involving insertion of an electrified needle to destroy the hair root and prevent any future growth. This should, of course, be done only by a trained, experienced practitioner; many states require licenses for people performing electrolysis. For all but the tiniest areas of the body, however, the procedure is time-consuming and expensive. For some small areas of unwanted hair, a bit of peroxide may be used, with care, to bleach them out of sight.

Another common hair problem is dandruff, excess flaking of dead skin from the scalp, often resulting (for unknown reasons) from overactivity of the skin's oil glands. When oil glands become plugged, dandruff and the hair itself may become dry and grayish. Scratching should be avoided, since the skin may be broken and invite infection. Several medicines can control dandruff and sometimes eliminate it.

The best protection for hair is to treat it gently, brushing it to remove surface dirt and distribute natural oils; wash the hair regularly; trim it every six weeks or so; use a conditioner to prevent tangling; wear a hat and/or sunblocking lotion to protect against ultraviolet rays; and be especially careful when combing hair immediately after washing, when hair can easily be pulled out of the softened scalp. In general, avoid chemicals that could damage hair or skin, or clog the pores. (See Skin, Hair, Nails, and Cosmetics Help, Information, and Ac-tion Guide on page 689; also skin.)

Hall, Radclyffe (1883–1943), a British novelist and psychic researcher, best known by far for her novel *The Well of Loneliness* (1928), her straightforward and open story of lesbians living their lives honestly in the largely inimical Brit-ish society of that time. An unsuccessful attempt to ban the book in United States failed in 1929, but it was banned in Britain until 1949.

Harris **v.** *McRae*, the 1980 U.S. Supreme Court decision that upheld the so-called Hyde Amendment, providing that Medicaid should not be used to pay for medically necessary abortions.

hCG, an abbreviation for human chorionic gonadotropin.

health equity, sex neutrality in the whole range of activities relating to health and medical care, including not only a doctor's examination, testing, treatment, and advice, but also research, study, funding, and analysis of medical data. In all these areas, it has become increasingly clear that men's bodies have been the standard, and that women's special physical concerns have been disregarded and ultimately shortchanged. This does not mean that all male doctors are biased against women, though some may be, but rather that male-oriented bias has per-meated and actually been built into doctors' training and delivery of medical care.

At its most basic, this bias means women generally have to go to two doctors—one for general health and one for the reproductive system—while men need to go to just one. Unless the woman's two doctors work closely together, neither has a full picture of her health. And if she relies on just one, she may get less-than-top-notch care (see gynecological examination). To eliminate this split, some doctors—many of them women—have proposed the development of a new medical specialty in women's health. As with pediatrics for children, the women's health specialist would be trained to treat the whole woman and would be especially attuned to overarching health concerns, such as menopause and os-teoporosis, and to special questions, such as signs of abuse (see battered women). Other doctors—again, many of them women—stress that the two sexes are physically more alike than different and prefer to focus on bringing women's health concerns more fully into mainstream medical training. They are con-cerned that women's health may become isolated and that emphasis on differ-ences may be turned against women, so that not only women but medical care in general may lose, rather than gain. In practice, of course, some doctors with-out formal medical specialties are specializing in total care—a sort of one-stop shopping—for women.

Another major area of concern is that until recently, a great deal of the clinical research on diseases and disorders, and of testing of new drugs and treatments, was carried out on men. Women were generally left out. In the case of drugs, this was often because of concerns about possible BIRTH DEFECTS in case of PREGNANCY or that the hormonal fluctuations of MENSTRUATION might throw off drug results. Both are legitimate concerns, and to meet those objections *additional* testing needs to be done, which is costly. But the result was that women (sometimes including pregnant women) later were given drugs that had been tested, and the dosages calibrated, only or primarily with men, with no studies of their effects in women; however, women's bodies often react differently to drugs from men's. For example, they have more adverse drug reactions and also more fatal drug reactions, for reasons yet unknown and only beginning to be explored. Not only that, the men tested were mostly in the prime of life. As has become ever clearer, elderly people respond to drugs differently, and the increasing majority of the elderly are women, creating a double medical bias against older women. Also, medical devices intended for women have not always been tested properly; the most controversial one is BREAST IMPLANTS.

Similarly, much of what doctors believe they know about diseases and disorders comes from studies primarily or solely on men. Massive studies of heart disease and cholesterol, for example, have been conducted with nary a woman in the sample. Beyond the lack of medical information, such discrimination could have other consequences. Many women with AIDS did not fit the classical definition of the disease based on male symptoms until it was changed in 1992, so they were judged ineligible for much-needed public assistance. Also, treatments that sometimes work well with men may have adverse effects on women (see HEART AND CIRCULATORY SYSTEM).

In addition, many diseases or issues that primarily or solely affect women, such as osteoporosis or the menstrual cycle, have until recently received surprisingly little attention from researchers. Many feminists and women's rights activists, including women in Congress, have lobbied the National Institutes of Health for more equitable distribution of funding to cover women's health issues and for inclusion of women in more studies, ideally in the proportions of men and women who have the particular disease in the general population. Promises were made but broken, prompting the introduction of a Women's Health Equity Act to put the promises into legislation. While passage of such a bill continues to be sought, others have been pressing the National Institutes of Health, which has established the Office on Research on Women's Health. The **PHS ACTION PLAN FOR WOMEN'S HEALTH** lays out priorities among women's health issues for the 1990s.

Various studies have also shown that some disorders, notably heart disease (see HEART AND CIRCULATORY SYSTEM), are treated much less aggressively in women than in men. Sometimes, however, the result is that women are treated when they do not need it; for example, a recent study produced the surprising result that high blood pressure is less dangerous in women than in men and so may not require treatment. The confusion over such vital and fundamental questions highlights the lack of proper information.

In some parts of the world where there is strong SON PREFERENCE, poorer medical treatment of women has been so widespread as to reduce their LIFE EX-

PECTANCY to less than that of men, when historically the reverse has been true. In rural India, for example, not only do boy children get better food, they are also more likely to be taken to the nearest city for medical treatment, where girls are fed leftovers and generally are treated by the local "wise woman."

Many women have also been concerned about what they call the "medicalization" of women's health. In particular, they have been concerned that doctors consider menstruation, PREGNANCY, and menopause as medical problems to be treated rather than as natural events in women's lives. For many women this has been bound up with a feeling that medicine was too impersonal, sterile, and male-dominated, with the woman in a passive, dependent, often uninformed role. Women also charged that many surgeons performed unnecessary operations (see HYSTERECTOMY).

One reaction to that was the burgeoning of natural CHILDBIRTH, often using midwives (see CERTIFIED NURSE–MIDWIFE), in which women and also men began to take a more active role in the DELIVERY process. A widespread advocacy movement also took shape, made up of organizations, such as many of those mentioned in this book, formed by patients faced with particular medical concerns.

Another result, from the late 1960s, in the United States and many other developed countries, was the women's health movement, stressing women "taking back" their own routine gynecological care. Often working together in clinics, women learned how to give each other breast and pelvic examinations (see GYNE-COLOGICAL EXAMINATION), perform simple laboratory tests, fit and insert some kinds of BIRTH CONTROL devices, and give themselves other routine care. The Boston Women's Health Collective is probably the best-known, largely because of their book *Our Bodies, Ourselves.* It was in a similar feminist health center that women developed the technique of *menstrual extraction,* a home version of a technique used in a medically performed ABORTION. Some of these stress home remedies and nonmedical approaches, including NATURAL FAMILY PLANNING.

The main hazard with such approaches is that women will overlook early signs of disease that a doctor might spot and so will miss the chance to deal with the disease in its early stages; one advantage of routine gynecological examinations is precisely that medical problems are often detected earlier in women than in men, who do not have such regularly scheduled checkups. The other hazard with self-help centers is that they may introduce infections and *cause* problems, while seeking independence from the "male medical establishment."

In such clinics, gynecological examinations may be performed by a specially trained nurse practitioner or by a physician, often a woman. In general, professionals perform those procedures that only they are licensed to perform, such as prescribing drugs or inserting IUDs (see INTRAUTERINE DEVICE), but otherwise act as consultants to the clinic. In some cases, clinics came under fire from the medical community for dispensing medical care and drugs without proper authority; some women were arrested and some clinics closed. Sometimes pressure was brought to bear on their physician consultants as well. Still, women's health centers, also called feminist health centers or clinics, have survived.

The main result of women's health advocacy, however, seems to be that the medical community itself is beginning to respond to pressure from—and *education* from—the no longer silent majority. In addition, more resources are now being turned toward specific testing involving large groups of women. (See WOM-EN's HEALTH HELP, INFORMATION, AND ACTION GUIDE, below.)

WOMEN'S HEALTH

Help, Information, and Action Guide

Organizations

▶ NATIONAL WOMEN'S HEALTH NETWORK (NWHN) (202-347-1140). Operates the **Women's Health Information Service**. Publishes *Research to Improve Women's Health: An Agenda for Equity, Turning Things Around: A Women's Occupational and Environmental Health Resource Guide;* books, booklets, and papers such as *Abortion Then and Now: Creative Responses to Restricted Access, Women, AIDS, and Public Health Policies, AIDS: What Every Women Needs to Know, Childbearing Policies Within a National Health Program: An Evolving Consensus for New Directions, Research to Improve Women's Health: An Agenda for Equity, Taking Hormones and Women's Health: Health Choices, Risks and Benefits, Women and the Crisis in Sex Hormones,* and *Hearts, Bones, Hot Flashes, and Hormones;* and information packets on specific topics, from ABORTION to YEAST INFECTIONS.

▶ AMERICAN COLLEGE OF OBSTETRICIANS AND GYNECOLOGISTS (ACOG) (202-638-5577). Maintains a resource center on obstetrical and gynecological questions; publishes ACOG Patient Education Pamphlets and a Healthy Mother's Food Wheel.

▶ NOW LEGAL DEFENSE AND EDUCATION FUND (NOW LDEF) (212-925-6635). Publishes the Legal Resource Kit *Women and Health.*

▶ FEDERATION OF FEMINIST WOMEN'S HEALTH CENTERS (916-737-0260). Publishes *A New View of a Woman's Body* and *How to Stay Out of the Gynecologist's Office.*

▶ STOP ABUSE BY COUNSELORS (STOP ABC) (206-243-2723). Publishes an attorney's list, a resource list, an organizing packet, and *What to Do When Psychotherapy Goes Wrong.*

▶ 9 TO 5, NATIONAL ASSOCIATION OF WORKING WOMEN (216-566-1699; Job Survival Hotline 800-522-0925). Publishes *VDT Syndrome: The Physical and Mental Trauma of Computer Work.*

▶ WOMEN'S LEGAL DEFENSE FUND (WLDF) (202-887-0364).

◪ ON OLDER WOMEN'S HEALTH

▶ NATIONAL COUNCIL ON THE AGING (NCOA) (202-479-1200 or 800-424-9046). Includes HEALTH PROMOTION INSTITUTE (HPI). Publishes

Eating Well to Stay Well, Keeping the Pressure Down, Medicine Is No Mystery, A New Medicine Man: A Different Kind of Health Care for Elders, Health Promotion and Aging: A National Directory of Selected Programs, Health Promotion and Aging: Strategies for Action, Health Promotion for Older Persons: A Selected Annotated Bibliography, Psychological Functioning of Older People, A Resource Guide for Injury Control Programs for Older Persons, A Resource Guide for Nutrition Management Programs for Older Persons, Update on Health Aging: Reading Material on Health Topics for the New Reader and Tutor, Long-Term Care Choices, and the videotape *The Sixth Sense* (with learning guide and handout booklets).

▶ OLDER WOMEN'S LEAGUE (OWL) (202-783-6686; OWL POWERLINE, 202-783-6689, a weekly update on congressional activities). Publishes *The Picture of Health: For Midlife and Older Women in America, Report on the Status of Midlife and Older Women in America, Caring for Caregivers: Addressing the Employment Needs of Long-Term Care Workers, In Search of a Solution: The American Health Care Crisis, Death and Dying: Staying in Control to the End of Our Lives, Health Care Financing and Midlife Women: A Sick System, Universal Health Care Action Kit, Taking Charge of the End of Your Life: Proceedings of a Forum on Living Wills and other Advance Directives, Women's Health Organizing Kit, Women's Health Briefing Packet,* and *Critical Condition: Midlife and Older Women in America's Health Care System.*

☑ GOVERNMENT HEALTH INFORMATION SOURCES

▶ ODPHP NATIONAL HEALTH INFORMATION CENTER (ONHIC) (301-565-4167, in Maryland; or 800-336-4797).
▶ OFFICE ON RESEARCH ON WOMEN'S HEALTH (ORWH) (301-402-1770).
▶ NATIONAL INSTITUTE OF ALLERGY AND INFECTIOUS DISEASES (NIAID) (301-496-5717).
▶ NATIONAL INSTITUTE OF CHILD HEALTH AND HUMAN DEVELOPMENT (NICHD) (301-496-5133).
▶ CENTERS FOR DISEASE CONTROL (CDC) (404-329-3534).
▶ FOOD AND DRUG ADMINISTRATION (FDA) (301-443-3170).

☑ SOCIAL AND POLICY CONCERNS

▶ NATIONAL CENTER FOR POLICY ALTERNATIVES (202-387-6030). Publishes *Health: Access and the Quality of Life, Leadership Brief on Low-Income Women and Health Care.*
▶ CLEARINGHOUSE ON WOMEN'S ISSUES (CWI) (301-871-6016 or 202-363-9795).
▶ CONGRESSIONAL CAUCUS FOR WOMEN'S ISSUES (202-225-6740).

▶ FEDERALLY EMPLOYED WOMEN (FEW) (202-898-0994).
▶ FUND FOR THE FEMINIST MAJORITY (617-695-9688; or 703-522-2214; or 213-651-0495). Publishes *Empowering Women in Medicine.*
▶ COMMISSION FOR WOMEN'S EQUALITY (CWE) (212-879-4500).
▶ MS. FOUNDATION FOR WOMEN (MFW) (212-353-8580).
▶ AMERICAN ASSOCIATION OF RETIRED PERSONS (AARP) (202-434-2277).

◪ INTERNATIONAL PERSPECTIVES

▶ INTERNATIONAL CENTER FOR RESEARCH ON WOMEN (ICRW) (202-797-0007). Publishes *Understanding and Evaluating Traditional Practices: A Guide for Improving Maternal Care* and *Better Health for Women: Research Results from the Maternal Nutrition and Health Care Program.*
▶ WOMEN'S INTERNATIONAL NETWORK (WIN) (617-862-9431).

Other resources

◪ GENERAL GUIDES

The Woman's Guide to Good Health. Consumer Reports Books Editors. Consumer Reports, 1991.
The A–Z of Women's Health, 2nd ed. Derek Llewellyn-Jones. Oxford University Press, 1990.
Everywoman's Health: The Complete Guide to Body and Mind, 4th ed. Douglas S. Thompson. Prentice-Hall, 1990.
The New A-to-Z of Women's Health: A Concise Encyclopedia. Christine Ammer. Facts on File, 1989; Hunter House, 1991.
Everywoman's Medical Handbook. Miriam Stoppard. Ballantine, 1989.

◪ OTHER GENERAL WORKS

Women's Health. Charles B. Clayman, ed. RD Assn, 1992.
In Sickness and in Health—What Every Man Should Know About the Woman He Loves. Mary E. O'Brien. Health Press, 1991.
Women's Bodies, Women's Dreams. Patricia Garfield. Ballantine, 1991.
Woman: Your Body, Your Health. Josleen Wilson. Harcourt Brace Jovanovich, 1990.
Women's Health Book. Loretta Kurban. Libra Press, 1990.
Women's Health Counts. Helen Roberts, ed. Routledge, 1990.
Womanhealth. Elaine L. Willis. Found Wellness, 1989.
One Thousand Two Hundred Fifty Health-Care Questions Women Ask. Joe S. McIlhaney, Jr. Baker Books, 1988.

◪ ON THE REPRODUCTIVE SYSTEM

It's Your Body: A Woman's Guide to Gynecology. Niels H. Lauersen and Steven Whitney. Berkley, 1992.

No Need to Be Afraid . . . First Pelvic Exam: A Handbook for Young Women and Their Mothers. Ellen Curro. Linking Ed Med, 1991.

Take This Book to the Gynecologist with You. Gale Malesky. Addison-Wesley, 1991.

Women's Reproductive Health: The Silent Emergency. Jodi L. Jacobson. Worldwatch Institute, 1991.

Women and Hormones: An Essential Guide to Being Female. Alice T. MacMahon. Family Publications, 1990.

Women and the Life Cycle: Transitions and Turning Points. Patricia Allatt and others, eds. St. Martin's, 1988.

Hormones: The Woman's Answerbook. Lois Jovanovic and Genell J. Subak-Sharpe. Fawcett, 1988.

(See also PREGNANCY AND CHILDBIRTH HELP, INFORMATION, AND ACTION GUIDE on page 580.)

◪ ON OLDER WOMEN'S HEALTH

Health Care for Older Women. Julie George and Shah Ebrahim, eds. Oxford University Press, 1992.

Choice Years: How to Stay Healthy, Happy and Beautiful Through Menopause and Beyond. Judith Paige and Pamela Gordon. Villard/Random, 1991.

Health and Fitness for Older Persons: Answers to Important Questions. James H. Humphrey. AMS Press, 1991.

A Search for Wellness: How to Turn Back Your Biological Clock. F. Kanses Mattson. Hampton Roads, 1990.

How to Avoid Old Age. Stanley L. Robinson. Remington (NJ), 1990.

Healthy Aging: New Directions in Health, Biology and Medicine. Joseph Bonner and William Harris. Borgo Press, 1990.

Secrets for Women in Their Prime, rev. ed. Betty Wand. Barr, 1989. Reprint of 1988 ed.

◪ ON OTHER SPECIAL CONCERNS

Doctor Discusses Female Surgery. Paul Neimark and Samuel Matlin. Budlong, 1989.

A Woman's Guide to Alternative Medicine. Liz Grist. Contemporary, 1988.

Alive and Well: A Lesbian Health Guide. Cuca Hepburn and Bonnie Gutierrez. Crossing Press, 1988.

◪ ON SOCIAL AND POLITICAL CONCERNS

Women and Doctors: A Physician's Explosive Account of Women's Medical Treatment—and Mistreatment—in America Today. John M. Smith. Atlantic Monthly, 1992.

Feminist Perspectives in Medical Ethics. Helen B. Holmes and Laura M. Purdy, eds. Indiana University Press, 1992.

No Longer Patient: Feminist Ethics and Health Care. Susan Sherwin. Temple University Press, 1991.

Women's Health: Readings on Social, Economic and Political Issues. Whatley Worcester. Kendall-Hunt, 1991.

Health Care and Gender. Charlotte F. Muller. Russell Sage, 1990.

Women's Health Alert: What Most Doctors Won't Tell You About. Sidney M. Wolfe. Addison-Wesley, 1990.

The Politics of Women's Biology. Ruth Hubbard. Rutgers University Press, 1990.

Women, Health, and Poverty. Cesar A. Perales and Lauren S. Young, eds. Haworth Press, 1989.

Healing Technology: Feminist Perspectives. Kathryn S. Ratcliff. University of Michigan Press, 1989.

Too Little, Too Late: Dealing with the Health Needs of Women in Poverty. Cesar A. Perales and Lauren S. Young, eds. Harrington Park, 1988.

◪ BACKGROUND WORKS

Women's Health from Womb to Tomb. Penny Kane. St. Martin's, 1991.

The Politics of Women's Biology. Ruth Hubbard. Rutgers University Press, 1990.

Women and Health in Africa. Meredeth Turshen, ed. Africa World, 1990.

Women, Health and Medicine in America: A Historical Handbook. Rima D. Apple. Garland, 1990.

Women and Health: Cross-Cultural Perspectives. Patricia Whelehan. Bergin & Garvey/Greenwood, 1988.

Healthy Mother, Healthy Babies National Coalition (HMHB), (409 12th Street, SW, Room 253, Washington, DC 20024-2188; 202-638-5577 or 202-863-2458; Lori Cooper, executive director), an "association of over one hundred national professional, voluntary, and governmental organizations with a common interest in maternal and infant health," housed in the offices of the AMERICAN COLLEGE OF OBSTETRICIANS AND GYNECOLOGISTS. HMHB seeks to promote preventive health education for all pregnant women and their families, develop networks for sharing information among organizations concerned about maternal and infant health, help develop state coalitions, and distribute public education materials, with special emphasis on reducing infant mortality and low birth weight; fostering healthy habits for pregnant women and women planning pregnancy; teaching how to ensure regular PRENATAL CARE and good NUTRITION; increasing women's understanding of risks and responsibilities of healthy child-bearing; immunization; and helping men better understand their supportive role in pregnancy and infant care. HMHB publishes various general materials, including a quarterly newsletter, and also materials developed by its seven subcommittees on priority areas: adolescent pregnancy, breast-feeding promotion, genetics, injury prevention, outreach to low-income women, oral health, and substance use. Some of these are distributed through the NATIONAL CENTER FOR EDUCATION IN MATERNAL AND CHILD HEALTH's National Maternal and Child Health Clearinghouse. HMHB also distributes materials produced directly by or in cooperation with some member organizations and state coalitions.

heart and circulatory system, the network through which vital oxygen-carrying BLOOD is carried throughout the body. The system is powered by a fist-shaped pump called the *heart,* made up largely of muscle called *myocardium,* which normally contracts about seventy times a minute throughout a lifetime.

The heart contains four chambers, with a vertical wall called the *septum* dividing it into two sides, each with an upper chamber (*atrium*) and a lower one (*ventricle*). The four chambers pump in a timed sequence to move blood. One-way "doors" called *valves,* at each of the entrances and exits to the chambers, prevent blood from flowing backward; if any of these valves open and close improperly, they make slightly abnormal sounds known as *heart murmurs,* which can be heard through a stethoscope.

Blood picks up oxygen from the lungs and pours through *pulmonary veins* into the heart's left atrium and then, when the valve opens, into the left ventricle. From there the blood—bright red from the *hemoglobin* that actually carries the oxygen—flows into the body's main artery, the *aorta,* and then through a network of smaller arteries, carrying fresh oxygen throughout the body. In the process, the blood picks up the waste product carbon dioxide, which makes the blood darker, and then flows through a parallel network of veins. Finally the blood gathers into the body's two main veins, the *vena cava,* which pour it into the right atrium of the heart. When the valve opens, the blood is pumped into the right ventricle and through the pulmonary artery into the lungs to receive fresh oxygen, beginning the process over again. The arteries that nourish the heart tissue itself are the *coronary arteries.*

Blood pressure is the force that blood exerts on the walls of the heart and the blood vessels—arteries and veins—as it circulates in the body; this is measured by two readings, one at the highest pressure, following a heart contraction, and one between contractions. The *pulse* is the push of blood at each contraction of the heart. On its return route, blood moves under lower pressure; normally valves in the veins prevent backflow; if these fail, a condition called *varicose veins* results. The blood vessels near the SKIN expand and contract to help regulate the body's temperature, though the system may malfunction in RAYNAUD'S DISEASE.

During PREGNANCY, the FETUS gets oxygen not from its own lungs, which are still developing, but from the MOTHER, whose heart enlarges and increases its pumping power by as much as 40 percent to provide blood for the developing being as well as for herself. This increased blood pressure also tends to increase body heat, so many women are far warmer during pregnancy than normally.

The fetus's still-developing heart also works differently to pump blood throughout the body. Blood from the mother goes through the placenta and umbilical cord to the fetus's liver and then into the lower (*inferior*) vena cava and right atrium; then it is pumped through a hole in the septum, called the *foramen ovale*, which normally closes at birth, though sometimes shortly after. After circulating in the upper part of the fetus's body, the blood flows back into the right atrium, through the upper (*superior*) vena cava, and then into the right ventricle, where it is pumped through the pulmonary artery and into the *ductus arteriosus,* a connecting tube found only in the fetus, and then into the lower part of the body, before exiting with its waste products through the umbilical cord and back to the placenta. Pregnant women are advised not to sleep or EXERCISE lying on their backs, since the weight of the developing fetus can press on the vena cava and cut off blood flow—and fresh oxygen. During CHILDBIRTH, maintenance of oxygen flow is also of vital importance. If fetal monitoring indicates that the oxygen flow to the fetus is compromised, doctors may perform an emergency delivery, such as a CESAREAN SECTION.

The heart is subject to a variety of disorders, including many BIRTH DEFECTS, some of which are repaired by the body itself after birth, and infections of various kinds. Most of these do not affect one sex more than another. However, later in life, heart disease shows up very differently in men and women. This has begun to be understood only in the last few decades, as the medical community has been pressed to provide more equitable medical research and testing (see HEALTH EQUITY).

The major concern for adults of middle years and older is a variety of disorders that impair the flow of blood through the arterial system. In *arteriosclerosis,* the artery walls thicken and lose their elasticity, producing what is commonly called *hardening of the arteries.* This may stem from or sometimes cause another problem, *hypertension* or high blood pressure (see below). The other main problem is *atherosclerosis,* in which arteries become clogged with fatty deposits and increase blood clotting as well. The resulting condition goes by various names, including *arteriosclerotic, ischemic* or *coronary heart disease.*

As the twin processes of arteriosclerosis and atherosclerosis continue, the blood flow is gradually constricted. If a major artery becomes blocked, the result can be serious and possibly fatal. If the coronary arteries supplying the heart are involved in the blockage, it is called a *heart attack, myocardial infarction, coronary occlusion,* or *coronary thrombosis.* It is lack of blood that causes the chest and arm pain so characteristic of a heart attack. The main concern then is to get prompt treatment, to minimize damage to the heart muscle.

If artery blockage interrupts blood supply to the brain—from a blood clot (*cerebral thrombosis*) or other foreign matter, including an air bubble (*cerebral embolism*)—or if the walls of blood vessels weaken and leak blood into the brain (*cerebral hemorrhage*), the result is a *stroke* or *cerebrovascular accident* (CVA), what was traditionally called *apoplexy.* Strokes are a leading cause of death in developed countries, killing one out of three people, though women less often than men. For the survivors, the damage depends on what part of the brain was deprived of oxygen and for how long. Sometimes the damage will be minimal, affecting speech or facial muscles, for example, but in some cases an arm, leg, or half the body may be paralyzed, and sometimes the victim may go into a coma. Again, prompt treatment and physical therapy are important to the patient's ability to recover some, if not all, use of the affected areas.

Arteriosclerosis is part of the aging process, though it can be slowed by proper NUTRITION and healthful exercise; but atherosclerosis is much more in human control. For a time in the mid–twentieth century it was the main cause of death in America. Since the mid–1960s the mortality rates have declined, though heart disease is still the leading cause of death in women over sixty-six. The decline is due partly to changes in life-style—quitting SMOKING; reducing OBESITY; cutting down on fat, cholesterol, and salt; lowering blood pressure; controlling DIABETES; and so on. However, some researchers feel that other factors, as yet unknown, have contributed to the decline.

Whatever the specific causes, they affect men and women differently. Citing recent studies of heart attacks in women, the director of the National Heart, Lung, and Blood Institute in 1991 noted several important differences in the way coronary heart disease develops and progresses in women:

- Women tend to show signs of coronary heart disease a decade later than men and to experience a heart attack two decades later, on the average.
- Women often learn that they have heart disease when they feel chest pains called *angina,* but in men the first sign is often a heart attack.
- In women, the first heart attack is more often fatal, and their death rate is higher in the first year after the attack.
- Women are more likely to experience painless heart attacks.
- Clot-dissolving drugs, which are injected into the body in the first few hours after a heart attack, work equally well in men and women. However, more women have bleeding as a complication of the treatment.
- Women have strokes from bleeding into the brain more often than men do. This is a crucial point, since many women take aspirin—which accelerates bleeding—because male-based studies have shown that aspirin reduced the incidence of a first heart attack, though it was unclear whether more strokes resulted. Studies of the effects of aspirin are being carried out on women.

Other research has indicated that cigarette smoking sharply increases a woman's risk of heart attack. Women who take BIRTH CONTROL PILLS after age thirty-five, and those who are overweight (see OBESITY) also have a greater risk of heart disease; so do women who have high levels of the fatty substance *triglycerides,* even if their cholesterol levels are low. Women also seem to fare less well than men after some kinds of heart surgery, such as bypass surgery, which constructs an artificial detour around a blockage.

Some researchers have believed that the later onset of heart disease in women was related to the ESTROGEN produced in the body in large amounts before MENOPAUSE. But since estrogen supplements given to men have shown no such protection, the question seems much more complicated.

Other circulatory problems involve blood pressure. People may have different blood pressure at different times, depending on their level of activity, the time of day, or the action of medications, for example. Too little blood pressure, or *hypotension,* can cause dizziness or fainting, from reduced blood flow to the brain; this can result from a variety of causes, including illness, shock, blood loss, certain drugs, adrenal gland problems, and heart attacks. Too much blood pressure, or *hypertension,* can increase the risk of heart attacks and stroke, as well as kidney damage (see URINARY TRACT) and EYE problems, especially *retinopathy.* A tendency to high blood pressure runs in families but also results from excess salt use, smoking, stress, birth control pills and other drugs, and disorders such as obesity, kidney problems, heart disorders, and adrenal gland problems. Hypertension can also develop during pregnancy and can increase the risk of complications, such as PREECLAMPSIA and eclampsia. Hypertension can be controlled by life-style changes supplemented with drugs. (See HEART AND CIRCULATORY SYSTEM HELP, INFORMATION, AND ACTION GUIDE, below.)

HEART AND CIRCULATORY SYSTEM

Help, Information, and Action Guide

Organizations

▶ NATIONAL HEART, LUNG, AND BLOOD INSTITUTE (301-496-4236). Publishes *Exercise and Your Heart, A Handbook of Heart Terms, Heart Attacks: Medicine for the Layman,* and such fact sheets as *Arteriosclerosis, Diabetes and Cardiovascular Disease,* and *Venous Thrombosis and Pulmonary Embolism.*

▶ NATIONAL INSTITUTE OF NEUROLOGICAL DISORDERS AND STROKE (NINDS) (301-496-5751).

▶ **American Heart Association (AHA)** (7320 Greenville Avenue, Dallas, TX 75231; 214-750-5300 or 800-AHA-USA1 [242-8721] [see telephone directory White Pages for local number]; Edward S. Cooper, president), an organization focusing on heart disease. It provides information; encourages formation of mutual-support groups; offers services to heart patients and their families; and publishes many print and audiovisual materials, including *E is for Exercise* and *High Blood Pressure.*

▶ NATIONAL WOMEN'S HEALTH NETWORK (NWHN) (202-347-1140). Operates the **Women's Health Information Service.** Publishes the information packet *Heart Disease.*

Other resources

■ **ON PREVENTION**

Beating the Odds Against Heart Disease and High Cholesterol: Reducing Your Hereditary Risk. C. Richard Conti and Diana Tonnessen. Addison-Wesley, 1992.

Lower Your Blood Pressure and Live Longer. Marvin Moser. Berkley, 1992.

Preventing Silent Heart Disease: How to Protect Yourself from America's No. 1 Killer. Harold L. Karpman. Holt, 1991.

Take Heart: Cut Your Inherited Risks of Heart Disease. Edward D. Frohlich and Genell J. Subak-Sharpe. Crown, 1990.

The Love-Your-Heart Guide for the 1990s: The Most Up-to-Date Information for Complete Heart Health. Lee Belshin. Contemporary, 1990.

The Swiss Nature Doctor's Guide to a Healthier Heart and Circulatory System. A. Vogel. Keats, 1990.

A Stronger Pump. Julia A. Purcell and others. Pritchett and Hull, 1990.

■ **ON TREATMENT**

The Heart Surgery Trap: Why Most Invasive Procedures Are Unnecessary and How to Avoid Them. Julian Whitaker. Poseidon Press, 1992.

Heart Illness and Intimacy: How Caring Relationships Aid Recovery. Wayne M. Sotile. Johns Hopkins, 1992.

Eight Steps to a Healthy Heart: The Complete Guide to Recovering from Heart Attack, Bypass Surgery, and Heart Disease. Robert E. Kowalski. Warner, 1992.

Dr. Dean Ornish's Program for Reversing Heart Disease Without Drugs or Surgery. Dean Ornish. Ballantine, 1992.

Heart Attack: What's Ahead? rev. ed. Julia A. Purcell and others. Pritchett and Hull, 1991.

Going for Heart Surgery: What You Need to Know. Carole A. Gassert. Pritchett and Hull, 1990.

Heart Disease: Thorsons New Self-Help Series. Leonard Mervyn. Thorsons SF, 1990.

Living with Heart Disease. Steve Parker. Watts, 1989.

■ **BACKGROUND WORKS**

Heart Talk: Understanding Cardiovascular Diseases. Mark V. Barrow. Cor-Ed Publications, 1992.

Heart to Heart: Understanding the Emotional Aspects of Heart Disease. Herbert N. Budnick. Health Press, 1991.

Understanding Heart Disease. Arthur Selzer. University of California Press, 1991.

A Parent's Guide to Heart Disorders. James H. Moller and others. University of Minnesota Press, 1988.

(See also WOMEN'S HEALTH HELP, INFORMATION, AND ACTION GUIDE on page 334.)

hemorrhoids, swollen veins in the rectum (see DIGESTIVE SYSTEM).

Herland: See Charlotte Perkins GILMAN.

hermaphrodite, a person who has the physical attributes of both male and female (see SEXUAL IDENTITY).

herpes, infection with either of two types of *herpes simplex virus* (HSV); often transmitted through sexual contact and so considered one of the SEXUALLY TRANSMITTED DISEASES (STDs). HSV type 1 causes oral herpes, which is commonly known as cold sores or "fever blisters"; but both types 1 and 2 can cause genital herpes. This involves sores in and around the VAGINA, VULVA, PENIS, anus (see DIGESTIVE SYSTEM), buttocks, or thighs, as well as other parts of the body that have been directly in contact with the virus, including the CERVIX and (mostly in men) the urinary passage (see URINARY TRACT).

These sores are visible to the naked eye but can sometimes be mistaken for symptoms of other STDs, notably the *hard chancre* of SYPHILIS or the *soft chancre* of CHANCROID, so various laboratory tests are used to make a firm diagnosis of herpes. Like many viral diseases, herpes has active and inactive states; it is generally transmitted only when the disease is in an active state, though it can be spread by someone with no noticeable symptoms. However, the NATIONAL INSTITUTE OF ALLERGY AND INFECTIOUS DISEASES (NIAID) says: "It is unlikely that the virus can be spread by contact with an object such as a toilet seat."

The first symptoms of herpes usually appear two to ten days from exposure to the virus, and this *primary episode* lasts an average of two to three weeks. The person at first may have a burning sensation; pain in the legs, buttocks, or GENITALS; a vaginal discharge; or a feeling of pressure in the abdominal region. Sores, also called *lesions*, appear within a few days, at first as small red bumps, later as blisters or painful open sores, which over some days become crusted and then heal over, without scarring. Other symptoms common during this primary episode are fever, headache, muscle aches, painful or difficult urination, and swollen glands.

After the initial infection, the virus settles in the sensory nerves at the base of the SPINE and becomes inactive. The virus reactivates from time to time, sometimes once or twice during a lifetime but in some people several times a year, for unknown reasons, though some feel reactivation is linked with MENSTRUATION, stress, or other illnesses. During these *recurrent episodes,* the virus returns to the SKIN surface at or near the original infection site, sometimes causing new sores but sometimes without visible symptoms. Symptoms are milder and last about a week. Early warning of a herpes reactivation are *prodromal symptoms* such as tingling sensation in the genitals or pain in the buttocks or running down the legs.

To speed healing and avoid spreading the infections to other people—or to other parts of the body—people with an active herpes episode should

- keep the infected area clean and dry to prevent the development of secondary infections.
- try to avoid touching the sores directly; if that is unavoidable, wash your hands carefully afterward.
- avoid sexual contact from the first recognized symptoms until the sores are completely healed.

The drug acyclovir has been used to speed healing time and limit severity of the symptoms and sometimes to prevent recurrences. Use of CONDOMS and possibly also SPERMICIDES containing nonoxynol-9 may also lessen the likelihood of spreading the disease. However, no cure exists.

The main hazard of herpes is to babies infected during CHILDBIRTH, on their passage through the birth canal, when their mothers have active herpes. In infected babies the virus can cause blindness, brain damage, and even death. Because the risk of infection is high and the results so serious, where a pregnant woman has herpes, doctors will often recommend weekly testing during the last several weeks of pregnancy—though some tests take seventy-two hours or longer for results to be obtained—and will do a careful examination before DELIVERY for any visible signs of infection. If there is any doubt about whether herpes is active, CESAREAN SECTION is recommended to protect the baby from possible infection. A woman who is herself first infected during PREGNANCY also has a higher-than-normal risk of having a MISCARRIAGE or premature delivery. Herpes can also have severe health consequences in people with impaired or suppressed IMMUNE SYSTEMS, such as those with AIDS. (See SEXUALLY TRANSMITTED DISEASES; also WHAT YOU CAN DO TO AVOID STDs on page 660; SEXUALLY TRANSMITTED DISEASES HELP, INFORMATION, AND ACTION GUIDE on page 658.)

heterosexism, the assumption that heterosexuality, or sex and love between people of the opposite sex, is both natural and superior to homosexuality, or sex and love between people of the same sex. Many LESBIANS regard heterosexism as a systematic working-out of *homophobia*—fear and loathing of same-sex relationships.

heterosexual, a person who receives sexual and emotional fulfillment from a person of the opposite sex. In practice, an unknown but substantial proportion of heterosexuals have had at least some HOMOSEXUAL experiences in their lives and in that sense may be called BISEXUAL. (See SEXUAL INTERCOURSE; MARRIAGE; COHABITATION; LESBIAN.)

Heymann, Lida (1867–1943), a German feminist, active from the 1890s in a wide range of women's organizations. She emerged as a leader of the radical wing of the German women's movement, co-founding the Women's Welfare Association in 1900 and, with her companion, Anita AUGSPURG, the German Union for Women's Suffrage in 1902. Heymann and Augspurg in 1907 became active in the German Women's Suffrage League, which engaged in the kinds of mass demonstrations then under way on behalf of WOMAN SUFFRAGE in Britain and the United States. From its formation in 1904, they were also leaders of the INTERNATIONAL WOMAN SUFFRAGE ALLIANCE. Both were also pacifists who opposed World War I and attended the 1915 International Congress of Women at The Hague (see PACIFISM AND NONVIOLENCE). In 1916 their suffrage league was closed by the German government. Heymann spent the rest of the war in hiding. During the Weimar period, Heymann became vice-president of the WOMEN'S INTERNATIONAL LEAGUE FOR PEACE AND FREEDOM. She and Augspurg fled to exile in Switzerland after the Nazi takeover of their country.

Hidden Face of Eve: Women in the Arab World, The: See Nawal EL SAADAWI.

high-risk pregnancy, a PREGNANCY in which MOTHER or FETUS has known complications, or when some factors in their health or life history or situation make complications or difficulty in DELIVERY more likely (see CHILDBIRTH).

Hill, Anita Faye (1956–), a politically conservative African-American law professor who became the center of the most spectacular SEXUAL HARASSMENT controversy of the century, and who won much for the world's women even while losing the specific battle on which the issue was joined.

A Yale Law School graduate, Hill worked as a lawyer in private practice in Washington, then as personal assistant to Clarence Thomas at the Office for Civil Rights of the U.S. Education Department. She moved to the EQUAL EMPLOYMENT OPPORTUNITY COMMISSION when he did. In 1983 she left government to teach law at Oral Roberts University, moving in 1986 to the University of Oklahoma, where she became a tenured full professor in 1990.

Judge Clarence Thomas was nominated to the Supreme Court by President George Bush on July 1, 1991. On September 27, 1991, the Senate Judiciary Committee members, deadlocked 7–7, sent the nomination to the full Senate for confirmation. They did so without publicly exposing sexual harassment charges leveled at Thomas by Hill during a routine FBI investigation. Just before the Senate vote, on October 7, the news media revealed Hill's multiple and specific charges, which triggered a massive storm of publicity and protest. The Senate postponed its vote, and the committee reopened hearings, which were held and broadcast worldwide from October 11 to 13.

The hearing became a partisan affair, with the committee's Republicans attacking Hill; most bitter were senators Arlen Specter, Orrin Hatch, and Alan Simpson. Specter even publicly accused Hill of perjury, a charge he did not follow up. Hill brought witnesses to prove that she had made these charges against Thomas privately years earlier. Thomas denied all charges and brought character witnesses. The Republicans won the battle; Thomas was confirmed by the Senate on October 15, by a 52–48 vote. Hill, having emerged as an international WOMEN'S RIGHTS celebrity, and with her dignity intact, went home to teach law in Oklahoma.

On the national scene, Anita Faye Hill's example, the issue, and an enormous sense of outrage remained. Some had thought that losing the specific battle would have a chilling effect, and that the blistering attacks on Hill for making her charges would discourage women from pursuing sexual harassment matters. Quite the contrary occurred. In the years that followed, the filing of sexual harassment charges multiplied, as more and more women refused to silently bear harassment any longer. In mid-1992 the U.S. Navy's TAILHOOK SCANDAL became public, opening the issue even further. The Hill-Thomas confrontation also had very direct multiple political impacts and, along with the ABORTION rights issue, brought new vitality and much-increased membership to such militant groups as the NATIONAL ORGANIZATION FOR WOMEN (NOW); spurred formation of others such as the WOMEN'S ACTION COALITION; and helped the nomination and election campaigns of many women then moving into positions of political power. (See also SEXUAL HARASSMENT; also SEXUAL DISCRIMINATION AND SEXUAL HARASSMENT HELP, INFORMATION, AND ACTION GUIDE on page 642.)

History of Woman Suffrage, The, a massive six-volume history of the American WOMAN SUFFRAGE movement published in 1886. It was conceived by Susan B. ANTHONY, Elizabeth Cady STANTON, and Matilda Joslyn GAGE, who wrote and compiled the first three volumes, totaling three thousand pages and covering the movement through 1883. Anthony and Ida Husted Harper edited the fourth volume at the turn of the century, and Harper wrote the final two volumes, taking the story through the winning of woman suffrage in 1920. The first three volumes are widely recognized as a valuable historical resource, the last three as useful but far too concerned with creating an acceptable conservative image of the people and organizations involved, rather than a rounded view of a multifaceted movement whose leaders were some of the most radical women of their day.

Hodgkin's disease, a type of CANCER affecting the lymphatic system (see IMMUNE SYSTEM).

home birth, delivery of a baby at home, generally under the care of a midwife (see CHILDBIRTH).

Home: Its Work and Influence, The: See Charlotte Perkins GILMAN.

homemaker, a woman who stays at home, doing HOUSEWORK and often caring for family members, generally children but sometimes also elderly or disabled adult relatives. In the traditional view of MARRIAGE, homemaking was a woman's role, her status sometimes enshrined in lore and law (see MARRIAGE), while the man was the *provider* who supported the household. For some women the traditional role continues to be right, proper, acceptable, satisfactory, and fulfilling.

For many others, times have changed, and the structure of the family and society as a whole with them. Both the drive for equality and tighter economic circumstances have led many women to work outside the home as well as in it (see WORK AND WOMEN), though often in lower-paying, less-demanding jobs that leave them more time to be with the family and to care for the home, which—despite decades of movement toward sharing of housework by marital partners—continues to be primarily the woman's responsibility. Such women often work a *double shift*, one paid, one unpaid. Women with high-earning jobs are often able to afford help with both housework and in-house CHILD CARE, but for most women it is hard enough—and sometimes impossible—to meet the fees for regular day care.

One serious problem facing homemakers today is that many of them will sooner or later find themselves on their own. In the United States today, approximately one out of every two or three marriages ends in DIVORCE. With changes in ALIMONY, CHILD SUPPORT and CUSTODY, women may find themselves at a distinct disadvantage in some separation-related disputes, often forced out of the family home and obliged to care for themselves and their children with a small fraction of what they formerly had for family support. Many women are countering these trends by using newer approaches to assess the homemaker's contribution to the marriage, in order to get the support they will need. Even if a woman is among the 15 percent of divorced women to be awarded alimony, in today's climate it may be paid only for two to three years, until she is presumed to have had time to train and prepare for the job market; often that holds true even if she is in her mid-fifties and has never before been employed outside the home. Such women are known as DISPLACED HOMEMAKERS. Another large group of displaced homemakers are found among WIDOWS, since women live longer than men and so are likely to outlive their mates, even if they remarry. (See CAREGIVER'S HELP, INFORMATION, AND ACTION GUIDE on page 454; COUPLES AND FAMILIES HELP, INFORMATION, AND ACTION GUIDE on page 418; THE WORLD'S WOMEN on page 822; AMERICAN WOMEN: AT HOME AND IN THE WORK FORCE on page 349.)

AMERICAN WOMEN:
AT HOME AND IN THE WORK FORCE

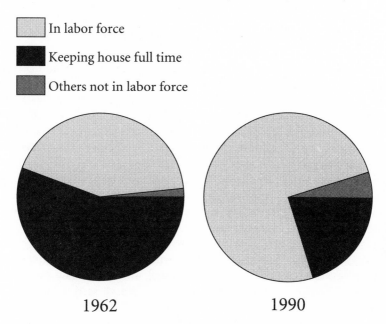

In labor force

Keeping house full time

Others not in labor force

1962   1990

Source: *Working Women: A Chartbook.* U.S. Department of Labor, Bureau of Labor Statistics, Bulletin, 2385, August 1991.

homophobia, an attitude of fear and loathing toward people attracted to others of the same sex (see LESBIAN).

homosexual, a person who receives sexual and emotional fulfillment from a person of the same sex. In practice, many homosexuals have HETEROSEXUAL experiences at various times in their lives and in that sense may be called BISEXUAL. (See LESBIAN.)

hormones, a range of chemicals produced by various organs or tissues in the body to trigger, regulate, or otherwise help control key functions within the body—in effect, to send chemical "messengers" throughout the body. Among the many functions regulated by hormones are metabolism (breakdown and use of substances for energy), growth, the composition of BLOOD, blood pressure (see HEART AND CIRCULATORY SYSTEM), the transmission of information in the BRAIN AND NERVOUS SYSTEM, and the development of SECONDARY SEX CHARACTERISTICS at PUBERTY. Among the specifically female functions controlled by hormones are

MENSTRUATION, OVULATION, MENOPAUSE, and numerous changes during PREGNANCY and lactation. In men the functions include the production of SPERM.

Most hormones are produced by *endocrine glands,* which secrete their chemicals directly into the bloodstream for circulation within the body. Among the many endocrine glands are the pituitary, thyroid, parathyroid, and adrenal glands, the pancreas, the hypothalamus, and the pineal body; also the female and male sex glands, the OVARIES and TESTES respectively, together called GONADS. During PREGNANCY, the placenta—the lining of the UTERUS that nourishes the FETUS—also secretes hormones, as part of the endocrine system. A smaller number of glands secrete their hormones through short tubes called *ducts* into the inner surface of an organ or directly to the outer surface of the body. These include the salivary glands in the mouth; the lacrimal glands in the EYES, which release tears; and the sweat glands on the SKIN.

These glands, especially the endocrine system, are strongly interdependent, and imbalances in the amount of hormones produced by one can have a profound impact on the others and on the overall health of the body. Many diseases or disorders result from relatively minute dysfunctions in one or more of the endocrine glands and are therefore treated with hormones. People with DIABETES, for example, may receive injections of the hormone *insulin.* Similarly, women (or men) whose INFERTILITY is caused by hormonal imbalance may be treated with appropriate sex hormones. Some sex hormones are also used to help control the reproductive cycle, such as BIRTH CONTROL PILLS, DEPO-PROVERA, or NORPLANT.

The female sex hormones ESTROGEN and PROGESTERONE, and the male sex hormones, or *androgens,* especially TESTOSTERONE, are produced primarily in the ovaries and testes respectively, but each sex produces small amounts of the hormones linked with the other's sexuality—a process that can sometimes go awry, on its own or because of outside intervention. Among the many protein-based hormones are FOLLICLE-STIMULATING HORMONE (**FSH**), LUTEINIZING HORMONE (**LH**), PROLACTIN, OXYTOCIN, HUMAN CHORIONIC GONADOTROPIN (**hCG**), GONADOTROPIN-RELEASING HORMONE (**GnRH**), insulin, and somatotropin (growth hormone). (See separate entries on specific sex-related hormones; also TESTES; OVARIES; see also WOMEN'S HEALTH HELP, INFORMATION, AND ACTION GUIDE on page 334.)

housewife: See HOUSEWORK; HOMEMAKER; DISPLACED HOMEMAKER; WORK AND WOMEN; also CAREGIVER'S HELP, INFORMATION, AND ACTION GUIDE on page 454.

housework, a general description for a wide range of familiar home tasks, including food supply preparation, CHILD CARE, cleaning, and general maintenance. Throughout the world, women and men alike regard these tasks as women's work—a status even codified in traditional law (see MARRIAGE)—even after a century of attempts to share the work more equally and in spite of some very large communal programs carried out over many years.

Charlotte Perkins GILMAN, in *Women and Economics* (1898), advocated abolishing the idea of women's work and replacing it with fully shared, communal housekeeping and child raising, as a prerequisite for the equality of women.

Taken up by many socialists, huge communal enterprises were later developed throughout the communist world; some still exist, most notably in China, often as adjuncts to large-scale farming and factories. Smaller experiments were undertaken elsewhere.

Even as women moved into the world's workplaces, old ideas about housework, especially child care, survived, essentially unchanged, although at least a century full of WOMEN'S RIGHTS crusaders have held the view that housework as woman's work perpetuates women's oppression.

One recent feminist approach to the matter has been to campaign for recognition that housework and other unpaid work performed by women has a palpable, measurable economic weight, a set of values that can be tallied in the world's system of accounts. Another has been to provide enhanced social services to reduce that unpaid work, at home and on the job. Yet another has been the development of flex-time at work, allowing men and women to choose their own working hours so they can divide unpaid work more equally. All of these proposals were included in the United Nations–sponsored 1985 NAIROBI FORWARD-LOOKING STRATEGIES FOR THE ADVANCEMENT OF WOMEN (summarized on page 804). Yet implementation of these principles country by country has been nonexistent or, at best, very, very slow, and the campaign to help transform the lives of masses of the world's women by transforming the treatment of their unpaid labor has barely begun. (See WOMEN'S WORK on page 352.)

The MARITAL CONTRACT has been adopted by some couples, largely in some of the advanced industrial countries. The SPOUSES or other partners living together enter into formal or informal work-sharing agreements. The approach, discussed considerably in feminist circles, has in some instances worked in practice but has not yet found wide acceptance and remains to be proven as a valid approach for large numbers of women and men.

"Wages for housework," the payment of money wages for those doing presently unpaid home-related tasks, has been considerably publicized, but has had very few real effects on women, men, or the question of unpaid labor.

One change that has had some impact, however, is assessing the value of housework in MARITAL PROPERTY. Traditionally, the HOMEMAKER's efforts were regarded legally as a "gift," but women's advocates and organizations have had some success in having the courts consider such work as contributions to the "marital community," and so considered worthy of value, especially in cases of SEPARATION or DIVORCE, in those states where division of marital property is at the discretion of the court (see MARITAL PROPERTY). (See HOMEMAKER; DISPLACED HOMEMAKER; MARITAL PROPERTY; also CAREGIVER'S HELP, INFORMATION, AND ACTION GUIDE on page 454; COUPLES AND FAMILIES HELP, INFORMATION, AND ACTION GUIDE on page 418; THE WORLD'S WOMEN on page 822.)

WOMEN'S WORK

Women in most regions spend as much or more time working than men when unpaid housework is taken into account.

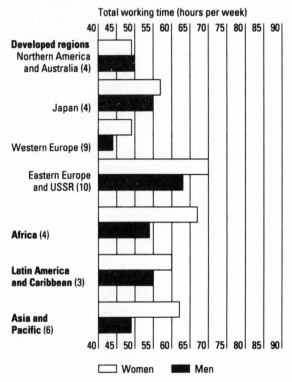

Total working time (hours per week)

Note: Numbers in parentheses refer to the number of studies in each region.

Source: *The World's Women 1970-1990: Trends and Statistics.* United Nations, 1991.

"I hate discussions of feminism that end up with who does the dishes," she said. So do I. But at the end, there are always the damned dishes.

MARILYN FRENCH, 1977
IN THE WOMEN'S ROOM

●

Howe, Julia Ward (1819–1910), author of "The Battle Hymn of the Republic" (1862) and a leading abolitionist before the Civil War, as was her husband, Samuel Gridley Howe. After the war she emerged as a leader of the WOMAN SUFFRAGE movement, co-founding in 1868 the New England Woman Suffrage Association; she was its first president (1868–1877) and served again from 1893 to 1910. In 1869 she helped found the moderate AMERICAN WOMAN SUFFRAGE ASSOCIATION and was a leader of that organization until its merger in 1890 with the more militant NATIONAL WOMAN SUFFRAGE ASSOCIATION, led by Susan B. ANTHONY and Elizabeth Cady STANTON, when both wings of the the woman suffrage movement united in the NATIONAL AMERICAN WOMAN SUFFRAGE ASSOCIATION. From 1871, Howe was also president of the American affiliate of the Women's International Peace Association. Howe's work included poetry, essays, travel books, and a popular biography of Margaret FULLER.

human chorionic gonadotropin (hCG), a group of HORMONES produced from early in PREGNANCY by the PLACENTA, the tissue in the UTERUS that nourishes a FETUS. Most kinds of pregnancy tests look for high levels of hCG in urine as a standard sign of pregnancy. Though its actions are not understood thoroughly, hCG apparently stimulates the OVARIES, including the CORPUS LUTEUM, to produce ESTROGEN and PROGESTERONE, both needed for a healthy pregnancy. It is also suspected of triggering gestational DIABETES in some women.

Sometimes hCG is given by injection as a treatment for INFERTILITY, to stimulate OVULATION in women and SPERM production in men; and, in some cases of impaired function of the pituitary gland, to stimulate development of SECONDARY SEX CHARACTERISTICS that normally develop at PUBERTY. For unknown reasons, some tumors have also been found to secrete high levels of hCG.

Human Life International (HLI) (7845 East Airpark Road, Gaithersburg, MD 20879; 301-670-7884; Paul Marx, president), an organization that opposes artificial intervention into the reproductive and life processes, including ABORTION and euthanasia, encouraging natural family planning (NFP). It maintains a library and publishes *Death Without Dignity* and various publications on NFP.

Human Rights Campaign Fund (1012 14th Street, NW, Suite 607, Washington, DC 20005; 202-628-4160 or 800-777-HRCF [4723]), an organization seeking full civil rights for gays and lesbians and responsible federal policies for combating AIDS. It lobbies and supports members of Congress who support these aims and publishes various materials, including the periodical *Momentum* and *Capitol Hill Update*.

Human Sexual Response (1966), the trailblazing book by sex researchers and therapists William H. Masters and Virginia Johnson, which exploded some of the myths surrounding sexual acts and roles. In particular, it pointed out that women, far from being passive and often unable to enjoy sex, are capable of quite "normally" experiencing multiple orgasms; that sexual life does not necessarily diminish and disappear with advancing age; and that sexual response is not dependent upon such male-centered matters as PENIS size and the then-standard missionary position for sexual intercourse (male above and dominant). Among other works by Masters and Johnson are *Human Sexual Inadequacy* (1966) and *The Pleasure Bond: A New Look at Sexuality and Commitment* (1974). (See SEXUAL INTERCOURSE; SEXUAL RESPONSE.)

husband, the male partner in a traditional MARRIAGE.

husband-coached childbirth, an alternative name for the Bradley method (see CHILDBIRTH).

hymen, a thin membrane that almost completely covers the external opening of the VAGINA. Normally it has a small opening in the center, through which menstrual blood will be released after PUBERTY. On rare occasions the hymen will have no opening, so blood cannot be released; this condition, called *imperforate hymen*, is sometimes the cause when a girl seems not to have begun MENSTRUATION at a normal time. The hymen is stretched or torn the first time the vagina is penetrated, as with SEXUAL INTERCOURSE, use of tampons during menstruation, or a GYNECOLOGICAL EXAMINATION, though it can also be torn by physical activity. At this tearing, small amounts of blood are generally released; in societies that value chastity, these are taken as a sign of VIRGINITY, and the breaking of the hymen is celebrated as a defloration or deflowering of the woman.

hypermenorrhea, menstrual periods with excessively heavy flow (see MENSTRUATION).

hypomenorrhea, menstrual periods with very little flow (see MENSTRUATION).

hysterectomy, the surgical removal of a woman's UTERUS. One of the most commonly performed operations in the United States, it is a source of considerable controversy in the medical community and among women themselves, because of disagreements about when hysterectomy is advisable or necessary and about its long-term effects.

The surgical procedures involved are relatively simple. In an *abdominal hysterectomy*, a horizontal incision is made in the lower abdomen (much as in a CESAREAN SECTION); the blood vessels leading to and from the uterus are cut and tied, as are the FALLOPIAN TUBES leading from the OVARIES, then the uterus (including the CERVIX, the "neck" extending into the VAGINA) is lifted out and the incision stitched up. This procedure is sometimes termed a *simple hysterectomy*, or when done at the same time as a cesarean, a *cesarean hysterectomy*. Often the fallopian tubes and ovaries are removed at the same time, in a *salpingectomy* and *oophorectomy*, the whole procedure then being medically termed a *hysterosalpingo-oophorectomy*, or more generally a *total* or *complete hysterectomy*. When the pelvic lymph nodes are also removed, as in advanced stages of cancer, it is called a *radical hysterectomy*.

In an alternative procedure, the *vaginal hysterectomy*, the incision is made in the vagina, through which the uterus is removed, and the vaginal incision then repaired by stitching. This approach has the advantage of leaving no external scars but cannot be used when the ovaries and fallopian tubes must be removed.

Despite the simplicity of the procedures, a hysterectomy is a major operation, requiring general or spinal anesthesia. The death rate from hysterectomy is approximately one to two per one thousand patients, and perhaps half can have postoperative complications, including adverse reaction to ANESTHESIA, hemorrhaging or life-threatening blood clots (see BLOOD), infection in the abdomen or URINARY TRACT, adhesions (scar tissue binding together normally separate internal surfaces), and damage to blood vessels in the urinary, intestinal, or pelvic area. The recovery also takes time, perhaps a week in the hospital (during which time a drainage tube may be inserted in the incision), a month or more at home, and several months or even a year before full strenuous work can be resumed.

Other effects are longer-term and vary widely from person to person. After surgery a woman has no more MENSTRUATION and no more ability to bear a child; for some that is highly desirable, for others a trigger for DEPRESSION, especially where a woman wants to retain her childbearing capability. Muscular contractions of the uterus are part of ORGASM, so their loss may change the quality of a woman's physical SEXUAL RESPONSE. For some women, loss of the uterus is "female castration"; for others the loss is outweighed by freedom from concern about possible PREGNANCY, from the cyclical side effects of menstruation, and from the condition that led to the hysterectomy.

Loss of the uterus also means loss of the hormones produced there, inducing instantaneous MENOPAUSE. Hormone replacement therapy is often used to maintain the benefits of these hormones, which (apart from their role in menstruation and the REPRODUCTIVE CYCLE) help keep the cardiovascular system healthy, regulate blood pressure, and keep bones strong, forestalling OSTEOPOROSIS (see ESTROGEN REPLACEMENT THERAPY). The desirability of natural hormone production is a key reason to have a hysterectomy only when absolutely necessary, and even then to have the most limited form, leaving in the ovaries where possible, for example. However, some surgeons feel that a woman at or past menopause undergoing abdominal hysterectomy anyway should have her ovaries removed also, since (over forty) she has a 1 percent chance of developing ovarian cancer, which is hard to detect and treat.

Other effects of hysterectomy are less clear-cut. In decades past, some studies and "old wives' tales" suggested that after a hysterectomy many women experienced depression, other MENTAL DISORDERS, headaches, dizziness, insomnia, and fatigue. Those views have been modified by some more recent studies finding that most women who had hysterectomies were pleased that they had done so. In one, a majority said they had "less inconvenience, more energy, better sex life, [and] less pain," while those who were depressed afterward were generally those depressed before.

Whether or not to have a hysterectomy—and if so, what kind—are major questions many women face at some time in their lives. Some 650,000 hysterectomies a year are performed in the United States alone. Among the serious conditions for which doctors often recommend hysterectomy are

- CANCER or precancerous conditions in the uterus, fallopian tubes, or ovaries.
- severe, chronic PELVIC INFLAMMATORY DISEASE (**PID**).
- heavy bleeding from the uterus that does not respond to hormone therapy or a D&C (*dilatation and curettage*).
- large FIBROIDS (benign growths), when they cause pressure or excessive bleeding.
- severe, painful ENDOMETRIOSIS, or growth of uterine tissue in abnormal places.

More controversial are recommendations of hysterectomy for conditions that are not immediately life-threatening or incapacitating, or for which less drastic alternatives exist. Among these are

- fibroids causing no medically worrisome symptoms. Rather than operate, some doctors prefer to closely monitor such fibroids through periodic examinations, especially when the woman is at or near MENOPAUSE, after which fibroids tend to shrink on their own. Even when an operation is indicated, some recommend a MYOMECTOMY, which involves removing only the fibroids themselves, not the whole uterus, though some procedures have additional hazards. (See MYOMECTOMY for a discussion of alternatives, including *ablation*, or *functional hysterectomy*, involving destruction of only the lining of the uterus.)
- *uterine prolapse*, or the sagging of the uterus into the vagina due to weakening of the pelvic muscles and ligaments. Instead of a hysterectomy, many doctors recommend Kegel EXERCISES (as done during PREGNANCY; see page 565) to strengthen the pelvic muscles, and sometimes use of a *pessary* (a device something like a DIAPHRAGM) to hold the uterus in place.
- *endometrial hyperplasia*, or excessive growth of the lining of the uterus, the *endometrium* (see UTERUS). Many doctors feel that although hyperplasia needs close follow-up, surgery may be unnecessary, since the hyperplasia sometimes reverses itself.
- *in situ* cervical CANCER, affecting the outermost layer of the cervix only (see UTERINE CANCER). While many doctors prefer hysterectomy in such cases, be-

cause cancer is life-threatening and can spread, some feel that in-situ cervical cancer can be treated effectively by removing only the affected superficial cell layer, by traditional surgery, *laser surgery* (using high-intensity light beams as "knives"), or *cryosurgery* (using extreme cold to freeze and kill the dangerous cells).

- cancer prevention. Most doctors regard the risk of surgery too great to make hysterectomy a recommended choice for cancer prevention, but some feel it is justified in women who face a high risk of developing uterine cancer, such as a woman whose grandmother, mother, and sisters all developed the condition.

- STERILIZATION. Far more dangerous than other methods of female sterilization, such as TUBAL LIGATION, hysterectomy is sometimes chosen as an option by women and doctors attempting to circumvent a religious prohibition against voluntary sterilization or BIRTH CONTROL, as among Roman Catholics.

These and other such "gray areas" are where the main controversy over hysterectomy lies. Feminists, consumer groups, and health care economists have noted that the number of hysterectomies performed varies widely, with studies from the mid-1970s showing that the rate of hysterectomies in the United States was twice as high in the South as in the Northeast; higher if a doctor was paid directly, rather than under a prepaid health plan; and lower when a second medical opinion was sought before surgery. For many observers, such studies suggested that perhaps a third of all hysterectomies in the United States were being performed unnecessarily. Sometimes the woman did not even know before the operation that the uterus might be removed. But other observers pointed out that some women insist on having a hysterectomy, to relieve discomfort, provide 100 percent effective birth control, or quell their fears of cancer, even where there is no compelling medical reason to have the operation.

Since the 1970s, "second opinions" have become more widespread and under some medical plans even mandated. Unlike emergency operations such as appendectomies, most hysterectomies are done on a nonemergency or "elective" basis, so many women can now explore more carefully the pros and cons of the surgery before making a decision. In response to pressure from women's and consumer groups, some states, such as California, have passed a law requiring that women be told of the side effects of a hysterectomy and alternatives to it and must give oral and written consent to the operation. Some medical groups, such as the AMERICAN COLLEGE OF OBSTETRICIANS AND GYNECOLOGISTS, oppose such informed-consent laws, though they encourage more public education on the matter.

The most important point for a woman to consider is the reason for the recommendation of a hysterectomy. Is it a life-threatening condition? Is it a major question of quality of life, involving a personal or social disability? Is it a minor annoyance? The overall decision will involve weighing the reasons for the surgery, its risks, and the woman's individual condition and life-style; the aim is to avoid undergoing unnecessary surgery, but not to forgo surgery that has substantial medical and other benefits.

HYSTERECTOMY

Help, Information, and Action Guide

Organizations

▶ HYSTERECTOMY EDUCATION RESOURCES AND SERVICES (**HERS**) FOUNDATION (422 Bryn Mawr Avenue, Bala Cynwyd, PA 19004; 215-667-7757; Nora Coffey, founder and president), an organization that aims to educate the public, seeking informed decisions about hysterectomies. The HERS Foundation provides referral services for second medical opinions and legal advice and also matches women one to one with others who have had similar experiences. HERS maintains a library and publishes various materials, including a quarterly newsletter, proceedings of the HERS Annual Hysterectomy Conference, reading lists, article reprints, and audiovisual materials.

▶ NATIONAL WOMEN'S HEALTH NETWORK (**NWHN**) (202-347-1140). Operates the WOMEN'S HEALTH INFORMATION SERVICE. Publishes the information packet *Hysterectomy*.

▶ AMERICAN COLLEGE OF OBSTETRICS AND GYNECOLOGY (**ACOG**) (202-638-5577).

▶ INSTITUTE FOR REPRODUCTIVE HEALTH (**IRH**) (213-854-6483). IRH's executive director, Dr. Vicki Georges Hufnagel, has helped analyze government data on rate of hysterectomies.

Other resources

Well-Informed Patient's Guide to Hysterectomy. Kathryn Cox. Dell, 1991.

Women's Health Alert: What Most Doctors Won't Tell You About. Sidney M. Wolfe. Addison-Wesley, 1991.

No Hysterectomy Option: Your Body, Your Choice. Herbert Goldfarb. Wiley, 1990.

No More Hysterectomies. Vickie G. Hufnagel and Susan K. Golant. NAL-Dutton, 1989.

Hysterectomy—Before and After: A Comprehensive Guide to Preventing, Preparing for, and Maximizing Health After Hysterectomy—With Essential Information on Menopause. Winnifred B. Cutler. Harper & Row, 1988.

Hysterectomy: The Positive Recovery Plan. Anne Dickson and Nikki Henriques. Harper & Row, 1987.

How to Avoid Hysterectomy. Lynn Payer. Pantheon, 1987.

The Castrated Woman: What Your Doctor Won't Tell You About Hysterectomy. Naomi M. Stokes. Watts, 1986.

> *Hysterectomy: Learning the Facts, Coping with the Feelings, Facing the Future.* Wanda Wigfall-Williams. Kesend, 1986.
> *Coping with a Hysterectomy.* Suzanne Morgan. NAL-Dutton, 1986; *Coping with a Hysterectomy: Your Own Choice Your Own Solution.* Doubleday, 1981.
> *Hysterectomy and You.* Delthia T. Ricks. Budlong, 1985.
> *Hysterectomy: A Book to Help You Deal with the Physical and Emotional Aspects.* Lorraine Dennerstein and others. Oxford University Press, 1982.
> (See also UTERUS; also WOMEN'S HEALTH HELP, INFORMATION, AND ACTION GUIDE on page 334.)

hysterosalpingography, an X-ray of a woman's reproductive organs (see INFERTILITY).

hysterosalpingo-oophorectomy, a combined operation involving surgical removal of the UTERUS (HYSTERECTOMY), FALLOPIAN TUBES (*salpingectomy*), and OVARIES (OOPHORECTOMY).

hysteroscopy, a surgical procedure that involves passing a long, thin viewing device known as a *hysteroscope* through the VAGINA and CERVIX into the UTERUS, often performed under regional or general ANESTHESIA. It allows direct viewing of the uterus and its lining, the *endometrium,* for both diagnosis and surgery, unlike a D&C (*dilatation and curettage*), which is largely a "blind" operation, since the surgeon is unable actually to see the area being worked on. Various surgical tools may be used with the hysteroscope, including the laser, surgical knife (*curette*), or razorlike tools (see MYOMECTOMY).

Hysteroscopy requires special training and skills and is generally performed by INFERTILITY specialists. It may be used in a wide variety of procedures, including checking for possible causes of infertility, location and removal of an INTRAUTERINE DEVICE (IUD), securing of a sample of tissue for a biopsy (as in checking for UTERINE CANCER), removing cervical polyps, performing a TUBAL LIGATION with a cauterizing instrument, or removing FIBROIDS or adhesions in the uterus. It is not, however, to be used during PREGNANCY, in cases of active or chronic infection or acute PELVIC INFLAMMATORY DISEASE, or where CANCER of the cervix is suspected or known. (See WOMEN'S HEALTH HELP, INFORMATION, AND ACTION GUIDE on page 334.)

I

immune system, a complex internal network that defends the body from attack by invaders such as bacteria, viruses, fungi, and parasites. At the heart of the immune system is a network of vessels called the *lymphatic system*, which carries a milky fluid called *lymph* through various filtering mechanisms, such as the *lymph nodes* in the groin and underarm areas, and organs such as the spleen (on the lower left side of the chest), tonsils, and adenoids. The foreign substances are trapped and neutralized or destroyed; during an infection, "swollen glands" may result, when large amounts of foreign matter are trapped. Though the body can function without these filtering organs, if necessary, they are an important part of the body's defenses. A ruptured spleen is a life-threatening emergency, a particular concern for BATTERED WOMEN, who, in the emergency situation of physical abuse, should try to protect the chest and abdominal areas from blows, as much as they can.

The immune system operates by distinguishing between "self" and "not-self." The body's own cells normally carry markers that identify them as part of the self; anything without such a marker is regarded as not-self and attacked. Any substance that triggers such an attack response is called an *antigen* (see ALLERGIES; BLOOD). To counter such foreign substances, lymph fluid contains specialized cells called *lymphocytes;* the two main kinds are called B cells and T cells, both originally formed in bone marrow (see SKELETAL SYSTEM).

B cells trigger creation of substances called *antibodies,* which target and destroy antigens. If a person has been exposed to a disease or been vaccinated against it, the body will contain antibodies to that disease, and the person is said to be *immune* to it. Babies receive temporary natural immunity from their MOTHERS, which is enhanced during BREASTFEEDING—a benefit withheld from children fed on formula. Antibodies are a kind of immune system molecule called *immunoglobulins;* sometimes such substances are injected directly into the body to provide temporary immunity, as when a pregnant woman has been exposed to rubella (German measles). ALLERGIES and asthma (see RESPIRATORY SYSTEM) are triggered primarily by *immunoglobulin E* (IgE).

T cells protect the body by directly attacking cells that have been taken over by foreign organisms, such as viruses, or have become somehow abnormal, as in CANCER. Different kinds include *suppressor cells,* which turn off, or suppress, abnormal cells; others may trigger growth of beneficial cells, destroy abnormal cells, or enhance the action of other cell destroyers. It is T cells that cause bodies to reject organ transplants; to counter their action, patients may be given *immunosuppressive drugs.*

If the immune system fails to function properly, a person is said to have *immunodeficiency*. Some children are born with defective immune systems, making them highly susceptible to infections; this is called an *inherited immunodeficiency*. It can sometimes be treated by injections of immunoglobulin, transplants of thymus gland tissue that contains T cells, or bone marrow transplants (see CANCER).

Immunodeficiency can also appear during a lifetime, as an *acquired immunodeficiency*. It can occur on a temporary or partial basis with some viral infections, such as measles, mononucleosis, or flu; with some anticancer therapies, such as radiation or chemotherapy; or in some other situations, such as severe malnutrition, stress, or surgery. It can also occur in a (so far) more permanent way in the disease called AIDS, or *acquired immune deficiency syndrome*, in which a virus destroys helper T cells and is harbored by other immune cells; as a result, the body is left defenseless against infections and cancers. Another long-term and possibly permanent immune disorder of as-yet-unknown origin seems to be CHRONIC FATIGUE IMMUNE DYSFUNCTION SYNDROME (CFIDS).

Sometimes the immune system itself is affected by cancer, such as *leukemia*, abnormal proliferation of the white blood cells (see BLOOD); *multiple myeloma*, abnormal growth of the cells that produce antibodies; or *lymphoma*, cancer of the lymph organs, including Hodgkin's disease.

The immune system can also malfunction and mistakenly attack part of the body itself, as if it were a foreign invader. The result is an *autoimmune disorder*, such as rheumatoid ARTHRITIS, Type I DIABETES, pernicious anemia (see BLOOD), or LUPUS. Allergies result when the body responds in an excessive and harmful way to antigens, in this case sometimes called *allergens*.

For more help, information, and action

▶ **Immune Deficiency Foundation (IDF)** (Courthouse Square, 3565 Ellicott Mills Drive, Unit B2, Ellicott City, MD 21043; 410-461-3127; Marcia Boyle, president), an organization concerned with immune deficiency diseases. It gathers and disseminates information; supports research; makes referrals; and publishes various materials, including the annual *IDF Newsletter, Immune Deficiency Diseases: An Overview, Patient and Family Handbook, List of Suggested Readings in Immunology,* and various audiovisuals.

▶ NATIONAL INSTITUTE OF ALLERGY AND INFECTIOUS DISEASES (NIAID) (301-496-5717). Publishes *Understanding the Immune System.*

▶ NATIONAL WOMEN'S HEALTH NETWORK (NWHN) (202-347-1140). Operates the **Women's Health Information Service.** Publishes the information packet *Autoimmune Disorders* and *Chronic Fatigue Immune Deficiency Syndrome.*

Other resources

Defending the Body: Unraveling the Mysteries of Immunology. Joel Davis. Atheneum, 1990.
The Immune System. Edward Edelson. Chelsea House, 1990.

The Body at War: The Miracle of the Immune System. John M. Dwyer. NAL, 1989.
Immunity and Survival: Keys to Immune System Health. Sylvia S. Greenberg. Plenum, 1989.
Your Immune System, rev. ed. Alan E. Nourse. Watts, 1989.
(See also specific disorders noted in article.)

implantation, the attachment of a fertilized egg—at that point often called an EMBRYO—in the lining of a woman's UTERUS early in PREGNANCY after traveling from the point of FERTILIZATION in the FALLOPIAN TUBES. If implantation takes place not in the uterus, but in the fallopian tubes or elsewhere in the pelvic area, the result can be a potentially life-threatening ECTOPIC PREGNANCY, generally requiring emergency surgery. (See PREGNANCY.)

incest, in law, SEXUAL INTERCOURSE or MARRIAGE between a man and a woman who are such close relatives that they cannot legally marry; more generally, societal prohibition of sexually oriented activity of any kind, including genital touching, genital exhibition, and verbal propositioning, between close relatives.

Prohibition against incest is virtually universal in human cultures. The precise relations prohibited vary, though almost all include the closest blood relations. In the United States, for example, state incest laws generally bar a person from incestuous relations with parents, children, brothers and sisters, half-brothers and half-sisters (with one parent in common), uncles and aunts, nieces and nephews, grandparents, great-grandparents, grandchildren, and great-grandchildren. Some states may also bar relationships with first cousins, stepchildren, stepparents, parents-in-law, children-in-law, brothers-in-law, sisters-in-law, or a spouse's grandchildren or grandparents. Prohibitions based on marital connections, called *affinity,* rather than blood relations, often end with DIVORCE or the death of the person connecting the two. For example, sexual relations or marriage between a husband and his late wife's daughter by another husband might no longer be considered incest after her death.

Incest is a criminal offense and may be punished by a prison sentence. Incest laws are relatively narrow, applying where sexual relations or marriage have occurred. Where incest involves a child under the AGE OF CONSENT, generally age sixteen or eighteen, child sexual abuse laws may be applied (see CHILD ABUSE AND NEGLECT); these are broader and include genital touching. If the incest takes place without the consent of one party—usually, but not always, the woman—it may be charged as RAPE; if the woman is underage, statutory rape may be charged, regardless of whether or not she gave her consent or had had sexual relations with other men previously.

Because incest is generally kept silent, it is unclear how common it is; certainly the overwhelming amount of child sexual abuse takes place in the home and frequently involves incest. Of females abused incestuously, the American Psychological Association estimates that approximately 25 percent involves fathers with their daughters; 25 percent involves stepfathers and their stepdaughters; and the remaining 50 percent involves adoptive fathers, grandfathers, brothers, half-brothers, uncles, and cousins of the young girls. Many people see such incest as an outgrowth of PATRIARCHY and the related view that women and children are property of the family's male members.

Many women acknowledge past incest only when they are adults, sometimes after years of repression; and many today are helped by open acknowledgment and support from other victims of incest. Though women are victimized by males primarily, in a small proportion of cases—which some researchers estimate as under 5 percent—the woman is the incestuous abuser. Many organizations and publications are now available to incest victims. Because they are so often linked to child abuse, readers seeking aid should see Child Abuse and Neglect Help, Information, and Action Guide on page 152. (See also child abuse and neglect.)

incompetent cervix, a condition in which a woman's cervix is formed so as to be unable to enable her to hold a child in the uterus for the full term.

incontinency: See urinary tract.

infanticide, the deliberate killing of a baby, a term sometimes extended by pro-life activists to refer to abortion, which would more properly be called *feticide*. History, archaeology, and anthropology all indicate that the practice of infanticide has been widespread among people around the world from the earliest times. Often, babies unwanted for any reason were left out in the open, a practice called *exposure;* there they would die, unless adopted by someone else. But in many cultures, unwanted infants would be killed outright, acts that were variously rationalized among different peoples, often with the notion that the infant is not fully human for some period of time after its birth—in some cultures a few hours or a few days, but sometimes as long as three years. Most societies today have set aside such notions.

The reasons for infanticide seem to have varied remarkably little over the centuries. They include birth defects in babies; disputed parentage, where the father (or partner of the mother) does not accept the child as his; situations where the mother or family is too ill, weak, poor, busy with other work, or burdened with other children to care for the child; where the mother is unable or unwilling to face social criticism for an out-of-wedlock child; and where the child is female—in many societies sufficient cause in itself for infanticide (see son preference).

Generally it is the mother who commits infanticide and faces possible criminal prosecution. But where an infant will overburden a mother, family, or community, infanticide has sometimes been mandated and carried out by the society itself, not only in cases of birth defects, but also when a mother has died in childbirth, when a child is born too soon after a previous child, in multiple births (one, both, or all sometimes being killed), or where a child is born too late in a season to survive a regular migration.

Though not officially acknowledged or condoned, the practice of infanticide still continues in some parts of the world. In south and east Asia, notably, female infants are exposed or killed in large enough numbers to create a marked disparity in the proportion of males and females in society. In China, some of that disparity, but only part, is accounted for by female infants being unregistered and shunted into a shadow life of PROSTITUTION. In many areas, especially where nutritional, economic, and other social resources are limited, infanticide continues under the guise of intentional neglect, "underinvestment" (see SON PREFERENCE), or engineered accidents, in which a child is left in a dangerous situation.

In developed countries, a tacit kind of infanticide took place until recently in neonatal hospitals. Infants with severe deformities, disabilities, or disorders were often left to die through minimal care or deliberate neglect. That changed substantially only with advances in neonatal medicine, especially since the 1960s. In the United States, medical care—including appropriate nutrition, hydration (fluids), and medication—for such infants was mandated under the 1984 Baby Doe Law, except where the infant was in a chronic, irreversible coma; treatment would be inhumane or futile; or treatment would merely prolong dying, while not improving a life-threatening condition.

With the development of various PRENATAL TESTS, such as AMNIOCENTESIS, CHORIONIC VILLUS SAMPLING (CVS), CORDOCENTESUS, or ULTRASOUND—which often indicate not only birth defects, but also the sex of the fetus—and with the legalization of ABORTION in many countries, the reasons that once led to infanticide now lead to abortion. These also disproportionately affect female fetuses, so that in some countries with strong son preference, the birth rate has been noticeably skewed toward more male births. (See also SEXUAL DISCRIMINATION; ABORTION; and SEXUAL DISCRIMINATION AND SEXUAL HARASSMENT HELP, INFORMATION, AND ACTION GUIDE on page 642.)

infertility, the inability to have a baby, including the inability to conceive and also the inability to carry a child full term to a healthy birth. Absolute, irreversible, and permanent inability to have a child is relatively rare and is generally called *sterility*. Infertility, by contrast, is temporary and reflects a decrease in the odds of conception and is often reversible with treatment; it is actually more properly called *subfertility*. Among *fertility specialists*, also called *sterologists*, infertility is generally defined as the inability to conceive after one to two years of trying, with unprotected sex (that is, with no use of BIRTH CONTROL devices) and without medical help. If the couple have never had a PREGNANCY, the condition is called *primary infertility*; but if they have had a previous pregnancy, it is called *secondary infertility*.

The most common problem is that the couple is not timing SEXUAL INTERCOURSE with OVULATION in a way that will maximize the chances of CONCEPTION. The techniques of NATURAL FAMILY PLANNING can be used successfully by many couples on their own, without necessity for medical intervention. And, in fact, many couples who have been consulting infertility specialists conceive on their own, even before any treatment has been given.

Because of their complicated REPRODUCTIVE SYSTEM, women may experience infertility for a wide variety of reasons. In men, the problems generally involve SPERM production. But in many cases infertility is caused by problems in both partners, and in at least one case out of ten the cause is never fully determined.

Many kinds of problems and conditions are associated with infertility, among them

▶ *poor physical condition* in general, but especially being overweight (see OBE-SITY), severely underweight (see ANOREXIA NERVOSA), or anemic (see BLOOD).

▶ *abuses of the body,* including SMOKING, AND ALCOHOL AND DRUG ABUSE; in men these can lower sperm count.

▶ *hostile conditions in the woman's reproductive system,* including a woman's allergic reaction to her partner's sperm (see ALLERGIES); a too acidic or impenetrable mucus in the VAGINA or CERVIX; or the presence of antibodies (see IM-MUNE SYSTEM) that cause sperm to clump together.

▶ GENETIC DISORDERS, such as TURNER'S SYNDROME, in which a girl has only one X chromosome; Klinefelter's syndrome, in which a boy has one or more extra X chromosomes; and cystic fibrosis in the man.

▶ HORMONE *problems,* especially affecting the pituitary, thyroid, or adrenal glands.

▶ *problems with the* OVARIES, including irregularity of ovulation or failure to produce eggs (see OVUM), a condition called *anovulation* (see ANOVULATORY PE-RIODS). Anovulation is increasingly common later in a woman's childbearing years and accounts for much of the gradual decrease in a woman's fertility.

▶ *problems with the sperm,* such as low sperm count or sperm that are too inactive or have too short a life span. Total lack of sperm, or *azoospermia,* is rare; more common is too few sperm, called *oligospermia.*

▶ *physical malformations,* such as a lacking or deformed UTERUS, lacking FALLO-PIAN TUBES, or undeveloped ovaries in the woman; or undeveloped or unde-scended TESTES in the man. The woman may also have an *incompetent cervix,* which makes her unable to hold a child in the uterus for the full term, even if conception does occur.

▶ *problems getting the sperm into the vagina normally,* including problems holding an erection, called *impotence,* and problems with EJACULATION (see PE-NIS; SEXUAL INTERCOURSE).

▶ *problems with sperm development,* generally because the testes are over-heated, as in cases of *varicocele,* a swollen vein in a testicle, easily treated by surgery; excess use of hot tubs or saunas; work involving exposure to heat; and sometimes simply pants that are too tight, causing testes to be carried too close to the body. Changing any of these conditions, such as wearing looser briefs and pants or temporarily changing work, can solve the problem.

▶ *infections,* especially SEXUALLY TRANSMITTED DISEASES affecting various repro-ductive organs, such as CHLAMYDIA and GONORRHEA. Untreated, these may cause PELVIC INFLAMMATORY DISEASE, with infertility resulting from current in-fections or damage from previous infections, including scar tissue.

▶ *blockage of tubes or ducts* through which the sperm and egg travel to meet for fertilization, sometimes due to infection (see above), injury, or other con-ditions. In women these include ENDOMETRIOSIS, scarring or adhesions in the fallopian tubes, polyps (small benign growths) in the cervix, FIBROIDS, or scars or damage from an INTRAUTERINE DEVICE (IUD) or from gynecological operations, such as previous ABORTION or ECTOPIC PREGNANCY.

▶ *the effects of various other disorders,* current or past, including mumps, measles, rubella (German measles), whooping cough, diphtheria, DIABETES, tuberculosis, and epilepsy.

▶ *medications for other disorders,* including HORMONES, antibiotics, aspirin, ibuprofen, antidepressants, antihypertensive medications, hallucinogens, and alcohol, any of which can in some cases lessen fertility.

In dealing with an infertility problem, the first stop for a couple should be their regular doctor, to determine if the cause is a general health problem unrelated to the reproductive system, such as a tumor in a pituitary gland or a thyroid disorder. The next step would be for the woman to see a gynecologist and the man a urologist, to check their respective reproductive systems, looking for obvious problems such as malformations or unrecognized sexually transmitted diseases. Only after exhausting the possibilities at this level should a couple generally move on to a fertility specialist, in practice usually a team.

At this stage a *fertility workup,* or a battery of tests, is performed. Precisely which tests are given depends on what previous doctors have done and on the particulars of the couple's situation, though the first three tests below are done in most cases.

▶ *semen analysis,* laboratory analysis of the man's semen produced by MASTURBATION usually after two days of sexual abstinence. Technicians note the number of sperm and their shape and "swimming power." In case of a low sperm count, further tests may be ordered to identify the cause.

▶ *postcoital test or Sims-Huhner test,* laboratory analysis of mucus samples from the woman's cervix a few hours after intercourse, to see if sperm are dead or alive, active or sluggish.

▶ *endometrial biopsy,* laboratory analysis of a sample of the *endometrium* (lining of the uterus) late in the reproductive cycle (see MENSTRUATION). The aim is to identify whether ovulation has occurred and whether the endometrium is being properly developed or not, perhaps because of a hormonal imbalance.

▶ *infection or antibody test,* laboratory analysis of semen or cervical mucus for signs of bacteria or antibodies. Sometimes a man will produce antibodies against his own sperm, or a woman will produce antibodies against the man's sperm, in both cases a malfunctioning of the immune system, in which the body mistakenly identifies the sperm as a foreign, potentially disease-causing invader. The presence of antibodies can be confirmed by a blood test called a *Duke's test.* Steroid therapy may be used to suppress the antibodies; or the sperm might be "washed" (see below).

▶ *ovulation tests,* to see if, in fact, ovulation has occurred. If ovulation is the problem, various types of hormonal treatments may be tried to induce it.

▶ *basal body temperature charts,* a daily temperature record, using a specially calibrated thermometer to pinpoint if and when ovulation occurs (see NATURAL FAMILY PLANNING).

▶ *blood tests,* a variety of laboratory analysis to monitor the pattern of hormonal secretions, especially for a woman with irregular or no menstruation. Some such tests are quite special and expensive and are normally used with other tests that have not provided adequate information.

▶ ULTRASOUND *scan,* to detect evidence of ovulation, if possible.

▶ HYSTEROSCOPY, a procedure that allows direct viewing of the uterus, often performed under spinal ANESTHESIA.

▶ LAPAROSCOPY, a minor surgical procedure involving insertion of a device called a *laparoscope* through a small incision in the abdominal wall, allowing doctors to examine directly the reproductive organs for evidence of ovulation, scarring, or blockage of fallopian tubes, and to assess what corrective procedures might be possible.

▶ *hysterosalpingogram,* an X-ray of a woman's reproductive organs, especially the uterus and fallopian tubes, which are highlighted by injection of a special dye pumped in through the vagina and cervix. The aim is to identify abnormalities, blockages, or other structural problems that might be preventing conception. Sometimes the blockage is sufficiently minor that the pumping of the dye into the tubes clears it. This is best performed in the early part of a woman's menstrual cycle, generally on an outpatient basis. Some discomfort is involved, especially from dilatation of the cervix. Some physicians prefer laparoscopy or hysteroscopy, since the hysterosalpingography directs radiation on the ovaries. Others disagree, arguing that the X-ray is less invasive and does not carry the risks of ANESTHESIA.

Many infertility problems found can be corrected by use of so-called *fertility drugs,* which act on the glands that produce key hormones. Because they may cause more than one egg to be produced, these drugs are associated with a significantly increased incidence of multiple births. Surgery is often possible, to correct minor malformations or unblock tubes and ducts, sometimes even to remove part of an ovary containing cysts in order to restart ovulation (see OVARIES).

For many sperm problems, one solution is to "wash" the sperm, separating them out of the semen and then depositing them directly in the uterus, in *intrauterine insemination* (see ARTIFICIAL INSEMINATION), or employing IN VITRO FERTILIZATION, depositing the embryo in the uterus. This is often used where the man, woman, or both have developed antibodies to the sperm or where the semen is so thick that it hinders movement of the sperm.

Various other techniques—all going under the general heading of *reproductive technology*—include EMBRYO TRANSFER, GAMETE INTRAFALLOPIAN TUBE TRANSFER (GIFT), IN VITRO FERTILIZATION (IVF), and SURROGATE PARENTING. These approaches are still relatively new, generally expensive, and have a low success rate, in addition to posing a wide variety of legal, ethical, and social problems. But they will continue to be widely used, as they offer opportunities never before available for infertile couples to have a child of their own.

ADOPTION remains an option for some people who have philosophical, religious, or other objections to reproductive technology, including surrogate parenting, and for others for whom infertility treatments are unsuccessful. Other people accept a childless state. (See INFERTILITY AND REPRODUCTIVE TECHNOLOGY HELP, INFORMATION, AND ACTION GUIDE on page 368.)

INFERTILITY AND REPRODUCTIVE TECHNOLOGY

Help, Information, and Action Guide

- **RESOLVE, Inc.** (617-643-2424). Mutual-support groups for couples dealing with infertility. Publishes a newsletter and fact sheets *Choosing a Specialist, Artificial Insemination, In Vitro Fertilization, Laparoscopy: What to Expect, Medical Evaluation of the Couple, Medical Management of Male Infertility, Semen Analysis, Surgical Techniques for Tubal Repair,* and *Varicocele: Surgical and Medical Treatment.*
- **Center for Surrogate Parenting (CSP)** (8383 Wilshire Boulevard, Suite 750, Beverly Hills, CA 90211; 213-655-1974; William W. Handle, president), an organization that arranges for surrogate parenting, "beginning with the initial consultation and following through to the finalization of the legal status between parents and child." Founded in 1981, it stresses that "psychological screening and counseling are an integral part of the program and mandatory through the postpartum period" and that "both surrogate mothers/egg donors and prospective parents must have medical, legal, criminal, and psychological clearance" to participate in the program. In addition to the traditional surrogate parenting program, CSP also offers in vitro fertilization/embryo implantation and an egg donor program.
- **de Miranda Institute for Infertility and Modern Parenting Issues** (3535 East Coast Highway, Box 95, Corona del Mar, CA 92625; 714-833-9898), an organization concerned with infertility and reproductive technology. It offers pamphlets and news updates on in vitro fertilization and related procedures.
- **NATIONAL INSTITUTE OF CHILD HEALTH AND HUMAN DEVELOPMENT (NICHD)** (301-496-5133).
- **NATIONAL WOMEN'S HEALTH NETWORK (NWHN)** (202-347-1140). Operates the **Women's Health Information Service.** Publishes the information packets *Infertility, New Reproductive Technology,* and *Pelvic Inflammatory Disease (PID).*
- **AMERICAN FERTILITY SOCIETY (AFS)** (205-933-8494). Publishes *Fertility and Sterility Journal* and professional materials such as *How to Organize a Basic Study of the Infertile Couple* and *Report of the Ad Hoc Committee on Artificial Insemination.*
- **INSTITUTE ON WOMEN AND TECHNOLOGY** (413-367-9725).
- **SINGLE MOTHERS BY CHOICE (SMC)** (212-988-0993).
- **Endometriosis Association (EA)** (414-962-8972; toll-free number 800-992-ENDO). (See ENDOMETRIOSIS.)

■ ON SPECIAL LESBIAN CONCERNS

▶ NATIONAL CENTER FOR LESBIAN RIGHTS (NCLR) (415-621-0674). Publishes *Lesbians Choosing Motherhood: Legal Issues in Donor Insemination.*
▶ LESBIAN MOTHERS NATIONAL DEFENSE FUND (LMNDF) (206-325-2643). Provides information on donor insemination.

Other resources

■ GENERAL WORKS

The Fertility Solution: A Revolutionary Approach to Reversing Infertility. A. Toth. Atlantic Monthly, 1992.
The Infertility Book: A Comprehensive Medical and Emotional Guide. Carla Harkness. Celestial Arts, 1992.
Conquering Infertility: A Guide for Couples, rev. ed. Stephen L. Corson. Prentice-Hall, 1991.
A Baby of Your Own: New Ways to Overcome Infertility. William G. Karow. Taylor, 1991.
Missed Conceptions: Overcoming Infertility. Anne Mullens. Shapolsky, 1991.
Overcoming Infertility. Robert Nachtigall. Thorsons (SF), 1991.
What You Can Do About Infertility. Pamela P. Novotny. Dell, 1991.
In Pursuit of Fertility: A Consultation with a Specialist. Robert R. Franklin and Dorothy Kay Brockman. Holt, 1990.
The Couple's Guide to Fertility: How New Medical Advances Can Help You Have a Baby. Gary S. Berger and Mark Fuerst. Doubleday, 1989.
Without Child: Experiencing and Resolving Infertility. Ellen S. Glazer and Susan L. Cooper. Free Press, 1989.
Infertility: A Guide for the Childless Couple, rev. ed. Barbara Eck Manning. Prentice-Hall, 1988.
The Infertility Maze: Finding Your Way to the Right Help and the Right Answers. Kassie Schwan. Contemporary, 1988.
Having Your Baby by Donor Insemination: A Complete Resource Guide. Elizabeth Noble. Houghton Mifflin, 1987.

■ ON REPRODUCTIVE TECHNOLOGY

New Options for Fertility: A Guide to In Vitro Fertilization and Other Assisted Reproduction Methods. Arthur L. Wisot and David R. Meldrum. Pharos, 1990.
How to Choose the Sex of Your Baby, rev. ed. Landrum B. Shettles and David Rorvick. Doubleday, 1989.
The New Fertility and Conception: Today's Essential Guide for Childless Couples. John J. Stangel. New American Library, 1988.

Reproductive Technologies: Gender, Motherhood, and Medicine, by Michelle Stanworth, ed. Minneapolis: University of Minnesota Press, 1988.

■ ON EXPERIENCING INFERTILITY

Never to Be a Mother: A Guide for All Women Who Didn't—or Couldn't— Have Children. Linda H. Anton. Harper San Francisco, 1992.

Surviving Infertility: A Compassionate Guide Through the Emotional Crisis of Infertility, rev. ed. Linda P. Salzer. HarperCollins, 1991.

Without Child: A Compassionate Look at Infertility, rev. ed. Martha Stout Shaw, 1990.

Sweet Grapes: How to Stop Being Infertile and Start Living Again, Jean W. Carter and Michael Carter. Perspectives Press, 1989.

A Hope Deferred: A Couple's Guide to Coping with Infertility. Jill Baughan. Multnomah, 1989.

Infertility: A Practical Guide to Coping. Alexander Gunn. Trafalgar Square, 1989.

■ BACKGROUND WORKS

Alternatives to Infertility: Is Surrogacy the Answer? Lita L. Schwartz. Brunner-Mazel, 1991.

Legal Aspects of Infertility. John Yeh and Mollie U. Yeh. Medical Economics, 1990; Blackwell, 1991.

Infertility: Medical and Social Choices. U.S. Government Printing Office, 1988.

■ PERSONAL STORIES

Waiting for Baby: One Couple's Journey Through Infertility to Adoption. Mary Earle Chase. McGraw-Hill, 1990.

Searching for the Stork: One Couple's Struggle to Start a Family. Marion Lee Wasserman. New American Library, 1988.

infibulation, a form of female genital mutilation involving surgical removal of the CLITORIS and LABIA *minora,* and the sealing of the *labia majora* (see FEMALE CIRCUMCISION).

inflammatory bowel disease (IBD), a type of digestive disorder (see DIGESTIVE SYSTEM).

inheritance rights, the legal right to inherit a share of a dead person's estate. If a will exists, and is properly validated by a *probate court,* that legal document spells out who inherits what share of the property. But if the person died *intestate* (without a will), the estate will be divided according to state *intestate succession laws.* Inheritance laws vary state by state but mostly allow inheritance rights to a SPOUSE and blood relatives, including a surviving husband or wife, children, parents, siblings, grandparents, and also often adopted children and adoptive parents. In general the laws lay out *descent,* outlining who has the right to inherit what share of property from a person, based on blood relationship; and *distribution,* the shares or portions that are to be allocated to each of the heirs and successors. If no near-enough relatives are found, the estate goes to the state.

A wife and husband have the right to inherit from each other. Under English common law, their traditional inheritance shares were called DOWER and CURTESY, respectively. Some states still retain dower and curtesy provisions, but most states today have laws that guarantee a certain proportion of a spouse's estate to the surviving spouse. In some states the survivor has the option of choosing between the state-mandated portion and the amount left in a will; this is called the RIGHT OF ELECTION. A wife and husband may waive their right to inherit from each other, as in a PRENUPTIAL AGREEMENT; often this is done to protect the inheritance rights of children from previous MARRIAGES. Inheritance rights of a wife and husband generally end when a SEPARATION or DIVORCE becomes final, though either may still inherit under the other's will.

Under intestate succession laws, legitimate children—that is, children in a marriage relationship—have the right to inherit from a parent, including a child born after the father's death. Usually, but not always, an adopted child has similar rights. If it is the child who dies, the estate generally goes to one or both parents, in some states shared with the surviving siblings.

A special case is an *illegitimate child,* now sometimes called a *nonmarital child,* born outside marriage or in a marriage that was not legal (see ANNULMENT). Traditionally, a nonmarital child could inherit only from the mother and her relatives, and vice versa. However, some states now accept a nonmarital child's right to inherit from the father who dies without a will, where paternity has been established (see FATHER). (See COUPLES AND FAMILIES HELP, INFORMATION, AND ACTION GUIDE on page 418; DIVORCE AND SEPARATION HELP, INFORMATION, AND ACTION GUIDE on page 238; OLDER WOMEN'S HELP, INFORMATION, AND ACTION GUIDE on page 374.)

Institute on Women and Technology (P.O. Box 338, North Amherst, MA 01059; 413-367-9725; H. Patricia Hynes, director), an organization founded in 1987 to assess technology and public policy that affect women, in areas such as BIRTH CONTROL, reproductive technology, office computers, genetic screening, and household technologies; more specifically, "to analyze the effects of new and existing technologies on women; to bring a feminist perspective to public policy on specific technologies and technology-based issues; and to advocate for technology that empowers women and sustains the natural world." Its work combines "scientific and ethical research, legal action, consulting, lectures, and education." The institute's current and planned projects focus on areas such as SURROGATE PARENTING, IN VITRO FERTILIZATION, lead contamination, Black women and birth control, cancer and women, environmental and chemical sources of infertility, militarism and PROSTITUTION, and SMOKING and adolescent girls. It publishes various materials, including *RU486: Misconceptions, Myths, and Morals*; its *The Recurring Silent Spring* is available from Teachers College Press (Colchester, VT); *Reconstructing Babylon: Women and Technology* is available from Indiana University Press.

insurance and pension equity, sex-neutral handling of the various means by which people attempt to ensure financial support for themselves and their families in case of illness and retirement. Women have traditionally been shortchanged in insurance and retirement coverage in several key ways: cost, availability, and benefits.

Most insurance and retirement plans are available through employers, so women who are not employed outside the home are generally unable to get insurance and pension coverage for the HOUSEWORK they perform. In the United States, the spousal Individual Retirement Account (IRA) can be used to provide limited protection for homemakers, but of course the family must have sufficient income to pay into it. Overall, a 1987 U.S. Census survey found that only about 20 percent of all women over sixty-five had pension rights, compared with 45 percent of men over sixty-five.

Even when women are employed outside the home, many work part-time and so may be denied access to insurance and pension plans. Many women also drop out of the workforce periodically to care for children or other family members and often forfeit pension contributions if they have less than five years' service. In the United States, a 1980 presidential commission found that women were half as likely as men to be employed in positions that provide pension rights; similarly, 42 percent of all part-time workers had no employer-provided health insurance, two-thirds of them women. Women can buy insurance privately—and, in fact, buy over half of the individually purchased health insurance policies in the United States—but private insurance is much more expensive than group insurance, and women are least able to afford it. Some women are able to arrange for group insurance through an affiliation of some sort, such as with the NATIONAL ASSOCIATION OF FEMALE EXECUTIVES or an alumnae organization.

In addition, women who have insurance or pension rights only through their husbands may lose them if they are divorced or widowed (see DIVORCE; WIDOW). Women should be sure they know not only their *own* pension rights, but also their husband's. In 1984 the U.S. General Accounting Office found that only 27 percent of all widows aged sixty-five or older received income from private or public pensions, as compared with 53 percent of married couples. Often the husband's pension stops at his death, sometimes because he did not choose a survivor benefit for his wife. The 1984 Retirement Equity Act (REA) required a retiring worker to obtain written consent from his or her SPOUSE if there are to be no survivor benfits in a pension. If presented with such a spousal consent form, a woman should explore carefully what it means for her financial present and future. This new law will help some women, though the poorest will benefit least.

The REA also made it possible for state courts to make pensions joint MARITAL PROPERTY in DIVORCE cases and to direct that pension payments go to wives and children in domestic relations cases, and several other provisions favorable to women were included in the law. If a woman is getting a divorce, she should get information about her husband's pension rights (see PREPARING FOR DIVORCE: A WOMAN'S GUIDE on page 236), since they may be regarded as marital property. She should also arrange in the SEPARATION AGREEMENT to ensure continuation of health insurance, to cover medical emergencies, and maintenance of life insurance, to provide for the FAMILY in case the father dies. When figuring costs for purposes of ALIMONY or CHILD SUPPORT, she should also include the cost of home, liability, and auto insurance.

Traditionally, insurance costs and benefits have been determined on the basis of various categories, including sex. Young men have paid higher rates for auto insurance than young women and have paid higher life insurance premiums because women generally have a higher LIFE EXPECTANCY than men. On the other hand, women have had to pay more for disability insurance than men of the same age and comparable health. They have also received lower payments from pensions, partly because—statistically, as a sex—they live longer and also because pension rights are based on salaries, and women on the average earn less than men. Sometimes women take less demanding outside jobs so they can fulfill a continuing role as HOMEMAKERS, but often the lower responsibility and lower pay result from SEXUAL DISCRIMINATION (see EQUAL PAY FOR EQUAL WORK).

In the United States, TITLE VII OF THE CIVIL RIGHTS ACT OF 1964 prohibits discrimination in employment, including health insurance, life insurance, or retirement plans that differentiate on the basis of sex. In firms with fifteen or more employees, this means, for example, that women cannot be asked to pay more into the pension fund and receive lower benefits out of the fund, on the assumption that—as a class—they live longer than men. Firms with under fifteen employees are not covered by the law, but two states—Montana and Massachusetts—have led the way by passing *sex-neutral* laws banning sexual discrimination in all lines of insurance, including life, auto, medical, disability, and pensions. Some other states have similar laws that cover only some types of insurance. Where such unisex laws have operated, the lifetime insurance costs for a woman—which the NOW LEGAL DEFENSE AND EDUCATION FUND has estimated as $20,176 more than for a similarly situated man—has dropped to near equity. Sex-based auto insurance rates have also sometimes been challenged successfully under state forms of the EQUAL RIGHTS AMENDMENT

Racial minorities and poor people of every background are also often discriminated against in insurance coverage, and many are covered by similar laws. Homosexual couples (see LESBIAN) often seek to have their unions recognized legally, not just for social acceptance, but also so that they can share in benefits meant to cover a spouse. (See SEXUAL DISCRIMINATION AND SEXUAL HARASSMENT HELP, INFORMATION, AND ACTION GUIDE on page 642; DIVORCE AND SEPARATION HELP, INFORMATION, AND ACTION GUIDE on page 238; OLDER WOMEN'S HELP, INFORMATION, AND ACTION GUIDE on page 374.)

OLDER WOMEN'S

Help, Information, and Action Guide

Organizations

▶ OLDER WOMEN'S LEAGUE (OWL) (202-783-6686; OWL POWERLINE, 202-783-6689, a weekly update on congressional activities). Publishes *Making Ends Meet: Midlife and Older Women's Search for Economic Self-Sufficiency through Job Training and Employment, Divorce and Older Women, Paying for Prejudice: Midlife and Older Women in America's Labor Force, Older Women and Job Discrimination: A Primer, Employment Discrimination Against Older Women, Death and Dying: Staying in Control to the End of Our Lives, Taking Charge of the End of Your Life: Proceedings of a Forum on Living Wills and other Advance Directives, Building Public/Private Coalitions for Older Women's Employment, Women and Pensions: Catch 22, Heading for Hardship: Retirement Income for American Women in the Next Century, The Road to Poverty: Report on the Economic Status of Midlife and Older Women in America,* and *Building Public/Private Coalitions for Older Women's Employment.*

▶ NATIONAL COUNCIL ON THE AGING (NCOA) (202-479-1200 or 800-424-9046). Includes **National Institute on Financial Issues and Services for Elders (NIFSE), Institute on Age, Work, and Retirement**, and **Senior Community Service Employment Program (SCSEP).** Publishes *Preparing for an Aging Society: Changes and Challenges, The Reality of Retirement, Design for Living, A Guide for Selection of Retirement Housing, Housing and Living Arrangements for the Elderly: A Selected Bibliography, Housing for Older Adults: Options and Answers, Project Independence, Home Safety, Housing Options, Home Service, Home Security,* and *Report on the Housing Choices of Older Americans: Summary of Survey Findings and Recommendations.* (See also CAREGIVER'S HELP, INFORMATION, AND ACTION GUIDE on page 454.)

▶ PENSION RIGHTS CENTER (202-296-3776). Has Women's Pension Project, National Pension Assistance Project, and Pensioners' Empowerment Project; publishes professional legal information packets on the main federally regulated retirement systems.

▶ Inter-National Association for Widowed People (IAWP) (P.O. Box 3564, Springfield, IL 62708; 217-787-0886; Dorothy L. Doering, president), an organization for widows or widowers and their families. It gathers and disseminates information; makes referrals to mutual-support programs; and offers special programs in travel, living arrangements, job placement, and social contact. It also publishes materials such as the bimonthly *The Survivors* and the pamphlet *Grief Curve.*

▶ NATIONAL DISPLACED HOMEMAKERS NETWORK (NDHN) (202-467-6346). Publishes *Success Over Forty: Strategies for Serving Older Displaced Homemakers.*

▶ WOMEN'S BUREAU, U.S. DEPARTMENT OF LABOR (202-523-6667). Operates Work and Family Clearinghouse (202-523-4486).

▶ NATIONAL CENTER ON WOMEN AND FAMILY LAW (NCOWFL) (212-674-8200).

▶ AMERICAN ASSOCIATION OF RETIRED PERSONS (AARP) (202-434-2277).

▶ CLEARINGHOUSE ON WOMEN'S ISSUES (CWI) (301-871-6016 or 202-363-9795).

▶ CONGRESSIONAL CAUCUS FOR WOMEN'S ISSUES (202-225-6740).

▶ NATIONAL CENTER FOR POLICY ALTERNATIVES (202-387-6030). Publishes *The Federal Employee Retirement and Income Security Act.*

▶ NATIONAL ASSOCIATION OF FEMALE EXECUTIVES (NAFE) (212-645-0770 or 800-669-1002).

▶ NOW LEGAL DEFENSE AND EDUCATION FUND (NOW LDEF) (212-925-6635). Publishes the *State Index of Women's Legal Rights, Attorney Referral Services List,* and the Legal Resource Kits *Insurance* and *Pensions.*

Other resources

◪ ON GROWING OLDER

Geroethics: A New Vision of Growing Old in America. Gerald A. Larue. Prometheus, 1992.

Ageing: The Facts, 2nd ed. Nicholas Coni. Oxford University Press, 1992.

Look Me in the Eye: Old Women, Aging, and Ageism, 2nd ed. Barbara Macdonald and Cynthia Rich. Spinsters Books, 1991.

Portraits of Passion: Aging Defying the Myth. Marshall B. Stearn. Park West, 1991.

Live Long and Love It. Win Arn and Charles Arn. Tyndale, 1991.

Older and Wiser. Nonie Birkedahl. New Harbinger, 1991.

The Second Spring of Your Life: How You Can Make Your Middle Years Joyous and Productive. Mel London. Continuum, 1990.

◪ ON RETIREMENT AND ECONOMIC SECURITY

Creating Your Own Future: A Woman's Guide to Retirement Planning. Judith A. Martindale and Mary J. Moses. Sourcebooks, 1991.

Keys to Living with a Retired Husband. Gloria B. Goodman. Barron's, 1991.

Women and Social Security: Progress Towards Equality of Treatment. Anne-Marie Brocas and others, eds. International Labour Office, 1990.

Retiring on Your Own Terms: Your Total Retirement Planning Guide to Fi-

nances, Health, Life-Style, and Much, Much More. James W. Ellison and others. Crown, 1989.

◪ ON FACING LOSS

Surviving Grief . . . and Learning to Live Again. Catherine Sanders. Wiley, 1992.
Understanding and Coping with Bereavement. Warner F. Bowers. Carlton, 1992.
I Don't Know What to Say: How to Help and Support Someone Who Is Dying. Robert Buckman. Random House, 1992.
Gentle Closings: How to Say Goodbye to Someone You Love. Ted Menten. Running Press, 1992.
Keys to Dealing with the Loss of a Loved One. Mary K. Kouri. Barron's, 1991.
Living with Dying: A Loving Guide for Family and Close Friends, rev. ed. David Carroll. Paragon House, 1991. Reprint of 1985 ed.
How to Survive the Loss of a Love. Melba Colgrove and others. Prelude Press, 1991.
The Survivor's Guide: Coping with the Details of Death. S. Sijpson. Firefly Books Ltd, 1990.
When Your Spouse Dies: A Concise and Practical Source of Help and Advice. Cathleen L. Curry. Ave Maria Press, 1990.
More Than Surviving: Caring for Yourself While You Grieve. Kelly Osmont. Centering Corp., 1990.
Grief: Rebuilding Your Life After Bereavement. R. M. Youngson. Sterling, 1990; Borgo Press, 1990.
Living with Dying: A Guide for Relatives and Friends, rev. ed. Glen W. Davidson. Augsburg Fortress, 1990.
Death in the Family: The Importance of Mourning. Lily Pincus. Schocken, 1988.
Grieving: How to Go on Living When Someone You Love Dies. Therese A. Rando. Lexington Books, 1988.

◪ ON FACING DEATH

Making End-of-Life Decisions. Lee E. Norrgard and Jo DeMars. ABC-CLIO, 1992.
Confrontations with the Reaper: A Philosophical Study of the Nature and Value of Death. Fred Feldman. Oxford University Press, 1992.
Being Human in the Face of Death. Deborah Roth and Emily LeVier, eds. IBS Press, 1990.
Meeting Death. Margaret Hyde and Lawrence Hyde. Walker, 1989.

■ BACKGROUND WORKS

How Old Are You? Age Consciousness in American Culture. Howard P. Chudacoff. Princeton University Press, 1992.

The Encyclopedia of Aging and the Elderly. F. Hampton Roy and Charles Russell. Facts on File, 1992.

The Journey of Life: A Cultural History of Aging in America. Thomas R. Cole. Cambridge University Press, 1991.

Growing Old in America, rev. ed. Patricia Von Brook. Information Plus (TX), 1990.

(See also WOMEN'S HEALTH HELP, INFORMATION, AND ACTION GUIDE on page 334; DIVORCE AND SEPARATION HELP, INFORMATION, AND ACTION GUIDE on page 238; WORKING WOMEN'S HELP, INFORMATION, AND ACTION GUIDE on page 779; EXERCISE AND FITNESS HELP, INFORMATION, AND ACTION GUIDE on page 270.)

intercourse: See SEXUAL INTERCOURSE.

International Bill of Rights for Women, a popular name for the CONVENTION ON THE ELIMINATION OF ALL FORMS OF DISCRIMINATION AGAINST WOMEN (see page 796 for the text).

International Center for Research on Women (ICRW) (1717 Massachusetts Avenue, NW, Suite 302, Washington, DC 20036; 202-797-0007; Mayra Buvinic, director), an organization founded in 1976, with both Washington, D.C., and London offices, to promote "social and economic development with women's full participation." ICRW works with policy makers and other people and organizations in the field to formulate policy and actions concerning "the economic, social, and health status of women in developing countries; women's critical contributions to development, given their dual productive and reproductive roles, and policy and program features that can improve the situation of poor women while making development interventions more effective." It provides policy-oriented research, program support, analysis services, and communications forums, "focusing on economic policies, family and household structure, health and nutrition, and agriculture and the environment," especially seeking to increase women's participation in credit and training programs for "microentrepreneurs," aiding women subsistence farmers and guiding international development agencies in addressing women's issues in their projects.

ICRW publishes numerous reports, reprints, and other publications, some in Spanish and French, such as *Women, Poverty and Environment in Latin America, Women on Their Own: Global Patterns of Female Headship, Mothers on Their*

Own: Policy Issues for Developing Countries, Women, Work, and Child Welfare in the Third World, Understanding and Evaluating Traditional Practices: A Guide for Improving Maternal Care, Better Health for Women: Research Results from the Maternal Nutrition and Health Care Program, and *Low-Income Housing: A Woman's Perspective.*

International Council of Women (ICW), a network of national councils of women, founded in 1888 and today including councils from approximately seventy-five countries, from Argentina to Zimbabwe. The American branch, which sparked the formation of the world network, was the NATIONAL COUNCIL OF WOMEN OF THE UNITED STATES (NCW/US), founded earlier that same year.

International Woman's Day, March 8; a day on which the campaign for WOMEN'S RIGHTS is honored by many groups. It originated formally in 1910, as a socialist holiday, and was celebrated by the international socialist movement until the Russian Revolution, when it became an official holiday in the Soviet Union and later in other communist countries and largely lost its attraction for most groups elsewhere. The day was taken up by some women's groups in the late 1960s and proved popular in many countries; in the United States it was included in the Women's History Week and Month celebrations each March.

International Woman Suffrage Alliance (IWSA), an organization formed in 1904 as a split-off from the INTERNATIONAL COUNCIL OF WOMEN (ICW) founded by Susan B. ANTHONY in 1888. The ISWA focused on WOMAN SUFFRAGE, rather than the wider range of issues pursued by the ICW. Carrie Chapman CATT was IWSA president from its founding until 1923, then becoming honorary chairman.

International Women's Health Coalition (IWHC) (24 East 21st Street, New York, NY 10010; 212-979-8500; Jane Ordway, contact), a "North American organization working in alliance with women's health advocates, women's organizations, health professionals, and government officials in Southern countries, and Northern institutions", formerly the **National Women's Health Coalition**. IWHC's primary aim is to promote and act as an advocate for women's reproductive health and rights in the United States and internationally. Its main "professional, moral, and financial support" goes to "colleagues in eight countries of Asia, Africa, and Latin America," with IWHC supporting individuals and projects that promote reproductive rights and high-quality health services, including safe abortion service and management of reproductive tract infections, in resource-poor communities. IWHC also documents the incidence and consequences of reproductive health problems, such as clandestine abortion and SEXUALLY TRANSMITTED DISEASES; holds international conferences; and provides an international communications network in the field.

Among IWHC's various publications, including conference reports, are *Reproductive Tract Infections: Global Impact and Priorities for Women's Reproductive Health, Special Challenges in Third World Women's Health: Reproductive Tract Infections, Cervical Cancer, and Contraceptive Safety, Women's Health in the Third World: The Impact of Unwanted Pregnancy, Population Control and Women's Health: Balancing the Scales, Reproductive Health and Dignity: Choices by Third World Women, Reproductive Choice in Jeopardy: International Policy Perspectives, The Contraceptive Development Process and Quality in Reproductive Health Services, Women and the Earth Debate,* and *Creating Common Ground: Report of a Meeting Between Women's Health Advocates and Scientists on Women's Perspectives on the Introduction of Fertility Regulation Technologies.*

International Women's Tribune Centre (IWTC) (777 United Nations Plaza, 3rd Floor, New York, NY 10017; 212-687-8633; Anne S. Walker, executive director), an organization founded in 1976 following INTERNATIONAL WOMEN'S YEAR and at the beginning of the United Nations Decade for Women (1975–1985). IWTC acts as a communications link for individuals and groups working on women's issues around the world and a source of information, technical assistance, and support from women's organizations. IWTC publishes various materials in areas of particular interest.

▶ *on women organizing:* the newsletters *Women and Law* and *Violence Against Women: Action Strategies Worldwide,* and manuals for fieldworkers;

▶ *on communications:* the newsletters *Women and Alternative Media* and *Participatory Media and Development,* the Women's International Micro-Computer Network, and a series of workshops, as on desktop publishing;

▶ *on community economic development:* the newsletter *Marketing Skills for Women* and the workbook *Marketing: A Manual of Training Activities for Women's Groups;*

▶ *on science and technology:* the newsletters *Women and the Environment* and *Strategies for Communicating Appropriate Technologies,* workbooks such as *Communicating Appropriate Technology with Rural Women* and *Women and Water: Issues, Activities, and Resources,* and workshops.

IWTC also manages the Women, Ink, program, to distribute resource materials on women and development, for the UNITED NATIONS DEVELOPMENT FUND FOR WOMEN (UNIFEM).

International Women's Year (1975), the beginning of what was designated by the United Nations as the Decade for Women (1975–1985), with a world conference at Mexico City in the summer of 1975. The participating countries agreed to study world women's rights issues country by country and to hold another meeting in Copenhagen (see COPENHAGEN WORLD CONFERENCE FOR WOMEN). But the conference largely mirrored the worldwide political issues of the time, spending far more time on Cold War, Middle East, and North-South issues than on women's rights. Some additional information and focus were developed in the years that followed, as at the Nairobi Conference in 1985 (see NAI-

robi Forward-Looking Strategies for the Advancement of Women), but little resulted. A further World Conference for Women was scheduled for 1995. Founded at the first conference, and still active, is the International Women's Tribune Centre.

intraductal papillomas, small, benign, wartlike growths in the lining of ducts near the nipple on a woman's breast.

intrapartal care, medical care of a woman and baby during labor.

intrauterine device (IUD), a metal or plastic device inserted into a woman's uterus, designed to prevent implantation of a fertilized egg, as a form of birth control. Some also contain hormones that aid in contraception; these must be replaced annually. A string attached to the IUD extends outside the body, so a woman can tell if the device is still in place.

The main attraction of IUDs is that some types can remain in place for up to five years, so the woman has no pills to take, no devices to put in or take out, and no calculations to make. Not only that, but they are 95–96 percent effective at preventing pregnancy, though precisely how they work is not known.

The problem is that some types of IUDs, notably the Dalkon Shield, were associated with increased risk of some serious health problems, including infection in the reproductive system, abortion combined with severe infection (called *septic abortion*), pelvic inflammatory disease, ectopic pregnancy, perforation of the uterus, and infertility. Many women also experienced less serious side effects, generally shortly after insertion, including cramps, dizziness, backache, bleeding, and heavy menstruation. In the United States, the Dalkon Shield was removed from the market in 1974, and its manufacturer agreed to pay medical costs of women injured by the device. In the wake of this settlement, most manufacturers ceased making IUDs in the United States, though some women continued to use them. Elsewhere in the world, notably in Europe, IUDs continued to be widely used, and their long-term experience has been more favorable. Indeed, in 1991 a new study based on the original data questioned whether IUDs in general were associated with increased pelvic infections, though it did not exonerate the Dalkon Shield in particular. Around the world, IUDs are the most widely used reversible form of contraception. In the late 1980s, for example, IUDs were used by nearly 84 million women, 60 million of them in China.

In the United States, the Food and Drug Administration recommends that the IUD be used only by women who have had children and who are involved in a monogamous relationship (see monogamy). Unlike several other forms of contraception, IUDs offer no protection against sexually transmitted diseases, such as aids. (See Birth Control and Family Planning Help, Information, and Action Guide on page 81.)

intrauterine insemination (IUI), a type of ARTIFICIAL INSEMINATION.

introitus, a medical term for the external opening of the VAGINA.

in utero **surgery**, an alternative term for FETAL SURGERY.

in vitro **fertilization (IVF)**, a complicated and delicate procedure for achieving FERTILIZATION outside the woman's body, in a laboratory dish; also called *test-tube fertilization*. *In vitro* actually means "in glass," as opposed to *in vivo*, in the living body, though today plastic dishes are often used. The technique was developed in 1963 by British obstetrician Patrick Steptoe and British reproductive physiologist Robert Edwards.

An attempt to circumvent INFERTILITY, IVF is commonly used when a woman's FALLOPIAN TUBES—the place where the women's egg (OVUM) and the man's SPERM normally meet—are blocked or damaged but the rest of her reproductive organs are functioning normally. In particular, the woman must be capable of ovulating in at least part of one OVARY, and the ovary must be accessible. It may also be used in unresponsive cases of ENDOMETRIOSIS, infertility resulting from a woman's antibodies to the sperm (see IMMUNE SYSTEM), and other types of infertility of known or unknown causes, where other treatments have failed.

In IVF a woman is generally given fertility drugs during the first week of her reproductive cycle, at the beginning of MENSTRUATION, to stimulate the ripening of eggs (see OVUM). This process, which sometimes involves injections of additional HORMONES, is monitored by ULTRASOUND and various blood tests. About fourteen days into the cycle, just before OVULATION, the doctor removes as many ripe eggs as possible, using either LAPAROSCOPY (involving an incision in the abdomen) or *aspiration* (using a hollow needle inserted into the abdomen), either way generally guided by ULTRASOUND.

In the actual fertilization, sperm are added to the dish containing the eggs. This sperm most often comes from the woman's husband or sex partner, generally produced by MASTURBATION in the doctor's office and used fresh, though sometimes frozen. However, sperm from a donor may also be used (see ARTIFICIAL INSEMINATION). If fertilization occurs, usually within twelve hours, the fertilized eggs, or ZYGOTES, will begin to divide. The doctor removes several of these from the dish, drawing them into a hollow tube called a *catheter*. This is then inserted through the woman's CERVIX and used to deposit the fertilized eggs, now often called EMBRYOS, into the UTERUS. If all goes well, one or more of the embryos will implant themselves and begin to grow. To increase this likelihood, the woman often remains in bed for some days. The failure rate is high—eggs often fail to implant or are aborted spontaneously in the next few weeks—so several eggs are used. However, where implantation is successful, multiple births often result. Many of the spontaneous ABORTIONS are due to GENETIC DISORDERS or CHROMOSOMAL ABNORMALITIES; new, still-experimental techniques may allow doctors to identify eggs with obvious defects and correct the defect or remove the defective cells, all before inserting the embryos in the woman's body. In about ten to fourteen days after the procedure, a pregnancy test will be performed to see if it "took"; if not, the procedure may be repeated; if so, the pregnancy will be carefully monitored. The woman will often be given PROGESTERONE (normally produced after natural ovulation) to help support the pregnancy.

Though *in vitro* fertilization has captured much public attention, it is a procedure that still has limited use. It has a low success rate—an average of only 10–20 percent, often takes several attempts, is emotionally and physically taxing, is done only in a relatively few specialist clinics, is very expensive, and is not covered by most insurance policies. In addition to the medical expenses themselves, except for those who happen to live near such a clinic, costs include travel to the clinic, cost of accommodations, and loss of pay from time off work, involving at least two weeks each time the procedure is tried. Because of this, IVF is generally regarded as a last-resort procedure, to be tried only after a woman and her partner have gone through full infertility workups and other options, such as TUBOPLASTY, have failed. One variation on IVF is GAMETE INTRAFALLOPIAN TUBE TRANSFER (GIFT).

IVF clinics also vary widely. Women considering the procedure should get precise information on the actual number of *live births* that have resulted from the clinic's work; at some clinics the actual success rate is near zero. Many clinics are so far relatively unregulated, though that may change as some have been found to distort and lie about their records. Women should also explore the success rate for other women of their age group, since FERTILITY declines gradually. Most programs accept women up to age forty, occasionally to forty-four, and some give priority to women over thirty-five.

Another concern is the legal status of fertilized eggs that have not been implanted, some of which may be stored for future use. Many doctors feel that a pregnancy has not been started until the embryo is implanted into a woman's uterus. However, some people argue that the embryo is a human being. In some places they have tried to pass laws declaring that failure to implant a fertilized egg is murder or that the physician caring for the embryo should be subject to child abuse penalties if any harm comes to it; or to force the physician to implant the frozen embryos into a surrogate mother (see SURROGATE PARENTING). Some people have gone to court over "ownership" of frozen embryos, and questions of INHERITANCE RIGHTS to a dead parent's estate have also been raised. Because of ethical and legal questions involving such out-of-the-body embryos, some states have even barred *in vitro* fertilization.

Another alternative, when a woman can produce eggs but is unable to carry a pregnancy to term, is a procedure called *in vitro fertilization/embryo implant*. In this case the egg and sperm of the wife and husband are mixed in a laboratory dish and the fertilized egg is then implanted in a *host surrogate mother*, who actually bears the child.

Conversely, excess eggs produced by women in IVF programs are sometimes donated to other women, who cannot produce eggs but can carry a pregnancy to term. Some organizations have established *egg donor* programs; the CENTER FOR SURROGATE PARENTING, for example, has a program in which egg donors are specifically solicited, screened, and matched with prospective recipients, like that of a sperm bank. (See INFERTILITY; also INFERTILITY AND REPRODUCTIVE TECHNOLOGY HELP, INFORMATION, AND ACTION GUIDE on page 368).

irritable bowel syndrome (IBS), a type of digestive disorder (see DIGESTIVE SYSTEM).

IUD, abbreviation for INTRAUTERINE DEVICE.

"I Was a Playboy Bunny": See Gloria STEINEM.

Janeway, Elizabeth (1913–), an American writer, a feminist whose *Man's World, Woman's Place* (1971) became a centerpiece of the emerging modern American women's movement, with particular impact on the large numbers of women then moving from definition as wives and mothers into the much wider world of work and status-building achievement of many kinds. Janeway examined and rejected the "social mythology" that the wider world was a "man's world," with women relegated to home and family. Her thinking provided a theoretical basis and justification for those women already on the move and for the millions more becoming conscious that current SEX ROLES were most emphatically not ordained by society or deity. Janeway's work also includes the essays in *Between Myth and Morning: Women Awakening* (1972) and *Powers of the Weak* (1980).

jejunoileal bypass, an operation to promote weight loss (see DIETING).

Kinsey Report, The, a pair of reports based on large-scale studies of human sexual response—*Sexual Behavior in the Human Male* (1948) and *Sexual Behavior in the Human Female* (1953). Both studies together provided much of the basis for a wide-ranging reexamination of what had been a far too narrow view of what was "normal" in sexual life. They redefined as entirely normal a considerable range of "perversions," including homosexuality (see LESBIAN), and previously taboo or illegal practices such as oral sex (see SEXUAL INTERCOURSE), MASTURBATION, premarital sex, and ADULTERY, all clearly common. Kinsey's work on the human female also made it quite clear that much of sexual practice and pleasure rested on mores rather than biology; for example, after Kinsey the clitoral ORGASM was accepted as normal, and women's SEXUAL RESPONSES were seen to have a considerably wider range than had commonly been thought possible.

labia, folds of flesh in a woman's VULVA; Latin for "lips." Two sets of lips protect the vaginal opening and are part of the female external GENITALS.

The smaller, inner lips—the *labia minora*—cover the VAGINA and urethra (see URINARY TRACT); the lips meet at the upper end to form a sort of hood (see FORESKIN) over the CLITORIS, the main organ of female SEXUAL RESPONSE. Both the labia minora and the clitoris are covered with moist mucous membrane and are highly sensitive to the touch and sexual arousal (see EROGENOUS ZONES; SEXUAL RESPONSE).

The larger, outer lips—the *labia majora*—are thicker. Their moist inner surfaces contain many sebaceous (oil) glands and have little or no hair. The labia majora's outer surfaces are covered with dry SKIN; after PUBERTY, these are covered with HAIR.

The labia change during a woman's lifetime. At birth the labia are often enlarged, due to the influence of HORMONES from the mother, but become smaller over the next few weeks. The labia may also be joined together at birth; normally they will separate naturally, without medical intervention. In a young girl, especially a virgin (see VIRGINITY), the labia minora are small and completely hidden by the labia majora, which lie so close together that when the girl's legs are together, they completely cover the GENITALS underneath. In the form of genital mutilation called FEMALE CIRCUMCISION, these labia majora are sometimes stitched to literally grow together, after removal of the clitoris.

In a sexually active mature woman, the labia majora gape somewhat. After childbearing, the labia minora often grow larger, sometimes extending beyond the labia majora, which shrink somewhat after MENOPAUSE. CANCER of the vulva most often affects the labia (see VULVA; CANCER). (See WOMEN'S HEALTH HELP, INFORMATION, AND ACTION GUIDE on page 334.)

labor, in PREGNANCY, the proximate events and actions that result in the DELIVERY of a baby; also the period in which these occur. Labor proceeds in stages, from the widening (*dilation*) of the CERVIX to the expulsion of the PLACENTA (afterbirth), and is the culmination of the approximately nine-month period of GESTATION, though what actually triggers the onset of labor is unclear.

Several events take place in the weeks and days before the stages of labor actually start. A woman often feels a burst of energy in the days before labor and may have a dull ache, similar to menstrual cramps, in the lower back or pelvis. Somewhat more obvious indicators of impending labor are

- the baby settles into its FETAL PRESENTATION, preparatory for birth. This *engagement, dropping,* or *falling* is generally quite noticeable to the mother, easing pressure on the upper abdomen and so making breathing easier, though it may increase pressure on the bladder (see URINARY TRACT). It may not occur until labor has actually started, however.
- The mucus that has plugged the cervix is expelled, resulting in a bloody discharge called *show* or *bloody show.*
- A watery fluid leaks out of the woman's VAGINA, in small or large amounts. This amniotic fluid results from the rupture of the AMNIOTIC SAC, or "bag of waters," that protects the FETUS during development. Labor often starts within twelve hours of this "rupture of the membranes," also called the "breaking of the bag of waters," so a woman should immediately report the time of the first fluid release to her doctor or midwife. Since the baby is no longer protected by the amniotic sac, the mother may be brought to the hospital or birthing center at this time. However, the amniotic membranes may not rupture until the woman is deep into labor.

These signs can indicate that labor will start in a matter of days or hours, but they may not be not clear cut.

Also, before labor begins, many women experience *Braxton-Hicks contractions,* often called *false labor.* These are irregular contractions that occur on occasion through pregnancy but are most obvious later in gestation, as the body prepares for labor, and are often mistaken for true labor. Felt primarily in the lower abdomen, Braxton-Hicks contractions are intermittent and relatively mild, rather than increasing in regularity, intensity, and frequency as with true contractions. They can easily be confused, however; the only sure distinction is that in true labor, the cervix begins to widen (dilate) after some hours.

Once labor *does* start, it generally proceeds in three stages, though even these vary widely from woman to woman and especially from a first birth to subsequent births.

▶ In the ***first stage,*** the muscles of the UTERUS begin to contract rhythmically, spasmodically, and painfully, in response to various HORMONES, notably OXYTO-CIN. Contractions are often relatively mild, irregular, and brief in the beginning but gradually settle into a regular rhythm, coming more frequently, lengthening, and intensifying. These contractions first widen the birth canal, formed by the CERVIX and the vagina, and then (in later stages) will propel the baby through it. In this first state the cervix becomes softer and thinner, a process called *effacement,* and also wider, in what is called *dilation.* At full dilation, the cervix will be about four inches wide; the baby's soft-boned head, though larger than that, will be compressed on its passage through. Contractions become even stronger, sometimes accompanied by nausea, vomiting, or trembling, toward the end of this process, in what is called the *transition.* This whole first stage may take twelve to thirteen hours or more in a first birth but may be shorter in subsequent births.

Once contractions start, the mother should promptly go to where the baby will be delivered. If to a hospital, she will generally be sent to a *labor room,* where the dilation of the cervix will be monitored, and then moved into a *delivery room* during the second stage of labor, though some hospitals have less disruptive combination *labor/delivery recovery* (LDR) rooms. Sometimes, especially in high-risk pregnancies, fetal monitoring will be used from this stage on.

▶ The *second stage* is when the baby is actually delivered, starting when the baby's head reaches the pelvic floor muscles. In the usual headfirst (*vertex*) presentation, the baby's head is moved through the birth canal by continuing contractions, pushed along by pressure from the abdominal muscles and diaphragm—the focus of so many classes (see CHILDBIRTH). Ideally the baby's head leads the way, appearing at the opening of the vagina in what is called *crowning.* In a hospital a woman will now be moved into the delivery room, if she is not there already. This is the time of maximum stretching for the *perineum,* the tissue between the vagina and the anus; and now is when doctors may surgically cut that tissue, in an EPISIOTOMY, the aim being to prevent ragged tearing, which is harder to heal.

When the head emerges, the doctor or midwife checks to see that the UMBILICAL CORD is not wrapped around the baby's neck and may also clear the baby's nose and mouth with a suction bulb to facilitate the baby's first breath. At this point the baby normally rotates the head and body somewhat, which eases passage of the rest of the body; if not, the doctor or midwife may do so, angling the shoulders so first one, then the other, comes out. After that, the rest of the body follows readily, along with the rest of the amniotic fluid. This whole second stage generally takes one to two hours for a first birth, but more like twenty minutes or even less in subsequent births.

When other parts of the body, rather than the head, appear first in the birth canal, various delivery problems can result (see FETAL PRESENTATION). The main concerns are that the baby's oxygen supply be maintained; if that is questionable, special procedures may be required, including CESAREAN SECTION, if necessary.

The new baby is often placed on the mother's abdomen and massaged lightly. Within a few minutes the umbilical cord is clamped and cut. At one minute after birth and again four minutes later, the newborn's condition is evaluated using a five-factor rating scale, called an *Apgar score,* the aim being to quickly identify babies with special problems that call for immediate treatment. To prevent damage (including blindness) from possible infection, notably with GONORRHEA, silver nitrate or erythromycin may be put in the baby's eyes, and injection of vitamin K may also be given to aid blood clotting. In some states such actions are required by law and in many recommended by medical experts; however, some people strongly object to them as invasive. In a hospital the baby's footprint may be taken and both mother and baby given identification bands. The baby may also be placed in a warmer briefly, before being returned to the mother.

▶ In the *third stage,* the PLACENTA separates from the uterine wall and is expelled along with the remaining amniotic membranes, in what is called the *afterbirth,* by continuing contractions. If the tissue is not expelled readily, the doctor or midwife may press on the upper part of the uterus to stimulate further contractions; drugs may also be given to help expel the afterbirth and to control subsequent bleeding. This last stage may take no more than ten minutes. Afterward, while the mother holds the baby, the doctor or midwife cleans the mother's GENITALS and stitches up any tears or cuts.

The process is shorter and easier in second and subsequent births because the cervix dilates and the muscles relax more readily. But in any birth, labor may take longer if special problems are encountered that make it harder for a woman to push the baby out on her own. Among these are abnormal fetal presentation, failure of the cervix to dilate sufficiently, a pelvis too small to accommodate the baby's head (called *cephalopelvic disproportion*), multiple births, or any sign that the fetus is getting insufficient oxygen, a condition called *fetal distress*. Some of these problems require some form of *assisted delivery,* such as *forceps delivery* or *vacuum extraction,* to help bring the child through the birth canal.

Forceps are a hinged device with curved arms, something like tongs. These are inserted into a woman's vagina and placed on either side of a child's head, being used to help pull the baby out and sometimes to turn the baby for easier delivery. Several centuries ago, when forceps were first invented, they were life-saving devices, since before then women unable to give birth unassisted generally died, often along with their babies, who were sometimes cut out of their bodies. Forceps are still used today, but they can do temporary and sometimes permanent damage to the baby's head and to the mother's reproductive organs. As a result, many doctors today opt for using a vacuum extractor or cesarean section as less risky.

A vacuum extraction employs one or more suction cups placed on the baby's head; these are attached by a long tube to a machine called a *vacuum extractor* or *ventouse.* The pump in the extractor produces suction, timed so that it pulls on the baby's head in unison with the mother's contractions. This procedure is less damaging to the baby and mother, though it may cause temporary swelling on the baby's scalp, and also eases difficult birth by not taking up space in the narrowest part of the birth canal, as forceps do. A similar machine is used to perform some kinds of ABORTIONS.

If at any time before the actual birth the mother is hemorrhaging or has eclampsia (see PREECLAMPSIA), or if the baby's oxygen supply is impaired or threatened, immediate surgical intervention may be required to save the life and health of mother, child, or both. Then a cesarean section would be performed, as it would in some other situations, as when the mother's pelvis is too small for the baby.

In some special situations the doctor must induce labor, to start or speed up the process of delivery. This is common, for example, where the baby is postmature (see GESTATION), where mother and baby have Rh incompatibility (see BLOOD), or where the mother has preeclampsia or eclampsia. It may also be done in cases of *dystocia,* or difficult (sometimes impossible) labor, as when a mother is too weak to continue. If the cervix is *ripe*—that is, if it has softened, thinned, and dilated sufficiently—the doctor may break the amniotic sac (if it is still unbroken), which may bring on contractions, as may dislodging the membranes in the uterus. (Labor may also be induced earlier in pregnancy as a form of ABORTION, by injection of saline solution or hormones into the amniotic fluid.)

The other main way of inducing labor is to give hormones, notably oxytocin, either by vaginal suppositories or intravenous injections. However, this, too, can be done only if the cervix is ripe, and only when the baby is in the proper headfirst postion and there is no abnormality in the woman's pelvis. If the baby is positioned badly, if the baby is too large for the mother's pelvis, if the baby shows any sign of fetal distress, or if the mother has had several children, oxytocin is not used. The problem is that contractions can be strong enough to rupture the uterus and kill the baby and by speeding up contractions can limit oxygen delivery to the baby as well. In the past, oxytocin was sometimes administered for the doctor's or mother's convenience, to speed up labor; but many medical experts, including the FOOD AND DRUG ADMINISTRATION, now feel that should never be done, and that oxytocin should be given only where the dangers of delay outweigh the risks of use. Induction of labor may be used in cases of STILLBIRTH, however. (See also PREGNANCY; CHILDBIRTH; also PREGNANCY AND CHILDBIRTH HELP, INFORMATION, AND ACTION GUIDE on page 580.)

lactation, production of milk (see BREASTFEEDING; BREAST).

lactose intolerance, a type of digestive disorder involving inability to digest the sugar *lactose* in milk and dairy products (see DIGESTIVE SYSTEM).

Lamaze method, a popular natural childbirth approach (see CHILDBIRTH).

Lambda Legal Defense and Education Fund (LLDEF)

(666 Broadway, New York, NY 10012; 212-995-8585; Kevin Cathcart, executive director), an organization to defend the civil rights of lesbians and gay men, including housing, child custody, and AIDS. It acts as an information resource and referral service; aids individual homosexuals and their attorneys and also litigates test cases; seeks to influence public policy; maintains a library; and publishes the periodicals *Lambda Update* and *AIDS Update*.

language and sexism, concern over the many patterns of language that convey the assumption of male dominance and traditional SEX ROLES. Spoken and written language carries much of the substance of cultures, and in matters of SEXISM and women's freedom, it reflects and reinforces old sexist attitudes; but when desexed or equalized, it is capable of reflecting and reinforcing new nonsexist attitudes. People conditioned by the Adam and EVE story and by centuries of usage, in which "he" represents all of humanity and "she" represents only specific women, unknowingly refresh their whole bundle of sexist attitudes every day. But writers, broadcasters, and all who work with words—including politicians, educators, and the clergy—are learning how to retire sexist language, and there is continuing social pressure to do so. In fact, the attempt to "desex"—that is, to equalize—language, has been a much-discussed matter in the latter part of the twentieth century; in recent years the focus has often been on making language "inclusive" of all peoples and both sexes, rather than exclusive in traditional ways. Actually, the importance of desexing language has sometimes been obscured by those who focus on awkward and sometimes almost unworkable campaigns for alternative forms of language, rather than continuing what has actually been a startlingly successful campaign.

Advocates of language desexing point out that it is easy enough to accomplish, with a few small basic changes; all that is required is the will to do it and to resist those usage purists who have not yet grasped that languages are in a constant process of change and development. In English, much is accomplished by introducing the interchangeable use of plurals for singulars, with "he" becoming "they," or by going around the question, for instance, substituting nonsexual pronouns like "a" and "an" for "he" and "his," and using "she" alternatively or instead of "he" where either is quite accurate and usable. Compound words that include man, like "salesman," "chairman," and "manpower," are also easily desexed, as to sales representative, chair, or workforce. And women (like men) need not be described by their sexual characteristics. Very little was accomplished by such early (now mostly jettisoned) approaches as the constant, awkward "he or she" and "him or her," or by such hopelessly unrealistic constructs as "he/she" and "himer." Those who try to build a new feminist language only isolate themselves. Some languages are more resistant to change than others, of course, such as those Latin-derived languages in which gender is built into the language, with nouns being masculine, feminine, or neutral, and the forms of accompanying words varying accordingly.

Even so, in a world that is more and more bound together by a single communications net, it has become possible to introduce new nonsexist usages throughout the world that help change that world, and in an astonishingly short time, measured by decades rather than the centuries usually taken for language changes of this magnitude. (See WOMEN'S RIGHTS HELP, INFORMATION, AND ACTION GUIDE on page 767.)

If the men in the room would only think how they would feel graduating with a "spinster of arts" degree, they would see how important this [language reform] is.

GLORIA STEINEM, 1981
————————— *IN A SPEECH AT YALE UNIVERSITY* —————————

•

laparoscopy, a type of medical procedure that allows the doctor to visually examine and sometimes to work on organs in the abdomen. A small incision is made in the patient's abdomen, commonly near the navel or just above the pubic bone; carbon dioxide is pumped in to inflate the abdominal cavity; then a thin, rigid, lighted, periscopelike device is passed through the abdominal wall, with the physician being guided by ULTRASOUND.

Laparoscopy may be used on either men or women to view organs such as the GALLBLADDER or liver but is used most commonly to explore internal female reproductive organs: the FALLOPIAN TUBES, OVARIES, and UTERUS. It is sometimes used as a general diagnostic procedure, as in exploring reasons for INFERTILITY, unexplained abdominal pain, or vaginal bleeding. It may also have more specific purposes, such as in checking for possible FIBROIDS, CYSTS (see HYSTERECTOMY), ECTOPIC PREGNANCY, or ENDOMETRIOSIS; to check whether CONCEPTION has occurred; or to perform a type of STERILIZATION called TUBAL LIGATION. Where any type of operation is being performed, such as tubal ligation, a second incision is generally required for surgical instruments to be inserted. A special form of laparoscopy is used to explore the fetus (see FETOSCOPY). A smaller incision, sometimes used in tubal ligation or ectopic pregnancy, is called *laparotomy*.

For more help, information, and action

▶ RESOLVE, INC. (617-643-2424). Publishes the fact sheet *Laparoscopy: What to Expect.*
(See also WOMEN'S HEALTH HELP, INFORMATION, AND ACTION GUIDE on page 334; INFERTILITY AND REPRODUCTIVE TECHNOLOGY HELP, INFORMATION, AND ACTION GUIDE on page 368.)

laparotomy, a type of surgical procedure used in TUBAL LIGATION or ECTOPIC PREGNANCY (see LAPAROSCOPY).

last menstrual period (LMP), the date used in calculating a woman's due date or delivery date in pregnancy (see GESTATION; PREGNANCY).

Lawyers' Committee for Civil Rights Under Law (1400 Eye [I] Street, NW, Suite 400, Washington, DC 20005; 202-371-1212; Barbara R. Arnwine, executive director), a "nonpartisan, nonprofit organization . . . formed in 1963 at the request of President John F. Kennedy to involve the private bar in the provision of legal services to victims of racial discrimination." It seeks "equal justice under the law" in both the United States and South Africa, by "providing legal resources for the needs of minorities and the poor, ensuring fair and equitable political participation, and eliminating all barriers to equal opportunities for all disadvantaged minorities and women." Through the *pro bono* resources of the private bar, it offers "legal representation, public policy advocacy, and public education on civil rights matters." It had independent affiliate offices in Boston, Chicago, Dallas, Denver, Los Angeles, Philadelphia, San Francisco, and Washington, D.C.

League of Women Voters (1730 M Street, NW, Washington, DC 20036; 202-429-1965; Gracia Hillman, executive director), the organization that succeeded the NATIONAL AMERICAN WOMAN SUFFRAGE ASSOCIATION (**NAWSA**), which had been the main American vehicle in the successful fight for WOMAN SUFFRAGE. In 1919, when women achieved the vote, NAWSA president Carrie Chapman CATT called for the formation of a successor organization; in February 1920 the league was formed, directly after the one-issue NAWSA was dissolved.

The league was conceived of as a multi-issue organization and has from the first functioned very effectively on such matters as voter registration and voter education; it sponsors highly visible presidential candidate television debates, and seeks to defend voting rights, monitor and influence government activities, and promote campaign finance reform. In this it has been more a national "good government" group than a hard-driving major WOMEN'S RIGHTS MOVEMENT vehicle in the modern period, as NAWSA had been in its time. It states its mission as "to encourage the active participation of citizens in government and to influence public policy through education and advocacy," as through its recent Take Back the System campaign, designed "to empower voters to build grass-roots citizen action." The league is nonpartisan, supporting no political parties or candidates, but it does advocate some issues and positions, as determined by its grass-roots membership, as regarding privacy in reproductive choice, health care, and environmental issues.

The league and its League of Women Voters Education Fund conduct research and publish many works, including the quarterly *The National Voter*, the periodic newsletter *League Action Service (LAS): Report from the Hill*, Action Alerts on topical issues before Congress, the book *In the Public Interest* (about the league's first fifty years), the booklet *Changed Forever: The League of Women Voters and the Equal Rights Amendment*, and a host of other publications in areas such as How to Be Politically Effective, Election Services, Debates, National Government, State and Local Government, International Relations, Natural Resources, Social Policy, Public Relations, and local voter guides.

Among the publications directly on women's issues are *The Women's Vote: Beyond the Nineteenth Amendment, Public Policy on Reproductive Choices, Coping with Conflict: Reproductive Choices and Community Controversy, Expanding School-Age Child Care: A Community Action Guide, Take Action on Child Care, Responding to the Health Care Crisis, Pay Equity: Issues and Answers*, and *Meeting the Employment Needs of Women: A Path out of Poverty?* The league also produces the Voter Service Guide available through the on-line computer service Prodigy.

LeBoyer method, a popular natural childbirth approach (see CHILDBIRTH).

lesbian, a woman who finds sexual and emotional fulfillment from other women. The name comes from the Mediterranean island of Lesbos, home of the early Greek poet Sappho, a woman who loved women. Some lesbians have relationships only with other women; some are BISEXUAL, having relations with both men and women, though often favoring one over the other.

Women have had intensely close relationships through history, not necessarily always involving sexual relations (see SEXUAL INTERCOURSE). The term *lesbian*, however, is fairly recent. Many HOMOSEXUAL women bear the name *lesbian* openly and proudly, asserting their rights in modern society, often in partnership with male homosexuals, or *gay* men. Some feminists charge that the label *lesbian* was developed as a tool of oppression by a heterosexual society; they argue that love between women has traditionally been regarded as natural and has only been termed "abnormal" as women have become more independent of men. And, indeed, many antifeminists have attempted to divide their opponents with charges of lesbianism (see ANTIFEMINIST). By contrast, other feminists have adopted lesbianism not simply as a sexual preference, or a civil rights cause, but as a political response to male oppression (see LESBIAN FEMINISM; RADICAL FEMINISM).

Indeed, it is unclear to what extent the lesbian life-style in modern society is a choice that reflects biologically driven sexual preferences and to what extent politically or socially driven preferences stem from antimale, feminist-separatist convictions. Nor is it clear how many women feel themselves to be lesbian or bisexual; some researchers estimate as many as 10–20 percent of all women, of all backgrounds and ages, in the United States. Figures are imprecise because so many women have hidden their feelings for other women.

Certainly being a lesbian is not easy. Women-loving women are subject to a wide range of direct verbal and physical attacks or are treated as invisible, both of which they regard as stemming from *homophobia,* fear and loathing of same-sex relationships, and *heterosexism,* the assumption that opposite-sex relationships are superior and the only natural form of human sexuality. Lesbians who hide their sexual preference may be shielded temporarily from open attack and from social and economic repercussions, but they bear the tremendous stress that comes with living a lie. Society's views also cause many women to react to their sexual feelings with self-hatred and low self-esteem, which is reflected in higher rates of suicide and ALCOHOL AND DRUG ABUSE. Alcoholism has been common partly because lesbian bars have traditionally been primary meeting places and "safe areas." Largely to provide a sense of support and community, and an alternative to the bar-centered life-style, many lesbians have—again, often with gay men—established lesbian and gay community centers for political and social events and also as places for referrals to whatever kinds of services might be needed, including therapy and medical advice (see below). They also help individual women with the difficult and complicated question of when and how to openly declare their sexual orientation, an often painful but also freeing process called *coming out.* Lesbians and gay men have also found a haven and place of community in many religious groups, though in some churches they are still outcasts.

More specifically, lesbians face discrimination in a number of areas. They continue to experience very widespread discrimination throughout the workplace, stemming from homophobia little restricted by law, custom, or practice. In the United States, in the early 1990s, the general rule in the private sector is that lesbians (and gay males) are employed at the sole discretion of their employes and are not protected by antidiscrimination laws, unless a specific employment contract exists. Attempts to construct such a contract by reference to an employer's nondiscrimination pledge, as in an employee handbook, have not been upheld in the courts. By 1990 Wisconsin and several localities, including such major cities as New York and Chicago, had passed laws prohibiting employment discrimination directed against lesbians and gay males, and at least a dozen states had issued executive orders to the same effect, but as a practical matter the new laws have so far afforded little real protection. Lesbians and gay males have traditionally also been barred from military service and discharged when found or when they declared their sexual preferences, though that has changed in many European countries and change began in the United States under the Clinton administration; they have also generally been barred from public employment connected with national security matters. Only in other federal employment might there be some constitutional protection, and even that has not yet been fully adjudicated, although federal policy states that homosexuality alone does not justify dismissal.

Many lesbian couples wish to marry, both to publicly solemnize their relationship and to gain legal rights associated with MARRIAGE, including availability of insurance, pensions, tax benefits, SOCIAL SECURITY benefits, hospital visitation rights, INHERITANCE RIGHTS, MARITAL PROPERTY, DIVORCE, and CUSTODY. As of 1992, in the United States, same-sex marriages were prohibited in every state. However, some cities allow lesbian or gay couples to register as *domestic partners,* to receive at least some such benefits. Many couples try to establish their legal relationships through a written contract, though such documents are not always upheld by the courts. In particular, a *durable power of attorney* is designed to allow one partner to have legal power to act for the other, if she becomes incapacitated. Without it, a lesbian may become involved in a bitter and nasty battle with her disabled partner's family for custody. Where a lesbian decides to have a child by ARTIFICIAL INSEMINATION of one partner, that partner is considered the biological mother; the other partner often has no legal right to custody or VISITATION RIGHTS, should the couple later split. (See COHABITATION; CUSTODY.)

Many lesbians have been married at one time in their lives. Sometimes this was because the woman only later in life recognized a sexual orientation toward women. However, in the past many women who were attracted to women married men because they were also attracted to men, because they denied their lesbian leanings, or as a means of outward conformity. Indeed, in decades past, lesbians and gay men would sometimes make marriages of convenience that were intended to give each a semblance of conforming to traditional convention while actually leaving them free to pursue same-sex relationships. That has become less common today, with many more couples seeking to be open about their sexual orientation and, where possible, to establish a long-term same-sex relationship.

Whatever the nature of their heterosexual relationships, lesbians have traditionally been at a considerable disadvantage in contested custody of their own children, as they have also in ADOPTION, VISITATION RIGHTS, foster care, housing, and guardianship rights. In bitter divorce battles, a lesbian's former husband has often been able to successfully use his ex-wife's lesbian activities against her in battles over custody, visitation, and financial settlements—or to use threats to expose her sexual orientation as a way to obtain unfair divorce settlements (see SEP-

ARATION AGREEMENT). Lesbian orientation is no longer an absolute bar to a favorable decision in many courts, and in some states courts are instructed to disregard a parent's sexual orientation unless it affects her fitness as a parent or caretaker. However, custody and related questions are still highly subjective and are likely to require any lesbian to stage a hard fight for a successful ruling. In addition, if a woman openly becomes a lesbian after receiving a favorable court decision, many courts consider that a "change of circumstance" sufficient to re-open the question of custody—necessitating another court battle.

Lesbians are also commonly targets of abuse and violence. The **NOW LEGAL DEFENSE AND EDUCATION FUND** reports that in the United States, recent surveys have shown that 92 percent of all lesbians and gay men have been subjected to verbal abuse or threats, and approximately 24 percent have been attacked physically because of their sexual orientation—a rate seven times that of the general adult population. Much activity among lesbian and gay rights groups in recent years has been focused on passage of laws against such attacks, but also more fundamentally on making the police and judicial systems more sensitive to such hate crimes, educating the public to reduce homophobia, and forming self-help patrol groups in largely homosexual neighborhoods.

Unfortunately, lesbians can also turn their violence on each other; BATTERED WOMEN are found in homosexual, not just heterosexual, relationships. However, a battered lesbian receives even less support from the outside world than her heterosexual counterpart; police are less likely to intervene, state protective laws often do not apply, and frequently victims do not even try to seek help, afraid that exposure as a lesbian would cost them their jobs or children or alienate them from their families and friends.

Many lesbians mistakenly feel that they are not subject to the same SEXUALLY TRANSMITTED DISEASES that affect heterosexuals. Nothing could be farther from the truth. Even if a woman has relationships only with other women, some of those partners may have had sexual relations with men. But even if both women have had only lesbian contacts, they still may pass diseases to each other through sexual contact; penetration by a PENIS is not necessary for that. Many lesbian women today use CONDOMS on their fingers or on sexual toys, or barriers between one woman's tongue and her partner's GENITALS (see SEXUAL INTERCOURSE), to prevent passing infections to each other. (See LESBIAN HELP, INFORMATION, AND ACTION GUIDE on page 397.)

Refusal to make herself the object is not always what turns women to homosexuality; most lesbians, on the contrary, seek to cultivate the treasures of their femininity. . . .

SIMONE DE BEAUVOIR, 1949
———————————— IN THE SECOND SEX ————————————

•

LESBIAN

Help, Information, and Action Guide

☑ HOTLINES

▶ **Gay and Lesbian Switchboard** (212-777-1800), an all-volunteer, New York City–based hotline, serving as a de facto national hot line, providing legal referrals, counseling, and referrals for general information.

▶ **Lesbian Switchboard** (212-741-2610; M–F 6–10 P.M.), an all-woman volunteer telephone service, providing information, referrals, and crisis counseling; run by the **Lesbian and Gay Community Services Center** (208 West 13th Street, New York, NY 10011; 212-620-7310).

▶ **National Hate Crime Reporting Hotline** (Department of Justice, Community Relations Service; 800-347-HATE [4283]).

☑ GENERAL LESBIAN AND GAY RIGHTS ORGANIZATIONS

▶ NATIONAL CENTER FOR LESBIAN RIGHTS (**NCLR**) (415-621-0674). *Publishes NCLR Newsletter, A Lesbian and Gay Parents' Legal Guide to Child Custody, Lesbians Choosing Motherhood: Legal Issues in Donor Insemination, Lesbian Mother Litigation Manual, Partnership Protection Documents, Preserving and Protecting the Families of Lesbians and Gay Men, Recognizing Lesbian and Gay Families: Strategies for Obtaining Domestic Partners Benefits.*

▶ **National Gay and Lesbian Task Force (NGLTF)** (1734 14th Street, NW, Washington, DC 20009-4309; 202-332-6483; TTY for hearing-impaired, 202-332-6219), the oldest national gay and lesbian civil rights advocacy organization. It works for such rights though lobbying, organizing, public education, and direct action and has various projects, including the Anti-Violence Project, the Privacy/Civil Rights Project, the Lesbian and Gay Families Project, the Campus Project, the Media Project, and the Gay and Lesbian Military Freedom Project.

▶ LAMBDA LEGAL DEFENSE AND EDUCATION FUND (**LLDEF**) (212-995-8585 or 213-629-2728). Publishes *Lesbians Choosing Motherhood.*

▶ **Lesbian and Gay Rights Project** (American Civil Liberties Union, 132 West 43rd Street, New York, NY 10036; 212-944-9800, ext. 545), an organization that defends lesbian and gay rights, through direct litigation and as co-counsel with other organizations. It publishes various materials, including *The Rights of Gay People: An American Civil Liberties Union Handbook.*

▶ **International Gay and Lesbian Human Rights Commission** (540 Castro Street, San Francisco, CA 94114; 415-255-8680; Julie Dorf, executive

L

director), an organization that monitors human rights conditions for lesbians and gays internationally and publicizes and acts against abuses.

▶ **Gay and Lesbian Advocates and Defenders (GLAD)** (P.O. Box 218, Boston, MA 02112; 617-426-1350; Jan Platner, executive director), a "New England lesbian and gay public interest legal organization [that] does litigation and educational work on lesbian and gay civil rights issues. It also has an AIDS Law Project and publishes the newsletter *GLAD Briefs*.

▶ **Gay and Lesbian Alliance Against Defamation (GLAAD)** (150 West 26th Street, Suite 503, New York, NY 10001; 212-807-1700; Ellen Carton, executive director), an organization that fosters fair, accurate, and inclusive representations of the lives of lesbians and gays. It monitors media treatment of lesbians and gays and operates the **GLAAD Phone Tree** and the **GLAAD Mediagram Campaign** (both: 80 Varick Street, Suite 3E, New York, NY 10013; 212-966-1700), an organized network of telephone and telegram contacts to fight homophobia. It also publishes a newsletter and bulletin.

▶ **ASTRAEA National Lesbian Action Foundation** (666 Broadway, Suite 520, New York, NY 10012; 212-529-8021; Katherine Acey, executive director), a grass-roots-oriented nationwide lesbian organization founded in 1977 by multiracial and multicultural feminist activists. Astraea ("starry one"), from the Roman name for the goddess of justice or holy law, supports projects that "contribute to the well-being of women and girls," addressing "issues related to heterosexism, homophobia, and sexism" and working to "eliminate *all* forms of oppression."

▶ **Gay and Lesbian Victory Fund** (1012 14th Street, NW, 7th floor, Washington, DC 20005; 202-VIC-TORY [842-8679]; William Waybourn, executive director), an organization that supports qualified gay and lesbian candidates for political office; actually a nationwide network of donors to help such candidates win elections. Members make a membership contribution of $100 or more and agree to contribute $100 or more to their choice of at least two candidates recommended by the fund, its basic criteria being that the candidate be openly gay or lesbian, endorse the proposed Federal Gay/Lesbian Civil Rights Bill, have aggressive positions on AIDS funding and antidiscrimination issues, be pre-choice, and be a viable candidate. It publishes the newsletter *Victory*.

▶ **DIGNITY/USA** (202-861-0017 or 800-877-8797).

▶ **Friends for Lesbian and Gay Concerns (FLGC)** (P.O. Box 222, Sumneytown, PA 18084; 215-561-1700 [ask for Lyle]; Bruce Birchard, general secretary), an association of lesbian, gay, and nongay people who "gather for worship after the manner of Friends (Quakers)," though many are from another (or no) religious group. It sponsors gatherings, retreats, and other events; supports same-sex MARRIAGES; and publishes a quarterly newsletter.

◪ OTHER ORGANIZATIONS

▶ **NOW** Legal Defense and Education Fund (**NOW LDEF**) (212-925-6635). Publishes the Legal Resource Kit *Lesbian Rights*.
▶ National Coalition Against Domestic Violence (**NCADV**) (303-839-1857). Publishes *Naming the Violence: Speaking Out About Lesbian Battering*.
▶ Human Rights Campaign Fund (202-628-4160 or 800-777-HRCF [4723]).
▶ National Women's Health Network (**NWHN**) (202-347-1140). Operates the **Women's Health Information Service**. Publishes the information packet *Lesbian Health Issues*.
▶ Ms. Foundation for Women (**MFW**) (212-353-8580).

◪ ON FRIENDS, PARENTS, AND PARENTING

▶ Lesbian Mothers National Defense Fund (**LMNDF**) (206-325-2643).
▶ **Federation of Parents and Friends of Lesbians and Gays (ParentsFLAG)** (P.O. Box 27605, Washington, DC 20038; 202-638-4200; Mitzi Henderson, president), a network of mutual-support groups for parents of homosexuals. It fosters parent-child communication and publishes various materials including *About Our Children* and *Coming Out to Your Parents*.
▶ **National Federation of Parents and Friends of Gays (NF/PFOG)** (8020 Eastern Avenue, NW, Washington, DC 20012; 202-726-3223; Eugene M. Baker, executive secretary), a network of peer-counseling groups, aimed at helping families and friends of homosexuals understand the problems faced by gay men and lesbians; seeks to educate public and professionals, and to change public policy and legislation; publishes various materials, including recommended reading list.

Other resources

◪ GENERAL WORKS

Being—Being Happy—Being Gay: Pathways to a Rewarding Life for Lesbians and Gay Men. Bert Herrman. Alamo Square Press, 1990.
Loving Boldly: Issues Facing Lesbians. Esther D. Rothblum and Ellen Cole. Harrington Park, 1989.
Lesbianism: Affirming Nontraditional Roles. Esther D. Rothblum and Ellen Cole. Haworth Press, 1989.
Woman Plus Woman. Dolores Klaich. Naiad Press, 1989
Inventing Ourselves: Lesbian Life Stories. The Hall Carpenter Archives Staff. Routledge, 1989.

Invisible Lives: The Loving Alternative of Millions of Women. Martha B. Barrett. Morrow, 1989.

◪ ON LONG-TERM RELATIONSHIPS

Staying Power: Long-Term Lesbian Couples. Susan E. Johnson. Naiad Press, 1990.
Ceremonies of the Heart: Celebrating Lesbian Unions. Becky Butler, ed. Seal Press Feminist, 1990.
Lesbian Couples. D. Merilee Clunis and G. Dorsey Green. Seal Press, 1988.

◪ ON YOUNG LESBIANS

Coping With Your Sexual Orientation. Deborah A. Miller and Alex Waigand. Rosen, 1990. For adolescents.
Gay and Lesbian Youth. R.C. Williams Savin. Hemisphere, 1990.
Gay and Lesbian Youth. Gilbert Herdt, ed. Haworth Press, 1989.
One Teenager in Ten. Ann Heron, ed. Alyson, 1982.

◪ ON OLDER LESBIANS

Lesbians at Midlife: The Creative Transition. Barbara Sang and others, eds. Spinsters Books, 1991.
Lesbians over Sixty Speak for Themselves. Monika Kehoe, ed. Harrington Park, 1989; Haworth Press, 1989.
Long Time Passing: Lives of Older Lesbians. Mary Adelman, ed. Alyson, 1986.

◪ ON LESBIANS AND THEIR FAMILIES

Different Mothers: Sons and Daughters of Lesbians Talk About Their Lives. Louise Rafkin, ed. Cleis Press, 1990.
Coming Out to Parents. Mary V. Bornoh. Pilgrim Press, 1990. (Address: 475 Riverside Drive, New York, NY 10715)
There's Something I've Been Meaning to Tell You: An Anthology About Lesbians and Gay Men Coming Out to Their Children. Loralee MacPike, ed. Naiad Press, 1989.
Different Daughters: A Book by Mothers of Lesbians. Louise Rafkin, ed. Cleis Press, 1987; Doubleday, 1989.
Considering Parenthood. Cheri Pies. Spinsters/Aunt Lute Press [San Francisco], 1988.
Mother, I Have Something to Tell You. Joe Brans. Doubleday, 1987.
Gay and Lesbian Parents. Fredrick W. Bozett. Praeger, 1987.
Politics of the Heart: A Lesbian Parenting Anthology. Sandra Pollace and Jeanne Vaughn. Firebrand Books, 1987.
The Complete Guide to Gay Parenting. Joy Schulenburg. Doubleday, 1985.

A Lesbian and Gay Parent's Guide to Child Custody. National Lawyers Guild Anti-Sexism Committee [San Francisco, CA], 1985.

☑ ON LEGAL RIGHTS

The Rights of Lesbians and Gay Men: The Basic ACLU Guide to a Gay Person's Rights, 3rd ed. Nan D. Hunter and others. Southern Illinois University Press, 1992.

Sexual Orientation and the Law. Harvard Law Review editors. Harvard University Press, 1990

A Legal Guide for Lesbian and Gay Couples, 5th ed. Hayden Curry and Denis Clifford. Nolo, 1989.

Lovers, Doctors, and the Law: Your Legal Rights and Responsibilities in Today's Health Care Crisis. Margaret Davis and Robert Scott. Harper & Row, 1989.

☑ ON PERSONAL AND PRACTICAL CONCERNS

The Advocate Adviser. Pat Califia. Alyson Publications, 1991. From a lesbian and gay advice column.

Coming Out: Another Fun 'n Games Book for Lesbians. Elizabeth Dean and others. New Victoria, 1991.

Lesbian Queries: The Book of Lesbian Questions. Jennifer Hertz and Martha Ertman. Naiad Press, 1990.

Lesbian Survival Manual. Rhonda Dicksion. Naiad Press, 1990.

More Lesbian Etiquette. Gail Sausser. Crossing Press, 1990.

A Lesbian Love Advisor. Celeste West. Cleis Press, 1989.

☑ ON HEALTH AND SEXUALITY

An Intimate Wilderness: Lesbian Writers on Sexuality. Judith Barrington, ed. Eighth Mount Press, 1991.

Susie Sexpert's Lesbian Sex World. Susie Bright. Cleis Press, 1991.

The Lesbian Erotic Dance: Butch, Femme, Androgyny, et al. JoAnn Loulan. Spinsters Books, 1990.

New, Improved! Dykes to Watch Out For. Alison Bechdel. Firebrand Books, 1990.

Alive and Well: A Lesbian Health Guide. Grace Hepburn, with Bonnie Gutierrez. (Available from The Crossing Press, Freedom, CA 95019.)

Alternative Health Care for Women. Party Westcott and Leyardia Black. Healing Arts Press, 1987. (Address: One Park Street, Rochester, NY 05767)

Lesbian Health Matters! Santa Cruz (CA) Women's Health Center, 1987.

◪ ON ETHNIC OR RACIAL CONCERNS

Chicana Lesbians: The Girls Our Mothers Warned Us About. Carla Trujillo, ed. Third Woman, 1991.
Twice Blessed: On Being Lesbian or Gay and Jewish. Christie Balka. Beacon Press, 1991.
Nice Jewish Girls: A Lesbian Anthology, rev. ed. Evelyn T. Beck, ed. Beacon Press, 1989.
Living the Spirit: A Gay American Indian Anthology. Will Roscoe, ed. St. Martin's, 1988.
Companeras: Latina Lesbians (An Anthology). Juanita Ramos, ed. Latina Lesbian History Project, 1987.
Home Girls. Barbara Smith, ed. Kitchen Table: Women of Color Press (Latham, NY), 1983.

◪ ON RELIGIOUS CONCERNS

A Book of Revelations: Lesbian and Gay Episcopalians Tell Their Own Stories. Louie Crew, ed. Integrity (DC), 1991.
The Welcoming Congregation: Resources of Affirming Gay, Lesbian and Bisexual Persons. Scott W. Alexander, ed. Unitarian University, 1990.
Let My People In: A Lesbian Minister Tells of Her Struggles to Live Openly and Maintain Her Ministry. Rose M. Denman. Morrow, 1990.
A Faith of One's Own: Explorations by Catholic Lesbians. Barbara Zanotti, ed. The Crossing Press, 1989. (Address: Trumansburg, NY 14886)

◪ ON SPECIAL CONCERNS

Lesbians and Gays in the Military. Defense Personnel Security Research and Education Center [Washington, DC], 1988.
The Lesbian in Front of the Classroom. Caroline Skidway and others. HerBook, 1988. (Address: P.O. Box 7467, Santa Cruz, CA 95061)
Naming the Violence: Speaking Out About Lesbian Violence. Kerry Lobel, ed. Seal Press, 1986.

◪ BACKGROUND WORKS

Odd Girls and Twilight Lovers: A History of Lesbian Life in Twentieth-Century America. Lillian Faderman. Columbia University Press, 1991.
Lesbian—Woman, 1991, rev. ed. Del Martin and Phyllis Lyon. Volcano Press, 1991.
Encyclopedia of Homosexuality. Wayne R. Dynes and others, eds. Garland, 1990.
Lesbian Texts and Contexts: Radical Revisions. Karla Jay and Joanne Glasgow, eds. New York University Press, 1990.

Another Mother Tongue: Gay Words, Gay Worlds, rev. ed. Judy Grahn. Beacon Press, 1990.

Lesbian Lists. Dell Richards. Alyson Publications, 1990.

Lesbian Philosophies and Cultures. Jeffner Allen. State University of New York Press, 1990.

Love and Politics: Radical Feminist and Lesbian Theories. Carol A. Douglas. Ism Press, 1990.

In Search of Gay America: Women and Men in a Time of Change. Neil Miller. Atlantic Monthly, 1989.

Gay Men and Women Who Enriched the World. Thomas Cowan. W. Mulvey, 1989.

Identity Politics: Lesbian Feminism and the Limits of Community. Shane Phelan. Temple University Press, 1989.

lesbian feminism, the view, shared by many but not all women who are lesbians, that to be a lesbian is to make a contribution to the cause of feminism and that only in a lesbian society can women be fully empowered—in essence, free (see EMPOWERMENT). Some lesbian feminists feel that HETEROSEXUAL women can join in the struggle for what Jill Johnston called the "lesbian nation," but most assert that women who have heterosexual relationships harm the feminist cause; and many take the fully separatist position that only lesbians or women-centered female celibates can be feminists. The latter view is seen by mainstream feminists as a self-isolating point of view. (See also FEMINISM; LESBIAN.)

Lesbian Mothers National Defense Fund (LMNDF) (P.O. Box 21567, Seattle, WA 98111; 206-325-2643; Nancy Rickerson, executive officer), an organization to help lesbians who are or wish to be mothers. It provides information on alternatives, such as donor insemination and adoption, and on lesbian and gay men custody cases; offers legal, psychological, and financial support to lesbian mothers in contested child custody situations; makes referrals to lawyers; and publishes quarterly *Mom's Apple Pie*.

Letters on the Equality of the Sexes and the Condition of Women. See Angelina and Sarah GRIMKÉ.

leukemia, a type of CANCER affecting the bone marrow (see BLOOD).

LH, an abbreviation for LUTEINIZING HORMONE.

liberal feminism: See FEMINISM.

liberated woman, someone who sees herself as wholly or largely free of the attitudes common to the male supremacist culture in which she finds herself. The term is seriously applicable only to a view of self and values, having less to do with any combination of specific accomplishments than with a more general refusal to submit, to assume stereotypical gender roles (see SEX ROLES), or to limit personal expectations. The term is also used by some men and women, often as an epithet, to describe a woman who lives a free sex life. A few highly political and utopian feminists deny the possibility of meaningful personal freedom until a women's revolution has succeeded. (See WOMEN'S LIBERATION MOVEMENT.)

life expectancy, an estimate of the number of years a person can be expected to live from a given time, such as birth, age twenty-one, age thirty-five, or age seventy. Such estimates are based on statistical studies of large numbers of people, and are affected by a variety of factors, including genetic background, physical condition, nutrition, social class, occupation, place of residence (which includes environmental factors), and perhaps most of all sex.

Most obviously, women generally live longer than men. During the twentieth century, life expectancy in most parts of the world has been increasing for both sexes, but more for women than for men, so that in the developed world, girls born today can be expected to live approximately 6.5 years more than boys of the same age. In the developing world, though the life expectancy is considerably lower for the whole population, women generally still have an advantage of four to five years in life expectancy at birth.

Women and men do not follow the same patterns, however. Rather, life expectancy varies at different times of life. Between the ages of fifteen and twenty-four, males are 2.7 times more likely than females to die, according to data summarized in Penny Kane's *Women's Health: From Womb to Womb* (St. Martin's, 1991); over age forty-five, men are twice as likely to die as women are. The main area of vulnerability for females has always been between the ages of one and eight, and during the prime reproductive years of twenty to thirty-five. It is in the middle years that women have made the greatest gains in life expectancy. The data strongly suggest that this is due in large part to their increasing control over their own reproduction, through BIRTH CONTROL and safely performed ABORTIONS. As a result, women can choose to have children when they are best able to bear them and care for them, with fewer overall pregnancies; better spacing of pregnancies, giving the body time to regain its strength; and few pregnancies in the more risky early and late childbearing years. Women's advantage in life expectancy continues strongly into their older years as well, though it is unclear why that is so.

Though life expectancy has improved generally, it has not done so in all parts of the world; in Hungary and in the countries that made up the former Soviet Union, in fact, the picture has worsened in recent decades for both men and women, possibly in part because of poor industrial safety, affecting workers of both sexes. Also, where women and men are increasingly involved in the same hazardous activities, such as SMOKING, ALCOHOL AND DRUG ABUSE, driving automobiles, and working in industrial plants, the differences between their life expectancies tends to lessen.

In some impoverished areas, notably in South Asia, the general pattern differs markedly; there young girls and women of childbearing age have a lower life expectancy than men of the same age. This may reflect the continuance of more traditional reproductive patterns, but may also result partly from SON PREFERENCE, in which male children from birth into adulthood are given the best of whatever the family can afford, from food to education to medical care.

But in most developed countries, the life expectancy is continuing to lengthen, though it is unclear whether there is a natural limit to the age that humans can reach, and women are making up an increasingly large proportion of the older population. Length of life does not always equal quality of life; and many women find themselves subject to chronic, disabling conditions exacerbated by longevity, such as OSTEOPOROSIS, ARTHRITIS, and hearing disorders (see EARS). A 1992 report from the National Institute on Aging (see OLDER WOMEN'S HELP, INFORMATION, AND ACTION GUIDE on page 374) found that, in the United States, among people seventy-five and older, more than 30 percent of the women required help with basic activities such as eating, dressing, bathing, cooking, managing finances, and going outside; for men, the percentage was much lower, at 17.2 percent. Increasingly, older people and their advocates have been seeking to provide services and living arrangements that will allow older people, many of them women, and many of them poor, to maintain their physical independence, with modest assistance. (See OLDER WOMEN'S HELP, INFORMATION, AND ACTION GUIDE on page 374; WOMEN'S HEALTH HELP, INFORMATION, AND ACTION GUIDE on page 334.)

lipomas, benign lumps of fatty tissue, as in the BREAST.

liposuction, an operation to remove fat by literally sucking it out of small incisions in the body (see COSMETIC SURGERY).

liver, a key organ in the DIGESTIVE SYSTEM.

living together agreement, a document drawn up by unmarried couples to protect themselves in case of illness, SEPARATION, disputes, or death (see COHABITATION).

LMP, an abbreviation for last menstrual period; the date used in calculating a woman's due date or delivery date in PREGNANCY (see GESTATION).

lone parent, an alternative term for SINGLE PARENT.

love: See MATE SELECTION.

lumpectomy, a type of mastectomy or breast surgery involving removal of a small section, rather than the whole breast (see BREAST CANCER).

lung cancer, malignancies affecting the RESPIRATORY SYSTEM, since 1987 the leading cause of CANCER deaths in women. In fact, the American Cancer Society estimates that from the mid-1950s to the mid-1980s, lung cancer deaths increased by an astounding 425 percent among women. Not only that, but while the incidence rate for men began to decline in the mid-1980s, the rate for women continued to increase. In all, an estimated 53,000 women were estimated to lose their lives to lung cancer in 1992, in the United States alone.

One of the main causes for these increases is the rise in women SMOKING. The scientific links between smoking and cancer are strong and growing stronger. Smoking causes specific damage to bronchial lining tissue, but early precancerous cellular changes can heal themselves and return to normal once smoking has stopped. But if smoking continues, abnormal growth patterns can lead to cancer. Other causes also contribute to lung cancer, among them exposure to various kinds of industrial chemicals, such as asbestos, arsenic, and organic chemicals; and exposure to radiation, from occupational, medical, or environmental sources, including the radioactive gas radon, which in recent years has been shown to be common in many households, seeping in from underground rocks. All of these dangers are magnified in smokers. In addition, increasing evidence shows that nonsmokers who are routinely exposed to smoke, in what is called *passive smoking*, also show increased risk of lung cancer.

Symptoms of lung cancer include a persistent cough, blood-streaked sputum, chest pain, and recurrent pneumonia or bronchitis (see RESPIRATORY SYSTEM). Unfortunately, symptoms often do not appear until the disease is in its advanced stages. As a result, the American Cancer Society places the five-year survival rate at only 13 percent overall. Although the survival rate is 41 percent for cases where the cancer is still localized, less than one case in five is diagnosed this early. Diagnosis can be aided by chest X-rays, analysis of cells from sputum, and fiberoptic examination of bronchial passages.

For localized cancers, surgery is generally performed. However, for most cancers, radiation and chemotherapy will be used in addition, to deal with the spread (*metastasis*). In some kinds of lung cancer, surgery is inappropriate, and chemotherapy and sometimes radiation are used, with some success, to achieve remission of the disease. (See CANCER; RESPIRATORY SYSTEM; also CANCER HELP, IN-FORMATION, AND ACTION GUIDE on page 133.)

lupus, an autoimmune disorder in which the body's IMMUNE SYSTEM mistakenly attacks connective tissue in the body; more formally called *lupus erythematosus* or *systemic lupus erythematosus* (SLE). Its causes are unclear, but some believe susceptibility is inherited and then triggered by some outside agent, such as a virus or medication.

For unknown reasons lupus is far more common in women than in men, appearing most often in late childhood through the early childbearing years and in some ethnic groups, especially Blacks. Symptoms may be mild, but can be life-threatening if vital organs are attacked, such as the heart (see HEART AND CIRCU-LATORY SYSTEM), kidneys (see URINARY TRACT), and central nervous system (see BRAIN AND NERVOUS SYSTEM). The most characteristic symptom is a reddish butterfly-shaped patch on the cheeks and nose, but other common symptoms include ARTHRITIS, anemia (see BLOOD), and *pleurisy,* inflammation of the lining of the lungs (see RESPIRATORY SYSTEM).

The course of development is also highly variable. Lupus may develop slowly and intermittently, over months or even years, with occasional fever or fatigue, or it may come on suddenly with a high fever. In its early stages it is often confused with other disorders, such as rheumatoid ARTHRITIS. It is normally diagnosed by finding specific antibodies in blood tests and biopsies. Some drugs help control inflammation, and patients are instructed to avoid the sun, which can worsen the condition. With early diagnosis and careful treatment, the death rate has been cut for severe cases of lupus. A mild form, called *discoid lupus erythematosus* (DSE), primarily affects the skin and appears mostly among women in their thirties. Circulatory problems are sometimes associated with LU-PUS (see REYNAUD'S DISEASE).

If vital organs are not affected, women with lupus may decide to have children. They have an increased likelihood of MISCARRIAGE and of flare-up of the disease after DELIVERY, however, so theirs would be consider a high-risk PREG-NANCY. Some studies have, in fact, shown that miscarriages that occur for unknown reasons are sometimes linked with undiagnosed lupus.

For more help, information, and action

▶ **Lupus Foundation of America (LFA)** (4 Research Place, Suite 180, Rockville, MD 20850; 301-690-9292 or 800-558-0121; John Huber, executive director), an organization that provides support to people with lupus, encouraging patient-to-patient contact; gathers and disseminates information; supports research; and publishes various materials, including the *Lupus News* and *Lupus Erythematosus: A Handbook for Physicians, Patients and their Families.*

▶ **American Lupus Society** (3914 Del Amo Boulevard, Suite 922, Torrance, CA 90503; 310-542-8891 or 800-331-1802; Joan Lavelle, executive director), a network of mutual-support groups for lupus patients and their families. It offers information and referrals, and publishes various materials including the newsletter *Lupus Erythematosus* (in English and Spanish) and *The Butterfly Mask*.

▶ NATIONAL INSTITUTE OF ARTHRITIS AND MUSCULOSKELETAL AND SKIN DISEASES (NIAMS) (301-496-8188). It publishes *Update: Lupus Erythematosus Research and Arthritis, Rheumatic Diseases, and Related Disorders*.

▶ Arthritis Foundation (404-872-7100). Publishes *Systemic Lupus Erythematosus*. (See ARTHRITIS HELP, INFORMATION, AND ACTION GUIDE on page 65.)

▶ NATIONAL INSTITUTE OF NEUROLOGICAL DISORDERS AND STROKE (NINDS) (301-496-5751).

▶ NATIONAL WOMEN'S HEALTH NETWORK (NWHN) (202-347-1140). Operates the **Women's Health Information Service**. Publishes the information packet *Autoimmune Disorders*.

Other resources

Lupus: My Search for a Diagnosis. Eileen Radziunas. Hunter House, 1990.
Embracing the Wolf: A Lupus Victim and Her Family Learn to Live with Chronic Disease. Joanna Baumer Permut. Cherokee Publishing, 1989.
Coping with Lupus. Robert H. Phillips. Avery, 1984.
(See also WOMEN'S HEALTH HELP, INFORMATION, AND ACTION GUIDE on page 334.)

luteal phase, an alternate name for SECRETORY PHASE, the middle portion of the reproductive cycle (see MENSTRUATION).

luteinizing hormone (LH), a HORMONE released by the pituitary gland that triggers the release of an egg (OVUM) from the OVARIES, in the process called OVULATION. More precisely, at about fourteen days before the beginning of the next reproductive cycle, marked by MENSTRUATION, a surge of LH triggers an egg to burst forth from the GRAAFIAN FOLLICLE in which it grew. This LH surge is measured in the *ovulation method* of NATURAL FAMILY PLANNING, whether a couple is seeking BIRTH CONTROL or CONCEPTION.

lymphatic system: See IMMUNE SYSTEM.

lymphogranuloma venereum (LGV), one of the SEXUALLY TRANSMITTED DISEASES (see CHLAMYDIA).

lymphoma, a type of CANCER affecting the lymphatic system (see IMMUNE SYSTEM).

makeup: See COSMETICS.

malignant hyperthermia, a genetically inherited, potentially life-threatening reaction to ANESTHESIA.

mammary gland, medical name for BREAST.

mammogram, an X-ray picture of the BREASTS, used in screening for BREAST CANCER. Each breast is placed separately between plastic plates and flattened, with some brief minor discomfort, to provide a clear picture of the internal tissue. With modern mammography equipment, the amount of radiation used is very low and the amount of detail far surpasses that of the past.

Mammography is designed to detect CANCER in its earliest stages—as much as two years before it is large enough to be felt manually by either the woman or her doctor—to increase the chances of successful treatment and to lessen the likelihood that a breast may be lost to surgery. As of this writing, the National Cancer Institute and several other major U.S. medical organizations recommend that, beginning at age forty, a woman should have a mammogram every one to two years and every year after age fifty, along with a physical examination by a doctor. The American Cancer Society also recommends a "baseline" mammogram for women age thirty-five to thirty-nine, to provide a basis for comparison. Some other medical groups, notably in Canada and Europe, disagree about the benefits of mammography to women forty to forty-nine; one Canadian study even suggested a slightly increased risk of cancer among screened women age forty to forty-nine, but critics of the study note that the mammographies in the study were done by unspecialized technologists using outdated equipment. A woman should discuss with her doctor how often she should be screened, depending on her age and personal and family history. Note that screening guidelines are only for women who have *no suspicious signs or symptoms,* such as ones that might show up in a BREAST SELF-EXAMINATION (see page 104). Women who notice any unusual lumps or other changes in their breasts should consult a doctor immediately.

Mammograms are done at offices or centers with the required special equipment, sometimes at screening programs in health clinics, hospitals, or even mobile vans. Women are recommended, however, to use mammography facilities that have extensive experience in using the procedure and that use a machine dedicated solely to mammographies (in the United States, these should be accredited by the American College of Radiology). Women who have BREAST IM-PLANTS should be sure that the facility uses the special mammography techniques designed for women with implants (see IF YOU HAVE IMPLANTS . . . on page 119). For referrals to a nearby mammography facility, women can check with their doctors or call the Cancer Information Service (800-4-CANCER [422-6237]). (See BREAST CANCER.)

mammoplasty, breast surgery (see COSMETIC SURGERY).

marital contract, a document developed and signed by MARRIAGE partners after the WEDDING; a *postnuptial* rather than PRENUPTIAL AGREEMENT. Such agreements are meant to define the main plans, intentions, expectations, and living arrangements of the couple, so each knows what to expect of the other.

It covers many of the same areas as a *living together contract* (see COHABI-TATION) but differs from that in two important ways. First, the marriage relationship is already defined in many ways in the law, as cohabitation generally is not. Second, while cohabiting partners need an agreement precisely because laws do not cover them, married partners are primarily expressing *intentions* toward each other, since traditionally courts did not honor *post*nuptial contracts between wife and husband, and courts are still highly variable in their handling of them. Some tend to deal with such an agreement as a legal contract and uphold or modify it if it is reasonable and fair and the partners were acting voluntarily and were not being deceived on some central points. But other courts follow the traditional practice forbidding contracts between married partners as being for "illicit sexual services," on the old assumption that the woman is serving the man, sexually and otherwise. This ignores the fact that most marital contracts are written with the view of establishing, by mutual consent, a more egalitarian relationship.

Among the many kinds of topics that might be covered in a marital agreement are

- handling of income, assets, and expenses, including budgeting and entertainment expenses.
- handling of property acquired during the relationship, specifically as to whether it will be held as separate property or treated as community property.
- handling of debts incurred, including whether they will have separate or joint liability and whether they have some guidelines on maximum levels of debt.
- furnishing, decorating, maintaining, provisioning, and cleaning the home (see HOUSEWORK), including not only who takes responsibility for what and on

what basis—equal, balanced, or rotating, for example—but also the life-style the partners envision.

- intentions regarding childbearing and child-rearing responsibilities, including handling of unintended, unwanted PREGNANCY.
- expectations of either party regarding support from the other (such as while getting a professional degree or while children are very young).
- where the couple's legal domicile will be established, and any special considerations, such as the possible need for a separate domicile, for professional or other purposes, or either's right to veto a proposed move.
- plans for leisure time, including handling of holidays.
- intentions regarding monogamy and possible sexual relationships with other people.
- support for any third party, such as a child, parent, or ex-spouse.
- commitments to family, friends, community, and business associates, including whether the couple want to set certain times to be wholly alone.
- access to the home by others, especially family and friends.
- handling of names for the partners and for any children (see NAMES IN MARRIAGE), during the marriage and in case of a DIVORCE.
- religious commitments, including the religion in which any child will be raised.
- the parties' individual need for privacy.
- handling of long-term security questions such as health insurance, life insurance, and wills (see INSURANCE AND PENSION EQUITY).
- any other areas of potential contention, such as use of a shared car or responsibility for pets or plants.
- arrangements for modifying the agreement, perhaps with scheduled reviews.
- how the relationship might be dissolved, if desired, especially whether it can be ended by one person or mutually, whether conciliation will be required, and how CUSTODY, CHILD SUPPORT, VISITATION RIGHTS, ALIMONY, and similar questions will be treated.
- conflict resolution, such as an agreement to use MEDIATION or ARBITRATION to solve disputes, if they should occur, without going to court, including (where desired) specification of fines or penalties for breach of contract.

Such a contract is, in truth, only as strong as the relationship between the two people. As in many areas of the law, if people are likely to break a contract, a piece of paper will not keep them from doing so. But a marriage contract can serve as a guide—an idealized model of their intentions in their life together. (See COUPLES AND FAMILIES HELP, INFORMATION, AND ACTION GUIDE on page 418.)

marital property, the combined assets of the partners in a MARRIAGE, a matter of considerable controversy and changing interpretation, especially with widespread changes in DIVORCE and in subsequent division of such property.

Historically, under English common law, most property belonged to the husband; in fact, legally, his wife and children were also, in essence, his property (see COVERTURE). With various Married Women's Property Acts from the mid-nineteenth century on, women became legally entitled to own property in their own names. However, much of the property was judged to be owned by the person who held title to it—if the house was in the husband's name, it belonged solely to the husband, for example. Vestiges of that attitude still remain but are gradually retreating as differing strategies are developed to assess ownership of marital property.

The concept of *community property* holds that all property acquired during marriage—except that acquired separately by inheritance or gift—is owned not by either individual, but by the "marital community." If that marriage breaks up, the property is divided equally between the marital partners. This can cause problems, however, since to divide the property, the major assets—frequently including the family home—must often be sold, leading to further disruption for the children, not to mention the MOTHER, who often has CUSTODY. The concept of community property is found especially in some lands of Spanish heritage, and in the United States in several western states, including California, Arizona, Louisiana, Nevada, Idaho, New Mexico, Texas, and Washington.

The other main strategy in the United States is a modification of common law, in which all assets (except gifts and inheritances) are divided on principles of "equitable distribution." The guidelines for division vary state by state, by law and practice, but take into account such matters as the parties' age, health, economic circumstances, and future earning capacity; the ages of children; who has custody of the children and whether it is desirable for that person to work outside the home; the length of the marriage; and the contributions and sacrifices made to the marriage by each, including the HOMEMAKER's services. Also a change from previous times, fault (see DIVORCE) is generally not considered in dividing marital property. In the United States, the model Uniform Marital Property Act regards marriage as an economic partnership, in which the work of both partners, including HOUSEWORK, is recognized as equal. The act breaks new ground in specifying that shared rights in marital property are "in place at divorce or death" and so do not require a court order or "transfer." So far, however, the act has not been widely adopted.

The main focus of change in the late twentieth century is on what constitutes marital property. Some things are clear: the house, the car, the furnishings, the land, the stocks and bonds, the business, and so on. However, some states are now considering other assets as part of marital property. Among those that have been included in some states—though sometimes rejected in others—are pension rights and retirement benefits (at least the portion that has accrued during the marriage (see INSURANCE AND PENSION EQUITY), disability pay, personal injury awards, life insurance policies, and the value of a professional degree. This is a rapidly changing area of the law, so women will want to engage an attorney who is experienced and up-to-date in the field and knows where new gains might be made. To help in this process, women contemplating separation or divorce should gather and make copies of all documents available on the family's financial assets (see PREPARING FOR A DIVORCE: A WOMAN'S GUIDE on page 236). (See also COUPLES AND FAMILIES HELP, INFORMATION, AND ACTION GUIDE on page 418; DIVORCE AND SEPARATION HELP, INFORMATION, AND ACTION GUIDE on page 238.)

marital status, the legal position of an adult as to whether they are or have ever been married. Specifically, adults are classified as

▶ *married,* if they are currently in a legal MARRIAGE. For census and other purposes, this classification is sometimes divided into two groups, *spouse present* and *spouse absent,* as when a couple has a SEPARATION or one SPOUSE has abandoned the other (see ABANDONMENT.)

▶ *widowed,* if their spouse has died (see WIDOW). This usually applies to current status only; if a woman was widowed and then remarried, she would be classified as married.

▶ *divorced,* if their previous marriage ended in a DIVORCE but the party in question has not remarried.

▶ *single,* if they have never been married (see SINGLE WOMAN). This generally includes couples who are living together unmarried (see COHABITATION), though not for all purposes.

More generally, however, a person may be classified as either single or married, with single also encompassing people who have been widowed or divorced.

Traditionally, a never-married woman was addressed as "Miss" and a married, separated, divorced, or widowed woman was "Mrs." Many woman in the twentieth century, however, have instead preferred to use "Ms.," emphasizing their independent status rather than any marital status (see **Ms.**).

marriage, the legal union of two people, generally a man and a woman; also the WEDDING ceremony at which most such unions are legally formed. A marriage is a socially sanctioned sexual relationship, generally between a single woman, called the *wife,* and a single man, the *husband,* in which children may be born and raised. Marriage between one woman and one man, called MONOGAMY, is expressly intended to last for life, though it can be broken by SEPARATION and terminated by ANNULMENT, DIVORCE, or death (see WIDOW).

Marriage carries with it various rights and obligations (see page 414). The wife and husband may agree to change these, before the marriage by prior agreement, in a PRENUPTIAL AGREEMENT; if the marriage is broken or terminated, in a SEPARATION AGREEMENT; or during the marriage, often after a dispute, in a RECONCILIATION *agreement.* Couples may also draw up a MARITAL CONTRACT regarding their rights and duties in the relationship, though these have less certain legal standing.

Societies have various formal and informal rules regarding who can marry (see MATE SELECTION). In some societies marriages can legally involve one woman or more and one man or more (see POLYGAMY), though in most countries, having multiple husbands or wives at once is generally illegal (see BIGAMY). Where divorce and remarriage is common, having a series of spouses is sometimes called *serial monogamy.*

Most marriages are formed at a special ceremony called a *wedding,* which may be civil or religious. But some are created without formalities, resulting from the parties living together openly as husband and wife or stating publicly their words of consent to and acknowledgment of their marriage. Many states no longer accept such COMMON-LAW MARRIAGES, however, and living together openly is now more generally called COHABITATION and often does not imply marriage, though some legal obligations may develop (see COHABITATION). One kind of marriage not generally permitted, but which has been allowed in some special circumstances such as wartime, is a *proxy marriage,* in which someone stands in for a missing partner, and having both partners' consent, speaks the words of the ceremony.

For a formal marriage, a license is required, valid for a limited period of time, such as thirty to sixty days. Traditionally, prospective marriages were also announced publicly ahead of time, in Christian communities on the three consecutive Sundays before the wedding, in what was called the reading of the *banns.* Today most states have only a brief waiting period. Parties to the marriage must also be old enough (see AGE OF CONSENT) and must have certain blood tests before marriage, as for SEXUALLY TRANSMITTED DISEASES (STDs), and sometimes a more general medical examination designed so that both parties are aware of any existing physical problems before a marriage. If a person is found to have an STD, the clerk can refuse a license.

Some LESBIANS and gay men, seeking to express before society their lifetime commitment to each other, have formed same-sex marriages. Such unions have been recognized in some communities and are sometimes solemnized in religious services. In most places these have no legal status, however, and in some states are expressly forbidden by law. As a result, same-sex marital partners—often called *domestic partners*—lack some of the rights and benefits normally involved in marriage, such as INHERITANCE RIGHTS and insurance benefits; also they may face complicated legal questions if they later break up, since normal divorce laws may not apply (see CUSTODY, for example).

In earlier times marriage was a grossly unequal relationship, in which the wife, all of her property, and any children, all became—effectively, in the law— the property of the husband. A woman moved from her parents' household to her husband's and from one legal and financial dependency to another. Whatever power women might wield in the marriage relationship itself—and on occasion that could be considerable—depended largely on the individual woman's strength, ability, aggressiveness, and perhaps family connections, and to some extent on the husband's weakness or his willingness to share power, in a situation where the law was almost completely on his side. That is still the case in many parts of the world, and in many individual marriages, but in countries where fights for WOMEN'S RIGHTS have been strongly waged, notably in the industrialized countries, the law is somewhat more evenhanded on such matters as married women's property rights (see COVERTURE); women's ability to obtain a legal separation or divorce; and their right to share in the assets of the marriage (see MARITAL PROPERTY).

In the law, marriage is not only a person's status, but also a form of contract, in which each partner has certain rights and obligations. These can vary widely from society to society and from one time period to another. Traditionally, under English common law, the husband was obliged to support his wife (see SPOUSAL SUPPORT), while the wife was obliged to serve the husband by keeping the home, cooking, and washing (see HOUSEWORK; HOMEMAKER). If either did not fulfill these basic duties, others might deplore the situation, but generally no one—not even the state—could interfere legally, except in extreme situations (see DIVORCE). Husband and wife also have the right to inherit from each other if one should die (see INHERITANCE RIGHTS; DOWER; CURTESY; RIGHT OF ELECTION).

In addition, the wife and husband have CONJUGAL RIGHTS—rights to the other's companionship, love, comfort, and sexual relations—also called *consortium* (see below). Traditionally, this meant that a wife had the duty to have sexual relations when her husband desired them and to bear and raise any children of their union. But, as the law is coming to recognize, conjugal rights are mutual. An annulment or divorce may be granted if one party refuses to have sex, is physically incapable of having sex, or has fraudulently concealed an inability to have children.

In the United States, the Supreme Court has found that the *right of privacy* largely protects the marital bedroom from intrusion by the state, in such matters as BIRTH CONTROL. Some states, however, have intruded into marital sexual relations by barring some kinds of sexual acts, such as *sodomy* and *fellatio* (see SEXUAL INTERCOURSE). Even birth control is not unrestricted, for if one partner uses CONTRACEPTION or has STERILIZATION against the other's will, that can be grounds for an annulment or divorce. However, the decision of whether or not to have an ABORTION is solely the woman's; her husband cannot legally bar or force an abortion.

Traditionally, forcible sexual intercourse between husband and wife was not a crime. The law regarding marital RAPE seems to be changing, though even if it changes in principle, it is still hard to prove. In some cases, however, rape may be chargeable as assault. This is, of course, part of the much wider question of domestic abuse (see BATTERED WOMEN; CHILD ABUSE AND NEGLECT), a developing area of the law, in which the courts—forcefully prodded by WOMEN'S RIGHTS organizations—are taking a new look at the balance between the traditional view of the husband-wife relationship and the need to protect women from assault.

A husband and wife occupy a special position in the law, since traditionally they were, legally, one. As a result, they could not sue each other or be sued for conspiracy. Today both kinds of suits can take place, though the right to sue each other is still limited in some places. This change allows one spouse to sue another for intentionally violating property rights—selling shares of stock without authority, for example—or to collect from an insurance company in an accident in which one injured the other.

By the same token, and to protect the confidentiality of marital communications, husbands and wives were traditionally not allowed to testify against one another. Various exceptions to that rule are now allowed. Most important, one partner can testify against the other in cases involving the family relationship itself, including domestic violence, ADULTERY, rape, and BIGAMY. In addition, in some states, one partner can *voluntarily* testify against another, though sometimes only with the other's consent. Such prohibitions generally end with divorce.

Also special in the law is the handling of cases involving injuries to wives or husbands. Some of these involve *consortium* or *conjugal rights*, including company, cooperation, affection, and sexual companionship. Traditionally only a husband could sue someone else for *loss of consortium*, if his wife was injured in some way that damaged her ability as a companion—sexual and otherwise—and homemaker. Not until 1950 did a woman get the right to sue for loss of consortium in the United States; now she can do so in most, but not all, states.

Traditionally, also, a husband could sue someone who interfered with the marriage, especially by inducing his wife to leave him; this could apply not just to a lover, but to any meddler, including a mother-in-law. Comparable suits today are rare but are sometimes called *heart-balm actions*. If a man feels his wife's heart has been "won away" by another man, he might charge *alienation of affections*. A suit charging a man with seducing his wife into adultery is called *criminal conversation*.

Traditionally, the place where the husband lives has been the married couple's legal residence, or *domicile* (though either husband or wife might have other residences). But today many states recognize that a woman may need to establish a separate domicile, as when running for public office or establishing eligibility for lower tuition at a state university, though in some states she is still obliged to establish that she is living separate from her husband "for cause."

It is the traditional legal position of married women—their sexual obligations and their total dependency—that has made some women call marriage "legal PROSTITUTION" (as Mary WOLLSTONECRAFT did as early as the eighteenth century) or "sexual slavery." Much has changed since then in the legal standing of women, individually and in marriage, but to some women marriage is still so much an instrument of PATRIARCHY, inequality, and oppression that they call for the total abolition of the legal union of men and women, seeking more equal, alternative forms of male-female relationship without the patriarchal baggage. Certainly that has been the motivation for some couples who choose cohabitation instead of marriage and of many who have written marital contracts. Some women have gone even farther, asserting that equal relationships between men and women are impossible in any formal or informal structure, and call for women's separatist movements, involving either *celibacy* or LESBIAN relationships.

Marriage and FAMILY are deeply intertwined with human history, however, and will remain so, though they may change in both private life and public perception. Whatever the pace of legal change, change on a social and personal level comes slowly. Some men have come to accept—and some have embraced and strongly fought for—an ideal of equal relationships between men and women, in marriage and out of it. More often, however, men are conflicted and confused about the changes; sometimes their intellectual ideals are at war with their more traditional training, while some men accept no changes at all. Frustration over these clashes, and a need to try to reassert or establish their power in the marriage relationship, is thought by many to contribute to violence directed at wives and their children (see BATTERED WOMEN, and CHILD ABUSE AND NEGLECT).

Whatever the strains, marriage remains a central part of the lives of most women. Around the world, many women are married before they are twenty, especially in sub-Saharan Africa and southwest Asia; among some traditional cultures, girls are married at or even before PUBERTY. In developed countries women tend to marry later, on average at about age twenty-three, and early marriages are today the exception. At whatever age, however, women tend to marry men older than themselves, and the resulting age gap tends to reinforce the traditional de-

FIRST MARRIAGES

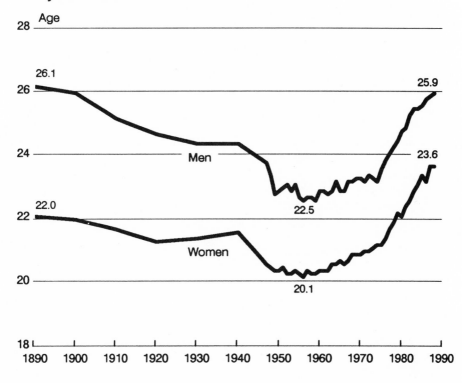

Median Age at First Marriage, by Sex: 1890 to 1988

Source: "Singleness in America," by Arlene F. Saluter, from U.S. Bureau of the Census, Current Population Reports, Series P-23, No. 162, *Studies in Marriage and the Family.* Government Printing Office, 1989.

M
·———·

pendent stance of the woman. In the United States, as of 1990, the median age of women at first marriage was 23.9 years, with that for men 26.1 years. In the period between 1970 and 1990, the proportion of women thirty to thirty-four years old who had never married nearly tripled, from 6 to 16 percent; those numbers may, however, have been skewed by the increase in the number of couples living together unmarried in that period (see COHABITATION).

In general, women tend to marry men of their own general background, though they often seek to marry into a higher socioeconomic background (see MATE SELECTION). Where they marry across some racial, religious, and ethnic lines, the marital partners have to deal with more than usual strains in the marriage, as they deal with the social expectations of others. (See COUPLES AND FAMILIES HELP, INFORMATION, AND ACTION GUIDE on page 418.)

ON THE RIGHT TO MARITAL PRIVACY

We deal with a right of privacy older than the Bill of Rights—older than our political parties, older than our school system. Marriage is a coming together for better or for worse, hopefully enduring, and intimate to the degree of being sacred.

WILLIAM O. DOUGLAS
U.S. SUPREME COURT JUSTICE
——————— GRISWOLD V. CONNECTICUT (1965) ———————

•

COUPLES AND FAMILIES
Help, Information, and Action Guide

Organizations

▶ **Family Resource Coalition (FRC)** (230 North Michigan Avenue, Suite 1625, Chicago, IL 60601; 312-726-4750; Gail C. Christopher, executive director), a network of community-based family support organizations, aiming to strengthen families and enhance the quality of child development. It acts as an information clearinghouse for family resource programs, attempts to influence public policy and legislation; and publishes materials including *Program to Strengthen Families: A Resource Guide.*

▶ **United Families of America (UFA)** (220 I Street, NE, Suite 150, Washington, DC 20002; 202-546-1600; Gordon S. Jones, executive director), an organization focusing families in society. It seeks to influence public policy and legislation to maintain the strength of the family. It conducts seminars and training sessions about lobbying; and publishes *National Family Reporter.*

▶ NATIONAL CENTER FOR YOUTH LAW (NCYL) (415-543-3307).

▨ ON SPECIAL FAMILY SITUATIONS

▶ **Stepfamily Association of America (SAA)** (215 Centennial Mall S., Suite 212, Lincoln, NE 68508; 402-477-7837 or 800-735-0329; Bill Munn, executive director), a network of mutual-support groups for stepfamilies. It has programs and meetings, some especially for children; acts as an advocate for stepfamily rights; makes referrals; and publishes various materials, including *Learning to Step Together.*

▶ **Step Family Foundation (SFF)** (333 West End Avenue, New York, NY 10023; 212-877-3244 or 800-SKY-STEP [759-7837]; Jeannette Lofas, executive director), an organization focusing on stepfamily relationships. It gathers and disseminates information; offers counseling and training groups; and publishes various materials.

▶ NATIONAL CENTER FOR LESBIAN RIGHTS (NCLR) (415-621-0674). Publishes *Lesbians Choosing Motherhood: Legal Issues in Donor Insemination, Lesbian Mother Litigation Manual, Partnership Protection Documents, Preserving and Protecting the Families of Lesbians and Gay Men, Recognizing Lesbian and Gay Families: Strategies for Obtaining Domestic Partners Benefits.*

Other resources

▨ GENERAL WORKS

Marriages and Families: Making Choices and Facing Change. 4th ed. Mary A. Lamanna and Agnes Riedmann. Wadsworth, 1991.

Marriage and Family Quest for Intimacy. Robert Lauer and Jeanette C. Lauer. William C. Brown, 1991.

Choices in Marriage and Family: 2nd ed. J. Gipson Wells. Collegiate Press, 1991.

The Family Contract: A Parent's Bill of Rights. Howard Leftin. PIA Press, 1990.

Families: Crisis and Caring. T. Berry Brazelton, M.D. Reading, MA: Addison-Wesley; New York: Ballantine, 1990.

What's Happening to the American Family, rev. ed. Sar A. Levitan and others. John Hopkins, 1988.

⊿ PRACTICAL GUIDES

The Survival Guide for Women: Single • Married • Divorced: Protecting Your Future. Renee Martin and Don Martin. Regnery, 1991.

The Living Together Kit: A Detailed Guide to Help Unmarried Couples Deal with Legal Realities. 6th ed. Toni Ihara and Ralph Warner. Nolo Press, 1990.

A Guide to a Happier Family: Overcoming the Anger, Frustration, and Boredom that Destroy Family Life. by Andrew Schwebel and others. Los Angeles: Tarcher, 1990.

The Complete Legal Guide to Marriage, Divorce, Custody, and Living Together. Steven M. Sack. Fisher Books, 1988.

⊿ ON BLENDED OR NONTRADITIONAL FAMILIES

Divorce and New Beginnings: An Authoritative Guide to Recovery and Growth, Solo Parenting, and Stepfamilies. Genevieve Clapp. Wiley, 1992.

Love in the Blended Family: Step-Families: A Package Deal. Angela N. Clubb. Health Communications, 1991.

Wider Families: New Traditional Family Forms. Theresa D. Marciano and Marvin B. Sussman, eds. Haworth Press, 1991.

Becoming a Stepfamily: Stages of Development in Remarried Families. Frank Cardelle. Gardner Press, 1989.

Remarriage and Blended Families. Stephen R. Treat. Pilgrim Press, 1988.

The Good Stepmother: A Practical Guide. Karen Savage and Patricia Adams. Crown, 1988.

⊿ ON INTERMARRIAGE

Raising Your Jewish/Christian Child: How Interfaith Parents Can Give Children the Best of Both Their Heritages. Lee F. Gruzen. Newmarket, 1990.

Intermarriage: The Challenge of Living with Differences. Susan Weidman Schneider. Free Press, 1989.

Happily Intermarried: Authoritative Advice for a Joyous Jewish-Christian Marriage. Rabbi Roy A. Rosenberg, Father Peter Meehan, and Reverend John Wade Payne. Macmillan, 1988.

The Rainbow Effect: Interracial Families. Kathlyn Gay. Franklin Watts, 1987.

⊿ ON PROBLEM FAMILIES

Family That Fights. Sharon C. Bernstein. A. Whitman, 1991.

Family Secrets. Harriet Webster. Addison-Wesley, 1991.

The Anti-Social Family. Michele Barrett and Mary McIntosh. Routledge Chapman & Hall, 1991.

Breaking Free of Addictive Family Relationships. Barry Weinhold. Stillpoint, 1991.

Overcoming Relationship Addiction: A Workshop for Women Who Love Too Much. Kathryn Apgar. Families International, 1991.

Making Peace with Your Adult Children. S. L. Smith. Plenum, 1991.

Wholing the Heart, Good News for Those Who Grew Up in Troubled Families. Rachel Callahan. Paulist Press, 1991.

Family Passages. Glenn H. Asquith, Jr. Nashville, TN: Broadman, 1990. On dealing with family crises.

When Families Fight: How to Handle Conflict with Those You Love. Jeffrey Rubin and Carol Rubin. Morrow, 1988.

(See also VIOLENCE AGAINST WOMEN HELP, INFORMATION, AND ACTION GUIDE on page 612; also CHILD ABUSE AND NEGLECT HELP, INFORMATION, AND ACTION GUIDE on page 152.)

◪ SPECIAL RELATIONSHIPS

In-Laws Books: Coping with the Strangers You're Related To. Leah S. Averick. Shapolsky, 1991.

In-Laws, Out-Laws: How to Make Peace with His Family and Yours. Penny Bilofsky. Villard/Random House, 1991.

◪ BACKGROUND BOOKS

Next of Kin: An International Reader on Changing Families. Lorne Tepperman and Susannah J. Wilson. Prentice-Hall, 1992.

Taking Sides: Clashing Views on Controversial Issues in Family and Personal Relationships. Gloria Bird and Michael Sporakowski. Dushkin, 1992.

Family: Personal Cultural and Archetypal Dimensions. Louis Steward. Sigo Press, 1991.

Family Mirrors: What Our Children's Lives Reveal About Ourselves. Elizabeth Fishel. Houghton Mifflin, 1991.

Divorce and Remarriage: Religious and Psychological Perspectives. William P. Roberts. Sheed and Ward (MO), 1990.

The Encyclopedia of Marriage, Divorce and Family. Margaret DiCanio. Facts on File, 1989.

Parents Divided, Parents Multiplied. Margaret O. Hyde and Elizabeth H. Forsyth. Westminster John Knox, 1989.

(See also SINGLE PARENT; DIVORCE.)

marriage squeeze, the social strain that results when people who wish to marry have too few potential suitable mates. Sociologists have long observed that women tend to marry men two to three years older than they are. When population patterns are holding relatively steady, that poses no problem. But in periods when demographics have been significantly changed, the number of potential mates may be too small. For example, this happened after World War I in Britain, after millions of young men were killed. In the United States the term has been applied to the bulge of population known as the *baby boom,* people born between 1945 and 1960, a time of large families. The number of children born in preceding years, during World War II, was much smaller, so women baby boomers have had a smaller pool of potential mates to draw from, and the disproportion grows greater throughout their lives, given the increasing difference in women's and men's LIFE EXPECTANCY.

A marriage squeeze can also result from deliberate changes in birth patterns. It is in the cards for India, China, and other countries with strong SON PREFERENCE; the ABORTION of female FETUSES and the killing of female infants (see FEMALE INFANTICIDE) is leaving far too few women available for the men who will want mates. (See MATE SELECTION.)

Married Love: See Marie STOPES.

Married Women's Property Acts, the series of nineteenth-century bills that first allowed married women to hold property in their own names (see COVERTURE).

Marxist feminism, an attempt to ingest FEMINISM into Marxist theory and practice; its theory was based largely on Friedrich Engels's *The Origin of the Family, Private Property and the State* (1884), and its practice during the twentieth century developed under the conditions of Soviet communism. Marxists then and now assert the primacy of the relations of production as the motor of social and political change and insist that the claims of the Marxist revolution must precede the claims of the WOMEN'S RIGHTS MOVEMENT. All but a few WOMEN'S RIGHTS advocates outside the communist world disagreed; nor did many inside that world find that women's rights remained a major goal for very long after the Bolshevik revolution of 1917. But the argument has had little modern relevance since the collapse of Soviet communism. (See also FEMINISM.)

Mary: See VIRGIN MARY.

mastectomy, removal of a breast; a general term for various kinds of operations (see BREAST CANCER).

Masters and Johnson: See *HUMAN SEXUAL RESPONSE.*

mastitis, inflammation of the BREAST.

mastoplexy, breast lift (see COSMETIC SURGERY).

masturbation, self-stimulation of one's GENITALS, often leading to the climactic, intensely pleasurable experience called ORGASM (see SEXUAL RESPONSE). Most women focus primarily on stimulating the CLITORIS, commonly rubbing it by hand but also stimulating it in other ways, with a stream of water, a small vibrator (see SEXUAL INTERCOURSE), various other objects, actions such as "riding" the arm of a chair or bicycle, or even crossing and rhythmically pressing one's legs together. At the same time, the woman may insert into her VAGINA and rhythmically move a penis-shaped object, such as a *dildo* (see SEXUAL INTERCOURSE).

Self-stimulation was long frowned upon, mistakenly linked with MENTAL DISORDERS or blindness, or simply regarded as "wrong." In some cultures the idea of *any* sexual feeling in a woman was so abhorred that her prime organs of sexual pleasure were removed or mutilated (see FEMALE CIRCUMCISION), practices that in some areas continue today.

Masturbation is now widely recognized as a common practice among humans of all ages. Genital stimulation is part of children's exploration of their bodies, and some children and even infants are believed to reach orgasm. The main period of sexual response begins with PUBERTY, however, and masturbation is common during adolescence and continues throughout adulthood and into old age. Indeed, for older women who have little or no sexual contact, some doctors today even recommend masturbation, for release of sexual tension as an aid to general health and also specifically to maintain lubrication of the tissues of the VAGINA, which might otherwise dry out, especially in the years after MENOPAUSE.

Many adult women who have sexual partners feel no need to masturbate privately, though some may do so to achieve a satisfaction lacking in the partnership. Sometimes sex therapists will recommend that a woman try masturbation, to discover what arouses and satisfies her the most so she can then explain her desires to her partner. But some couples—both HETEROSEXUAL and LESBIAN—use masturbation as part of their mutual sexual experience, watching each other masturbate or performing mutual masturbation on each other. They may turn to it as a variation, but also in special circumstances, such as during a woman's menstrual period (see MENSTRUATION), as a means of BIRTH CONTROL during a fertile period (see NATURAL FAMILY PLANNING), or when one or both partners have a physical problem that makes other sexual activity awkward, difficult, or impossible. Even without vaginal penetration, couples should be careful about the possibility of transmitting infection, including AIDS (see SEXUAL INTERCOURSE). (See SEX AND SEXUALITY HELP, INFORMATION, AND ACTION GUIDE on page 665.)

mate selection, a process of choosing of a long-term partner, often with the immediate or ultimate view toward MARRIAGE, and usually by applying formal or informal customs or rules. Modern women and men are largely used to selecting their own partners, though parents often have influence and sometimes veto power; but traditionally and still in many parts of the world the selection has often been made by parents or other interested parties, especially where money and power are involved. Sometimes the wishes of the partners might be taken into consideration, but in some times and places, the prospective couple never met each other before the WEDDING. No matter who makes the selection, however, the process takes place within a complicated, subtle, and often unwritten set of guidelines.

The most basic guidelines include societies' various restrictions on people who are allowed to marry. There are almost universal bans on marriage between close relatives, called INCEST. Particularly in traditional cultures, societies often have elaborate rules on whom a person is forbidden to marry (EXOGAMY) and others describing characteristics of people one is allowed to marry (ENDOGAMY). In some times and places certain groups of people have not been permitted to marry, such as people with severe MENTAL DISORDERS, mental retardation (called "feeblemindedness"), criminals, or alcoholics; in many parts of the world such laws continue today.

Beyond formal restrictions, people often have an informal set of "specifications" for a potential mate. Traditionally, women have been urged by their parents to look for a good "provider," while men have been enjoined to look for a woman who will be a good HOMEMAKER. Mate seekers themselves have often had a more elaborate list of specifications. These may include race, caste, or ethnic background; religion, socioeconomic status, life-style, and educational level; age; physical attractiveness, including height and weight; general health, including freedom from reproductive diseases and disabilities; and general "reputation." However, the greater the specifications, the fewer possibilities to meet them, and in practice a person's unconscious "want list" grows shorter in time.

Marriage is a major way that people can improve their socioeconomic position in the world. This has been especially true for women, who have traditionally had few other routes for upward mobility, and this continues to be so, even though both women and men today have other avenues for social mobility through education and careers. Sociologists have noted the tendency of females to date, and therefore to marry, higher-status (rather than lower-status) males, to at least maintain or improve their social status; this pattern is called the *mating and dating gradient*. Women also generally tend to marry men older than they are.

In general, people tend to marry people of their own general background or "circle," especially for a first marriage. This tendency is reinforced in traditional societies by the giving of a DOWRY or BRIDEGIFT, generally by people of comparable socioeconomic status, but continues so in modern, more mobile societies as well. Even where laws have been changed to allow for intermarriage between distinct social classes called *castes* in India, or between races in the United States, most people do not cross such boundaries readily. Other boundaries, such as religion and socioeconomic status, are somewhat less important in modern, mobile societies. But crossing any such boundaries, as in *intermarriage* between religious faiths or *interracial marriage,* adds at least some additional strain for the partners to deal with, especially where children are involved.

Finding a range of appropriate dates and mates has seldom been easy. In traditional cultures, and still in rural settings, people often found potential mates through a variety of social patterns and events, such as dances, games, churches, organizations, or festivals—though in modern times many potential mates in rural areas have been drawn away to the cities. But the task is more difficult in modern, fragmented urban and suburban settings, since there are fewer natural meeting places. Many traditional cultures have had some variety of *matchmaker,* a woman (usually) whose job it was to find appropriate marriage partners and introduce them to each other, for a fee. Some societies, such as those in India, still use matchmakers. The modern equivalent is a *dating service,* which arranges introductions of people who meet the specifications outlined by each. In some such services, people make brief videotapes talking about themselves and the kind of person and relationship they are looking for. Many people have chosen direct advertisement, through *personals ads* in newspapers and periodicals. A big difference in these tactics is that, for the first time, women have been more actively involved in the search, instead of waiting passively to be selected by someone else.

Even in modern times, some such dating and advertising services operate internationally. In recent years some women have been imported into the United States as *mail-order brides* from other countries such as Russia. This has been common during many periods in places where men heavily outnumbered women, such as late-nineteenth- and early-twentieth-century immigrant or mining communities, but this may also reflect men's desire to find a more "traditional" kind of wife.

Many businesses have also responded to the need for meeting places by organizing evenings and events targeted specifically to singles; so have some organizations, such as local chapters of PARENTS WITHOUT PARTNERS. And, of course, there are inevitably the bars that make up the *singles scene*—not so popular in an AIDS-conscious era—where men and women "cruise around," looking for potential partners. Apart from the "meat market" aspect of these bars, the lack of any kind of screening means that women are often at potential risk of meeting a violence-minded male—though that is a problem in other settings as well. For many women the best way to meet potential dates and mates is still through a network of friends and acquaintances around shared activities, such as at cultural, religious, or political organizations, and especially in schools.

Workplaces are also good meeting places but pose hazards as well, with possible complications involving conflict of interest where a women and man work closely together. Many companies formally bar such relationships, and others frown on them. If the relationship goes sour, the woman has traditionally been the person fired or pushed out, and that is still largely the case, though the man's career may also be damaged in the process.

To attract a mate, women traditionally have been taught to emphasize their physical attractiveness, their homemaking skills, and their "femininity," especially in a role supportive to men. With the drive toward equal rights and equal position in society, many feminists and career women have been emphasizing their own physical and intellectual skills rather than deferring to men in those areas. For many women that means adding another, vitally important "specification" to the list of characteristics for potential mates: someone with a compatible view of the relationship between women and men in modern society. In traditionally minded regions, highly educated women may have particular problems finding a suitable mate, since many men prefer their wives to be less well educated than they are.

Once a man and woman have met and established a relationship, they are in the complicated period known by the now quaint term of *courtship*. For couples who find "love at first sight," the courtship period may be so short as to be indistinguishable. But for many other couples it is a long, slow, complex process of getting to know one another and assessing whether or not they suit one another in a long-term way. The new sexual freedom since the 1960s has complicated matters in some ways, for though it has eased many relationships of its sexually "teasing" aspects, and has kept many couples from mistaking sexual chemistry for the makings of a long-term relationship, it has sometimes made relationships *too* facile, bringing couples together sexually before they hardly know each other.

Psychologists have focused on mate selection as a fulfillment of needs. Some suggest that people choose partners who complement them, so a dominant woman might choose a submissive man, for example, or a talkative man may be drawn to a woman who is a good listener. Others view mate selection as a multi-stage process involving an unconscious weighing up of one's own personal assets and attributes against the potential partner's and an evaluation of the extent to which the other person holds the same or complementary values, attitudes, and principles. Though many couples, in the end, seem to meet accidentally, perhaps the explanation is in the old adage: Chance favors the prepared mind.

And where is love in all this? That depends greatly on the individuals involved, their culture, and their circumstances. Surprisingly, for something so central to our lives and our literature, romantic love has been very little studied by social scientists. Until the twentieth century, that was partly because romantic love was considered a "luxury" only the more affluent could afford. And it is true that, traditionally and still in many cultures, economic and social considerations were powerful factors in selecting a mate. But even social scientists have now come to understand that love, far from being a luxury, is found the world around. Even in cultures where arranged marriages are still common, some couples find ways to make love matches, where the attraction is strong enough. Sometimes where a match is made for socioeconomic reasons, one or both partners may seek a love match outside the marriage, in extramarital affairs or in another marriage after a DIVORCE or the death of a partner. In most Western countries, where individuals make their own choices, the importance of love depends primarily on their own priorities. Where the partners regard the mutual relationship as the prime consideration, love is central in mate selection. Where the partners are—consciously or not—primarily making a socioeconomic decision, love may be a lesser priority.

But, in fact, individuals do not always fall in love wisely. In these days many are able to have a relationship with someone on a trial basis (see COHABITATION); if the first flush of love does not survive the rough-and-tumble of daily life, no great harm is done. If the parties are married, the result may be a bitter SEPARA-

TION and DIVORCE, sometimes with children involved. Where divorce is readily available, the ex-partners will be free to use their gained wisdom in selecting another mate, as most do sooner or later. But where it is not, a truly horrific situation can be created. This is especially true where women lack the right to choose their own mates, as in many of India's child marriages. (See COUPLES AND FAMILIES HELP, INFORMATION, AND ACTION GUIDE on page 418.)

maternity center, a free-standing birthing center (see CHILDBIRTH).

maternity cycle: the period from CONCEPTION to about six weeks after childbirth (see PREGNANCY), including PRENATAL CARE (before birth), *intrapartal care* (during labor), and *postnatal* or *postpartal care* (after the birth), sometimes *perinatal care* (in the twenty-eight days after the birth).

mating and dating gradient: See MATE SELECTION.

matriarchy, a kinship group or other social or political structure in which succession passes through the female line, with power, status, and property passing to successive generations of women—that is, in *matrilineal* fashion. The term *matriarchy* is also often encountered colloquially, to describe an extended family in which there are women who are or seem to be the strongest figures in the FAMILY.

Some European nineteenth-century system builders developed a considerable body of theory regarding the existence of women-dominated societies—that is, matriarchies—"early" in human history, in the Mediterranean and the Near East, probably in the third and fourth millennia B.C. Perhaps the most prominent of these was Johann Bachofen, who in *Mother Right* (1861) accepted biblical dating and thought that human history began approximately six thousand years ago, in the fourth millennium B.C., therefore putting his "dawn" matriarchies into the fourth and third millennia B.C. Anthropologist Lewis Henry Morgan in *Ancient Society* (1877) developed a sequential theory of societal development based upon his work in North American Indian history, particularly with the Iroquois. Friedrich Engels adapted some of Morgan's thinking in his *The Origin of the Family, Private Property and the State* (1884).

But these theorists were very early; Bachofen had no idea of the length and diversity of human history, which is now measured in tens of thousands of years. Morgan had no idea of the long, complex cultural history of the far-from-primitive North Americans he studied, stretching far back into East Asian history and south to the great cultures of the Mississippi Valley and Central America. Engels followed, his far-too-simple and ungrounded historical model built on flawed information and equally oversimplified economic determinism.

Some early-twentieth-century feminist theorists also developed matriarchy theories; Robert BRIFFAULT based his theory in *The Mothers* (1927) largely on what he believed to be mother-goddess figures found on several archaeological

sites, and Helen Diner built a theory of Amazonian societies on the evidence provided by Bachofen and Briffault, with her own inferences added. In the recent
period, their work has been carried on by such theorists as Elizabeth Gould
DAVIS, who in *The First Sex* (1971) predicted an early return of matriarchy;
Evelyn Reed, who in *Woman's Evolution* (1975) took a Marxist approach; and
Merlin Stone, who in *When God Was a Woman* (1976) restated the early-
matriarchy theory and linked it with GODDESS WORSHIP theory.

Modern "primitive" societies are not survivals and cannot be studied as
such; nor is there any but the most fragmentary data about the older societies.
The little information that is available about a few of the societies in older human history seems to indicate male domination much farther back than the
fourth millennium B.C. There is little hard evidence to support any theory about
either matriarchy or PATRIARCHY, only poorly supported inferences on both sides
of an argument that can have no resolution without information. But the so far
unprovable argument need not be resolved; overwhelming modern evidence supports the view that women and men can, if given a chance, live equally with respect to status, power, and social, economic, political, and legal position, however
similar or different they may be intrinsically. (See also GODDESS WORSHIP.)

matrifocal family, a rather uneasy current term describing a FAMILY in which
the role of the MOTHER is very substantial and highly respected, while at the same
time often being used to generalize about families stemming from some kinds of
ethnic and economic backgrounds; for example, poor African-Caribbean-
American households in U.S. cities are sometimes described as "matrifocal." The
truth is often far less simple than the descriptor; poverty and racism also strongly
affect women, men, and children in such families. Nor can the term easily be applied to single mothers (see SINGLE PARENT), although they may be the entire
adult focus of the family. A matrifocal or any other kind of family is characterized by the passage of attitudes through the generations and through many kinds
of social and economic circumstances. (See FAMILY.)

matriliny: See MATRIARCHY; FAMILY.

matrilocality, in some cultures, the settling of families along matriarchal
lines, with new families living in the extended families and clans of the wife (see
FAMILY).

mediation, a procedure in which two people in conflict present their dispute
to a neutral third party for resolution, an increasingly popular alternative to a
court suit. The mediator has no power to impose a solution but instead is
charged with trying to help the disputants find common ground and reach a solution acceptable to both of them. The result is a written agreement, in CUSTODY
situations sometimes called a *parenting plan*.

The main advantages of mediation are that the people in conflict solve the problem themselves, and in private, and that the whole procedure is faster, cheaper, and less stressful than litigation and often ARBITRATION as well. Mediation is increasingly being used in disputes over child custody, VISITATION RIGHTS, division of MARITAL PROPERTY, and other DIVORCE and FAMILY law disputes; in some states, such as California, mediation is mandatory in relation to custody and visitation. Many SEPARATION AGREEMENTS and living-together agreements (see COHABITATION) also include mediation and arbitration clauses. If mediation fails, the disputants sometimes turn to ARBITRATION.

Mediation is not a cure-all, however, and can put women at a significant disadvantage in some situations, especially BATTERED WOMEN. In particular, the mediation process is not fully confidential, so a woman may be unable to shield her address, phone number, or employer from an abusive ex-partner; nor does a mediator have the legal power to instruct the abuser to stop the abuse, as a judge does. In addition, battered women may too afraid or too emotionally troubled by the abuse to be able to speak up strongly in their own behalf; but they need to do so, because the mediator's position is designed to be neutral. Many women, battered or not, are so anxious to end a relationship that they agree to much less in CHILD SUPPORT and property than they and their children are entitled to have and truly need.

For such reasons, many women's organizations—and many mediators as well—stress that both parties in mediation should be represented by lawyers and should certainly not sign anything without having it reviewed by an attorney. Remember: Even if the mediator is a lawyer, he or she is not *your* lawyer.

Custody is another area of concern. Many mediated settlements result in joint custody, but that often means no or lower child support payments, is difficult to enforce, and creates an extremely difficult situation where domestic abuse has been involved.

Whatever their situation, women should not be cowed into an agreement by the situation. Even where courts mandate that the parties must *try* mediation, that does not mean that the parties *must* agree to a settlement—in general, less than 40 percent do. If a woman believes that the proposed settlement is not in her or her children's best interests, she should decide to try for a court-ordered settlement. If a mediated settlement is reached, she should be sure to have the agreement approved by a court, otherwise it may not have the status of an enforceable court order. (See DIVORCE AND SEPARATION HELP, INFORMATION, AND ACTION GUIDE on page 238.)

medical care: See HEALTH EQUITY.

melanoma, a highly dangerous type of CANCER affecting the SKIN.

menarche, the onset of MENSTRUATION in a woman, generally between the ages of ten and sixteen; if earlier, generally considered precocious PUBERTY.

menopause, the cessation of MENSTRUATION, and so of a woman's reproductive capability; popularly called "the change" or "change of life." Menopause does not occur at a precise, recognizable moment, like an on-off switch; rather, it is a process that begins years before the actual ending of menstrual periods, during a period called the CLIMACTERIC.

In general, the range of several months to years at the beginning of the climacteric, generally in a woman's forties, is called *premenopause.* The time around her last menstrual period is called *perimenopause.* The actual date of a woman's last menstrual period is regarded as the formal date at which menopause begins. After a woman goes at least a year without having a menstrual period, she is considered to be in *postmenopause.* However neat this may sound, in practice medical authorities disagree about when menopause has actually occurred; many doctors say not until a woman has gone for a full year without a period, some say two years, some say more.

Menopause may be induced medically, as when a woman's OVARIES are removed; may occur prematurely, as when a woman has a hormonal imbalance; and may occur temporarily, as under conditions of great stress or serious illness (such as ANOREXIA NERVOSA). But for most women in Western countries, menstruation stops between the mid-forties and mid-fifties, with the average age gradually rising during the twentieth century; in the United States, the usual range by the late 1980s was 48–55, with the median 51.4 years. Cessation of periods before age thirty-five is generally termed "premature." For unknown reasons, women who start menstruating early generally have late menopause, patterns usually running true among women in the same family.

On rare occasions the periods stop abruptly; more often they become lighter and irregular in the months and years before they completely stop. Changes in menstrual patterns, especially if bleeding occurs more often, more heavily, or in between periods, can be signals of physical problems, so a woman should always consult her doctor about menstrual changes and always about any kind of bleeding after menopause has been established. Throughout these years a woman can still become pregnant and so should continue using BIRTH CONTROL.

Women are advised to keep a regular menstrual record, showing not just the date a period begins, but always its length and the number of days since the previous period. They should keep this even if—perhaps especially if—they have begun to experience premenopausal changes. This chart will give a woman—and her doctor—an accurate picture of her menstrual history. Many women experience premenstrual symptoms even when they fail to have a period (see ANOVULATORY PERIOD); such women may find it instructive to note the date and nature of such symptoms, to see if they are indeed related to a menstrual cycle. This will, later on, give a sense of whether or not menopause has actually been completed. Women on BIRTH CONTROL PILLS will not so readily recognize the onset of the climacteric, since the pills themselves regulate the cycle, with bleeding caused by going off the pill.

Menopause, like PUBERTY, involves great changes in the balances of HORMONES in the body, primarily the female hormone ESTROGEN but also others as well. Eventually an equilibrium is established between the lower level of estrogen and the other hormones of the body. Indeed, tests of hormone levels, especially

LUTEINIZING HORMONE (LH) and FOLLICLE-STIMULATING HORMONE (FSH), are given to assess whether or not a woman is in menopause, though such tests do not indicate if the change is permanent or a temporary response to stress or weight loss, for example.

Women may begin noticing signs of hormonal changes as early as their mid-thirties, though more often in their forties; for some, in fact, the changes bring welcome relief from painful periods. For some women this process takes place almost unnoticed; this is especially true of overweight women (see OBESITY), since fatty tissue itself makes estrogen, thus stabilizing levels; it is also associated with later-than-usual menopause. However, many women experience a wide variety of side effects stemming from unevenness in hormonal production during this transition.

The best-known and most commonly experienced of these is *hot flashes,* temporary waves of heat and flushes, especially to face, neck, chest, and arms, often accompanied by shallow breathing and sweating. Many women also experience chills and heavy sweating, especially during the night, which can disturb sleep. Medically these are all considered types of *vasomotor instability,* or instability in the temperature regulation mechanisms of the body. Many other women experience a general range of symptoms similar to those of premenstrual syndrome (see MENSTRUATION), including headaches, nervousness, irritability, anxiety, excitability, and swollen, tender BREASTS. Still other women may experience symptoms such as generalized aches, notably in the back, legs, or joints; feelings of vertigo, faintness, or dizziness; appetite changes—increases or decreases; constipation (see DIGESTIVE SYSTEM); and frequent need to urinate, sometimes with incontinence (see URINARY TRACT). Many women find that they gain weight or tend to bloat, but some researchers now feel that this stems not from menopausal changes, but from a more sedentary life. Some longer-term changes result, including accelerated bone loss (see OSTEOPOROSIS) and a general drying out of body tissues (see SKIN, VAGINA). In addition, women who have early menstruation and late menopause are at somewhat increased risk of estrogen-fueled cancers (see BREAST CANCER; UTERINE CANCER). Women who have early menopause are more likely to experience osteoporosis.

Much has been written about problems associated with menopause. However, it is not entirely clear to what extent the problems are related to biochemical changes in the body and to what extent they stem from the individual woman's life situation. Especially where a woman has been a traditional HOMEMAKER, menopause means the end of a woman's reproductive functions and often coincides with the end of her need as a MOTHER as well, as children grow up and move out on their own, and sometimes also with a DIVORCE, retirement (or a husband's retirement), or need to care for an aging parent. In addition, the time of menopause may coincide with a "mid-life crisis," in which a woman is reevaluating her life, itself a sometimes painful and turbulent process. Sometimes this is mixed up with concerns they are "losing their looks."

For many women, the symptoms of menopause are sufficiently disruptive to call for treatment. This usually involves ESTROGEN REPLACEMENT THERAPY. But many other women object to such treatment as "medicalization" of a natural process. One new factor in the picture is the much increased LIFE EXPECTANCY of modern women; because many live so much longer than in the past, usually decades beyond menopause, the after-effects of menopause, especially bone thinning and generally drying, have many more years in which to take their toll on the body. It has been widely observed that although women live longer, their quality of life is often impaired, and many older women are too frail or disabled to live independently. For some women, therapies aimed at forestalling such effects can be immensely important. For other women, such as those with FIBROIDS or a family or personal history of CANCER, treatment with estrogen is not recommended, as the risks are too great. In general, a healthful diet and regular EXERCISE can ease many symptoms of menopause; some women also find it helpful to eliminate or drastically cut the amount of caffeine, sugar, and alcohol they consume. Some find help from vitamins B or E (see KEY VITAMINS AND MINERALS on page 502) or from a cup of milk at bedtime.

Many women have postmenopausal problems with SEXUAL INTERCOURSE because thinning and drying of the vaginal walls can make sex physically uncomfortable (see VAGINA), as tissues become raw and itchy. The best way to forestall such drying out is to maintain an active sex life. However, where drying is a problem, doctors often recommend water-soluble lubricants, such as creams, gels, or suppositories, or estrogen replacement therapy, where not contraindicated.

Despite all the focus on the problems of menopause, many women today are ready and even anxious to move on to the next stage of life, unhampered by birth control, childbearing, menstruation, and—in cultures that still have them—menstrual taboos. In some traditional cultures, especially where historically most women died in their late forties, the postmenopausal women frequently found a new, enhanced status as a "wise woman," often with considerable respect and authority in her local community. (See MENOPAUSE HELP, INFORMATION, AND ACTION GUIDE, below.)

MENOPAUSE

Help, Information, and Action Guide

Organizations

▶ NATIONAL WOMEN'S HEALTH NETWORK (NWHN) (202-347-1140). Operates the **Women's Health Information Service**. Publishes *Taking Hormones and Women's Health; Choices, Risks and Benefits, Women and the Crisis in Sex Hormones, Hearts, Bones, Hot Flashes and Hormones,* and the information packet *Menopause ERT/HRT.*

Other resources

⊠ GENERAL WORKS

Choice Years: How to Stay Healthy, Happy and Beautiful Through Menopause and Beyond. Judith Paige and Pamela Gordon. Random House, 1991.

Menopause and the Years Ahead. rev. ed. Mary Beard and Lindsay Curtis. Fisher Books, 1991.

The Menopause Handbook. Susan F. Trien. Ballantine, 1991.

Menopause Self-Help Book. Susan M. Lark. Celestial Arts, 1990.

Managing Your Menopause. Wulf H. Utian. Prentice-Hall, 1990.

What's Stopped Happening to Me? Gail Parent and others. Lyle Stuart/Carol, 1990.

Stay Cool Through Menopause: Answers to Most Frequently Asked Questions. Melvin Frisch. Body Press-Perigee/Putnam, 1989.

Menopause: A Self-Care Manual. rev. ed. Judy Costlow and others. Santa Fe Health, 1989.

⊠ ON NATURAL APPROACHES

Natural Menopause: The Complete Guide to a Woman's Most Misunderstood Passage. Susan Perry and Katherine O'Harlan. Addison-Wesley, 1992.

Menopause, Naturally; Preparing for the Second Half of Life. Sadja Greenwood. Instant Improve, 1991. Reprint of 1984 ed. Volcano Press, rev. ed., 1989.

Second Spring: A Guide to Healthy Menopause Through Traditional Chinese Medicine. Honora L. Wolfe. Blue Poppy, 1990.

Menopause Without Medicine: Feel Healthy, Look Younger, Live Longer. Linda Ojeda. Borgo Press, 1989; Hunter House, 1989.

⊠ ON MEDICAL TREATMENTS

The Menopause and Hormonal Replacement Therapy, Facts and Controversies. Regine Sitruk-Ware, ed. Dekker, 1991.

A Portrait of the Menopause: Expert Reports on Medical and Therapeutic Strategies for the 1990's. H. Burger and M. Boulet, eds. Parthenon (NJ), 1991.

Doctor Discusses Menopause and Estrogen. M. Edward Davis and Dona Meilach. Budlong, 1991.

⊠ PERSONAL AND INTERPRETIVE WORKS

The Silent Passage. Gail Sheehy. Random House, 1992.

The Change: Women, Ageing and the Menopause. Germaine Greer. Knopf, 1992.

Women of the 14th Moon: Writings on Menopause. Dena Taylor and Amber
Sumrall, eds. Crossing Press, 1991.
The Meanings of Menopause: Historical, Medical, and Clinical Perspectives.
Ruth Formanek, ed. Analytic Press, 1990.
Women on Menopause: A Change for the Better. Anne Dickson and Nikki
Henriques. Healing Arts/Inner Traditions, 1989.
Menopause: A Time for Positive Change. Judi Fairlie and others. Sterling,
1988; Borgo Press, 1989.
Journey Through Menopause: A Personal Rite of Passage. Christine Downing.
Crossroad (NY), 1989.
(See also WOMEN'S HEALTH HELP, INFORMATION, AND ACTION GUIDE on page
334; OLDER WOMEN'S HELP, INFORMATION, AND ACTION GUIDE on page 374.)

menorrhagia, menstrual periods with excessively heavy flow (see MENSTRUA-
TION).

men's liberation movement, a catch-all sort of term, including several
quite differently motivated tendencies. In the late 1960s and early 1970s, small
men's groups formed in Britain and the United States paralleling the development of the radical feminist WOMEN'S LIBERATION MOVEMENT groups of the time
and using some of the same CONSCIOUSNESS-RAISING techniques for group self-
analysis and to attract and hold like-minded people. Most members were young
Whites active in peace and civil rights movements, and in NEW LEFT activities,
who sought simultaneously to help the emerging women's liberation movement
and to find and cultivate aspects of themselves that were not male-supremacist.
For some, the men's liberation movement was a phase in transit to less radical
and confrontational lives; for a few, it meant continuing ties with the women's
movement.

For others, it was the beginning a long journey that led them into the quite
different men's liberation movement of the 1990s, which developed considerable
momentum around publication of Robert Bly's *Iron John: A Book About Men*
(1990). Bly's consciousness-raising groups pursued his construct of the repressed
"inner warrior"; the encounter groups of the new movement, relying on Bly's
view of Jung's theory of archetypes, sought to release the "king" and "wild man"
said to be buried deep in the psyche of all men. Some of his disciples organized
group exercises, often outdoors, featuring drum playing, grunting, and shouting
together, a rather flamboyant aspect of the movement that received much play in
the mass media. For many of the men involved, the movement apparently did
seem an agreeable experience, though its long-term benefits had yet to be experienced. Many of the feminists who observed the transmutation of the men's liberation movement were dismayed, feeling that they were witnessing an

about-face, a glorification of the old patriarchal male values, now described as ar-chetypes. (See PATRIARCHY.)

menstrual extraction, a women's self-help procedure using suction to re-move the contents of the UTERUS, a homemade version of the medical procedure called *vacuum extraction* (see ABORTION; MENSTRUATION).

menstrual phase, the beginning portion of the reproductive cycle that in-volves MENSTRUATION, the clearing out of the unused egg (OVUM) and uterine lin-ing from the previous cycle, and also sees a new group of eggs begin to ripen. Both events are triggered by the secretion of the FOLLICLE-STIMULATING HORMONE (FSH), itself triggered by a fall of other HORMONES, primarily the female sex hor-mones ESTROGEN and PROGESTERONE.

menstruation, the periodic flow of a bloody fluid out of a woman's VAGINA. It actually originates in the UTERUS and consists of an unfertilized egg (OVUM) and the unused *endometrium,* the uterine lining that is prepared for a possible PREG-NANCY. More generally called a "period," menstruation occurs roughly once every twenty-four to thirty-five days and generally lasts four to five days, though it may be as brief as a single day or last over a week. The length, regularity, and heav-iness of the flow vary not only from woman to woman, but with various times in an individual woman's life.

Menstruation is actually the beginning and ending of the *menstrual* or *re-productive cycle,* which occurs in phases orchestrated by various of the body's HORMONES:

▶ In the ***proliferative or follicular phase,*** the endometrium begins to thicken in response to ESTROGEN, ready to provide nourishment if a fertilized egg later ar-rives.

▶ In the ***secretory or luteal phase,*** roughly midway through the cycle, an egg is released in the process called OVULATION, triggered by LUTEINIZING HORMONE (LH) from the pituitary gland. Also in this phase, the woman's body begins to produce the hormone PROGESTERONE, which brings further thickening and swelling of the endometrium. This is the phase during which a woman can become pregnant, often signaled by a slight rise in temperature after ovulation (see NATURAL FAMILY PLANNING).

▶ The ***menstrual phase*** follows only if no pregnancy occurs. Estrogen and pro-gesterone production declines, and the uterus begins contractions to expel the unused endometrium and unfertilized egg. Then the process begins again, the first day of the period being the start of the new cycle. Even as menstrual flow continues, the body begins to secrete more estrogen to trigger the next phase, and the pituitary gland secretes FOLLICLE-STIMULATING HORMONE (FSH), which triggers the development of a new ovum.

This cycle repeats itself throughout a woman's reproductive life. A girl's first menstrual cycle normally occurs between ages ten and sixteen, as part of PU-

BERTY; the onset of menstruation, called *menarche,* is a sign of fertility and sexual maturity. With occasional breaks and irregularities, as for a pregnancy or in times of severe illness or stress, the cycle will recur for decades, to approximately age forty-five to fifty-five, ending with MENOPAUSE, itself part of a wider set of changes called the CLIMACTERIC.

After CHILDBIRTH, menstruation does not normally return as long as a mother is lactating (see BREASTFEEDING), in past eras providing a common kind of CONTRACEPTION. For that matter, past social prohibitions aside, menstruation itself poses no bar to SEXUAL INTERCOURSE and indeed carries little risk of pregnancy, since an egg is unlikely to be present, though some women may wish to use a DIAPHRAGM to contain the flow and reduce messiness. Sexual activity may cause discomfort to women who have difficult periods, but some women find that an ORGASM can bring relief to menstrual discomfort. However, a major modern concern is that AIDS is more readily transmitted during menstruation, if either partner is infected (see AIDS).

Menstruation poses practical problems, especially for women with active lives. In past eras, women have used diaperlike pads of absorbent material to soak up the flow; these would generally be washed and reused. In the twentieth century, most women in affluent countries have turned to disposable products, especially pads called *sanitary napkins* and later compact, absorbent cylinders called *tampons,* which have the distinct advantage of being placed *inside* the body, though they carry some risk of TOXIC SHOCK SYNDROME.

Other alternatives also exist. Some women use a soft, plastic menstrual cup, which fits over the CERVIX, held by suction, and collects the menstrual fluid; a diaphragm (see BIRTH CONTROL) can serve the same purpose. Others employ a reusable, unbleached natural sponge (not artificial or chemically treated) to which a string has been attached, though this may also increase the risk of toxic shock syndrome. Such alternatives are especially attractive to environmentalists concerned about waste from disposables and avoidance of bleach and chemicals in commercial products.

In the early 1970s, some women developed a procedure called *menstrual extraction,* using a thin tube (*cannula*) inserted into the cervix and a syringe that uses suction or aspiration to remove the menstrual fluid all at once, avoiding possible cramps or inconvenience. Attractive as the notion might be, it also carries the risk of infection and damage to the uterus, and research on its long-term effects on the body and on a woman's reproductive ability is lacking. Another disadvantage is that it requires the help of someone else trained in the procedure, since it cannot be done by the woman herself, though it may be performed at home or at a self-help clinic. A similar procedure, *vacuum aspiration,* is used in some ABORTIONS, but a larger instrument is used. Though some women recommend using menstrual extraction as a way of ending a possible PREGNANCY even before it is verified, one significant hazard (as with any abortion) is that fragments will remain and become infected.

Apart from the physical inconvenience and the sometime social taboos that have occasionally led it to be called "the curse," menstruation can cause various kinds of problems. Most common are the cramps and general discomfort that come under the heading of *dysmenorrhea.* Generally concentrated early in, or just before, the period, cramps are spasms and aches in the lower abdominal area, with pain sometimes transferred to the GENITALS, lower back, thighs, and pelvic area and in severe cases also involving nausea, vomiting (see DIGESTIVE SYSTEM), dizziness, and fainting. The precise cause is unknown but presumably results from uterine contractions to expel the endometrium and slight dilation of the cervix. Though some women rarely, if ever, have dysmenorrhea, many do, and perhaps one in ten is significantly discommoded by it for a few hours to several days. Cramps generally become less severe after age thirty.

Women on BIRTH CONTROL PILLS often gain relief from menstrual cramps. Some drugs administered to ease cramps can cause problems if there is a possibility that a woman may become pregnant and pass the drugs on to the FETUS. Most women rely on home remedies, such as heating pads, hot water bottles, hot baths, hot drinks, alcoholic drinks, deep breathing, back massage, and gentle muscle-relaxing EXERCISES. Some women even find that energetic exercise is helpful, in both the short and long term. Proper NUTRITION should also help, and some people find a high-fiber diet just before a period eases the constipation that often accompanies and worsens dysmenorrhea.

Dysmenorrhea can also result from various kinds of disorders, such as ENDOMETRIOSIS, FIBROIDS, PELVIC INFLAMMATORY DISEASE (PID), or effects from an INTRAUTERINE DEVICE (IUD). Any women experiencing dysmenorrhea for the first time, or more severely than in the past, should have the doctor check to be sure it is not a sign of an underlying physical problem.

Lack of menstruation is also a concern. Absence of a period is often one of the first outward signs of pregnancy, but if a pregnancy test proves negative, a woman should have a complete medical examination, since cessation of menstruation can be an early warning of a serious physical problem.

Cessation of menstruation in a woman who is not pregnant or in menopause is called *secondary amenorrhea* and can be caused by a wide variety of problems, including a tumor in the REPRODUCTIVE SYSTEM, hormonal disorders, and, of course, removal of the uterus (see HYSTERECTOMY). Periods can also stop during times of stress and starvation or significant nutritional deficiency; it is, in fact, often an early sign of ANOREXIA NERVOSA, even before extreme weight loss, and is also common among young women who exercise strenuously, such as gymnasts and ballet dancers. Secondary amenorrhea is associated with increased risk of OSTEOPOROSIS later in life, because the estrogen that is so important in the menstrual cycle inhibits bone loss. Perhaps 1–3 percent of women fail to resume normal periods after stopping use of BIRTH CONTROL PILLS.

Primary amenorrhea is when a girl fails to begin menstruating by age sixteen. Late onset of menstruation is not in itself a problem, if the girl has shown normal development of SECONDARY SEX CHARACTERISTICS, since the range of menarche is widely variable. But physicians will generally want to check for the possibility of disorders, including hormonal disorders, a tumor in the pituitary gland, and on rare occasions absence of one or more reproductive organs. Sometimes the girl has indeed been menstruating, but the HYMEN has not been perforated, so the flow has been retained in the body and simply absorbed over time. This condition, called *cryptomenorrhea,* is easily corrected.

Periods can also be abnormal in other ways. They may arrive in cycles of under twenty-two days (*polymenorrhea*) or over thirty-eight days (*oligomenorrhea*); come with very little flow (*hypomenorrhea*); produce excessively heavy flow (*hypermenorrhea* or *menorrhagia*); or involve irregular bleeding. Variation is normal. Depending on the individual woman, these are not *necessarily* problems, though they may make CONCEPTION more difficult. Slight staining or spotting in midcycle, around the time of ovulation, is also common and normal. And changes in the period are common near menarche and menopause, with hormonal changes in the body. In particular, many women in the few years after menarche and before menopause experience ANOVULATORY PERIODS—vaginal bleeding without release of an egg (*ovulation*)—which throws off the hormonal balance that controls the menstrual cycle; so do women on oral contraceptives, which suppress ovulation.

But bleeding *can* result from physical problems, such as hormonal imbalances, FIBROIDS or polyps, CANCER, or an IUD. Scanty flow can be linked with EC-TOPIC PREGNANCY. Any woman who experiences vaginal bleeding *between* periods, or a marked changed in the heaviness or length of periods, should have a physical examination to check for potentially serious disorders. Sometimes problematic bleeding can be treated with hormones or corrected by a D&C.

Another problem that has received great attention in recent years is *premenstrual syndrome* (PMS), also called *congestive dysmenorrhea* or *premenstrual tension*. This is an umbrella name for a set of responses that a woman's body makes to the hormonal changes in the latter half of the menstrual cycle, between ovulation and menstruation, especially a few days before bleeding begins. Many women experience fluid buildup (*edema*), which involves weight gain and bloating, especially of the abdomen, BREASTS, ankles, and fingers; this is often associated with aches in the back and lower abdomen, muscles, and joints, as well as headaches, acne and other SKIN lesions, irritability, fatigue, and tension. One theory suggests that estrogen inhibits the kidneys' normal flushing of excess sodium from the body. Whatever the cause, it normally ends as the period starts.

Many women have little or no premenstrual symptoms, but for some PMS can be seriously disruptive, causing them to lose time from work or school; on occasion it has even been used successfully as a defense for a violent crime committed by a woman. For women with PMS, some doctors prescribe diuretic pills to counteract fluid buildup or birth control pills or hormonal supplements to smooth out hormonal swings. Individual women should monitor their responses to different foods and eliminate those that trigger fluid retention or headaches (see ALLERGIES); common culprits are caffeine, chocolate, and salty foods.

From the earliest times in human history, the uniquely female process of menstruation has been regarded with some awe. In many cultures, menstrual blood was regarded as having special creative powers, and contact with it—real or symbolic, as through red paint or dirt—was thought to enhance a man's creative potential. In other cultures, menstrual blood was feared and regarded as taboo; women were sometimes segregated from the rest of the community during menstruation and required to undergo special cleansing rites afterward. Many modern feminists have pointed out that the "specialness" of menstruation, its association with taboos or the more modern focus on hormonal swings, has often been used against women as part of a wider SEXUAL DISCRIMINATION, as a means

of denying them access to means of social, economic, and political power. (See
MENSTRUATION HELP, INFORMATION, AND ACTION GUIDE, below.)

MENSTRUATION

Help, Information, and Action Guide

Organizations

▶ NATIONAL WOMEN'S HEALTH NETWORK (**NWHN**) (202-347-1140). Operates the **Women's Health Information Service.** Publishes the information packets *Premenstrual Syndrome (PMS)* and *Menstrual Bleeding.*
▶ FEDERATION OF FEMINIST WOMEN'S HEALTH CENTERS (**FFWHC**) (916-737-0260). Stresses self-help procedures, such as menstrual extraction.

Other resources

Dragon Time: Magic and Mystery of Menstruation. Luisa Francia. Ash Tree, 1991.
Menstrual Health in Women's Lives. Alice J. Dan and Linda L. Lewis, eds. University of Illinois Press, 1991.
The Curse: A Cultural History of Menstruation, rev. ed. Janice Delaney and others. University of Illinois Press, 1988.
Red Flower: Rethinking Menstruation. Dena Taylor. Crossing Press, 1988.
The Wise Wound: Myths, Realities, and Meanings of Menstruation, rev. ed. Penelope Shuttle and Peter Redgrove. Grove Weidenfeld, 1988; Bantam, 1990.

▰ FOR YOUNG GIRLS

Period. JoAnn Gardner-Loulan and others. Volcano Press, 1990; reprint of 1979 ed.
Getting Your Period: A Book About Menstruation. Jean Marzollo. Dial, 1989.
Life Blood. Margaret Sheffield. Knopf, 1989.

▰ BACKGROUND BOOKS

Blood Relations: Menstruation and the Origins of Culture. Chris Knight. Yale University Press, 1991.

Blood Magic: The Anthropology of Menstruation. Thomas Buckley and Alma Gottlieb, eds. University of California Press, 1988.
(See also WOMEN'S HEALTH HELP, INFORMATION, AND ACTION GUIDE on page 334.)

mental disorders, any of a large number of conditions characterized by patterns of behavior that cause distress, possible harm, or death (to self or others); grossly impaired functioning; or disability. If the patterns of behavior, or *syndromes,* continue or recur over a long period of time, or if the symptoms are so severe as to make the person unable to function in society, the mental disorder comes to be regarded as a clinical problem.

Professionals in psychiatry and psychology try to define more precisely what is, or is not, a mental disorder, and to describe its nature and possible treatment, but in fact the area is still enormously muddy, confused, and subjective. Traditionally, many individuals who felt themselves to be in conflict with society's norms, and who exhibited behavior that was nonstandard, have been labeled as "mentally ill." These have included HOMOSEXUALS, people with a different GENDER IDENTITY than the one assigned to them by society, and many women who fought against and failed to perform actions regarded as appropriate to their SEX ROLES. Though professional opinion is changing in some of these areas, many LESBIANS and feminists have in the past found themselves labeled as mentally ill, and such attitudes often persist, even if professional associations no longer classify homosexuality as a mental illness.

The area of mental illness is also a quagmire in another way, because so little is known about the genesis and development of mental disorders. Some, especially Freudians, focus on events in early childhood as crucial to mental health or illness (see PENIS ENVY; ELECTRA COMPLEX). Others stress the physical bases of mental illness, including faulty biochemistry stemming from genetic defects (see GENETIC DISORDERS) and imbalance of HORMONES (see DEPRESSION; MENOPAUSE; MENSTRUATION). The problem comes when someone who has a biochemical imbalance is treated not with medications but only with "talking therapy"; or, conversely, when a person is treated only with drugs, leaving untouched trauma from events such as RAPE or childhood sexual abuse (see CHILD ABUSE AND NEGLECT). In truth, mental illness has a number of interlocking and interactive causes, which science has yet to unravel.

The most widely accepted definitions, classifications, and descriptions of mental disorders and their treatments are those in the American Psychiatric Association's *Diagnostic and Statistical Manual of Mental Disorders* (see MENTAL HEALTH HELP, INFORMATION, AND ACTION GUIDE on page 442), though even these are highly controversial within the psychiatric community. Among the disorders of most concern to women are:
• various kinds of EATING DISORDERS, which in this book are dealt with in sep-

arate articles, under: ANOREXIA NERVOSA; BULIMIA; BINGE EATING DISORDER; OBE-SITY; PICA.

- mood disorders, including DEPRESSION and *bi-polar disorders* (manic-depression).
- anxiety disorders, including phobias and panic attacks, characterized by excessive fear, tension, worry, and uneasiness, often involving physical changes such as sweating, accelerated heartbeat, and disturbed breathing. Phobias involve persistent, powerful, unbased fear of an object, such as dogs, cats, snakes, insects, or blood, or situations, such as enclosed spaces *(claustrophobia)* and open spaces *(agoraphobia)*. Reactions can be so extreme as to involve nausea and vomiting, incontinence, choking sensations, trembling or shaking, temporary loss of identity, fear of going crazy, fear of losing control, or fear of dying.
- *gender identity disorders* or *identity disorders,* a matter of considerable controversy, where (as traditionally) women have been forced into male-determined roles, with any deviance from those roles labeled as a "disorder."

Beyond these are a wide range of disorders of unknown origin, though often with a strong suggestion of physical or biochemical problems at base, including dissociative disorders, such as multiple personality disorders; and various dysfunctional personality styles, including dependent, paranoid, and passive–aggressive personality disorders.

Some women have emotional problems or turmoil, short of a clinical disorder, which they believe stem primarily from their conflict with social norms of female behavior; many such women prefer feminist therapists, feeling that male therapists are unable to properly understand their problems. Women should not be misled, however, into thinking that *any* feminist therapist will be appropriate. With any therapist, male or female, a woman should be sure she feels comfortable, and that she and the therapist share long-term goals about the aims and process of therapy.

One major concern for women with male therapists is the widespread problem of sexual abuse within a doctor-patient relationship. If a woman is forced or coerced into submission, it would, of course, be RAPE. However, far more common is a sexual relationship that develops seemingly by mutual consent between male doctor and female patient. In fact, such a relationship is a gross violation of the proper doctor-patient relationship, with the doctor failing to maintain professional distance and therefore both failing to help the patient and often harming her, especially because he stands in a position of power and authority regarding her. Such relationships are contrary to all professional standards, and are supposedly sufficient reason for a therapist to lose a license; in fact, though figures are hard to come by, studies suggest that the practice is widespread, the profession having dismally failed to police itself. Organizations like STOP ABUSE BY COUNSELORS is among those calling for change. In the meantime, women should beware of sexual relationships in such a setting. If they have problems they are working through, the process will not be helped by allowing themselves to be drawn—or by the doctor allowing himself to be drawn—into a sexual relationship, thereby destroying any therapeutic possibilities.

Laws vary widely, but in some places, long-term insanity can sometimes be grounds for DIVORCE, as when a person has been diagnosed as incurable, or sometimes when the condition has been so severe over a specified number of years (often including hospitalizations) as to make normal marital life impossible. The person obtaining the divorce, however, is still responsible for supporting the mentally disabled spouse.

Though, traditionally, communications between a patient and a psychologist or psychiatrist are confidential, patients should be aware that they are not completely so. Some kinds of treatment for some mental illnesses are covered by health insurance plans, though many are not; when therapy is covered, insurance companies have the right to "audit" the therapist's notes of sessions. In certain situations psychotherapists can also be called to testify in court about confidential matters, as in some child abuse or murder cases. (See MENTAL HEALTH HELP, INFORMATION, AND ACTION GUIDE, below.)

MENTAL HEALTH

Help, Information, and Action Guide

Organizations

✓ GENERAL ORGANIZATIONS

▶ National Institute of Mental Health (NIMH) (Parklawn Building, 7-103, 5600 Fishers Lane, Rockville, MD 20857; public affairs 301-443-4536; publications 301-443-4513; Frederick Goodwin, director), an arm of the National Institutes of Health concerned with mental health and illness. It sponsors research and provides information to health professionals and the general public, through materials such as *A Consumer's Guide to Mental Health Services, Schizophrenia: Questions and Answers,* and series of "Useful Information On" booklets on topics such as anorexia nervosa and bulimia, paranoia, phobias and panic, sleep disorders, obsessive-compulsive disorder, and medications for mental illness.

▶ National Mental Health Association (NMHA) (1021 Prince Street, Alexandria, VA 22314-2971; 703-684-7722 or 800-969-NMHA [6642]; John Horner, executive director), an organization that acts as an advocate for people with mental disorders, by pushing for improvements in care and prevention. It publishes various print and audiovisual materials, including *Women's Changing Roles: Finding a Balance.*

▶ Anxiety Disorders Association of America (ADAA) (6000 Executive Boulevard, Rockville, MD 20852; 301-231-9350 or [at a charge of $2.00/min.] 900-737-3400; Norman Klombers, president), an organization concerned with anxiety disorders. It acts as an information clearinghouse; encourages the formation of local mutual-support groups; and publishes various materials, including *Breaking the Panic Cycle* and *Phobia: A Comprehensive Summary of Modern Treatments.*

▶ **National Alliance for the Mentally Ill (NAMI)** (2101 Wilson Boulevard, Suite 302, Arlington, VA 22201; 703-524-7600 or helplines 800-950-6264; Laurie M. Flynn, executive director), a network of mutual-support groups of families and friends of people with serious mental illnesses. It seeks to educate the public; provides information; and publishes various materials, including a bimonthly newsletter, *Anti-Stigma Handbook, Consumer's Guide to Mental Health Services,* and brochures on mental illnesses.

◪ ON DEPRESSION

▶ **Depression and Related Affective Disorders Association (DRADA)** (DRADA-Meyer 3-181, Johns Hopkins Hospital, 601 North Wolfe Street, Baltimore, MD 21205; 301-987-4647 or 301-955-5756; Paul Hoegberg, president), an organization focusing on clinical depression. It publishes the quarterly newsletter *Smooth Sailing,* the brochure *I Am the Greatest, I Am Depressed,* and other materials.

▶ **National Depressive and Manic-Depressive Association (NDMDA)** (730 North Franklin, Suite 501, Chicago, IL 60610; 312-642-0049; Susan Dime-Meenan, executive director), an organization focusing on depression and bipolar disorders. It provides information.

▶ **National Foundation for Depressive Illness** (P.O. Box 2257, New York, NY 10116; 800-248-4344), an organization focusing on depression. It provides information and referrals to mutual-support groups.

▶ **Depression After Delivery** (P.O. Box 1282, Morrisville, PA 19067; 215-295-3994), an organization focusing on postpartum depression.

▶ **NATIONAL WOMEN'S HEALTH NETWORK (NWHN)** (202-347-1140). Operates the **Women's Health Information Service.** Distributes the information packets *Depression/Manic Depression* and *Postpartum Depression.*

◪ SELF-HELP GROUPS

▶ **Emotional Health Anonymous (EHA)** (P.O. Box 429, Glendale, CA 91770; 818-240-3215), a network of mutual-support groups for people recovering from emotional illness, modeled on Alcoholics Anonymous. It publishes various materials, including the bimonthly *Hang-Up.*

▶ **Emotions Anonymous (EA)** (P.O. Box 4245, St. Paul, MN 55104; 612-647-9712; Karen Crawford, executive director), a network of mutual-support groups for people recovering from emotional illness, modeled on Alcoholics Anonymous. It publishes various materials including *Emotions Anonymous World Directory.*

Other reference sources

◪ ON WOMEN'S PSYCHOLOGY

The Psychology of Women. Michele A. Paludi. Brown and Benchmark, 1991.
Always Daddy's Girl: Understanding Your Father's Impact on Who You Are.
H. Norman Wright. Regal, 1991.
Trusting Ourselves: The Complete Guide to Emotional Well-Being for Women.
Karen Johnson. Atlantic Monthly, 1991.
Trusting Ourselves: The Sourcebook on Psychology for Women. Karen Johnson. Atlantic Monthly, 1990. A survey of different psychological schools' stance toward women.
Understanding Woman's Behaviour. Parveen Kumar. Aegina Press, 1990.

◪ ON DEPRESSION

I Don't Know Who You Are Anymore: A Family's Struggle with Depression.
Kellie Branson and Dale A. Babcock. Legendary, 1992.
Straight Talk About Anxiety and Depression. Michael Maloney and Rachel Kranz. Facts on File, 1991. For teens.
Banish the Post-Baby Blues: All the Advice, Support and Encouragement You Need to Cope with Post-Natal Depression. Anne-Marie Sapsted. Thorsons, 1990.
Encyclopedia of Depression. Roberta Roesch. Facts on File, 1990.
Teenage Depression. Herma Silverstein. Watts, 1990.
You Can Beat Depression: A Guide to Recovery. John Preston. Impact, 1989.
The Good News About Depression: New Breakthrough Medical Treatments That Can Work for You. Mark S. Gold and Lois B. Morris. Bantam, 1988.
Do You Have a Depressive Illness? How to Tell, What to Do. Donald F. Klein and Paul H. Wender. New American Library, 1988.
Blow Away the Black Clouds: A Woman's Answer to Depression. Florence Littauer. Walker, 1988.

◪ ON FEMINIST THERAPY

Healing Voices: Feminist Approaches to Therapy with Women. Toni A. Laidlaw. Jossey-Bass, 1990.
A Guide to Feminist Family Therapy. Lois Braverman, ed. Harrington Park, 1988.

◪ GENERAL WORKS

The Anxiety and Phobia Workbook. Ed Bourne. New Harbinger, 1990.
The Family Mental Health Encyclopedia. Frank J. Bruno. Wiley, 1989.

The Encyclopedia of Phobias, Fears, and Anxieties. Ronald M. Doctor and
Ada P. Kahn. Facts on File, 1989.
The New Harvard Guide to Psychiatry. Armand M. Nicholi, Jr., ed. Belknap/
Harvard, 1988.
Diagnostic and Statistical Manual of Mental Disorders. 3rd ed. (DSM-III-R).
American Psychiatric Association, 1987. Descriptions of currently recog-
nized mental disorders, in understandable language.
Health Care U.S.A. Jean Carper. Prentice Hall Press, 1987. Lists centers for
treatment or research.

☑ PERSONAL AND PRACTICAL GUIDES

Reclaiming Woman's Voice: Becoming Whole. Lesley I. Shore. Llewellyn,
1992.
Feeling Good, Feeling Bad. Diane Langberg. Servant, 1991.
*Prisoner of Another War: A Remarkable Journey of Healing from Childhood
Trauma.* Marilyn Murray. PageMill Press, 1991.
*Slay Your Own Dragons: How Women Can Overcome Self-Sabotage in Love
and Work.* Nancy Good. St. Martin's, 1990.
*My Life Is Great, Why Do I Feel So Awful? Successful Women, Hidden Pas-
sions.* Steve Pieczenik. Warner Books, 1990.
*The Empowered Woman: New Directions for Overcoming Obstacles to Success
and Happiness.* Riki Robbins Jones. Lifetime, 1990.
Knowing Herself: Women Tell Their Stories in Psychotherapy. J. H. Robbins,
ed. Plenum, 1990.
*The Emotionally Abused Woman: Overcoming Destructive Patterns and Re-
claiming Yourself.* Beverly Engel. Lowell House, 1990.
*Courage to Be Yourself: A Woman's Guide to Growing Beyond Emotional De-
pendence.* Sue P. Thoele. Pyramid Press, 1989.
The Superwoman Syndrome. Marjorie H. Shaevitz. Warner Books, 1988.
Supermom: "The Lost Child." Linda DeBlanco. Forget Me Not, 1988.
The Indispensable Woman: Beating the Perfection Addiction. Ellen S. Stern.
Bantam, 1988.
(See also CHILD ABUSE AND NEGLECT HELP, INFORMATION, AND ACTION GUIDE
on page 152, for books on recovering from, and breaking the cycle of,
childhood abuse.)

☑ BACKGROUND WORKS

Freud, Women and Society. J. O. Wisdom. Transaction, 1992.
Troubled Women: Roles and Realities in Psychoanalytic Perspective. Reuben
Fine. Jossey-Bass, 1992.
Beyond Female Masochism. Frigga Haug. Routledge Chapman and Hall,
1991.

Exploring—Teaching the Psychology of Women: A Manual of Resources. Michele A. Paludi. State University of New York Press, 1990.

Psychiatric Skeletons: Tracing the Legacy of Mental Illness in the Family. Steven D. Targum. PIA Press, 1989.

Psychiatric Disorders in America. Lee Robins and Darrel A. Regier, eds. Free Press, 1989.

Women in Therapy. Harriet G. Lerner. Aronson, 1988.

The Bonds of Love: Psychoanalysis, Feminism, and the Problem of Domination. Jessica Benjamin. Pantheon, 1988.

Treating Women's Fear of Failure. Esther D. Rothblum and Ellen Cole, eds. Haworth Press, 1988.

Feminist Counselling in Action. Jocelyn Chaplin. Sage, 1988.

The Psychopathology of Everyday Racism and Sexism. Lenora Fulani, ed. Harrington Park, 1988.

The Politics of Race and Gender in Therapy. Lenora Fulani, ed. Haworth Press, 1988.

Female Authority: Empowering Women Through Psychotherapy. Polly Young-Eisendrath and Florence Wiedemann. Guilford Press, 1987.

Meritor v. *Vinson*, the 1986 U.S. Supreme Court decision that established a hostile workplace as constituting SEXUAL HARASSMENT.

metabolic disorders, a group of digestive disorders (see DIGESTIVE SYSTEM).

metaphysical feminism, as used by Robin MORGAN in her book *Going Too Far* (1977), a concept of FEMINISM as an all-embracing religious belief, which affirms the primacy of all life, of planet Earth's ecosystem, and of the creation of a heaven-on-earth kind of worldwide Utopia, with all freed of all of the afflictions that have so far been part of the human condition. (See also FEMINISM.)

Mexico City Conference (1975): See INTERNATIONAL WOMEN'S YEAR.

midwife, an attendant at a birth, today usually a CERTIFIED NURSE–MIDWIFE (CNM) (see CHILDBIRTH).

Mill, John Stuart (1806–1873), a leading nineteenth-century English philosopher-economist and free-thinking rationalist, after Jeremy Bentham the chief exponent of utilitarianism. His major works included *A System of Logic* (1843), *Principles of Political Economy* (1848), *On Liberty* (1859), *Considerations on Representative Government* (1861), *Utilitarianism* (1863), and *The Subjection of Women* (1869). His long relationship with Harriet TAYLOR, then married to someone else, began in 1830; Mill and Taylor married in 1851, after her first husband's death in 1849. They collaborated in *On Liberty,* though she was uncredited.

Mill was a leader in the long fight for WOMEN'S RIGHTS. *The Subjection of Women,* which was built entirely rationally from his preceding body of work, called for complete legal, economic, and social equality for all persons, a truly revolutionary call in its time, and became a cornerstone of the worldwide WOMEN'S RIGHTS MOVEMENT then beginning to develop.

Mill was also a practical feminist. While a Member of Parliament, he presented the first British WOMAN SUFFRAGE petition, in 1866, and introduced the first British woman suffrage resolution in 1867.

Millett, Kate (1934–), a sculptor and teacher who in 1970 emerged as a leading radical feminist with the publication of her book *Sexual Politics.* That work depends greatly on her literary criticism of such authors as D. H. Lawrence, Norman Mailer, and Henry Miller as patriarchal, woman-hating authors tied to what she perceives as antiwoman Freudian psychology; her position was that male domination in patriarchal societies was the cause of almost all societal and personal ills. She called for a sexual revolution to sweep all that away and with it the FAMILY, Freudian psychology, and all the forms of SEXUAL DISCRIMINATION and violent abuse. She has also published *The Loony Bin Trip* (1991), telling her side of a series of events that included her commitment by members of her family to mental hospitals in 1973 and 1980. (See also WOMEN'S LIBERATION MOVEMENT.)

minilaparotomy, a type of TUBAL LIGATION.

minituck, a type of abdominoplasty (see COSMETIC SURGERY).

misandry, hatred of men in general, by women; a term recently introduced into the language.

miscarriage, the loss of a FETUS before the twenty-eighth week of GESTATION. It is an involuntary termination of a PREGNANCY, often medically termed a *spontaneous abortion,* unlike the voluntary termination called simply ABORTION. If the fetus dies at a later stage, it is called a STILLBIRTH.

Miscarriages are far more common than is generally recognized, because many occur in the first ten weeks of pregnancy, often before a woman is even aware that she is pregnant. They occur in at least one of every ten pregnancies and perhaps in as many as three in ten. Most result from GENETIC DISORDERS, CHROMOSOMAL ABNORMALITIES, or other BIRTH DEFECTS so severe that they are incompatible with life. However, a severe illness in the MOTHER, an autoimmune disorder (see IMMUNE SYSTEM), or exposure to environmental hazards, such as poisons and radiation, can also cause a spontaneous abortion. Other causes of miscarriages, generally farther into the pregnancy, can be the presence of FIBROIDS in the UTERUS, an incompetent CERVIX that is unable to hold the fetus in the uterus, and structural abnormalities in the mother. Injury and overactivity alone rarely cause miscarriage, according to most public health experts (see EXERCISE).

Signs of an impending miscarriage include bleeding, cramping, and dizziness. If such warning signs are recognized early enough, the pregnancy can sometimes be saved with bed rest. However, once a spontaneous abortion starts, it cannot be stopped. In what is called a *complete abortion,* the cervix dilates (widens), fluid from the AMNIOTIC SAC spills out, bleeding becomes heavier, and the fetus and pregnancy-related tissues, such as the PLACENTA and amniotic sac, are expelled.

Sometimes, however, the fetus and its associated tissues die but are not expelled, though symptoms of pregnancy end and the uterus returns to its normal size. This is called a *missed abortion* and poses a threat of serious infection and other disorders in the mother, if the tissues are not removed. Because doctors cannot otherwise be sure that an abortion is fully complete, in most cases they will perform an operation called a D&C *(dilatation and curettage)* to clean out any remaining tissue.

A single miscarriage does not necessarily mean that later pregnancies will be troubled; they will, however, be medically treated as high-risk pregnancies, for safety. Doctors often advise that a woman allow herself to recover physically and emotionally for a few months after a miscarriage, before attempting another CONCEPTION. (See also PREGNANCY AND CHILDBIRTH HELP, INFORMATION, AND ACTION GUIDE on page 580.)

misogyny, hatred of women in general, by men (see SEXISM; SEXUAL DISCRIMINATION).

Mittelschmerz, the cramping pain in the lower abdomen that some women feel at the time of OVULATION; a German word meaning "middle pain." The pain can sometimes be quite severe and may be mistaken for the onset of acute appendicitis, but it generally lasts only a few hours, sometimes accompanied by slight bleeding. Many women do not experience Mittelschmerz, and its causes are unclear.

molluscum contagiosum, a viral infection common among young children; in adults, one of the SEXUALLY TRANSMITTED DISEASES. In adults the infection produces painless, wartlike bumps on the GENITALS, lower abdomen, or inner thighs; most often these go unnoticed but can become itchy or irritated. Often these heal without treatment, though doctors may treat them with chemicals or by scraping them off. (See SEXUALLY TRANSMITTED DISEASES; also WHAT YOU CAN DO TO AVOID STDs on page 660.)

mommy track, a set of covert discriminatory promotion practices, aimed at women who raise families while continuing their careers. The practice often occurs in high-pressure jobs and organizations, as in the litigation department of a law firm or the acquisitions and mergers department of a business firm, but it is far from limited to these kinds of situations. Although such discrimination is prohibited by law in the United States, many men—and a few women, too—still believe that women with young children, and especially currently employed women who take leave to have children, are not fully committed to their work and so are not as promotable as men—or as women who do not have children but stay without interruption. This unsupported view has nothing to do with reality and far more often than not is used merely as an excuse to discriminate against promotable women in favor of men. Litigation on this aspect of job discrimination proceeds, although proving the existence of a mommy track is seldom easy. (See also SEXUAL DISCRIMINATION; WORK AND WOMEN; FAMILY AND MEDICAL LEAVE; also WORKING WOMEN'S HELP, INFORMATION, AND ACTION GUIDE on page 779; CAREGIVER'S HELP, INFORMATION, AND ACTION GUIDE on page 454.)

monogamy, the condition of a woman having a single husband at one time, or a man a single wife; in the expressed intention of MARRIAGE vows, a union for life. When divorces and remarriages are common, having a sequence of spouses is said to be *serial monogamy*. By contrast, having two spouses at one time is called BIGAMY and two or more is POLYGAMY. In general usage, however, *bigamy* is used to refer to illegally having two or more husbands or wives, while *polygamy* is more often applied to the legal practice of having multiple husbands or wives, where that is an accepted cultural tradition. (See MARRIAGE.)

monoliasis, a main type of YEAST INFECTION.

mons veneris (mound of Venus), the triangular mound of fatty tissue covering the pubic bone (*pubis symphysis*), which sits over the CLITORIS and the rest of the external female GENITALS, called the VULVA. From PUBERTY, the mons veneris is covered with HAIR, in a triangular pattern sometimes called the *escutcheon*.

Morgan, Robin (1941–), an American writer and editor, active in the peace and civil rights movements of the 1960s. She emerged as a leading radical feminist in 1970 with publication of her essay "Goodbye to All That," in which she attacked those movements, asserting they were dominated by sexist men, and announced her affiliation thereafter to women-only movements. In the same year she edited the very popular feminist anthology *Sisterhood Is Powerful.* She later published several poetry collections and the essays collected in *Going Too Far: The Personal Chronicles of a Feminist* (1978), *The Anatomy of Freedom* (1982), and *Sisterhood Is Global* (1984). She became editor of *Ms.* magazine in 1990. (See also WOMEN'S LIBERATION MOVEMENT.)

morning after pill (MAP), popular name for any type of drug given after SEXUAL INTERCOURSE that is designed to block a PREGNANCY, notably by preventing a fertilized egg (OVUM) from implanting in the UTERUS; also called *postcoital contraception.* It is not intended to be used as a regular form of CONTRACEPTION, but rather as an emergency backup, when other BIRTH CONTROL methods have failed, such as when a CONDOM has broken or come off, or a DIAPHRAGM has become dislodged; or when no birth control methods have been used, as during a RAPE. The pill must be taken within seventy-two hours, and so operates in the "gray" area between FERTILIZATION and IMPLANTATION in the uterus wall, which many doctors regard as the beginning of a pregnancy. As one doctor put it, the morning after pill therefore is not contraception, not ABORTION, but what might be called *interception.*

The first morning after pill in the United States—and the only one ever specifically approved *for that use* by the FOOD AND DRUG ADMINISTRATION (FDA)—was DES *(estrogen diethylstilbestrol);* when the strongly adverse side effects of DES became known (such as increased risk of vaginal CANCER), it was withdrawn from the market, though it was still given on college campuses into the early 1980s.

By the mid-1970s, Canadian and Dutch studies showed that a BIRTH CONTROL PILL with lower doses of ESTROGEN and progestin was effective as a morning after pill. Since then, it and other variants have since been used widely, with a success rate of 92 percent or higher. The widespread use of the morning after pill (MAP) is cited as one reason that the abortion rate in the Netherlands is one-fifth that in the United States. A 1992 report by the Alan Guttmacher Institute (see PLANNED PARENTHOOD) estimated that general availability of morning after pills in the United States could cut unintended pregnancies by 1.7 million a year, and halve the annual number of abortions, from 1.6 million to 800,000.

Drugs prescribed as morning after pills all have FDA approval, but *for other uses;* that means that doctors can legally prescribe them, but that they cannot be advertised and promoted as morning after pills. U.S. drug companies have not sought approval for MAP use for a variety of reasons.

- They fear an outcry from antiabortion groups, even though the MAP is technically not an abortion pill. Indeed, under the Reagan and Bush administrations, at least, clinics receiving federal funds were barred from prescribing or even discussing the possibility of morning after pills.
- The expense of going through the testing process is very great, considering that women will take the pills only occasionally (unlike some other pills that are taken for long periods of time).

- Drug companies are concerned about legal liability, not surprisingly since many major lawsuits involve birth defects.

This question of birth defects is a legitimate concern, since if implantation occurs in spite of the MAP, or if a woman is already pregnant before taking the pill, the FETUS may be damaged. Because of this, doctors and clinics who offer the morning after pill generally do so only after the woman receives counseling that covers such questions, and signs an informed consent statement, sometimes specifying that an ABORTION will be sought if a pregnancy results in spite of the morning after pill. Many also conduct a pregnancy test to be sure the woman is not *already* pregnant from previous sexual relations.

In addition, some women's groups, notably the NATIONAL WOMEN'S HEALTH NETWORK, have strongly criticized the FDA for insufficiently testing estrogen-based drugs before releasing them in the market. Indeed, some such groups regard the danger from large doses of hormones, even on a one-time basis, as posing an unknown and therefore unacceptable risk. Certainly any women who have conditions that make taking birth control pills not advisable—such as those with high BLOOD pressure or BREAST CANCER (see BIRTH CONTROL PILLS for a fuller discussion)—should not take morning after pills. Women should also be aware that the morning after pill provides no protection from ECTOPIC PREGNANCY (implantation somewhere outside the uterus) or from SEXUALLY TRANSMITTED DISEASES (STDs), as barrier methods do. The MAP should not be regarded as a regular method of contraception, since the long-term effects of large doses of hormones are unknown.

But for increasing numbers of doctors and women, the morning after pill has become an important type of *emergency* backup method of contraception. The MAP has been made widely available to college students and has been given routinely to rape victims in many hospitals (other than Catholic ones). Many private clinics—including since the late 1980s many Planned Parenthood offices—have also been prescribing MAP for emergency contraception.

Women who know immediately that they face the possibility of an unwanted pregnancy, and who would not wish to carry such a pregnancy to term, but would rather seek an abortion, may be candidates for the morning after pill. They must act quickly, seeing their doctor or clinic and taking the pill within seventy-two hours. They should discuss with their doctor the pros and cons, and the possible long-term side effects, understanding that more is being learned as new studies are done. Short-term side effects from the medically induced hormonal swings include tenderness of the BREASTS, nausea, and vomiting; indeed, some women are unable to keep the pills down, though others have only modest side effects. As of late 1992, the drug RU486 was shown to have potential as a morning after pill. (See BIRTH CONTROL; DES; RU486; see also BIRTH CONTROL AND FAMILY PLANNING HELP, INFORMATION, AND ACTION GUIDE on page 81.)

morning sickness, nausea and vomiting associated with PREGNANCY (see DIGESTIVE SYSTEM).

mother, the woman who legally exercises PARENTS' RIGHTS regarding a child. In the narrowest sense, the mother is the woman who contributed half of the child's genes (see GENETIC INHERITANCE); she is known as the child's *biological mother, natural mother,* or *birth mother.* If she gives up her parental rights and places her child up for ADOPTION, the woman who adopts the child is called the *adoptive mother;* if the placement is temporary or pending final adoption, the woman may be called the *foster mother.* If a woman married a man with children, she is their *stepmother.* However, though she may have informal authority over them in the home, she is not their legal mother unless she formally adopts the children.

A woman who agrees to become pregnant with the SPERM from another woman's husband and bear the child is called a *surrogate mother* (see SURROGATE PARENTING). In a newer form of reproductive technology, *IN VITRO FERTILIZATION/* embryo implant, the egg and sperm come from the husband and the wife, who is unable to carry a child; the fertilized egg is then implanted in a *host surrogate mother,* who carries it to term. In this situation the host surrogate mother is the birth mother, but the infertile wife is the biological mother. The Center for Surrogate Parenting (see INFERTILITY AND REPRODUCTIVE TECHNOLOGY HELP, INFORMATION, AND ACTION GUIDE on page 368) reports that it has successfully petitioned the courts to enter the biological mother's name, rather than the birth mother's name, on the birth certificate. (The biological mother's husband is already the biological FATHER.) In an earlier, more traditional use, *surrogate mother* referred to a woman in the child's life who played a quasi-motherly role, such as a beloved teacher or neighbor.

If a woman has an unplanned, unwanted PREGNANCY, she can choose to carry the child full term or to have an ABORTION, without consent from her husband or the *unwed father* (if she is unmarried). However, governments have tried to restrict her REPRODUCTIVE RIGHTS in various ways. Depending on the state law, a pregnant girl under the AGE OF CONSENT may be required to notify or obtain the consent of her parents, or of the court, before having an abortion. In addition, going beyond the role of educating women about proper PRENATAL CARE and attempting to persuade them to care for themselves and their baby, the state has attempted in various ways to hold women legally responsible for the health of the FETUS they are carrying. Some women have even been charged in criminal court for failing to follow medical advice and doing things that could harm or kill the fetus, such as taking drugs (see ALCOHOL AND DRUG ABUSE). Such issues are relatively new in the courts, and the resolution of such questions is far from clear.

Once the child is born, the mother becomes and generally remains the primary caregiver, though fathers are increasingly involved with raising their children, especially when the family remains intact. The special ties between mother and baby—often called *bonding* or *maternal-infant attachment*—generally begin at birth. Often the newborn is placed on the mother's abdomen to begin the process of interaction through which the child learns to "make contact" with the world, developing the feelings of trust and security necessary for normal growth and development, including learning the many skills necessary for functioning. If this bonding fails, as it sometimes does for unknown reasons—including DEPRESSION in the mother—and if the baby does not bond with someone else, such as the father or another caregiver, its physical and mental development may be significantly retarded and it may develop emotional problems later. Mothers who fail to develop bonds with their children are more likely to abuse and neglect them (see CHILD ABUSE AND NEGLECT). It is the development of such early bonding that causes some surrogate mothers such difficulty and has caused some mothers to change their minds and keep the children they bore.

During this early *symbiotic stage* of bonding, the child is believed to see the mother as part of self. But, gradually, as the child begins to move around in the environment and especially to walk, this child begins to see the mother as distinct from self, a stage psychologists call *separation-individuation*. Even so, bonds between mother and child are often so strong that a child experiences *separation anxiety*, or fear that a temporary separation—as when the child is left in CHILD CARE—will be permanent. In most cases children pass through these phases normally and develop a distinct sense of self. From infancy to adolescence, however, the mother generally remains the child's *psychological parent*, the person who has the strongest emotional ties to the child and is closest to the child's day-to-day activities, hopes, and fears. This is one key reason that, other reasons aside, mothers are generally granted CUSTODY of children in case of SEPARATION or DIVORCE.

In the past, mothers generally stayed in the home, working as HOMEMAKERS and caring for their children as they grew. In recent centuries, however, that pattern has changed markedly as women have moved into the workforce in large numbers (see WORK AND WOMEN). Today women have some difficult decisions to make when they have young children. Do they stay at home or continue working? If they stay at home, do they do so permanently or until some specific time, such as when the child enters nursery school, enters primary school, or enters junior high or high school? If they continue working, do they follow a fast promotion track, with all the high pressure and long hours that entails? Or do they go for a job that has more flexibility in hours or days or allows work at home? Do they opt for (or are they shunted onto) a less demanding career path (see MOMMY TRACK)? Not every woman has or wants all such options. But her range of choices depends on many things, especially the extent to which her partner will be sharing the caregiving chores. For SINGLE PARENTS, choices are more limited, and many married women find that—when it comes to parenting—they are very nearly single parents. The other main factors in a woman's choices are her own earning ability—and therefore ability to pay for CHILD CARE; the availability of reliable, flexible child care; the availability of FAMILY AND MEDICAL LEAVE that will allow women to take time off when necessary for caregiving functions; her employer's willingness to accommodate her needs as a mother; and the flexibility and portability of her work skills, as for work at home. Many women prefer to stay at home, especially in the early months and years of a child's development; others find or feel they would grow "stir crazy" doing so and much prefer to continue independent employment, in one form or another. Each woman must think through her own desires and options to find the decision that is right for herself and her life situation—with no need to feel "guilty," whatever the choice. (See CAREGIVER'S HELP, INFORMATION, AND ACTION GUIDE on page 454.)

CAREGIVER'S

Help, Information, and Action Guide

Organizations

▶ **Mothers at Home** (P.O. Box 2208, Merrifield, VA 22116; 703-352-2292), an organization for mothers who stay in the home to raise their children. It aims to raise their morale and image; gathers and disseminates information; and publishes the monthly *Welcome Home*.

▶ **The Children's Foundation** (TCF) (725 15th Street NW, Suite 505, Washington, DC 20005; 202-347-3300; Kay Hollestelle, executive director), an organization that focuses on the social and economic welfare of families with children. It supplies food for children of low- or moderate-income families at child care and family day care centers; and also publishes the *National Directory of Family Day Care Associations and Support Groups, Fact Sheet on Family Day Care, A Guide for Parents Using or Seeking Home-Based Child Care,* and *Better Baby Care: A Book for Family Day Care Providers.*

▶ **National Association for Family Day Care (NAFDC)** (1331-A Pennsylvania Avenue, NW, Suite 348, Washington, DC 20004; or P.O. Box 71268, Murray, UT 84107; 801-268-9148; Linda Geigle, president), an organization focused on day care in household settings for children. It sets standards for day care centers and publishes newsletter and other publications, including the brochure *What Is Family Day Care?*

▶ **International Nanny Association** (P.O. Box 26522, Austin, TX 78755; 512-454-6462; Donna Leet Dixon, contact), an organization of nannies, employment agencies, and training schools. It sets professional standards and maintains a directory of placement agencies.

▶ **National Association for the Education of Young Children (NAEYC)** (1834 Connecticut Avenue, NW, Washington, DC 20009; 202-232-8777 or 800-424-2460; Marilyn M. Smith, executive director), an organization concerned with high-quality care and education of young children. It supplies accreditation for early childhood programs and provides information and referrals. It also publishes numerous materials, including the bimonthly magazine *Young Children;* the quarterly *Early Childhood Research;* resource guides, policy reports, and books on child care and other topics, including *Opening Your Door to Children: How to Start a Family Day Care Program;* video training tapes; and brochures on child care and early education (some also in Spanish), such as *Finding the Best Care for Your Infant and Toddler, How to Choose a Good Early Childhood Program,* and *So Many Goodbyes: Ways to Ease the Transition Between Home and Groups for Young Children.*

▶ PARENTS WITHOUT PARTNERS (PWP) (301-588-9354; toll-free number 800-637-7974).
▶ FAMILY SERVICE ASSOCIATION OF AMERICA (FSA) (414-359-2111). Publishes *The Family Guide to Child Care: Making the Right Choices.*

☑ POLITICAL AND SOCIAL ORGANIZATIONS

▶ 9 TO 5, NATIONAL ASSOCIATION OF WORKING WOMEN (216-566-1699; Job Survival Hotline 800-522-0925). Publishes the *9 to 5 Newsline, Wage Replacement for Family Leave: Is It Necessary? It Is Feasible?, New Work Force Politics and the Small Business Sector: Is Parental Leave Good for Small Business: A Multivariate Analysis of Business Employment Growth.*
▶ WOMEN'S BUREAU, U.S. DEPARTMENT OF LABOR (202-523-6667). Operates Work and Family Clearinghouse (202-523-4486). Publishes *Employers and Child Care: Benefiting Work and Family* (1990) and *State Maternity/Parental Leave Laws* (1990).
▶ FAMILIES AND WORK INSTITUTE (212-465-2044). Publishes *The Corporate Reference Guide to Work-Family Programs, The State Reference Guide to Work-Family Programs for State Employees, Beyond the Parental Leave Debate: The Impact of Laws in Four States, Parental Leave and Productivity: Current Research, Public-Private Partnerships for Child Care: A Feasibility Study for New York State, The Six Stages of Parenthood, The Preschool Years, The Family in Transition: An International Symposium.*
▶ NATIONAL CENTER FOR POLICY ALTERNATIVES (202-387-6030). Publishes *The Child Care Challenge: Creating Solutions Through Employer-Supported Programs and Public-Private Initiatives, Leadership Brief on Childcare, Reinvesting in Childcare, Family and Medical Leave: Strategies for Success, Leadership Brief on Family and Medical Leave, Legislative Sourcebook on Family and Medical Leave, Policy Choices in Family Leave: Best Practices in the States,* and *History and Summary of the Federal Family and Medical Leave Act,* and the audiotape *Families, Feminism and the Future.*
▶ NOW LEGAL DEFENSE AND EDUCATION FUND (NOW LDEF) (212-925-6635). Publishes the Legal Resource Kit *Employment—Pregnancy and Parental Leave.*
▶ WOMEN'S RESEARCH AND EDUCATION INSTITUTE (WREI) (202-328-7070. Publishes *Family and Medical Leave: Who Pays for the Lack of It?* and *Parental Leave and "Woman's Place": The Implications and Impact of Three European Approaches to Family Leave Policy.*
▶ LEAGUE OF WOMEN VOTERS (202-429-1965). Publishes *Expanding School-Age Child Care: A Community Action Guide* and *Take Action on Child Care.*
▶ WOMEN'S LEGAL DEFENSE FUND (WLDF) (202-887-0364). Publishes *State Leave Laws Chart.*
▶ **Child Care Action Campaign (CCAC)** (330 Seventh Ave, 18th Floor,

New York, NY 10001; 212-239-0138; Barbara Reisman, executive director), an organization seeking to improve child care, especially by influencing legislative action. It publishes a newsletter and other materials, including audiocassettes.

▶ WOMEN'S MINISTRY UNIT (WMU) (502-569-5382). Distributes *Parental Leave Guidelines for Governing Bodies*.

▶ CATALYST (212-777-8900). Publishes *Perspective on Current Corporate Issues* and *The Corporate Guide to Parental Leaves*.

▶ CONGRESSIONAL CAUCUS FOR WOMEN'S ISSUES (202-225-6740).

▶ MS. FOUNDATION FOR WOMEN (MFW) (212-353-8580).

▶ INSTITUTE ON WOMEN AND TECHNOLOGY (413-367-9725).

▶ CHILD WELFARE LEAGUE OF AMERICA (CWLA) (202-639-2952).

▶ NATIONAL CENTER FOR YOUTH LAW (NCYL) (415-543-3307).

▶ FEDERALLY EMPLOYED WOMEN (FEW) (202-898-0994).

Other resources

◪ ON MOTHERHOOD

Mothering Heights: Reclaiming Motherhood from the Experts. Sonia Taitz. Morrow, 1992.

Having a Baby in Your Forties: An Intimate, Touching Account of a Career-Minded Woman Adjusting to Becoming a Mother. Patricia Mellon-Elibol. Lifetime, 1992.

Mothers Talk Back. Susan Swan and others, eds. Coach House/InBook, 1992.

Motherhood and Representation. E. Ann Kaplan. Routledge, 1992.

The Stay-at-Home Mom: For Women at Home and Those Who Want to Be. Donna Otto. Harvest House, 1991.

Mothering: A Complete Guide for Mothers of All Ages. Grace Ketterman. Oliver-Nelson, 1991.

Terrible Angel: Surviving the First Five Years of Motherhood. Patricia H. Clifford. Paulist Press, 1991.

The Unofficial Mother's Handbook. Art Peterson and Norma Peterson. NAL-Dutton, 1991.

One Thousand Mother's Questions Answered: All You Need to Know About Child Care from Conception to School. Davina Lloyd and Ann Rushton. Thorsons (SF), 1991.

Motherhood. Philadelphia: Running Press, 1990.

Motherhood: What It Does to Your Mind. Jane Price. Unwin Hyman, 1989.

Mother's First Year: A Coping Guide for Recent and Prospective Mothers. Hanns G. Pieper. Betterway, 1989.

The Mother's Survival Guide. Shirley R. Radl. Steve Davis, 1989.

Too Long a Child: The Mother-Daughter Dyad. Nini Herman. Columbia University Press, 1989.

◪ ON WORKING MOTHERS

Women's Two Roles: A Contemporary Dilemma. Phyllis Moen. Auburn House/Greenwood, 1992.

Making It Work: Finding the Time and Energy for Your Career, Marriage, Children, and Self. Victoria Houston. Contemporary, 1990.

Working Parent/Happy Child: You Can Balance Job and Family. Caryl Waller Krueger. Abingdon, 1990.

Answers to the Mommy Track: How Wives and Mothers in Business Reach the Top and Balance Their Lives. Trudi Ferguson. New Horizon, 1990.

The Phantom Spouse: Helping Your Family Survive Business Travel or Relocation. Denise V. Lang. Betterway, 1990.

Tips for Working Parents: Creative Solutions to Everyday Problems. Kathleen McBride. Storey/Garden Way, 1989.

The Second Shift: Working Parents and the Revolution at Home. Arlie Hochschild. Viking, 1989.

Sequencing: A New Solution for Women Who Want Marriage, Career, and Family. Arlene Rossen Cardozo. Collier/Macmillan, 1989.

Remaking Motherhood: How Working Mothers Are Shaping Our Children's Future. Anita Shreve. Fawcett, 1988.

Time Out for Motherhood: A Guide to the Financial, Emotional, and Career Aspects of Having a Baby. Lucy Scott and Meredith Joan Angwin. Tarcher, 1988.

The Working Parent Dilemma: How to Balance the Responsibilities of Children and Careers. Earl Grollman and Gerri L. Sweder. Beacon Press, 1988.

The Woman Who Works, The Parent Who Cares: A Revolutionary Program for Raising Your Child. Sirgay Sanger and John Kelly. Harper & Row, 1988.

◪ PRACTICAL GUIDES ON CHILD CARE

Day Care: Looking for Answers. Kathlyn Gay. Enslow, 1992.

Shopping for Quality Daycare. Claudia Bischoff. Round Lake, 1992.

All About Child Care. rev. ed. Marilyn Segal. Nova University Family Center, 1991.

Child Care: A Parent's Guide. Sonja Flating. Facts on File, 1991.

Keys to Choosing Child Care. Stevanne Auerbach. Barron's, 1991.

Home-Alone Kids: A Parent's Guide to Providing the Best Care for Your Child. Bryan E. Robinson and others. Lexington Books, 1989.

Child Care That Works: How Families Can Share Their Lives with Child Care and Thrive. Ann Muscari and Wenda Wardell Morrone. Doubleday, 1989.

Day-Care: A Parent's Choice. James Hollingsworth and others. D/B Trust, 1989.

◪ ON MAKING CHILD CARE A BUSINESS

Profitable Child Care: How to Establish a Successful Business. Nan L. Howkins and Heidi Kane. Facts on File, 1992.

Careers in Child Care. Alma L. Visser and Patricia A. Woy. Betterway, 1991.

Little People: Big Business: A Guide to Successful In-Home Day Care. Margaret M. Gillis and others. Betterway, 1991.

Start Your Own At Home Child Care Business. Patricia Gallagher. Doubleday, 1989.

◪ PRACTICAL GUIDES ON MATERNITY AND FAMILY LEAVE

Maternity Leave: The Working Woman's Practical Guide to Combining Pregnancy, Motherhood and Career. Eileen L. Casey. Green Mountain, 1992.

Family and Medical Leave: Strategies for Success. Lisa Sementilli-Dann. CPA Washington, 1991.

Your Maternity Leave: How to Leave Work, Have a Baby and Go Back to Work Without Getting Lost, Trapped or Sandbagged Along the Way. Jean Marzollo. Poseidon, 1989.

(See also PREGNANCY DISCRIMINATION ACT.)

◪ ON HOMEMAKERS

What's a Smart Woman Like You Doing in a Place Like This? Homemaking on Purpose. Mary A. Froehlich, ed. Wolgemuth and Hyatt, 1989.

The Dual Disadvantage of Displaced Homemakers: Findings from the Study, Low-Wage Jobs and Workers: Trends and Options for Change. Roberta M. Spalter-Roth. Institute for Women's Policy Research, 1989.

Have Skills Women's Workbook: Finding Jobs Using Your Homemaking and Volunteer Work Experience. Ruth B. Ekstrom. Educational Testing Service, 1988.

Women and Home-Based Work. Kathleen E. Christensen. Holt, 1988.

Just a Housewife: The Rise and Fall of Domesticity in America. Glenna Matthews. Oxford University Press, 1987.

◪ BACKGROUND WORKS

Equal Parenthood and Social Policy: A Study of Parental Leave in Sweden. Linda Haas. State University New York Press, 1992.

Parental Leave and Child Care: Setting a Research and Policy Agenda. Janet S. Hyde and Marilyn J. Essex. Temple University Press, 1991.

Science and Politics: The Dual Vision of Feminist Policy Research, the Example of Family and Medical Leave. rev. ed. Roberta M. Spalter-Roth and Heidi Hartmann. Institute for Women's Policy Research, 1991.

Negotiated Care: The Experience of Family Day Care Providers. Margaret K. Nelson. Temple University Press, 1991.

Current Issues in Day Care for Young Children. Peter Moss and Edward Melhuish. Unipub, 1991.

Family Support, Day Care and Educational Provisions for Young Children. Unipub, 1991.

Child Care, Parental Leave, and the Under Three's: Policy Innovation in Europe. Sheila B. Kamerman and Alfred J. Kahn, eds. Greenwood, 1991.

The Day Care Dilemma: Critical Concerns for American Families. Angela Browne Miller. Plenum/Insight, 1990.

Costs to Americans of Lack of Family Leave. Roberta M. Spalter-Roth and Heidi Hartmann. Institute for Women's Policy Research, 1989.

Unneccessary Losses: The Costs to Workers in the States of the Lack of Family and Medical Leave. Roberta M. Spalter-Roth and others. Institute for Women's Policy Research, 1989.

mother goddess: See GODDESS WORSHIP.

mother right, another name for the whole body of rights stemming from a matrilineal line of succession; that is, through successive generations of women. (See MATRIARCHY.)

Mothers, The (1927), Robert BRIFFAULT's three-volume study of what he felt to be the matriarchal early history of human culture (see MATRIARCHY), which he described as later supplanted by PATRIARCHY. He based much of his thinking on the female figurines found on several European archaeological sites, positing wide-scale GODDESS WORSHIP. His work and theory proved very attractive to many twentieth-century feminists and provided much of the basis of early goddess theories, although subsequent anthropological research and historical thinking has cast great doubt on his data and theory.

Mott, Lucretia Coffin (1793–1880), a Quaker minister who became a leading abolitionist in the 1830s and founder of the Philadelphia Female Anti-Slavery Society. She became a pioneer American WOMEN'S RIGHTS leader in the

1840s, after she and Elizabeth Cady STANTON were refused seating at the 1840 World Anti-Slavery Convention in London. In 1848 she and Stanton organized the landmark SENECA FALLS WOMEN'S RIGHTS CONVENTION.

Mott focused much of her attention on the antislavery movement before and during the Civil War, from 1850 as an organizer of the Underground Railroad and of aid to escaped slaves and after the war to newly freed African-Americans.

In 1866 she chaired the Equal Rights Convention. She also continued her work in the WOMEN'S RIGHTS MOVEMENT, attempting to bridge the gap that opened up in 1869, with the organization of the relatively conservative AMERICAN WOMAN SUFFRAGE ASSOCIATION as an alternative to the more militant NATIONAL WOMAN SUFFRAGE ASSOCIATION, led by Susan B. ANTHONY and Stanton. (See also WOMEN'S RIGHTS MOVEMENT.)

mound of Venus, an alternative name for MONS VENERIS.

Ms., a form of address connoting the independent status of the woman being addressed, rather than referring to her MARITAL STATUS, as do the addresses "Miss" and "Mrs." It was adopted by a few women as early as the 1940s and became widely used in the late 1960s and early 1970s, also generating the title of the magazine *Ms.* Proponents note that the address "Mr." for males does not reflect marital status, which is—or should be—irrelevant in professional, legal, work-oriented, or formal situations where such titles are most often used.

Ms., a popular American WOMEN'S RIGHTS and feminist magazine, founded in 1971; Gloria STEINEM was a founder and was chief editor until 1987. The magazine covered a wide range of women's special concerns and cultural and historical interests and proved very appealing, its circulation quickly moving into the 300,000–350,000 range in the early 1970s. But although it appealed to more than its core of feminist readers, it depended on that core, and when in the 1980s the women's movement encountered difficulties, so did *Ms.* Sagging income ultimately forced repeated sales of the magazine and ultimately a brief shutdown. But the magazine revived in the early 1990s, adopting a new no-advertisement policy, installing Robin MORGAN as its new editor, and taking a somewhat more radical feminist path than it had in the days of its mass circulation.

Ms. Foundation for Women (MFW) (141 Fifth Avenue, Suite 6-S, New York, NY 10010; 212-353-8580; Marie C. Wilson, executive director), an organization founded in 1972 to "support the efforts of grassroots women who typically have limited access to traditional funding sources." Among the categories for which grants are provided are

▶ *Collaborative Fund for Women's Economic Development,* stressing job creation projects, including self-employment and "micro-businesses" for women, especially low-income women and women of color.

▶ *Economic Justice,* providing training for nontraditional jobs, cooperatives, and self-employment opportunities and seeking fair employment practices and safe working environments for those hardest hit by economic decline, such as immigrant and nonunionized women, DISPLACED HOMEMAKERS, office workers, women farmworkers, and women "hard-hats."

▶ *Empowerment,* seeking social justice for immigrant and refugee women and LESBIAN civil rights, acting as advocates for imprisoned mothers and welfare mothers, and "cultivating indigenous leadership and protesting war."

▶ *Girls,* supporting projects that nurture "the developing identities of adolescent girls" and address "their specific needs and problems," through its National Girls Initiative, including a Girls Project focusing on sexual abuse, building self-esteem, and challenges to sex-role stereotyping.

▶ *Safety,* focusing on child sexual abuse, RAPE, sexual assault, and hate violence against women, including lesbians, with programs including shelters, self-defense training, and advocacy for imprisoned BATTERED WOMEN and abused children.

▶ *Reproductive Rights, Health, and AIDS,* stressing "universal health care campaigns for women, AIDS education in communities or color, and reproductive safety in the workplace" and concerned with "lack of medical research on diseases affecting women."

▶ *Reproductive Rights Coalition Fund,* supporting a wide range of initiatives to guarantee reproductive rights, especially for minors, low-income women, and women of color.

▶ *Leadership Enrichment Fund,* supporting previous grantees in obtaining technical assistance and skills training.

Grants are funded by volunteer donations and grants from major foundations and corporations.

multiple sclerosis (MS), a disorder involving disruption of communication in the nervous system, caused by damage or destruction of *myelin,* a fatty substance that protects nerve cells in the BRAIN and spinal cord (see SKELETAL SYSTEM), and its replacement with scar tissue (*sclerosis*). It is considered a type of *autoimmune disease,* in which the body mistakenly attacks its own tissue (see IMMUNE SYSTEM). Why this happens is unclear. One speculation is that a virus picked up early in life triggers the autoimmune reaction.

The disease is most common in the world's temperate zones (rather than tropical climates) and often comes on in young childhood; in fact, the likelihood of contracting MS is affected by where a person spends the first fifteen years of life. Like many autoimmune disorders, it affects women more often than men. For unknown reasons, it also affects people of Caucasian background more often than others. MS is not a GENETIC DISORDER, nor is it contagious; in some cases more than one family member may contract it, but that is believed to be because of a hereditary vulnerability and/or the result of being exposed to the same environmental factors.

Symptoms vary considerably, depending on which parts of the body are affected and the severity of the damage, but include numbness, tingling sensations, weakness or cramping of muscles (see MUSCULAR SYSTEM), lack of coordination, paralysis, abnormal fatigue, blurred or double vision, confusion, absentmindedness, inability to control bowels and bladder, and diminished sexual functioning. MS also follows highly variable patterns. Some people may have a single attack, without any recurrence. Others have alternating periods of active symptoms, called *exacerbations*, and symptom-free periods, called *remissions*. In others, MS is chronic and becomes increasingly severe. Because symptoms are so variable, diagnosis is difficult, and normally involves a variety of tests, such as sampling of spinal fluid or scans.

Recent studies with animals indicate that some kinds of antibodies in the immune system help repair myelin—suggesting a basis for the highly variable symptoms. Inspired by this, researchers are working on ways to try to increase the number and effectiveness of such antibodies in the system, in search of a treatment or cure. At present, though drugs and therapy can help alleviate symptoms, no cure exists.

MS does not, however, affect LIFE EXPECTANCY, so it need not be a bar to a relatively normal life. Traditionally, women with MS were advised that a PREGNANCY could cause their condition to worsen; but according to the National Multiple Sclerosis Society (see below), more recent studies do not support that idea, and "in general pregnancy is no longer held to be necessarily detrimental." The society does caution, however, that a woman with MS should carefully assess whether or not she will have the physical stamina to care for a baby and later an active youngster, and whether she will have the resources needed to help her do so.

For help, information, and action

▶ **National Multiple Sclerosis Society (NMSS)** (205 East 42nd Street, New York, NY 10017; 212-986-3240; Thor Hanson, president), an organization concerned with multiple sclerosis. It offers information and referrals; provides community services, including counseling, vocational rehabilitation, and medical equipment on loan; publishes various materials, including the quarterly magazine *Plain Talk: A Book About Multiple Sclerosis for Families*, and brochures *Someone You Know Has Multiple Sclerosis: A Book for Families, What Everyone Should Know About Multiple Sclerosis, Emotional Aspects of MS*, and *Living with MS: A Practical Guide.*

▶ NATIONAL INSTITUTE OF NEUROLOGICAL DISORDERS AND STROKE (NINDS) (301-496-5751). Publishes the brochure *Multiple Sclerosis: Hope Through Research.*

Other resources

Multiple Sclerosis: A Self-Help Guide to Its Management, rev. ed. Judy Graham. Inner Traditions, 1989.

All of a Piece: A Life with Multiple Sclerosis. Barbara D. Webster. Johns Hopkins University Press, 1989.

Multiple Sclerosis: A Guide for Patients and Families. Labe C. Scheinberg. Raven Press, 1983.

muscular system, part of the internal architecture of the body, with the SKEL-ETAL SYSTEM providing shape, support, stability, strength, support, and motion. Muscles are bundles of fibers of various structure and texture, which allow bones and other parts of the body to move. The three main types of muscle are

▶ *smooth muscles,* which control movement of the internal organs such as the intestines or bladder. These are largely involuntary muscles, controlled by impulses from the brain. Some operate continually, such as those involved in breathing, digestion, and circulation. Others are used seldom or never, such as those that contract the UTERUS during CHILDBIRTH.

▶ *cardiac muscle (myocardium),* the specially designed pump that contracts approximately one hundred thousand times a day, to power BLOOD through the body (see HEART AND CIRCULATORY SYSTEM).

▶ *skeletal muscle,* the voluntary muscles that are used to move parts of the body or to maintain them in a fixed position.

Unlike the other two types of muscle, skeletal muscles require use to maintain their proper state of partial contraction, called *muscle tone.* Regular EXERCISE keeps the muscles toned up and ready to use; builds the size and strength not only of muscles, but also of bone, important in forestalling OSTEOPOROSIS; and helps protect against problems such as lower back pain (see SPINE) or prolapsed UTERUS. If muscles are not used, they slacken, or *atrophy.* Conversely, muscles may remain excessively contracted, a condition called *spasticity.* The muscles themselves are linked to specialized connective tissue called *tendons,* which link muscle to bones or other muscles, and *ligaments,* which connect and stabilize bones at the joints and also help support various organs or body parts, including the uterus, bladder, liver, DIAPHRAGM, and BREASTS. On the average, women have less muscle mass and strength than men, though of course individual women may be more muscular than individual men.

Skeletal muscles vary by the type of function they perform: an *extensor muscle* opens an angle, as of an arm of leg; a *flexor* closes it; an *adductor muscle* moves part of the body toward the center; an *abductor* moves it out from the body; a *levator muscle* raises a body part; a *depressor* lowers it; *constrictor* or *sphincter muscles* surround or close off openings, as of the anus (see DIGESTIVE SYSTEM).

Each muscle, however small or large, is linked with nerves that carry messages from the brain, specifically releasing a chemical called *acetylcholine.* This *neurotransmitter* triggers a sequence of biochemical events, involving vital minerals such as sodium, potassium, and calcium (see KEY VITAMINS AND MINERALS on page 502), to stimulate the muscle to perform its particular movement. In the process, information from the muscles and tendons is transmitted back to the brain, which may limit the length of the muscle's stretch accordingly. The availability of vital nutrients also affects this process. A lack of potassium, for example, may cause weakness of the muscle, while lack of calcium can cause muscle spasms. If overused, muscles may use up their energy supply, primarily in the form of the sugar *glycogen*, and build up lactic acid. Lack of oxygen in the system can also cause spasms and cramps in the muscles, which are starved of necessary oxygen.

Soreness following strenuous exercise may also be caused by small tears in the related tendons and ligaments; biochemical by-products collect in the area of the injury, and as these are picked up by the blood and dispersed throughout the system, the soreness goes away. If the ligaments are actually torn or damaged, often near where they meet the bone, it is called a *sprain*. Problems with the SPINE, such as the twisting called *scoliosis* or problems with disks, can also cause muscle ache, pain, or spasm, as can poor posture in general, which unnaturally strains muscles so much that they become fatigued and cramp. Muscle spasms may actually be a protective device, acting almost like a splint, to prevent movements that can cause harm, as around the spine.

Sometimes such spasms result from overuse, especially where the muscles are being used to repeat the same motions over and over again, in what is called *repetitive motion stress disorder*. This has become a widespread type of disorder in offices and assembly lines and as such affects many women. Closely related is *carpal tunnel syndrome*, involving painful and debilitating inflammation of the muscles that pass through a narrow bone-and-tissue passageway in the wrist called the *carpal tunnel;* this especially affects women because of their smaller bones.

Muscles are subject to a wide variety of disorders—many of them relatively rare and mostly appearing during childhood and adolescence—involving muscle destruction or degeneration, often with fatty tissues replacing the atropied, or wasted, muscle. Some forms are mild and progress slowly, but others can be fatal. Grouped together under the general name of *muscular dystrophy* (MD), these are typically GENETIC DISORDERS believed to result from abnormality in the production of one or another key protein. Some forms are found in both men and women; some result only when both mother and father pass on defective genes; and some are found only in men but are sex-linked disorders passed on by their mothers, unaffected carriers of the defective gene (see PATTERNS OF GENETIC INHERITANCE on page 311). Women with any personal or family history of muscular dystrophy may want to seek GENETIC COUNSELING before planning a PREGNANCY. Tests given before pregnancy can detect whether a potential parent carries a defective gene. Other tests during pregnancy, such as AMNIOCENTESIS and CHORIONIC VILLUS SAMPLING, can detect some forms of muscular dystrophy.

For more help, information, and action

▶ NATIONAL INSTITUTE OF ARTHRITIS AND MUSCULOSKELETAL AND SKIN DISEASES (NIAMS) (301-496-8188); AMS Clearinghouse, (301-495-4484); Office of Research on Women's Health (301-402-1770).

▶ 9 TO 5, NATIONAL ASSOCIATION OF WORKING WOMEN (216-566-1699; Job Survival Hotline 800-522-0925). Publishes *VDT Syndrome: The Physical and Mental Trauma of Computer Work.*

▶ Muscular Dystrophy Association (MDA) (810 Seventh Avenue, 27th Floor, New York, NY 10019; 212-586-0808; Robert Ross, executive director), an organization concerned with muscular dystrophy and related neuromuscular diseases. It operates a nationwide network of diagnostic, research, and treatment clinics, providing free care to uninsured families. It also offers genetic counseling and other services to patients and families; undertakes public education; and publishes a news quarterly and many other materials, such as *What Everyone Should Know About Muscular Dystrophy*, *Who Is At Risk? The Genetics of Duchenne Muscular Dystrophy*, and *The CPK Test for Detection of Female Carriers of Duchenne Muscular Dystrophy*.

Other resources

The Musculoskeletal System. Dale C. Garell and Solomon H. Snyder, eds. Chelsea House, 1993.
Muscle Management: A New and Revolutionary Technique for Maximizing Potential. Elizabeth Andrews. Thorsons (SF), 1991.
Chronic Muscle Pain Syndrome. Paul Davidson. Berkley, 1991.
Relief from Carpal Tunnel Syndrome and Other Repetitive Motion Disorders. Nora Tennenhaus. Dell, 1991.
The One Minute Muscle Manager: Seven Simple Steps to Relax Muscle and Relieve Pain. Gary A. Young. General Publications, 1990.
(See also EXERCISE; SKELETAL SYSTEM; also EXERCISE AND FITNESS HELP, INFORMATION, AND ACTION GUIDE on page 270; WOMEN'S HEALTH HELP, INFORMATION, AND ACTION GUIDE on page 334).

mycoplasmas, a type of tiny bacteria that cause infections; one of the SEXUALLY TRANSMITTED DISEASES. Mycoplasmas are widely found, even sometimes in the GENITALS of people who are not sexually active, and doctors do not fully understand how they work in infections. The main concern is that, in women, mycoplasmas may be associated with BACTERIAL VAGINOSIS, MISCARRIAGE, and PELVIC INFLAMMATORY DISEASE, which can lead to INFERTILITY and potentially life-threatening ECTOPIC PREGNANCY. Some researchers have also suggested that mycoplasmas may have a role in the spread and development of AIDS infections. Mycoplasmas are treated with antibiotics; both partners need to be treated to avoid reinfection. (See SEXUALLY TRANSMITTED DISEASES; also WHAT YOU CAN DO TO AVOID STDS on page 660; SEXUALLY TRANSMITTED DISEASES HELP, INFORMATION, AND ACTION GUIDE on page 658.)

myomectomy, a surgical procedure that involves removal of FIBROIDS from a woman's UTERUS, as an alternative to a HYSTERECTOMY, which is removal of the whole uterus. Myomectomy is especially attractive to younger women who still wish to be able to bear children, as well as to women who wish to retain the uterus for reasons of long-term health and SEXUAL RESPONSE. It is only an alternative when the fibroids are relative small, for excessively large fibroids are extremely difficult and risky to remove by myomectomy.

Women considering a myomectomy should be aware of several risks and cautions. A standard myomectomy is as serious an operation as a hysterectomy and requires a higher degree of skill in the surgeon, as well as considerable patience in trying to get all the sites of fibroid growth. A myomectomy also has a higher complication rate, especially chances of hemorrhage and infection. In addition, adhesions—scar tissue binding internal organs together abnormally—may form, and the fibroids may recur. Either adhesions or new fibroids might cause INFERTILITY, and if PREGNANCY does occur, a CESAREAN SECTION may be required for DELIVERY.

In some cases a surgeon performs a myomectomy but finds complications, such as excessive fibroids, cancerous or precancerous conditions, or hemorrhaging. Many in that instance will then routinely perform a hysterectomy. Most gynecologists will discuss this possibility with a woman before an operation. If a woman wants to avoid a hysterectomy, she should discuss thoroughly the conditions under which she would want a hysterectomy, such as when bleeding places her life in danger or when CANCER is found.

A newer procedure called a *hysteroscopic myomectomy* can be used for fibroids *inside* the uterus, the least common kind, not for those outside or within the uterine wall. Using a *hysteroscope* (see HYSTEROSCOPY), a long, thin, lighted tube inserted through the VAGINA and CERVIX into the uterus, the surgeon is able to see into the uterus without abdominal incisions. Fibroids can then be removed by various surgical procedures, including the knife or *laser surgery*. Microsurgery can also be used in some cases, using tools inserted through tiny incisions in the abdomen (see LAPAROSCOPY). These procedures are less dangerous, have a shorter recovery time, and may have fewer adverse effects, in particular reducing blood loss and formation of adhesions.

A related procedure called *ablation* involves destruction of the *endometrium*, the lining of the uterus, including any *submucous* fibroids on the inner surface. This results in what is called a *functional hysterectomy*, since the uterus remains but will no longer support a pregnancy. Ablation can be performed with a surgical knife (*curette*), as during a D&C (*dilatation and curettage*). However, a newer method employs a laser (concentrated beam of light) to destroy and simultaneously seal and sterilize the *endometrium* (lining of the uterus), including any fibroids, and effectively destroys a woman's childbearing capacity while retaining the uterus. This procedure is too new and lacking in long-term data, so it is not generally regarded as a form of STERILIZATION, though it may have that effect. Its main advantages are that it produces less bleeding and goes deeper than a curette could. The operation is performed at a hospital under general or regional ANESTHESIA. Another relatively new, still experimental alternative is *hysteroscopic resection* in which razor-sharp tools are used with a hysteroscope to "shave" fibroids off, rather than cut them out.

Myomectomy is not recommended where there is cancer, precancerous tissue, or active PELVIC INFLAMMATORY DISEASE. If necessary, a myomectomy may be attempted during pregnancy but often causes a MISCARRIAGE. (See also HYSTERECTOMY; also HYSTERECTOMY HELP, INFORMATION, AND ACTION GUIDE on page 358.)

nails, the hard covers that grow atop the ends of fingers and toes, made of specialized SKIN cells and consisting largely of the protein *keratin.* The nail tissue on the surface is made up of dead cells, but under the *cuticle,* the crescent-shaped, skin-covered area, the nail is not only alive but very sensitive, with a rich blood supply.

Because of their long growing time—about six to nine months—nails are actually a window on a person's well-being. Health problems of various kinds are reflected in lines, ridges, pits, spots, and other marks or changes in shape, which can speak volumes to a physician. Anemia (see BLOOD) may show itself in spoon-shaped nails, for example; and a woman with ARTHRITIS in her finger joints will often have split or misshaped nails. Traumatic events—a serious infection, a surgical operation, even a prolonged period of insomnia—may also show up on the nails. Manicuring or pedicuring too often can cause splitting of the nails, as can poor NUTRITION and also reactions to substances such as detergents, nail polish, or nail-hardening agents.

Common nail problems include

▶ *fungal infections,* which may need to be treated medically for some months, until the diseased nail has been replaced by healthy growth.

▶ *bacterial infections,* when bacteria invade through cuts, hangnails, or other openings, a condition called *paronychia.* These are treated with soaking, and sometimes lancing and antibiotics.

▶ *ingrown toenails,* a condition common when people wear shoes so tight that they force distorted growth of the nail. Caught early, the problem can be eased by inserting a cotton swab under the problem corner of the nail and lifting it slightly so it can grow normally. If severe, and if infection has set in, medical treatment may be necessary. The problem can be prevented by cutting nails straight across, rather than on a curve, and by wearing shoes with sufficient toe room.

Healthy nails should be smooth and shiny, and should evenly show the color of the skin beneath them. Softening creams can help decrease splitting of the cuticles or the likelihood of hangnails. Women who paint their nails should be sure not to push the cuticle back too far and so expose live tissue to the nail polish. (See SKIN, HAIR, NAILS, AND COSMETICS HELP, INFORMATION, AND ACTION GUIDE on page 689.)

Nairobi Forward-Looking Strategies for the Advancement of Women

, a program adopted by the July 1985 final world conference of the United Nations Decade for Women (see INTERNATIONAL WOMEN'S YEAR), held at Nairobi, Kenya. The conference was dominated by Middle East and North-South political and economic issues, rather than by the establishment of a powerful worldwide campaign for the advancement of women. However, it did pass a document, endorsed by the U.N. General Assembly in December 1985 but wholly advisory in nature, calling for a long series of reforms. (See NAIROBI FORWARD-LOOKING STRATEGIES FOR THE ADVANCEMENT OF WOMEN: A SUMMARY on page 804.)

names in marriage, the choice of what last name to use after MARRIAGE, a question that confronts most women at least once during their lives and for many more than once. Until the twentieth century, except for rulers, women upon marriage generally lost the family names they were born with, called their *maiden names,* and adopted those of their husbands—therefore for all practical purposes losing their independent identities. Sometimes they effectively lost their first names in public as well, so Amelia Smith might become Mrs. Joseph Jones. When WOMEN'S RIGHTS leader Lucy STONE and abolitionist Henry Blackwell married in 1855, she kept her name and both partners publicly stated their belief in equal rights in marriage, a trailblazing set of actions in their day. But that was far from the norm; although a few professional women, among them actresses, doctors, and writers, kept their names after marriage, women continued to routinely lose their names and identities as late as the mid-1960s, with very many keeping their former husbands' names even after DIVORCE.

With the advent of the modern women's movement, far more women began to keep their names on marriage and throughout their lives. New societal trends also fed the development of name holding, including the tendency of many people to live together without marrying (see COHABITATION) and the enormously increased numbers of DIVORCES and SINGLE PARENTS. Many working women building careers saw the desirability of keeping their own names and the inconvenience and professional peril of fracturing their identities by tying themselves to the identities of men. Many women now keep their identities simply as a matter of self-respect, and some make the act symbolic of the emergence of a new day in a previously male-dominated society. Others, making their way through several relationships and absences of relationships with men, keep their names as a now socially acceptable matter of convenience. For some feminists, the matter of identity and name has played a more central role and made it desirable to adopt new names, sometimes in an attempt to recognize their mothers' lost names, sometimes signifying a complete break with a male-dominated past.

Some women have adopted a middle course, combining the family names of each partners in a hyphenated form used by both, a pattern that had been used for centuries among some in the European upper classes. If Mary Smith marries Joe Brown, for example, she would be Mary Smith-Brown, and he would be Joe Smith-Brown. That still leaves somewhat unsettled the question of the name used for the children of the family; in such cases a child might be Elizabeth Smith-Brown but more often is Elizabeth Brown. In Hispanic regions a child normally carries both parents' names, but in reverse order, with the father's name first and the mother's name second; for example Juan Suarez Garcia, often shortened informally to Juan Suarez. One option that some modern couples use, though infrequently, is for both to change their names to a new name acceptable to both.

The **NOW LEGAL DEFENSE AND EDUCATION FUND** (NOW LDEF) notes that in the United States state laws do not currently require a woman to take her husband's last name as her own. If a woman has been using her husband's name and wishes to revert to using her own, she has no legal bar to doing so, but she will need to go through the time-consuming process of changing all of her legal documents, such as SOCIAL SECURITY card, driver's license, car registration, payroll and income tax records, passports, credit, and the like. In such situations, as when a woman adopted her husband's family name in the years when to do otherwise was rare, some women have chosen to use their husband's last name in private life but their own name in their work, much as an actor does. To limit social confusion, some groups such as NOW LDEF recommend that women be consistent, whichever form they adopt, especially for legal and financial documents. (See WOMEN'S RIGHTS HELP, INFORMATION, AND ACTION GUIDE on page 767.)

It would have saved trouble had I remained Perkins from the first; this changing of women's names is a nuisance we are now happily outgrowing.

CHARLOTTE PERKINS GILMAN, 1935
IN THE LIVING OF CHARLOTTE PERKINS GILMAN

•

National Adoption Information Clearinghouse (NAIC)

(1400 Eye [I] Street, NW, Suite 600, Washington, DC 20005; 202-842-1919), an organization founded in 1987 to act as an information center on all aspects of adoption, including international adoptions or special-needs adoptions. It maintains a library and computerized data base; provides information on state and federal adoptions laws; and makes referrals to adoption agencies, crisis pregnancy centers, or support groups; but does not itself provide counseling or placement. It publishes various materials, including the *National Adoption Directory* and *National Crisis Pregnancy Centers Directory*, fact sheets, and reprints.

National American Woman Suffrage Association (NAWSA),

an organization formed in 1890 by the merger of the two wings of the American WOMAN SUFFRAGE movement, which had in 1869 split into the small, relatively conservative AMERICAN WOMAN SUFFRAGE ASSOCIATION and the larger, more militant NATIONAL WOMAN SUFFRAGE ASSOCIATION. Elizabeth Cady STANTON was NAWSA's first president (1890–1892), succeeded by Susan B. ANTHONY

(1892–1900). By the early twentieth century, the organization was perceived as too conservative by some of its younger members; it suffered a new split in 1916, when Alice PAUL founded the NATIONAL WOMAN'S PARTY, but retained enough strength to mount a powerful campaign for the vote that in 1919 resulted in the NINETEENTH AMENDMENT. It then dissolved, its single issue won, to be partially succeeded by the LEAGUE OF WOMEN VOTERS. (See also WOMEN'S RIGHTS MOVEMENT.)

National Association of Cuban-American Women (NACAW)

(2119 South Webster, P.O. Box 10538, Fort Wayne, IN 46802; 219-745-5421; Graciela Beecher, president), an organization founded in 1977 to help Cuban-American women and other Spanish-speaking people adjust to and benefit from life in the United States. NACAW seeks to increase awareness of opportunities and services available and to provide direct services as needed. Among its projects are English as a second language programs; basic skills classes; programs and materials on educational equity for women, especially non-English-speaking and educational aid sources; international cultural awareness programs, including radio and television; and various bilingual materials. Its affiliated **Cuban American Legal Defense and Education Fund (CALDEF)** (same address and phone), founded in 1980, works to "gain equal treatment and equal opportunity for Cuban Americans and other Latin Americans in the fields of education, employment, housing, politics, and justice," through mediation or, if needed, litigation. It supports women's equity, bilingual education, and employment programs.

National Association of Female Executives (NAFE)

(127 West 24th Street, 4th Floor, New York, NY 10011-1914; 212-645-0770; 800-669-1002 for membership information; Wendy Reid Crisp, national director), an organization founded in 1972 to help women—current and *future* executives—achieve their career and financial goals. NAFE (pronounced NAFF-ee) offers career development seminars, regional conferences, and "insider breakfasts," linking women with a network of contacts, locally and nationally; it also acts as an advocate for women executives in public policy discussions. NAFE members receive numerous benefits, including a Gold MasterCard group insurance coverage (including life, medical, dental, disability, homeowners, and automobile), a career options test, résumé services, discounts on books and cassettes from the NAFE Bookshelf, discount shopping services, and travel center services. For members who want to start their own business, the NAFE Venture Capital Fund provides funds (5,000–$50,000) for approved business plans, as well as a credit line of $35,000. NAFE publishes the bimonthly magazine *Executive Female* and the *NAFE Network Directory.*

National Association of Women Business Owners (NAWBO)

(600 South Federal Street, Suite 400, Chicago, IL 60605; 312-922-0465 or 800-272-2000; Barbara Mardo, administrative director), the "only organization

for women business owners," founded in 1974, open to "sole proprietors, partners, and corporate owners with day-to-day management responsibility." Its stated mission is to provide "a strong and continuing voice and vision for women business owners within the economic, social, and political communities." It is the official U.S. member of Les Femmes Chefs d'Entreprises Mondiales (FCEM), the World Association of Women Entrepreneurs, an international network of women business owners representing nearly thirty thousand businesses in more than twenty-three countries.

NAWBO gives women support and encouragement, through networking of business owners and chapters, and also management and technical assistance, through workshops, seminars, retreats on business issues, the Leadership Institute and Fast-Track Management Assistance Program, and regular FCEM international conferences. NAWBO acts as a public policy advocate, playing a key role in the passage of the Women's Business Ownership Act of 1988, encouraging loans and training as well as collection of data on women-owned businesses. It also sponsors a Public Affairs Day, with updates and discussions on current issues and training on how to lobby Congress; works with major corporations "in programs and issues of mutual benefit;" which increases the likelihood of women business owners being named to corporate, government, and nonprofit boards; offers a direct discount program on insurance, car rentals, airfares, and fax machines as well as member-to-member discounts on business-to-business services and a NAWBO MasterCard; and maintains the National Foundation for Women Business Owners (NFWBO) for education and research. NAWBO members receive the national newsletter *Statement*, the international newsletter *Pragmatica*, local chapter newsletters focusing on community, state, and regional topics, and a national roster of members and special mailings on important legislative developments.

National Black Women's Health Project (NBWHP) (1237 Ralph David Abernathy Boulevard, SW, Atlanta, GA 30310; 404-681-4554; Cynthia Newbille Marsh, executive director), a self-help and advocacy organization founded in 1981, initially as a project of the NATIONAL WOMEN'S HEALTH NETWORK. NBWHP is "committed to improving the health of black women," especially those living on low incomes, through its national headquarters in Atlanta and offices in other major cities, including New York, Philadelphia, Oakland (CA), and Washington, D.C. Through grass-roots self-help groups, it seeks to improve "health first by improving self-esteem in adult and teenaged Black women," so they are "empowered to use the information and services available to them." Through its Washington, D.C., office it seeks to help shape public policies and the agenda for reproductive health and rights in ways that improve the health status of African-American women and children. NBWHP has sponsored conferences on Black women's health; founded various centers (sometimes working with other groups), focusing on matters such as maternal and infant mortality, teen pregnancy, and general health; promoted programs such as Walking for Wellness; founded the internationally oriented SisteReach program to help Third World women work for better health; and produced a documentary film on sex-

uality and reproduction from a Black women's perspective, *On Becoming a Woman: Mothers and Daughters Talking Together.*

National Black Women's Political Leadership Caucus
(3005 Bladensburg Road, NE, #217, Washington, DC 20018; 202-529-2806; Juanita Kennedy Morgan, executive secretary), an organization founded in 1971 that works "to include and educate Black women in the political process to the benefit of minorities and the entire nation" and to help all women understand "how to accomplish goals within the legislative process and maintain a place for women in the political arena." The caucus operates as an organized network for change, helping develop and promote legislation based on analysis of the needs and priorities of the community, and especially seeks to bring more Black women into politics at all levels.

National Center for Education in Maternal and Child Health (NCEMCH) (703-524-7802), and National Maternal and Child Health Clearinghouse (NMCHC) (703-821-8955)
(NCEMCH/NMCHC, Georgetown University, 2000 15th Street N, Suite 701, Arlington, VA 22201-2617; Rochelle Mayer, director), affiliated federally funded organizations that supply education and information on all aspects of maternal and child health and available services and programs. They make referrals to appropriate hot lines and publish many materials for the public and professionals, including newsletters, directories, bibliographies, resource guides, and brochures.

National Center for Lesbian Rights (NCLR)
(1370 Mission Street, 4th Floor, San Francisco, CA 94103; 415-621-0674; Elizabeth Hendrickson, executive director), a public-interest law firm, formerly the Lesbian Rights Project (LRP), that "works through the courts, the legal system, and in the community to eradicate discrimination against lesbians and gay men" through a "unique combination of legal representation and community education." It offers direct legal services, including telephone counseling, preparation of legal documents, and representation at court, as well as technical assistance to legal professionals and advocates nationwide. Among its many concerns are ADOPTION, donor paternity in ARTIFICIAL INSEMINATION cases, child CUSTODY, VISITATION RIGHTS, co-parenting, housing, and employment discrimination; it also has a Lesbian of Color Project.

NCLR publishes various materials, including the quarterly *NCLR Newsletter, A Lesbian and Gay Parent's Legal Guide to Child Custody, Lesbians Choosing Motherhood: Legal Issues in Donor Insemination, Lesbian Mother Litigation Manual, Partnership Protection Documents, Preserving and Protecting the Families of Lesbians and Gay Men, Recognizing Lesbian and Gay Families: Strategies for Obtaining Domestic Partners Benefits, AIDS and Child Custody: A Guide to Advocacy,* and *Boy Scouts/Anti-Gay Discrimination Resource Package;* it also distributes other materials, including books and reprints.

National Center for Policy Alternatives (1875 Connecticut Avenue, NW, Suite 710, Washington, DC 20009; 202-387-6030; Linda Tarr-Whelan, president/executive director), an organization that "promotes progressive policies in all fifty states." The center works with "a bipartisan network of state legislators, officials, and advocates to create policy models, draft legislation, convene conferences, and serve as a clearinghouse for policies and programs," working in four main areas:

▶ *economic development,* including public/private capital partnerships, affordable housing and CHILD CARE, access to capital for rural and inner-city areas, and reinvestment of defense resources for domestic use.

▶ *environment,* including environmentally sustainable economic policies, alternative energy use, recycling, and citizen power to "fight local environmental degradation, especially in poor communities or communities of color."

▶ *women's economic justice,* including "economic empowerment and self-sufficiency for women, justice in the workplace, universal family policy including child care and family leave, and full reproduction choices from family planning to maternal and infant care and abortion."

▶ *governance,* promoting citizen participation through more accessible voter registration and balloting, more candidate accountability, cleaner campaign financing, and better public information on candidates and issues.

The center coordinates a group of more than two hundred legislators, called policy alternative leaders (PALs), sponsors a state issues forum, develops leadership programs, and works in states to introduce policy ideas, develop strategies, and testify before legislative committees. The center publishes a quarterly newsletter, *Ways & Means*; regular *State Reports* for each main area of work, detailing new legislation and analyzing policy trends; and various policy readers and compendiums. Among the center's publications specifically on women's issues are

• on child care: *The Child Care Challenge: Creating Solutions Through Employer-Supported Programs and Public–Private Initiatives,* and *Leadership Brief on Childcare, Reinvesting in Childcare.*

• on abortion: *Choice After* Webster: *An Overview of State Abortion Legislation, Comprehensive Reproductive Choice Legislation: Examples from the States, Eroding the Constitutional Right to Abortion: The* Webster *Decision of 1989 and Minors' Access Decisions of 1990, Health Care Access for Low-Income Women, Minors' Access to Abortion: 1990 Supreme Court Decisions, The Politics of RU486: States Look for Ways to Counter Anti-Choice Opposition, The State Legislative Agenda of the National Anti-Choice Movement, Update on the Title X "Gage Rule": Implications for the States.*

• on substance abuse: *Women, Babies, and Drugs: Family-Centered Treatment Options* and *Public Health Solutions to the Problem of Drug Use by Pregnant Women: A Review of the 1991 Legislative Sessions.*

• on family and medical leave: *Family and Medical Leave: Strategies for Success, Leadership Brief on Family and Medical Leave, Legislative Sourcebook on Family and Medical Leave, Policy Choices in Family Leave: Best Practices in the States,* and *History and Summary of the Federal Family and Medical Leave Act.*

Other publications include *The Women's Economic Justice Agenda: Ideas for the States, Health: Access and the Quality of Life, Leadership Brief on Low-Income*

Women and Health Care, The Federal Employee Retirement and Income Security Act, and the audiotapes *Families, Feminism and the Future* and *Human Capital: The Third Deficit.*

National Center for Youth Law (NCYL) (114 Sansome Street, Suite

900, San Francisco, CA 94104-3820; 415-543-3307; John F. O'Toole, director), an organization "devoted to improving the lives of poor children in the United States," specifically by increasing "the quality and scope of legal representation for poor children"; insuring the "establishment and enforcement of legal rights for poor children, including the right of access to necessary government services"; and insuring "that government provides services to poor families with children in the least restrictive manner and with minimum interference in their lives." NYCL was founded in 1970 as the Youth Law Center, which in 1978 merged with the National Juvenile Law Center, and has helped organize local child advocacy organizations. It works to support those who can best represent America's poor children, providing assistance to legal and other professionals regarding youth law and juvenile court procedures, through litigation, consultation, training programs, various support services, and publications, including the bimonthly *Youth Law News* and numerous reprints on topics such as abuse, neglect, and termination of parental rights; adoption; adolescent pregnancy and parenting; child care; child support; housing discrimination against families with children; juvenile justice and institutions; public benefit programs for children; sexual abuse; and general youth law.

National Center on Women and Family Law (NCOWFL) (799

Broadway, Room 402; New York, NY 10003; 212-674-8200; Laurie Woods, director), a national legal organization founded in 1979 that directly litigates and seeks to influence policy and practices on issues concerning poor women and also assists lawyers and advocates on legal problems relating to poor women and children, including "battery of women, the economic consequences of divorce, child custody, child support enforcement, legal safeguards for older women, economic and sex discrimination, rape, sexual abuse of children, parental kidnapping, and single mothers' rights." NCOWFL provides education for judges, lawyers, and advocates through conferences, seminars, workshops, and training sessions on women's legal issues, such as custody, mediation, battery, child support, incest, and wife support. It also operates a special **National Battered Women's Law Project**, which assists advocates, policy makers, and attorneys; serves as an information clearinghouse, analyzing developments and issues; and produces various materials, including a legal subscription service.

NCOWFL publishes numerous materials, including the bimonthly newsletter *The Women's Advocate;* manuals such as *Protecting Confidentiality: A Legal Manual for Battered Women's Programs, Representation in Interstate Child Custody Disputes and Parental Kidnapping: Policy, Practice and Law, Guide to Interstate Custody Disputes for Domestic Violence Advocates, Custody Litigation on Behalf of Battered Women, Battered Women: The Facts, Child Support: A Manual for Attor-*

neys, *Child Support and You, Mediation and You* (on why it may be inappropriate for battered women), *Mediator's Guide to Domestic Abuse, Effects of Battery of the Mother on Children: Psychological and Legal Authority, Mediation—A Guide for Advocates and Attorneys Representing Battered Women, Child Sexual Abuse, Legal Issues and Legal Options in Civil Child Sexual Abuse Cases: Representing the Protective Parent*; and more than one hundred resource packets on family law issues such as automatic cost-of-living increases for child support awards, studies on the economic impact of divorce on women and children, civil suits by rape victims, wife and child support for military wives, child support guidelines, and sex and economic discrimination in child custody awards.

National Coalition Against Domestic Violence (NCADV)

(P.O. Box 18749, Denver, CO 80218-0749; 303-839-1852; Rita Smith, office coordinator), an organization founded in 1978 to "assist and empower battered women and their children." Its members are grass-roots organizations and individuals in both rural and urban areas, with formerly battered women forming "a significant portion" of the board. NCADV provides information, advocates increased federal funding for battered women's programs, plans strategies for increasing public and policy-maker awareness, and organizes regional training programs for battered women's advocates. It publishes various materials, including the quarterly newsletter *NCADV Voice*, the information bulletin *NCADV Update, A Current Analysis of the Battered Women's Movement, National Director of DV [Domestic Violence] Programs, Guidelines for Mental Health Practitioners in Domestic Violence Cases, Rural Task Force Resource Packet, Naming the Violence: Speaking Out About Lesbian Battering*, and *Domestic Violence Awareness Month Packet.*

National Committee on Pay Equity (NCPE)

(1126 16th Street, NW, Suite 411, Washington, DC 20036; 202-331-7343; Susan Bianchi-Sand, executive director), a "national coalition of labor, women's, and civil rights organizations, professional associations and religious organizations working to eliminate sex- and race-based wage discrimination and to achieve pay equity," advocating "fair pay practices based on skill, effort, responsibility, and working conditions." Founded in 1979, NCPE acts as a clearinghouse on pay equity information, provides technical assistance, training sessions, and conferences for pay equity advocates; acts as a guide to resources such as the Ontario (Canada) Pay Equity Commission's *Implementing Pay Equity in the Workplace*; and publishes numerous materials, including the newsletter *Newsnotes, Raising Awareness About Pay Inequities, Pay Equity Bibliography and Resource List, Pay Equity Makes Good Business Sense, The Pay Equity Sourcebook*, and *Legislating Pay Equity to Raise Women's Wages: A Progress Report on the Implementation of the Ontario, Canada, Pay Equity Act, Bargaining for Pay Equity: A Strategy Manual.*

National Conference of Puerto Rican Women (NACOPRW), (Conferencia Nacional de Mujeres Puertorriqueñas, Inc.)

(5 Thomas Circle, Washington, DC 20005; 202-387-4716; Nydia I. Santiago, executive director), an organization founded in 1972 "to promote the full participation of Puerto Rican and other Hispanic women in their economic, social, and political life in the United States and Puerto Rico." Through its national and local offices, NACOPRW acts as advocate for Puerto Rican and other Hispanic women; offers workshops, training seminars, and conferences on topics such as health, leadership training, economic development, education, technology, mentoring, and political empowerment; provides scholarships; and "constitutes a network of concerned Puerto Rican women and serves as a support system." It publishes a quarterly newsletter, *Ecos Nacionales.*

National Council for Children's Rights (NCCR)

(721 2nd Street, NE, Washington, DC 20002; 202-223-6227 or 800-787-KIDS [5437]; David L. Levy, president), an organization supporting more equitable divorce, custody, and child support arrangements, especially favoring joint custody, visitation enforcement, and mediation. It gathers research data, offers seminars, and publishes various materials, including the newsletter *Speak Out for Children.* (See CHILDREN'S RIGHTS COUNCIL.)

National Council for Research on Women (NCRW)

(Sara Delano Roosevelt Memorial House, 47–49 East 65th Street, New York, NY 10021; 212-570-5001; Mary Ellen S. Capek, executive director), an "independent association of centers and organizations that provide resources for feminist research, policy analysis, and education programs for women and girls." Founded in 1981, the council seeks to bridge distinctions among scholarship, policy, and action programs by facilitating research, communication, and cooperative exchange among member centers and affiliates; promoting visibility for feminist research; building links between individuals and organizations doing research, policy, and grass-roots work on women; expanding international networks; and serving as a "clearinghouse for current information about research, policy initiatives, funding opportunities, and other resources."

It maintains a national on-line Work-in-Progress Database, holds seminars, and publishes various materials, including the quarterly *Women's Research Network News (WRNN)*; directories such as *A Women's Mailing List Directory, Directory of National Women's Organizations, Directory of Women's Media, Opportunities for Research and Study,* and *International Centers for Research on Women*; reports such as *Sexual Harassment: Research and Resources, A Report-in-Progress* and *Risk, Resiliency, and Resistance: Current Research on Adolescent Girls*; and other works such as *A Women's Thesaurus: An Index of Language Used to Describe and Locate Information by and About Women, Women in Academe: Progress and Prospects, A Task Force Report, Mainstreaming Minority Women's Studies, Transforming the Knowledge Base,* and *A Declining Commitment to Research About Women.*

National Council of Negro Women (NCNW)

(16647 K Street, NW, Suite 700, Washington, DC 20006; 202-659-0006; Dorothy I. Height, president), an organization founded in 1935 by Mary McLeod Bethune to act as an "organization of organizations," to "harness the power and extend the leadership of Black women." From the beginning it has included and welcomed "women of all racial and cultural backgrounds"; its membership now includes 33 national affiliated organizations and 250 community-based sections, and NCNW also works with other national organizations and in 10 African countries. It serves as a clearinghouse for the activities of women, sponsoring "educational, economical, social, cultural, and scientific self-help projects" and striving to "achieve equality of opportunity and eliminate prejudice and discrimination based upon race, creed, color, sex, or national origin."

National Council of Women of the United States (NCW/US)

(777 United Nations Plaza, New York, NY 10017; 212-697-1278; Alicia Paolozzi, president), a "nonsectarian, nonpartisan" organization founded in 1888, spurring the foundation of the INTERNATIONAL COUNCIL OF WOMEN formed by the joinder of similar national councils from around the world. Among the original founders were some key early figures in the fight for WOMEN'S RIGHTS, including Susan B. ANTHONY, Elizabeth Cady STANTON, Lucy STONE, Julia Ward HOWE, Clara Barton, May Wright Sewell, and Frances Willard, many of whom had earlier worked in the fight against slavery. As NCW/US, they and their successors—both individuals and member organizations—worked for WOMAN SUFFRAGE, abolition of child labor, and improvement of working conditions, as today the organization "works for the education, participation, and advancement of women," acting "as a forum to bring all sides of an issue before women so that they may make informed decisions," also providing "opportunities for women to be involved, to speak out, to be heard."

NCW/US holds many programs, workshops, and seminars and works with committees and organizations on every level, including the United Nations, as a chartered U.N. Non-Governmental Organization since 1945. As part of ICW it seeks to promote "equal rights and responsibilities, peace efforts through negotiation, and the integration of women into decision bodies," maintaining standing committees in numerous areas, including arts and letters/music, child and family, economics, education, environment and habitat, health, home economics, international relations and peace, laws and the status of women, mass media, migration, social welfare, and women and employment. It publishes periodic newsletters.

NATIONAL COUNCIL OF WOMEN— A STATEMENT OF PURPOSE

We, women of the United States of America, believing that the best good of humanity will be advanced by efforts toward greater unity of sympathy and purpose, and that a voluntary association of individuals so united will best serve the highest good of the family, the community, the state, do hereby freely band ourselves together into a federation of all races, creeds, and traditions, to further the application of the Golden Rule to society, custom, and law.

Source: Founding document of the National Council of Women of the United States, 1888.

National Council on Child Abuse and Family Violence

(NCCAFV) (1155 Connecticut Avenue, NW, Suite 300, Washington, DC 20036; 202-429-6695 or Helpline, 800-222-2000; Alan Davis, president), an organization supporting community centers for prevention and treatment of violence and abuse in families. It acts as a clearinghouse for information on and funding for such centers and publishes a newsletter and other materials.

National Council on the Aging (NCOA)

(409 Third Street, SW, Washington, DC 20024; 202-479-1200 or 800-424-9046; Daniel Thursz, president), an organization founded in 1950 "to help professionals and volunteers in aging's many disciplines better serve older Americans," on the principle that "life's options—whether for employment, education, suitable housing, and for much more—should remain undiminished *throughout lifetimes.*" Its toll-free hot line provides information and publication on topics such as family caregivers, senior employment, and long-term care. NCOA has various *constituent units* that focus on specific areas of concern:

► **National Institute of Senior Centers (NISC)**, which focuses on senior centers as bases for community services; it publishes guidelines for center operations and goals.

► **National Voluntary Organizations for Independent Living for the Aging (NVOILA)**, a coalition of national organizations from various areas, such as optometry or home economics, that include but are not limited to aging, to develop programs directed at older people.

► **National Center on Rural Aging (NCRA)**, a project that seeks to develop and replicate community programs for the elderly in rural areas.

► **National Institute on Adult Daycare (NIAD)**, an arm that promotes adult day care programs to "help promote and maintain independent living at home rather than in institutions."

▶ **National Association of Older Worker Services (NAOWS),** which seeks "to increase employment for older workers—men and women in their forties, fifties, and up who want to enter or reenter the workforce," by encouraging their participation, for instance, in the Job Training Partnership Act (JTPA) project and by protecting them under the Age Discrimination in Employment Act.

▶ **National Institute of Senior Housing (NISH),** seeking ways to help people stay in their own homes—a concept called "aging in place"—where possible and also providing appropriate housing, as under the 1990 National Affordable Housing Act.

▶ **National Institute on Community-based Long-term Care (NICLC),** working for better provision of long-term care, not just nursing homes but also health care, meal services, homemaker aides, accessible transportation, grocery shopping, adult day care, and respite and training for family caregivers.

▶ **Health Promotion Institute (HPI),** promoting "optimal quality of life, including physical, mental, and emotional health, emphasizing empowerment of older adults to take positive actions toward personal goals."

▶ **National Interfaith Coalition on Aging (NICA),** seeking "to inform the religious community about the 'aging revolution,' while focusing the nation's attention on the spiritual dimensions of growing old."

▶ **National Institute on Financial Issues and Services for Elders (NIFSE),** a unit focusing on the financial well-being of older Americans, seeking to "become an authoritative source of education and guidance on retirement and midlife planning.

▶ **National Center for Voluntary Leadership in Aging (NCVLA),** a newly formed unit "intended to link and assist volunteers serving on boards, commissions, and committees of organizations seeking to meet the needs of older adults and their families."

In addition, NCOA's **Institute on Age, Work, and Retirement** promotes midlife reassessment of circumstances, plans, and aspirations, as a basis for decisions about the rest of life; and the **Senior Community Service Employment Program (SCSEP)** helps assess, train, and assist low-income women and men fifty-five years and older reenter—or enter for the first time—the workforce, a project funded through the U.S. Department of Labor.

The institute has a wide range of publications on these and other concerns, including the magazine *Perspective on Aging,* the bimonthly newsletter *NCOA Networks,* the quarterly journal *Abstracts in Social Gerontology: Current Literature on Aging,* and general works such as *Preparing for an Aging Society: Changes and Challenges, The Reality of Retirement, Cumulative Subject Index to Current Literature on Aging, 1980–1988, A Memory Retention Course for the Aged,* and the videotape *Coming of Age in America.* Other publications in specific areas include

▶ *on caregivers: Caregiver Support Groups in America, Caregiving Tips, Family Home Caring Guides,* and *Respite Resource Guide.*

▶ *on living places: Design for Living, A Guide for Selection of Retirement Housing, Housing for Older Adults: Options and Answers, Home Safety, Housing Options, Home Service,* and *Home Security.*

▶ **on adult day care:** *Adult Day Care in America: Summary of a National Survey, Eldercare in the Work Place, Developing Adult Day Care: An Approach to Maintaining Independence for Impaired Older Persons, Issues for an Aging America: Employees and Eldercare—A Briefing Book,* "Why Adult Day Care?" and the videotapes *Sharing the Caring: Adult Day Care* and *Taking the Lead— Workplace Responses to Eldercare.*

▶ **on work and the aging:** *Commitment to an Aging Work Force: Strategies and Models for Helping Older Workers Achieve Full Potential,* and *Mature/Older Job Seeker's Guide.*

▶ **on health and the aging:** *Eating Well to Stay Well, Health Promotion and Aging: Strategies for Action, Medicine Is No Mystery, A New Medicine Man: A Different Kind of Health Care for Elders, Psychological Functioning of Older People, Update on Health Aging: Reading Material on Health Topics for the New Reader and Tutor, Long-Term Care Choices,* and the videotape *The Sixth Sense* (with learning guide and handout booklets).

▶ **on community services:** *Senior Centers and the At-Risk Older Person, Start Your Own Latchkey Program,* "What Is a Multipurpose Senior Center?" and the videotape *Senior Center Standards: Commitment to the Future.*

▶ **on arts and humanities:** *Arts and Aging Media Sourcebook: Films, Videos, Slide-Tape Shows, Arts, the Humanities and Older Americans: A Catalogue of Program Profiles, A Resource Guide to People, Places and Programs in Arts and Aging, Tutoring Older Adults in Literacy Programs,* and a series of anthologies for elder discussion groups, *funded by the National Endowment for the Humanities.*

National Displaced Homemakers Network (NDHN) (1625

K Street, NW, Suite 300, Washington, DC 20006; 202-467-6346; Jill Miller, executive director), an organization established in 1979, aimed at helping DISPLACED HOMEMAK-ERS become financially independent. NDHN acts as an advocate for displaced homemakers and other mature women, seeking to influence public policy and legislation affecting them, and educating employers to the value of employing them, gaining a signal victory with the passage of the 1990 Displaced Homemakers Self-Sufficiency Assistance Act (see DISPLACED HOMEMAKERS). NDHN is actually a network of more than 1,100 programs around the country, which include mutual-support groups, exploration of career options, academic or vocational training programs, special programs for women of color, and job placement programs.

NDHN has a computer software management information system, a subscription service (for programs or for organizations and agencies), and many publications, including the quarterly *Network News*; the biannual *Transition Times, the NHDN Program Directory,* manuals such as *Overcoming Obstacles, Winning Jobs: Tools to Prepare Displaced Homemakers for Paid Employment, Success over Forty: Strategies for Serving Older Displaced Homemakers,* and *A Program for Everyone: Serving Women of Color;* guides such as *Network Know How: Everything You Need to Know to Start a Program and Keep It Going, Guide to the Displaced Homemakers Self-Sufficiency Assistance Act,* and *Displaced Homemakers' Guide to the Carl D. Perkins Vocational and Applied Technology Education Act of 1990;* reports such as *The More Things Change . . . A Status Report on Displaced Homemakers and Single Par-*

ents in the 1980s; the *Handbook on State Displaced Homemaker Legislation*; brochures such as *A New Law That Helps Displaced Homemakers: Health Insurance Continuation*; and videos such as *Partners in Change* (co-produced with the AMERICAN ASSOCIATION OF RETIRED PERSONS).

National Federation of Business and Professional Women's Clubs, Inc.: See BUSINESS AND PROFESSIONAL WOMEN/USA (BPW/USA).

National Heart, Lung, and Blood Institute (NHLBI) (9000 Rockville Pike, Building 31, Room 4A21, Bethesda, MD 20892; 301-496-4236; Claude Lenfant, director), one of the National Institutes of Health. It sponsors research, provides information and referrals, and publishes a wide range of general and technical materials. It also sponsors the information clearinghouse **High Blood Pressure Information Center** (120/80 National Institutes of Health, Bethesda, MD 20892; 301-496-1809) and has a special **Sickle-Cell Disease Branch** (301-496-6931).

National Hook-Up of Black Women (NHBW) (c/o Wynetta Frazier, 5117 South University Avenue, Chicago, IL 60615; 312-643-5866; Wynetta Frazier, president), an organization formed in 1975 to act as a "communications network between women's organizations and individuals, to support the Congressional Black Caucus Legislative efforts and to provide a national forum to articulate the needs and concerns of Black Women and families . . . regardless of economic, educational and social status." It also seeks to highlight the achievement and contributions of Black women and "provide a support base for all Black women who serve in political office, organizational leadership, and those seeking self-improvement through educational and career goals." The National Hook-Up is not itself an action organization, but a communications resource for existing organizations and individuals, providing "informational and educational services to Black women who are involved with critical issues," such as racial and SEXUAL DISCRIMINATION.

National Institute of Allergy and Infectious Diseases (NIAID) (9000 Rockville Pike, Building 31, Room 7A50, Bethesda, MD 20892; 301-496-5717; Anthony Fauci, director), an arm of the U.S. National Institutes of Health, focusing on researching the causes, diagnosis, prevention, and treatment of allergies and infectious diseases. It maintains a network of **Asthma and Allergic Disease Centers**. The NIAID publishes numerous materials, including research reports for professionals and more generally oriented brochures.

National Institute of Arthritis and Musculoskeletal and Skin Diseases (NIAMS) (9000 Rockville Pike, Building 31, Room 4C05, Be-

thesda, MD 20892; 301-496-8188; Connie Raab, director), one of the U.S. National Institutes of Health. It sponsors research and educates both professionals and the public, through the **Arthritis and Musculoskeletal and Skin Diseases (AMS) Clearinghouse** (P.O. Box AMS, 9000 Rockville Pike, Building 31, Room 4C05, Bethesda, MD 20892; 301-495-4484), which supplies numerous materials.

National Institute of Child Health and Human Development (NICHD)

(9000 Rockville Pike, Building 31, Room 2A32, Bethesda, MD 20892; 301-496-5133; Duane Alexander, director), one of the U.S. National Institutes of Health, focusing on child health and human development, from CONCEPTION through ADOLESCENCE, and including INFERTILITY. Founded in 1962, it sponsors research and provides information through various publications such as *Pregnancy Basics, Understanding Gestational Diabetes,* and a series of "Facts About" booklets on topics such as *Anorexia Nervosa, Down's Syndrome, Endometriosis, Oral Contraceptives, Precocious Puberty, Cesarean Childbirth,* and *Premature Birth;* and research reports for health professionals.

National Institute of Diabetes, Digestive and Kidney Diseases (NIDDK)

(9000 Rockville Pike, Building 31, Room 9A04, Bethesda, MD 20892; 301-496-3583), one of the U.S. National Institutes of Health. It sponsors research, provides information, and publishes materials for the public and health professionals. For the public, it operates the **National Kidney and Urologic Disease Information Clearinghouse (NKUDIC)** (Box NKUDIC, Bethesda, MD 20892; 301-468-6345); **National Diabetes Information Clearinghouse** (Box NDIC, Bethesda, MD 20892; 301-468-2162); and **National Digestive Disease Information Clearinghouse** (Box NDDIC, Bethesda, MD 20892; 301-468-6344), which answer questions, make referrals, and distribute NIDDK materials.

National Institute of Mental Health (NIMH)

(Parklawn Building, 15C-05, 5600 Fishers Lane, Rockville, MD 20857; public affairs 301-443-4536; publications 301-443-4513), one of the National Institutes of Health. It sponsors research and gathers and disseminates information, through various publications, including *A Consumer's Guide to Mental Health Services, Schizophrenia: Questions and Answers,* and a series of booklets titled "Useful Information On . . ." covering topics such as ANOREXIA NERVOSA and BULIMIA, paranoia, phobias and panic, sleep disorders, obsessive-compulsive disorders, and medications for mental illness.

National Institute of Neurological Disorders and Stroke (NINDS)

(9000 Rockville Pike, Building 31, Room 8A16, Bethesda, MD 20892; 301-496-5751; Marian Emr, chief, Office of Scientific Health Reports), one of the National Institutes of Health. It focuses on the brain, strokes, and related disorders, publishing numerous materials for both the public and health professionals.

National Legal Resource Center for Child Advocacy and Protection (American Bar Association, 1800 M Street, NW, South Lobby, Washington, DC 20036; 202-331-2200), a professional organization dedicated to using the legal system to protect children. It gathers resources and provides information on topics such as child custody, child abuse, and missing children.

National Organization for Victim Assistance (NOVA) (757 Park Road, NW, Washington, DC 20010; 202-232-6682; Marlene A. Young, executive director), an organization concerned with victims of crime, focusing especially on juvenile victimization, minority victims, sexual assault, and domestic violence. It advocates claims for relief and recovery; provides crisis intervention, short-term counseling, and medical and legal advice; makes referrals to assistance programs and other services, including rape crisis centers and battered women's shelters nationwide; acts as an information clearinghouse; and publishes various materials, including the *NOVA Newsletter* and the *Victim Service Program Directory*.

National Organization for Women (NOW) (1000 16th Street, NW, Suite 700, Washington, DC 20036; 202-331-0066; Patricia Ireland, president), one of the key organizations of the modern WOMEN'S RIGHTS MOVEMENT in the United States, founded in 1966 to promote full equality and equal partnership between men and women and to end prejudice and discrimination against women in the society. To these ends, NOW has been extremely active in lobbying, litigation, and organized activism on women's issues, especially in promoting the EQUAL RIGHTS AMENDMENT (ERA) and the passage and enforcement of legislation banning discrimination on the basis of sex. National NOW publishes the bimonthly newspaper *NOW Times*, while various local groups publish monthly newsletters alerting NOW's members—both men and women—about issues and actions of importance to these goals.

Under its first president, Betty FRIEDAN, NOW both rode and helped swell the new wave of FEMINISM that rose in the mid-1960s. It identified itself especially with support for the Equal Rights Amendment, ABORTION rights, CHILD CARE programs, EQUAL PAY FOR EQUAL WORK, and INSURANCE AND PENSION EQUITY; it also worked to ban SEXUAL DISCRIMINATION, as through the PREGNANCY DISCRIMINATION ACT, and to elect more women in key political positions. High points of NOW history were the congressional passage of the ERA in 1971, the nomination of Geraldine Ferraro as Walter Mondale's vice-presidential running mate in the 1984 presidential race (during which NOW directly supported the Democratic ticket), and the blocking of Robert Bork's nomination to the Supreme Court in 1986, largely because of his history of opposition to abortion rights and even access to BIRTH CONTROL. But the ERA ultimately failed to be ratified nationwide, and Ferraro's candidacy became embroiled in and tarnished by investigations of her husband's finances, leaving NOW (like other feminist groups) facing a troubled and uncertain future, its own finances deeply in the red.

In 1985 the NOW membership was split sharply by a bitter fight, as activism-oriented former president Eleanor Smeal (1977–1982) came back to oust her hand-picked successor, Judy Goldsmith, who had focused more on grass-roots and mainstream political activity. Wounds were somewhat healed by the election in 1987 of Molly Yard, a New Deal–style liberal much influenced by Eleanor ROOSEVELT, who was charged with finding a new focus for the women's movement in a more conservative time, when many felt that feminism was passé. Retiring after a stroke in 1991, Yard was herself replaced by Patricia Ireland. Throughout it all, NOW's work in the legal arena continued unabated and may ultimately prove to be the organization's most valuable long-term contribution to the cause of women's rights. Much of this work has been carried on through NOW's litigation and educational arm, the **NOW LEGAL DEFENSE AND EDUCATION FUND**. (See also WOMEN'S RIGHTS MOVEMENT; WOMEN'S LIBERATION MOVEMENT.)

National Union of Women's Suffrage Societies (NUWSS), the

major moderate organization of the British WOMAN SUFFRAGE movement, from its formation in 1897 as a coalition of many regional groups. It was led by Millicent Garrett Fawcett from 1897 to 1919; she retired after the fight had been won. Fawcett and the NUWSS did not join the Pankhursts and their **WOMEN'S SOCIAL AND POLITICAL UNION (WSPU)** in their militant, highly confrontational battle for suffrage, instead continuing to apply wide-scale mass pressure for the vote. Both wings of the woman suffrage movement, however, supported the British war effort during World War I, probably partly in return for the promise of suffrage at war's end.

National Woman's Party (NWP) (Sewall-Belmont House, 144 Consti-

tution Avenue, NE, Washington, DC 20002; 202-546-1210; Sharon F. Griffith, executive director), an organization that started life as the Congressional Union for Woman Suffrage in 1913, a militant offshoot of the **NATIONAL AMERICAN WOMAN SUFFRAGE ASSOCIATION (NAWSA)**, the chief vehicle of the American WOMAN SUFFRAGE movement, taking its present name in 1916. It was founded by Alice PAUL, who, radicalized by her work with the militant British suffrage movement, left the NAWSA in 1913 to form the organization that developed into the National Woman's Party and began a series of demonstrations and other actions that in 1917 grew into a major campaign. But as pro-war, antiradical hysteria grew, NWP pickets were met by violence and mass arrests, paralleling the antiradical attacks of the time, which jailed Eugene Debs and hundreds of other dissenters.

During 1918 and 1919, as the campaign for woman suffrage grew, the NWP gained a good deal of strength. But, like the NAWSA, it was largely a one-issue organization; with passage of the **NINETEENTH AMENDMENT**, its membership dropped to only a few hundred. In the early 1920s it moved to take up a wide range of WOMEN'S RIGHTS matters, its few remaining militants from 1923 campaigning for Alice Paul's first version of the **EQUAL RIGHTS AMENDMENT (ERA)**. It had the ERA reintroduced into every session of Congress until 1972, and again since 1982, after failure of state ratification.

NWP's current national goals include "eliminating violence against females;

retaining reproductive choice; securing legislative relief to minimize poverty among women; achieving pay equity for women; increasing the number of women running for and holding public office; increasing career opportunities for women in leadership positions in government; supporting child care and family and medical leave laws; ensuring fair media coverage of the Equal Rights Amendment and other National Woman's Party issues; aligning federal and state equality laws; heightening awareness of women to the hazards of teen pregnancy, AIDS, drug abuse, and addiction; and securing an official U.S. Alice Paul commemorative stamp."

Among its international goals are restoring U.S. support for and membership in UNESCO, with its work for equality of the sexes and the improvement of women's status; ratifying the CONVENTION ON THE ELIMINATION OF ALL FORMS OF DISCRIMINATION AGAINST WOMEN, sometimes called the International Bill of Rights for Women (see page 796 for the text); coordinating global efforts to abolish worldwide female sexual slavery and PROSTITUTION; and educating women in other countries about the history and status of American women and maintaining a dialogue with them. NWP works with other organizations and governments toward these ends and acts as a clearinghouse on suffrage and the Equal Rights Amendment, maintaining a microfilm library on the history of the NWP and the ERA, films on Alice Paul and on the contemporary women's rights movement and the quest for the ERA. It publishes the quarterly *Equal Rights* and *The Equal Rights Amendment: Answers to Your Questions*. NWP also conducts tours of its headquarters building, one of the oldest in Washington.

National Woman Suffrage Association (NWSA),

the main organization of the American WOMAN SUFFRAGE movement, founded in May 1869 by Elizabeth Cady STANTON and Susan B. ANTHONY; it had many state and local affiliates and an annual convention in Washington, D.C., that focused national attention on the issue. NWSA, a for-women-only successor to the Equal Rights Association, signaled a post–Civil War split in the antislavery and women's movement coalition that had developed in the decades prior to the war. From 1878 on, NWSA caused a woman suffrage amendment to be introduced annually into Congress and also took up a wide range of other WOMEN'S RIGHTS issues, unlike AMERICAN WOMAN SUFFRAGE ASSOCIATION (AWSA), formed as an alternative in 1869, which focused solely on woman suffrage. Stanton was president of the more militant NWSA from 1869 to 1890, the year it merged with the relatively conservative AWSA. The merged organizations went on together as the NATIONAL AMERICAN WOMAN SUFFRAGE ASSOCIATION. (See also WOMEN'S RIGHTS MOVEMENT.)

National Women's Health Network (NWHN)

(1325 G Street, NW, Washington, DC 20005; 202-347-1140; Beverly F. Baker, executive director), an advocacy organization founded in 1976 to give "women a greater voice in the health care system." It operates the **Women's Health Information Service** as a clearinghouse of women's health information to help women make well-informed health decisions, responding to written or telephoned questions; it also seeks to shape public policy and legislation, as by supporting passage of the proposed Health Equity Act and pressing for research on health issues of special concern to women. It works in concert with other groups, such as the NATIONAL BLACK WOMEN'S HEALTH PROJECT (originally an NWHN project).

NWHN publishes or distributes numerous materials, including the bimonthly newsletter *Network News*; books, booklets, and papers such as *Abortion Then and Now: Creative Responses to Restricted Access, Women, AIDS, and Public Health Policies, AIDS: What Every Women Needs to Know, Childbearing Policies Within a National Health Program: An Evolving Consensus for New Directions, Research to Improve Women's Health: An Agenda for Equity, Turning Things Around: A Women's Occupational and Environmental Health Resource Guide, Taking Hormones and Women's Health: Health Choices, Risks and Benefits, Women and the Crisis in Sex Hormones*, and *Hearts, Bones, Hot Flashes and Hormones*; and reprints of information on specific topics, from *Abortion* to *Yeast Infections*, also including *National Health Plan, New Reproductive Technology*, and *Occupational/ Environmental Health*.

National Women's Political Caucus (NWPC) (1275 K Street, NW, Suite 750, Washington, DC 20005; 202-898-1100; Jody Newman, executive director), a "multipartisan, grassroots organization" founded in 1971, focused on getting pro-choice, pro-equality women elected and appointed to public office at all levels, seeking equality for all women and focusing on issues such as child care, family and medical leave, reproductive freedom, pay equity, expansion of educational opportunities, prevention of teen pregnancies, access to quality health care, and safe, affordable housing. NWPC identifies and recruits pro-choice women candidates; mobilizes voters; trains them and their staff in running campaigns, raising funds, and getting out the vote; and also works with political parties at all levels as an advocate for women's issues. NWPC publishes various materials, including the monthly newsletter *Women's Political Times, Fact Sheet on Women's Political Progress, Political Campaigning: A New Decade, Mobilizing the Pro-Choice Vote: A Basic Phonebanking Guide, The Appointment of Women: A Survey of Governors' Cabinets 1989-1991, Don't Miss That Appointment!, Voting Record of the 101st Congress* (and previous Congresses), *National Directory of Women Elected Officials 1991, How to Change the World: A Woman's Guide to Grassroots Lobbying*, and *Your Campaign and Abortion Rights*.

Native American feminism: See FEMINISM.

natural childbirth, an approach to LABOR and DELIVERY that seeks to minimize medical intervention in the birthing process (see CHILDBIRTH).

natural family planning (NFP), an approach to BIRTH CONTROL that avoids the use of artificial or mechanical means. The various NFP approaches use various signs and changes in the woman's body to identify the time of OVULATION, when she has produced an egg (OVUM) available to be fertilized.

If the aim is to avoid CONCEPTION, the couple may abstain from SEXUAL INTERCOURSE from the time of ovulation to the beginning of the woman's period (see MENSTRUATION). This approach is also called *periodic abstinence.* If the aim is to achieve conception, as when INFERTILITY is a concern, the couple will be sure to have sexual intercourse in the period of maximum fertility, just after ovulation; this would also be the prime time for ARTIFICIAL INSEMINATION or for extracting an egg for *IN VITRO* FERTILIZATION.

There are three main NFP approaches:

▶ *calendar (rhythm) method,* in which a woman tracks the successive dates of her menstrual cycle, calculating when ovulation is likely to occur. This method depends for its effectiveness on the woman's having a regular menstrual cycle and on the assumption that, whatever the length of the cycle, ovulation takes place about fourteen days before the beginning of the next period. As a form of birth control, this traditional method is highly unreliable. The U.S. Public Health Service concludes: "It is now generally agreed that this method is effective only when used in conjunction with one or both of the other methods [below]."

▶ *basal body temperature method,* in which a woman takes her temperature every morning, using a specially calibrated thermometer called a basal thermometer, designed to measure very small temperature changes. The *basal body temperature*—the temperature of the body at rest—is taken at about the same time each day, before arising. Ovulation is assumed to be taking place when the temperature rises one-half to one degree and remains elevated for three days.

▶ *cervical (vaginal) mucus method,* or *Billings method,* which involves observing and charting changes in the color and texture of the mucus in the VAGINA, secreted by the CERVIX. At around the time of ovulation, the cervical mucus changes from thick and opaque to clear and slippery, much like raw egg white, allowing easier passage for SPERM. From the time the mucus changes until at least three days afterward is the most fertile period. For contraception, couples are advised to avoid intercourse during this time, while for couples wishing to conceive, this is the target period. Women must receive training, from doctors or NFP groups (see BIRTH CONTROL AND FAMILY PLANNING HELP, INFORMATION, AND ACTION GUIDE on page 81), in what to look for. Some use a supplemental home medical test, based on the knowledge that at ovulation, the mucus has more sugar; special fertility kits are sold that show whether glucose is elevated in the cervical mucus.

A related approach is the *ovulation method,* in which a woman uses a home medical test to monitor her urine for levels of LUTEINIZING HORMONE (LH). Since LH triggers ovulation, an LH surge suggests that ovulation will probably occur in twenty-four to thirty-six hours. (See OVULATION.)

When couples use all three, or the latter two, methods together, the Public Health Service reports that the effectiveness rate for preventing conceptions "can approach 76–98 percent"; this is called the *symptothermal method.*

A related form of natural family planning is the *withdrawal method,* also called *coitus interruptus* or *coitus incompletus* (see SEXUAL INTERCOURSE), in which the male withdraws his penis from his partner's VAGINA before EJACULATION. In use at least since biblical times, withdrawal requires no supplies or medical visits—but it does require enormous self-control and motivation on the part of the male. But even with a maximum of goodwill and experience, it is a rather unreliable method, since some semen is released into the vagina even before ejaculation. Some other varieties of sexual activity that do not require vaginal penetration are also part of many couple's sexual repertoire, with incidental or deliberate contraceptive benefits (see SEXUAL INTERCOURSE).

Another traditional form of natural contraception is prolonged BREASTFEEDING.

New Left, a quite diverse body of radical activists and organizations that developed as part of the United States civil rights and anti–Vietnam War movements of the 1960s, which for a time in the mid-1960s functioned as a Left coalition dominated by the Students for a Democratic Society (SDS) and the Student Non-Violent Coordinating Committee (SNCC). Most of the participants were young, middle class to affluent, and college-educated. In structure and ideology, its leading early activists showed most affinity for the activists of the European and American anarchist movements, with more than a dash of home-grown utopian socialism. By the late 1960s some of the Maoist-oriented activists of the Progressive Labor party, a communist splinter group, also played a substantial role, as did some young communist-affiliated activists.

The New Left, with its tactics of confrontation and its anarchist and utopian-socialist ideological roots, was the matrix from which came many activists of the radical feminist portion of the WOMEN'S RIGHTS MOVEMENT. But the New Left was also a movement dominated by male leaders, some of them outspoken sexists, as was quite evident from the mid-1960s. With the unfolding of a large mainstream women's movement, as with the formation of the NATIONAL ORGANIZATION FOR WOMEN in 1966, many of the radical women of the day departed from the New Left organizations to form such radical feminist women's organizations as RADICAL WOMEN, WOMEN'S INTERNATIONAL TERRORIST CONSPIRACY FROM HELL (WITCH), REDSTOCKINGS, and RADICALESBIANS, all part of the emerging WOMEN'S LIBERATION MOVEMENT.

NFP, an abbreviation for NATURAL FAMILY PLANNING.

Nineteenth Amendment (Woman Suffrage Amendment), an addition to the U.S. Constitution, stating that "the right of citizens of the United States to vote shall not be denied or abridged by the United States or by any state on account of sex." The historic amendment was first introduced in 1878; it passed both houses of Congress in 1919 and was ratified on August 26, 1920, with Tennessee providing the necessary thirty-sixth-state ratification vote.

Passage of the amendment was a major event in the worldwide campaign for WOMAN SUFFRAGE that had started in the United States and Europe early in the nineteenth century and had been powerfully and formally initiated by Elizabeth Cady STANTON'S DECLARATION OF SENTIMENTS AND RESOLUTIONS at the landmark 1848 SENECA FALLS WOMEN'S RIGHTS CONVENTION. New Zealand, Australia, and several Scandinavian countries adopted woman suffrage before World War I. In Britain, partial suffrage came in 1918, and full suffrage in 1928. Woman suffrage also came in many other countries after World War I, though many countries did not adopt woman suffrage until after World War II, and some have yet to do so. For an overview, see WOMEN IN POLITICAL LIFE: AN UPDATE on page 806. (See also POLITICAL PARTICIPATION.)

9 to 5, National Association of Working Women (614 Superior Avenue, NW, Cleveland, OH 44113; 216-566-1699; Job Survival Hotline 800-522-0925; Karen Nussbaum, executive director), an advocacy organization for working women, especially office workers, founded in 1973. Among 9 to 5's special concerns are SEXUAL HARASSMENT; equity in pay, health and safety protection, and career advancement; health problems from office automation; abuses of electronic monitoring of computer or telephone workers; CHILD CARE; and FAMILY AND MEDICAL LEAVE. It operates a hot line, offering counseling on such topics as workers' rights, dealing with harassment, and coping with office politics; holds a Summer School for Working Women; and offers basic legal assistance and referrals, plus discounts on various products and services.

It publishes various materials, including the *9 to 5 Newsline*; books such as *The 9 to 5 Guide to Combating Sexual Harassment, Candid Advice from 9 to 5, the National Association of Working Women, Wage Replacement for Family Leave: Is It Necessary? Is It Feasible?*, *"Business as Usual": Stories from the 9 to 5 Job Survival Hotline, 9 to 5–The Working Women's Guide to Office Survival, VDT Syndrome: The Physical and Mental Trauma of Computer Work, Unequal Justice: Why Women Need Stronger Civil Rights Protections, a Brief Analysis, Stories of Mistrust and Manipulation: The Electronic Monitoring of the American Work Force, Solutions for the New Work Force: Policies for a New Social Contract, White Collar Displacement: Job Erosion in the Service Sector*, and *High Performance Office Work: Improving Jobs and Productivity: An Overview with Case Studies of Clerical Job Redesign*; fact sheets such as *9 to 5 Profile of Working Women* (annual) and on office health and safety issues.

nonspecific vaginitis, an alternate name for BACTERIAL VAGINOSIS.

Non-Traditional Employment for Women Act (NEW), a U.S. federal law passed in 1991 to help women move into nontraditional training and occupations, it is an extension of the earlier Job Training Partnership Act (JTPA). Under NEW, each service delivery area (SDA) must write into its Job Training Plan goals for training and placing women in nontraditional employment and apprenticeships, as in traditionally all-male construction jobs, and must report to

the state in detail on its success in meeting those goals. The state sets its own goals and must report to the U.S. Department of Labor (DOL) on how well it has succeeded in training, placing, and retaining women in nontraditional occupations. The extent of funding for NEW and the enforcement of reporting requirements remains to be seen. (See WORK AND WOMEN.)

Noonan's syndrome, a condition similar to TURNER'S SYNDROME.

Norplant, a form of BIRTH CONTROL that involves implantation of capsules in a woman's arm. These contain *progestin,* a synthetic form of PROGESTERONE and a HORMONE used in BIRTH CONTROL PILLS. Whether in pill or implant form, progestin inhibits OVULATION and also thickens the mucus of the CERVIX, making it more hostile to SPERM; it may also have other contraceptive actions, but they are not proven.

Norplant consists of six matchstick-size silicone rubber capsules, arrayed like a small fan. These are implanted under a woman's skin, normally on the inside of the upper arm, where they can be felt, though not seen. For up to five years, these release small amounts of progestin into the bloodstream. The main advantage is that, once the capsules are in place, the woman need not be concerned about birth control for nearly five years. If she wishes to become pregnant before then, the implants can be removed at any time; her FERTILITY will be restored within a short time—BLOOD levels of progestin become undetectable within five to fourteen days.

Norplant is inserted during an outpatient procedure requiring approximately ten to fifteen minutes. After local ANESTHESIA is used to numb the upper-arm area of insertion, the doctor makes a small incision, about one-eighth-inch long, and uses a special instrument to insert the six capsules under the skin. The area is then covered with gauze and a bandage; no stitches are needed. After the anesthetic wears off, the woman may experience tenderness or itching in the area, as well as possible discoloration, bruising, and swelling, all temporary, and occasionally infection. Norplant becomes effective within twenty-four hours.

Removal is slightly more complicated and generally takes longer. Sometimes it requires two visits, with the second perhaps a week later, because there may be difficulty locating and removing all the capsules in one visit, since the area puffs up with the anesthetic. A new set of capsules can be inserted at the same time, if desired, either in the same site or elsewhere on either arm. As of mid-1991, the cost to health professionals of a set of capsules and insertion apparatus was $350; the costs of the insertion and removal depend on the woman's physician. Implantation is covered by Medicaid, and some states also subsidize costs to make the procedure more widely available.

In development and experimental use since the late 1960s, Norplant has been used in Finland since 1983 and was approved for use in the United States in 1990. Studies have shown Norplant to be more than 99 percent effective in preventing PREGNANCY, and in fact, a 1991 report by the Alan Guttmacher Institute showed it to be the most effective form of birth control, with a pregnancy rate of 0.05–0.5 percent, compared to permanent STERILIZATION, at 0.2–0.5 percent. Original reports indicated that after two years of use, Norplant was slightly less effective in women more than 150 pounds, but capsules have since been made softer, so that may no longer be so.

Some women using Norplant have experienced side effects; the most common, affecting approximately 45 percent of women in the studies, is irregular menstrual bleeding (see MENSTRUATION). Another 10 percent have periods three to four months apart. Other common side effects are headache, DEPRESSION, nervousness, dizziness, nausea, SKIN rash or acne, change of appetite, tenderness of the BREASTS, weight gain, enlargement of the OVARIES, and excessive growth of body or facial HAIR. Some other women have experienced discharge from the breasts or VAGINA, inflammation of the CERVIX, abdominal discomfort, and muscle and skeletal pain, but it was unclear whether these symptoms were linked to Norplant, since they are such common experiences.

Norplant is not recommended for everyone. It is not advised for women with unexplained vaginal bleeding, BREAST CANCER, blood clots (especially in the legs, lungs, or eyes), acute liver disease, or liver tumors, whether malignant or benign. In addition—even though most of the adverse side effects of oral contraceptives (see BIRTH CONTROL PILLS) are believed to result from ESTROGEN, not progesterone—the FDA advises physicians to "consider the possible increased risks associated with oral contraceptives, including elevated blood pressure, thromboembolic disorders [blood clots obstructing blood vessels], and other vascular problems that might occur with use of the contraceptive implant." Concern about silicone in BREAST IMPLANTS should also cause close monitoring of the site for any adverse local effects as well.

In general, Norplant will be most attractive to women who want long-term contraception without the permanency of STERILIZATION and are unhappy with other forms of contraception, including those who cannot use estrogen. It will be less attractive to women who are satisfied with other forms of contraception; would be unhappy with possible irregular menstrual bleeding; are put off by the cost of the procedure; and want to have a birth control method that they can stop at any time, without the necessity of one or more visits for removal.

Although designed for voluntary birth control, Norplant has the potential of being used as an instrument of social control. In the United States, for example, some legislators have proposed measures that would pay women on welfare if they agreed to have Norplant inserted and maintained it, or would require insertion of Norplant in women convicted of certain drug offenses, as has been ordered by at least one judge. Although the proposed measures died a quick death, such ideas tend to resurface, and the fate of judicial orders of Norplant implantation are still pending. Certainly the availability of Norplant revives old controversies about the social control of reproduction (see EUGENICS, STERILIZATION). (See BIRTH CONTROL; also BIRTH CONTROL AND FAMILY PLANNING HELP, INFORMATION, AND ACTION GUIDE on page 81.)

Northwest Women's Law Center (119 South Main Street, Suite 330, Seattle, WA 98104-2515; 206-682-9552; for information and referral, 206-621-7691),

a public-interest law center focusing exclusively on women's legal issues, in areas such as "discrimination in employment and education; violence against women; threats to reproductive freedom; and inequities resulting from divorce." The law center provides general legal information and referrals; undertakes some cases involving significant legal issues; testifies on proposed legislation; provides education through community workshops and continuing legal education and through training on issues such as sexual harassment. It also publishes various materials, including the quarterly newsletter *Equal Times*; books such as *Sexual Harassment in Employment and Education* and *Justifiable Homicide: Battered Women, Self-Defense, and the Law*; the booklet *Family Law in Washington State*; fact sheets on numerous topics and videos such as *Breaking the Cycle: Domestic Violence and the Law* and *Her Day in Court: Women and Justice in Washington State*.

NOW Legal Defense and Education Fund (NOW LDEF)

(99 Hudson Street, New York, NY 10013; 212-925-6635; Helen R. Neuborne, executive director), an organization affiliated with and founded by the NATIONAL ORGANIZATION FOR WOMEN in 1970, as a litigation and educational arm. Its main areas of concern are

▶ *workplace issues,* "gender-based discrimination in the hiring, training, promoting, and firing of women in all fields of employment," including equal employment opportunity, access to traditionally male jobs, and SEXUAL HARASSMENT. This is a main focus of the fund's legal program.

▶ *economic support: insurance and pension,* including insurance company discrimination against women, many of them part-time workers, and "discriminatory gender-based insurance rates." NOW LDEF has litigated or joined others in insurance discrimination cases, including one that upheld Massachusetts's unisex insurance regulations. It also works for "fair and equal distribution of pensions and other forms of retirements benefits between married couples at the time of divorce." (See INSURANCE AND PENSION EQUITY.)

▶ *education,* seeking equal educational opportunities as a basis for more general equality, as in economic opportunity. Since 1974 it has sponsored the PROJECT ON EQUAL EDUCATION RIGHTS (PEER), (202-332-7337), which seeks to eliminate SEXUAL DISCRIMINATION in schools. (See EDUCATION EQUITY.)

▶ *family law,* including the economics of homemaking (see HOMEMAKER), ALIMONY and CHILD SUPPORT, CHILD CARE, and FAMILY AND MEDICAL LEAVE. It seeks public recognition of the economic value of a homemaker's work, educating the courts and the public to understand that a homemaker loses "opportunities to establish or increase her own earning potential," increasing "her husband's earning capacity at the expense of her own." It works to change public laws and policies to provide adequate support for woman and family in case of divorce and of the family as a whole in case of illness and disability, as well as adequate child care in general.

▶ *domestic violence,* including BATTERED WOMEN and childhood sexual abuse (see CHILD ABUSE AND NEGLECT; INCEST). It works to educate the public and to change laws and public policy, also litigating cases. It also acts as a clearinghouse for information on child sexual abuse victims/survivors, their family members and friends, attorneys who represent them, and mental health professionals.

▶ *reproductive choices,* including the rights to bear children, to use CONTRACEPTION, and to terminate PREGNANCY, again working to educate the public and litigate cases. NOW LDEF significantly expanded its legal program in this area after the *Webster* v. *Reproductive Health Services* Supreme Court decision. (See REPRODUCTIVE RIGHTS; BIRTH CONTROL; ABORTION.)

▶ *court reform,* seeking to eliminate gender bias in the court system itself, especially "stereotyped thinking about sex roles, society's judgment on the relative worth of women and men, and myths and misconceptions about the social and economic realities of women's and men's lives." It seeks to implement reforms and, in 1980, founded the National Judicial Education Program to Promote Equality for Women and Men in the Courts (NJEP), in cooperation with the National Association of Women Judges (NAWJ), to educate judges, lawyers, and law students about "unspoken and unrecognized prejudice" in cases involving child support awards and enforcement, custody, the value of homemaker work in damages and divorce, sexual assault, domestic violence, employment, perceptions of witness credibility, and general behavior of judges, lawyers, and court staff toward women in the courtroom.

NOW LDEF also publishes numerous materials, including the *State Index of Women's Legal Rights, Facts on Reproductive Rights: A Resource Manual, Protectng Young Women's Right to Abortion: A Guide to Parental Notification and Consent Laws, Divorce Mediation: A Guide for Women, Divorce Planning: A Guide for Women,* and *Child Support Guidelines: How You Can Make a Difference;* an *Attorney Referral Services List;* a video training program *Sexual Harassment: Walking the Corporate Fine Line;* a series of Legal Resource Kits, including *Child Custody, Child Support, Education, Employment—General, Employment—Pay Equity, Employment—Pregnancy and Parental Leave, Employment—Sexual Harassment, Equal Rights Amendment, Incest and Child Sexual Abuse, Insurance and Pensions, Lesbian Rights, Male-Only Clubs, Reproductive Rights, Separation and Divorce—General, Separation and Divorce—Pensions, Violence Against Women,* and *Women and Health;* and *Myths of Equality,* statistical fact sheets on women's issues, including sexual harassment in employment, education, child sexual abuse, and separation and divorce.

Publications of the National Judicial Education Program (available from Women Judges' Fund for Justice, 733 15th Street, NW, Suite 700, Washington, DC 20005; 202-783-2073, include the training program *Judicial Discretion: Does Sex Make a Difference?, Operating a Task Force on Gender Bias in the Courts: A Manual for Action, Learning from the New Jersey Supreme Court Task Force on Women in the Courts: Evaluation, Recommendations, and Implications for Other States, Promoting Gender Fairness Through Judicial Education: A Guide to Issues and Resources, Planning for Evaluation: Guidelines for Task Forces on Gender Bias in the Courts.*

nuptials, an alternative word for a WEDDING or MARRIAGE ceremony. Agreements entered into before marriage are called PRENUPTIAL AGREEMENTS or *antenuptial agreements.*

Nurturing Network, The (TNN) (910 Main Street, Suite 360, P.O. Box 2050, Boise, ID 83701; 208-344-7200 or 800-TNN-4MOM [866-4666]; Mary Cunningham Agee, executive director and founder), a charitable organization to assist women faced with a crisis PREGNANCY—unplanned, unwanted, or disruptive of the woman's life. Offering an alternative to ABORTION, TNN provides a "professional, medical, counseling, and residential network across the country which enables a college or working woman to continue the life of her unborn child *without sacrificing her own educational or career goals,*" serving "pregnant women, regardless of age, race, or creed," including not just young, SINGLE WOMEN, but also older women and BATTERED WOMEN.

Founded in 1986, TNN provides social workers, health professionals, and volunteers for counseling, guidance, and medical services; aids in maintaining continuity of education or career plans and goals, sometimes by arranging school transfers, job relocations, or supportive temporary homes; financial aid; PRENATAL CARE; parenting and CHILD CARE classes and workshops; and ADOPTION services, if desired. Such services are organized locally by volunteer members called *cluster coordinators.* Because TNN's focus is firmly on assisting women with crisis pregnancies, its work has received support from people and organizations on both sides of the abortion issue.

nutrition, the process of providing enough of the right kinds of foods so that the body functions in a healthy way; also the study of the proper amounts and kinds of foods for daily consumption, how the body uses foods in general, and the food itself.

The body requires several kinds of necessary nutritive elements every day:

► *proteins,* complex chemicals formed of *amino acids* that form the basic structure of many basic body tissues, HORMONES, and vital constituents of BLOOD and also promote most of the body's biochemical reactions. Foods rich in protein include meat, poultry, fish, eggs, milk, and cheese; these contain all the essential amino acids and so are called *complete proteins.* Nuts, beans, and peas are also good sources of protein but do not contain all amino acids, so they must be mixed with other foods to provide all necessary amino acids, as in a vegetarian diet.

► *carbohydrates,* foods such as sugar and starch that provide the body's main source of energy, primarily in the form of *glucose.* Carbohydrates are found in many common, inexpensive foods, including bread and other baked goods, potatoes, pasta and rice, candies, fruits, and vegetables. For maximum nutrients and fiber, nutritionists recommend getting carbohydrates from whole-grain products and fresh fruits and vegetables (these are *complex carbohydrates* or *polysaccharides,* made up of many sugar molecules), rather than less nutritious refined foods, such as sugar and white flour, which are *simple carbohydrates.*

► *fats,* chemical compounds formed primarily of carbon and hydrogen that are the body's most concentrated source of energy and are also vital in helping the body absorb certain types of vitamins (see below). Fats that contain as many hydrogen atoms as possible are called *saturated.* Solid at room temperature, saturated fats come mainly from animal sources, including meat and dairy products, but also from some plant products, such as coconut and palm kernel oils. Unsaturated fats are those with a carbon atom unoccupied by hydrogen at one site (*monounsaturated*) or more sites (*polyunsaturated*); these are more healthful for the body, though intake should still be limited. Liquid at room temperature, unsaturated fats are found in plant-derived oils, such as the polyunsaturated sunflower, corn, soybean, cottonseed, and safflower oils, and the monounsaturated olive, canola, and peanut oils. Closely related to fats, and generally found in the same sources as saturated fats, is a substance called *cholesterol.* This is an important part of cell structure and is also used in the body's formation of vitamin D and some HORMONES. But in the bloodstream, cholesterol travels in huge molecules of fat and protein, called *lipoproteins,* which tend to clog up the circulatory system, causing severe and possibly life-threatening health problems (see HEART AND CIRCULATORY SYSTEM). (See FIGURE OUT YOUR FAT on page 496.)

▶ *fiber,* the portion of food (such as cellulose in carbohydrates) that is indigestible but performs vital functions in the DIGESTIVE SYSTEM, helping to maintain normal bowel movements by soaking up water and easing passage of feces. High-fiber diets have been linked to lower rates of colon CANCER and can ease some digestive problems, such as *irritable bowel syndrome* and *constipation;* because it gives a sensation of fullness, fiber may also be helpful in DIETING. Good sources of fiber are whole-grain products, vegetables, and fruits, as well as rice, corn, and oat bran. To avoid abdominal discomfort, gas, and diarrhea, fiber should be increased in the diet slowly. The National Cancer Institute (see CANCER) recommends an upper limit of 35 grams of fiber a day; more than that could interfere with the body's ability to absorb iron and other minerals (see below).

▶ *vitamins,* a group of complex chemical compounds that do not themselves provide energy but are required in minute amounts for the transformation of food into the energy required for normal functioning, including body building. The various vitamins are formed largely of the same elements—carbon, hydrogen, oxygen, and sometimes nitrogen—but each has a unique structure and performs different functions in the body. Some types, such as B and C vitamins, are *water-soluble;* these need to be resupplied every day, since if they are not used immediately, they are quickly excreted in urine or perspiration. Some other vitamins, notably A, D, E, and K, are *fat-soluble* and if not used immediately build up in body fat, sometimes to damaging levels (see page 496). In general, the fresher and the more lightly cooked the foods, the more vitamins they will retain. Leaving the peel on vegetables and steaming instead of boiling, for example, will keep vitamins from leaching away. (For an overview of vitamins and minerals, their functions, good sources of them, results of deficiency and excess, and special cautions, see KEY VITAMINS AND MINERALS on page 502.)

▶ *minerals,* chemical elements that are required for the healthy functioning of the body. The so-called *macrominerals* or *macronutrients* needed in relatively large amounts include *calcium, potassium, magnesium, sodium, chloride, phosphorus,* and *sulfur. Microminerals* or *micronutrients,* needed in only relatively small amounts, include *iron, copper, iodine, zinc, selenium,* and *fluoride.* Though these are vital in small amounts, excess amounts of minerals can cause severe health problems (see page 497).

▶ *water,* the liquid of life, formed of hydrogen and oxygen. Though not generally regarded as part of a diet, water is vital to the functioning of the digestive system and to the biochemical processes that build, energize, and activate the body.

FIGURE OUT YOUR FAT

The recommendation is that no more than 30 percent of total calories come from fat. Food labels list food in grams. To find out what *your* total intake of fats in grams should be, multiply your daily calories (in this example 2,200) by 0.30 (30 percent) and divide by 9 (the number of calories in a gram of fat).

Example:

$$2,200 \text{ calories} \times 0.30 = 660 \text{ calories from fat}$$
$$660 \text{ calories} \div 9 = 73 \text{ grams of fat}$$

Source: "Women and Nutrition." Dori Stehlen. *FDA Consumer,* Jan.–Feb. 1991.

In most cases a person's entire nutritional needs can be met by a balanced diet, with no need for dietary supplements. Based on nutrition research, government sources recommend that people follow these dietary guidelines for good health:

• eat a variety of foods;
• maintain a desirable weight;
• avoid too much fat, especially saturated fat and cholesterol;
• eat foods with an adequate amount of starch and fiber;
• avoid too much sugar;
• avoid too much sodium;
• drink alcohol only in moderation.

Beyond these general guidelines, government agencies make specific recommendations as to the kinds and amounts of food that should form the daily diet (see RECOMMENDED DAILY DIET on page 498.)

In addition, the government has identified in the Recommended Daily Amounts (RDAs)—now often called Reference Daily Values (RDVs)—the amounts of essential vitamins and minerals believed to be necessary for the normal functioning of the body (see RECOMMENDED DAILY ALLOWANCES [RDAS] FOR WOMEN AGE 19 TO 50 on page 501). These RDAs are designed to "be adequate to meet the known nutritional needs of practically all healthy persons." However, they are averages, which means that some individuals who have unusually high requirements may need more, as will people who are ill or injured. Some other nutrients are known to be essential, but research has not supplied sufficient data for RDAs to be established. Among these are the vitamins K, biotin, and pantothenic acid; the minerals copper, manganese, fluoride, chromium, selenium, and molybdenum; and also sodium, potassium, and chloride. For these the government makes estimates only. Balance is important; since many nutrients work together, too little of some may make others useless.

Inadequate amounts of vitamins and minerals can lead to serious disorders called *deficiency diseases,* though more often the problem is unrecognized *depletion.* The elderly are at special risk; many lose much of their ability to smell and taste food with age, and those who live alone often do not or cannot provide themselves with properly nutritious meals. Indeed, many behavior patterns diagnosed as "senility" or even "Alzheimer's disease" have been found to result from nutritional deficiencies. Pregnant women with poor nutrition are also at risk; vitamin deficiencies are believed to be linked with various BIRTH DEFECTS and possibly MISCARRIAGES.

However, excess vitamins can also cause problems; some are toxic in large amounts and may interfere with the absorption of other nutrients. The FOOD AND DRUG ADMINISTRATION stresses that a well-balanced diet should meet all the body's vitamin needs, so it does not recommend vitamin supplements, except for people recovering from certain illnesses or vitamin deficiencies. However, many people do take vitamin supplements, so a word of caution is in order: More is not better. So-called *megadoses* of vitamins, or amounts greatly in excess of the Recommended Daily Allowance (RDA), can be dangerous, causing serious health problems, birth defects during PREGNANCY, and even death. In any case, supplements should not be substitutes for a balanced diet, which they cannot replace.

Excess amounts of essential minerals can also threaten overall health, possibly resulting in poisoning; disruption, damage, or failure of vital organs such as the heart, kidneys, and liver; and, in extreme cases, death. The recommended amounts are so small that poisonous overdoses can readily result from talking too much. Increased amounts of some minerals, such as calcium, are sometimes recommended for pregnant women or young children; but health officials urge that before taking any mineral supplements (and before giving any to a child), a woman should consult her doctor or clinic.

The general nutritional recommendations are also designed to meet all the body's daily energy needs, measured in *calories (kilocalories).* But individuals vary. Women with large bodies who lead very active lives will, of course, need more energy than women with small bodies who lead sedentary lives. In general, an adult woman needs about 1,000–1,300 calories a day *just to stay alive*—to pump the blood, supply the oxygen, process the food into energy, excrete waste products, keep the body's structures in good repair, and maintain the body's chemical balance. *Any* activities beyond that, even ones as simple as dressing or brushing teeth, require additional calories. Each woman must judge her energy needs based on her own body structure and activity level and what she has learned about her own *metabolism,* or the way the body uses the energy, which varies greatly from person to person.

When the energy intake and energy needs are roughly equal, body weight remains fairly stable. EXERCISE can use up excess calories by raising energy requirements. But if the person eats food containing more calories than are required for the body's energy needs, the excess is stored in fat cells *(adipose tissues).* These are the body's long-term energy reserves and are stored at various sites around the body—in women for the most part in the hips, thighs, and breasts (see SECONDARY SEX CHARACTERISTICS)—with various health implications (see OBESITY). People who are 10 percent above the weight considered ideal for their sex and age (see SUGGESTED WEIGHTS FOR ADULTS on page 516) are generally considered *overweight,* while some 20 percent above that target is called *obese.*

In affluent Western societies, or those with fat-rich diets, excess fat is a national malady and the focus of various slimming activities (see DIETING). When these are carried on by people who are already near their ideal weight, or carried out in a dangerous way, severe health problems can result, including various EATING DISORDERS such as ANOREXIA NERVOSA and BULIMIA. Weight significantly *under* the ideal for age or height is also associated with health problems, leaving the body without necessary reserves and with possibly life-threatening chemical imbalances if the body draws on tissues for the energy it needs. If unconnected with dieting or eating disorders, weight loss—especially if sudden—is a sign of health problems. (See DIET AND NUTRITION HELP, INFORMATION, AND ACTION GUIDE on page 513.)

RECOMMENDED DAILY DIET

The recommended diet for adults is as follows. Pregnant women or those with special health needs may, of course, need to modify this to meet their individual needs, with advice from their doctors.

▶ *whole-grain or enriched breads, cereals, and cereal products:*
6 to 11 servings daily. Breads and cereal foods provide minerals and vitamins, particularly the B vitamins and iron, as well as protein. Whole-grain breads and cereals provide essential trace elements such as zinc and also fiber, a natural laxative. Check the labels on breads and cereals to make sure that they are made with whole-wheat or whole-grain flour or are enriched with minerals and vitamins.
Count as 1 serving:
   1 slice bread
   1 muffin

> 1 roll or biscuit
> 1 tortilla or taco shell
> ½ to ¾ cup cooked or ready-to-eat cereal, such as oatmeal, farina, grits, raisin bran, shredded wheat
> 1 cup popcorn (1½ tablespoons unpopped)
> ½ to ¾ cup noodles, spaghetti, rice, bulgar, macaroni
> 2 small pancakes
> 1 section waffle
> 2 graham crackers or 4 to 6 small crackers

Count as 2 servings:

> 1 hamburger bun or hot dog roll
> 1 English muffin

▶ *vegetables:* 3 to 5 servings of one-half cup of vegetables or one-half cup of juice daily. The dark green leafy vegetables and deep yellow vegetables are rich in vitamin A. The dark green leafy vegetables are also valuable for iron, vitamin C, magnesium, folic acid, and vitamin B₂ (riboflavin).

▶ *fruits:* 2 to 4 servings of one-half cup of fruit or vegetable or one-half cup of juice daily. Both fruits and vegetables contain vitamins, minerals, and fiber, a natural laxative.

Specific recommendations for fruits and vegetables:

at least 1 serving of a good source of vitamin A every other day, such as apricots, broccoli, cantaloupe, carrots, dark green leafy vegetables (beet greens, chard, collards, kale, mustard greens, spinach, turnip greens), pumpkin, sweet potatoes, or winter squash.

at least 1 serving of a good source of vitamin C every day, such as broccoli, Brussels sprouts, cantaloupe, cauliflower, green or sweet red pepper, grapefruit or grapefruit juice, orange or orange juice, tomatoes, dark green leafy vegetables (beet greens, chard, collards, kale, mustard greens, spinach, turnip greens), cabbage, strawberries, or watermelon.

2 servings of other vegetables and fruits every day, such as beets, corn, eggplant, green and wax beans, lettuce, peas, potatoes, squash, apples, bananas, cherries, grapes, pears, pineapple, or plums.

▶ *meat, fish, poultry, eggs, dried beans and peas, nuts:* 2–3 servings daily. These products supply protein as well as vitamins and minerals, to maintain the health of body cells. During pregnancy, 3 servings of these foods will supply the protein needed to help build new tissues for the baby. When you use dried beans, dried peas, or cereals as main dishes, combine them with a small amount of cheese, milk, or meat to increase the protein value of the meal. Some examples include chile con carne, black-eyed peas and ham, chicken and rice, pizza, macaroni and cheese, and spaghetti and meatballs. Also, by combining grains and beans and nuts, you will increase the amounts of protein your body can use. Some examples would be beans and rice or peanut butter on whole-wheat bread.

Count as 1 serving:

> 2 or 3 ounces lean meat. (Remove the extra fat when possible.) Some examples: 1 hamburger, 2 thin slices of beef, pork, lamb, or veal, 1 lean pork chop, 2 slices luncheon meat, 2 hot dogs.
>
> 2 or 3 ounces fish. Some examples: 1 whole small fish, 1 small fish fillet, ⅓ of a 6½-ounce can of tuna fish or salmon.
>
> 2 or 3 ounces chicken, turkey, or other poultry. Some examples: 2 slices light or dark meat turkey, 1 chicken leg, ½ chicken breast.

Count as ½ serving:

> ½ to ¾ cup cooked dried beans, peas, lentils, or garbanzos (chick peas)
>
> 2 to 3 tablespoons peanut butter
>
> 1 or 2 slices cheese
>
> 1 egg
>
> 1 cup tofu
>
> 4 to 6 tablespoons nuts or seeds

▶ *milk and milk products:* 2 to 3 eight-ounce glasses of milk or milk products daily (general recommendation); 4 for pregnant women, elderly women, or those at special risk of osteoporosis. These have the calcium and other nutrients needed for strong bones and teeth, including the baby's during a pregnancy. Choose milks that have vitamin D added. You may select whole milk, buttermilk, lowfat milk, or dry or fluid skim milk. Low-fat milk and skim milk have fewer calories than whole milk. Milk or cheese used in making soup, pudding, sauces, and other foods count toward the total amount of milk you use.

These amounts equal the calcium in one 8-ounce glass of milk:

> 1 cup liquid skim milk, low-fat milk, or buttermilk
>
> ½ cup evaporated milk (undiluted)
>
> 2 one-inch cubes or 2 slices of cheese
>
> ⅓ cup instant powdered milk
>
> 1 cup plain yogurt, custard, or milk pudding

These amounts equal the calcium in ⅓ cup of milk:

> ⅔ cup cottage cheese
>
> ½ cup ice cream

Note: If you cannot drink milk, discuss this problem with your doctor.

▶ *fats, oils, and sweets:* Use sparingly, according to calories needed. This group of foods includes margarine, butter, candies, jellies, sugars, syrups, desserts, soft drinks, snack foods, salad dressings, vegetable oils, and other fats used in cooking. Most of these foods are high in fat, sugar, or salt. Use them to meet additional caloric needs after basic nutritional needs have been met. Eating too much fat and too many sweets may crowd out other necessary nutrients.

Some nutrients should be limited in the daily diet. General guidelines to follow are

- Limit total fat to 30 percent of your total calorie consumption, with no more than 10 percent from saturated fats. Limit cholesterol intake to less than 300 milligrams a day. (See FIGURE OUT YOUR FAT on page 496.)
- Limit the amount of salt (sodium chloride) to 6 grams (a little more than 1 teaspoon) or less per day; the equivalent in prepared foods is approximately 2,400 milligrams of sodium, as indicated on food labels. Eat sparingly of very salty foods, in general; limit use of salt in cooking and at table.
- Avoid taking dietary supplements that, for any one day, contain more than the U.S. Recommended Daily Allowances, except where advised by a doctor for special circumstances.
- If you drink alcohol, limit the amount in any one day to no more than 2 cans of beer, 2 small glasses of wine, or 2 average cocktails. Pregnant women should drink no alcoholic beverages.

In addition, to maintain appropriate body weight, balance the amount of food you eat with a corresponding amount of exercise, to reduce health risks associated with obesity.

Source: Adapted from *Prenatal Care*. (1989), prepared for the Public Health Service by the Bureau of Health Care Delivery and Assistance, Division of Maternal and Child Health; *Food Guide Pyramid: A Guide to Daily Food Choices*, as reprinted in *FDA Consumer*, July–Aug. 1992; *Nutrition and the Elderly*, by Alexandra Greeley, *FDA Consumer*, Oct. 1990; *Diet and Health: Implications for Reducing Chronic Disease Risk*, Committee on Diet and Health of the Food Nutrition Board, National Academy Press, 1989.

RECOMMENDED DAILY ALLOWANCES (RDAs) FOR WOMEN AGE 19 TO 50

Vitamins

A	800 micrograms
D	10 micrograms (age 19–24); 5 micrograms (age 25–50)
E	8 milligrams

K	60 micrograms (age 19–24); 65 micrograms (25–50)
C	60 milligrams
Thiamine	1.1 milligrams
Riboflavin	1.3 milligrams
Niacin	15 milligrams
B_6	1.6 milligrams
Folate	180 micrograms
B_{12}	2 micrograms

Minerals

Calcium	1,200 milligrams (age 19–24); 800 milligrams (age 25–50)*
Phosphorus	1,200 milligrams (age 19–24); 800 milligrams (age 25–50)
Magnesium	280 milligrams
Iron	15 milligrams
Zinc	12 milligrams
Iodine	150 micrograms
Selenium	55 micrograms

*More during pregnancy; check with your doctor.
Source: National Academy of Science/National Research Council RDAs (1989), as reprinted in *FDA Consumer,* Jan.–Feb. 1991.

KEY VITAMINS AND MINERALS

► *Vitamins*

vitamin A (retinol)

Functions: Helps in growth of new cells and healthy tissue; important in normal vision, especially at night.
Sources: Liver, egg yolks, and dairy products. Made in the body from carotene-containing green and yellow vegetables and yellow fruits, including apricots, carrots, sweet potatoes, squash, and leafy green vegetables.

Results of deficiency: Night blindness, diarrhea, dry skin, dry eyes, susceptibility to intestinal infections, impaired growth.

Results of excess: Nausea, blurred vision, headaches, loss of hair, dry skin, irregular menstruation, impaired growth, enlarged liver and spleen, bone pain, and increased skull pressure.

Special caution: Large doses during pregnancy, especially first trimester, are known to cause birth defects. Women who are pregnant or likely to become so should avoid taking supplements containing more than the Recommended Daily Allowance (RDA) for pregnant women.

vitamin B₁ (thiamine)*

Functions: Helps in normal digestion, growth, fertility, lactation, functioning of nerve tissue, and carbohydrate metabolism (breaking down for energy use).

Sources: Meats such as pork and liver; whole-grain and fortified-grain products, such as breads, cereals, and pasta; nuts and beans.

Results of deficiency: Loss of appetite, fluid buildup (edema), heart problems, nausea and vomiting, spastic muscle contractions. Causes *beriberi,* a deficiency disease involving disruption of the nervous system.

Results of excess: Unknown; water-soluble and excess excreted in urine.

vitamin B₂ (riboflavin)*

Functions: Helps the body obtain energy from carbohydrates and proteins.

Sources: Leafy vegetables, enriched and whole-grain breads, liver, lean meats, eggs, dairy products.

Results of deficiency: Lip sores and cracks; dim vision.

Result of excess: Unknown; water-soluble and excess excreted in urine.

Special caution: Deficiency may result from use of certain kinds of drugs used to treat depression and other mental disorders, and of estrogen-containing contraceptive pills. May also result from digestive disorders affecting intestinal absorption of nutrients, and from serious illness, injury, or surgery.

vitamin B₆ (pyridoxine, pyridoxal, or pyridoxamine)*

Functions: Important in the body's use of protein and in proper growth and maintenance of body functions. Exists in three forms.

Sources: Liver, whole-grain cereals, red meats, green vegetables, yellow corn.

Results of deficiency: Soreness of the mouth, nausea, dizziness, weight loss, sometimes neurological disorders and a kind of anemia, and in infants possible seizures.

Results of excess: Unknown; water-soluble and excess excreted in urine, though extreme excess has been linked with nerve inflammation, or *neuritis.*

vitamin B₁₂ (folate or cyanocobalamin)

Functions: Important to normal development of red blood cells in the bone marrow and to general cell functioning, especially in the nervous system and intestines.

Sources: Lean meats, organ meats such as liver, kidneys, and heart; fish and shellfish; eggs; diary products.

Results of deficiency: Pernicious anemia and neurological disorders, in extreme cases including degeneration of the spinal cord. During pregnancy, may be associated with the development of neural tube defects, such as spina bifida, in the baby.

Results of excess: Unknown; water-soluble and excess excreted in urine.

Special caution: Americans often have low intake of vitamin B₁₂ and are sometimes given supplements to reduce the risk of neural tube defects, though links with deficiency are not proven. Very little vitamin B₁₂ is present in fruits and vegetables, so people on a vegetarian diet are advised to take vitamin B₁₂ supplements.

vitamin C (ascorbic acid)

Functions: Important in promoting growth, especially of teeth and bones; repairing tissue, and healing wounds. Acts as a preservative in foods.

Sources: Abundant in many fruits and vegetables, notably turnip greens, green peppers, kale, broccoli, mustard greens, citrus fruits, strawberries, currants, and tomatoes.

Results of deficiency: The deficiency disease *scurvy,* involving bleeding of gums, bruises, weakness, loss of weight, lassitude, and irritability.

Results of excess: Unknown, but if megadoses (much in excess of the RDA) are taken and then discontinued, deficiency symptoms can occur, not only in adults but also in newborns if the excess occurred during the pregnancy.

Special caution: Some people believe that megadoses of vitamin C can protect against the common cold, but that thesis has not been confirmed by scientific research. Some researchers recommend that smokers take vitamin C supplements, because smoking makes them more susceptible to respiratory infections.

vitamin D (calciferol)

Functions: Important to the absorption of calcium and phosphorus to form bones. In the body, converted to a substance acting somewhat like a hormone. Exists in several forms, all vital.

Sources: Formed in the skin by ultraviolet rays. Abundant in canned and fresh fish, especially from salt water; egg yolks; and foods fortified with vitamin D, such as milk and margarine.

Results of deficiency: The deficiency disease called *rickets* in children and *osteomalacia* in adults, involving deformations of the skeleton, including spine, bowed legs, and flat feet, also pot-belly appearance.

Results of excess: Nausea, weight loss, weakness, excessive urination, hypertension (high blood pressure), hardening (calcification) of soft tissues, including blood vessels and kidneys, bone deformities, and multiple fractures.

Special caution: For infants and people of all ages with chronic illnesses, with little exposure to the sun, fortified foods are especially important. Too much sun can cause other health problems (see SKIN).

vitamin E

Functions: Actually a group of substances, it is important for formation of red blood cells and normal cell structure and for maintaining activities of some enzymes. Helps prevent oxygen from destroying other substances in the body, including other vitamins; called an *antioxidant.* May slow aging of cells, and promote healing of skin. Used in treating a rare form of anemia in infants.

Sources: Vegetable oils, beans, eggs, whole grains, liver, nuts, and green leafy vegetables.

Results of deficiency: Not clearly known. Possible reduction of blood clotting and destruction of red blood cells, causing anemia. In infants, irritability and fluid buildup (edema).

Results of excess: Abdominal pain, nausea, vomiting, and diarrhea; also reduction of absorptions of other vitamins, notably A, D, and K, leading to vitamin deficiencies.

Special caution: Deficiencies are rare but may result from digestive disorders, disrupting absorption of nutrients in the intestinal system.

vitamin K

Functions: Essential for blood clotting. Exists in several forms, including one manufactured by bacteria in the intestines.
Sources: Abundant in spinach, lettuce, kale, cabbage, cauliflower, liver, and egg yolk. Also available in synthetic form.
Results of deficiency: Hemorrhage and liver problems.
Results of excess: None known.
Special caution: May result from long-term treatment with antibiotics, which kill vitamin K–producing bacteria in the intestines, or from digestive disorders disrupting intestinal absorption of vitamins. Human milk is low on vitamin K, so the American Academy of Pediatrics recommends that vitamin K be given at birth to infants, to prevent bleeding disorders.

niacin (nicotinamide or nicotinic acid)*

Functions: Important to the health of tissue and nerve cells; to normal appetite and digestion, especially of carbohydrates and fats; and to the manufacture of sex hormones.
Sources: Poultry; fish; meat, especially liver; whole-grain or fortified grain products; nuts; peas and beans.
Results of deficiency: Weakness, dizziness, changes in skin and intestinal lining, loss of appetite, and irritability. In severe cases, the deficiency disease *pellagra,* involving mouth sores, rough skin, diarrhea, and mental disorders.
Results of excess: Headaches, cramps, and nausea.
Special caution: Deficiencies may result from long-term heavy alcohol consumption and from digestive disorders affecting intestinal absorption of nutrients.

folic acid (folacin)*

Functions: Important in the manufacturing of red blood cells and in general energy metabolism.
Sources: Abundant in liver, beans, and green leafy vegetables; also found in nuts, fresh oranges, and whole-wheat products.
Results of deficiency: Diarrhea and a form of anemia, causing fatigue, pallor, and depression.
Results of excess: May obscure symptoms of pernicious anemia.
Special caution: Very important in development of the fetus, especially of the nervous system and red blood cells. Pregnant women are sometimes

given folic acid supplements, especially during the last three months of pregnancy. Some researchers recommend folic acid supplements for smokers.

biotin (formerly vitamin H)*

Functions: Important in the metabolism (breaking down for energy) of carbohydrates, proteins, and fats.
Sources: Abundant in eggs, milk, meats, peanuts, dried beans, mushrooms, and bananas, though it can be destroyed by a factor in raw egg whites. Also produced by bacteria in the intestinal tract.
Results of deficiency: Fatigue, depression, nausea, insomnia, and muscle pain.
Results of excess: Unknown; water-soluble and excess excreted in urine and feces.
Special caution: May occur with long-term use of antibiotics or sulfa drugs.

pantothenic acid*

Functions: Important in the body's growth, maintenance, and energy metabolism.
Sources: Many foods, including meats (especially liver and kidneys), milk and dairy products, egg yolks, whole-grain products, peanuts, white and sweet potatoes, peas, and most other vegetables.
Results of deficiency: Headache, fatigue, poor muscle coordination, nausea, and cramps.
Results of excess: Unknown; water-soluble and excess excreted in urine.
Special caution: May result from digestive disorders affecting intestinal absorption of nutrients; long-term heavy alcohol use; or severe illness, injury or surgery.

*These form part of a group of vitamins known as vitamin B complex.

▶ **Minerals**

calcium

Functions: Important in building and maintenance of strong bones and teeth; proper functioning of nerves and muscles; blood clotting; and the body's metabolism.

Sources: Milk and other dairy products, eggs, fish (especially sardines and shellfish), green leafy vegetables, dried peas and beans, and fruits, especially citrus.

Results of deficiency: The deficiency disease called *rickets* in children and *osteomalacia* in adults, involving deformations of the skeleton, including spine, bowed legs, and flat feet; also pot-belly appearance. General calcium deficiency is called *hypocalcemia.*

Results of excess: Calcium deposits in tissues, depression.

Special caution: Levels in the blood are controlled by vitamin D and hormones produced by the thyroid and parathyroid glands. Lack of vitamin D, problems with those glands, or kidney problems can produce deficiency. Pregnant women, elderly women, and those at risk for osteoporosis must be sure to have adequate calcium, taking supplements (often antacid tablets primarily of calcium) when indicated.

potassium

Functions: Important in maintaining the body's normal heart rhythm, water balance, and nerve and muscle functioning, often working together with sodium and calcium.

Sources: Many foods, especially oranges, bananas, dried fruits, peanut butter, and potatoes.

Results of deficiency: Muscle weakness and irregular heartbeat, potentially life-threatening. General potassium deficiency is called *hypokalemia.*

Results of excess: Heart irregularities and possible cardiac arrest. General potassium excess is called *hyperkalemia.*

Special caution: Potassium deficiency often results in loss of body fluids, as through vomiting and diarrhea, and so is a danger to people with bulimia. It is also associated with diabetes and Cushing's syndrome, a disorder of the adrenal glands. Too much potassium can result from kidney problems or taking excess potassium supplements.

magnesium

Functions: Important in the formation of bones and teeth; proper functioning of nerves and muscles; and proper action of enzymes orchestrating biochemical reactions in the body.

Sources: Abundant in green leafy vegetables, nuts, whole-grain products, and soy beans. Also in some antacids and laxatives.

Results of deficiency: Muscle weakness.

Results of excess: Nausea, confusion, and disruption of normal heart function.

Special caution: Magnesium deficiency is associated with diarrhea, diabetes, long-term heavy alcohol consumption, and kidney problems. Also found in infants fed on cow's milk or on formula with too little magnesium. Excess can result from overuse of magnesium-rich antacids and laxatives.

sodium

Functions: Important in maintaining the body's balance of water and electrolytes (electrically charged particles of minerals and other compounds) and proper functioning of nerves and muscles.

Sources: Found in many foods and often added in cooking in the form of sodium chloride (table salt) or sodium bicarbonate. Abundant in processed foods, ham, cheese, breads and cereals, and pickled, smoked, or cured meats, fish, and vegetables. Also in water treated with water softeners.

Results of deficiency: Muscle cramps, weakness, headache, and, in severe cases, low blood pressure, confusion, and fainting.

Results of excess: High blood pressure (hypertension), water buildup (edema), kidney damage, and heart problems.

Special caution: Deficiency can result from overuse of diuretic drugs, persistent diarrhea or vomiting (and so associated with bulimia), and disorders of the kidneys (which control sodium blood levels), cystic fibrosis, and adrenal gland problems. Excess is a substantial problem in Western countries, and nutritionists urge consumers to check prepared foods for sodium levels and to exercise restraint in adding salt.

chloride

Functions: Key component of the body's digestive juices, as in hydrochloric acid.

Sources: Table salt (sodium chloride).

Results of deficiency: Disruption of the body's chemical balance.

Results of excess: Disruption of the body's chemical balance.

phosphorus

Functions: Important in the body's metabolism; works with calcium to build strong bones and teeth.

Sources: Milk, cheese, meats, egg yolks, fish, poultry, whole-grain products, beans, and nuts.

Results of deficiency: Weakness, bone pain, and abnormal growth.

Results of excess: Blocking of the body's use of calcium. Chronic phosphorus poisoning can cause anemia, cirrhosis of the liver, and kidney problems. Severe acute phosphorus poisoning can lead to vomiting and bloody diarrhea; failure of vital organs, such as the heart, kidneys, or liver; delirium and seizures; and death.

Special caution: Phosphorus is common in agricultural and industrial chemicals, including pesticides, and constitutes a major environmental hazard.

sulfur

Functions: Important in several key amino acids, the protein building blocks, and so to the body's building and maintenance of bones, tendons, and connective tissues.

Sources: Wheat germ, dried beans, beef, clams. Also used in sulfa drugs or sulfonamides to treat some infections, especially of the urinary tract and skin.

Results of deficiency: Weakness, tiredness.

Results of excess: Unknown.

Special caution: Sulfur deficiency may result from a vegetarian diet with insufficient protein.

iron

Functions: Vital in the making of blood substances, notably *hemoglobin*, which transports oxygen from the lungs to the cells, and *myoglobin*, which stores oxygen in muscles.

Sources: Many foods, including meats, especially liver; egg yolks; shellfish; green leafy vegetables; dried fruits such as prunes; raisins, and apricots; whole-grain and enriched breads and cereals; and beans.

Results of deficiency: Iron-deficiency anemia.

Results of excess: Accumulating of iron in internal organs, causing cirrhosis of the liver.

Special caution: Women are often advised to take iron supplements during and after pregnancy, throughout lactation, and when experiencing very heavy menstruation. Small amounts of meat or foods containing vitamin C can increase the total amount of iron absorbed from the meal.

copper

Functions: Helps form red blood cells, proteins, and enzymes that orchestrate the body's biochemical reactions.

Sources: Organ meats, such as liver, kidneys, and heart; shellfish; dried beans and peas; nuts and fruits, especially raisins; and mushrooms.

Results of deficiency: Rare.

Results of excess: Nausea, vomiting, and diarrhea. With long-term buildup, serious health problems, such as hepatitis and cirrhosis of the liver.

Special caution: Copper poisoning can result from food cooked in unlined copper pots or alcohol distilled with copper tubing. Copper can also build up in some diseases, such as Wilson's disease.

iodine

Functions: Vital for normal functioning of the thyroid gland, which produces hormones important in the body's metabolism, growth, and development.

Sources: Seafood and iodized salt—sodium chloride with iodine added.

Results of deficiency: Goiter (enlarged thyroid gland), underactive thyroid gland *(hypothyroidism)*, and, in infants, a type of mental retardation called *cretinism*. Radioactive forms of iodine are used to treat or diagnose some thyroid problems; iodine is also used in some antiseptics and cough medicines.

Results of excess: Possible allergic reactions, including rash, swollen face, abdominal pain, vomiting, and headache.

zinc

Functions: Important in normal growth and development, especially of the reproductive system, the manufacture of proteins, and healing wounds.

Sources: High-protein foods, such as meats, especially liver; seafood; milk and other dairy products; nuts; dried beans and peas; and whole-grain or enriched breads and cereals.

Results of deficiency: Loss of taste and appetite; slowed growth, including sexual maturation; slow healing of wounds; and susceptibility to infection and injury.

Results of excess: Gastrointestinal problems, including nausea, vomiting, and diarrhea, which can cause associated loss of iron and copper.

Special caution: Excess during pregnancy, as from too much mineral supplements, can lead to premature delivery or stillbirth. Deficiency is rare, except in cases of malnutrition and disorders that hinder the body's ability to use zinc, including some digestive disorders, cystic fibrosis, and cirrhosis of the liver. Burns and sickle-cell anemia can cause the body to need significantly more zinc.

fluorine (fluoride)

Functions: Important in the proper formation and maintenance of bone, especially for children, and for preventing tooth decay.
Sources: Widely used in fluoridation programs, either added to water or given as rinses, drops, tablets, or toothpaste.
Results of deficiency: Tooth decay.
Results of excess: Mottled discoloration of teeth.
Special caution: Fluorine is most effective at fighting cavities when given to children, so it is incorporated as tooth enamel if actually formed. Sodium fluoride has been tested as a treatment for osteoporosis. Recent scientific studies have not supported concerns that fluoridation is associated with increased cancer risk, Down's syndrome, gastrointestinal problems, or diseases of the genital, urinary, and respiratory systems.

selenium

Functions: Important in maintaining the elasticity of body tissues and thus slowing the aging process. Aids oxygen supply to the heart and helps form *prostaglandins,* which counter high blood pressure and abnormal blood clotting.
Sources: Meat, fish, whole grains, and dairy products, and some vegetables, if selenium was present in the soil where they were grown. Selenium is also used in some dandruff shampoos.
Results of deficiency: Premature aging, muscle pain, increased risk of heart disease.
Results of excess: Baldness, loss of nails and teeth, fatigue, vomiting, and, in severe cases, death.
Special caution: Selenium poisoning can result from taking excess mineral supplements or eating vegetables grown in some intensively irrigated areas with extremely high selenium content in the soil. Selenium has only recently been recognized as an environmental poison, and its widespread effects are as yet unknown.

DIET AND NUTRITION

Help, Information, and Action Guide

Organizations

▶ **Human Nutrition Information Service** (Room 325A, Federal Building, Hyattsville, MD 20782; 301-436-8498; Neal Opsen, director), a service of the U.S. Department of Agriculture (USDA). It answers information and distributes various materials, including *Dietary Guidelines for Americans.*
▶ Food and Drug Administration **(FDA)** (301-472-4750).
▶ National Center for Education in Maternal and Child Health **(NCEMCH)** (703-524-7802), and National Maternal and Child Health Clearinghouse **(NMCHC)** (703-821-8955). Publish *Nutrition Resources for Early Childhood—Resource Guide.*
▶ National Women's Health Network **(NWHN)** (202-347-1140). Operates the **Women's Health Information Service.** Publishes *The Diet Your Doctor Won't Give You.*
▶ Women's Sports Foundation **(WSF)** (212-972-9170; Women's Sports Infoline, 800-227-3988). Publishes expert packet on *Nutrition/Weight Control.*
▶ **Center for Science in the Public Interest (CSPI)** (1501 16th Street, NW, Washington, DC 20036; 202-332-9110; Michael Jacobsen, executive director), an organization of people concerned about the adverse effects of scientific technology on food safety and nutrition. It seeks to educate the public and change government policy concerning testing, labeling, and advertising. It publishes various materials, including *Nutrition Action Healthletter.*
▶ **American Home Economics Association (AHEA)** (1555 King Street, Alexandria, VA 22314; 703-706-4600; Mary Jane Kolar, executive director), an organization of professional home economists. It publishes various materials.

Other resources

◪ **GENERAL WORKS**

Everywoman's Guide to Nutrition. Judith E. Brown, University of Minnesota Press, 1990.
The Nutrition Desk Reference, rev. ed. Robert H. Garrison, Jr., and Elizabeth Somer. Keats Publishing, 1990.

The Tufts University Guide to Total Nutrition. Stanley Gershoff with Catherine Whitney. Harper & Row, 1990.

Jean Mayer's Diet and Nutritional Guide. Jean Mayer and Jeanne P. Goldberg. Pharos, 1990.

New Theories on Diet and Nutrition. Sally Lee. Watts, 1990.

The Columbia Encyclopedia of Women's Nutrition. Carlton Fredericks. Putnam, 1989.

The Surgeon General's Report on Nutrition and Health. Prima, 1988.

◪ VITAMINS AND MINERALS

The Vitamin and Mineral Encyclopedia. Sheldon Saul Hendler. Simon & Schuster, 1990.

Good Health with Vitamins and Minerals: A Complete Guide to a Lifetime of Safe and Effective Use. John Gallagher. Summit, 1990.

Drugs, Vitamins, Minerals in Pregnancy. Ann Karen Henry and Jill Feldhausen. Fisher Books, 1990.

The People's Guide to Vitamins and Minerals from A to Zinc. rev. ed. Dominick Bosco. Contemporary, 1989.

The Complete Book of Vitamins and Minerals for Health. Rodale Books, 1988.

◪ BACKGROUND WORKS

Nutrition During Pregnancy, Part 1: Weight Gain, Part 2: Nutrient Supplements. Washington, DC: National Academy Press, 1990.

Prescription for Nutritional Healing: A Practical A–Z Reference to Drug-Free Remedies. James Balch and Phyllis Balch. Avery, 1990.

Nutritional Influences on Illness: A Sourcebook of Clinical Research. Melvyn R. Werbach. Keats Publishing, 1989.

obesity, the condition of weighing considerably more than is considered ideal for a person's height and age. Put simply, obesity results from eating more calories in food than the body requires for its energy needs; the excess is stored in fat cells (*adipose tissue*). Obesity is associated with increased risk of various health problems, including DIABETES, gallstones (see GALLBLADDER), heart disease and hypertension (see HEART AND CIRCULATORY SYSTEM), BREAST CANCER, and other types of CANCER, such as of the UTERUS, OVARIES, and colon and rectum (see DIGESTIVE SYSTEM). Even someone mildly or moderately overweight is at some increased risk of such disorders and has a lessened LIFE EXPECTANCY.

Traditionally obesity has been defined as being 20 percent or more above the weight considered optimal for a person's weight and age—that being the weight correlated with the lowest death rates in actuarial statistics (see SUGGESTED WEIGHTS FOR ADULTS on page 516). Recognizing that as the body ages, fat cells become less metabolically active, and have less harmful effects in the body, such lists now generally have higher weight ranges for older people. As footnote 3 of the table outlines, the higher weights in the ranges are generally applied to men and the lower to women, who are presumed to have generally smaller body frames and less muscle. Such assignments are arbitrary, however; George Washington University medical professor and obesity expert C. Wayne Callaway noted in 1991: "There is no evidence showing that women live longer if they weigh less than men of equal stature."

SUGGESTED WEIGHTS FOR ADULTS

Height[1]	Weight (in lbs.) Age 19–34[2]	Weight (in lbs.) Age 35 and Over
5'0"	97–128[3]	108–138
5'1"	101–132	111–143
5'2"	104–137	115–148
5'3"	107–141	119–152
5'4"	111–146	122–157
5'5"	114–150	126–162
5'6"	118–155	130–167
5'7"	121–160	134–172
5'8"	125–164	138–178
5'9"	129–169	142–183
5'10"	132–174	146–188
5'11"	136–179	151–194
6'0"	140–184	155–199
6'1"	144–189	159–205
6'2"	148–195	165–210
6'3"	152–200	168–216
6'4"	156–205	173–222
6'5"	160–211	177–228
6'6"	164–216	182–234

1 Without shoes.
2 Without clothes.
3 The higher weights in the ranges generally apply to men, who tend to have larger body frames and more muscle; the lower weights more often apply to women, who have smaller body frames and less muscle. Weights even below the range may be appropriate for some small-boned people.
Source: National Research Council (1989), as reprinted in *FDA Consumer*, Jan.–Feb. 1991.

Some health experts now view the weight-range yardstick as both imprecise and too restrictive and feel that more emphasis should be placed on where the fat is carried on the body. Fat in the hips and thighs—though perhaps the bane of those who strive for slimness—poses much less hazard to health than fat stored in the abdomen. Researchers believe that this is partly because when fat is called on for use by the body, fatty acids from the hips and thighs go right into general circulation, while those from the abdomen go first to the liver; there they interfere with the body's balancing of insulin and glucose (sugar) levels in the blood and set the stage for diabetes, hypertension, and heart disease. Some obesity experts propose that a better definition of obesity is the *waist-to-hip ratio*, calculated by dividing the waist measurement by the hip measurement; for example, a 27-in. waist / 38-in. hips = 0.71. A woman whose ratio is 0.8 or higher would be considered at high risk for weight-related health problems (for men, with their different bodily fat distribution, the problem ratio would be 0.95).

Another approach to defining obesity is by percent of body fat, with above 20 percent body fat being considered obese for a woman (10–15 percent for a man). The fat/body weight ratio requires sophisticated laboratory equipment for accurate measurement, so it has limited practical use. However, clearly if two women of the same height weigh 150 pounds, and one has increased muscle from EXERCISE and the other is completely out of shape, the second has a much higher percent of body fat. A related approach is called the *body mass index,* in which body weight is divided by the body height squared and then compared with a given table.

More vexing is the question of why some people become obese and others do not. The answer is complex and seems to involve heredity, environment, metabolism, and level of physical activity. Though diet and life-style are important, recent studies indicate that the most important factor seems to be GENETIC INHERITANCE, which affects what proportion of excess food calories is used and what stored, and where. In fact, some researchers report finding evidence of a gene for obesity, with inheritance following the classic pattern for recessive inheritance, in which a child must receive the gene from both parents. But many other genes also seem to be involved, including those affecting appetite and metabolism—the biochemical reactions that provide energy for the body.

Several studies have indicated that many people become obese not because they eat too much, but because their bodies burn calories too slowly, storing any unused food energy as fat. Whether infants or adults, in general people with the slowest metabolisms are more likely to become overweight; and this low metabolic rate seems to run in families. Worse, when many overweight or obese people diet, their bodies slow their metabolism even more, making it even harder to lose fat.

The different patterns of fat distribution between the sexes (see SECONDARY SEX CHARACTERISTICS) result from an interplay between SEX HORMONES and *lipoprotein lipase* (LPL), an enzyme produced by fat cells *(adipose tissue)* to help store calories as fat. Women store many excess calories in the hips, thighs, and BREASTS, where fat cells secrete LPL, while in men LPL production and fat storage take place more commonly in the abdominal region. Women may lose weight more slowly than men partly because fat in the thighs and buttocks is used for long-term energy reserves, while abdominal fat is drawn on for quick energy. The gene that codes for LPL is the target of much research.

Fat cells store fat to be used when other shorter-term sources of energy, primarily glucose, are used up or unavailable. The body can store virtually limitless amounts of fat; each fat cell can expand to more than ten times its original size, and new ones form to store even more fat. The problem is that as people diet and exercise to lose weight, their fat cells produce higher levels of LPL, as if to retain or regain their larger size. In addition, dieting slows the body's metabolic rate, and as fat cells shrink they release their contents less readily, both of which retard weight loss. Basically, a diet is an attempt to overcome this resistance of the body (see DIETING).

Whatever the cause or definition of obesity, everyone who is overweight faces the same problems—how to get rid of the excess fat. The problems are considerable, as the body gains weight easily and resists loss strongly. However, studies indicate that for obese people even relatively small weight losses—say, ten to twenty-five pounds, rather than the needed one hundred—can have significant health benefits and are easier to maintain. Obesity is sometimes considered a type of EATING DISORDER and may be associated with other such disorders, such as BULIMIA or BINGE EATING DISORDER. (See EATING DISORDERS HELP, INFORMATION, AND ACTION GUIDE on page 58.)

occupational segregation: See WORK AND WOMEN.

ODPHP National Health Information Center (ONHIC) (P.O. Box 1133, Washington, DC 20013-1133; 301-565-4167, in Maryland, or 800-336-4797), a health information referral service established in 1979 by the U.S. Department of Health and Human Service's Office of Disease Prevention and Health Promotion (ODPHP). The center's aims are to "identify health information resources; channel requests for information to these resources; and develop publications on health-related topics of interest to health professionals, the health media, and the general public." It maintains a library, open to the public by appointment, and a computer data base, available on-line through DIRLINE, part of the National Library of Medicine's MEDLARS system. Also part of the center is the **National Information Center for Orphan Drugs and Rare Diseases (NICODARD),** sponsored by the **Food and Drug Administration,** focusing on diseases affecting fewer than two hundred thousand people in the country and medicines not widely researched or available. Among the center's many publications are *Healthfinders*, a series of resource lists on current health concerns; *Health Information Resources in the Federal Government, Locating Funds for Health Promotion Projects*; and other directories, resource guides, and bibliographies on various health topics.

Oedipus complex, the supposed sexual feelings of a son for his MOTHER; in Freudian psychology, a normal stage that is resolved by the son identifying with the FATHER and adopting his appropriate SEX ROLE. In girls, the analogous theoretical relationship with the father is called an ELECTRA COMPLEX. Both names are taken from characters in Greek tragedies.

Office of Disease Prevention and Health Promotion National Health Information Center: See ODPHP NATIONAL HEALTH INFORMATION CENTER (ONHIC).

Office of Women's Health: See PHS ACTION PLAN FOR WOMEN'S HEALTH.

Office on Research on Women's Health (ORWH) (National Institutes of Health, Building 1, Room 201, Bethesda, MD 20892; 301-402-1770, Vivian W. Pinn, director), an office established in 1990, within the Office of the Director of the National Institutes of Health (NIH), to "strengthen and enhance research related to diseases, disorders, and conditions that affect women and ensure that research conducted and supported by the NIH adequately addresses issues regarding women's health; to ensure that women are appropriately represented in biomedical and biobehavioral research studies supported by the NIH; and to develop opportunities and support for recruitment, retention, reentry, and advancement of women in biomedical careers." Women's health issues are defined as "diseases, disorders, and conditions that are unique to, more prevalent among, or more serious in women, or for which there are different risk factors or interventions for women than for men." The office is also charged with collaborating on the **Women's Health Initiative,** a "prevention study to examine the major causes of death, disability, and frailty—heart disease and stroke, cancers (particularly breast and colorectal), and osteoporosis—in older women of all races and socioeconomic strata."

Ohio v. *Akron Center for Reproductive Health*, the 1990 U.S. Supreme Court ruling upholding a state law that required a teenager to notify one parent before obtaining an ABORTION.

Older Women's League (OWL) (666 11th Street, NW, Suite 700, Washington, DC 20001; 202-783-6686; OWL POWERLINE, 202-783-6689, a weekly update on congressional activities; Lou Glasse, president), an organization founded in 1980 to "focus exclusively on women as they age." It works to "achieve economic and social equity and to improve the image and status of midlife and older women through education, research, and public advocacy" with membership open to people of all ages. OWL seeks a universal health care system, a more equitable and more adequate Social Security system, expanded employer-sponsored pension coverage, and increased access to safe and affordable housing; it also works to combat discrimination in the workplace and to protect the individual's right to maintain control of quality-of-life decisions through the end of life. Members have access to long-term care insurance.

OWL publishes the bimonthly *The OWL Observer* and various other materials, including

- books such as *Making Ends Meet: Midlife and Older Women's Search for Economic Self-Sufficiency Through Job Training and Employment, Women and Money: The Independent Women's Guide to Financial Security for Life, Caring for Caregivers: Addressing the Employment Needs of Long-Term Care Workers,* and *Employment Discrimination Against Older Women.*
- Mother's Day reports, such as *Critical Condition: Midlife and Older Women in America's Health Care System, Paying for Prejudice: Midlife and Older Women in America's Labor Force, Heading for Hardship: Retirement Income for American Women in the Next Century, Failing America's Caregivers: A Status Report*

on *Women Who Care, The Road to Poverty: Report on the Economic Status of Midlife and Older Women in America, The Picture of Health: For Midlife and Older Women in America,* and *Report on the Status of Midlife and Older Women in America.*

- Gray papers, such as *In Search of a Solution: The American Health Care Crisis, Divorce and Older Women, Women and Pensions: Catch-22, Death and Dying: Staying in Control to the End of Our Lives,* and *Till Death Do Us Part: Caregiving Wives of Severely Disabled Husbands.*
- Model bills such as *Universal Health Care, COBRA* (continuation of group health care benefits), and *Spousal Impoverishment. Medicaid Antidiscrimination, Respite for Caregivers,* and *Osteoporosis;*
- videotapes such as *A Matter of Life and Death* and *Working Together—Creating Change.*
- miscellaneous publications such as *Universal Health Care Action Kit* and *Older Women and Job Discrimination: A Primer.*

It also publishes reprints of testimony before Congress on the above topics and many others, including the EQUAL RIGHTS AMENDMENT, adult day care, the Family and Medical Leave Act, and home and community-based long-term care.

oligomenorrhea, menstrual periods that arrive in cycles longer than thirty-eight days (see MENSTRUATION).

oligospermia, a condition involving too few SPERM (see INFERTILITY).

On Understanding Women (1931): See Mary Ritter BEARD.

oophorectomy, a surgical procedure to remove one or both OVARIES, as in cases of ovarian CANCER, painful or persistent cysts (see OVARIES), or PELVIC INFLAMMATORY DISEASE. If one ovary is removed, the procedure is called *unilateral oophorectomy;* if both, *bilateral oophorectomy.* The operation requires incisions in the lower abdomen (similar to those in an abdominal HYSTERECTOMY or CESAREAN SECTION); is generally done under general ANESTHESIA; and requires a month to six weeks of healing before resumption of most normal activities, including SEXUAL INTERCOURSE.

If only part of an ovary is removed, as in treatment of STEIN-LEVENTHAL SYNDROME (*polycystic syndrome* or *ovaries*), it is called a *wedge resection.* Often when the ovaries are removed, so are the uterus (in a HYSTERECTOMY) and the fallopian tubes (SALPINGECTOMY), the combined operation being called a *hysterosalpingo-oophorectomy.*

For some decades surgeons performing a hysterectomy routinely also removed the ovaries and fallopian tubes as well. They reasoned that because the woman's childbearing was over, the ovaries had no further function, and removal would eliminate the risk of ovarian cancer. It now seems, however, that premature menopause has other adverse health effects, and the small amounts of hormones that ovaries continue to produce after menopause may confer some health benefits. As a result, that practice is somewhat less common. A woman facing an operation on any part of her internal REPRODUCTIVE SYSTEM should discuss the pros and cons with her doctor. (See OVARIES; HYSTERECTOMY.)

oophoritis, inflammation of the OVARIES.

oral contraceptives, an alternate term for BIRTH CONTROL PILLS.

Organization of Chinese American Women (OCAW) (1300 N

Street, NW, Suite 100, Washington, DC 20005; 202-638-0330; Pauline W. Tsui, executive director), an organization established in 1977 "to advance the cause of Chinese American women in the United States and to foster public awareness of their special needs and concerns," and to promote their equal participation in "all aspects of life through the advancement of equal rights, responsibilities, and opportunities," stressing integration into the mainstream of women's activities, programs, and groups. Among OCAW's main concerns are "equal employment opportunities at both the professional and nonprofessional levels; overcoming stereotypes, racial discrimination, and restrictive traditional beliefs; assistance to poverty-stricken recent immigrants; and access to leadership and policy-making positions. OCAW sponsors forums, seminars, conferences, and exchange programs with Asian Pacific rim countries; serves as a clearinghouse on Chinese American women's issues; provides grants and training; and publishes various materials, including the newsletter *OCAW Speaks* and *Brief History and Bibliography on Chinese American Women.*

orgasm, the intensely pleasurable climactic release of tension that follows sexual activity, such as SEXUAL INTERCOURSE or MASTURBATION. Orgasm is actually part of a whole cycle of feelings and physiological changes moving from excitement to plateau then to orgasm and resolution (see SEXUAL RESPONSE).

osteoporosis, a disorder of the SKELETAL SYSTEM leading to severe loss of bone density and strength; literally "porous bone." The weakening results in pain, injury, and sometimes deformities.

Bone reaches its peak mass at about age thirty-five and after that begins slowly to lose density and strength. This is a normal process, and almost half of all women and men over age seventy-five experience a form of osteoporosis— though women do so disproportionately, because they tend to live longer. This is called *age-related* or *Type II osteoporosis.*

However, Type I osteoporosis is found only among women and typically appears in the years following MENOPAUSE. The continual breakdown and rebuilding of bone (see SKELETAL SYSTEM) is controlled by various HORMONES, among them ESTROGEN; with sharply decreased estrogen, much more bone is broken down than rebuilt. Among the bones most affected are the vertebrae of the spine, hipbones, flat bones such as the pelvis, and long bones such as those in the arms and legs. The result is an increasing risk of fractures, often of the wrist, hip, or spinal vertebrae, which partially collapse to form the curved upper spine once popularly known as "dowager's hump" (see SPINE).

The problem is widespread. In the United States alone, osteoporosis causes an estimated 1.3 million fractures a year, and 20–25 percent of all postmenopausal women are considered at risk for fractures from osteoporosis. Hip fractures are the most dangerous, because the body is immobilized for so long. An estimated one out of five postmenopausal women with a hip fracture will die within a year, generally from pneumonia (see RESPIRATORY SYSTEM), blood clots in the lung, or heart failure (see HEART AND CIRCULATORY SYSTEM), all triggered or exacerbated by impaired circulation due to enforced immobility. Fewer than two out of the five will ever again be able to walk unaided or to resume their previous level of activity, though advances in surgery may increase their numbers. Even in less severe cases, the average woman will lose height, perhaps inches, as she grows older because of crush fractures of the spinal vertebrae.

Osteoporosis is initially a "silent disease." It develops over years with few symptoms, except sometimes chronic pain in the spine or muscle spasms in the back. Many cases are diagnosed only in an X-ray for an unrelated problem or when a fracture occurs, sometimes suddenly and with minimal trauma. Though bone thinning can be diagnosed by various imaging techniques, such procedures are generally used only for women at significant risk of osteoporosis, partly because they are not generally covered by most insurance plans—and partly because by the time osteoporosis has been diagnosed, the damage has been done. No medical technology now available has been able to restore bone mass once it has been lost, though a number of approaches are being explored to do just that.

Prevention constitutes the main approach for now, and it starts in childhood. The more bone mass a woman builds up during childhood and early maturity, the less likely she will be to develop osteoporosis. This means maintaining a consistently adequate level in the body of calcium and of other vital nutrients needed for the proper use of calcium (see NUTRITION; also KEY VITAMINS AND MINERALS on page 502). Women need to pay special attention to nutrition during PREGNANCY, when calcium is needed for the growing baby, and especially during an adolescent pregnancy, when the bone-building process has not yet been completed in the mother (see SKELETAL SYSTEM). Other factors that may increase risk of osteoporosis, or worsen its effects, are

▶ *sedentary life-style,* since weight-bearing EXERCISE promotes bone deposition.
▶ SMOKING, since cigarette smokers have lower levels of estrogen in the blood.
▶ *heavy alcohol intake,* because alcohol inhibits absorption of calcium (see ALCOHOL AND DRUG ABUSE).
▶ *exercise* so strenuous that MENSTRUATION stops.
▶ HYSTERECTOMY, which, especially if the OVARIES are also removed, causes a premenopausal woman to go into premature "surgical menopause."

▶ *Paget's disease of the bone,* which causes excessive rebuilding of bone and consequent dense but fragile bones.

▶ *some hormone disorders,* such as Cushing's syndrome.

▶ *some lung disorders,* such as bronchitis and emphysema (see RESPIRATORY SYSTEM).

▶ *general nutritional deficiency or imbalance,* as in ANOREXIA NERVOSA or BULIMIA.

Osteoporosis can also result as a side effect from drugs, such as corticosteroids (see STEROIDS) and heparin, and from various disorders, including hyperthyroidism, rheumatoid ARTHRITIS, kidney disease (see URINARY TRACT), and some kinds of CANCER, especially leukemia (see BLOOD) and lymphoma (see IMMUNE SYSTEM).

Women at highest risk of osteoporosis are thin, small-boned women, especially those of Caucasian or Asian ancestry and those with a family history of the condition; women of Hispanic or African descent have fewer problems. All women should discuss their personal and family history with their doctor *the earlier the better,* to assess their vulnerability to osteoporosis, and plan accordingly—especially to determine the best daily amount of calcium for their individual needs. Some controversy exists about the need for and proper amount of calcium for women of various ages (see RECOMMENDED DAILY ALLOWANCES on page 501), since too much calcium can have adverse side effects, especially on the kidneys. ESTROGEN REPLACEMENT THERAPY may be appropriate for some, but it has side effects that make it inappropriate for others, especially women at risk for BREAST CANCER or other cancer.

Researchers are studying the effectiveness of taking *calcitonin,* a thyroid hormone that inhibits bone breakdown, but whether it can prevent fractures is so far unclear. Similarly, early studies showed that sodium fluoride can spur rebuilding of bone, but it remains weak, and does not lessen the number of fractures. In some countries, such as Japan, a vitamin D hormone called *calcitriol* is given to help the body absorb calcium from food through the intestines; but in countries with high-calcium diets, such as the United States, this poses the danger of kidney damage from excess calcium. A still newer vitamin D variation, *1-alpha hydroxy-vitamin D_2,* holds the promise of inhibiting bone loss without causing calcium buildup. Researchers are working on a test that would use calcium levels from temporarily simulated menopause to indicate a woman's susceptibility to osteoporosis. No treatments currently being explored can undo damage caused by fractures. (See OSTEOPOROSIS HELP, INFORMATION, AND ACTION GUIDE on page 524.)

OSTEOPOROSIS

Help, Information, and Action Guide

Organizations

▶ **National Osteoporosis Foundation (NOF)** (2100 M Street, NW, Suite 602, Washington, DC 20037; 202-223-2227; Sandra C. Raymond, executive director), an organization of people concerned about osteoporosis. It provides information and referrals, supports research, and educates the public. It publishes a quarterly newsletter, the book *Osteoporosis: A Woman's Guide*, and various booklets.
▶ NATIONAL INSTITUTE OF ARTHRITIS AND MUSCULOSKELETAL AND SKIN DISEASES **(NIAMS)** (301-496-8188). Publishes *Osteoporosis: Causes, Prevention, Treatment.*
▶ NATIONAL WOMEN'S HEALTH NETWORK **(NWHN)** (202-347-1140). Operates the **Women's Health Information Service.** Publishes the information packet *Osteoporosis.*

Other resources

Keys to Understanding Osteoporosis. Jan Rozek. Barron's, 1992.
Healthy Bones: What You Should Know About Osteoporosis. Nancy Appleton. Avery, 1991.
Osteoporosis and You. Elizabeth K. White. Budlong, 1989.
Osteoporosis. Langer. Keats, 1989.
Osteoporosis: The Silent Thief. William A. Beck and Louis V. Avioli. American Assocation of Retired Persons, 1988.
Osteoporosis. William A. Peck. Scott Foresman, 1988.
Osteoporosis. David F. Fardon. Price Stern, 1987.
Osteoporosis. Margot J. Fromer. Pocket Books, 1986.

◪ **ON PREVENTION AND TREATMENT**

Prevention of Postmenopausal Osteoporosis: Dream or Reality? W. A. Peck, ed. Parthenon (NJ), 1990.
Preventing Osteoporosis: The Kenneth Cooper Method. Kenneth H. Cooper. Bantam, 1989.
The Reliable Healthcare Companions: Understanding and Managing Osteoporosis. John L. Decker, ed. Avon, 1988.

O

Dealing with Osteoporosis. Partha Banerjee. Dorrance, 1988.
Osteoporosis: Prevention and Treatment. Felix Kolb. Better Health, 1986.

---

otoplasty, ear surgery (see COSMETIC SURGERY).

ovarian ablation, surgical removal or deactivation of a woman's OVARIES (see MYOMECTOMY), in an attempt to prevent recurrence of CANCER (see BREAST CANCER).

ovariectomy, an alternative name for *oophorectomy*, a surgical procedure to remove one or both OVARIES.

ovaries, the pair of female sex glands (GONADS) that manufacture eggs (see OVUM) and also ESTROGEN and PROGESTERONE, the key female sex HORMONES. These small, oval glands lie on either side of the UTERUS and just under the FALLOPIAN TUBES, in the lower abdomen. Each ovary contains, from the time of birth, several hundred thousand to a million egg-producing structures called *follicles*. These remain immature, however, until PUBERTY, when a girl's pituitary gland begins to produce FOLLICLE-STIMULATING HORMONE (FSH); this periodically signals the ovaries to ripen eggs, a process that signals the onset of sexual maturity in a woman.

Normally once a month, as part of the reproductive cycle (see MENSTRUATION), secretions of FSH signal follicles in one of the two ovaries to ripen a group of eggs—perhaps twenty or so. These follicles also produce estrogen, which triggers thickening of the *endometrium,* the lining of the uterus, to prepare for a possible fertilized egg; this is the *proliferative* or *follicular phase* of the menstrual cycle. Unlike all other cells in the body, the egg cells in these follicles subdivide into two identical cells, each with half the number of chromosomes (twenty-three, instead of forty-six) needed for the new and unique human being that will emerge if the egg is fertilized (see FERTILIZATION; GENETIC INHERITANCE); in the male, SPERM cells do the same. From each subdivided egg, one-half—called the *polar body*—shrivel up and disintegrate.

Of the remaining egg cells, one becomes dominant—though how and why is unknown—and the rest also generally disintegrate. The surviving dominant egg cell grows prodigiously—though still smaller than the dot over an "i" in absolute terms—and develops a protective coating of four layers. (On occasion two or more egg cells grow; if fertilized, these will lead to twins or multiple births; see FERTILIZATION.) Once mature, the egg awaits the hormonal signal to burst out of its growth site, called the *Graafian follicle.*

That signal comes at about fourteen days before the beginning of the next reproductive cycle—that is, before the onset of the next menstrual period—when the pituitary gland secretes LUTEINIZING HORMONE (LH). This breaks down the outer wall of the Graafian follicle, releasing the mature egg, or *ovum*, in the process called OVULATION. At this time, the egg sheds its outer two protective layers, which are left behind in the ovary; these form what is called the CORPUS LUTEUM (Latin for "yellow body") and trigger the release of progesterone. This triggers further thickening of the endometrium; it is called the *secretory* or *luteal phase* of the menstrual cycle. Meanwhile, if all goes normally, the egg—still with two protective layers—is drawn into the fallopian tube that is suspended above each ovary. (See THE FEMALE REPRODUCTIVE SYSTEM on page 621 for an illustration.) It is in the fallopian tubes, during those few days when the egg is mature and readily accessible, that fertilization will take place (see NATURAL FAMILY PLANNING).

If an egg *is* fertilized, it will normally move down the fallopian tubes into the uterus and will implant itself in the uterine wall. In that case, the corpus luteum will continue producing progesterone, forestalling the ripening of more eggs in the ovaries. Gradually the PLACENTA that forms to nourish the new FETUS in the uterus takes over production of progesterone, and the corpus luteum dwindles away. However, if fertilization does *not* take place, the corpus luteum ceases to produce progesterone within about two weeks, shrinking away to a trace. The fall in progesterone and estrogen is a signal for the expulsion of the unused egg and endometrium, in the *menstrual phase* of the cycle; it also triggers the secretion of more follicle-stimulating hormone, to start ripening a new group of eggs.

Except during PREGNANCY, BREASTFEEDING (in which hormones suppress the egg-ripening cycle), or in times of severe illness and stress, this cycle will recur month after month for decades, from the onset of menstruation, called MENARCHE, to its cessation, called MENOPAUSE. Of the up to two million possible eggs in a newborn girl's ovaries, only a few hundred will ever fully mature and be available for possible fertilization. Though many are potentially available, the number of eggs that ripen seems to diminish as a woman grows older; in fact, during the CLIMACTERIC, the long set of changes that precedes actual menopause, many women have ANOVULATORY PERIODS, where they have menstruation even though no egg was ripened. As a result, a woman has more difficulty conceiving in the latter years of her reproductive life. In perhaps 5 percent of all women, the ovaries cease their functioning early, for unknown reasons, inducing a premature menopause. After menopause, the ovaries shrink to about one-third their former size, as the remaining egg follicles disintegrate.

The ovaries are complicated and delicate mechanisms. *Palpation*—manual feeling of the size and shape—of the ovaries is an important part of every GYNE-COLOGICAL EXAMINATION. Any enlargement of the ovaries, or significant difference in their sizes, is cause for further exploration. The ovaries warrant this special attention because they cannot readily be directly examined, and some disorders can threaten FERTILITY and even life before being detected.

Among the most common disorders affecting the ovaries is *oophoritis*, a general inflammation of the ovaries. This may result from common infections, such as mumps, or from various SEXUALLY TRANSMITTED DISEASES, such as GONOR-

RHEA. If a woman has general PELVIC INFLAMMATORY DISEASE, she may experience INFERTILITY or possible life-threatening ECTOPIC PREGNANCY. Oophoritis is generally treated with medications such as antibiotics.

Also common are *ovarian cysts*, sacs filled with a fluid or gelatinous material, some as small as raisins but others as large as an orange. Often they cause no symptoms and are found only during a routine gynecological examination. However, they can cause a feeling of pressure or fullness in the abdomen and sometimes pain during SEXUAL INTERCOURSE.

Many cysts occur due to minor malfunctions in the reproductive cycle: a *follicle* or *follicular cyst* forms when a Graafian follicle fails to release a ripened egg; a *corpus luteum cyst* forms when the corpus luteum fails to dwindle away. These often disappear on their own over several months, a process sometimes hastened by administering BIRTH CONTROL PILLS. Such cysts rarely occur in women already taking oral contraceptives. However, if the cysts are large, if they rupture and bleed, or cause severe pain, they may be removed surgically, in a *cystectomy*. Only in cases where a very large cyst is involved need the whole ovary be removed, in an operation called an OOPHORECTOMY or *ovariectomy*.

When symptoms are not severe, the main concern is to rule out possible ectopic pregnancy and CANCER (see below); to do so, a physician may call for an ULTRASOUND scan or perform a LAPAROSCOPY, making a tiny incision in the abdomen to directly view or take a biopsy of the ovaries. A special case is STEIN-LEVENTHAL SYNDROME, also called *polycystic syndrome*, in which women have numerous small cysts in their ovaries.

Less common, but much more dangerous, is *ovarian cancer*, a type of CANCER that causes special concern because it is "silent"; often no obvious symptoms surface until late in development. In more than three-quarters of all cases it is diagnosed only after it has spread beyond the localized stage and is less treatable. Perhaps the most common sign is fullness or swelling of the abdomen (from accumulation of fluid), often mistaken for vague or generalized digestive upset, and sometimes abnormal bleeding. Ovarian cancer may strike at any age, but women over sixty are at greatest risk, and those who have never borne a child have at least double the risk, as do women with BREAST CANCER. A somewhat lower risk is found among women who had a first pregnancy early, had early menopause, or have used birth control pills, which reduce the frequency of ovulation. Internationally, ovarian cancer is more common among industrialized countries, except Japan.

The American Cancer Society recommends that a woman over forty should have a cancer-related checkup, including a pelvic examination, every year. Unfortunately, the PAP SMEAR only detects cancer of the CERVIX, not of the ovaries. Radiation and chemotherapy are used to treat ovarian cancer, along with surgery. Except in early stages, when only the affected ovary may be removed, surgery will often involve removal of both ovaries, the uterus (HYSTERECTOMY), and the fallopian tubes (SALPINGECTOMY), the combined operation being called a *hysterosalpingo-oophorectomy*. (See also CANCER.)

More rarely, women may have structural defects, abnormalities in, or absence of the ovaries; these are generally associated with CHROMOSOMAL ABNORMALITIES, such as TURNER'S SYNDROME.

When a premenopausal woman has both ovaries removed (see OOPHOR-OECTOMY), she may experience severe menopausal symptoms (see MENOPAUSE) because of the suddenness of the hormonal changes. ESTROGEN REPLACEMENT THERAPY is sometimes used to ease the symptoms, though it is not appropriate for all women. If only one ovary is removed, a woman can still become pregnant as long as the other ovary is functioning normally, though her chances of conceiving are lessened significantly.

For help, information, and action

▶ NATIONAL WOMEN'S HEALTH NETWORK (NWHN) (202-347-1140). Operates the **Women's Health Information Service.** Publishes the information packet *Ovarian Cysts.*
(See also OVULATION; OOPHORECTOMY; HYSTERECTOMY; REPRODUCTIVE SYSTEM; MENOPAUSE; also WOMEN'S HEALTH HELP, INFORMATION, AND ACTION GUIDE on page 334.)

ovulation, the release of a mature OVUM—the female reproductive cell, or egg—from a woman's OVARIES into the FALLOPIAN TUBES, where FERTILIZATION may take place. Ovulation is a key part of the menstrual cycle and normally occurs monthly, from the onset of MENSTRUATION to MENOPAUSE.

Regular menstruation does not necessarily mean that a woman is ovulating, however. In the early and last years of menstruating, and occasionally at other times, a woman may have ANOVULATORY PERIODS, with bleeding but no egg release. One of the first questions explored in an INFERTILITY workup is whether or not the woman is actually ovulating.

When ovulation occurs, the woman's temperature rises slightly; the mucus in the CERVIX changes color and texture; and her body produces a surge of LU-TEINIZING HORMONE (LH), triggering the actual release of the egg, which occurs twenty-four to thirty-six hours later. She may also experience slight abdominal pain, called MITTELSCHMERZ. These signs can be used to aid in BIRTH CONTROL, as indications of when to avoid SEXUAL INTERCOURSE, or to identify when prospective parents have the best chances for CONCEPTION, through intercourse or other methods such as ARTIFICIAL INSEMINATION or *IN VITRO* FERTILIZATION. To determine when they are ovulating, women may routinely take their temperature, using an especially sensitive thermometer to detect the rise; examine samples of cervical mucus for changes; or use a home medical test to track the amount of LH in their urine (see NATURAL FAMILY PLANNING).

ovum, the egg produced in a woman's OVARIES, about 0.04 inches (0.1 mm) across; the female reproductive cell. All the ova a woman will ever have are present in immature form when she is born, up to one million in each of the two ovaries. Of these, only about four hundred will ever mature and be released (see OVULATION) for possible FERTILIZATION by a SPERM, the male sex cell. In that case, the fertilized egg normally travels from the FALLOPIAN TUBES to the UTERUS and develops into an EMBRYO. The rest of the ova degenerate in the body.

oxytocin, a HORMONE that stimulates contractions of the UTERUS during LABOR and also the ducts in the BREASTS, forcing milk toward the nipple (see BREASTFEEDING). Oxytocin is secreted by the pituitary gland, after it is stimulated by other hormonal secretions from the hypothalamus; during breastfeeding its release is also stimulated by the baby's nursing or by the mother's anticipation of breastfeeding. Synthetic forms of oxytocin have sometimes been used to induce LABOR or to strengthen uterine contractions during labor, though excess use can cause adverse effects, such as threatening the baby's supply of oxygen. It may also be given to empty the UTERUS of the PLACENTA after DELIVERY or of the fetal remains in case of incomplete MISCARRIAGE or ABORTION. Lesser amounts of oxytocin may also be involved in the expulsion of uterine contents during MENSTRUATION, with the contractions—milder and less regular than those of labor—known generally as *cramps*.

pacifism and nonviolence, opposition to the use of violence in resolving disputes and support of peaceful means of conflict resolution. Such causes have engaged many of the world's leading women, some of them also WOMEN'S RIGHTS leaders, especially since the outbreak of World War I. Emily Greene Balch, who lost her teaching position at Wellesley for opposing U.S. participation in World War I, went on to become a founder, with Jane ADDAMS, of the very durable WOMEN'S INTERNATIONAL LEAGUE FOR PEACE AND FREEDOM; both were awarded the Nobel Peace Prize. Women's rights leader Carrie Chapman CATT spent much of her later life during the interwar period as a peace and disarmament advocate. In Germany, feminists Anita AUGSPURG and Lida HEYMANN worked for pacifism during both world wars. Jeannette RANKIN, the first U.S. congresswoman, opposed World War I, was the only House member to vote against entry into World War II, and demonstrated against the Vietnam War. Bella Abzug was a prime organizer of the Woman's Strike for Peace during the Vietnam War. Many Friends (Quakers) refused to participate in wars from the formation of their society in 1652, including many leading women.

Some women, including some feminists, feel that women are naturally peace-loving, and so are uniquely qualified to be exponents of pacifism and nonviolence. Others, however, have pointed out that women are not unique in supporting peace movements, noting that George Fox, founder of the Society of Friends, Mohandas K. Gandhi, and Martin Luther King, among others, have been leading pacifists and exponents of nonviolence. In fact, women hold opinions across the whole political spectrum. Certainly many support pacifism and nonviolence; however, the main WOMAN SUFFRAGE organizations supported World War I, and more recently many U.S. women were proud to have been in the U.S. armed forces during the Persian Gulf War and are seeking full combat status. (See POLITICAL PARTICIPATION; also POLITICAL PARTICIPATION HELP, INFORMATION, AND ACTION GUIDE on page 547.)

As a woman I can't go to war, and I refuse to send anyone else.

———————————— *JEANNETTE RANKIN, 1941* ————————————

•

Paglia, Camille (1947–)

Paglia, Camille (1947–), an American teacher and author who emerged as a celebrity with the publication of her book *Sexual Personae: Art and Decadence from Nefertiti to Emily Dickinson* (1990). The highly controversial work took up a wide range of matters, many of them aspects of popular culture and education, a common theme being attacks on many trends in modern education, in favor of a classics-based curriculum: a very familiar argument, but put forward in Paglia's book in an extraordinary combative fashion that drew considerable media attention.

Even more sensational was Paglia's equally combative attack on many people and trends and especially the trend in modern feminist movements toward "political correctness," as part of her more general iconoclastic stance. Her arguments proved very attractive to many conservatives, although she has consistently described herself as a feminist and declared herself opposed to anti-PORNOGRAPHY movements. Her flamboyant personal style, abrasive to some, has garnered wide attention on the lecture circuit.

palimony, a popular term for a form of ALIMONY, paid voluntarily or under court order, to a companion on dissolution of an unmarried couple's relationship; the term stems from a highly publicized court case involving Michele Triola and film star Lee Marvin (see COHABITATION).

Pankhurst, Emmeline (1858–1928), Christabel (1880–1958), and Sylvia (1882–1960)

Pankhurst, Emmeline (1858–1928), **Christabel** (1880–1958), and **Sylvia** (1882–1960), militant suffragists, a mother and her daughters, who were key leaders of the successful British WOMAN SUFFRAGE movement of the early twentieth century. Emmeline Pankhurst and her husband, barrister Richard Pankhurst, worked together as liberals and then socialists and as WOMEN'S RIGHTS activists from their MARRIAGE in 1879 through his death in 1898. She then moved from London to Manchester, where she and her daughter Christabel in 1903 founded the WOMEN'S SOCIAL AND POLITICAL UNION (WSPU), the direct-action organization that spearheaded the militant side of the British fight for woman suffrage.

During the next eleven years she led an increasingly powerful and bitter struggle for woman suffrage; she was frequently arrested and in 1913 began to encourage arson and other violence directed against property in a highly successful campaign to focus public attention on the suffrage issue. Her leadership also survived splits in the woman suffrage movement; she and her daughter Christabel were criticized sharply for their rather autocratic leadership style and in 1912 for removing their early colleagues Emmeline and Richard PETHICK-LAWRENCE from the WSPU leadership.

In 1914, with the outbreak of World War I, Emmeline Pankhurst's militant activities came to a stop. She fully supported the British war effort, breaking with her daughter Sylvia and many other feminist militants, who opposed the war. There is considerable evidence suggesting that she had at least a tacit government promise of postwar woman suffrage in return for her war support; whether suffrage would have come after the war in any event is still a matter of some debate. She did not go on in the women's movement after the war and the winning of partial woman suffrage in 1918. She lived abroad in the early 1920s and was active in the Conservative party on her return to Britain in 1926.

Christabel Pankhurst was the leading organizer of the WSPU; often arrested, she led the organization from exile in France from 1912, as she was under threat of prosecution in Britain. A lawyer and writer, she edited *The Suffragette* and published a series of articles on venereal diseases (see SEXUALLY TRANSMITTED DISEASES), issued in 1913 as the book *The Great Scourge and How to End It*. She joined her mother in supporting World War I, and did not rejoin the women's movement after the war, turning after 1920 toward Christianity and the Second Coming.

Sylvia Pankhurst, an artist, was active in the WSPU. In 1914, she broke with her mother and sister over her opposition to the war, and founded the socialist periodical *Worker's Dreadnought* (1914–1924); she was a communist for a short time after the war. An antifascist during the interwar period, she became deeply involved in the Ethiopian resistance to Italian invasion, beginning a lifelong interest in that country; she lived in Ethiopia from 1956 to 1960. (See also WOMAN SUFFRAGE.)

You have to make more noise than anybody else, you have to make yourself more obtrusive than anybody else, you have to fill the papers more than anybody else, in fact you have to be there all the time to see that they do not snow you under, if you are really going to get your reform realized.

EMMELINE PANKHURST, 1913
————————— IN THE SPEECH "WHEN CIVIL WAR IS WAGED BY WOMEN" —————————

•

Pap smear, a test designed to detect cancerous or precancerous cells in a woman's CERVIX; also called the *cervical smear*, or more fully *Papanicolaou test*, after its developer. Simplicity itself, the test requires a small sample of cells and mucus that is painlessly scraped away from the end of the cervix and then analyzed under a microscope for signs of abnormal cells *(cervical dysplasias)* that might be warnings of current or developing CANCER. The samples can also be analyzed to assess a woman's ESTROGEN production and for some common vaginal infections, such as CHLAMYDIA. If abnormalities are found, the doctor will generally follow up with a biopsy (sample) of the questionable tissue.

Women are advised to have a Pap test regularly, from the beginning of sexual activity, every 2 to 3 years after three consecutive normal tests, but at least annually for women with many sex partners. Women with a history of HERPES or those at high risk for cervical cancer may be tested more often, as their doctor recommends. (See UTERINE CANCER.)

parent, the FATHER or MOTHER of a child of any age. PARENTS' RIGHTS and associated responsibilities are generally defined by law, in the United States also protected by the Constitution. Related CHILDREN'S RIGHTS are still a developing area of the law, in such areas as CHILD ABUSE AND NEGLECT or ABANDONMENT.

parental access, an alternative term for VISITATION RIGHTS.

Parental Locator Service (PLS), a U.S. federal branch that helps locate absent PARENTS, generally to obtain CHILD SUPPORT but also to pursue cases of parental kidnapping (see CUSTODY). It is a service of the Office of Child Support Enforcement (OCSE), an arm of the U.S. Department of Health and Human Services. (Call the Federal Information Center, 800-347-1997, for the nearest regional office.) The federal PLS (FPLS) conducts computer searches through income tax records, SOCIAL SECURITY records, and the like, while on the state level the PLS scans voter registration, car registration, driver's license, welfare, prison and worker's compensation records. Though slow, these services are a boon to women without the resources to pay for a private investigator. Women should not neglect to try other avenues first, however, including friends, relatives, colleagues, and their own personal knowledge about the missing parent's interests, habits, and associations.

parents' rights, parents' legal rights to have CUSTODY and supervision of their children and to make basic decisions affecting their welfare, including their medical care, whether children are minors or adults sufficiently disabled not to be able to care for themselves. Associated with these rights (though less clearly defined legally) are parents' responsibilities, among them to provide the basic necessities of life, such as food, clothing, shelter, and medical treatment; to see that the child is educated; to provide supervision, discipline, and control; to protect and guide the child; and more generally to show love and concern.

In the United States, parents' rights are protected under the Constitution. They are not absolute, however. Parents can voluntarily give up their parental rights, as when they place a child for ADOPTION. In cases of SEPARATION OR DIVORCE, one parent may lose custody, though retaining VISITATION RIGHTS.

Parents can also lose their parental rights by failing to provide proper care or supervision, as in cases of ABANDONMENT or CHILD ABUSE AND NEGLECT. The legal proceeding that negates parents' claims on their child is called *termination of parental rights (TPR);* if TPR succeeds, the child can be placed for adoption without formal consent from the parents. TPR is undertaken generally by the state, but sometimes by foster parents who wish to adopt a child in their care. In a landmark 1992 case, a child—twelve-year-old Gregory Kingsley—successfully initiated termination of parental rights in his own name so that he could be adopted by his foster parents. As of 1993, the case was still under review.

If parents are unable to exercise control over children—such as juvenile delinquents, chronic truants, or runaways—the court may legally label the children *incorrigible,* take them under court supervision, and place them in foster care or an institution. Sometimes parents will voluntarily transfer their parents' rights to the state in such cases. The court can also declare a child a temporary ward of the state, to see that a child receives lifesaving medical treatment, when parents refuse consent (often for religious reasons). (See CHILD ABUSE AND NEGLECT HELP,

INFORMATION, AND ACTION GUIDE on page 152; DIVORCE AND SEPARATION HELP, IN-
FORMATION, AND ACTION GUIDE on page 238.)

Parents Without Partners (PWP) (8807 Colesville Road, Silver Spring, MD 20910; 301-588-9354 or 800-637-7974; ask for the information center), an organization of parents, with or without custody, who are single for whatever reason. It serves as a clearinghouse for information on single parenting and the special concerns associated with it, including child support, custody, and visitation rights, providing referrals for help. Members are referred to local chapters or, if none is nearby, can become members-at-large. PWP publishes many materials, including the magazine *The Single Parent;* the book *My Mom and Dad Are Getting a Divorce;* brochures such as *40 Tips for Better Single Parenting, Are You a Single Parent?, Single Parenting and Education,* and *Single Parenting and Legislation;* and bibliographies on divorce and single parenthood for various groups, including parents never married, widowed, separated, or divorced and children and teens. It also has information kits on family law for parents in varying situations such as noncustodial fathers, noncustodial mothers, never married mothers, and parents raising children alone; and information sheets on topics of concern to them, such as resource organizations, child support, visitation, and rights to examine school records.

paternity suit, a court proceeding to establish the legal FATHER of a child.

Patriarchal Attitudes (1970), Eve Figes's centerpiece work of the emerging British women's movement of the early 1970s, a history-based study that attacked male dominance, female subservience, and in particular the institution of MARRIAGE, which Figes felt was the greatest bar to real equality between the sexes.

patriarchy, in the widest sense, the domination of women as a group by men as a group, in families, clans, and other social units and in all of the other institutions and organizations of a culture, as well, from the smallest hamlet to the largest national or supernational body. That dominance expresses itself in every aspect of culture, notably *patriliny*—that is, the male-dominated line of succession in families and institutions—and equally notably the definition of women's sole legitimate roles as those of wives and MOTHERS.

In some cultures, including those loosely defined as "Judeo-Christian" in religious and philosophical origin, patriarchy has also been described as the domination of older men over younger, the model being the patriarchs of the Bible. That age distinction is still generally accepted for families and clan structures; an oldest man in a family may still be described as a patriarch, with great moral authority surviving the loss of economic and physical dominance.

But in the modern period, with the advent of democracy, the end of the dynasties, and the institution of early retirement, it is far harder to ascribe dominance to the older men in a culture, and patriarchy is often redefined as the domination of all mature men over all others in the culture. It is in this sense that the term *patriarchy* is most commonly used, in essence, as a synonym for "male supremacy" or "male chauvinism" and the modern continuation of very old male-centered attitudes and legal, economic, and social relationships destructive of women.

In this sense, every advance in the long fight for WOMEN'S RIGHTS, and for equality and full independence for women, is a victory over male supremacy, over patriarchal attitudes and structures. In this sense, Anita Faye HILL lost a battle when Clarence Thomas became a Supreme Court justice but made a powerful contribution to the fight against male supremacist SEXUAL HARASSMENT and for equality in the workplace and beyond. In this sense, the long road from SENECA FALLS in 1848 to the WOMAN SUFFRAGE amendment in 1920 was a massive victory in the fight for equality and against patriarchy.

For some feminist and antifeminist theorists, "patriarchy" is far more than a synonym for "male supremacy"; it is a formal description of a social, economic, legal, and political system designed to perpetuate male domination and the exploitation of women, especially the exploitation of women's bodies, basically meaning reproductive functions. Some feminists see formal patriarchy as a constant in human history; others see it as—however long—a passing phase in human history, to be replaced by either equality or MATRIARCHY. Some socialists, starting with Friedrich Engels, thought socialism a necessary prerequisite for women's equality. Other socialists, like radical feminist Shulamith FIRESTONE, thought the end of patriarchy would require both socialism and the end of the biological FAMILY. And some radical feminists, like Andrea DWORKIN and Marilyn FRENCH, have felt patriarchal domination and the victimization of women to be at the center of all human societies and describe the history of all societies as what French calls a very literal "war against women" that has been going on for at least four thousand years and includes epidemic mass RAPE and mass murder of women by men.

On the other hand, many antifeminists believe patriarchy is rooted in the differing biologies of the sexes, in allegedly aggression-producing testosterone levels and immutable sex-determined social roles (see SEX ROLES).

Modern historians and anthropologists generally consider formal historical patriarchy theories to be highly speculative, for there is very little solid and useful information to apply in the area, given the impossibilities of viewing live and current "primitive" societies as survivals from the past. What continues to be quite clear, however, is that all major human societies are dominated by men, who hold an overwhelming proportion of the positions of temporal and religious power, and that male supremacy—or patriarchy, if that is one's preferred term—is a fact, as is the continued dominance of male supremacist attitudes throughout the world. Many countries in the modern period have made substantial changes in such areas as woman suffrage, property and marital rights, and workplace rights; but male-supremacist or patriarchal ideas and institutions continue to hamper independence and progress for women in many spheres of life. (See SEXUAL DISCRIMINATION AND SEXUAL HARASSMENT HELP, INFORMATION, AND ACTION GUIDE on page 642.)

patriliny: See PATRIARCHY; FAMILY.

patrilocality, the settling of families along patriarchal lines, with new families living in the extended families and clans of the husband (see FAMILY; PATRIARCHY).

Paul, Alice (1885–1977), an early-twentieth-century leader in the fight for WOMAN SUFFRAGE, who continued and widened her equal rights work in the decades following passage of the NINETEENTH AMENDMENT. An American social worker and lawyer, Paul became a radical feminist while a student in Britain (1907–1912), joining the British suffrage movement and becoming an often arrested militant. She brought that militancy home with her in 1912, leaving the NATIONAL AMERICAN WOMAN SUFFRAGE ASSOCIATION to found the radical activist Congressional Union in 1913. With Lucy Burns she founded the NATIONAL WOMAN'S PARTY in 1916. Paul wrote the first version of the EQUAL RIGHTS AMENDMENT (**ERA**) in 1923, helping to keep it before Congress in some form until both houses passed the ERA in 1972.

pay equity, equal pay for work of comparable value; a hotly contested WOMEN'S RIGHTS issue from the late 1970s. Although the Equal Pay Act of 1963 mandated EQUAL PAY FOR EQUAL WORK—that is, equal pay for all people doing jobs calling for substantially equal skill, effort, and responsibility—if left untouched the massive wage discrimination created by the sex-segregated jobs held by more than two-thirds of American working women (see WORK AND WOMEN). The NATIONAL COMMITTEE ON PAY EQUITY has reported that "nearly half of all employed women are in occupations where at least 80 percent of the workers are woman," that "women of color are further clustered within female-dominated occupations into the lowest-paying," and that "the more women in an occupation, the lower the pay." (See THE WAGE GAP BY SEX AND RACE on page 537.)

Some feminists have proposed the setting of standards that equalize quite different kinds of jobs, by means of job evaluations that compare such factors as responsibility, skill, training, hazards, and working conditions. A few have gone much farther, advocating that jobs also be graded and pay set according to "social value," though they did address the question of who was to define or judge social value. Even without this question, however, pay equity evaluations are very hard to achieve, as for example between nurses and lawyers, managers and teachers, or for that matter between managers of nursing homes and law practices and managers of boutiques and golf clubs.

Difficult or not, many localities have passed comparable pay laws, which as of 1992 had yet to go through the entire process of court review, or adjudication. No U.S. federal statute has yet been adopted. Canada's Ontario legislature is regarded as the first to require pay equity in both public and private sectors through its 1987 Pay Equity Act. The question of pay equity is also a live one in the European community and several of its member states, most notably in the form of a 1979 nonbinding European Commission directive urging the adoption of pay equity policies. (See WORKING WOMEN'S HELP, INFORMATION, AND ACTION GUIDE on page 779; and SEXUAL DISCRIMINATION AND SEXUAL HARASSMENT HELP, INFORMATION, AND ACTION GUIDE on page 642.)

We want rights. The flour-merchant, the house-builder, and the postman charge us no less on account of our sex; but when we endeavor to earn money to pay all these, then, indeed, we find the difference.

—————————— *LUCY STONE, 1855* ——————————

•

THE WAGE GAP BY SEX AND RACE

Median† Annual Earnings Year-Round, Full-Time U.S. Workers (1990):

White Men	$28,881	100.0%
Black Men	$21,114	73.1%
White Women	$20,048	69.4%
Hispanic Men*	$19,136	66.3%
Black Women	$18,040	62.5%
Hispanic Women*	$15,672	54.3%

Note: The wage gap is a statistical indicator that is often used as an index of the status of women's earnings relative to men's and the status of African-American and Hispanics' earnings relative to White men's. White men's earnings are used as the basis for the comparison because they are workers not subject to race- or sex-based wage discrimination. The wage gap is often expressed as a percentage, as in "women are paid 71 percent of what men are paid" or "women earn seventy-one cents for every dollar paid to men," when the gap is stated as women's earnings relative to men's earnings. This figure is obtained by dividing women's median annual earnings by men's median annual earnings.

†The median is the midpoint; the number of people with income above the median is the same as the number below it.
*Persons of Hispanic origin can be of any race.

Source: Census Bureau, U.S. Department of Commerce, Current Population Reports, Consumer Income, Series P-60, no. 174, as reprinted in the National Committee on Pay Equity's *Newsnotes*, April 1992.

Pediculosis pubis, the formal name for PUBIC LICE.

PEER, an acronym for PROJECT ON EQUAL EDUCATION RIGHTS.

pelvic floor muscles, abdominal muscles that help hold the UTERUS in place. (See UTERUS; EXERCISES DURING AND AFTER PREGNANCY on page 561.)

pelvic inflammatory disease (PID), an infection of the upper parts of a woman's REPRODUCTIVE SYSTEM, including the UTERUS, OVARIES, FALLOPIAN TUBES, and nearby structures. Often caused by SEXUALLY TRANSMITTED DISEASES, most notably GONORRHEA and CHLAMYDIA (often together), PID results when disease-causing organisms travel from the VAGINA and CERVIX into the upper genital tract. The resulting infections can be acute, announcing themselves with noticeable symptoms such as fever or sharp pain, or they can be chronic, doing their damage silently and undetected over a long period of time, though often with some abdominal or pelvic pain.

Among the frequent results of PID is scarring of the narrow fallopian tubes. This is one of the most common causes of INFERTILITY, since scar tissue blocks the normal passage of the egg (OVUM) into the uterus. Such blockage leads to six to ten times the risk of an ECTOPIC PREGNANCY, a potentially life-threatening situation in which a fertilized egg becomes implanted in the fallopian tubes and starts to grow there. The amount of damage done depends on the number of episodes of PID—because infections can recur—and their severity; risk of complications increases with a woman's age.

Though a woman's symptoms and laboratory tests can indicate the presence of infection in the body, generally a LAPAROSCOPY is needed to confirm a tentative diagnosis of PID. Antibiotics and other medications are used in treatment, the type depending on the disease-causing organism involved. Sex partners are generally treated as well, even if they show no symptoms, to prevent reinfection of the original patient. In acute cases, and where ectopic pregnancy is suspected, a woman with PID may be hospitalized. In general, a woman who has had PID is advised not to use an INTRAUTERINE DEVICE (IUD) for CONTRACEPTION. (See SEXUALLY TRANSMITTED DISEASES; INFERTILITY; ECTOPIC PREGNANCY; also WOMEN'S HEALTH HELP, INFORMATION, AND ACTION GUIDE on page 334.)

penis, the main male organ for SEXUAL RESPONSE and for delivery of SPERM for possible FERTILIZATION of an egg (OVUM); also called a *phallus*. The penis is actually a shaft of spongy tissue that fills with BLOOD and becomes erect during sexual arousal, and that serves as the passageway for SEMEN and urine, both of which exit at the tip, called the *glans*. Made of the same tissue as a woman's CLITORIS, the penis is richly supplied with blood vessels and nerves and is extremely sensitive to stimulation, especially the glans (see EROGENOUS ZONES). The tip of the penis is protected by a partly retractable "hood" of skin called the FORESKIN or *prepuce.* For hygienic, medical, or religious reasons, the foreskin is sometimes removed, generally soon after birth, in an operation called *circumcision.*

During arousal, three longitudinal areas of spongy tissue within the penis fill with blood, while muscles tighten to prevent outflow. The two largest, the *corpora cavernosa,* lie on the upper part of the penis; on the lower side is the *corpus spongiosum,* through which runs the urethra, closed off to prevent passage of urine during sexual activity. When full of blood, the penis is firm and juts out from the body, in what is called an *erection,* rather than hanging down loosely. Some amount of erection is required for vaginal or anal penetration during SEXUAL INTERCOURSE and must be maintained for intercourse to continue and to proceed to ORGASM and EJACULATION of the sperm. On rare occasions a man may experience persistent erection, even in the absence of sexual arousal; this condition, called *priapism,* is potentially serious and can indicate presence of an infection or blood disease.

More common is the inability to achieve or maintain an erection; in fact, this generally temporary condition, called *impotence,* is believed to affect most men at some time during their lifetimes. It may be caused by a variety of psychological disorders, including stress, fatigue, and DEPRESSION; physical disorders, including DIABETES, hormonal imbalance (HORMONES), ALCOHOL AND DRUG ABUSE, and neurological problems; or medications, especially diuretics, blood pressure medications, antidepressants, and antipsychotics. Impotence is more common in older men; the causes are unclear but may include impaired blood circulation (see HEART AND CIRCULATORY SYSTEM), lower levels of the male sex hormone TESTOSTERONE, or lack of stimulation from a longtime sex partner. In cases of impotence, the first step should be a medical examination to determine if there are any underlying long-term and possibly serious physical causes, or if a change in medication might solve the problem. If not, counseling or sex therapy can often help a couple overcome temporary impotence (see SEXUAL RESPONSE).

When impotence does not respond to treatment or is permanent, as in cases of nerve damage, a *penile implant* may be employed. One type involves insertion of a silicone splint into the penis; this provides an erection sufficient to allow vaginal intercourse, though the penis does not increase in size. One concern is the possibility of reactions to silicone (see BREAST IMPLANTS; COSMETIC SURGERY). Another alternative is the insertion of an inflatable implant, with a small pump in the scrotum that can fill the penis with fluid, to allow for an erection and therefore intercourse; afterward, a small release valve allows the water to flow out. Such implants allow the male and his partner to continue pleasurable sexual activity, though without normal ejaculation. (See SEXUAL RESPONSE; SEX AND SEXUALITY HELP, INFORMATION, AND ACTION GUIDE on page 665.)

penis envy, in Freudian psychology, the theory that when young girls discover the anatomical differences between themselves and boys (see REPRODUCTIVE SYSTEM), they develop strong feelings of envy and desire to have a penis themselves, for which the longing for a child becomes a substitute.

pension equity: See INSURANCE AND PENSION EQUITY.

Pension Rights Center (918 16th Street, NW, Suite 704, Washington, DC 20006; 202-296-3776; Barbara Coleman, newsletter editor), the "only organization in the country that works full-time to protect the pension interests of workers and retirees." Founded in 1976, the center seeks to "educate the public about pension issues, protect and promote the pension interests of workers and retirees, and develop solutions to the nation's pension problems." The center acts as a pension advocate, aiding grass-roots groups and individuals to secure benefits often wrongly denied. Among the Center's current projects are

▶ *Women's Pension Project,* focusing on fairer pension policies for older women through its Women's Pension Advocacy Council. It operates the Clearinghouse on Pensions and Divorce, providing legal assistance to divorcing women and their lawyers on pension problems, and works with women's and retirees' groups for greater equity in pension laws, as with the OLDER WOMEN'S LEAGUE and the National Senior Citizen Law Center on a Women's Pension Policy Consortium. It also publishes booklets on pension issues for women, including *Your Pension Rights at Divorce: What Women Need to Know,* and professional legal information packets on the main federally regulated retirement systems, and maintains a computerized index of state court cases dealing with pensions and divorce.

▶ *Pensioners' Empowerment Project,* working to organize retirees to work for adequate pensions, seeking cost-of-living adjustments and stricter oversight of pension investments.

▶ *National Pension Assistance Project,* offering legal assistance to individuals with pension problems. It also conducts legal seminars, offers an information and referral service, and publishes a newsletter and fact sheets.

Center publications include *Protecting Your Pension Money, Can You Count on Getting a Pension?,* and *The Pension Plan [Almost] Nobody Knows About,* on Simplified Employee Pensions (SEPs).

percutaneous umbilical cord sampling, an alternative name for the PRENATAL TEST called CORDOCENTESUS.

perinatal care, medical care of a woman and new baby in the first twenty-eight days after CHILDBIRTH. More generally, care of a woman and her new baby after childbirth may be called *postnatal* or *postpartal care.*

perineum, the area of skin between the VAGINA and the ANUS and the associated muscles of fibrous tissues that lie underneath. During CHILDBIRTH, the perineum is stretched to allow DELIVERY of the baby. This process often causes tears in the skin; to prevent ragged tears and promote healing, obstetricians often make a clean cut in the perineum, a controversial procedure called an EPISIOTOMY.

period, a popular term for MENSTRUATION.

Perkins Act, a bill passed in 1990 by the U.S. Congress to provide equitable vocational education opportunities for women and girls, more formally called the Carl D. Perkins Vocational and Applied Technology Education Act. (See ED-UCATION; DISPLACED HOMEMAKERS.)

Persons of Opposite Sex Sharing Living Quarters (POSSLQ),

a census designation for couples living together (see COHABITATION).

Pethick-Lawrence, Emmeline (1867–1954), a British feminist and

social worker who emerged as a WOMAN SUFFRAGE movement leader when she and her husband, Frederick Lawrence, joined Emmeline PANKHURST in the WOMEN'S SOCIAL AND POLITICAL UNION (WSPU) in 1906. She became treasurer of the WSPU and a key and often arrested figure in the direct action and mass demonstrations of the period. She and her husband founded the periodical *Votes for Women* in 1907.

In 1912 the Pethick-Lawrences were ejected from the WSPU by the Pankhursts, after an internal power struggle. Without contesting their expulsion, they then joined the United Suffragists and continued their work. Emmeline became a leading pacifist and was later president of the Women's Freedom League, while Frederick became a Labour Member of Parliament.

phallocentric, like ANDROCENTRIC, a term describing anything that places the male at the center of things; "phallus" being a synonym for penis, the term—often used negatively—connotes an overbearing emphasis on male issues. Some who use the term *phallocentric* trace it more specifically to Freudian psychology.

PHS Action Plan for Women's Health, a document drafted by the

Public Health Service (PHS) Committee on Women's Health Issues, intended to establish which women's health issues should receive priority during the decades of the 1990s. Developed by the Federal Office of Women's Health (see page 542), itself established by pressure from women's advocates, the action plan calls for various kinds of programs, including

- a comprehensive survey of health care services and (personnel effectiveness) and availability for women.
- exploration of ways to improve access to medical care, especially for minority and underserved women.
- research to ensure the safety of drugs and medical devices used by women.
- identification of health hazards.
- prevention and control of diseases.
- promotion of healthy life-styles.

The plan specifically targets certain kinds of diseases and disorders of concern to women, including heart disease (see HEART AND CIRCULATORY SYSTEM), AIDS and other SEXUALLY TRANSMITTED DISEASE, autoimmune diseases (see IMMUNE SYSTEM; ARTHRITIS; LUPUS; MULTIPLE SCLEROSIS), OSTEOPOROSIS, and CANCER of various types, including LUNG CANCER and BREAST CANCER, which are increasingly serious among women. Other health concerns are reproductive health, MENOPAUSE, ALCOHOL AND DRUG ABUSE, SMOKING, and female participation as research subjects, where appropriate (see HEALTH EQUITY). As part of this effort, the FOOD AND DRUG ADMINISTRATION is developing health education programs to "support women in their efforts to learn about sound health practices and the safe use of products such as oral contraceptives." (For a copy of the plan, or more information, contact the Federal Office of Women's Health, Office of the Assistant Secretary for Health, 200 Independence Avenue, SW, Room 730-B, Washington, DC 20201; 202-690-7650.)

pica, a type of EATING DISORDER involving a compulsive desire to eat nonfood substances, such as dirt, clay, paint, laundry starch, chalk, wood, glue, or hair. This kind of craving often stems from a deficiency in NUTRITION and sometimes occurs during PREGNANCY, though it may also be linked with some MENTAL DISORDERS. (See EATING DISORDERS HELP, INFORMATION, AND ACTION GUIDE on page 58.)

pill, the, a popular name for BIRTH CONTROL PILLS (oral contraceptives).

pink ghetto, a sex-segregated occupation. (See WORK AND WOMEN.)

placenta, an organ that develops in the UTERUS during PREGNANCY to provide oxygen and other nourishment for the developing FETUS and to remove fetal waste products. After the fertilized egg is implanted in the lining of the uterus, (see IMPLANTATION), approximately a week after FERTILIZATION, its outer layer (the *chorion*) begins to develop into the placenta; it is connected to the fetus by a tube called the UMBILICAL CORD, which develops around the fifth week of pregnancy.

The blood of mother and baby do not meet directly, but oxygen, nutrients, and waste products are passed between them in the placenta, through minuscule fingerlike projections of tiny blood vessels. It is samples from these "fingers," called *chorionic villi*, that are analyzed in the PRENATAL TEST called CHORIONIC VILLUS SAMPLING.

The placenta also produces HORMONES, including ESTROGEN, PROGESTERONE, and HUMAN CHORIONIC GONADOTROPIN (**hCG**); several types of pregnancy tests test a woman's urine for signs of hCG. The placenta functions until the baby is born and is then expelled from the uterus, in what is called the *afterbirth*.

Normally IMPLANTATION and therefore growth of the placenta takes place in the upper central or side parts of the uterus. But sometimes the placenta is placed so low that it partially or completely covers the CERVIX, the neck of the uterus. One serious result of this condition, called *placenta previa,* is bleeding, including the possibility of a potentially life-threatening hemorrhage. Complete bed rest and even hospitalization may be recommended, and the baby is often delivered by CESAREAN SECTION, especially when the cervix is completely blocked.

The other main problem is *abruptio placentae,* in which the placenta separates prematurely from the uterine wall, an event often signaled by vaginal bleeding. The degree of separation is often assessed through an ULTRASOUND scan. If bleeding is light and separation only partial, the pregnancy may continue, though bed rest may be recommended for the duration of GESTATION. But if bleeding is heavy and the separation is great, the baby is often delivered immediately, either by induction of LABOR, where appropriate, or CESAREAN SECTION. Women with PREECLAMPSIA, anemia (see BLOOD), and high blood pressure (see HEART AND CIRCULATORY SYSTEM) are more likely to have abruptio placentae; SMOKING and physical trauma, such as an accident, can also increase the risk of premature separation. (See PREGNANCY.)

placenta previa, a PLACENTA placed abnormally low in a woman's UTERUS during PREGNANCY (see PLACENTA).

Planned Parenthood (Planned Parenthood Federation of America [PPFA], 810 Seventh Avenue, New York, NY 10019; 212-541-7800 or 800-829-7732; Pam Maraldo, president), a key organization in BIRTH CONTROL and REPRODUCTIVE RIGHTS. It is the successor of America's first birth control clinic, founded by Margaret SANGER in 1916, and of her American Birth Control League (founded in 1921) and the Birth Control Clinical Research Bureau (1923), renamed the Planned Parenthood Federation in 1942. Both historically and currently, the PPFA has been important in providing medical, educational, and counseling services relating to family planning and has proved a strong advocate of reproductive rights in general. Through its network of hundreds of centers, staffed by trained health professionals aided by thousands of volunteers, it provides information about CONTRACEPTION, spacing of children, and so-called safe sex and the avoidance of SEXUALLY TRANSMITTED DISEASES, including AIDS; since *Roe* v. *Wade* it also makes ABORTION available, as well as contraceptive devices and instructions on how to use them, PREGNANCY tests, INFERTILITY diagnoses, PRENATAL CARE, ADOPTION referrals, voluntary STERILIZATION, screening for BREAST CANCER or CANCER of the CERVIX (see UTERINE CANCER), anonymous or confidential testing for HIV (the virus that causes AIDS), and counseling in these and related areas. More recently, the PPFA has begun training doctors in abortion techniques, no longer taught in some medical schools.

In the United States alone, Planned Parenthood served nearly three million people in more than nine hundred clinics in 1991. Among its special emphases are the First Things First program, aimed at "too early childbirth" among American teenagers; African-American Men for Choice, seeking to "more fully engage African-American men in the struggle to preserve American's reproductive rights"; and sex education, working to help parents, schools, and others to provide young people with comprehensive education on sexuality.

The PPFA also supports and monitors development of new methods of CONTRACEPTION, as through the **Alan Guttmacher Institute (AGI)** (2010 Massachusetts Avenue, NW, Washington, DC 20036; 202-296-4012; Jeannie Rosoff, executive director), which it partly supports; provides ongoing medical training for its staff; and campaigns to educate the public and influence legislators and policy makers on related matters, as through its **Planned Parenthood Action Fund,** working on topics such as overturning the Title X "gag rule" designed to restrict health professionals from providing information on abortion; advocating widespread availability of the so-called abortion pill, RU486; and participating in legal action to maintain and widen abortion rights.

Planned Parenthood publishes many materials, including the biweekly internal newsletter *INsider;* the bimonthly newsletter *LINKLine; Current Literature in Family Planning,* a monthly annotated bibliography of works on family planning; *Adolescent Sexuality,* an annual annotated bibliography of works on teens and sexuality; *Guidelines for Comprehensive Sexuality Education;* numerous pamphlets and booklets on topics such as AIDS, abortion, and birth control in general; and a resource catalog of publications, videos, and other materials on birth control, sexuality, and reproductive health and rights. PPFA also maintains a data base of audiovisual materials related to family planning, and PPXNET, a national telecommunications network linking its offices.

In addition to its national office in New York City, a legislative and public information office in Washington, D.C., and regional offices in the United States (in Atlanta, San Francisco, and Chicago), it has three international regional offices, in Bangkok, Thailand, for Asia and the Pacific; in Miami, Florida, for Latin America; and in Nairobi, Kenya (with a suboffice in Lagos, Nigeria), for Africa; and also aids developing countries through its **Family Planning International Assistance (FPIA).** PPFA is a member of the London-based **International Planned Parenthood Federation (IPPF)** (Halfdan Mahler, secretary-general), which includes family planning associations from more than 130 countries; and the **International Service Agencies (ISA)** (Richard J. Leary, executive director), a federation of nonprofit groups that provide medical, emergency, relief, development, and other such services overseas. During 1992, Planned Parenthood extended its activities to Russia, where the previous lack of family-planning services had led to the health-endangering practice of abortion as the main means of birth control.

A REASON FOR BEING:
THE MISSION STATEMENT OF THE
PLANNED PARENTHOOD FEDERATION OF AMERICA

Planned Parenthood believes in the fundamental right of each individual, throughout the world, to manage his or her fertility, regardless of the individual's income, marital status, age, national origin, or residence. We believe that reproductive self-determination must be voluntary and preserve the individual's right to privacy. We further believe that such self-determination will contribute to an enhancement of the equality of life, strong family relationships, and population stability.

Based on these beliefs, the mission of Planned Parenthood is

- to provide comprehensive reproductive and complementary health care services in settings that preserve and protect the essential privacy and rights of each individual;
- to advocate public policies that guarantee these rights and ensure access to such services;
- to provide educational programs that enhance understanding of individual and societal implications of human sexuality;
- to promote research and the advancement of technology in reproductive health care and encourage understanding of their inherent bioethical, behavioral, and social implications.

Adopted by the Planned Parenthood Federation of America in 1984.

Planned Parenthood* v. *Casey, a 1992 U.S. Supreme Court ruling on a Pennsylvania ABORTION law that specifically reaffirmed *Roe* v. *Wade,* indicating that laws prohibiting all or most abortions would be considered unconstitutional; but it also affirmed the states' rights to place restrictions on the providing of abortions, as long as they do not pose an "undue burden." (See ABORTION; also THE U.S. SUPREME COURT ON ABORTION on page 9.)

Planned Parenthood* v. *Danforth, the 1976 U.S. Supreme Court ruling that struck down a Missouri law requiring a married woman to obtain her husband's consent for ABORTION.

plastic surgery, surgical procedures to repair or reconstruct SKIN and underlying tissue, cartilage, and bone. Such work may be done for medical reasons, to correct BIRTH DEFECTS, or repair damage from injury or disease; this is generally called *reconstructive surgery*. But a large proportion of plastic surgery operations are discretionary, done primarily to improve appearance, and are generally called COSMETIC SURGERY.

PMS, an abbreviation for *premenstrual syndrome* (see MENSTRUATION).

polar body, the segment of genetic material that is cast aside in the making of an egg (OVUM); it disintegrates quickly (see OVARY).

political participation, the ability for any group to vote in elections to all public offices, to be eligible to all public offices, to have access to jobs at every governmental level, and to participate in making and carrying through public policy, with men and women operating on equal terms in every respect; it is a major worldwide concern and goal for modern women.

Women's participation in political processes has developed greatly in the past two centuries, with women reformers and revolutionaries alike emerging in many countries as highly visible, increasingly powerful forces on specific social issues and on issues facing entire societies. From SENECA FALLS in 1848 to the winning of suffrage in the United States, Britain, and many other countries in the twentieth century, hundreds of thousands of women have entered the political process worldwide, campaigning on WOMAN SUFFRAGE and a wide range of other WOMEN'S RIGHTS matters and led by women such as Elizabeth Cady STANTON, Susan B. ANTHONY, Lucy STONE, Sojourner TRUTH, Emmeline PANKHURST, Margaret SANGER, Julia Ward HOWE, Carrie Chapman CATT, Emma GOLDMAN, Lucretia MOTT, Anita AUGSPURG, Lida HEYMANN, and Nawal EL SAADAWI. From the first they were active on a wide range of other issues, as well: the antislavery movement, the TEMPERANCE MOVEMENT, the campaign for equal marital and property rights (see MARRIAGE; MARITAL PROPERTY), the campaign against child labor, and the many anarchist and socialist movements.

In the twentieth century, women quickly moved into the mainstream political parties and began to emerge in leadership roles, as did Eleanor ROOSEVELT, British Labour party leader Jennie Lee, Spanish Communist party leader Dolores Ibarruri ("La Pasionaria"), and Argentinian fascist Evita Perón. Women peace movement leaders also became world figures, as did Nobel Peace Prize winners Jane ADDAMS, Emily Greene Balch, and Alva Reimer Myrdal (see PACIFISM AND NONVIOLENCE).

The latter part of the twentieth century saw the emergence of several powerful women national leaders, including such world figures as India's Indira Gandhi and Britain's Margaret Thatcher, and such well-known world figures as Pakistan's Benazir Bhutto, the Philippines' Corazon Aquino, South Africa's Winnie Mandela, Nicaragua's Violeta Chamorro, and Burma's (Myanmar's) Aung San Suu Kyi. These leaders have been associated with large numbers of highly polit-

ically active women, including many leaders of the second wave women's movement and large numbers of elected and appointed officeholders.

The number of women candidates in the 1992 United States elections
signaled a very wide movement of women into national-level American politics.
That move had already occurred at the state and local levels and was accelerating;
the percentage of women in state legislatures went from 4.8 percent in 1971 to
18.2 percent in 1991 (in absolute numbers, from 362 to 1369), and the percentage of women mayors in cities with populations of more than 30,000 went from
1.1 percent to 17.1 percent (from 7 to 151) in the same period. (See PERCENTAGE
OF FEMALE AND MALE OFFICEHOLDERS IN AMERICAN POLITICS on page 549.) The EM-
POWERMENT of women in politics was developing even more quickly in several
European countries, most notably in Norway (led by Prime Minister Gro Harlem
Brundtland), Sweden, Denmark, Iceland, and the Netherlands. Millions of
women are also active in the whole range of issue-oriented political groups, as in
social justice and environmental organizations. A view of the entire world shows
progress in women's political participation in many countries—but also shows
that a great deal has yet to be done, and that much of the world is as yet little
touched by women's political participation. (See POLITICAL PARTICIPATION HELP,
INFORMATION, AND ACTION GUIDE, below.)

WE'VE COME A LONG WAY . . .

Were our state a pure democracy, there would still be excluded from our
deliberations women, who, to prevent depravation of morals and ambiguity
of issues, should not mix promiscuously in gatherings of men.

Thomas Jefferson

POLITICAL PARTICIPATION

Help, Information, and Action Guide

Organizations

▶ CENTER FOR AMERICAN WOMAN AND POLITICS (CAWP) (908-828-2210).
Has a Subscriber Information Service (SIS), and publishes *CAWP News
& Notes;* fact sheets on women in office and on special topics such as the

gender gap, sex differences in voter turnout, and women of color in elective office; and reports such as *Gender and Policymaking: Studies of
Women in Office, The Impact of Women in Public Office,* and *Reshaping
the Agenda: Women in State Legislatures.*

▶ LEAGUE OF WOMEN VOTERS (202-429-1965). Publishes the quarterly *The
National Voter,* the periodic newsletter *League Action Service (LAS): Report from the Hill,* Action Alerts on topical issues before Congress, and
a host of other publications in areas such as How to Be Politically Effective, Election Services, Debates, National Government, State and Local
Government, International Relations, Natural Resources, Social Policy,
Public Relations, and local voter guides.

▶ CONGRESSIONAL CAUCUS FOR WOMEN'S ISSUES (202-225-6740).

▶ FUND FOR THE FEMINIST MAJORITY (617-695-9688; or 703-522-2214; or
213-651-0495). Publishes *Feminist Majority Report, Empowering Women,
The Feminization of Power: 50/50 by the Year 2000, The Feminization of
Power: An International Comparison.*

▶ NATIONAL BLACK WOMEN'S POLITICAL LEADERSHIP CAUCUS (202-529-2806).

▶ NATIONAL HOOK-UP OF BLACK WOMEN (NHBW) (312-643-5866).

▶ CLEARINGHOUSE ON WOMEN'S ISSUES (CWI) (301-871-6016; or
202-363-9795).

▶ LAWYERS' COMMITTEE FOR CIVIL RIGHTS UNDER LAW (202-371-1212).

▶ NATIONAL CONFERENCE OF PUERTO RICAN WOMEN (NACOPRW) (CONFER-
ENCIA NACIONAL DE MUJERES PUERTORRIQUEÑAS, INC.) (202-387-4716).

▶ COMMISSION FOR WOMEN'S EQUALITY (CWE) (212-879-4500).

▶ HUMAN RIGHTS CAMPAIGN FUND (202-628-4160; or 800-777-HRCF
[4723]).

▶ MS. FOUNDATION FOR WOMEN (MFW) (212-353-8580).

▶ CHURCH WOMEN UNITED (CWU) (212-870-2347). Publishes the quarterly
newsletter *UN Update* and action alerts on national legislation affecting
women and children.

◪ FOR DIRECT SUPPORT OF CANDIDATES

▶ WOMEN'S CAMPAIGN FUND (WCF) (202-544-4484). Bipartisan, pro-choice.

▶ NATIONAL WOMEN'S POLITICAL CAUCUS (NWPC) (202-898-1100). Biparti-
san, pro-choice. Publishes the newsletter *Women's Political Times, Fact
Sheet on Women's Political Progress, Political Campaigning: A New Decade,
The Appointment of Women: A Survey of Governors' Cabinets 1989–1991,
Don't Miss That Appointment!, National Directory of Women Elected
Officials 1991,* and *How to Change the World: A Woman's Guide to Grass-
roots Lobbying.*

▶ EMILY'S LIST (202-887-1957). Democrats, pro-choice.

▶ WISH LIST (WOMEN IN THE SENATE AND HOUSE) (908-747-4221). Republicans, pro-choice.

■ ON INTERNATIONAL CONCERNS

► WOMEN'S ENVIRONMENT AND DEVELOPMENT ORGANIZATION (WEDO) (212-759-7982).

► UNITED NATIONS DEVELOPMENT FUND FOR WOMEN (UNIFEM) (212-906-6400). Publishes *The World's Women: Trends and Statistics 1970–1990.*

► WOMEN'S INTERNATIONAL RESOURCE EXCHANGE (WIRE) (212-741-2955). Publishes *Women at War: Peru's Shining Path, Women and the Gulf War, Women in the Intifada, Jewish Women's Call for Peace: A Handbook for Jewish Women on the Israeli-Palestinian Conflict, On the Questions of Women in South Africa,* and *Women in the Algerian Liberation Struggle.*

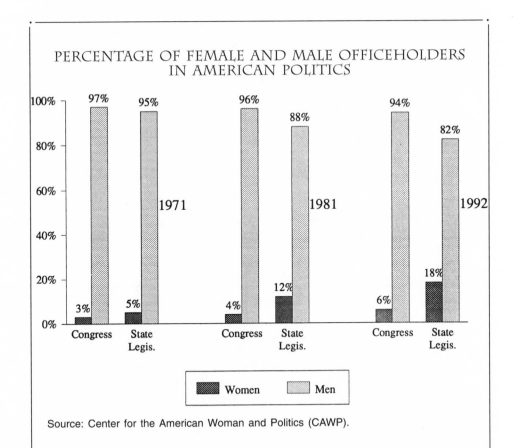

PERCENTAGE OF FEMALE AND MALE OFFICEHOLDERS IN AMERICAN POLITICS

Source: Center for the American Woman and Politics (CAWP).

polyandry, the condition of a woman having several husbands (see POLYGAMY).

polycystic syndrome (ovaries), an alternative name for STEIN-LEVENTHAL SYNDROME.

polygamy, the condition of a woman having two or more husbands at the same time *(polyandry)*, or a man two or more wives *(polygyny)*. In places where that is a crime, the term BIGAMY is more often used, even though *bigamy* more precisely refers to having two spouses simultaneously. In all parts of the United States, and in most of the rest of the world, polygamy is illegal.

In some cultures and religious groups, polygamy is still accepted and quite legal, though the social and legal trend is certainly against it. The Mormons, once polygamous, have generally adopted MONOGAMY, except for some small groups that exist outside the law. Polygamy still occurs in Muslim cultures, but its existence is declining. Usually it has not been banned outright, despite women's movements against it; more often laws have been instituted to protect WOMEN'S RIGHTS to a greater extent in polygamous MARRIAGES. Because these often required that all wives be treated equally, and therefore required more financial support from the husband, polygamy is generally restricted to a small, affluent elite; in Egypt, for example, less than 3 percent of marriages involve polygamy. (See MARRIAGE; also COUPLES AND FAMILIES HELP, INFORMATION, AND ACTION GUIDE on page 418.)

polygyny, the condition of a man with several wives (see POLYGAMY).

polymenorrhea, periods that arrive in cycles shorter than twenty-two days (see MENSTRUATION).

pornography, in general, material created with the intent to arouse sexual feelings; but in practice, a term whose very definition has been a major social and legal battleground. In the United States, various liberal, moderate, and conservative Supreme Courts, returning to the questions again and again, have found pornography extremely difficult to define, much less regulate.

Those who accord primacy to the First Amendment, liberals and conservatives alike, have in the modern period insisted with some success that pornography is impossible to define, and that the principle of freedom of expression demands that such books as *Ulysses, Lady Chatterley's Lover, Tropic of Cancer,* and *Fanny Hill*—all at one time barred from publication in the United States—be published, although all continue to be objectionable to large numbers of Americans. They also had to resist censorship for a remarkably large range of other works, from *Catcher in the Rye* and *Huckleberry Finn,* both sometimes banned, to print and broadcast works of highly sexual content, to WOMEN'S RIGHTS MOVE-

MENT works, especially those relating to BIRTH CONTROL, ABORTION, or other sexual matter, which have also been banned often, and in many countries.

On the other side of the issue have been those conservatively inclined Americans who wish to ban all or some of the above for a variety of reasons, including what they felt were lewdness, obscenity, indecency, immorality, and deviation from religious teachings. Many of these people, often sincerely and devoutly religious, felt that they had no difficulty at all in understanding what pornography was and what to do about it.

First Amendment advocates deplored much of the sexually explicit material they felt forced to defend and even more strongly deplored all steps toward its censorship, feeling that any censorship was the thin edge of the antidemocratic wedge. Conservative antipornography crusaders hailed all attempts at censorship of sexually explicit materials as blows struck for FAMILY and country and deplored the successes of First Amendment defenders.

Starting in the mid-1970s, the American women's rights movement experienced quite a severe breach, which continues today. A group of radical feminists, led by writer Andrea DWORKIN and lawyer Catharine MacKinnon, strongly advanced the position that pornography was, in essence, an attack on women's civil rights and that such "injurious speech" was not protected by the First Amendment. They felt that what they saw as pornography was SEXUAL DISCRIMINATION that debased women and led to physical attacks upon them. MacKinnon and Dworkin proposed a model law that defined and prohibited a very wide range of words and pictures, from depictions of sexual torture to depictions of women "dehumanized as sexual objects" or "presented in postures or positions of sexual submission, servility, or display." They were supported by a number of other radical feminists and by a few who went beyond the law to vandalize and burn bookstores they called pornographic. They were sharply opposed by the main body of the woman's movement and its leadership, some of them organized into the Feminist Anti-Censorship Task Force, and by the AMERICAN CIVIL LIBERTIES UNION. In 1983 the conservative-dominated City Council of Indianapolis (of which William H. Hudnut III was then mayor) adopted a law based on the MacKinnon-Dworkin model. In 1986, in *American Booksellers Association* v. *Hudnut,* the Supreme Court responded by declaring the Indianapolis law (and others on the same model) unconstitutional violations of the freedom of expression guaranteed by the First Amendment.

The long argument continues, on many fronts. For example, in February 1992 the Supreme Court of Canada upheld an antiobscenity law and redefined obscenity as including that which subordinated or degraded women. But in the United States, the Supreme Court in a related June 1992 landmark case voided a St. Paul, Minnesota, law that criminalized speech or behavior that "caused anger or alarm" because of its treatment of "race, creed, color, religion, or gender."

The argument also has its ironies: In 1990, artists Karen Finley, Holly Hughes, John Fleck, and Tim Miller were denied National Endowment for the Arts (NEA) grants by NEA chairman John Frohnmayer because of their allegedly obscene work. Finley, a feminist, had created a work that attacked sexual abuse but was barred because it included strongly sexual, violent, and bloody scenes that depicted women and children experiencing sexual abuse. The case became a major feminist and civil liberties cause. (Ironically, in 1991 Frohnmayer lost his job, largely because he defended a grant for a very explicit and antiviolence film on HOMOSEXUAL themes, which the same radical conservatives who had attacked Finley attacked as homosexual pornography.) (See SEXUAL DISCRIMINATION AND SEXUAL HARASSMENT HELP, INFORMATION, AND ACTION GUIDE on page 642; SEX AND SEXUALITY HELP, INFORMATION, AND ACTION GUIDE on page 665.)

POSSLQ, an acronym for "Persons of Opposite Sex Sharing Living Quarters," a census designation for unmarried couples living together (see COHABITATION); pronounced "POSS-ul-cue."

postcoital test, one of a battery of tests in a *fertility workup*, performed to discover the causes of INFERTILITY; also called the *Sims-Huhner test*.

postfeminist, a self-description adopted by many women in the 1980s, to differentiate their view of FEMINISM from the radical feminist tactics of the late 1960s and early 1970s, reflecting a desire not to be identified with militant direct action in a period of antifeminist backlash. With the revitalization of the U.S. women's movement in the early 1990s, "postfeminist" fell into disuse, although "feminist" did not make much of a comeback, either; the term *women's movement* was heard more and more. (See also FEMINISM; RADICAL FEMINISM.)

postnatal care, medical care of a woman and new baby after CHILDBIRTH; also called *postpartal care*. Care offered during the first twenty-eight days after birth is also called *perinatal care*.

power: See EMPOWERMENT.

preeclampsia, a potentially serious condition, its cause unknown, that affects 5–7 percent of women during PREGNANCY, generally after the twentieth week. Among the symptoms are high BLOOD pressure (see HEART AND CIRCULATORY SYSTEM), *edema* (fluid buildup in the body), protein in the urine *(proteinuria)*, headaches, nausea and vomiting (see DIGESTIVE SYSTEM), abdominal pain, and blurred vision.

If unchecked, preeclampsia can cause severe, even life-threatening problems. The PLACENTA may separate prematurely, a condition called *abruptio placentae*, cutting off nourishment to the FETUS. Also, preeclampsia may develop into the much more serious *eclampsia*, in which symptoms become more severe, and seizures may develop, which can result in coma or death for both mother and baby. In fact, if the disorder reaches the stage of eclampsia, one out of ten mothers and one out of four babies will die. Eclampsia develops late in pregnancy, sometimes during LABOR or even shortly after DELIVERY. Its causes are unknown, but some have suggested that it results from a toxin (poison) produced by the placenta; in fact, some consider preeclampsia and eclampsia to be mild and severe forms of a condition they call *toxemia of pregnancy.*

Preeclampsia occurs most often in first pregnancies, in women between twenty and forty, especially those with a personal or family history of related disorders, such as DIABETES or kidney problems (see URINARY TRACT). Good NUTRITION, rest, and regular EXERCISE help lessen the risk of developing the disorder. Even if it does develop, it can be held in check with proper PRENATAL CARE, though the pregnancy would be considered a high-risk one. If severe symptoms do develop late in pregnancy, an emergency delivery is often performed—by CESAREAN SECTION, if necessary. Otherwise the woman is at risk for serious problems, such as kidney failure, liver damage, cerebral hemorrhage, convulsions, blood disorders, and hemorrhaging in the EYES, which can cause temporary blindness. The condition generally clears up quickly after CHILDBIRTH; however, body systems severely damaged by the condition may not be reparable. (See PREGNANCY; also PREGNANCY AND CHILDBIRTH HELP, INFORMATION, AND ACTION GUIDE on page 580.)

pregnancy, the growth of a new being in a woman's body and the changes the body makes in order to carry out its reproductive functions, from the moment of FERTILIZATION—the union of a woman's egg (OVUM) and a man's SPERM—to the baby's emergence, normally some nine months later, as a fully formed individual. In size, the new being will grow from a tiny speck to a baby approximately twenty inches long, normally weighing seven to eight pounds.

The growth takes an average of 266 days, a period known as GESTATION or *full term.* However, because the precise date of fertilization is generally unknown or uncertain, doctors traditionally calculate the *due date* or *delivery date* from the woman's *last menstrual period* (LMP). This is often two weeks before fertilization, so gestation is generally considered to be 9 ⅓ months, 40 weeks, or 280 days. Changes occur daily, but in general the term of pregnancy is divided into three periods of three months each, called *trimesters.* (For an overview of the changes, see WHAT HAPPENS DURING PREGNANCY on page 557.)

Normally, sperm and egg unite in the FALLOPIAN TUBES following vaginal SEXUAL INTERCOURSE. However, various other methods can be used to achieve fertilization, such as ARTIFICIAL INSEMINATION or *IN VITRO* FERTILIZATION, when a woman or her partner has problems that prevent her from conceiving normally (see INFERTILITY), or she wishes to have a child without a male sex partner (see SINGLE PARENT; LESBIAN). The new EMBRYO then normally moves to the UTERUS, where it implants itself and grows. If implantation takes place outside the uterus, it is called an ECTOPIC PREGNANCY and is a potentially life-threatening condition.

Most women first suspect they are pregnant when they miss a menstrual period, though monthly bleeding can stop for other reasons (see MENSTRUATION) and can continue during the early stages of pregnancy. Other common signs of pregnancy are sore or tender BREASTS; nausea, vomiting, heartburn, and reflux of stomach acids (see DIGESTIVE SYSTEM); fatigue, weight gain, and abdominal swelling; and fluid buildup *(edema)*. A woman's basal body temperature during pregnancy also remains steadily high, rather than varying in a monthly cycle, as is normal (see NATURAL FAMILY PLANNING). Pregnancy can be confirmed most reliably by various pregnancy tests, which usually measure the level of certain HORMONES—especially HUMAN CHORIONIC GONADOTROPIN, or hCG—in the urine or blood. Most home pregnancy tests involve urine testing, but blood testing done by doctors is generally considered more reliable, especially for older women. The U.S. Public Health Service recommends: "It is important to have a pregnancy test as soon as possible after you miss your first period or as soon as you think you might be pregnant. Some tests can be done as early as a few days after a single missed period." The PHS stresses that a woman should see her doctor *whatever* the result of the test, if the period does not arrive, since cessation of menstruation can be the signal of other health problems, some of them quite serious, such as ectopic pregnancy.

Early testing is important because the first two to three months of the baby's development are crucial. The sooner a woman knows she is pregnant, the sooner she can take steps to maximize her chances of having a healthy baby and to minimize risks to herself (see PRENATAL CARE). She will, for example, want to cease any activities that could cause BIRTH DEFECTS in the developing FETUS, such as SMOKING; drinking or taking "recreational" drugs (see ALCOHOL AND DRUG ABUSE for more on the dangers); taking any prescribed or over-the-counter medications, except when a doctor has specifically indicated that they are safe during pregnancy; exposing herself to radiation or poisons, as at work, which could damage the fetus; or engaging in potentially dangerous physical activities, such as downhill skiing (see EXERCISE). At the same time, she will want to identify quickly and treat any health problems that may adversely affect the pregnancy or her own health, including DIABETES (one form of which can be triggered by pregnancy); high blood pressure (see HEART AND CIRCULATORY SYSTEM); BLOOD disorders such as anemia and Rh incompatibility; lack of immunity to rubella (German measles); PREECLAMPSIA; and any SEXUALLY TRANSMITTED DISEASES, such as GONORRHEA, SYPHILIS, HERPES, and AIDS. In addition, a woman will need to adjust her daily diet to be sure that she is providing sufficient NUTRITION for two, following guidelines from her doctor (see NUTRITION; PRENATAL CARE).

And indeed, prenatal care concerns itself with not only the baby's healthy development, but also the woman's own long-term health. Pregnancy is not risk free. Maternal mortality—the number of deaths per a specified number of pregnancies—has declined significantly in recent centuries and especially in the twentieth century, but even in affluent countries with modern medical facilities, CHILDBIRTH, miscarriage, abortion, or pregnancy-related conditions cause the death of approximately eight women for every one hundred thousand pregnancies. In addition to better prenatal care and nutrition, the decline has been due to the availability of antibiotics to treat infections; blood transfusions to treat hemorrhaging or blood-type incompatibility; and information on and access to BIRTH CONTROL, important because it allows women to limit and space their pregnancies, giving their bodies time to recover fully in between. In fact, access to CONTRACEPTION has been a major factor in increasing women's LIFE EXPECTANCY in this century. Women most at risk during a pregnancy are those who lack proper prenatal care, especially those who are poor and not well educated; women under twenty; women over thirty; those having their first pregnancy; and those having over four pregnancies. Among the conditions that most often cause maternal death are high blood pressure (hypertension), eclampsia (see PREECLAMPSIA), ectopic pregnancy, and hemorrhaging before or after birth or abortion. Abortion, MISCARRIAGE, and CESAREAN SECTION are also associated with increased mortality risk.

Beyond mortality risk, pregnancy takes a toll on the body. The old saw "For every baby, a woman loses a tooth" is not true, but a woman can increase the likelihood of long-term health problems, such as OSTEOPOROSIS, if she has too many children too close together; has irreversible damage from pregnancy-related illnesses, such as eclampsia (see PREECLAMPSIA); or has inadequate nutrition, since her body will deplete its own reserves to provide for the baby. These are special concerns for teenage women, who have not yet completed their own physical growth, which may be limited by the drain on the body's reserves during pregnancy.

Because such questions are so important, some couples plan a pregnancy in advance, getting physical examinations to be sure they are in good health and starting exercise programs to see that they are physically fit before conceiving. When appropriate, some parents must also act beforehand to limit their exposure to potential environmental hazards, often job-related, such as chemicals or radiation (as for pilots and flight attendants); they may want to arrange for different work, if possible, before conceiving and during pregnancy. (See INFERTILITY.)

As part of their pregnancy planning, before or soon after conception, many couples will want to receive GENETIC COUNSELING. This focuses on the couples' personal and family medical history, especially any history of GENETIC DISORDERS, CHROMOSOMAL ABNORMALITIES, or difficulties during pregnancy, such as miscarriage or STILLBIRTH. After tests confirm a pregnancy, many couples have various other tests often as part of prenatal care, to screen for possible genetic disorders. Among these are AMNIOCENTESIS, ALPHA FETOPROTEIN, CHORIONIC VILLUS SAMPLING, and ULTRASOUND scans. If the fetus is found to have physical defects, the couple—though sometimes the MOTHER alone—must make some difficult decisions: whether to bear the baby with its defects and provide for its special needs; whether to have an elective ABORTION; or whether to see if the problem can be corrected through FETAL SURGERY, as some now can. Because time and planning are involved, the earlier such testing can be performed, the better.

Not all pregnancies are planned, of course. Because adolescent pregnancy is so common today—involving one in eight pregnancies in the United States—many people think of unexpected pregnancies primarily in terms of young, unmarried women. But unanticipated pregnancies can occur in women of any age or MARITAL STATUS. Unplanned does not necessarily mean unwanted, but it does mean that the woman is going to have a major, unexpected life-style change. The question of REPRODUCTIVE RIGHTS relates to precisely this question: Is the unanticipated life-style change that a pregnancy would bring acceptable, and can she cope with it? That basic question must be answered individually by each woman.

Many situations exist in which a woman could feel she is *not* able to cope with having a child: she might still be a teenager, growing herself, without job skills, often unmarried and still dependent on parents; she might not yet have completed her high school or college education; she might be a BATTERED WOMAN, who fears to bring into the world another child who may be abused; the pregnancy may be the result of sexual abuse (see RAPE; INCEST; CHILD ABUSE AND NEGLECT); she might already have more children they she can feed and provide for; she might not be making enough money at her job to provide for a baby, as a SINGLE PARENT, without going on welfare; she might fear that a pregnancy will break into and limit her career; or she might fear having a baby will endanger her own health. In these and other such situations, women sometimes choose to have an abortion, or to complete the pregnancy but then place the child for ADOPTION. Various organizations exist to help women in such difficult situations, often working confidentially (see PREGNANCY AND CHILDBIRTH HELP, INFORMATION, AND ACTION GUIDE on page 580; ABORTION HELP, INFORMATION, AND ACTION GUIDE on page 10; ADOPTION HELP, INFORMATION, AND ACTION GUIDE on page 19).

Whether the pregnancy is planned or unplanned, women who choose to bear and keep their babies have some months in which to make the plans necessary to reorient their lives. After the initial confirmation of pregnancy, a woman will need to make a whole range of decisions, sometimes on her own but often with her partner, on how she wants the birth to be handled and who she wants to oversee it (for a discussion of decisions in this regard, see CHILDBIRTH; DELIVERY). If she is still in school, she needs to think about when she should leave school and for how long and generally how she will complete her education or obtain needed job skills.

If a woman is employed, as today so many are, she needs to decide what her own long-term desires are regarding employment before discussing the pregnancy with anyone at work. In particular, she will need to decide whether she plans (assuming the birth proceeds normally) to return to work immediately, take a longer-term leave, continue in the labor force but in more flexible work (such as out of home), or leave the labor force and stay at home for a time (see MOMMY TRACK; HOMEMAKER). Once she has decided what she wants, she should explore how her firm or institution has handled other pregnancies, to determine the likelihood that her desires will be honored. She will also want to have her body in shape to meet the demands of pregnancy and LABOR (see EXERCISES DURING AND AFTER PREGNANCY on page 561). Many companies have liberal FAMILY AND MEDICAL LEAVE policies (broader versions of what used to be called *maternity leave*) and flexible work arrangements for new mothers, while others may summarily fire or demote a woman who announces that she is pregnant, despite the fact that in many areas such a response is against the law (see PREGNANCY DISCRIMINATION ACT). Women who plan to continue out-of-the-home employment will also have to make arrangements for CHILD CARE, which itself can take some months to put into place.

Beyond that, a woman will need to prepare herself for a new role as a MOTHER, understanding that today—even if she is married at the time—she may very well later become a SINGLE PARENT. (See PREGNANCY AND CHILDBIRTH HELP, INFORMATION, AND ACTION GUIDE on page 580.)

WHAT HAPPENS DURING PREGNANCY

At the start, the fertilized egg formed by the union of egg (OVUM) and SPERM is no larger than the dot over this letter *i*. This new being will normally grow for about nine months, a period known as GESTATION. Changes take place constantly, but traditionally gestation is divided into three periods of three months, called *trimesters*.

First Trimester

This is the most critical period of a pregnancy. During this first three months, the new being will grow to about three inches long and one ounce in weight and will develop all major organs, though these will not function independently for many months yet. At this early stage, alcohol and drugs (see ALCOHOL AND DRUG ABUSE), SMOKING, medications (including BIRTH CONTROL PILLS and SPERMICIDES), environmental hazards such as radiation or toxic chemicals, poor NUTRITION, untreated illnesses and diseases, and many other factors can harm a baby for life. That is why a woman should avoid such influences if she even suspects a pregnancy and should quickly schedule PRENATAL CARE. In case of BIRTH DEFECTS or GENETIC DISORDERS so severe as to be incompatible with life, a pregnancy may end spontaneously soon after it begins, often without a woman even knowing it. The new being's GENETIC INHERITANCE is determined at the point of FERTILIZATION.

During the first trimester, the mother will begin to experience the early signs of pregnancy. These include "morning sickness," or nausea (see DIGESTIVE SYSTEM; also TIPS FOR FIGHTING MORNING SICKNESS on page 229); tenderness and heaviness in the BREASTS, as glands develop for their milk-producing function; darkening and sensitivity of the nipples; frequent urination (see URINARY TRACT), triggered partly by hormonal changes; a weight gain of three to four pounds, usually around the waist, as the body begins to build up reserves; and lethargy and tiredness, due partly to sleeplessness from the hormonal changes and partly from the HORMONES themselves.

◪ FIRST MONTH

As soon as FERTILIZATION takes place, the fertilized egg begins to grow through division of its cells, moving slowly down the fallopian tubes and into the UTERUS. There, in roughly a week, it implants itself in the uterine wall and begins to grow there. Many health professionals regard that pregnancy only starts at the point of implantation, and that so-called MORNING AFTER PILLS act as neither CONTRACEPTION nor ABORTION, but as "interception." During implantation, some blood may be released, which can be mistaken for a period. Hormonal changes triggered by implantation are assessed in many early pregnancy tests.

Shortly after implantation, the AMNIOTIC SAC begins to form around the developing being, now generally called an EMBRYO. This sac fills gradually with amniotic fluid, which cushions the embryo from injury and pressure. This first trimester also sees the development of tissue called the PLACENTA, which supplies nourishment to the embryo, and the UMBILICAL CORD, which carries nourishment to and waste products away from the embryo. Samples of fluid or tissue from these organs are examined in PRENATAL TESTS such as AMNIOCENTESIS and CHORIONIC VILLUS SAMPLING. By the end of this first month, the head (including nose, mouth, and wide-apart fishlike eyes), heart, lungs, brain, spinal column, and genitals are beginning to develop, and the tiny heart is beating.

◪ SECOND MONTH

During this month the embryo comes to be known as a FETUS, a word meaning "young one." Arms and legs are developing from "limb buds," forming tiny hands, fingers, elbows, knees, ankles, and toes. Internal organs such as the stomach and liver develop. The head grows very large, compared to the rest of the body, and develops tiny ears and the beginnings of HAIR on the head.

◪ THIRD MONTH

Fingernails and toenails develop, as do external SIGNS of the new being's sexual organs. Movements of the hands, legs, and head, including opening and closing of the mouth, can be seen on ULTRASOUND though not yet felt by the mother.

The mother will generally feel warmer than usual, since the heart will have increased its amount of circulation by about a third, to supply the uterus and fetus. Her clothes will feel a little tight, as fat reserves are laid down not only in the midsection, but also in the arms and thighs.

Second Trimester

During these three months, many of the minor discomforts of pregnancy will disappear, and pregnant women often feel very good physically. They will often gain three to four pounds during each of these months, and during the fourth month they will usually begin to "show" and to feel more comfortable in maternity clothes, including a maternity bra. The fetus's heartbeat can be heard through a special instrument called a fetoscope. If she has not done so already, the mother will want to make her final decisions as to various CHILDBIRTH options during this trimester.

▨ FOURTH MONTH

Growing fast, the fetus weighs about six ounces and reaches about eight to ten inches long by the end of the month and begins to develop sucking and swallowing reflexes. The umbilical cord continues to develop, to provide enough blood and nourishment. During this month the mother usually feels a slight fluttering or "bubbling" sensation in the lower abdomen; this is movement of the baby, called *quickening*. The mother should write down the date she first feels this movement, as it helps the doctor to determine the due date.

▨ FIFTH MONTH

By the end of this month the fetus will weigh about a pound and be about a foot long. The heartbeat can be strongly heard, and movements become more noticeable. Nipples grow darker and wider, as breasts prepare to make milk. Many women will find themselves beginning to breathe more deeply and more frequently during this period.

▨ SIXTH MONTH

By the end of this sixth month, the second trimester, the fetus is a fully formed baby, about 1.5 pounds and fourteen inches long. It needs much more growth and development but, if born now, has a chance to survive with special care (see page 560). Skin is red and wrinkled, with virtually no fat underneath the skin. Movement picks up, and the baby can be seen to suck its thumb. The mother may develop a backache from the weight gain and pressure of the pregnancy. Low-heeled shoes provide balance and comfort; exercises can also help. (See **EXERCISES DURING AND AFTER PREGNANCY** on page 561.)

Third Trimester

This is the time during which the baby completes its growth and the development of its internal systems, such as the HEART AND CIRCULATORY SYSTEM and the RESPIRATORY SYSTEM. With the growth, the mother will generally experience discomfort—indigestion and frequent urination—from pressure on the stomach and bladder. Smaller meals and more frequent urination can ease symptoms. She will be gaining another three to four pounds a month. During this period, if not before, the mother should be making final preparations for the arrival of the baby.

◪ SEVENTH MONTH

The baby grows to about 2–2.5 pounds and 15 inches long and may suck its thumb, cry, and respond to external stimuli. The volume of fluid in the amniotic sac begins to decline, as does the nourishing function of the placenta. The baby becomes stronger and more active, as it kicks, stretches, and changes position, with movements that can sometimes even be seen on the abdomen. If born during this month, the baby has a relatively good chance of surviving. Women will often experience some swelling of the ankles, which can be eased by propping the feet up during the day or lying down.

◪ EIGHTH MONTH

With its eyes now open, the baby has grown to about four to five pounds and sixteen to eighteen inches long. Most organs and systems are well developed, except for the lungs; this can cause problems with premature birth (see below), but a baby born now has an excellent chance of surviving. During most of the pregnancy, the fetus lies in a head-up position in the uterus, but during this month the baby changes to a head-down position in preparation for birth, though some do not adopt an ideal position (see FETAL PRESENTATION). If she has not done so already, the mother will want to stop any heavy lifting or other work that causes strain and may want to take rest periods during the day, if possible.

◪ NINTH MONTH

As birth approaches, the baby settles farther down in the mother's pelvis, or "drops" (see LABOR for a fuller discussion). Once this takes place, the mother will often feel more comfortable and especially be able to breathe easier, though pressure on the bladder may increase the need for frequent urination and can cause incontinence (see URINARY TRACT). A baby born in the ninth month—that is, thirty-six to forty weeks from the mother's last menstrual period (LMP)—is considered to be a "full-term" baby, generally weighing six to nine pounds and being about nineteen to twenty inches long.

A baby born before the ninth month is described as *premature*. Why early birth occurs is unclear, but the risk of premature delivery is increased in adolescent pregnancies, with poor NUTRITION and with smoking, drinking, and use of DRUGS. Sometimes doctors may administer drugs to try to prevent or halt premature labor. Labor may be induced prematurely because the health of infant or mother is endangered, as in cases of PRE-ECLAMPSIA or DIABETES. Because their organs are small and not fully developed, premature babies often have health problems, and in the past many died; however, with modern medical technology, approximately four out of five babies born after twenty-eight weeks of development can be saved, and even some babies born after twenty-three weeks and weighing under two pounds have survived.

A baby born after forty-two weeks or more is called *postmature*. Because the placenta works less efficiently late in pregnancy, the baby will generally look gaunt and have wrinkled, peeling skin, since much fat has been lost from the body. The baby may also have serious chemical imbalances in the blood, especially of the minerals calcium and potassium (see KEY VITAMINS AND MINERALS on page 502), which require immediate treatment, to prevent neurological damage. Because the child is larger and its bones less malleable, a postmature birth is more difficult and damaging for the mother. Risk of STILLBIRTH increases. To avoid such problems, doctors will often induce LABOR or perform a CESAREAN SECTION by the forty-second week of gestation.

EXERCISES DURING AND AFTER PREGNANCY

Exercise

Exercise is very important to you and your baby. If you stay active you will feel better. Outdoor exercise and recreation give you a chance to get sunshine and fresh air. Walking is particularly good because it strengthens some of the muscles you will use in labor.

If you normally are active in sports, continue to enjoy them. However, it's wise to stop when you get tired. Also, try team activities instead of individual games, and avoid strenuous workouts. Do things with your friends and family—swim in a pool, dance, go on a picnic, and participate in light sports that pose no danger of falling or being bumped. If you are thinking of trying a new sport or exercise, or have been using a specific exercise routine, talk it over with your doctor or someone at the clinic.

Avoid lifting heavy objects and moving furniture while you are pregnant. Stretching will not harm you or your baby, but don't reach for things from a chair or ladder because you might lose your balance and fall. During the latter part of your pregnancy, you will probably begin to feel awkward because your balance is affected by your increasing size. At this point you may want to substitute walking for more active sports.

Here are some exercises that are useful for strengthening muscles used in labor and delivery. They are quite simple to do and can be practiced whenever you have an opportunity to sit for a few minutes.

Tailor Sitting

While seated on the floor, bring your feet close to your body, and cross your ankles. Maintain this position as long as it is comfortable to do so.

Tailor Press

While seated on the floor, bring the soles of your feet together as close to your body as is comfortable. Place your hands under your knees and press down with your knees while resisting the pressure with your hands. Count slowly to three, then relax. Gradually increase the number of presses until you are doing them ten times, twice each day.

Tailor Stretch

While seated on the floor and keeping your back straight, stretch your legs in front of you with your feet about a foot apart. Allow your feet to flop outward. Stretch your hands forward toward your left foot, then back; toward the center, then back; toward the right foot, then back. Gradually increase the sets of stretches until you are doing ten of them twice a day.

Kegel Exercise

This is sometimes called the Pelvic Floor Exercise because it is designed to strengthen the muscles in your pelvis. After you have practiced it, you will be able to relax your pelvic muscles for delivery. First, sit down. Then contract the lowest muscles of the pelvis as tightly as you can. Tighten muscles higher in the pelvis until you are contracting the muscles at the top. Counting slowly to 10 helps, tightening additional muscles at each number. Release slowly, as you count back from 10 to 1. You are developing control of the muscles so that you can stop at any point.

These muscles are the same ones you use to stop the flow of urine. To see if you are doing the Kegel exercise correctly, try stopping the flow of urine while you are urinating. Practice the exercise for several minutes two or three times a day.

An alternate method of doing the Kegel exercise is to tighten first the pelvic muscles, then the anal muscle. Hold a few seconds, then release slowly in reverse order.

Breathing Techniques

There are breathing techniques that you can practice while you are pregnant to help you relax during labor. They also help reduce muscle tension that works against the contractions and causes pain. If you are able to relax, you will be able to use the rest periods between labor contractions to reduce fatigue and build up your energy.

Relaxation

Lie down with your knees bent and feet on the floor. Breathe in once as deeply as possible, then hiss or blow the air out slowly through your mouth. Let yourself completely relax.

Practice Contraction

Pretend that you are having a contraction that lasts about 30 to 45 seconds. At the beginning of the contraction, take a complete breath and blow it out. Then breathe deeply, slowly, and rhythmically through the remainder of the practice contraction. Have your partner or coach go through this technique with you.

Abdominal Breathing

This exercise helps keep the abdominal wall relaxed and keeps the uterus from pressing against the lining of the abdomen. Lie down and place your hands on your abdomen. Breathe in slowly and fully, allowing your abdominal wall to rise gently. Hold this position for four to six heartbeats. Breathe out slowly and smoothly through the mouth, allowing your abdomen to fall. Relax. Repeat four or five times.

You can learn about other breathing techniques in prenatal classes or from your doctor.

Rest

Rest is just as important as exercise during pregnancy. Be sure to get plenty of sleep at night. Most pregnant women need about 8 hours of sleep but your needs may be different. You may also need to rest during the day.

There are some things you can do to keep from getting too tired. If your work requires you to be on your feet most of the day, try to sit down, put your feet up, and close your eyes whenever it is convenient. But if you spend most of your time sitting, get up and walk around for a few minutes every hour. When you are at home, take a nap during the day, especially if you have children who take naps. Plan a short rest period and really relax about the same time every day. When resting, you may find it more comfortable to use an extra pillow as shown in the illustration.

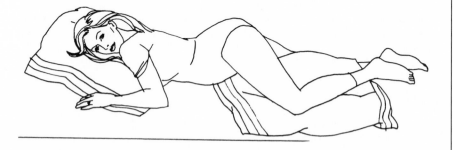

Try to find easier ways to do things. And ask other members of the family to share the workload. Perhaps someone else can help with the grocery shopping, laundry, and housework.

You should also know the best way to get out of bed:

a. Turn onto your side.

b. While bending your knees, use your arms to raise yourself up.

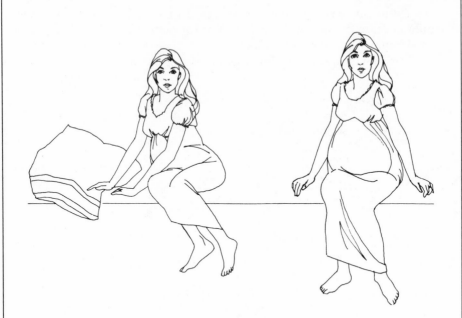

c. Lower your feet to the floor.

d. Sit upright for a few
moments and hold onto
the side of the bed.

e. Lean forward.

f. Use the muscles in your legs to rise.

Backache

As your pregnancy progresses, your posture changes because your uterus is growing and pulls on your back muscles. Your pelvic joints also loosen. This may cause backache. To help prevent strain, wear low-heeled supporting shoes. Your doctor may suggest a maternity girdle that gives support without binding.

Good posture is important in preventing backache. Try not to lift heavy objects, particularly if there is someone around who can lift them for you.

Here are several exercises that should help your back. Ask the nurse or someone at the clinic to help you do the exercises if you are not sure you are doing them correctly.

This squatting exercise helps avoid backstrain and strengthens muscles you will use in labor. This position is a good one for reaching low drawers or for lifting a child or an object weighing 15 to 30 pounds:

- Holding on to a heavy piece of furniture, squat down on your heels and allow your knees to spread apart. Keep your heels flat on the floor and your toes straight ahead. You may pick up the object from the floor by squatting, holding the object close to your body, and rising slowly, using your leg muscles.

The following exercise, called the "Pelvic Rock," increases the flexibility of your lower back and strengthens your abdominal muscles. It not only relieves backache, but will help improve your posture and appearance. Practice all the versions several times every day. Try walking and standing with your pelvis lifted forward as described below.

- When you practice the pelvic rock standing up, use a sturdy chair. Stand back 2 feet away from the back of the chair and bend slightly forward from your hips. Place your hands on the chair back and keep your elbows straight. Thrust your hips backward and relax your abdominal muscles. You now have a sway back. Bend your knees slightly, then slowly pull your hips forward. Tuck your buttocks under as if someone were pushing you from behind. Repeat.

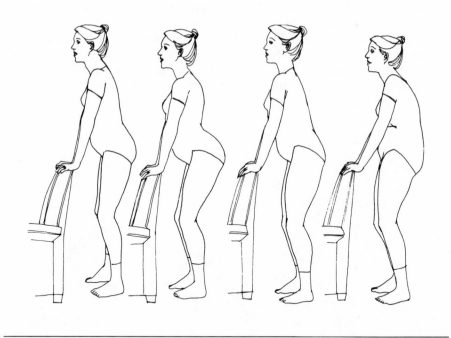

- Also practice the pelvic rock lying on your back with your knees bent and feet flat on the floor. Tighten your lower abdominal muscles and muscles of the buttocks. This elevates your tailbone and presses the small of your back to the floor. Then relax your abdominal and buttock muscles. As you do this, arch your back as high as you can. Rest for a minute, then repeat.

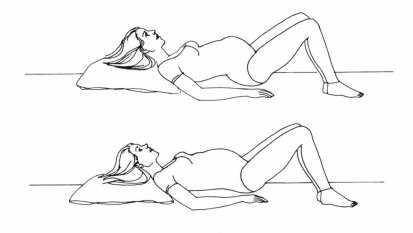

- In the third version of the pelvic rock, get down on all fours with your legs slightly apart and your elbows and back straight. While inhaling, arch your back using the muscles in your lower abdomen. As you exhale, slowly relax, allowing your back to sag. Return to the original position. Then repeat.

If you have a problem or pain doing these exercises, tell your doctor, nurse, or teacher.

Many community agencies, hospitals, and clinics offer special exercise classes for pregnant women. Exercises are also a part of most childbirth preparation classes. Talk to your doctor or nurse about the benefits of such classes and how you can enroll.

Getting Back into Shape

Getting out of bed and walking around is the first "exercise" you will do after childbirth. Do this as soon as you feel up to it.

With the approval of your doctor or nurse-midwife, exercises may be started 24 hours after a normal delivery. Regular mild exercising will strengthen your muscles and help you get back into shape. Lying on your abdomen will help your uterus return to its normal position. Your doctor or nurse may give you some exercises, or you may want to try some of these.

Lie flat. Breathe in deeply from your abdomen. Exhale all the air. Rest. Repeat 5 times.

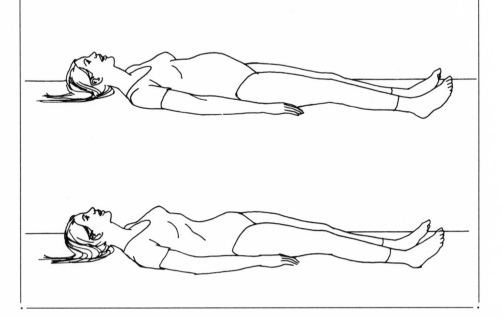

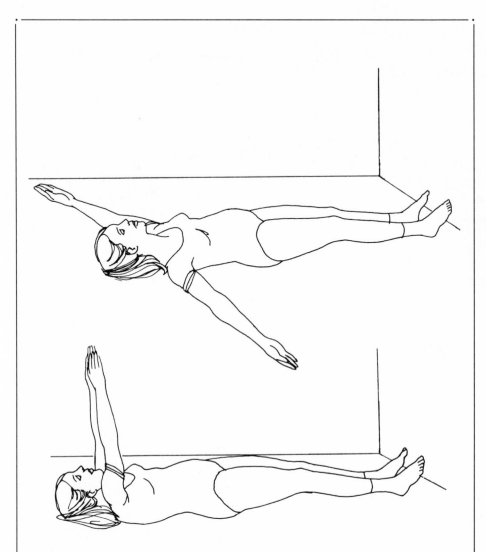

Lie flat with your arms out at your sides. With your elbows stiff, raise your arms until they are straight over your head. Bring your palms together. Lower your arms. Rest. Repeat 5 times.

Lie flat with your legs straight. Raise your head and one knee slightly. Reach toward that knee with the opposite hand. Relax, then repeat with the other hand and knee. Repeat the sequence 5 times.

The following exercises are designed to strengthen your abdominal muscles. You should begin by repeating each exercise about 3 times and gradually increasing the number as you feel more comfortable.

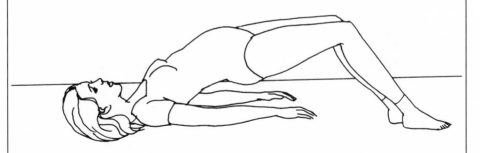

Lie flat with your arms at your sides. Slide your feet toward your buttocks. Arch your back while supporting yourself with arms, shoulders, and feet. Relax.

Lie flat with your knees raised. Then lift your head while raising the pelvis and tightening the buttocks muscles. Relax.

Lie on your back. Raise one knee and pull your thigh down onto your abdomen. Lower your foot to your buttock. Then raise the leg and straighten it. Lower slowly to the floor. Rest and repeat with the other leg.

Lie flat on your back with toes extended outward. Raise the left leg using your abdominal muscles. Lower your leg slowly, then repeat with the right leg.

Resting on all fours, arch your back while contracting the muscles in your buttocks and abdomen. Relax, then breathe deeply.

Lie flat on your back as shown. Lift both legs at once using the muscles in your abdomen. Lower your legs slowly.

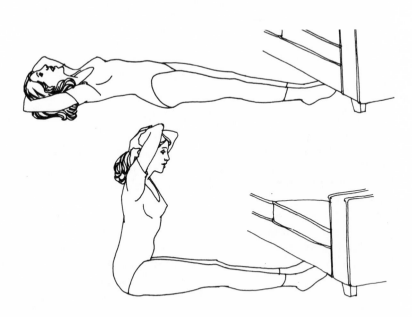

Lie flat on your back using a piece of furniture to brace your feet. Place your hands behind your head and slowly sit up. Lie back slowly using your abdominal muscles.

Source: *Prenatal Care.* Prepared for the Public Health Service by the Health Resources and Services Administration, Bureau of Health Care Delivery and Assistance, Division of Maternal and Child Health, 1989.

PREGNANCY AND CHILDBIRTH

Help, Information, and Action Guide

Organizations

◪ **ON PREGNANCY AND CHILDBIRTH IN GENERAL**

▶ **Pregnancy Helpline** (800-228-0332).
▶ National Center for Education in Maternal and Child Health (**NCEMCH**) (202-625-8400). Publishes numerous materials, including *Caring for Our Future: The Content of Prenatal Care, Prenatal Care, Infant Care, Preterm and Low Birthweight Infants: Cost and Effectiveness, Adolescent Pregnancy—Resource Guide, Healthy Foods, Healthy Baby, Environmental Exposures and Pregnancy—Resource Guide,* and *Pregnancy and Childbearing Among Homeless Adolescents.*
▶ National Institute of Child Health and Human Development (**NICHD**) (301-496-5133). Publishes *Pregnancy Basics (What You Need to Know and Do to Have a Good Healthy Baby),* and a series of "Facts About" booklets on topics such as *Cesarean Childbirth* and *Premature Birth.*
▶ American College of Obstetricians and Gynecologists (**ACOG**) (202-638-5577). Publishes Patient Education Pamphlets and maintains a resource center for the general public, on obstetrical and gynecological questions.
▶ Healthy Mother, Healthy Babies National Coalition (**HMHB**) (202-638-5577 or 202-863-2458).
▶ National Women's Health Network (**NWHN**) (202-347-1140). Operates the **Women's Health Information Service.** Publishes *Childbearing Policies Within a National Health Program: An Evolving Consensus for New Directions* and the information packets *Pregnancy/Childbirth, Teen Pregnancy, Cesarean Childbirth,* and *Home Pregnancy Tests.*
▶ Federation of Feminist Women's Health Centers (916-737-0260). Publishes *Woman-Centered Pregnancy and Birth.*
▶ Women's Sports Foundation (**WSF**) (212-972-9170; Women's Sports Infoline, 800-227-3988). Publishes an expert packet on *Pregnancy and Exercise.*

◪ **ON UNWANTED PREGNANCY**

▶ Nurturing Network, The (**TNN**) (208-344-7200 or 800-TNN-4MOM [866-4666]. Provides counseling and aid for women of any age who decide *against* having an abortion.
▶ Child Welfare League of America (**CWLA**) (202-639-2952). Its

Florence Crittenton Division offers a national adolescent pregnancy service.

▶ NATIONAL ADOPTION INFORMATION CLEARINGHOUSE (**NAIC**) (202-842-1919). Publishes *National Crisis Pregnancy Centers Directory.*

▶ BIRTHRIGHT, UNITED STATES OF AMERICA (609-848-1819; Birthright Hotline 800-848-LOVE [5683]). Urges alternatives to abortion. Offers childbirth and parenting classes.

☑ ON POLITICAL, LEGAL, OR SOCIAL CONCERNS

▶ CENTER FOR WOMEN POLICY STUDIES (**CWPS**) (202-872-1770).

▶ NATIONAL CENTER FOR POLICY ALTERNATIVES (202-387-6030).

▶ NOW LEGAL DEFENSE AND EDUCATION FUND (**NOW LEDF**) (212-925-6635).

▶ WOMEN'S MINISTRY UNIT (**WMU**) (502-569-5382). Publishes *Problem Pregnancy/Keeping the Covenant: Guidelines for Ministry.*

▶ WOMEN'S INTERNATIONAL NETWORK (**WIN**) (617-862-9431). Publishes *A Picture Story of Reproduction from a Woman's View* and *The Childbirth Picture Book* for use internationally.

(See also PREGNANCY DISCRIMINATION ACT.)

☑ ON PRENATAL CARE

▶ MARCH OF DIMES BIRTH DEFECTS FOUNDATION (**MDBDF**) (914-428-7100; local chapters in telephone directory White Pages). Some chapters have available certified midwives and prenatal services for high-risk pregnancies. Publishes numerous materials.

▶ **Positive Pregnancy and Parenting Fitness** (51 Saltrock Road, Baltic, CT 06330; 203-822-8573 or 800-433-5523; Sylvia Klein Olkin, executive director), an organization that seeks to train and support pregnant women and new mothers, through pregnancy and parenting fitness classes. It trains instructors; has a mail-order catalog; and publishes a newsletter.

▶ **DES Action** (415-826-5060). Publishes *Every Woman's Guide to Tests During Pregnancy, Preventing Preterm Birth: A Parents' Guide, Fertility and Pregnancy Guide for DES Daughters and Sons,* and *Natural Remedies for Pregnancy Discomforts.* (See DES.)

☑ ON CHILDBIRTH IN GENERAL

▶ **International Association of Parents and Professionals for Safe Alternatives in Childbirth** (NAPSAC) (Route 1, Box 646, Marble Hill, MO 63764; 314-238-2010; David Stewart, executive director), an international organization of childbirth professionals supporting alternatives to traditional hospital-based childbirth. It provides information and referrals on such topics as natural childbirth, parental education about childbirth alternatives, midwifery, breast-feeding, and nutrition of pregnant women; and publishes *Directory of Alternative Birth Services and Consumer Guide.*

▶ **International Childbirth Education Association (ICEA)** (P.O. Box 20048, Minneapolis, MN 55420; 612-854-8660; Trudy Keller, president), an organization concerned with the education of parents for childbirth and breastfeeding, supporting parental choice with safe, low-cost alternatives. It provides information about doctors sympathetic to vaginal birth after a cesarean; organizes classes for women who have had a C-section; and publishes various materials.

▶ **National Association of Childbearing Centers (NACC)** (3123 Gottschall Road, Perkiomenville, PA 18074; 215-234-8068; Eunice K. M. (Kitty) Ernst, executive director), an organization concerned with birth centers. It sets standards; acts as an information clearinghouse for the public and professionals; makes referrals; and publishes various materials, including a quarterly newsletter.

▶ **Childbirth Education Foundation (CEF)** (P.O. Box 5, Richboro, PA 18954; 215-357-2792; James C. Peron, executive director), an organization concerned with reform of childbirth methods. It promotes certified nurse–midwives, birthing centers, and similar alternatives; provides training for childbirth educators, including Lamaze and La Leche instructors. Originally the **Non-Circumcision Educational Foundation (NCEF),** it also seeks to educate the public against circumcision and other routine perinatal procedures, through seminars and workshops. CDEF publishes various print and film materials.

▶ **Maternity Center Association (MCA)** (48 East 92nd Street, New York, NY 10128; 212-369-7300; Ruth Watson Lubic, general director), an organization concerned with maternity centers. It seeks to improve maternity care; provides information and education; sponsors research; and publishes a quarterly newsletter *Special Delivery,* various pamphlets, and books such as *Preparation for Childbearing* and *Newborn Needs.*

▶ **American College of Nurse Midwives (ACNM)** (1522 K Street, NW, Suite 1000, Washington, DC 20005; 202-289-0171; Ronald Nitzsche, chief operating officer), a professional organization of certified nurse-midwives. It accredits a nurse-midwife education program; provides information and referrals; seeks to educate the public and influence social policy; and publishes various materials.

◪ ON SPECIAL APPROACHES TO DELIVERY

▶ **American Academy of Husband-Coached Childbirth (AAHCC)** (P.O. Box 5224, Sherman Oaks, CA 91413; 818-788-6662 or Pregnancy Hotline 800-423-2397 or 800-42-BIRTH [422-4784]; Jay and Marjie Hathaway, executive directors), a for-profit organization dedicated to spreading use of the Bradley Method of natural childbirth. It trains instructors, makes referrals, provides information, and publishes various materials.

▶ **American Society for Prophylaxis in Obstetrics (ASPO/Lamaze)** (1101 Connecticut Avenue, NW, Suite 700, Washington, DC 20036; 202-857-1128 or 800-368-4404; Linda Harmon, executive director), an organization of health professionals supporting the Lamaze method of natural childbirth. It trains and certifies instructors, makes referrals, provides information, and publishes various materials.

▶ **Read Natural Childbirth Foundation (RNCF)** (P.O. Box 150956, San Rafael, CA 94915; 415-465-8462; Margaret B. Farley, president), an organization of health professionals supporting the Grantly Dick-Read approach to natural childbirth. It publishes various materials, including *Preparation for Childbirth* and the film *A Time to Be Born*.

▶ **National Association of Childbirth Education (NACE)** (3940 11th Street, Riverside, CA 92501; 714-686-0422; Rebecca Smith, president), an organization of childbirth educators supporting the Pavlov-Lamaze method. (See also CESAREAN SECTION.)

▧ **ON PERINATAL CARE**

▶ **National Perinatal Association (NPA)** (101 ½ South Union Street, Alexandria, VA 22314; 703-549-5523; Sandra Butler Whyte, executive director), an organization focusing on perinatal health care. It publishes a newsletter.

▶ **National Perinatal Information Center** (One Blackstone Place, 688 Eddy Street, Providence, RI 02903; 401-274-0650; David Gagnon, executive director), an organization that provides information on perinatal care to both the public and professionals.

▧ **AGAINST CIRCUMCISION AND OTHER PERINATAL PROCEDURES**

▶ **National Organization of Circumcision Information Resource Centers (NO-CIRC)** (731 Sir Francis Drake Boulevard, San Anselmo, CA 94960; 415-454-5669; Marilyn Fayre Milos, executive director), an organization of groups against circumcision. It seeks to educate the public and publishes a newsletter and other materials.

▶ **Newborn Rights Society (NRS)** (P.O. Box 48, St. Peters, PA 19470; 215-323-6061; Paul Zimmer, executive director), an organization opposing circumcision and other routine perinatal procedures. It gathers and disseminates information.

▶ **Remain Intact Organization (RIO)** (Airport Route 2, Box 86, Larchwood, IA 51241; 712-477-2256; Russell Zanggner, director), an organization opposing routine circumcision. It distributes printed, audio, and video materials.

◪ ON POSTNATAL CARE

▶ **National Center for Clinical Infant Programs (NCCIP)** 733 15th Street, Suite 912, Washington, DC 20005; 202-347-0308; Eleanor S. Szanton, executive director), an organization that seeks to improve the care of infants and young children. It supports the development of clinics focusing on early intervention and prevention and publishes various materials, including *Zero to Three* and *Clinical Infant Reports.*

▶ **Parent Care (PC)** (1010 ½ South Union Street, Alexandria, VA 22314; 703-836-4678; Nan Streeter, administrative liaison), an organization of parents and health professionals concerned about premature or high-risk babies. It encourages formation of local support groups, seeks to educate the public, maintains a library, and publishes a newletter and *Parents of Prematures Resource Directory.*

(See also BREASTFEEDING.)

◪ ON MULTIPLE BIRTHS

▶ **Twins Foundation** (P.O. Box 9487, Providence, RI 02940; 401-274-TWIN [8946]; Kay Cassill, president), an organization focusing on multiple births. It seeks to enhance the welfare of twins in general.

▶ **National Organization of Mothers of Twins Clubs (NOMOTC)** (P.O. Box 23188, Albuquerque, NM, 87112-1188; 505-275-0955; Lois Gallmeyer, executive secretary), a network of clubs for parents of twins and other multiple births. NOMOTC facilitates the exchange of information on the raising of twins among parents, teachers, and medical professionals; aims to educate the public about the individuality of twins; maintains a library; and aids in research on twins. It publishes *MOTC's Notebook.*

▶ **Twin Services** (P.O. Box 10066, Berkeley, CA 94709; 510-524-0863; Patricia M. Malmstrom, executive director), a partly state-funded family service agency concerned with multiple births. It offers the Twinline phone counseling service, provides information and referrals, and publishes various materials, packaged by age group.

▶ **Triplet Connection (TC)** (P.O. Box 99571, Stockton, CA 95209; 209-474-0885; Janet Bleyl, president), a mutual-support group for parents of triplets. It help parents prepare for high-risk birth; shares information and experiences of mutual interest; operates a Tender Hearts program for mothers who lost one or more children in a multiple birth; and publishes a newsletter.

☑ ON PREGNANCY OR INFANT LOSS

▶ **Pregnancy and Infant Loss Center (PILC)** (1421 East Wayzata Boulevard, Suite 30, Wayzata, MN 55391; 612-473-9372; Gail Staltes, executive director), an organization for people who have had a miscarriage, stillbirth, or infant death. It encourages formation of mutual-support groups, provides information, makes referrals, maintains a help line, and publishes various materials, including the newsletter *Loving Arms.*

▶ **SHARE—Pregnancy and Infant Loss Support Inc.** (National Office, St. Joseph's Health Center, 300 First Capitol Drive, St. Charles, MO 63301-2893; Cathi Lammert, director), a network of mutual-support groups for families who have lost a baby, through stillbirth, miscarriage, or early infant death. It provides information about resources for surviving family members; and publishes various materials, including the newsletter *Share.*

▶ COMPASSIONATE FRIENDS, THE (TCF) (312-990-0010).

Other resources

What Happens If You Have a Baby? Ann Redpath. Capstone Press, 1992.
What to Expect When You're Expecting, 2nd ed. Arlene Eisenberg and others. Workman, 1991.
Complete Guide to Pregnancy, Childbirth and the Newborn. Penny Simkin. Meadowbrook, 1991.
The Illustrated Book of Pregnancy and Childbirth. Margaret Martin. Facts on File, 1991.
From Here to Maternity: Your Guide for the Nine-Month Journey Toward Motherhood. Connie C. Marshall. Prima, 1991.
The Mother's Guide to a Healthier Pregnancy and Easier Birth. Jeanine L. LaBaw and Mary M. Lepley. Lifesounds, 1991.
Guide to Pregnancy and Childbirth. William G. Birch. Budlong, 1991.
Natural Pregnancy, Janet Balaskas. Interlink, 1990.
Pregnancy Day by Day. Sheila Kitzinger. Random House, 1990.
The Illustrated Dictionary of Pregnancy and Childbirth. Carl Jones. Meadowbrook, 1990.
Doctor Discusses Pregnancy. William G. Birch and Dona Z. Meilach. Budlong, 1990.
The Complete Book of Pregnancy and Childbirth, rev. ed. Sheila Kitzinger. Schocken, 1989.
Dr. Miriam Stoppard's Pregnancy and Birth Book. Miriam Stoppard. Ballantine, 1989.
The Columbia University College of Physicians and Surgeons Complete

Guide to Pregnancy. Donald F. Tapley and W. Duane Todd, eds. Crown, 1988.

ON PLANNING FOR PREGNANCY

Preconception: A Woman's Guide to Pregnancy and Parenthood. Brenda E. Aikey-Keller. John Muir, 1990.

Getting Pregnant: How Couples Can Protect Their Reproductive Powers Throughout Their Childbearing Years. Niels H. Lauersen and Colette Bouchez. Rawson, 1990.

Before You Conceive: The Complete Prepregnancy Guide. John R. Sussman and B. Blake Levitt. Bantam, 1989.

Preconceptions: Preparation for Pregnancy. John T. Queenan and Kimberly K. Leslie. Little, Brown, 1989.

Pre-Conceptions: What You Can Do Before Pregnancy to Help You Have a Healthy Baby. Norra Tannenhaus. Contemporary, 1988.

How to Get Pregnant. Sherman J. Silber. Warner, 1988.

The Baby Makers. Diana Frank and Marta Vogel. Carrol & Graf, 1988.

ON TEEN PREGNANCY

Facing Teenage Pregnancy: A Handbook for the Pregnant Teen. Patricia Roles. Child Welfare, 1990.

Teen Guide to Childbirth. Fern G. Brown. Watts, 1990.

ON UNPLANNED PREGNANCY

Bitter Fruit: Women's Experiences of Unplanned Pregnancy, Abortion, and Adoption. Ann Perkins and Rita Townsend. Hunter House, 1992.

Pregnant by Mistake: The Stories of Seventeen Women, rev. ed. Katrina Maxtone-Graham. Remi, 1990. Reprint of 1973 ed.

Having Your Baby When Others Say No: Overcoming the Fears About Having Your Baby. Madeline Nugent. Avery, 1991.

Coping with an Unplanned Pregnancy. Carolyn Simpson. Rosen, 1990.

Pregnant and Single: Help for the Tough Choices. Carolyn Owens and Linda M. Roggow. Pyranee/Zondervan, 1990.

ON EXERCISE AND COMFORT

The Pregnant Woman's Comfort Guide: Safe, Quick and Easy Relief from the Discomforts of Pregnancy and Postpartum. Sherry L. Jimenez. Avery, 1992.

Easy Pregnancy with Yoga. Stella Weller. Thorsons (SF), 1991.

Elisabeth Bing's Guide to Moving Through Pregnancy: Advice from America's Foremost Childbirth Educator on Making Pregnancy as Physically Comfortable as Possible, at Home and at Work. Elisabeth Bing. Noonday/Farrar, Straus & Giroux, 1991.

(See also EXERCISE: EXERCISE AND FITNESS HELP, INFORMATION, AND ACTION GUIDE on page 270.)

◪ ON OTHER SPECIAL CONSIDERATIONS

Pregnancy: The Psychological Experience. Libby L. Colman. Noonday/Farrar, Straus & Giroux, 1991.

Psychological Processes of Childbearing. Joan Raphael-Leff. Chapman and Hall, 1990.

Pregnancy over Thirty-Five. Kathryn Schrotenboer-Cox and Joan Weiss. Ballantine, 1989.

Having a Baby After 30. Elisabeth Bing and Libby Colman. Farrar, Straus & Giroux, 1989.

Making Love During Pregnancy. Elisabeth Bing and Libby Colman. Farrar, Straus & Giroux, 1989.

How to Choose the Sex of Your Baby: The Newly Revised Edition of the Method Best Supported by the Scientific Evidence. Landrum B. Shettles and David Rorvick. Doubleday, 1988.

◪ ON PRENATAL CARE AND CONCERNS

Mother and Fetus: Changing Notions of Maternal Responsibility. Robert H. Blank. Greenwood, 1992.

Everyday Drugs and Pregnancy: Alcohol, Tobacco, and Caffeine, rev. ed. Do It Now, 1991.

Birth-Tech: Tests and Technology in Pregnancy and Birth. Ann Charlish and Linda H. Holt. Facts on File, 1990.

A Child Is Born, rev. ed. Photographs, Lennart Nilsson; text Lars Harnberger. Delacorte, 1990. Color photos of life before birth, from conception.

Caring for Your Unborn Child. Roy Ridgway. Thorsons (SF), 1990.

Alcohol, Tobacco, and Other Drugs May Harm the Unborn. Paddy S. Cook and Tineke Haase. U.S. Government Printing Office, 1990.

Loving Your Preborn Baby. Carol Van Klompenburg and Elizabeth Siitari. Shaw, 1990.

How Your Baby Grows in Pregnancy. Glade B. Curtis. Fisher Books, 1989.

The Secret Life of the Unborn Child. Thomas Verny and John Kelly. Delta, 1988.

Prenatal Tests: What They Are, Their Benefits and Risks, and How to Decide Whether to Have Them or Not. Robin J. R. Blatt. Vintage, 1988.

Prenatal Care: Reaching Mothers, Reaching Infants. Sarah S. Brown, ed. National Academy Press, 1988.

The Tentative Pregnancy: Prenatal Diagnosis and the Future of Motherhood. Barbara K. Rothman. Penguin, 1986.

◪ ON MULTIPLE BIRTHS

Having Twins: A Parent's Guide to Pregnancy, Birth, and Early Childhood, 2nd ed. Elizabeth Noble. Houghton Mifflin, 1990.
The Parents Guide to Raising Twins, 2nd ed. Elizabeth Griedrich and Cherry Rowland. St. Martin's, 1990.
Twins. Roxanne Pulitzer. Villard Books, 1990.
The Joy of Twins: Having, Raising, and Loving Babies Who Arrive in Groups. Pamela Patrick Novotny. Crown, 1988.
Twins: From Conception to Five Years. Averil Clegg and Anne Woolett. Van Nostrand, 1983; Ballantine, 1988.
Make Room for Twins: A Complete Guide to Pregnancy, Delivery, and the Childhood Years. Terry Pink Alexander. Bantam, 1987.

◪ ON OTHER HIGH-RISK PREGNANCIES

Getting Pregnant and Staying Pregnant: Overcoming Infertility and Managing Your High-Risk Pregnancy, 2nd ed. Diana Raab. Hunter House, 1991.
Intensive Caring: New Hope for High-Risk Pregnancy. Dianne Hales and Timothy R. B. Johnson. Brown, 1990.
Pregnancy Bedrest: A Guide for the Pregnant Woman and Her Family. Susan H. Johnston. Holt, 1990.
Past Due: A Story of Disability, Pregnancy and Birth. Anne Finger. Seal Press Feminist, 1990.
How to Prevent Miscarriages and Other Crises of Pregnancy. Stefan Semchyshyn. Macmillan, 1989.

◪ ON CHILDBIRTH

The Working Woman's Essential Lamaze Handbook: Everything You Need to Know About Lamaze and Childbirth. O. Robin Sweet and Patty Bryan. Disney, 1992.
The Water Birth Handbook: Everything You Need to Know about Waterbirths. Roger Lichy and Eileen Herzberg. Atrium, 1992.
Childbirth with Love. Niels H. Lauersen. Berkley, 1991.
Alternative Birth: The Complete Guide. Carl Jones. Tarcher, 1991.
Methods of Childbirth: The Completely Updated Version of a Classic Work for Today's Woman, rev. ed. Constance A. Bean. Morrow, 1990.
A Wise Birth: Bringing Together the Best of Natural Birth with Modern Medicine. Penny Armstrong and Sheryl Feldman. Morrow, 1990.
An Easier Childbirth: A Mother's Workbook for Health and Emotional Well-Being During Pregnancy and Delivery. Gayle Peterson. Tarcher, 1991.
The Midwife's Pregnancy and Childbirth Book: Having Your Baby Your Way. Marion McCartney and Antonia Van der Meer. Holt, 1990.

The Lamaze Ready Reference Guide for Labor and Birth, 2nd ed. Harriet R. Shapiro and others. Shapiro Kuba, 1990.

Partners in Birth: Your Complete Guide to Helping a Mother Give Birth. Kathy Cain. Warner, 1990.

Good Birth: A Safe Birth, rev. ed. Diana Korte. Bantam, 1990.

Doctor Discusses Prepared Childbirth. Lou Joseph and Ulisse Cucco. Budlong, 1990.

Childbirth Choices in Mothers' Words. Kim Selbert. Mills Sanderson, 1990.

Birth Without Violence. Frederick Leboyer. Fawcett, 1990.

Preparation for Birth: The Complete Guide to the Lamaze Method. Beverly Savage and Diana Simkin. Ballantine, 1989.

The Birth Partner: Everything You Need to Know to Help a Woman Through Childbirth. Penny Simkin. Harvard Common Press, 1989.

The Birth Partner's Handbook. Carl Jones with Jan Jones. Meadowbrook Press, 1989.

Labor Pains. Kate Klimo. Ivy/Ballantine, 1989. Following women from Lamaze class through birth.

Birth. Nancy Durrell McKenna. David & Charles, 1989. Photographs of birth.

Your Child's First Journey: A Guide to Prepared Birth from Pregnancy to Parenthood, 2nd ed. Ginny Brinkley and others. Avery, 1988.

Fritzi Kallop's Birth Book. Fritzi Kallop and Julie Houston. Vintage, 1988.

The Birth Partner's Handbook. Penny Simkin. Meadowbrook Press, 1988.

Mind over Labor. Carol Jones. Viking, 1987.

Childbearing: A Book of Choices. Ruth Watson Lubic and Gene R. Hawes. McGraw-Hill, 1986. Lubic is general director of the Maternity Center Association (see page 582).

(See also CESAREAN SECTION.)

◪ AFTER CHILDBIRTH

Parenting Your Premature Baby: A Complete Guide to Birth, Postpartum Care, and Early Childhood. Janine Jason and Antonia van der Meer. Holt, 1989; Delacorte, 1990.

What to Expect the First Year. Arlene Eisenberg and others. Workman, 1988.

The New Mother's Body: A Complete Postpartum Guide to the Body After Birth. Paula M. Siegel. Bantam, 1988.

◪ ON PREGNANCY OR INFANT LOSS

Empty Cradle, Broken Heart: Surviving the Death of Your Baby. Deborah L. Davis. Fulcrum, 1991.

Waiting: A Diary of Loss and Hope in Pregnancy. Ellen J. Reich. Haworth Press, 1991.

Hidden Loss: Miscarriage and Ectopic Pregnancy. Valerie Hey. Quartet, 1990.
Recovering from the Loss of a Child. Katherine Fair Donnelly. Dodd, Mead, 1988.
Beyond Endurance: When a Child Dies. Ronald J. Knapp. Schocken, 1986.
When Your Child Is Gone: Learning to Live Again. Francine Roder. Capital Publishing, 1986.

◪ BACKGROUND BOOKS

The Nature of Birth and Breastfeeding. Michel Odent. Bergin & Garvey/ Greenwood, 1992.
Safer Childbirth? A Critical History of Maternity Care. Marjorie Tew. Chapman and Hall, 1990.
Jewish Laws of Childbirth. Y. Silverstein. Feldheim, 1990.
The Woman in the Body: A Cultural Analysis of Reproduction. Emily Martin. Beacon Press, 1989.
Lying-In: A History of Childbirth in America. Richard W. Wertz and Dorothy C. Wertz. Yale University Press, 1989.
Beyond Conception: The New Politics of Reproduction. Patricia Spallone. Bergin & Garvey, 1989.
Cradle and All: Women Writers on Pregnancy and Birth. Laura Chester, ed. Faber and Faber, 1989.
The Midwife Challenge. Sheila Kitzinger, ed. Pandora/Thorsons (SF), 1989.
Labor Pains: Modern Midwives and Home Birth. Deborah A. Sullivan and Rose Weitz. Yale University Press, 1988.
(See also PREGNANCY DISCRIMINATION ACT; BREASTFEEDING.)

Pregnancy Discrimination Act of 1978 (PDA), a U.S. federal law barring discrimination against a woman because of her PREGNANCY, CHILDBIRTH, or related medical conditions. The statute is an amendment to TITLE VII OF THE CIVIL RIGHTS ACT OF 1964, extending to women who work in firms with more than fifteen employees the same civil rights protection as people with "other" disabilities. The immediate spur to the PDA's passage was a 1976 U.S. Supreme Court decision finding that no civil rights laws were violated by an employer's health insurance plan that provided benefits for accidents and nonemployment-related accidents, but not for pregnancy-related conditions.

The PDA bars firms of fifteen or more from discriminating against a woman because she is pregnant, specifically from refusing to hire, firing, demoting, or penalizing her. However, contrary to popular opinion, it does not guarantee any particular benefits, specifying only that employers' benefit plans may not discriminate against women—that is, if health insurance, disability leave, and fringes such as vacations, seniority, and raises are available to the firm's disabled employees, then they must be made available to pregnant women as well. In some states laws do mandate specific kinds of benefits or protections for pregnant women, such as FAMILY AND MEDICAL LEAVE and related fringe benefits, although these vary widely; a federal bill was not passed and signed until 1993 (see FAMILY AND MEDICAL LEAVE). How the existing laws are interpreted by the courts is always open to question, and at times employers have tried to use them to *limit* the rights of women, under the cloak of protection (see below). Several key cases turning on the Pregnancy Discrimination Act and related laws have been decided in federal courts in recent years, and others no doubt will follow.

One of the most important of these was *Automobile Workers* v. *Johnson Controls, Inc.* (1991), in which the Supreme Court (affirming a California State court ruling) unanimously held that employers could not use gender as a reason to bar a woman from holding a specific job. Johnson Controls' "fetus-protection policy" barred all women—even those with no plans to have children, unless they could prove they were infertile—from work involving exposure to lead. The Court held that the policy's "bias is obvious," noting that lead also harms the male REPRODUCTIVE SYSTEM. Johnson argued that the policy fell under a safety exception in the Civil Rights Act, allowing an employer to discriminate on the basis of sex, religion, or national origin in cases where there is a *bona fide occupational qualification* (BFOQ), "reasonably necessary to the normal operation of that particular business or enterprise." But writing for the Court, Justice Harry A. Blackmun said that exception was allowed only in extremely narrow circumstances, noting that the Pregnancy Discrimination Act contains its own BFOQ standard: that unless pregnant employees differ from others "in their ability or inability to work," they must be "treated the same" as other employees "for all employment related purposes." He concluded: "In other words, women as capable of doing their jobs as their male counterparts may not be forced to choose between having a child and having a job."

Blackmun noted that in many states a woman can bring suit for "prenatal injury based either on negligence or on wrongful death," but said that if "the employer fully informs the woman of the risk, and the employer has not acted negligently, the basis for holding an employer liable seems remote at best." Businesses are still concerned about such liability, especially from children born with defects linked to a mother's work, while some other observers fear that a company's warnings of danger may be taken to absolve them of proper liability for injury to their employees.

Another major case was *California Federal Savings and Loan Association* v. *Guerra* (1987), in which the U.S. Supreme Court upheld the legality of a California state law (and by extension similar laws in other states) providing unpaid pregnancy disability leave of up to four months to female workers, guaranteeing the availability of their jobs on return. In the specific case, Lillian Garland, a receptionist at the Los Angeles bank, was fired after taking three months' pregnancy leave. Business groups (and the Reagan administration) argued that pregnant workers must be treated the same as, but not better than, workers with other disabilities. However, as Justice Thurgood Marshall expressed it, the Congress intended the Pregnancy Discrimination Act to be "a floor beneath which pregnancy disability benefits may not drop—not a ceiling above which they may not rise," noting that the Congress never "intended to prohibit such [preferential] treatment." He also pointed out that the California law was extremely narrow, providing not paid leave, but only a general right to reinstatement.

Many people and groups hailed the decision as a step forward and urged passage of specific benefits laws in other states. Others, including some civil rights and women's groups, were concerned that if special treatment is allowed, employers will be discouraged from hiring women, having the unwanted effect of constricting their job opportunities. Some, such as the NATIONAL ORGANIZATION FOR WOMEN, suggested that the solution would be to give all workers—men and women, pregnant or not—the same unpaid leave for all medical disabilities.

The EQUAL EMPLOYMENT OPPORTUNITY COMMISSION (EEOC) has also played a role, as in its late 1990 interpretation of the Pregnancy Discrimination Act, noting that companies with parental leave programs only for females may be open to charges of SEXUAL DISCRIMINATION, unless the usually more generous maternal leave is linked specifically to disability relating to pregnancy or CHILDBIRTH. The new policy came in response to a U.S. Court of Appeals ruling on a case in which a male Pittsburgh teacher successfully charged discrimination regarding a policy that allowed female employees (but not males) to use up to one year of sick leave combined with unpaid leave for child rearing. The EEOC suggested that the "clearest safe harbor policy" for employers is for pregnancy disability leave to be separated from parental leave, so that

> ... employees may take disability leave based upon medical documentation. The policy defines disability to include pregnancy disability. It also provides for four weeks of parental leave for men and women following the birth or adoption of a child. Under this policy, a new mother who documents disability for six weeks could take six weeks of disability leave followed by four weeks of parental leave. A new father could take four weeks of parental leave.

Individual women who are or may in the future become pregnant can take some comfort from such rulings, that strengthen and clarify the Pregnancy Discrimination Act. However, in practice, individuals have an extremely difficult time bringing a pregnancy discrimination case (like other civil rights cases) to court and winning. As a result, many women still find themselves harassed or fired during their pregnancy, either immediately, as the pregnancy develops, or later while out on leave.

When contemplating a pregnancy or before announcing one, a working woman would be wise to review the pregnancy discrimination laws in her own state, perhaps contacting one of the groups (such as those on page 593) that are active in seeking stronger protection for pregnant women in the workplace. They may also want to explore discreetly how other pregnant women in their firm have fared, learning from their experience and preparing for possible problems. More personally, they will want to think through their own plans and desires, regarding the length of maternity leave, CHILD CARE arrangements, BREASTFEEDING vs. bottlefeeding, and future intentions regarding work—whether to return to work full-time or part-time (and if so, how quickly), to work at home (for the same firm or another), or to leave employment and stay at home with the child. Having the answers to these questions before any announcement of a pregnancy will put a woman in the strongest possible position to protect her own interests.

At least for corporate settings, some observers recommend that women lay out their plans and requests in writing, to present to their managers.

For more help, information, and action

- ► 9 TO 5, NATIONAL ASSOCIATION OF WORKING WOMEN (216-566-5420; 9 to 5 Office Survival Hotline 800-245-9865). Operates hot line on legal questions relating to pregnancy discrimination.
- ► EQUAL RIGHTS ADVOCATES (ERA) (415-621-0672; advice and counseling line, 415-621-0505). A national women's law center. Publishes the "Know Your Rights" brochure *Pregnancy Discrimination* (in English and Spanish).
- ► NATIONAL ORGANIZATION FOR WOMEN (NOW) (202-331-0066).
- ► NOW LEGAL DEFENSE AND EDUCATION FUND (NOW LDEF) (212-925-6635). Publishes the Legal Resource Kit *Employment—Pregnancy and Parental Leave.*
- ► WOMEN'S RIGHTS PROJECT, AMERICAN CIVIL LIBERTIES UNION (ACLU) (212-944-9800).
- ► WOMEN'S LEGAL DEFENSE FUND (202-887-0364). Publishes *Sex Discrimination in the Workplace: A Legal Handbook.*
- ► FAMILIES AND WORK INSTITUTE (212-465-2044).

Other Resources

Pregnant and Working: What Are Your Rights? (1986). Available from New York Committee on Occupational Safety and Health (NYCOSH), 275 Seventh Avenue, New York, NY 10001.

The Rights of the Pregnant Parent, rev. ed. Valmai H. Elkins and Elisabeth Bing. Schocken, 1985.

(For more sources of information, or for legal advice and referrals, see also SEXUAL DISCRIMINATION AND SEXUAL HARASSMENT HELP, INFORMATION, AND ACTION GUIDE on page 642.)

ON PREGNANCY DISCRIMINATION

Concern for a woman's existing or potential offspring historically has been the excuse for denying women equal employment opportunities. Congress in the PDA [Pregnancy Discrimination Act] prohibited discrimination on the basis of a woman's ability to become pregnant. We do no more than hold that the Pregnancy Discrimination Act means what it says. It is no more appropriate for the courts than it is for individual employers to decide whether a woman's reproductive role is more important to herself and her family than her economic role. Congress has left this choice to the woman as hers.

Supreme Court Justice Harry A. Blackmun
Automobile Workers v. *Johnson Controls, Inc.* (1991)

premarital sex, SEXUAL INTERCOURSE before MARRIAGE. Sex before marriage is a matter of great concern in those societies that highly regard VIRGINITY but less so where unmarried couples commonly live together (see COHABITATION). Agreements about MARITAL PROPERTY, made before marriage, are called *premarital* or PRENUPTIAL AGREEMENTS.

premenstrual syndrome (PMS), an umbrella term for a series of bodily responses that occur in women, to a greater or lesser extent, a week or more before a period (see MENSTRUATION).

prenatal care, medical care of a pregnant women and FETUS throughout PREGNANCY; also called *antepartal care*. As more has been learned about the influence of a woman's health and actions on the child she is carrying, especially in the crucial early weeks of development, prenatal care has become ever more important. In general, the sooner prenatal care begins, the better for both mother and baby; a woman is advised to see her doctor or clinic as soon as she suspects she might be pregnant.

Prenatal care starts with pregnancy tests to confirm pregnancy and continues with exploration of a woman's personal and family medical history for signs of any problems. Various tests identify possible health problems or threats to the continuation of the pregnancy (see PRENATAL TESTS). The doctor or clinic staff will also give advice on what to do—such as have good NUTRITION and EXERCISE moderately—and what not to do—such as SMOKING, drinking, and taking drugs (see ALCOHOL AND DRUG ABUSE), whether illegal or prescribed, except when the doctor has evidence that they are not harmful to a FETUS.

The results of a woman's history and tests will determine whether the pregnancy is classed as normal, with all delivery options open (see CHILDBIRTH), or *high-risk,* which may require extra observation and care from a specially trained *maternal and fetal specialist,* and delivery in a relatively sophisticated hospital. The first visit generally will take a long time, as the history is taken and tests are done. Later visits will be briefer, generally monthly for the first six months; bimonthly through the eighth month; and then weekly until the birth, with more frequent visits to monitor special problems, if required. At appropriate times other tests may be performed, including genetic screening tests, such as AMNIOCENTESIS, CHORIONIC VILLUS SAMPLING, FETOSCOPY, and ULTRASOUND scanning, and follow-up tests to check for any pregnancy-related health problems, such as DIABETES or PREECLAMPSIA. (See PRENATAL VISITS: WHAT TO EXPECT, below; also PREGNANCY; PREGNANCY AND CHILDBIRTH HELP, INFORMATION, AND ACTION GUIDE on page 580.)

PRENATAL VISITS: WHAT TO EXPECT

Your First Visit

Your first visit will probably take more time than later appointments. In addition to a physical examination, you will need to give information about yourself and your pregnancy.

☑ FIRST THERE WILL BE QUESTIONS ABOUT YOU:

- About your previous pregnancies, miscarriages, or abortions.
- About your periods—when they started, what they are like.
- About your medical history—illnesses you have had, illnesses the father has had, illnesses in members of either family.
- About your diet and life-style.

☑ THEN THERE WILL BE A PHYSICAL EXAMINATION:

- The measurement of your height and weight and blood pressure.
- An examination of your eyes, ears, nose, throat, and teeth.
- An examination of your heart, lungs, breasts, and abdomen.
- An internal examination (pelvic examination) of the growth of your uterus and the amount of room in your pelvis for the baby.

☑ *IN ADDITION, SEVERAL LABORATORY TESTS WILL BE PERFORMED.*

- A Pap smear to detect any signs of cervical cancer.
- A pregnancy test (even if you have done a test with a home urine kit).
- A culture of the cervix to check for gonorrhea.
- Blood tests:
  - to see if you are anemic
  - to learn your blood type and Rh factor
  - to check for syphilis
  - to check if you have had rubella (German measles)
- Urine tests:
  - for diabetes
  - for kidney function and toxemia
  - to check for the possibility of infection

It is very important that you ask the doctor or nurse any questions you have about your pregnancy, your general health, or your examination and tests. If you don't ask, they may assume you understand. Remember, there is no such thing as a foolish question.

Tell your doctor if you have any physical problems, if you are under stress, or if you have any other special concerns. It is important for your doctor to understand how your pregnancy is affecting you and your family. In some instances the doctor or nurse may refer you to someone else [a specialist] for help with certain problems.

Later Visits

Usually you will return about once a month during the first six months of pregnancy. During the seventh and eighth months, you will make visits every two weeks and after that every week until delivery. During these visits, your weight, blood pressure, and urine will be checked. Your abdomen may be measured to see how the baby is growing. These examinations help insure that your pregnancy is progressing normally. Internal (pelvic) examinations and blood tests are not performed on every routine visit. If you have questions or concerns between visits, write them down and bring them to your next appointment.

Remember, it's important for your doctor to know about any medical problems you or your family may have had, particularly such chronic conditions as diabetes, kidney disorders, thyroid problems, heart conditions, and respiratory illnesses. Once the doctor knows about them, the necessary steps can be taken to reduce any risk to you or to the baby.

Source: *Prenatal Care.* Prepared for the Public Health Service by the Health Resources and Services Administration, Bureau of Health Care Delivery and Assistance, Division of Maternal and Child Health, 1989.

prenatal test, a type of medical test given to a woman during PREGNANCY but before CHILDBIRTH, generally to assess the health and condition of the FETUS, especially to identify any serious BIRTH DEFECTS, GENETIC DISORDERS, or CHROMOSOMAL ABNORMALITIES. Such tests may be given at differing times but are performed as early as possible during the pregnancy, so the options of ABORTION or FETAL SURGERY are open, if serious defects are found. Some tests—such as AMNIOCENTESIS, CHORIONIC VILLUS SAMPLING (CVS), CORDOCENTESUS, or ALPHA FETOPROTEIN (AFP)—involve taking samples of cells shed by the fetus and analyzing their genetic content for information about possible abnormalities. Other prenatal tests involve visually examining the fetus for signs of defects, directly, as in FETOSCOPY, or indirectly, as in ULTRASOUND.

The selection of tests depends on the woman's personal and family medical history (see PRENATAL CARE), the reasons for suggesting the tests, and the strengths and weaknesses of each test. Women should understand, however, that no single test and not all the known tests given together can identify all birth defects.

Similarly, no test is 100 percent accurate. As with all medical tests, the information given is often fragmentary and susceptible to different interpretations. Some tests (such as the alpha fetoprotein test) give only very general indications of problems, which may not in fact be affecting the fetus. Tests can often give *false positives,* indicating a disorder exists when it actually does not, or *false negatives,* indicating that a disorder does *not* exist when it actually does. A test that is 80 percent accurate, for example, would give false readings—positive or negative—one out of every five times. In fact, many tests have an accuracy or reliability rating of less than 80 percent. So the result of *any* test—prenatal or otherwise—should not be considered as absolute. Balanced against the possible gain in knowledge are the potential risks, which vary from virtually nonexistent to substantial.

Medical personnel should give patients information about medical tests and procedures—what is actually entailed, and the risks as well as the benefits; obtain *informed consent* before the test or procedure is carried out; and give full, understandable explanations of test results. In some places this is a "consumer right" backed by law. Law or not, women must be their own advocates when it comes to getting full explanations of medical tests. Among the questions they should ask about a prenatal test—or virtually any medical test—are

▶ *What is the test designed to show?* Is it to screen for a possible disorder, for example, or to confirm a diagnosis already tentatively made?

▶ *How accurate is the test?* How likely is it to give a false negative or false positive result?

▶ *How definitive is the test?* Will the answer be specific and reliable? Or will it just give a general indication, which will need to be followed up by other tests, if a positive result is obtained?

▶ *Where will it be done?* Can the test be performed in a doctor's office, clinic, hospital as an outpatient, or hospital as an impatient? If alternatives exists, how do they differ in the balance of safety, accuracy, and cost?

▶ *How much will it cost?* Will there be a single fee or separate charges for physician, anesthetist (if necessary), nurse, laboratory work, and hospital room?

▶ *Is the test covered by insurance?* Insurance policies vary, of course, but most doctors and clinics will have some idea of which procedures are routinely covered and which are questionable. Some insurance companies also require information before a test and insist on prior permission to have a test for it to be covered; some may also cover procedures performed in a hospital, but not in a doctor's office.

▶ *When should it be done?* Some can and should be done early in pregnancy; others can be performed only later.

▶ *What must be done to prepare for the test?* You may, for example, have to fast for some hours or drink large amounts of water before the test.

▶ *What kinds of side effects might result, and how long might they last?* Some tests, such as ULTRASOUND, have only the most modest discomfort from a full bladder, while others can involve pain and significant discomfort.

▶ *What are the risks of taking the test, to the fetus or to the mother?* Quite different from temporary side effects, these serious risks include the possibility of infection, injury, allergic reaction, loss of the fetus, even death of the mother, depending on the test.

▶ *What are the risks of not taking the test?* Women need to weigh the risks, side effects, and costs against the value of the knowledge to be gained. Knowing that a woman has a multiple PREGNANCY or that mother and child have an Rh incompatibility (see BLOOD) can help doctors make special preparations for CHILDBIRTH, for example. But if a woman has no intention of acting on the results—for example, if she has no intention of seeking an ABORTION or exploring possible FETAL SURGERY in case BIRTH DEFECTS are found, then some prenatal tests will have little value.

▶ *How long will it take to get the test results?* In some cases, as with ultrasound, the woman can actually see the fetus on a screen; in others, laboratory analysis can take some days.

▶ *What does the test result mean?* Once the test is completed, do the results indicate that a disorder actually exists, that it does not exist, or that it *may* exist? If the results are numerical, how do they compare to "normal" numerical results? Are the results clear-cut or ambiguous? Do they suggest action, retesting, or inaction?

With the answers to such questions in hand, women are prepared to make informed decisions if prenatal testing is recommended. (See specific tests mentioned above; also GENETIC INHERITANCE AND BIRTH DEFECTS HELP, INFORMATION, AND ACTION GUIDE on page 314; PREGNANCY AND CHILDBIRTH HELP, INFORMATION, AND ACTION GUIDE on page 580.)

prenuptial agreement, a document drawn up and agreed to by a couple in contemplation of MARRIAGE, with or without the aid of a lawyer, which does not actually take effect until the WEDDING; also called *premarital agreement* or, in the law, *antenuptial agreement*. Most, though not all, states recognize such agreements as valid, as long as the agreement was voluntary and basically fair, with neither party trying to "get the better" of the other through deceit. Prenuptial agreements preempt state laws that generally apply to marriage and DIVORCE, on such matters as ownership, management, and control of property; how MARITAL PROPERTY shall be distributed or disposed of at SEPARATION, DIVORCE, or death; AL-IMONY; wills and trusts (see INHERITANCE RIGHTS); and beneficiaries of life insurance (see INSURANCE AND PENSION EQUITY).

In the United States, some states have adopted a Uniform Pre-Marital Agreement Act as to how courts will deal with issues related to such agreements, while other states have individual laws covering prenuptial agreements. They generally agree in confirming that CHILD SUPPORT may not be affected adversely by the prenuptial agreement. In some states, where unmarried couples have had *living together agreements* (see COHABITATION), they can convert these to prenuptial agreements, if they wish. (See COUPLES AND FAMILIES HELP, INFORMATION, AND ACTION GUIDE on page 418; DIVORCE AND SEPARATION HELP, INFORMATION, AND ACTION GUIDE on page 238.)

prepared childbirth, an approach to LABOR and DELIVERY that seeks to minimize medical intervention in the birthing process (see CHILDBIRTH).

prepuce, an alternative term for FORESKIN.

primary sex characteristics, the reproductive organs and structures that are present from birth and that determine an infant's sex; sometimes called *primal sex characteristics*. In a girl or woman, the VULVA (including the CLITORIS and LABIA), VAGINA, CERVIX, UTERUS, FALLOPIAN TUBES, and OVARIES—all key elements of the female REPRODUCTIVE SYSTEM—are considered primary characteristics. By contrast, SECONDARY SEX CHARACTERISTICS are those that develop at PUBERTY, such as pubic hair or growth of BREASTS and LABIA to adult form. In males, primary sex characteristics include possession of a PENIS and TESTES. In rare cases, primary sex characteristics are ambiguous; a person may lack some primary organs, have undeveloped organs, or have organs belonging to each sex (see SEX IDENTITY).

progesterone, a female sex HORMONE produced in women after OVULATION, or release of an egg (OVUM), primarily by the discarded outer layers of the egg, which together are called the CORPUS LUTEUM. Its production is triggered, in a sense, by LUTEINIZING HORMONE (LH), which spurs the egg to burst out of the ovary. The progesterone surge causes an approximately 1° F increase in body temperature, which is measured during NATURAL FAMILY PLANNING. Progesterone is also produced in small amounts by the adrenal glands of both men and women and by the TESTES in men.

Progesterone's main function is to spur further buildup of the *endometrium,* the lining of the UTERUS, to prepare for a possible fertilized egg. In the absence of FERTILIZATION, the corpus luteum stops producing progesterone after about two weeks; the drop in progesterone and also ESTROGEN triggers the onset of MENSTRUATION and the end and beginning of another cycle. If fertilization *does* take place, the corpus luteum continues progesterone production until the PLACENTA—the uterine tissue that nourishes a growing FETUS—begins to produce large amounts of the hormone. Higher levels of progesterone during PREGNANCY stimulate BREAST development, inhibit movements of muscles in the uterus, and block ovulation.

Synthetic progesterone, called *progestin*, is often used as a medication, in cases of ANOVULATORY PERIODS, ENDOMETRIOSIS, for some kinds of INFERTILITY, and in some cases of endometrial cancer (see UTERINE CANCER). It is also used along with estrogen in some kinds of contraceptive medications, including BIRTH CONTROL PILLS, NORPLANT, and DEPO-PROVERA. Progestin-laden INTRAUTERINE DEVICES (IUDs) or vaginal rings may also be used. Progesterone or progestin can cause significant SIDE EFFECTS, however, and should be used only after careful consideration of a woman's total medical situation (see BIRTH CONTROL PILLS for more on the pros and cons).

progestin, a synthetic form of PROGESTERONE, used in some BIRTH CONTROL PILLS, NORPLANT, and DEPO-PROVERA.

Project on Equal Education Rights (PEER) (c/o NOW Legal Defense and Education Fund, 99 Hudson Street, 12th Floor, New York, NY 10013; 212-925-6635; Walteen Grady Truely, director), a project of the **NOW LEGAL DEFENSE AND EDUCATION FUND,** itself originally established as a litigation and education arm of the **NATIONAL ORGANIZATION FOR WOMEN.** Established in 1974, PEER seeks to eliminate sex discrimination in schools, especially by making the goals of Title IX of the Education Amendments of 1972 a reality in schools. PEER gathers and disseminates information on the treatment of girls and women in education; holds conferences and sponsors programs to ensure that girls have equal sports opportunities and equal access to training in science, mathematics, and computers; and has special programs for girls at risk for dropping out of school, including its Project SISTER (Stay in School to Earn Rewards), which seeks to prevent adolescent PREGNANCY, and in some states Project TEAM (The Education of Adolescent Mothers), which helps teen parents.

PEER also publishes various materials, including the newsletter *Equal Education Alert;* and also:

- PEER Reports, such as *Learning Her Place—Sex Bias in the Elementary Classroom, Ties That Bind: The Price of Pursuing the Male Mystique, Black Women in a High-Tech World, "Like She Owns the Earth"—Women and Sports, The Heart of Excellence: Equal Opportunities and Educational Reform,* and *The Report Card on Educating Hispanic Women;*
- PEER Policy Papers, such as *Fulfilling the Promise: A Guide to the Sex Equity Provisions of the Vocational Education Act, The New Women's Educational Equity Act: Still Alive and Making a Difference, The PEER Report Card: Update on Women and Girls in America's Schools: A State-by-State Survey,* and *Equity in Middle School: Mathematics, Science & Computer Education—A Survey of Teachers' Perceptions;*

- PEER Computer Equity Reports, such as *Sex Bias at the Computer Terminal— How Schools Program Girls* and *Programming Equity into Computer Education: Today's Guide to the Schools of the Future;*
- PEER Training and Organizing Manuals, such as *Cracking the Glass Slipper: PEER's Guide to Ending Sex Bias in Your Schools* and *Sharpening Advocacy Skills: A Guide to Organizing for Change;*
- the Project SISTER Report *In Their Own Voices: Young Women Talk About Dropping Out;*
- Title IX materials such as *Beyond Title IX: PEER's State-by-State Guide to Women's Educational Equity Laws* and *Title IX Packet,* including *Anyone's Guide to Filing a Title IX Complaint.*

prolactin, a HORMONE secreted by the pituitary gland that stimulates milk production in a woman's BREASTS. Prolactin also stimulates the production of other pituitary hormones—LUTEINIZING HORMONE (**LH**) and FOLLICLE-STIMULATING HORMONE (**FSH**)—which in turn stimulate OVULATION, or, release of an egg (OVUM). Because of this, prolactin is sometimes called a *luteotrophin* or *luteotropic hormone* (LTH).

The secretion of prolactin is itself regulated by other hormones, including the *prolactin-inhibiting factor* (PIF) and the *thyrotropic release hormone* (TRH), both produced by the hypothalamus. Sometimes a problem in either the hypothalamus or pituitary can lead to prolactin production—and lactation—in a woman who has not just given birth. That condition is called *galactorrhea* and should always trigger a medical examination, as it may be the symptom of a serious diseases, such as a tumor *(prolactinoma)*. Such tumors are often benign and readily treatable.

proliferative phase (follicular phase), the portion of the reproductive cycle (see MENSTRUATION) during which eggs start to ripen in a woman's OVARIES and the *endometrium,* the lining of the UTERUS, begins to thicken, to prepare for a possible fertilized egg. This phase is triggered by production of FOLLICLE-STIMULATING HORMONE (**FSH**).

prostate gland, a gland that produces secretions that form part of a man's SEMEN (see REPRODUCTIVE SYSTEM).

prostitution, the practice of having SEXUAL INTERCOURSE, in whatever form, for pay, often related to sexual slavery or the condition of being forced to have sex. Both are sources of women's oppression that continue to be encountered in several forms in the modern world.

In many countries the wholly legal, often government-regulated prostitution of the nineteenth century has given way to a situation in which a nominally illegal system of prostitution is selectively enforced by corrupt police and judiciary and dominated by male criminals engaged in a wide range of illegal activities. Britain has decriminalized prostitution, but not solicitation, while in the United States only Nevada has decriminalized prostitution. Prostitution was for some decades seriously outlawed throughout the communist world, though never entirely prohibited in fact; since the end of the Soviet Union and the independence of Eastern Europe, the region has moved toward the kind of semilegal criminally run system that prevails in much of Europe and the Americas. China continues to outlaw prostitution, but in practice not as sharply as in Maoist times, while it is entirely accepted in the rest of Asia, Africa, and Oceania, outside the communist countries. Male Japanese and other international tourists still engage in the infamous "sex tours" to other countries, especially in southeast Asia, that have engaged media attention for some decades, even in the face of the lethal sexually transmitted AIDS.

Female children and young women are still being sold and otherwise tricked or coerced into sexual slavery throughout the world, perhaps most freely in some portions of south and east Asia and Africa—indeed child-buying for prostitution seems to be increasing as clients seek sexual contacts with people less likely to have AIDS—and many governments in fact tolerate this slave trade, despite a series of international agreements now in force. The 1949 United Nations–sponsored Convention for the Suppression of the Traffic in Persons and of the Exploitation of the Prostitution of Others superseded a series of other international agreements, beginning with the "white slave" treaties of 1904 and 1910. So did the 1956 Supplementary Convention on the Abolition of Slavery, the Slave Trade, and Institutions and Practices Similar to Slavery, but neither has been fully ratified or effectively enforced throughout the world.

With the rise of the modern women's movement, some United States and European prostitutes led a fight for recognition of their work as a trade like any other trade, deserving of full legalization and protection from criminals. Most notable was the San Francisco–based COYOTE (Call Off Your Old Tired Ethics) organization, founded by Margo St. James in 1973, which served as a model for several other prostitutes' groups.

In truth, many women drift into prostitution—often to pay for a drug habit or because they have left abusive homes and have few other marketable skills and job prospects—then become effectively enslaved. Health problems are also a major concern. Prostitution, always a high-risk occupation, has become even more so with the advent of the worldwide AIDS epidemic. Many prostitutes, especially intravenous drug users, have become carriers of the disease and as such potentially deadly sources of mass infection.

Many WOMEN'S RIGHTS advocates—among the first, if not the first, being Mary WOLLSTONECRAFT in 1792—have seen MARRIAGE in general as a kind of legalized prostitution, involving the sale of a woman's body to a single man instead of many, and some have chosen to call marriage sexual slavery. Current DIVORCE rates date those comments for many countries, and many couples have in the modern era established egalitarian relationships of which no such characterization could be made, but individual women in some marriages and in many parts of the world might find their lot little better than that of a prostitute or sexual slave. (See SEX AND SEXUALITY HELP, INFORMATION, AND ACTION GUIDE on page 665; see also RAPE; INCEST.)

protective legislation, a group of laws, interpreted by regulations and court cases, intended to protect children and women, who were believed least able to defend themselves, from the kind of workplace exploitation so typical of the early days of industrialism in Europe and North America.

In England from the 1830s, the United States from the 1850s, and then in much of Western and Central Europe, trade unionists and reformers of both sexes and WOMEN'S RIGHTS leaders fought for and to a limited extent won laws that regulated the age, hours, working conditions, and occupations of children and women. Early in the twentieth century, such American women as the International Ladies Garment Workers Union and Women's Trade Union League leader Rose Schneiderman, Grace ABBOTT, Secretary of Labor Frances Perkins, and Eleanor ROOSEVELT were in the forefront of that fight. And it was a hard fight: it took the deaths of 146 workers in the 1911 Triangle Shirtwaist Company fire—most of them young Jewish-American and Italian-American immigrant women who were burned or jumped to their deaths because the exit doors of their unsafe factory were locked—to win effective factory health and safety legislation in New York, which served as a model for later New Deal legislation.

But there were costs, too, some of them hidden, as pointed out by a few women's rights leaders. For women there were sexist restrictions, most notably on night work and on the holding of some kinds of industrial jobs, and an effective presumption that women were weaker and less fit than men for many kinds of work. Many of those restrictions disappeared with the passage of the New Deal 1938 Fair Labor Standards Act, as did the presumption of weakness during World War II, when women held all kinds of industrial jobs and demonstrated their ability to do¯them as well as men. But much protective and some limiting legislation remained in force.

During the postwar period, workplace discrimination against women reappeared, to be prohibited only in 1964 with passage of TITLE VII OF THE CIVIL RIGHTS ACT and establishment of the EQUAL EMPLOYMENT OPPORTUNITY COMMISSION (EEOC). The question of protective—and restrictive—legislation affecting women is far from fully resolved, however, and continues to arise in such areas as health and safety regulations protecting pregnant women that come into conflict with their right to freely choose their jobs (see PREGNANCY DISCRIMINATION ACT).

Protectiveness has often muffled the sound of doors closing against women.

BETTY FRIEDAN, 1963
IN THE FEMININE MYSTIQUE

●

psychoprophylaxis, an alternative name for the Lamaze method of natural childbirth (see CHILDBIRTH).

puberty, the series of physiological changes that gradually transform a child into an adult. In girls these changes usually start between ages ten and twelve, triggered by a set of hormonal signals.

A master HORMONE called *luteinizing hormone-releasing hormone* (LHRH) is released by the brain in periodic bursts, which trigger the pituitary gland to produce hormones called *gonadotropins*. These stimulate the development of sex glands, or *gonads,* which produce the special cells required for reproduction. In women the sex glands are the OVARIES, which produce eggs (see OVUM); in men they are the TESTES, which produce SPERM. As they prepare for their adult functions, the sex glands themselves are stimulated to produce *other* hormones, in girls primarily ESTROGEN and in boys TESTOSTERONE.

It is these sex hormones that trigger the development of physical changes, called SECONDARY SEX CHARACTERISTICS, that indicate a young person is approaching sexual maturity. In girls the BREASTS, LABIA, and UTERUS all develop; hair begins to grow in the underarm and pubic regions; MENSTRUATION and OVULATION begin; and the hips widen as fat is deposited around the body in a characteristic adult female distribution, providing long-term energy reserves, to be tapped in case of a PREGNANCY. (It is these changes that some girls with ANOREXIA NERVOSA may be trying, consciously or unconsciously, to halt or reverse.) At the same time, and often becoming apparent before the other changes, the girl begins a growth spurt that continues into the late teens, when growth generally ends. Girls generally begin puberty earlier than boys, so in this in-between stage are often taller than boys of their own age, though boys tend to grow taller in the long run. In boys the comparable set of changes include development of the PENIS and TESTES; widening of the shoulders; growth of hair on the face, underarms, and pubic area; deepening of the voice; production of sperm; and the occurrence of spontaneous erections (see SEXUAL RESPONSE).

These physiological changes lay the basis for the social and psychological period called *adolescence.* In various cultures puberty has traditionally been celebrated with a social rite, often celebrating the attainment of womanhood or manhood, but in some cases the occasion for forcing a woman into a culturally determined SEX ROLE, as most graphically in the case of FEMALE CIRCUMCISION.

In rare cases—perhaps one out of ten thousand, affecting more girls than boys—the child begins puberty abnormally early, before age nine for girls and age ten for boys. The causes of this *precocious puberty* are unclear and probably various. Some cases are caused by tumors, hormonal disorders, or other diseases that trigger release of LHRH. At least some cases of precocious puberty seem to be inherited by young boys from their unaffected carrier mothers (see GENETIC INHERITANCE). The main problem of precocious puberty is that while production of sex hormones is initially speeded up, it often stops more quickly, leaving adult height shorter than normal; and that children who become sexual beings before their peers are at a significant social disadvantage. Researchers are experimenting with therapies to halt or slow precocious puberty and have had some early success in desensitizing the pituitary gland to the effects of LHRH. (See SEX AND SEXUALITY HELP, INFORMATION, AND ACTION GUIDE on page 665.)

pubic lice, tiny parasitic mites *(Pediculosis pubis* or *crab lice)* that infest pubic hair, feeding on human blood. These are generally spread by sexual contact and so are considered one of the SEXUALLY TRANSMITTED DISEASES, though they can also spread by contact with infested clothing or bedding. The main symptoms are itching; scratching should be avoided, if possible, since that may spread lice elsewhere on the body. The lice and their tiny white eggs *(nits)* can be diagnosed by sight under a microscope. Various lotions and shampoos are available to kill pubic lice; however, pregnant women should use no such products without consulting a doctor. Itching may persist for a time afterward, until the SKIN heals. Any clothing or bedding that has been in contact with an infected person should be dry-cleaned or washed in very hot water (125° F). Once off the body, pubic lice die within twenty-four hours, but eggs can live for up to six days. (See SEXUALLY TRANSMITTED DISEASES; also WHAT YOU CAN DO TO AVOID STDs on page 660.)

pudenda, an alternative name for external GENITALS, generally referring to women (see VULVA).

putative spouse doctrine, the legal principle that in some states protects a person who has been deceived into thinking that a legal marriage exists when in fact it does not, as in a case of BIGAMY. Depending on the laws of the state, the putative spouse may share, at least to some extent, in the division of the couple's MARITAL PROPERTY. (See also COHABITATION.)

Radicalesbians, a small radical LESBIAN feminist group formed in New York City in 1970, which in its position paper *The Woman-Identified Woman* asserted that the goal of women's liberation could not be achieved without women making themselves, as women, the center of their own concerns. The statement attempted to expand the common definition of lesbian beyond sexual orientation to include political orientation; as a practical matter, it was more a statement of separatism and an invitation to nonlesbian women to join the radical lesbian group in forming a united front for action, on the group's terms. Although the Radicalesbian group remained small, its thinking later became important to many lesbians and lesbian organizations. (See also WOMEN'S LIBERATION MOVEMENT.)

radical feminism, a body of theory developed by a relatively small group of activists who broke away from the American NEW LEFT of the 1960s to form a series of small revolutionary organizations in the late 1960s and early 1970s, their groups most resembling the anarchist-oriented New Left organizations from which they had come. Active in the WOMEN'S LIBERATION MOVEMENT of the day, they advocated the development of an entirely new body of women-organized and -run institutions and of a new women-oriented society. All men were seen as enemies, as were such institutions as the FAMILY and motherhood, along with all the other institutions of what was described as a woman-murdering patriarchal society, by such authors as Andrea DWORKIN, Kate MILLETT, Ti-Grace ATKINSON, and Robin MORGAN. (See also FEMINISM; CULTURAL FEMINISM.)

Radical Women, an early New York City–based radical feminist organization founded in 1967 by Shulamith FIRESTONE and Pam Allen. Its journal was *Notes from the First Year*. But the first year was its only year; the small organization split into three even smaller splinters in October 1968. (See also WOMEN'S LIBERATION MOVEMENT.)

Rankin, Jeannette Pickering (1880–1973), an American social worker who became a WOMAN SUFFRAGE campaigner in her native Montana and other western states from 1910, winning the fight in Montana in 1914, the year she became legislative secretary of the NATIONAL AMERICAN WOMAN SUFFRAGE ASSOCIATION. In 1916, standing as a Montana Republican, she became the first woman to be elected to the House of Representatives—four years before national ratification of the NINETEENTH AMENDMENT. A pacifist, Rankin opposed American entry into World War I and did not run for reelection (see PACIFISM and NONVIOLENCE); instead in 1918, she ran for the Senate as an independent and lost. History repeated: she ran for Congress again in Montana in 1940, as an isolationist; won a second term in the House; and was on December 8, 1941, the only member of Congress to vote against American entry into World War II. Her electoral career ended with that vote; she never again ran for political office. She did, however, continue to be an active pacifist; her final major appearance was at the head of the Jeannette Rankin Brigade at the 1968 Washington, D.C., anti–Vietnam War demonstration.

Men and women are like right and left hands;
it doesn't make sense not to use both.

———————————————— *JEANNETTE RANKIN* ————————————————

•

rape, the act of compelling someone to have sexual acts unwillingly or unknowingly; also called *sexual assault*. The definition of what actually constitutes rape has been undergoing a significant change in recent decades, since sexual assault has been a major WOMEN'S RIGHTS issue. It is an issue facing all women, of any age, because rape is in some significant ways less about sex than it is about power, with the behavior often designed to show control over the woman and to humiliate her, not "simply" to relieve biological urges.

SEXUAL INTERCOURSE with a female under the AGE OF CONSENT is labeled *statutory rape*, literally because she is regarded by law as unable to give consent. In practice, with the change of sexual mores since the 1970s, statutory rape is less often charged these days, especially between consenting adolescents, except when the male is significantly older than the female and in a position of trust or authority over her. If the sexual activity is in a family setting, the charge may instead be INCEST or CHILD ABUSE AND NEGLECT, depending on state laws.

Today most attention is focused on rape as sexual activity *without* the woman's consent. Traditionally, only violent or forcible attacks by a man on a woman other than this wife were regarded as rape. In centuries past, a woman had virtually no independent legal status, instead being "covered" by her husband (see COVERTURE), so rape was in the law actually seen as a crime not against the woman, but against her husband and "owner" and, through him, the state. The woman was often perceived as having brought the attack on herself, as being not victim but seductress, to be accused and hammered by the defense attorneys, whose main defense usually consisted in damaging the woman's character.

Though women's legal status has changed, unfortunately this pattern of assumption and treatment survives.

In fact, many women who have brought charges of assault talk of a *second rape*: their abusive treatment by police and in the courts. In those institutions, traditionally dominated by men, views of rape were shaped by masculine myths, such as

- the woman unconsciously wanted to be raped;
- the woman "asked for it" by the way she dressed, spoke, or acted;
- women like to be "taken" forcibly;
- some women accuse a man of rape out of malice, guilt, or revenge;
- women "deserve" to be raped;
- women say "no" when they mean yes;
- no woman can be raped unless she wants to be.

In the past the police and the courts also felt that if a woman had once consented to sexual relations with a man, she forfeited her right ever to refuse him and charge rape at any time later on. That has only begun to change.

It is no wonder that rape was so seldom even reported. Even when women brought charges, very few rape cases ever went to trial, and of these only a few resulted in conviction. Rape has traditionally been a crime suffered by women in silence, largely because society gave them little or no protection from such attacks. That began to change dramatically in the 1970s with the rise of the latest wave of the women's movement and works like Susan BROWNMILLER's *Against Our Will: Men, Women, and Rape* (1975). Regarding rape as emblematic of society's degradation of women, women began to develop groups that not only helped women give each other mutual support, but also helped educate the public about the frequency of rape and the *second* crime in society's treatment of rape victims.

What constitutes rape is still a matter of considerable controversy. The traditional definition of the Federal Bureau of Investigation (FBI) was that rape is "carnal knowledge of a female forcibly and against her will," including attempts to commit rape by force or threats of force. In some states "carnal knowledge" has been narrowly defined as involving actual or attempted vaginal SEXUAL INTERCOURSE. Other states have a wider view of the definition, including vaginal penetration by objects, including fingers; oral or anal sex; and also rape of men, not just women, though females continue to be the main victims. Some states may consider rape to have occurred if the woman was unconscious or otherwise incapable of giving or withholding consent, as if she were under the heavy influence of drugs or was mentally retarded, or if she were faced with the *threat* of irresistible force. Many women's rights organizations are today focusing precisely on the question of what constitutes rape and especially are opening to public scrutiny and protection two new areas: *martial rape* and *date rape*.

Traditionally, a married woman was supposedly obliged to be available for sexual intercourse at any time her husband wished. Since that was one of the legal foundations of MARRIAGE, the law did not recognize forcible sex within marriage as rape. Also since a woman was legally her husband's "property," rape was conceived of as legally impossible. Marital or spousal rape occurred, however, though in what frequency is unclear. In one 1980–1981 study, one out of ten

Boston-area women said their husbands had used force or threats to compel sex at least once, in a current or previous marriage.

Despite the also traditional reluctance of courts to meddle in marital affairs (see MARRIAGE), in the late 1970s some states changed the laws that exempted husbands from charges of marital rape. Typically, a woman must prove that physical force was used, that the threats were such that she could not resist the assault, or that she was unconscious at the time. Marital rape is still not recognized in most of the world, however, and is difficult to prove. In many cases rape is part of a wider pattern of family violence (see BATTERED WOMEN; INCEST; CHILD ABUSE AND NEGLECT.)

With date or acquaintance rape, women are sexually assaulted by people known to them—a manager, a fellow student, a co-worker, a neighbor, a relative, and, yes, a date. In fact, the 1990 National Crime Survey estimates that of the *known* rapes 58 percent were committed by someone the victim knew, including a husband or boyfriend, and 35 percent took place in the woman's own home. Date rape is especially painful to women, because—in addition to the violation of their bodies and their "space"—it involves abuse from people they regarded with some trust. Sometimes that trust is gone by the time of the rape, as with an ex-lover, but often the attack comes out of the blue in what had seemed, before it, a perfectly normal relationship. In fact, many women have only in recent years openly acknowledged or even recognized their experiences of date rape, partly because the common stereotype of a rapist is that of a crazed sadist, who tortures and perhaps kills his victim—a terrifying but always small percentage of rapists. Many men carry the same stereotype and fail to see their actions as rape.

Many date rape cases go unreported. Indeed, women raped by acquaintances are believed less likely to seek help at a crisis center, much less report the attack. One 1980s study for *Ms.* magazine found that one out of every four women (in a sample of more than three thousand at thirty-two colleges) had been a victim of rape or attempted rape, and in 84 percent of the cases knew their attacker, but only 27 percent of these women realized that the sexual assault they had experienced met the legal definition of rape. Many meet with disbelief when they tell others what happened. On campuses, *gang rapes* of women by groups such as fraternities are an increasingly acknowledged problem.

A related concern is *stalking,* in which a man—sometimes a stranger—follows a woman constantly, wherever she goes, often with implied menace. The problem has become sufficiently widespread that some states have passed antistalking laws.

Also a substantial concern is *custodial rape,* committed by men in positions of power, such as police officers, doctors, soldiers, prison officers, and hostel staff. This is a widespread problem all over the world, though it is only in recent years that it has been acknowledged.

Treatment of rape cases has improved markedly. Many communities have rape crisis centers that offer support; police forces often have officers specially trained to deal with rape cases; many courts have struck down sex-biased rules of evidence; and many district attorney's offices have added witness support services. (For an ideal picture, see RIGHTS OF RAPE VICTIMS on page 611.) Rape victims are no longer routinely sent for psychiatric examination, as was once common, and some states have enacted *rape shield laws,* which limit the court's inquiry into the victim's sexual history, often also keeping her name confidential. Even so, most rape cases still go unreported, many are not brought to trial for weak evidence, and many that go to trial do not achieve a conviction.

For individual rape victims, social and psychological counselors have identified a *rape trauma syndrome* that commonly results from the attack. Initially many women feel shock and fear, but also embarrassment, humiliation, and even guilt, with associated psychological and physical reactions such as DEPRESSION, headaches, insomnia, nausea, sexual dysfunction, and loss of appetite. Some of these symptoms will remain for long periods of time, even as the woman gradually goes about the process of reorganizing her life, when appropriate moving to another residence or changing her phone number. Many women are helped in this process by the social, psychological, and legal counseling available in rape crisis centers. Some never do recover fully, and find that the event casts a permanent shadow over their lives.

Women who become pregnant through rape often seek an ABORTION, and except in areas where abortion is unavailable or limited to saving the mother's life, most areas will grant an abortion for a child of rape or incest. As late as 1992, however, a fourteen-year-old Irish woman, raped by a friend of the family, was initially denied the right to go to England for an abortion, until the Irish government responded to public outcry.

Another special concern regarding rape is the possibility of catching a SEXUALLY TRANSMITTED DISEASE, especially AIDS. When force is, indeed, involved, the chances of transmitting AIDS are increased, because it can enter through the resulting cuts and tears in the skin. That appears to be especially true for anal sex (see SEXUAL INTERCOURSE). In a 1992 case, one woman about to be raped pleaded with the rapist to use a CONDOM and gave him one; that act may have reduced her risk of catching AIDS, if the rapist was infected, but was later found to bar her from bringing rape charges against the man; the jury found that this implied consent. Such cases will surely proliferate, and how future prosecutors and courts will respond to them is uncertain. One observer suggested that judges and juries need to understand that *submission* is not *permission.*

For many women, a major focus is on prevention of sexual assault. Women can avoid being in places where they are targets, for example. With dates or acquaintances, unless you know a man *very* well, you would be wise not to

- bring a man home, even if other adults are there.
- go to the man's home; even if he says others are there, many men take this as an implicit assent to have sex.
- go in the car with him to an isolated area.
- depend solely on him for a ride home; be prepared with other alternatives, such as a cab.
- become intoxicated and so seem more vulnerable; alcohol can also loosen the man's inhibitions.

Women should also be alert to signs of excessive control, inappropriate anger, or extreme possessiveness. However, if people could always *see* danger, there would be no problem. (See VIOLENCE AGAINST WOMEN HELP, INFORMATION, AND ACTION GUIDE on page 612.)

Perhaps it [rape] is the only crime in which the victim becomes the accused.

———————— FREDA ADLER, 1975, IN SISTERS IN CRIME ————————

•

RIGHTS OF RAPE VICTIMS

Ideally, every victim of sexual assault should have the right
- to be treated with dignity and respect during questioning.
- to be educated about procedures and the law in a rape case and her role as witness for the state.
- to free medical and psychological treatment by sensitive, trained personnel.
- to choose what preventative medical measures will be taken.
- to the best possible collection of evidence for court.
- to have support resources like rape crisis groups, to be accompanied by sympathetic friends, etc.
- to legal representation that supports the victim, since the victim cannot have legal counsel of her choice as the defendant can (because it is the *state,* not the woman, who is prosecuting the rapist).
- to a preliminary hearing in each case when an arrest is made.
- to personal privacy (prior sexual experience should not be admissible as evidence).
- to be considered a credible witness equal to one in any other crime.
- to consent to sexual relations with the spouse without violence and without coercion.
- to be protected from any violent assault regardless of the weapon used and regardless of which part of the body is violated.
- to submit to rape from fear alone without this being seen as consent, or to ward off the attack without being liable to prosecution itself.

Source: Rape Crisis Center, Washington, D.C., as quoted in *Encyclopedia of Feminism.* Lisa Tuttle. Facts on File, 1986.

VIOLENCE AGAINST WOMEN

Help, Information, and Action Guide

Organizations

▶ NATIONAL CENTER ON WOMEN AND FAMILY LAW (NCOWFL) (212-674-8200). Operates the **National Battered Women's Law Project.** Publishes the newsletter *The Women's Advocate, Protecting Confidentiality: A Legal Manual for Battered Women's Programs, Guide to Interstate Custody Disputes for Domestic Violence Advocates, Custody Litigation on Behalf of Battered Women, Battered Women: The Facts, Mediation and You* (on why it may be inappropriate for battered women), *Mediator's Guide to Domestic Abuse, Mediation—A Guide for Advocates and Attorneys Representating Battered Women,* and resource packets on family law issues such as civil suits by rape victims.

▶ NATIONAL COALITION AGAINST DOMESTIC VIOLENCE (NCADV) (202-638-6388). Publishes the newsletter *NCADV Voice,* the information bulletin *NCADV Update, A Current Analysis of the Battered Women's Movement, National Director of DV (Domestic Violence) Programs, Guidelines for Mental Health Practitioners in Domestic Violence Cases, Rural Task Force Resource Packet, Naming the Violence: Speaking Out About Lesbian Battering,* and *Domestic Violence Awareness Month Packet.*

▶ NOW LEGAL DEFENSE AND EDUCATION FUND (NOW LDEF) (212-925-6635). Co-sponsors the National Judicial Education Program to Promote Equality for Women and Men in the Courts (NJEP). Publishes the *State Index of Women's Legal Rights* and *Attorney Referral Services List;* a statistical fact sheet on child sexual abuse; and the Legal Resource Kit *Incest and Child Sexual Abuse* and *Violence Against Women.*

▶ NATIONAL COUNCIL ON CHILD ABUSE AND FAMILY VIOLENCE (NCCAFV) (202-429-6695 or Helpline, 800-222-2000).

▶ NATIONAL ORGANIZATION FOR VICTIM ASSISTANCE (NOVA) (202-232-6682). Publishes the *NOVA Newsletter* and the *Victim Service Program Directory.*

▶ NATIONAL WOMEN'S HEALTH NETWORK (NWHN) (202-347-1140). Operates the **Women's Health Information Service,** including health effects of violence.

▶ CLEARINGHOUSE ON WOMEN'S ISSUES (CWI) (301-871-6016 or 202-363-9795).

▶ CENTER FOR WOMEN POLICY STUDIES (CWPS) (202-872-1770).

▶ CONGRESSIONAL CAUCUS FOR WOMEN'S ISSUES (202-225-6740).

▶ NATIONAL CENTER FOR YOUTH LAW (NCYL) (415-543-3307).

▶ FEDERALLY EMPLOYED WOMEN (FEW) (202-898-0994).

► COMMISSION FOR WOMEN'S EQUALITY (CWE) (212-879-4500).
► Ms. FOUNDATION FOR WOMEN (MFW) (212-353-8580).
► WOMEN'S ACTION COALITION (WAC) (WAC voice mail 212-967-7711, ext. WACM [9226]).

▣ FOR LEGAL ADVICE AND REFERRALS

► EQUAL RIGHTS ADVOCATES (ERA) (415-621-0672; advice and counseling line, 415-621-0505). A national women's law center.
► LAWYERS' COMMITTEE FOR CIVIL RIGHTS UNDER LAW (202-371-1212).
► NORTHWEST WOMEN'S LAW CENTER (206-682-9552; for information and referral, 206-621-7691). For Washington State area.
► WOMEN'S JUSTICE CENTER (WJC) (313-961-5528; domestic violence shelter 24-hour crisis lines, 313-921-3900 or 313-921-3901; after-school dating violence hot line, 313-921-0420). For Detroit area.

▣ RELIGIOUS PERSPECTIVES

► COMMISSION FOR WOMEN (CW), EVANGELICAL LUTHERAN CHURCH IN AMERICA (ELCA) (312-380-2860). Publishes *If You Have Been Sexually Abused or Harassed ... A Guide to Getting Effective Help in the ECLA* and a bibliography on sexual abuse and sexual harassment.
► WOMEN'S MINISTRY UNIT (WMU) (502-569-5382). Publishes or distributes *Myths and Facts About Rape and Battering, Family Violence: A Religious Issue,* and *The Doorway to Response* (on helping battered women).

▣ INTERNATIONAL PERSPECTIVES

► UNITED NATION'S DEVELOPMENT FUND FOR WOMEN (UNIFEM) (212-906-6400). Publishes *The World's Women: Trends and Statistics 1970–1990* and *Freedom from Violence: Women's Strategies from Around the World.*
► WOMEN'S INTERNATIONAL RESOURCE EXCHANGE (WIRE) (212-741-2955). Publishes *A Developing Legal System Grapples with an Ancient Problem: Rape in Nicaragua.*
► INTERNATIONAL WOMEN'S TRIBUNE CENTRE (IWTC) (212-687-8633). Publishes the newsletter *Violence Against Women.*

Other resources

▣ PERSONAL GUIDES ON RAPE

If You Are Raped, 2nd abridged ed. Kathryn M. Johnson. Learning Publications, 1992.

Everything You Need to Know About Date Rape, rev. ed. Frances Shuker-Haines. Rosen, 1992.

Rape: What Would You Do If? rev. ed. Dianne D. Booher. Simon & Schuster, 1991.

◪ GENERAL WORKS ON RAPE

The Second Rape: Society's Continued Betrayal of the Victim. Lee Madigan, Lee and Nancy Gamble. Free Press, 1991.

The Female Fear: The Social Cost of Rape. Margaret T. Gordon and Stephanie Riger. University of Illinois Press, 1991.

Acquaintance Rape: The Hidden Crime. Andrea Parrot and Laurie Bechhofer, eds. Wiley, 1991.

Rape Within Marriage. HMSO Staff. Unipub, 1990.

Rape in Marriage. rev. ed. Diana E. Russell. Indiana University Press, 1990.

The Voices of Rape. Janet Bode. Watts, 1990.

I Never Called It Rape: The Ms. Report on Recognizing, Fighting, and Surviving Date Rape. Robin Warshaw. HarperCollins, 1988.

◪ BACKGROUND WORKS ON RAPE

The Victim of Rape: Institutional Reactions. Lynda L. Holmstrom and Ann W. Burgess. Transaction, 1991.

The Law of Rape. Irving J. Sloan, ed. Oceana, 1991.

Rape and Criminal Justice: The Social Construction of Sexual Assault. Gary LaFree. Wadsworth, 1989.

Theories of Rape: Recent Inquiries into the Causes of Sexual Aggression. Lee Ellis, ed. Hemisphere, 1989.

Brutal Intimates: Rapists. Zulma Gonzalez-Parker. Heartfelt Press, 1989.

Four Theories of Rape in American Society. Larry Baron and Murray Straus. Yale University Press, 1989.

Rape: The Evidential Examination and Management of the Sexual Assault Survivor. William M. Green. Free Press, 1988.

The Rape Controversy. Melissa Benn and others. State Mutual Books, 1988.

◪ ON OTHER SEXUAL ABUSE

Sex in the Parish. Karen Lebacqz and Ronald G. Barton. Westminster/John Knox Press, 1991.

Sex in the Forbidden Zone: When Men in Power—Therapists, Doctors, Clergy, Teachers and Others—Betray Women's Trust. Peter Rutter. Tarcher, 1990.

Is Nothing Sacred? When Sex Invades the Pastoral Relationship. Marie Fortune. HarperSanFrancisco, 1989.

Sexual Assault and Child Sexual Abuse: A Directory of Survivor Services and Programs. Linda Webster. Oryx Press, 1989.

Sexual Exploitation: Rape, Child Sexual Abuse, and Workplace Harassment. Diana Russell. Sage Publications, 1984.

◢ ON FAMILY VIOLENCE IN GENERAL

Family Violence: A Special Issue of Families in Society. Families International, 1991.

The Presence of the Past: Male Violence in the Family. Jan Horsfall. Paul & Co., 1991.

Family Violence: Coping with Modern Issues. Janie E. Rench. Lerner, 1991.

Family Violence and the Chemical Connection. Sally A. Baker. Health Communications, 1991.

Domestic Violence: No Longer Behind the Curtains. Alison Landes, ed. Information Plus (TX), 1991.

Family Violence and the Women's Movement. Gillian A. Walker. University of Toronto Press, 1990.

Breaking Free from Domestic Violence. Jerry L. Brinegar and Howard Pearson. Valet, 1990.

Domestic Violence: The Criminal Justice Response. Eve S. Buzawa and Carl G. Buzawa. Sage, 1990.

Domestic Violence and Occupation of the Family Home. UNIPUB, 1989.

Policing "Domestic" Violence: Women, the Law, and the State. Susan S. Edwards. Sage, 1989.

Feminist Perspectives on Wife Abuse. Kersti Yilo and Michele Bograd, eds. Sage, 1988.

◢ BACKGROUND BOOKS ON SEXUAL VIOLENCE

Violent Attachments. J. Reid Meloy. Aronson, 1992.

Understanding Sexual Violence: A Study of Convicted Rapists. Diana Scully. Unwin Hyman, 1990.

Sex, Love, and Violence: Strategies for Transformation. Cloe Madanes. Norton, 1990.

Violence in Dating Relationships: Emerging Social Issues. Maureen A. Pirog-Good and Jan E. Stets, eds. Greenwood, 1989.

The Lust to Kill: A Feminist Investigation of Sexual Murder. Deborah Cameron and Elizabeth Frazer. New York University Press, 1989.

Violence in Intimate Relationships. Gordon Russell, ed. PMA, 1988.

◢ ON RECOVERY

Do Tell Someone! Inner Turmoils Surrounding Sexual Abuse Victims. Yvonnia M. Houston. Shane (CA), 1992.

Quest for Respect: A Healing Guide for Survivors of Rape. Linda Braswell. Pathfinder (CA), 1990.

New Beginnings, rev. ed. Beth Haseltine and Lynn Peterson. Rape Abuse Crisis, 1990.

Free of the Shadows: Recovery from Sexual Violence. Caren Adams and Jennifer Fay. New Harbinger, 1989.

(See also CHILD ABUSE AND NEGLECT HELP, INFORMATION, AND ACTION GUIDE on page 152; COUPLES AND FAMILIES HELP, INFORMATION, AND ACTION GUIDE on page 418.)

Raynaud's disease, a condition in which the BLOOD vessels (see HEART AND CIRCULATORY SYSTEM) in the fingers, and sometimes toes, are so sensitive to cold that they go into spasm. Fingers feel numb, tingling, or burning and go through changes of color, first white, then blue; later, when circulation returns, they become red and painful. In some cases the walls of arteries thicken, permanently reducing blood flow to the tips of the fingers and leading to ulceration or even death of skin tissue. Raynaud's disease is especially common in women. Sufferers are advised to protect their hands and feet from the cold as much as possible, staying inside altogether in extremely cold weather; and to stop SMOKING, which constricts circulation. Medications called vasodilators are sometimes prescribed to relax the walls of the blood vessels; a bit of alcohol may have the same effect. In some cases surgery is used to cut the nerves that control constriction and dilation of the arteries. Sometimes the condition is associated with other disorders, including autoimmune disorders (see IMMUNE SYSTEM) such as ARTHRITIS and LUPUS; if that is the case, it is called *Raynaud's phenomenon.* (See HEART AND CIRCULATORY SYSTEM; also WOMEN'S HEALTH HELP, INFORMATION, AND ACTION GUIDE on page 334.)

Read method, a popular natural childbirth approach (see CHILDBIRTH).

reconciliation, in MARRIAGE, the resumption of amicable relations between a husband and wife who had been separated or otherwise in battle. The term implies that the parties "lay down their arms," forgive mutual injuries, and resume their marriage relationship. Some courts require attempts to reconciliation before ruling on certain suits, such as ANNULMENT, SEPARATION, DIVORCE, or related CUSTODY, ALIMONY, CHILD SUPPORT, OR MARITAL PROPERTY questions; sometimes these involve marriage counseling. If a couple has been separated, and especially if they previously filed a formal SEPARATION AGREEMENT, they may want or need to reaffirm the rights and obligations of marriage in a *reconciliation agreement.*

recrimination, a traditional defense in an adversarial DIVORCE.

Redstockings, an early CONSCIOUSNESS-RAISING radical feminist organization founded in 1969 by Shulamith FIRESTONE and Ellen Willis; one of the splinter groups developed after the demise of the RADICAL WOMEN group. Redstockings lasted only one year, dissolving in 1970. (See also WOMEN'S LIBERATION MOVEMENT.)

reduction mammoplasty, BREAST reduction (see COSMETIC SURGERY).

reform feminism: See FEMINISM.

religion and women's rights, a set of concerns that arise because of the tension between much organized religious belief and the principle of women's equality; these have drawn several kinds of responses from WOMEN'S RIGHTS advocates during the past two centuries.

For some, like Quakers and Reform Jews, whose faiths are far from fundamentalist, the issue of a patriarchal deity has perhaps posed less contradiction with women's rights than for Catholics, fundamentalist Protestants, or Orthodox Jews. But for women affiliated with religions that have at the center the single, patriarchal deity of the Bible, there have been problems asserting equality in the framework of organized religion.

Women in the nineteenth and early twentieth century attempted to change patriarchal attitudes and church structures, in part by a feminist reinterpretation of the Bible, as in Matilda GAGE's *Woman, Church, and State* (1893) and Elizabeth Cady STANTON's *The Women's Bible* (1895, 1898). Late in the twentieth century, Mary DALY called for similar reforms in the Catholic church, in her book *The Church and the Second Sex* (1968). Several twentieth-century reform movements, on such specifics as the ordination of women, have also developed and have had some success, as in the ordination of Barbara Harris, who in 1989 became the first woman bishop of the Episcopal church and of the worldwide Anglican communion; in 1992 Anglicans in Britain decided to allow ordination of women. But the success has been quite limited. In late 1992 all attempts to secure the ordination of women on any level had so far been defeated within the Catholic church, as had been attempts to alter the Anglican liturgy. For women church reformers, a century-long struggle was, in the early 1990s, still just beginning.

Many women rationalists simply "voted with their feet," leaving religion for agnosticism or atheism—a little-publicized but wide response. Many others adopted political beliefs that were at odds with their previous religious beliefs, such as many who became socialists and anarchists; where in power, communists tended to severely restrict or outlaw all religions. But this response has been described as more a substitution of another set of religious beliefs than a move to rationalism.

Others developed alternative feminist religious beliefs, sometimes cast directly as religions and sometimes as a set of rationally derived convictions. Mary Daly, moving away from the Catholic church, joined in developing the alternative religion of SPIRITUAL FEMINISM. In her *Gyn/Ecology: The Metaethics of Radical Feminism* (1978), she spoke for a group of radical feminists who had rejected all existing major churches as patriarchal and substituted a monotheistic Goddess, based on what they believed to be the religious system of earlier matriarchal cultures (see GODDESS WORSHIP; MATRIARCHY).

Another spiritual feminist variant, ECOFEMINISM, is built around the belief that women are best able to solve the world's ecological problems created by men and the nature of PATRIARCHY. The related METAPHYSICAL FEMINISM conceived of FEMINISM itself as a pantheistic religious belief that could lead to a worldwide utopia, as put forward by Robin MORGAN in her book *Going Too Far* (1977). Some feminists approached the matter of alternative religious belief by becoming self-described WITCHES, a term covering a wide range of quite diverse beliefs and practices, as variously developed in many cultures. (See RELIGION AND WOMEN'S RIGHTS HELP, INFORMATION, AND ACTION GUIDE, below.)

I recognize no rights but human rights—I know nothing of men's rights and women's rights; for in Christ Jesus there is neither male nor female. It is my solemn conviction that, until this principle of equality is recognized and embodied in practice, the church can do nothing effectual for the permanent reformation of the world.

———————————— *ANGELINA GRIMKÉ, 1836* ————————————

•

RELIGION AND WOMEN'S RIGHTS

Help, Information and Action Guide

▶ COMMISSION FOR WOMEN'S EQUALITY (CWE) (212-879-4500).
▶ COMMISSION FOR WOMEN (CW), EVANGELICAL LUTHERAN CHURCH IN AMERICA (ELCA) (312-380-2860). Publishes *Call the Laborers: A Congregational Resource on Women and Ordained Ministry. Twenty Years After the Ordination of Women: Reports on the Participation of Ordained Women,* and a bibliography of the ordination of women.
▶ CHURCH WOMEN UNITED (CWU) (212-870-2347). Publishes the magazine *Churchwoman.*
▶ GENERAL COMMISSION ON THE STATUS AND ROLE OF WOMEN IN THE UNITED METHODIST CHURCH (GCSRW-UMC) (708-869-7330).
▶ NATIONAL COUNCIL ON THE AGING (NCOA) (202-479-1200 or 800-424-9046). Includes **National Interfaith Coalition on Aging (NICA).**

▶ Women's International Resource Exchange (WIRE) (212-741-2955). Publishes *Women Doing Theology in Latin America.*
▶ Dignity/USA (202-861-0017 or 800-877-8797).

Other resources

Can Women Re-Image the Church? Rosemary Chinnici. Paulist Press, 1992.
A Dangerous Delight: Women and Power in the Church. Monica Furlong. SPCK (London), 1991.
In Whose Image? God and Gender. Jann Aldredge Clanton. Crossroad, 1990.
The Male-Female Church Staff: Celebrating the Gifts, Confronting the Challenges. Anne Marie Nuechterlien and Celia Allison Hahn. The Alban Institute, 1990.
Sex, Race and God: Christian Feminism in Black and White. Susan Brooks Thistlethwaite. Crossroad, 1989.
Worship: Searching for Language. Gail Ramshaw. Pastoral Press, 1988. (Address: 225 Sheridan Street, NW, Washington, DC 20011.)
Creating Inclusive Community: Women Talk Race, Class, Gender and Sexual Identity. Packet of resources for 8-session group use. (Available from National Assembly of Religious Women, 529 South Wabash, Room 404, Chicago, IL 60605; 312-663-1980).

▨ BY OR ABOUT WOMEN OF COLOR

Speaking for Ourselves: Bible Studies and Discussion Starters for Women. Wendy S. Robins and Musimbi R. A. Kanyoro. World Council of Churches Publications (Geneva, Switzerland), 1990.
White Women's Christ and Black Women's Jesus: Feminist Christology and Womanist Response. Jacqueline Grant. Scholar's Press (Atlanta, GA), 1989.
We Dare to Dream: Doing Theology as Asian Women. Virginia Fabella and Sun Ai Lee Park, eds. Orbis, 1989.
Inheriting Our Mother's Gardens: Feminist Theology in Third World Perspective. Letty Russell and others, eds. Westminster Press, 1988.
Hispanic Women: Prophetic Voice in the Church. Ada Mara Isasi-Diaz and Yolanda Tarango. Harper & Row, 1988.
Just a Sister Away: A Womanist Vision of Women's Relationships in the Bible. Renita J. Weems. Lauramedia (San Diego), 1988.

▨ ON RELIGIOUS LANGUAGE AND WOMEN

Our Naming of God: Problems and Prospects of God-Talk Today. Carl E. Braaten, ed. Fortress Press, 1989.

What Language Shall I Borrow? God Talk in Worship: A Male Response to Feminist Theology. Brian Wren. Crossroad, 1989.

Excellent Words: Inclusive Language in Liturgy and Scripture. Lutheran Episcopal Campus Ministry at the Massachusetts Institute of Technology, 1988.

The Divine Feminine: Biblical Imagery of God as Female. Virginia Molenkott. Crossroad, 1983.

Faithful and Fair: Transcending Sexist Language in Worship. Keith Watkins. Abingdon, 1981.

(See also LANGUAGE AND SEXISM.)

reproductive cycle, another term for menstrual cycle (see MENSTRUATION).

reproductive rights, a woman's ability to control her own FERTILITY, safely and effectively, without interference from the state or any individual; a matter of considerable controversy historically and today, it is a developing area of the law both nationally and internationally.

"Reproductive rights" is most generally taken to mean access to BIRTH CONTROL information and contraceptive devises so a woman (or couple) can conceive when desired; to ABORTION so she can terminate an unwanted PREGNANCY; to voluntary STERILIZATION when she wishes to end possible childbearing; and to the whole range of reproductive technology to achieve conception, such as ARTIFICIAL INSEMINATION and *IN VITRO* FERTILIZATION. But reproductive rights might also properly include access to reproductive health care, so a woman can remain free of the diseases and disabilities that may endanger her sexuality and her ability to carry a healthy baby to term. In this sense reproductive rights would include access to sex education; counseling on hygiene, SEXUALLY TRANSMITTED DISEASES, and MENSTRUATION; INFERTILITY treatments; PRENATAL CARE; trained supervision for CHILDBIRTH and postpartum care; and infant and child health services.

In addition, in those parts of Africa and the Middle East where it exists, reproductive rights must include freedom from FEMALE CIRCUMCISION, which not only destroys a woman's sexuality, but also endangers her reproductive ability and indeed her life. (See topics noted above, and also BIRTH CONTROL AND FAMILY PLANNING HELP, INFORMATION, AND ACTION GUIDE on page 81; ABORTION HELP, INFORMATION, AND ACTION GUIDE on page 10; PREGNANCY AND CHILDBIRTH HELP, INFORMATION, AND ACTION GUIDE on page 580; and INFERTILITY AND REPRODUCTIVE TECHNOLOGY HELP, INFORMATION, AND ACTION GUIDE on page 368.)

reproductive system, the sexual organs, or GENITALS, that allow men and women to have SEXUAL INTERCOURSE; to produce the eggs (see OVUM) and SPERM required to make up a new being, with a unique GENETIC INHERITANCE; and, in the woman, to develop the growing FETUS and give birth.

The main parts of the woman's reproductive system (discussed more fully in separate entries) are

- the OVARIES, which produce the egg (ovum) required for CONCEPTION, or FERTILIZATION.
- the FALLOPIAN TUBES, narrow passageways through which the ovum travels and where the egg and sperm normally meet.
- the UTERUS, at the other end of the fallopian tubes, through which the sperm pass on the way to the egg; where the fertilized egg is implanted and grows; or from which, if the egg is not fertilized, the lining is shed in periodic MENSTRUATION.
- the CERVIX, the narrow end of the uterus, through which the sperm pass on the way to the uterus; which changes biochemically at around the time of maximum fertility (see NATURAL FAMILY PLANNING); and which helps hold the growing FETUS in place, until it widens at the end of GESTATION to allow for CHILDBIRTH.
- the VAGINA, through which the sperm pass; and which with the widened cervix forms the birth canal for the baby's passage to independent life.

These parts of the reproductive system also play a role in the pleasures of sexual intercourse (see SEXUAL RESPONSE), in the process enhancing the process of reproduction, as do the external genitals, in women known as the VULVA, and including the CLITORIS, LABIA, and BARTHOLIN'S GLANDS. In addition, various HORMONES control the stages of the reproductive cycle (see MENSTRUATION).

THE FEMALE REPRODUCTIVE SYSTEM

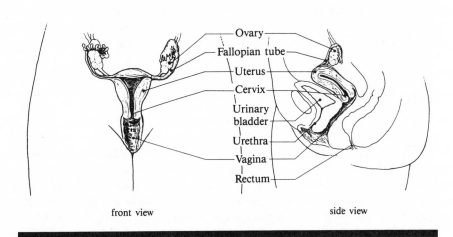

front view   side view

Source: *Pelvic Inflammatory Disease.* U.S. Department of Health and Human Services, Public Health Service, National Institute of Allergies and Infectious Diseases (NIAID), 1987.

The male reproductive system includes

▶ the TESTES, the pair of sex glands (GONADS) where sperm are actually manufactured and which also produce various hormones. The testes (testicles) are normally suspended outside the body in a protective SKIN sac called the *scrotum*, which hangs between the anus and the PENIS.

▶ the *epididymis,* two long, coiled tubes, one behind each testicle; actually a holding area into which immature sperm pass, by way of small tubes called *vas efferentia,* and where they mature.

▶ the *seminal vesicles,* structures that produce the fluid that makes up most of SEMEN, the sperm-containing fluid released at EJACULATION during ORGASM.

▶ the *prostate gland,* a chestnut-size organ that produces secretions forming part of semen; it is situated under the bladder and in front of the rectum. It grows to adult size during PUBERTY and enlarges further in older men, sometimes causing urinary problems.

▶ the *vas deferens,* one of a pair of tubes through which mature sperm pass on their way from the epididymis; the two loop up out of the scrotum in a kind of open-ended "figure 8" to the base of the bladder. It is the vas deferens that are cut during the type of male STERILIZATION called VASECTOMY.

▶ the *ejaculatory duct,* a short tube in which—shortly before ejaculation— sperm from the vas deferens and fluids from the seminal vesicles and prostate gland mix to form semen. This duct actually passes through the prostate gland.

▶ the *penis,* the main male organ of sexual response, through which semen passes. During sexual intercourse, the *urethra* through which urine normally passes becomes a passageway for semen, which is ejaculated as part of the male orgasm; some semen may leak out before ejaculation, so natural family planning techniques that rely on withdrawal of the penis before ejaculation are relatively unreliable.

In a newborn male, the penis and testes are relatively large, because of the effect of hormones from the mother; they soon grow smaller and then during PUBERTY gradually grow to their adult size. (See CONCEPTION; OVUM; SPERM; also SEX AND SEXUALITY HELP, INFORMATION, AND ACTION GUIDE on page 665.)

repudiation, a traditional form of DIVORCE.

RESOLVE, Inc. (1310 Broadway, Dept. GM, Somerville, MA 02144-1731; 617-623-0744; Beverly Freeman, executive director), a network of mutual-support groups, with trained counselors, for couples dealing with infertility. It makes referrals and publishes a newsletter and fact sheets on specific topics, including *Adoption, Artificial Insemination, Choosing a Specialist, Endometriosis,* In Vitro *Fertilization, Laparoscopy: What to Expect, Medical Evaluation of the Couple, Medical Management of Male Infertility, Miscarriage: Medical Facts, Semen Analysis, Surgical Techniques for Tubal Repair, Varicocele: Surgical and Medical Treatment.*

respiratory system, the lungs and network of air passages that bring in oxygen-laden air, pass oxygen on to the bloodstream, and expel unwanted carbon dioxide. The whole process of breathing in and out, exchanging oxygen and carbon dioxide in blood, is called *respiration*. It not only supplies the body with vital oxygen, but also helps maintain the body's chemical balance.

More specifically, air passes from the nose and mouth through the *trachea* (windpipe), bronchial tubes *(bronchi)* branching right and left toward the two lungs in the upper chest, narrower tubes in the lungs *(bronchioles)*, and finally into tiny air sacs called *alveoli*. Oxygen passes through the membranes of the alveoli and is picked up by the BLOOD and circulated throughout the body (see HEART AND CIRCULATORY SYSTEM). At the same time, carbon dioxide is picked up from the blood and moved out of the same set of air passages, being exhaled from the nose and mouth. The process is controlled by muscles operated by the central nervous system (see MUSCULAR SYSTEM; BRAIN AND NERVOUS SYSTEM), which helps the lungs expand during inhalation and contract for exhalation. If this process is disrupted in any way—if the bronchial tubes are blocked, for example, or if the air being breathed contains insufficient oxygen—the person's life can be in immediate danger.

The respiratory system is subject to a variety of disorders, among them

▶ *infection,* by bacteria, viruses, or fungi, all of which can infect air passages or lungs in general and can sometimes form life-threatening inflammation, including inflammation of the trachea *(tracheitis)*, bronchial tubes *(bronchitis)*, bronchioles *(bronchiolitis)*, or lungs *(pneumonia*; double pneumonia involves both lungs), and irreversible expansion of and structural damage to the bronchial tubes*(bronchiectasis)*, generally the result of long-term disorders. Some, though not all, respiratory infections are treatable with antibiotics.

▶ *allergies,* excessive reactions to foreign substances in the body (see ALLERGIES), often resulting in what is called *asthma*. In an asthma attack, the bronchial tubes are partly choked off by muscle spasms and swelling of bronchial tissue, and mucus clogs the smaller tubes, so little or no fresh air can enter. In a severe attack, the person may turn pale or blue, especially around the lips and NAILS, break out in a cold sweat, and have an accelerated heartbeat. Though it is not usually fatal, the number of fatalities is increasing, for unknown reasons. Asthma has traditionally been treated with bronchodilators, but recently doctors have turned to chemical treatments, which aim to block the swelling that may occur even *after* use of bronchodilators.

▶ *toxic substances,* inhalation of poisonous or damaging gases or dusts, such as asbestos or SMOKING, which can injure delicate lungs, often producing scarring and fibrous tissue that hampers the ability to breathe.

▶ *inhalation of foreign matter* directly into the lungs or indirectly (as from vomiting), causing pneumonia. This is especially common among newborns after a difficult birth, or in cases of ALCOHOL AND DRUG ABUSE.

▶ *blockage of air passages,* where the body produces mucus or other substances in abnormal amounts, blocking air passages and decreasing breathing capacity, as in the GENETIC DISORDER cystic fibrosis. If the condition is chronic or progressive, it may be called *chronic obstructive lung disease* (COLD), *chronic obstructive pulmonary disease* (COPD), or *chronic obstructive respiratory disease* (CORD).

- **injury,** in which something penetrates the respiratory area, possibly causing a lung to collapse.
- **damage to muscles and nerves** controlling respiration. If they fail, a person may be placed on an artificial respirator to continue breathing mechanically.
- **impaired blood and oxygen supply,** which can result from various causes. For example, a blood clot may block an artery feeding the lungs, or heart problems can cause fluids to collect in the lungs, a condition called *edema.* People who smoke or have chronic bronchitis or asthma often have a condition called *emphysema,* in which the lung's elastic tissue is scarred and the walls of the alveoli are damaged, limiting their ability to exchange oxygen and carbon dioxide. The result is chronic shortness of breath and significant limitation of activity.
- **tumors,** benign or cancerous, often associated with SMOKING (see LUNG CANCER).

Women have special breathing problems during PREGNANCY, because the growing FETUS presses on the diaphragm, the large muscle vital for breathing that separates the chest and abdominal cavities. By late in pregnancy, women may often become breathless from even modest exertion; depending on the fetal position, breathing in the last weeks of pregnancy can also sometimes be painful. To ease the discomfort when lying down, many women pile several pillows on a slant, to keep them on an incline instead of lying flat.

For more help, information, and action

- **American Lung Association (ALA)** (National Headquarters, 1740 Broadway, New York, NY 10019; 212-315-8700; James A. Swomley, executive director), an organization concerned with lung disorders. It gathers and disseminates information and publishes various print and audiovisual materials, such as *About Lungs and Lung Diseases, As You Live . . . You Breathe, Histo Facts, Health Hazards in the Arts, In Defense of the Lung,* and *Tuberculosis Facts.*
- NATIONAL HEART, LUNG, AND BLOOD INSTITUTE **(NHLBI)** (301-496-4236). Publishes *The Lungs: Medicine for the Layman* and *Chronic Obstructive Pulmonary Disease.*

Other resources

The Chronic Bronchitis and Emphysema Handbook. François Haas and Sheila Sperber Haas. Wiley, 1990.

The Breath Connection: How to Reduce Psychosomatic and Stress-Related Disorders with Easy-to-Do Breathing Exercises. Robert Fried. Plenum, 1990.

Health Care U.S.A. Jean Carper. Prentice Hall Press, 1987. Lists key lung disease specialists and treatment and research centers. (See also ALLERGIES; LUNG CANCER; CANCER.)

Retirement Equity Act of 1984 (REA), a U.S. federal law aimed at correcting inequities in federal and state pension laws (see INSURANCE AND PENSION EQUITY).

Revolution, The, a magazine edited by Susan B. ANTHONY.

Revolution from Within: A Book of Self-Esteem: See Gloria STEINEM.

rhinoplasty, nose surgery (see COSMETIC SURGERY).

rhytidectomy, a facelift (see COSMETIC SURGERY).

Rich, Adrienne Cecile (1929–), a U.S. poet and radical feminist, best known to wide audiences for such poetry collections as *A Change of World* (1951), *Snapshots of a Daughter-in-Law* (1953), *Diamond Cutters* (1955), *Necessities of Life and Other Poems* (1969), *Diving into the Wreck* (1973), *The Dream of a Common Language* (1978), *A Wild Patience Has Taken Me This Far* (1981), and *Time's Power* (1989). Her major radical feminist works include *Of Woman Born* (1976), *Women and Honour* (1977), *On Lives, Secrets, and Silences* (1979), and *Blood, Bread, and Poetry* (1989). In 1974 she refused to accept personally a National Book Award, choosing instead to accept it with Alice WALKER and Audrey Rich as a symbol of her solidarity with womankind.

right of election, in inheritance, the ability of a surviving wife or husband to choose between the amount granted in the decedent's will, called the *distributive share*, and the minimum amount provided by law, often one-third to one-half of the estate. Laws giving the right of election take the place of the more traditional common law practices of DOWER and CURTESY; these continue in some areas, however, as the right of election does not exist in all states. (See INHERITANCE RIGHTS.)

Roe v. Wade, the landmark 1973 U.S. Supreme Court decision that for the first time legalized abortion in the United States. (see ABORTION).

Roosevelt, Eleanor (Anna Eleanor Roosevelt; 1884–1962), an American political leader, who while the wife of President Franklin Delano Roosevelt became a national and world figure in her own right and after his death went on to become the leading woman of her time. Hers was the most central

American political family of the twentieth century. She was the niece of President Theodore Roosevelt, married Franklin Roosevelt in 1905, took him through his crippling bout with polio in the early 1920s, and went to the White House with him as his colleague as well as wife, the person he called his "eyes and ears." She was instrumental in forming his "New Deal" policies that helped sustain the country through the Great Depression and made great strides for women and disenfranchised people in general.

Eleanor Roosevelt worked with the Red Cross during World War I, with the LEAGUE OF WOMEN VOTERS from 1920, and from the early 1920s in the Democratic Party. After Franklin Roosevelt's election in 1932 she strongly influenced the development of the new administration's social programs and also took them to the country, as lecturer and writer, most notably in her nationally syndicated daily column *My Day*. She also brought many leading women into the federal government and was herself a symbol of women's achievement during the Great Depression and World War II.

She was a member of the United States delegation to the United Nations (1945–1953) and chaired the U.N. Commission on Human Rights, in 1948 accomplishing passage of the landmark U.N. Declaration of Human Rights. She also continued to be active as a leading reformer in the Democratic Party, while still writing and lecturing. Her three autobiographies were *This Is My Story* (1937), *This I Remember* (1949), and *On My Own* (1958).

Too often the great decisions are originated and given form in bodies made up wholly of men, or so completely dominated by them that whatever of special value women have to offer is shunted aside without expression.

ELEANOR ROOSEVELT, 1952
IN A SPEECH BEFORE THE UNITED NATIONS

•

Rubyfruit Jungle: See Rita Mae BROWN.

RU486, a drug used to induce ABORTION; named for Roussel-Uclaf, the French company that developed the pill. It is sometimes called the "abortion pill," but its developer, Étienne-Émile Baulieu, prefers to call it a *contragestive*, because it acts to prevent GESTATION, or growth of an EMBRYO in the UTERUS.

RU486 has been the subject of enormous controversy, with many antiabortion activists totally opposed to its use and many pro-choice activists hailing it as a breakthrough. However, the pill is neither so easy to use nor as totally free of possible side effects as has been popularly thought. Some women's organizations, such as the NATIONAL WOMEN'S HEALTH NETWORK, have raised significant questions about whether tests have been sufficiently thorough and long-term for widespread use, even if the pill is approved for use where it has previously been banned, as in the United States.

RU486, also called *mifepristone* or *mifegyne,* works by blocking the action of PROGESTERONE, which is vital for maintaining a PREGNANCY; the lining of the uterus breaks down, preventing or weakening implantation, and is then sloughed off, the result being an induced MISCARRIAGE or MENSTRUATION. RU486 is effective only during the first seven weeks of pregnancy; the embryo is at that stage no larger than a pea. RU486 alone is effective only 80 percent of the time, but effectiveness rises to 95 percent when it is used in combination with a synthetic drug called *prostaglandin,* which causes uterine contractions and helps ensure complete expulsion.

Far from being a pill that a woman can take in the privacy of her own home, as has been the popular conception, RU486 involves a several-stage process. In France, where it was approved for use in 1988, a woman goes to a BIRTH CONTROL center for a pregnancy test and a GYNECOLOGICAL EXAMINATION, and then registers her decision to have an abortion. She returns a week later, where she is given an oral dose of RU486. She returns again two days later for a dose of prostaglandin, either as an injection or a vaginal suppository; at that point she stays in the clinic for about four hours, so the doctors can monitor and treat side effects from the prostaglandin, including pain, nausea, vomiting, and diarrhea. In three out of four women, the blood flow of the abortion begins while they are in the clinic; in others it starts later. A week later the woman returns to the clinic to be sure the abortion is complete. If it is not—if some matter is left in the uterus or if no abortion took place—she is scheduled to have a surgical abortion; this occurs in about one woman out of twenty and is necessary to avoid possibly life-threatening infections. In France, a woman signs a form agreeing to have a surgical abortion if RU486 fails, as a condition of being given the pill, because of concerns about damage to the FETUS if the pregnancy is then taken to term.

At this checkup also, doctors monitor the woman's bleeding, which can last from a few days to over a month; in about one to two women per one thousand it can be so heavy as to require a transfusion (see BLOOD). In one case, in 1991, a thirty-one-year-old Frenchwoman died of cardiovascular shock, because of a life-threatening drop in blood pressure. As a result, France issued new guidelines for RU486, barring its use in women who smoke (see SMOKING), as that woman did, or are over age thirty-four. Also advised to avoid RU486 are women who have had a recent CESAREAN SECTION or have various health problems, including circulatory problems or high blood pressure (see HEART AND CIRCULATORY SYSTEM), FIBROIDS, bronchial asthma (see ALLERGIES; RESPIRATORY SYSTEM), glaucoma (see EYES), ulcers or colitis (see DIGESTIVE SYSTEM), anemia (see BLOOD), gynecological infections (see SEXUALLY TRANSMITTED DISEASES), or problems with the adrenal glands.

One thing seems clear: As it now stands, RU486 does not "demedicalize" the process of abortion. While it can be prescribed and administered anonymously in a doctor's office, and so (unlike abortion clinics) would not make either the woman or her doctor subject to the antiabortion protests of recent years, it still requires several visits to the doctor. That poses special problems for young women, rural women, poor women, and those with young children and inadequate CHILD CARE. In some European countries, where abortion frequently requires a hospital stay (for which there is often a several-week wait) and is performed under general ANESTHESIA, RU486 may be an attractive alternative; in many such countries health care costs are covered by the government, so any difference in cost is also not a factor. In the United States, however, where surgical abortions are less major procedures, even with increased restrictions on their availability, RU486 may be both more expensive and less convenient for many women—and in 5 percent of the cases may need to be followed by a surgical abortion as well.

Another drawback is that RU486 is effective only in the first seven weeks of pregnancy, or up to five weeks after a missed period. However, many women barely know they are pregnant by this time, and even if they do, most are not prepared to make a decision on abortion so quickly. This is especially true of young women, who tend to leave the decision longer than most and who therefore are more likely to have a second trimester abortion.

Many people have held out the hope of RU486 to solve population problems in the developing world. Certainly the need is great, given the number of women who die each year from unskilled, unsanitary abortions. If a simple pill existed, it would seem to be ideal. But the realities of several visits, careful monitoring for bleeding problems and incomplete abortion, and the need for refrigeration of prostaglandin all make RU486—at the present stage of development—so cumbersome to administrate as to be unlikely to help the poor women, rural or urban, who need it most.

A wider concern is the question of long-term effects. Though studies have been done following women after a single abortion, there has not been time to monitor them for any long-term changes. More worrisome, little or nothing is known of the potential effects on the body if a woman has several RU486 abortions during her lifetime. Critics point to the problems with DES (diethylstibestrol), which was later found to damage the REPRODUCTIVE SYSTEM, with adverse effects being passed on to the next generation. Even many who support access to the drug, in the United States and elsewhere, are concerned over a possible rush to use RU486 widely before it has had thorough testing for long-term effects.

In practice, the ban on RU486 will probably be lifted gradually, and its use then will be subject to what the argument is all about: choice. Women will then be able to make informed decisions about whether or not to have an abortion and, if so, what method to use. It is likely, too, that RU486 and similar drugs will continue to be improved and developed. Down the line, as Baulieu himself has predicted, many women may take a once-a-month pill to prevent implantation and gestation; if that happens, the line between CONCEPTION and abortion will dissolve. In fact, a 1992 Scottish study indicated that RU486 was safe and effective as a MORNING AFTER PILL. RU486 has also shown promise for other uses, such as slowing development of BREAST CANCER and brain tumors and relaxing the CERVIX during difficult deliveries, to lessen cesarean sections, especially in STILLBIRTHS. (See ABORTION; DES; BIRTH CONTROL; also ABORTION HELP, INFORMATION, AND ACTION GUIDE on page 10; and BIRTH CONTROL AND FAMILY PLANNING HELP, INFORMATION, AND ACTION GUIDE on page 81.)

salpingectomy, surgical removal of the FALLOPIAN TUBES, as in cases of ECTOPIC PREGNANCY.

Sanger, Margaret Higgins (1879–1966), an American public health nurse who became one of the leading women of the twentieth century in the course of her long battle to legalize and spread information on CONTRACEPTION; it was Sanger who coined the term BIRTH CONTROL in 1914.

Sanger's interest in contraception stemmed from her work with poor mothers as a visiting nurse in the slums that made up New York's Lower East Side shortly after the turn of century and also through her long association with such radical feminists as Emma GOLDMAN. Some of her earliest articles were published in the Socialist party organ *The Call*. In 1914 she founded the magazine *Woman Rebel* and was in that year indicted on obscenity charges for sending contraceptive information through the mail, as articles in her magazine. The indictment was dropped. In that year she also founded the National Birth Control League.

In 1916, in the Brownsville section of Brooklyn, Sanger founded the first birth control clinic. She was arrested and jailed for thirty days in 1917 but on appeal won a landmark New York State Court of Appeals decision that made it possible for doctors to give patients birth control information; another court case, in 1936, provided much of the basis for granting doctors the right legally to prescribe birth control devices.

Her wider work developed with her founding of the American Birth Control League in 1921, followed in 1923 by the Birth Control Clinical Research Bureau, the first such clinic staffed by doctors. The league ultimately, in 1942, became the PLANNED PARENTHOOD Federation. Her worldwide work also proceeded; in 1953 she became president of the International Planned Parenthood Federation. Her books include *What Every Woman Should Know* (1917), *Women, Morality, and Birth Control* (1922), and *My Fight for Birth Control* (1931).

sanitary napkins, disposable products used during MENSTRUATION to absorb blood flow.

scabies, infestation of the SKIN by tiny mites called *Sarcoptes scabiei*. These are often spread through sexual contact and so are considered one of the SEXUALLY TRANSMITTED DISEASES, but they may also be spread by contact with infested skin, linens, even furniture. Symptoms include intense itching in the most commonly affected areas, including hands (especially between the fingers), wrists, elbows, lower abdomen, and GENITALS. Where the female scabies burrows into the skin to lay eggs, small red humps or lines appear—but perhaps not for a month or more, during which time a person can unknowingly transmit the disease. The skin irritation can be mistaken for poison ivy or eczema but can be diagnosed by examining a skin scraping under a microscope.

Scabies can be treated with various kinds of creams or lotions, but pregnant women should not use any without consulting a doctor. Sex partners and family members are also advised to be treated. Clothing or bedding that has been in contact with an infected person should be dry-cleaned, washed in very hot water, dried at a high setting, and ironed—or boiled—to get rid of mites. (See SEXUALLY TRANSMITTED DISEASES; also WHAT YOU CAN DO TO AVOID STDs on page 660.)

Schlafly, Phyllis Stewart (1924–), an author, broadcaster, and political activist, best known as the antifeminist who spearheaded the successful campaign against ratification of the EQUAL RIGHTS AMENDMENT (ERA). Active in conservative Republican politics from the early 1950s, she came to national prominence with her self-published 1964 book, *A Choice Not an Echo,* supporting Barry Goldwater's presidential campaign. Schlafly established herself as a national leader by founding several conservative women's groups, the core of the audience for her *Phyllis Schlafly Report.*

From this newsletter she launched her first written public attack on the Equal Rights Amendment in 1972, later founding the national Stop-ERA and Eagle Forum organizations, which worked with other ANTIFEMINIST organizations nationwide to block ratification of the ERA. Though initially discounted, Schlafly and her supporters did indeed stop the ERA in its tracks. Their main weapons were charges that the ERA was a threat to FAMILY life and would be a "step down" for women, who Schlafly said were "extremely well treated," and that under the ERA women would be obliged to serve in the military and would lose protection under various financial support laws (see SPOUSAL SUPPORT; ALIMONY).

Throughout her career Schlafly has portrayed herself as a housewife coordinating her activities on her kitchen table, but many observers have pointed out that she is a professional politician, with full-time domestic and office staff to back her up while she raised the six children she bore starting in 1950 and while she returned to law school, gaining her J.D. in 1978. Among her other books on female-related issues are *The Power of the Positive Woman* (1977), *Child Abuse in the Classroom* (1984), and *Pornography's Victims* (1987).

The claim that American women are downtrodden and unfairly treated is the fraud of the century.

PHYLLIS SCHLAFLY, AS QUOTED
IN MS. MAGAZINE, MARCH 1974

•

scrotum, the loose sac of SKIN that holds a man's TESTES (see REPRODUCTIVE SYSTEM).

secondary sex characteristics, physical aspects of the body that develop during PUBERTY, as the body responds to various HORMONES, especially the sex hormones—ESTROGEN in women, TESTOSTERONE in men. Among the secondary sex characteristics in women are the development of BREASTS and LABIA; the growth of hair in an adult pattern, notably in the pubic area and under the arms; and the laying down of fat deposits in various parts of the body to give the characteristic figure of an adult woman. The corresponding secondary sex characteristics in men include development of the PENIS and TESTES; hair in the pubic and underarm areas and on the face; and general bodily development to adult form. (See PRIMARY SEX CHARACTERISTICS.)

Second Sex, The: See Simone de BEAUVOIR.

Second Stage, The: See Betty FRIEDAN.

secretory phase (luteal phase), the middle portion of the reproductive cycle (see MENSTRUATION), beginning with the release of an egg (OVUM) during OVULATION, which is itself triggered by the production of LUTEINIZING HORMONE (LH) from the pituitary gland.

seduction, an inducement to surrender CHASTITY, generally a man seducing a woman but sometimes the other way around. Traditionally, a father could bring a *seduction suit* against a man who seduced an unmarried daughter. In Western countries such suits are rarely brought today, partly because the revolution in sexual mores has rendered them obsolete and also because women are increasingly taking and being given responsibility for their own sexual activity. Seduction, then, is more often an inducement to have SEXUAL INTERCOURSE by mutual consent. If the girl or boy seduced is under the AGE OF CONSENT, however, an older person can be charged with statutory RAPE, child sexual abuse (see CHILD ABUSE AND NEGLECT), or, within a family, INCEST.

semen, the fluid forcefully released from a male's PENIS on EJACULATION during ORGASM. The fluid is largely made up of secretions from structures called *seminal vesicles*, but it also contains secretions from the *prostate gland* and SPERM; they are mixed together in a short tube called the *ejaculatory duct* (see REPRODUCTIVE SYSTEM; TESTES; SPERM).

semen analysis, one of a battery of tests in a *fertility workup*, performed to discover the causes of INFERTILITY.

Seneca Falls Women's Rights Convention, the landmark first

meeting of the first American WOMEN'S RIGHTS MOVEMENT, organized by Elizabeth Cady STANTON and Lucretia MOTT at Seneca Falls, New York, July 19–20, 1848. The meeting is variously reported as having been attended by one hundred to more than three hundred people and included at least forty men, among them former slave and abolitionist Frederick Douglass and Henry Stanton, husband of Elizabeth Cady Stanton. In the end, sixty-eight women and thirty-two men signed the DECLARATION OF SENTIMENTS AND RESOLUTIONS (see page 793 for full text), written by Stanton, which became in essence the founding document of the American women's rights movement. All but one of the resolutions incorporated in the declaration passed unanimously; the WOMAN SUFFRAGE resolution passed very narrowly. Some of the signers later withdrew their endorsements, faced with the storm of public abuse generated by those who opposed the declaration.

With the Declaration of Sentiments and Resolutions, the full movement for WOMEN'S RIGHTS began; almost a century and a half later, the document retains its power and current relevance, many of the issues it addresses still at the center of the worldwide fight for women's rights. In 1980, the 1848 convention site, including the Elizabeth Cady Stanton home, became the Women's Rights National Historic Park. Nearby is the privately funded Women's Hall of Fame.

separation, in MARRIAGE, the end of living together (see COHABITATION), either by mutual agreement or as provided by court ruling. Legally this is called a *divorce a mensa et thoro* (divorce from bed and board) or a *limited divorce*. Separation is generally a prelude to DIVORCE but may continue indefinitely, as when divorce is precluded by religious conviction. Either way, a SEPARATION AGREEMENT should be drawn up to lay out the changes in the rights and obligations of wife and husband to each other, since the fundamentals of their marital relationship have been changed (see MARRIAGE). If a couple later reconciles and again lives together as wife and husband, the separation agreement would end, unless otherwise provided in the agreement itself; the couple would need to draw up a RECONCILIATION agreement. If another separation occurred later, a new separation agreement would be required. (See SEPARATION AGREEMENT; RECONCILIATION; DI-VORCE; also DIVORCE AND SEPARATION HELP, INFORMATION, AND ACTION GUIDE on page 238.)

separation agreement, a document that specifies the changes in the legal rights and obligations of a wife and husband to each other, when a MARRIAGE is broken by SEPARATION or terminated by DIVORCE and sometimes ANNULMENT.

Though the breaking-up period is one of great turbulence and strain, a woman should arrange with her husband and their respective lawyers to draw up a written separation agreement quickly, even before the actual separation if possible. It is important that wife and husband each have separate legal representation, since their interests are different. On no account should the couple—even if both are lawyers—try to draw up the document themselves, since the result may affect the rest of their lives. Cool, dispassionate heads are needed.

Among the many areas that may be covered in a separation agreement are

▶ ALIMONY, also called *maintenance* or *spousal support,* payments to provide for the continuing support of a spouse, today usually for limited periods. Traditionally, and still most often, made by a husband to a wife, though payments by a rich or high-earning wife to a husband are increasingly common.

▶ CHILD SUPPORT, payments to provide for continuing support for children of the marriage. Child support should be clearly distinguished from alimony, and both should continue year-round, even during times when the child is living with the paying parent, for the maintenance of the child's home.

▶ CUSTODY, the main rights and responsibilities to care for children. If parents are unable to agree, the court may mandate custodial arrangements.

▶ VISITATION RIGHTS, the basic arrangements for a noncustodial parent to see a child. The arrangements should be as specific as possible, including everything from travel costs to out-of-state trips to safety concerns.

▶ *division of* MARITAL PROPERTY, an equitable distribution of marital assets between the partners, taking into account the past and present contributions of each, the length of the marriage, the background and employment prospects of a nonemployed spouse, the present and future needs of the children, and sometimes questions of fault. This is one of the most complicated, contentious, and difficult areas covered by a separation agreement.

▶ CHILD CARE costs, where a parent who has custody is a working parent, since this may not be covered by child support payments above.

▶ *education costs,* especially the cost of a college education. This, too, is not covered by child support; judges cannot mandate that a parent contribute to a child's college education, and in a surprising number of cases, noncustodial parents—generally fathers—have stopped paying child support when the child reached eighteen and have failed to contribute at all to college expenses. This leaves the child disadvantaged and places the whole burden on the custodial parent.

▶ *health care costs,* including health insurance coverage and also routine medical care, including eye exams and glasses, dental work and orthodontia, psychological counseling, and the like.

▶ *life insurance costs,* to provide for the children. Some experts recommend that the policy on the noncustodial parent (usually the father) be owned by the custodial parent, who also maintains the responsibility for making premium payments, in trust for the children. (See INSURANCE AND PENSION EQUITY.)

▶ *family debts,* covering who shall be responsible for which debts.

▶ *income-tax deduction,* indicating who shall take a deduction for the children.

▶ *attorney fees,* covering who shall pay for the two attorneys, including later fees, if necessary to enforce the agreement, such as obtaining child support or visitation rights.

▶ *warranty of full disclosure of all income and assets,* so that both parties are assuring that all property has been included.

▶ *mutual covenant to execute documents,* a legal promise to put the terms of the separation agreement into effect, such as assigning insurance benefits or changing property deeds.

▶ *mutual waiver of* INHERITANCE RIGHTS not otherwise covered in the agreement.

▶ *a provision that* RECONCILIATION *will not negate the agreement.* However, if the parties reconcile after a time of separation, a *reconciliation agreement* should replace the separation agreement and lay out the terms of the new relationship. And should another separation occur, a new separation agreement should be made.

Both parties should also sign a statement that they understand the agreement and are not under duress to sign it. Many people also include a clause specifying that MEDIATION and ARBITRATION may be used to settle disputes arising from the agreement; some states, notably California, mandate mediation in cases involving custody and visitation. (See DIVORCE AND SEPARATION HELP, INFORMATION, AND ACTION GUIDE on page 238; also PREPARING FOR DIVORCE: A WOMAN'S GUIDE on page 236).

separatism, in the widest sense, a move within a social or political movement to "go it alone," as in the wave of nationalist movements and civils wars that swept Eastern Europe after the collapse of Soviet communism. In social movements, examples are Marcus Garvey's "Back to Africa" movement of the 1920s, the Black separatist movement of the 1960s and 1970s, or the many attempts to create fully autonomous utopian socialist or sectarian religious communities. In the feminist movement, separatism appeared perhaps most notably as a fictive model in the 1915 Charlotte Perkins GILMAN novel *Herland*—and in the real world in several 1970s and 1980s utopian feminist communities, seeming an especially attractive model for some radical LESBIAN groups who wished to create a world totally independent from men.

Serious Proposal to the Ladies for the Advancement of their True and Greatest Interest, A (1701), a book by English writer Mary Astell (1668–1731), proposing establishment of an educational institution for women. Radical in its time, the proposal is thought to have come close to adoption, although it ultimately failed. (See EDUCATION EQUITY.)

Women are from their very Infancy debarr'd those advantages [of education] with the want of which they are afterwards reproached, and nursed up in those vices which will hereafter be upbraided them. So partial are Men as to expect Bricks when they afford no straw.

MARY ASTELL, 1694
IN A SERIOUS PROPOSAL TO THE LADIES FOR THE
ADVANCEMENT OF
———————————— THEIR TRUE AND GREATEST INTEREST ————————————

•

Sex and Destiny: The Politics of Human Fertility: See Germaine
GREER.

sex change, a surgical operation to change a person's external GENITALS, and a set of hormonal treatments, all designed to change the person's biologically in-dicated sex; also called *sex reassignment surgery.* The still-rare operation, widely publicized after it was performed on Christine (born George) Jorgenson in 1962, is sought by *transsexuals,* people who feel that their GENDER IDENTITY—their in-ternal feeling of their sex—does not match the body they inhabit.

For perhaps a year before surgery, patients are given HORMONES, which are continued after surgery as well. Transsexual males are given female hormones, such as ESTROGEN, which cause various bodily changes, including BREAST develop-ment and softening of the SKIN. The actual surgical procedure involves removal of the PENIS and TESTES and construction of LABIA and a VAGINA. Some electrolysis is used to remove facial and body hair; COSMETIC SURGERY may be performed to make the face more "feminine" looking; and the person learns to wear female clothing and to talk in a higher-pitched voice. Conversely, transsexual females are given male hormones, such as TESTOSTERONE, which deepen their voices and in-crease their muscular build. Skin and tissue from the abdomen and labia are used to form a penis and scrotum. The latter procedure is performed less often. Most people undergoing a sex change also receive extensive counseling before, during, and after the actual surgery. (See SEX AND SEXUALITY HELP, INFORMA-TION, AND ACTION GUIDE on page 665.)

sexism, a catch phrase popular from the late 1960s, referring to the whole spec-trum of male-dominant actions, attitudes, and assumptions, analogous to "rac-ism" in matters of race and racial discrimination. In the widest sense, sexism is that whole body of attitudes and behavior based on acceptance of stereotypical male-dominant and female-submissive SEX ROLES. The belief that males are natu-rally superior and therefore fulfilling their destined archetypal roles is—for the vast majority of men—unexamined, implicit, and seldom accessible to reason, built as it is deep into the structures, folkways, mores, language, and religious beliefs of their cultures.

Sexism is pervasive, touching many aspects of life; the treatment of women as SEX OBJECTS rather than individuals, the description of a working woman as a "girl," discriminatory hiring and promotion practices, and the assumption that women will do the HOUSEWORK and be unpaid for it—all display sexist assumptions, attitudes, and behavior, however overt or subtle, direct or indirect. So, too, are the assumptions that women are less able to reason than men, are intrinsically more emotional than men, should be expected from infancy to achieve less than men in many areas and occupations, and many other such limiting assumptions and the multifold discriminations that spring from them. And so, too, are the outright hates expressed by misogynists, who view women as sex receptacles or as subversive destroyers of men, or any other of a range of negative attitudes.

Some would have it that sexism is somehow limited to, or more prevalent in, cultures dominated by White males, as in Europe and North America, but that is not so. It is equally present in such minority groups as African-Americans and Hispanic-Americans and often far more overtly the rule elsewhere, as throughout the Muslim world, in sub-Saharan Africa, and in east and south Asia.

The term *sexist* has also been applied to equally unprovable theories of women's intrinsic superiority, though some feminists prefer to call them examples of "reverse sexism." In such matters as hiring and promotion, though, it is increasingly clear that sexism is a double-edged charge, that can successfully be used to frustrate preferential hiring and promotion in pursuit of affirmative action goals. (See SEXUAL DISCRIMINATION AND SEXUAL HARASSMENT HELP, INFORMATION, AND ACTION GUIDE on page 642; also LANGUAGE AND SEXISM; SEXUAL DISCRIMINATION; SEX ROLE.)

sex object, the focus of sexual attention and arousal. Women are quite properly angry and resentful when men treat them primarily or solely as objects for sexual gratification, not as whole, independent human beings; such attitudes generally spring from unquestioned assumptions about women's roles (see SEXISM; SEX ROLE).

sex role, the pattern of behaviors, attitudes, and mental and emotional characteristics that a society associates with females or males. Many feminists and WOMEN'S RIGHTS advocates prefer to use the term *gender role,* regarding *sex* to refer only to biologically based differences between women and men, such as that women can bear children and men cannot; they reserve *gender* to refer to culturally derived distinctions. Their point is that most so-called *sex differences* in society are, in fact, not biologically determined but are determined and taught by the culture, and that they vary in different societies and at different times in history. In some times and places, for example, spinning has been regarded as a male activity and in others a female one—witness the old name *spinster* for a SINGLE WOMAN. In fact, much of the WOMEN'S RIGHTS MOVEMENT at every stage has been an attempt to allow women a wider range of roles. And at the heart of much of the women's movement from its earliest days has been the conviction that traditional sex roles are unnecessarily limiting; that women should be free to fulfill a wider range of roles; and, more fundamentally, that social roles in society should be assigned not on the basis of sex, but on the basis of individual choice and merit. By contrast, what we call SEXISM is essentially a social attempt to restrict women to their traditionally defined roles.

Sex roles are learned at an early age. Young boys and girls are taught by direction, by a complex and only partly conscious system of rewards and punishments, and by example—from *role models*—what behavior and activities are considered appropriate for their sex. At every stage of life, in the home, in CHILD CARE, in school, in the community, on television and in movies, young girls and boys learn what "little girls and little boys do" and do *not* do; how females and males are expected to dress (see CROSS-DRESSING); what is considered "feminine" or "masculine"; and what is the predominant SEXUAL DIVISION OF LABOR. In seeking freedom from constricting sex roles for themselves and their children, many modern women have looked toward an ideal of ANDROGYNY, or a combination of both male and female attributes in one. (See SEXUAL DISCRIMINATION AND SEXUAL HARASSMENT HELP, INFORMATION, AND ACTION GUIDE on page 642; SEX AND SEXUALITY HELP, INFORMATION, AND ACTION GUIDE on page 665.)

In our steady insistence on proclaiming sex-distinction we have grown to consider most human attributes as masculine attributes, for the simple reason that they were allowed for men and forbidden to women.

CHARLOTTE PERKINS GILMAN, 1900
—— IN WOMEN AND ECONOMICS ——

•

sex selection, the use of a procedure aimed at controlling or influencing the sex of a child in PREGNANCY, whether before or after FERTILIZATION. Before CONCEPTION, one of the main techniques used is called *sperm splitting*. It is a man's SPERM that determines the sex of offspring; if the sperm carries an X chromosome, the offspring will be a girl (XX); if it carries a Y chromosome, a boy (XY). When desired, some of the Y-bearing or X-bearing chromosomes are separated out of the sperm, increasing the likelihood of the sex desired. The sperm is then used for fertilization in techniques such as ARTIFICIAL INSEMINATION or *IN VITRO* FERTILIZATION.

Similarly, some approaches try to make the fluids in a woman's VAGINA more acid by using a mildly acid DOUCHE; since Y-bearing sperm are more vulnerable to acid, this attempts to increases the likelihood of conceiving a girl. Conversely, making a woman's vaginal fluids more alkaline by using a somewhat alkaline douche attempts to make a boy more likely. Also, if the woman has an ORGASM near the time of insemination, her vagina becomes slightly more alkaline.

None of these techniques is widely used, nor is any very successful; though it is possible that they may increase the chances of having a child of the desired sex, sound scientific evidence of such effects is lacking. New, still experimental techniques allow doctors to determine the sex of an EMBRYO before insertion into a woman's body, in *in vitro* fertilization.

In general, X-bearing sperm seem to live longer, and some people suggest, therefore, that having SEXUAL INTERCOURSE one to two days *before* ovulation may increase chances of having a girl. However, the factors involved are extremely complex, and some researchers have come to an opposite recommendation, concluding that intercourse before ovulation tends to increase the likelihood of having a boy.

Postconception sex selection relies on the results of various PRENATAL TESTS, such as AMNIOCENTESIS, ULTRASOUND, or CHORIONIC VILLUS SAMPLING (**CVS**). Many such tests show the sex of a FETUS, in addition to desired information on GENETIC DISORDERS or CHROMOSOMAL ABNORMALITIES. One main reason for attempting sex selection is to avoid serious genetic disorders, especially those that affect mostly boys, such as hemophilia (see BLOOD) or some types of muscular dystrophy (see MUSCULAR SYSTEM).

Sometimes a woman or couple will choose an ABORTION if the fetus is not of the desired sex. Occasionally a couple desires a female baby, but most often it is female fetuses that are aborted, the preference being for male children (see SON PREFERENCE). In some countries, notably India, this is such a widespread practice that the proportion of males to females in the society is being totally distorted. In some countries, also, sex selection of a sort may take place after birth, generally in the form of female INFANTICIDE.

Some population planners recommend sex selection to help limit population growth, since many couples have larger families than desired because they are hoping to have a mix of sexes but instead have had all boys or all girls. The corollary is that, if boys are preferred, the next generation will have fewer women to bear children. (See PREGNANCY AND CHILDBIRTH HELP, INFORMATION, AND ACTION GUIDE on page 580; INFERTILITY AND REPRODUCTIVE TECHNOLOGY HELP, INFORMATION, AND ACTION GUIDE on page 368.)

sexual abuse: See RAPE; SEXUAL HARASSMENT, BATTERED WOMEN; CHILD ABUSE AND NEGLECT.

Sexual Behavior in the Human Male; Sexual Behavior in the Human Female: See *THE KINSEY REPORT*.

sexual discrimination, in the widest sense, all biased actions against people of one sex or the other. As generally understood, these are specific kinds of discrimination, the kinds that can therefore be quite specifically attacked by laws and new kinds of nondiscriminatory practices.

Among the most prominent of these types of sexual discrimination against women worldwide are

- The denial of or restrictions on the right to vote, hold office, make policy, and hold public and private jobs fully equally with men. (See POLITICAL PARTICIPA-TION.)
- Restrictions on women's free and equal choice of nationality, as when it is tied to their husband's nationality.
- Workplace discrimination, in hiring, choice of work, promotion, job security, training, equal pay for work of equal value, unemployment and disability insurance, public and private pension rights, health and safety, and because of exercise of reproductive functions. (See WORK AND WOMEN; EQUAL PAY FOR EQUAL WORK; PAY EQUITY; OCCUPATIONAL SEGREGATION; EDUCATION EQUITY; GLASS CEILING; MOMMY TRACK; PROTECTIVE LEGISLATION; INSURANCE AND PENSION EQUITY; PREGNANCY DISCRIMINATION ACT.)
- Damaging and unequal medical and sometimes religious practices. (See HEALTH EQUITY; FEMALE CIRCUMCISION; SON PREFERENCE.)
- Discrimination in the granting of credit. (See EQUAL CREDIT OPPORTUNITY ACT.)
- A wide range of discriminatory laws and practices in the areas of marital and family rights, including a woman's choice of SPOUSE, number of children, and spacing of children; her access to family planning information, including CONTRACEPTION and ABORTION; legal rights such as ADOPTION, guardianship, property rights, and choice of family name. (See MARRIAGE; COHABITATION; FAMILY; BIRTH CONTROL; REPRODUCTIVE RIGHTS; NAMES IN MARRIAGE.)
- Subjection to violent and degrading treatment, in the home or the wider culture, whether at peace or at war. (See RAPE; BATTERED WOMEN; SEXUAL HARASSMENT; CHILD ABUSE AND NEGLECT.)

Freedom from the abuses listed above constitutes, in effect, WOMEN'S RIGHTS. On the international front, these have been outlined in the 1979 United Nations *Convention on the Elimination of All Forms of Discrimination Against Women* (see page 796 for full text).

In the United States, the most prominent current sexual discrimination issues are found in the workplace. SEXUAL HARASSMENT has been by far the most highly publicized of these, because of the Anita Faye HILL–Clarence Thomas confrontation and her treatment before the Senate Judiciary Committee, and because of the TAILHOOK SCANDAL and other armed forces harassment and discrimination cases. Also of great importance is the issue of OCCUPATIONAL SEGREGATION, the grouping of by far the largest numbers of women in the workforce in low-paid administrative support and service occupations. Although women are moving into higher-paying occupations in large numbers, segregated training and placement patterns continue to be the norm. The related question of EQUAL PAY FOR EQUAL WORK, while guaranteed by law, has also become the sharply contested question of PAY EQUITY. The issue of illegal discrimination in hiring remains a practical problem, as does the question of discriminatory firing and other job security patterns, brought sharply to the fore during the depression of the early

1990s. Discriminatory promotion practices, at their high end popularity called the GLASS CEILING, are widespread, as is covert promotion discrimination against those women who raise families while continuing their careers, popularly called being placed on the MOMMY TRACK. And the question of pregnancy discrimination, although taken up by the PREGNANCY DISCRIMINATION ACT and its accompanying body of regulations and cases, continues to be a matter of contention. So, too, are a number of health and safety questions and associated insurance rights (see INSURANCE AND PENSION EQUITY; HEALTH EQUITY). The practical and legal implications of the substitution of equal rights laws for PROTECTIVE LEGISLATION are still being explored, with new laws, regulations, and cases continuing to flow in a considerable stream from the intersection of women's rights, labor, and employer interests. Very widespread sexual orientation discrimination also continues throughout the workplace, with LESBIANS and gays often facing homophobia that is, in practical terms, extraordinarily resistant to antidiscrimination laws.

Sexual discrimination cases, like other kinds of discrimination cases, are difficult to bring to court and win. There are so many different ways of discriminating that no set of laws could possibly cover them all. However, many cases can be resolved before court is reached, by working through a firm's personnel procedures or through state or federal agencies. The procedures are long and tedious, however, and women need a great deal of help in carrying them through. They can help themselves by preparing their own case immediately from when the discrimination starts (see SEXUAL DISCRIMINATION ON THE JOB: WHAT YOU CAN DO on page 641). If a woman is deciding to refer her case to the EQUAL EMPLOYMENT OPPORTUNITY COMMISSION (EEOC), she may want to look at HOW TO FILE AN EEOC COMPLAINT on page 262, for an overview. For organizations that can help women fight discrimination, see SEXUAL DISCRIMINATION AND SEXUAL HARASSMENT HELP, INFORMATION, AND ACTION GUIDE on page 642. (See also TITLE VII OF THE 1964 CIVIL RIGHTS ACT; EQUAL EMPLOYMENT OPPORTUNITY ACT OF 1972; TITLE IX OF THE 1972 EDUCATION ACT AMENDMENTS.)

It is interesting that many women do not recognize themselves as discriminated against; no better proof could be found of the totality of their conditioning.

KATE MILLETT, 1969

IN SEXUAL POLITICS

•

SEXUAL DISCRIMINATION ON THE JOB: WHAT YOU CAN DO

When deciding what to do about discrimination on the job, it is important to remember that antidiscrimination laws are not perfect and do not cover every type of violation or injustice at the workplace. Furthermore, pursuing a claim may be difficult if you are still working for the employer that discriminated against you. Thus, strategies for resolving a conflict will vary according to your particular employment situation. Often, going through the internal administrative process [of the organization] is sufficient. Other times it is necessary to file a complain with a state or federal agency or, as a last resort, pursue legal action in court. It is always good to consult a lawyer or legal services organization to determine what claims you have and to assess the strengths and weaknesses of your case. When fighting discrimination, keep in mind the following tips:

▶ *Document your case:* As soon as you encounter any form of sex/race discrimination, begin keeping records. Write down dates, places, times, and possible witnesses to the conflicts you have encountered. If possible, ask your co-workers to write statements supporting your allegations, especially if they have suffered similar treatment by supervisors or co-workers.

▶ *Create a paper trail:* Make your complaints to supervisors and administrators in writing. Describe the problem and ways to resolve it. This creates a detailed written record of the incidents or conflicts that you have tried to settle informally.

▶ *Use the grievance procedure:* If internal channels exist, you may be able to resolve the problem informally through grievance procedures at your workplace. Many employers have specific policies for handling discrimination problems. Find out what they are. A personnel or affirmative action officer should have this information available.

▶ *Involve your union:* If you are a union member, file a formal grievance through the union and try to get a shop steward or other union official to help you work through the grievance process.

▶ *File a discrimination complaint:* File a formal charge of discrimination with [the appropriate state or local agency] or the federal EQUAL EMPLOYMENT OPPORTUNITY COMMISSION (EEOC). If you are a federal employee, follow federal guidelines on how to lodge a discrimination complaint. Remember, federal employees have a limited time frame in which to file a complaint. Check with the EEO officer at your worksite.

▶ *Don't miss filing deadlines:* In order to preserve the timeliness of your complaint, you must file a formal discrimination charge with either the EEOC or [the appropriate state or local agency]. The importance of filing on time cannot be overemphasized. In most instances, courts will not consider a discrimination case unless a charge was filed first with the appropriate agency and the proper procedures were followed. Consult with a community legal organization or an attorney to find out about specific filing requirements and deadline.

Source: "Sex Discrimination" and "Pregnancy Discrimination," both "Know Your Rights" brochures from Equal Rights Advocates. (See also **How to File an EEOC Complaint** on page 262.)

SEXUAL DISCRIMINATION AND SEXUAL HARASSMENT

Help, Information, and Action Guide

Organizations

▶ **NOW** Legal Defense and Education Fund (**NOW LDEF**) (212-925-6635). Co-sponsors the National Judicial Education Program to Promote Equality for Women and Men in the Courts (NJEP). Publishes the *State Index of Women's Legal Rights* and *Attorney Referral Services List;* the Legal Resources Kits *Employment—Sexual Harassment* and *Male-Only Clubs;* a statistical fact sheet on sexual harassment in employment; and a video training program *Sexual Harassment: Walking the Corporate Fine Line.* (See other publications on judicial bias at main entry, **NOW Legal Defense and Education Fund.**)

▶ National Organization for Women (**NOW**) (202-331-0066).

▶ Women's Legal Defense Fund (**WLDF**) (202-887-0364). Publishes *Sex Discrimination in the Workplace: A Legal Handbook.*

▶ Older Women's League (**OWL**) (202-783-6686; OWL POWERLINE, 202-783-6689, a weekly update on congressional activities). Publishes *Employment Discrimination Against Older Women.*

▶ National Council for Research on Women (**NCRW**) (212-570-5001). Publishes *Sexual Harassment: Research and Resources. A Report-in-Progress.*

▶ Fund for the Feminist Majority (617-695-9688; 703-522-2214; or 213-651-0495).

▶ Congressional Caucus for Women's Issues (202-225-6740).

▶ CLEARINGHOUSE ON WOMEN'S ISSUES (CWI) (301-871-6016 or 202-363-9795).

▶ WOMEN'S ACTION COALITION (WAC) (WAC voice mail 212-967-7711, ext. WACM [9226]).

▶ NATIONAL HOOK-UP OF BLACK WOMEN (NHBW) (312-643-5866).

▶ WOMEN AND FOUNDATIONS/CORPORATE PHILANTHROPY (WAF/CP) (212-463-9934. Publishes *Getting It Done: From Commitment to Action of Funding for Women and Girls*, *Making a Difference: The Impact of Women in Philanthropy*, *Working in Foundations: Career Patterns of Women and Men*, *Far from Done: The Challenge of Diversifying Philanthropic Leadership*, and *Far from Done: The Status of Women and Girls in America*.

▶ MS. FOUNDATION FOR WOMEN (MFW) (212-353-8580).

▶ CENTER FOR WOMEN POLICY STUDIES (CWPS) (202-872-1770). Has *Educational Equity Policy Studies* (EEPS).

▶ NATIONAL ASSOCIATION OF CUBAN-AMERICAN WOMEN (NACAW) (219-745-5421).

▶ NATIONAL COUNCIL OF NEGRO WOMEN (NCNW) (202-659-0006).

◩ IN EDUCATION AND SPORTS

▶ PROJECT ON EQUAL EDUCATION RIGHTS (PEER) (212-925-6635). Publishes *Equal Education Alert*; Peer Reports and Policy Papers such as *Learning Her Place—Sex Bias in the Elementary Classroom*, *"Like She Owns the Earth"—Women and Sports*, *The Heart of Excellence: Equal Opportunities and Educational Reform*, and *Fulfilling the Promise: A Guide to the Sex Equity Provisions of the Vocational Education Act*; PEER Computer Equity Reports, such as *Sex Bias at the Computer Terminal—How Schools Program Girls*; PEER's Training and Organizing Manuals, such as *Cracking the Glass Slipper: PEER's Guide to Ending Sex Bias in Your Schools*; and Title IX materials such as *Beyond Title IX: PEER's State-by-State Guide to Women's Educational Equity Laws* and *Title IX Packet*, including *Anyone's Guide to Filing a Title IX Complaint*.

▶ WOMEN'S SPORTS FOUNDATION (WSF) (212-972-9170); Women's Sports Infoline, 800-227-3988). Publishes *Women's Athletic Scholarship Guide* and *Playing Fair: A Guide to Title IX in College and High School Sports*; expert packets on various topics such as *General Careers* [in sports] and *Participation Statistics*; videotapes such as *Aspire Higher: Careers in Sports for Women*: and research reports such as *The Women's Sports Foundation Report: Minorities in High School Sports*, and *Miller Lite Report on Women in Sports*.

◪ ON THE JOB

▸ **Women's Bureau, U.S. Department of Labor** (202-523-6667; on sexual harassment, 202-523-6652; TDD [Telecommunication Devices for the Deaf] 800-326-2577). Publishes *A Working Woman's Guide to Her Job Rights* (1992), *Preventing Sexual Harassment in the Workplace, Directory of Nontraditional Training and Employment Programs Serving Women* (1991), and *Women in the Skilled Trades and Other Manual Occupations* (1990).

▸ **9 to 5, National Association of Working Women** (216-566-1699; Job Survival Hotline 800-522-0925). Offers hot-line counseling on dealing with harassment. Publishes the *9 to 5 Newsline* and *The 9 to 5 Guide to Combating Sexual Harassment: Candid Advice from 9 to 5, the National Association of Working Women, Unequal Justice: Why Women Need Stronger Civil Rights Protections, a Brief Analysis.*

▸ **National Association of Female Executives (NAFE)** (212-645-0770 or 800-669-1002).

▸ **Federally Employed Women (FEW)** (202-898-0994). Publishes *News & Views* and the videotape *Balancing the Scales of Equality.*

▸ **National Conference on Pay Equity (NCPE)** (202-331-7343). Publishes *Raising Awareness About Pay Inequities.*

◪ ON RELIGION

▸ **Women's Ministry Unit (WMU)** (502-569-5382). Publishes and distributes *Sexual Misconduct* and *Naming the Unnamed: Sexual Harassment in the Church.*

▸ **Commission for Women (CW), Evangelical Lutheran Church in America (ELCA)** (312-380-2860). Publishes a bibliography on inclusive language.

▸ **Commission for Women's Equality (CWE)** (212-879-4500). (See also **religion and women's rights**.)

◪ FOR LEGAL ADVICE AND REFERRALS

▸ **Equal Rights Advocates (ERA)** (415-621-0672; advice and counseling line, 415-621-0505). A national women's law center. Publishes the "Know Your Rights" brochure *Sex Discrimination.*

▸ **Lawyers' Committee for Civil Rights Under Law** (202-371-1212).

▸ **Northwest Women's Law Center** (206-682-9552; for information and referral, 206-621-7691). For Washington State area.

▸ **Women's Justice Center (WJC)**, (313-961-5528). For Detroit area. (For sexual orientation discrimination, see **Lesbian Help, Information, and Action Guide** on page 397.)

Other resources

■ ON SEXUAL DISCRIMINATION IN GENERAL

Coping with Discrimination, rev. ed. Gabrielle I. Edwards. Rosen, 1992.
Taking a Stand Against Sexism and Sex Discrimination, Trudy J. Hanmer. Watts, 1990.
(See also WORKING WOMEN'S HELP, INFORMATION, AND ACTION GUIDE on page 779; WOMEN'S RIGHTS HELP, INFORMATION, AND ACTION GUIDE on page 767.)

■ ON SEX/GENDER ROLES

Gender: Stereotypes and Roles, 3rd ed. Susan Basow. Brooks-Cole, 1992.
Race, Class, and Gender in the United States, 2nd ed. Paula S. Rothenberg. St. Martin's, 1992.
Gender Constructs and Social Issues. Tony L. Whitehead and Barbara V. Reid, eds. University of Illinois Press, 1992.
Gendered Spaces. Daphne Spain. University of North Carolina Press, 1992.
Women, Men and Society. 2nd ed. Claire M. Renzetti and Daniel Curran. Allyn, 1992.
Dress and Gender: Making and Meaning in Cultural Contexts. Ruth Barnes and Joanne B. Eicher. Berg, 1992.
Gender Matters from School to Work. Jane Gaskell. Taylor and Francis, 1991.
Sex and Gender in Society. 2nd ed. Jean Stockard and Miriam M. Johnson. Prentice-Hall, 1991.
The Gender Reader. Evelyn Ashton-Jones and Gary A. Olson. Allyn, 1991.
The Beauty Myth: How Images of Beauty Are Used Against Women. Naomi Wolf. Morrow, 1991.
Sex and Gender: The Human Experience, 2nd ed. James A. Doyle and Michele A. Paludi. Wm. C. Brown, 1991.
There's a Good Girl: Gender Stereotyping in the First Three Years of Life—A Diary. Marianne Grabrucker. Quartet Books, 1990.
Gender, Power and Sexuality. Pamela Abbott and Clara Wallace, eds. International Special Books, 1990.
The Social Construction of Gender. Judith Lorber and Susan A. Farrell, eds. Sage, 1990.
Mothers, Leadership, and Success. Guy R. Odom. Polybius, 1990.
Sex Roles and the School, 2nd ed. Sara Delamont. Routledge, 1990.
Unleashing Our Unknown Selves: An Inquiry into the Future of Feminity and Masculinity. France Morrow. Praeger/Greenwood, 1990.
Love in America: Gender and Self-Development. Francesca M. Cancian. Cambridge University Press, 1990.

Gender Trouble: Feminism and the Subversion of Identity. Judith Butler. Routledge (NY), 1989.

How Are Sex Roles Established? Greenhaven, 1989.

Androgyny: The Opposites Within. June Singer. Sigo Press, 1989.

Gender in Transition: A New Frontier. J. Offerman-Zuckerberg, ed. Plenum, 1989.

Male-Female Roles: Opposing Viewpoints. Terry O'Neill and Neal Bernards. Greenhaven, 1989.

Gender Blending: Confronting the Limits of Duality. Holly Devor. Indiana University Press, 1989.

Male-Female Roles. David L. Bender and Bruno Leone, eds. Greenhaven, 1988.

Genda Agenda. Evans. Paul and Co., 1988.

◪ ON SEX/GENDER IN LANGUAGE AND COMMUNICATION

He Says, She Says: Closing the Communication Gap Between the Sexes. Lillian Glass. Putnam, 1992.

Constructing and Reconstructing Gender: The Links Among Communication, Language, and Gender. Linda A. Perry and others, eds. State University of New York Press, 1992.

Distorted Images: Misunderstandings Between Men and Women. Anne Borrowdale. Westminster John Knox, 1991.

You Just Don't Understand: Women and Men in Conversation. Deborah Tannen. Morrow, 1990; Ballantine, 1991.

Gender Communication. Laurie Arliss. Prentice-Hall, 1990.

Communication Between the Sexes: Sex Differences and Sex-Role Stereotypes, 2nd ed. Lea P. Stewart and others. Gorsuch Scarisbrick, 1990.

How to Talk So Men Will Listen. Marian K. Woodall. Professional Business Communications, 1990.

Language, Gender, and Professional Writing: Theoretical Approaches and Guidelines for Nonsexist Usage. Francine W. Frank and Paula Treichler, eds. Modern Language, 1989.

Language and Gender: Making the Difference. Cate Poynton. Oxford University Press, 1989.

Down with Stereotypes: Eliminating Sexism from Children's Literature and School Textbooks. Michel Andree. UNIPUB, 1987.

That's Not What I Meant: How Conversational Style Makes or Breaks Relationships. Deborah Tannen. Morrow, 1986; Ballantine, 1987.

◪ ON SEXUAL HARASSMENT IN GENERAL

Harassed: One Hundred Women Define Inappropriate Behavior in the Workplace. Nancy D. McCann and Thomas A. McGinn. Business One Irwin, 1992.

Sexual Harassment on the Job. Bill Petrocelli and Barbara K. Repa. Nolo Press, 1992.

Ivory Power: Sexual Harassment on Campus. Michele A. Paludi, ed. State University of New York Press, 1991.

The Lecherous Professor: Sexual Harassment on Campus, 2nd ed. Billie W. Dziech and Linda Weiner. University of Illinois Press, 1990.

Corporate Attractions: An Inside Account of Sexual Harassment with the New Sexual Roles for Men and Women on the Job. Kathleen Neville. Acropolis, 1990.

Sexual Harassment in the Workplace, rev. ed. Ralph H. Baxter, Jr. Executive Enterprises, 1989.

Rape, Incest, and Sexual Harassment: A Guide for Helping Survivors. Kathryn Quina and Nancy Carlson. Greenwood, 1989.

Talking of Silence: The Sexual Harassment of Schoolgirls. Carrie M. Herbert. Taylor and Francis, 1989.

Sexual Harassment at Work. Ann Sedley and Melissa Benn. State Mutual Books, 1988.

☑ BACKGROUND WORKS ON SEXUAL HARASSMENT

Capitol Games: Clarence Thomas, Anita Hill, and the Behind-the-Scenes Story of a Supreme Court Nomination. Timothy M. Phelps and Helen Winternitz. Disney, 1992.

Academic and Workplace Sexual Harassment: A Resource Manual. Michele A. Paludi and Richard B. Barickman. State University of New York Press, 1991.

Sexual Harassment in the Workplace: Law and Practice. Alba Conte. Wiley, 1990.

☑ ON SEX DIFFERENCES

The Mismeasure of Women: Why Women Are Not the Better Sex, the Inferior Sex, or the Opposite Sex, and How Using Men as the Yardstick for Normalcy Has Given Women the Short End of the Stick. Carol Tavris. Simon & Schuster, 1992.

The Great Sex Divide: A Study of Male-Female Differences. Glenn Wilson. Scott-Townsend, 1992.

Theoretical Perspectives on Sexual Difference. Deborah L. Rhode. Yale University Press, 1990.

Sex Differences: Modern Biology and the Unisex Fallacy. Yves Christen. Transaction, 1990.

■ INTERNATIONAL AND HISTORICAL PERSPECTIVES

Gender in Gross-Cultural Perspective. Caroline Brettell and Carolyn Sargent, eds. Prentice-Hall, 1992.

The New Soviet Man and Woman: Sex Role Socialization in the U.S.S.R. Lynne Attwood. Indiana University Press, 1991.

Sex in China: Studies in Sexology in Chinese Culture. F. F. Ruan and M. Matsumura. Plenum, 1991.

Sex and Gender in Historical Perspective. Edward Muir and others, eds. Johns Hopkins, 1990.

Making Sex: Body and Gender from the Greeks to Freud. Thomas Laqueur. Harvard University Press, 1990.

Transcending Boundaries: Multi-Disciplinary Approaches to the Study of Gender. Pamela R. Frese and John M. Coggeshall, eds. Bergin & Garvey/ Greenwood, 1990.

Sex and Psyche: Gender and Self—Viewed Cross-Culturally. John E. Williams and Deborah L. Best. Sage, 1990.

Gender and the Politics of History. Joan W. Scott. Columbia University Press, 1989.

■ BACKGROUND BOOKS

Gender, Interaction and Inequality. C. L. Ridgeway, ed. Springer-Verlag, 1991.

Deceptive Distinctions: Sex, Gender and the Social Order. Cynthia F. Epstein. Yale University Press, 1990. Reprint of 1988 ed.

Gender at the Crossroads of Knowledge: Feminist Anthropology in the Postmodern Era. Micaela Di Leonardo, ed. University of California Press, 1991.

Gender Differences: Their Impact on Public Policy. Mary L. Kendrigan, ed. Greenwood, 1991.

On Peace, War, and Gender: A Challenge to Genetic Explanations. Anne E. Hunter, ed. Feminist Press, 1991.

Sex Law: A Legal Sourcebook on Critical Sexual Issues for the Non-Lawyer. Scott E. Friedman. McFarland, 1990.

Justice and Gender. Deborah L. Rhode. Harvard University Press, 1989.

Race, Gender, and Class. Larry Davis and Enola Proctor. Prentice-Hall, 1989.

sexual division of labor, a pervasive pattern of SEX ROLES that determines which types of work in a society are to be done by women and which by men. Though in virtually every culture these divisions are considered traditional, time-honored, unchanging, fixed, and all but set into concrete, in fact they vary widely from culture to culture, and time to time. Work done by men in one culture is done by women in another. In many cultures, men and women alike perform work that elsewhere is regarded as the province of one or the other. And throughout history, task assignments change as social change or crisis have called for them to do so. During World War II, Rosie the Riveter and millions of her sisters did work that had previously been regarded as "men's work," as millions of other women have run shops, farms, and whole kingdoms throughout history whenever need loosened the bonds of the sexual division of labor. Similarly, a few men in recent decades have broken the bonds in a different way, to become house-husbands and take primary care of their young children. Even so, the pattern of male dominance in many spheres of work continues (see WORK AND WOMEN; SEXISM).

Traditional analyses of sexual division of labor, largely written by males on the assumption that PATRIARCHY was virtually a divine right, have focused on the idea that the male was the hunter and prime provider and so the basis of all economic and social development. Many other analysts, including many feminists, suggest that such a theory greatly distorts human development, failing to take into account women's fundamental economic and social contributions as gatherers, and so also prime providers, and also failing to include in their analyses the vital PREGNANCY and child-rearing roles played primarily by women but also by men. (See WORK AND WOMEN; HOUSEWORK; SEXUAL DISCRIMINATION; SEX ROLES; also SEXUAL DISCRIMINATION AND SEXUAL HARASSMENT HELP, INFORMATION, AND ACTION GUIDE on page 642; SEX AND SEXUALITY HELP, INFORMATION, AND ACTION GUIDE on page 665.)

sexual harassment, in general, "unwelcome sexual advances, requests for sexual favors, and other verbal or physical conduct of a sexual nature," as defined by the EQUAL EMPLOYMENT OPPORTUNITY COMMISSION (EEOC); a problem long encountered, though not necessarily articulated as such. Women, and especially those with little or no power or defense, have for at least some thousands of years been pressured by men to have unwanted sexual relations—and have suffered greatly from both refusal and acquiescence. Women slaves, domestic workers, farm laborers, industrial workers, young women at home or on their own, students and teachers, indeed women in all walks of life have experienced everything from the threat of murder, the fact of RAPE, and death in unwanted CHILDBIRTH to the covert pawing and sexist talk of the modern workplace, replete with quite respectable and sometimes eminent men who ingenuously express surprise when accused of SEXISM and harassment, claiming that they "just didn't know that women didn't like what they were doing to them." For women and female children, sexual harassment has been and still is a fact of life, part of living in any male-dominated culture.

What is quite new, however, is the modern articulation of the concept of sexual harassment, which has occurred only since the early 1960s, and the developing worldwide campaign to illuminate and destroy it. Everywhere this involves the development of new social attitudes, side by side with the development of a new body of laws that outlaw a widening range of sexual harassments. So it was

that the landmark 1991 sexual harassment confrontation between Anita Faye
HILL and then–Supreme Court nominee Clarence Thomas focused on the moral
issue of whether or not he was fit to serve on the U.S. Supreme Court and occurred in the form of televised U.S. Senate hearings before a worldwide audience,
rather than in a courtroom. The equally notable establishment of a hostile workplace as constituting sexual harassment came in the 1986 *Meritor* v. *Vinson* U.S.
Supreme Court decision (see below).

Employment discrimination, including SEXUAL DISCRIMINATION, was barred
by TITLE VII OF THE 1964 CIVIL RIGHTS ACT, which set up the EQUAL EMPLOYMENT
OPPORTUNITY COMMISSION (EEOC). A series of other laws, regulations, and cases
followed, interpreting and expanding the new law, including the EQUAL EMPLOY-
MENT OPPORTUNITY ACT OF 1972; TITLE IX OF THE 1972 EDUCATION ACT AMEND-
MENTS, denying federal aid to discriminatory educational institutions; and the
1978 Civil Service Reform Act. Attempts to define sexual harassment as discrimination began to succeed in the late 1970s, most notably with a 1979 Executive
Branch Office of Personnel Management policy statement that defined and called
for an end to harassment.

In 1980, at least a decade late, the EEOC issued its first sexual harassment
regulations, stating that the behaviors described above "constitute sexual harassment when

1. submission to such conduct is made either explicitly or implicitly a term or
   condition of an individual's employment,
2. submission to or rejection of such conduct by an individual is used as the
   basis for employment decisions affecting such individual, or
3. such conduct has the purpose or effect of unreasonably interfering with an
   individual's work performance or creating an intimidating, hostile, or offensive working environment."

Six years later, in *Meritor* v. *Vinson,* the Supreme Court ruled in its first
sexual harassment case that a woman bank employee who had submitted to a supervisor's sexual demands for fear of losing her job, even though her fear was
groundless and her promotions based solely on merit, had been functioning in
a sexually harassing "hostile environment" and that the bank was responsible for
the acts of its supervisor. In 1991 the Supreme Court went even further, defining
nude pinups in a workplace as the creation of a hostile environment and therefore as actionable sexual harassment.

The Court also began to rule on sexual harassment cases in education,
brought under Title IX of the 1972 Education Act Amendments. In 1979 it ruled
that cases could be brought under the act but recognized no right to collect damages. But in 1992, in *Franklin* v. *Gwinnett County Public Schools,* it ruled that a
former Georgia high school student, who had been sexually harassed and had ultimately submitted to SEXUAL INTERCOURSE with a male teacher, could collect
money damages.

Sexual harassment court cases began to be brought in lower courts
throughout the United States in the early 1990s, many of them on issues that (as
of late 1992) had yet to be reviewed by the Supreme Court. One notable "first"
was the award of $15,000 to high school student Katy Lyle because of her sexual
harassment by male students at the Duluth (Minnesota) Central High School.

Another notable "first" was permission to bring a workplace sexual harassment case into a Minnesota federal court as a class action, an approach not previously allowed. And in a highly publicized case, reporter Lisa Olsen, who charged that she had been sexually harassed by football players while working in the team's dressing room, settled her sexual harassment suit against the New England Patriots for a reported $500,000.

For workplace sexual harassment complaints, a major vehicle continued to be the filing of charges with the EEOC (see How to File an EEOC Complaint on page 262). Many had felt that women would be far less willing to file charges after the failure of Anita Faye Hill to stop Clarence Thomas's nomination, coupled with the highly personal nature of the attacks made on her by the Republican members of the Senate Judiciary Committee. But even though it was widely recognized that EEOC sexual harassment complaints took a great deal of time and seldom succeeded, large numbers of American women turned out to be so enraged and energized by the distasteful affair that they greatly increased their numbers of sexual harassment complaints. By the middle of 1992, EEOC sexual harassment complaints had risen from 3,135 for the first six months of 1991 to 4,754 for the first six months of 1992, an increase of more than 50 percent.

Sexual harassment also emerged as a major issue in the armed forces, very notably with the September 1991 Tailhook Scandal, in which serving and retired naval aviators sexually harassed and criminally physically abused at least twenty-six women, most of them serving naval officers, at a Las Vegas convention of the Tailhook Association, a professional association of aviators; the event was followed by an attempted cover-up, public exposure, the resignation of Navy Secretary H. Lawrence Garrett III, and a massive investigation that was still proceeding in late 1992. The extraordinary public scandal generated many other accounts of sexual harassment and rape in several military services.

Beyond the court, agency, and other institutional cases, the idea of sexual harassment began to find much wider public acceptance. A strongly backed sexual harassment charge began to be enough to damage a career in public life. In 1992 Washington State U.S. Senator Brock Adams decided not to seek re-election to a second term after the Seattle Times ran sexual harassment and abuse charges made by eight women. Civil libertarians voiced concerns on this aspect of the matter, pointing out that trial in the media was by no means due process, and that much has yet to be worked out in this fast-developing field.

And beyond the issue of sexual harassment itself, the anger generated by the treatment of Anita Faye Hill in her appearances before the Senate Judiciary Committee propelled many American women into renewed and very vigorous political action on women's rights issues and a much wider range of social justice matters, as attested to by the greatly increased number of women candidates in the 1992 elections. (See political participation; also Political Participation Help, Information, and Action Guide on page 547.)

Sexual harassment also emerged as a worldwide set of issues in the early 1990s. In September, 1991, for example, France joined Spain in criminalizing sexual harassment, defining it as "to solicit sexual favors from subordinates at work" by "order, constraint, or pressure." In October 1991 the European Community proposed a general, nonbinding code covering sexual harassment in the workplace, to serve as a model for member states. Even Japan, a bastion of male supremacy with a very weak women's rights movement, saw a historic "first" in April 1992, when a woman who had been subjected to verbal sexual harassment won a $12,500 lower court award. (See SEXUAL HARASSMENT: WHAT EVERY WORKING WOMAN NEEDS TO KNOW, below; SEXUAL DISCRIMINATION AND SEXUAL HARASSMENT HELP, INFORMATION, AND ACTION GUIDE on page 628.)

SEXUAL HARASSMENT: WHAT EVERY WORKING WOMAN NEEDS TO KNOW

Have you experienced any of the following at work:

- Suggestive comments about your appearance?
- Unwanted touching or other physical contact?
- Unwanted sexual jokes or comments?
- Sexual advances?
- Exposure to pornographic pictures?

If you have experienced any unwanted *verbal* or *physical* conduct of a sexual nature, **you are not alone.** This behavior is considered *sexual harassment.*

It's not only offensive—*it's against the law.*

Sexual harassment is illegal even if the harasser is not your boss, even if he is not threatening that you will lose your job if you don't go along.

What the law says:

- Sexual harassment is *unwanted, repeated* sexual attention at work.
- Sexual harassment is *illegal* if
  - your job depends on your going along with this behavior, or
  - the conditions of your employment (such as pay, promotion, vacation) depend on your going along with this behavior, or
  - the harassment creates a hostile or offensive work environment that interferes with your ability to do your job.
- Everyone has the right to a workplace free of harassment.

What you can do:

Sexual harassment is *not your fault.*

Sexual harassment is not about sex. It's about *power.* Typically such behavior is designed to humiliate and control.

Here are some steps to take if you are being sexually harassed on the job:

1. **Say no clearly.** Inform the harasser that his attentions are unwanted. Make clear you find the behavior offensive. If it persists, write a memo to the harasser asking him to stop; keep a copy.

2. **Document the harassment.** Write down each incident, including date, time, and place. Detail what happened and include your response. Keep a copy at home. This information will be useful if you need to take legal action.

3. **Get emotional support** from friends and family.

4. **Document your work.** Keep copies of performance evaluations and memos that attest to the quality of your work. The harasser may question your job performance in order to justify his behavior.

5. **Look for witnesses and other victims.** You are probably not the first person who has been mistreated by this individual. Ask around; you may find others who will support your charge. Two accusations are much harder to ignore.

6. **Explore company channels.** Use any grievance procedures or channels detailed in your employee handbook. If you're in a union, get the union steward involved right away.

7. **File a complaint.** If you need to pursue a legal remedy, contact your state discrimination agency or the federal Equal Employment Opportunity Commission (look in your phone book for the field office closest to you). The federal agency covers workplaces of fifteen or more. State law may protect you if you're in a smaller workplace.

8. **Attorneys.** You do not need an attorney to file a claim, but you may want to speak with a legal service or private attorney specializing in employment discrimination.

Under the new Civil Rights Act of 1991, victims of sexual harassment are entitled to damages for pain and suffering as well as to any lost pay. If you win, you may also recover legal fees.

Source: *Sexual Harassment: What Every Woman Needs to Know.* 9 to 5. National Association of Working Women.

sexual identity, the assignment of a person as either male or female, based on biologically determined attributes; by contrast to one's inner sexual identification, called GENDER IDENTITY.

Where a child has the external GENITALS of either female or male (see REPRODUCTIVE SYSTEM), the assignment is obvious. But it is not always so. A child can have both female and male attributes, including sometimes both male and female sex organs, with or without any CHROMOSOMAL ABNORMALITIES. Such a child is called a *hermaphrodite* or *bisexual* and may be "assigned" to one sex or the other for purposes of dressing, training, and rearing but may later show some ambivalence as to gender identity.

Some children are born with what are termed *ambiguous genitalia,* not clearly one sex or the other, a condition sometimes called *pseudohermaphroditism.* A child who has the chromosomes of a female may, for example, have a CLITORIS so large as to resemble a PENIS, or LABIA that are fused and resemble the male scrotum; while a child with male chromosomes may have a VAGINA-like opening under the penis. In some cases, children have unknowingly been reared as one sex (see SEX ROLE) when, at PUBERTY, their development showed them to be another. If the child's sexual ambiguity is properly recognized, the parents or doctor will "assign" the child a sex on the basis of chromosomes, and the child is raised with that gender identity. The ambiguous genitals can be corrected surgically, and hormonal treatment is often given to enhance the gender assigned. (See SEX AND SEXUALITY HELP, INFORMATION, AND ACTION GUIDE on page 665.)

sexual intercourse, in general, contact and activity involving the GENITALS of the participants, also called *sexual relations.* Sometimes the term is used in a very limited sense, to refer to the insertion of a man's erect PENIS into a woman's VAGINA; this is more specifically called *coitus.* But, more generally, sexual intercourse or relations can refer to a wide range of activities, involving various partners—HETEROSEXUAL, HOMOSEXUAL, or groups—and many other parts of the body as well.

Whatever the variations, where the activity is mutual and pleasurable, the partners will experience a cycle of SEXUAL RESPONSE that often, but not always, includes a climactic experience called ORGASM. However, when someone has been forced into sexual activity, the action may be classed in a variety of ways, depending on the circumstance (see RAPE; INCEST; CHILD ABUSE AND NEGLECT; SEXUAL HARASSMENT; BATTERED WOMEN).

The traditional form of sexual intercourse is coitus, also called *copulation* or *vaginal intercourse,* in which the man's penis penetrates the vagina. The couples' complementary rhythmic movements, with alternating penetration and partial withdrawal, grow deeper and faster as excitement builds and the woman's vaginal area deepens to receive the penetration; these continue generally until one or both reach an orgasm, which for a man involves EJACULATION of SEMEN, which contain SPERM.

The *man-above,* or *missionary, position,* is the most common and in some areas the only publicly "acceptable" position for what is a most private act. However, couples may have sex in a variety of different positions, sometimes called *figurae veneris,* including the woman above, side by side, sitting, standing, kneeling, and rear entry (variously called *coitus à la vache,* "in cow fashion"; *coitus à tergo,* "from behind"; or *coitus more ferarum,* "in the manner of beasts"). Coitus in such positions may sometimes increase the pleasure of one or both partners, prolong the pleasure, add variety, ease the physical strain (as when one partner has a disability or health problem), and sometimes allow partners to suit the sizes of their sexual equipment better to one another. Couples are advised to be open and experiment, to see what works best for them and their needs. Sometimes, a male nearing orgasm may suppress it deliberately, to enhance his own and his partner's pleasure, an approach called *coitus reservatus* or *coitus prolongatus;* however, the male may sometimes pass the peak of excitement and lose the erection, leaving one or both partners unsatisfied.

Among couples who use the *withdrawal method* of BIRTH CONTROL (see NATURAL FAMILY PLANNING), the man removes his penis before ejaculating, or "coming"; this is also called *coitus interruptus* or *coitus incompletus.* Some couples also use alternative positions that make the penis penetrate less deeply into the vagina and therefore keeps it farther away from the CERVIX through which SPERM must pass in order to reach and fertilize the egg (OVUM), if any is present. This method is unreliable, however, since some semen is leaked before orgasm.

Coitus may also involve other parts of the body. Before birth control methods were known or widely available, or where their use was proscribed by law or religion, some couples avoided CONCEPTION by various alternatives. One is moving the penis between a woman's thighs, a practice variously called *coitus ante portas* ("before the door"), *interfemoral intercourse, coitus inter femora,* or *intracrural intercourse.* This was often used by adolescents to prevent breaking the HYMEN. It is not fully satisfactory as a contraceptive technique, however, since some semen may still be carried to the vagina. The penis may also be moved back and forth in the partner's armpit *(coitus in axilla)* or between a woman's breasts *(coitus intra mammas* or *intermammarius).* But the two most widely used alternative orifices are the anus and the mouth.

Anal intercourse involves insertion of the penis in the anus (see DIGESTIVE SYSTEM); this activity also goes by other names, including *coitus in ano, coitus analis, anogenital intercourse,* or *sodomy* (see below). Anal sex is common among HOMOSEXUALS but is also used by many HETEROSEXUALS. Some find it a highly pleasurable alternative to vaginal intercourse. In some cultures, where birth control is either unavailable or barred by religion, anal sex is used for birth control. It carries significant health hazards, however. The BLOOD vessels of the anus are delicate and easily damaged; in particular, they bleed, so AIDS may readily be spread, if one partner is infected. CONDOMS provide some protection but are more likely to become damaged and ineffective from the powerful strains involved in anal intercourse. In addition, anal sex can spread to the GENITALS many other diseases caused by bacteria that live in the digestive tract (see URINARY TRACT; VAGINA; SEXUALLY TRANSMITTED DISEASES). If vaginal intercourse is to follow anal intercourse, couples are advised first to remove and discard the condom, wash the penis carefully, and put on a new condom.

The mouth is also widely used in intercourse. Mouth-to-mouth kissing is often an important part of foreplay. When the penis is moved in the mouth, and the lips and tongue are used for additional stimulation, it is generally called *fellatio, coitus in os* ("in the mouth"), or more popularly *blowing,* a *blow job,* or *going down.* Conversely, the tongue or mouth can be used on the woman's VULVA, an act called *cunnilingus* (literally "to lick vulva"). Either partner may also use the tongue to stimulate the sensitive area around the anus, in what is called *rimming.* Together, such activities are known as *oral sex* or *oral-genital sex;* they are widely used for stimulation and sexual satisfaction by men and women of all sexual orientations. Among heterosexuals, oral-genital sex is often part of foreplay to vaginal or anal intercourse but may also be the main experience leading to orgasm. Cunnilingus is widely used by female homosexuals, or LESBIANS, as fellatio is by male homosexuals. Where partners simultaneously perform oral sex on each other, it is called "69," for the analogy to the way the numbers fit together.

Fingers and hands are also widely used for sexual pleasure, caressing, arousing, and stimulating the body, often focusing on the EROGENOUS ZONES, including the external genitals. Where a man or woman is manually stimulated to orgasm, it is popularly called a *hand job* (see MASTURBATION). Fingers and hands are sometimes inserted into body orifices, including the vagina, anus, and mouth, as one or two fingers *(digital penetration)* or a whole fist *(fisting)*. For many lovers, manual stimulation is an important part of the overall sexual experience, both during foreplay and in the postorgasm period of resolution and relaxation. Some use oils or lubricants for a sensual, massagelike experience; however, perfumes should be avoided, as they can be irritating to the SKIN.

Many couples also use various stimulative devices. The most common is a *dildo,* an artificial tool shaped like an erect penis. Some women use them for self-stimulation during MASTURBATION; lesbians may use dildos for mutual stimulation; and couples may use them for variety or when a man is unable to maintain an erect penis. Also widely used is a *vibrator,* an electrical- or battery-powered device that causes vibrations. These may be applied to the area around the CLITORIS; penis-shaped vibrators may be inserted into the upper part of the vagina. Vibrators can provide intense orgasms, even among older women who have never experienced one before. Sex therapists sometimes prescribe them to help women identify what brings them to orgasm, information that can than be translated to a sex partner for more satisfying mutual sexual experiences.

In discussions of how to avoid AIDS and other sexually transmitted diseases, most attention has been focused on "safer sex" in vaginal or anal intercourse, especially on using a condom on the penis (see **CONDOMS: WHAT WOMEN NEED TO KNOW** on page 188; **WHAT YOU CAN DO TO AVOID STDS** on page 660) and a DIAPHRAGM and SPERMICIDE in the woman's vagina. These are extremely important for all women to keep in mind. However, women are at risk of getting infected with AIDS or STDs from other kinds of sex as well, whether their partners are male or female. *Any activity that can result in mixing of blood or semen is potentially unsafe.* For example, a woman who has just brushed her teeth, and has unknowingly had slight bleeding, may be exposed to AIDs during fellatio with a partner. Similarly, someone could be exposed to AIDS from a woman's vaginal juices during cunnilingus. So can a woman who tongues the anus of her partner, if there is any bleeding. Menstrual bleeding, even in minute amounts, also poses a danger. So do tiny cracks, cuts, hangnails, chapping, and abrasions on the hands. In addition, vibrators and other sexual items can transfer bodily fluids from one person or place to another.

To try to prevent such transmissions, many heterosexual and homosexual couples use various protective measures in addition to condoms. They wear disposable surgical latex gloves (such as those used in a GYNECOLOGICAL EXAMINATION) or reusable gloves (if carefully washed) for hand-genital contact—being careful also not to move the covered fingers to other orifices. They use condoms on dildos, vibrators, and other sexual devices, just as on the penis, for any activity.

For oral sex involving the vulva and anus, they use various kinds of barriers. One common choice is to take a condom, cut off the tip, cut up one side, and roll it out flat to use as a barrier between one person's mouth and the other's genitals. Some people use a rubber dam such as those used in dental offices; they caution that it should be washed first, since one side is often coated with talc, which can irritate sensitive body parts. Double layers of household plastic wrap have also been used; though cheaper and handier, this has not been shown scientifically to be safe for these purposes and is not as strong. Lubricants are often spread on the side of the barrier opposite the tongue or indeed on any condom to ease friction, but only water-based lubricants should be used, as petroleum-based products can damage and weaken such barriers, as well as condoms and diaphragms.

In some times and places, some kinds of sexual activity have been labeled "unnatural" and sometimes made illegal, under the general name of *sodomy*. What has been regarded as "wrong" has changed over time; however, in the United States, the label *sodomy* has traditionally been applied to anal intercourse, fellatio, and bestiality (sex with an animal), and outlawed. Many states no longer have sodomy laws, and those that do rarely bring prosecution when mutually consenting adults are involved. (See Sex and Sexuality Help, Information, and Action Guide on page 665.)

sexually transmitted diseases (STDs), a group of diseases spread primarily through sexual contact, generally some form of sexual intercourse, vaginal or anal; by hand or mouth contact with the genitals of an infected person; or from mother to child during childbirth. Some such diseases have severe and even life-threatening consequences; these include some of the long-known STDs, such as syphilis and gonorrhea, formerly called *venereal diseases*. The most serious and frightening of them all is one of the most recently discovered: aids. Medical researchers now know that there are many other STDs as well. Some of these are not severe or life-threatening in themselves, but they can make the body more vulnerable to entry by the virus that causes AIDS, or they can also cause infections serious enough to cause infertility, an example being chlamydia. Some are not curable, so patients can only be treated for symptoms; these include AIDS and herpes. Others can be treated easily, if caught early, before damage has been done, although the microorganisms causing some kinds of STDs are becoming resistant to antibiotics, and higher doses or newer types are needed to cure them.

STDs can affect anyone—men and women, from any background or economic level. Anyone who has sexual relations is potentially at risk for developing STDs; the only absolutely "safe sex" is no sex. STDs are most prevalent, however, among people with frequent multiple sex partners. The incidence of STDs is rising because in recent decades multiple sex partners have become more common and also because young people have become sexually active earlier. Today, nearly one-third of all cases of STDs involve teenagers. Unfortunately, many STDs cause no symptoms initially, or the early symptoms may be mistaken for another disorder, but the STD can still be passed from an infected person to a sex partner. Use of CONDOMS, DIAPHRAGMS, and SPERMICIDES can reduce the risk somewhat, providing at least *safer* sex. But doctors recommend that women who have more than one sex partner be tested periodically for STDs.

Quite apart from AIDS, which threatens the lives of both sexes, other STDS often cause more severe and more frequent health problems for women. Some can cause PELVIC INFLAMMATORY DISEASE **(PID),** which can cause both infertility and potentially life-threatening ECTOPIC PREGNANCY. At least one, GENITAL WARTS, and perhaps other STDs increase the risk of cervical CANCER (see CERVIX). Among those passed from mother to baby during childbirth, some can be cured easily, but others can cause permanent disability or death of the newborn. Some kinds of gastrointestinal infections, caused by bacteria or parasites and potentially quite severe, can also be spread during sexual activity involving the anus, such as oral-anal contact; these include hepatitis, colitis, enteritis, giardiasis, and amebiasis.

Women can be completely safe from STDs only by complete sexual abstinence, or if both sex partners have sex only with each other from the beginning of their sexual activity, at whatever age. In the latter case, and in other sexual relationships, women (like men) are obliged to trust their partners to be honest about their sexual activity and to warn them and protect them from any known STD. In fact, lovers and spouses have on occasion filed lawsuits for negligence, fraud, emotional distress, and the like when their partners have knowingly or wantonly infected them (*Lovers, Doctors, and the Law,* below, reviews landmark cases and a state-by-state review of applicable laws). On their own, however, women can take steps to reduce the risk of contracting an STD (see WHAT YOU CAN YOU DO TO AVOID STDs on page 660; see also SEXUAL INTERCOURSE). For information on some STDs of prime concern, see AIDS, BACTERIAL VAGINOSIS, CHANCROID, CHLAMYDIA, CYTOMEGALOVIRUS INFECTION **(CMV),** GENITAL WARTS, GONORRHEA, GRANULOMA INGUINALE, GROUP B STREPTOCOCCAL INFECTIONS **(GBS),** HEPATITIS, HERPES, MOLLUSCUM CONTAGIOSUM, MYCOPLASMAS, PUBIC LICE, SCABIES, SYPHILIS, and TRICHOMONIASIS. Also transmissible sexually are YEAST INFECTIONS.

SEXUALLY TRANSMITTED DISEASES

Help, Information, and Action Guide

▶ CENTERS FOR DISEASE CONTROL NATIONAL STD HOTLINE (800-227-8922).
▶ NATIONAL INSTITUTE OF ALLERGY AND INFECTIOUS DISEASES **(NIAID)** (301-496-5717). Publishes *Sexually Transmitted Diseases* and *Genital Herpes.*
▶ **American Social Health Association (ASHA)** (260 Sheridan Avenue, Suite 307, Palo Alto, CA 94306; 415-321-5134), an organization that seeks to prevent, control, and eliminate sexually transmitted diseases. It

provides information, makes referrals, and publishes various quarterlies and brochures. ASHA also operates the **Herpes Resource Center** (Box 100, Palo Alto, CA 94302; 415-328-7710), an organization for people with genital herpes, which provides support, especially through local chapters.

▶ NATIONAL WOMEN'S HEALTH NETWORK **(NWHN)** (202-347-1140). Operates the **Women's Health Information Service.** Publishes the information packets *Sexually Transmitted Diseases (STDs)* and *Pelvic Inflammatory Disease (PID).*

▶ INTERNATIONAL WOMEN'S HEALTH COALITION **(IWHC)** (212-979-8500). Publishes *Reproductive Tract Infections: Global Impact and Priorities for Women's Reproductive Health, Special Challenges in Third World Women's Health: Reproductive Tract Infections.*

Other resources

◪ **PERSONAL AND PRACTICAL GUIDES**

Sexually Transmitted Diseases. Mark McCauslin. Crestwood/Macmillan, 1992.
Sexually Transmitted Diseases. Alan E. Nourse, M.D. Watts, 1991.
Sexually Transmitted Diseases. Marjorie Little. Chelsea House, 1991.
VD Blues, rev. ed. Do It Now, 1990.
Coping with Venereal Disease, rev. ed. Gabrielle Edwards. Rosen Group, 1988.

◪ **ON HERPES**

Herpes Perplex, rev. ed. Do It Now, 1989.
The Truth About Herpes, 3rd ed. Stephen L. Sacks. Gordon Soules Books, 1988.

◪ **BACKGROUND WORKS**

Sexuality and Sexually Transmitted Diseases: A Doctor Confronts the Myth of "Safe" Sex. Joe S. McIlhaney, Jr. Baker Books, 1990.
Syphilis as AIDS. Robert B. Mitchell. Edward-William Austin, 1990.
Lovers, Doctors and the Law: Your Legal Rights and Responsibilities in Today's Sex-Health Crisis. Margaret Davis and Robert S. Scott. HarperCollins, 1988.
Sexually Transmitted Diseases and Society. Sylvia Cerel Brown, ed. Stanford University Press, 1988.

(See also WOMEN'S HEALTH HELP, INFORMATION, AND ACTION GUIDE on page 334.)

WHAT YOU CAN DO TO AVOID STDS

Although there is no sure way for a sexually active person to avoid exposure to STDs, there are many things he or she can do to reduce the risk.

A person who has decided to begin a sexual relationship should take the following steps to reduce the risk of developing an STD:

- Be direct and frank about asking a new sex partner whether he or she has an STD, has been exposed to one, or has any unexplained physical symptoms.
- Learn to recognize the physical signs of STDs and inspect a sex partner's body, especially the genital area, for sores, rashes, or discharges.
- Learn to use a condom (rubber) correctly and use it during sexual intercourse. Diaphragms or spermicides (particularly those containing nonoxynol-9), alone or in combination, also may reduce the risk of transmission of some STDs.

Anyone who is sexually active with someone other than a long-term monogamous partner should

- have regular checkups for STDs even in the absence of symptoms. These tests can be done during a routine visit to the doctor's office.
- learn the common symptoms of STDs. Seek medical help immediately if any suspicious symptoms develop, even if they are mild.

Anyone diagnosed as having an STD should

1. notify all recent sex partners and urge them to get a checkup.
2. follow the doctor's orders and complete the full course of medication prescribed. A follow-up test to ensure that the infection has been cured is often an important final step in treatment.
3. avoid all sexual activity while being treated for an STD.

Sometimes people are too embarrassed or frightened to ask for help or information. Most STDs are readily treated, and the earlier a person seeks treatment and warns sex partners about the disease, the less likely it is that the disease will do irreparable physical damage, be spread to others, or, in the case of a woman, be passed on to a newborn baby.

Private doctors, local health departments, and family planning clinics have information about STDs. In addition, the American Social Health Association (ASHA) [see SEXUALLY TRANSMITTED DISEASES HELP, INFORMATION, AND ACTION GUIDE on page 658] provides free information and keeps lists of clinics and private doctors who provide treatment for people with STDs.

[Note: See also SEXUAL INTERCOURSE for more suggestions on avoiding transmission of STDs, especially for forms of sex other than vaginal or anal intercourse.]

Source: *An Introduction to Sexually Transmitted Diseases* (1987). Prepared by the National Institute of Allergy and Infectious Diseases, for the Public Health Service.

sexual orientation discrimination: See LESBIAN.

Sexual Personae: See Camille PAGLIA.

Sexual Politics: See Kate MILLETT.

sexual response, a pattern of physiological changes that occur in the body during sexual activity, whether SEXUAL INTERCOURSE or MASTURBATION. The response varies widely with the person and the situation, since sexual attraction is very individual and in many people, especially women, is closely tied to feelings of love and affection with the partner. But sex researchers have found that sexual response follows the same general cycle, divided for convenience into four phases, but in reality a continuous flow of feeling. The four phases are
- ▶ *excitement phase.* This is the period of arousal, which may result from simply thinking about sex or seeing a sexually desirable person, or from a wide range of activities, including kisses or other caresses. Some such activities are general, such as hugging or backrubs, but others are directed at the body's sexually sensitive EROGENOUS ZONES, especially with manual or oral stimulation of a woman's VULVA and BREASTS, or a men's PENIS (see SEXUAL INTERCOURSE). Such activities are generally called *foreplay.* This is important to prepare the body for sexual activity; women who have not been sexually aroused can experience discomfort during intercourse and may fail to achieve satisfaction from it.

   During arousal, BLOOD vessels widen, or *dilate,* and blood flows into the area of the GENITALS, a process called *vasocongestion;* at the same time muscles contract, especially in the genitals, a process called *myotonia.* In women these processes cause the VAGINA to release a lubricant; the tip (*glans*) and body of the CLITORIS enlarges and becomes very sensitive; nipples become erect; the outer, larger LABIA (*labia majora*) spread apart and flatten, while the inner labia (*labia minora*) swell and open up; the upper part of the *vagina* widens and the UTERUS and CERVIX pull up, making a larger area to house the penis; blood pressure and pulse rate increase; the breasts swell; and some women develop a light rash, or *sex flush,* on the upper abdomen and chest. In men these processes cause the penis (and sometimes also the nipples) to become erect and the blood pressure and pulse rate to rise; also, the TESTES are pulled up closer to the body.

▶ *plateau phase.* During this phase, vasocongestion continues and peaks. In both men and women, breathing rate, pulse rate, and blood pressure continue to rise.

In women the tissues surrounding the vaginal opening swell and thicken, to form what is called the *orgasmic platform.* The breasts swell further; the uterus enlarges; and BARTHOLIN'S GLANDS secrete a lubricating liquid. Also the clitoris draws back, or *retracts,* into the body and under a fold of tissue called the *clitoral hood;* various kinds of sexual activity stimulate the clitoris by moving the hood back and forth over it. Just before orgasm, the color of the inner labia changes, in women who have not had children, from pink to bright red; in those who have, from bright red to a deeper purplish red.

In men, the ridge around the tip of the penis (*glans*) swells and the testes fill with blood and pull even closer to the body. During vaginal intercourse, a man may withdraw his penis at this stage, just before orgasm, as in the withdrawal method of NATURAL FAMILY PLANNING, but some sperm still may be in the VAGINA. This is because sperm are contained in a liquid, secreted from Cowper's glands, which appears at the tip of the penis during this phase.

▶ *orgasm.* This is the climactic phase, when voluntary and semivoluntary movements are replaced by involuntary movements in the body, which force the accumulated blood out of the genitals and bring release of the sexual tension that has been building in the first two phases. Blood pressure and heart rate peak and then subside.

In women the orgasm involves rhythmic muscular contractions of the vagina's orgasmic platform (on the average 3–12 contractions, .7–.8 second apart), the sphincter muscles of the anus and urethra (see MUSCULAR SYSTEM), and to some extent the UTERUS as well, following often by sudden relaxation and a flood of warmth. Some sex researchers note that some women ejaculate a fluid (not believed to be urine) from the urethra at orgasm; but little is known about female ejaculation. It was not, for example, covered in Masters and Johnson's *HUMAN SEXUAL RESPONSE.*

Orgasms differ markedly from time to time and woman to woman. Some women may have intense pleasure from not just one but several orgasms, while others experience release of sexual tension without experiencing anything like what is described by others as a "peak experience." Women often take longer to reach an orgasm than men do—according to sex researchers William Masters and Virginia Johnson, an average of fifteen minutes as compared with three—but over time, partners can learn to match their timing to their mutual satisfaction, sometimes through sex therapy. A woman's partner may not always be aware that she has had an orgasm and so should be told, to increase the satisfaction.

In men, the contractions of orgasm serve to move sperm-containing fluid from the male REPRODUCTIVE SYSTEM into a holding area called the *urethral bulb;* this and the penis itself then contract rhythmically to ejaculate the semen.

▶ **resolution.** After the orgasm, the body returns gradually to its previous state. Blood leaves the engorged tissues; breathing, pulse rate, and blood pressure return to normal. There often follows a time of emotional and physical relaxation, sometimes called *afterglow* or *afterplay,* which within a relationship can be a treasured, shared private time.

During a time called the *refractory period,* neither men nor women are able to be aroused again. In women this period can be short indeed, and some women can have multiple orgasms if stimulation continues. In men, the period may last a few minutes or a whole day, and it generally lengthens with age. Even if a man has no erection after orgasm, he can continue to provide pleasure to a woman by stimulating her genitals by hand or mouth (see SEXUAL INTERCOURSE). However, if a woman has not had an orgasm, her return to normal takes longer, and the pelvic congestion that remains can sometimes bring discomfort similar to menstrual cramps (see MENSTRUATION). A woman may often enjoy sexual activity for itself and for the pleasure of her partner, without orgasm.

For women, the question of sexual response has been a complicated one. In some cultures women were—and in some cases still are—mutilated to destroy their capacity for sexual pleasure (see FEMALE CIRCUMCISION). In many other cultures women's capacity has been destroyed or damaged in other ways, such as by rigid antisex teachings; by trauma such as sexual abuse (see INCEST; RAPE; CHILD ABUSE AND NEGLECT; BATTERED WOMEN; SEXUAL HARASSMENT); by undiagnosed physical problems (see VAGINA); by ignorance of how their own body responds; by lack of attraction to a partner; or by lack of knowledgable stimulation by a partner. Traditionally, women who were unable to achieve satisfaction, especially orgasm, from sex were termed *frigid;* that term has largely been replaced by the cumbersome but less loaded *female orgasmic dysfunction.*

But even women who *did* have orgasms were sometimes told that theirs was the "wrong kind." This idea stemmed from Sigmund Freud's notion that women could experience two types of orgasm: the *clitoral orgasm* (see CLITORIS), which he termed "immature," and the *vaginal orgasm,* achieved during sexual intercourse, which he labeled "mature." That notion was countered in 1966 with the publication of Masters and Johnson's *Human Sexual Response.* These sex researchers reported that the clitoris was the site of all female orgasms, and that some women simply received sufficient stimulation from the normal movement of intercourse, while others required more direct stimulation, by her own hand or her partner's, sometimes during intercourse, sometimes before or after. However, some other sex researchers believe that orgasm can result from various kinds of stimulation. In particular, some feel that the G SPOT, which is noticeable in at least some women, may help produce a vaginally centered orgasm. Others note that some women can reach orgasm—though rarely—just from stimulation of the breasts or even being in an especially erotic situation. Some women report that orgasms reached through manual stimulation of the clitoris are more intense and localized, though not necessarily more satisfying, than orgasms that occur during intercourse.

The most important thing for a woman is to come to know her own *individual* pattern of sexual response and to understand what gives her pleasure, rather than trying to match some described average or ideal. For some women, the key to having an orgasm is MASTURBATION, sometimes with a vibrator (see SEXUAL INTERCOURSE). Sex therapists find that once women get to know the responses of their own bodies, they can more readily convey to their partners what is needed to satisfy them.

For a woman who has never experienced orgasm, called *primary orgasmic dysfunction* or *anorgasmia,* or who once did but no longer does, called *situational orgasmic dysfunction,* the first stop is her regular doctor or gynecologist, to rule out any anatomical, physiological, or medical problems. Malformation of the vagina or excess dryness, for example, can cause painful intercourse, called *dyspareunia.* Various kinds of infections (see VAGINA; SEXUALLY TRANSMITTED DISEASES) can cause discomfort, as can ALCOHOL AND DRUG ABUSE, which changes the body chemistry.

Once medical problems have been ruled out or handled, if the problem persists, many couples find help in sex therapy. Many sexual problems can be linked to problems within the relationship, to conflicts, to disagreement about what sex "should" be like, to fear of PREGNANCY, to loss or lack of desire for one's partner, and the like. Not all such problems can be solved, at least not by sex therapy. But if the couple are committed to solving their sexual problems, sex therapy can often help, sometimes as part of more general marital therapy. Often the "problem" is simply that the partners are too anxious, concentrating all their energy and attention on "achieving" an orgasm rather than enjoying the sexual experience of which orgasm becomes simply a natural part.

One of the main approaches in sex therapy is to help a couple overcome various anxieties and taboos about sex, and to help increase their ability to communicate regarding sex, by having them engage in a series of exercises. For example, with the *sensate focus* technique, couples are advised to spend a quarter hour several times a week touching, caressing, and massaging the body but avoiding erogenous zones such as the genitals and breasts, to gain increasing comfort with each other's—and their own—bodies. Then they progress to stimulating the genitals and breasts, stopping short of orgasm and still without intercourse. Only then do they proceed to intercourse, still keeping focus on sharing enjoyment of the whole sexual experience, not on an orgasm as such.

This approach is also used sometimes to reawaken sexual desire or to help remedy male sexual problems, such as

▶ *impotence,* or inability to develop or maintain an erection.
▶ *retarded ejaculation* or *ejaculatory incompetence,* or inability to ejaculate while the penis is in the vagina, which can be a cause of INFERTILITY.
▶ *premature ejaculation,* or ejaculating too quickly, within a minute or two, or before his partner is fully aroused. Some couples work together to retard ejaculation; when the man signals that he is approaching ejaculation, his partner takes hold of the penis, just below the ridge of the tip, with the thumb below and the first two fingers close together on the top side, and presses firmly for a few seconds. This *squeeze technique* usually halts the immediate desire to ejaculate, while not affecting the erection.

Another problem, which does not affect sexual response, is *retrograde ejaculation,* in which semen flows backward into the bladder, merging with urine, instead of forward through the penis. This occurs in some men who have DIABETES, are taking medications for high blood pressure, have had prostate surgery, or are paraplegics; and is correctable by surgery or, sometimes, with decongestant medications. It is not harmful, however, except that it may cause temporary INFERTILITY.

Though much therapy is directed toward couples, often with male and female co-therapists, some other therapists treat individuals without a partner as well, in some cases using surrogate partners. Women who have fears about being "too small" for a penis and experiencing pain during intercourse may learn more about their bodies (see VAGINA), to prepare themselves for future relationships. Sometimes sexual fears stem from earlier traumas, and deeper therapy—or therapy that moves beyond exclusively sexual issues—may be needed to deal with the wrongs of the past.

Many sexual problems are temporary and may disappear as other problems are resolved or other life changes occur. Many women, for example, find that they have very little interest in sex in the weeks or even months after a child's birth. Whether this relates to hormonal changes in the body or simply to the stress of dealing with a new baby, and all that entails, the desire for sex generally returns as life settles into a new normality. (See SEX AND SEXUALITY HELP, INFORMATION, AND ACTION GUIDE, below.)

When modern woman discovered the orgasm it was (combined with modern birth control) perhaps the biggest single nail in the coffin of male dominance.

EVA FIGES, AS QUOTED IN ELAINE MORGAN'S
——————— THE DESCENT OF WOMEN, 1972 ———————

•

SEX AND SEXUALITY
Help, Information, and Action Guide

Organizations

▶ **Sex Information and Education Council of the United States (SIECUS)**
130 West 42nd St., Suite 2500, New York, NY 10036-7901; 212-819-9770; Ann Welbourne-Moglia, executive director), an organization concerned

with sex education and health care. It seeks free access to information on human sexuality; acts as an information clearinghouse; and publishes various materials, including the bimonthly *SIECUS Report,* bibliographies, and books such as *Winning the Battle for Sex Education* and *Oh NO! What Do I Do Now?*

▶ PLANNED PARENTHOOD (212-541-7800). A primary source of information about and access to birth control and reproductive rights, and by extension about sexuality.

▶ **American Association of Sex Educators, Counselors, and Therapists** (11 Dupont Circle, NW, Suite 220, Washington, DC 20036; 202-462-1171), an organization of professionals in sex education, counseling, and therapy. It seeks to set and maintain high standards of training and ethics and certifies professionals in the field; provides information to the public and professionals; and publishes various materials, including a national directory of certified sex educators and the *Journal of Sex Education and Therapy.*

▶ NATIONAL WOMEN'S HEALTH NETWORK (**NWHN**) (202-347-1140). Operates the **Women's Health Information Service.**

▶ MS. FOUNDATION FOR WOMEN (**MFW**) (212-353-8580).

▶ INSTITUTE ON WOMEN AND TECHNOLOGY (413-367-9725).

▶ WOMEN'S INTERNATIONAL NETWORK (**WIN**) (617-862-9431).

▶ WOMEN'S INTERNATIONAL RESOURCE EXCHANGE (**WIRE**) (212-741-2955). Publishes *Virginity and Premarital Sex in Contemporary China.*

Other resources

The Erotic Impulse: Honoring the Sensual Self. David Steinberg, ed. Tarcher, 1992.

Peak Sexual Experience. John Selby. Warner, 1992.

Safely Sexual. Robert A. Hatcher. Irvington, 1992.

Dictionary of Sexual Slang: Words, Phrases, and Idioms from AC–DC to Zig-Zag. Alan Richter. Wiley, 1992.

The Kinsey Institute New Report on Sex. June M. Reinisch and Ruth Beasley. St. Martin's, 1991.

Questions You've Asked About Sexuality. Alberta Mazat. Pacific Press, 1991.

What Do You Know About Sex? Diane Zahler. Prentice-Hall, 1991.

Love Cycles: The Science of Intimacy. Winnifred B. Cutler. Random House, 1991.

Does Anyone Still Remember When Sex Was Fun? Anderson. Kendall-Hunt, 1991.

The New Kinsey Institute Report on Sex: Up-to-Date Answers to Questions About Sex. June M. Reinisch. Pharos (NY), 1990.

Couple Sexual Awareness: Building Sexual Happiness. Barry McCarthy and Emily McCarthy. Carroll and Graf, 1990.

Sex from the Inside Out. Tom Melton. JTM Press, 1990.

Your Complete Guide to Sexual Health. Elizabeth T. Ortiz. Prentice-Hall, 1989.

The Love Triangle: Sex, Dating and Love. Ronald L. Kotesky. SP Publications, 1989.

◪ FOR ADOLESCENT GIRLS

The Sexual Dictionary: Terms and Expressions for Teens and Parents. Kathryn T. Johnson and others. Larksdale, 1992.

Tell It Like It Is: Straight Talk About Sex. Annamaria Formichella and others. Avon, 1991.

Kerry's Thirteenth Birthday: Everything Your Parents and Their Friends Know About Sex but Are Too Polite to Talk About. Mary J. Rachner. Oxner Institute, 1991.

Sex Is Not a Four-Letter Word. James N. Watkins. Tyndale, 1991.

Love in Your Life: A Jewish View of Teenage Sexuality. Roland B. Gittelsohn. UAHC, 1991.

Drugs, Sex, and Integrity: What Does Judaism Say? Daniel F. Polish. UAHC, 1991.

Teen Guide to Safe Sex. Alan E. Nourse. Watts, 1990.

Love and Sex and Growing Up. Eric W. Johnson. Bantam, 1990.

Coping with Your Sexual Orientation. Deborah A. Miller and Alex Waigandt. Rosen, 1990. (See also **LESBIAN HELP, INFORMATION, AND ACTION GUIDE** on page 397.)

Be Smart About Sex: Facts for Young People. Jean Fiedler and Hal Fiedler. Enslow, 1990.

The Sex Education Dictionary for Today's Teens and Preteens. Dean Hoch and Nancy Hoch. Landmark, 1990.

The Dating Dilemma: Handling Sexual Pressures. Bob Stone and Bob Palmer. Baker Books, 1990.

Sex: A Christian Perspective. Group Publishing, 1990.

Becoming a Woman: Basic Information, Guidance and Attitudes on Sex for Girls. Valerie R. Dillon. Twenty-Third Publications, 1990. From a Christian moral point of view.

Sex and the Teenager: Choices and Decisions. Kieran Sawyer. Ave Maria, 1990.

The Gift of Sexuality: A Guide for Young People. Robert J. Fox. Our Sunday Visitor, 1989.

Love, Dating and Sex: What Teens Want to Know. George B. Eager. Mailbox, 1989.

What's Happening to My Body? Book for Girls, rev. ed. Lynda Madaras. Newmarket Press, 1988.

A Young Woman's Guide to Sex. Jacqueline Voss and Jay Gale. The Body Press (LA), 1988.
Teen Sex. Margaret O. Hyde. Westminster John Knox, 1988.
Girltalk About Guys. Carol Weston. Harper & Row, 1988.

◪ ON SEX EDUCATION

Living Smart: Understanding Sexuality in the Teen Years. Pennie Core-Gebhart and others. University of Arkansas Press, 1991.
What's Wrong with Sex Education? Preteen and Teenage Sexual Development and Environmental Influences. Melvin Anchell. Hoffman Center, 1991.
Healthy Sex Education in Your Schools: A Parent's Handbook. Anne Newman. Focus Family, 1990.
Has Sex Education Failed Our Teenagers? A Research Report. Dinah Richard. Focus on the Family, 1990.
Sex Respect: The Option of True Sexual Freedom: A Public Health Guide for Parents, rev. ed. Coleen K. Mast. Respect, 1990.

◪ ON SEXUAL PROBLEMS AND THERAPIES

Naked Ghosts: Intimate Stories from the Files of a Sex Therapist. Carol G. Wells. Prentice-Hall, 1991.
Sexual Dysfunction: A Guide for Assessment and Treatment. John P. Wincze and Michael P. Carey. Guilford Press, 1991.
Sexual Healing: A Self-Help Program to Enhance Your Sensuality and Overcome Common Sexual Problems. Barbara Keesling. Hunter House, 1990.
Disorders of Desire: Sex and Gender in Modern American Sexology. Janice M. Irvine. Temple University Press, 1990.
Sex by Prescription: The Startling Truth About Today's Sex Therapy. Thomas Szasz. Syracuse University Press, 1990. Reprint of 1980 ed.
Sexocize: A Female Genitourinary Program, 2nd ed. Janan Clark. West Pine, 1989.
Hope and Recovery: A Twelve Step Guide for Healing from Compulsive Sexual Behavior. CompCare, 1989.
Women and Sex Therapy. Ellen Cole and Esther D. Rothblum, eds. Harrington Park, 1988.
The Illustrated Manual of Sex Therapy, 2nd ed. Helen S. Kaplan. Brunner-Mazel, 1988.

◪ LEGAL PERSPECTIVES

Litigating Morality: American Legal Thought and Its English Roots. Alice F. Bartee and Wayne C. Bartee. Praeger/Greenwood, 1992.
Sexual Orientation and the Law. Editors of the *Harvard Law Review.* Harvard University Press, 1990.

Sex and the Law. Fenton Bresler. Trafalgar Square, 1989.

The Sexual Rights of Adolescents: Competence, Vulnerability, and Parental Control. Hyman Rodman and others. Columbia University Press, 1988.

■ INTERNATIONAL AND HISTORICAL PERSPECTIVES

The World of Sex: Customs and Beliefs. Edgar A. Gregersen. Irvington, 1992.

Against Nature: And Other Essays on History, Sexuality and Identity. Jeffrey Weeks. Paul and Co., 1991.

A History of Sexuality, Vol. 1. Michel Foucault. Random House, 1990.

Sex and Sexuality: From Repression to Expression. Mildred W. Weil. University Press of America, 1990.

Passion and Power: Sexuality in History. Kathy Peiss, eds. Temple University Press, 1989.

Love and Sex in Twelve Cultures. Robert Endleman. Psyche Press (NY), 1989.

Sexuality: An Illustrated History. Sander L. Gilman. Wiley, 1989.

A Women's History of Sex. Harriet Gilbert and Christine Roche. Unwin Hyman, 1988.

■ RELIGIOUS AND MORAL PERSPECTIVES

Catholic Sex for the Multitudes. Augustos B. Flowers. Catholic Arts Society, 1991.

Love Without Shame: Sexuality in Biblical Perspective. David Wyrtzen. Discovery House, 1991.

Restoring Innocence. Alfred Ells. Oliver-Nelson, 1991.

Church Fathers, Independent Virgins. Joyce E. Salisbury. Routledge Chapman and Hall, 1991.

Lust for Enlightenment: Buddhism and Sex. John Stevens. Shambhala, 1990.

Shattering the Silence: Telling the Church the Truth About Kids and Sexuality. David Lewis and others. Gospel Advocate, 1990.

Purity: The Mystery of Christian Sexuality. Dietrich Von Hildebrand. Franciscan University Press, 1989.

Carnal Knowing: Female Nakedness and Religious Meaning in the Christian West. Margaret Miles. Beacon Press, 1989.

A Sense of Sexuality: Christian Love and Intimacy. James D. Whitehead and Evelyn E. Whitehead. Doubleday, 1989.

Sins of the Body. Terry Muck, ed. Christianity Today, 1989.

With All Purity: What You Need to Know About Sexual Ethics, rev. ed. Stanley Rickard. Regular Baptist Press, 1989.

Sexual Values: Opposing Viewpoints. Lisa Orr. Greenhaven, 1989.

Toward the Fullness of Life and the Fullness of Love. Arnaud Desjardins. Threshold (VT), 1989.

Creative Love: The Ethics of Human Reproduction. John F. Boyle, ed. Christendom Press, 1989.
Marital Intimacy: A Catholic Perspective. Joan Anzia and Mary Durkin. Loyola, 1989. Reprint of 1980 ed.
Whole and Holy Sexuality. William F. Kraft. Abbey, 1989.
Sex and Morality: Who Is Teaching Our Sex Standards? Dr. Ruth Westheimer and Louis Lieberman. Harcourt Brace Jovanovich, 1988.
Sex and the New You. Richard Bimier. Concordia, 1988.
Living in Sin? A Bishop Rethinks Human Sexuality. John S. Spong. Abingdon, 1988.
Sexual Chaos: The Personal and Social Consequences of the Sexual Revolution. John S. Vertefeuille. Good News, 1988.
Human Sexuality: A Christian View. John C. Dwyer. Sheed and Ward (MO), 1988.
Contemporary Sexual Morality. John F. Dedek. Sheed and Ward (MO), 1988.

◪ ON PROSTITUTION AND EXPLOITATION

Enslaved. Gordon Thomas. Pharos (NY), 1991.
Uneasy Virtue: The Politics of Prostitution and the American Reform Tradition. Barbara M. Hobson. University of Chicago Press, 1990.
A Vindication of the Rights of Whores: The International Movement for Prostitutes' Rights. Gail Pheterson, ed. Seal Press Feminist, 1989.
Sex Work: Writings by Women in the Sex Industry. Frederique Delacoste and Priscilla Alexander, eds. Cleis Press, 1991. Reprint of 1987 ed.
Children Enslaved. Roger Sawyer. Routledge, 1988.
The Call Girl. Harold Greenwald. Libra, 1988.

◪ ON PORNOGRAPHY

On Pornography: Literature, Sexuality, and Obscenity Law. Ian Hunter and others. St. Martin's, 1992.
Pornography, Feminism and the Individual. Alison Assiter. Westview, 1991.
Feminism and Pornography. Ronald J. Berger. Greenwood, 1991.
Porn: Myths for the Twentieth Century. Robert J. Stoller. Yale University Press, 1991.
Pornography: The Other Side. F. M. Christensen. Greenwood, 1990.
Pornography in a Free Society. Gordon Hawkins and Franklin E. Zimring. Cambridge University Press, 1989.
Freedom and Taboo: Pornography and the Politics of a Self Divided. Richard S. Randall. University of California Press, 1989.
The New Politics of Pornography. Donald A. Downs. University of Chicago Press, 1989.
For Adult Users Only: The Dilemma of Violent Pornography. Susan Gubar and Joan Hoff, eds. Indiana University Press, 1989.

Pornography. Carol Gorman. Watts, 1988.

Perspectives on Pornography: Sexuality in Film and Literature. Gary Day and Clive Bloom, eds. St. Martin's, 1988.

Pornography and Civil Rights: A New Day for Women's Equality. Andrea Dworkin and Catharine A. MacKinnon. Organizing Porn, 1988.

◪ **BACKGROUND BOOKS**

Embattled Eros: Sexual Politics and Ethics in Contemporary America. Steven Seidman. Routledge (NY), 1992.

Sex and Reason. Richard A. Posner. Harvard University Press, 1992.

Dangerous Passage: The Social Control of Sexuality in Women's Adolescence. Constance Nathanson. Temple University Press, 1991.

The Philosophy of (Erotic) Love. Robert C. Solomon and Kathleen M. Higgins, eds. University Press of Kansas, 1991.

Encyclopedia of Erotic Wisdom: A Reference Guide to the Symbolism, Techniques, Rituals, Sacred Texts, Anatomy, and History of Sexuality. Rufus C. Camphausen. Inner Traditions, 1991.

Taking Sides: Clashing Views on Controversial Issues in Human Sexuality, 3rd ed. Robert Francoeur. Dushkin, 1991.

Sexuality Spirituality: A Study of Feminine-Masculine Relationships. John Moore. Element (MA), 1990.

Romanced to Death: The Sexual Seduction of American Culture. Paul DeParrie. Wolgemuth and Hyatt, 1990.

Untangling the Sexual Revolution. Henry W. Spaulding, II. Beacon Hill, 1989.

True Love and Perfect Union: The Feminist Reform of Sex and Society, 2nd ed. William Leach. Wesleyan University Press/University Press of New England, 1989.

sexual slavery: See PROSTITUTION.

significant other, a now somewhat outdated term for a person with whom one has a close and special relationship, but not necessarily one with formal standing, such as an ENGAGEMENT, MARRIAGE, or even COHABITATION.

silicone: See BREAST IMPLANTS.

Sims-Huhner test, one of a battery of tests in a *fertility workup*, performed to discover the causes of INFERTILITY; also called a *postcoital test*.

Sims position, a position during CHILDBIRTH where the mother lies on her left side, rather than on her back.

Single Mothers by Choice (SMC) (P.O. Box 1642, Gracie Square Station, New York, NY 10028; 212-988-0993; Jane Mattes, founder and director), an organization founded in 1981 to "provide support and information to single women who have chosen or who are considering single motherhood," deliberately or by accident, through SEXUAL INTERCOURSE, ADOPTION, or ARTIFICIAL INSEMINATION. SMC facilitates exchange of information and resources locally and nationally; offers meetings and workshops, such as mothers who adopted or those who conceived with donor insemination, including some for those considering single motherhood, to help clarify issues toward making a decision. It also publishes various materials, including a quarterly newsletter, a membership directory, and an information packet containing articles on single mothers by choice, and on donor insemination and adoption.

SINGLE MOTHERS BY CHOICE
PHILOSOPHY

1. A single mother by choice is a woman willing to take the initiative. Her child might have been conceived or adopted. What we all share is the decision to take on the responsibility of raising our babies knowing that, at least at the outset, there will be no primary paternal caretaker.

   We do not include women who were widowed or divorced after they had children because the emotional and practical aspects of their situation are usually quite different.

2. Our goals are to offer support and information to single mothers by choice and to single women considering motherhood, to provide a peer group for our children, and to clarify the public's understanding of single mothers by choice.

3. SMC is not an advocacy group. It is not fair to a child or woman to urge her to get into an impractical or overextended situation, or one where there are a great many unresolved issues or deep concerns. Single parenting is difficult enough for the woman who is sure and prepared.

4. In general, our members feel that it is preferable to raise a child with two loving parents. However, in the absence of a good partnership, and with the rate of divorce as high as it is, we feel that being raised by a caring single parent is definitely a viable option.

5. The majority of us are well established in our careers and are able to support a child without recourse to public funds.
6. The word *choice* in our title has two implications: we have made a serious and thoughtful decision to take on the responsibility of raising a child by ourselves, and we have chosen not to be in a relationship rather than be in one that does not seem satisfactory.

Source: SINGLE MOTHERS BY CHOICE.

single parent, a MOTHER or FATHER who is raising one or more children without a partner; in Canada called a *lone parent*. In the last twenty years the percentage of one-parent families with children has risen dramatically, in the United States from 12.9 percent of families with children in 1970 to 27.3 in 1988. In single-parent families headed by mothers, the rise is even greater, from 11.5 to 23.7 percent; among Black single mothers, the comparable figures are from 33.0 in 1970—already high—to an astounding 55.6 in 1988. Overall, mothers head more than 87 percent of all one-parent families. (See CHANGES IN ONE- AND TWO-PARENT FAMILIES on page 678.) Among all single-parent families in the United States, more than 39 percent resulted from DIVORCE and more than 21 percent from SEPARATION, formal or informal (see ABANDONMENT); more than 31 percent are headed by never married mothers; and more than 6 percent result from the death of a SPOUSE. The specifics differ elsewhere in the world, but in most countries—at least where divorce laws have been liberalized—the trend is the same.

On the average, single parents tend to be younger than their two-parent counterparts, with single mothers younger than single fathers. This has significant economic implications, because younger single parents have fewer job skills and life experience and are more likely to need help from others, including parents or other relatives, the absent parent, or aid organizations, public or private. Even when they have training, women who are single parents tend to earn less in the workforce than men (see SEXUAL DISCRIMINATION; EQUAL PAY FOR EQUAL WORK; OCCUPATION SEGREGATION). Also, in a world where two family incomes are often needed to make ends meet, the single-parent family has only one. In theory CHILD SUPPORT and ALIMONY should help make up the difference, but in practice many mothers receive little or no support.

Those are two very strong reasons why, of all families with children who live below the poverty line, approximately 60 percent are single-parent families. Looking at it another way, among all families headed by single mothers, more than 45 percent live below the poverty line (as compared with approximately 17 percent of male single-parent families). Many such families receive government support, such as food stamps, Medicaid, and SOCIAL SECURITY. When they are lucky, they also have available help such as job training that will allow them to support themselves.

Single parents lack the mutual help and support that, ideally, a partner would provide. They must make, on their own, all the crucial medical, social, legal, financial, and other decisions that affect the child, as well as day-to-day decisions such as where to live, how to support the family, and how to care for the child when at work or school. And they must handle all alone the chores involved in keeping a household going, though older children are generally drafted to help with these.

Difficult though all this may be, single-parent families can as healthy and happy as any other family. Indeed, studies have shown that a single-parent family can be better for children than a two-parent family with great discord. Children in single-parent families can grow strong and confident from their experience in helping to solve day-to-day problems. Single parents simply have to work harder at parenting. CHILD CARE and FAMILY AND MEDICAL LEAVE are vital to free them to care for their family while holding a job as most must do. Though single parents have no one at hand to share directly in their burden, many groups and organizations have formed to help them cope with their special concerns; among the best known is PARENTS WITHOUT PARTNERS (for others, see SINGLE PARENT'S HELP, INFORMATION, AND ACTION GUIDE on page 676). Such organizations offer advice on single parenting, including information on special legal concerns, and also give single parents a chance to share their experiences with others in small groups.

Never married or unmarried single mothers face special decisions once they have decided to bear and raise the child, rather than to have an ABORTION or give the child up for ADOPTION. If she has not already done so, a single mother will need to decide whether or not to tell the father of the child, if he is known. Legally the father is obliged to give child support; if the single mother seeks some kinds of government aid, she will generally be required to initiate a paternity suit to establish the father's child support obligations (see CHILD SUPPORT). Indeed, some single mothers have chosen to seek little or no child support, in order to avoid legal entanglements with the father.

In the past, many never married or unmarried mothers pretended to others that they were divorced or widowed, to avoid social ostracism for themselves or the child; this is much less common today, especially in urban areas. Indeed, some single women now deliberately choose to have babies on their own, through ARTIFICIAL INSEMINATION or *adoption,* though such options are difficult or illegal to exercise in some states. This allows them to become mothers while retaining their independence, rather than living with an unsuitable partner just to give the child a legal father. They have the advantage of avoiding quarrels with a partner about child rearing. More commonly, the PREGNANCY is unplanned, and the mother chooses to have and keep the baby. Much attention has focused on adolescent pregnancy, and indeed almost 45 percent of unmarried mothers are under twenty; but many older women decide to bear and raise their child alone. Having a baby "out of wedlock" can still be highly controversial, however; witness the 1992 flap over then–Vice President Dan Quayle's criticism of television's unmarried Murphy Brown (played by Candice Bergen) having a baby on her own.

Never married or unmarried mothers need to think ahead to any possible social problems and prepare themselves and the child for them. In particular they are advised to explain the circumstances of the birth and single-parent family to the child themselves, when the child is young; this should be done in terms as simple and understandable as possible, stressing that a one-parent family is one of many kinds of families. That will spare the child hurt or shock on learning about the family from others and will also prepare her or him to counter possible negative comments from others.

When the father has been part of the family but then is gone—as through divorce, abandonment, or death—the single parent must help children with the transition. This is not always easy, because the mother may have her own grief to deal with. But it is important to be sure that children do not feel they are to blame for the father's departure, and that they do not carry unrealistic fantasies about a possible RECONCILIATION. Children will not always talk about such things, but single parents will be wise to discuss such matters with them occasionally.

In the brochure *40 Tips for Better Single Parenting*, Parents Without Partners recommends the following:
- If divorced, say that divorce is a decision made by adults, not by children.
- If you did not marry, your child may develop some fantasy to explain not having a parent present, so you should find ways to reassure your child. For example: "I didn't believe your father and I could be happy together, but I wanted you very much."
- Widowed parents may need to deal with a child's fantasy that an angry thought or word caused the death of a parent. Make sure your child knows this cannot happen.

Both divorced and never married mothers must deal with VISITATION RIGHTS, should the father wish to exercise them, and sometimes the grandparents as well (see GRANDPARENTS RIGHTS). If so, they should try to make visitation as easy and abrasion-free as possible, allowing the child to respect and love the other parent (see TIPS FOR MAKING VISITATION WORK on page 744), without becoming involved in a parental battle or feeling they must choose between one or the other. In particular, a single parent should try not to inject negative feelings such as bitterness, jealousy, blame, revenge, or anger into the child's relationship with the other parent. When the father does not visit, single mothers must try to explain the absence in a way that will ease the child's hurt and feelings of rejection.

Single mothers must certainly assure their children that they will not be abandoned and that they are still loved and will continue to be cared for. But mothers should be sure they do not invest *too* much time and emotion in their children. For their long-term mutual health, both need to have a life beyond the parent-child relationship. Single mothers should never forget that they have their own lives as individuals, not just in relation to their children. It is important for both parent and child to reach out to others for friendship; indeed, many single-parent families establish informal networks to ease the burdens that each carries. Single mothers should recognize that *all* parents—not just single parents—can sometimes resent the sacrifices they make for their children. When that happens—preferably before that happens—they should reach out to others for help in coping. Whatever the situation, it is important for single mothers to keep in mind that the child did not make the decision to be raised in a single-parent family and to not rely too heavily on the child—no matter how strong and supportive—in dealing with their own problems.

Family experts recommend that single parents resolve any legal questions as smoothly and quickly as possible. Prolonged separations, on-again/off-again relationships, child support, custody, visitation, paternity suits, and other such matters can, if left uncertain, undermine the sense of permanence and security that a parent strives to give a family. Even if the family will be undergoing long-term changes—for example, if a single mother is going to school part-time to prepare for a better job—the children will feel most secure if they understand that this is all part of a plan. Similarly, predictable household routines will provide a sense of order and responsibility.

Many single mothers marry later, or remarry. While new relationships can occur at any age, they are most likely when women—and their children—are young. Significantly, in at least one study, one-third of all single parents *preferred* to remain single, especially older mothers. When beginning new relationships, single parents are advised to introduce potential partners slowly, discussing them before introducing them, stressing that the new person will not replace their absent parent, and making sure that they maintain time for the children alone. (See SINGLE PARENT'S HELP, INFORMATION, AND ACTION GUIDE, below.)

SINGLE PARENT'S

Help, Information, and Action Guide

Organizations

▶ PARENTS WITHOUT PARTNERS (PWP) (301-588-9354 or 800-637-7974). Publishes the magazine *The Single Parent;* brochures such as *40 Tips for Better Single Parenting, Are You a Single Parent?, Single Parenting and Education,* and *Single Parenting and Legislation;* a bibliography on single parenthood; and information kits for never-married mothers or parents raising children alone.

▶ SINGLE MOTHERS BY CHOICE (SMC) (212-988-0993).

▶ NURTURING NETWORK, THE (TNN) (208-344-7200 or 800-TNN-4MOM [866-4666]).

▶ NATIONAL CENTER ON WOMEN AND FAMILY LAW (NCOWFL) (212-674-8200).

▶ NATIONAL CENTER FOR YOUTH LAW (NCYL) (415-543-3307).

▶ NATIONAL DISPLACED HOMEMAKERS NETWORK (NDHN) (202-467-6346).

Publishes the *NHDN Program Directory* and *The More Things Change ... A Status Report on Displaced Homemakers and Single Parents in the 1980s.*

▶ INTERNATIONAL CENTER FOR RESEARCH ON WOMEN (ICRW) (202-797-0007). Publishes *Women on Their Own: Global Patterns of Female Headship, Mothers on Their Own: Policy Issues for Developing Countries,* and *Women, Work, and Child Welfare in the Third World.*

Other resources

Lone Parenthood: Coping with Constraints and Making Opportunities in Single-Parent Families. Michael Hardey and Graham Crow, eds. University of Toronto Press, 1992.

Never a Day Off: Surviving Single Parenthood. Elizabeth H. Rigdon. Beacon Hill, 1991.

Complete Financial Guide for Single Parents. Larry Burkett. Dandelion House, 1991.

The Two-Parent Family Is Not the Best. June Stephenson. Diemer-Smith, 1991.

The Single Mother's Book: A Practical Guide to Managing Your Children, Career, Home, Finances and Everything Else. Joan Anderson. Peachtree, 1990.

Single Moms, Single Dads: Help and Hope for the One-Parent Family. David R. Miller. Accent Books, 1990.

Daughters Without Dads. Lois Mowday. Nelson, 1990.

Handbook for Single Parents. William Rabior and Vicki W. Bedard. Liquori Publications, 1990.

The Single Parent Family. Thomas D. Yawkey and Georgianna M. Cornelius. Technomic, 1989.

Successful Single Parenting. Gary Richmond. Harvest House, 1989.

Just One of Me: Confessions of a Less-Than-Perfect Single Parent. Dandi D. Knorr. Shaw Publishers, 1989.

Teen Guide to Single Parenting. Herma Silverstein. Watts, 1989.

Women as Single Parents: Confronting Institutional Barriers in the Courts, the Workplace, and the Housing Market. Elizabeth A. Mulroy, ed. Auburn House/Greenwood, 1988.

Single Mothers Raising Sons. Bobbie Reed. Nelson, 1988.

Survival Skills for Single Parents. Paul J. Ciborowski. Stratmar Educational Systems, 1988.

Survival Tips for a Single Parent. Jeanette Johnson. Review & Herald, 1988.

A Single Black Mother. Thelma Williams. A-Town Publishing, 1988.

Mothers Alone: Strategies for a Time of Change. Sheila B. Kamerman and Alfred J. Kahn. Auburn House/Greenwood, 1988.

CHANGES IN ONE- AND TWO-PARENT FAMILIES

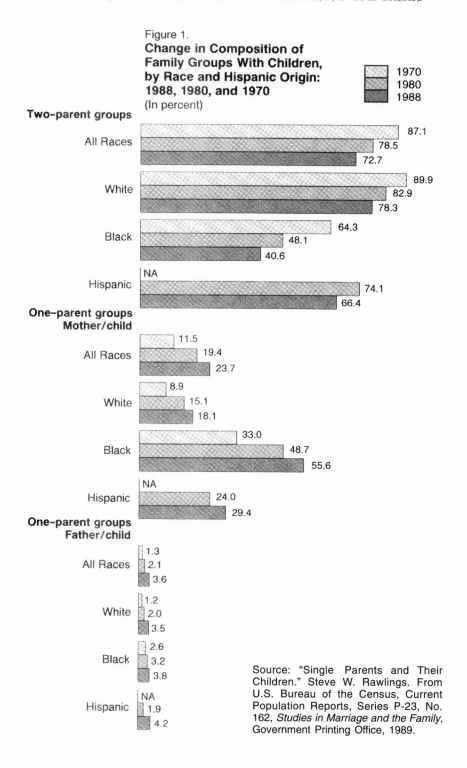

Figure 1.
Change in Composition of Family Groups With Children, by Race and Hispanic Origin: 1988, 1980, and 1970
(In percent)

1970
1980
1988

Two-parent groups

All Races
87.1
78.5
72.7

White
89.9
82.9
78.3

Black
64.3
48.1
40.6

Hispanic
NA
74.1
66.4

One-parent groups Mother/child

All Races
11.5
19.4
23.7

White
8.9
15.1
18.1

Black
33.0
48.7
55.6

Hispanic
NA
24.0
29.4

One-parent groups Father/child

All Races
1.3
2.1
3.6

White
1.2
2.0
3.5

Black
2.6
3.2
3.8

Hispanic
NA
1.9
4.2

Source: "Single Parents and Their Children." Steve W. Rawlings. From U.S. Bureau of the Census, Current Population Reports, Series P-23, No. 162, *Studies in Marriage and the Family*, Government Printing Office, 1989.

The Single Parent Survival Guide: The Hilarious Handbook of Fractured Families. Michael Sack and Marion Keen. Price Stern, 1988.
(See also CAREGIVER'S HELP, INFORMATION, AND ACTION GUIDE on page 454; COUPLES AND FAMILIES HELP, INFORMATION, AND ACTION GUIDE on page 418; DIVORCE AND SEPARATION HELP, INFORMATION, AND ACTION GUIDE on page 238.)

single woman, the legal MARITAL STATUS of an adult female who has never been married; in a wider sense, as for census purposes, also including a woman who has been previously married but is divorced or widowed.

Historically, society rather looked down on single women, except in approved settings, such as religion. An unmarried male, or *bachelor*, might be sought after by hostesses looking for "an extra man," but an unmarried female—formerly and in some places legally still called a *spinster*—was seen as a burden and a social embarrassment. Young girls were warned about the horrors of becoming an *old maid*—and the horrors could be real in the days when a woman had few reputable ways of earning her own living and maintaining her independence. Many an unmarried woman was condemned to a dependence—often reluctant—on a male relative for support and possibly work in a domestic venue, as a governess or maid.

However, never married and formerly married women had some distinct advantages over married women. Married women traditionally had no legal standing (see COVERTURE; MARRIAGE), but were "covered" by their husbands, and so called *feme covert*; by contrast, single women were legally independent. The *feme sol*, or single woman, could own property, make contracts, leave an estate, and serve as a legal guardian or estate administrator, things that married women generally could not do until after the Married Women's Property Acts of the mid-nineteenth century. The legal distinctions between a married and single woman have largely eroded, but even today single women continue to have somewhat more independence under the law.

With the rise of WOMEN'S RIGHTS MOVEMENTS from the mid-nineteenth century onward, some women have stayed single by choice—as they always have, to some extent—from the start or after a previous marriage or DIVORCE. Certainly there have always been some women who were unable to find an appropriate partner (see MATE SELECTION; MARRIAGE SQUEEZE) or who did not wish a heterosexual union (see LESBIAN). But many were drawn to the independent life, and some devoted their lives to causes or careers in place of marriage.

In recent decades many more adults have been spending a larger proportion of their lives single, especially in developed countries, but in significant parts of the developing world as well. This is the result of many social trends, among them that

• both women and men are tending to marry later (see MARRIAGE), so the proportion of people age twenty to forty who have never married has been increasing.

- adults frequently find themselves becoming single again one or more times in midlife, because of DIVORCE.
- women tend to live longer, and the difference in LIFE EXPECTANCY between men and women is growing wider in many parts of the world, so many WIDOWS live alone after the death of a spouse.
- single women today are freer to earn their own livings and often to get an education and so are increasingly able to support themselves independently—and often prefer to do so—rather than join another household in a dependent status.
- many heterosexual couples are living together in long-term relationships, rather than—or preparatory to—marrying (see COHABITATION).
- many homosexual couples have "come out" about their sexual orientation and instead of living in sham marriages are living openly with same-sex partners (see LESBIAN).

Many single women have led full, happy, satisfied lives, despite continuing stereotypes of the single woman as warped spinster or cold career woman, both of whom melt internally at the sight of a baby. This does not mean that single women—like other humans of both sexes—do not necessarily have ambivalence or even regrets about some of their choices. In the 1980s and early 1990s, for example, many women—single or married—who had forgone children for career decided late in their reproductive lives to have a baby, characterized as "listening to their biological clock tick." Others, despite media hype on these questions, felt no such urges.

Many women who are classed as "single" for legal or census purposes do not actually live alone. Many are, in fact, SINGLE PARENTS, raising one or more young children; among woman-headed households in developing countries, this is the dominant pattern (see FAMILY). Many single women in all countries are young people still living with their parents, or adults living with, and often caring for, an older relative (see HOMEMAKER). Many people who appear to be single are only legally so but are actually living with someone (see COHABITATION). Where money is tight, especially among young people, several single people may share the costs of a house or apartment.

However, many single women do actually live alone, in what census takers call *one-person households*. That is true of the majority of woman-headed households in developed countries, and especially of many elderly women the world over. Many are women who have put off marriage, are between marriages, or are postmarriage or -divorce. In the United States, nearly 95 percent of all women are married at some point in their lives, but the likelihood of their being married drops off sharply as they grow older, as the ratio of men to women drops (see RATIO OF UNMARRIED MEN PER 100 UNMARRIED WOMEN: 1990 on page 682). As a result, older women are more likely to live alone; as of the 1990 U.S. census, 42 percent of all women over sixty-five live alone; over age eighty-five, the proportion is two-thirds.

Older women are also more likely than older men to be poor; over age eighty-five, three times more likely. One key reason for this is that many women now over sixty-five worked as homemakers, and because they did not get paid for doing HOUSEWORK, they were unable to build up pensions and SOCIAL SECURITY on their earnings; as a result, they do not have benefits in their own names, relying instead on whatever benefits (if any) were passed on from their husbands. Even when women were employed outside the home, their earnings were less, so they had less in the way of later benefits (see INSURANCE AND PENSION EQUITY; EQUAL PAY FOR EQUAL WORK; PAY EQUITY; WORK AND WOMEN; SEXUAL DISCRIMINATION).

As they get older, men and women—single or married—experience a different quality of life. Though elderly men are more likely to have short-term, fatal diseases—as reflected in their shorter life expectancy—elderly women tend to have long-term, chronic, disabling diseases. As a result, more than 30 percent of women over age seventy-five need help from someone with basic tasks such as eating, dressing, bathing, preparing meals, managing money, and getting outside. This is, of course, the largest-growing segment of the population and will continue to be so as the Baby Boomers age. In the United States, for example, the 1990 census found that the proportion of people over eighty-five in the population had increased sixfold from 1900 to 1990. Many elderly single women gradually find themselves unable to live alone without help. Though some may need to go into nursing homes or special retirement communities with assistance available, many find themselves able to maintain their independence with small amounts of aid, such as Meals on Wheels programs or day help.

Given women's longer lifetimes, and the current demographics, single women in their middle years are sometimes finding themselves in what sociologists have dubbed a *sandwich*. While still raising children, they may also find themselves having to provide at least some care and supervision for an elderly parent, often a mother.

For more help, information, and action

When Women Choose to Be Single. Rita Robinson. IBS Press, 1991.
Women Without Husbands: An Exploration of the Margins of Marriage. Joan Chandler. St. Martin's, 1991.
Wake Up, Sleeping Beauty: How to Start Living Happily Ever After—Right Now. Jane Adams. Morrow, 1990.
Beating the Marriage Odds: When You Are Smart, Single, and Over Thirty-Five. Barbara Lovenheim. Morrow, 1990.
Why Women Shouldn't Marry. Cynthia S. Smith. Ivy Books, 1989.
A Guide for a Single Woman in Relationship to Men. Anthony C. Renfro. Renfro Publishers, 1988.
(See also WORKING WOMEN'S HELP, INFORMATION, AND ACTION GUIDE on page 779; SINGLE PARENT'S HELP, INFORMATION, AND ACTION GUIDE on page 676; OLDER WOMEN'S HELP, INFORMATION, AND ACTION GUIDE on page 374.)

RATIO OF UNMARRIED MEN PER
100 UNMARRIED WOMEN: 1990

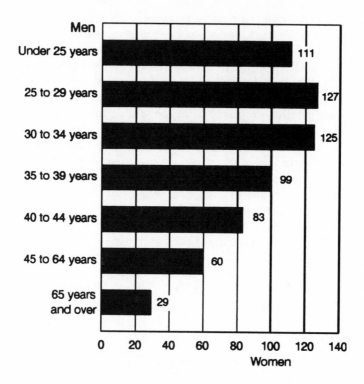

Source: U.S. Bureau of the Census, Current Population Reports, Series P-20, No. 450. *Marital Status and Living Arrangements: March 1990* U.S. Government Printing Office, 1991.

skeletal system, the internal framework of the body, providing shape, support, stability, strength, and (with the MUSCULAR SYSTEM) motion.

The 206 bones of various shapes and sizes that make up the skeleton are generally made up of three layers: the thin outer membrane (*periosteum*) containing blood vessels and nerves; the dense hard shell made largely of calcium phosphate in a protein structure (the *osteoid matrix*); and the spongy internal tissue, including the *bone marrow,* where vital red BLOOD cells are produced. The central, or *axial,* skeleton is made up of the skull, the ribs, the breastbone (*sternum*), and the SPINE. The rest of the bones, including the shoulder bones (*scapulae* and *clavicle*), arms, legs, and pelvis, make up the *appendicular skeleton.*

Bones are connected to muscles by a type of connective tissue called *tendons.* Bones meet and connect at junctions called *joints;* to reduce the friction of bones grinding against each other, the ends of the bones are covered with cartilage and the joints themselves have a special lining, the *synovial membrane.* Special connective tissue called *ligaments* hold the joints in place and stabilize them. Some joints do not move, such as those that join in the skull; some have relatively little movement, as in the spine; while some are highly movable. These mobile joints come in several different types: *ball-and-socket joints,* allowing backward, forward, sideways, and rotating movements, as in the hip and shoulder; *hinge joints,* allowing bending and straightening, as in fingers, sometimes with some rotation built in as well, as with knees and elbows; *pivot joints,* allowing rotation, as in some vertebrae; and *ellipsoidal joints,* allowing various types of movement, except pivotal, as in the wrist.

Skeletons are roughly the same in men and women. On the average, men's skeletons have somewhat longer and heavier bones, with broader shoulders and longer rib cages, than women's, though of course individual women may be bigger-boned than individual men. The main differences are that women have wider pelvic bones, allowing for PREGNANCY and CHILDBIRTH, and that the thigh bones attached to the pelvis are set somewhat wider apart and at a slightly inward angle, making the walk somewhat different.

Though it seems unchanging and lifeless, bone is actually living tissue. Old cells are continually being broken down, or *resorbed,* and replaced by new ones, in a bone-rebuilding process called *remodeling.* This process is controlled by various HORMONES, which regulate the level of calcium in the blood.

Bone not only grows but also changes during a lifetime. An EMBRYO has no bone, only a tough, resilient material called *cartilage.* By about the seventh to eighth week of PREGNANCY, this cartilage begins to turn into bone; this process of *ossification* takes years, ending only in early adulthood. A newborn's skull is soft, easing childbirth, and contains gaps called *fontanelles,* which are by about age eighteen months closed with bone. During the first year of life, the infant's head grows dramatically, starting at only about one-quarter of the body's length and ending almost full adult size. During early childhood, most growth occurs in the long bones of the arms and legs, primarily at the ends, called *epiphyses* or more popularly *growth plates* or *growth centers.* Normally growth occurs steadily, at a rate of two to three inches a year from age two to PUBERTY, though various kinds of growth disorders or poor NUTRITION can slow that rate, which is more generally determined by GENETIC INHERITANCE.

Then, with puberty, a growth spurt occurs, with not only the limbs but also the trunk growing faster through adolescence; this spurt normally starts between ages eight and twelve in girls (ten and sixteen in boys), generally before *menarche,* or onset of MENSTRUATION. A person reaches full skeletal dimensions when the epiphyses turn to bone, at about ages fourteen to sixteen in girls (sixteen to eighteen in boys). By that time the legs account for about one-half of the body's height and the head only about one-eighth.

However, bones continue to grow in both size and strength into a person's mid-thirties, with calcium being deposited into bone faster than it is taken out. This process is enhanced by weight-bearing EXERCISE, which tends to promote deposition of bone. After that peak of bone mass, bone begins to decline in both strength and density, a process that accelerates in women following the great hormonal shift called MENOPAUSE.

Healthy bone depends on an adequate supply of calcium, especially during the growing years. That is especially true of women, since they have somewhat less bone mass to start with and lose it faster later in life. Pregnant women must be especially careful to maintain proper levels of calcium, so their bones will not be "robbed" of their strength. One of the hazards of adolescent pregnancy is that the girl is still growing, and the calcium demands on her body may weaken her general bone mass; it also may end her growth prematurely, leading to shorter stature. Moderate weight-bearing exercise is also valuable in building or maintaining bone mass.

Bone is subject to a variety of disorders, including fractures; infections of the bone (*osteomyelitis*) or bone marrow (as in tuberculosis); tumors (see CANCER); and various disorders that affect the formation of bone, as by malformation, excessive turnover, or premature ossification, among them GENETIC DISORDERS such as *osteogenesis imperfecta, achondroplasia,* and *osteopetrosis,* and others of unknown origin, such as *craniosynostosis* or *Paget's disease of the bone.* Among the bone disorders of special concern to women are OSTEOPOROSIS, literally "porous bone," and ARTHRITIS, literally "inflammation of the joints," both of which are common in some form among many older people but affect women disproportionately and can be very debilitating. The SPINE is subject to a variety of special disorders, such as scoliosis (see SPINE).

Bone marrow is playing an increasingly important role in the treatment of some types of cancer that spread (*metastasize*). Healthy marrow is "harvested" and stored; the body is bombarded with drugs and radiation designed to kill the cancer, which also kills the remaining bone marrow; the previously harvested marrow is then reinserted into the bone (see CANCER). Bone marrow can also be transplanted from one person to another, though finding a donor who is an appropriate "match" can be very difficult.

For more help, information, and action

▶ NATIONAL INSTITUTE OF ARTHRITIS AND MUSCULOSKELETAL AND SKIN DISEASES (NIAMS) (301-496-8188); **AMS Clearinghouse,** (301-495-4484); **Office of Research on Women's Health** (301-402-1770).

▶ **American Society for Bone and Mineral Research (ASBMR)** (1101 Connecticut Avenue, NW, Suite 700, Washington, DC; 202-857-1161; Judith Thomas, executive director), an organization of professionals concerned with bone and mineral diseases. It publishes a newsletter and the *Journal of Bone and Mineral Research.*

Other resources

Bones and Joints: A Guide for Students, 2nd ed. Christine Gunn. Churchill, 1992. (See also OSTEOPOROSIS; SPINE; ARTHRITIS; TEETH.)

Skene's glands, a pair of small glands that open in the VULVA just below the urethra (see URINARY TRACT); also called *Skene's ducts* or *paraurethral ducts.* Their

function is unknown, though some think they may be analogous to a male's prostate glands (see REPRODUCTIVE SYSTEM). They are notable mainly for often becoming infected; if GONORRHEA is involved, the glands may have to be removed to completely rid the body of the infectious organisms.

skin, the thin outer covering of the human body, considered the body's largest organ. The skin is a protective shield that has a wide variety of functions; it

- protects the body against dirt, chemicals, and disease-causing organisms;
- recognizes "foreign" substances attempting to breach its defenses and stimulates production of cells to fight off the attack, as in a poison ivy rash;
- produces the pigment *melanin* to protect against the sun's ultraviolet rays, in the process called *tanning*;
- acts like the body's umbrella, causing most water simply to run off;
- includes sense receptors for heat, cold, touch, and pain;
- stretches as the body inside it moves and changes shape and orientation, later resuming its original shape through a natural elasticity provided by a substance called *collagen*;
- produces vitamin D, vital for strong teeth and bones, in the presence of sunlight;
- cushions the body from injury;
- helps regulate body temperature, by producing sweat that will evaporate and cool the body or by constricting surface blood vessels to retain body heat.

In addition, the skin has the capacity to repair itself, after cuts, burns, and other such injuries.

The skin is actually made up of three layers, a thin outer layer called the *epidermis* (literally meaning "upon skin"); a thicker middle layer called the *dermis;* and an even thicker bottom layer, *subcutaneous tissue,* consisting mostly of fat but also including muscle fibers, such as are used in changing facial expression. The epidermis varies in thickness, generally being thinnest in the eyelids and thickest on the soles of the feet. Epidermal cells are made up primarily of a protein called *keratin;* specialized versions of this substance form the HAIR and NAILS.

Growing through the epidermis are several types of structures that originate in the dermis, including hair follicles, sweat glands, BLOOD vessels, nerve endings, muscles, and oil (*sebaceous*) glands, which produce oils (*sebum*) to keep the skin and hair moist and supple. The dermis also anchors the epidermis to the underlying subcutaneous tissue of the body. This fatty tissue, important not only as a cushion but also in conserving body heat, also varies considerably in thickness, being quite thin in some places, such as the shins or scalp, and quite thick in others, such as the buttocks or a mature woman's BREASTS.

Skin varies widely in color. The color at birth depends on a person's GENETIC INHERITANCE; the more and larger the melanin particles produced, the darker the skin. Within each individual, skin color also varies; most people have at least some clumps of melanin particles, called *freckles,* or even denser clumps, called *moles.* These often increase in size, number, or darkness with exposure to the sun. In fact, the so-called *liver spots* commonly associated with aging are often the result of long-term exposure to the sun, though sometimes to hormonal changes, as during PREGNANCY. Variations in color may also result from birthmarks, which are unusual collections of blood vessels near the skin's surface. Raised, strawberrylike marks—generally red, but sometimes blue, if fed by a vein—often grow during early childhood, but gradually disappear by school age. Flatter marks are generally permanent, though some techniques are being explored to remove them.

During pregnancy, and sometimes while on BIRTH CONTROL PILLS, a woman's body may produce excess amounts of melanin, forming brownish patches, often on the face, which may be further darkened by the sun. This is called *melasma gravidarum, mask of pregnancy,* or, more generally, *hyperpigmentation.* On rare occasions the body produces little or no melanin, leaving the skin unprotected, a condition generally called *hypopigmentation;* usually this results from a type of GENETIC DISORDER, such as *albinism,* which involves failure of the cells to produce melanin; or *vitiligo,* which involves an absence of melanin-producing cells. Some diseases show themselves partly by their effect on the skin, including SEXUALLY TRANSMITTED DISEASES (STDs) that may cause sores or blisters, the most common being HERPES. Similarly, liver diseases may produce a yellowish cast called *jaundice* (see DIGESTIVE SYSTEM).

Skin also changes over time. A baby's skin is smooth and sensitive and often heals quickly and tracelessly from cuts and other minor injuries. During PUBERTY, under the influence of hormonal changes, oil glands begin to produce more actively; they slow production decades later, in women starting around age forty. The skin then gradually becomes drier and less elastic, causing it to sag. Throughout a lifetime skin is renewing itself constantly, with dead cells sloughing off and being replaced by new ones. This process slows with age, so cuts and other such injuries often take longer to heal in older people.

By far the most common skin disorder is *contact dermatitis,* which involves a superficial skin inflammation called *eczema,* ranging from a red, itchy rash to blisters or ulcers to chronic thickening, drying, cracking, and hardening of the skin. Sometimes contact dermatitis is caused by ALLERGIES, when the body becomes sensitized to a substance such as poison ivy or tomatoes, but it often results from direct damage to the skin by irritating substances. If a substance is very damaging, such as an acid, the trigger for the dermatitis is clear, but often the reaction is mild and builds up over time, so some considerable detective work may be needed to find the culprit. To all the natural products in the world have been added many artificially created substances, making the modern world a kind of minefield for people with sensitive skin (see PREVENTING SKIN INFLAMMATION on page 691). Sometimes the site of the inflammation gives clues; a rash under the ears, for example, may suggest irritation by a perfume, or an inflamed line around the wrist or neck may point to jewelry containing nickel, a common irritant. Sometimes medications applied for self-treatment can themselves cause further inflammation. People with persistent skin inflammation should see a *dermatologist,* a skin specialist who can help identify the source of the problem and recommend treatment.

Another widespread skin problem is *acne,* the epidemic of pimples that is the bane of adolescence. Acne results when the skin's oil (sebaceous) glands work overtime; in some gland ducts, dead cells and oil form a plug called a *comedo.*

If the plug is below the skin's surface, it is medically called a *closed comedo,* popularly a *whitehead;* if the plug emerges at the top of the duct, it is an *open comedo,* or *blackhead,* the color resulting from a buildup of melanin. Generally acne is triggered by hormonal changes, as during PUBERTY or before MENSTRUATION, and sometimes by drugs, COSMETICS, industrial chemicals, some bacteria, and even birth control pills. Susceptibility and severity depend largely on genetic inheritance, though it may also be linked to stress, emotions, and diet—not junk food as such, studies have shown, but specific foods that trigger acne in individuals (see ALLERGIES). Dermatologists recommend that patients *not* squeeze or pick at pimples, since this can injure the skin; instruments called *comedo extractors* may be used to remove them. Antibiotics are sometimes used to treat persistent infected pimples. Drugs derived from vitamin A have also been found effective against acne; however, they make the skin more sensitive to sun; may cause drying, irritation, or peeling of the skin; may cause inflammation of the lips; and, most important, can cause MISCARRIAGE and BIRTH DEFECTS in pregnant women.

Far more serious is skin CANCER, of which there are three main types:
- ▶ **basal cell carcinoma,** the most common form of skin CANCER, which develops very slowly, often as a white or flesh-colored lump or a patch or red flaky skin that may ooze blood or scab over but never quite heal. Linked with exposure to sunlight, these cancers are usually found on the face, hands, and other parts of the body routinely exposed to the sun.
- ▶ **squamous cell carcinoma,** an irregularly shaped clump of cancerous cells, also linked with exposure to the sun.
- ▶ **malignant melanoma,** a fast-spreading tumor, frequently arising from a pigmented spot on the skin, such as a freckle or mole. Unless caught very quickly, it spreads (*metastasizes*) so rapidly that it is often fatal.

For basal cell or squamous cell cancers, the American Cancer Society (ACS) reports that "cure is highly likely if detected and treated early." Malignant melanoma is also labeled "highly curable" if detected and quickly treated in its earliest stages. About four out of five melanomas are diagnosed at the local stage and have a five-year survival rate of 90 percent, according to the ACS. Survival rates for "regional and distant disease" are 50 percent and 14 percent, respectively (see CANCER), where the cancer has spread beyond the original site.

Because melanomas are so dangerous, women should routinely scan their skin for any changes, paying special attention to freckles and moles, looking for darkening or other color change; growth, especially beyond previously established "borders" to produce irregular edges; and oozing, bleeding, or other ulceration. Many doctors summarize the warning signs of melanoma with the ABCD rule:
- A is for asymmetry. One half of the mole does not match the other half.
- B is for border irregularity. The edges are ragged, notched, or blurred.
- C is for color. The pigmentation is not uniform.
- D is for diameter greater than 6 millimeters. Any sudden or progressive increase in size should be of special concern.

Any new mole that appears after puberty bears close watching. Any suspicious change calls for an immediate visit to the doctor, so any cancer can be identified and cut out before it spreads and becomes lethal.

Age is no protection. In years past melanoma was rare under age forty, but doctors are increasingly finding melanoma in patients in their twenties. Skin cancers of all kinds are increasingly common. In the United States the rate has been rising 3–5 percent annually in recent years. In 1991 alone approximately 600,000 people were found to have some form of skin cancer, 32,000 of them with melanoma, and about 8,000 people die annually, or twice as many as in the previous decade. People with fair skin who have had heavy sun exposure are at special risk. This is because many cancers are triggered by accumulated skin damage from the sun's rays, particularly *ultraviolet radiation.*

In fact, one of the greatest dangers to skin health is long-term daily exposure to the sun, which causes not only immediate damage such as sunburns, but also long-term damage such as drying, loss of elasticity, and resulting wrinkling. The modern fashion of tanning is ironic because it not only triggers life-threatening problems such as cancers, but also ages the skin prematurely. Skin experts put it bluntly: Tanning is actually the body's way of trying to prevent skin damage; tanned skin is damaged skin, and the deeper the color—that is the more *melanin* produced in attempts to block out ultraviolet rays—the more extensive the damage. This is true of people with all types and colors of skin, but especially so for the fair-skinned, who have fewer melanin-producing cells.

Women concerned about their skin health will limit their exposure to the sun at all latitudes and all times of the year, but especially during midday, in the warmer months, or at the equator, when the rays are most direct, and at higher altitudes, where the atmosphere is thinner. When they are outdoors they should wear a hat to shade the face and clothing of a tight weave to cover body, arms, and legs—loosely woven, gauzy, or wet clothes help very little. Just as much protection is needed on cool, overcast days as on hot sunny days; the sun's warming infrared rays are screened out by clouds in the atmosphere, but ultraviolet rays pass right through. Shade also offers only an illusion of safety, because ultraviolet rays bounce off bright surfaces, such as sand, water, and light concrete and can even penetrate glass and underwater, to cause damage.

Experts recommend that—even for a casual exposure, such as driving a car or walking to the store—any exposed part of the body should be covered with a sunscreen of a *sun protection factor* (SPF) of 15 or more. A waterproof sunscreen is recommended where people sweat heavily or are going in and out of water. The SPF is intended as an indication of how long a person can remain in the sun without burning; for example, if a person would normally get a sunburn after 10 minutes' unprotected sun exposure, she could expect to stay in the sun for 150 minutes before getting a sunburn. Sunscreens as high as 50 are on the market and may be valuable for people with very fair skin, but (as of this writing) the FDA has not yet developed tests to determine the effectiveness of sunscreen with SPFs over 15. The sunscreen should be applied liberally—an ounce or two per application at the beach, for example—and every two hours (or immediately after being in the water, if the sunscreen is not waterproof). Studies have shown that most people use only about half as much as recommended, leaving them with half the protection, or the equivalent of an SPF 7 from an SPF 15 sunscreen.

Sunscreens primarily block out type B ultraviolet (UVB) rays. Some sunscreens block out some type A (UVA) rays as well, but none blocks out all UVAs, and the FDA has not developed ways to evaluate UVA protection. Another wild card is the type C (UVC) ray, which is the most dangerous; at present type C rays are mostly screened out in the earth's upper atmosphere, but one of the fears about the thinning of the ozone layer is that more UVC rays will reach the earth, causing extensive damage.

As with other skin preparations, women will want to test a sunscreen on a small part of their body before using it widely. Many people are sensitive to the substance PABA (*paraaminobenzoic acid*) used in sunscreens and may want to use a PABA-free, hypoallergenic sunscreen. Irritation may also be increased with higher SPF strengths. Some drugs, including certain antibiotics and birth control pills, can also increase sensitivity to sunscreen ingredients; women taking medications will want to check with their doctor.

In general, the skin reflects the health of the body. Doctors use the paleness or pinkness, slackness or tautness, of the skin as early indicators of a patient's physical condition. In general the best skin care is a healthy life, with a balanced diet, proper rest and exercise, and good hygiene. Individual women will have to sort out for themselves conflicting advice about whether or not to wash with soap and water and what moisturizers to use, if any. Much depends on the individual's skin characteristics—particularly oiliness or dryness—and the conditions at home or work; central heating or air-conditioning, for example, may cause more dryness and call for a moisturizer to ease flaking or cracking of skin.

Some types of skin damage, including acne scars and sagging or wrinkling due to aging, can be treated by various types of COSMETIC SURGERY, including *dermabrasion, chemical peels,* injections, and various kinds of "lifts" of skin in the face and elsewhere. There, too, but on a much more serious level, women will need to weigh the possible benefits against the risks of surgery, some of them substantial. (See SKIN, HAIR, NAILS, AND COSMETICS HELP, INFORMATION, AND ACTION GUIDE, below.)

SKIN, HAIR, NAILS, AND COSMETICS
Help, Information, and Action Guide

Organizations

▶ NATIONAL INSTITUTE OF ARTHRITIS AND MUSCULOSKELETAL AND SKIN DISEASES (NIAMS) (301-496-8188).
▶ FOOD AND DRUG ADMINISTRATION (301-443-3170 or 2410). To report adverse reactions to cosmetics write to the FDA's **Center for Food Safety and Applied Nutrition, Division of Colors and Cosmetics** (200 C Street, SW, Washington, DC 20204).

▶ **American Academy of Dermatology** (930 North Meacham Road, Schaumburg, IL 60173-4965; Mailing address: P.O. Box 4014, Schaumburg, IL 60168-4014; 708-869-3954; Brad Claxton, executive director), a professional organization for dermatologists. It publishes consumer-oriented booklets on various skin disorders.

Other resources

Healthy Skin: The Facts: Good Skin Care Throughout Life. Rona M. MacKie. Oxford University Press, 1992.

Saving Your Skin: Secrets of Healthy Skin and Hair. Anne E. Hunt. ARE Press, 1991.

Cosmetics and Toiletries. Wilfried Umbach. Prentice-Hall, 1991.

Don't Go to the Cosmetic Counters Without Me. Paula Begoun. Beginning Press, 1991.

Safe in the Sun: Your Skin Survival Guide for the 1990s. Mary E. Siegel. Walker, 1990.

Skin Disorders. Lynn Lamberg. Chelsea House, 1990.

Overcoming Acne: The How and Why of Healthy Skin Care. Alvin Silverstein and Robert Silverstein. Morrow, 1990.

How to Cut, Curl, and Care for Your Hair. Charles Booth and Sharon Esche. Outlet, 1990.

Take Care of Your Skin. Elaine Brumberg. HarperCollins, 1989.

The New Medically Based No-Nonsense Beauty Book. Deborah Chase. Holt, 1989.

Fornay's Guide to Skin Care and Makeup for Women of Color. Alfred Fornay. Simon & Schuster, 1989.

Take Care of Your Skin: The Truth about Buying and Using Today's Skin Care Products. Elaine Brumberg. HarperCollins, 1989.

Smart Face: A Dermatologist's Guide to Cosmetics and Skin Care. Thomas Goodman and Stephanie Young. Prentice-Hall, 1988.

The Consumer's Dictionary of Cosmetic Ingredients, rev. ed. Ruth Winter. Crown, 1988.

PREVENTING SKIN INFLAMMATION

Sensitive-skinned people—and even those with tougher hides—would be well to follow a number of measures to prevent contact dermatitis:

- Read the labels on cosmetics. FDA requires that all ingredients in cosmetics be listed on the label in descending order of predominance. If a cosmetic causes a problem, note the ingredients—fragrances and preservatives are the most likely suspects—and avoid similar cosmetic formulations in the future. (Specific fragrance components are not listed, so a switch to fragrance-free products should be tried if dermatitis persists.)
- Wash new clothing and bed linens several times before using. Contact dermatitis caused by clothing is usually due to formaldehyde released by chemicals in the finishing of fabrics and sometimes to the dyes. Avoid polyester blends and cottons that are labeled "permanent press" and "wrinkle-resistant," and stick to natural fibers, such as cotton, linen, and silk. (Though wool is a natural fiber, it can be irritating.)
- Use soaps or detergents formulated specifically for babies' wash if laundry products are under suspicion. Avoid fabric softeners and antistatic products and double-rinse the wash.
- Wear heavy-duty vinyl gloves with cotton liners, if possible, when hands are in contact with harsh cleansers at home or chemical irritants at work. Avoid abrasive soaps for removing grease and oil. Remove rings when using soaps and detergents, because these materials can become trapped under rings and cause irritation. Keep the hands well moisturized with a bland cream or lotion.
- Learn to recognize the leaves of poison ivy and poison oak, each three-leaved, and poison sumac, with its oval leaves and white berries. If exposed to them, wash hands and skin thoroughly after exposure, using any kind of soap. Before applying over-the-counter poison ivy preparations, read the labels and use with caution medications containing zirconium, benzocaine, and diphenhydramine hydrochloride. Although most people have no problem with these, sometimes they may be sensitive and produce a dermatitis on top of the poison ivy rash. Dermatitis can result from handling other plants, including vegetables such as parsnips, garlic, onions, tomatoes, carrots, and ginger.
- Don't self-treat too long. If the dermatitis is not better after a week or ten days, see the doctor. The topical medications may be the problem, or the itching and rash may be symptoms of something quite different. An intolerable itch may be a sign of Hodgkin's disease, or of scabies, transmitted by the itch mite, a parasite. Red, itchy rashes can also be caused by superficial fungal infections, such as candidiasis, or impetigo and other bacterial infections.

Source: *FDA Consumer,* May 1990, "Contact Dermatitis: Solutions to Rash Mysteries," by Eelyn Zamula.

slavery, sexual: See PROSTITUTION.

smoking, inhalation of fumes of burning plants, primarily tobacco but also other plants (see ALCOHOL AND DRUG ABUSE). Smoking is a major and growing problem among women. Even while evidence has been mounting of the enormous health problems related to smoking, cigarettes have continued to be attractive to women, because they have been symbols of liberation from past strictures—some have called them an "equal opportunity killer"—and have been linked with sophistication and slimness. Also, as many adults quit smoking in the face of health risks, tobacco companies have successfully targeted young people, and especially young women for their advertising campaigns; in the United States, young women under age twenty-three are the fastest-growing groups of smokers.

Many women's organizations find themselves in a peculiar bind over this. Tobacco companies have given substantial funding to many women's groups and activities, when few other sources of funding were available, so some organizations now find it hard to take as strong a stand as needs to be taken against smoking, for the protection of women's health. Many are doing so, however. In 1989, for example, the NATIONAL ORGANIZATION FOR WOMEN held a conference on smoking as a feminist health issue; members of the AMERICAN MEDICAL WOMEN'S ASSOCIATION often boycott magazines featuring cigarette ads, and others are protesting tobacco-company sponsorship, such as the Virginia Slims tennis tournament.

The medical facts are these: Smoking increases the risk of CANCER and cardiovascular disease (see HEART AND CIRCULATORY SYSTEM), the two leading causes of death in women. More specifically, LUNG CANCER in 1987 surpassed BREAST CANCER as the most lethal type of CANCER for women. But smoking also increases the likelihood of other cancers, especially those of the bladder, kidney, pancreas, and CERVIX (see UTERINE CANCER). Oral cancer, affecting the lips, mouth, tongue, and pharynx, is still relatively uncommon among women but is growing in those who smoke. Smoking lowers women's levels of ESTROGEN, undercutting the effects of ESTROGEN REPLACEMENT THERAPY and making women more vulnerable to OSTEOPOROSIS; it also increases the levels of male HORMONES in the body. Two recent studies show that a woman who smokes has a 60 percent greater risk of developing cataracts (see EYES).

Other adverse effects include an increased risk of problems with MENSTRUATION, earlier and more difficult MENOPAUSE, and accelerated dryness and aging of the SKIN. Women (and men) who smoke are more infertile (see INFERTILITY), and when they do conceive they have a higher risk of MISCARRIAGE, STILLBIRTH, ECTOPIC PREGNANCY, placenta previa and abruptio placentae (see PLACENTA), low-birth-weight babies, and infant mortality, especially from sudden infant death syndrome (SIDS). Why this happens is not entirely clear, but it is believed that nicotine and carbon monoxide slow the delivery of vital oxygen to the FETUS in the womb. Moreover, breast milk can be contaminated with nicotine (see BREASTFEEDING). In addition, a recent study shows that the more a mother smokes after birth, the more behavioral problems her children are likely to have.

As studies are continuing to show, nonsmokers are also affected by breathing in "secondhand smoke" from others. A major multinational 1992 study found that nonsmoking women married to smoking spouses had a significantly higher risk of lung cancer than those married to nonsmokers, confirming earlier, more limited research. A 1991 study of nonsmoking women even found nicotine in their cervical mucus, with levels highest among women exposed to smoke at home. Nonsmoking women who live or work with smokers should do their best to obtain a smoke-free environment.

And the problem is still growing. In the United States, for example, only 18 percent of women smoked in 1935, but that figure had jumped to 30 percent 50 years later; by contrast, the figures for men had dropped from 52 to 35 percent. Though these percentages are down from all-time highs in the 1970s, as anti-smoking campaigns have had some effect, one great concern is that many of these smokers are young women, who begin to smoke at a higher rate than young men and a quarter of whom continue to smoke throughout a PREGNANCY. And the more and the longer they smoke, the worse for the developing baby. Elsewhere in the world, the rate of smoking is generally between 24 and 40 percent in industrialized countries, and from 2 to 10 percent in developing countries.

Much attention is focused on stopping the habit before it starts, because once established it is very hard to break. Researchers have found that nicotine, the main addictive substance, acts on the brain within seconds of inhalation to trigger the release of certain chemicals and hormones that stimulate alertness and improve thinking and also offer brief feelings of pleasure. Withdrawal symptoms include craving, anxiety, irritability, and sleep disturbances; while acute symptoms may wear off in days or months, the craving—even though diminished—can last for years or even a lifetime.

Though some people are able to make a decision to quit and stick to it, most cannot. For them the most successful approach to quitting smoking has proved to be some kind of organized program, often offering counseling, relaxation training, behavioral therapy, and sometimes hypnosis. In the 1980s a nicotine gum was federally approved for use; however, it was often misused, since people were supposed to "park" the wad of gum between the jaw and cheek periodically, to get the proper dose. In the 1990s came *transdermal patches,* which were placed on the skin and released small amounts of nicotine into the blood. These provided proper doses and also gradually reduced the doses; users of some patchers were also offered some counseling besides.

But researchers have found that the patches are best used *with,* not instead of, a quit-smoking program, to deal with associated behavioral patterns, such as the impulse to smoke when drinking alcohol or coffee. Some patch users have suffered insomnia and unusual nightmares, but a newer patch to be used only during waking hours may ease that problem—though it won't deal with the immediate craving for a cigarette upon waking. Patches should not be used while people are still smoking, because they will then get an extra dose—possibly overdose—of nicotine that has been connected with HEART AND CIRCULATORY SYSTEM problems. Though nicotine gum and patches are generally not to be taken during pregnancy, some doctors have recommended them for women who were otherwise unable to stop smoking, arguing that they pose less risk to the fetus than smoking itself does. (See ALCOHOL AND DRUG ABUSE HELP, INFORMATION, AND ACTION GUIDE on page 37.)

SMOKING

Help, Information, and Action Guide

Organizations

▶ **Office on Smoking and Health** (U.S. Department of Health and Human Services, Centers of Disease Control, Mail Stop K-50, 4770 Buford Highway NE, Atlanta, GA 30341-3724; 301-443-1575), a federal office that gathers and disseminates information on the effects of cigarette smoking, as by publishing various materials, including an annual review of research findings.

▶ MARCH OF DIMES BIRTH DEFECTS FOUNDATION (914-428-7100; local chapters in telephone directory White Pages). Publishes *Drugs, Alcohol and Tobacco Abuse During Pregnancy* and *Babies Don't Thrive in Smoke-Filled Wombs.*

▶ **American Cancer Society** (212-599-8200 or 800-552-7996). Publishes *Dangers of Smoking, Benefits of Quitting and Relative Risks of Reduced Exposure, Quitter's Guide: A 7-Day Plan to Help You Stop Smoking Cigarettes, Fifty Most-Often-Asked Questions About Smoking,* and *The Decision Is Yours.* (See CANCER.)

▶ **American Lung Association** (212-315-8700; see telephone White Pages for local number). Publishes *Freedom from Smoking® in 20 Days, A Lifetime of Freedom from Smoking®, Help a Friend Stop Smoking, Stop Smoking/Stay Trim,* and the videocassette *In Control: A Home Video Freedom from Smoking® Program.* (See RESPIRATORY SYSTEM.)

▶ **National Cancer Institute (NCI)** (800-4-CANCER [422-6237]). Publishes *Clearing the Air: A Guide to Quitting Smoking, Why Do You Smoke?* and *You've Kicked the Smoking Habit for Good.* (See CANCER.)

▶ NATIONAL INSTITUTE OF DIABETES, DIGESTIVE, AND KIDNEY DISEASES **(NIDDK)** (301-496-3583) Publishes *Smoking and Your Digestive System.*

Other resources

◨ PRACTICAL GUIDES

Butt Out: A Guide to Helping a Loved One or Friend Kick the Smoking Habit; Part 2: A Guide to Helping Yourself Kick the Smoking Habit. David O. Antonuccio. R & E Publishers, 1992.

What's Tough About Smoking Is Quitting: An Interactive Approach to Getting You Through the Tough Times. Donna Cohn. Detroit St, 1991.

The Quitter's Companion: Becoming a Happy Nonsmoker. Jon Seigel. S&W Press, 1990.

QuitSmart: A Guide to Freedom from Cigarettes, rev. ed. Robert H. Shipley. J. B. Press, 1990.

Women Smokers Can Quit: A Different Approach. Sue F. Delaney. Women's Healthcare Press, 1989.

No Butts About It: How to Want to Stop Smoking, 3rd ed. John R. Parker. Johmax Books, 1989.

The Smoke-Free Guide: How to Eliminate Tobacco Smoke from Your Environment. Arlene Galloway. Gordon Soules, 1988.

No-Nag, No-Guilt, Do-It-Your-Own-Way Guide to Quitting Smoking. Tom Ferguson. Ballantine, 1988.

Quitsmart: A Guide to Freedom from Cigarettes, rev. ed. Robert H. Shipley. J. B. Press, 1988.

Stop Smoking Workbook: It's Easy to Stop Smoking, It Takes Recovery to Stay Stopped. David C. Jones. Dolphin, 1990.

Hooked—But Not Helpless: Ending Your Love-Hate Relationship with Nicotine. Patricia Allison and Jack Yost. BridgeCity Books, 1990.

Quit and Stay Quit: Medical Treatment Program for Smokers, 4th ed. Terry A. Rustin. Discovery (TX), 1989.

■ GENERAL WORKS

The Facts About Smoking. Consumer Reports Books Editors, C. Barr Taylor, and Joel D. Killen. Consumer Reports, 1991.

Smoking: The Artificial Passion. David Krogh. W. H. Freeman, 1991.

The Last Puff: Ex-Smokers Share the Secrets of Their Success. John W. Farquhar and Gene A. Spiller. Norton, 1990.

(See also LUNG CANCER; CANCER; HEART AND CIRCULATORY SYSTEM.)

socialist feminism, an attempt to synthesize MARXIST FEMINISM and RADICAL FEMINISM into a coherent analysis of all human societies and a guide to action in support of a feminist revolution. Social feminists see the repression and exploitation of women at the heart of what they believe to be a male-supremacist world system. They call for the end of the unpaid labor of women in the home (see HOUSEWORK) and the communalizing of all other labor in a new socialist system. Their analysis is structured around Karl Marx's nineteenth-century systemic analysis and ideal system construct, seen even by many former adherents as an antique ideology since the collapse of Soviet communism. (See also FEMINISM; MARXIST FEMINISM.)

Social Security, the basic United States social insurance coverage for most working people over sixty-two, though full benefits start at age sixty-five, and at age sixty-seven for those born after 1937. Social Security carries with it elegibility for Medicare, later-years health insurance. It also provides coverage in a number of the kinds of special situations encountered by women, beyond the basic coverage envisioned, for paid women workers and unpaid HOMEMAKERS when the law became effective in 1935. Among these are benefit payments available for surviving SPOUSES; for parents of disabled children; to some formerly married women, including some of those who remarry; to those who have valid COMMON-LAW MARRIAGES; to some who are disabled or become disabled after becoming WIDOWS; to some who care for surviving children; and to the survivors of women who are covered by Social Security. Also considered Social Security is the AID TO FAMILIES WITH DEPENDENT CHILDREN program, primarily providing aid when such families are deprived of one parent's CHILD SUPPORT.

The rules are by no means simple and may in some instances call for advance planning. For example, remarriage before age sixty may disqualify someone from receiving benefits as a divorced spouse. Also, eligibility for federal Social Security survivors' benefits may depend on a woman's state of residence. Social Security benefits are available to surviving spouses in common-law marriages, but not all states recognize these as valid. A couple living together for the specified period of time in a state that *does* recognize common-law marriages may, however, later be able to claim benefits, no matter where they live, because other states—and the federal government—will then recognize the marriage.

Social Security rules do change, and it is worthwhile to keep up with those changes. One very good source of information is *The Social Security Book,* issued by the AMERICAN ASSOCIATION OF RETIRED PERSONS and revised periodically. (See OLDER WOMEN'S HELP, INFORMATION, AND ACTION GUIDE on page 374.)

Society for the Advancement of Women's Health Research (SAWHR) (1601 Connecticut Avenue, NW, Suite 801, Washington, DC; 202-328-2200; Joanne Howes, project manager), an organization established in 1990 "as a result of mounting concern that the health of all American women was at risk due to biases in medical and health research." It has focused on several main areas: "failure to include women in major clinical research trials; inadequate attention to gender differences and analysis in medical research; inadequate funding for research of diseases and conditions primarily affecting women; and dearth of women investigators in senior positions in the scientific community." The society convenes scientific advisory meetings (SAMs), round-table discussions, and corporate advisory councils (CACs) to bring these issues to national prominence and help bring about changes through, for example, the proposed Women's Health Equity Act. The Society's publications include the *Journal of Women's Health,* and the reports *Towards a Women's Health Research Agenda: Findings of the Scientific Advisory Meeting, Women's Health Research: Opportunities and Strategies for Change,* and *Towards a Woman's Health Research Agenda: Findings of the 1991 Women's Health Research Roundtables.*

"Solitude of Self, The": See Elizabeth Cady STANTON.

son preference, the desire to have and the favoring of boy children over girl children; a sometimes life-and-death form of SEXUAL DISCRIMINATION directed at children. Families in many societies in many times and places have distinct son preference; such patterns lie deep in many cultures, especially where inheritance patterns run through the male line (see PATRIARCHY) and where males have a significantly higher status than women, including a greater ability to earn money and so to care for parents later in life—and where a female child costs heavily in terms of a DOWRY paid out at her marriage. A particular family, of course, may prefer female children; individual girl children may be treasured; and patterns of discrimination may be more common or more subtle in some countries than others. But, worldwide, son preference remains common, most notably in India and China.

Son preference has adverse effects at all stages of life. During PREGNANCY, more female than male FETUSES are selected for ABORTION; more are subject to ABANDONMENT or INFANTICIDE, once born; more get a smaller share of nutritional and medical resources, especially when these are limited (see HEALTH EQUITY); fewer receive education, especially where it is limited and costly (see EDUCATION EQUITY). Once adulthood is reached, this son preference merges into a societywide sexual discrimination.

sperm, the male sex cell that can unite with the female sex cell, the egg (OVUM), to form a fertilized egg at CONCEPTION; shorthand for *spermatozoon,* or plural *spermatozoa.* These tiny cells are made and released by the millions although only one is able to fertilize a single egg.

Sperm are manufactured in the male sex glands, called the TESTES, within numerous tiny coiled tubes called *seminiferous tubules.* Special cells called *spermatogonia* duplicate and divide, "mixing and matching" to form a sperm that has just *half* of the genetic material needed to make a full human being (see GENETIC INHERITANCE). When newly formed and immature, they are called *spermatids;* they already contain the all-important genetic material but must move into a "holding area" called the *epididymis,* where they mature and grow tails to help them move through a woman's REPRODUCTIVE SYSTEM. They are stored in the epididymis until needed. This process of *spermatogenesis* starts at PUBERTY and continues throughout life.

In the EJACULATION that is part of a male's ORGASM, perhaps 200 million to more than 500 million sperm are released into a woman's REPRODUCTIVE SYSTEM. There they face an obstacle course in the forty-eight hours that remain of their life:

- Acidic secretions in the woman's VAGINA kill many sperm.
- Secretions of hostile mucus in the CERVIX, which become more hospitable only around the time of the woman's OVULATION.
- Many sperm become entrapped and die on the walls of the cervix.
- In the UTERUS, the microscopic sperm—about .002 in. or .05 mm across— must cross the relatively vast expanse of three to four inches, and many fail to do so.
- In the FALLOPIAN TUBES, many sperm become entrapped in mucus-covered walls.
- The egg itself is protected by two hard-to-breach outer layers.

During the journey, which takes one to a few hours, most sperm are lost; estimates are that only a few thousand generally survive to reach the fallopian tubes. There they can remain alive and active for up to forty-eight hours, moved around by tadpolelike tails. The sperm also carry stores of chemicals that, on arrival, help one, and only one, sperm make its way through the egg's protective shields. With all these obstacles, the wonder is that a woman can sometimes become pregnant from just a single "shot" of sperm, not that things occasionally go wrong with the process.

One of the main causes of INFERTILITY is that a man has too few sperm in his semen—called a low *sperm count* because a sample is actually examined and the sperm counted in the laboratory—or his sperm do not have enough propulsion to swim upstream to the egg. Sometimes the mucus in a woman's reproductive system is so acidic that it kills all or most of the sperm. In such cases couples may try alternative methods for fertilization, such as *IN VITRO* FERTILIZATION and ARTIFICIAL INSEMINATION.

Some organizations collect sperm, sometimes for a fee, and sell it for use in alternative fertilization procedures (see ARTIFICIAL INSEMINATION). In such donations the donor's identity is normally kept confidential (except when both donor and donee agree to reveal it), but a full medical history is generally gathered and kept on file, for later reference by the mother or child.

Sperm determine the sex of a child in fertilization: each egg carries an X chromosome; if the sperm also carries an X, the offspring will be a girl (XX); if it carries a Y, a boy (XY). In general, X-carrying sperm prefer slightly acidic environments, swim more slowly, and live longer than Y-carrying sperm, which prefer slightly alkaline settings. When a woman or couple wish to try to predetermine the sex of their child, a procedure called *sperm splitting* can be used, separating out X or Y chromosomes from the sperm used in artificial insemination (see SEX SELECTION).

When the object is to avoid conception, many couples use a variety of BIRTH CONTROL methods, such as CONDOMS or DIAPHRAGMS, often supplemented by SPERMICIDES, designed to kill sperm before they can reach and fertilize an egg.

Women who think they may be pregnant, however, may want to avoid using spermicides, since they are suspected of causing BIRTH DEFECTS when used early in a PREGNANCY. (See FERTILIZATION; BIRTH CONTROL; INFERTILITY; GENETIC INHERITANCE; ARTIFICIAL INSEMINATION.)

spermicide, any of a range of substances—including contraceptive foams, creams, jellies, gels, and suppositories—that are used as a chemical form of BIRTH CONTROL, the first being developed in Britain in 1927. Such substances contain ingredients designed to kill sperm, such as *nonoxynol-9* or *octoxynol.* The spermicide is placed in the woman's VAGINA no more than an hour before SEXUAL INTERCOURSE and should be left in place—that is, not douched—for at least six hours afterward. Used alone, spermicides are only 70–80 percent effective at preventing PREGNANCY, according to the FOOD AND DRUG ADMINISTRATION (FDA), but, used with a DIAPHRAGM, CERVICAL CAP, CONDOM, or contraceptive SPONGE, they can be much more effective.

On rare occasions spermicides can cause irritation or allergic reactions. Some people feel they may cause BIRTH DEFECTS if used by a woman who does not yet know she is pregnant. In at least one case, a woman won a suit against a spermicide manufacturer for birth defects in her child. However, the FDA has noted: "Although the judge found in favor of the woman and her child, FDA has not found scientific data to support an association between spermicides and birth defects. The agency continues to monitor the situation." Women who use or are considering using spermicides may want to consult their doctor or clinic, or the FDA, for current information. One advantage to spermicides is that they offer some protection against some SEXUALLY TRANSMITTED DISEASES, though spermicide alone should not be considered protection against AIDS. (See BIRTH CONTROL AND FAMILY PLANNING HELP, INFORMATION, AND ACTION GUIDE on page 81.)

spine, a specialized part of the SKELETAL SYSTEM; a column of small, roughly cylindrical bones *(vertebrae)* and cartilage that extends from the skull to the pelvis, supporting the head and trunk. It encloses and protects the *spinal cord,* a column of nerve tissue that transmits signals between the brain and various parts of the body (see BRAIN AND NERVOUS SYSTEM) and is itself enclosed by three membranes—the *dura mater, arachnoid,* and *pia mater,* together called the *meninges*—and by encircling ligaments that help give the spine support and stability.

The top seven spinal bones, directly supporting the head, are the *cervical vertebrae;* below that are the *thoracic vertebrae,* twelve bones to which the ribs are attached; below that, in the lower back area, come the *lumbar vertebrae,* which bear much of the strain of lifting; then come five fused vertebrae, together called the *sacrum;* and finally four fused vertebrae called the *coccyx.* Between the vertebrae lie disks, gel-filled cushions of cartilage that act as shock absorbers.

The spinal cord is the "central switching point" for the body's communication network and so is a vital and delicate mechanism. The spine itself is subject to a variety of disorders. Sometimes part of the spinal cord may be incomplete or exposed at birth, in what is called a *neural tube defect*, such as *spinal bifida* (see BIRTH DEFECTS). The spinal cord may also be injured in an accident, leading to temporary or permanent paralysis of part or all of the body.

Among women the most common spinal disorders involve abnormal curvature of the spine, the three main types being

▶ *scoliosis*, an abnormal sideways curvature of the spine, sometimes shaped almost like an "S." This condition often appears in children, in infancy more common among boys than girls, but equally common in both sexes by school age. Though often part of a child's GENETIC INHERITANCE, scoliosis can also result from unequal leg length, which causes the body to tilt; from tumors or injuries; or from diseases such as polio.

▶ *kyphosis*, excessive curving of the upper spine, sometimes called a *humpback*. This is common in adults, especially older women, with OSTEOPOROSIS, as vertebrae fracture and partially collapse and so the condition was traditionally called *dowager's hump*. It may also appear in children, from an injury or as a GENETIC DISORDER, such as Hunter's syndrome.

▶ *lordosis* or *hyperlordosis*, excessive curving of the lower spine, sometimes called *swayback*. This, too, is common in women with osteoporosis, though (like kyphosis) it may appear in children. It can be exaggerated by poor posture.

In fact, these disorders often appear together. While kyphosis and lordosis are readily apparent, scoliosis is less obvious to the eye in its early stages, though it may be diagnosed by X-rays. If recognized early, it can be treated relatively simply, by using exercises or orthopedic devices, such as shoe lifts, to make the legs of even length. However, if undiagnosed as growth continues, the deformity may become more severe and painful. Treatment then may require braces, casts, and even surgery, with bone grafts to bring the spinal vertebrae into a straight line. Early diagnosis, treatment, and careful monitoring are important, to prevent the disorders from becoming disabling. Women should also avoid life-style choices that might increase their risk of osteoporosis.

Women as well as men often also have more generalized back problems. Some of them stem from muscle problems (see MUSCULAR SYSTEM), but others may result from problems with the disks, as—with age, injury, and some diseases—the disk fibers wear away. The degenerated disk may protrude from between the vertebrae, causing pain or loss of feeling when the protruding parts press against nerves, sometimes called a "pinched nerve"; sometimes a disk can even break the ligament, called *extrusion*, or fragments may break off and move, called *sequestration*. Many disk problems respond to rest, traction, physical therapy, and anti-inflammatory drugs. A drug called *chymopapain*, from the papaya plant, has been used with some success to dissolve problematic disk fragments, though the injection by needle poses some risks. Sometimes surgery may be required to remove the disk fragments or, in severe cases, to remove the whole disk and fuse the adjacent vertebrae.

For more help, information, and action

▶ **Scoliosis Association (SA)** (P.O. Box 51353, Raleigh, NC 27609; 919-846-2639; Barbara M. Shulman, president), an organization concerned with scoliosis, affiliated with the International Federation of Scoliosis Associations. It encourages screening programs in school and public education; sponsors local mutual-support groups; maintains a film library; and publishes various materials, including the quarterly *Backtalk* and the *Scoliosis Screening Manual.*

▶ **National Scoliosis Foundation (NSF)** (72 Mt. Auburn Street, Watertown, MA 02172; 617-926-0397; Laura B. Gowen, president), an organization concerned with scoliosis, kyphosis, and lordosis. It aids volunteers in setting up local screening programs and publishes various print and audiovisual materials, including the newsletter *The Spinal Connection,* educational booklets, brochures, and resource lists.

▶ **Scoliosis Research Society (SRSO)** (222 South Prospect, Park Ridge, IL 60068; 708-698-1628; Carole Murphy, executive director), an organization of health professionals, fostering research on spinal deformities.

Other resources

Sex and Back Pain: Advice on Restoring Comfortable Sex Lost to Back Pain. Lauren Andrew Hebert. IMPACC ME, 1992.

Back in Shape: A Back Owner's Manual. Stephen Hochschuler. Houghton Mifflin, 1991.

Stopping Scoliosis: The Complete Guide to Diagnosis and Treatment. Nancy Schommer. Avery, 1991.

Safe Sex for Bad Backs. Stephen H. Hochschuler, ed. TBI Press, 1991.

Healing Back Pain: The Mind-Body Connection. John E. Sarno. Warner, 1991.

More Advice from the Back Doctor. Hamilton Hall. Firefly, 1990.

Your Aching Back: A Doctor's Guide to Relief, rev. ed. Augustus White. Simon & Schuster, 1990.

Backpower Program. David Imrie. Wiley, 1990.

No More Aching Back: Dr. Root's New 15-Minute-a-Day Program for a Healthy Back. Leon Root. Random House, 1990.

Doctor Discusses Care of the Back. Paul Neimark and Gerald Berkowitz. Budlong, 1990.

Back Pain: A Practical Guide to Coping. David Tagg and Linda Tagg. Trafalgar Square, 1989.

Good-Bye to Bad Backs: A Proven Program of Simple Stretching and Strengthening Exercises for Better Body Alignment and Freedom from Lower Back Pain. Judith Scott. Scribner/Macmillan, 1988.

(See also SKELETAL SYSTEM; OSTEOPOROSIS.)

spiritual feminism, a term describing a considerable spectrum of religious beliefs and practices among women.

In its older and by far widest form, it is an attempt to bring the spirit and practice of full equality for women into the world's churches and their doctrines (see RELIGION AND WOMEN'S RIGHTS), by reinterpreting such basic documents as the Bible and attempting to completely change patriarchal attitudes and church structures. To those ends, Elizabeth Cady STANTON wrote her feminist *The Women's Bible* (1895, 1898) and Matilda GAGE wrote her *Woman, Church, and State* (1893). Three-quarters of a century later, Mary DALY pursued similar ends in the Catholic church, in her book *The Church and the Second Sex* (1968). It was also to these ends that a group of twentieth-century reform movements developed within several Christian and Jewish religious institutions, on such issues as the ordination of women, with breakthroughs beginning to occur late in the century.

With the WOMEN'S LIBERATION MOVEMENT came development of separatist sentiments in the women's religious movement, although reform-minded spiritual feminists continued to be by far more numerous. Daly, in *Gyn/Ecology: The Metaethics of Radical Feminism* (1978), became a spokeswoman for the portion of the spiritual feminist movement that rejected all existing major churches as hopelessly patriarchal and turned instead to GODDESS WORSHIP, based on what they believed to be a widespread set of beliefs in early, matriarchal cultures (see MATRIARCHY).

Some spiritual feminists also define themselves as *ecofeminists,* who apply their religious beliefs to environmental problems, feeling that with matriarchy and goddess worship would come a better ability to heal the wounds of planet Earth. (See also FEMINISM; ECOFEMINISM; RELIGION AND WOMEN'S RIGHTS.)

sponge (cervical sponge), a soft sponge shaped like a shallow cup, saturated with SPERMICIDE and designed to fit over the CERVIX as a BIRTH CONTROL device. Like the DIAPHRAGM and CERVICAL CAP, the cervical sponge offers both a physical and chemical barrier to SPERM, though the FOOD AND DRUG ADMINISTRATION estimates that at 80–87 percent, it is somewhat less effective at barring PREGNANCY. Unlike those devices, however, the sponge requires neither special fitting nor prescriptions but can be purchased over-the-counter and is disposable. The sponge can be inserted hours before intercourse and should remain in place for at least six hours afterward; it can stay in place up to twenty-four hours, with no additional spermicide needed if intercourse is repeated.

Some women—such as those with ARTHRITIS in their hands—may experience difficulty in inserting and positioning the sponge and later removing it. The sponge on occasion may fragment on removal, possibly causing infection from any parts left in the vagina. Some women or their partners may experience irritation or allergic reactions (see ALLERGIES) and should discontinue use in case of genital burning or irritation. Spermicide may also be linked with BIRTH DEFECTS, if used when the woman is already pregnant (see SPERMICIDE); however, it gives some protection against SEXUALLY TRANSMITTED DISEEASES, though it should not be regarded as any protection against AIDS. The sponge also carries some increased risk of TOXIC SHOCK SYNDROME. But, all in all, many women find the cervical sponge a safe, convenient method of birth control. (See BIRTH CONTROL AND FAMILY PLANNING HELP, INFORMATION, AND ACTION GUIDE on page 81.)

spousal consent: See INSURANCE AND PENSION EQUITY.

spousal support, the obligation of partners in a MARRIAGE to contribute to the support of the other; sometimes also an alternative term for ALIMONY.

Traditionally, spousal support was a one-way street. In the generally accepted division of marital rights and responsibilities (see MARRIAGE), it was regarded as a husband's duty to support his wife—to provide a house, furniture, utensils, food, clothing, and other daily necessities. Indeed, for centuries MATE SELECTION for women had as a major goal to find a good *provider*. A husband's failure to support his wife (except when he proved he was *unable* to do so) was grounds for DIVORCE should she wish one—regardless of whether or not she could support herself. The converse was not true. It was extremely rare for a man to try or succeed in divorcing his wife on the grounds of nonsupport.

Spousal support could be a bare and stingy thing, however. Though the husband was obliged to support his wife, the state did not become involved in assessing the level of support to be allowed. In fact, many women have lived lives of extreme penury, being granted no money of their own and managing the household on a very limited allowance; in some cases they received not even that, but ran the house on "egg and chicken" money. Nor did a woman automatically have the right to spend her husband's money; if she bought on credit, it was because her husband allowed her to do so. Courts traditionally refused to intervene in questions of spousal support on the grounds of protecting "family privacy," except to confirm the "necessary doctrine," that the husband was obliged to pay for household necessaries purchased by the wife. As a result, the family's credit was in the husband's name, and many a woman found at DIVORCE or her husband's death (see WIDOW) that she had no credit history, even though she might have had the prime responsibility for handling the family's money and credit throughout the marriage. Today most states have laws guaranteeing a woman's right to her own credit (see EQUAL CREDIT OPPORTUNITY ACT), and many states have written new laws that require both spouses to support each other. In community property states (see MARITAL PROPERTY), debts by either husband or wife are to be paid for out of their jointly held property.

Today, where two-career families are common, many states allow husbands and wives to claim support from each other. This more equitable principle has carried over into alimony, with some men these days claiming postmarital support from their wives, such as high-earning celebrities or executives. Indeed, many wives have worked as the main FAMILY breadwinner in the early years of a marriage, while the husband was attending school, especially obtaining professional degrees. This contribution to the family has increasingly been considered in assessing equitable division of MARITAL PROPERTY during SEPARATION or divorce. (See COUPLES AND FAMILIES HELP, INFORMATION, AND ACTION GUIDE on page 418; DIVORCE AND SEPARATION HELP, INFORMATION, AND ACTION GUIDE on page 238.)

spouse, a general term for either wife or husband—that is, for either member of a married couple (see MARRIAGE). As a move toward legal equity between the sexes, the term *spouse* is used in many laws and rulings referring to the rights and responsibilities of married parties, where once laws would specify *husband* or *wife*, in relation to such questions as ALIMONY or SPOUSAL SUPPORT.

spouse abuse, an alternative term for wife battering (see BATTERED WOMEN).

Stanton, Elizabeth Cady (1815–1902), a pioneer American WOMEN'S RIGHTS leader. In 1848 she and Lucretia MOTT organized the landmark SENECA FALLS WOMEN'S RIGHTS CONVENTION; the meeting resulted in the notable DECLARA-TION OF SENTIMENTS AND RESOLUTIONS (see full text on page 793), written and in-troduced by Stanton, a key document in the history of women and the worldwide fight for WOMEN'S RIGHTS.

In the two decades before the Civil War, Stanton's women's rights work de-veloped side by side with her abolitionist work, the latter joined with that of her husband, Henry Stanton. In 1851 she met and began her lifelong association with Susan B. ANTHONY; their first major shared work was founding the New York Women's State Temperance Society (1852–1853).

After the war she and Anthony focused on building the women's rights movement, founding the periodical *The Revolution* (1868–1870) and the NA-TIONAL WOMAN SUFFRAGE ASSOCIATION (**NWSA**) in 1869. Stanton was the first president of the NWSA (1869–1890). The somewhat more conservative AMERI-CAN WOMAN SUFFRAGE ASSOCIATION had been organized as an alternative to the NWSA in 1869; when the two wings of the American women's movement re-joined, in 1890, Stanton became the first president of the unified NATIONAL AMER-ICAN WOMAN SUFFRAGE ASSOCIATION (1890–1892). With Matilda Gage, Stanton wrote the DECLARATION OF THE RIGHTS OF WOMEN, presented at the 1876 centen-nial celebration of the Declaration of Independence, in Philadelphia.

Anthony, Stanton, and Gage wrote *The History of Woman Suffrage* (1886). Stanton, who late in her life turned some of her attention to equality within re-ligious institutions, also wrote *The Women's Bible* (1895, 1898), a feminist inter-pretation of what she considered a patriarchal, often sexist work. Her last public speech, "The Solitude of Self," at the 1892 convention of the National American Woman Suffrage Association, was regarded by many as her greatest work.

Her daughter, **Harriet Stanton Blatch** (1856–1940), became a leading early-twentieth-century women's rights activist, founding the American Political Union in 1908 and later working in the NATIONAL WOMAN'S PARTY. (See also WOMEN'S RIGHTS MOVEMENT.)

Steinem, Gloria (1934–), an American feminist journalist who became a popular figure in 1963 with publication of her investigative article "I Was a Play-boy Bunny," on the lives of women working in the sexist, very popular Playboy clubs of the time. She moved into reform feminist activism in the late 1960s and in 1971 was a founder and first editor (1971–1987) of *Ms.* magazine, which quickly became a major women's movement publication. Steinem was also a women's movement celebrity, for more than two decades a highly visible presence in print and broadcast media, as well as a sought-after lecturer. Her works include the essays in *Outrageous Acts and Other Rebellions* (1983); her study of Marilyn Monroe, *Marilyn* (1986); and *Revolution from Within: A Book of Self-Esteem* (1991), a popular psychology book aimed at helping women to feel better through self-analysis and resultant resolution of inner conflicts.

I have met brave women who are exploring the outer edge of human possibility, with no history to guide them, and with a courage to make themselves vulnerable that I find moving beyond words.

GLORIA STEINEM, 1972
IN "SISTERHOOD"

•

Stein-Leventhal syndrome

Stein-Leventhal syndrome, a condition in which a woman's OVARIES contain many small CYSTS, sacs filled with fluid or gelatinous material; also called *polycystic syndrome* or *polycystic ovaries*. This relatively rare syndrome seems to be caused by a hormonal imbalance, involving overproduction of male sex HORMONES by the woman's adrenal glands, for unknown reasons. The cysts are actually eggs (see OVUM) that are unable to burst out of the follicles in which they grew; the capsules that form over the follicles produce more male hormones. As a result, women with the syndrome release no eggs and are infertile without treatment; they menstruate rarely, if at all (see MENSTRUATION); and they often are obese and have excess body and facial HAIR, a condition called *hirsutism*.

The condition is sometimes treated with female sex hormones, ESTROGEN and PROGESTERONE. Alternatively, in an operation called *wedge resection*, surgeons may cut out only the affected part of the ovary. This can sometimes restore OVULATION; but in some cases it can *reduce* fertility by also removing egg-bearing tissue and by causing scar tissue that may itself inhibit ovulation. Laser surgery holds some promise for destroying the individual cysts without scar tissue and leaving the rest of the ovary untouched. (See INFERTILITY AND REPRODUCTIVE TECHNOLOGY HELP, INFORMATION, AND ACTION GUIDE on page 368; WOMEN'S HEALTH HELP, INFORMATION, AND ACTION GUIDE on page 334.)

sterility, the absolute, permanent, and irreversible inability to have a baby, occurring sometimes for unknown reasons (such as possible exposure to various environmental hazards), sometimes by choice, as in STERILIZATION. This is actually a relatively rare condition; much more common is a decreased likelihood of being able to conceive and carry to term a healthy child because of temporary, treatable, or reversible conditions (see INFERTILITY).

sterilization, in a general sense, the process of making something unreproductive or incapable of supporting life; more specifically, a permanent form of BIRTH CONTROL (see below).

Medical tools, and special settings such as operating and delivery rooms, are generally treated to prevent growth of disease-causing microorganisms, by the use of antiseptics, disinfectants, boiling, steaming (if under high pressure, called *autoclaving),* or radiation, including X-rays and ultraviolet radiation. One of the main medical advantages of hospital-based CHILDBIRTH is precisely that it takes place in a setting that should—if all procedures have been properly followed—be disease free. Some women object that the setting is, in *personal* terms, "too sterile" and prefer less hospitallike settings, even with somewhat higher risk of disease.

Some are also concerned that in hospitals women and their babies may be exposed to diseases not present in their homes. Their fears were given some support by a 1992 study that showed a sizable proportion of doctors and nurses failed to cleanse their hands with antiseptic between examination of one patient and another. Individual women should look hard and skeptically at the cleanliness of their doctor's office and hospital, as part of making their choice about where and how to deliver their child.

Sterilization is also a form of birth control, referring to any medical or surgical procedure intended to prevent a person from ever reproducing, specifically by blocking normal passage of the woman's egg (OVUM) and the man's SPERM. Sterilization is regarded as a permanent procedure; though some kinds can be reversed, the success rate of such operations is very low.

Sterilization today is generally a voluntary choice. For women this usually involves TUBAL LIGATION, literally tying or clamping of the FALLOPIAN TUBES; for men the main choice is *vasectomy,* the severing of the *vas deferens,* the tubes that normally carry sperm to the penis. For both surgical procedures, the effectiveness rate for preventing pregnancy is more than 99 percent, with vasectomy being the more minor type of surgical procedure. Some other operations may have sterilization as a side effect, such as HYSTERECTOMY, OOPHORECTOMY, and *ablation,* destruction of the lining of the uterus (see MYOMECTOMY).

At some times and places, governments have used involuntary sterilization to prevent some people—notably those thought to have physical or mental defects—from bearing children. That is less common today, being widely regarded as infringements on human freedom in general and on REPRODUCTIVE RIGHTS in particular, though the impulse to social control of reproduction remains, generally by governmental pressure to use contraception (see EUGENICS BIRTH CONTROL; NORPLANT; DEPO-PROVERA).

However, as late as the 1970s, the U.S. Department of Health and Human Services (HHS) had to issue regulations to curb abuses related to sterilization, such as social services departments threatening to end PREGNANCY benefits or deny payment for PRENATAL CARE or DELIVERY to women who would not agree to be sterilized. The HHS guidelines require that sterilization be barred for anyone under twenty-one years old; that the procedure, its risks, and its permanence must be described in the person's native language; that the person give written consent while not impaired or under duress—for example, *not* just before, during, or after an ABORTION or LABOR, or while under the influence of drugs and alcohol; and that a thirty-day waiting period be mandatory after written consent. The guidelines call for fines or imprisonment as punishment for any threats to terminate benefits. These are primarily an ideal, however, since such guidelines are difficult to enforce. (See BIRTH CONTROL; BIRTH CONTROL AND FAMILY PLANNING HELP, INFORMATION, AND ACTION GUIDE on page 81.)

steroids, a group of HORMONES, formed from cholesterol, that include *corticosteroids*, produced by the cortex of the adrenal glands, and the male and female sex hormones, including TESTOSTERONE, ESTROGEN, and PROGESTERONE. Some steroids are legitimately used for medical purposes; corticosteroids may, for example, be used on a limited basis to promote healing in a joint (see ARTHRITIS).

But many steroids are widely used and abused for their body-building, muscle-recovery, injury-healing, bone-strengthening effects. The most widely abused are *anabolic steroid* drugs, the name referring to their protein-building effect; these are usually synthetic forms of male sex hormones, especially testosterone. And the greatest abusers are athletes, seeking to build up their muscle mass and strength despite medical warnings against the practice and increasing testing and penalties in sports competition. The main clearly evident side effects of anabolic steroids are high cholesterol in the BLOOD, a depressed IMMUNE SYSTEM, and serious liver disorders (see DIGESTIVE SYSTEM). For women, effects may also include development of HAIR on the face, acne, diminishing of the BREASTS, deepening of the voice, enlarging of the CLITORIS, and irregularities in MENSTRUATION. (See HORMONES; EXERCISE; also WOMEN'S HEALTH HELP, INFORMATION, AND ACTION GUIDE on page 334.)

sterologists, an alternative name for *fertility specialists*, who specialize in treating INFERTILITY.

stillbirth, the birth of a FETUS that has died before or during DELIVERY; also called *late fetal death*. The term is usually applied to a fetus that was beyond the twenty-eighth week of GESTATION and weighed at least 2.2 pounds (1,000 g) and so would normally have been expected to live. Death of a fetus before this point is called MISCARRIAGE, or *spontaneous abortion*. After lack of a heartbeat is detected, the child is delivered vaginally, sometimes with induced LABOR, or by CESAREAN SECTION, if necessary. The doctor is then required to examine the child and report the cause of death, if it can be determined, on a death certificate.

A stillbirth can have many causes. Sometimes the problem is obvious, as when the UMBILICAL CORD has become wrapped around the baby's neck and cut off the oxygen supply, or the PLACENTA has malfunctioned, cutting off nourishment. Severe malfunctions of or damage to the BRAIN AND NERVOUS SYSTEM, such as anencephaly (partial or complete absence of the brain) or spina bifida (incompletely closed spinal cord), can also cause stillbirth, as can incompatibility of the Rh factors between mother and child (see BLOOD). Stillbirth is also more common with extremely low birth weight or premature delivery. In addition, disorders affecting the mother may cause stillbirth, among them DIABETES, measles, chicken pox, toxoplasmosis, HERPES, SYPHILIS, CYTOMEGALOVIRUS, and influenza. However, in perhaps one case out of three the cause of death is unknown.

A stillbirth does not necessarily mean that a woman will have problems with later pregnancies; they would, however, be medically treated as high-risk pregnancies, for safety. A woman should allow herself to heal emotionally and give her body time to rebuild physical reserves before attempting another CONCEPTION, and she may want to discuss with her doctor how long to wait. (See PREGNANCY AND CHILDBIRTH HELP, INFORMATION, AND ACTION GUIDE on page 580.)

stomach stapling, a popular name for two operations, *gastroplasty* or *gastric bypass*, to promote weight loss (see DIETING).

Stone, Lucy (1818–1893), a pioneering American feminist and abolitionist who emerged as a speaker for the Anti-Slavery Society in 1848. She and abolitionist Henry Brown Blackwell married and joined forces in 1855, maintaining a then unusual equality in MARRIAGE. Especially notable was that Lucy Stone kept her own name (see NAMES IN MARRIAGE) and both partners publicly stated their opposition to women's subservient legal position in marriage.

Stone became a leading figure on the relatively conservative side of the American women's rights movement after the Civil War. She was an organizer of the Equal Rights Association in 1866 and in 1869 was a key figure in the organization of the AMERICAN WOMAN SUFFRAGE ASSOCIATION, formed as an alternative to the more militant NATIONAL WOMAN SUFFRAGE ASSOCIATION, led by Susan B. ANTHONY and Elizabeth Cady STANTON. Stone also founded and edited the *Woman's Journal.* In 1890 the two wings of the women's movement joined in the NATIONAL AMERICAN WOMAN SUFFRAGE ASSOCIATION, with Stone becoming part of the new organization's executive. (See also WOMEN'S RIGHTS MOVEMENT; NAMES IN MARRIAGE.)

The right to vote will yet be swallowed up in the real question, viz: has woman a right to herself? It is very little to me to have the right to vote, to own property, etc., if I may not keep my body, and its uses, in my absolute right.

———— *LUCY STONE, 1855* ————

•

Stop Abuse by Counselors (STOP ABC) (P.O. Box 68292, Seattle, WA 98169; 206-243-2723; Shirley Siegel, contact), a "consumer organization whose primary goal is to prevent the exploitation of clients by health and mental health care practitioners." STOP ABC encourages research into the incidence of unethical counseling practices; seeks to educate the public on ways to select a counselor and identify problems in a counseling relationship; advocates notification of employers and licensing boards and civil action when appropriate; makes referrals to attorneys experienced in counseling abuse cases; and supports legislation to curb counseling abuse. It publishes various materials, including an attorney's list, a computer printout of relevant resources, an organizing packet, and *What to Do When Psychotherapy Goes Wrong* (ordering address: STOP ABC Publishing, 5651 South 144th Street, Tukwila, WA 98168).

Stopes, Marie (1880–1958), a British BIRTH CONTROL advocate who emerged as a major figure in 1918 with publication of her very popular best-sellers *Married Love* and *Wise Parenthood,* in which she advocated birth control and sex education as means by which women could achieve sexual satisfaction, by negating much of the fear of PREGNANCY. She published several other books on the same theme, including *Radiant Motherhood* (1920) and *Enduring Passion* (1928).

storage disorders, a group of digestive disorders (see DIGESTIVE SYSTEM).

Subjection of Women, The: See John Stuart MILL.

substance abuse: See ALCOHOL AND DRUG ABUSE.

suction-assisted lipectomy, an alternative name for liposuction (see COSMETIC SURGERY).

suffragist or **suffragette**, one who was active in the campaign for WOMAN SUFFRAGE. The two terms are essentially synonyms, but for many people on both sides of the issue, a suffragette was a direct-action militant, and the label was usually therefore either an epithet or a badge of honor. (See also WOMAN SUFFRAGE.)

Supermom: See WORK AND WOMEN.

surgical delivery, an alternative name for CESAREAN SECTION.

surrogate parenting, an approach to INFERTILITY in which a woman bears a child for a couple who are unable to have one themselves, usually for a fee and by legal contract; sometimes called *noncoital collaborative reproduction*. In general, the surrogate mother is inseminated by a man, usually through ARTIFICIAL INSEMINATION, bears the child that grows from her own egg (OVUM), and then gives up the child for ADOPTION by the husband and wife.

The physical procedure is deceptively simple. But for the surrogate MOTHER, the arrangement can be a legal, emotional, and social quagmire. The legal status of the child and of the surrogacy contract may be uncertain, depending on state laws and judicial rulings; interest groups and public opinion variously praise and attack the surrogate mother; and the surrogate mothers themselves are often caught off-guard by their own feelings for the child and confusion about whether or not to honor the contract to give the child up for adoption.

The classic case, of course, involved surrogate mother Mary Beth Whitehead, who refused to give up "Baby M" and sought in court to retain her PARENTS' RIGHTS, regardless of her contract with William and Elizabeth Stern. In that case the court gave CUSTODY to the Sterns, with broad VISITATION RIGHTS to Whitehead, a ruling that was confirmed, even though a later New Jersey court ruled that commercial surrogate mother contracts were illegal and that the surrogate mother was the legal mother of the child.

Many surrogacy arrangements have worked quite satisfactorily, however. Many surrogate mothers stress being pleased to have been able to bring a child to a childless couple. Often the surrogate mother and the adoptive parents all express the feeling that the child is truly the couple's child in the sense that the child would not have come into being without their desire and perseverance.

The surrogate mother approach is most often chosen when the husband is fertile but his wife either is not, is too ill to bear a child, or bears a GENETIC DISORDER that would be passed on to her children. For prospective parents, the main concern is that the surrogate mother will, in the end, not release the child for adoption. The couple should thoroughly explore the possible ramifications of surrogacy before proceeding; in particular they should review the current status of surrogacy contracts in this developing and highly variable area of the law and consider whether they are prepared to deal with the situation that might develop if the contract is broken. In that case, though the husband would be the child's biological FATHER, having contributed half of the child's GENETIC INHERITANCE, he might or might not be considered the *legal* father (see FATHER), depending on state law.

Another approach to surrogate parenting uses *IN VITRO* FERTILIZATION, where the wife has healthy eggs but for some reason cannot carry the child. Eggs are removed from the infertile wife and fertilized in a laboratory dish with the husband's sperm. Then the fertilized egg or eggs are implanted into a *host surrogate mother;* she bears the child, but the child's GENETIC INHERITANCE comes from the husband and wife. The Center for Surrogate Parenting (see below) reports that it has successfully petitioned the courts, in this situation, to enter the biological mother's name, rather than the birth mother's name, on the birth certificate.

In an earlier, more traditional use, a surrogate mother or father was an adult in the child's life who played a quasi-parental role, such as a beloved teacher or neighbor.

For help, information, and action

▶ **Center for Surrogate Parenting (CSP)** (8383 Wilshire Boulevard, Suite 750, Beverly Hills, CA 90211; 213-655-1974; William Handle, president), an organization of health and legal professionals working with surrogate parenting. CSP provides information; seeks to influence public policy and laws regarding surrogacy; and publishes various materials. An associated organization, at the same address and telephone number is the **National Association of Surrogate Mothers.**

▶ **National Coalition Against Surrogacy (NCAS)** (c/o Foundation on Economic Trends, 1130 17th Street, NW, Suite 630, Washington, DC 20036; 202-466-2823), an organization of people against surrogate parenting. NCAS provides support for women unhappy in a surrogate role and seeks to bar surrogate maternity contracts.

Other resources

The Case of Baby M: And the Facts of Life. Rochelle Sharpe. Prentice-Hall, 1989.
Surrogate Motherhood. Martha A. Field. Harvard University Press, 1988.
Surrogate Parenting. Amy Z. Overvold. Pharos (NY), 1988.
Surrogate Mothers. Elaine Landau. Watts, 1988.
Sacred Bond: The Legacy of Baby M. Phyllis Chesler. Random House, 1988.

◪ **BACKGROUND WORKS**

Surrogate Motherhood: Politics and Privacy. Larry Gostin, ed. Indiana University Press, 1990.
Birth Power: The Case for Surrogacy. Carmel Shalev. Yale University Press, 1989.
Surrogate Motherhood: The Ethics of Using Human Beings. Thomas A. Shannon. Crossroad (NY), 1988.
Families with a Difference: Varieties of Surrogate Parenthood. Michael Humphreys and Heather Humphreys. Routledge, 1988.
Surrogate Parenting and the Law of Adoption. Irving J. Sloan. Oceana, 1988.

◪ **PERSONAL EXPERIENCES**

A Mother's Story. Mary Beth Whitehead. St. Martin's, 1989.
Sacred Bond: The Legacy of Baby M. Phyllis Chesler. Random House, 1988.
Birth Mother: America's First Legal Surrogate Mother Tells the Story of Her Change of Heart. Elizabeth Kane. Harcourt Brace Jovanovich, 1988.

syphilis, infection with the bacterium *Treponema pallidum;* a type of SEXUALLY TRANSMITTED DISEASE that was dreaded for centuries but is now readily treated with antibiotics, *if properly recognized, diagnosed, and treated.*

Syphilis proceeds in four stages. In *primary syphilis* the main symptom is a usually painless open sore called a *chancre,* which appears ten days to three months—though normally two to six weeks—after exposure. The chancre usually appears on the VULVA or VAGINA in women and the penis in men, though it may also appear on the tongue or lips, fingertips, or inside the body on the CERVIX. This sore is called a *hard chancre* to distinguish it from the so-called *soft chancre* of CHANCROID or sores in HERPES. Though the syphilis chancre disappears within a few weeks, often before the person is aware of infection, the disease continues.

Secondary syphilis involves a SKIN rash that appears two to twelve weeks after the chancre disappears. The rash may be in just a few areas, such as the palms of the hands or soles of the feet, or it may cover the whole body. Bacteria are present in the sores that form the rash and can be spread to others through physical contact—not necessarily sexual. Accompanying symptoms may include mild fever, fatigue, headache, sore throat, and other flulike symptoms, as well as patchy HAIR loss and swollen lymph glands throughout the body. Symptoms subside in several weeks or months, coming and going for perhaps one to two years. Again, these are often so mild as to go unnoticed and therefore untreated.

Then syphilis moves into a *latent stage.* Symptoms cease, and the infected person is no longer contagious. Many people have no further consequences. But 15–40 percent of people with syphilis then develop the complications characteristic of the *tertiary* or *late stage,* which can last for years, even decades. During this time the bacteria progressively damage virtually every part of the body, leading finally to blindness, heart disease, mental illness, and eventually death.

It is this terrible progression that caused the disease to be so feared for centuries. Today it can be readily treated with penicillin or other antibiotics. However, no treatment can undo damage already done. That is why it is so vital for syphilis to be diagnosed and treated early. This is easier said than done. Because so many of its early symptoms are mild and similar to those of other diseases, syphilis is called the "great imitator" and often goes undiagnosed. Doctors are trained to recognize the symptoms and can confirm diagnosis with microscopic examination and BLOOD tests—but the patient must first arrive for testing. Any suspicious rash or sore in the genital area should trigger a visit to a doctor or clinic.

Syphilis is spread by direct contact with open sores on someone with an active infection (in one of the first two stages). It is usually transmitted through the mucous membranes of the GENITALS, mouth, or anus (see DIGESTIVE SYSTEM) but can also enter through broken skin anywhere on the body. Women should avoid any physical contact with any person believed to be infected with syphilis, which can be spread not just through sores, but also through other infected tissues and body fluids. Use of CONDOMS and SPERMICIDES containing nonoxynol-9 can reduce the risk, as can limiting the number of sex partners. Cure of one infection gives no protection against another, since the body does not build up immunity to the syphilis bacteria.

A pregnant woman has special risks with syphilis. If she is in the primary or secondary stage, she has an increased risk of MISCARRIAGE or STILLBIRTH. If the disease is untreated, she can infect the baby, who may be born with skin sores, mental retardation, meningitis (infection of the membranes covering the brain and spinal cord), and various physical defects (see BIRTH DEFECTS); the infected newborn can also transmit syphilis to others. However, if the syphilis is diagnosed and treated before the fourth month of pregnancy, the baby may be unaffected. After the fourth month, by which time the bacteria have generally reached and infected the baby, treatment can cure the infection in both mother and baby but cannot undo damage to the baby's development. It is for these reasons that a syphilis test is routine on the first visit in PRENATAL CARE. (See SEXUALLY TRANSMITTED DISEASES; also WHAT YOU CAN DO TO AVOID STDs on page 660; SEXUALLY TRANSMITTED DISEASES HELP, INFORMATION, AND ACTION GUIDE on page 658.)

systemic lupus erythematosus, the full medical name for LUPUS.

Tailhook scandal, a major SEXUAL HARASSMENT and sexual assault case, involving at least seventy serving and retired U.S. Navy aviators who assaulted at least twenty-six women, most of them serving naval officers, at the September 1991 convention of the Tailhook Association.

The thirty-five-year-old naval aviators' organization was privately run, but the Navy had flown a reported 1,500 naval officers to Las Vegas at government expense to attend the convention. One of those present was Navy Secretary H. Lawrence Garrett III; many senior officers also attended.

On September 7, the last night of the convention at the Hilton Hotel in Las Vegas, large numbers of drunken naval officers who were gathered on the third floor of the hotel committed criminal physical assaults on women leaving the elevators, including many whom they knew to be naval officers. The men forced women to run gauntlets, grabbing at their BREASTS, GENITALS, and other body parts and tearing off their clothes; later investigations established that such gauntlets had been a standard feature at all Tailhook conventions since at least 1989, and senior officers were aware of this. Navy Secretary Garrett, who was nearby, denied knowing anything at all about the practice or the September 7 assaults, though later investigations established that one of his top aides had known about the assaults that night, after one of the attacked woman officers, helicopter pilot and admiral's aide Lieutenant Paula Coughlin, had told him about them. Garrett had also been close to the scene of the crime, as established when a suppressed portion of the original Navy investigative report on the matter later surfaced. Ms. Coughlin also reported the mass assault to her superior, Rear Admiral John W. Snyder, who was later relieved of his command for failure to respond adequately to her charges.

On October 7, exactly one month later, Anita Faye HILL went public with the sexual harassment charges against then-nominee for Supreme Court justice Clarence Thomas, which led to the riveting Hill-Thomas hearings before the Senate Judiciary Committee, broadcast to a worldwide television audience. Coincidentally or otherwise, the Navy began an investigation of the Tailhook assaults on October 11; a second inquiry was ordered three weeks later. The inquiry established that there had been many assaults, but its April 30 report turned up a total of two suspects, clearly indicating a massive cover-up in the Navy.

In late June Coughlin went public with her story in an interview with Peter Jennings on ABC News and in *The Washington Post*. In the highly charged anti-sexual-harassment atmosphere that had been created by Hill's treatment before the Senate Judiciary Committee, and with a presidential campaign under way, her entirely credible, easily verifiable charges, coupled with her status as a Navy pilot with an unblemished reputation, out of a Navy family, had an enormous impact. Women, led by many congressional women, reacted explosively; so did many men, appalled by the ugliness of the incident and the subsequent cover-up attempt. The Senate Armed Services Committee quickly froze more than 4,500 pending promotions, retirements, and command changes, announcing that it would ultimately handle them one by one to determine any possible connection with the Tailhook scandal. On June 27 Navy Secretary Garrett resigned.

In the aftermath of the scandal, the Navy and the other armed forces mounted massive public relations efforts, aimed at indicating commitment to educate the armed forces in order to create a new sensitivity on sexual abuse matters. In direct response to the Tailhook scandal, Rear Admiral Duvall Williams, commander of the Naval Investigation Service, and Rear Admiral John E. Gordon, the Navy's Judge Advocate General, took early retirement; Rear Admiral George W. Davis, Jr., Naval Inspector General, was relieved of his duties and re assigned; and some other senior naval officers were denied promotion. In related events, several aviators were disciplined because of sexually offensive skits at an air base; sensitivity training materials were supplied to commanders; and new procedures were introduced to handle Navy sexual harassment complaints. Quite notably, those complaints were to be handled by naval commanders, rather than any kind of independent authority, sharply calling into question the real extent of the reforms.

Meanwhile, as the Tailhook scandal continued, the armed services were revealed to have a wide and deep range of sexual abuse problems, and armed forces women at many levels and their families came forward with accounts of sexual harassment, all the way from insulting talk to repeated RAPES. (See SEXUAL HARASSMENT; SEXUAL DISCRIMINATION AND SEXUAL HARASSMENT HELP, INFORMATION, AND ACTION GUIDE on page 642.)

tampons, disposable products used during MENSTRUATION to absorb flow. They are linked with risk of the rare TOXIC SHOCK SYNDROME.

tattooing, injection of indelible dye into the SKIN (see COSMETIC SURGERY).

taxol, a drug that has shown promise in the treatment of BREAST CANCER and some other types of CANCER.

Taylor, Harriet (1808–1858), an English feminist who collaborated with John Stuart MILL in writing *On Liberty* (1859), as he always stated, although she was at the time uncredited. She was probably also the author of the article "On the Enfranchisement of Women," published anonymously in the *Westminster Review* (1851). Her long relationship with Mill began in 1830; she was then married to John Taylor and remained so until his death in 1849; she and Mill married in 1851.

teeth, the set of enamel-covered bony structures set into the jaw, important for chewing and all-around health and also for speaking and the shape and look of the face. Children have a set of twenty *primary teeth,* also called *baby* or *milk teeth,* or, medically, *deciduous teeth,* since they fall out (like the leaves of deciduous trees). They are replaced by the thirty-two *permanent teeth* that begin to appear at around age six to seven and complete their emergence by the late teens, though in some people the last four teeth, the *wisdom teeth,* do not fully appear or may cause problems that require their removal.

Each tooth extends one or more roots into the jawbone. Its central core of living pulp, including blood vessels and sensitive nerves, is housed in a hard substance called *dentin,* which in turn is surrounded by a bonelike sensitive material called *cementum. Periodontal ligaments* anchor the cementum to the *gums,* fleshy tissue that acts as a shock absorber for the teeth. The part of the tooth that extends above the gum line is covered by a hard layer of enamel called the *crown.*

The main dental problem is, of course, cavities, which dentists call *caries.* This is decay in the tooth, often caused by bacteria that, when sugar is available, form an acid that eats away at the tooth surface. Some people are more susceptible to tooth decay than others, because of their GENETIC INHERITANCE or personal history, to some extent related to their mother's diet during PREGNANCY. People with BULIMIA have special problems, because stomach acids from frequent vomiting also attack the teeth. Decay can be largely prevented, however, through good health; proper dental care; the use of fluorides in toothpaste, water, or special rinses to harden the tooth surface; and periodic dental cleaning and checkups.

Unlike infections in other parts of the body, tooth decay cannot be either cured or reversed; it can only be halted—the decayed matter is removed and the remaining cavity filled. If that is not done, the bacteria may reach the pulp, producing a pocket of infection called an *abscess,* and can, if unchecked, cause general infection in the blood, possibly even affecting the heart. An abscessed tooth is treated by *root canal therapy,* which involves removal of the pulp and its replacement with a filling; if treatment fails, the tooth will need to be extracted.

Another common dental problem is *plaque,* accumulated hard material deposited around the edges of the teeth, formed by the action of chemicals in saliva and food. This provides a place for bacteria to multiply, infecting both the teeth and the gums. Regular brushing and flossing and cleaning at semiannual checkups—or more often, if plaque buildup is heavy—can hold down plaque buildup, a process that accelerates with age. The main concern, apart from tooth decay, is that—in a condition called *gingivitis*—swollen or infected gums will loosen their hold on teeth, making chewing difficult and, if unchecked, eventually allowing teeth to fall out. If gums bleed during eating or brushing, a visit to the dentist is in order.

Because of hormonal and biochemical changes in the body, women are especially susceptible to plaque and gingivitis during pregnancy (as are people with DIABETES) and so are advised to be particularly meticulous about oral hygiene and to see their dentist to remove plague buildup. The old wives' notion that the baby takes all the calcium from a mother's teeth or "a tooth is lost for every pregnancy" has no basis in fact, but poor dental care during pregnancy can lead to lost teeth later on.

The mother's diet during pregnancy is extremely important to the child's dental health (see NUTRITION); at birth a child's primary teeth are largely formed, though they have not yet erupted from the jawbone. The American Dental Association recommends that dental X-rays should be given during pregnancy only in case of emergency; however, the standard lead shield protects both mother and unborn child if an X-ray is needed.

Several new procedures are available to help improve the look of damaged, discolored, or mispositioned teeth, among them

▶ *bleaching,* using a warm peroxide solution to remove stains.
▶ *bonding,* painting a plastic or resin layer on the teeth, which covers stains and also can be used to build up teeth that are damaged or too far apart.
▶ *laminate veneer,* bonding a layer of plastic or porcelain to the tooth, akin to false fingernails.

Since these procedures are still relatively new, it is unclear how they will stand up in the long run. They are, however, more conservative approaches to fixing the "look" of teeth, alternatives to the traditional, more drastic method of cutting down the top of the tooth and replacing it with an artificial *cap* or *crown* made of acrylic, porcelain, gold or other metals, or a combination of these. Crowns are still used, of course, when a tooth has been broken or severely decayed. Another approach to the "look" of teeth is *orthodonture,* which uses braces and wires to reposition teeth into proper alignment, a process started ideally in the early teens; when the jaw and teeth are still developing.

If a tooth is lost, it may be replaced by a removable or fixed *bridge,* which places an artificial tooth in the socket and attaches it to neighboring natural teeth, or sometimes by a *dental implant,* in which the artificial tooth is attached directly to the jawbone. If many teeth have been lost, *partial* or *full dentures* are used to replace them.

Especially among older people, reduced saliva flow can result in *dry mouth,* a problem often associated with some medications, such as antihistamines and diuretics. The problem is that saliva is needed to lubricate the mouth, wash away food, and neutralize acids. Sugar-free candy or gum can stimulate saliva flow, or oral rinses can be used to replace moisture.

Another problem related to teeth, affecting both men and women, is *temporomandibular joint (TMJ) disorder,* which results in headaches, earaches, facial pain, "clicking" or "popping" of the jaw, and difficulty or pain in opening the mouth wide, yawning, or chewing. It is sometimes called the "painful pretender" because it is hard to diagnose and easily mistaken for other medical problems. Apparently it results when the jaw and its supporting muscles and ligaments fail to work together properly and the muscles used in chewing go into spasm. Heat and muscle-relaxing drugs can ease the spasms, but long-term treatment involves changing the patterns that led to the disorder. (See SKELETAL SYSTEM; ARTHRITIS.)

For more help, information, and action

▶ **National Institute of Dental Research (NIDR)** (9000 Rockville Pike, Building 31, Room 2C35, Bethesda, MD 20892; 301-496-4261), one of the National Institutes of Health, focusing on dental health and disorders. It provides information and publishes technical reports for specialists and more general brochures such as *A Healthy Mouth for You and Your Baby, Tooth Decay, Periodontal Disease and Diabetes—A Guide for Patients,* and *Dental Tips for Diabetics.*

▶ **American Dental Association (ADA)** (211 East Chicago Avenue, Chicago, IL 60611; 312-440-2500 or 800-621-8099, John S. Zapp, executive director), a dental professionals' organization. It sponsors research, accredits dental schools, and publishes many professionals materials, including *Dentist's Desk Reference* and dental health education materials.

▶ **NATIONAL WOMEN'S HEALTH NETWORK (NWHN)** (202-347-1140). Operates the **Women's Health Information Service.** Publishes the information packet *TMJ (Temporomandibular Joint Disorder).*

Other resources

The Mount Sinai Medical Center Family Guide to Dental Health. Jack Klatell and others. Macmillan, 1991.
The Oral Report: The Consumer's Common Sense Guide to Better Dental Care. Jerry F. Taintor with Mary Jane Taintor. New York: Facts on File, 1988.

◪ **ON TEMPOROMANDIBULAR JOINT (TMJ) DISORDER**

No More Pain: A Self-Help Program for TMJ. Sharon Carr and Terry L. Daugherty. S. Carr, 1989.
TMJ Book. Andrew S. Kaplan and Gray Williams, Jr. Pharos (NY), 1988.

temperance movement, an anti-alcohol movement that in the United States attracted many female and male social reformers, most of them devout middle-class Protestants, from the 1790s through the early 1930s, until the repeal of Prohibition. It was also a means through which many American women entered political life as social reformers (see POLITICAL PARTICIPATION) and remained a major vehicle for many women even as the WOMEN'S RIGHTS MOVEMENT grew.

The link between the temperance movement and the women's movement was strong from the first. For example, starting in 1849 Elizabeth Cady STANTON wrote articles for *The Lily,* the temperance periodical issued by her Seneca Falls neighbor, women's rights activist Amelia Bloomer, who with Stanton had attended the historic SENECA FALLS WOMEN'S RIGHTS CONVENTION only a year earlier; and Stanton and Susan B. ANTHONY worked together (1852–1853) in the New York State Women's Temperance Society.

From its formation in 1874, the WOMEN'S CHRISTIAN TEMPERANCE UNION (WCTU) played a major role in developing what eventually became the failed

Prohibition experiment of the 1920s. From 1879 to 1898, during the presidency of Emma Frances E. Willard, the WCTU was also a major women's rights organization, supporting WOMAN SUFFRAGE and a wide range of other reforms affecting women, but in the twentieth century it came to focus almost entirely on its campaign for Prohibition, which ultimately proved unworkable.

testes (testicles), the pair of male sex glands (GONADS) that manufacture SPERM and also produce TESTOSTERONE, the key male sex HORMONE. In a male FETUS the testes lie inside the abdomen, but in response to hormones produced by the MOTHER they gradually descend through a passageway called the *inguinal canal* to hang outside the body, suspended in a pouch of SKIN called the *scrotum*. Failure of one or both testicles to descend into the scrotum can result in INFERTILITY, since the internal body temperature is too high for sperm to live; undescended testicles are also associated with an increased risk of CANCER.

A fibrous covering called the *tunica albuginea* further protects the testes; they are nourished through the *spermatic cord*, which passes through an opening called the *inguinal ring* and contains arteries, veins, nerves, and other structures. Within the testes are many tiny coiled tubes, called *seminiferous tubules*, in which SPERM are generated by special cells called *spermatogonia*, starting during PUBERTY. (See also REPRODUCTIVE SYSTEM.)

testosterone, the most important of the male sex HORMONES, or *androgens*, which helps regulate bone and muscle growth and sexual development. It is produced primarily in the male and female sex glands (GONADS), by the TESTES in men and OVARIES in women, as well as in the adrenal glands. Testosterone is produced only in small amounts in young boys and women, but from PUBERTY larger secretions of testosterone in males lead not just to a growth spurt, but also to the development of SECONDARY SEX CHARACTERISTICS, including HAIR on the face and body, larger muscles, deeper voice, and the growth of the testes and PENIS to adult sizes. The same kinds of characteristics can be found among women who—against most medical advice—take testosterone for body development (see STEROIDS); liver damage can also result. However, testosterone is sometimes used medically to treat disorders involving testosterone deficiency. Testosterone was for a time used to treat BREAST CANCER, but such use is rare today. (See HORMONES.)

test-tube fertilization, an alternative name for *IN VITRO* FERTILIZATION.

Thornburgh* v. *American College of Obstetricians and Gynecologists, the 1986 U.S. Supreme Court ruling that struck down an earlier version of Pennsylvania's Abortion Control Act, restricting abortion rights, later revised and largely affirmed in *PLANNED PARENTHOOD* v. *CASEY* (1992). (See ABORTION; also THE U.S. SUPREME COURT ON ABORTION on page 9.)

Title IV-D of the Social Security Act, a U.S. federal law passed in 1975 that established the Office of Child Support Enforcement (OCSE) (see CHILD SUPPORT; PARENT LOCATOR SERVICE).

Title VII of the Civil Rights Act of 1964, the basic U.S. federal law barring discrimination in any phase of employment because of sex, race, color, religion, or national origin. Title VII covers all private employers of fifteen or more people, including federal employees, but with somewhat different complaint-filing rules. The law does not bar discrimination against LESBIANS and gay males. The EQUAL EMPLOYMENT OPPORTUNITY COMMISSION (EEOC) was provided by the law to enforce its provisions, though it was not until the Equal Employment Opportunity Act of 1972 became law that the EEOC had the authority to initiate complaints, greatly enhancing its power. The EEOC also enforces such anti-gender-discrimination laws as the Equal Pay Act (see EQUAL PAY FOR EQUAL WORK), the PREGNANCY DISCRIMINATION ACT, and the Age Discrimination Act, and is responsible for SEXUAL HARASSMENT complaints filed pursuant to Title VII. Title VII also applies to questions of INSURANCE AND PENSION EQUITY.

Title IX of the 1972 Education Act Amendments, the basic U.S. federal law barring discrimination in federally assisted educational programs and related activities, very notably including sports, in all educational levels, public and private, preschool to doctoral level. Compliance procedures are set forth in the law, which is enforced by several federal agencies, though mainly by the Department of Education and the Justice Department. These procedures and enforcing departments can be bypassed by a complainant who chooses to go directly to court; complainants can come from a wide range of interested parties, as well as from directly aggrieved individuals and groups. Some significant exceptions are provided by the law, in such areas as single-sex schools, military schools, undergraduate admissions policies, some religious schools, fraternities and sororities, and such organizations as the Boy Scouts and Girl Scouts, but Title IX does cover the vast majority of federally assisted schools and has brought major changes to American education.

Some of the most highly visible changes have come in sports and have resulted in a huge increase in women's participation. Less dramatic, but very basic and centrally important to the development of full equality, have been the moves toward full sexual integration and equality in the classroom and in all school-related activities, and the development of sex neutrality in such areas as counseling and disciplinary procedures, though dress codes are still a notable matter of contention. The law also prohibits sex-segregated dormitories and other live-in and working facilities. It also prohibits any form of discrimination against pregnant students and teachers, though it does not make any provision for CHILD CARE. Title IX-based interference with curricula and textbooks is prohibited, as an unconstitutional violation of First Amendment academic freedom guarantees.

The law has brought significant improvements, but great disparity still exists between males and females in educational opportunity (see EDUCATION EQ-

UITY). According to the WOMEN'S SPORTS FOUNDATION, for example, of all athletes in United States high schools only 35 percent are women, and in colleges only 33 percent, although male/female enrollments are roughly fifty–fifty. Less than one-third of athletic scholarship dollars goes to women—much more than before the law was passed, but still a meaningful gap—and less than one-quarter of the college sports budgets is allocated to women's sports. (See EDUCATION EQUITY; SEXUAL DISCRIMINATION; also SEXUAL DISCRIMINATION AND SEXUAL HARASSMENT HELP, INFORMATION, AND ACTION GUIDE on page 642.)

tokenism, the inclusion of small numbers of people who are discriminated against in order to demonstrate falsely the inclusion of people from such groups, as when a lone woman or African-American is placed on a corporate board that has traditionally had no women or minority group members and the person is from the start powerless to shape board decisions. But inclusion has to start somewhere, and trailblazers can sometimes be mistaken for tokens. Indeed, some who may have been seen as tokens by those who appointed them have turned out instead to be trailblazers. Even Thurgood Marshall and Sandra Day O'Connor, respectively the first African-American and the first woman on the U.S. Supreme Court, were seen as tokens by some, rather than the historic figures they really were.

toxemia of pregnancy, an alternative name for PRECLAMPSIA and eclampsia.

toxic shock syndrome (TSS), a rare but serious, potentially life-threatening condition that results from infection by *staphylococcus aureus* bacteria, which produces a toxin (poison) in the body. Initial symptoms include high fever and skin rash, followed by *shock,* a condition in which BLOOD flow (see HEART AND CIRCULATORY SYSTEM) is so drastically reduced that blood-starved tissues can be severely damaged. Symptoms of shock include cold, clammy skin; paleness; rapid, weak pulse and breathing; dizziness; and weakness. Emergency medical help should be summoned immediately. If unchecked, the infection and shock can cause collapse, fainting, coma, liver and kidney failure, and death. Toxic shock syndrome is treated with antibiotics and intravenous therapy; even so, a small percent of people with TSS may die.

TSS can affect men, children, and menopausal women, since the infection can enter the body in various ways, but it is most common in women during their menstrual years. The disease was first widely recognized in the 1970s, when it was linked with the use of superabsorbent tampons (see MENSTRUATION); when these were removed from the shelves, the incidence of the disease dropped sharply. However, TSS is still linked to the use of tampons and contraceptive devices, such as CERVICAL CAPS, SPONGES, and DIAPHRAGMS. Women should be sure not to leave any of these in the body for longer than necessary. To lessen risk of infection, tampons should be changed frequently and ideally alternated at some times during the day with sanitary napkins. (See also **Women's Health Help, In-formation, and Action Guide** on page 334.)

transsexualism, the inner feeling that one's GENDER IDENTITY is different from one's assigned sex (SEXUAL IDENTITY), a feeling that causes some people to seek a SEX CHANGE operation.

transvestite, a person who wears clothing culturally assigned to the opposite sex (see CROSS-DRESSING).

trichomoniasis, infection with a tiny parasite, *Trichomonoas vaginalis;* gener-ally spread through sexual contact and so classed as one of the SEXUALLY TRANS-MITTED DISEASES (STDs). Like several other STDs, "trich" often occurs without symptoms. When infection does bring symptoms, they usually appear four to twenty days from exposure but can sometimes appear years after infection. In women, symptoms include a heavy yellowish-green or gray vaginal discharge, ab-dominal pain, discomfort during SEXUAL INTERCOURSE, itching in the GENITALS, and painful urination. Men are more often symptomless but may have a thin, whitish discharge from the penis and painful or difficult urination. Many women learn they have trichomoniasis when they have a PAP SMEAR; it can also be diag-nosed by microscopic examination of vaginal fluid. While not in itself serious, trichomoniasis can lead to chronic inflammation of the URINARY TRACT; some sug-gest that, like other STDs, it may make people more vulnerable to AIDS infection. Both partners should be treated to prevent reinfection of the woman, though men may otherwise recover within a few weeks without treatment. Use of CON-DOMS, DIAPHRAGMS, and SPERMICIDES containing nonoxynol-9 can help prevent the spread of trichomoniasis. (See SEXUALLY TRANSMITTED DISEASES; also WHAT YOU CAN DO TO AVOID STDs on page 660; SEXUALLY TRANSMITTED DISEASES HELP, IN-FORMATION, AND ACTION GUIDE on page 658.)

Truth, Sojourner (Isabella Van Wegener; 1797–1883), an African-American abolitionist and WOMEN'S RIGHTS advocate, born in slavery. She became a free woman in New York State in the late 1820s and moved to New York City, reclaiming one of her children from slavery in a landmark legal case. In 1843, in response to a religious call, she changed her name to Sojourner Truth and became a traveling evangelical preacher. In the late 1840s she emerged as a leading speaker for abolition and women's rights, and especially for WOMAN SUF-FRAGE. At the 1851 Akron women's rights convention, confronting male harassers shouting about the weakness of women, she made her famous "Ain't I a woman?" response (see page 723). She often accompanied her speeches with sales of her biography, *The Narrative of Sojourner Truth.* Truth worked for the Freed-men's Bureau during Reconstruction. (See WOMEN'S RIGHTS MOVEMENT.)

AIN'T I A WOMAN?

The man over there says women need to be helped into carriages and lifted over ditches, and to have the best place everywhere. Nobody ever helps me into carriages or over puddles, or gives me the best place—and ain't I a woman? Look at my arm! I have ploughed and planted and gathered into barns, and no man could head me—and ain't I a woman? I could work as much and eat as much as a man—when I could get it—and bear the lash as well! And ain't I a woman? I have born thirteen children, and seen most of them sold into slavery, and when I cried out with my mother's grief, none but Jesus heard me—and ain't I a woman?

> Sojourner Truth, at an 1851 women's rights convention in Akron, Ohio, responding to male hecklers

tubal ligation, the tying *(ligation)* of a woman's FALLOPIAN TUBES so no sperm can reach any egg (OVUM); a form of STERILIZATION, or permanent BIRTH CONTROL. The National Center for Health Statistics reports that in the United States, tubal ligation is the most common single type of CONTRACEPTION used by women over thirty and that of all women who use birth control, 41 percent have their "tubes tied" by age thirty-nine.

The operation is usually performed under general ANESTHESIA, using one of several different procedures:

▶ *laparotomy,* which involves a three- to five-inch incision in the abdomen, takes about thirty minutes, and requires a hospital stay of several days and home recovery of about four weeks. This is the oldest form of tubal ligation, today rarely used, except in women who have already had some type of abdominal surgery or immediately after CHILDBIRTH.

▶ *minilaparotomy,* which involves a shorter one-inch incision and takes twenty to thirty minutes, with a shorter recovery time than a laparotomy.

▶ LAPAROSCOPY, which involves a half-inch incision near the navel and so is popularly called *Band-Aid* or *belly-button surgery.* A special needle and a thin, rigid, lighted, tube-and-lens device, called a *laparoscope,* are introduced through the incision. Through the needle, the doctor pumps an inert gas to push the intestines away from the UTERUS and fallopian tubes, and uses the laparoscope to see the operating site. Using instruments inserted at the same site, or at a second small incision at the pubic hairline, the doctor then seals off the fallopian tubes. Often done on an outpatient basis, though under general anesthesia, the procedure takes about an hour and requires one to two days' recovery.

▶ *vaginal tubal ligation,* which involves incisions through the vagina and involves higher risk of infection and bleeding, as well as a higher failure rate. As a result, this procedure is today less commonly performed.

Whatever the type of procedure, the end result is that the tubes are sealed. Today they are not actually tied but are generally clipped, clamped, or burned with electrocauterization, though that carries the risk of burning abdominal organs, such as the intestines and bladder, and destroying the blood supply to the OVARIES. One alternative is a *fimbrectomy*, in which the petal-like ends of the fallopian tubes are removed, so they cannot draw eggs into the tubes.

Women generally experience some pain and discomfort after all of these operations. The complication rate depends on the surgeon and the type of procedure but may be as low as 1 percent and as high as 15.3 percent. Some researchers have reported that women who have had tubal ligation with electrocauterization later have higher rates of HYSTERECTOMY, as well as premenstrual syndrome (PMS), heavy menstrual bleeding, and irregular bleeding (see MENSTRUATION); other studies have failed to confirm those results, however.

Attempts to surgically reopen tubes after ligation have had little success (see TUBOPLASTY), so tubal ligation should be regarded as permanent. However, researchers are exploring various approaches not only to lessen the risk of complications, but also to make the operation more readily reversible. One possible approach involves insertion of silicone plugs into the fallopian tubes, which could later be removed if a woman decided she wanted children. (See STERILIZATION; also BIRTH CONTROL AND FAMILY PLANNING HELP, INFORMATION, AND ACTION GUIDE on page 81.)

tuboplasty, a surgical operation to open and sometimes rebuild a woman's FALLOPIAN TUBES, where blockage has prevented CONCEPTION; also called *tuberoplasty*. When the blockage in the tubes results from scar tissue, surgeons will try to remove damaged tissue using microsurgery or laser surgery. When the blockage is near the petal-like ends (*fimbriae*) of the tubes, lying just above the OVARIES, sometimes the scar tissue is removed and a small plastic hood inserted to keep the ends open; the hoods are removed later in a second operation several months later.

Microsurgery is also used to reopen tubes after a TUBAL LIGATION, the operation popularly described as having one's "tubes tied." No woman should have a tubal ligation unless she expects it to be permanent—because it may well be irreversible. If the tubes were burned in the original operation, the chances of reopening them successfully are only about one in ten; if the fimbriae were removed, near zero. Chances are somewhat better if some other techniques are used, though much still depends on the skill of the surgeon. Sometimes a narrow tube is inserted to keep the fallopian tubes open. Even if fertilization takes place, however, a woman still has a relatively high risk of possibly life-threatening ECTOPIC PREGNANCY, where the growth takes place in the tube instead of the uterus.

For more help, information, and action

▶ RESOLVE, Inc. (617-643-2424). Publishes the fact sheet *Surgical Techniques for Tubal Repair*.

(See **INFERTILITY AND REPRODUCTIVE TECHNOLOGY HELP, INFORMATION, AND ACTION GUIDE** on page 368.)

tummy tuck, a type of abdominoplasty (see **COSMETIC SURGERY**).

tumors, abnormal growths (see **CANCER**).

Turner's syndrome, a type of **GENETIC DISORDER** that results from a **CHROMOSOMAL ABNORMALITY**, in which a girl is born with only one X chromosome instead of the usual two (see **GENETIC INHERITANCE**). Women with Turner's syndrome lack normal **OVARIES** and so are unable to bear children. **MENSTRUATION** comes late, if at all; if menstrual periods do not start by age sixteen to eighteen, Turner's syndrome is one of the conditions a doctor may check for. Similarly, **SECONDARY SEX CHARACTERISTICS** may develop late or not at all, though **HORMONES** may be used to foster development. Short stature and a characteristic additional membranous skin, called webbing, in the neck are common with Turner's syndrome, which is often associated with **EAR** and hearing problems and **HEART AND CIRCULATORY SYSTEM** problems. Characteristics of Turner's syndrome are found among some women (and also some men) who have apparently normal sex chromosomes; their condition is called *Noonan's syndrome*.

For more help, information, and action

▶ **Turner's Syndrome Society of the United States** (c/o Lynn-Georgia Tesch, 3539 Tonkawood Road, Minnetonka, MN 55345; 612-938-3118), an organization concerned with Turner's syndrome. It provides family support and gathers and disseminates information, as in a quarterly newsletter, the audiovisual *Turner's Syndrome, The X's and O's of Turner's Syndrome*, and other materials. (See also **GENETIC INHERITANCE AND BIRTH DEFECTS HELP, INFORMATION, AND ACTION GUIDE** on page 314.)

21st Century Party, a U.S. national political party founded in 1992, with strong ties to the **NATIONAL ORGANIZATION FOR WOMAN (NOW)**. The stated political agenda of the party included a very wide range of feminist, civil rights, environmental, and other liberal and radical issues, as part of an attempt to develop an equally wide set of constituencies; from the first, though, it had a largely feminist agenda, conceived in a period of setbacks and **ANTIFEMINIST** backlash. Party initiators included Eleanor Smeal of the **FUND FOR THE FEMINIST MAJORITY**, Dolores Huerta, and NOW president Patricia Ireland. A previous attempt to develop a feminist political party was the **NATIONAL WOMAN'S PARTY**, founded by Alice **PAUL** in 1916, which gained strength during 1918 and 1919, in the final stages of the campaign for **WOMAN SUFFRAGE**, but dwindled to a small militant group in the early 1920s.

Twenty Years at Hull House: See Jane **ADDAMS**.

$\mathscr{U}$

ulcers, a type of digestive disorder (see DIGESTIVE SYSTEM).

ultrasound, a type of medical test designed to produce an image of internal organs, and also of a FETUS, on a special screen. High-frequency sound waves are emitted as a special device called a *transducer* is passed over the "target" portion of the body, over which a gel has been rubbed, to improve penetration of the sound waves, which bounce off internal tissues and organs, producing echoes of various distinctive strength and timing. Data from the varying echoes are used by a computer to form instantly a moving picture, called a *sonogram,* on a special television screen. The picture is somewhat muddy and unclear—though many MOTHERS and FATHERS have delighted in viewing a fetus move in the womb (see below)—but to the experienced eye it can be extremely useful, in addition to viewing a fetus, for showing the size of internal organs and detecting everything from tumors, BLOOD clots, detached retinas (see EYES), gallstones (see GALLBLAD-DER), and kidney stones to arteriosclerosis, aneurysms, and heart abnormalities (see HEART AND CIRCULATORY SYSTEM), in heart-oriented procedures called *echocardiography.*

Special wand-shaped ultrasound probes have been developed for use in the rectum and VAGINA, allowing physicians to watch for release of eggs (see OVUM) for use in *IN VITRO* FERTILIZATION. And miniature probes in thin, flexible tubing are used to study the URINARY TRACT and gastrointestinal tract (see DIGESTIVE SYS-TEM), showing abnormalities in those systems, and can even be threaded into ar-teries. Doppler ultrasound, involving changes in pitch as well as sound, is used to trace blood flow and heartbeat, to detect fetal heartbeats, or even to show whether a body is beginning to reject a transplanted organ. Ultrasound is not useful for imaging the lungs or SKELETAL SYSTEM, and the image quality can be ad-versely affected by excess fat or large scars.

When used during a woman's PREGNANCY, ultrasound can provide obstetri-cians with some enormously useful information:

- the size and number of the fetuses in the UTERUS, as well as a quite accurate indication of age from the overall length, or the thigh-bone length and head circumference.
- the presence of some types of BIRTH DEFECTS, such as anencephaly (absence of a brain) or polydactyly (excess fingers or toes).
- the position of the fetus and PLACENTA, especially important in cases of breech

birth (see FETAL PRESENTATION; CHILDBIRTH); it will indicate if prebirth intervention is necessary for the health of mother or fetus.

- fetal movement, including breathing and heartbeat.
- the amount of amniotic fluid in the uterus, important in the assessment of fetal health.

Ultrasound is also used during numerous other medical tests and procedures common among women, including AMNIOCENTESIS, CHORIONIC VILLUS SAMPLING, CORDOCENTESUS, FETAL SURGERY, FETOSCOPY, *in vitro* fertilization, TUBAL LIGATION, and LAPAROSCOPY in general. It can also help physicians identify possible structural causes of INFERTILITY.

Ultrasound has become an enormously popular medical tool, because little or no discomfort is involved, apart from the need for women to have a full bladder during examinations of the uterus. Unlike X-rays, it can distinguish lumps that are probably benign, fluid-filled CYSTS from solid, possibly malignant tumors; and it can indicate penetration of cancerous tumors into nearby organs and systems. Ultrasound is also considered generally safe. Ultrasound waves can generate heat, microscopic bubbles, and vibrations, but these have not been shown to cause harm to humans; most studies also indicate that ultrasound is not harmful to the fetus, either. For maximum safety, however, the FOOD AND DRUG ADMINISTRATION (FDA) recommends that ultrasound be used *not* solely to get a picture of the fetus or determine its sex, but only for specific medical reasons, such as family history of birth defects, unexplained vaginal bleeding, or indications that the fetus is not growing properly.

Ultrasound waves are also used in some kinds of treatment, many of them experimental, including for glaucoma, to speed the healing of bone fractures, to ease the pain and stiffness of ARTHRITIS and other inflammatory disorders, some dental procedures, and experimental CANCER therapies. Ultrasound therapies carry somewhat greater risks, because they use larger doses of sound waves and so can destroy tissue. To prevent birth defects, the FDA recommends that ultrasound therapy not be delivered to any organs in the male or female REPRODUCTIVE SYSTEM. (See also PRENATAL TESTS; also GENETIC INHERITANCE AND BIRTH DEFECTS HELP, INFORMATION, AND ACTION GUIDE on page 314.)

umbilical cord, the long tube that connects a developing FETUS and the nourishing PLACENTA during PREGNANCY, normally developing by about the fifth week after FERTILIZATION. Through two arteries and one vein, it supplies oxygen and nutrients to the fetus and removes fetal waste products. If the cord has only one artery, the fetus may get insufficient oxygen, possibly leading to BIRTH DEFECTS.

The cord, 1.5–2 feet in length, often wraps around the fetus, which can cause problems, especially if it circles around the neck. If that occurs during DELIVERY, it can often be untwined. If the long cord slips down through the mother's CERVIX during delivery, a condition called *prolapse*, the flow of oxygen-rich BLOOD to the baby may be cut off; to prevent damage to the baby, an emergency CESAREAN SECTION may be performed, or forceps may be used (see DELIVERY). Both problems are more common in cases of abnormal FETAL PRESENTATION.

After delivery the baby begins to rely on its own heart and lungs for oxygen and blood circulation (see HEART AND CIRCULATORY SYSTEM; RESPIRATORY SYSTEM). The umbilical cord is clamped and cut off; the stump later falls off, leaving behind the *navel, umbilicus,* or *belly button.* (See PREGNANCY; CHILDBIRTH.)

UNIFEM, acronym for UNITED NATIONS DEVELOPMENT FUND FOR WOMEN.

unisex rates: See INSURANCE AND PENSION EQUITY.

United Nations Development Fund for Women (UNIFEM)

(304 East 45th Street, 6th Floor, New York, NY 10017; 212-906-6400; Sharon Capeling-Alakija, director), an organization founded in 1976 as the Voluntary Fund for the United Nations Decade for Women, becoming UNIFEM in 1985. Seeking to be a "catalyst for economic and social advancement in the developing world," it provides direct support for women's projects and promotes "the inclusion of women in the decision-making processes of mainstream development programs," often working with government planning bodies, women's affairs bureaus, and women's organizations at the national and grass-roots levels, including National Committees for UNIFEM. In addition to its Women, Environment, Development (WED) program, it worked with several other United Nations branches to produce the report *The World's Women: Trends and Statistics 1970–1990.*

UNIFEM also sponsors the Women, Ink. project, managed by the INTERNATIONAL WOMEN'S TRIBUNE CENTRE **(IWTC),** which publishes resource materials on DEVELOPMENT AND WOMEN'S RIGHTS, such as *Freedom from Violence: Women's Strategies from Around the World, Legal Literacy: A Tool for Women's Empowerment, Empowerment and the Law: Strategies of Third World Women, Women, Law and Development: Action for Change, Tools for Community Participation, Women Working Together for Personal, Economic, and Community Development, Navamaga: Training Activities for Group Building, Health, and Income Generation, Learning to Teach, Women and World Development: An Education and Action Handbook,* and handbooks on business skills for "microenterprises."

unmarried status, the legal status of someone who has never been married; a term also sometimes applied to someone who has been married but is now either divorced or widowed. (See SINGLE WOMAN; WIDOW; DIVORCE.)

urinary tract, the system by which the body extracts and disposes of its liquid waste products and maintains the proper chemical balance in the body. Urinary problems are common among women.

The system consists of the kidneys—a pair of organs shaped like the kidney beans named for them—in the back above the waistline, on either side of the spinal column; two long tubes called *ureters,* which connect the kidneys with the *bladder,* a sac in the lower abdomen; and a single tube called the *urethra* through which liquids are emptied to the outside, from an opening just above the VAGINA.

With each beat of the heart, one-quarter of the body's BLOOD is pumped directly to the kidneys. There it is pushed through the fine *mesangial membrane* into minute structures called *nephrons,* of which each kidney has about one million. These consist of clusters of tiny blood vessels called *glomeruli* that filter out relatively large particles such as blood cells and proteins and send the rest through other filtering structures called *tubules.* These help regulate the body's delicate chemical balance by selecting out certain chemicals and some water—depending on the blood's chemistry at the time—and returning them to the system. The unwanted (and sometimes toxic) substances and excess water are sent down the ureters and stored until the bladder is full and the person decides to empty it.

In the process, the kidneys regulate the amounts of key substances in the body, such as calcium, sodium, potassium, and the like, to ensure that the body has the nutrients it requires for normal function, but not so much of any substance as to be harmful (see KEY VITAMINS AND MINERALS on page 502). They also produce HORMONES that help regulate blood pressure and red blood cell count.

By far the most common urinary problem among women is *urinary tract infection (UTI),* partly because the urethra is so short and infectious organisms have a relatively short distance to the bladder. In the healthy body, urine is sterile, containing fluid, salts, and other waste products, but not microorganisms. However, bacteria from the DIGESTIVE SYSTEM—often spread inadvertently from the anus nearby—can readily colonize the opening to the urethra and spread upward. Similarly, CHLAMYDIA and MYCOPLASMAS, both microorganisms causing SEXUALLY TRANSMITTED DISEASES, can spread from the nearby vaginal opening.

Infection limited to the urethra is called *urethritis;* if infectious organisms travel to the bladder, it is called *cystitis.* Common symptoms of such infections are a frequent urge to urinate, though often only small amounts are passed; a burning, even painful feeling during urination; an uncomfortable pressure above the pubic bone; and general fatigue. Pregnant women are particularly susceptible to UTIs, because various changes in the body—including pressure on the urinary tract causing retention of small amounts of stagnant urine, and relaxing of the urethral muscles in response to HORMONES—increase the risk of urinary infections. UTIs are also common after MENOPAUSE, prolapse of the UTERUS, and sometimes with the wearing of sanitary napkins during MENSTRUATION, though use of tampons may also irritate the area.

The infection is easily diagnosed by testing a sample of urine for signs of pus, bacteria, or other microorganisms. The sample must be a "clean catch," meaning that the genital area has been washed beforehand and some urine is released before the sample is taken, to avoid contamination by bacteria from the external genitals. *Chlamydia* and *mycoplasmas* require special cultures for detection. UTIs are treated with antibacterial drugs of various kinds, depending on the source of infection and the patient's medical history. It is important to take the full course of treatment, even after symptoms disappear, to be sure the infection is cleared up, as in most cases it is. Heating pads and warm baths may help ease discomfort. Many doctors also recommend drinking plenty of water—good preventive advice, also, since it helps flush out the system—or cranberry juice, which makes urine more acidic and so inhibits bacteria growth; they also suggest avoiding possible irritants such as coffee, alcohol, and spicy foods. (See TIPS FOR PREVENTING URINARY TRACT INFECTIONS on page 732.)

However, if the infection is not diagnosed promptly or is unresponsive to treatment, the microorganisms can travel up the ureters to the kidneys, causing *pyelonephritis*. Symptoms of this more serious condition include milky, cloudy, or reddish (from blood) urine; pain in the back or side below the ribs; nausea and vomiting; and high fever. Untreated pyelonephritis can lead to further serious illnesses, including blood poisoning *(septicemia)*, scarring damage of the kidneys, and eventually kidney failure. If the kidneys fail, a *dialysis* machine must be used to temporarily take over the kidney's functions, if the person is to survive.

When kidney infection is suspected, or when a woman has persistent urinary infections, a doctor may order an *intravenous pyelogram* (IVP), an X-ray picture of the kidneys, ureters, and bladder, taken after the patient has been injected with an opaque dye; or a *cystoscopy*, a small hollow tube with lenses and a light, through which the doctor can examine the inside of the bladder.

Cystitis and urethritis—which mean simply "inflammation of the bladder and urethra"—can also result from pounding on or bruising of the area. They may result, for example, from strenuous SEXUAL INTERCOURSE (as in some cases of what has been called *honeymoon cystitis*), RAPE, beatings (see BATTERED WOMEN), and even from wearing too tight jeans or panty hose. Cystitis can also result from an overuse of or sensitivity to vaginal douches (see DOUCHING), vaginal deodorants, and antiseptic in the bathwater.

Another common problem among women is involuntary release of urine, or *incontinence*. Though once "unmentionable," this is now understood to be a widespread problem among women of all ages but especially among women who have borne children and older women. A ring of muscle, or *sphincter* (see MUSCULAR SYSTEM), normally tightens to block the passage of urine from the bladder into the urethra, and another operates at the external end of the urethra. In some circumstances, as when a woman laughs, coughs deeply, or picks up something heavy, and during some strenuous athletic activity, one or both of these muscles relaxes, allowing urine to escape. Incontinence may also result when the muscles have been overly stretched or lost some elasticity, as during PREGNANCY, because of OBESITY, with displacement of pelvic organs (as with a prolapsed UTERUS), or with age, especially after menopause. Many women can regain much of their lost bladder control by doing regular pelvic floor EXERCISES to strengthen those muscles (see EXERCISES DURING AND AFTER PREGNANCY on page 561), or by changing their diet to eliminate irritants (see above); medications also work for many people.

CANCER in the kidneys and urinary tract are also a substantial concern. Cancer of the bladder and of kidneys are the ninth and eleventh most common cancers among women. Bladder cancer in particular is strongly associated with SMOKING, believed to be responsible for approximately 37 percent of the bladder cancer deaths among women, according to the American Cancer Society, though it is significantly more common among men. Higher risk of bladder cancer is also associated with living in urban areas and working with dyes, rubber, or leather. (See URINARY PROBLEMS HELP, INFORMATION, AND ACTION GUIDE, below.)

URINARY PROBLEMS

Help, Information, and Action Guide

Organizations

▶ NATIONAL WOMEN'S HEALTH NETWORK (NWHN) (202-347-1140). Operates the **Women's Health Information Service.** Publishes the information packets *Urinary Tract Infections (UTIs)* and *Interstitial Cystitis.*

▶ NATIONAL INSTITUTE OF DIABETES, DIGESTIVE AND KIDNEY DISEASES (NIDDK) (301-496-3583). Operates the **National Kidney and Urologic Disease Information Clearinghouse (NKUDIC)** (301-468-6345). Distributes *Understanding Urinary Tract Infections* and *When Your Kidneys Fail ... A Handbook for Patients and Their Families*, 2nd ed.

▶ HIP (Help for Incontinent People) (P.O. Box 544, Union, SC 29379; 803-579-7900; Katherine F. Jeter, executive director), an organization that focuses on problems of people with loss of bladder or bowel control. It gathers and disseminates information on treatment approaches, responds personally to questions, provides referrals, and publishes various materials, including the quarterly newsletter *HIP Report, Resource Guide of Continence Products and Services*, a directory of incontinence specialists, and various audio and visual programs and exercises to help build control.

▶ Simon Foundation for Continence (P.O. Box 835-S, Wilmette, IL 60091; 800-23-SIMON [237-4666] for patient information or 708-864-3913 for professional information; Cheryle B. Gartley, president), an organization that focuses on continence awareness, research, and education to teach people that "incontinence can be cured, treated, or managed." It publishes the quarterly newsletter *The Informer*, the book *Managing Incontinence: A Guide to Living with Loss of Bladder Control: Products and Devices • Emotional Adjustment • Sexuality • Coping Through Humor • Personal Experiences • Medical Information*, and the videotape series *Understanding and Treating Incontinence*; and it distributes the brochure *Incontinence: Everything You Wanted to Know but Were Afraid to Ask* (from **Alliance for Aging Research,** 2021 K Street NW, Suite 305, Washington, DC 20006; 202-293-2856).

▶ American Kidney Fund (AKF) (301-881-3052 or 800-638-8299 [U.S. except MD] or 800-492-8361 [MD only]). Publishes the pamphlets *Facts*

About Kidney Diseases and Their Treatment, Dialysis Patient, and *Give a Kidney.*

▶ **National Kidney Foundation (NKF)** (30 East 33rd Street, Suite 1100, New York, NY 10016; John Davis, executive director), an organization concerned with kidney disease. It provides information and makes referrals, offers patient services, operates an organ donor program, and publishes various materials including a quarterly newsletter, a medical journal, and pamphlets such as *What Everyone Should Know About Kidneys, How Can Urinary Tract Obstructions Affect You?, Transplantation, Dialysis,* and *If You Needed a Kidney or Other Vital Organ to Live, Would You Be Able to Get One?*

Other resources

Kidney Disorders. Martha Miller. Chelsea House, 1992.

Urinary Incontinence and How to Overcome It. Gordon Press, 1991.

The Kidney Patient's Book: New Treatment, New Hope. Timothy P. Ahlstrom. Great Issues Press, 1991.

Resource Guide of Continence Products and Services. Revisionist Press, 1991.

Overcoming Bladder Disorders: Compassionate, Authoritative Medical and Self-Help Solutions for Incontinence, Cystitis, Interstitial Cystitis, Prostate Problems, Bladder Cancer. Rebecca Chalker and Kristene E. Whitmore. HarperCollins, 1990.

Urine Testing, rev. ed. Do It Now, 1990.

Waking Up Dry: How to End Bedwetting Forever. Martin B. Scharf. Writer's Digest Books, 1986.

(See also **WOMEN'S HEALTH HELP, INFORMATION, AND ACTION GUIDE** on page 334.)

TIPS FOR PREVENTING URINARY TRACT INFECTIONS

- Drink plenty of water every day. Some doctors suggest drinking cranberry juice, which in large amounts inhibits the growth of some bacteria by acidifying the urine.
- Don't put off urinating when you feel the need.

- Wipe from front to back to prevent bacteria around the anus from entering the vagina or urethra.
- Cleanse the genital area before sexual intercourse.
- Empty the bladder shortly before and after sexual intercourse.
- Avoid using feminine hygiene sprays and scented douches.
- Wear loose-fitting underclothes of breathable materials such as cotton, rather than moisture-retaining synthetic materials or tight-fitting jeans or panty hose.

Source: Adapted from *Understanding Urinary Tract Infections*, National Institute of Diabetes & Digestive & Kidney Diseases (NIDDK), 1988.

uterine cancer, CANCER affecting the endometrium (the lining of the UTERUS) and the CERVIX, the neck of the uterus. It is one of the most common cancers among women—the fourth most common in the United States—though much less deadly than in the past in regions where women have regular medical examinations and a periodic PAP SMEAR to detect cancerous or, better yet, precancerous tissue. In fact, the American Cancer Society notes that the death rate for uterine and cervical cancer has declined more than 70 percent over the last four decades in the United States.

Early detection is the key. If cervical cancer is detected in the extremely localized *carcinoma in situ* stage (see CANCER), the five-year survival rate is almost 100 percent; the survival rate for early stages of cervical cancer in general is 88 percent, while the rate for all cervical cancer patients is 66 percent. The comparable rates for endometrial cancer are 100, 93, and 83 percent.

If a Pap smear indicates any abnormal cells, the next step is for the doctor to take a *biopsy* (sample) of tissue for more thorough analysis. Using a special low-power microscope called a *colposcope* to view cervical tissue, the doctor can pinpoint questionable areas. If these are on the surface or are only mildly questionable, the doctor may take a small *punch biopsy*, often in an office or clinic. If the area extends out of sight, the doctor will take a larger cone-shaped sample, in what is called a *cone biopsy* or *conization*. Lasers are sometimes used to destroy abnormal tissue.

To obtain samples of endometrial tissue, doctors may employ *vacuum aspiration* (as in an early ABORTION), using suction to remove a sample of tissue, in an office or clinic; or *curettage*, using a small scraper *(curette)* inserted through the cervical canal to remove tissue samples, often an outpatient procedure (see D&C). The Pap test is most effective at detecting cervical cancer, less so at detecting endometrial cancer. As a result, doctors often take a biopsy of endometrial tissue from women who are at high risk for endometrial cancer, even when Pap tests are normal.

Women most at risk for cervical cancer include those who become sexually active when quite young; have multiple sex partners; smoke cigarettes (see SMOK-ING); are daughters of mothers who took the drug DES during PREGNANCY; or have some kinds of SEXUALLY TRANSMITTED DISEASES, such as HERPES or GENITAL WARTS. Women at special risk for endometrial cancer are those with a history of INFER-TILITY, OBESITY, FIBROIDS, lack of OVULATION, or prolonged treatment with ESTRO-GEN (see ESTROGEN REPLACEMENT THERAPY).

The main warning signs of uterine or cervical cancer are any abnormal bleeding, as between menstrual periods (see MENSTRUATION) or after MENOPAUSE, or any unusual vaginal discharge. Because these signs are so general, if a woman is not tested regularly, the cancer may not be diagnosed until it has spread to other areas, including the VAGINA, VULVA, bladder, and rectum, and is far harder to treat.

Precancerous endometrial conditions are sometimes treated with the hor-mone PROGESTERONE. Cervical cancer *in situ* can be destroyed by *cryotherapy* (ex-treme cold), *electrocoagulation* (burning of affected tissues with electric current), *laser* (use of high-intensity light beams), or local surgery, including *conization* (removal of only part of the cervix; see above). With these treatments a woman is still able to bear children, if she so desires. Beyond that, the main treatment is surgical removal of cervix and uterus (see HYSTERECTOMY), radiation, or both.

For more help, information, and action

▶ **National Cancer Institute (NCI)** (Cancer Information Service 800-4-CANCER [422-6237]). Publishes *What You Need to Know About Cancer of the Uterus.* (See CANCER.)

▶ NATIONAL WOMEN'S HEALTH NETWORK (NWHN) (202-347-1140). Operates the **Women's Health Information Service.** Publishes the information packet *Cer-vical Cancer/Pap Smears.*

(See also CANCER; UTERUS; CERVIX; also WOMEN'S HEALTH HELP, INFORMATION, AND ACTION GUIDE on page 334.)

uterus, a hollow, muscular organ in a woman's lower abdomen; also called the *womb.* Situated above and behind the bladder, the uterus is shaped roughly like an upside-down pear and is a little larger than a pear even in an adult woman who has borne no children. The main portion of the uterus is called the *corpus;* connecting to it near the top on either side are the two FALLOPIAN TUBES that lead from the OVARIES. At the bottom is a narrow neck called the CERVIX, which leads into the VAGINA. (For an illustration, see THE FEMALE REPRODUCTIVE SYSTEM on page 621.)

The main function of the uterus is to provide a place for a FETUS to grow. Even if a woman never becomes pregnant, every month from the beginning of MENSTRUATION to MENOPAUSE the uterus prepares itself for that function. Its walls are thick to provide both protection and nourishment; most of that thickness is muscular tissue called *myometrium,* all richly supplied with blood vessels and nerves. On the outside, the uterus is lined by the *peritoneum* (tissue that lines the whole abdominal-pelvic area); on the inside is a special lining called the *endometrium.*

During the monthly reproductive cycle (see MENSTRUATION), the endometrium thickens in response to various HORMONES, especially ESTROGEN and PROGESTERONE. If no egg is fertilized, other hormones will trigger the uterus to contract and expel the unused egg and endometrial lining, in the menstrual period. But if an egg *is* fertilized, it will—if all goes normally—pass from the fallopian tube into the uterus, where it will become *implanted* in the uterus. There it will grow for approximately thirty-eight to forty-two weeks, with the uterus expanding to accommodate the fetus. Then, apparently triggered by the hormone called OXYTOCIN, the uterine muscles begin an involuntary series of regular contractions, called LABOR, which push the baby down through the widened cervix and vagina into independent life. After birth the uterus shrinks, though never to as small as before pregnancy, until after menopause.

Uterine muscles also play a role in the pleasurable release of sexual tension called ORGASM. In addition, the uterus also secretes some hormones that can have beneficial health effects, perhaps helping to decrease risk of heart attack (see HEART AND CIRCULATORY SYSTEM).

Though a sturdy workhorse of an organ, the uterus is subject to a number of problems, among them

▶ *tipped* or *retroverted uterus,* in which the uterus is oriented slightly backward. The uterus is anchored only at the cervix; the rest of the uterus is free to move, though held generally in place by various ligaments and muscles, notably the *pelvic floor muscles.* In newborn girls the uterus is usually tipped backward; by sexual maturity the uterus has tipped forward at an angle to the vagina in most women. In 25–30 percent, however, the uterus stays tipped backward. Sometimes it tips backward after a pregnancy, as supporting ligaments are stretched; when scar tissue or adhesions have formed after surgery or infections such as PELVIC INFLAMMATORY DISEASE or SEXUALLY TRANSMITTED DISEASES; or in cases of FIBROIDS (benign uterine growths), or ENDOMETRIOSIS, overgrowth of the endometrium. Though some women have no symptoms with a tipped uterus, others have a generalized backache and pain during vaginal SEXUAL INTERCOURSE. They also may have more difficulty with CONCEPTION and are often advised to try a variety of positions for intercourse. A special device called a *pessary* (similar to a DIAPHRAGM) may be inserted into the vagina to help hold the uterus in a better position. Surgery to "fix" the uterus in position is seldom performed today.

▶ *structural abnormalities,* a wide variety of anomalies, including partitions and sometimes even a double uterus and cervix. Such problems are rare and generally present from birth but can make pregnancy and delivery difficult or impossible.

▶ *endometritis,* inflammation of the uterine lining, often with abdominal pain and a yellowish discharge. This may result from PELVIC INFLAMMATORY DISEASE (PID), including infection following an ABORTION or irritation from an INTRAUTERINE DEVICE (IUD). It is generally treated with antibiotics.

▶ *cancer,* which can affect both the endometrium and cervix. This is a common kind of cancer in women, but testing and early diagnosis have led to a significant decline in death from these cancers. (See UTERINE CANCER.)

▶ *endometrial problems,* disorders involving abnormal growth of the endometrium, most notably ENDOMETRIOSIS, growth of endometrial tissue outside the uterus; small benign growths called *polyps;* and *endometrial hyperplasia,* abnormal thickening of the endometrial lining, which can cause heavy bleeding. To check for conditions affecting the cervix and the interior of the uterus, doctors often perform a minor operation called a D&C *(dilatation and curettage),* or a HYSTEROSCOPY. If all or part of the uterus must be removed, they will perform a HYSTERECTOMY—an operation about which much controversy swirls. (See WOMEN'S HEALTH HELP, INFORMATION, AND ACTION GUIDE on page 334.)

vacuum extraction, a procedure that uses suction to remove the contents of the UTERUS; it can be used in cases of ABORTION and may also be used to aid in CHILDBIRTH.

vagina, the muscular passageway that forms a connection between a woman's external GENITALS and her other internal reproductive organs. More specifically, the vagina is the canal between the VULVA and the CERVIX, itself the neck of the UTERUS. During CHILDBIRTH the cervix and vagina both widen to form the *birth canal* for the baby's DELIVERY. During vaginal SEXUAL INTERCOURSE, it houses the PENIS and receives the man's SPERM, which make their way through the cervix and uterus to the FALLOPIAN TUBES, where FERTILIZATION normally takes place. During MENSTRUATION the vagina provides an outlet for menstrual flow. In some kinds of HYSTERECTOMY the uterus is removed through the vagina.

About four inches long in a mature woman, the vagina has ridged muscular walls that, when relaxed, are collapsed on each other. The opening, called the *introitus*, is partly covered by a membrane called the HYMEN, until it is first penetrated, as in SEXUAL INTERCOURSE or use of a tampon; it is in this area that nerves are most concentrated. Richly supplied with BLOOD vessels, the vaginal walls fill with blood during sexual arousal and widen apart for intercourse. Near the introitus is a *sphincter* muscle, which contracts during ORGASM and also serves to hold in tampons. At least some women have a highly sensitive G SPOT inside the vagina, a subject under some debate.

A mucous membrane covers the vaginal walls and keeps the region moist and clean, as old cells are shed and replaced with new ones. The mucus normally varies from thin and transparent to opaque and jellylike, changes monitored in some forms of BIRTH CONTROL (see NATURAL FAMILY PLANNING); it is thick and white during pregnancy. The amount of mucus increases during sexual intercourse, to lubricate the vagina, and may vary if the woman is taking BIRTH CONTROL PILLS or antibiotics, has DIABETES, or is under stress. A greenish, yellowish, or bad-smelling discharge; a thick white (except during pregnancy) discharge; or any noticeable increase in normal vaginal secretions—especially if accompanied by any itching, burning, low back pain, or abdominal pain—may be a sign of infection, such as various SEXUALLY TRANSMITTED DISEASES, including some form of PELVIC INFLAMMATORY DISEASE, or a YEAST INFECTION, and should be checked medically. Leaving a tampon (see MENSTRUATION) or DIAPHRAGM in the body too long can promote growth of infection, notably TOXIC SHOCK SYNDROME. A brownish or blood-spotted discharge may indicate a problem with the CERVIX and should also be checked. The vagina has a slightly acidic environment, which helps fight disease-causing organisms. Acid also makes the vagina inhospitable to sperm; in excess, this can lead to INFERTILITY, as can some infections.

Women have two main kinds of vaginal problems:

▶ **vaginitis,** inflammation of the vagina. Often this is caused by one of the types of infections noted above and is accompanied by a discharge, itching, burning, sores, and the like. Sometimes these are caused by changes in the woman's body introduced by medications, including a reaction to SPERMICIDES; an illness such as DIABETES; DOUCHING, including a reaction to chemicals; and a reaction to soaps or bath oils. But often the infection has spread to the vagina from the outside, as in BACTERIAL VAGINOSIS. Women can partly protect themselves from infection by using devices such as CONDOMS and VAGINAL POUCHES. (See SEXUALLY TRANSMITTED DISEASES. For preventive advice, see WHAT YOU CAN DO TO AVOID STDS on page 660; CONDOMS: WHAT WOMEN NEED TO KNOW on page 188; and TIPS FOR PREVENTING URINARY TRACT INFECTIONS on page 732.)

Vaginitis can also result when the mucous membrane lining the vagina becomes thin, dry, and readily inflamed. This is very common among women near and after MENOPAUSE, as the body dries out with the reduction in ESTROGEN, a condition called *atrophic vaginitis.* Women with some kinds of autoimmune disorders (see IMMUNE SYSTEM) also are troubled with dryness in the vagina and elsewhere in the body. In some women, ESTROGEN REPLACEMENT THERAPY (ERT) can easily ease the problem. Where ERT is not indicated, as when a woman has FIBROIDS, the doctor may recommend use of a lubricant; women should be sure that it is sterile and water-soluble, however, so that it will neither introduce infection nor damage protective devices such as a CONDOM, DIAPHRAGM, and VAGINAL POUCH.

▶ **vaginismus,** involuntary spasms of muscles in and around the vagina, sometimes also causing the legs to straighten and come tightly together. This prevents entry, or makes it extremely difficult and painful, whether by a man's PENIS, a tampon (see MENSTRUATION), or a *speculum* used in a GYNECOLOGICAL EXAMINATION. In extreme cases sexual intercourse is impossible and physical examination can be conducted only under ANESTHESIA.

Vaginismus is generally associated with nervousness, tension, guilt, and fear. In an unknown number of cases, it is linked with a past trauma, such as INCEST, child molestation (see CHILD ABUSE AND NEGLECT), or RAPE. Many times it results when a woman has had little or no sex education and has been taught to react to sex with fear, guilt, disgust, or other negative feelings. Some amount of vaginismus is common in the first few experiences with intercourse; if those were painful, especially if the partners were ill suited and the penetration was rough, fear of more pain can set up a cycle of increasing tension.

A woman experiencing vaginismus should first consult her gynecologist, to check for any possible anatomical or physiological abnormalities and also for signs of any conditions that might cause pain, such as various kinds of *vagi-*

V

nitis, which might be treated. If these have been ruled out, a woman may then be referred to a sex therapist.

Often therapy starts with some basic education about the normal workings of the sex organs. More specific treatment involves learning how to alternately relax and tighten her vaginal muscles and learning to introduce dilators into the vagina and removing them. The dilators are graded in size, and over several sessions the woman will learn to relax her muscles so she can introduce increasingly larger-size dilators, until she reaches the size of an erect penis. Sometimes treatment will also start with, or at least include, the women introducing her own fingertip and then a whole finger into her vagina, as part of familiarizing herself with her own GENITALS.

On rare occasions a woman has no vagina, or no opening to her vagina, a condition called *vaginal atresia,* or the hymen may have no opening (see HYMEN). When other internal reproductive organs are functioning normally, this may mean that menstrual fluid has no outlet, and the accumulation may eventually become painful. A vaginal opening can be surgically created for such women. Also rare is CANCER of the vagina. (See also SEXUAL INTERCOURSE; also SEX AND SEXUALITY HELP, INFORMATION, AND ACTION GUIDE on page 665; WOMEN'S HEALTH HELP, INFORMATION, AND ACTION GUIDE on page 334.)

vaginal pouch, a soft, loose-fitting, seven-inch-long, prelubricated polyurethane sheath designed to fit inside a woman's VAGINA to act as a physical barrier against a man's SPERM and other fluids. Sometimes called a *female condom,* it is a form of BIRTH CONTROL that combines some aspects of the traditional male CONDOM and the DIAPHRAGM.

Attached to the sheath are two flexible polyurethane rings; the one inside the closed end of the sheath fits over the CERVIX like a diaphragm, while the outer ring at the open end lies outside the body, anchoring the sheath in place over the LABIA. Like the condom, the vaginal pouch can be bought over-the-counter (in the United States approved by the FOOD AND DRUG ADMINISTRATION only in 1993), requires no special fitting or prescription, is easy to use, is disposable, and can be used with a SPERMICIDE. Also like a condom, it provides a barrier against SEXUALLY TRANSMITTED DISEASES, although no birth control device can offer 100 percent protection against AIDS. In Europe the pouch is marketed under the name Femidom; in the United States and Canada, as Reality.

The main advantages of the vaginal pouch are that the woman is in control of her own birth control and sexual health; it is also less disruptive of sexual activity than a condom, since it can be put into place before arousal. Because it is both looser and made of thinner material, many couples report more satisfaction than with a condom. Clinical trials show that the pouch is as effective as the diaphragm or SPONGE in preventing PREGNANCY, with an effectiveness rate of about 85 percent, making it also more effective than condoms. It also seems to be more effective than condoms in preventing AIDS and other sexually transmitted diseases, since pouches are significantly less likely to tear, break, or slip during use, with a tear rate of 1 percent (as opposed to 1–14 percent for condoms), and a rate of exposure to SEMEN through either breakage or slippage of 3 percent (as compared with 11 percent for condoms). Nor does the pouch (so far) seem associated with allergic reactions (see ALLERGIES) or increased risk of vaginal or URI-NARY TRACT infections (see VAGINA). Some, however, find the device cumbersome or dislike the appearance of the ring outside the vagina. As with condoms and diaphragms, women should be careful of sharp nails and rings during handling or insertion and should use only water-based lubricants, if additional lubrication is desired, since petroleum-based lubricants can damage the material.

Under development are other variations on this theme. The *Woman's Choice Female Condomme* is a heavier latex pouch, with an umbrella-like cap, inserted with a plastic applicator. The *Unisex Condom Garment,* or *Bikini Condom,* is a pair of polyurethane bikini-style pants with an attached sheath, which works as either a condom or vaginal pouch, depending on whether the person wearing it is a man or a woman. (See BIRTH CONTROL AND FAMILY PLANNING HELP, INFORMATION, AND ACTION GUIDE on page 81.)

varicose veins, a condition in which BLOOD flowing through the body (see HEART AND CIRCULATORY SYSTEM) collects in the veins, often because of failure of tiny one-way doors called *valves,* which are supposed to prevent backflow. The result is bluish distended veins that appear through the SKIN surface, especially of the legs (though hemorrhoids result from a similar problem). The tendency toward varicose veins seems to be inherited (see GENETIC INHERITANCE). They are more common among women than men, especially those who are overweight (see OBESITY) or who spend a lot of time standing in one place. Varicose veins often develop during PREGNANCY but may disappear with weight loss and EXERCISE. Warning symptoms include swollen ankles, muscles cramps during the night, and generalized soreness in the legs.

Varicose veins are best treated preventively and in early stages, since they can become progressively worse and in serious cases can ulcerate and hemorrhage. The main therapy for mild cases is to raise the feet whenever possible; sit, rather than stand, when possible; move around as much as possible, if standing is necessary; and avoid blockage of circulation in the legs, as from crossing the legs or constricting elastic tops or bottoms on socks, stockings, girdles, or garters. Leg exercises are also helpful, as well as walking, swimming, and bicycling. Many women who are on their feet a lot wear elasticized support stockings, to limit distension of the veins. In more severe cases medications may be injected into the veins to cause them to harden, rerouting circulation to healthier veins. Alternatively, a surgical operation may be performed to tie off or remove some of the veins. (See HEART AND CIRCULATORY SYSTEM; also WOMEN'S HEALTH HELP, INFORMATION, AND ACTION GUIDE on page 334.)

vas deferens, tubes through which SPERM pass before EJACULATION during ORGASM (see REPRODUCTIVE SYSTEM). These are the tubes that are cut in the form of male STERILIZATION called *vasectomy.*

venereal diseases (VD), a somewhat outdated term for some kinds of SEX-UALLY TRANSMITTED DISEASES, notably SYPHILIS and GONORRHEA.

venereal warts, an alternative name for GENITAL WARTS.

vestibule, the boat-shaped area that contains the female external GENITALS—that is, the VULVA, including the LABIA, the CLITORIS, the opening to the VAGINA, BARTHOLIN'S GLANDS, and SKENE'S GLANDS. Lining the vestibule is mucous membrane, and lying underneath are clusters of veins. When a woman is sexually aroused, these veins fill with blood, becoming congested and firm to the touch.

Vindication of the Rights of Women, A: See Mary WOLLSTONECRAFT.

virginity, the state of a person, female or male, who has never had SEXUAL INTERCOURSE. Traditionally a woman was supposed to remain a virgin until married, though the number of premarital pregnancies throughout history has shown that many were not. In more recent decades, and especially since the introduction of BIRTH CONTROL PILLS, sex among unmarried women has become openly far more common. The related term CHASTITY may refer to a virgin or to a married woman of sexual fidelity and virtue.

The term *virgnity* can be interpreted very loosely or narrowly, depending on the time and the place. To some, a woman may participate in a wide range of sexual activity (see SEXUAL INTERCOURSE), but if her vagina has not been penetrated, she is still technically a virgin. In other places, and especially in Islamic countries, the woman must be absolutely untouched sexually for her to be regarded as a virgin. To assure this, the traditional cultural norm in some regions is even to remove from some women the capacity for sexual pleasure (see FEMALE CIRCUMCISION). On the WEDDING night, cloth showing blood from the breaking of the hymen is often brandished aloft before waiting friends and family, as proof of the husband's prowess and the wife's virginity.

Virgin Mary, the mother of Jesus, a central figure in the New Testament and in several Christian faiths. She has been variously viewed by feminist theoreticians and theologians. For some she is an archetypically powerless figure in a patriarchal landscape (see PATRIARCHY). For others she reflects the image of an earlier time, when women were supposedly treated with far more respect than in biblical times. And for others, perhaps most notably Catholic-turned-spiritual-feminist Mary DALY, she is the embodiment of an earlier Goddess, her Christian status a revival or survival of an earlier period of primacy as deity (see GODDESS WORSHIP; MATRIARCHY; RELIGION AND WOMEN'S RIGHTS; SPIRITUAL FEMINISM.)

V

visitation rights, the legal right of a parent not living in the FAMILY home to see his or her children on some basis agreed upon with the custodial parent or guardian (see CUSTODY). Some noncustodial parents prefer to use the term *parental access,* which does not carry the implication that they are only "visitors" to their own children.

Visitation rights are basic PARENTS' RIGHTS, held by legal parents, whether separated, divorced, or otherwise absent. If the child was born to unmarried parents, the biological FATHER has visitation rights if he acknowledges that the child is his or if a successful PATERNITY SUIT is brought against him. He is not, however, obligated to exercise such rights.

In some states, grandparents have legally protected visitation rights, and various organizations have been lobbying for extension of such rights (see GRAND-PARENTS' RIGHTS.). In such a state, for example, a grandmother would have visitation rights, even if she and the child's parents are estranged. Similarly, if the parents have separated and the child is in the custody of the MOTHER, the paternal grandmother would have visitation rights.

In some cases, people may be granted visitation rights even if they have no legally recognized relationship with the child. For example, someone who acts as a *psychological parent*—such as a neighbor who has given day-to-day care and is closer to the child's hopes and fears than either biological parent—might be granted visitation rights, either informally by the parents or even formally by the court. Similarly, in a LESBIAN relationship, if one of the partners bears a child, as through ARTIFICIAL INSEMINATION, and the couple later splits, the other partner may be given visitation rights, again either informally or on some occasions formally by a court.

One or both parents can lose visitation rights under some circumstances. For example, a parent's life-style may be considered so harmful to a child because of heavy ALCOHOL AND DRUG ABUSE that the court will bar any contact between parent or child. In cases of ABANDONMENT or severe CHILD ABUSE AND NEGLECT, the court may even terminate parents' rights. Parents may also give up their parental rights by placing the child for ADOPTION. If parental rights are lost or relinquished, both parents and grandparents generally lose visitation rights, with the standard form of adoption, in which identities of the original and adoptive parents are sealed. Visitation rights may be retained, however, if the child is adopted by another family member, such as a stepfather or aunt, and in some forms of open adoption.

The court does not lightly terminate parents' rights, however, and tends instead to set conditions for visitation. If one parent has been violent or abusive in the past, for example, the court may require that parent and child can meet only in the presence of a third party appointed by the court, in what is called *supervised visitation.* If one parent objects to a child's visiting with the other parent and an unmarried partner, the court may restrict visits to daytime hours only. A parent can also petition the court to change visitation arrangements, if, for example, the other parent begins to use drugs heavily. Some also use an ex-partner's openly acknowledged homosexuality to reopen court consideration of visitation (see LESBIAN). Court responses to such petitions vary widely from state to state.

Parents who have *joint custody* do not have visitation rights, in strict legal terms, because they share custody. But all parents have to work out visitation schedules to try to accommodate the needs of both parents and children—and sometimes grandparents as well. Even when the separation or divorce was relatively amicable, this task requires considerable skill, forbearance, and tact, but when the split and custody fight were bitter, it sometimes becomes impossible. In such cases the court may become involved in setting custody and visitation arrangements, such as every other weekend and part of the summer with the noncustodial parent.

The court may also place some restrictions on visitation. If it feels, for example, that shuttling back and forth between parents every weekend involves so much travel as to be an undue hardship for the child, the court may restrict the number of visits or the total distance the child may travel. Or if the custodial parent is moving so far away as to effectively deny visitation rights to the other parent, the court may require that the custodial parent live within a certain geographical area, to retain visitation rights. In such cases the court may also bar the custodial parent from moving without giving written notice to the noncustodial parent in time to allow possible court modification of the visitation arrangements.

More often, however, the court simply orders that visitation be scheduled at "reasonable" times and places. Where that is the case, family experts recommend that parents make specific arrangements at the start, to limit areas of potential misunderstanding and resentment (see TIPS FOR MAKING VISITATION WORK on page 744). With clearly set-out arrangements, if the custodial parent denies visitation, the noncustodial parent can be specific about when and where visitation was denied. This is important when the noncustodial parent may need to go to court and prove that "reasonable visitation" was not allowed, in violation of a court order. If visitation is persistently denied, family experts recommend that the noncustodial parent carefully document each attempt to arrange for visitation, recording each meeting time and failure to make the child available, when possible having a third party as a witness who can testify to the facts.

Some custodial parents deny visitation in an attempt to obtain overdue CHILD SUPPORT; and conversely, some noncustodial parents withhold child support payments when denied visitation. However, in most states the two are legally separate issues, and a parent who denies visitation is theoretically subject to fines or jail for being in *contempt of court,* for disobeying a court order. In practice, courts rarely jail or fine custodial parents, since that could harm the child. Some states have special agencies to mediate visitation disputes and aid in gaining visitation rights. In some cases, one or the other parent has hidden or abducted the child, to completely bar the other from access (see CUSTODY). If they are found, however, such parents risk losing custody and perhaps all access to their children. (See DIVORCE AND SEPARATION HELP, INFORMATION, AND ACTION GUIDE on page 238.)

TIPS FOR MAKING VISITATION WORK

For both parents

- Be flexible and reasonable in making visitation arrangements.
- If the child must travel between parents, agree as part of your original visitation arrangements on which parent pays which travel expenses.
- Do not try to pump the children about your ex's activities and friends.
- Do not try to turn the children against your ex.
- Do not use the children to pass messages between you and your ex.
- Do not use the visitation to talk to or argue with your ex.
- Do not make unrealistic promises to children or try to outdo your ex by promising something you cannot fulfill.
- Do not undermine the other parent's discipline or feed any tendency for the children to play one parent off against another.
- Understand that children may carry confusion and resentment into visitation and do not try to make such feelings the basis of argument with your ex; if such feelings persist, consider counseling for both child and parents.
- Keep a separate date book purely for visitation arrangements, noting in it any visitation problems, such as failure to keep an appointment or denial of visitation; this can act as a record should there be future disputes over visitation.

For noncustodial parents

- Suggest reasonable visiting hours that do not put undue strain on the children or the custodial parent.
- Understand that older children increasingly have their own activities, and take them into account when arranging visitation.
- Pick up children promptly or, if necessary, call as soon as possible to alter arrangements.
- Return children promptly at the agreed-upon time.
- See the children regularly, so the children know they can count on you, rather than letting long stretches go by without contact.
- Spend at least some time with the children yourself alone, rather than always involving other relatives or friends or dropping your children off with others.
- Do not insist that a new partner always be present during visitation.

- Try to bring the children into your everyday life and interests, rather than taking the children on a constant whirlwind of outings.
- Do not drink alcohol or use drugs while with the children; apart from the danger to the child, problems in this area can cause you to lose visitation rights.
- See that children are kept reasonably clean and properly cared for—for example, that cuts and scrapes are treated rather than left untended.
- If the child is taking medication, make sure it is taken at the proper times.
- If a child has a rash or some other problem that seems to require a physical examination, protect yourself from possible charges of child abuse and neglect by having a third person present or taking the child to a doctor.
- If the child becomes ill or is injured, seek medical attention and contact the other parent.
- If you are unable to avoid disagreeable discussion with your ex when picking up the children, try arranging to pick them up elsewhere, as at a friend or relative's house or at school, or have a mutual friend pick them up for you.
- Do not tell the child you will have custody someday; if you wish to seek a change, take the proper legal steps.
- Do not drink or use drugs, since visitation may not be allowed.
- Stay up-to-date with your child support, even if you are having problems with visitation.

For custodial parents

- Have children ready when agreed for pickup by your ex or, if necessary, call as soon as possible to alter arrangements.
- Be available at the agreed-upon time for the children's return.
- See that the children are reasonably clean and cared for at the time of visitation.
- Supply proper clothes for the custodial period.
- Tell the other parent if the child is ill, and call off the visitation, if necessary.
- If your child is on medication, be sure to send the medication with instructions on timing and proper amounts.
- Let your child enjoy and have fun being with the other parent.
- Let your child enjoy having gifts from the other parent.
- If you are not receiving child support, you must still let your child spend time with your ex.
- If your ex has been drinking or using drugs, you do not have to let the

child go on the visitation. If you do not, you should keep track of the date and occasion and when appropriate notify the court.

- Do not drink alcohol or use drugs while with the children; apart from the danger to the child, problems in this area can cause the court to reconsider custody.

Source: Parents Without Partners and other sources, as adapted for *Parent's Desk Reference* (1990), Irene Franck and David Brownstone.

vulva, all of a female's external GENITALS, which lie in the crotch between the thighs; also called *pudenda*. At the center is the opening of the VAGINA, or *introitus*. In a young girl this opening is almost completely covered by a membrane called a HYMEN, which stretches and ruptures with the first penetration of the vagina. On either side of the vaginal opening are BARTHOLIN'S GLANDS, which secrete mucus on sexual excitement, to ease SEXUAL INTERCOURSE.

Behind the vagina is the *anus*, the opening of the rectum (see DIGESTIVE SYSTEM). The area between the vagina and anus is called the PERINEUM, which must stretch to allow for CHILDBIRTH; it is sometimes surgically cut in an EPISIOTOMY to ease DELIVERY. Above the vagina is the opening of the *urethra* (see URINARY TRACT), called the *urethral meatus*. On either side of this are SKENE'S GLANDS.

Above the urethra is the CLITORIS, the main organ of female sexual response, analogous to a man's PENIS. Partly enclosing and protecting the vagina and urethra are folds of fatty tissue, or "lips," called LABIA. The small inner lips— the *labia minora*—meet to cover and protect the urethra and vagina, when the legs are together; the upper ends of the labia minora meet to form a sort of hood over the clitoris, called the *prepuce* or FORESKIN. The clitoris and the labia minora are covered with moist mucous membrane and are sensitive to sexual arousal and touch.

The larger, outer lips—the *labia majora*—form the vulva's outer protective layer. The inner surfaces of the labia majora are moist and have abundant sebaceous (oil) glands, with little or no hair. The outer surfaces are covered with dry SKIN that contain sweat glands and, from PUBERTY on, HAIR.

The boat-shaped area that contains the labia, the clitoris, the vagina, and Bartholin's glands is called the VESTIBULE. Further protecting the vulva is the MONS VENERIS, which is the pubic bone covered by a mound of fatty tissue, sitting above the clitoris; this, too, is covered with hair from puberty on.

In a newborn girl the labia and clitoris are rather large, because of the HORMONES she got from her mother; these assume what will be their normal size within a few weeks. Sometimes the labia are joined at birth, but usually they separate on their own. A slight white or pinkish creamy fluid may be discharged from the vagina in the first few weeks; this, too, should gradually decline in a week or two. At any time after these first few weeks, any new discharge, bulge, or lump in the vulva should trigger an examination by a doctor or clinic staff.

The main disorders affecting the vulva are infections. Many of these are transmitted between the various openings—the vagina, the urethra, and the rectum—and may be treated with relative ease. However, many infections are SEXUALLY TRANSMITTED DISEASES, some of which can be life-threatening, and which require early detection and treatment to prevent lasting damage.

General inflammation of the vulva—*vulvitis*—is a common symptom of such infections, but inflammation can also result from allergic reactions (see SKIN; ALLERGIES). Among the common triggers of such reactions are soap, DOUCHING, vaginal foams or sprays, sanitary napkins, CONDOMS, and DIAPHRAGMS. On rare occasions, reactions to condoms, diaphragms, and other latex rubber products can cause life-threatening allergic shock; anyone who has any burning or irritation associated with the use of contraceptives should discontinue use and consult a doctor or clinic, as well as switch to other forms of protection. Reactions to some medicines, including antibiotics, can also trigger vulvitis.

Lumps, sores, or other lesions on the vulva should also be examined promptly. Many are benign, but some may be cancerous. Vulvar CANCER, actually a type of skin cancer (see SKIN), usually affects the labia, generally in women after MENOPAUSE. Like many such cancers, it is best treated if diagnosed early. Warning signs of vulvar cancer include persistent itching, redness, sores, or wartlike growths, changes in molelike growths, and thickening of the skin. Precancerous lesions are removed locally; but if cancer is involved, more extensive surgery is involved. In a *vulvectomy*, the surgeon removes the labia, clitoris, Bartholin's glands, the outer part of the vagina, and the skin surrounding the vulva. SEXUAL INTERCOURSE can still take place and can be satisfactory, though some of the area's main EROGENOUS ZONES have been removed. In the traditional genital mutilation called FEMALE CIRCUMCISION, the clitoris and labia minora are partly or completely removed, and the labia majora may be abraded and stitched to grow together. (See SEX AND SEXUALITY HELP, INFORMATION, AND ACTION GUIDE on page 665; WOMEN'S HEALTH HELP, INFORMATION, AND ACTION GUIDE on page 334.)

Walker, Alice (1944–), Black American writer active in both the civil rights movement and the feminist movement, though she prefers the term WOMANISM. Walker's main work has explored the experience of African-American women, their African cultural roots, and the dual impact of sexism and racism in their lives, in fictions such as *You Can't Keep a Good Woman Down* (1981); the Pulitzer Prize–winning *The Color Purple* (1982), later an Oscar-winning film; *The Temple of My Familiar* (1989), and *Possessing the Secret of Joy* (1992), exploring the effects of the ritual genital mutilation called FEMALE CIRCUMCISION. Early a contributing editor to *Ms.* magazine, she has also published numerous essays, two notable collections being *In Search of Our Mother's Gardens* (1983) and *Living By the Word* (1991).

War Against Women, The: See Marilyn FRENCH.

Webster v. Reproductive Health Services, the 1989 U.S. Supreme Court ruling upholding a Missouri law that barred the use of public hospitals or clinics for ABORTIONS.

wedding, the formal ceremony or ritual that solemnizes most MARRIAGES, which signifies public recognition of the sexual relationship between a man and woman, their formation of a FAMILY, and their socially accepted right to have children. It comes at the end of a process of MATE SELECTION, by the couple themselves or their families, and generally of an ENGAGEMENT, in some traditional cultures itself a process that may include several stages, including elaborate exchanges of gifts between families and clans (see BRIDEGIFT).

Weddings vary widely the world over. In some places they may extend over several days and involve hundreds of people; but sometimes the couple will be married privately, with simply the required two witnesses. In many Westernized countries, the wedding has traditionally been arranged and paid for by the bride's family. However, in some areas (such as Poland) the costs are routinely shared; for example, the bride's family traditionally supplies the meals, while the groom's pays for alcoholic drinks and music. Where the prospective groom's family is much more affluent than the prospective bride's, his family may arrange the wedding. In recent years, especially among high-earning couples, the man and woman have sometimes elected to pay for their own wedding and keep complete control over the event—they may, for example, tend to invite more of their own friends and business associates than distant relatives and their *parents'* business associates. Wedding consultants recommend that a couple plan the kind of wedding *they* envision before discussing it with either set of parents, who may bring pressure to have quite a different-style affair. But when times are lean, some couples choose to forgo the elaborate wedding celebration and put their money toward a house instead. Indeed, some parents offer their children a choice of a wedding or the cash that would have gone to pay for it. Second weddings tend to be simple, private affairs.

Couples who elect to have a "big" wedding have months of planning ahead of them. The traditional wedding, following a pattern set in the nineteenth century, involves a ceremony in a church, synagogue, or (more recently) a hall hired in a hotel or restaurant, with the bride in white gown and veil and the groom waiting at the altar, with bridesmaids and best man in attendance. Following the ceremony comes a reception for the guests, with wedding cake, much music, and, finally, showers of rice, confetti, and sometimes tin cans and old shoes as the couple depart for a honeymoon. One major change from the traditional ceremony has been that many couples, in recent decades, have been editing and rewriting the old "love, honor, and obey" sections to suit the relationships they see for themselves (see MARRIAGE).

In other parts of the world, premarital preparations may be quite different. In those parts of Africa and the Middle East where women have *infibulation,* the kind of FEMALE CIRCUMCISION that involves removing the CLITORIS and sealing the LABIA, the premarital preparations include cutting apart a woman's labia so she is able to have SEXUAL INTERCOURSE. In these areas, where VIRGINITY and CHASTITY are zealously prized, women are kept in close confinement by their parents, to ensure that they have no sexual contact before marriage. There, the new husband, on the wedding night, traditionally brandishes before his friends a cloth showing blood, as evidence of his sexual prowess and his new wife's virginity at marriage. (See COUPLES AND FAMILIES HELP, INFORMATION, AND ACTION GUIDE on page 418.)

wedge resection, a type of operation involving surgical removal of only part of an ovary or other organ, rather than the whole. (See OOPHORECTOMY; OVARIES.)

Well of Loneliness, The: See Radclyffe HALL.

What Every Woman Should Know: See Margaret SANGER.

widow, a woman whose husband has died; a man whose wife has died is called a *widower*. Because women tend to live longer than men (see LIFE EXPECTANCY), women are more likely to become widowed—and to remain so—than men are, especially in the later years of life. The figures are striking. In 1988, among people over sixty-five years old in the United States, 51 percent of women were widowed after their first marriage, and only 18 percent of these had remarried at the time of the survey. By contrast, 19 percent of men had been widowed, but 41 percent of them remarried. Because of the difference in life expectancy, the ratio of men to women in various age groups falls sharply (see RATIO OF UNMARRIED MEN PER 100 UNMARRIED WOMEN: 1990 on page 682). Many women, however, prefer not to remarry, after the initial loss coming to value their new freedom and independence as single women.

Traditionally, the widow's share in her husband's estate, called a DOWER, was set by common law. Today many states have replaced the dower system with laws of their own that protect the woman's INHERITANCE RIGHTS. Various laws also work—though imperfectly—to protect a widow's rights to her husband's insurance, pension, and SOCIAL SECURITY benefits (see INSURANCE AND PENSION EQUITY). (See SINGLE WOMAN; also OLDER WOMEN'S HELP, INFORMATION, AND ACTION GUIDE on page 374.)

wife, the female partner in a traditional MARRIAGE.

wife abuse, an alternative term for BATTERED WOMEN.

WISH List (Women in the Senate and House) (210 West Front Street, Red Bank, NJ 07701; 908-747-4221; Glenda Greenwald, president), a national network of political donors, created to help elect pro-choice Republican women to higher office; modeled on the Democratic women's EMILY'S LIST. WISH List screens qualified candidates and selects those for support early in campaigns; members agree to contribute $100 to the WISH List and $100 or more to at least two candidates in each election cycle. WISH List publishes a newsletter, periodic updates, and current candidate profiles.

witches, a wide range of believers in alternative religions and healing practices, including people and movements in many cultures, often as an integral part of their dominant religious beliefs, as in Haiti, some sub-Saharan African areas, and some portions of Indonesia. Witchcraft is practiced by women and by men, variously called witches, shamans, sorcerers, medicine women, and medicine men. A considerable range of motives are ascribed to them, from the baleful sorcerer found in some cultures to the benign "witchcraft" of the herbal healer.

During the fourteenth to seventeenth centuries, witches—and many people called witches by their prosecutors—were objects of persecution in the Christian portions of Europe and then in the European American colonies. The torture and murder of accused witches was, almost from the beginning, part of the Inquisition carried on by the Catholic Church, with Jews and "witches" being the main (though far from the only) targets of attack. "Witches"—like Jews then, earlier, and later—were very convenient scapegoats for a religious organization facing Renaissance-generated questions, the rise of national leaders who denied continentwide Catholic authority, and the emergence of "heresy"—defined as anything other than Church dogma—culminating in the rise of Protestantism. In those centuries Europe was always in ferment; in the fourteenth century alone, its peoples experienced massive peasant revolts, religious wars, and in midcentury the Black Death.

Women, largely poor country women, many of them healers, were persecuted as witches throughout the period, their numbers growing as the witch-hunts turned into a continentwide craze. One of the most notable was Joan of Arc, a country woman turned political leader, burned as a witch for quite obviously political reasons, and later posthumously rehabilitated and declared a saint. It should also be noted that the Protestants also participated in the later stages of the witch-hunting craze, as in the notable Salem witch trials of the 1690s, which resulted in twenty murders.

As to the numbers ultimately murdered as "witches" during the witch-hunting centuries, no serious estimate is possible. Guesses have run from several hundred thousand to as many as nine million, the overwhelming majority of them women. Some modern feminists, most notably Margaret Murray in *The Witch-Cult in Western Europe* (1921), have believed the witchcraft craze to be, in essence, an attack by patriarchal authorities on women practicing an "Old Religion." However, that is very much a minority view among historians and anthropologists, including those self-defined as feminists.

Witchcraft has achieved something of a comeback in modern Europe and the United States, intertwined with the development of a group of alternative religions self-defined as pagan and also intertwined with some feminist alternative religions. From the early 1970s, all-woman covens began to develop, along with all-woman witchcraft practices, very different from standard practices, which have historically involved both women and men. Many women who defined themselves as witches also became believers in GODDESS WORSHIP. (See RELIGION AND WOMEN'S RIGHTS; SPIRITUAL FEMINISM.)

Wollstonecraft, Mary (1759–1797), a pioneer British feminist and the author of the landmark *A Vindication of the Rights of Women* (1792), a very full and clear statement of what was to become the main reform position for the following two centuries regarding the need for the equal status of women.

Wollstonecraft defined and identified male oppression and wrote of the fallacy of male supremacy (see PATRIARCHY); the need for comprehensive women's education, far beyond the education for charm, beauty, and elegant submissiveness so prized by men and therefore by most women in her time; the rightness of opening up the professions and wider world to women; and the overriding need to develop a society in which women and men were truly free and equal. Though she was among the first, perhaps *the* first, to call MARRIAGE legalized PROSTITUTION, she did not attack the institution of marriage and woman's role as wife and MOTHER, as many later feminists would, and as an author took a rather puritanical view of sex.

Her own life, however, was free enough to encompass liaisons without marriage, including the birth of her daughter Fanny while she was unmarried. She and William Godwin married in 1796, when she became pregnant again; her death followed the birth of her second daughter, Mary, who became Mary Wollstonecraft Shelley, author of *Frankenstein* and wife of Percy Bysshe Shelley.

Wollstonecraft's work also included *Thoughts on the Education of Daughters* (1787), the novel *Mary* (1788), and *Historical and Moral View of the Origin and Progress of the French Revolution* (1794). (See also WOMEN'S RIGHTS MOVEMENT.)

Would man but generously snap our chains, and be content with rational fellowship instead of slavish obedience, they would find us more observant daughters, more affectionate sisters, more faithful wives, more reasonable mothers—in a word, better citizens. We should then love them with true affection, because we should learn to respect ourselves....

MARY WOLLSTONECRAFT, 1792
———————————— IN A VINDICATION OF THE RIGHTS OF WOMEN ————————————

•

Woman in the Nineteenth Century: See Margaret FULLER.

womanism, a nineteenth-century term, preceding and synonymous with FEMINISM, meaning advocacy of the rights of women or, in its widest sense, support of the works, achievements, and advances made by women. In the late 1970s, African-American writer Alice WALKER introduced a related use of the term to describe a group of qualities she believed was characteristic of African-American women, most notably an ebullient self-confidence in pursuit of African-American feminist and related goals, which to her include a wide range of reformist and revolutionary goals that can also be pursued by women and men together.

woman movement: See FEMINISM.

Woman Rebel: See Margaret SANGER.

woman suffrage, the full and equal enfranchisement of women; that is, the ability of women to vote. This emerged as the great issue of the nineteenth-century WOMEN'S RIGHTS MOVEMENT in July 1848, when it was demanded in the founding document of the American women's rights movement, Elizabeth Cady STANTON's DECLARATION OF SENTIMENTS AND RESOLUTIONS, signed by sixty-eight women and thirty-two men, including Stanton, Susan B. ANTHONY, Lucretia MOTT, Frederick Douglass, and Henry Stanton, at the historic SENECA FALLS WOMEN's RIGHTS CONVENTION.

The issue was joined in England in 1866 with the first mass petition for women's enfranchisement, gathered by the suffragists of the Kensington Society and presented to Parliament by John Stuart MILL, who introduced the first woman suffrage resolution to that same body the following year. A worldwide movement developed. Susan B. Anthony founded the INTERNATIONAL COUNCIL OF WOMEN in 1888, and in 1904 suffragists from many countries founded the INTERNATIONAL WOMAN SUFFRAGE ALLIANCE.

Stanton, Anthony, Mott, and other leading U.S. suffragists were also leading abolitionists who gave primacy to the fight against slavery over the fight for the vote until the end of the Civil War. They had hoped that when the right to vote was extended to African-Americans it would also be extended to women; but when the Fourteenth Amendment granted African-American suffrage, in 1868, women of all colors found they were still denied the vote. In 1869 Stanton and Anthony formed the militant, women-only NATIONAL WOMAN SUFFRAGE ASSOCIATION (NWSA); in the same year Lucy STONE and others founded the more moderate AMERICAN WOMAN SUFFRAGE ASSOCIATION. Both organizations pursued the fight for women suffrage, merging in 1890 to form the NATIONAL AMERICAN WOMAN SUFFRAGE ASSOCIATION (NAWSA). In 1878 the first Woman Suffrage Amendment to the Constitution was introduced in Congress; it came to be known as the Anthony Amendment and ultimately in 1920 became the successful NINETEENTH AMENDMENT.

But the suffrage fight began to be won in the United States before 1920, with woman suffrage being adopted in the Wyoming and Utah territories in 1869. In 1890, on its incorporation into statehood, Wyoming became the first state to introduce woman suffrage. Colorado followed in 1893 and Utah and Idaho in 1896. Half the world away, New Zealand introduced woman suffrage in 1893 and Australia in 1902, followed by several Scandinavian countries and the new Soviet Union before and during World War I.

In Britain, the petition of 1866 began a campaign that grew throughout the balance of the century, led by Lydia Becker from 1867 to 1890 and then by Millicent Garrett Fawcett as president of the National Union of Women's Suffrage Societies (1890–1919). In 1903 Emmeline and Christabel PANKHURST founded the WOMEN's SOCIAL AND POLITICAL UNION (WSPU), their highly visible direct-action organization that spearheaded the militant side of the British fight for woman suffrage, until they abruptly turned around to support the war effort during World War I, as did the moderate suffragists. Other key figures in this final push included Sylvia PANKHURST, Emmeline PETHICK-LAWRENCE and her husband, Richard Pethick-Lawrence, Emily Wilding DAVISON, and English trade unionist and suffrage activist Annie Kenney. Suffrage for women over thirty was won in Britain in 1920 and full suffrage in 1928. After World War I woman suffrage also came in many other European countries, though delayed in others until after World War II. In some countries around the world it is yet to be won. For an overview, see **WOMEN IN POLITICAL LIFE: AN UPDATE** on page 806. (See also **POLITICAL PARTICIPATION; WOMEN'S RIGHTS MOVEMENT.**)

What we suffragettes aspire to be when we are enfranchised is ambassadors of freedom to women in other parts of the world, who are not so free as we are.

CHRISTABEL PANKHURST, 1915

—————————— IN THE SPEECH "AMERICA AND THE WAR" ——————————

•

Woman's Christian Temperance Union (WCTU) (National Office,

1730 Chicago Ave., Evanston, IL 60201; 708-864-1396 or 800-755-1321; Rachel B. Kelly, president), an interdenominational Christian women's organization founded in 1874; one of the organizations in the nineteenth- and early-twentieth-century **TEMPERANCE MOVEMENT,** closely affiliated in its early years with the **WOMEN'S RIGHTS MOVEMENT.** Today part of an international organization, the WCTU still urges abstinence, not only from alcohol but also from narcotic drugs and tobacco (see **ALCOHOL AND DRUG ABUSE; SMOKING**), especially focusing on educating young people about the dangers of these activities. It publishes various materials, including the newsletter *National Happenings*, the magazine *The Union Signal*, the children's magazine *The Young Crusader*, an annual directory, and films, and also sponsors abstinence training camps for young people.

Woman Suffrage Amendment, an alternative name for the NINETEENTH

AMENDMENT to the U.S. Constitution, also called the Anthony Amendment, granting women the right to vote.

womb, an alternate name for the **UTERUS**, though a term that contains much more of the connotation of warmth, nourishment, and security—as in the phrase *return to the womb*—than does the more neutral term *uterus*.

Women and Economics: See Charlotte Perkins GILMAN.

Women and Foundations/Corporate Philanthropy (WAF/CP)

(322 Eighth Avenue, Room 702, New York, NY 10001; 212-463-9934), an organization founded in 1977; a "national association of grantmakers ... who have a particular concern for the economic, social, and physical well-being of women of all ages, races, and social class." Their goals include increasing funding for programs for all women and girls and to increasing the number of women and peo-

ple of color holding positions of philanthropic leadership. WAF/CP conducts internship programs; sponsors regional conferences; and runs special services projects, such as the National Network of Women's Funds (NNWF) and the Far from Done Fund.

WAF/CP publishes a three-times-a-year newsletter and various other materials, including *WAF/CP Membership Directory, Directory of Women's Funds, Getting It Done: From Commitment to Action of Funding for Women and Girls, Making a Difference: The Impact of Women in Philanthropy, Working in Foundations: Career Patterns of Women and Men, Statements from the Grass Roots: Women Breaking the Continuum of Poverty, Far from Done: The Challenge of Diversifying Philanthropic Leadership, Far from Done: The Status of Women and Girls in America,* and *Survey of Grantmakers Concerned with Adolescent Pregnancy.*

Women and Madness (1972), Phyllis Chesler's powerful study of assigned SEX ROLES and the questions of "deviance" and "madness," in which she took the position that strong, independent women who reach beyond passive roles find themselves labeled deviant and can sometimes even be driven mad by societal expectations and psychiatric misperception (see MENTAL DISORDERS). In this respect her work is closely related to the theories developed by Simone de BEAUVOIR in *The Second Sex* (1949).

Women and Sex: See Nawal EL SAADAWI.

Women as a Force in History (1946): See Mary Ritter BEARD.

Women's Action Coalition (WAC) (P.O. Box 1862 Chelsea Station, New York, NY 10011; WAC voice mail 212-967-7711, ext. WACM [9226]); Tracy Essoglou, contact), an organization founded in New York in January 1992 in response to the 1991 Hill-Thomas hearings (see Anita Faye HILL), committed to "direct action on issues affecting the rights of all women." WAC supports the EQUAL RIGHTS AMENDMENT, and seeks "economic parity and representation for all women," and an end to "homophobia, racism, religious prejudice, and violence against women," while asserting "every woman's right to quality health care, child care, and reproductive freedom." WAC is actually a loose network of chapters in various cities of the United States, Canada, and Europe, with no formal hierarchy, but using a "telephone tree" to reach and mobilize members to appear at action sites sometimes within hours, as to defend abortion clinics or support sexual abuse victims, and to use telephoning, faxing, letter writing, and other human resources and professional expertise to direct public attention to issues of concern—local, national, or international. Their slogan is "WAC is watching. We will take action."

WHY WAC?

Current legislation fails to reflect the experience of women

- Women earn 33% less than men for equal work.
- Up to 85% of women experience sexual harassment during their working lives.
- Women are 66% of the adult poor, and 7 out of 10 women over age 65 live in poverty.
- Over $30 billion in child support remains unpaid since 1976.
- 44 states have no laws prohibiting discrimination based on sexual orientation, thus denying lesbians protection of their civil rights.
- The cost of day care forces many families headed by single working women below the poverty line.
- Though not considered a women's health issue, AIDS is the leading killer of women in New York City.
- 30% of women who need legal, timely, affordable abortions can't get them.
- Every 15 seconds a woman is battered in the U.S., and 1 woman in 5 is raped in her lifetime.

That's why

Source: WOMEN'S ACTION COALITION.

Women's Bible, The: See Elizabeth Cady STANTON.

Women's Bureau (U.S. Department of Labor, 200 Constitution Avenue, NW, Room S3002, Washington, DC 20210; 202-219-6606 or 202-523-6652 for ordering materials), a federal agency created by the U.S. Congress in 1920, at the urging of women's organizations, "to formulate standards and policies which shall promote the welfare of wage-earning women, improve their working conditions, increase their efficiency, and advance their opportunities for profitable employment." Early efforts were directed at reforming working conditions and wages, and, during World War II, dealt with women's entry into the labor force. The bureau urged passage of the Equal Pay Act (see EQUAL PAY FOR EQUAL WORK) and establishment of the President's Commission on the Status of Women in 1961, and has continued to gather and disseminate information on the status of women.

Especially since the 1970s, it has emphasized greater access of women to training and employment in "nontraditional jobs in the trades, professional specialties, and the upper levels of corporate management." With increasing emphasis on the family-care needs of working women, the bureau founded the **Work and Family Clearinghouse,** a computerized data base of information called **CHOICES: Clearinghouse on Implementation of Child Care and Eldercare Services** (202-523-4486 or 800-827-5335).

The bureau publishes the newsletter *women&work;* the booklets *Women's Bureau: What It Is, What It Does, A Working Woman's Guide to Her Job Rights, Directory of Nontraditional Training and Employment Programs Serving Women, Employers and Child Care: Benefiting Work and Family, Women on the Job: Careers in the Electronic Media, Flexible Workstyle: A Look at Contingent Labor,* and *Employment-Focused Programs for Adolescent Mothers;* and various fact sheets, such as *Milestones: The Women's Bureau Celebrates 70 Years of Women's Labor History, 20 Facts on Women Workers, Women Workers: Outlook to 2005, Earnings Differences Between Women and Men, State Maternity/Parental Leave Laws, Women in Management, Working Mothers and Their Children, Women Who Maintain Families, Women in the Skilled Trades and in Other Manual Occupations, Black Women in the Labor Force, Women of Hispanic Origin in the Labor Force, Women in Labor Organizations, Women with Work Disabilities, Women Business Owners,* and individual sheets on women business owners of various backgrounds, including Hispanic, Black, Asian American, and American Indian/Alaska Native.

Women's Campaign Fund (WCF)

Women's Campaign Fund (WCF) (120 Maryland Avenue, NE, Washington, DC 20002; 202-544-4484; Jane Danowitz, executive director), a bipartisan organization founded in 1974 supporting pro-choice women candidates in their campaigns for public office at every political level, often helping to recruit women in targeted seats. WCF contributes money directly, notably including vital start-up money; provides access to a national funding network; and offers other strategic and technical assistance, in areas such as polling, fund-raising, direct mail, issue development, voter contact, advertising, and media relations. It also maintains the Women's Campaign Research Fund to provide political and policy-making skills to women candidates officeholders.

Women's Environment and Development Organization (WEDO)

Women's Environment and Development Organization (WEDO) (WEDO/Women USA Fund, Inc., 845 Third Avenue, 15th Floor, New York, NY 10022; 212-759-7982; Bella Abzug, co-founder and USA co-chair), an organization founded in 1989 as an international network of women that seeks to "monitor implementation of governments' Earth Summit commitments," especially recommendations for women. WEDO (pronounced *"wee doo"*) also aims to provide leadership and advocacy training, mentor programs, and the like, to strengthen women as policymakers. It gathers, and disseminates news of women's issues and activities through its bimonthly newsletter *News & Views,* reports, and audiotapes of international congresses.

Women's Health Information Service, an information clearinghouse on women's health, a service of the NATIONAL WOMEN'S HEALTH NETWORK.

women's health movement: See HEALTH EQUITY.

Women's History Month: See INTERNATIONAL WOMAN'S DAY.

Women's International League for Peace and Freedom (WILPF) (1213 Race Street, Philadelphia, PA 19107-1691; 215-563-7110; Jane Midgley, executive director; International Office: Centre International, 1 Rue de Varembe, 1211 Geneva 20, Switzerland), an international women's peace organization, stemming from the WOMEN'S PEACE PARTY founded by Jane ADDAMS in 1915, during World War I, and then organized internationally in 1919. Addams become the first president of the WILPF and shared a Nobel Peace Prize in 1931 for her work. Another founder and the first secretary of the WILPF was Emily Green Balch, who shared a 1946 Nobel Peace Prize.

The WILPF, in the early 1990s still a vital force in women's and peace movements, is an adviser and consultant to several United Nations bodies and continues to pursue a wide range of peace initiatives while also remaining active in the full range of WOMENS' RIGHTS issues. Describing itself as "grass-roots and community based," the U.S. arm seeks a "just and peaceful world," with "equality of all people in a world free of sexism, racism ... and all other oppression," organizing "to eradicate the root causes of war," including such problems as "poverty, homelessness, unemployment, and lack of health care." Its main action priorities are "disarmament, racial justice, women's rights, and ending U.S. foreign intervention." Among the main action campaigns are women vs. violence; a women's peace and justice treaty between the women of North and Latin America; a comprehensive test ban treaty and comprehensive Middle East peace negotiations; economic justice, under a women's budget; women's rights in general, including REPRODUCTIVE RIGHTS, EMPOWERMENT, and undoing SEXISM; and racial justice, ending racism in budget priorities and foreign policy.

On the rights of women specifically, WILPF seeks to combat all "legal restrictions and sexist attitudes [that] have kept women from full participation and a rightful share of power in our society," in particular seeking elimination of all discriminatory laws, passage of the EQUAL RIGHTS AMENDMENT, freedom of choice concerning ABORTION, an end to enforced STERILIZATION, equal opportunity for education (see EDUCATION EQUITY) and job opportunities, and EQUAL PAY FOR EQUAL WORK. It publishes the U.S. magazine *Peace and Freedom*; the international quarterly *Pax et Libertas*; the bimonthly bulletin *Program and Legislative Action*; and various brochures and fliers on issues and campaigns, such as *The Women's Budget*. (See PACIFISM AND NONVIOLENCE.)

Women's International Network (WIN)

Women's International Network (WIN) (187 Grant Street, Lexington, MA 02173; 617-862-9431; Fran P. Hosken, coordinator/editor), an organization founded in 1975, during INTERNATIONAL WOMEN'S YEAR, "working for women's health and development worldwide," serving "the general public, institutions, and organizations by transmitting international information about women and women's groups." WIN has a gift and sponsorship program, so people can sponsor or support a women's organization in a developing country, and supplies technical assistance and consulting services for women's development. It publishes the quarterly *Women's International Network News (WIN News)* as a "worldwide open participatory communication system by, for, and about women of all backgrounds, beliefs, nationalities, and age groups," providing a free issue to those who send news or sponsorships. Regular coverage includes sections entitled Women and Health, Female Circumcision/Genital Mutilation, Women and Development, Women and Environment, Women and Violence, Women and Media, and Women and International Affairs, a clearinghouse of career opportunities for women working in the international field. WIN also provides educational materials, at cost, such as *A Picture Story of Reproduction from a Woman's View*, *Nutrition Supplement* (in English, French, and Spanish), and *The Childbirth Picture Book*, with a USA reading and resource list, and also English, Spanish, French, and Arabic versions for worldwide use by community health workers.

Women's International Resource Exchange (WIRE)

Women's International Resource Exchange (WIRE) (122 West 27th Street, 10th Floor, New York, NY 10001-6202; 212-741-2955; Sybil Wong, administrator), a small women's collective, founded in 1979, that reprints and distributes, "in monograph and booklet format, information on and analyses of the problems, struggles and achievements of women in the Third World," mostly in English but some also in Spanish. Among its recent publications are *A Developing Legal System Grapples with an Ancient Problem: Rape in Nicaragua*, *The Literacy Issue: Feminine Perspectives on Reading and Writing*, *Women at War: Peru's Shining Path*, *Women Doing Theology in Latin America*, *Women and the Gulf War*, *Women in the Intifada*, *Jewish Women's Call for Peace: A Handbook for Jewish Women on the Israeli-Palestinian Conflict*, *On the Questions of Women in South Africa*, *Women in the Algerian Liberation Struggle*, *Virginity and Premarital Sex in Contemporary China*, and *The Struggle of the Indian Woman, Feminism in Sri Lanka: 1975–1985*.

Women's International Terrorist Conspiracy from Hell (WITCH)

Women's International Terrorist Conspiracy from Hell (WITCH), a New York radical women's movement group that briefly (1968–1969) gained a great deal of media attention through its theatrical style of demonstration, beginning with its Halloween 1968 New York Stock Exchange demonstration, in which the protesting women dressed as witches. The group pulled back and quickly disappeared after its 1969 anti–Bridal Fair demonstrations were widely taken to be a demonstration against brides, rather than as the intended demonstration against the bridal industry. (See also WOMEN'S LIBERATION MOVEMENT.)

Women's Justice Center (WJC) (23 East Adams, Detroit, MI 48226;

313-961-7073; Legal Services, 313-961-5528), an organization established in 1975 to provide legal services for low-income residents in the metropolitan Detroit area. It provides information on legal rights, offers free "attorney-facilitated divorce overview meetings," makes referrals, runs community outreach programs, and encourages mutual-support groups. It also operates My Sister's Place (MSP) (P.O. Box 13500, Detroit, MI 48213; 313-921-3902; 24-hour crisis lines, 313-921-3900 or 313-921-3901), a domestic violence shelter for abused women and their children. WJC also runs Teens Networking Together (TNT), a program to help teens deal with dating violence; it also operates an after-school dating violence hot line (313-921-0420).

Women's Legal Defense Fund (WLDF) (2000 P Street NW, Suite 400,

Washington, DC 20036; 202-887-0364), an organization that focuses on issues involving women, such as family and medical leaves, reproductive health, sex discrimination in the workplace, and custody disputes. It acts as advocate for women's rights and publishes various materials, including *State Leave Laws Chart* (regarding family and medical leave), *Sex Discrimination in the Workplace: A Legal Handbook*, and *Custody Handbook*.

women's liberation movement, a term often used during the late 1960s

and until the mid-1970s to describe the whole worldwide WOMEN'S RIGHTS MOVE-MENT and the entire spectrum of feminist thought and organizations. The term is still used by many on the revolutionary side of the modern women's movement and by many ANTIFEMINISTS who attack "women's libbers," depicting them much as "bomb-throwing anarchists" were depicted a century ago. But the world has moved on. To the overwhelming majority of WOMEN'S RIGHTS advocates, the term *women's liberation* is now only a thoroughly respectable antique that does not quite accurately describe themselves and their beliefs.

The women's liberation movement was a relatively small but quite influential and very highly visible segment of the emerging new women's movement of the late 1960s. The main movement had been initiated by Betty FRIEDAN and others after the appearance of Friedan's 1963 book *The Feminine Mystique;* by 1966 Friedan had been a founder and was first president of the NATIONAL ORGANIZA-TION FOR WOMEN, and a new women's movement was under way involving millions of women in the United States and Western Europe.

Among those joining that movement from 1967 were many young women from the NEW LEFT, leaving their old organizations in response to the mainstream initiatives of Friedan and others. These included some who would become founders and leaders of the amorphous movement called women's liberation, modeling their scattered, loosely affiliated groups on the anarchist-oriented New Left organizations from which they came. They organized such groups as RADI-CAL WOMEN, founded in 1967 by Shulamith FIRESTONE and Pam Allen; WOMEN'S INTERNATIONAL TERRORIST CONSPIRACY FROM HELL (WITCH), founded in 1968; REDSTOCKINGS, founded in 1969 by Firestone and Ellen Willis; and

RADICALESBIANS, founded in 1970. None of the women's liberation groups was very large, and few lasted very long; in all there were an estimated 10,000–15,000 activists in the movement. But though small in number, they made a considerable impact, stressing confrontational tactics, introducing the concept of CONSCIOUSNESS-RAISING, gaining much media attention, and sharply raising some issues that were later taken up by the mainstream of the feminist movement. Some women's liberationist authors also reached very wide audiences, including Firestone, Andrea DWORKIN, Kate MILLETT, and Robin MORGAN. (See also WOMEN'S RIGHTS MOVEMENT.)

Women's Ministry Unit (WMU) (Presbyterian Church [U.S.A.], 100 Witherspoon Street, Louisville, KY 40202; 502-569-5382), an arm of the Presbyterian church that "coordinates the planning and developing of programs and resources related to women's issues," helping to prepare women for effective leadership; "acting as a coordinating center for issues of concern to women"; and seeking to "eliminate racism, sexism, classism, and ageism in church structures and in the society at large." It includes several special groups: **Committee of Women of Color** (502-569-5380); **Justice for Women (JFW),** (502-569-5380); **Presbyterian Women (PW)** (502-569-5844); and **Women Employed by the Church** (502-569-5845). PW publishes the magazine *Horizons.*

WMU in general publishes many materials, including the newsletter *Women;* the video *Tying the Thread;* and brochures about the unit and its committees; and it also publishes or distributes other materials, including booklets such as *Sisters in the Streets: Planning for Ministry with Women Who Are Prostitutes, Problem Pregnancy/Keeping the Covenant: Guidelines for Ministry,* and *Women Elders: Sinners or Servants;* brochures such as *Sexual Misconduct, Women and AIDS,* and *Myths and Facts About Rape and Battering;* reports such as *Naming the Unnamed: Sexual Harassment in the Church;* manuals such as *The Doorway to Response* (on helping battered women) and *Women in Jail and Prison: A Training Manual for Volunteering Advocates;* pamphlets such as *Where to Go When She Says No;* fliers such as *Parental Leave Guidelines for Governing Bodies;* study papers such as *All the Livelong Day: Women and Work* and *Pornography: Far from the Song of Songs;* study action guides such as *Family Violence: A Religious Issue;* packets such as *What It Means to Be for Choice, Christian Reflection on the Issues of Abortion, Child Advocacy Packets,* and *Women's Rights: Human Rights* (on the U.N. Convention on the Eliminations of All Forms of Discrimination Against Women); books such as *The Motherhood of God;* and videos such as *Whose Choice?* (a pro-choice video).

Women's Party, The: See WOMEN'S SOCIAL AND POLITICAL UNION (WSPU).

Women's Peace Party (WPP), an American women's pacifist organization, formed in January 1915 in opposition to World War I and to any American participation in the war then consuming Europe. Jane ADDAMS was its first pres-

ident. In May 1915 its leaders extended their activities abroad, attending the International Congress of Women, at The Hague. In the United States, the WPP lasted until 1919, then merging with the WOMEN'S INTERNATIONAL LEAGUE FOR PEACE AND FREEDOM (WILPF).

Women's Research and Education Institute (WREI) (1700 18th

Street, NW, Suite 400, Washington, DC 20009; 202-328-7070; Betty Parsons Dooley, executive director), an organization founded in 1977 to provide "nonpartisan information and policy analysis on women's equity issues." WREI serves as a clearinghouse of information on women's issues, for public officials and agencies, advocacy organizations, reporters, and researchers, as well as for individual women. It encourages researchers to "consider the public policy implications of their work" and seeks to "strengthen the links between researchers, policy makers, and opinion leaders so that research will be translated into action." It spotlights emerging issues with conferences, symposia, and briefings; carries out special projects such as the Women in the Military Project; and offers congressional fellowships on women and public policy.

WREI publishes numerous materials, such as the periodical *The American Woman*, a comprehensive report on the social, economic, and political status of U.S. women; reports such as *This Recession's Invisible Victims: Women Sales and Service Workers, Family and Medical Leave: Who Pays for the Lack of It?, Parental Leave and "Woman's Place": The Implications and Impact of Three European Approaches to Family Leave Policy*, and *Home-Based Employment; Implications for Working Women*; and fact sheets such as *Women in the U.S. Armed Services: The War in the Persian Gulf, Women in the Military 1980–1990*, and *Women and Housing*.

women's rights, a considerable body of legal, social, economic, and political

rights and issues, which vary from age to age and from culture to culture. To a large extent, women's rights are defined either by their absence or by the continual need to fight for them, even though previously won. For example, WOMAN SUFFRAGE was the greatest women's rights issue of the nineteenth and early twentieth centuries but is now so well established in many countries that it is recognized as simply a democratic right, though a whole body of women's rights to full POLITICAL PARTICIPATION still must be won in every country, and even the basic right to vote has not yet been won in all countries. Similarly, and at least as obviously, SEXUAL DISCRIMINATION in hiring may be illegal in some countries, as it is in the United States, but equal hiring rights and practices are vital legal rights that are still notably impaired in practice. Generally recognized women's rights also stem from special needs, as in the area of workplace discrimination against pregnant women (see PREGNANCY DISCRIMINATION ACT).

In addition, some rights have been recognized as such only after long struggles, and may no longer seem necessary in some countries but may yet be missed. An example often cited is the United States women workers' PROTECTIVE LEGISLATION fought through by the Progressives before World War I and ex-

panded and consolidated by the New Deal in the 1930s. Most of these were invalidated by passage of equal rights laws in the 1960s, which seemed—and still
seem—a far better way to address the inequities and exploitation involved. But
that presupposes aggressive enforcement of equal rights laws. In practice, gutted
equal rights enforcement and the removal of protective legislation can combine
to seriously damage and endanger woman workers, and especially poor Hispanic-
American, African-American, and Asian-American woman workers, some of
them recent immigrants.

Beyond the generally accepted human rights spelled out in the United Nations Declaration of Human Rights, we describe below some of the key women's
rights generally recognized as worldwide goals by the U.N. and to some considerable extent by many countries. It should be noted here that "generally recognized goals" in practice often translate into massive battles, when goals are
transformed into specific action—as in the extraordinary resistance put up by
many "men's clubs" to admitting women as members, on the entirely specious
grounds that these obviously centrally important loci of economic, social, and
political power are entirely "private."

Among the key women's rights currently fought for are

- the right to vote in all elections, on terms equal in every respect to those enjoyed by men. (See POLITICAL PARTICIPATION.)
- the right to be eligible for election to all public offices, on terms equal in every
respect to those enjoyed by men.
- the right to completely equal participation in all public policy making and
carry-through, including access to every job level, right to the top, nationally
and internationally.
- the right to fully equal participation in all private organizations concerned
with public matters.
- the right to fully equal nationality, completely independent of and in no way
tied to the nationality of husbands.
- the right to equal employment, in terms of hiring, choice of work, promotion,
job security, training, equal pay for work of equal value, unemployment and
disability insurance, public and private pension rights, and health and safety.
The health and safety right includes protection of reproductive functions, a
source of conflict between the right to hold any job and special legal protections so that women may not be forced into jobs damaging or potentially
damaging to the reproductive function. (See WORK AND WOMEN; EQUAL PAY FOR
EQUAL WORK; PAY EQUITY; OCCUPATIONAL SEGREGATION; EDUCATION EQUITY; GLASS
CEILING; MOMMY TRACK; PROTECTIVE LEGISLATION; INSURANCE AND PENSION EQ-
UITY; PREGNANCY DISCRIMINATION ACT.)
- the right not to be discriminated against because of PREGNANCY, the need for
maternity leave, or marital status; and the right to receive family economic
and social support, including compensated maternity leave. (See PREGNANCY
DISCRIMINATION ACT; FAMILY AND MEDICAL LEAVE.)
- the right to health care in relation to pregnancy, CHILDBIRTH, and the postnatal
period and, more generally, the rights to equal health care and not to be subjected to damaging medical practices. The last has in recent years been in-
voked in an attempt to bring an end to such practices as ritual genital surgery

(see FEMALE CIRCUMCISION), a religious rite in some cultures. (See HEALTH EQUITY; PRENATAL CARE; SON PREFERENCE.)

- the right of equal access to credit. (See EQUAL CREDIT OPPORTUNITY ACT.)
- the right to fully equal educational opportunity, including participation in sports. (See EDUCATION EQUITY; TITLE VII OF THE CIVIL RIGHTS ACT OF **1964**.)
- fully equal marital and family rights, including choice of spouse, number and spacing of children, family planning information including CONTRACEPTION (see BIRTH CONTROL), and such legal rights as guardianship and ADOPTION, property rights, and choice of family name. The question of information on and access to contraception continues to be highly controversial in the United States and some other countries, though it is a settled one in many parts of the world. (See MARRIAGE; COHABITATION; FAMILY; BIRTH CONTROL; REPRODUCTIVE RIGHTS; NAMES IN MARRIAGE.)

In more general terms, women have the right not to be subjected at any time to violent and degrading treatment, in the home or the wider culture, whether at peace or at war. (See RAPE; BATTERED WOMEN; SEXUAL HARASSMENT; CHILD ABUSE AND NEGLECT.)

Many of these rights are outlined in the 1979 United Nations CONVENTION ON THE ELIMINATION OF ALL FORMS OF DISCRIMINATION AGAINST WOMEN, reprinted on page 796. (See WOMEN'S RIGHTS MOVEMENT; also WOMEN'S RIGHTS HELP, INFORMATION, AND ACTION GUIDE on page 767.)

Men their rights and nothing more;
women their rights and nothing less.

MOTTO OF THE WOMEN'S RIGHTS PERIODICAL
THE REVOLUTION *(1868–1870)*,
———— EDITED BY SUSAN B. ANTHONY AND ELIZABETH CADY STANTON ————

•

women's rights movement, the two-centuries-long campaign for the full equality of women in every aspect of human life. Although many women had become powerful figures in earlier times, it was the ideal of total equality for all, as expressed in great documents of the American and French revolutions, that infused the WOMEN'S RIGHTS movement. Pioneer women's rights thinkers, among them Olympe de GOUGES and her *Declaration of the Rights of Women and Citizens* (1790), Mary WOLLSTONECRAFT in her *A Vindication of the Rights of Women* (1792), Margaret FULLER in her *Woman in the Nineteenth Century* (1845), and Elizabeth Cady STANTON, in her landmark DECLARATION OF SENTIMENTS AND RESOLUTIONS (1848), laid the rational and ethical basis for the movement. With passage of Stanton's Declaration of Sentiments at the historic SENECA FALLS WOMEN'S RIGHTS CONVENTION of 1848, a worldwide movement began.

Side by side with that very formal call for women's rights, other actions were taking place, as in the growing pressure for married women's property rights in the United States and England, leading to state-by-state Married Women's Property Acts beginning in 1839 and the British Married Women's Property Bill in 1857 (see COVERTURE). Campaigns also began to improve the conditions of women and children workers, as in the French campaign led by socialist and women's rights crusader Jeanne DEROIN in the 1840s.

The rise of the nineteenth-century international Socialist movement, while focusing attention on the oppression of women, also gave primacy to socialist economic, social, and political issues and to socialist organizations led by men. With socialists taking the position that the question of women's rights in a male-dominated society could not really be addressed until after the victory of socialism, the women's rights movement as such went slowly on the European continent until it caught up in the worldwide fight for WOMAN SUFFRAGE late in the century; that fight was pursued most vigorously in the United States and England. To some extent, that difference in emphasis continued through much of the twentieth century and even into the current period, with some Marxists who are also feminists still asserting the primacy of socialist goals over women's rights goals.

In the United States and England the women's rights movement developed rather independently, each for somewhat different reasons. For women's rights activists in the United States, the central issue preceding the creation of the women's rights movement was the abolition of slavery; women such as Stanton, Lucretia MOTT, Susan B. ANTHONY, Sojourner TRUTH, and Julia Ward HOWE were all leading abolitionists, many of them antislavery lecturers and participants in the Underground Railroad (the informal network to aid former slaves) along with male abolitionists such as Frederick Douglass and Henry Stanton.

But after the Civil War the American women's rights movement split. Stanton, Anthony, and others formed the militant women-only NATIONAL WOMAN SUFFRAGE ASSOCIATION (NWSA), with Stanton as its first president (1869–1890). The other wing of the woman suffrage movement, led by Lucy STONE and later Howe, and including men, became the moderate AMERICAN WOMAN SUFFRAGE ASSOCIATION (AWSA). The two wings rejoined in 1890 to help develop a national and international woman suffrage movement that won major victories following World War I, including passage of the NINETEENTH AMENDMENT in 1920.

The organized women's rights movement sagged after the suffrage fight was won. In the 1920s, with the vote and new sexual and social freedoms, large bodies of women in the industrial nations of the West felt that they had won their war, as did most of the younger women who had inherited the gains made. Farther east, the new Soviet system seemed to many to have legalized massive gains for women's rights, though most of those gains were quickly negated by the Stalin dictatorship. Then, in the 1930s and through the Great Depression, the worldwide fight against fascism, and World War II, women's rights issues were pushed aside, even by many who had been and would again be women's rights activists.

The sag in the organized women's rights movement continued through the early years of the Cold War, until the emergence of a revived women's rights movement in the 1960s. Not that the fight for women's rights had died in those years: the work of the WOMEN'S BUREAU, and of Eleanor ROOSEVELT during the

New Deal years and as chief architect of the 1948 United Nations Declaration of Human Rights, testifies to the continuing vitality of that movement.

A new wave of women's rights activity began in the 1960s, its ideas fueled by the work of such writers as Simone de BEAUVOIR and Betty FRIEDAN, taking organizational form in the United States with the formation of the NATIONAL ORGANIZATION FOR WOMEN (NOW) in 1966 and raising what became a very wide spectrum of women's rights issues, as had the founders of the first women's movement at Seneca Falls in 1848. From the late 1960s through the 1970s, a highly visible segment of the new movement was the WOMEN'S LIBERATION MOVEMENT, composed of some thousands of revolutionary and other radical women, many of them formerly part of the NEW LEFT, seeking a new society as a complete solution to the issues being raised.

The new women's rights movement, sometimes called the *second wave*, made the fight for the EQUAL RIGHTS AMENDMENT a central focus during the 1970s—and lost that fight to the swing toward conservatism that resulted in the Reagan and Bush administrations of the 1980s and early 1990s. With a newly conservative U.S. Supreme Court that seemed intent on reversing the course of recent history, as in its rulings restricting ABORTION rights, and dwindling support in the country, the women's rights movement sagged during the 1980s; it revived again with the fight to protect ABORTION rights clinics and to save the rights granted under *ROE v. WADE*; and was galvanized by the riveting confrontation between Anita Faye HILL and then–Supreme Court nominee Clarence Thomas, which brought the issue of SEXUAL HARASSMENT to a worldwide audience. The overt assault on women in the TAILHOOK SCANDAL proved another rallying point.

As of this writing, the revitalized and greatly expanded women's movement has moved to elect many more women to political office and to take up a wide range of continuing issues, including abortion rights and the fight to legalize the so-called abortion pill, RU486; employment discrimination and workplace equality (see WOMEN AND WORK); equal credit (see EQUAL CREDIT OPPORTUNITY ACT) and business ownership opportunities; equal educational opportunities (see EDUCATION EQUITY); RAPE and other kinds of violence against women (see BATTERED WOMEN; CHILD ABUSE AND NEGLECT; INCEST); DIVORCE, child CUSTODY, CHILD SUPPORT, division of MARITAL PROPERTY, and other marital questions; and LESBIAN rights. (See WOMEN'S RIGHTS HELP, INFORMATION, AND ACTION GUIDE on page 767; also WOMEN'S LIBERATION MOVEMENT.)

WOMEN'S RIGHTS

Help, Information, and Action Guide

Organizations

▶ NATIONAL ORGANIZATION FOR WOMEN (**NOW**) (202-331-0066).
▶ **NOW** LEGAL DEFENSE AND EDUCATION FUND (**NOW LDEF**) (212-925-6635). Published the Legal Resource Kit *Equal Rights Amendment.*
▶ WOMEN'S LEGAL DEFENSE FUND (**WLDF**) (202-887-0364).
▶ FUND FOR THE FEMINIST MAJORITY (617-695-9688; 703-522-2214; or 213-651-0495). Publishes the quarterly newsletter *Feminist Majority Report, Empowering Women, The Feminization of Power: 50/50 by the Year 2000, The Feminization of Power: An International Comparison, Empowering Women in Business, Empowering Women in Medicine, Empowering Women in Philanthropy.*
▶ FEMINISTS CONCERNED FOR BETTER FEMINIST LEADERSHIP (**FCBFL**) (212-796-1467). Distributes *Feminism: Freedom from Wifism.*
▶ NATIONAL COUNCIL FOR RESEARCH ON WOMEN (**NCRW**) (212-570-5001). Publishes the quarterly *Women's Research Network News (WRNN), Directory of National Women's Organizations, Directory of Women's Media, A Women's Thesaurus: An Index of Language Used to Describe and Locate Information by and About Women.*
▶ 9 TO 5, NATIONAL ASSOCIATION OF WORKING WOMEN (216-566-1699; Job Survival Hotline 800-522-0925). Publishes *Unequal Justice: Why Women Need Stronger Civil Rights Protections, a Brief Analysis.*
▶ MS. FOUNDATION FOR WOMEN (**MFW**) (212-353-8580).
▶ NATIONAL CENTER ON WOMEN AND FAMILY LAW (**NCOWFL**) (212-674-8200). Publishes the newsletter *The Women's Advocate.*
▶ ORGANIZATION OF CHINESE AMERICAN WOMEN (**OCAW**) (202-638-0330).
▶ COMMISSION FOR WOMEN'S EQUALITY (**CWE**) (212-879-4500). Publishes the *International Directory of Jewish Feminists.*
▶ COMMISSION FOR WOMEN (**CW**), EVANGELICAL LUTHERAN CHURCH IN AMERICA (**ELCA**) (312-380-2860).
▶ NATIONAL COUNCIL OF NEGRO WOMEN (**NCNW**) (202-659-0006).

◪ **ON INTERNATIONAL CONCERNS**

▶ UNITED NATIONS DEVELOPMENT FUND FOR WOMEN (**UNIFEM**) (212-906-6400). Publishes *The World's Women: Trends and Statistics 1970–1990, Legal Literacy: A Tool for Women's Empowerment, Empow-*

erment and the Law: Strategies of Third World Women, Women, Law and Development: Action for Change.
▶ WOMEN'S INTERNATIONAL RESOURCE EXCHANGE (WIRE) (212-741-2955). Publishes *The Struggle of the Indian Woman* and *Feminism in Sri Lanka: 1975–1985.*
▶ WOMEN'S INTERNATIONAL NETWORK (WIN) (617-862-9431). Publishes the quarterly *Women's International Network News (WIN News).*
(See also many other organizations throughout this book, such as those listed under SEXUAL DISCRIMINATION AND SEXUAL HARASSMENT HELP, INFORMATION, AND ACTION GUIDE on page 642; WORKING WOMEN'S HELP, INFORMATION, AND ACTION GUIDE on page 779; VIOLENCE AGAINST WOMEN HELP, INFORMATION, AND ACTION GUIDE on page 612.)

Other resources

◪ CONTEMPORARY PERSPECTIVES ON FEMINISM AND WOMEN'S RIGHTS

Engaging Feminism: Students Speak Up and Speak Out. Jean O'Barr and Mary Wyer. University Press of Virginia, 1992.
Backlash: The Undeclared War Against American Women. Susan Faludi. Crown, 1991.
Feminist Fatale: Voices from the "Twentysomething" Generation Explore the Future of the "Women's Movement." Paula Kamen. Fine, 1991.
Women in Protest. Karina Smith. Trafalgar Square, 1991.
Women's Rights in the U.S.A.: Policy Debates and Gender Roles. Stetson. Brooks-Cole, 1991.
What Policies Would Promote Social Justice for Women? Greenhaven, 1990.
Conflicts in Feminism. Marianne Hirsch and Evelyn F. Keller, eds. Routledge, 1990.
The Sexual Liberals and the Attack on Feminism. Dorchen Leidholdt and Janice G. Raymond. Pergamon, 1990.
Have Women's Roles Changed for the Better? Greenhaven, 1989.
A Lesser Life: The Myth of Women's Liberation in America. Sylvia A. Hewlett. Warner, 1989.
Women and Counter-Power. Yolande Cohen, ed. Black Rose/Paul and Co., 1989.
Feminism, 2nd ed. Angela Miles and Geraldine Finn, eds. Paul and Co., 1989.
For and Against Feminism. Ann Curthoys. Paul and Co., 1989.
Rights of Women. Mandy Wharton. Watts, 1989.
Women's Issues. Laura Stempel. Salem Press, 1989.
The Failure of Feminism. Nicholas Davidson. Prometheus, 1988.

◪ ON MODERN MOVEMENTS FOR WOMEN'S RIGHTS

Women's Movements in America: Their Successes, Disappointments, and Aspirations. Rita J. Simon and Gloria Danziger. Praeger/Greenwood, 1991.

Moving On: New Perspectives on the Women's Movement. Tayo Andreasen, ed. Coronet, 1991.

In Pursuit of Equality: Women, Public Policy, and the Federal Courts. Susan G. Mezey. St. Martin's, 1991.

More Joy Than Rage: Crossing Generations with the New Feminism. Caryl Rivers. University Press of New England, 1991.

American Feminism: A Contemporary History. Ginette Castro. New York University Press, 1990.

British Feminism in the Twentieth Century. Harold L. Smith, ed. University of Massachusetts Press, 1990.

Survival in Doldrums: The American Women's Rights Movement, 1945 to the 1960's. Leila J. Rupp and Verta Taylor. Ohio State University Press, 1990. Reprint of 1987 ed.

The Power Players: Parity: Organization for Women's Equality and Rights. Bonnie Huval. Aegina Press, 1990.

Women and Social Protest. Guida West and Rhoda L. Blumberg, eds. Oxford University Press, 1990.

Women Together, Women Alone: The Legacy of the Consciousness-Raising Movement. Anita Shreve. Viking Penguin, 1989.

Conceived in Conflict: The Politics of the Women's Movement and the Crusade for the ERA. Elisabeth Griffithe. Random House, 1989.

Sixty-Eight, Seventy-Eight, Eighty-Eight: From Women's Liberation to Feminism. Amanda Sebestyen. Prism/Avery, 1989.

Daring to Be Bad: Radical Feminism in America, 1967–75. Alice Echols. University of Minnesota Press, 1989.

The Grounding of Modern Feminism. Nancy F. Cott. Yale University Press, 1989. Reprint of 1987 ed.

The Sisterhood: The Inside Story of the Women's Movement and the Leaders Who Made It Happen. Marcia Cohen. Columbine/Fawcett, 1989. Reprint.

Women's Struggles and Strategies. Saskia Wieringa. Ashgate, 1988.

◪ ON THE EQUAL RIGHTS AMENDMENT

Legacy: The Equal Rights and Feminist Movements. Ross S. Kidde. Center for Family Development, 1992.

Sex, Gender, and the Politics of ERA: A State and the Nation. Donald G. Mathews and Jane S. De Har. Oxford University Press, 1991.

Conceived in Conflict: The Politics of the Women's Movement and the Crusade for the ERA. Elisabeth Griffithe. Random House, 1989.

◪ OTHER LEGAL CONCERNS

Law, Gender, and Injustice: A Legal History of U.S. Women. Joan Hoff. New York University Press, 1991.
At the Boundaries of Law: Feminism and Legal Theory. Martha A. Fineman and Nancy S. Thomadsen, eds. Routledge (NY), 1990.
Feminism and the Power of Law. Carol Smart. Routledge, 1989.
(See also SEXUAL DISCRIMINATION AND SEXUAL HARASSMENT HELP, INFORMATION, AND ACTION GUIDE on page 642; WORKING WOMEN'S HELP, INFORMATION, AND ACTION GUIDE on page 779; VIOLENCE AGAINST WOMEN HELP, INFORMATION, AND ACTION GUIDE on page 612.)

◪ ON OTHER SPECIAL CONCERNS

White Political Women: Paths from Privilege to Empowerment. Diane L. Fowlkes. University of Tennessee Press, 1992.
Segregated Sisterhood: Racism and the Politics of American Feminism. Nancie Caraway. University of Tennessee Press, 1991.
La Chicana and the Intersection of Race, Class and Gender. Irene I. Blea. Praeger/Greenwood, 1991.
Black Feminist Thought: Knowledge, Consciousness, and the Politics of Empowerment. Patricia H. Collins. Unwin Hyman, 1990.
Love and Politics: Radical Feminist and Lesbian Theories. Carol A. Douglas. Ism Press, 1990.
Identity Politics: Lesbian Feminism and the Limits of Community. Shane Phelan. Temple University Press, 1989.

◪ HISTORICAL PERSPECTIVES

Victorian Feminists. Barbara Caine. Oxford University Press, 1992.
Women and Sisters: The Antislavery Feminists in American Culture. Jean F. Yellin. Yale University Press, 1992. Reprint of 1989 ed.
Handbook of American Women's History. Angela Howard Zophy with Frances M. Kavenik, eds. Garland, 1990.
Women's Rights and the Rights of Man. A. J. Arnaud and E. Kingdom. Aberdeen University Press/Macmillan, 1990.
Hidden from History: Three Hundred Years of Women's Oppression and the Fight Against It. Sheila Rowbotham. Paul and Co., 1989.
Feminism in America: A History, 2nd ed. William L. O'Neill. Transaction, 1989.
Victorian Feminism, 1850 to 1900. Philippa Levine. University Presses of Florida, 1989.
The History of Feminism. Marcia Cohen. Simon & Schuster, 1988.

◪ INTERNATIONAL PERSPECTIVES

Women's Work and Women's Lives: The Continuing Struggle Worldwide. Hilda Kahne and Janet Giele. Westview, 1992.

Women Transforming Politics: Worldwide Strategies for Empowerment. Jill M. Bystydzienski. Indiana University Press, 1992.

Contemporary Western European Feminism. Gisela Kaplan. New York University Press, 1992.

Rights of Women in Islam. Asghar A. Engineer. St. Martin's, 1992; Apt, 1992.

Women and Gender in Islam: Historical Roots of a Modern Debate. Leila Ahmed. Yale University Press, 1992.

Family, Household and Gender Relations in Latin America. Elizabeth Jelin, ed. Routledge Chapman and Hall, 1992.

Women in Cross-Cultural Perspective. Leonore L. Adler, ed. Praeger/ Greenwood, 1991.

Veil and the Male Elite: A Feminist Interpretation of Women's Right in Islam. Fatima Mernissi. Addison-Wesley, 1991.

Indian Women's Movement. Maitryee Chaudhuri. Advent (NY), 1991.

The Women's Liberation Movement in Russia: Feminism, Nihilism and Bolshevism, 1860–1930. Richard Stites. Princeton University Press, 1991.

Calling the Equality Bluff: Women in Israel. Barbara Swirski and Marilyn P. Safir. Pergamon, 1991.

Both Right and Left Handed: Arab Women Talk About Their Lives. Bouthaina Shaaban. Indiana University Press, 1991.

The Social and Legal Status of Women: A Global Perspective. Winnie Hazou. Praeger/Greenwood, 1990.

Gender Inequality: An International Study of Discrimination and Participation. Mino Vianello and Renata Siemienska. Sage, 1990.

Discrimination Against Women: A Global Survey of the Economic, Educational, Social and Political Status of Women. Eschel M. Rhoodie. McFarland, 1989.

Women's Movements of the World. Longman Group Inc., Staff. Oryx Press, 1988.

Sex and Power: The Rise of Women in America, Russia, Sweden, and Italy, 2nd ed. Donald Meyer. University Press of New England, 1989.

Russian Women's Studies: Essays on Sexism in Soviet Culture. Tatyana Mamonova. Pergamon, 1988.

◪ ON FEMINISM AND POLITICAL CONCERNS

Freedom, Feminism and the State: An Overview of Individualist Feminism, 2nd ed. Wendy McElroy, ed. Holmes and Meier, 1991.

Modern Political Theory and Contemporary Feminism: A Dialectical Analysis. Jennifer Ring. State University of New York Press, 1991.

Feminism and Political Theory. Cass R. Sunstein, ed. Center for the Study of Language, 1990.

The Disorder of Women: Democracy, Feminism, and Political Theory. Carole Pateman. Stanford University Press, 1990.

Beyond Oppression; Feminist Theory and Political Strategy. Mary E. Hawkesworth. Continuum, 1990.

Toward a Feminist Theory of the State. Catharine A. MacKinnon. Harvard University Press, 1989.

Feminism and Politics: A Comparative Perspective. Joyce Gelb. University of California Press, 1989.

Feminism and Institutions: Dialogues on Feminist Theory. Linda Kauffman, ed. Blackwell, 1989.

Learning About Women: Gender, Politics, and Power. Jill K. Conway and others, eds. University of Michigan Press, 1989.

Feminist Perspectives on Peace and Peace Education. Birgit Brock-Utne. Pergamon, 1989.

Woman, Culture and Politics. Angela Y. Davis. Random House, 1989.

◪ ON FEMINISM AND SOCIAL/ENVIRONMENTAL CONCERNS

Ecological Feminism. Karen J. Warren and Jim Cheney. Westview, 1993.

Reweaving the World: The Emergence of Ecofeminism. Irene Diamond and Gloria Orenstein. Sierra Club, 1990.

Women and Social Welfare: A Feminist Analysis. Dorothy C. Miller. Greenwood, 1990.

Finding Our Way: Rethinking Eco-Feminist Politics. Janet Biehl. Black Rose, 1990.

Healing the Wounds: The Promise of Ecofeminism. Judith Plant, ed., New Society, 1989.

Women, Class, and the Feminist Imagination: A Socialist-Feminist Reader. Karen V. Hansen and Ilene J. Philipson, eds. Temple University Press, 1989.

Social Feminism. Noami Black. Cornell University Press, 1988.

Feminism vs. Familism: Research and Policy for the 1990's. Roberta M. Spalter-Roth. Institute for Women's Policy Research, 1988.

◪ ON FEMINISM AND ETHICAL/MORAL CONCERNS

Speaking from the Heart: A Feminist Perspective on Ethics. Rita C. Manning. Rowman, 1992.

Explorations in Feminist Ethics: Theory and Practice. Eve B. Cole and Susan Coultrap-McQuin, eds. Indiana University Press, 1992.

Feminist Ethics. Claudia Card, ed. University Press of Kansas, 1991.

Feminist Perspectives: Philosophical Essays on Method and Moral. Lorraine Code and others, eds. University of Toronto Press, 1988.

◪ ON FEMINISM AND SCIENTIFIC/TECHNOLOGICAL CONCERNS

Feminism Confronts Technology. Judy Wajcman. Pennsylvania State University Press, 1991.
Feminism and Science. Nancy Tuana, ed. Indiana University Press, 1989.
Body-Politics: Women and the Discourses of Science. Mary Jacobus and others, eds. Routledge, 1989.

◪ ON FEMINISM AND CULTURAL CONCERNS

Feminine Sentences: Essays on Women and Culture. Janet Wolff. University of California Press, 1991.
Gender and Genius: Towards a Feminist Aesthetics. Christine Battersby. Indiana University Press, 1990.
Women, Art and Society. Whitney Chadwick. Thames and Hudson, 1989.
Into the Mainstream: How Feminism Has Changed Women's Writing. Nicci Gerrard. Unwin Hyman, 1989.
Feminist Interventions: Politics, History, Literature. Elizabeth Fox-Genovese. Wesleyan University Press/University Press of New England, 1989.
Visibly Female: Feminism and Art. Hilary Robinson, ed. Universe, 1988.
Vision and Difference: Femininity, Feminism and the Histories of Art. Griselda Pollock. Routledge, 1988.

◪ ON OTHER FEMINIST PERSPECTIVES

Feminism Without Illusions: A Critique of Individualism. Elizabeth Fox-Genovese. University of North Carolina Press, 1991.
Telling It Like It Is: Reflections of a Not So Radical Feminist. Elayne Clift. Knowledge Ideas and Trends, 1991.
Throwing Like a Girl and Other Essays in Feminist Philosophy and Social Theory. Iris M. Young. Indiana University Press, 1990.
Inessential Woman: Problems of Exclusion in Feminist Thought. Elizabeth Spelman. Beacon, 1990.
Feminist Theory in Practice and Process. Micheline R. Malson and others, eds. University of Chicago Press, 1989.
Transforming Feminism. Maria Riley. Sheed and Ward (MO), 1989.
Women, Knowledge, and Reality: Explorations in Feminist Philosophy. Ann Garry and Marilyn Pearsall, eds. Unwin Hyman, 1989.
Loving and Working: Reweaving Women's Public and Private Lives. Rosemary C. Barciauskas and Debra B. Hull. Meyer Stone, 1989.
A Leisure of One's Own: A Feminist Perspective on Women's Leisure. Karla Henderson and others. Venture (PA), 1989.

Essentially Speaking: Feminism, Nature and Difference. Diana Fuss. Routledge, 1989.

Feminist Frontiers. Laurel W. Richardson and Verta Taylor. Random House, 1989.

Is the Future Female? Troubled Thoughts on Contemporary Feminism. Lynne Segal. Bedrick, 1988.

▨ ON WOMEN AND SOCIAL CHANGES

Balancing Acts: Women and the Process of Social Change. Patricia L. Johnson, ed. Westview, 1992.

The Paradox of Change: American Women in the 20th Century. William H. Chafe. Oxford University Press, 1992. A revision of *The American Woman: Her Changing Social, Economic, and Political Roles, 1920–1970* (1972).

Prisoners of Men's Dreams: Striking Out for a New Feminine Future. Suzanne Gordon. Little, Brown, 1991.

Retrieving Women's History: Changing Perceptions of the Role of Women in Politics and Society. S. Jay Kleinberg, ed. Berg Publishers, 1991.

Chocolate Ain't Enough . . . No More: Every Woman's Choice. Arnie Wallace and Adryan Russ. Challenger (CA), 1991.

Fearful Kingdom: Women's Flight from Equality. Wendy Kaminer. Addison-Wesley, 1991.

Women's Changing Role, rev. ed. Carol Foster and others. Information Plus (TX), 1990.

On Her Own: Growing Up in the Shadow of the American Dream. Ruth Sidel. Viking Penguin, 1990.

Tender Power. Sherry S. Cohen. Addison-Wesley, 1990.

Suburban Lives. Margaret Marsh. Rutgers University Press, 1990.

Narrowing the Gender Gap. Geeta Somjee. St. Martin's, 1989.

▨ REFERENCES ON WOMEN

Encyclopedia of Women's Associations Worldwide. Lesley Ripley Greenfield, ed. Gale, 1993.

Women: Challenges to the Year 2000. United Nations, 1992.

European Women's Almanac. Paula Snyder, ed. Columbia University Press, 1992. A sourcebook, with statistics and addresses for further information.

Women's Information Directory: A Guide to Approximately 6,000 Organizations, Agencies, Institutions, Programs, and Publications Concerned with Women in the United States. Shawn Brennan, ed. Gale, 1992.

The World's Women 1970–1990: Trends and Statistics. United Nations, 1991.

Statistical Record of Women Worldwide. Linda Schmittroth, ed. Gale, 1991.

Women's Rights in International Documents: A Sourcebook with Commentary.
Winston E. Langley, ed. McFarland, 1991.
American Woman, 1990–91: A Status Report. Sara Rix. Norton, 1990.
The Dictionary of Feminist Theory. Maggie Humm. Ohio State University
Press, 1990.
Women's Studies Encyclopedia, 3 vols. Helen Tierney. Greenwood,
1989–1991.
Encyclopedia of Feminism. Lisa Tuttle. Facts on File, 1986.

◪ BACKGROUND WORKS

*Inviting Women's Rebellion: A Political Process Interpretation of the Women's
Movement.* Anne N. Costain. Johns Hopkins, 1992.
*Against the Tide: "Pro-Feminist Men" in the United States: 1776–1990, a Doc-
umentary History.* Michael S. Kimmel and Thomas Mosmiller, eds. Bea-
con Press, 1992.
Modern Woman and Her Shadow. Silvia Di Lorenzo. Sigo Press, 1992.
Uncertain Terms: Negotiating Gender in American Culture. Faye Ginsberg,
ed. Beacon Press, 1991.
Sexual Democracy: Women, Oppression, and Revolution. Ann Ferguson.
Westview, 1991.
Women, Theory and Society: From Private to Public Patriarchy. Sylvia Walby.
Blackwell, 1990.
Putting on Appearances: Gender and Advertising. Diane Barthel. Temple Uni-
versity Press, 1989.
Gender and the Politics of History. Joan W. Scott. Columbia University Press,
1989.
Imaging American Women: Idea and Ideals in Cultural History. Martha
Banta. Columbia University Press, 1989.
The Social Identity of Women. Suzanne Skevington and Deborah Baker, eds.
Sage, 1989.
Feminism and the Contradictions of Oppression. Caroline Ramazanoglu.
Routledge, 1989.

Women's Room, The: See Marilyn FRENCH.

Women's Social and Political Union (WSPU), the direct-action or-
ganization that spearheaded the British fight for WOMAN SUFFRAGE. It was founded
by Emmeline and Christabel PANKHURST in Manchester in 1903; its central figures also included Sylvia PANKHURST, Emmeline PETHICK-LAWRENCE and her husband, Richard Pethick-Lawrence, and Annie Kenney. The WSPU's powerful and
highly visible campaign for WOMAN SUFFRAGE lasted eleven years, until the out-

break of World War I, and included, especially from 1913 on, a wide range of defiant acts, toward the end including arson and the bombing of property. Many of its militants were arrested and imprisoned again and again, went on hunger strikes in prison, were force-fed, and attracted enormous public attention to the woman suffrage fight. When Emmeline and Christabel Pankhurst supported the war and renounced militant action, much of the WSPU's membership dropped away. The WSPU became the Women's Party in 1917; that organization dissolved in 1919. (See also WOMAN SUFFRAGE.)

Women's Sports Foundation (WSF) (342 Madison Avenue, Suite 728, New York, NY 10173-0728; 212-972-9170; Women's Sports Infoline, 800-227-3988; Donna Lopiano, executive director), an "educational organization dedicated to promoting and enhancing the sports and fitness experience for all girls and women." Founded in 1974, WSF "advocates change in policies, laws, and social patterns that discourage female sports participation." It sponsors an annual conference on women in sports; offers grants to individuals, for travel and training or leadership development, and to institutions, for funding sports programs; sponsors award programs; and offers information and referrals on the Women's Sports Infoline.

WSF publishes various educational materials, including the newsletter *The Women's Sports Experience*; brochures such as *A Parent's Guide to Girls' Sports*, *Women's Athletic Scholarship Guide*, *A Woman's Guide to Coaching*, and *Playing Fair: A Guide to Title IX in College and High School Sports*; expert packets on topics such as *Drug Use*, *Eating Disorders*, *General Fitness*, *Nutrition/Weight Control*, *General Careers* (in sports), *Participation Statistics*, *Pregnancy and Exercise*, *Psychology*, and *Kid's Packet*; videotapes such as *Aspire Higher: Careers in Sports for Women*, *Surer, Swifter, Stronger*, and *Girls in Sports: The Winning Combination*; and research reports such as *The Wilson Report: Moms, Dads, Daughters & Sports*, *The Women's Sports Foundation Report: Minorities in High School Sports*, and *Miller Lite Report on Women in Sports*.

women's studies, an academic field that has developed since the late 1960s largely in the United States, in the context of the new WOMEN'S RIGHTS MOVEMENT, and in response to a widespread belief that all but a few women in world history had until then been left out of the study of history and many other academic disciplines. This perception ultimately led to the development of a powerful women's studies movement on thousands of U.S. campuses. A distinct duality marked the women's studies movement; some women academics stressed integration of women's studies into the whole range of curricula, while others urged development of separate women's studies groups and departments, to function as independent sources of power and funding in academe.

As the movement became more settled, however, the two tended to influence each other, and some were able to advocate strongly both an independent core of women's studies and integration into the academic whole. With increasing financial pressure on American higher education in the 1980s and early 1990s, coupled with a certain amount of ANTIFEMINIST backlash, women's studies came under attack in many institutions, encouraging defensive and separatist tendencies.

The women's studies movement to some extent mirrors the fragmentation and issues in the larger modern women's movement, with African-American, Chicana, spiritual, eco-, Marxist, LESBIAN, Jewish, Asian-American, and several other kinds of feminists calling for attention to be paid to their special concerns within women's studies programs.

For more help, information, and action

▶ NATIONAL COUNCIL FOR RESEARCH ON WOMEN (NCRW) (212-570-5001). Publishes the quarterly *Women's Research Network News (WRNN)*, *Directory of Women's Media*, *Opportunities for Research and Study*, *International Centers for Research on Women*, *Mainstreaming Minority Women's Studies*, *Transforming the Knowledge Base*, and *A Declining Commitment to Research About Women*. (See also EDUCATION EQUITY; SEXUAL DISCRIMINATION.)

Work and Family Clearinghouse, an arm of the WOMEN'S BUREAU.

work and women, the whole range of activities at which women are employed, whether paid or not; a matter that needs illumination, for while the vast majority of the world's women work, much of their output is not measured and factored into the world's accounts. A woman who is a domestic worker employed by others is a member of the workforce, but the vital HOUSEWORK she does as a HOMEMAKER, in caring for her own home and family, is literally not counted, because she is not paid for it. Similarly, a CHILD CARE center is quite obviously part of an economic system, but MOTHERS who do precisely the same work in their own home for their own families are treated as if they were not part of the system—they are not counted. All over the globe, only a few women are, in fact, entirely removed from the world of work.

On the contrary, the United Nations tables reproduced on page 822 show that, with unpaid HOUSEWORK factored in, the real average work week of women in most of the world is considerably *longer* than that of men. This revealing fact is the basis for much feminist activity aimed at bringing women's unpaid work into the world's accounts and securing pay for women's unpaid work—some of the goals stated in the United Nations document, the NAIROBI FORWARD-LOOKING STRATEGIES FOR THE ADVANCEMENT OF WOMEN: A SUMMARY (for full text, see page 804). Pay for unpaid labor is seen by many feminists as a matter of simple social justice, but also by many as an indispensable basis for equal rights for women throughout the world. Former housewives who are forced by circumstance into the workforce without skills also have very serious problems (see DISPLACED HOMEMAKERS).

But changing the patterns of the SEXUAL DIVISION OF LABOR will be a very long-term struggle, requiring a decades-long worldwide campaign that is only now beginning. What is happening far more swiftly is that women in many countries are moving into the recognized economic workplace in greatly increased numbers, and generating national and international campaigns for workplace equality. This is especially true in the United States, where the percentage of women in the civilian workforce climbed by 41 percent between 1950 and 1990, while the percentage of men in the workforce dropped by a reported 10 percent. The huge increase was accompanied by a surge of women into such previously male bastions as the law, medicine, dentistry, financial management, marketing and outside selling, and general management. Growth is expected to continue in these and other such fields, although women in these fields continue to average far less pay than men.

Sexual segregation continues to be the major workforce fact for most women. More than two-thirds of employed American women continue to hold what have become during the twentieth century traditional, sex-segregated, low-paying jobs in administrative support and service occupations of many kinds: secretaries, typists, clerks, retail sellers, nurses, health aides, teachers, waitresses, low-paid industrial workers, and a wide range of other such economic dead ends, sometimes called the "pink ghetto." This continuing occupational segregation has generated a call for PAY EQUITY that goes beyond the guarantee of EQUAL PAY FOR EQUAL WORK secured by the 1963 Equal Pay Act. It has also generated calls for laws and programs to help women move into jobs classified as traditionally male—in the United States, as in the 1991 NON-TRADITIONAL EMPLOYMENT FOR WOMEN ACT.

Large numbers of women have also become small business owners in recent years. During the 1980s, the percentage of United States businesses owned by women rose from 26.1 to more than 30. But most women-owned businesses were small, grossing all together only approximately 15 percent of the nation's total receipts; and many, with their small resources, did not survive the depression of the early 1990s.

The armed forces also saw a major influx of women, although much smaller than the increase in the civilian workforce; in the United States their numbers topped 11 percent in the late 1980s. Pervasive SEXISM in the military was exposed by the TAILHOOK SCANDAL and its several aftermaths, but women continued to move toward a sexually integrated set of armed forces.

This wave of working women in all occupations encountered a wide range of new and old problems in the workplace. Chief among them was discrimination, in all its forms (see SEXUAL DISCRIMINATION). Many also encountered a federal, state, and local social service network that did not even come close to taking into account their need—and the need of millions of other women and men— for an effective system of CHILD CARE and FAMILY AND MEDICAL LEAVE, as part of a meaningful national health insurance plan. Instead they found a starved social services system, gutted by budget cuts rather than expanded to meet much new and larger needs.

The great majority of working women in the United States and throughout the world also found themselves the victims of the traditional sexual division of labor: they were expected to work full-time and *still* do all the unpaid household work, including child care, that they had done before—work that, for women the world over, has come to be called a "second shift." For a woman with children and a demanding, time-consuming career, that often meant trying to become a "supermom," with a ninety- to one-hundred-hour work week and a mass of conflicting expectations to meet—one certain result being that she would feel intense guilt over failing to perform the impossible day after day.

But even for women with less demanding jobs, the combination of paid work and unpaid housework in a two-job household meant, in essence, handling two full-time jobs and at least a sixty- to seventy-hour workweek. For many SINGLE PARENTS, it could be far, far worse: a low-paying job, children, no decent place to live after a DIVORCE, inadequate and often nonexistent health insurance, and life below the poverty level, even with work.

For an overview of women and work today, see AMERICAN WORKING WOMEN: A STATISTICAL PORTRAIT on page 808 and THE WORLD'S WOMEN: INDICATORS ON TIME USE on pages 822 and 823. For more information and guidance on personal and practical concerns, see WORKING WOMEN'S HELP, INFORMATION, AND ACTION GUIDE, below, and specific topics noted above.

WORKING WOMEN'S
Help, Information, and Action Guide

Organizations

▶ 9 TO 5, NATIONAL ASSOCIATION OF WORKING WOMEN (216-566-1699; Job Survival Hotline 800-522-0925). Offers a Summer School for Working Women. Offers Hotline counseling on such topics as workers' rights, dealing with harassment, and coping with office politics. Publishes the *9 to 5 Newsline*, the annual *9 to 5 Profile of Working Women*, *"Business As Usual": Stories from the 9 to 5 Job Survival Hotline, 9 to 5—The Working Women's Guide to Office Survival, VDT Syndrome: The Physical and Mental Trauma of Computer Work, New Work Force Politics and the Small Business Sector: Is Parental Leave Good for Small Business: A Multivariate Analysis of Business Employment Growth, Stories of Mistrust and Manipulation: The Electronic Monitoring of the American Work Force, Solutions for the New Work Force: Policies for a New Social Contract, White Collar Displacement: Job Erosion in the Service Sector*, and *High Performance Office Work: Improving Jobs and Productivity: An Overview with Case Studies of Clerical Job Redesign*.

▶ FAMILIES AND WORK INSTITUTE (212-465-2044). Publishes *The Corporate*

Reference Guide to Work-Family Programs, The State Reference Guide to Work-Family Programs for State Employees, Beyond the Parental Leave Debate: The Impact of Laws in Four States, and *Parental Leave and Productivity: Current Research;* and internationally oriented works such as *The Family-Friendly Employer: Examples from Europe, Families at Work: Practical Examples from 140 Businesses, The Implementation of Flexible Time and Leave Policies: Observations from European Employers,* and *The Relevance of British Career Break Schemes for American Companies.*

▶ WOMEN'S BUREAU, U.S. DEPARTMENT OF LABOR (202-523-6667). Publishes *Working Woman's Guide to Her Job Rights* and *Earnings Differences Between Women and Men.*

▶ NATIONAL ASSOCIATION OF FEMALE EXECUTIVES (NAFE) (212-645-0770 or 800-669-1002). Publishes the magazine *Executive Female* and the *NAFE Network Directory.*

▶ NATIONAL ASSOCIATION OF WOMEN BUSINESS OWNERS (NAWBO) (312-922-0465 or 800-272-2000).

▶ WOMEN'S RESEARCH AND EDUCATION INSTITUTE (WREI) (202-328-7070. Publishes *Home-based Employment: Implications for Working Women;* and fact sheets such as *Women in the Military 1980–1990.*

▶ WOMEN'S LEGAL DEFENSE FUND (WLDF) (202-887-0364). Publishes *Expanding Employment Opportunities for Women: A Blueprint for the Future.*

▶ CLEARINGHOUSE ON WOMEN'S ISSUES (CWI) (301-871-6016 or 202-363-9795).

▶ CONGRESSIONAL CAUCUS FOR WOMEN'S ISSUES (202-225-6740).

▶ FUND FOR THE FEMINIST MAJORITY (617-695-9688; or 703-522-2214; or 213-651-0495). Publishes *Feminist Majority Report, Empowering Women, The Feminization of Power: 50/50 by the Year 2000, The Feminization of Power: An International Comparison, Empowering Women in Business,* and *Empowering Women in Philanthropy.*

▶ LEAGUE OF WOMEN VOTERS (202-429-1965). Publishes *Pay Equity: Issues and Answers* and *Meeting the Employment Needs of Women: A Path Out of Poverty?*

▶ COMMISSION FOR WOMEN'S EQUALITY (CWE) (212-879-4500).

▶ INSTITUTE OF WOMEN AND TECHNOLOGY (413-367-9725).

▶ MS. FOUNDATION FOR WOMEN (MFW) (212-353-8580).

▶ NATIONAL CENTER FOR POLICY ALTERNATIVES (202-387-6030). Publishes *The Women's Economic Justice Agenda: Ideas for the States.*

▶ NATIONAL DISPLACED HOMEMAKERS NETWORK (NDHN) (202-467-6346). Publishes *Network News, Transition Times, Overcoming Obstacles, Winning Jobs: Tools to Prepare Displaced Homemakers for Paid Employment,* and *Success over Forty: Strategies for Serving Older Displaced Homemakers.*

▶ FEDERALLY EMPLOYED WOMEN (FEW) (202-898-0994). Publishes *News &*

Views and *Report of a Survey on Women and the Federal Women's Program in the Federal Government.*

▶ WOMEN'S MINISTRY UNIT (WMU) (502-569-5382). Publishes and distributes *All the Livelong Day: Women and Work.*

▶ NATIONAL ASSOCIATION OF CUBAN-AMERICAN WOMEN (NACAW) (219-745-5421).

▶ NATIONAL WOMEN'S HEALTH NETWORK (NWHN) (202-347-1140). Operates the **Women's Health Information Service.** Publishes the information packet *Occupational/Environmental Health.*

▶ CENTER FOR WOMEN POLICY STUDIES (CWPS) (202-872-1770). Has *Work and Family Policy Program.* Publishes *Women of Color in Science, Mathematics, and Engineering: A Review of the Literature.*

(See also SEXUAL DISCRIMINATION AND SEXUAL HARASSMENT HELP, INFORMATION, AND ACTION GUIDE on page 642; for more on women in developing countries, see POVERTY AND WOMEN HELP, INFORMATION, AND ACTION GUIDE on page 287.)

☑ ON PAY AND BENEFITS

▶ NATIONAL COMMITTEE ON PAY EQUITY (NCPE) (202-331-7343). Publishes *Raising Awareness About Pay Inequities, Pay Equity Bibliography and Resource List, Pay Equity Makes Good Business Sense, The Pay Equity Sourcebook, Legislating Pay Equity to Raise Women's Wages: A Progress Report on the Implementation of the Ontario, Canada Pay Equity Act,* and *Bargaining for Pay Equity: A Strategy Manual.*

▶ PENSION RIGHTS CENTER (202-296-3776). Publishes *Protecting Your Pension Money, Can You Count on Getting a Pension?,* and *The Pension Plan (Almost) Nobody Knows About,* on Simplified Employee Pensions (SEPs).

▶ NOW LEGAL DEFENSE AND EDUCATION FUND (NOW LDEF) (212-925-6635). Publishes the Legal Resource Kits *Employment—General Employment—Pay Equity, Employment—Pregnancy and Parental Leave,* and *Employment—Sexual Harassment.*

▶ CATALYST (212-777-8900). Publishes the monthly *Perspective on Current Corporate Issues* and *The Corporate Guide to Parental Leaves.* (See also CAREGIVER'S HELP, INFORMATION, AND ACTION GUIDE on page 454.)

☑ ON OLDER WORKING WOMEN

▶ NATIONAL COUNCIL ON THE AGING (NCOA) (202-479-1200 or 800-424-9046). Includes **National Association of Older Worker Services (NAOWES), Institute on Age, Work, and Retirement,** and **Senior Community Service Employment Program (SCSEP).** Publishes *The Reality of Retirement, Commitment to an Aging Work Force: Strategies and Models* *for Helping Older Workers Achieve Full Potential,* and *Mature/Older Job Seeker's Guide.*

▶ **NOW** Legal Defense and Education Fund (**NOW LDEF**) (212-925-6635). Publishes the *State Index of Women's Legal Rights, Attorney Referral Services List,* and the Legal Resource Kits *Insurance and Pensions.*

▶ Older Women's League (**OWL**) (202-783-6686; OWL POWERLINE, 202-783-6689, a weekly update on congressional activities). Publishes *Employment Discrimination Against Older Women, Paying for Prejudice: Midlife and Older Women in America's Labor Force, Heading for Hardship: Retirement Income for American Women in the Next Century, The Road to Poverty: Report on the Economic Status of Midlife and Older Women in America, Older Women and Job Discrimination: A Primer, Women and Pensions: Catch 22,* and *Building Public/Private Coalitions for Older Women's Employment.*

▶ American Association of Retired Persons (**AARP**) (202-434-2277).
(See also Older Women's Help, Information, and Action Guide on page 374.)

🔲 **FOR LEGAL ADVICE AND REFERRALS**

▶ Equal Rights Advocates (**ERA**) (415-621-0672) advice and counseling line, 415-621-0505). A national women's law center.
▶ Lawyers' Committee for Civil Rights Under Law (202-371-1212).
▶ Northwest Women's Law Center (206-682-9552; for information and referral, 206-621-7691). For Washington State area.
▶ Women's Justice Center (**WJC**) (313-961-5528). For Detroit area.

Other resources

Women and Working Lives. Sara Arber and Nigel Gilbert. St. Martin's, 1991.
The Book for Working Women: Is There Any Other Kind? J. P. Kilbourn, ed. Aha, 1991.
The Working Woman. Joanne Wallace. J. Wallace, 1990.
Managing Lives: Corporate Women and Social Change. Sue J. Freeman. University of Massachusetts Press, 1990.
Women at Work: Unity in Diversity. James A. Walsh, ed. Women's World, 1990.
Women's Leisure, What Leisure? Eileen Green and others. New York University Press, 1990.
Spouse, Parent, Worker: On Gender and Multiple Roles. Faye J. Crosby. Yale University Press, 1990. Reprint of 1987 ed.
Women and Work. Tom Cox, ed. Taylor and Francis, 1988.

◪ PERSONAL AND PRACTICAL GUIDES

Childhood Dreams—Career Answers: A Woman's Practical and Playful Guide to the Career Puzzle. Marti Chaney and Vicki Thayer. Life Works Press, 1992.

The Women's Job Search Handbook: Identifying and Getting the Job You Want. Gerri Bloomberg and Margaret Holden. Williamson, 1991.

The Smart Woman's Guide to Résumés and Job-Hunting, Julie A. King and Betsy Sheldon. Career Press, 1991.

Stress First Aid for the Working Woman: How to Keep Cool When You're Under Fire! Bee Epstein. Becoming Press, 1991.

Congratulations! You've Been Fired: Sound Advice for Women Who've Been Terminated, Pink-Slipped, Downsized or Otherwise Unemployed. Emily Koltnow and Lynne S. Dumas. Columbine/Fawcett, 1990.

The Résumé Guide for Women of the Nineties. Kim Marino. Tangerine Press, 1990.

Single Solutions—An Essential Guide for the Single Career Woman. Charlotte E. Thompson. Branden, 1990.

Job Sharing: A Practical Guide for Women. Pam Walton. Beekman, 1990.

The Working Woman's Guide to (Real) Success. Elsa Houtz. Harvest House, 1990.

Returning to Work: A Practical Guide for Women. Alec Reed. Beekman, 1989.

Smart Women at Work: Twelve Steps to Career Breakthroughs. Terry Ward. Ballantine, 1989.

Survive the Nine to Five: Get on Top of Your Job and Achieve Health and Happiness. Diana Lamplugh and others. Borgo Press, 1989.

(For more on working mothers, see CAREGIVER'S HELP, INFORMATION, AND ACTION GUIDE on page 454.)

◪ ON WOMEN AND CAREERS

The Third Sex: The New Professional Woman. Patricia A. McBroom. Paragon House, 1992. Reprint of 1986 ed.

Lives of Career Women: Approaches to Work, Marriage, and Children. F. M. Carp, ed. Plenum, 1991.

Taking Control of Your Life: The Secrets of Successful Enterprising Women. Gail Blanke and Kathleen Walas. MasterMedia Ltd, 1990.

Women and Careers: Success and Orientations. Millicent E. Poole and Janice Langan-Fox. Taylor and Francis, 1990.

The Female Advantage: Women's Ways of Leadership. Sally Helgeson. Currency Book/Bantam Doubleday Dell, 1990.

Paths to Power: A Woman's Guide from First Job to Top Executive. Natasha Josefowitz. Addison-Wesley, 1990.

Sisterhood Betrayed. Jill Barber. St. Martin's, 1990.

Power Failure: Why Some Women Short Circuit Their Careers and How to Avoid It. Barbara Bools and Lydia Swan. St. Martin's, 1989.

ON PAY EQUITY

European Community Sex Equality Law. Evelyn Ellis. Oxford University Press, 1992.

Doing Comparable Worth: Gender, Class, and Pay Equity. Joan Acker. Temple University Press, 1991.

Between Feminism and Labor: The Significance of the Comparable Worth Movement. Linda M. Blum. University of California Press, 1991.

The Economics of Comparable Worth. Mark R. Killingsworth. W. E. Upjohn, 1990.

Pay Equity in Ontario: A Manager's Guide. David Conklin and Paul Bergman, eds. Ashgate, 1990.

Wage Justice: Comparable Worth and the Paradox of Technocratic Reform. Sara M. Evans and Barbara J. Nelson. University of Chicago Press, 1989.

A Secretary and a Cook: Challenging Women's Wages in the Courts of the United States and Great Britain. Steven Willborn. ILR Press, 1989.

The Revaluation of Women's Work. Sheila Lewenhak. Routledge, 1988.

No More Peanuts. Jo Morris. State Mutual Books, 1988.

Equity and Gender: The Comparable Worth Debate. Ellen F. Paul. Transaction, 1988.

ON SEX SEGREGATION OF WORK

Women, Work, and School: Occupational Segregation and the Role of Education. Leslie R. Wolfe. Westview, 1991. By the executive director of the **CENTER FOR WOMEN POLICY STUDIES.**

Poor Work: Disadvantages and the Division of Labor. Philip Brown and Richard Scase, eds. Taylor and Francis, 1991.

Secretaries Talk: Sexuality, Power and Work. Rosemary Pringle. Routledge Chapman and Hall, 1989.

Revolving Doors: Sex Segregation and Women's Careers. Jerry A. Jacobs. Stanford University Press, 1989.

Women's Work: Development and the Division of Labor by Gender. Eleanor Leacock and Helen I. Safa. Bergin & Garvey/Greenwood, 1988.

Gender Segregation at Work. Sylvia Walby. Taylor and Francis, 1988.

ON MALE-FEMALE RELATIONS AT WORK

Working with Men: Professional Women's Stories of Power, Sexuality and Ethics. Beth Milwid. Beyond Words, 1990.

Men and Women: Partners at Work. George Simons and Gene Weissman. Crisp Publications, 1990.

Women in the Workplace: A Man's Perspective. Lloyd S. Lewan and Ronald G. Billingsley. Remington Press, 1988.
(See also SEXUAL DISCRIMINATION AND SEXUAL HARASSMENT HELP, INFORMATION, AND ACTION GUIDE on page 642.)

▱ ON WOMEN IN NONTRADITIONAL WORK

Gender Differences at Work: Women and Men in Nontraditional Occupations. Christine L. Williams. University of California Press, 1991.
Directory of Non-Traditional Training and Employment Programs Serving Women. U.S. Department of Labor, Women's Bureau, 1991.
Job Queues, Gender Queues: Explaining Women's Inroads into Male Occupations. Barbara F. Reskin and Patricia A. Roos. Temple University Press, 1990.
Exploring Nontraditional Jobs for Women, rev. ed. Rose Neufid. Rosen, 1989.
Women, Work, and Computerization: Forming New Alliances. K. Tijdens and others, eds. North Holland/Elsevier, 1989.
Pleasure, Power, and Technology: Some Tales of Gender, Engineering, and the Cooperative Workplace. Sally Hacker. Unwin Hyman, 1989.
Hard-Hatted Women: Stories of Struggle and Success in the Trades. Molly Martin, ed. Seal Press Feminist, 1988.

▱ OTHER SPECIAL CONSIDERATIONS

Women, Work, and Health. M. Frankenhauser, ed. Plenum, 1991.
Bitter Choices: Blue-Collar Women In and Out of Work. Ellen I. Rosen. University of Chicago Press, 1990.
Women Changing Work. Patricia W. Lunneborg. Bergin & Garvey/Greenwood, 1990.
The Other Women: A Workbook for Women Who Work with Women. Carolyn S. Duff and others. WomenWorks, 1989.
Temporary Work. Heidi Hartmann and June Lapidus. Institute for Women's Policy Research, 1989.
Low Wage Jobs and Workers: Trends and Options for Change. Displaced Homemakers Network Staff and Institute for Women's Policy Research Staff. Institute for Women's Policy Research, 1989.
Women, Work, and Divorce. Richard R. Peterson. State University of New York Press, 1989.
Homeworking: Myths and Realities. Sheila Allen and Carol Wolkowitz. New York University Press, 1988.

▱ INTERNATIONAL AND HISTORICAL PERSPECTIVES

Working Women: International Perspectives on Labour and Gender Ideology. Nanneke Redclift and M. Thea Sinclair, eds. Routledge, 1991.

Social Justice for Women: The International Labor Organization and Women. Carol R. Lubin and Anne Winslow. Duke, 1991.

Understanding the Gender Gap: An Economic History of American Women. Claudia Goldin. Oxford University Press, 1990.

Women's Work and the Family Economy in Historical Perspective. Pat Hudson and W. R. Lee, eds. St. Martin's, 1990.

Women, Employment and Family in the International Division of Labour. Sharon Stichter and Jane L. Parpart, eds. Temple University Press, 1990.

Homework: Historical and Contemporary Perspectives on Paid Labor at Home. Eileen Boris and Cynthia R. Daniels, eds. University of Illinois Press, 1989.

Women Working: Comparative Perspectives in Developing Areas. Alma T. Junsay and Tim B. Heaton. Greenwood, 1989.

Women Workers in Multinational Enterprises in Developing Countries, 2nd ed. International Labour Office, 1988.

A Home Divided: Women and Income in the Third World. Daisy Dwyer and Judith Bruce, eds. Stanford University Press, 1988.

Womanpower: The Arab Debate on Women at Work. Nadia Hijab. Cambridge University Press, 1988.

Rosie the Riveter Revisited: Women, the War, and Social Change. Sherna B. Gluck. NAL-Dutton, 1988.

(See also **POVERTY AND WOMEN HELP, INFORMATION, AND ACTION GUIDE** on page 287.)

◪ **BACKGROUND WORKS**

Circles of Care: Work and Identity in Women's Lives. Emily K. Abel and Margaret K. Nelson, eds. State University of New York Press, 1990.

Women at Work: Psychological and Organizational Perspectives. Jenny Firth-Cozens and Michael West, eds. Taylor and Francis, 1990.

A Woman's Wage: Historical Meanings and Social Consequences. Alice Kessler-Harris. University Press of Kentucky, 1990.

Doing It the Hard Way: Investigations of Gender and Technology. Sally L. Hacker and others, eds. Unwin Hyman, 1990.

Gendered Jobs and Social Change. Rosemary Crompton and Kay Sanderson. Unwin Hyman, 1990.

Tapestries of Life: Women's Work, Women's Consciousness, and the Meaning of Daily Experience. Bettina Aptheker. University of Massachusetts Press, 1989.

Women, Work, and Technology: Transformations. Barbara D. Wright, ed. University of Michigan Press, 1988.

Feminization of the Labor Force: Paradoxes and Promises. Jane Jenson and others. Oxford University Press, 1988.

Women's Work, Economic Trends and Policy Issues. Heidi Hartmann. Institute for Women's Policy Research, 1988.
Women's Quest for Economic Equality. Victor R. Fuchs. Harvard University Press, 1988.
Women and Work. Angela Coyle and Jane Skinner, eds. New York University Press, 1988.

World Association of Women Entrepreneurs, the English name of the Femmes Chefs D'Entreprises Mondiales (FCEM), of which NATIONAL ASSOCIATION OF WOMEN BUSINESS OWNERS (**NAWBO**) is the official U.S. member.

World Conference for Women, a United Nations–sponsored international conference scheduled for 1995; a follow-up to previous conferences in 1975, 1980, and 1985. (See INTERNATIONAL WOMEN'S YEAR; COPENHAGEN WORLD CONFERENCE FOR WOMEN; NAIROBI FORWARD-LOOKING STRATEGIES FOR THE ADVANCEMENT OF WOMEN.)

X–Y–Z

yeast infection, infection with a type of fungus, most often *Candida (Monilia) albicans,* which produces an infection called *candidiasis* or *moniliasis.* Other names for such yeast infections include *vaginal thrush, vaginal mycosis,* and *mycotic vaginitis.* The body normally houses many such fungi, generally in the DI-GESTIVE SYSTEM and VAGINA, but these are normally kept in check by "friendly" bacteria in the body and by the slight acidity of the vagina. However, changes in the natural balances within the body can cause overgrowth of candida and related organisms. Such changes can occur with DIABETES, PREGNANCY, use of antibiotics and STEROIDS, BIRTH CONTROL PILLS, and with low ESTROGEN levels, such as after MENOPAUSE. At least one study suggested that at least some persistent yeast infections may be linked to an allergic reaction to the partner's SEMEN (see ALLERGIES).

Symptoms of vaginal yeast infection include a thick, white, curdlike vaginal discharge; burning, itching, or irritation in the VULVA; sometimes a rash on the thighs; pain *(dyspareunia)* during SEXUAL INTERCOURSE. Infection of the mouth, called *oral thrush,* produces white, cheeselike patches on the tongue, inside the mouth, and the throat. In the gastrointestinal tract, yeast infections produce bloating, abdominal distress, and changes in bowel habits. Infection can be passed from mother to infant at birth, or back and forth between sexual partners. Because of that, both sex partners should be treated simultaneously.

The immediate infection is generally treated with fungicidal creams or suppositories and sometimes pills to reduce yeast growth in the intestinal tract. But for long-term treatment, the underlying cause must be treated. For some women that means changing from birth control pills to some other form of CONTRACEPTION. On their own, some women have found that eating yogurt or DOUCHING with a mildly acidic douche can control their yeast infections. Some women have treated yeast infections on their own by introducing yogurt into their vagina; however, unpasteurized yogurt—the only kind with active ingredients that might attack the yeast infection—can also introduce *other* infections.

For more help, information, and action

▶ NATIONAL WOMEN'S HEALTH NETWORK (NWHN) (202-347-1140). Operates the **Women's Health Information Service.** Publishes the information packet *Yeast Infections.*

(See also SEXUALLY TRANSMITTED DISEASES; also WOMEN'S HEALTH HELP, INFORMATION, AND ACTION GUIDE on page 334.)

zygote, the scientific name for the fertilized egg created from the union of a woman's egg (OVUM) and a man's SPERM. Some use the term *zygote* only until cell division starts, in a matter of hours, calling the resulting ball of cells a *blastocyte* or *blastocyst*. Most people use the term *zygote* until the tiny ball of cells is implanted in the UTERUS, after about a week. Still others use the terms *zygote* or *fertilized egg* for another four weeks, until organs begin to develop.

The zygote or fertilized egg grows into an EMBRYO. If more than one being results from a single egg, these twins or multiple births are called *monozygotic*, or *identical*. But if beings grow at the same time but from separate fertilized eggs, they are termed *dizygotic, nonidentical*, or *fraternal*. (See FERTILIZATION; PREGNANCY; for a stage-by-stage description of growth, see WHAT HAPPENS DURING PREGNANCY on page 557.)

SPECIAL

INFORMATION

SECTION

DECLARATION OF SENTIMENTS

AND RESOLUTIONS

Following is the complete text of Elizabeth Cady STANTON'*s key feminist document, inspired by the Declaration of Independence and presented at the* SENECA FALLS WOMEN'S RIGHTS CONVENTION *in July 1848.*

When, in the course of human events, it becomes necessary for one portion of the family of man to assume among the people of the earth a position different from that which they have hitherto occupied, but one to which the laws of nature and of nature's God entitle them, a decent respect to the opinions of mankind requires that they should declare the causes that impel them to such a course.

We hold these truths to be self-evident: that all men and women are created equal; that they are endowed by their Creator with certain inalienable rights; that among these are life, liberty, and the pursuit of happiness; that to secure these rights governments are instituted, deriving their just powers from the consent of the governed. Whenever any form of government becomes destructive of these ends, it is the right of those who suffer from it to refuse allegiance to it, and to insist upon the institution of a new government, laying its foundations upon such principles, and organizing its powers in such form, as to them shall seem most likely to effect their safety and happiness. Prudence, indeed, will dictate that governments long established should not be changed for light and transient causes; and accordingly all experience hath shown that mankind are more disposed to suffer, while evils are sufferable, than to right themselves by abolishing the forms to which they are accustomed. But when a long train of abuses and usurpations, pursuing invariably the same object, evinces a design to reduce them under absolute despotism, it is their duty to throw off such government, and to provide new guards for their future security. Such has been the patient sufferance of the women under this government, and such is now the necessity which constrains them to demand the equal station to which they are entitled.

The history of mankind is a history of repeated injuries and usurpations on the part of man toward woman, having in direct object the establishment of an absolute tyranny over her. To prove this, let facts be submitted to a candid world.

He has never permitted her to exercise her inalienable right to the elective franchise.

He has compelled her to submit to laws, in the formation of which she had no voice.

He has withheld from her rights which are given to the most ignorant and degraded men—both natives and foreigners.

Having deprived her of this first right of a citizen, the elective franchise, thereby leaving her without representation in the halls of legislation, he has oppressed her on all sides.

He has made her, if married, in the eye of the law, civilly dead.

He has taken from her all right in property, even to the wages she earns.

He has made her, morally, an irresponsible being, as she can commit many crimes with impunity, provided they be done in the presence of her husband. In the covenant of marriage, she is compelled to promise obedience to her husband, he becoming, to all intents and purposes, her master—the law giving him power to deprive her of her liberty, and to administer chastisement.

He has so framed the laws of divorce, as to what shall be the proper causes, and in case of separation, to whom the guardianship of the children shall be given, as to be wholly regardless of the happiness of women—the law, in all cases, going upon the false supposition of the supremacy of man, and giving all power into his hands.

After depriving her of all rights as a married woman, if single, and the owner of property, he has taxed her to support a government which recognizes her only when her property can be made profitable to it.

He has monopolized nearly all the profitable employments, and from those she is permitted to follow, she receives but a scanty remuneration. He closes against her all the avenues to wealth and distinction which he considers most honorable to himself. As a teacher of theology, medicine, or law, she is not known.

He has denied her the facilities for obtaining a thorough education, all colleges being closed against her.

He allows her in Church, as well as State, but a subordinate position, claiming Apostolic authority for her exclusion from the ministry, and, with some exceptions, from any public participation in the affairs of the Church.

He has created a false public sentiment by giving to the world a different code of morals for men and women, by which moral delinquencies which exclude women from society, are not only tolerated, but deemed of little account in man.

He has usurped the prerogative of Jehovah himself, claiming it as his right to assign for her a sphere of action, when that belongs to her conscience and to her God.

He has endeavored, in every way that he could, to destroy her confidence in her own powers, to lessen her self-respect, and to make her willing to lead a dependent and abject life.

Now, in view of this entire disfranchisement of one-half the people of this country, their social and religious degradation—in view of the unjust laws above mentioned, and because women do feel themselves aggrieved, oppressed, and fraudulently deprived of their most sacred rights, we insist that they have immediate admission to all the rights and privileges which belong to them as citizens of the United States.

In entering upon the great work before us, we anticipate no small amount of misconception, misrepresentation, and ridicule; but we shall use every instrumentality within our power to effect our object. We shall employ agents, circulate tracts, petition the State and National legislatures, and endeavor to enlist the pulpit and the press in our behalf. We hope this Convention will be followed by a series of Conventions embracing every part of the country.

Resolutions

Whereas, the great precept of nature is conceded to be, that "man shall pursue his own true and substantial happiness." Blackstone in his Commentaries remarks, that this law of Nature being coeval with mankind, and dictated by God himself, is of course superior in obligation to any other. It is binding over all the globe, in all countries and at all times; no human laws are of any validity if contrary to this, and such of them as are valid, derive all their force, and all their validity, and all their authority, mediately and immediately, from this original; therefore,

Resolved That such laws as conflict, in any way, with the true and substantial happiness of woman, are contrary to the great precept of nature and of no validity, for this is "superior in obligation to any other."

Resolved That all laws which prevent woman from occupying such a station in society as her conscience shall dictate, or which place her in a position inferior to that of man, are contrary to the great precept of nature, and therefore of no force or authority.

Resolved That woman is man's equal—was intended to be so by the Creator, and the highest good of the race demands that she should be recognized as such.

Resolved That the women of this country ought to be enlightened in regard to the laws under which they live, that they may no longer publish their degradation by declaring themselves satisfied with their present position, nor their ignorance, by asserting that they have all the rights they want.

Resolved That inasmuch as man, while claiming for himself intellectual superiority, does accord to woman moral superiority, it is preeminently his duty to encourage her to speak and teach, as she has an opportunity, in all religious assemblies.

Resolved That the same amount of virtue, delicacy and refinement of behavior that is required of woman in the social state, should also be required of man, and the same transgressions should be visited with equal severity on both man and woman.

Resolved That the objection of indelicacy and impropriety, which is so often brought against woman when she addresses a public audience, comes with a very illgrace from those who encourage, by their attendance, her appearance on the stage, in the concert, or in feats of the circus.

Resolved That woman has too long rested satisfied in the circumscribed limits which corrupt customs and a perverted application of the Scriptures have marked out for her, and that it is time she should move in the enlarged sphere which her great Creator has assigned her.

Resolved That it is the duty of the women of this country to secure to themselves their sacred right to the elective franchise.

Resolved That the equality of human rights results necessarily from the fact of the identity of the race in capabilities and responsibilities.

Resolved, therefore, That, being invested by the Creator with the same capabilities, and the same consciousness of responsibility for their exercise, it is demonstrably the right and duty of woman, equally with man, to promote every righteous cause by every righteous means; and especially in regard to the great subjects of morals and religion, it is self-evidently her right to participate with her brother in teaching them, both in private and in public, by writing and by speaking, by any instrumentalities proper to be used, and in any assemblies proper to be held; and this being a self-evident truth growing out of the divinely implanted principles of human nature, any custom or authority adverse to it, whether modern or wearing the hoary sanction of antiquity, is to be regarded as a self-evident falsehood, and at war with mankind.

Resolved That the speedy success of our cause depends upon the zealous and untiring efforts of both men and women, for the overthrow of the monopoly of the pulpit, and for the securing to woman an equal participation with men in the various trades, professions, and commerce.

CONVENTION ON THE

ELIMINATION OF ALL FORMS

OF DISCRIMINATION

AGAINST WOMEN

[Adopted and opened for signature, ratification, and accession by the U.N. General Assembly resolution 34/180 of 18 December 1979]

The States Parties to the present Convention,

Noting that the Charter of the United Nations reaffirms faith in fundamental human rights, in the dignity and worth of the human person and in the equal rights of men and women,

Noting that the Universal Declaration of Human Rights affirms the principle of the inadmissibility of discrimination and proclaims that all human beings are born free and equal in dignity and rights and that everyone is entitled to all the rights and freedoms set forth therein, without distinction of any kind, including distinction based on sex,

Noting that the States Parties to the International Covenants on Human Rights have the obligation to ensure the equal right of men and women to enjoy all economic, social, cultural, civil and political rights,

Considering the international conventions concluded under the auspices of the United Nations and the specialized agencies promoting equality of rights of men and women,

Noting also the resolutions, declarations and recommendations adopted by the United Nations and the specialized agencies promoting equality of rights of men and women,

Concerned, however, that despite these various instruments extensive discrimination against women continues to exist,

Recalling that discrimination against women violates the principles of equality of rights and respect for human dignity, is an obstacle to the participation of women, on equal terms with men, in the political, social, economic and cultural life of their countries, hampers the growth of the prosperity of society and the family and makes more difficult the full development of the potentialities of women in the service of their countries and of humanity,

Concerned that in situations of poverty women have the least access to food, health, education, training and opportunities for employment and other needs,

Convinced that the establishment of the new international economic order based on equity and justice will contribute significantly towards the promotion of equality between men and women,

Emphasizing that the eradication of *apartheid*, all forms of racism, racial discrimination, colonialism, neo-colonialism, aggression, foreign occupation and domination and interference in the internal affairs of States is essential to the full enjoyment of the rights of men and women,

Affirming that the strengthening of international peace and security, the relaxation of international tension, mutual co-operation among all States irrespective of their social and economic systems, general and complete disarmament, in particular nuclear disarmament under strict and effective international control, the affirmation of the principles of justice, equality and mutual benefit in relations among countries and the realization of the right of peoples under alien and colonial domination and foreign occupation to self-determination and independence, as well as respect for national sovereignty and territorial integrity, will promote social progress and development and as a consequence will contribute to the attainment of full equality between men and women,

Convinced that the full and complete development of a country, the welfare of the world and the cause of peace require the maximum participation of women on equal terms with men in all fields,

Bearing in mind the great contribution of women to the welfare of the family and to the development of society, so far not fully recognized, the social significance of maternity and the role of both parents in the family and in the upbringing of children, and aware that the role of women in procreation should not be a basis for discrimination but that the upbringing of children requires a sharing of responsibility between men and women and society as a whole,

Aware that a change in the traditional role of men as well as the role of women in society and in the family is needed to achieve full equality between men and women,

Determined to implement the principles set forth in the Declaration on the Elimination of Discrimination Against Women and, for that purpose, to adopt the measures required for the elimination of such discrimination in all its forms and manifestations,

Have agreed on the following:

PART I

Article 1

For the purposes of the present Convention, the term "discrimination against women" shall mean any distinction, exclusion or restriction made on the basis of sex which has the effect or purpose of impairing or nullifying the recognition, enjoyment or exercise by women, irrespective of their marital status, on a basis of equality of men and women, of human rights and fundamental freedoms in the political, economic, social, cultural, civil or any other field.

Article 2

States Parties condemn discrimination against women in all its forms, agree to pursue by all appropriate means and without delay a policy of eliminating discrimination against women and, to this end, undertake:

(a) To embody the principle of the quality of men and women in their national constitutions or other appropriate legislation if not yet incorporated therein and to ensure, through law and other appropriate means, the practical realization of this principle;

(b) To adopt appropriate legislative and other measures, including sanctions where appropriate, prohibiting all discrimination against women;

(c) To establish legal protection of the rights of women on an equal basis with men and to ensure through competent national tribunals and other public institutions the effective protection of women against any act of discrimination;

(d) To refrain from engaging in any act or practice of discrimination against women and to ensure that public authorities and institutions shall act in conformity with this obligation;

(e) To take all appropriate measures to eliminate discrimination against women by any person, organization or enterprise;

(f) To take all appropriate measures, including legislation, to modify or abolish existing laws, regulations, customs and practices which constitute discrimination against women;

(g) To repeal all national penal provisions which constitute discrimination against women.

Article 3

States Parties shall take in all fields, in particular in the political, social, economic and cultural fields, all appropriate measures, including legislation, to ensure the full development and advancement of women, for the purpose of guaranteeing them the exercise and enjoyment of human rights and fundamental freedoms on a basis of equality with men.

Article 4

1. Adoption by States Parties of temporary special measures aimed at accelerating *de facto* equality between men and women shall not be considered discrimination as defined in the present Convention, but shall in no way entail as a consequence the maintenance of unequal or separate standards; these measures shall be discontinued when the objectives of equality of opportunity and treatment have been achieved.

2. Adoption by States Parties of special measures, including those measures contained in the present Convention, aimed at protecting maternity shall not be considered discriminatory.

Article 5

States Parties shall take all appropriate measures:

(a) To modify the social and cultural patterns of conduct of men and women, with a view to achieving the elimination of prejudices and customary and all other practices which are based on the idea of the inferiority or the superiority of either of the sexes or on stereotyped roles for men and women;

(b) To ensure that family education includes a proper understanding of maternity as a social function and the recognition of the common responsibility of men and women in the upbringing and development of their children, it being understood that the interest of the children is the primordial consideration in all cases.

Article 6

States Parties shall take all appropriate measures including legislation, to suppress all forms of traffic in women and exploitation of prostitution of women.

PART II

Article 7

States Parties shall take all appropriate measures to eliminate discrimination against women in the political and public life of the country and, in particular, shall ensure to women, on equal terms with men, the right:

(a) To vote in all elections and public referenda and to be eligible for election to all publicly elected bodies;

(b) To participate in the formulation of government policy and the implementation thereof and to hold public office and perform all public functions at all levels of government;

(c) To participate in non-governmental organizations and associations concerned with the public and political life of the country.

Article 8

States Parties shall take all appropriate measures to ensure to women, on equal terms with men and without any discrimination, the opportunity to represent their Governments at the international level and to participate in the work of international organizations.

Article 9

1. States Parties shall grant women equal rights with men to acquire, change or retain their nationality. They shall ensure in particular that neither marriage to an alien nor change of nationality by the husband during marriage shall automatically change the nationality of the wife, render her stateless or force upon her the nationality of the husband.

2. States Parties shall grant women equal rights with men with respect to the nationality of their children.

PART III

Article 10

States Parties shall take all appropriate measures to eliminate discrimination against women in order to ensure to them equal rights with men in the field of educations and in particular to ensure, on a basis of equality of men and women:

(a) The same conditions for career and vocational guidance, for access to studies and for the achievement of diplomas in educational establishments of all categories in rural as well as in urban areas; this equality shall be ensured in pre-school, general, technical, professional and higher technical education, as well as in all types of vocational training;

(b) Access to the same curricula, the same examinations, teaching staff with qualifications of the same standard and school premises and equipment of the same quality;

(c) The elimination of any stereotyped concept of the roles of men and women at all levels and in all forms of educations by encouraging coeducation and other types of education which will help to achieve this aim and, in particular, by the revision of textbooks and school programmes and the adaptation of teaching methods;

(d) The same opportunities to benefit from scholarships and other study grants;

(e) The same opportunities for access to programmes of continuing education, including adult and functional literacy programmes, particularly those aimed at reducing at the earliest possible time, any gap in education existing between men and women;

(f) The reduction of female student drop-out rates and the organization of programmes for girls and women who have left school prematurely;

(g) The same opportunities to participate actively in sports and physical education;

(h) Access to specific educational information to help to ensure the health and well-being of families, including information and advice on family planning.

Article 11

1. States Parties shall take all appropriate measures to eliminate discrimination against women in the field of employment in order to ensure, on a basis of equality of men and women, the same rights, in particular:

(a) The right to work as an inalienable right of all human beings;

(b) The right to the same employment opportunities, including the application of the same criteria for selection in matters of employment;

(c) The right to free choice of profession and employment, the right to promotion, job security and all benefits and conditions of service and the right to receive vocational training and retraining, including apprenticeships, advanced vocational training and recurrent training;

(d) The right to equal remuneration, including benefits and to equal treatment in respect of work of equal value, as well as equality of treatment in the evaluation of the quality of work;

(e) The right to social security; particularly in cases of retirement, unemployment, sickness, invalidity and old age and other incapacity to work, as well as the right to paid leave;

(f) The right to protection of health and to safety in working conditions, including the safeguarding of the function of reproduction.

2. In order to prevent discrimination against women on the grounds of marriage or maternity and to ensure their effective right to work, States Parties shall take appropriate measures:

(a) To prohibit, subject to the imposition of sanctions, dismissal on the grounds of pregnancy or of maternity leave and discrimination in dismissals on the basis of marital status;

(b) To introduce maternity leave with pay or with comparable social benefits without loss of former employment, seniority or social allowances;

(c) To encourage the provision of the necessary supporting social services to enable parents to combine family obligations with work responsibilities and participation in public life, in particular through promoting the establishment and development of a network of child-care facilities;

(d) To provide special protection to women during pregnancy in types of work proved to be harmful to them.

3. Protective legislation relating to matters covered in this article shall be reviewed periodically in the light of scientific and technological knowledge and shall be revised, repealed or extended as necessary.

Article 12

1. States Parties shall take all appropriate measures to eliminate discrimination against women in the field of health care in order to ensure, on a basis of equality of men and women, access to health care services, including those related to family planning.

2. Notwithstanding the provisions of paragraph 1 of this Article, States Parties shall ensure to women appropriate services in connexion with pregnancy, confinement and the postnatal period, granting free services where necessary, as well as adequate nutrition during pregnancy and lactation.

Article 13

States Parties shall take all appropriate measures to eliminate discrimination against women in other areas of economic and social life in order to ensure, on a basis of equality of men and women, the same rights, in particular:

(a) The right to family benefits;

(b) The right to bank loans, mortgages and other forms of financial credit;

(c) The right to participate in recreational activities, sports and all aspects of cultural life.

Article 14

1. States Parties shall take into account the particular problems faced by rural women and the significant roles which rural women play in the economic survival of their families, including their work in the non-monetized sectors of the economy, and shall take all appropriate measures to ensure the application of the provisions of the present Convention to women in rural areas.

2. States Parties shall take all appropriate measures to eliminate discrimination against women in rural areas in order to ensure, on a basis of equality of men and women, that they participate in and benefit from rural development and, in particular, shall ensure to such women the right:

(a) To participate in the elaboration and implementation of development planning at all levels;

(b) To have access to adequate health care facilities, including information, counselling and services in family planning;

(c) To benefit directly from social security programmes;

(d) To obtain all types of training and education, formal and non-formal, including that relating to functional literacy, as well as *inter alia,* the benefit of all community and extension services, in order to increase their technical proficiency;

(e) To organize self-help groups and co-operatives in order to obtain equal access to economic opportunities through employment or self-employment;

(f) To participate in all community activities;

(g) To have access to agricultural credit and loans, marketing facilities, appropriate technology and equal treatment in land and agrarian reform as well as in land resettlement schemes;

(h) To enjoy adequate living conditions, particularly in relation to housing, sanitation, electricity and water supply, transport and communications.

PART IV

Article 15

1. States Parties shall accord to women equality with men before the law.

2. States Parties shall accord to women, in civil matters, a legal capacity identical to that of men and the same opportunities to exercise that capacity. In particular, they shall give women equal rights to conclude contracts and to administer property and shall treat them equally in all stages of procedure in courts and tribunals.

3. States Parties agree that all contracts and all other private instruments of any kind with a legal effect which is directed at restricting the legal capacity of women shall be deemed null and void.

4. States Parties shall accord to men and women the same rights with regard to the law relating to the movement of persons and the freedom to choose their residence and domicile.

Article 16

1. States Parties shall take all appropriate measures to eliminate discrimination against women in all matters relating to marriage and family relations and in particular shall ensure, on a basis of equality of men and women:

(a) The same right to enter into marriage;

(b) The same right freely to choose a spouse and to enter into marriage only with their free and full consent;

(c) The same rights and responsibilities during marriage and at its dissolution;

(d) The same rights and responsibilities as parents, irrespective of their marital status, in matters relating to their children; in all cases the interests of the children shall be paramount;

(e) The same rights to decide freely and responsibly on the number and spacing of their children and to have access to the information, education and means to enable them to exercise these rights;

(f) The same rights and responsibilities with regard to guardianship, wardship, trustee-ship and adoption of children, or similar institutions where these concepts exist in national legislation; in all cases the interests of the children shall be paramount;

(g) The same personal rights as husband and wife, including the right to choose a family name, a profession and an occupation;

(h) The same rights for both spouses in respect of the ownership, acquisition, management, administration, enjoyment and disposition of property, whether free of charge or for a valuable consideration.

2. The betrothal and the marriage of a child shall have no legal effect, and all necessary action, including legislation, shall be taken to specify a minimum age for marriage and to make the registration of marriages in an official registry compulsory.

Part V

Article 17

1. For the purpose of considering the progress made in the implementation of the present Convention, there shall be established a Committee on the Elimination of Discrimination Against Women (hereinafter referred to as the Committee) consisting, at the time of entry into force of the Convention, of eighteen and after ratification of or accession to the Convention by the thirty-fifth State Party, of twenty-three experts of high moral standing and competence in the field covered by the convention. The experts shall be elected by States Parties from among their nationals and shall serve in their personal capacity, consideration being given to equitable geographical distribution and to the representation of the different forms of civilization as well as the principal legal systems.

2. The members of the Committee shall be elected by secret ballot from a list of persons nominated by States Parties. Each State Party may nominate one person from among its own nationals.

3. The initial election shall be held six months after the date of the entry into force of the present Convention. At least three months before the date of each election the Secretary-General of the United Nations shall address a letter to the States Parties inviting them to submit their nominations within two months. The Secretary-General shall prepare a list in alphabetical order of all persons thus nominated, indicating the States Parties which have nominated them, and shall submit it to the States Parties.

4. Elections of the members of the Committee shall be held at a meeting of States Parties convened by the Secretary-General at United Nations Headquarters. At that meeting, for which two-thirds of the States Parties shall constitute a quorum, the persons elected to the Committee shall be those nominees who obtain the largest number of votes and an absolute majority of the votes of the representatives of States Parties present and voting.

5. The members of the Committee shall be elected for a term of four years. However, the terms of nine of the members elected at the first election shall expire at the end of two years; immediately after the first election the names of these nine members shall be chosen by lot by the Chairman of the Committee.

NAIROBI FORWARD-LOOKING

STRATEGIES FOR THE

ADVANCEMENT OF WOMEN:

A SUMMARY

The Nairobi Forward-Looking Strategies for the Advancement of Women were adopted by the World Conference to Review and Appraise the Achievements of the United Nations Decade for Women: Equality, Development and Peace, held in Nairobi, Kenya, 15–26 July 1985, and endorsed by the General Assembly in its resolution 40/108 on 13 December 1985. They call for:

Sexual equality
- the elimination of all forms of discrimination against women
- equal rights under the law
- equal rights to marriage and divorce
- the establishment, in every country, of a high-level governmental body to monitor and implement progress towards equality.

Women's autonomy and power
- the right of all women—irrespective of marital status—to buy, sell, own and administer property and other resources independently
- the protection of women's rights to land, credit, training, investment and income as an integral part of all agrarian reform and agricultural development
- the equal involvement of women, at every stage and level of development
- the promotion of women to positions of power at every level within all political and legislative bodies in order to achieve parity with men
- measures to promote equal distribution of productive resources and reduce mass poverty among women, particularly in times of economic recession.

Recognition of women's unpaid work
- recognition of the extent and value of women's unpaid work, inside and outside the home

- inclusion of women's paid and unpaid work in national accounts and economic statistics
- the sharing of domestic responsibilities
- the development of services, to reduce women's child-care and domestic workload, including introduction of incentives to encourage employers to provide child-care facilities for working parents
- the establishment of flexible working hours to encourage the sharing of child-care and domestic work between parents.

Advances in women's paid work
- equal employment opportunities
- equal pay for work of equal value
- recognition of the extent and value of women's work in the informal sector
- measures to encourage women to work in male-dominated occupations and vice versa, in order to desegregate the work place
- preferential treatment in hiring of women so long as they are a disproportionate share of the unemployed
- adequate social security and unemployment benefits.

Health services and family planning
- equal access to health services
- adequate health facilities for mothers and children
- every woman's right to decide on the number and spacing of her children, and access to family planning for every woman
- discouragement of child-bearing at too early an age.

Better educational opportunities
- equal access to education and training
- efforts to have more girls study subjects usually selected by boys, and vice versa, in order to desegregate curricula
- efforts to ensure that girls don't drop out of school
- the provision of adult education for women.

Promotion of peace
- the involvement of women, in promoting peace and disarmament.

Minimum targets for the year 2000
- enforcement of laws guaranteeing implementation of women's equality
- an increase in the life expectancy of women to at least 65 years in all countries
- the reduction of maternal mortality
- the elimination of women's illiteracy
- the expansion of employment opportunities.

WOMEN IN POLITICAL LIFE: AN UPDATE

Selected Countries	Date of Right to Vote	Date of Right to Be Elected	% Women in Parliament 1991
Algeria	1962	1962	2.4
Argentina	1947	1947	4.7
Australia	1901/1967*	1901/1967*	6.7
Bangladesh	1947	1947	10.3
Brazil	1934	1934	6.0
Bulgaria	1944	1944	8.5
Cameroon	1946	1946	14.4
Canada	1917/1918/1950*	1920/1960/1969*	13.2
Chile	1931/1949*	1931/1949*	5.8
China	1949	1949	21.3
Cuba	1934	1934	33.9
Czechoslovakia	1920	1920	8.7
Denmark	1915	1915	33.0
Ecuador	1946	1946	5.5
Egypt	1956	1956	2.2
El Salvador	1961	1961	8.3
Equatorial Guinea	1963	1963	0.0
Finland	1906	1906	38.5
France	1944	1944	5.7
Gabon	1956	1956	4.2
Germany	1918	1918	20.4
Greece	1952	1952	5.3
Hungary	1945	1945	7.0
Iceland	1915	1915	23.8
India	1950	1950	7.1
Indonesia	1945	1945	12.4
Iraq	1980	1980	10.8
Iran	1963	1963	1.5
Ireland	1918	1918	7.8
Israel	1948	1948	6.7
Italy	1945	1945	12.8
Ivory Coast	1952	1952	4.6
Jamaica	1944	1944	5.0
Japan	1945/1947*	1945/1947*	2.3
Jordan	1974	1974	0.0
Kenya	1963	1963	1.1
Korea (North)	1946	1946	20.1
Korea (South)	1948	1948	2.0
Laos	1958	1958	8.9
Kuwait	NOT YET	NOT YET	0.0
Luxembourg	1919	1919	13.3

Selected Countries	Date of Right to Vote	Date of Right to Be Elected	% Women in Parliament 1991
Madagascar	1959	1959	6.5
Malaysia	1957	1957	5.0
Mexico	1947	1953	12.4
Mongolia	1923/1924*	1923/1924*	2.1
Morocco	1963	1963	0.0
Mozambique	1975	1975	15.7
Nepal	1951	1951	3.4
New Zealand	1893	1919	16.5
Nicaragua	1955	1955	16.3
Norway	1907/1913*	1907/1913*	35.8
Pakistan	1937	1937	0.9
Papua New Guinea	1975	1975	0.0
Peru	1950	1956	5.5
Philippines	1937	1937	9.0
Poland	1918	1918	13.5
Portugal	1931/1976*	1931/1976*	7.6
Romania	1929/1946*	1929/1946*	3.6
Rwanda	1961	1961	17.1
South Africa	1930/1984*	1930/1984*	2.6
Spain	1931	1931	14.6
Sweden	1918/1921*	1918/1921*	38.1
Switzerland	1971	1971	14.0
Syria	1949	1953	8.4
Thailand	1932	1932	3.8
Togo	1956	1956	3.9
Tonga	1960	1960	0.0
Tunisia	1959	1959	4.2
Turkey	1930/1934*	1930/1934*	1.3
United Arab Emirates	NOT YET	NOT YET	0.0
United Kingdom	1918/1928*	1918/1928*	6.3
United States	1920	1788	6.4
Venezuela	1947	1947	9.9
Vietnam	1946	1946	17.7
Zambia	1962	1964	5.1
Zimbabwe	1957	1978	12.0

Source: Adapted from material from the Inter-Parliamentary Union (Geneva) annual report on the status of women in leadership positions worldwide, as reported in *National NOW Times, June 1992.*
*Where several dates are shown, full suffrage for all adult women came only in several stages.

AMERICAN WORKING

WOMEN:

A STATISTICAL PORTRAIT

Table 1. Labor force status and occupation of the employed by sex, 1990 annual averages

(Numbers in thousands)

Characteristic	Total	Women		Men	
		Number	Percent of total	Number	Percent of total
LABOR FORCE STATUS					
Civilian noninstitutional population	188,049	98,399	52.3	89,650	47.7
Civilian labor force	124,787	56,554	45.3	68,234	54.7
Employed	117,914	53,479	45.4	64,435	54.6
Full-time workers	97,994	40,011	40.8	54,982	59.2
Unemployed..	6,874	3,075	44.7	3,799	55.3
Not in labor force..................................	63,262	41,845	66.1	21,417	33.9
OCCUPATION					
Executive, administrative, and managerial	14,839	5,943	40.0	8,897	60.0
Professional specialty	15,818	8,095	51.2	7,723	48.8
Technicians and related support	3,842	1,888	49.1	1,954	50.9
Sales occupations..................................	14,191	6,983	49.2	7,208	50.8
Administrative support, including clerical	18,641	14,870	79.8	3,771	20.2
Service occupations...............................	15,759	9,470	60.1	6,288	39.9
Precision production, craft, and repair....	13,641	1,159	8.5	12,482	91.5
Operators, fabricators, and laborers	17,775	4,526	25.5	13,249	74.5
Farming, forestry, and fishing.................	3,408	544	16.0	2,864	84.0

Table 2. Civilian labor force participation rates of all persons, teenagers, and adults by sex, 1960–90 annual averages

(Percent of population in labor force)

Year	Women			Men		
	Total, 16 years and over	16 to 19 years	20 years and over	Total, 16 years and over	16 to 19 years	20 years and over
1960	37.7	39.3	37.6	83.3	56.1	86.0
1961	38.1	39.7	38.0	82.9	54.6	85.7
1962	37.9	39.0	37.8	82.0	53.8	84.8
1963	38.3	38.0	38.3	81.4	52.9	84.4
1964	38.7	37.0	38.9	81.0	52.4	84.2
1965	39.3	38.0	39.4	80.7	53.8	83.9
1966	40.3	41.4	40.1	80.4	55.3	83.6
1967	41.1	41.6	41.1	80.4	55.6	83.4
1968	41.6	41.9	41.6	80.1	55.1	83.1
1969	42.7	43.2	42.7	79.8	55.9	82.8
1970	43.3	44.0	43.3	79.7	56.1	82.6
1971	43.4	43.4	43.3	79.1	56.1	82.1
1972	43.9	45.8	43.7	78.9	58.1	81.6
1973	44.7	47.8	44.4	78.8	59.7	81.3
1974	45.7	49.1	45.3	78.7	60.7	81.0
1975	46.3	49.1	46.0	77.9	59.1	80.3
1976	47.3	49.8	47.0	77.5	59.3	79.8
1977	48.4	51.2	48.1	77.7	60.9	79.7
1978	50.0	53.7	49.6	77.9	62.0	79.8
1979	50.9	54.2	50.6	77.8	61.5	79.8
1980	51.5	52.9	51.3	77.4	60.5	79.4
1981	52.1	51.8	52.1	77.0	59.0	79.0
1982	52.6	51.4	52.7	76.6	56.7	78.7
1983	52.9	50.8	53.1	76.4	56.2	78.5
1984	53.6	51.8	53.7	76.4	56.0	78.3
1985	54.5	52.1	54.7	76.3	56.8	78.1
1986	55.3	53.0	55.5	76.3	56.4	78.1
1987	56.0	53.3	56.2	76.2	56.1	78.0
1988	56.6	53.6	56.8	76.2	56.9	77.9
1989	57.4	53.9	57.7	76.4	57.9	78.1
1990	57.5	51.8	57.9	76.1	55.7	77.8

Table 3. Civilian labor force participation rates by age and sex, 1960 and 1990 annual averages

(Percent of population in labor force)

Age	Women		Men	
	1960	1990	1960	1990
Total 16 years and over........................	37.7	57.5	83.3	76.1
16 to 19 years	39.3	51.8	56.1	55.7
20 to 24 years	46.1	71.6	88.1	84.3
25 to 34 years	36.0	73.6	97.5	94.2
35 to 44 years	43.4	76.5	97.7	94.4
45 to 54 years	49.9	71.2	95.7	90.7
55 to 64 years	37.2	45.3	86.8	67.7
65 years and over	10.8	8.7	33.1	16.4

Table 4. Civilian labor force participation rates of persons 20 years and over by sex, race, and Hispanic origin, 1973–90 annual averages

(Percent of population in labor force)

Year	Women, 20 years and over			Men, 20 years and over		
	White	Black	Hispanic origin	White	Black	Hispanic origin
1973	43.5	51.6	41.3	81.6	78.4	85.9
1974	44.4	51.4	42.7	81.4	77.6	86.0
1975	45.3	51.1	43.8	80.7	76.0	85.5
1976	46.2	52.5	44.6	80.3	75.4	84.2
1977	47.3	53.6	45.1	80.2	75.6	84.8
1978	48.7	55.5	47.2	80.1	76.2	84.9
1979	49.8	55.4	48.0	80.1	76.3	85.3
1980	50.6	55.6	48.5	79.8	75.1	84.9
1981	51.5	56.0	49.7	79.5	74.5	84.7
1982	52.2	56.2	49.3	79.2	74.7	84.0
1983	52.5	56.8	49.0	78.9	75.2	84.1
1984	53.1	57.6	50.5	78.7	74.8	84.3
1985	54.0	58.6	50.6	78.5	74.4	84.0
1986	54.9	58.9	51.7	78.5	74.8	84.6
1987	55.6	60.0	53.3	78.4	74.7	84.5
1988	56.3	60.1	54.2	78.3	74.6	85.0
1989	57.2	60.6	54.9	78.5	74.4	85.0
1990	57.6	60.0	54.6	78.3	73.8	84.1

NOTE: Data for persons of Hispanic origin, beginning in 1980, are not strictly comparable with data for prior years because of revisions in the estimation procedures.

Table 5. Civilian labor force participation rates of women in nine industrialized countries, annual averages, selected years, 1970–90

(Percent of population in labor force)

Country	1970	1975	1980	1985	1990
United States	43.3	46.3	51.5	54.5	57.5
Australia	40.4	44.5	45.5	47.0	53.1
Canada	38.3	44.4	50.4	54.6	58.4
France	39.8	41.7	44.3	45.5	45.9
Italy	26.4	26.8	30.1	30.7	32.6
Japan	48.7	44.8	46.6	47.6	49.1
Netherlands	(¹)	29.5	34.3	38.6	42.2
Sweden	50.0	55.2	59.3	61.5	63.9
United Kingdom	42.2	46.2	47.8	49.6	53.3

¹Data not available
NOTE: Data for 1990 for France, Italy, Sweden, and the United Kingdom are preliminary. Data for the Netherlands are for 1988, the latest year available.

Table 6. Employed persons by sex, 1960–90 annual averages

(in thousands)

Year	Total, 16 years and over	Women	Men
1960	65,778	21,874	43,904
1961	65,746	22,090	43,656
1962¹	66,702	22,525	44,177
1963	67,762	23,105	44,657
1964	69,305	23,831	45,474
1965	71,088	24,748	46,340
1966	72,895	25,976	46,919
1967	74,372	26,893	47,479
1968	75,920	27,807	48,114
1969	77,902	29,084	48,818
1970	78,678	29,688	48,990
1971	79,367	29,976	49,390
1972¹	82,153	31,257	50,896
1973¹	85,064	32,715	52,349
1974	86,794	33,769	53,024
1975	85,846	33,989	51,857
1976	88,752	35,615	53,138
1977	92,017	37,289	54,728
1978¹	96,048	39,569	56,479
1979	98,824	41,217	57,607
1980	99,303	42,117	57,186
1981	100,397	43,000	57,397

(Continued on next page)

Year	Total, 16 years and over	Women	Men
1982..	99,526	43,256	56,271
1983..	100,834	44,047	56,787
1984..	105,005	45,915	59,091
1985..	107,150	47,259	59,891
1986[1]	109,597	48,706	60,892
1987..	112,440	50,334	62,107
1988..	114,968	51,696	63,273
1989..	117,342	53,027	64,315
1990..	117,914	53,479	64,435

[1]Not strictly comparable with prior years because of revisions in the population levels and/or estimation procedures used in the Current Population Survey (CPS). For an explanation, see the original report.

Table 7. Employed full- and part-time workers, 20 years and over, by sex, 1968–90 annual averages

(Numbers in thousands)

Year	Total	Employed women, 20 years and over				Total	Employed men, 20 years and over			
		Full time		Part time			Full time		Part time	
		Number	Percent of total	Number	Percent of total		Number	Percent of total	Number	Percent of total
1968	25,281	19,600	77.5	5,681	22.5	44,859	42,720	95.2	2,139	4.8
1969	26,397	20,454	77.5	5,944	22.5	45,388	43,100	95.0	2,288	5.0
1970	26,952	20,654	76.6	6,297	23.4	45,581	43,138	94.6	2,443	5.4
1971	27,246	20,769	76.2	6,477	23.8	45,912	43,321	94.4	2,591	5.6
1972[1]	28,276	21,536	76.2	6,741	23.8	47,130	44,476	94.4	2,654	5.6
1973[1]	29,484	22,495	76.3	6,991	23.7	48,310	45,637	94.5	2,673	5.5
1974	30,424	23,181	76.2	7,243	23.8	48,922	46,158	94.3	2,765	5.7
1975	30,726	23,242	75.6	7,484	24.4	48,018	45,051	93.8	2,967	6.2
1976	32,226	24,406	75.7	7,820	24.3	49,190	46,175	93.9	3,015	6.1
1977	33,775	25,587	75.8	8,187	24.2	50,555	47,402	93.8	3,152	6.2
1978[1]	35,836	27,326	76.3	8,511	23.7	52,143	49,007	94.0	3,136	6.0
1979	37,434	28,623	76.5	8,812	23.5	53,308	50,174	94.1	3,133	5.9
1980	38,492	29,391	76.4	9,102	23.6	53,101	49,698	93.6	3,403	6.4
1981	39,590	30,041	75.9	9,549	24.1	53,582	50,092	93.5	3,490	6.5
1982	40,086	30,007	74.9	10,079	25.1	52,891	48,895	92.4	3,996	7.6
1983	41,004	30,680	74.8	10,324	25.2	53,487	49,264	92.1	4,223	7.9
1984	42,793	32,404	75.7	10,388	24.3	55,769	51,624	92.6	4,145	7.4
1985	44,154	33,604	76.1	10,551	23.9	56,562	52,425	92.7	4,137	7.3
1986[1]	45,556	34,812	76.4	10,744	23.6	57,569	53,317	92.6	4,252	7.4
1987	47,074	36,121	76.7	10,953	23.3	58,726	54,381	92.6	4,345	7.4
1988	48,383	37,299	77.1	11,084	22.9	59,781	55,353	92.6	4,427	7.4
1989	49,745	38,408	77.2	11,337	22.8	60,837	56,386	92.7	4,451	7.3
1990	50,455	39,036	77.4	11,419	22.6	61,198	56,640	92.6	4,558	7.4

[1] Not strictly comparable with prior years because of revisions in the population levels and/or estimation procedures used in the Current Population Survey (CPS). For an explanation, see the original report.

Table 8. Percent distribution of the employed by occupation and sex, 1972 and 1990 annual averages

Occupation	Women		Men	
	1972	1990	1972	1990
Total, 16 years and over (thousands)	31,257	53,479	50,896	64,435
Percent	100.0	100.0	100.0	100.0
Executive, administrative, and managerial	4.6	11.1	11.5	13.8
Professional specialty	12.4	15.1	9.7	12.0
Technicians and related support	2.4	3.5	2.3	3.0
Sales occupations	11.1	13.1	10.0	11.2
Administrative support, including clerical	31.5	27.8	6.4	5.9
Service occupations	21.2	17.7	8.3	9.8
Precision production, craft, and repair	1.6	2.2	19.4	19.4
Operators, fabricators, and laborers	13.4	8.5	25.9	20.6
Farming, forestry, and fishing	1.9	1.0	6.4	4.4

Table 9. Employed women in selected occupations, 1972 and 1990 annual averages

(Numbers in thousands)

Occupation	1972		1990	
	Total employed	Percent women	Total employed	Percent women
Assemblers	1,022	46.8	1,130	43.5
Bartenders	202	27.9	307	55.6
Bus drivers	253	34.1	443	51.6
Computer programmers	188	19.9	594	36.0
Lawyers	305	4.0	729	20.6
Physicians	332	10.1	575	19.3
Registered nurses	807	97.6	1,673	94.5
Secretaries	2,964	99.1	3,956	99.0
Teachers, except college and university	2,852	70.0	3,993	73.7
Telephone installers and repairers	312	1.9	193	11.3

NOTE: Data for 1972 and 1990 are not strictly comparable due to changes in the occupational classification system beginning in 1983.

Table 10. Women on nonfarm payrolls by industry, 1990 annual averages

(Numbers in thousands)

Industry	Employees		
	Total	Women	
		Number	Percent of total
Total nonfarm..	109,971	52,147	47.4
Total private	91,649	42,423	46.3
Mining..	711	96	13.5
Construction	5,136	554	10.8
Manufacturing..	19,111	6,297	33.0
Durable goods..	11,115	2,969	26.7
Nondurable goods..	7,995	3,329	41.6
Transportation and public utilities............................	5,826	1,711	29.4
Wholesale trade	6,205	1,903	30.7
Retail trade[1]..	19,683	10,462	53.2
General merchandise stores....................................	2,516	1,727	68.6
Food stores	3,229	1,640	50.8
Apparel and accessory stores...............................	1,178	891	75.6
Eating and drinking places....................................	6,565	3,659	55.7
Finance, insurance, and real estate......................	6,739	4,259	63.2
Services[1]..	28,240	17,141	60.7
Business services	5,241	2,493	47.6
Health services..	7,844	6,456	82.3
Educational services	1,652	934	56.5
Social services	1,811	1,409	77.8
Government	18,322	9,725	53.1
Federal	3,085	1,258	40.8
State..	4,303	2,139	49.7
Local..	10,934	6,328	57.9

[1] Includes other industries, not shown separately.

Table 11. Median weekly earnings ratios for full-time wage and salary workers by age, race, and sex, 1979 and 1990 annual averages

Age and race	1979			1990		
	Women	Men	Ratio of women's to men's earnings	Women	Men	Ratio of women's to men's earnings
TOTAL						
16 years and over.............................	$182	$291	62.5	$348	$485	71.8
16 to 24 years...................................	154	196	78.6	254	283	89.8

Age and race	1979			1990		
	Women	Men	Ratio of women's to men's earnings	Women	Men	Ratio of women's to men's earnings
25 years and over............................	194	314	61.8	370	514	72.0
25 to 54 years.................................	196	315	62.2	374	512	73.0
25 to 34 years.............................	199	295	67.5	357	452	79.0
35 to 44 years.............................	195	335	58.2	391	563	69.4
45 to 54 years.............................	192	337	57.0	377	592	63.7
55 years and over..........................	187	305	61.3	342	526	65.0
55 to 64 years.............................	188	312	60.3	348	545	63.9
65 years and over.........................	170	219	77.6	300	402	74.6
White						
16 years and over............................	184	298	61.7	355	497	71.4
16 to 24 years.................................	155	199	77.9	257	287	89.5
25 years and over...........................	197	321	61.4	378	529	71.5
25 to 54 years.............................	198	322	61.5	382	525	72.8
55 years and over.........................	190	313	60.7	348	554	62.8
Black						
16 years and over............................	169	227	74.4	308	360	85.6
16 to 24 years.................................	144	167	86.2	234	249	94.0
25 years and over...........................	177	245	72.2	320	386	82.9
25 to 54 years.............................	179	249	71.9	321	387	82.9
55 years and over.........................	159	216	73.6	303	381	79.5

Table 12. Unemployment rates of all persons, teenagers, and adults by sex, 1960–90 annual averages

(Percent of labor force that is unemployed)

Year	Women			Men		
	Total, 16 years and over	16 to 19 years	20 years and over	Total, 16 years and over	16 to 19 years	20 years and over
1960	5.9	13.9	5.1	5.4	15.3	4.7
1961	7.2	16.3	6.3	6.4	17.1	5.7
1962	6.2	14.6	5.4	5.2	14.7	4.6
1963	6.5	17.2	5.4	5.2	17.2	4.5
1964	6.2	16.6	5.2	4.6	15.8	3.9
1965	5.5	15.7	4.5	4.0	14.1	3.2
1966	4.8	14.1	3.8	3.2	11.7	2.5
1967	5.2	13.5	4.2	3.1	12.3	2.3
1968	4.8	14.0	3.8	2.9	11.6	2.2
1969	4.7	13.3	3.7	2.8	11.4	2.1

(Continued on next page)

Year	Women			Men		
	Total, 16 years and over	16 to 19 years	20 years and over	Total, 16 years and over	16 to 19 years	20 years and over
1970	5.9	15.6	4.8	4.4	15.0	3.5
1971	6.9	17.2	5.7	5.3	16.6	4.4
1972	6.6	16.7	5.4	5.0	15.9	4.0
1973	6.0	15.3	4.9	4.2	13.9	3.3
1974	6.7	16.6	5.5	4.9	15.6	3.8
1975	9.3	19.7	8.0	7.9	20.1	6.8
1976	8.6	18.7	7.4	7.1	19.2	5.9
1977	8.2	18.3	7.0	6.3	17.3	5.2
1978	7.2	17.1	6.0	5.3	15.8	4.3
1979	6.8	16.4	5.7	5.1	15.9	4.2
1980	7.4	17.2	6.4	6.9	18.3	5.9
1981	7.9	19.0	6.8	7.4	20.1	6.3
1982	9.4	21.9	8.3	9.9	24.4	8.8
1983	9.2	21.3	8.1	9.9	23.3	8.9
1984	7.6	18.0	6.8	7.4	19.6	6.6
1985	7.4	17.6	6.6	7.0	19.5	6.2
1986	7.1	17.6	6.2	6.9	19.0	6.1
1987	6.2	15.9	5.4	6.2	17.8	5.4
1988	5.6	14.4	4.9	5.5	16.0	4.8
1989	5.4	14.0	4.7	5.2	15.9	4.5
1990	5.4	14.7	4.8	5.6	16.3	4.9

Table 13. Unemployment rates by age and sex, 1990 annual averages

(Percent of labor force that is unemployed)

Age	Women	Men
Total, 16 years and over	5.4	5.6
16 to 19 years	14.7	16.3
20 years and over	4.8	4.9
20 to 24 years	8.5	9.1
25 to 34 years	5.6	5.5
35 to 44 years	4.2	4.0
45 to 54 years	3.4	3.7
55 to 64 years	2.8	3.8
65 years and over	3.1	3.0
65 to 69 years	3.4	3.2
70 to 74 years	2.4	3.3
75 years and over	3.0	1.8

Table 14. Unemployment rates by race, Hispanic origin, age, and sex, 1990 annual averages

(Percent of labor force that is unemployed)

Age, race, and Hispanic origin	Women	Men
White, 16 years and over	4.6	4.8
16 to 19 years	12.6	14.2
20 years and over	4.1	4.3
20 to 24 years	6.8	7.6
25 to 34 years	4.5	4.7
35 to 44 years	3.7	3.5
45 to 54 years	3.2	3.4
55 to 64 years	2.7	3.6
65 years and over	2.8	2.8
Black, 16 years and over	10.8	11.8
16 to 19 years	30.0	32.1
20 years and over	9.6	10.4
20 to 24 years	19.7	20.2
25 to 34 years	11.9	11.5
35 to 44 years	7.2	8.5
45 to 54 years	4.4	6.3
55 to 64 years	3.7	5.5
65 years and over	5.8	4.6
Hispanic origin, 16 years and over	8.3	7.8
16 to 19 years	19.5	19.6
20 years and over	7.4	7.0
20 to 24 years	10.4	8.3
25 to 34 years	8.0	6.8
35 to 44 years	6.6	6.5
45 to 54 years	6.0	6.8
55 to 64 years	4.2	6.5
65 years and over	6.4	5.8

Table 15. Employment status of women by race and household relationship, 1990 annual averages

(Numbers in thousands)

Sex and household relationship	Civilian noninsti- tutional popula- tion	Civilian labor force Total	Percent of popula- tion	Employed	Unemployed Number	Unemployed Percent of labor force	Not in labor force
TOTAL							
Wives	51,365	30,005	58.4	28,912	1,093	3.6	21,360
Women who maintain families[1]	11,154	6,925	62.1	6,357	568	8.2	4,229
Women who live alone.........................	13,952	5,949	42.6	5,753	196	3.3	8,002
16 to 24 years....................................	572	502	87.7	481	21	4.2	70
25 to 59 years....................................	5,022	4,291	85.4	4,155	136	3.2	731
60 years and over..............................	8,359	1,157	13.8	1,117	40	3.4	7,202
Women who live with nonrelatives	5,369	4,178	77.8	3,930	248	5.9	1,191
16 to 24 years....................................	1,707	1,354	79.3	1,254	100	7.4	353
25 to 59 years....................................	3,273	2,740	83.7	2,594	146	5.3	533
60 years and over..............................	389	84	21.7	82	3	3.2	305
White							
Wives	46,223	26,724	57.8	25,801	923	3.5	19,499
Women who maintain families[1]	7,448	4,761	63.9	4,463	298	6.3	2,687
Women who live alone.........................	12,215	5,117	41.9	4,967	150	2.9	7,098
16 to 24 years....................................	491	437	89.1	421	16	3.6	54
25 to 59 years....................................	4,179	3,634	86.9	3,532	102	2.8	545
60 years and over..............................	7,545	1,046	13.9	1,014	32	3.1	6,499
Women who live with nonrelatives	4,597	3,657	79.6	3,461	197	5.4	940
16 to 24 years....................................	1,506	1,219	80.9	1,138	81	6.7	287
25 to 59 years....................................	2,773	2,370	85.5	2,256	113	4.8	403
60 years and over..............................	318	68	21.5	66	2	(2)	250
Black							
Wives	3,471	2,279	65.7	2,158	121	5.3	1,191
Women who maintain families[1]	3,360	1,967	58.5	1,710	257	13.1	1,393
Women who live alone.........................	1,483	696	46.9	656	40	5.7	788
16 to 24 years....................................	62	50	(2)	46	4	(2)	12
25 to 59 years....................................	708	546	77.1	518	29	5.2	162
60 years and over..............................	713	100	14.0	92	7	7.4	613
Women who live with nonrelatives	554	381	68.8	338	43	11.2	173
16 to 24 years....................................	138	97	70.2	82	15	15.7	41
25 to 59 years....................................	359	273	76.1	246	27	9.9	86
60 years and over..............................	57	11	(2)	11	–	(2)	46

[1]Refers to never-married, widowed, divorced, or separated women.
[2]Data not shown where base is less than 75,000.

Table 16. Labor force status and reason not in labor force for persons 25 to 54 years of age by sex, annual averages, selected years, 1962–90

Sex, labor force status, and reason	1962	1965	1970	1975	1980	1985	1990
WOMEN							
Civilian noninstitutional population (thousands)	34,458	34,856	36,371	39,700	43,603	48,493	53,856
Percent	100.0	100.0	100.0	100.0	100.0	100.0	100.0
In the civilian labor force	43.4	45.2	50.1	55.0	63.9	69.6	74.1
Employed	41.2	43.3	47.8	51.0	60.1	65.3	70.7
Not in the labor force	56.6	54.8	49.9	45.0	36.1	30.4	25.9
Keeping house	55.5	53.4	47.9	41.9	32.2	26.1	21.1
Other reasons	1.1	1.3	2.1	3.2	3.9	4.3	4.9
Going to school	.2	.3	.4	.7	.9	1.1	1.2
Unable to work	.3	.3	.4	.6	.6	.5	1.0
All other reasons	.6	.7	1.2	1.9	2.4	2.7	2.7
MEN							
Civilian noninstitutional population (thousands)	31,758	32,121	33,612	37,071	41,095	45,973	51,641
Percent	100.0	100.0	100.0	100.0	100.0	100.0	100.0
In the civilian labor force	96.8	96.7	95.8	94.4	94.2	93.9	93.4
Employed	92.9	94.1	93.2	89.0	89.4	88.7	89.2
Not in the labor force	3.2	3.3	4.2	5.6	5.8	6.1	6.6
Keeping house	.1	.1	.1	.2	.2	.3	.5
Other reasons	3.1	3.2	4.0	5.4	5.5	5.7	6.1
Going to school	.4	.4	.6	.8	.8	.8	.8
Unable to work	1.0	.9	1.5	1.9	1.6	1.3	1.9
All other reasons	1.8	1.9	2.0	2.7	3.2	3.6	3.3

Table 17. Families by type of family and labor force status of members, March, selected years, 1960–90

Type of family and labor force status of members	1960	1965	1970	1975	1980	1985	1990
	Number of families (in thousands)						
Married-couple families	39,335	41,648	44,436	47,438	49,132	50,395	52,385
Husband in labor force, not the wife	23,864	23,060	21,715	20,066	17,179	14,747	13,081
Husband and wife in labor force	11,177	13,485	16,924	19,355	22,728	25,041	28,043
Wife in labor force, not the husband	813	985	1,217	1,755	1,942	2,345	2,451
Neither husband nor wife in labor force	3,477	4,118	4,579	6,262	7,284	8,263	8,810
Families maintained by women[1]	4,494	5,006	5,580	7,330	9,009	10,524	11.309
Householder in labor force	2,243	2,548	2,952	3,988	5,377	6,419	7,088
Householder not in labor force	2,248	2,458	2,628	3,342	3,632	4,105	4,221

(Continued on next page)

Type of family and labor force status of members	1960	1965	1970	1975	1980	1985	1990
	Number of families (in thousands)						
Families maintained by men[1]	1,233	1,182	1,221	1,513	1,769	2,313	2,929
Householder in labor force	908	850	877	1,127	1,312	1,786	2,285
Householder not in labor force	325	332	344	386	457	527	644
	Percent distribution						
Married-couple families	100.0	100.0	100.0	100.0	100.0	100.0	100.0
Husband in labor force, not the wife	60.7	55.4	48.9	42.3	35.0	29.3	25.0
Husband and wife in labor force	28.4	32.4	38.1	40.8	46.3	49.7	53.5
Wife in labor force, not the husband	2.1	2.4	2.7	3.7	4.0	4.7	4.7
Neither husband nor wife in labor force	8.8	9.9	10.3	13.2	14.8	16.4	16.8
Families maintained by women[1]	100.0	100.0	100.0	100.0	100.0	100.0	100.0
Householder in labor force	49.9	50.9	52.9	54.4	59.7	61.0	62.7
Householder not in labor force	50.1	49.1	47.1	45.6	40.3	39.0	37.3
Families maintained by men[1]	100.0	100.0	100.0	100.0	100.0	100.0	100.0
Householder in labor force	73.6	71.9	71.8	74.5	74.2	77.2	78.0
Householder not in labor force	26.4	28.1	28.2	25.5	25.8	22.8	22.0

[1] Refers to families maintained by never-married, widowed, divorced, or separated men or women.
NOTE: Data include families where the husband, wife, or male maintaining the family is in the Armed Forces, either living off post or with their families on post.

Table 18. Civilian labor force and labor force participation rates of mothers by marital status and age of youngest child, March, selected years, 1975–90

(Numbers in thousands)

Category and year		Civilian labor force					Civilian labor force participation rate			
		With children:					With children:			
	Total	Under 2 years old	2 to 3 years old	4 to 5 years old	6 to 17 years old	Total	Under 2 years old	2 to 3 years old	4 to 5 years old	6 to 17 years old
TOTAL										
1975	14,121	1,727	1,830	1,817	8,750	47.2	31.8	41.0	45.4	54.7
1980	17,391	2,293	2,190	1,825	11,081	56.7	39.1	51.0	54.8	64.4
1985	19,068	2,839	2,562	2,168	11,500	62.4	48.0	54.6	61.7	69.9
1990	21,156	3,309	2,915	2,515	12,418	67.0	52.0	61.2	65.8	74.7
Married										
1975	11,447	1,526	1,512	1,428	6,984	45.0	31.0	39.3	42.8	52.4
1980	13,558	2,024	1,768	1,375	8,390	54.3	39.0	49.6	51.9	61.8
1985	14,766	2,562	2,097	1,639	8,469	61.0	49.4	54.5	60.8	67.8
1990	16,296	2,828	2,351	1,924	9,192	66.4	53.6	61.5	64.7	73.6
Single parent[1]										
1975	2,674	201	318	389	1,766	60.0	39.0	52.0	58.5	66.2
1980	3,833	269	422	450	2,691	67.0	40.1	57.8	66.4	74.0
1985	4,302	277	465	529	3,031	67.8	38.0	55.3	64.4	76.6
1990	4,860	481	564	591	3,226	69.2	44.0	60.1	69.9	77.9

[1] Includes never-married, widowed, divorced, and separated mothers.
NOTE: Children refer to own children of the husband, wife, or person maintaining the family and include sons and daughters, stepchildren, and adopted children. Excluded are other related children such as grandchildren, nieces, nephews, and cousins, and unrelated children.

Source: *Working Women: A Chartbook.* U.S. Department of Labor, Bureau of Labor Statistics, Bulletin, 2385, August 1991.

THE WORLD'S WOMEN

The following tables are drawn from the United Nations report *The World's Women 1970–1990: Trends and Statistics* (United Nations, 1991). Note that the original tables included various notes that have not been included here.

Indicators on Time Use
▶ *A. Time use of women and men in selected country studies*

Time use in selected activities (hours per week)

Country or area	Year	Economic activity f	m	Unpaid housework Household chores f	m	Child care f	m	Total f	m	Personal care and free time f	m
Northern America and Australia											
Australia	1987	16.9	35.5	27.2	13.8	5.8	1.6	33.0	15.3	118	117
Canada	1971	18.8	41.2	29.5	8.9	6.2	1.5	35.7	10.4	114	116
	1981	17.2	30.7	23.0	11.1	4.3	1.5	27.3	12.5	124	125
	1986	17.5	32.9	24.6	12.1	4.3	1.4	28.9	13.5	121	121
United States	1965	18.7	48.3	32.1	8.8	5.7	1.3	37.8	10.0	111	109
	1975	16.7	37.6	27.6	9.6	4.4	1.3	32.0	10.9	119	119
	1986	24.5	41.3	29.9	17.4	2.0	0.8	31.9	18.1	112	109
Western Europe											
Belgium	1966	19.3	50.8	34.7	6.0	3.6	0.8	38.4	6.9	110	111
Finland	1979	21.8	30.0	22.5	10.8	3.0	0.9	25.6	11.7	122	125
France	1965	21.7	51.8	35.0	9.9	7.6	1.3	42.6	11.3	104	105
Germany (Federal Rep. of Germany)	1965	13.3	42.4	39.3	10.2	4.9	0.9	44.2	11.1	111	115
Netherlands	1975	5.8	27.3	27.1	7.1	5.3	1.6	32.4	8.7	130	132
	1980	7.1	23.9	27.9	7.4	5.5	1.5	33.4	8.8	130	135
Norway	1972	14.4	40.0	32.8	5.7	4.4	1.2	37.2	6.9	117	121
	1981	17.1	34.2	25.1	7.1	4.8	2.0	29.8	9.2	121	125
United Kingdom	1961	16.5	45.7	31.3	4.3	2.6	0.4	33.9	4.8	118	118
	1975	17.2	39.6	27.1	4.9	2.4	0.6	29.5	5.5	121	123
	1984	14.1	26.8	26.4	10.3	3.6	1.1	30.0	11.4	124	130
Eastern Europe and USSR											
Bulgaria	1965	42.6	52.9	25.6	11.1	2.9	1.4	28.6	12.5	97	103
	1988	37.7	46.9	29.3	14.3	4.3	1.1	33.7	15.3	97	106
Czechoslovakia	1965	29.8	44.4	36.0	12.7	4.7	2.5	40.7	15.1	97	109
Hungary	1965	34.0	56.6	36.3	5.5	4.7	2.5	41.0	7.9	93	103
	1976	26.7	41.5	30.2	10.9	3.0	1.4	33.3	12.3	108	114
Poland	1965	30.5	52.2	33.5	9.7	5.3	2.7	38.9	12.4	99	103
	1984	24.9	42.2	30.5	7.7	4.4	2.0	34.9	9.7	108	116
Yugoslavia	1965	19.5	49.5	37.0	8.1	3.8	1.4	40.7	9.5	108	109
USSR	1965	43.0	53.2	32.3	14.0	3.6	1.4	35.9	15.4	89	99
	1986	38.5	49.0	25.7	14.6	4.4	1.5	30.1	16.1	99	103
Latin America											
Guatemala	1977	29.4	56.7	39.9	6.3	9.8	4.6	49.7	10.9	89	101
Peru	1966	15.1	52.1	36.0	5.6	4.5	0.5	40.5	6.1	112	110
Venezuela	1983	15.5	42.2	28.2	3.0	4.0	0.7	32.2	3.7	120	122
Asia											
Indonesia (Java)	1973	41.3	55.3	28.9	3.0	7.2	2.6	36.1	5.6	..	..
Nepal	1979	32.3	40.7	38.5	10.8	4.8	1.1	43.3	11.9	..	..

▶ B. Distribution between women and men of unpaid housework

Country or area	Year	Unpaid housework (% share of women and men)									
		Preparing meals		Child care		Shopping		Other housework		Total	
		f	m	f	m	f	m	f	m	f	m
Northern America and Australia											
Australia	1987	76	24	78	22	60	40	53	47	68	32
Canada	1971	87	13	80	20	58	42	78	22	77	23
	1981	74	26	75	25	61	39	66	34	69	31
	1986	81	19	76	24	58	42	67	33	68	32
United States	1965	90	10	82	18	66	34	78	22	79	21
	1975	87	13	77	23	62	38	69	31	75	25
	1986	78	22	73	28	60	40	61	39	64	36
Western Europe											
Belgium	1966	94	6	81	19	76	24	83	17	85	15
Finland	1979	82	18	77	23	57	43	54	46	69	31
France	1965	87	13	85	15	70	30	76	24	79	21
Germany (Federal Rep. of Germany)	1965	94	6	84	16	75	25	74	26	80	20
Netherlands	1975	83	17	77	23	65	35	84	16	79	21
	1980	80	20	79	21	63	37	86	14	79	21
Norway	1972	89	11	79	21	67	33	86	14	84	16
	1981	81	19	70	30	57	43	82	18	76	24
United Kingdom	1961	90	10	86	14	79	21	89	11	88	12
	1975	89	11	81	19	69	31	87	13	84	16
	1984	74	26	76	24	60	40	76	24	72	28
Eastern Europe and USSR											
Bulgaria	1965	89	11	68	32	53	47	64	36	70	30
	1988	88	12	81	19	70	30	58	42	69	31
Czechoslovakia	1965	85	15	66	34	70	30	69	31	73	27
Germany (former German Dem. Rep.)	1966	80	20	75	25	67	33	75	25	75	25
Hungary	1965	91	9	66	34	74	26	87	13	84	16
	1976	90	10	68	32	65	35	64	36	73	27
Poland	1965	86	14	66	34	75	25	73	27	76	24
	1984	90	10	69	31	70	30	76	24	78	22
Yugoslavia	1965	94	6	73	27	63	37	80	20	81	19
USSR	1965	87	13	72	28	50	50	67	33	70	30
	1986	75	25	75	25	62	38	59	41	65	35
Latin America											
Guatemala	1977	99	1	68	32	58	42	73	27	82	18
Peru	1966	94	6	90	10	69	31	86	14	87	13
Venezuela	1983	98	2	85	15	70	30	87	13	90	10
Asia											
Indonesia (Java)	1973	96	4	74	26	88	13	80	20	87	13
Nepal	1979	88	12	81	19	41	59	76	24	78	22

Indicators on Housing, Human Settlements, and Environment

	Urban and rural population						Safe water, sanitary facilities, and electricity, 1980/85						
Country or area	% of women living in urban areas		Annual change in population, 1985–1990 (%)		Females per 100 males, latest year		F/100 M, rural-urban migration 1965/75	Population without safe water (%)		Population without adequate sanitation (%)		Households without electricity (%)	
	1970	latest	Urban	Rural	Urban	Rural		Urban	Rural	Urban	Rural	Urban	Rural
Developed regions													
Albania	..	35	2.6	1.4	96	93	..	..	..	..	..	..	..
Australia	87	87	1.2	1.2	103	89	90	..	..	..	..	..	..
Austria	53	56	0.5	-0.8	117	105	117	..	..	..	..	..	..
Belgium	..	95	0.2	-3.7	105	99	..	..	..	..	..	..	..
Bulgaria	..	65	1.2	-2.3	101	102	107	..	..	..	..	..	..
Canada	77	77	1.0	0.4	106	94	..	..	..	..	..	..	..
Czechoslovakia	56	66	1.1	-1.7	107	103	..	..	..	..	..	..	..
Denmark	47	85	0.3	-1.8	106	88	..	..	..	..	..	..	..
Finland	66	61	1.5	-2.0	111	100	102	..	..	..	..	..	..
France	..	74	0.5	-0.1	107	100	110	..	..	..	..	..	..
Germany; Federal Rep. of Germany	..	..	0.0	-1.3	..	..	..	..	..	..	..	..	..
former German Dem. Rep.	74	77	0.3	-0.9	112	107	110	..	..	..	..	..	..
Greece	53	59	1.1	-1.1	106	100	105	..	..	..	..	..	..
Hungary	46	59	1.0	-1.8	109	104	175	..	..	..	..	..	..
Iceland	..	90	1.2	-1.2	100	86	..	..	..	..	..	..	..
Ireland	55	58	1.6	0.0	106	91	116	..	..	..	..	..	..
Italy	..	..	0.4	-0.7	..	..	..	..	..	..	..	..	..
Japan	72	77	0.5	0.2	103	105	117	..	..	..	..	..	..
Luxembourg	68	..	0.6	-2.9	..	..	101	..	..	..	..	..	..
Malta	94	84	0.9	-1.9	110	104	..	..	..	..	..	..	..
Netherlands	..	89	0.4	0.2	103	97	..	..	..	..	..	..	..
New Zealand	70	85	0.9	0.2	104	89	251	..	..	..	..	..	..
Norway	..	61	0.7	-1.0	111	100	..	..	..	..	..	..	..
Poland	..	61	1.3	-0.5	108	100	..	..	..	..	..	..	..
Portugal	27	30	1.6	-0.4	113	105	..	..	..	..	..	..	..
Romania	40	49	1.0	-0.1	102	103	..	..	..	..	..	..	..
Spain	..	92	1.1	-1.9	104	98	..	..	..	..	..	..	..
Sweden	83	84	0.1	-0.7	105	89	176	..	..	..	..	..	..
Switzerland	59	62	0.6	-0.5	109	100	..	..	..	..	..	..	..
USSR	..	66	1.4	-0.4	113	114	..	..	..	..	..	..	..
United Kingdom	79	89	0.3	-1.8	109	99	..	..	..	..	..	..	..
United States	74	74	0.9	0.7	108	100	..	..	..	..	..	..	..
Yugoslavia	39	47	2.3	-0.9	105	100	..	..	..	..	..	..	..
Africa													
Algeria	45	61	4.2	2.4	102	100	..	30	5	30	..	..	..
Angola	..	..	5.7	1.7	..	..	..	10	88	71	85	..	..
Benin	..	31	6.9	1.0	98	111	..	55	91	55	96	..	..
Botswana	9	20	7.9	2.4	95	115	..	2	28	21	88	..	..
Burkina Faso	..	..	5.5	2.4	..	..	..	50	74	62	95	..	..
Burundi	2	4	8.7	2.5	79	108	..	67	78	10	75	..	..
Cameroon	..	27	5.8	0.0	93	104	..	54	70	..	..	81	99
Cape Verde	..	..	5.8	-1.0	..	..	..	1	79	64	91	..	..
Central African Rep.	..	35	4.4	1.0	109	108	..	76	95	64	91	..	..
Chad	..	..	6.9	0.7	..	..	..	73	70	..	..	..	..

Indicators on Housing, Human Settlements, and Environment [cont.]

Country or area	% of women living in urban areas		Annual change in population, 1985–1990 (%)		Females per 100 males, latest year		F/100 M, rural-urban migration 1965/75	Population without safe water (%)		Population without adequate sanitation (%)		Households without electricity (%)	
	1970	latest	Urban	Rural	Urban	Rural		Urban	Rural	Urban	Rural	Urban	Rural
Comoros	..	23	5.1	2.5	101	100	..	1	48	..	..	..	..
Congo	..	35	4.2	1.8	92	110	..	58	93	83	..	..	..
Côte d'Ivoire	..	..	6.4	2.5	..	..	..	70	90	87	80	..	..
Djibouti	..	..	3.8	0.1	..	..	..	47	80	57	81	..	..
Egypt	..	44	3.6	1.7	95	96	..	7	39	5	51	23	81
Equatorial Guinea	..	..	4.0	-0.2	..	..	..	53	..	72	..	..	..
Ethiopia	..	11	4.4	1.7	115	98	..	7	58	..	95	..	..
Gabon	..	33	5.8	1.8	90	112	..	25	66	..	..	..	..
Gambia	..	..	5.2	2.2	..	..	..	0	67	..	..	..	..
Ghana	..	..	4.1	2.7	..	..	100	28	61	53	83	..	..
Guinea	..	18	5.5	1.6	95	104	..	9	98	46	99	..	..
Guinea-Bissau	..	..	4.7	1.1	..	..	..	79	63	79	87	..	..
Kenya	8	14	8.2	3.3	82	105	78	39	79	25	61	..	..
Lesotho	..	5	6.9	2.0	118	100	..	63	86	78	89	..	..
Liberia	24	31	5.5	1.7	..	..	..	50	76	76	80	..	..
Libyan Arab Jamahiriya	..	..	5.5	0.2	..	..	..	0	23	..	..	..	..
Madagascar	..	17	6.2	2.3	103	99	..	27	91	92	..	..	..
Malawi	..	8	7.7	2.7	86	110	..	18	46	..	..	..	..
Mali	..	17	4.3	2.7	103	105	..	42	80	10	95	..	..
Mauritania	..	21	6.8	0.3	85	104	..	20	84	93	..	..	..
Mauritius	45	41	1.3	1.2	100	99	..	0	2	0	5	..	..
Morocco	..	43	4.2	1.2	99	100	125	..	..	..	..	..	..
Mozambique	..	12	9.5	0.7	88	108	..	18	98	..	..	..	..
Namibia	..	43	5.4	0.7	90	112	..	..	..	..	..	..	..
Niger	..	..	7.0	2.2	..	..	..	52	66	64	97	..	..
Nigeria	..	19	6.1	2.2	93	105	..	40	70	70	..	..	..
Reunion	..	..	3.1	-0.4	..	..	..	..	..	..	..	..	..
Rwanda	3	4	7.9	3.1	82	107	..	45	40	40	40	..	..
Sao Tome and Principe	..	..	..	..	..	..	..	..	..	..	..	..	..
Senegal	..	34	3.9	2.0	103	102	..	37	73	13	98	..	..
Seychelles	27	38	..	..	102	97	..	..	..	..	..	..	..
Sierra Leone	..	..	5.2	1.4	..	..	..	42	92	57	90	..	..
Somalia	..	..	5.7	2.2	..	..	..	40	80	40	95	..	..
South Africa	45	55	3.3	0.8	99	107	..	..	..	..	..	..	..
Sudan	..	19	4.3	2.6	88	99	..	..	..	80	99	..	..
Swaziland	7	..	8.3	1.5	..	..	..	..	..	38	90	..	..
Togo	13	17	6.3	2.2	..	..	..	32	74	66	92	..	..
Tunisia	..	53	2.9	1.8	97	96	113	2	21	34	71	32	94
Uganda	7	11	5.7	3.3	86	104	..	55	88	60	90	..	..
United Rep. Tanzania	5	13	10.1	1.3	93	106	91	15	53	9	24	..	..
Western Sahara	..	..	..	..	..	..	..	..	..	..	..	..	..
Zaire	..	17	4.8	2.3	97	105	..	57	95	92	90	..	..
Zambia	..	39	6.3	1.2	97	109	..	30	68	44	59	..	..
Zimbabwe	14	22	5.6	2.4	88	110	..	0	90	0	95	..	..
Latin America and Caribbean													
Antigua and Barbuda	34	..	..	..	..	..	..	..	..	..	..	..	..
Argentina	..	85	1.7	-0.9	105	86	..	28	81	7	63	..	..

Indicators on Housing, Human Settlements, and Environment [cont.]

	Urban and rural population						Safe water, sanitary facilities and electricity, 1980/85					
	% of women living in urban areas		Annual change in population, 1985–1990 (%)		Females per 100 males, latest year		F/100 M, rural-urban migration	Population without safe water (%)		Population without adequate sanitation (%)		Households without electricity (%)	
Country or area	1970	latest	Urban	Rural	Urban	Rural	1965/75	Urban	Rural	Urban	Rural	Urban	Rural
Bahamas	59	76	..	..	107	102	..	41	..	36	..	..	..
Barbados	..	..	1.8	-0.3	..	..	..	0	80	0	..	..	..
Belize	..	..	..	..	..	..	..	..	..	..	..	..	..
Bolivia	..	50	4.3	1.3	105	100	..	22	88	59	91	24	94
Brazil	..	72	3.2	-1.3	103	93	105	..	48	67	99	..	..
Chile	78	85	2.2	-1.0	107	84	111	0	82	0	90	..	..
Colombia	..	70	2.9	0.2	110	88	197	0	24	4	86	..	..
Costa Rica	43	46	4.2	1.1	109	93	120	7	14	0	60	..	..
Cuba	..	73	1.6	-1.6	103	89	106	..	..	..	..	1	54
Dominica	..	..	..	..	..	..	..	..	..	..	..	..	..
Dominican Republic	..	..	3.9	0.0	..	..	115	15	67	59	90	..	..
Ecuador	43	53	4.6	0.7	103	94	101	2	79	36	74	..	..
El Salvador	40	41	2.8	1.3	110	99	146	29	57	48	66	..	..
French Guiana	71	..	..	..	..	..	..	..	..	..	..	..	..
Grenada	..	..	..	..	..	..	..	..	..	..	..	..	..
Guadeloupe	..	..	1.5	-0.7	..	..	..	..	..	..	..	..	..
Guatemala	..	38	3.9	2.2	105	93	132	10	74	47	72	..	..
Guyana	..	23	3.2	1.0	108	98	105	0	39	46	19	..	..
Haiti	..	28	4.1	1.0	125	101	..	27	75	46	88	..	..
Honduras	..	41	5.2	1.9	107	95	122	9	45	56	60	..	..
Jamaica	..	43	2.7	0.3	114	98	..	1	7	8	10	..	..
Martinique	..	..	1.2	-2.5	..	..	..	..	..	..	..	..	..
Mexico	60	67	3.1	0.2	105	97	107	10	60	7	88	..	..
Netherlands Antilles	..	..	..	..	..	..	..	..	..	..	..	..	..
Nicaragua	50	56	4.6	1.9	116	92	..	2	91	27	84	..	..
Panama	49	54	3.0	1.1	105	88	..	3	74	39	29	9	67
Paraguay	..	44	4.3	1.8	107	94	..	54	90	8	5	..	..
Peru	..	68	3.4	0.7	100	96	..	27	82	43	98	83	96
Puerto Rico	59	68	2.4	-0.9	109	99	..	..	..	..	..	..	..
St. Kitts and Nevis	35	36	..	..	110	106	..	..	..	..	..	..	..
St. Lucia	..	..	..	..	..	..	..	..	..	..	..	..	..
St. Vincent/Grenadines	..	..	..	..	..	..	..	..	..	..	..	..	..
Suriname	..	..	2.3	0.8	..	..	..	7	13	0	4	..	..
Trinidad and Tobago	13	48	3.2	-1.5	103	98	..	3	23	0	2	8	24
Uruguay	..	86	1.0	-0.4	110	76	290	5	73	41	41	11	66
US Virgin Islands	25	40	..	..	113	106	..	..	..	..	..	..	..
Venezuela	79	84	3.3	-2.7	100	87	119	12	35	43	94	..	..
Asia and Pacific													
Afghanistan	..	17	6.0	1.8	94	94	..	70	90	..	..	..	..
Bahrain	77	80	4.0	2.3	70	76	..	0	0	0	0	..	..
Bangladesh	8	14	5.6	2.3	79	97	75	71	57	79	98	..	..
Bhutan	..	..	5.6	2.0	..	..	..	60	86	..	..	..	..
Brunei Darussalam	..	59	..	..	88	87	..	..	..	..	..	..	..
Cambodia	..	14	4.0	2.3	97	101	..	..	..	..	..	..	..
China	..	20	2.2	1.2	91	96	..	..	..	..	..	..	..
Cyprus	..	46	2.4	-0.3	98	103	..	0	0	0	0	..	..
East Timor	..	..	4.6	1.9	..	..	..	..	..	..	..	..	..

Indicators on Housing, Human Settlements, and Environment [*cont.*]

Country or area	% of women living in urban areas 1970	% of women living in urban areas latest	Annual change in population, 1985–1990 (%) Urban	Annual change in population, 1985–1990 (%) Rural	Females per 100 males, latest year Urban	Females per 100 males, latest year Rural	F/100 M, rural-urban migration 1965/75	Population without safe water (%) Urban	Population without safe water (%) Rural	Population without adequate sanitation (%) Urban	Population without adequate sanitation (%) Rural	Households without electricity (%) Urban	Households without electricity (%) Rural
Fiji	33	39	3.0	0.6	100	95	131	..	..	..	..	7	49
French Polynesia	38	..	..	..	..	..	..	..	..	..	..	..	..
Guam	25	..	..	..	..	..	..	..	..	..	..	..	..
Hong Kong	..	93	1.5	-0.7	95	90	..	..	..	..	..	..	..
India	19	25	4.0	1.4	89	96	86	20	53	70	99	..	..
Indonesia	17	26	4.3	0.7	101	101	104	60	68	70	70	53	94
Iran (Islamic Rep. of)	..	46	4.7	2.2	91	97	79	10	48	5	65	..	..
Iraq	57	67	4.6	0.9	92	99	89	0	54	0	85	..	..
Israel	86	89	1.9	-1.4	101	94	..	..	..	..	..	..	..
Jordan	..	59	5.2	1.7	93	94	..	0	10	0	5	..	..
Kiribati	23	..	..	..	..	..	..	..	..	..	..	..	..
Korea, D. People's R.	..	..	3.5	0.3	..	..	..	0	0	0	0	..	..
Korea Republic of	41	66	3.2	-3.1	101	98	108	..	..	..	..	..	..
Kuwait	..	..	4.5	-3.1	..	..	..	0	0	0	0	..	..
Lao People's Dem. Rep.	15	..	5.9	1.8	..	..	..	..	..	..	..	..	..
Lebanon	..	76	3.0	-1.6	104	103	..	2	2	6	82	..	..
Macau	97	..	..	..	..	..	..	..	..	..	..	..	..
Malaysia	27	35	4.4	0.9	99	100	..	..	..	..	..	..	..
Maldives	12	23	..	..	78	99	..	47	92	31	99	..	..
Mongolia	44	52	3.3	2.9	101	98	..	0	0	..	..	..	..
Myanmar	..	24	2.7	1.9	101	102	..	64	79	66	85	..	..
Nepal	4	6	7.1	2.1	87	96	..	29	89	84	99	..	..
New Caledonia	..	42	..	..	99	93	..	..	..	..	..	..	..
Oman	..	..	7.3	3.0	..	..	..	30	90	40	..	..	..
Pacific Islands	32	30	..	..	96	95	..	..	..	..	..	..	..
Pakistan	26	28	5.0	2.9	87	92	..	16	72	44	95	29	85
Papua New Guinea	9	12	4.8	2.3	73	94	..	46	90	49	97	..	..
Philippines	..	38	3.9	1.6	105	96	..	..	..	..	..	..	..
Qatar	..	..	4.6	1.6	..	..	..	2	50	30	..	..	..
Samoa	22	22	..	..	96	92	..	..	..	..	..	..	..
Saudi Arabia	..	..	5.2	0.5	..	..	..	0	32	0	67	..	..
Singapore	..	75	1.1	..	98	91	..	..	..	..	..	..	..
Solomon Islands	5	7	..	..	64	95	..	9	..	14	..	..	..
Sri Lanka	22	21	1.6	1.3	91	98	..	24	74	..	..	53	92
Syrian Arab Republic	..	49	4.6	2.6	94	98	91	23	35	30	..	..	..
Thailand	13	17	4.3	0.8	104	100	111	30	30	50	56	8	88
Tonga	..	..	..	..	..	..	..	..	..	..	..	..	..
Turkey	..	43	3.1	1.1	91	102	86	..	..	..	..	42	88
United Arab Emirates	..	84	3.3	3.3	47	36	..	0	0	7	78	..	..
Vanatu	10	17	..	..	84	89	..	..	..	..	..	..	..
Viet Nam	..	18	3.8	1.9	94	109	..	10	70	..	..	..	..
Yemen	31	35	6.6	1.8	90	111	..	10	76	27	67	..	..

Sources: *Demographic Yearbook, 1974, 1977, 1983* and *1987* (United Nations publications); *Prospects of World Urbanization 1988*, Population Studies No. 112 (United Nations publication,

Sales no. E.88.XIII.8); *World Population Trends and Policies, 1987 Monitoring Report*, Population Studies No. 103 (United Nations publication, Sales. No. E.88.XIII.3); *Age and Sex Structure of Urban and Rural Populations, 1970–2000: The 1980 Assessment* (United Nations, ESA/P/WP.81); World Health Organization, "Evaluation of the Strategy for Health for all 1985–1986: Detailed Analysis of Global Indicators" (Geneva, WHO/HST/87.2/1987); *Compendium of Human Settlements Statistics 1983* (United Nations publication, Sales No. E/R.84,XVII.5).

WOMEN'S WORDS:

BOOKS BY WOMEN WHOSE

WORDS HAVE CHANGED

THE WORLD

For its seventy-fifth anniversary in 1992, the Women's National Book Association—founded in 1917, three years before women gained the vote, by women booksellers barred from membership in the all-male Bookseller's League—prepared a list of seventy-five books "by women whose words have changed the world" and "have brought insight, awe, and pleasure to countless readers over the years." Their list, organized alphabetically by author, is reprinted with their permission.

Jane Addams, *Twenty Years at Hull House*
Louisa May Alcott, *Little Women*
Isabel Allende, *The House of the Spirits*
Maya Angelou, *I Know Why the Caged Bird Sings*
Hannah Arendt, *The Human Condition*
Jane Austen, *Pride and Prejudice*
Simone de Beauvoir, *The Second Sex*
Ruth Benedict, *Patterns of Culture*
Boston Women's Health Book Collective Staff, *Our Bodies, Ourselves*
Charlotte Brontë, *Jane Eyre*
Emily Brontë, *Wuthering Heights*
Susan Brownmiller, *Against Our Will: Men, Women, and Rape*
Pearl S. Buck, *The Good Earth*
Rachel Carson, *Silent Spring*
Willa Cather, *My Ántonia*
Mary Boykin Chesnut, *A Diary from Dixie*
Kate Chopin, *The Awakening*
Agatha Christie, *The Murder of Roger Ackroyd*
Emily Dickinson, *The Complete Poems of Emily Dickinson*
Mary Baker Eddy, *Science and Health*
George Eliot [Mary Ann or Marian Evans], *Middlemarch*
Fannie Farmer, *The Boston Cooking-School Cook Book*
Frances FitzGerald, *Fire in the Lake*
Dian Fossey, *Gorillas in the Mist*
Anne Frank, *Diary of a Young Girl*
Betty Friedan, *The Feminine Mystique*

Emma Goldman, *Living My Life*
Germaine Greer, *The Female Eunuch*
Radclyffe Hall, *The Well of Loneliness*
Edith Hamilton, *Mythology*
Betty Lehan Harragan, *Games Mother Never Taught You*
Karen Horney, *Our Inner Conflicts*
Zora Neale Hurston, *Their Eyes Were Watching God*
Helen Keller, *The Story of My Life*
Maxine Hong Kingston, *The Women Warrior*
Elisabeth Kubler-Ross, *On Death and Dying*
Frances Moore Lappé, *Diet for a Small Planet*
Harper Lee, *To Kill a Mockingbird*
Doris Lessing, *The Golden Notebook*
Anne Morrow Lindbergh, *Gift from the Sea*
Audre Lorde, *The Cancer Journals*
Carson McCullers, *The Heart Is a Lonely Hunter*
Katherine Mansfield, *The Garden Party*
Beryl Markham, *West with the Night*
Margaret Mead, *Coming of Age in Samoa*
Golda Meir, *My Life*
Edna St. Vincent Millay, *Collected Poems*
Margaret Mitchell, *Gone With the Wind*
Marianne Moore, *Complete Poems of Marianne Moore*
Toni Morrison, *Song of Solomon*
Lady Shikibu Murasaki, *The Tales of Genji*
Anaïs Nin, *The Early Diary of Anaïs Nin*
Flannery O'Connor, *The Complete Stories*
Zoe Oldenbourg, *The World Is Not Enough*
Tillie Olsen, *Silences*
Elaine Pagels, *The Gnostic Gospels*
Emmeline Pankhurst, *My Own Story*
Sylvia Plath, *The Bell Jar*
Katherine Anne Porter, *Ship of Fools*
Adrienne Rich, *Of Woman Born*
Margaret Sanger, *Margaret Sanger: An Autobiography*
Sappho, *Sappho: A New Translation*
May Sarton, *Journal of a Solitude*
Mary Shelley, *Frankenstein*
Susan Sontag, *Illness as Metaphor*
Gertrude Stein, *The Autobiography of Alice B. Toklas*
Harriet Beecher Stowe, *Uncle Tom's Cabin*
Barbara Tuchman, *A Distant Mirror*
Sigrid Undset, *Kristin Lavransdatter*
Alice Walker, *The Color Purple*
Eudora Welty, *Delta Wedding*
Edith Wharton, *Ethan Frome*
Phillis Wheatley, *The Collected Works of Phillis Wheatley*
Mary Wollstonecraft, *A Vindication of the Rights of Women*
Virginia Woolf, *A Room of One's Own*

Source: Women's National Book Association (WNBA), 160 Fifth Avenue, New York, NY 10010; 212-675-7805. Reprinted by permission.

HIGHLIGHTS IN THE FIGHT

FOR WOMEN'S RIGHTS

1701   *A Serious Proposal to the Ladies for the Advancement of their True and Greatest Interest*, by English writer Mary Astell, regarded as the first public call for women's education.

1787   *Thoughts on the Education of Daughters*, by English writer Mary Wollstonecraft. Massachusetts allows women abandoned by their husbands to sell property.

1790   *Declaration of the Rights of Women and Citizens*, by French revolutionary Olympe de Gouges.

1792   *A Vindication of the Rights of Women*, a key argument for women's equal status, by Mary Wollstonecraft.

1821   Emma Willard introduces a revolutionary curriculum, including mathematics, science, history, and literature, at her Troy Female Seminary, in New York.

1823   Catharine Beecher founds the Hartford Academy for women.

1837   Mary Lyon founds Mt. Holyoke Seminary (later College).

1838   *Letters on the Equality of the Sexes and the Condition of Women*, by Angelina and Sarah Grimké, their defense against criticism of women's participation in political action.

1839   The first Married Women's Property Act is passed in Mississippi, allowing women to hold property in their own name.

1840s   Jeanne Deroin leads campaigns to improve conditions for women and children workers in France.

1843   "The Great Lawsuit: Man versus Men, Woman versus Women," by American writer Margaret Fuller.
Isabella Van Wegener adopts the name Sojourner Truth and becomes a traveling preacher, urging women's rights and the abolition of slavery.

1845   *Woman in the Nineteenth Century*, by Margaret Fuller.

1848   Seneca Falls Women's Rights Convention, organized by Elizabeth Cady Stanton and Lucretia Mott, introduces Stanton's Declaration of Sentiments and Resolutions, a key document in women's rights, beginning the full women's rights movement.
Cours de droit social pour les femmes, by French feminist Jeanne Deroin.

1849   Jeanne Deroin becomes the first women candidate to France's National Assembly, after the 1848 Revolution.

1851   "On the Enfranchisement of Women" is published anonymously in the *Westminster Review*, probably by Harriet Taylor.
"Ain't I a Woman?" speech by Sojourner Truth at an Akron, Ohio, women's rights convention.

1852   Barbara Leigh-Smith Bodichon opens Portland Hall, an experimental coeducational school in Britain.

1854   *A Brief Summary in Plain Language of the Most Important Laws Concerning*

Women, a key document in the fight for women's property rights, by British feminist Barbara Leigh-Smith Bodichon.

1854 *Almanach des femmes*, by French feminist Jeanne Deroin, written from exile in Britain.

1855 Lucy Stone keeps her own name on marriage to Henry Brown Blackwell.

1856 *Lettre aux travailleurs*, by French feminist Jeanne Deroin.

1857 Married Women's Property Bill is passed in Britain, recognizing women's rights within marriage.

New York Infirmary for Indigent Women and Children is opened by Drs. Elizabeth and Emily Blackwell.

1858 *English Woman's Journal* is founded by Barbara Leigh-Smith Bodichon.

1861 *Mother Right*, by Johann Bachofen, posits "dawn" matriarchies.

1865 Vassar College is founded as the first of the top-ranked American women's colleges.

1866 The first petition for woman suffrage, organized by Emily Davies, Barbara Leigh-Smith Bodichon, and others, is presented to the British Parliament by John Stuart Mill.

Lucretia Coffin Mott chairs the U.S. Equal Rights Convention.

1867 The first British woman suffrage resolution is presented to Parliament by John Stuart Mill.

Lydia Becker leads a woman suffrage campaign in Britain (1867–1890).

1868 *The Revolution*, the leading United States women's rights periodical, is founded by Susan B. Anthony and Elizabeth Cady Stanton.

New England Woman Suffrage Association is founded by Julia Ward Howe.

1869 Wyoming and Utah, then territories, grant woman suffrage.

American Women's Suffrage Association and National Woman Suffrage Association are founded, splitting the U.S. women's rights movement.

Emily Davies founds the college for women that in 1874 ultimately becomes Girton College.

Elizabeth Blackwell founds the London School of Medicine for Women.

The Subjection of Women, by John Stuart Mill, a work he explained had developed out of discussions with his late wife, Harriet Taylor.

1871 Julia Ward Howe becomes president of the Women's International Peace Association.

1874 Girton College is established for women's education at Cambridge, by Emily Davies with the aid of Barbara Leigh-Smith Bodichon.

1876 Declaration of the Rights of Women, by Elizabeth Cady Stanton and Matilda Joslyn Gage, is introduced at U.S. centennial celebration in Philadelphia.

1878 Woman Suffrage Amendment, later called the Anthony Amendment, is first introduced in U.S. Congress.

1886 *The History of Woman Suffrage* (first three volumes) is published by Susan B. Anthony, Elizabeth Cady Stanton, and Matilda Joslyn Gage.

1887 Woman Suffrage Amendment (Anthony Amendment) brought to vote in Congress but defeated.

1888 International Council of Women founded.

1889 Jane Addams and Ellen Gates Starr found Chicago's Hull House.

1890 Wyoming becomes the first state to introduce woman suffrage.

National American Woman Suffrage Association is founded, as U.S. women's rights movement reunited.

1892 "The Solitude of Self," by Elizabeth Cady Stanton.

1893 Colorado grants woman suffrage.

New Zealand grants woman suffrage.

Woman, Church, and State, by Matilda Gage.

1895 *The Women's Bible*, by Elizabeth Cady Stanton.

1896 Utah and Idaho grant woman suffrage.

1897 National Union of Women's Suffrage Societies (NUWSS) is founded as the main moderate wing of the British woman suffrage movement by Millicent Garrett Fawcett.

1898 *Women and Economics*, by Charlotte Perkins Gilman.

1900 Women's Welfare Association is founded in Germany, by Lida Heymann and others.

Concerning Children, by Charlotte Perkins Gilman.

1902 Australia grants woman suffrage.

German Union for Women's Suffrage is founded by Lida Heymann and Anita Augspurg.

1903 Emmeline and Christabel Pankhurst found the militant Women's Social and Political Union (WSPU) in Britain.

The Home: Its Work and Influence, by Charlotte Perkins Gilman.

1904 International Woman Suffrage Alliance is founded.

1905 Austrian novelist Bertha von Suttner, whose pacifist activities inspired the Nobel Peace Prize, becomes the first woman to receive it.

1906 Emmeline and Frederick Pethick-Lawrence join the Women's Social and Political Union.

Emma Goldman founds the magazine *Mother Earth*.

1907 Emmeline and Frederick Pethick-Lawrence found the British periodical *Votes for Women*.

German Women's Suffrage League begins organizing mass demonstrations (c. 1907).

1909 Charlotte Perkins Gilman founds the magazine *The Forerunner*.

1910 *Twenty Years at Hull House*, by Jane Addams.

Women in Industry, by Edith Abbott.

1911 *The Man-Made World, or Our Androcentric Culture*, by Charlotte Perkins Gilman.

1912 Emmeline and Frederick Pethick-Lawrence are ejected from the Women's Social and Political Union (WSPU) by the Pankhursts.

1913 British suffragists begin an arson and property-violence campaign.

Congressional Union for Woman Suffrage is founded by Alice Paul.

Emily Wilding Davison commits suicide before King George V's horse at Britain's Epsom Derby, in protest over lack of woman suffrage.

1914 Margaret Sanger coins the term *birth control*, founds the National Birth Control League, and is indicted on obscenity charges for sending contraceptive information through the mail, as articles in her just-founded magazine *Woman Rebel*.

Montana grants woman suffrage.

1915 *Herland*, a feminist utopian novel, by Charlotte Perkins Gilman.

International Congress of Women is held at The Hague.

1916 Jeannette Pickering Rankin becomes the first woman member of the U.S. House of Representatives, representing Montana.

Margaret Sanger founds the first birth control clinic, in Brooklyn, New York.

National Woman's Party is founded by Alice Paul and Lucy Burns.

1917 Margaret Sanger is arrested and jailed for giving out birth control information; during the appeal of her case, the court establishes the right of doctors to give patients information on contraceptives. She also publishes *What Every Woman Should Know*.

1918   Women receive partial suffrage in Britain.

      Married Love and *Wise Parenthood*, by Marie Stopes, advocating birth control and sex education for sexual satisfaction.

      Jeannette Pickering Rankin runs for Senate from Montana as a pacifist independent but loses.

1919   Nineteenth Amendment (Anthony Amendment) passed by U.S. Congress.

      Virginia-born Nancy Langhorne Astor becomes the first woman to sit in the British House of Commons (1919–1945).

      Women's International League for Peace and Freedom founded.

1920   Nineteenth Amendment (Anthony Amendment) to the U.S. Constitution, granting the vote to adult women citizens, is ratified by the states and becomes law.

      League of Women Voters is founded; Eleanor Roosevelt becomes an active member.

      Britain grants suffrage to women over age thirty.

1921   Margaret Sanger founds the American Birth Control League, forerunner of Planned Parenthood.

      The Witch-Cult in Western Europe, by Margaret Murray, theorizing that witch trials were patriarchal attacks on women practicing an "old religion."

1922   *Women, Morality, and Birth Control*, by Margaret Sanger.

1923   Equal Rights Amendment (ERA) is first proposed by Alice Paul, reading: "Equality of rights under the law shall not be denied or abridged by the United States or by any State on account of sex."

      His Religion and Hers: A Study of the Faith of Our Fathers and the Work of Our Mothers, by Charlotte Perkins Gilman.

      Margaret Sanger founds the Birth Control Clinical Research Bureau.

1927   *The Mothers*, by Robert Briffault, theorizing early matriarchies, based on finds of mother-goddess figures.

1928   Britain extends suffrage to all adult women.

      The Well of Loneliness, a novel about lesbian life, by Radclyffe Hall.

1931   Jane Addams wins the Nobel Peace Prize (shared with Nicholas Murray Butler).

      My Fight for Birth Control, by Margaret Sanger.

      On Understanding Women, by Mary Ritter Beard.

1932   *Mothers and Amazons*, by Helen Diner.

1936   A court case involving birth-control advocate Margaret Sanger establishes the right of doctors to legally prescribe birth control devices.

1940   Jeannette Pickering Rankin, the first woman member of the U.S. Congress (1916–1918), is elected to Congress again.

1941   Jeannette Pickering Rankin casts the only vote in the U.S. Congress against entering World War II.

1942   Planned Parenthood Federation is established.

1945   Eleanor Roosevelt serves as a member of the U.S. delegation to the United Nations (1945–1953).

1946   American professor Emily Greene Balch, cofounder and longtime leader of the Women's International League for Peace and Freedom, wins the Novel Peace Prize.

      United Nations Commission on the Status of Women is formed, to foster women's rights and monitor women's status internationally.

      Women as a Force in History, by Mary Ritter Beard.

1948   Eleanor Roosevelt chairs the United Nations Commission on Human Rights, which passes the landmark U.N. Declaration of Human Rights.

Sexual Behavior in the Human Male, the first Kinsey report on human sexual response.

1949 *The Second Sex*, by Simone de Beauvoir.

Convention for the Suppression of the Traffic in Persons and of the Exploitation of the Prostitution of Others is passed by the United Nations.

Ban on British publication is lifted for *The Well of Loneliness* (1928), a novel about lesbian life.

1952 International Convention of the Political Rights of Women calls for all women to have equal political rights, in voting, holding office, and exercising public functions.

1953 Margaret Sanger becomes president of the International Planned Parenthood Federation.

Sexual Behavior in the Human Female, the second Kinsey report on human sexual response.

1957 International conventions call for women's equal rights within marriage and in dissolving marriage (1957–1962).

1959 Siramoro Bandaranaike becomes the world's first woman prime minister, elected in Sri Lanka to replace her assassinated husband.

1963 Equal Pay Act, the first federal law against sexual discrimination, is passed by the U.S. Congress, requiring the payment of equal amounts to women and men doing jobs calling for substantially equal skill, effort, and responsibility.

The Feminist Mystique, a key work in the modern American women's movement, by Betty Friedan.

"I Was a Playboy Bunny," an investigative article by Gloria Steinem.

1964 U.S. Congress passes Title VII of the Civil Rights Act, prohibiting employment discrimination based on race, color, religion, sex, or national origin, and creating the Equal Employment Opportunity Commission (EEOC).

1965 In *Griswold* v. *Connecticut*, the U.S. Supreme Court strikes down a law that would have banned use of contraceptives by married couples and establishes the right of privacy between them and their doctor.

1966 National Organization for Women (NOW) is founded, with Betty Friedan as president.

Indira Gandhi becomes prime minister of India.

Human Sexual Response and *Human Sexual Inadequacy*, by sex researchers and therapists William H. Masters and Virginia Johnson.

1967 The National Organization for Women declares itself for the Equal Rights Amendment (ERA), beginning the modern campaign for its passage.

International Declaration on the Elimination of All Forms of Discrimination Against Women is passed.

Radical Women is founded in the United States by Shulamith Firestone and Pam Allen; it splinters in 1968.

An executive order bans employment discrimination based on sex by U.S. federal contractors.

1968 *The Church and the Second Sex*, by Mary Daly, criticizing Catholic attitudes toward women.

Women's International Terrorist Conspiracy from Hell (WITCH) is founded in New York, and demonstrates at the New York Stock Exchange on Halloween.

1969 An executive order directs U.S. federal agencies to establish affirmative action programs.

Golda Meir becomes prime minister of Israel.

New York Radical Feminists is founded.

Redstockings, an early consciousness-raising radical feminist group, is founded by Shulamith Firestone and Ellen Willis; it dissolves in 1970.

Women's International Terrorist Conspiracy from Hell (WITCH) holds an anti–Bridal Fair demonstration.

1970 *Patriarchal Attitudes*, by Eva Figes.

Sexual Politics, by Kate Millett.

The Coming of Age, by Simone de Beauvoir.

The Female Eunuch, by Germaine Greer.

The Dialectic of Sex: The Case for Feminist Revolution, by Shulamith Firestone.

"Goodbye to All That," on the superiority of women-only movements, and *Sisterhood Is Powerful*, a feminist anthology, both by Robin Morgan.

Our Blood: Prophecies and Discourses on Sexual Politics, by Andrea Dworkin.

Radicalesbians is founded in New York and issues the position paper *The Woman-Identified Woman*.

1971 U.S. House of Representatives passes the Equal Rights Amendment (ERA) by a vote of 354 to 23.

Ms. magazine is founded by Gloria Steinem.

In *Reed* v. *Reed*, the U.S. Supreme Court declared that women are "persons" and that state laws classifying them on the basis of sex are invalidated.

Man's World, Woman's Place, by Elizabeth Janeway.

The First Sex, by Elizabeth Gould Davis, posits early matriarchies and predicts a return of matriarchy.

1972 Equal Rights Amendment (ERA) is passed in the U.S. Senate by a vote of 84 to 8.

In *Eisenstadt* v. *Baird*, the U.S. Supreme Court extends to unmarried people the legal right to use contraceptives and the right of privacy between them and their doctor.

U.S. Congress passes Title IX of the Educational Amendments Act, barring discrimination on the basis of sex in all public undergraduate schools and in most private and public graduate and vocational schools that receive public funds.

Women and Madness, Phyllis Chesler's influential study of "deviance" from assigned sex roles.

Rape Crisis Center, considered the first in the United States, is founded in Washington, D.C.

Women and Sex, over which Egyptian feminist and doctor Nawal El Saadawi loses her job at the Egyptian Health Ministry, is published.

1973 In *Roe* v. *Wade*, the U.S. Supreme Court for the first time legalizes abortion in the United States.

Thirty states ratify the Equal Rights Amendment (ERA).

Rubyfruit Jungle, Rita Mae Brown's largely autobiographical novel about lesbianism.

1974 *The Pleasure Bond: A New Look at Sexuality and Commitment*, by William H. Masters and Virginia Johnson.

Woman Hating, by radical feminist Andrea Dworkin.

Beyond God the Father, Mary Daly's critical work on Catholicism.

1975 *Against Our Will: Men, Women and Rape*, by Susan Brownmiller, on rape as a means of subjugating all women.

Equal Credit Opportunity Act passed by U.S. Congress, from 1977 prohibiting creditor discrimination on the basis of race, ethnic origin, religion, age, sex, marital status, or welfare status.

In *Taylor* v. *Louisiana*, the Supreme Court invalidates state laws that restrict jury duty on the basis of sex.

International Women's Year, and United Nations Decade for Women: Equality, Development, Peace, both begin with the World Conference on Women in Mexico City.

U.S. Congress passes Title IV-D of the Social Security Act establishing the Office of Child Support Enforcement (OCSE).

Women's Evolution, by Evelyn Reed, taking a Marxist approach to matriarchy.

1976 In *Planned Parenthood* v. *Danforth*, the U.S. Supreme Court strikes down a Missouri law requiring a married woman to obtain her husband's consent for abortion.

Mairead Corrigan and Betty Williams, cofounders of the Northern Irish Peace Movement, win the Nobel Peace Prize.

When God Was a Woman, by Merlin Stone, linking early matriarchy and goddess-worship theories.

1977 In *Carey* v. *Population Services International*, the U.S. Supreme Court extends to minors the legal right to use contraceptives and the right of privacy between them and their doctor.

In *Beal* v. *Doe*, the U.S. Supreme Court rules that states are not required to use public funds to pay for abortions.

The Women's Room, by Marilyn French.

1978 Pregnancy Discrimination Act (PDA) is passed by the U.S. Congress, defining pregnancy as a "disability" and requiring employers to make available the same benefits for pregnant women as for "other" disabled employees.

In *Los Angeles Department of Water and Power* v. *Manhart*, the U.S. Supreme Court rules that women are to be treated equally with men in terms of retirement benefits and cannot be required to make larger contributions for the same monthly benefits.

Gyn/Ecology: The Metaethics of Radical Feminism, Mary Daly's work on spiritual feminism and radical feminist theology.

The Dinner Party, an art work honoring 999 women, some mythical, by Judy Chicago.

Going Too Far: The Personal Chronicles of a Feminist, essays by Robin Morgan.

Woman at Point Zero, by Egyptian feminist Nawal El Saadawi, a sympathetic view of a woman imprisoned for killing a pimp.

1979 Margaret Thatcher becomes prime minister of Britain, that country's first elected woman leader, and its longest-serving of the twentieth century (1979–1990).

United Nations General Assembly adopts the Convention on the Elimination of All Forms of Discrimination Against Women.

In *Bellotti* v. *Baird*, the U.S. Supreme Court rules that a state cannot require a teenager to get her parents' consent for an abortion, unless an alternative is provided, such as getting consent from a judge.

The Obstacle Race: The Fortunes of Women Painters and Their Work, by Germaine Greer.

The Hidden Face of Eve: Women in the Arab World, by Egyptian feminist Nawal El Saadawi.

U.S. Congress granted a three-year extension for state ratification of the Equal Rights Amendment (ERA).

Mother Teresa, founder of the Missionaries of Charity, serving the poor in India and elsewhere, wins the Nobel Peace Prize.

European Community adopts a nonbinding directive urging the adoption of pay equity policies.

1980 World Conference on Women is held in Copenhagen.

Vigdis Finnbogadóttir is elected President of Iceland.

In *Harris* v. *McRae*, the U.S. Supreme Court decision upholds the so-called Hyde Amendment, providing that Medicaid cannot be used to pay for medically necessary abortions.

Women's Rights National Historic Park is established in Seneca Falls, New York.

1981   *The Second Stage*, by Betty Friedan.

Nawal El Saadawi, Egyptian feminist and editor of feminist magazine *Confrontation*, is jailed for her work.

Pornography: Men Possessing Women, by radical feminist Andrea Dworkin.

1982   Equal Rights Amendment (ERA) fails to be ratified by enough states to become part of the U.S. Constitution, being passed by only thirty-five out of the then required thirty-eight states.

Political Swedish economist and peace activist Alva Reimer Myrdal wins Nobel Peace Prize.

Egyptian feminist Nawal El Saadawi founds a Pan-Arab women's group.

The Anatomy of Freedom, essays by Robin Morgan.

1983   Equal Rights Amendment is reintroduced in Congress but fails to gain the required two-thirds votes in the House of Representatives. It continues to be introduced annually.

In *City of Akron* v. *Akron Center for Reproductive Health*, the U.S. Supreme Court strikes down a law requiring a twenty-four-hour wait before an abortion, because the statute asserted "the unborn child is a human life from the moment of conception."

In *AFSCME* v. *State of Washington*, a U.S. federal district court rules that women are entitled to be compensated by the state, if they are paid less than men for jobs of comparable worth.

Indianapolis passes a model antipornography law earlier developed by Catharine MacKinnon and Andrea Dworkin, based on the premise that pornography is a violation of women's civil rights.

Outrageous Acts and Other Rebellions, essays by Gloria Steinem.

1984   U.S. Congress passes the Child Support Enforcement Amendments to the Title IV-D of the Social Security Act, giving women means to collect delinquent child support payments.

Retirement Equity Act is passed by U.S. Congress, requiring a retiring worker to obtain written consent from the spouse, if there are to be no survivor benefits in a pension.

In *Hishon* v. *King and Spalding*, the U.S. Supreme Court rules that law firms under Title VII (see **1964**) cannot discriminate on the basis of sex in promoting lawyers to partnership.

Sex and Destiny: The Politics of Human Fertility, by Germaine Greer.

Sisterhood Is Global, essays by Robin Morgan.

1985   World Conference on Women in Nairobi, adopts the Nairobi Forward-Looking Strategies for the Advancement of Women.

Beyond Power: On Women, Men and Morals, by Marilyn French.

1986   U.S. Supreme Court's *Meritor Savings Bank* v. *Vinson* decision establishes that a hostile workplace constituted sexual harassment, and that sexual harassment violates laws against sexual discrimination.

In *American Booksellers Association* v. *Hudnut*, the U.S. Supreme Court strikes down an Indianapolis antipornography ordinance as an unconstitutional violation of First Amendment free speech guarantees.

In *Thornburgh* v. *American College of Obstetricians and Gynecologists*, the U.S. Supreme Court strikes down Pennsylvania's Abortion Control Act, restricting abortion rights, later revised and largely affirmed in *Planned Parenthood* v. *Casey* (1992).

Corazon Aquino becomes president of the Philippines.

1987 Canada's Ontario legislature passes the first Pay Equity Act, requiring pay equity in both public and private sectors.

In *California Federal Savings and Loan Association* v. *Guerra*, the U.S. Supreme Court upholds the legality of a law providing unpaid pregnancy disability leave to female workers, guaranteeing availability of their jobs on return.

Gro Harlem Brundtland chairs the World Commission on Environment and Development, producing the global report *Our Common Future.*

1988 Benazir Bhutto becomes prime minister of Pakistan.

Ecumenical Decade of Churches in Solidarity with Women called for by the World Council of Churches begins.

1989 In *Webster* v. *Reproductive Health Services*, the U.S. Supreme Court upholds a Missouri law that bars the use of public hospitals or clinics for abortions.

1990 In *Ohio* v. *Akron Center for Reproductive Health*, the U.S. Supreme Court upholds a state law requiring a teenager to notify one parent before obtaining an abortion.

U.S. Congress passes the Displaced Homemakers Self-Sufficiency Assistance Act (DHSSA), establishing the first federal training program specifically designed for displaced homemakers and single parents, and the Perkins Act, intended to provide equal vocational education opportunities for women and girls.

Violetta Chamorro is elected president of Nicaragua.

Performance artist Karen Finley is denied a National Endowment for the Arts (NEA) grant for a work on sexual abuse, on the grounds that it is obscene.

Sexual Personae: Art and Decadence from Nefertiti to Emily Dickinson, by Camille Paglia.

Mary Robinson is elected president of Ireland.

Robin Morgan becomes editor of *Ms.* magazine.

1991 Anita Faye Hill charges U.S. Supreme Court nominee Clarence Thomas with sexual harassment, in internationally televised Senate Judiciary Committee hearings, revitalizing the women's movement.

Aung San Suu Kyi, under house arrest as leader of the democratic opposition to dictatorship in her homeland of Burma (Myanmar), is awarded the Nobel Peace Prize.

In *Automobile Workers* v. *Johnson Controls, Inc.*, the U.S. Supreme Court unanimously holds that employers cannot use gender as a reason to bar a woman from a specific job, holding that Johnson's "fetus-protection policy" had obvious bias, since it barred all women from jobs that were dangerous to the reproductive systems of males as well as females.

Backlash: The Undeclared War Against American Women, by Susan Faludi.

Revolution from Within: A Book of Self-Esteem, by Gloria Steinem.

The Loony Bin Trip, by Kate Millett.

1992 In *Planned Parenthood* v. *Casey*, the U.S. Supreme Court—by a tenuous 5–4 majority—reaffirms *Roe* v. *Wade*'s legalization of abortion, while allowing the states to place restrictions on the provision of abortions, as long as they do not pose an "undue burden."

The Tailhook scandal—involving molestation of numerous women at a Navy aviators' convention in 1991 and the subsequent cover-up—is made public, opening the wider scandal of sexual harassment and abuse toward women in the armed forces.

In *Franklin* v. *Gwinnett County Public Schools*, the U.S. Supreme Court holds, in a rare unanimous decision, that a sexually harassed student could collect damages from the school district.

21st Century Party founded in United States with an agenda of feminist, civil rights, environmental, and other liberal and radical issues.

In *R.A.V.* v. *St. Paul*, the U.S. Supreme Court overturns a St. Paul, Minnesota, law criminalizing speech or behavior that "caused anger or alarm" because of its treatment of "race, creed, color, religion, or gender."

U.S. Supreme Court bars the return of RU486—the so-called abortion pills—to a pregnant woman who imported them into the country for her personal use.

The War Against Women, by Marilyn French.

Rigoberta Menchú, a Quiché Indian seeking to end the civil war in her homeland of Guatemala, wins the Nobel Peace Prize.